INFORMATION PRIVACY LAW

INFORMATION PRIVACY LAW

Daniel J. Solove
Assistant Professor of Law
Seton Hall Law School

Marc Rotenberg
Executive Director
The Electronic Privacy Information Center
&
Adjunct Professor of Law
Georgetown University Law Center

PUBLISHERS

1185 Avenue of the Americas, New York, NY 10036
www.aspenpublishers.com

Printed in the United States of America

1 2 3 4 5 6 7 8 9 0

ISBN 0-7355-3382-2

Library of Congress Cataloging-in-Publication Data

Solove, Daniel J., 1972–
   Information privacy law / Daniel J. Solove, Marc Rotenberg.
      p. cm.
   Includes bibliographical references and index.
   ISBN 0-7355-3382-2
   1. Privacy, Right of—United States.   2. Data protection—
Law and legislation—United States.   3. Confidential commu-
nications—Law and legislation—United States   4. Personality
(Law)—United States.   I. Rotenberg, Marc.   II. Title.

KF1262 .S66 2003
342.73'0858—dc21   2002027776

About Aspen Publishers

Aspen Publishers, headquartered in New York City, is a leading information provider for attorneys, business professionals, and law students. Written by preeminent authorities, our products consist of analytical and practical information covering both U.S. and international topics. We publish in the full range of formats, including updated manuals, books, periodicals, CDs, and online products.

Our proprietary content is complemented by 2,500 legal databases, containing over 11 million documents, available through our Loislaw division. Aspen Publishers also offers a wide range of topical legal and business databases linked to Loislaw's primary material. Our mission is to provide accurate, timely, and authoritative content in easily accessible formats, supported by unmatched customer care.

To order any Aspen Publishers title, go to *www.aspenpublishers.com* or call 1-800-638-8437.

To reinstate your manual update service, call 1-800-638-8437.

For more information on Loislaw products, go to *www.loislaw.com* or call 1-800-364-2512.

For Customer Care issues, e-mail *CustomerCare@aspenpublishers.com;* call 1-800-234-1660; or fax 1-800-901-9075.

Aspen Publishers
A Wolters Kluwer Company

To my parents and grandparents—DJS

To Anna, Chaz and Chloe, my parents, and GG—MSR

SUMMARY OF CONTENTS

CONTENTS

2 PRIVACY AND THE MEDIA   63

5 *PRIVACY OF ASSOCIATIONS, ANONYMITY, AND IDENTIFICATION*

6   *PRIVACY, RECORDS, AND COMPUTER DATABASES*   459

7 *PRIVACY AND PLACE*   585

PREFACE

As the twenty-first century begins, it appears that few public policy issues will attract more attention in the years ahead than the protection of privacy. The rapid growth of the Internet, coupled with new business practices and new efforts by government to deploy technology for law enforcement and the administration of programs, have raised far-reaching questions about the future of privacy.

Central to many of these debates is the role of law. To what extent can the law safeguard the right of privacy in an era of rapidly evolving technology? What competing interests must be considered? What is the appropriate role of the courts and the legislatures? These questions are not new, but they have acquired greater urgency as the law is asked to evaluate an increasingly complex array of privacy matters.

For lawyers, this rapid growth has raised both new challenges and new opportunities. In the private sector, attorneys now routinely advise business clients about the development of privacy policies, compliance with privacy statutes, and privacy regulations in new markets. Attorneys litigate on behalf of clients who believe that their privacy has been violated while others defend against these allegations. State attorneys general have become leading champions of privacy rights. Policymakers in government evaluate new legislative proposals both to expand and to limit privacy claims. Legal advisors on trade policy, technology development, consumer protection, and national security all consider privacy issues in the course of their work.

The years ahead are likely to pose even greater challenges and opportunities for those versed in privacy law. The growing use of genetic information, the increasing transformation of the electronic marketplace, and new systems of identification will raise new privacy concerns that will eventually come before the courts and the lawmakers.

Clearly, privacy has emerged as one of the critical legal subjects in the modern era. Law schools will need to incorporate information privacy and related topics into the curriculum in order to prepare lawyers for the new challenges facing clients and the important policy decisions facing society.

This text provides a cornerstone for the study of information privacy law. Our goal is to provide a comprehensive and accessible introduction for the student and an authoritative reference for the practitioner. We have organized the book around the general topics and themes that are currently arising in the law. Information privacy law is a complicated and vast body of different types of legal protections, and our organizational choices reflect our aim of producing a clear and coherent synthesis of the field. When selecting cases, we have included the leading cases as well as endeavored to provide a solid historical background and a timely and fresh perspective on the major privacy issues facing lawyers in the twenty-first century. Important majority opinions are followed by equally important dissents. The text includes extensive notes and commentary, and it integrates cases and statutes with theoretical and policy perspectives. To facilitate discussion and debate, we have included excerpts from commentators with a wide range of viewpoints. Technical terms are clearly explained.

Information Privacy Law draws heavily on recent developments in the high-tech field as well as international law. We anticipate that these factors will contribute significantly to the development of privacy law in the near future. The text also explores the major themes in the development of the field — the meaning of privacy, the reasonable expectation of privacy, the application of constitutional principles to new technologies, and the transformation of norms into legal frameworks.

We hope that this text provides a useful introduction to the challenges of the field of information privacy now and in the future.

A NOTE ON THE EDITING

We have deleted many citations and footnotes from the cases to facilitate readability. The footnotes that have been retained in the cases have been renumbered. When discussing books, articles, and other materials in the notes and commentary, we have included full citations in footnotes in order to make the text easier to read. We have also included many citations to additional works in the footnotes that may be of interest to the reader.

Daniel J. Solove
Marc Rotenberg

December 2002

ACKNOWLEDGMENTS

Daniel J. Solove: I would like to thank Carl Coleman, John Jacobi, Orin Kerr, Raymond Ku, Joel Reidenberg, Michael Risinger, Paul Schwartz, Peter Swire, William Thompson, and Peter Winn for helpful comments and suggestions. Charlie Sullivan and Jake Barnes provided indispensable advice about how to bring this project to fruition. Special thanks to Richard Mixter at Aspen Publishing for his encouragement and faith in this project, to Jessica Barmack for her excellent editorial advice, to John Burdeaux for his superb managing of the project, and to Sandra Doherty for her careful copyediting. I would also like to thank my research assistants Peter Choy, Monica Contreras, Poornima Ravishankar, John Spaccarotella, Eli Weiss, and Kate Yannitte. My secretary, Linda Murph, provided much needed help during many phases of this project. Finally, I would like to thank Dean Kathleen Boozang and Dean Pat Hobbs for making sure that I had the resources I needed.

Marc Rotenberg: Thanks to the folks at EPIC, particularly Mikal Condon, Chris Hoofnagle, Adam Kessel, and Cédric Laurant, the members of the EPIC Advisory Board, particularly James Boyle, Anita Allen-Castellitto, Julie E. Cohen, Oscar Gandy, Jerry Kang, Pam Samuelson, Paul Schwartz, and Frank Tuerkheimer. Several people encouraged me to pursue work in this field back in the early days. Thanks to Dean Judy Areen, Dean Paul Brest, David Burnham, Morton Halperin, Judge A. Leon Higginbotham, Jr., Senator Patrick J. Leahy, John Podesta, Phil Stern, John Shattuck, and Harvey Silverglate.

We are grateful to the following sources for their permission to reprint excerpts of their scholarship:

Anita L. Allen, *Coercing Privacy*, 40 William & Mary L. Rev. 723, 729-730, 733-735, 737-741, 752-755 (1999). Used by permission. (c) 1999 by William & Mary Law Review and Anita L. Allen.

Anita L. Allen, *Minor Distractions: Children, Privacy and E-Commerce*, 38 Houston L. Rev. 751, 752-753, 768-769, 775-776 (2001). Reprinted with permission.

Colin J. Bennett, *Convergence Revisited: Toward a Global Policy for the Protection of Personal Data? in Technology and Privacy: The New Landscape* 99, 106-108

(Philip E. Agre & Marc Rotenberg eds. 1997). (c) 1997 by The MIT Press. Reprinted by the permission of The MIT Press and Colin Bennett.

Erwin Chemerinsky, *Protect the Press: A First Amendment Standard for Safeguarding Aggressive Newsgathering*, 33 U. Rich. L Rev. 1143, 1159, 1163-1164 (2000). Reprinted with permission.

Julie E. Cohen, *Examined Lives: Informational Privacy*, 52 Stan. L. Rev. 1371, 1423-1428, 1405-1407, 1416-1418, 1421 (2000). (c) 2000. Reprinted by permission of the Stanford Law Review in the format textbook via Copyright Clearance Center and Julie Cohen.

Julie E. Cohen, *A Right to Read Anonymously: A Closer Look at "Copyright Management" in Cyberspace*, 28 Conn. L Rev. 981, 1004-1005, 1007, 1012-1013 (1996). (c) 1996 by Connecticut Law Review and Julie E. Cohen. Reprinted with permission.

C. Thomas Dienes, *Protecting Investigative Journalism*, 67 Geo. Wash. L. Rev. 1139, 1143 (1999). (c) 1999 by the George Washington Law Review. Reprinted with permission.

Richard Epstein, *The Legal Regulation of Genetic Discrimination: Old Responses to New Technology*, 74 B.U. L. Rev. 1, 2-4, 8-13, 18-19 (1994). Reprinted with permission of Richard Epstein.

Amitai Etzioni, The Limits of Privacy 2-3, 213-214 (1999). (c) 1999 by Amitai Etzioni. Reprinted by permission of Basic Books, a member of Perseus Books, LLC and Amitai Etzioni.

Robert Gellman, *Does Privacy Law Work? in Technology and Privacy: The New Landscape* 193, 196-201 (Philip E. Agre & Marc Rotenberg eds. 1997). (c) 1997 by The MIT Press. Reprinted by permission of The MIT Press and Robert Gellman.

Lawrence O. Gostin, *Health Information Privacy*, 80 Cornell L. Rev. 451, 454-455, 457-458, 492-494 (1995). Reprinted with permission.

Simson Garfinkel, Database Nation: The Death of Privacy in the 21st Century 136-139 (2000). (c) 2000 by O'Reilly & Associates, Inc. Reprinted with permission.

Robert M. Gellman, *Prescribing Privacy: The Uncertain Role of the Physician in the Protection of Patient Privacy*, 62 N.C. L. Rev. 255, 292-294 (1984). Reprinted with permission of the North Carolina Law Review.

Steven Hetcher, *The FTC as Internet Privacy Norm Entrepreneur*, 53 Vand. L. Rev. 2041, 2042-2047, 2053-2055 (2000). Reprinted with the permission of Steven Hetcher.

Edward Janger & Paul M. Schwartz, *The Gramm-Leach-Bliley Act, Information Privacy, and the Limits of Default Rules*, 86 Minn. L. Rev. 1219 (2002). Reprinted with permission.

E. Judson Jennings, *Carnivore: U.S. Government Surveillance of Internet Transmissions* 6 Va. J.L. & Tech. 10 (2001). Reprinted with permission.

Scott Killingsworth, *Minding Your Own Business: Privacy Policies in Principle and in Practice* 7 J. Intell. Prop L. 57, 91-92 (1999). Reprinted with permission of the Journal of Intellectual Property Law and Scott Killingsworth.

Pauline T. Kim, *Privacy Rights' Public Policy, and the Employment Relationship*, 57 Ohio St. L.J. 671, 722, 724, 682, 703 (1996). Reprinted with permission.

Raymond S.R. Ku, *Think Twice Before You Type*, 163 N.J.L.J. 747 (Feb. 19, 2001). This excerpted article is reprinted with permission from the February 19, 2001, issue of the New Jersey Law Journal. (c) 2002 NLP IP Company.

Lawrence Lessig, Code and Other Laws of Cyberspace 159-161 (1999). (c) 1999 by Lawrence Lessig. Reprinted by permission of Basic Books, a member of Perseus Books, LLC and Lawrence Lessig.

Catharine MacKinnon, Toward a Feminist Theory of the State 190-193 (1989). (c) 1989 by Harvard University Press. Reprinted with permission.

Richard S. Murphy, *Property Rights in Personal Information: An Economic Defense of Privacy*, 84 Geo L.J. 2381, 2397-2398 (1996). Reprinted with permission of the publisher, Georgetown Law Journal (c) 1996.

Richard A. Posner, *The Right of Privacy*, 12 Ga. L. Rev. 393 (1978). Reprinted with permission.

Radhika Rao, *Property, Privacy and the Human Body*, 80 B.U. L Rev. 359, 434-440 (2000). Reprinted with permission of the Boston University Law Review and Radhika Rao.

Joel R. Reidenberg, *Setting Standards for Fair Information Practice in the U.S. Private Sector*, 80 Iowa L. Rev. 497 (1995). Reprinted with permission.

Joel R. Reidenberg, *Privacy in the Information Economy: A Fortress or Frontier for Individual Rights,* 44 Fed. Comm. L.J. 195, 211-213 (1992). Reprinted with permission.

Joel Reidenberg, *E-Commerce and Trans-Atlantic Privacy,* 38 Hous. L. Rev. 717, 739-740, 744-746 (2001). Reprinted with permission.

Marc Rotenberg, *Fair Information Practices and the Architecture of Privacy (What Larry Doesn't Get),* 2001 Stan. Tech. L. Rev. 1, 43-48 (2001). Reprinted with permission.

Paul M. Schwartz, *Privacy and Democracy in Cyberspace,* 52 Vand. L. Rev. 1609, 1655-1656, 1658-1662, 1611, 1633-1634, 1637-1638 (1999). Reprinted with the permission of Paul Schwartz.

Paul M. Schwartz, *Privacy and the Economics of Health Care Information,* 76 Tex. L. Rev. 1, 3, 4, 12-15, 46-47 (1997). (c) 1997 the Texas Law Review. Reprinted with permission.

Paul M. Schwartz, *Free Speech Versus Information Privacy: Eugene Volokh's First Amendment Jurisprudence,* 52 Stan. L. Rev. 1559, 1560-1564 (2000). Reprinted with the permission of the Stanford Law Review in the format textbook via Copyright Clearance Center and Paul Schwartz.

Reva B. Seigel, *The Rule of Love: Wife Beating as Prerogative of Privacy*, 105 Yale L.J. 2117, 2118, 2122-2123, 2128, 2137, 2141, 2151-2154, 2166, 2171, 2182 (1996). Reprinted by permission of the *Yale Law Journal* Company and the William S. Hein Company, from the *Yale Law Journal,* vol. 105, pages 2117-2207.

Spiros Simitis, *Reviewing Privacy in an Informational Society*, 135 U. Pa. L. Rev. 707, 709-710, 724-726, 732-738, 746 (1987). (c) 1987 by the University of Pennsylvania Law Review. Reprinted by permission of the University of Pennsylvania Law Review and Spiros Simitis.

David L. Sobel, *The Process That "John Doe" Is Due: Addressing the Legal Challenge to Internet Anonymity,* 49 Va. J.L. & Tech. 3, 13, 14 (2000). Reprinted with permission.

Richard Sobel, *The Degradation of the Moral Economy of Political Identity Under a Computerized National Identification System*, 8 B.U. J. Sci. & Tech. L. 37 (2002). Reprinted with permission.

Daniel J. Solove, *Access and Aggregation: Privacy, Public Records, and the Constitution*, 86 Minn. L. Rev. 1137 (2002). (c) 2002 by Daniel J. Solove and the Minnesota Law Review.

Daniel J. Solove, *Privacy and Power: Computer Databases and Metaphors for Informational Privacy*, 53 Stan. L. Rev. 1393, 1414-1423 (2001). (c) 2001 by the Stanford Law Review and Daniel J. Solove.

Jeff Sovern, *Opting In, Opting Out, or No Options at All: The Fight for Control of Personal Information*, 74 Wash. L. Rev. 1033, 1072-1075, 1081-1083, 1085-1088, 1090-1091, 1101-1103, 1106, 1118 (1999). Reprinted with permission.

Peter P. Swire, *Financial Privacy and the Theory of High-Tech Government Surveillance* 77 Wash. U.L.Q. 461, 464-465, 469-472 (1999). Reprinted with permission.

Richard C. Turkington, *Confidentiality Policy for HIV-Related Information: An Analytical Framework for Sorting Out Hard and Easy Cases*, 34 Vill. L Rev. 871, 904-905, 907 (1989). Reprinted with permission.

Rein Turn & Willis H. Ware, *Privacy and Security Issues in Information Systems* Ch. 1, RAND p. 568. Santa Monica, CA: RAND, July 1976. (c) RAND 1976. Reprinted by permission.

Alan Westin, Privacy and Freedom 7, 31-38 (1967). A study sponsored by the Association of the Bar of the City of New York. Reprinted with permission.

Diane L. Zimmerman, *Requiem for a Heavyweight: A Farewell to Warren and Brandeis's Privacy Tort*, 68 Cornell L. Rev. 291, 333-334, 340 (1983). Reprinted with permission.

INFORMATION
PRIVACY LAW

CHAPTER 1

INTRODUCTION

A. PRIVACY AND ITS LEGAL PROTECTION

We live in a world shaped by technology and fueled by information. Technological devices — such as telephones, video and audio recording devices, computers, and the Internet — have revolutionized our ability to capture information about the world and to communicate with each other. Information is the lifeblood of today's society. Increasingly our everyday activities involve the transfer and recording of information. The government collects vast quantities of personal information in records pertaining to an individual's birth, marriage, divorce, property, court proceedings, motor vehicles, voting activities, criminal transgressions, professional licensing, and so on. Private sector entities also amass gigantic databases of personal information for marketing purposes or to prepare credit histories. Wherever we go, whatever we do, we could easily leave behind a trail of data that is recorded and gathered together.

These new technologies, coupled with the increasing use of personal information by business and government, pose new challenges for the protection of privacy. This book is about the law's response to new challenges to privacy. A significant amount of law regulates information privacy in the United States and around the world. Is this law responsive to the present and future dangers to privacy? What duties and responsibilities must corporations, government agencies, and other private and public sector entities be aware of with regard to personal data? What rights do individuals have to prevent and redress invasions to their privacy? These are some of the questions that this text will address.

The topic of this book is information privacy law. Information privacy concerns the collection, use, and disclosure of personal information. Information privacy is often contrasted with "decisional privacy," which concerns the freedom to make decisions about one's body and family. Decisional privacy involves matters such as contraception, procreation, abortion, and child rearing, and is at the center of a series of Supreme Court cases often referred to as substantive due process or the constitutional right to privacy. But information privacy increasingly incorporates elements of decisional privacy as the use of data both expands and limits individual autonomy.

Information privacy law is an interrelated web of tort law, federal and state constitutional law, federal and state statutory law, evidentiary privileges, property law, contract law, and criminal law. Information privacy law is relatively new, although its roots reach far back. It is developing coherence as privacy doctrines in one area are being used to inform and structure privacy responses in other areas. Information privacy law raises a related set of political, policy, and philosophical questions: What is privacy? Why is privacy important? What is the impact of technology on privacy? What is the role of the courts, the legislatures, and the law in safeguarding privacy?

Why study information privacy law? First, in today's Information Age, privacy is an issue of paramount importance for freedom and democracy. One of the central issues of information privacy concerns the power of commercial and government entities over individual autonomy and decisionmaking. Understood broadly, information privacy is about the type of society we are constructing as we move forward in today's Information Age.

Second, information privacy is an issue of growing public concern. Information privacy problems are timely, frequently in the news, and often the subject of litigation and legislation. Information privacy has also become a priority on the legislative agenda of Congress and many state legislatures.

Third, there are many new laws and legal developments regarding information privacy. Increased litigation, legislation, regulation, as well as public concern over privacy are spurring corporations in a variety of commerce and services to address privacy. Lawyers are drafting privacy policies, litigating privacy issues, and are developing ways for dot-com companies, corporations, hospitals, insurers, and banks to conform to privacy regulations. For example, lawyers will be needed to help health care providers comply with the recently promulgated regulations under the Health Insurance Portability and Accountability Act (HIPAA). In short, attorneys increasingly will be grappling with privacy issues — either through litigation of privacy violations or through measures to comply with privacy regulations and to prevent litigation. All of these developments demand lawyers versed in the grand scheme and subtle nuance of information privacy law.

Fourth, information privacy law is an engaging and fascinating topic. The issues are controversial, complex, relevant, and current. Few areas of law are more closely intertwined with our world of rapid technological innovation. The study of privacy law also helps us understand how our legal institutions respond to change, and may help prepare us for other challenges ahead.

B. INFORMATION PRIVACY LAW: ORIGINS AND ROOTS

Information privacy law is a wide-ranging body of law, having roots in common law, constitutional law, statutory law, and international law.[1] This sec-

---

[1] For other works surveying the field of information privacy law, *see* Richard Turkington & Anita L. Allen, *Privacy Law: Cases and Materials* (2002); Paul M. Schwartz & Joel R. Reidenberg, *Data Privacy Law* (1996); Ken Gormley, *One Hundred Years of Privacy*, 1992 Wis. L. Rev. 1335. For an in-

tion will provide a brief introduction to the various strands of information privacy law that will be covered throughout this book.

1. COMMON LAW ROOTS

One of the most significant chapters in the history of privacy law is the common law's development of tort remedies to protect privacy. In the late nineteenth century, considerable concerns about privacy captured the public's attention, ultimately resulting in the 1890 publication of Samuel Warren and Louis Brandeis's influential article, *The Right to Privacy*.[2] According to Roscoe Pound, the article did "nothing less than add a chapter to our law."[3] Harry Kalven even hailed it as the "most influential law review article of all."[4] The clearest indication of the article's ongoing vitality can be found in the Supreme Court's recent decision, *Kyllo v. United States*, 533 U.S. 27 (2001). The Brandeis and Warren article is cited by the majority, those in concurrence, and those in dissent!

Several developments in the late nineteenth century created a growing interest in privacy. First, the press was increasingly sensationalistic. Prior to the Civil War, wide-circulation newspapers were rare. However, the development of a new form of sensationalistic journalism, known as "yellow journalism," made newspapers wildly successful. In 1833, Benjamin Day began publishing a newspaper called the *Sun* patterned after the "penny presses" in London (so named because they sold for a penny). The *Sun* contained news of scandals, such as family squabbles, public drunkenness, and petty crimes. In about four months, the *Sun* had a circulation of 4,000, almost the same as the existing New York daily papers. Just two months later, the *Sun* was reaching 8,000 in circulation. Other penny press papers soon followed.

Between 1850 and 1890, newspaper circulation increased about 1,000 percent — from 100 papers with 800,000 readers to 900 papers with more than 8 million readers. Joseph Pulitzer and William Randolph Hearst became the leading rivals in the newspaper business, each amassing newspaper empires. Their highly sensationalistic journalism became the paradigm for yellow journalism.[5]

Second, technological developments caused great alarm for privacy. In their article, Warren and Brandeis pointed to the invention of "instantaneous photography" as a new challenge to privacy. Photography had been around for many years before Warren and Brandeis penned their article. However, the equipment was expensive, cumbersome, and complicated to use. In 1884, the

---

teresting series of stories about various privacy cases and issues, *see* Ellen Alderman & Caroline Kennedy, *The Right to Privacy* (1997).

[2] Samuel Warren & Louis Brandeis, *The Right to Privacy*, 4 Harv. L. Rev. 193 (1890).

[3] Alpheus Mason, *Brandeis: A Free Man's Life* 70 (1946).

[4] Harry Kalven, Jr., *Privacy in Tort Law — Were Warren and Brandeis Wrong?*, 31 L. & Contemp. Probs. 326, 327 (1966).

[5] For more information about yellow journalism, *see generally* Gini Graham Scott, *Mind Your Own Business: The Battle for Personal Privacy* 37–38 (1995); Robert Ellis Smith, *Ben Franklin's Web Site: Privacy and Curiosity from Plymouth Rock to the Internet* 102–120 (2000).

Eastman Kodak Company introduced the "snap camera," a hand-held camera that was small and cheap enough for use by the general public. The snap camera allowed people to take candid photographs in public places for the first time. In the late nineteenth century, few daily newspapers even printed drawings, let alone photographs. Warren and Brandeis, however, astutely recognized the potential for the new technology of cameras to be used by the sensationalistic press.

The origin of Warren and Brandeis's article has been the subject of considerable debate. Some suggest that Warren and Brandeis were strongly influenced by an article written in 1890 by E.L. Godkin, a famous social commentator in his day.[6] In the article, Godkin observed:

> . . . Privacy is a distinctly modern product, one of the luxuries of civilization, which is not only unsought for but unknown in primitive or barbarous societies. . . .
>
> . . . [The law manifests] respect for [an individual's] personality as an individual, for that kingdom of the mind, that inner world of personal thought and feeling in which every man passes some time, and in which every man who is worth much to himself or others, passes a great deal of time. The right to decide how much knowledge of this personal thought and feeling, and how much knowledge, therefore, of his tastes and habits, of his own private doings and affairs, and those of his family living under his roof, the public at large shall have, is as much one of his natural rights as his right to decide how he shall eat and drink, what he shall wear, and in what manner he shall pass his leisure hours. . . .
>
> Personal dignity is the fine flower of civilization, and the more of it there is in a community, the better off the community is. . . .
>
> The chief enemy of privacy in modern life is that interest in other people and their affairs known as curiosity, which in the days before newspapers created personal gossip. . . . Nobody quite likes to confess that he is eager to know all he can about his neighbor's private life, and yet the private life of our neighbors form the staple topic of conversation in most circles in the absence of strong intellectual, political, or commercial interests. This eagerness may be defended on the ground that the love of gossip is after all human, and that everything that is human concerns us deeply. . . . But as long as gossip was oral, it spread, as regarded any one individual, over a very small area, and was confined to the immediate circle of his acquaintances. It did not reach, or but rarely reached, those who knew nothing of him. It did not make his name, or his walk, or his conversation familiar to strangers. And what is more to the purpose, it spared him the pain or mortification of knowing that he was gossiped about. A man seldom heard oral gossip about him which simply made him ridiculous, or trespassed on his lawful privacy, but made no positive attack on his reputation. His peace and comfort were, therefore, but slightly affected by it. . . .
>
> In other words, gossip about private individuals is now printed, and makes its victim, with all his imperfections on his head, known to hundreds or thousands miles away from his place of abode; and, what is worst of all, brings to his knowledge exactly what is said about him, with all its details. It thus in-

---

[6] *See* Elbridge L. Adams, *The Right to Privacy and its Relation to the Law of Libel*, 39 Am. L. Rev. 37 (1905); Dorothy J. Glancy, *The Invention of the Right to Privacy*, 21 Ariz. L. Rev. 1 (1979).

flicts what is, to many men, the great pain of believing that everybody he meets in the street is perfectly familiar with some folly, or misfortune, or indiscretion, or weakness, which he had previously supposed had never got beyond his domestic circle. . . .

In truth, there is only one remedy for the violations of the right to privacy within the reach of the American public, and that is but an imperfect one. It is to be found in attaching social discredit to invasions of it on the part of conductors of the press. At present this check can hardly be said to exist. It is to a large extent nullified by the fact that the offence is often pecuniarily profitable. . . .[7]

Warren and Brandeis cited to Godkin's article, and their article bears some similarities to Godkin's. However, although recognizing the growing threats to privacy, Godkin remained cynical about the possibility of a solution, expressing only the hope that attitudes would change to be more respectful of privacy. Warren and Brandeis had a different view, believing that the law could provide protection for privacy.

Another theory suggests that incursions into the privacy of Samuel Warren inspired the article. Warren, a wealthy and powerful attorney in Boston, practiced law with Louis Brandeis, who later went on to become a U.S. Supreme Court Justice. In 1883, Samuel Warren married Mabel Bayard, the daughter of a prominent senator from Delaware, and set up house in Boston's Back Bay. The Warrens were among the Boston elite and were frequently reported on in *The Saturday Evening Gazette*, "which specialized in 'blue blood items,'" and "reported their activities in lurid detail."[8]

According to William Prosser, Warren was motivated to write the article because reporters intruded upon his daughter's wedding. However, this certainly could not have been the reason because in 1890, Warren's oldest daughter was not even 10 years old![9] Most likely, the impetus for writing the article was Warren's displeasure about a number of stories in the *Gazette* about his dinner parties.[10]

Whatever inspired them to write, Warren and Brandeis published an article that profoundly shaped the development of the law of privacy.

SAMUEL WARREN AND LOUIS BRANDEIS,
THE RIGHT TO PRIVACY

---

4 Harv. L. Rev. 193 (1890)

It could be done only on principles of private justice, moral fitness, and public convenience, which, when applied to a new subject, make common law without a precedent; much more when received and approved by usage.
— Willes, J., in Millar v. Taylor, 4 Burr. 2303, 2312

---

[7] E.L. Godkin, *The Rights of the Citizen: IV. To His Own Reputation*, Scribner's Magazine (1890); *see also* E.L. Godkin, *The Right to Privacy*, The Nation (Dec. 25, 1890).

[8] Mason, *supra*, at 46.

[9] *See* James H. Barron, *Warren and Brandeis*, The Right to Privacy, 4 Harvard L. Rev. 193 (1890): *Demystifying a Landmark Citation*, 13 Suffolk L. Rev. 875 (1979).

[10] *See* Smith, *supra*, at 118–119. A more complete description of the circumstances surrounding the publication of the article can be found in M. Green, *The Mount Vernon Street Warrens: A*

That the individual shall have full protection in person and in property is a principle as old as the common law; but it has been found necessary from time to time to define anew the exact nature and extent of such protection. Political, social, and economic changes entail the recognition of new rights, and the common law, in its eternal youth, grows to meet the new demands of society. Thus, in very early times, the law gave a remedy only for physical interference with life and property, for trespasses *vi et armis*. Then the "right to life" served only to protect the subject from battery in its various forms; liberty meant freedom from actual restraint; and the right to property secured to the individual his lands and his cattle. Later, there came a recognition of man's spiritual nature, of his feelings and his intellect. Gradually the scope of these legal rights broadened; and now the right to life has come to mean the right to enjoy life, — the right to be let alone; the right to liberty secures the exercise of extensive civil privileges; and the term "property" has grown to comprise every form of possession — intangible, as well as tangible.

Thus, with the recognition of the legal value of sensations, the protection against actual bodily injury was extended to prohibit mere attempts to do such injury; that is, the putting another in fear of such injury. From the action of battery grew that of assault. Much later there came a qualified protection of the individual against offensive noises and odors, against dust and smoke, and excessive vibration. The law of nuisance was developed. So regard for human emotions soon extended the scope of personal immunity beyond the body of the individual. His reputation, the standing among his fellow-men, was considered, and the law of slander and libel arose. Man's family relations became a part of the legal conception of his life, and the alienation of a wife's affections was held remediable. Occasionally the law halted, as in its refusal to recognize the intrusion by seduction upon the honor of the family. But even here the demands of society were met. A mean fiction, the action per quod servitium amisit, was resorted to, and by allowing damages for injury to the parents' feelings, an adequate remedy was ordinarily afforded. Similar to the expansion of the right to life was the growth of the legal conception of property. From corporeal property arose the incorporeal rights issuing out of it; and then there opened the wide realm of intangible property, in the products and processes of the mind, as works of literature and art, goodwill, trade secrets, and trademarks.

This development of the law was inevitable. The intense intellectual and emotional life, and the heightening of sensations which came with the advance of civilization, made it clear to men that only a part of the pain, pleasure, and profit of life lay in physical things. Thoughts, emotions, and sensations demanded legal recognition, and the beautiful capacity for growth which char-

Boston Story, 1860–1910 (1989); Morris L. Ernst & Alan U. Schwartz, *Privacy: The Right to Be Let Alone* 45–46 (1962); Philippa Strum, *Brandeis: Beyond Progressivism* (1993); Lewis J. Paper, *Brandeis* (1983); Irwin R. Kramer, *The Birth of Privacy Law: A Century Since Warren and Brandeis*, 39 Cath. U. L. Rev. 703 (1990); Dorothy Glancy, *The Invention of the Right to Privacy*, 21 Ariz. L. Rev. 1, 25–27 (1979); Symposium, *The Right to Privacy One Hundred Years Later*, 41 Case W. Res. L. Rev. 643–928 (1991).

acterizes the common law enabled the judges to afford the requisite protection, without the interposition of the legislature.

Recent inventions and business methods call attention to the next step which must be taken for the protection of the person, and for securing to the individual what Judge Cooley calls the right "to be let alone."[11] Instantaneous photographs and newspaper enterprise have invaded the sacred precincts of private and domestic life; and numerous mechanical devices threaten to make good the prediction that "what is whispered in the closet shall be proclaimed from the house-tops." For years there has been a feeling that the law must afford some remedy for the unauthorized circulation of portraits of private persons; and the evil of invasion of privacy by the newspapers, long keenly felt, has been but recently discussed by an able writer. The alleged facts of a somewhat notorious case brought before an inferior tribunal in New York a few months ago, directly involved the consideration of the right of circulating portraits; and the question whether our law will recognize and protect the right to privacy in this and in other respects must soon come before our courts for consideration.

Of the desirability — indeed of the necessity — of some such protection, there can, it is believed, be no doubt. The press is overstepping in every direction the obvious bounds of propriety and of decency. Gossip is no longer the resource of the idle and of the vicious, but has become a trade, which is pursued with industry as well as effrontery. To satisfy a prurient taste the details of sexual relations are spread broadcast in the columns of the daily papers. To occupy the indolent, column upon column is filled with idle gossip, which can only be procured by intrusion upon the domestic circle. The intensity and complexity of life, attendant upon advancing civilization, have rendered necessary some retreat from the world, and man, under the refining influence of culture, has become more sensitive to publicity, so that solitude and privacy have become more essential to the individual; but modern enterprise and invention have, through invasions upon his privacy, subjected him to mental pain and distress, far greater than could be inflicted by mere bodily injury. Nor is the harm wrought by such invasions confined to the suffering of those who may be the subjects of journalistic or other enterprise. In this, as in other branches of commerce, the supply creates the demand. Each crop of unseemly gossip, thus harvested, becomes the seed of more, and, in direct proportion to its circulation, results in the lowering of social standards and of morality. Even gossip apparently harmless, when widely and persistently circulated, is potent for evil. It both belittles and perverts. It belittles by inverting the relative importance of things, thus dwarfing the thoughts and aspirations of a people. When personal gossip attains the dignity of print, and crowds the space available for matters of real interest to the community, what wonder that the ignorant and thoughtless mistake its relative importance. Easy of comprehension, appealing to that weak side of human nature which is never wholly cast down by the misfortunes and frailties of our neighbors, no one can be surprised that

---

[11] Cooley on Torts, 2d ed., p. 29.

it usurps the place of interest in brains capable of other things. Triviality destroys at once robustness of thought and delicacy of feeling. No enthusiasm can flourish, no generous impulse can survive under its blighting influence.

It is our purpose to consider whether the existing law affords a principle which can properly be invoked to protect the privacy of the individual; and, if it does, what the nature and extent of such protection is.

Owing to the nature of the instruments by which privacy is invaded, the injury inflicted bears a superficial resemblance to the wrongs dealt with by the law of slander and of libel, while a legal remedy for such injury seems to involve the treatment of mere wounded feelings, as a substantive cause of action. The principle on which the law of defamation rests, covers, however, a radically different class of effects from those for which attention is now asked. It deals only with damage to reputation, with the injury done to the individual in his external relations to the community, by lowering him in the estimation of his fellows. The matter published of him, however widely circulated, and however unsuited to publicity, must, in order to be actionable, have a direct tendency to injure him in his intercourse with others, and even if in writing or in print, must subject him to the hatred, ridicule, or contempt of his fellowmen,—the effect of the publication upon his estimate of himself and upon his own feelings nor forming an essential element in the cause of action. In short, the wrongs and correlative rights recognized by the law of slander and libel are in their nature material rather than spiritual. That branch of the law simply extends the protection surrounding physical property to certain of the conditions necessary or helpful to worldly prosperity. On the other hand, our law recognizes no principle upon which compensation can be granted for mere injury to the feelings. However painful the mental effects upon another of an act, though purely wanton or even malicious, yet if the act itself is otherwise lawful, the suffering inflicted is *dannum absque injuria*. Injury of feelings may indeed be taken account of in ascertaining the amount of damages when attending what is recognized as a legal injury; but our system, unlike the Roman law, does not afford a remedy even for mental suffering which results from mere contumely and insult, but from an intentional and unwarranted violation of the "honor" of another.

It is not however necessary, in order to sustain the view that the common law recognizes and upholds a principle applicable to cases of invasion of privacy, to invoke the analogy, which is but superficial, to injuries sustained, either by an attack upon reputation or by what the civilians called a violation of honor; for the legal doctrines relating to infractions of what is ordinarily termed the common-law right to intellectual and artistic property are, it is believed, but instances and applications of a general right to privacy, which properly understood afford a remedy for the evils under consideration.

The common law secures to each individual the right of determining, ordinarily, to what extent his thoughts, sentiments, and emotions shall be communicated to others. Under our system of government, he can never be compelled to express them (except when upon the witness stand); and even if he has chosen to give them expression, he generally retains the power to fix the limits of the publicity which shall be given them. The existence of this right does not depend upon the particular method of expression adopted. It is immaterial whether it be by word or by signs, in painting, by sculpture, or in music. Neither does the existence of the right depend upon the nature or value of the thought or emotions, nor upon the excellence of the means of expression. The same protection is accorded to a casual letter or an entry in a diary and to the most valuable poem or essay, to a botch or daub and to a masterpiece. In every such case the individual is entitled to decide whether that which is his shall be given to the public. No other has the right to publish his productions in any form, without his consent. This right is wholly independent of the material on which, the thought, sentiment, or emotions is expressed. It may exist independently of any corporeal being, as in words spoken, a song sung, a drama acted. Or if expressed on any material, as in a poem in writing, the author may have parted with the paper, without forfeiting any proprietary right in the composition itself. The right is lost only when the author himself communicates his production to the public, — in other words, publishes it. It is entirely independent of the copyright laws, and their extension into the domain of art. The aim of those statutes is to secure to the author, composer, or artist the entire profits arising from publication; but the common-law protection enables him to control absolutely the act of publication, and in the exercise of his own discretion, to decide whether there shall be any publication at all. The statutory right is of no value, unless there is a publication; the common-law right is lost as soon as there is a publication.

What is the nature, the basis, of this right to prevent the publication of manuscripts or works of art? It is stated to be the enforcement of a right of property; and no difficulty arises in accepting this view, so long as we have only to deal with the reproduction of literary and artistic compositions. They certainly possess many of the attributes of ordinary property; they are transferable; they have a value; and publication or reproduction is a use by which that value is realized. But where the value of the production is found not in the right to take the profits arising from publication, but in the peace of mind or the relief afforded by the ability to prevent any publication at all, it is difficult to regard the right as one of property, in the common acceptation of that term. A man records in a letter to his son, or in his diary, that he did not dine with his wife on a certain day. No one into whose hands those papers fall could publish them to the world, even if possession of the documents had been obtained rightfully; and the prohibition would not be confined to the publication of a copy of the letter itself, or of the diary entry; the restraint extends also to a publication of the contents. What is the thing which is protected? Surely, not the intellectual act of recording the fact that the husband did not dine with his wife, but that fact itself. It is not the intellectual product, but the domestic occurrence. A man writes a dozen letters to different people. No person would be permitted to publish a list of the letters written. If the letters or the contents of the diary were protected as literary compositions, the scope of the protection afforded should be the same secured to a published writing under the copyright law. But the copyright law would not prevent an enumeration of the letters, or the publication of some of the facts contained therein. The copyright of a series of paintings or etchings would prevent a reproduction of the paintings as pictures; but it would not prevent a publication of list or even a description of them. Yet in the famous case of *Prince Albert v. Strange*, the court held that the common-law rule prohibited not merely the reproduction of the etchings which the plaintiff and Queen Victoria had made for their own pleasure, but also "the publishing (at least by printing or writing), though not by copy or resemblance, a description of them, whether more or less limited or summary, whether in the form of a catalogue or otherwise." Likewise, an unpublished collection of news possessing no element of a literary nature is protected from privacy.

That this protection cannot rest upon the right to literary or artistic property in any exact sense, appears the more clearly when the subject-matter for which protection is invoked is not even in the form of intellectual property, but has the attributes of ordinary tangible property. Suppose a man has a collection of gems or curiosities which he keeps private: it would hardly be contended that any person could publish a catalogue of them, and yet the articles enumerated are certainly not intellectual property in the legal sense, any more than a collection of stoves or of chairs.

The belief that the idea of property in its narrow sense was the basis of the protection of unpublished manuscripts led an able court to refuse, in several cases, injunctions against the publication of private letters, on the ground that "letters not possessing the attributes of literary compositions are not property entitled to protection;" and that it was "evident the plaintiff could not have considered the letters as of any value whatever as literary productions, for a letter cannot be considered of value to the author which he never would consent to have published." But those decisions have not been followed, and it may not be considered settled that the protection afforded by the common law to the author of any writing is entirely independent of its pecuniary value, its intrinsic merits, or of any intention to publish the same and, of course, also, wholly independent of the material, if any, upon which, or the mode in which, the thought or sentiment was expressed.

Although the courts have asserted that they rested their decisions on the narrow grounds of protection to property, yet there are recognitions of a more liberal doctrine. Thus in the case of *Prince Albert v. Strange*, already referred to, the opinions of both the Vice-Chancellor and of the Lord Chancellor, on appeal, show a more or less clearly defined perception of a principle broader than those which were mainly discussed, and on which they both place their chief reliance. Vice-Chancellor Knight Bruce referred to publishing of a man that he had "written to particular persons or on particular subjects" as an instance of possibly injurious disclosures as to private matters, that the courts would in a proper case prevent; yet it is difficult to perceive how, in such a case, any right of privacy, in the narrow sense, would be drawn in question, or why, if such a publication would be restrained when it threatened to expose the victim not merely to sarcasm, but to ruin, it should not equally be enjoined, if it threatened to embitter his life. To deprive a man of the potential profits to be realized by publishing a catalogue of his gems cannot per se be a wrong to him. The possibility of future profits is not a right of property which the law ordinarily recognizes; it must, therefore, be an infraction of other rights which constitutes the wrongful act, and that infraction is equally wrongful, whether its results are to forestall the profits that the individual himself might secure by giving the matter a publicity obnoxious to him, or to gain an advantage at the expense of his mental pain and suffering. . . .

These considerations lead to the conclusion that the protection afforded to thoughts, sentiments, and emotions, expressed through the medium of writing or of the arts, so far as it consists in preventing publication, is merely an instance of the enforcement of the more general right of the individual to be let alone. It is like the right not be assaulted or beaten, the right not be imprisoned, the right not to be maliciously prosecuted, the right not to be defamed. In each of these rights, as indeed in all other rights recognized by the law, there inheres the quality of being owned or possessed — and (as that is the distinguishing attribute of property) there may some propriety in speaking of those rights as property. But, obviously, they bear little resemblance to what is ordinarily comprehended under that term. The principle which protects personal writings and all other personal productions, not against theft and physical appropriation, but against publication in any form, is in reality not the principle of private property, but that of an inviolate personality.

If we are correct in this conclusion, the existing law affords a principle from which may be invoked to protect the privacy of the individual from invasion either by the too enterprising press, the photographer, or the possessor of any other modern device for rewording or reproducing scenes or sounds. For the protection afforded is not confined by the authorities to those cases where any particular medium or form of expression has been adopted, not to products of the intellect. The same protection is afforded to emotions and sensations expressed in a musical composition or other work of art as to a literary composition; and words spoken, a pantomime acted, a sonata performed, is no less entitled to protection than if each had been reduced to writing. The circumstance that a thought or emotion has been recorded in a permanent form renders its identification easier, and hence may be important from the point of view of evidence, but it has no significance as a matter of substantive right. If, then, the decisions indicate a general right to privacy for thoughts, emotions, and sensations, these should receive the same protection, whether expressed in writing, or in conduct, in conversation, in attitudes, or in facial expression.

It may be urged that a distinction should be taken between the deliberate expression of thoughts and emotions in literary or artistic compositions and the casual and often involuntary expression given to them in the ordinary conduct of life. In other words, it may be contended that the protection afforded is granted to the conscious products of labor, perhaps as an encouragement to effort. This contention, however plausible, has, in fact, little to recommend it. If the amount of labor involved be adopted as the test, we might well find that the effort to conduct one's self properly in business and in domestic relations had been far greater than that involved in painting a picture or writing a book; one would find that it was far easier to express lofty sentiments in a diary than in the conduct of a noble life. If the test of deliberateness of the act be adopted, much casual correspondence which is now accorded full protection would be excluded from the beneficent operation of existing rules. After the decisions denying the distinction attempted to be made between those literary productions which it was intended to publish and those which it was not, all considerations of the amount of labor involved, the degree of deliberation, the value of the product, and the intention of publishing must be abandoned, and no basis is discerned upon which the right to restrain publication and reproduction of such so-called literary and artistic works can be rested, except the right to privacy, as a part of the more general right to the immunity of the person, — the right to one's personality.

It should be stated that, in some instances where protection has been afforded against wrongful publication, the jurisdiction has been asserted, not on the ground of property, or at least not wholly on that ground, but upon the ground of an alleged breach of an implied contract or of a trust or confidence. . . .

This process of implying a term in a contract, or of implying a trust (particularly where a contract is written, and where there is no established usage or custom), is nothing more nor less than a judicial declaration that public morality, private justice, and general convenience demand the recognition of such a rule, and that the publication under similar circumstances would be considered an intolerable abuse. So long as these circumstances happen to present a contract upon which such a term can be engrafted by the judicial mind, or to supply relations upon which a trust or confidence can be erected, there may be no objection to working out the desired protection through the doctrines of contract or of trust. But the court can hardly stop there. The narrower doctrine may have satisfied the demands of society at a time when the abuse to be guarded against could rarely have arisen without violating a contract or a special confidence; but now that modern devices afford abundant opportunities for the perpetration of such wrongs without any participation by the injured party, the protection granted by the law must be placed upon a broader foundation. While, for instance, the state of the photographic art was such that one's picture could seldom be taken without his consciously "sitting" for the purpose, the law of contract or of trust might afford the prudent man sufficient safeguards against the improper circulation of his portrait; but since the latest advances in photographic art have rendered it possible to take pictures surreptitiously, the doctrines of contract and of trust are inadequate to support the required protection, and the law of tort must be resorted to. The right of property in its widest sense, including all possession, including all rights and privileges, and hence embracing the right to an inviolate personality, affords alone that broad basis upon which the protection which the individual demands can be rested.

Thus, the courts, in searching for some principle upon which the publication of private letters could be enjoined, naturally came upon the ideas of a breach of confidence, and of an implied contract; but it required little consideration to discern that this doctrine could not afford all the protection required, since it would not support the court in granting a remedy against a stranger; and so the theory of property in the contents of letters was adopted. Indeed, it is difficult to conceive on what theory of the law the casual recipient of a letter, who proceeds to publish it, is guilty of a breach of contract, express or implied, or of any breach of trust, in the ordinary acceptation of that term. Suppose a letter has been addressed to him without his solicitation. He opens it, and reads. Surely, he has not made any contract; he has not accepted any trust. He cannot, by opening and reading the letter, have come under any obligation save what the law declares; and, however expressed, that obligation is simply to observe the legal right of the sender, whatever it may be, and whether it be called his right or property in the contents of the letter, or his right to privacy. . . .

We must therefore conclude that the rights, so protected, whatever their exact nature, are not rights arising from contract or from special trust, but are rights as against the world; and, as above stated, the principle which has been applied to protect these rights is in reality not the principle of private property, unless that word be used in an extended and unusual sense. The principle which protects personal writings and any other productions of the intellect of or the emotions, is the right to privacy, and the law has no new principle to formulate when it extends this protection to the personal appearance, sayings, acts, and to personal relation, domestic or otherwise.[12]

If the invasion of privacy constitutes a legal *injuria*, the elements for demanding redress exist, since already the value of mental suffering, caused by an act wrongful in itself, is recognized as a basis for compensation.

The right of one who has remained a private individual, to prevent his public portraiture, presents the simplest case for such extension; the right to protect one's self from pen portraiture, from a discussion by the press of one's private affairs, would be a more important and far-reaching one. If casual and unimportant statements in a letter, if handiwork, however inartistic and valueless, if possessions of all sorts are protected not only against reproduction, but also against description and enumeration, how much more should the acts and sayings of a man in his social and domestic relations be guarded from ruthless publicity. If you may not reproduce a woman's face photographically without her consent, how much less should be tolerated the reproduction of her face, her form, and her actions, by graphic descriptions colored to suit a gross and depraved imagination.

The right to privacy, limited as such right must necessarily be, has already found expression in the law of France.

It remains to consider what are the limitations of this right to privacy, and what remedies may be granted for the enforcement of the right. To determine in advance of experience the exact line at which the dignity and convenience of the individual must yield to the demands of the public welfare or of private justice would be a difficult task; but the more general rules are furnished by the

---

[12]The application of an existing principle to a new state of facts is not judicial legislation. To call it such is to assert that the existing body of law consists practically of the statutes and decided cases, and to deny that the principles (of which these cases are ordinarily said to be evidence) exist at all. It is not the application of an existing principle to new cases, but the introduction of a new principle, which is properly termed judicial legislation.

But even the fact that a certain decision would involved judicial legislation should not be taken against the property of making it. This power has been commonly exercised by our judges, when applying to a new subject principles of private justice, moral fitness, and public convenience. Indeed, the elasticity of our law, its adaptability to new conditions, the capacity for growth, which has enabled it to meet the wants of an ever changing society and to apply immediate relief for every recognized wrong, have been its greatest boast. . . .

legal analogies already developed in the law of slander and libel, and in the law of literary and artistic property.

1. The right to privacy does not prohibit any publication of matter which is of public or general interest. In determining the scope of this rule, aid would be afforded by the analogy, in the law of libel and slander, of cases which deal with the qualified privilege of comment and criticism on matters of public and general interest. There are of course difficulties in applying such a rule; but they are inherent in the subject-matter, and are certainly no greater than those which exist in many other branches of the law,—for instance, in that large class of cases in which the reasonableness or unreasonableness of an act is made the test of liability. The design of the law must be to protect those persons with whose affairs the community has no legitimate concern, from being dragged into an undesirable and undesired publicity and to protect all persons, whatsoever; their position or station, from having matters which they may properly prefer to keep private, made public against their will. It is the unwarranted invasion of individual privacy which is reprehended, and to be, so far as possible, prevented. The distinction, however, noted in the above statement is obvious and fundamental. There are persons who may reasonably claim as a right, protection from the notoriety entailed by being made the victims of journalistic enterprise. There are others who, in varying degrees, have renounced the right to live their lives screened from public observation. Matters which men of the first class may justly contend, concern themselves alone, may in those of the second be the subject of legitimate interest to their fellow-citizens. Peculiarities of manner and person, which in the ordinary individual should be free from comment, may acquire a public importance, if found in a candidate for public office. Some further discrimination is necessary, therefore, than to class facts or deeds as public or private according to a standard to be applied to the fact or deed per se. To publish of a modest and retiring individual that he suffers from an impediment in his speech or that he cannot spell correctly, is an unwarranted, if not an unexampled, infringement of his rights, while to state and comment on the same characteristics found in a would-be congressman could not be regarded as beyond the pale of propriety.

The general object in view is to protect the privacy of private life, and to whatever degree and in whatever connection a man's life has ceased to be private, before the publication under consideration has been made, to that extent the protection is likely to be withdrawn. Since, then, the propriety of publishing the very same facts may depend wholly upon the person concerning whom they are published, no fixed formula can be used to prohibit obnoxious publications. Any rule of liability adopted must have in it an elasticity which shall take account of the varying circumstances of each case,—a necessity which unfortunately renders such a doctrine not only more difficult of application, but also to a certain extent uncertain in its operation and easily rendered abortive. Besides, it is only the more flagrant breaches of decency and propriety that could in practice be reached, and it is not perhaps desirable even to attempt to repress everything which the nicest taste and keenest sense of the respect due to private life would condemn.

In general, then, the matters of which the publication should be repressed may be described as those which concern the private life, habits, acts, and relations of an individual, and have no legitimate connection with his fitness for a public office which he seeks or for which he is suggested, or for any public or quasi public position which he seeks or for which he is suggested, and have no legitimate relation to or bearing upon any act done by him in a public or quasi public capacity. The foregoing is not designed as a wholly accurate or exhaustive definition, since that which must ultimately in a vast number of cases become a question of individual judgment and opinion is incapable of such definition; but it is an attempt to indicate broadly the class of matters referred to. Some things all men alike are entitled to keep from popular curiosity, whether in public life or not, while others are only private because the persons concerned have not assumed a position which makes their doings legitimate matters of public investigation.

2. The right to privacy does not prohibit the communication of any matter, though in its nature private, when the publication is made under circumstances which would render it a privileged communication according to the law of slander and libel. Under this rule, the right to privacy is not invaded by any publication made in a court of justice, in legislative bodies, or the committees of those bodies; in municipal assemblies, or the committees of such assemblies, or practically by any communication in any other public body, municipal or parochial, or in any body quasi public, like the large voluntary associations formed for almost every purpose of benevolence, business, or other general interest; and (at least in many jurisdictions) reports of any such proceedings would in some measure be accorded a like privilege. Nor would the rule prohibit any publication made by one in the discharge of some public or private duty, whether legal or moral, or in conduct of one's own affairs, in matters where his own interest is concerned.

3. The law would probably not grant any redress for the invasion of privacy by oral publication in the absence of special damage. The same reasons exist for distinguishing between oral and written publications of private matters, as is afforded in the law of defamation by the restricted liability for slander as compared with the liability for libel. The injury resulting from such oral communications would ordinarily be so trifling that the law might well, in the interest of free speech, disregard it altogether.

4. The right to privacy ceases upon the publication of the facts by the individual, or with his consent.

This is but another application of the rule which has become familiar in the law of literary and artistic property. The cases there decided establish also what should be deemed a publication, — the important principle in this connection being that a private communication of circulation for a restricted purpose is not a publication within the meaning of the law.

5. The truth of the matter published does not afford a defence. Obviously this branch of the law should have no concern with the truth or falsehood of the matters published. It is not for injury to the individual's character that redress or prevention is sought, but for injury to the right of privacy. For the former, the law of slander and libel provides perhaps a sufficient safeguard. The

latter implies the right not merely to prevent inaccurate portrayal of private life, but to prevent its being depicted at all.

6. The absence of "malice" in the publisher does not afford a defence. Personal ill-will is not an ingredient of the offence, any more than in an ordinary case of trespass to person or to property. Such malice is never necessary to be shown in an action for libel or slander at common law, except in rebuttal of some defence, e.g., that the occasion rendered the communication privileged, or, under the statutes in this State and elsewhere, that the statement complained of was true. The invasion of the privacy that is to be protected is equally complete and equally injurious, whether the motives by which the speaker or writer was actuated are taken by themselves, culpable or not; just as the damage to character, and to some extent the tendency to provoke a breach of the peace, is equally the result of defamation without regard to motives leading to its publication. Viewed as a wrong to the individual, this rule is the same pervading the whole law of torts, by which one is held responsible for his intentional acts, even thought they care committed with no sinister intent; and viewed as a wrong to society, it is the same principle adopted in a large category of statutory offences.

The remedies for an invasion of the right of privacy are also suggested by those administered in the law of defamation, and in the law of literary and artistic property, namely:—

1. An action of tort for damages in all cases. Even in the absence of special damages, substantial compensation could be allowed for injury to feelings as in the action of slander and libel.

2. An injunction, in perhaps a very limited class of cases.

It would doubtless be desirable that the privacy of the individual should receive the added protection of the criminal law, but for this, legislation would be required. Perhaps it would be deemed proper to bring the criminal liability for such publication within narrower limits; but that the community has an interest in preventing such invasions of privacy, sufficiently strong to justify the introduction of such a remedy, cannot be doubted. Still, the protection of society must come mainly through a recognition of the rights of the individual. Each man is responsible for his own acts and omissions only. If he condones what he reprobates, with a weapon at hand equal to his defence, he is responsible for the results. If he resists, public opinion will rally to his support. Has he then such a weapon? It is believed that the common law provides him with one, forged in the slow fire of the centuries, and to-day fitly tempered to his hand. The common law has always recognized a man's house as his castle, impregnable, often, even to his own officers engaged in the execution of its command. Shall the courts thus close the front entrance to constituted authority, and open wide the back door to idle or prurient curiosity?

NOTES & COMMENTARY

1. The article argued for the creation of a new right—the right to privacy. Why did the authors believe that other legal claims were inadequate? For

example, why does the law of slander or the law of contracts not provide a sufficient remedy for the harm described by the authors? Why do Warren and Brandeis reject property rights and copyright as tools to protect privacy?

2. How do Warren and Brandeis derive a right to privacy from the common law? Under what principle do they locate this right? Look again at footnote 12, where Warren and Brandeis contend that they are not recommending "judicial legislation." Why do they include this footnote? Do you agree with their argument?

3. The authors describe privacy as not "the principle of private property but that of inviolate personality." What does that mean? What interests are protected by this right? Is this a unified view of privacy or are there differing interests?

4. *"The Right to Be Let Alone."* Warren and Brandeis refer to privacy as "the right to be let alone." This phrase was coined by Judge Thomas Cooley earlier in his famous treatise on torts.[13] Do Warren and Brandeis define what privacy is or elaborate upon what being "let alone" consists of? If so, what do they say privacy is? Is this a good account of what constitutes privacy?

5. The authors conclude: "The common law has always recognized a man's house as his castle, impregnable often, even to its own officers engaged in the execution of its commands. Shall the courts thus close the front entrance to constituted authority and open wide the back door to idle or prurient curiosity?" Which legal principles are contrasted in this description?

6. *The Scope of the Right to Privacy.* Brandeis and Warren were careful not to describe privacy as an absolute right. They set out six limitations on the right to privacy. Consider the first limitation and the relationship between the right to privacy and the need for publication on matters of public concern. What conclusions do the authors reach about these competing claims? According to Warren and Brandeis, would the reporting that a public official engaged in illegal business practices be protected by a right to privacy? What about illicit sexual activity?

7. *Oral and Written Communications.* What is the significance of distinguishing oral communication and written communication? In many parts of the article, Brandeis and Warren appear to argue against technology-based distinctions. Why not follow that approach here?

8. *The Nature of the Injury Caused by Privacy Invasions.* Warren and Brandeis argue that privacy invasions are more harmful than bodily injuries. Do you agree? Warren and Brandeis characterize the injury caused by the violation of privacy as an injury to the feelings. Do you agree? Or do you think that the injury extends beyond an injury to the feelings?

9. *Remedies.* Brandeis and Warren suggest two remedies for an invasion of privacy — an action in tort and injunction. These remedies are similar to those in defamation and copyright. What do the authors say about a criminal remedy?

---

[13] Thomas C. Cooley, *Law of Torts* 29 (2d ed. 1888).

10. *Criticisms.* Some have argued that the article is a defense of bourgeois values, i.e., the freedom of an elite group to avoid public scrutiny.[14] Which aspects of the article support this view? Are there parts of the article which suggest otherwise? Is privacy, as described in the Warren and Brandeis article, a class-based right?

THE DEVELOPMENT OF PRIVACY PROTECTION UNDER THE COMMON LAW

The Privacy Torts. Warren and Brandeis's article had a profound influence on the development of the law of privacy. In the early 1900s, courts and legislatures responded to the Warren and Brandeis article by recognizing a right of privacy in case law and statutory law. In 1960, William Prosser cataloged the several hundred cases decided since the Warren and Brandeis article and concluded that there were four distinct privacy torts.[15] Prosser's classification of these torts survives to this day. The privacy torts are:

(1) *Public Disclosure of Private Facts.* This tort creates a cause of action for one who publicly discloses a private matter that is "highly offensive to a reasonable person" and "is not of legitimate concern to the public." Restatement (second) of Torts § 652D (1977).

(2) *Intrusion upon Seclusion.* This tort provides a remedy when one intrudes "upon the solitude or seclusion of another or his private affairs or concerns" if the intrusion is "highly offensive to a reasonable person." Restatement (second) of Torts § 652B (1977).

(3) *False Light.* This tort creates a cause of action when one publicly discloses a matter that places a person "in a false light" that is "highly offensive to a reasonable person." Restatement (second) of Torts § 652E (1977).

(4) *Appropriation.* Under this tort, a plaintiff has a remedy against one "who appropriates to his own use or benefit the name or likeness" of the plaintiff. Restatement (second) of Torts § 652C (1977).

Today, most states recognize some or all of these torts. These torts will be discussed further in Chapter 2.

Defamation. The law of defamation existed long before Warren and Brandeis's article. Defamation law, consisting of the torts of libel and slander, creates liability when one makes a false statement about a person that harms the person's reputation. The Supreme Court has held that the First Amendment places certain limits on defamation law. Defamation will be discussed in greater detail in Chapter 2.

Infliction of Emotional Distress. The tort of intentional infliction of emotional distress can also serve as a remedy for certain privacy invasions.

---

[14] *See* Donald R. Pember, *Privacy and the Press* (1972).
[15] *See* William L. Prosser, *Privacy*, 48 Cal. L. Rev. 383 (1960).

This tort provides a remedy when one "by extreme and outrageous conduct intentionally or recklessly causes severe emotional distress to another." Restatement (second) of Torts §46 (1977). Since privacy invasions can often result in severe emotional distress, this tort may provide a remedy. However, it is limited by the requirement of "extreme and outrageous conduct."

Evidentiary Privileges. The law of evidence has long recognized privacy as an important goal that can override the truth-seeking function of the trial. Under the common law, certain communications are privileged, and hence cannot be inquired into during a legal proceeding. The law of evidence has recognized the importance of protecting the privacy of communications between attorney and client, priest and penitent, husband and wife, physician and patient, and psychotherapist and patient. Evidentiary privileges will be discussed in more detail in Chapter 3.

Property Rights. Although there are few property laws specifically governing privacy, these laws often implicate privacy. The appropriation tort is akin to a property right, and some commentators suggest that personal information should be viewed as a form of property.[16] Recall, however, that Warren and Brandeis rejected property as an adequate protection for privacy.

Contract Law. Sometimes specific contractual provisions protect against the collection, use, or disclosure of personal information. In certain contexts, courts have entertained actions for breach of implied contract or tort actions based on implicit duties once certain relationships are established, such as physician-patient relationships, which have been analogized to fiduciary relationships. Privacy policies as well as terms of service containing privacy provisions can sometimes be analogized to a contract.

Contract often functions as a way of sidestepping state and federal privacy laws. Many employers make employees consent to drug testing as well as e-mail and workplace surveillance in their employment contracts.

Some commentators advocate a contractual approach to privacy, such as Jerry Kang, who suggests a contractual default rule that limits the way personal information can be used but that can be contracted around by parties who do not desire to be governed by the rule.[17]

Criminal Law. Privacy is also protected by criminal law. The criminal law protects bodily invasions, such as assault, battery, and rape. The privacy of one's home is also protected by criminal sanctions for trespass. Stalking and harassing can give rise to criminal culpability. The crime of blackmail prohibits coercing an individual by threatening to expose her personal secrets. Many of the statutes protecting privacy also contain criminal penalties, such as the statutes pertaining to wiretapping and identity theft.

---

[16] *See, e.g.,* Alan Westin, *Privacy and Freedom* 324 (1967); *see also* Richard S. Murphy, *Property Rights in Personal Information: An Economic Defense of* Privacy, 84 Geo. L.J. 2381 (1996); Richard A. Posner, *The Economics of Justice* (1981); Lawrence Lessig, *Code and Other Laws of Cyberspace* 154–162 (1999).

[17] *See* Jerry Kang, *Information Privacy in Cyberspace Transactions*, 50 Stan. L. Rev. 1193 (1998).

2. CONSTITUTIONAL LAW ROOTS

Federal Constitutional Law. Although the United States' Constitution does not specifically mention privacy, it has a number of provisions that protect privacy, and it has been interpreted as providing a right to privacy. In some instances the First Amendment serves to safeguard privacy. For example, the First Amendment protects the right to speak anonymously. *See McIntyre v. Ohio Election Comm'n*, 514 U.S. 334 (1995). The First Amendment's freedom of association clause protects individuals from being compelled to disclose the groups to which they belong or contribute. Under the First Amendment: "Congress shall make no law . . . abridging . . . the right of the people peaceably to assemble. . . ." For example, the Court has struck down the compulsory disclosure of the names and addresses of an organization's members, *see NAACP v. Alabama*, 357 U.S. 449 (1958), as well as a law requiring public teachers to list all organizations to which they belong or contribute. *See Shelton v. Tucker*, 364 U.S. 479 (1960).

The Third Amendment protects the privacy of the home by preventing the government from requiring soldiers to reside in people's homes: "No Soldier shall, in time of peace be quartered in any house, without the consent of the Owner, nor in time of war, but in a manner to be prescribed by law."

The Fourth Amendment provides that people have the right "to be secure in their persons, houses, papers, and effects, against unreasonable searches and seizures. . . ." Almost 40 years after writing *The Right to Privacy*, Brandeis, then a Supreme Court Justice, wrote a dissent that has had a significant influence on Fourth Amendment law. The case was *Olmstead v. United States*, 277 U.S. 438 (1928), where the Court held that wiretapping was not an invasion of privacy under the Fourth Amendment because it was not a physical trespass into the home. Justice Brandeis dissented, contending that the central interest protected by the Fourth Amendment was not property but the "right to be let alone":

> The protection guaranteed by the amendments is much broader in scope. The makers of our Constitution undertook to secure conditions favorable to the pursuit of happiness. They recognized the significance of man's spiritual nature, of his feelings and of his intellect. They knew that only a part of the pain, pleasure and satisfactions of life are to be found in material things. They sought to protect Americans in their beliefs, their thoughts, their emotions and their sensations. They conferred, as against the government, the right to be let alone — the most comprehensive of rights and the right most valued by civilized men. To protect that right, every unjustifiable intrusion by the government upon the privacy of the individual, whatever the means employed, must be deemed a violation of the Fourth Amendment.

Brandeis's dissent demonstrated that the "right to be let alone" did not merely have common law roots (as he had argued in *The Right to Privacy*) but also had constitutional roots as well in the Fourth Amendment.

Modern Fourth Amendment law incorporates much of Brandeis's view. In *Katz v. United States*, 389 U.S. 347 (1967), the Court held that the Fourth

Amendment "protects people, not places" and said that the police must obtain a warrant when a search takes place in a public pay phone on a public street. The Court currently determines a person's right to privacy by the "reasonable expectations of privacy" test, a standard articulated in Justice Harlan's concurrence to *Katz*. First, a person must "have exhibited an actual (subjective) expectation of privacy" and, second, "the expectation be one that society is prepared to recognize as 'reasonable.'"

The Fifth Amendment guarantees that: "No person . . . shall be compelled in any criminal case to be a witness against himself. . . ." This right, commonly referred to as the privilege against self-incrimination, protects privacy by restricting the ability of the government to force individuals to divulge certain information about themselves.

In the landmark 1965 case *Griswold v. Connecticut*, 318 U.S. 479 (1965), the Court declared that an individual has a constitutional right to privacy. The Court located this right within the "penumbras" or "zones" of freedom created by an expansive interpretation of the Bill of Rights. Subsequently, the Court has handed down an inconsistent line of cases protecting certain fundamental life choices such as abortion but not the right to die, and protecting certain aspects of one's intimate sexual life such as contraception but not homosexual conduct.

In *Whalen v. Roe*, 433 U.S. 425 (1977), the Court extended its substantive due process privacy protection to information privacy, holding that the "zone of privacy" protected by the Constitution encompasses the "individual interest in avoiding disclosure of personal matters." This offshoot of the right to privacy has become known as the "constitutional right to information privacy." It will be covered in more depth in Chapter 3.

State Constitutional Law. A number of states have directly provided for the protection of privacy in their constitutions. For example, the Alaska Constitution provides: "The right of the people to privacy is recognized and shall not be infringed." Alaska Const. art. I, §22. According to the California Constitution: "All people are by their nature free and independent and have inalienable rights. Among these are enjoying and defending life and liberty, acquiring, possessing, and protecting property, and pursuing and obtaining safety, happiness, and privacy." Cal. Const. art. I, §1. Unlike most state constitutional provisions, the California constitutional right to privacy applies not only to state actors but also to private parties. *See, e.g., Hill v. NCAA*, 865 P.2d 638 (Cal. 1994). The Florida Constitution provides: "Every natural person has the right to be let alone and free from governmental intrusion into his private life except as otherwise provided herein." Fla. Const. art. I, §23.[18]

---

[18]For more examples, *see* Ariz. Const. art. II, §8; Mont. Const. art. II, §10; Haw. Const. art. I, §6; Ill. Const. art. I, §§6, 12; La. Const. art. I, §5; S.C. Const. art. I, §10; Wash. Const. art. I, §7. For a further discussion of state constitutional protections of privacy, *see* Timothy O. Lenz, *"Rights Talk" About Privacy in State Courts*, 60 Alb. L. Rev. 1613 (1997); Mark Silverstein, Note, *Privacy Rights in State Constitutions: Models for Illinois?*, 1989 U. Ill. L. Rev. 215.

3. STATUTORY LAW ROOTS

Federal Statutory Law. From the mid-1960s to the mid-1970s, privacy emerged as a central political and social concern. In tune with the heightened attention to privacy, philosophers, legal scholars, and others turned their focus on privacy, raising public awareness about the growing threats to privacy from technology.[19]

In the mid-1960s electronic eavesdropping erupted into a substantial public issue, spawning numerous television news documentaries as well as receiving significant attention in major newspapers. A proposal for a National Data Center in 1965 triggered public protest and congressional hearings. At this time, the computer was a new and unexplored technological tool that raised risks of unprecedented data collection about individuals, with potentially devastating effects on privacy. Indeed, toward the end of the 1960s, the issue of the collection of personal information in databases had become one of the defining social issues of American society.

During this time the Supreme Court announced a number of landmark decisions regarding the right to privacy, including *Griswold v. Connecticut* in 1965 and *Roe v. Wade* in 1973 which were landmark decisions regarding the right to decisional/reproductive privacy and autonomy. The famous reasonable expectations of privacy test in Fourth Amendment jurisprudence emerged in 1967 with *Katz v. United States.*

Due to growing fears about the ability of computers to store and search personal information, Congress devoted increasing attention to the issue of privacy. As Priscilla Regan observes:

> In 1965, a new problem was placed on the congressional agenda by subcommittee chairs in both the House and the Senate. The problem was defined as the invasion of privacy by computers and evoked images of *1984*, the "Computerized Man," and a dossier society. Press interest was high, public concern was generated and resulted in numerous letters being sent to members of Congress, and almost thirty days of congressional hearings were held in the late 1960s and early 1970s.[20]

In 1973, in a highly influential report, the United States Department of Health Education and Welfare (HEW) undertook an extensive review of data processing in the United States. Among many recommendations, the HEW report proposed that a Code of Fair Information Practices be established. The Fair Information Practices consist of a number of basic information privacy principles that allocate rights and responsibilities in the collection and use of personal information:

---

[19] *See, e.g.,* Vance Packard, *The Naked Society* (1964); Myron Brenton, *The Privacy Invaders* (1964); Alan Westin, *Privacy and Freedom* (1967); Arthur Miller, *The Assault on Privacy* (1971); *Nomos XII: Privacy* (J. Ronald Pennock & J.W. Chapman eds. 1971); Alan Westin & Michael A. Baker, *Databanks in a Free Society: Computers, Record-Keeping and Privacy* (1972); Aryeh Neier, *The Secret Files They Keep on You* (1975); Kenneth L. Karst, *"The Files": Legal Controls Over the Accuracy and Accessibility of Stored Personal Data,* 31 L. & Contemp. Probs. 342 (1966); Symposium, *Computers, Data Banks, and Individual Privacy,* 53 Minn. L. Rev. 211–245 (1968); Symposium, *Privacy,* 31 L. & Contemp. Probs. 251–435 (1966).

[20] Priscilla M. Regan, *Legislating Privacy: Technology, Social Values, and Public Policy* 82 (1995).

- There must be no personal-data record-keeping systems whose very existence is secret.
- There must be a way for an individual to find out what information about him is in a record and how it is used.
- There must be a way for an individual to prevent information about him obtained for one purpose from being used or made available for other purposes without his consent.
- There must be a way for an individual to correct or amend a record of identifiable information about him.
- Any organization creating, maintaining, using, or disseminating records of identifiable personal data must assure the reliability of the data for their intended use and must take reasonable precautions to prevent misuse of the data.[21]

As Marc Rotenberg observes, the Fair Information Practices have "played a significant role in framing privacy laws in the United States."[22]

Beginning in the 1970s, Congress has passed a number of laws protecting privacy in various sectors of the information economy:[23]

- Fair Credit Reporting Act of 1970, Pub. L. No. 90-32, 15 U.S.C. §§ 1681–1681t — provides citizens with rights regarding the use and disclosure of their personal information by credit reporting agencies. *See* Chapter 6.
- Privacy Act of 1974, Pub. L. No. 93-579, 5 U.S.C. § 552a — provides individuals with a number of rights concerning their personal information maintained in government record systems, such as the right to see one's records and to ensure that the information in them is accurate. *See* Chapter 6.
- Family Educational Rights and Privacy Act of 1974, Pub. L. No. 93-380, 20 U.S.C. §§ 1221 note, 1232g — protects the privacy of school records. *See* Chapter 7.
- Right to Financial Privacy Act of 1978, Pub. L. No. 95-630, 12 U.S.C. §§ 3401–3422 — requires a subpoena or search warrant for law enforcement officials to obtain financial records. *See* Chapter 6.
- Privacy Protection Act of 1980, Pub. L. No. 96-440, 42 U.S.C. § 2000aa — restricts the government's ability to search and seize the work product of the press and the media. *See* Chapter 4.
- Cable Communications Policy Act of 1984, Pub. L. No. 98-549, 47 U.S.C. § 551 — mandates privacy protection for records maintained by cable companies. *See* Chapter 6.
- Electronic Communications Privacy Act of 1986, Pub. L. No. 99-508 and Pub. L. No. 103-414, 18 U.S.C §§ 2510–2522, 2701–2709 — updates Fed-

---

[21] *See* U.S. Dep't of Health, Education and Welfare, *Secretary's Advisory Committee on Automated Personal Data Systems, Records, Computers, and Rights of Citizens* viii (1973).

[22] Marc Rotenberg, *Fair Information Practices and the Architecture of Privacy (What Larry Doesn't Get)*, Stan. Tech. L. Rev. 1, 44 (2001).

[23] For a comprehensive compendium of these statutes, *see Privacy Law Sourcebook* (Marc Rotenberg ed. 2001).

eral Wiretap Law to respond to the new developments in technology. *See* Chapters 4 and 7.

- Computer Matching and Privacy Protection Act of 1988, Pub. L. No. 100-503, 5 U.S.C. §§ 552a — regulates automated investigations conducted by government agencies comparing computer files. *See* Chapter 6.
- Employee Polygraph Protection Act of 1988, Pub. L. No. 100-347, 29 U.S.C. §§ 2001–2009 — governs the use of polygraphs by private sector employers. *See* Chapter 7.
- Video Privacy Protection Act of 1988, Pub. L. No. 100-618, 18 U.S.C. §§ 2710–2711 — protects the privacy of videotape rental information. *See* Chapter 6.
- Telephone Consumer Protection Act of 1991, Pub. L. No. 102-243, 47 U.S.C. § 227 — provides certain remedies from repeat telephone calls by telemarketers. *See* Chapter 6.
- Driver's Privacy Protection Act of 1994, Pub. L. No. 103-322, 18 U.S.C. §§ 2721–2725 — restricts the states from disclosing or selling personal information in their motor vehicle records. *See* Chapter 6.
- Health Insurance Portability and Accountability Act of 1996, Pub. L. No. 104-191 — gives the Department of Health and Human Services (HHS) the authority to promulgate regulations governing the privacy of medical records. *See* Chapter 3.
- Children's Online Privacy Protection Act of 1998, Pub. L. No. 106-170, 15 U.S.C. §§ 6501–06 — restricts the use of information gathered from children under age 13 by Internet web sites. *See* Chapter 6.
- Gramm-Leach Bliley Act of 1999, Pub. L. No. 106-102, 15 U.S.C. §§ 6801–6809 — requires privacy notices and provides opt-out rights when financial institutions seek to disclose personal data to other companies. *See* Chapter 6.

Not all of Congress's legislation regarding privacy has been protective of privacy. A number of statutes have mandated the government collection of sensitive personal data or facilitated government investigation techniques:

- Bank Secrecy Act of 1970, Pub. L. No. 91-508 — requires banks to maintain reports of people's financial transactions to assist in government white collar investigations. *See* Chapter 6.
- Communications Assistance for Law Enforcement Act of 1994, Pub. L. No. 103-414 — requires telecommunication providers to help facilitate government interceptions of communications and surveillance. *See* Chapter 4.
- Personal Responsibility and Work Opportunity Reconciliation Act of 1996, Pub. L. No. 104-193 — requires the collection of personal information (including Social Security numbers, addresses, and wages) of all people who obtain a new job anywhere in the nation, which will be placed into a national database to help track down deadbeat parents.

State Statutory Law. The states have passed statutes protecting privacy in many contexts, regulating both the public and private sectors. These laws cover a wide range of subjects, from employoment records and medical records to library records and student records. However, less than a third have enacted a general privacy law akin to the Privacy Act.[24] As Paul Schwartz observes, most states lack "omnibus data protection laws."[25]

4. INTERNATIONAL LAW ROOTS

Privacy is a global concern. International law, and more precisely, the privacy laws of other countries and international privacy norms, implicate privacy interests in the United States. For example, commercial firms in the United States must comply with the various standards for global commerce. The Organization of Economic Cooperation and Development (OECD) developed an extensive series of privacy guidelines in 1980 that formed the basis for privacy laws in North America, Europe, and East Asia. In 1995, the European Union issued the *European Community Directive on Data Protection*, which outlines the basic principles for privacy legislation for European Union member countries.[26] The Directive became effective on October 25, 1998.[27] International privacy law will be covered in more depth in Chapter 8.

C. PHILOSOPHICAL PERSPECTIVES

1. THE PHILOSOPHICAL DISCOURSE ABOUT PRIVACY

(a) The Concept of Privacy and the Right to Privacy

At the outset, it is important to distinguish between the concept of privacy and the right of privacy. As Hyman Gross observed, "[t]he law does not determine what privacy is, but only what situations of privacy will be afforded legal protection."[28] Privacy as a concept involves what privacy entails and how it is to be valued. Privacy as a right involves the extent to which privacy is (and should be) legally protected.

While instructive and illuminative, law cannot be the exclusive material for constructing a concept of privacy. Law is the product of the weighing of competing values, and it sometimes embodies difficult trade-offs. In order to determine what the law *should* protect, we cannot merely look to what the law *does* protect.

---

[24] *See* Smith, *Ben Franklin's Web Site, supra*, at 333. For a compilation of state privacy laws, *see* Robert Ellis Smith, *Compilation of State and Federal Privacy Laws* (2002).

[25] Paul M. Schwartz, *Privacy and Participation: Personal Information and Public Sector Regulation in the United States*, 80 Iowa L. Rev. 553, 605 (1995).

[26] *See* Directive of the European Parliament and the Council of Europe on the Protection of Individuals with Regard to the Processing of Personal Data and on the Free Movement of Such Data (1996).

[27] For more information about the EU Data Directive, *see* Paul M. Schwartz & Joel R. Reidenberg, *Data Privacy Law* (1996); Peter P. Swire & Robert E. Litan, *None of Your Business: World Data Flows, Electronic Commerce, and the European Privacy Directive* (1998); Colin J. Bennett, *Regulating Privacy: Data Protection of Public Policy in Europe and the United States* (1992); David H. Flaherty, *Protecting Privacy in Surveillance Societies* (1989).

[28] Hyman Gross, *The Concept of Privacy*, 42 N.Y.U. L. Rev. 34, 36 (1967).

(b) The Public and Private Spheres

A longstanding distinction in philosophical discourse is between the public and private spheres. Some form of boundary between public and private has been maintained throughout the history of Western civilization.[29]

Generally, the public sphere is the realm of life experienced in the open, in the community, and in the world of politics. The private sphere is the realm of life where one retreats to isolation or to one's family. At its core is the world of the home. The private sphere, observes Edward Shils, is a realm where the individual "is not bound by the rules that govern public life. . . . The 'private life' is a secluded life, a life separated from the compelling burdens of public authority."[30]

According to Hannah Arendt, both spheres are essential dimensions of human life:

> . . . In ancient feeling, the privative trait of privacy, indicated in the word itself, was all-important; it meant literally a state of being deprived of something, and even of the highest and most human of man's capacities. A man who lived only a private life, who like the slave was not permitted to enter the public realm, or like the barbarian had chosen not to establish such a realm, was not fully human. We no longer think primarily of deprivation when we use the word "privacy," and this is partly due to the enormous enrichment of the private sphere through modern individualism. . . .
>
> To live an entirely private life means above all to be deprived of things essential to a truly human life: to be deprived of the reality that comes from being seen and heard by others, to be deprived of an "objective" relationship with them that comes from being related to and separated from them through the intermediary of a common world of things, to be deprived of the possibility of achieving something more permanent than life itself. . . .
>
> . . . [T]he four walls of one's private property offer the only reliable hiding place from the common public world, not only from everything that goes on in it but also from its very publicity, from being seen and being heard. A life spent entirely in public, in the presence of others, becomes, as we would say, shallow. While it retains visibility, it loses the quality of rising into sight from some darker ground which must remain hidden if it is not to lose its depth in a very real, non-subjective sense. . . .[31]

John Stuart Mill relied upon a notion of the public/private dichotomy to determine when society should regulate individual conduct. Mill contended that there was a realm where people had social responsibilities and where society could properly restrain people from acting or punish them for their deeds. This realm consisted in acts which were hurtful to others or to which people "may rightfully be compelled to perform; such as to give evidence in a

---

[29] *See* Georges Duby, *Foreword*, in *A History of the Private Life I: From Pagan Rome to Byzantium* viii (Paul Veyne ed. & Arthur Goldhammer trans. 1987); *see also* Jürgen Habermas, *The Structural Transformation of the Public Sphere* (Thomas Burger trans. 1991).

[30] Edward Shils, *Privacy: Its Constitution and Vicissitudes*, 31 L. & Contemp. Probs. 281, 283 (1966).

[31] Hannah Arendt, *The Human Condition* (1958).

court of justice; to bear his fair share in the common defence, or in any other joint work necessary to the interest of the society of which he enjoys the protection."[32] However, "there is a sphere of action in which society, as distinguished from the individual, has, if any, only an indirect interest; comprehending all that portion of a person's life and conduct which affects only himself, or if it also affects others, only with their free, voluntary, and undeceived consent and participation."[33] Conduct within this sphere consists of "self-regarding" acts, and society should not interfere with such acts. As Mill further elaborated:

> . . . I fully admit that the mischief which a person does to himself may seriously affect, both through their sympathies and their interests, those nearly connected with him and, in a minor degree, society at large. When, by conduct of this sort, a person is led to violate a distinct and assignable obligation to any other person or persons, the case is taken out of the self-regarding class, and becomes amenable to moral disapprobation in the proper sense of the term. . . . Whenever, in short, there is a definite damage, or a definite risk of damage, either to an individual or to the public, the case is taken out of the province of liberty, and placed in that of morality or law.
>
> But with regard to the merely contingent, or, as it may be called, constructive injury which a person causes to society, by conduct which neither violates any specific duty to the public, nor occasions perceptible hurt to any assignable individual accept himself; the inconvenience is one which society can afford to bear, for the sake of the greater good of human freedom. . . .[34]

2. THE DEFINITION AND THE VALUE OF PRIVACY

The following excerpts explore the definition and value of privacy. Those who attempt to define privacy seek to describe what privacy constitutes. Over the past four decades, academics have defined privacy as a right of personhood, intimacy, secrecy, limited access to the self, and control over information. However, defining privacy has proven to be quite complicated, and many commentators have expressed great difficulty in defining precisely what privacy is. In the words of one commentator, "even the most strenuous advocate of a right to privacy must confess that there are serious problems of defining the essence and scope of this right."[35] According to Robert Post, "[p]rivacy is a value so complex, so entangled in competing and contradictory dimensions, so engorged with various and distinct meanings, that I sometimes despair whether it can be usefully addressed at all."[36]

Conceptualizing privacy not only involves defining privacy but articulating the value of privacy. The value of privacy concerns its importance — how privacy is to be weighed relative to other interests and values. The excerpts

---

[32] John Stuart Mill, *On Liberty* 12 (1859).

[33] *Id.* at 13

[34] *Id.* at 75-76. *See also* James Fitzjames Stephen, *Liberty, Equality, and Fraternity* 160–162 (1873).

[35] William M. Beaney, *The Right to Privacy and American Law*, 31 L. & Contemp. Probs. 253, 255 (1966).

[36] Robert C. Post, *Three Concepts of Privacy*, 89 Geo. L.J. 2087, 2087 (2001).

that follow attempt to grapple with the complicated task of defining privacy and explaining why privacy is worth protecting.

ALAN WESTIN, *PRIVACY AND FREEDOM*

(1967)

. . . Privacy is the claim of individuals, groups, or institutions to determine for themselves when, how, and to what extent information about them is communicated to others. Viewed in terms of the relation of the individual to social participation, privacy is the voluntary and temporary withdrawal of a person from the general society through physical or psychological means, either in a state of solitude or small-group intimacy or, when among larger groups, in a condition of anonymity or reserve. The individual's desire for privacy is never absolute, since participation in society is an equally powerful desire. Thus each individual is continually engaged in a personal adjustment process in which he balances the desire for privacy with the desire for disclosure and communication of himself to others, in light of the environmental conditions and social norms set by the society in which he lives. The individual does so in the face of pressures from the curiosity of others and from the processes of surveillance that every society sets in order to enforce its social norms. . . .

Recognizing the differences that political and sensory cultures make in setting norms of privacy among modern societies, it is still possible to describe the general functions that privacy performs for individuals and groups in Western democratic nations. Before describing these, it is helpful to explain in somewhat greater detail the four basic states of individual privacy [which are solitude, intimacy, anonymity, and reserve.] . . .

The first state of privacy is solitude; here the individual is separated from the group and freed from the observation of other persons. He may be subjected to jarring physical stimuli, such as noise, odors, and vibrations. His peace of mind may continue to be disturbed by physical sensations of heat, cold, itching, and pain. He may believe that he is being observed by God or some supernatural force, or fear that some authority is secretly watching him. Finally, in solitude he will be especially subject to that familiar dialogue with the mind or conscience. But, despite all these physical or psychological intrusions, solitude is the most complete state of privacy that individuals can achieve.

In the second state of privacy, the individual is acting as part of a small unit that claims and is allowed to exercise corporate seclusion so that it may achieve a close, relaxed, and frank relationship between two or more individuals. Typical units of intimacy are husband and wife, the family, a friendship circle, or a work clique. Whether close contact brings relaxed relations or abrasive hostility depends on the personal interaction of the members, but without intimacy a basic need of human contact would not be met.

The third state of privacy, anonymity, occurs when the individual is in public places or performing public acts but still seeks, and finds, freedom from identification and surveillance. He may be riding a subway, attending a ball game, or walking the streets; he is among people and knows that he is being observed; but unless he is a well-known celebrity, he does not expect to be personally identified and held to the full rules of behavior and role that would operate if he were known to those observing him. In this state the individual is able to merge into the "situational landscape." Knowledge or fear that one is under systematic observation in public places destroys the sense of relaxation and freedom that men seek in open spaces and public arenas. . . .

Still another kind of anonymity is the publication of ideas anonymously. Here the individual wants to present some idea publicly to the community or to a segment of it, but does not want to be universally identified at once as the author — especially not by the authorities, who may be forced to take action if they "know" the perpetrator. The core of each of these types of anonymous action is the desire of individuals for times of "public privacy."

Reserve, the fourth and most subtle state of privacy, is the creation of a psychological barrier against unwanted intrusion; this occurs when the individual's need to limit communication about himself is protected by the willing discretion of those surrounding him. Most of our lives are spend not in solitude or anonymity but in situations of intimacy and in group settings where we are known to others. Even in the most intimate relations, communication of self to others is always incomplete and is based on the need to hold back some parts of one's self as either too personal and sacred or too shameful and profane to express. This circumstance gives rise to what Simmel called "reciprocal reserve and indifference," the relation that creates "mental distance" to protect the personality. This creation of mental distance — a variant of the concept of "social distance" — takes place in every sort of relationship under rules of social etiquette; it expresses the individual's choice to withhold or disclose information — the choice that is the dynamic aspect of privacy in daily interpersonal relations. . . .

This analysis of the various states of privacy is useful in discussing the basic question of the functions privacy performs for individuals in democratic societies. These can also be grouped conveniently under four headings — personal autonomy, emotional release, self-evaluation, and limited and protected communication. . . .

Personal Autonomy. . . . Each person is aware of the gap between what he wants to be and what he actually is, between what the world sees of him and what he knows to be his much more complex reality. In addition, there are aspects of himself that the individual does not fully understand but is slowly exploring and shaping as he develops. Every individual lives behind a mask in this manner; indeed, the first etymological meaning of the word "person" was "mask," indicating both the conscious and expressive presentation of the self to a social audience. If this mask is torn off and the individual's real self bared to a world in which everyone else still wears his mask and believes in masked performances, the individual can be seared by the hot light of selective, forced exposure. . . .

The autonomy that privacy protects is also vital to the development of individuality and consciousness of individual choice in life. . . . This development of individuality is particularly important in democratic societies, since qualities of independent thought, diversity of views, and non-conformity are considered desirable traits for individuals. Such independence requires time for sheltered experimentation and testing of ideas, for preparation and practice in thought and conduct, without fear of ridicule or penalty, and for the opportunity to alter opinions before making them public. The individual's sense that it is he who decides when to "go public" is a crucial aspect of his feeling of autonomy. Without such time for incubation and growth, through privacy, many ideas and positions would be launched into the world with dangerous prematurity. . . .

Emotional Release. Life in society generates such tensions for the individual that both physical and psychological health demand periods of privacy for various types of emotional release. At one level, such relaxation is required from the pressure of playing social roles. Social scientists agree that each person constantly plays a series of varied and multiple roles, depending on his audience and behavioral situation. On any given day a man may move through the roles of stern father, loving husband, car-pool comedian, skilled lathe operator, union steward, water-cooler flirt, and American Legion committee chairman — all psychologically different roles that he adopts as he moves from scene to scene on the social stage. Like actors on the dramatic stage, Goffman has noted, individuals can sustain roles only for reasonable periods of time, and no individual can play indefinitely, without relief, the variety of roles that life demands. There have to be moments "off stage" when the individual can be "himself": tender, angry, irritable, lustful, or dream-filled. . . .

Another form of emotional release is provided by the protection privacy gives to minor non-compliance with social norms. Some norms are formally adopted — perhaps as law — which society really expects many persons to break. This ambivalence produces a situation in which almost everyone does break some social or institutional norms — for example, violating traffic laws, breaking sexual mores, cheating on expense accounts, overstating income-tax deductions, or smoking in rest rooms when this is prohibited. Although society will usually punish the most flagrant abuses, it tolerates the great bulk of the violations as "permissible" deviations. If there were no privacy to permit society to ignore these deviations — if all transgressions were known — most persons in society would be under organizational discipline or in jail, or could be manipulated by threats of such action. The firm expectation of having privacy for permissible deviations is a distinguishing characteristic of life in a free society. At a lesser but still important level, privacy also allows individuals to deviate temporarily from social etiquette when alone or among intimates, as by putting feet on desks, cursing, letting one's face go slack, or scratching wherever one itches.

Another aspect of release is the "safety-valve" function afforded by privacy. Most persons need to give vent to their anger at "the system," "city hall," "the boss," and various others who exercise authority over them, and to do this in the intimacy of family or friendship circles, or in private papers, without fear of being held responsible for such comments. . . . Without the aid of such release in accommodating the daily abrasions with authorities, most people would experience serious emotional pressure. . . .

Limited and Protected Communication. The greatest threat to civilized social life would be a situation in which each individual was utterly candid in his communications with others, saying exactly what he knew or felt at all times. The havoc done to interpersonal relations by children, saints, mental patients, and adult "innocents" is legendary. . . .

Privacy for limited and protected communication has two general aspects. First, it provides the individual with the opportunities he needs for sharing confidences and intimacies with those he trusts — spouse, "the family," personal friends, and close associates at work. The individual discloses because he knows that his confidences will be held, and because he knows that breach of confidence violates social norms in a civilized society. "A friend," said Emerson, "is someone before . . . [whom] I can think aloud." In addition, the individual often wants to secure counsel from persons with whom he does not have to live daily after disclosing his confidences. He seeks professionally objective advice from persons whose status in society promises that they will not later use his distress to take advantage of him. To protect freedom of limited communication, such relationships — with doctors, lawyers, ministers, psychiatrists, psychologists, and others — are given varying but important degrees of legal privilege against forced disclosure. . . .

NOTES & QUESTIONS

1. *Privacy as Control over Information.* A number of theorists, including Westin, conceive of privacy as a form of control over personal information.[37] Consider Charles Fried's definition of privacy:

> At first approximation, privacy seems to be related to secrecy, to limiting the knowledge of others about oneself. This notion must be refined. It is not true, for instance, that the less that is known about us the more privacy we have. Privacy is not simply an absence of information about is in the minds of others; rather it is the *control* we have over information about ourselves.
>
> To refer for instance to the privacy of a lonely man on a desert island would be to engage in irony. The person who enjoys privacy is able to grant or deny access to others. . . .
>
> Privacy, thus, is control over knowledge about oneself. But it is not simply control over the quantity of information abroad; there are modulations in the quality of the knowledge as well. We may not mind that a person knows a general fact about us, and yet feel our privacy invaded if he knows the details. . . .[38]

Is this a compelling definition of privacy?

2. *Privacy as Limited Access to the Self.* Another group of theorists view privacy as a form of limited access to the self. Consider Ruth Gavison:

> . . . Our interest in privacy . . . is related to our concern over our accessibility to others: the extent to which we are known to others, the extent to which others have physical access to us, and the extent to which we are the subject of others' attention. This concept of privacy as concern for limited accessibility enables us to identify when losses of privacy occur. Furthermore, the reasons for which we claim privacy in different situations are simi-

---

[37] *See also* Adam Carlyle Breckenridge, *The Right to Privacy* 1 (1970); Randall P. Bezanson, *The Right to Privacy Revisited: Privacy, News, and Social Change, 1810–1990*, 80 Cal. L. Rev. 1133 (1992). For a critique of privacy as control, *see* Anita L. Allen, *Privacy as Data Control: Conceptual, Practical, and Moral Limits of the Paradigm*, 32 Conn. L. Rev. 861 (2000).

[38] Charles Fried, *Privacy*, 77 Yale L.J. 475 (1968).

lar. They are related to the functions privacy has in our lives: the promotion of liberty, autonomy, selfhood, and human relations, and furthering the existence of a free society. . . .

The concept of privacy suggested here is a complex of these three independent and irreducible elements: secrecy, anonymity, and solitude. Each is independent in the sense that a loss of privacy may occur through a change in any one of the three, without a necessary loss in either of the other two. The concept is nevertheless coherent because the three elements are all part of the same notion of accessibility, and are related in many important ways. . . .[39]

How does this theory of privacy differ from the notion of privacy as "the right to be let alone"? How does it differ from privacy as control over information? How much control should individuals have over access to themselves? Should the decision depend upon each particular person's desires? Or should there be an objective standard—a reasonable degree of control over access?

3. ***Privacy as Intimacy.*** A number of theorists argue that "intimacy" appropriately defines what information or matters are private. For example, Julie Inness argues that "intimacy" is the common denominator in all the matters that people claim to be private. Privacy is "the state of the agent having control over decisions concerning matters that draw their meaning and value from the agent's love, caring, or liking. These decisions cover choices on the agent's part about access to herself, the dissemination of information about herself, and her actions."[40]

Jeffrey Rosen adopts a similar view when he writes:

> . . . Privacy protects us from being misdefined and judged out of context in a world of short attention spans, a world in which information can easily be confused with knowledge. True knowledge of another person is the culmination of a slow process of mutual revelation. It requires the gradual setting aside of social masks, the incremental building of trust, which leads to the exchange of personal disclosures. It cannot be rushed; this is why, after intemperate self-revelation in the heat of passion, one may feel something close to self-betrayal. True knowledge of another person, in all of his or her complexity, can be achieved only with a handful of friends, lovers, or family members. In order to flourish, the intimate relationships on which true knowledge of another person depends need space as well as time: sanctuaries from the gaze of the crowd in which slow mutual self-disclosure is possible.
>
> When intimate personal information circulates among a small group of people who know us well, its significance can be weighed against other aspects of our personality and character. By contrast, when intimate informa-

---

[39] Ruth Gavison, *Privacy and the Limits of Law*, 89 Yale L.J. 421 (1980); *See also* Edward Shils, *Privacy: Its Constitution and Vicissitudes*, 31 L. & Contemp. Probs. 281, 281 (1996); Sissela Bok, *Secrets: On the Ethics of Concealment and Revelation* 10–11 (1982); Ernest Van Den Haag, *On Privacy*, in *Nomos XII: Privacy* 149 (J. Ronald Pennock & J.W. Chapman eds. 1971); Sidney M. Jourard, *Some Psychological Aspects of Privacy*, 31 L. & Contemp. Probs. 307, 307 (1966); David O'Brien, *Privacy, Law, and Public Policy* 16 (1979); Hyman Gross, *The Concept of Privacy*, 42 N.Y.U. L. Rev. 34 (1967).

[40] Julie C. Inness, *Privacy, Intimacy, and Isolation* 56, 58, 63, 64, 67 (1992). For other proponents of privacy as intimacy, *see* Robert S. Gerstein, *Intimacy and Privacy*, in *Philosophical Dimensions of Privacy: An Anthology* 265, 265 (Ferdinand David Schoeman ed., 1984); James Rachels, *Why Privacy Is Important*, in *Philosophical Dimensions of Privacy: An Anthology* 290, 292 (Ferdinand David Schoeman ed., 1984); Tom Gerety, *Redefining Privacy*, 12 Harv. C.R.-C.L. L. Rev. 233 (1977).

tion is removed from its original context and revealed to strangers, we are vulnerable to being misjudged on the basis of our most embarrassing, and therefore most memorable, tastes and preferences. . . . In a world in which citizens are bombarded with information, people form impressions quickly, based on sound bites, and these impressions are likely to oversimplify and misrepresent our complicated and often contradictory characters. . . .[41]

Does "intimacy" adequately separate private matters from public ones? Can something be private but not intimate? Can something be intimate but not private?

JULIE E. COHEN, *EXAMINED LIVES:*
INFORMATIONAL PRIVACY AND THE SUBJECT AS OBJECT

52 Stan. L. Rev. 1373 (2000)

Prevailing market-based approaches to data privacy policy — including "solutions" in the form of tradable privacy rights or heightened disclosure requirements before consent — treat preferences for informational privacy as a matter of individual taste, entitled to no more (and often much less) weight than preferences for black shoes over brown or red wine over white. But the values of informational privacy are far more fundamental. A degree of freedom from scrutiny and categorization by others promotes important noninstrumental values, and serves vital individual and collective ends.

First, informational autonomy comports with important values concerning the fair and just treatment of individuals within society. From Kant to Rawls, a central strand of Western philosophical tradition emphasizes respect for the fundamental dignity of persons, and a concomitant commitment to egalitarianism in both principle and practice. Advocates of strong data privacy protection argue that these principles have clear and very specific implications for the treatment of personally-identified data: They require that we forbid data-processing practices that treat individuals as mere conglomerations of transactional data, or that rank people as prospective customers, tenants, neighbors, employees, or insureds based on their financial or genetic desirability. . . .

Autonomous individuals do not spring full-blown from the womb. We must learn to process information and to draw our own conclusions about the world around us. We must learn to choose, and must learn something before we can choose anything. Here, though, information theory suggests a paradox: "Autonomy" connotes an essential independence of critical faculty and an imperviousness to influence. But to the extent that information shapes behavior, autonomy is radically contingent upon environment and circumstance. . . . Autonomy in a contingent world requires a zone of relative insulation from outside scrutiny and interference — a field of operation within which to engage in the conscious construction of self. The solution to the paradox of contingent autonomy, in other words, lies in a second paradox: To exist in fact as well as in theory, autonomy must be nurtured.

A realm of autonomous, unmonitored choice, in turn, promotes a vital diversity of speech and behavior. The recognition that anonymity shelters

---

[41] Jeffrey Rosen, *The Unwanted Gaze: The Destruction of Privacy in America* 8–9 (2000).

constitutionally-protected decisions about speech, belief, and political and intellectual association — decisions that otherwise might be chilled by unpopularity or simple difference — is part of our constitutional tradition. . . .

The benefits of informational privacy are related to, but distinct from, those afforded by seclusion from visual monitoring. It is well-recognized that respite from visual scrutiny affords individuals an important measure of psychological repose. Within our society, at least, we are accustomed to physical spaces within which we can be unobserved, and intrusion into those spaces is experienced as violating the boundaries of self. But the scrutiny, and the repose, can be informational as well as visual, and this does not depend entirely on whether the behavior takes place "in private." The injury, here, does not lie in the exposure of formerly private behaviors to public view, but in the dissolution of the boundaries that insulate different spheres of behavior from one another. The universe of all information about all record-generating behaviors generates a "picture" that, in some respects, is more detailed and intimate than that produced by visual observation, and that picture is accessible, in theory and often in reality, to just about anyone who wants to see it. In such a world, we all may be more cautious.

The point is not that people will not learn under conditions of no-privacy, but that they will learn differently, and that the experience of being watched will constrain, ex ante, the acceptable spectrum of belief and behavior. Pervasive monitoring of every first move or false start will, at the margin, incline choices toward the bland and the mainstream. The result will be a subtle yet fundamental shift in the content of our character, a blunting and blurring of rough edges and sharp lines. . . . The condition of no-privacy threatens not only to chill the expression of eccentric individuality, but also, gradually, to dampen the force of our aspirations to it. . . .

. . . [T]he insulation provided by informational privacy also plays a subtler, more conservative role in reinforcing the existing social fabric. Sociologist Erving Goffman demonstrated that the construction of social facades to mediate between self and community is both instinctive and expected. Alan Westin describes this social dimension of privacy as "reserve." This characterization, though, seems incomplete. On Goffman's account, the construction of social personae isn't just about withholding information that we don't want others to have. It is about defining the parameters of social interaction in ways that maximize social ease, and thus is about collective as well as individual comfort. We do not need, or even want, to know each other that well. Less information makes routine interactions easier; we are then free to choose, consensually and without embarrassment, the interactions that we wish to treat as less routine. Informational privacy, in short, is a constitutive element of a civil society in the broadest sense of that term. . . .

NOTES & QUESTIONS

1. ***Privacy and Respect for Persons.*** Julie Cohen's theory locates the purpose of privacy as promoting the development of autonomous individuals and, more broadly, civil society. Compare her theory to the following theory by Stanley Benn:

Finding oneself an object of scrutiny, as the focus of another's attention, brings one to a new consciousness of oneself, as something seen through another's eyes. According to [Jean Paul] Sartre, indeed, it is a necessary condition for knowing oneself as anything at all that one should conceive oneself as an object of scrutiny. It is only through the regard of the other that the observed becomes aware of himself as an object, knowable, having a determinate character, in principle predictable. His consciousness of pure freedom as subject, as originator and chooser, is at once assailed by it; he is fixed as *something*—with limited probabilities rather than infinite, indeterminate possibilities. . . .

The underpinning of a claim not to be watched without leave will be more general if it can be grounded in this way on the principle of respect for persons than on a utilitarian duty to avoid inflicting suffering. . . . But respect for persons will sustain an objection even to secret watching, which may do no actual harm at all. Covert observation — spying — is objectionable because it deliberately deceives a person about his world, thwarting, for reasons that *cannot* be his reasons, his attempts to make a rational choice. One cannot be said to respect a man as engaged on an enterprise worthy of consideration if one knowingly and deliberately alters his conditions of action, concealing the fact from him. . . .[42]

How is Cohen's theory similar to and/or different from Benn's?

Benn argues that privacy is a form of respect for persons. By being watched, Benn contends, the observed becomes "fixed as *something*—with limited probabilities rather than infinite indeterminate possibilities." Does Benn adequately capture why surveillance is harmful? Is Benn really concerned about the negative consequences of surveillance on a person's behavior? Or is Benn more concerned about the violation of respect for another?

PAUL M. SCHWARTZ,
PRIVACY AND DEMOCRACY IN CYBERSPACE

52 Vand. L. Rev. 1609 (1999)

. . . Self-determination is a capacity that is embodied and developed through social forms and practices. The threat to this quality arises when private or government action interferes with a person's control of her reasoning process. . . . [P]erfected surveillance of naked thought's digital expression short-circuits the individual's own process of decisionmaking. . . .

The maintenance of a democratic order requires both deliberative democracy and an individual capacity for self-determination. . . . [T]he emerging pattern of information use in cyberspace poses a risk to these two essential values. Our task now is to develop privacy standards that are capable of structuring the right kind of information use. . . .

Most scholars, and much of the law in this area, work around a liberal paradigm that we can term "privacy-control." From the age of computer mainframes in the 1960s to the current reign of the Internet's decentralized net-

---

[42] Stanley I. Benn, *Privacy, Freedom, and Respect for Persons*, from *Nomos XIII: Privacy* (J. Ronald Pennock & J. W. Chapman eds., 1971).

works, academics and the law have gravitated towards the idea of privacy as a personal right to control the use of one's data. . . .

. . . [One flaw with the "privacy-control" paradigm is the "autonomy trap."] [T]he organization of information privacy through individual control of personal data rests on a view of autonomy as a given, preexisting quality. . . .

As a policy cornerstone, however, the idea of privacy-control falls straight into the "autonomy trap." The difficulty with privacy-control in the Information Age is that individual self-determination is itself shaped by the processing of personal data. . . .

To give an example of an autonomy trap in cyberspace, the act of clicking through a "consent" screen on a Web site may be considered by some observers to be an exercise of self-reliant choice. Yet, this screen can contain boilerplate language that permits all further processing and transmission of one's personal data. Even without a consent screen, some Web sites place consent boilerplate within a "privacy statement" on their home page or elsewhere on their site. For example, the online version of one New York newspaper states, "By using this site, you agree to the Privacy Policy of the New York Post." This language presents the conditions for data processing on a take-it-or-leave-it basis. It seeks to create the legal fiction that all who visit this Web site have expressed informed consent to its data processing practices. An even more extreme manifestation of the "consent trap" is a belief that an initial decision to surf the Web itself is a self-reliant choice to accept all further use of one's personal data generated by this activity. . . .

The liberal ideal views autonomous individuals as able to interact freely and equally so long as the government or public does not interfere. The reality is, however, that individuals can be trapped when such glorification of freedom of action neglects the actual conditions of choice. Here, another problem arises with self-governance through information-control: the "data seclusion deception." The idea of privacy as data seclusion is easy to explain: unless the individual wishes to surrender her personal information, she is to be free to use her privacy right as a trump to keep it confidential or to subject its release to conditions that she alone wishes to set. The individual is to be at the center of shaping data anonymity. Yet, this right to keep data isolated quickly proves illusory because of the demands of the Information Age. . . .

NOTES & QUESTIONS

1. *Privacy and Personhood.* Like Schwartz, a number of theorists argue that privacy is essential for self-development. According to Jeffrey Reiman, privacy "protects the individual's interest in becoming, being, and remaining a person."[43] The notion that privacy protects personhood or identity is captured in Warren and Brandeis's notion of "inviolate personality." How does privacy promote self-development?

---

[43]Jeffrey H. Reiman, *Privacy, Intimacy, and Personhood,* in *Philosophical Dimensions of Privacy: An Anthology* 300, 308 (Ferdinand David Schoeman, ed. 1984).

Consider the following: "Every acceptance of a public role entails the repression, channelizing, and deflection of 'private' or personal attention, motives, and demands upon the self in order to address oneself to the expectations of others."[44] Can we really be ourselves in the public sphere? Is our "public self" any less part of our persona than our "private self"?

2. ***Privacy and Democracy.*** Schwartz views privacy as essential for a democratic society. Why is privacy important for political participation? Do you agree with Schwartz?

3. ***Privacy and Role Playing.*** Recall Westin's view of selfhood:

> Each person is aware of the gap between what he wants to be and what he actually is, between what the world sees of him and what he knows to be his much more complex reality. In addition, there are aspects of himself that the individual does not fully understand but is slowly exploring and shaping as he develops. Every individual lives behind a mask in this manner; indeed, the first etymological meaning of the word "person" was "mask," indicating both the conscious and expressive presentation of the self to a social audience. If this mask is torn off and the individual's real self bared to a world in which everyone else still wears his mask and believes in masked performances, the individual can be seared by the hot light of selective, forced exposure.

Is there a "true" or "core" or "authentic" self? Or do we perform many roles and perhaps have multiple selves? Is there a self beneath the roles that we play?

4. Schwartz criticizes the conception of privacy as control over information. Why? What are the problems of viewing privacy as a right to control personal information?

5. What is the relationship, according to these authors, between privacy and autonomy? Can one exist without the other?

6. Is there a core characteristic common in all the things we understand as being "private"? If so, what do you think it is?

Daniel Solove contends that "most theorists attempt to conceptualize privacy by isolating one or more common 'essential' or 'core' characteristics of privacy." He critiques this method of conceptualizing privacy as yielding conceptions of privacy that are either too narrow or too broad. In contrast, Solove argues:

> . . . [P]rivacy is better understood by drawing from Ludwig Wittgenstein's notion of "family resemblances" in his famous work *Philosophical Investigations*. As Wittgenstein suggests, certain concepts might not have a single common characteristic; rather they draw from a common pool of similar elements, "a complicated network of similarities overlapping and criss-crossing; sometimes overall similarities, sometimes similarities of detail." . . .
>
> . . . [P]rivacy is not reducible to a set of neutral conditions that apply to all matters we deem private. Rather, to say that a particular matter is "private" or to talk about "privacy" in the abstract is to make a generalization

---

[44] Joseph Bensman & Robert Lilienfeld, *Between Public and Private: Lost Boundaries of the Self* 174 (1979).

about particular practices. These practices are a product of history and culture. Therefore, we should explore what it means for something to be private contextually by looking at particular practices.[45]

Can privacy be more adequately conceptualized by shifting away from the quest to find the common core characteristics of privacy?[46]

3. CRITICS OF PRIVACY

AMITAI ETZIONI, *THE LIMITS OF PRIVACY*

(1999)

. . . Although we cherish privacy in a free society, we also value other goods. Hence, we must address the moral, legal, and social issues that arise when serving the common good entails violating privacy.

When I mentioned the subject of this book to audiences of friends, students in my classes, and members of the public, initially they were all taken aback. Privacy, they pointed out, is under siege, if not already overrun. Given privacy's great importance to a free people, my listeners stressed, one should seek new ways to shore it up, not cast more aspersions on it.

To begin a new dialogue about privacy, I have asked these and similar audiences if they would like to know whether the person entrusted with their child care is a convicted child molester. I mention that when such screening is done, thousands are found to have criminal records, ones that include pedophilia. I further ask: Would they want to know whether the staff of a nursing home in which their mother now lives have criminal records that include abusing the elderly? I note that 14 percent of such employees are found to have criminal records, some of which include violent acts against senior citizens. And should public authorities be entitled to determine whether drivers of school buses, pilots, or police officers are under the influence of illegal drugs? Should the FBI be in a position to crack the encryption messages employed by terrorists before they use them to orchestrate the next Oklahoma City bombing? Addressing such concerns raises the question of if and when we are justified in implementing measures that diminish privacy in the service of the common good. . . .

Communitarianism holds that a good society seeks a carefully crafted balance between individual rights and social responsibilities, between liberty and the common good. . . .

. . . [T]he next step is to apply this principle to actual societies. We can then ask whether a particular society, in a given period, leans too far in one

---

[45] Daniel J. Solove, *Conceptualizing Privacy*, 90 Cal. L. Rev. 1087 (2002).

[46] For additional reading about philosophical theories of privacy, *see* Judith W. DeCew, *In Pursuit of Privacy: Law, Ethics, and the Rise of Technology* (1997) (surveying and critiquing various theories of privacy); Anita L. Allen, *Uneasy Access: Privacy for Women in a Free Society* (1988) (same); Ferdinand D. Schoeman, ed., *Philosophical Dimensions of Privacy* (1984) (anthology of articles about the concept of privacy).

direction or the other. In a society that strongly enforces social duties but neglects individual rights (as does Japan, for instance, when it comes to the rights of women, minorities, and the disabled), strenuously fostering the other side in order to achieve balance would entail the expansion of autonomy. Indeed, even in the West, when John Locke, Adam Smith, and John Stuart Mill wrote their influential works, and for roughly the first 190 years of the American republic, the struggle to expand the realm of individual liberty was extremely justified, and there was little reason to be concerned that social responsibilities would be neglected. However, as communitarians have repeatedly noted, the relationship between rights and responsibilities drastically shifted in American society between 1960 and 1990 as a new emphasis on personal autonomy and individualism gradually overwhelmed other societal considerations. . . .

. . . *[T]he best way to curtail the need for governmental control and intrusion is to have somewhat less privacy.* This point requires some elaboration.

The key to understanding this notion lies in the importance, especially to communitarians, of the "third realm." This realm is not the state or the market (or individual choices), but rather the community, which relies on subtle social fostering of prosocial conduct by such means as communal recognition, approbation, and censure. These processes require the scrutiny of some behavior, not by police or secret agents, but by friends, neighbors, and fellow members of voluntary associations. . . .

. . . [P]ublicness reduces the need for public control, while excessive privacy often necessitates state-imposed limits on private choices. . . .

NOTES & QUESTIONS

1. *Privacy and the Common Good.* Is Etzioni correct in viewing privacy as in tension with the common good? In what ways might privacy serve the common good? Consider the following argument from Priscilla Regan:

   . . . The philosophical basis of privacy policy overemphasizes the importance of privacy to the individual and fails to recognize the broader social importance of privacy. This emphasis of privacy as an individual right or an individual interest provides a weak basis for formulating policy to protect privacy. When privacy is defined as an individual right, policy formulation entails a balancing of the individual right to privacy against a competing interest or right. In general, the competing interest is recognized as a social interest. For example, the police interest in law enforcement, the government interest in detecting fraud, and an employer's interest in securing an honest work force are discussed and defined as societal interests. It is also assumed that the individual has a stake in these societal interests. As a result, privacy has been on the defensive, with those alleging a privacy invasion bearing the burden of proving that a certain activity does indeed invade privacy and that the "social" benefit to be gained from the privacy invasion is less important than the individual harm incurred. . . .

   Privacy is a *common value* in that all individuals value some degree of privacy and have some common perceptions about privacy. Privacy is also a *public value* in that it has value not just to the individual as an individual or to all individuals in common but also to the democratic political system. . . .

> A public value of privacy derives not only from its protection of the individual as an individual but also from its usefulness as a restraint on the government or on the use of power. . . .[47]

3. Consider once again the characterization of privacy set out by Brandeis and Warren. Does this strengthen or undermine the various communal interests described by Etzioni?

4. *Reductionists.* Some theorists, referred to as "reductionists," assert that privacy can be reduced to other concepts and rights. For example, Judith Jarvis Thomson contends that there is nothing particularly distinctive about privacy and to talk about things as violating the "right to privacy" is not all that useful. Privacy is really a cluster of other rights, such as the right to liberty, property rights, and the right not to be injured: "[T]he right to privacy is everywhere overlapped by other rights."[48] Is there something distinctive about privacy? Or can privacy be explained in terms of other, more primary rights and interests? What does privacy capture that these other rights and interests (autonomy, property, liberty, etc.) do not?

4. ECONOMIC ANALYSIS OF PRIVACY

Richard A. Posner, *The Right of Privacy*

12 Ga. L. Rev. 393 (1978)

. . . Prying enables one to form a more accurate picture of a friend or colleague, and the knowledge gained is useful in one's social or professional dealings with him. For example, in choosing a friend one legitimately wants to know whether he will be discreet or indiscreet, selfish or generous, and these qualities are not always apparent on initial acquaintance. Even a pure altruist needs to know the (approximate) wealth of any prospective beneficiary of his altruism in order to be able to gauge the value of a transfer to him.

The other side of the coin is that social, like business, dealings present opportunities for exploitation through misrepresentation. Psychologists and sociologists have pointed out that even in every day life people try to manipulate by misrepresentation other people's opinion of them. As one psychologist has written, the "wish for privacy expresses a desire . . . to control others' perceptions and beliefs vis-à-vis the self-concealing person." Even the strongest defenders of privacy describe the individual's right to privacy as the right to "control the flow of information about him." A seldom remarked corollary to a right to misrepresent one's character is that others have a legitimate interest in unmasking the deception. . . .

Much of the demand for privacy, however, concerns discreditable information, often information concerning past or present criminal activity or moral conduct at variance with a person's professed moral standards. And often the motive for concealment is, as suggested earlier, to mislead those with whom

---

[47] Priscilla M. Regan, *Legislating Privacy: Technology, Social Values, and Public Policy* 213, 225 (1995).

[48] Judith Jarvis Thomson, *The Right to Privacy*, 4 Philosophy & Public Affairs 295 (1975).

he transacts. Other private information that people wish to conceal, while not strictly discreditable, would if revealed correct misapprehensions that the individual is trying to exploit, as when a worker conceals a serious health problem from his employer or a prospective husband conceals his sterility from his fiancée. It is not clear why society should assign the property right in such information to the individual to whom it pertains; and the common law, as we shall see, generally does not. . . .

We think it wrong (and inefficient) that the law should permit a seller in hawking his wares to make false or incomplete representations as to their quality. But people "sell" themselves as well as their goods. They profess high standards of behavior in order to induce others to engage in social or business dealings with them from which they derive an advantage but at the same time they conceal some of the facts that these acquaintances would find useful in forming an accurate picture of their character. There are practical reasons for not imposing a general legal duty of full and frank disclosure of one's material. . . .

. . . [E]veryone should be allowed to protect himself from disadvantageous transactions by ferreting out concealed facts about individuals which are material to the representations (implicit or explicit) that those individuals make concerning their moral qualities.

It is no answer that such individuals have "the right to be let alone." Very few people want to be let alone. They want to manipulate the world around them by selective disclosure of facts about themselves. . . .

NOTES & QUESTIONS

1. What is Posner's definition of privacy? How does Posner determine the value of privacy (i.e., how it should be weighed relative to other interests and values)? In what circumstances is Posner likely to defend a privacy claim?

2. One economic argument for privacy is that sometimes people form irrational judgments based upon learning certain information about others. For example, an employer may not hire certain people based on their political views or associations, sexual orientation, mental illness, and prior criminal convictions — even though these facts may have no relevance to a potential employee's abilities to do the job. These judgments decrease efficiency. Posner, in his book, *The Economics of Justice*, offers a response:

   This objection overlooks the opportunity costs of shunning people for stupid reasons, or, stated otherwise, the gains from dealing with someone whom others shun irrationally. If ex-convicts are good workers but most employers do not know this, employers who do know will be able to hire them at a below-average wage because of their depressed job opportunities and will thereby obtain a competitive advantage over the bigots. In a diverse, decentralized, and competitive society, irrational shunning will be weeded out over time. . . .[49]

   Will the market be able to eradicate irrational judgments?

---

[49] Richard A. Posner, *The Economics of Justice* (1981). Posner further develops his theories about privacy in Richard A. Posner, *Overcoming Law* 531–551 (1995). Posner first set out his views on privacy in Richard A. Posner, *An Economic Theory of Privacy*, Regulations (May/June 1978).

3. Contrast Posner's view of gossip with the one set out by Brandeis and Warren. What are the costs and benefits of gossip?

4. Consider the following critique of Posner by Edward Bloustein:

> We must remember that Posner stated in *Economic Analysis of Law* that economics "cannot prescribe social change"; it can only tell us about the economic costs of managing it one way or another. . . . [Posner's] characterization of the privacy of personal information as a species of commercial fraud . . . [is an] extension[ ] of a social value judgment rather than implications or conclusions of economic theory. . . .
>
> Our society, in fact, places a very high value on maintaining individual privacy, even to the extent of concealing "discreditable" information. . . .[50]

RICHARD S. MURPHY, *PROPERTY RIGHTS IN PERSONAL INFORMATION: AN ECONOMIC DEFENSE OF PRIVACY*

84 Geo L.J. 2381 (1996)

. . . Privacy rules permit the satisfaction of private preferences. An activity that may generate embarrassment or reprobation from some sectors of society will not occur if the activity carries with it a significant risk of being disclosed. Purchasing contraceptives is one obvious example. Another is watching an X-rated video in a hotel. If the hotel identifies the video on the bill to the customer, that video will not be watched. . . .

Given anonymity, people will do what they want. The Internet provides us with a natural experiment in this regard. The extent of pornography and graphic conversation on the Internet is widely known. A brief tour of the World Wide Web will turn up hundreds of sex-based topics, from tame to unusual to hard-core, and apparently these topics are among the most popular on the Internet. When the cost — namely, reproach or embarrassment — of engaging in certain behavior is eliminated through privacy protection, the demand for that behavior skyrockets.

Is this a good thing or a bad thing? From an economic perspective, unless one makes an evaluation that a given subjective preference is detrimental (as with child pornography), the satisfaction of private preferences weighs on the positive side of the scale. True, the suppression of the fact that a person engages in such activity may permit deception, but only ex post. If I am correct that ex ante, the activity will not be engaged in in the absence of privacy protection, then there is no economic argument for disclosure.

Further, demarcating a relatively large sphere for the private self creates an opportunity for discovery or actualization of a "true" nature, which may have a value beyond the utility of satisfying preferences. In his latest book, Posner argues, in true pragmatic fashion, that there is no "true" self or at least that the private self is no more "true" than the public self. I do not agree, but, even accepting this statement, surely there is value in a purely, or almost purely, pri-

---

[50] Edward J. Bloustein, *Privacy Is Dear at Any Price: A Response to Professor Posner's Economic Theory*, 12 Ga. L. Rev. 429, 441 (1978). For another critique of Posner's approach, *see* Kim Lane Scheppele, *Legal Secrets: Equality and Efficiency in the Common Law* (1988).

vate self. For one thing, it fosters experimentation. As Roger Rosenblatt put it, "Out of our private gropings and self-inspections grow our imaginative values — private language, imagery, memory. In the caves of the mind one bats about to discover a light entirely of one's own which, though it should turn out to be dim, is still worth a life." Unless a person can investigate without risk of reproach what his own preferences are, he will not be able to maximize his own happiness. . . .[51]

NOTES & QUESTIONS

1. How would Murphy respond to Posner's argument that privacy is a way for people "to manipulate the world around them by selective disclosure of facts about themselves"? Can less information ever be economically efficient?

5. THE FEMINIST PERSPECTIVE ON PRIVACY

Reva B. Siegel, *"The Rule of Love":*
Wife Beating as Prerogative and Privacy

105 Yale L.J. 2117 (1996)

. . . The Anglo-American common law originally provided that a husband, as master of his household, could subject his wife to corporal punishment or "chastisement" so long as he did not inflict permanent injury upon her. During the nineteenth century, an era of feminist agitation for reform of marriage law, authorities in England and the United States declared that a husband no longer had the right to chastise his wife. Yet, for a century after courts repudiated the right of chastisement, the American legal system continued to treat wife beating differently from other cases of assault and battery. While authorities denied that a husband had the right to beat his wife, they intervened only intermittently in cases of marital violence: Men who assaulted their wives were often granted formal and informal immunities from prosecution, in order to protect the privacy of the family and to promote "domestic harmony." In the late 1970s, the feminist movement began to challenge the concept of family privacy that shielded wife abuse, and since then, it has secured many reforms designed to protect women from marital violence. . . .

Until the late nineteenth century, Anglo-American common law structured marriage to give a husband superiority over his wife in most aspects of the relationship. By law, a husband acquired rights to his wife's person, the value of her paid and unpaid labor, and most property she brought into the marriage. A wife was obliged to obey and serve her husband, and the husband was subject to a reciprocal duty to support his wife and represent her within the legal system. . . .

---

[51] Richard S. Murphy, *Property Rights in Personal Information: An Economic Defense of Privacy*, 84 Geo L.J. 2381, 2397–2398 (1996).

As master of the household, a husband could command his wife's obedience, and subject her to corporal punishment or "chastisement" if she defied his authority. In his treatise on the English common law, Blackstone explained that a husband could "give his wife moderate correction." . . . .

During the 1850s, woman's rights advocates organized numerous conventions throughout the Northeast and Midwest, published newspapers, and conducted petition campaigns seeking for women the right to vote and demanding various reforms of marriage law. And in time the movement did elicit a response. Legislatures and courts began to modify the common law of marital status — first giving wives the right to hold property in marriage, and then the right to their earnings and the rudiments of legal agency: the right to file suit in their own names and to claim contract and tort damages. . . .

. . . By the 1880s, prominent members of the American Bar Association advocated punishing wife beaters at the whipping post, and campaigned vigorously for legislation authorizing the penalty. Between 1876 and 1906, twelve states and the District of Columbia considered enacting legislation that provided for the punishment of wife beaters at the whipping post. The bills were enacted in Maryland (1882), Delaware (1901), and Oregon (1906). . . .

We are left with a striking portrait of legal change. Jurists and lawmakers emphatically repudiated the doctrine of marital chastisement, yet responded to marital violence erratically — often condoning it, and condemning it in circumstances suggesting little interest in the plight of battered wives. Given this record, how are we to make sense of chastisement's demise? . . .

A key concept in the doctrinal regime that emerged from chastisement's demise was the notion of marital privacy. During the antebellum era, courts began to invoke marital privacy as a supplementary rationale for chastisement, in order to justify the common law doctrine within the discourse of companionate marriage, when rationales rooted in authority-based discourses of marriage had begun to lose their persuasive power. . . .

To quote a North Carolina chastisement opinion:

> We know that a slap on the cheek, let it be as light as it may, indeed any touching of the person of another in a rude or angry manner — is in law an assault and battery. In the nature of things it cannot apply to persons in the marriage state, it would break down the great principle of mutual confidence and dependence; throw open the bedroom to the gaze of the public; and spread discord and misery, contention and strife, where peace and concord ought to reign. It must be remembered that rules of law are intended to act in all classes of society. . . .

In *Rhodes*, the defendant whipped his wife "three licks, with a switch about the size of one of his fingers (but not as large as a man's thumb)"; the trial court ruled that a husband had the right to chastise his wife and so was not guilty of assault and battery. On appeal, the North Carolina Supreme Court upheld the verdict but justified it on different grounds. Opening its opinion with the blunt observation that "[t]he violence complained of would without question have constituted a battery if the subject of it had not been the defendant's wife," the court explained why it would not find the defendant guilty:

> The courts have been loath to take cognizance of trivial complaints arising out of the domestic relations — such as master and apprentice, teacher and pupil,

parent and child, husband and wife. Not because those relations are not subject to law, but because the evil of publicity would be greater than the evil involved in the trifles complained of; and because they ought to be left to family government. . . .

. . . By now it should be clear enough how privacy talk was deployed in the domestic violence context to enforce and preserve authority relations between man and wife. . . .

. . . By the early twentieth century, numerous state supreme courts had barred wives from suing their husbands for intentional torts — typically on the grounds that "the tranquility of family relations" would be "disturb[ed]" . . . .

It was not until the late 1970s that the contemporary women's rights movement mounted an effective challenge to this regime. Today, after numerous protest activities and law suits, there are shelters for battered women and their children, new arrest procedures for police departments across the country, and even federal legislation making gender-motivated assaults a civil rights violation. . . .

There is remarkably little scholarship on the social history of privacy discourses; consequently, we know very little about the ways in which conceptions of privacy shaped popular understandings of marriage, or marital violence, in the nineteenth century. But there is no reason to assume that, before demise of the chastisement prerogative, married persons understood a traditional prerogative of marriage, rooted in notions of a husband's authority as master and head of his household, in a framework of "privacy" and "domestic harmony." It seems just as likely that legal elites devised the story linking "privacy" and "domestic harmony" to wife beating in the wake of chastisement's demise (or in anticipation of it). . . .

CATHARINE A. MACKINNON,
TOWARD A FEMINIST THEORY OF THE STATE

(1989)

The liberal ideal of the private holds that, as long as the public does not interfere, autonomous individuals interact freely and equally. Privacy is the ultimate value of the negative state. Conceptually, this private is hermetic. It means that which is inaccessible to, unaccountable to, unconstructed by, anything beyond itself. By definition, it is not part of or conditioned by anything systematic outside it. It is personal, intimate, autonomous, particular, individual, the original source and final outpost of the self, gender neutral. It is defined by everything that feminism reveals women have never been allowed to be or to have, and by everything that women have been equated with and defined in terms of men's ability to have. To complain in public of inequality within the private contradicts the liberal definition of the private. . . . Its inviolability by the state, framed as an individual right, presupposes that the private is not already an arm of the state. In this scheme, intimacy is implicitly thought to guarantee symmetry of power. Injuries arise through violation of the private sphere, not within and by and because of it.

In private, consent tends to be presumed. Showing coercion is supposed to avoid this presumption. But the problem is getting anything private to be perceived as coercive. This is an epistemic problem of major dimensions and explains why privacy doctrine is most at home at home, the place women experience the most force, in the family, and why it centers on sex. Why a person would "allow" force in private (the "why doesn't she leave" question raised to battered women) is a question given its insult by the social meaning of the private as a sphere of choice. For women the measure of the intimacy has been the measure of oppression. This is why feminism has seen the personal as the political. The private is public for those for whom the personal is political. In this sense, for women there is no private, either normatively or empirically. Feminism confronts the fact that women have no privacy to lose or to guarantee. Women are not inviolable. Women's sexuality is not only violable, it is — hence, women are — seen in and as their violation. To confront the fact that women have no privacy is to confront the intimate degradation of women as the public order. . . .

When the law of privacy restricts intrusions into intimacy, it bars changes in control over that intimacy through law. The existing distribution of power and resources within the private sphere are precisely what the law of privacy exists to protect. . . . [T]he legal concept of privacy can and has shielded the place of battery, marital rape, and women's exploited domestic labor. It has preserved the central institutions whereby women are deprived of identity, autonomy, control, and self-definition. It has protected a primary activity through which male supremacy is expressed and enforced. . . .

This right to privacy is a right of men "to be let alone" to oppress women one at a time. . . .

ANITA L. ALLEN, *UNEASY ACCESS: PRIVACY FOR WOMEN IN A FREE SOCIETY*

(1988)

Critiques of privacy such as MacKinnon's go wrong at the point where the historic unequal treatment of women and the misuse of the private household to further women's domination is taken as grounds for rejecting either the condition of privacy itself or the long-overdue legal rights to effective decisionmaking that promote and protect that condition. Privacy, here broadly defined as the inaccessibility of persons, their mental states, or information about them to the senses and surveillance devices of others . . . does not pose an inherent threat to women. Nor do sex, love, marriage, and children any longer presume the total abrogation of the forms of privacy a woman might otherwise enjoy. On the contrary, women today are finally in a position to expect, experience, and exploit real privacy within the home and within heterosexual relationships. The women's movement, education, access to affordable birth control, liberalized divorce laws, and the larger role for women in politics, government, and the economy have expanded women's opinions and contributed to the erosion of oppressively nonegalitarian styles of home life. These advances have enhanced the capacity of American men and women, but especially and for the first time women, to secure conditions of adequate and meaningful privacy at home paramount to moral personhood and responsible participation in families and larger segments of society. Instead of rejecting privacy as "male ideology" and subjugation, women can and ought to embrace opportunities for privacy and the exercise of reproductive liberty in their private lives.

NOTES & QUESTIONS

1. Reva Siegel points out the troubling use of privacy to protect the oppression of women in the home, which Catharine MacKinnon has discussed at length elsewhere. Is MacKinnon's negative response to the public/private distinction justifiable given the prior uses of this distinction? Or do you agree with Anita Allen that privacy can and should not be abandoned as a value despite its checkered past?[52]
2. Does the right to privacy described by Warren and Brandeis apply equally to men and women?[53]

D. PROTECTING PRIVACY: TECHNOLOGY AND POLICY

1. PRIVACY AND TECHNOLOGY

We live in a society of rapidly advancing technology. Many technologies enable new forms of monitoring and recording. In 1890, Warren and Brandeis were concerned about new technological developments in photography. Today's technological developments far outpace those that Warren and Brandeis considered. However, technology is not just a threat to privacy; it may also provide a means to protect privacy. Below is a brief survey of some of the technologies that threaten and enhance privacy:

VIDEO SURVEILLANCE TECHNOLOGIES

Surveillance Cameras. Video cameras are becoming smaller and more ubiquitous. People are increasingly using small "nanny cams" to monitor babysitters and childcare providers in their homes. Cities are experimenting with monitoring citizens with elaborate systems of surveillance cameras. Since the mid-1990s, many cities in Britain have established a system of surveillance cameras monitored by closed circuit television (CCTV). Recently, a similar type of system has been proposed for certain areas in Washington, D.C. *See* Chapter 4.

---

[52] For an overview of the feminist critique of privacy, *see generally* Judith W. DeCew, *In Pursuit of Privacy: Law, Ethics, and the Rise of Technology* 81–94 (1997); Patricia Boling, *Privacy and the Politics of Intimate Life* (1996); Anita L. Allen, *Uneasy Access: Privacy for Women in a Free Society* (1988); Frances Olsen, *Constitutional Law: Feminist Critiques of the Public/Private Distinction*, 10 Const. Commentary 327 (1993); Ruth Gavison, *Feminism and the Public/Private Distinction*, 45 Stan. L. Rev. 21 (1992).

[53] For an interesting feminist critique of the Warren and Brandeis article, *see* Anita L. Allen & Erin Mack, *How Privacy Got Its Gender*, 10 N. Ill. U. L. Rev. 441 (1990).

X-Ray Devices. X-rays can see through opaque surfaces — through bags, clothing, and skin. Traditionally, X-rays penetrate through both clothing and skin to provide images of bones and internal organs. Recently developed devices use low level X-rays to see an image of the naked body through one's clothing. Critics have called these devices a "virtual strip search." *See* Chapter 4.

Thermal Sensors. Thermal sensors are able to detect heat patterns at significant distances or through the walls of a building. *See* Chapter 4.

AUDIO SURVEILLANCE TECHNOLOGIES

Wiretapping. Wiretapping — the surreptitious interception of a person's telephone conversations — has become a prevalent practice for law enforcement. *See* Chapter 4.

Bugging. The use of hidden recording devices, or "bugs," has been facilitated by smaller and more sophisticated devices. *See* Chapter 4.

Parabolic Microphones. Parabolic microphones can amplify sound at large distances. They need not be placed near a person's mouth to record a conversation. *See* Chapter 4.

IDENTIFICATION AND TRACKING TECHNOLOGIES

Identification Cards. Following September 11, there have been proposals for national identification cards, which can be linked to databases of personal information about individuals. *See* Chapter 5.

DNA Identification and Databases. Advances in genetics have enabled the use of DNA to identify individuals. States are constructing DNA databases for this purpose. Study of the Human Genome has enabled us to figure out whether people are predisposed to certain genetic disorders. *See* Chapter 3.

Biometric Identification. Technology has enabled more sophisticated forms of identification, based on certain unique body characteristics. Increasingly, we are seeing the use of eye scanners, hand print scanners, and so on. *See* Chapter 5.

Face Recognition. Face recognition systems can purportedly match people's faces on surveillance cameras with photographs stored in a database. In January 2001, in Tampa Bay, the police used such a system to scan fans at SuperBowl XXXV. Additionally, a facial recognition system consisting of 36 surveillance cameras was set up in Ybor City, Tampa's entertainment district. *See* Chapter 4.

Tracking Devices. Miniature wireless transmitters can be secretly installed in vehicles or in people's accessories, such as clothing, a watch, or a purse, to track their movements. Satellites can assist in the constant tracking of one's whereabouts (e.g., the Global Positioning System used in some cars). It is now possible to track the location of a person making a cell phone call. Devices can now be surgically placed under the skin to identify people and possibly one day even track their whereabouts. *See* Chapter 4.

DATA PROCESSING TECHNOLOGIES

Computer Databases. Computers enable the easy storage and manipulation of data. Increasingly, marketers and other private sector entities are accumulating personal information about millions of individuals in large databases. Such data includes financial information, shopping activities, hobbies, interests, and book purchases. As people use the Internet with greater frequency, expressing themselves in web postings, chatrooms, and online questionnaires and polls, information is being archived. *See* Chapter 6.

Data Mining. Increasingly, companies and government agents are developing enhanced analytic tools to interpret the data that they collect. These tools make it possible to detect certain behavior patterns and develop psychological profiles. *See* Chapter 6.

INTERNET AND COMPUTER MONITORING TECHNOLOGIES

Cookies. Cookies are small text files secretly deployed from a web site to a visitor's computer. The cookie stores a code that can be read by the web site, and in some cases other web sites, when the visitor returns. This enables web sites to gather and store information about Internet users. *See* Chapter 6.

Web Bugs. Web bugs are named after "bugs"—hidden audio recording devices. A web bug is a hidden graphic, often a single pixel, that can be sent in an e-mail message. It can monitor when an e-mail message has been read and collect data about the computer that reads it. Further, the sender of a web bug can use it to link a visitor to a web site to her e-mail address.[54] *See* Chapter 6.

Carnivore. The FBI has developed a device that monitors the e-mail sent to and from an Internet Service Provider. The device, called "Carnivore" and later renamed DCS1000, can search through e-mail traffic to intercept specific messages. *See* Chapter 4.

Keystroke Loggers. These devices can be surreptitiously installed onto one's computer and can keep a log of all the keystrokes one types. *See* Chapter 4.

---

[54] *See generally* Richard M. Smith, *FAQ: Web Bugs*, <*http://www.privacyfoundation.org/resources/webbug.asp*>.

Magic Lantern. The FBI has developed a computer virus that sends a keystroke logging program in an e-mail message. The virus implants the program on the recipient's hard drive, and the program surreptitiously records the recipient's keystrokes and can transmit the information back to the FBI. This technology enables the FBI to place a keystroke logger without having to physically install it in a person's computer. *See* Chapter 4.

Internet Monitoring Technologies. Various screening technologies enable employers to scan through employees' e-mail for certain words or phrases. Further, employers can use programs to track employees' websurfing at work. *See* Chapter 7.

PRIVACY ENHANCING TECHNOLOGIES

Privacy enhancing technologies (PETs) are technologies that protect private activities or minimize or eliminate the collection of personally identifiable information. Some examples include:

Encryption. Encryption is a way to protect the confidentiality and security of communications. Encryption systems are methods of translating a communication into a code which is translated back to the original message by the intended recipient. Encryption keeps data (such as financial information) secure from unauthorized viewers and enables people to communicate without fear that their messages will be eavesdropped on by hackers or others. Encryption also enables authentication and verification. However, encryption raises concerns for law enforcement and national security, since being able to decrypt communications enables the government to catch criminals, monitor the communications of terrorists, and spy on other nations. *See* Chapter 4.

Anonymizing Technologies. Certain technologies enable people to send e-mail or surf the web without leaving traces of who they are. An anonymous remailer is a service that prevents one's e-mail messages from being traced back to the sender. Further, when one navigates the Internet, one's activity can also be traced. Anonymizing technologies can prevent the web sites from being able to trace the visitor.

Given this panoply of new technologies, how should a society go about protecting privacy? What are your thoughts about the relationship between law and technology as a means to protect privacy? Is one a substitute for the other or are there complementary roles? We will return to these issues later in this text.

Information privacy law is a very policy-oriented field, and throughout this book, you will often be asked to think about how to craft appropriate policy solutions to privacy problems. The articles in the next section offer perspectives on why and how privacy ought to be protected in a world of swiftly changing technology.

2. PRIVACY, POLICYMAKING, AND SOCIAL GOVERNANCE

ANITA ALLEN, *COERCING PRIVACY*

40 Wm. & Mary L. Rev. 723 (1999)

. . . The final decades of the twentieth century could be remembered for the rapid erosion of expectations of personal privacy and of the taste for personal privacy in the United States. . . . I sense that people expect increasingly little physical, informational, and proprietary privacy, and that people seem to prefer less of these types of privacy relative to other goods. . . .

One way to address the erosion would be to stop the avalanche of technology and commercial opportunity responsible for the erosion. We could stop the avalanche of technology, but we will not, if the past is any indication. In the United States, with a few exceptions like government-funded human cloning and fetal tissue research, the rule is that technology marches on.

We could stop the avalanche of commercial opportunity by intervening in the market for privacy; that is, we could (some way or another) increase the costs of consuming other people's privacy and lower the profits of voluntarily giving up one's own privacy. The problem with this suggested strategy is that, even without the details of implementation, it raises the specter of censorship, repression, paternalism, and bureaucracy. Privacy is something we think people are supposed to want; if it turns out that they do not, perhaps third parties should not force it on them, decreasing both their utility and that of those who enjoy disclosure, revelation, and exposure.

Of course, we force privacy on people all the time. Our elected officials criminalize public nudity, even to the point of discouraging breastfeeding. . . . It is one thing, the argument might go, to force privacy on someone by criminalizing nude sun-bathing and topless dancing. These activities have pernicious third-party effects and attract vice. It would be wrong, the argument might continue, to force privacy on someone, in the absence of harm to others, solely on the grounds that one ought not say too much about one's thoughts, feelings, and experiences; one ought not reveal in detail how one spends one's time at home; and one ought not live constantly on display. Paternalistic laws against extremes of factual and physical self-revelation seem utterly inconsistent with liberal self-expression, and yet such laws are suggested by the strong claims liberal theorists make about the value of privacy. Liberal theorists claim that we need privacy to be persons, independent thinkers, free political actors, and citizens of a tolerant democracy.

Walling off the avalanche of technology and commercial opportunity via regulation and prohibition may be violative of liberal, libertarian, and market values. Halting the erosion without bureaucracy and coercion may be a more promising route. Here the focus should be on strengthening individuals to stand up to the avalanche: empower fellow-citizens — through preaching and teaching — to hold on to their own privacy and to consume less of others'. This alternative approach — strengthening the moral foundation of the community — simply may be too difficult. The market for private facts not only feeds the taste for consuming the privacy of others; it simultaneously constructs such tastes. . . .

For people under forty-five who understand that they do not, and cannot, expect to have many secrets, informational privacy may now seem less important. As a culture, we seem to be learning how to be happy and productive — even spiritual — knowing that we are like open books, our houses made of glass. Our parents may appear on the television shows of Oprah Winfrey or Jerry Springer to discuss incest, homosexuality, miscegenation, adultery, transvestitism, and cruelty in the family. Our adopted children may go on television to be reunited with their birth parents. Our law students may compete with their peers for a spot on the MTV program The Real World, and a chance to live with television cameras for months on end and be viewed by mass audiences. Our ten-year-olds may aspire to have their summer camp experiences — snits, fights, fun, and all — chronicled by camera crews and broadcast as entertainment for others on the Disney Channel.

Should we worry about any of this? What values are at stake? Scholars and other commentators associate privacy with several important clusters of value. Privacy has value relative to normative conceptions of spiritual personality, political freedom, health and welfare, human dignity, and autonomy. . . .

Liberal moral philosophers maintain that respecting the many forms of privacy is paramount to respect for human dignity, personhood, moral autonomy, workable community life, and tolerant democratic political and legal institutions. . . .

To speak of "coercing" privacy is to call attention to privacy as a foundation, a precondition of a liberal egalitarian society. Privacy is not an optional good, like a second home or an investment account. . . .

A hard task seems to lay before us — namely, deciding which forms of privacy are so critical that they should become matters of coercion. . . .

As liberals, we should not want people to sell all their freedom, and, as liberals, we should not want people to sell all their privacy and capacities for private choices. This is, in part, because the liberal conceptions of private choice as freedom from governmental and other outside interference with decision-making closely link privacy and freedom. The liberal conception of privacy as freedom from unwanted disclosures, publicity, and loss of control of personality also closely links privacy to freedom. . . . [R]egulatory measures aimed at curbing the culture of exposure for the sake of "forcing" people to love privacy and live privately would be consistent with liberal values. . . .

Government will have to intervene in private lives for the sake of privacy and values associated with it. Protecting privacy, however, rarely will require government to proscribe specific categories of conduct. The men who sunbathe in the nude on warm Sundays in Berlin's Tiergarten are as morally autonomous as their friends and neighbors who do not. The threat to liberalism is not that individuals sometimes expose their naked bodies in public places, display affection with same-sex partners in public, or broadcast personal information on national television. The threat to liberalism is that in an increasing variety of ways our lives are being emptied of privacy on a daily basis, especially physical and informational privacy. . . .

NOTES & QUESTIONS

1. Allen argues that people regularly surrender their privacy and that we should "coerce" privacy. In other words, privacy must be seen as an inalienable right, one that people cannot give away. What if a person wants to live in the spotlight or to give away her personal information? Why shouldn't she be allowed to do so? Recall those who defined privacy as control over information. One aspect of control is that an individual can decide for herself how much privacy she desires. What would Allen say about such a definition of privacy? Recall Paul Schwartz's critique of privacy as control over information. Would Schwartz agree with Allen?

2. Consider also whether a desire for publicity and a desire for privacy can co-exist. Does the person who "tells it all" on the Jerry Springer talk show have any less expectation of privacy when she returns home to be with her family and friends or picks up the telephone to make a private call?

3. Allen contends that our society is changing by becoming more exhibitionistic and voyeuristic. The result is that expectations of privacy are eroding. If people no longer expect privacy in many situations, then why should we continue to protect it?

MARC ROTENBERG, *WE ARE ALL PRIVACY FUNDAMENTALISTS*

Should Individuals Have Absolute Control over the Secondary
Use of Their Personal Information? Alan Westin–Marc Rotenberg Debate
Proceeding of the First Conference on Computers,
Freedom and Privacy 47 (IEEE 1991)

We are all privacy fundamentalists about some aspects our personal lives. It may not be all aspects. It may not even be most aspects. But it is our ability to assert a fundamental privacy right that protects us as individuals. Sixty years ago Justice Brandeis wrote that "the makers of our Constitution undertook to secure conditions favorable for the pursuit of happiness. They recognized the significance of our spiritual nature, of our feelings and of our intellect. They knew that only part of the pain, pleasure, and satisfaction of life are to be found in material things. They sought to protect Americans and their beliefs, their thoughts, and their sensations."

Without the right of privacy, there could be no public life. Without the opportunity to form smaller communities within the larger community, diversity would collapse and dissent would be crushed. Privacy is the most fragile freedom, better defined not by the eloquent expression associated with the First Amendment but rather by the quiet contemplation that precedes the articulation of personal belief.

When we enter public life, we make judgments about how to disclose personal information based on the choices that are presented. A credit agency may well be entitled to know our annual income before deciding to grant us credit. But what could be the basis for allowing the credit agency to make use of this information, provided for the purpose of obtaining credit, to develop a direct-marketing product without the person's permission? Does mere possession constitute ownership?

[Equifax executive] John Baker spoke of "balancing," and rightly appealed to our deeply rooted sense of justice to resolve difficult problems through fairness. But there can be no balance between individuals and institutions when the currency of privacy is presumptively taken from us. We would all come to such an auction too poor to reclaim that which once was ours.

Some of us may freely consent to the secondary use, though many of us object. But don't all of us share a fundamental belief that we ought, at least, to be consulted about how personal information is used that we entrust to institutions? And there is nothing in this statement that precluded technological development or discourages innovative business practices. It merely asks that we be given the right — to the extent that our names are sold or personal information is disclosed to strangers — to decide whether we freely consent to that activity.

It is not sufficient to provide a notice and allow the consumer to opt-out. Such a measure places an onerous burden on consumers in the information age. We should not be required to tell companies that they may not do what they should not do.

Yes, personal information has commercial value and is used to promote businesses, both large and small. But this observation merely restates the question and does not begin to address how commercial value should be allocated. Shouldn't the individual have an interest in the commercial value, and shouldn't the individual come to the bargaining table in full possession of his or her identity?

And, yes, on balance, most of us are not that concerned about information privacy. Most of us list names and numbers in the phone book. Most of us do not object to the transfer of mailing lists from one company to another. But the right of privacy is not simply a ratification of a majority practice.

For if liberty is to mean anything, it must be the recognition of claims that individuals have against larger communities and the practices of those larger communities. You may not need the protection that an unlisted number provides, or the assurance of that information given for one purpose will not be used for another, but other people do.

We must fight to protect the right of privacy. Not simply those rights that we ourselves exercise, but those that we understand others may need. If we fail to do this, our technologies may continue to evolve and our material needs may continue to be satisfied, but the character of our political life, our public world and our private well-being will diminish greatly, and the promise of enrichment that progress offers will gradually subside. . . .

NOTES & QUESTIONS

1. Shortly after the Rotenberg–Westin debate at the first conference on Computers, Freedom, and Privacy, the Lotus Corporation proposed to release a new product called Marketplace based on credit record information maintained by Equifax. Westin worked as an advisor to Equifax. Rotenberg orga-

nized a public protest. Thirty thousand e-mail messages went to Lotus CEO Jim Manzi. In the end, Lotus dropped the plans for Marketplace.[55]

2. To what extent is privacy integral to promoting democracy and expression?

3. Rotenberg argues that without privacy, the "character of our political life, our public world" will diminish. How is privacy related to political life?

REIN TURN & W. H. WARE, *PRIVACY AND SECURITY ISSUES IN INFORMATION SYSTEMS*

(1976)

. . . Privacy is an issue that concerns the computer community in connection with maintaining personal information on individual citizens in computerized record-keeping systems. It deals with the rights of the individual regarding the collection of information in a record-keeping system about his person and activities, and the processing, dissemination, storage, and use of this information in making determinations about him. This last aspect is a long-standing legal and social problem that has become associated with the computer field mainly because computerized record-keeping systems are much more efficient than the manual systems they have replaced, and because they permit linkages between record-keeping systems and correlations of records on a much greater scale than previously possible in manual systems. Thus threats to individual privacy from manual record-keeping systems are potentially amplified in computerized systems. . . .

There is now a general consensus that the legislative approach, rather than reliance on self-policing by record-keeping agencies, is a preferred approach to solving the privacy problem in the United States.

Privacy is not a right explicitly enumerated in the United States Constitution, although it is in the California and Alaska constitutions. Furthermore, until recently the entire concept of privacy protection as it applies to personal information in record-keeping systems had not been developed. In related areas such as eavesdropping, wiretapping, and use of polygraphs, a series of court interpretations had applied various Amendments of the Constitution, such as the Fourth Amendment's right to security from unreasonable search and seizure. However, these were not readily and naturally applicable to information privacy.

A very different approach to individual privacy vis-à-vis record-keeping systems . . . is the concept of a Code of Fair Information Practices. It was conceived by the Special Advisory Committee on Automated Personal Data Systems to the Secretary of the Department of Health, Education, and Welfare, and rested on five principles that had been talked about by many people but not succinctly and comprehensively considered as a whole prior to the HEW Committee.

---

[55] *See* Langdon Winner, *Victory for Computer Populism*, Tech. Rev. (1990); Laura J. Gurak, *Persuasion and Privacy in Cyberspace: The Online Protests over Lotus Marketplace and the Clipper Chip* (1997).

Both the concept of a Code and its details are now widely used as the foundation of privacy legislation in the United States, and its applicability is being studied in other countries. The five basic principles of the Code are equally applicable to the personal information record-keeping systems in the government and in the private sector.

1. There must be no personal data record-keeping systems whose very existence is secret.
2. There must be a way for an individual to find out what information about him is on record and how it is used.
3. There must be a way for an individual to correct or amend a record of identifiable information about him.
4. There must be a way for an individual to prevent information about him that was obtained for one purpose from being used or made available for other purposes without his consent.
5. Any organization creating, maintaining, using, or disseminating records of identifiable personal data must guarantee the reliability of the data for their intended use and must take precautions to prevent misuse of the data.

Legislation based on these principles would deter the misuse of personal information by stipulating that any deviation from the Code would be an abuse of personal information subject to criminal and civil sanctions, recovery of punitive and actual damages, and injunctive relief. . . .

We must recognize, however, that the right of privacy vis-à-vis record-keeping systems is not more important than other individual rights that may be supported and strengthened by the same record-keeping systems. In many cases the objectives in providing privacy are in consonance with other rights, but at times they conflict. There is a central conflict between the legitimate need of public and private institutions for information about people and the need of individuals to be protected against harmful uses of information. There is also a conflict between an individual's desire for privacy and society's collective need to know about and to oversee government's operations. Furthermore, since privacy safeguards can delay access to information needed for making determinations about an individual or can increase the associated costs, privacy can be in conflict even with the individual's own interests. Yet it has been said that "freedom is what privacy is all about," and that without privacy protection the very existence of massive record systems in the government will have a chilling effect on the citizens' exercise of their rights and freedom of expression and of petitioning the government. Thus, it will not be easy to strike the right balance among the many dimensions of this issue. The Privacy Act of 1974 is a starting point on a learning curve which through amendments, court decisions, and new privacy laws, will hopefully lead toward such a balanced solution. . . .

NOTES & QUESTIONS

1. As Turn and Ware observe, the development of record systems gave rise to a series of new threats to privacy. What response do they propose?

2. Examine the Code of Fair Information Practices quoted in the excerpt above. Do these principles vary on the nature of technology? We will return to this question in Chapter 6.

JOEL R. REIDENBERG, *SETTING STANDARDS FOR FAIR INFORMATION PRACTICE IN THE U.S. PRIVATE SECTOR*

80 Iowa L. Rev. 497 (1995)

Despite the growth of the Information Society, the United States has resisted all calls for omnibus or comprehensive legal rules for fair information practice in the private sector. Legal rules have developed on an ad hoc, targeted basis, while industry has elaborated voluntary norms and practices for particular problems. Over the years, there has been an almost zealous adherence to this ideal of narrowly targeted standards. In other countries, the response to the Information Age has been quite different. Foreign nations have enacted broad, sweeping "data protection" laws to establish fair information practices in both public and private sectors.

In democratic society, information standards reflect specific conceptions of governance. An individual's desire for seclusion from the public realm opposes the societal value in a free flow of information for economic or political gain. Legal rules for the treatment of information set boundaries for state intrusion into a citizen's life and for state control of a citizen's conduct. For private interactions and the relationships between citizens, both law and practice set the balance between dignity and free flows of information. In American society, two powerful political values have driven the pursuit of narrowly targeted standards: (1) the desire to minimize restrictions on information flows and (2) the desire to disperse standards setting. . . .

At its founding, the American democracy faced two broad ideological commitments: one republican and the other (since termed) liberal. The republican commitment emphasized self-government, while the liberal commitment focused on individual rights. The Constitution of the United States reflected a synthesis of these two commitments. In the course of its development, American politics enshrined a belief in limited government distinct from foreign models of democracy. . . . Even as the role of government in society through regulation of social welfare increased during both the Progressive Era and the New Deal Era, American political philosophy still reflected a substantial degree of hostility toward the regulation of private relations. Elsewhere, namely in continental Europe, prevailing politics viewed the government more benevolently. Professor Glendon has aptly observed that the discourse of American politics is now cast in terms of "rights talk." This rhetoric of rights emphasizes limitations on government power over the citizen. While the emergence of an American welfare state during the twentieth century may have signaled a greater role for government in the marketplace, the idea that the government should not intervene in the marketplace of ideas in the absence of compelling needs remains dominant. Rather than government action, private relationships or private contracts, thus, become a principal source of regulation for information flows. . . .

As a corollary to minimal state regulation of information flows, the American system values a dispersion of standards for fair information practice. There are no universal rules and there is no discrete source, such as one sectoral rule or one industry norm or practice, to provide all the standards for a particular context. Fair treatment of personal information relies on the aggregation of standards from various sources. This diversity promotes the goal that no single actor, whether it be the government through its power to make legal rules or a private firm through market power and contractual relationships, should control information flows. . . .

Unlike the ad hoc, narrowly tailored standards of the United States, foreign standards often offer comprehensive legal norms for the treatment of personal information. Divergent norms among various countries in a global information economy are problematic. Global information processing, thus, requires the U.S. private sector to consider trends in foreign standards of fair information practice. . . .

NOTES & QUESTIONS

1. The United States has protected privacy sectorally — in particular sectors of the economy and other narrow contexts. More specifically, the United States has relied on a series of particularized statues and remedies that differ from context to context. In contrast, Europe has protected privacy in a more comprehensive way with rules and policies that apply across the board to all instances where personal data is collected and used. Thus, different countries have different rules for protecting privacy based on their ideological commitments and historical experiences.

   The Reidenberg excerpt illustrates that United States information privacy law does not exist in a vacuum. It has global implications and will increasingly be influenced by the law of other countries. As the economies of nations become more interdependent, personal data is increasingly flowing between different nations. There is significant potential that clashes in privacy policymaking will affect international commerce. Which nation's privacy rules should govern? As Reidenberg points out, the United States will need to take heed of the approaches to privacy adopted in other nations. To what extent should the United States bend its privacy policymaking approach in response from international pressure?

2. In another article, Reidenberg argues that policymaking with regard to privacy involves issues of social governance:

   > Data privacy rules are often cast as a balance between two basic liberties: fundamental human rights on one side and the free flow of information on the other side. Yet, because societies differ on how and when personal information should be available for private and public sector needs, the treatment and interaction of these liberties will express a specific delineation between the state, civil society, and the citizen.[56]

---

[56]Joel R. Reidenberg, *Resolving Conflicting International Data Privacy Rules in Cyberspace*, 52 Stan. L. Rev. 1315 (2000).

Privacy, according to Reidenberg, involves establishing a balance between protecting the rights of individuals and enabling information flow. Do you think these interests always exist in opposition? Consider financial services, communications networks, and medical care. Does privacy impair or enable information flow?

SPIROS SIMITIS,
REVIEWING PRIVACY IN AN INFORMATION SOCIETY

135 U. Pa. L. Rev. 707 (1987)

. . . The increased access to personal information resulting from modern, sophisticated techniques of automated processing has sharpened the need to abandon the search for a "neutral" concept in favor of an understanding free of abstractions and fully aware of the political and societal background of all privacy debates. Modern forms of data collection have altered the privacy discussion in three principal ways. First, privacy considerations no longer arise out of particular individual problems; rather, they express conflicts affecting everyone. The course of the privacy debate is neither determined by the caricature of a prominent golfer with a chocolate packet protruding out of his pocket, nor by the hints at the use of a sexual stimulant by a respected university professor, but by the intensive retrieval of personal data of virtually every employee, taxpayer, patient, bank customer, welfare recipient, or car driver. Second, smart cards and videotex make it possible to record and reconstruct individual activities in minute detail. Surveillance has thereby lost its exceptional character and has become a more and more routine practice. Finally, personal information is increasingly used to enforce standards of behavior. Information processing is developing, therefore, into an essential element of long-term strategies of manipulation intended to mold and adjust individual conduct. . . .

. . . [B]ecause of both the broad availability of personal data and the elaborate matching procedures, individual activities can be accurately reconstructed through automated processing. Surveillance becomes the order of the day. Significantly enough, security agencies were among the first to discover the advantages of automated retrieval. They not only quickly computerized their own data collections but also sought and obtained access to state and private data banks. Entirely new investigation techniques, such as computer profiling, were developed, enabling the agencies to trace wanted persons by matching a presumptive pattern of consumption habits against, for instance, the records of utility companies. The successful attempts at computer-based voice and picture identification will probably influence the work of security agencies even more. . . .

Both the quest for greater transparency and the defense of free speech are legitimated by the goal of allowing the individual to understand social reality better and thus to form a personal opinion on its decisive factors as well as on possible changes. The citizen's right to be "a participator in the government of affairs," to use Jefferson's terms, reflects a profoundly rational process. It presupposes individuals who not only disperse the necessary information but also have the capacity to transform the accessible data into policy expectations. Transparency is, in other words, a basic element of competent communicative action and consequently remains indispensable as long as social discourse is to be promoted, not inhibited.

Inhibition, however, tends to be the rule once automated processing of personal data becomes a normal tool of both government and private enterprises. The price for an undoubted improvement in transparency is a no less evident loss in competence of communication. Habits, activities, and preferences are compiled, registered, and retrieved to facilitate better adjustment, not to improve the individual's capacity to act and to decide. Whatever the original incentive for computerization may have been, processing increasingly appears as the ideal means to adapt an individual to a predetermined, standardized behavior that aims at the highest possible degree of compliance with the model patient, consumer, taxpayer, employee, or citizen. Furthermore, interactive systems do not, despite all contrary assertions, restore a long lost individuality by correcting the effects of mass production in a mass society. On the contrary, the telematic integration forces the individual once more into a preset scheme. The media supplier dictates the conditions under which communication takes place, fixes the possible subjects of the dialogue, and, due to the personal data collected, is in an increasingly better position to influence the subscriber's behavior. Interactive systems, therefore, suggest individual activity where in fact no more than stereotyped reactions occur.

In short, the transparency achieved through automated processing creates possibly the best conditions for colonization of the individual's lifeworld. Accurate, constantly updated knowledge of her personal history is systematically incorporated into policies that deliberately structure her behavior. The more routinized automated processing augments the transparency, however, the more privacy proves to be a prerequisite to the capacity to participate in social discourse. Where privacy is dismantled, both the chance for personal assessment of the political and societal process and the opportunity to develop and maintain a particular style of life fade. . . .

The processing of personal data is not unique to a particular society. On the contrary, the attractiveness of information technology transcends political boundaries, particularly because of the opportunity to guide the individual's behavior. For a democratic society, however, the risks are high: labeling of individuals, manipulative tendencies, magnification of errors, and strengthening of social control threaten the very fabric of democracy. Yet, despite the incontestable importance of its technical aspects, informatization, like industrialization, is primarily a political and social challenge. When the relationship between information processing and democracy is understood, it becomes clear that the protection of privacy is the price necessary to secure the individual's ability to communicate and participate. Regulations that create precisely specified conditions for personal data processing are the decisive test for discerning whether society is aware of this price and willing to pay it. If the signs of experience are correct, this payment can be delayed no further. There is, in fact, no alternative to the advice of Horace: Seize the day, put not trust in the morrow. . . .

NOTES & QUESTIONS

1. As Simitis and other authors in this section observe, privacy is an issue about social structure. What is the relationship between privacy and democracy according to Simitis?

2. Generally, one would assume that greater information flow facilitates democracy — it enables more expression, more political discourse, more information about the workings of government. Simitis, however, contends that privacy is "necessary to secure the individual's ability to communicate and participate." How are these two notions about information flow to be reconciled?

3. This chapter has explored privacy and its protection in law.[57] Briefly summarize the main legal theories that have been set out. To what extent are these theories dependent on the presence (or absence) of technology? Consider also the role of legal institutions. When should courts protect privacy? When should the legislatures?

---

[57] For additional perspectives on creating policy for the protection of privacy, *see* Colin J. Bennett & Rebecca Grant, eds., *Visions of Privacy: Policy Choices for the Digital Age* (2000); David H. Flaherty, *Protecting Privacy in Surveillance Societies: The Federal Republic of Germany, Sweden, France, Canada, and the United States* (1992); Fred H. Cate, *Privacy in the Information Age* (1997).

CHAPTER 2

PRIVACY AND THE MEDIA

Warren and Brandeis wrote about the increasing proliferation of gossip in the newspapers. Today, the problems Warren and Brandeis were concerned about are dramatically magnified by the vast expansion of the media. In addition to newspapers, there are magazines, movies, television, and the Internet. From marketers to movie-makers, from tabloids to 24-hour news channels, from talk shows to reality TV, we are witnessing an explosion in the demand for images, video, and stories about the personal lives of individuals both famous and obscure. Further, anybody with a web site can now disseminate information instantly around the world.

Warren and Brandeis were also concerned with photography, a new technology that had the potential to greatly facilitate information gathering by the media. Today, technologies of gathering data are significantly more sophisticated. Video cameras are in widespread use and exist in miniature forms for easy concealment; high-powered telephoto lenses can enable one to film or photograph from large distances.

This chapter focuses on legal remedies for the gathering and dissemination of personal information by media entities. "Media" is understood broadly in this chapter to include people and businesses that gather and disseminate information to inform, advertise, or entertain. The chapter then explores four general types of privacy incursion by the media: (1) intrusions and harassment in the course of gathering information; (2) the disclosure of truthful information; (3) the dissemination of misleading or false information; and (4) the appropriation of name or likeness. The principal remedies for media incursions into privacy are the four privacy torts inspired by Warren and Brandeis's article. This chapter begins with a brief overview of how the torts developed following the publication of the article. The privacy torts are not the only remedies for privacy invasions. The tort of defamation, discussed at length in this chapter, is an older remedy for a particular type of privacy intrusion — the dissemination of false information. Another remedy is the tort of infliction of emotional distress, which is discussed briefly in section C. Additionally, a number of states have enacted statutes protecting against particular forms of disclosure.

A. THE RECOGNITION OF WARREN AND BRANDEIS'S PRIVACY TORTS

Samuel Warren and Louis Brandeis's 1890 article, *The Right to Privacy*, suggested that the existing causes of action under the common law did not adequately protect privacy but that the legal concepts in the common law could be modified to achieve the task.

As early as 1903, courts and legislatures responded to the Warren and Brandeis article by creating a number of privacy torts to redress the harms that Warren and Brandeis had noted. In *Roberson v. Rocherster Folding Box Co.*, 64 N.E. 442 (N.Y. 1902), the New York Court of Appeals refused to recognize a common law tort action for privacy invasions. Franklin Mills Flour displayed a lithograph of Abigail Roberson (a teenager) on 25,000 advertisement flyers without her consent. Roberson claimed that the use of her image on the flyer caused her great humiliation and resulted in illness requiring medical help. The court, however, concluded:

> . . . There is no precedent for such an action to be found in the decisions of this court. . . . Mention of such a right is not to be found in Blackstone, Kent, or any other of the great commentators upon the law; nor, so far as the learning of counsel or the courts in this case have been able to discover, does its existence seem to have been asserted prior to about the year 1890. . . .
>
> . . . The courts, however, being without authority to legislate, are required to decide cases upon principle, and so are necessarily embarrassed by precedents created by an extreme, and therefore unjustifiable, application of an old principle. . . . [W]hile justice in a given case may be worked out by a decision of the court according to the notions of right which govern the individual judge or body of judges comprising the court, the mischief which will finally result may be almost incalculable under our system, which makes a decision in one case a precedent for decisions in all future cases which are akin to it in the essential facts. . . .

The court went on to say:

> The legislative body could very well interfere and arbitrarily provide that no one should be permitted for his own selfish purpose to use the picture or the name of another for advertising purposes without his general consent. In such event no embarrassment would result to the general body of law, for the law would be applicable only to cases provided for by statute. The courts, however, being without authority to legislate, are required to decide cases upon principle, and so are necessarily embarrassed by precedents created by an extreme, and therefore unjustifiable, application of an old principle.

Shortly after the decision, a note in the *Yale Law Journal* criticized the *Roberson* decision because it enabled the press "to pry into and grossly display before the public matters of the most private and personal concern."[1] One of the judges in the majority defended the opinion in the *Columbia Law Review*.[2]

In 1903, the New York legislature responded to the explicit invitation in *Roberson* to legislate by creating a privacy tort action by statute. *See* N.Y. Civ.

---

[1] *An Actionable Right to Privacy?*, 12 Yale L.J. 34 (1902).
[2] Denis O'Brien, *The Right to Privacy*, 2 Colum. L. Rev. 486 (1902).

Rights Act § 51. This statute is still in use today. As you will see again later on in this text, courts are frequently engaged in a dialogue with legislatures about the scope of privacy rights.

In the 1905 case *Pavesich v. New England Life Insurance Co.*, 50 S.E. 68 (Ga. 1905), Georgia became the first state to recognize a common law tort action for privacy invasions. There, a newspaper published a life insurance advertisement with a photograph of the plaintiff without the plaintiff's consent. The court held:

> . . . The right of privacy has its foundation in the instincts of nature. It is recognized intuitively, consciousness being the witness that can be called to establish its existence. Any person whose intellect is in a normal condition recognizes at once that as to each individual member of society there are matters private, and there are matters public so far as the individual is concerned. Each individual as instinctively resents any encroachment by the public upon his rights which are of a private nature as he does the withdrawal of those of his rights which are of a public nature. A right of privacy in matters purely private is therefore derived from natural law. . . .
>
> One who desires to live a life of partial seclusion has a right to choose the times, places, and manner in which and at which he will submit himself to the public gaze. Subject to the limitation above referred to, the body of a person cannot be put on exhibition at any time or at any place without his consent. . . .
>
> It therefore follows from what has been said that a violation of the right of privacy is a direct invasion of a legal right of the individual. . . .

In 1960, Dean William Prosser wrote his famous article, *Privacy*, examining the over 300 privacy tort cases decided in the 70 years since the Warren and Brandeis article.

WILLIAM PROSSER, *PRIVACY*

48 Cal. L. Rev. 383 (1960)

. . . The law of privacy comprises four distinct kinds of invasion of four different interests of the plaintiff, which are tied together by the common name, but otherwise have almost nothing in common except that each represents an interference with the right of the plaintiff, in the phrase coined by Judge Cooley, "to be let alone." Without any attempt at exact definition, these four torts may be described as follows:

1. Intrusion upon the plaintiff's seclusion or solitude, or into his private affairs.
2. Public disclosure of embarrassing private facts about the plaintiff.
3. Publicity which places the plaintiff in a false light in the public eye.
4. Appropriation, for the defendant's advantage, of the plaintiff's name or likeness.

NOTES & QUESTIONS

1. Prosser's analytical framework imposed order and clarity on the jumbled line of cases that followed the Warren and Brandeis article. The Restatement of Torts recognizes the four torts Prosser described in his article. These

torts are known collectively as "invasion of privacy." The torts include: (1) intrusion upon seclusion; (2) public disclosure of private facts; (3) false light; and (4) appropriation.

2. ***The Interests Protected by the Privacy Torts.*** In response to Prosser's assertion that the privacy torts have almost "nothing in common," Edward Bloustein replied that "what provoked Warren and Brandeis to write their article was a fear that a rampant press feeding on the stuff of private life would destroy individual dignity and integrity and emasculate individual freedom and independence." This underlying principle is a protection of "human dignity" and "personality."[3]

In contrast to Bloustein, Robert Post contends that the privacy torts do "not simply uphold the interests of individuals against the demands of the community, but instead safeguard[ ] rules of civility that in some significant measure constitute both individuals and community." Post argues that the torts establish boundaries between people, which when violated create strife. The privacy torts promote "forms of respect [for other people] by which we maintain a community."[4]

3. The Prosser taxonomy has provided a useful way to discuss the privacy torts. As you will see, courts often step through the provisions in the Restatement to determine the scope and character of a privacy claim. But as you will also see, the categories are not always so neatly defined. The appropriation tort, for example, has two very different interpretations: one that focuses on the privacy harm of unwanted disclosure, the other on commercial interests of people, somewhat paradoxically, who seek public exposure. We will examine this in more detail below. More broadly, we will consider the nature of personal information at issue in each of the tort claims, i.e., whether it is truthful, whether it is false, whether it creates commercial value, and also how it was obtained. We will follow this approach in our discussion throughout this chapter.

LAKE V. WAL-MART STORES, INC.

582 N.W.2d 231 (Minn. 1998)

BLATZ, C. J. . . . Elli Lake and Melissa Weber appeal from a dismissal of their complaint for failure to state a claim upon which relief may be granted. The district court and court of appeals held that Lake and Weber's complaint alleging intrusion upon seclusion, appropriation, publication of private facts, and false light publicity could not proceed because Minnesota does not recognize a common law tort action for invasion of privacy. We reverse as to the claims of intrusion upon seclusion, appropriation, and publication of private facts, but affirm as to false light publicity.

Nineteen-year-old Elli Lake and 20-year-old Melissa Weber vacationed in Mexico in March 1995 with Weber's sister. During the vacation, Weber's sister

---

[3] Edward J. Bloustein, *Privacy as an Aspect of Human Dignity: An Answer to Dean Prosser*, 39 N.Y.U. L. Rev. 962, 971, 1000–1001, 974 (1964).

[4] Robert C. Post, *The Social Foundations of Privacy: Community and Self in the Common Law Tort*, 77 Cal. L. Rev. 957 (1989).

took a photograph of Lake and Weber naked in the shower together. After their vacation, Lake and Weber brought five rolls of film to the Dilworth, Minnesota Wal-Mart store and photo lab. When they received their developed photographs along with the negatives, an enclosed written notice stated that one or more of the photographs had not been printed because of their "nature."

In July 1995, an acquaintance of Lake and Weber alluded to the photograph and questioned their sexual orientation. Again, in December 1995, another friend told Lake and Weber that a Wal-Mart employee had shown her a copy of the photograph. By February 1996, Lake was informed that one or more copies of the photograph were circulating in the community.

Lake and Weber filed a complaint against Wal-Mart Stores, Inc. and one or more as-yet unidentified Wal-Mart employees on February 23, 1996, alleging the four traditional invasion of privacy torts — intrusion upon seclusion, appropriation, publication of private facts, and false light publicity. . . . The district court granted Wal-Mart's motion to dismiss, explaining that Minnesota has not recognized any of the four invasion of privacy torts. The court of appeals affirmed.

Whether Minnesota should recognize any or all of the invasion of privacy causes of action is a question of first impression in Minnesota. . . .

This court has the power to recognize and abolish common law doctrines. The common law is not composed of firmly fixed rules. Rather, as we have long recognized, the common law:

> is the embodiment of broad and comprehensive unwritten principles, inspired by natural reason, an innate sense of justice, adopted by common consent for the regulation and government of the affairs of men. It is the growth of ages, and an examination of many of its principles, as enunciated and discussed in the books, discloses a constant improvement and development in keeping with advancing civilization and new conditions of society. Its guiding star has always been the rule of right and wrong, and in this country its principles demonstrate that there is in fact, as well as in theory, a remedy for all wrongs.

As society changes over time, the common law must also evolve:

> It must be remembered that the common law is the result of growth, and that its development has been determined by the social needs of the community which it governs. It is the resultant of conflicting social forces, and those forces which are for the time dominant leave their impress upon the law. It is of judicial origin, and seeks to establish doctrines and rules for the determination, protection, and enforcement of legal rights. Manifestly it must change as society changes and new rights are recognized. To be an efficient instrument, and not a mere abstraction, it must gradually adapt itself to changed conditions.

To determine the common law, we look to other states as well as to England.

The tort of invasion of privacy is rooted in a common law right to privacy first described in an 1890 law review article by Samuel Warren and Louis Brandeis. The article posited that the common law has always protected an individual's person and property, with the extent and nature of that protection changing over time. The fundamental right to privacy is both reflected in those protections and grows out of them:

Thus, in the very early times, the law gave a remedy only for physical inter-ference with life and property, for trespass vi et armis. Then the "right to life" served only to protect the subject from battery in its various forms; liberty meant freedom from actual restraint; and the right to property secured to the individual his lands and his cattle. Later, there came a recognition of a man's spiritual nature, of his feelings and his intellect. Gradually the scope of these legal rights broadened; and now the right to life has come to mean the right to enjoy life, — the right to be let alone; the right to liberty secures the exer-cise of extensive civil privileges; and the term "property" has grown to com-prise every form of possession — intangible, as well as tangible.

Although no English cases explicitly articulated a "right to privacy," sev-eral cases decided under theories of property, contract, or breach of confidence also included invasion of privacy as a basis for protecting personal violations. The article encouraged recognition of the common law right to privacy, as the strength of our legal system lies in its elasticity, adaptability, capacity for growth, and ability "to meet the wants of an ever changing society and to apply immediate relief for every recognized wrong.". . .

Today, the vast majority of jurisdictions now recognize some form of the right to privacy. Only Minnesota, North Dakota, and Wyoming have not yet recognized any of the four privacy torts. Although New York and Nebraska courts have declined to recognize a common law basis for the right to privacy and instead provide statutory protection, we reject the proposition that only the legislature may establish new causes of action. The right to privacy is in-herent in the English protections of individual property and contract rights and the "right to be let alone" is recognized as part of the common law across this country. Thus, it is within the province of the judiciary to establish pri-vacy torts in this jurisdiction.

Today we join the majority of jurisdictions and recognize the tort of inva-sion of privacy. The right to privacy is an integral part of our humanity; one has a public persona, exposed and active, and a private persona, guarded and preserved. The heart of our liberty is choosing which parts of our lives shall be-come public and which parts we shall hold close. . . .

We decline to recognize the tort of false light publicity at this time. We are concerned that claims under false light are similar to claims of defamation, and to the extent that false light is more expansive than defamation, tension between this tort and the First Amendment is increased.

False light is the most widely criticized of the four privacy torts and has been rejected by several jurisdictions. . . .

Thus we recognize a right to privacy present in the common law of Min-nesota, including causes of action in tort for intrusion upon seclusion, appro-priation, and publication of private facts, but we decline to recognize the tort of false light publicity. . . .

TOMLJANOVICH, J. dissenting. I would not recognize a cause of action for in-trusion upon seclusion, appropriation or publication of private facts. . . .

An action for an invasion of the right to privacy is not rooted in the Constitution. "[T]he Fourth Amendment cannot be translated into a general constitutional 'right to privacy.'" *Katz v. United States*, 389 U.S. 347, 350 (1967).

Those privacy rights that have their origin in the Constitution are much more fundamental rights of privacy — marriage and reproduction. *See Griswold v. Connecticut*, 381 U.S. 479, 485 (1965) (penumbral rights of privacy and repose protect notions of privacy surrounding the marriage relationship and reproduction).

We have become a much more litigious society since 1975 when we acknowledged that we have never recognized a cause of action for invasion of privacy. We should be even more reluctant now to recognize a new tort.

In the absence of a constitutional basis, I would leave to the legislature the decision to create a new tort for invasion of privacy.

NOTES & QUESTIONS

1. Today, most states recognize some or all of the privacy torts. Minnesota, a long holdout and one of the few states to refuse to recognize the privacy torts, finally did so, more than 100 years after the publication of the Warren and Brandeis article.
2. The dissent in *Lake* contends, in a similar way as *Roberson*, that it should be the legislature, not the courts, that recognize new tort actions to protect privacy. In New York, the statute passed in response to *Roberson* remains the state's source for privacy tort remedies. Like New York, some states have recognized the privacy torts legislatively; other states, like Georgia in *Pavesich* and Minnesota in *Lake*, have recognized them judicially. Which means of recognizing the torts do you believe to be most justifiable? Why?

B. INFORMATION GATHERING

In order to report the news, journalists must gather information. This often involves being nosy, inquisitive, and aggressive. Given the vast proliferation of media and the tremendous competition to get breaking information and live video or photographs, there is a great potential for media information gathering to become intrusive and harassing, especially when a person becomes the subject of a prominent story. A number of remedies are available for intrusions by the gatherers of information. The primary remedy is the tort of intrusion upon seclusion. Some states, such as California, have passed statutes providing remedies from aggressive photographers known as paparazzi. These two types of remedies will be the focus of this section. Other remedies include trespass (if the newsgatherer wrongfully entered one's home or property) and fraud (if the newsgatherer lied or used deceitful methods to obtain information). Additionally, the wiretapping laws of many states provide remedies when one records the conversations of others without their consent. In a number of states, consent is required from all participants to a conversation. In some states and under federal wiretap law, consent is only required from one of the parties, so a journalist could secretly record a conversation in which she participates. Wiretapping law will be discussed in more depth in Chapter 4.

1. INTRUSION UPON SECLUSION

(a) Introduction

RESTATEMENT (SECOND) OF TORTS § 652B:
INTRUSION UPON SECLUSION

One who intentionally intrudes, physically or otherwise, upon the solitude or seclusion of another or his private affairs or concerns, is subject to liability to the other for invasion of his privacy, if the intrusion would be highly offensive to a reasonable person.

NOTES & QUESTIONS

1. For the tort of public disclosure of private facts (*see* section C below), liability does not depend upon how the information is obtained. The information can be acquired lawfully and disclosure could still be tortious. In contrast, the tort of intrusion concerns the way that that information is obtained. Consider the following commentary to the Restatement:

> Comment (a): Intrusion "does not depend upon any publicity given to the person whose interest is invaded or to his affairs."
>
> Comment (b): "The intrusion itself makes the defendant subject to liability, even though there is no publication or other use of any kind of the photograph or information outlined."

(b) Intrusion upon the Solitude or Seclusion of Another

NADER v. GENERAL MOTORS CORP.

255 N.E.2d 765 (N.Y. Ct. App. 1970)

FULD, C. J. . . . The plaintiff [Ralph Nader], an author and lecturer on automotive safety, has, for some years, been an articulate and severe critic of General Motors' products from the standpoint of safety and design. According to the complaint—which, for present purposes, we must assume to be true—the appellant [General Motors Corporation], having learned of the imminent publication of the plaintiff's book "Unsafe at any Speed," decided to conduct a campaign of intimidation against him in order to "suppress plaintiff's criticism of and prevent his disclosure of information" about its products. To that end, the appellant authorized and directed the other defendants to engage in a series of activities which, the plaintiff claims in his first two causes of action, violated his right to privacy.

Specifically, the plaintiff alleges that the appellant's agents (1) conducted a series of interviews with acquaintances of the plaintiff, "questioning them about, and casting aspersions upon (his) political, social . . . racial and religious views . . . ; his integrity; his sexual proclivities and inclinations; and his personal habits"; (2) kept him under surveillance in public places for an unreasonable length of time; (3) caused him to be accosted by girls for the purpose of entrapping him into illicit relationships; (4) made threatening, harassing and obnoxious telephone calls to him; (5) tapped his telephone and eavesdropped, by means of mechanical and electronic equipment, on his private conversations with others; and (6) conducted a "continuing" and harassing investigation of him. [Nader's complaint, among other things, contained a cause of action for intrusion.]

. . . It should be emphasized that the mere gathering of information about a particular individual does not give rise to a cause of action under [the intrusion tort]. Privacy is invaded only if the information sought is of a confidential nature and the defendant's conduct was unreasonably intrusive. Just as a common-law copyright is lost when material is published, so, too, there can be no invasion of privacy where the information sought is open to public view or has been voluntarily revealed to others. In order to sustain a cause of action for invasion of privacy, therefore, the plaintiff must show that the appellant's conduct was truly "intrusive" and that it was designed to elicit information which would not be available through normal inquiry or observation. . . .

. . . At most, only two of the activities charged to the appellant are, in our view, actionable as invasions of privacy under the law of the District of Columbia. . . .

Turning, then, to the particular acts charged in the complaint, we cannot find any basis for a claim of invasion of privacy, under District of Columbia law, in the allegations that the appellant, through its agents or employees, interviewed many persons who knew the plaintiff, asking questions about him and casting aspersions on his character. Although those inquiries may have uncovered information of a personal nature, it is difficult to see how they may be said to have invaded the plaintiff's privacy. Information about the plaintiff which was already known to others could hardly be regarded as private to the plaintiff. Presumably, the plaintiff had previously revealed the information to such other persons, and he would necessarily assume the risk that a friend or acquaintance in whom he had confided might breach the confidence. If, as alleged, the questions tended to disparage the plaintiff's character, his remedy would seem to be by way of an action for defamation, not for breach of his right to privacy.

Nor can we find any actionable invasion of privacy in the allegations that the appellant caused the plaintiff to be accosted by girls with illicit proposals, or that it was responsible for the making of a large number of threatening and harassing telephone calls to the plaintiff's home at odd hours. Neither of these activities, howsoever offensive and disturbing, involved intrusion for the purpose of gathering information of a private and confidential nature. . . .

Apart, however, from the foregoing allegations which we find inadequate to spell out a cause of action for invasion of privacy under District of Columbia law, the complaint contains allegations concerning other activities by the appellant or its agents which do satisfy the requirements for such a cause of action. The one which most clearly meets those requirements is the charge that the appellant and its codefendants engaged in unauthorized wiretapping and eavesdropping by mechanical and electronic means. . . .

There are additional allegations that the appellant hired people to shadow the plaintiff and keep him under surveillance. In particular, he claims that, on one occasion, one of its agents followed him into a bank, getting sufficiently close to him to see the denomination of the bills he was withdrawing from his account. From what we have already said, it is manifest that the mere observation of the plaintiff in a public place does not amount to an invasion of his privacy. But, under certain circumstances, surveillance may be so "overzealous" as to render it actionable. Whether or not the surveillance in the present case falls into this latter category will depend on the nature of the proof. A person does not automatically make public everything he does merely by being in a public place, and the mere fact that Nader was in a bank did not give anyone the right to try to discover the amount of money he was withdrawing. On the other hand, if the plaintiff acted in such a way as to reveal that fact to any casual observer, then, it may not be said that the appellant intruded into his private sphere. In any event, though, it is enough for present purposes to say that the surveillance allegation is not insufficient as a matter of law. . . .

BRIETEL, J. concurring in the result. . . . [S]cholars, in trying to define the elusive concept of the right of privacy, have, as of the present, subdivided the common law right into separate classifications, most significantly distinguishing between unreasonable intrusion and unreasonable publicity. This does not mean, however, that the classifications are either frozen or exhausted, or that several of the classifications may not overlap.

Concretely applied to this case, it is suggested, for example, that it is premature to hold that the attempted entrapment of plaintiff in a public place by seemingly promiscuous ladies is no invasion of any of the categories of the right to privacy and is restricted to a much more limited cause of action for intentional infliction of mental distress. Moreover, it does not strain credulity or imagination to conceive of the systematic "public" surveillance of another as being the implementation of a plan to intrude on the privacy of another. Although acts performed in "public," especially if taken singly or in small numbers, may not be confidential, at least arguably a right to privacy may nevertheless be invaded through extensive or exhaustive monitoring and cataloguing of acts normally disconnected and anonymous.

These are but illustrations of the problems raised in attempting to determine issues of relevancy and allocability of evidence in advance of a trial record. The other allegations so treated involve harassing telephone calls, and investigatory interviews. It is just as important that while allegations treated singly may not constitute a cause of action, they may do so in combination, or serve to enhance other violations of the right to privacy.

It is not unimportant that plaintiff contends that a giant corporation had allegedly sought by surreptitious and unusual methods to silence an unusually effective critic. If there was such a plan, and only a trial would show that, it is unduly restrictive of the future trial to allocate the evidence beforehand based only on a pleader's specification of overt acts on the bold assumption that they are not connected causally or do not bear on intent and motive.

It should be observed, too, that the right to privacy, even as thus far developed, does not always refer to that which is not known to the public or is confidential. Indeed, the statutory right of privacy in this State and perhaps the most traditional right of privacy in the "common law sense" relates to the commercialized publicity of one's face or name, perhaps the two most public aspects of an individual. . . .

Accordingly, because of the prematurity of ruling on any other question but the sufficiency of the causes of action, I concur in result only.

NOTES & QUESTIONS

1. *Surveillance in Public Places.* Do you agree with the court that the "shadowing" of Nader — the following him around and monitoring of his day-to-day activities — constitutes a form of intrusion even though the acts took place in public?

Consider the following comment from the Restatement:

> Comment (c). The defendant is subject to liability under the rule stated in this Section only when he has intruded into a private place, or has otherwise invaded a private seclusion that the plaintiff has thrown about his person or affairs. Thus there is no liability for the examination of a public record concerning the plaintiff, or of documents that the plaintiff is required to keep and make available for public inspection. Nor is there liability for observing him or even taking his photograph while he is walking on the public highway, since he is not then in seclusion, and his appearance is public and open to the public eye. Even in a public place, however, there may be some matters about the plaintiff, such as his underwear or lack of it, that are not exhibited to the public gaze; and there may still be invasion of privacy when there is intrusion upon these matters.

The "shadowing" of Nader consisted of closely monitoring acts that were "exhibited to the public gaze." Consider the following statement in Judge Breitel's concurrence: "Although acts performed in 'public,' especially if taken singly or in small numbers, may not be confidential, at least arguably a right to privacy may nevertheless be invaded through extensive or exhaustive monitoring and cataloguing of acts normally disconnected and anonymous." Which approach is preferable — that of the Restatement or that manifested in Judge Breitel's concurrence?

2. *Wiretapping and Electronic Surveillance.* In *Hamberger v. Eastman*, 206 A.2d 239 (N.H. 1964), a husband and wife brought an intrusion action against their landlord for installing a secret recording device in their bedroom. The device had wires going into the landlord's residence. The court sided with the plaintiffs:

> The defendant contends that the right of privacy should not be recognized on the facts of the present case as they appear in the pleadings because there are no allegations that anyone listened or overheard any sounds or voices originating from the plaintiffs' bedroom. The tort of intrusion on the plaintiffs' solitude or seclusion does not require publicity and communication to third persons although this would affect the amount of damages, as Prosser makes clear. The defendant also contends that the right of privacy is not violated unless something has been published, written or printed and that oral publicity is not sufficient. Recent cases make it clear that this is not a requirement.

If the peeping Tom, the big ear and the electronic eavesdropper (whether ingenious or ingenuous) have a place in the hierarchy of social values, it ought not to be at the expense of a married couple minding their own business in the seclusion of their bedroom who have never asked for or by their conduct deserved a potential projection of their private conversations and actions to their landlord or to others. Whether actual or potential such "publicity with respect to private matters of purely personal concern is an injury to personality. It impairs the mental peace and comfort of the individual and may produce suffering more acute than that produced by a mere bodily injury." III Pound, Jurisprudence 58 (1959). The use of parabolic microphones and sonic wave devices designed to pick up conversations in a room without entering it and at a considerable distance away makes the problem far from fanciful.

3. **Collective Actions by Different Journalists.** Suppose a person is accosted by throngs of reporters. At any one moment, there is always one or more reporters on her trail. Groups of reporters camp outside her home. The impact from the collective actions of all the reporters is extremely disruptive to the person's life. Can she sue the reporters collectively? Bruce Sanford argues that each reporter should only be liable for his or her own behavior: "A stake-out by a group of unrelated reporters should be viewed as no more than the sum of its separate parts."[5] Do you agree?

DIETEMANN V. TIME, INC.

449 F.2d 245 (9th Cir. 1971)

HUFSTEDLER, C. J. . . . Plaintiff, a disabled veteran with little education, was engaged in the practice of healing with clay, minerals, and herbs — as practiced, simple quackery.

Defendant, Time, Incorporated, a New York corporation, publishes Life Magazine. Its November 1, 1963 edition carried an article entitled "Crackdown on Quackery." The article depicted plaintiff as a quack and included two pictures of him. One picture was taken at plaintiff's home on September 20, 1963, previous to his arrest on a charge of practicing medicine without a license, and the other taken at the time of his arrest.

Life Magazine entered into an arrangement with the District Attorney's Office of Los Angeles County whereby Life's employees would visit plaintiff and obtain facts and pictures concerning his activities. Two employees of Life, Mrs. Jackie Metcalf and Mr. William Ray, went to plaintiff's home on September 20, 1963. When they arrived at a locked gate, they rang a bell and plaintiff came out of his house and was told by Mrs. Metcalf and Ray that they had been sent there by a friend, a Mr. Johnson. The use of Johnson's name was a ruse to gain entrance. Plaintiff admitted them and all three went into the house and into plaintiff's den.

The plaintiff had some equipment which could at best be described as gadgets, not equipment which had anything to do with the practice of medi-

---

[5] Bruce W. Sanford, *Libel and Privacy* § 11.2, at 541 (2d ed. 1991).

cine. Plaintiff, while examining Mrs. Metcalf, was photographed by Ray with a hidden camera without the consent of plaintiff. One of the pictures taken by him appeared in Life Magazine showing plaintiff with his hand on the upper portion of Mrs. Metcalf's breast while he was looking at some gadgets and holding what appeared to be a wand in his right hand. Mrs. Metcalf had told plaintiff that she had a lump in her breast. Plaintiff concluded that she had eaten some rancid butter 11 years, 9 months, and 7 days prior to that time. Other persons were seated in the room during this time.

The conversation between Mrs. Metcalf and plaintiff was transmitted by radio transmitter hidden in Mrs. Metcalf's purse to a tape recorder in a parked automobile occupied by Joseph Bride, Life employee, John Miner of the District Attorney's Office, and Grant Leake, an investigator of the State Department of Public Health. While the recorded conversation was not quoted in the article in Life, it was mentioned that Life correspondent Bride was making notes of what was being received via the radio transmitter, and such information was at least referred to in the article.

The foregoing events were photographed and recorded by an arrangement among Miner of the District Attorney's Office, Leake of the State Department of Public Health, and Bride, a representative of Life. It had been agreed that Life would obtain pictures and information for use as evidence, and later could be used by Life for publication. . . .

Plaintiff, although a journeyman plumber, claims to be a scientist. Plaintiff had no listings and his home had no sign of any kind. He did not advertise, nor did he have a telephone. He made no charges when he attempted to diagnose or to prescribe herbs and minerals. He did accept contributions.

[The plaintiff was arrested at his home on a charge of practicing medicine without a license. After the plaintiff entered a plea of nolo contendere to the charges, Life's article was published. The plaintiff sued Life in federal district court. The district court concluded that the defendant had invaded the plaintiff's privacy and awarded $1,000 in damages.]

. . . In jurisdictions other than California in which a common law tort for invasion of privacy is recognized, it has been consistently held that surreptitious electronic recording of a plaintiff's conversation causing him emotional distress is actionable. Despite some variations in the description and the labels applied to the tort, there is agreement that publication is not a necessary element of the tort, that the existence of a technical trespass is immaterial, and that proof of special damages is not required. . . .

. . . [W]e have little difficulty in concluding that clandestine photography of the plaintiff in his den and the recordation and transmission of his conversation without his consent resulting in his emotional distress warrants recovery for invasion of privacy in California. . . .

Plaintiff's den was a sphere from which he could reasonably expect to exclude eavesdropping newsmen. He invited two of defendant's employees to the den. One who invites another to his home or office takes a risk that the visitor may not be what he seems, and that the visitor may repeat all he hears and observes when he leaves. But he does not and should not be required to take the risk that what is heard and seen will be transmitted by photograph or recording, or in our modern world, in full living color and hi-fi to the public at large or to any segment of it that the visitor may select. A different rule could have a most pernicious effect upon the dignity of man and it would surely lead to guarded conversations and conduct where candor is most valued, e.g., in the case of doctors and lawyers.

The defendant claims that the First Amendment immunizes it from liability for invading plaintiff's den with a hidden camera and its concealed electronic instruments because its employees were gathering news and its instrumentalities "are indispensable tools of investigative reporting." We agree that newsgathering is an integral part of news dissemination. We strongly disagree, however, that the hidden mechanical contrivances are "indispensable tools" of newsgathering. Investigative reporting is an ancient art; its successful practice long antecedes the invention of miniature cameras and electronic devices. The First Amendment has never been construed to accord newsmen immunity from torts or crimes committed during the course of newsgathering. The First Amendment is not a license to trespass, to steal, or to intrude by electronic means into the precincts of another's home or office. It does not become such a license simply because the person subjected to the intrusion is reasonably suspected of committing a crime.

Defendant relies upon the line of cases commencing with *New York Times Co. v. Sullivan* and extending through *Rosenbloom v. Metromedia, Inc.* to sustain its contentions that (1) publication of news, however tortiously gathered, insulates defendant from liability for the antecedent tort, and (2) even of it is not thus shielded from liability, those cases prevent consideration of publication as an element in computing damages. . . .

No interest protected by the First Amendment is adversely affected by permitting damages for intrusion to be enhanced by the fact of later publication of the information that the publisher improperly acquired. Assessing damages for the additional emotional distress suffered by a plaintiff when the wrongfully acquired data are purveyed to the multitude chills intrusive acts. It does not chill freedom of expression guaranteed by the First Amendment. A rule forbidding the use of publication as an ingredient of damages would deny to the injured plaintiff recovery for real harm done to him without any countervailing benefit to the legitimate interest of the public in being informed. The same rule would encourage conduct by news media that grossly offends ordinary men. . . .

DESNICK V. AMERICAN BROADCASTING CO., INC.

44 F.3d 1345 (7th Cir. 1995)

[Dr. Desnick owned an ophthalmic clinic known as the Desnick Eye Center. The Eye Center had 25 offices in four states and performed over 10,000 cataract operations each year, mainly on elderly persons under Medicare. In 1993, Entine, the producer of ABC's news program *PrimeTimeLive*, telephoned Dr. Desnick and told him that the show wanted to do a segment on cataract practices. Entine told Desnick that the segment would be "fair and balanced" and that it would not include undercover surveillance. Desnick permitted an ABC crew to videotape the Eye Center's Chicago office, to film a cataract operation, and to interview doctors and patients. However, unknown to Desnick,

Entine sent seven people with concealed cameras to the Eye Center's Wisconsin and Indiana offices. These seven people posed as patients and requested eye operations. Glazer and Simon are among the employees who were secretly videotaped examining these "test patients."

When the program aired, it was introduced by Sam Donaldson, who began by stating: "We begin tonight with the story of a so-called 'big cutter,' Dr. James Desnick. . . . [I]n our undercover investigation of the big cutter you'll meet tonight, we turned up evidence that he may also be a big charger, doing unnecessary cataract surgery for the money." The show included interviews with dissatisfied patients, evidence of potential fraud, as well as the experiences of the seven "test patients," many of whom were told they needed cataract surgery. *PrimeTimeLive*'s ophthalmology expert concluded, however, that it would be "near malpractice to do surgery on them." The show also mentioned that the Illinois Medical Board had charged Dr. Desnick with malpractice and deception. Additionally, the show contained an "ambush interview" of Dr. Desnick while he was at an airport, with Donaldson shouting out allegations of fraud to Desnick.

Among a number of causes of action raised by the plaintiffs, who included Desnick, Simon, and Glazer, is an action for intrusion upon seclusion.]

POSNER, C. J. . . . To enter upon another's land without consent is a trespass. The force of this rule has, it is true, been diluted somewhat by concepts of privilege and of implied consent. But there is no journalists' privilege to trespass. And there can be no implied consent in any nonfictitious sense of the term when express consent is procured by a misrepresentation or a misleading omission. The Desnick Eye Center would not have agreed to the entry of the test patients into its offices had it known they wanted eye examinations only in order to gather material for a television expose of the Center and that they were going to make secret videotapes of the examinations. Yet some cases, illustrated by *Martin v. Fidelity & Casualty Co.*, 421 So. 2d 109, 111 (Ala. 1982), deem consent effective even though it was procured by fraud. There must be *something* to this surprising result. Without it a restaurant critic could not conceal his identity when he ordered a meal, or a browser pretend to be interested in merchandise that he could not afford to buy. Dinner guests would be trespassers if they were false friends who never would have been invited had the host known their true character, and a consumer who in an effort to bargain down an automobile dealer falsely claimed to be able to buy the same car elsewhere at a lower price would be a trespasser in the dealer's showroom. Some of these might be classified as privileged trespasses, designed to promote competition. Others might be thought justified by some kind of implied consent — the restaurant critic for example might point by way of analogy to the use of the "fair use" defense by book reviewers charged with copyright infringement and argue that the restaurant industry as a whole would be injured if restaurants could exclude critics. But most such efforts at rationalization would be little better than evasions. The fact is that consent to an entry is often given legal effect even though the entrant has intentions that if known to the owner of the property would cause him for perfectly understandable and generally ethical or at least lawful reasons to revoke his consent.

The law's willingness to give effect to consent procured by fraud is not limited to the tort of trespass. The *Restatement* gives the example of a man who obtains consent to sexual intercourse by promising a woman $100, yet (unbeknownst to her, of course) he pays her with a counterfeit bill and intended to do so from the start. The man is not guilty of battery, even though unconsented-to sexual intercourse is a battery. Yet we know that to conceal the fact that one has a venereal disease transforms "consensual" intercourse into battery. Seduction, standardly effected by false promises of love, is not rape; intercourse under the pretense of rendering medical or psychiatric treatment is, at least in most states. It certainly is battery. Trespass presents close parallels. If a homeowner opens his door to a purported meter reader who is in fact nothing of the sort — just a busybody curious about the interior of the home — the homeowner's consent to his entry is not a defense to a suit for trespass. And likewise if a competitor gained entry to a business firm's premises posing as a customer but in fact hoping to steal the firm's trade secrets.

How to distinguish the two classes of case — the seducer from the medical impersonator, the restaurant critic from the meter-reader impersonator? The answer can have nothing to do with fraud; there is fraud in all the cases. It has to do with the interest that the torts in question, battery and trespass, protect. The one protects the inviolability of the person, the other the inviolability of the person's property. The woman who is seduced wants to have sex with her seducer, and the restaurant owner wants to have customers. The woman who is victimized by the medical impersonator has no desire to have sex with her doctor; she wants medical treatment. And the homeowner victimized by the phony meter reader does not want strangers in his house unless they have authorized service functions. The dealer's objection to the customer who claims falsely to have a lower price from a competing dealer is not to the physical presence of the customer, but to the fraud that he is trying to perpetuate. The lines are not bright — they are not even inevitable. They are the traces of the old forms of action, which have resulted in a multitude of artificial distinctions in modern law. But that is nothing new.

There was no invasion in the present case of any of the specific interests that the tort of trespass seeks to protect. The test patients entered offices that were open to anyone expressing a desire for ophthalmic services and videotaped physicians engaged in professional, not personal, communications with strangers (the testers themselves). The activities of the offices were not disrupted. . . . Nor was there any "inva[sion of] a person's private space," as in our hypothetical meter-reader case, as in the famous case of *De May v. Roberts*, 9 N.W. 146 (Mich. 1881) (where a doctor, called to the plaintiff's home to deliver her baby, brought along with him a friend who was curious to see a birth but was not a medical doctor, and represented the friend to be his medical assistant), as in one of its numerous modern counterparts, . . . and as in *Dietemann v. Time, Inc.*, 449 F.2d 245 (9th Cir. 1971), on which the plaintiffs in our case rely. *Dietemann* involved a home. True, the portion invaded was an office, where the plaintiff performed quack healing of nonexistent ailments. The parallel to this case is plain enough, but there is a difference. Dietemann was not in business, and did not advertise his services or charge for them. His quackery was private.

No embarrassingly intimate details of anybody's life were publicized in the present case. There was no eavesdropping on a private conversation; the testers recorded their own conversations with the Desnick Eye Center's physicians. There was no violation of the doctor-patient privilege. There was no theft, or intent to steal, trade secrets; no disruption of decorum, of peace and quiet; no noisy or distracting demonstrations. Had the testers been undercover FBI agents, there would have been no violation of the Fourth Amendment, because there would have been no invasion of a legally protected interest in property or privacy. . . .

NOTES & QUESTIONS

1. ***Investigative Reporting.*** As is illustrated by *Dietemann* and *Desnick*, investigative reporting often depends upon deception. Those cases are split on the issue of whether such investigative techniques can give rise to intrusion. Recall the *Dietemann* court's statement:

> Investigative reporting is an ancient art; its successful practice long antecedes the invention of miniature cameras and electronic devices. The First Amendment has never been construed to accord newsmen immunity from torts or crimes committed during the course of newsgathering. The First Amendment is not a license to trespass, to steal, or to intrude by electronic means into the precincts of another's home or office. It does not become such a license simply because the person subjected to the intrusion is reasonably suspected of committing a crime.[6]

However, investigative reporting has served an important function throughout history. In 1887, a reporter named Nellie Bly pretended to be mentally ill to gain access to a mental asylum. Her portrayal of the brutal conditions led to significant reforms. Upton Sinclair went undercover as a meatpacker to expose conditions in slaughterhouses for his book *The Jungle* in 1904.[7] C. Thomas Dienes argues:

> . . . Undercover journalism often serves the public interest. In the public sector, it allows the media to perform its role as the eyes and ears of the people, to perform a checking function on government. Especially at a time when citizens are often unable or unwilling to supervise government, this media role is critical to self-government. In the private sector, when the government fails in its responsibility to protect the public against fraudulent and unethical business and professional practices, whether because of lack of resources or unwillingness, media exposure of such practices can and often does provide the spur forcing government action.
> Nevertheless, the techniques of investigative reporting generally, and undercover journalism in particular, are controversial even within journalism.

---

[6] *See also Food Lion, Inc. v. Captial Cities/ABC, Inc.*, 194 F.3d 505 (4th Cir. 1999) (holding that ABC could be held liable for fraud, trespass, and breach of loyalty by having its reporters submit applications with false identities to a supermarket to get hired and investigate and secretly record the supermarket's food handling practices).

[7] *See* C. Thomas Dienes, *Protecting Investigative Journalism*, 67 Geo. Wash. L. Rev. 1139, 1141 (1999).

Many editors and journalists condemn the use of confidential sources, any misrepresentation or lying to get information, and the use of the new snooping technology to probe where eyes and ears cannot go.

Undercover reporting has sometimes been called "stunt journalism." But it is difficult to believe that many of the stories of public importance of the kind that I have noted could have been published without the use of undercover reporting. . . .[8]

2. *Intrusion Liability for the Receipt of Data Obtained by Intrusion.* In *Pearson v. Dodd*, 410 F.2d 701 (D.C. Cir. 1969), two former employees of Senator Thomas Dodd of Connecticut, with the assistance of two of Dodd's active staff members, entered Dodd's office without authorization and surreptitiously made copies of many documents in his files. These documents related to Dodd's relationship to lobbyists for foreign interests. Newspaper columnists Drew Pearson and Jack Anderson published articles containing information from these documents. Pearson and Anderson did not participate in or order the illegal copying; they only received copies of the documents knowing that they had been copied without authorization. Dodd sued Pearson and Anderson for invasion of privacy. The court held that intrusion could not extend to those who merely received the information:

> If we were to hold appellants liable for invasion of privacy on these facts, we would establish the proposition that one who receives information from an intruder, knowing it has been obtained by improper intrusion, is guilty of a tort. In an untried and developing area of tort law, we are not prepared to go so far. A person approached by an eavesdroppe with an offer to share in the information gathered through the eavesdropping would perhaps play the nobler part should he spurn the offer and shut his ears. However, it seems to us that at this point it would place too great a strain on human weakness to hold one liable in damages who merely succumbs to temptation and listens.

(c) Highly Offensive

SHULMAN V. GROUP W. PRODUCTIONS, INC.

955 P.2d 469 (Cal. 1998)

WERDEGAR, J. . . . On June 24, 1990, plaintiffs Ruth and Wayne Shulman, mother and son, were injured when the car in which they and two other family members were riding on interstate 10 in Riverside County flew off the highway and tumbled down an embankment into a drainage ditch on state-owned property, coming to rest upside down. Ruth, the most seriously injured of the two, was pinned under the car. Ruth and Wayne both had to be cut free from the vehicle by the device known as "the jaws of life."

A rescue helicopter operated by Mercy Air was dispatched to the scene. The flight nurse, who would perform the medical care at the scene and on the way to the hospital, was Laura Carnahan. Also on board were the pilot, a medic and

---

[8]*Id.* at 1143. For further background about investigative journalism and the use of deception, see Bernard W. Bell, *Secrets and Lies: News Media and Law Enforcement Use of Deception as an Investigative Tool,* 60 U. Pitt. L. Rev. 745 (1999).

Joel Cooke, a video camera operator employed by defendants Group W Productions, Inc., and 4MN Productions. Cooke was recording the rescue operation for later broadcast.

Cooke roamed the accident scene, videotaping the rescue. Nurse Carnahan wore a wireless microphone that picked up her conversations with both Ruth and the other rescue personnel. Cooke's tape was edited into a piece approximately nine minutes long, which, with the addition of narrative voice-over, was broadcast on September 29, 1990, as a segment of *On Scene: Emergency Response*.

The segment begins with the Mercy Air helicopter shown on its way to the accident site. The narrator's voice is heard in the background, setting the scene and describing in general terms what has happened. . . .

The videotape shows only a glimpse of Wayne, and his voice is never heard. Ruth is shown several times, either by brief shots of a limb or her torso, or with her features blocked by others or obscured by an oxygen mask. She is also heard speaking several times. Carnahan calls her "Ruth" and her last name is not mentioned on the broadcast.

While Ruth is still trapped under the car, Carnahan asks Ruth's age. Ruth responds, "I'm old." On further questioning, Ruth reveals she is 47, and Carnahan observes that "it's all relative. You're not that old." During her extrication from the car, Ruth asks at least twice if she is dreaming. At one point she asks Carnahan, who has told her she will be taken to the hospital in a helicopter: "Are you teasing?" At another point she says: "This is terrible. Am I dreaming?" She also asks what happened and where the rest of her family is, repeating the questions even after being told she was in an accident and the other family members are being cared for. While being loaded into the helicopter on a stretcher, Ruth says: "I just want to die." Carnahan reassures her that she is "going to do real well," but Ruth repeats: "I just want to die. I don't want to go through this."

Ruth and Wayne are placed in the helicopter, and its door is closed. The narrator states: "Once airborne, Laura and [the flight medic] will update their patients' vital signs and establish communications with the waiting trauma teams at Loma Linda." Carnahan, speaking into what appears to be a radio microphone, transmits some of Ruth's vital signs and states that Ruth cannot move her feet and has no sensation. The video footage during the helicopter ride includes a few seconds of Ruth's face, covered by an oxygen mask. Wayne is neither shown nor heard.

The helicopter lands on the hospital roof. With the door open, Ruth states while being taken out: "My upper back hurts." Carnahan replies: "Your upper back hurts. That's what you were saying up there." Ruth states: "I don't feel that great." Carnahan responds: "You probably don't."

Finally, Ruth is shown being moved from the helicopter into the - hospital. . . .

The accident left Ruth a paraplegic. When the segment was broadcast, Wayne phoned Ruth in her hospital room and told her to turn on the television because "Channel 4 is showing our accident now." Shortly afterward, several hospital workers came into the room to mention that a videotaped segment of her accident was being shown. Ruth was "shocked, so to speak, that this would be run and I would be exploited, have my privacy invaded, which is what I felt had happened." She did not know her rescue had been recorded in this manner and had never consented to the recording or broadcast. Ruth had the impression from the broadcast "that I was kind of talking non-stop, and I remember hearing some of the things I said, which were not very pleasant." Asked at deposition what part of the broadcast material she considered private, Ruth explained: "I think the whole scene was pretty private. It was pretty gruesome, the parts that I saw, my knee sticking out of the car. I certainly did not look my best, and I don't feel it's for the public to see. I was not at my best in what I was thinking and what I was saying and what was being shown, and it's not for the public to see this trauma that I was going through."

Ruth and Wayne sued the producers of *On Scene: Emergency Response*, as well as others. The first amended complaint included two causes of action for invasion of privacy, one based on defendants' unlawful intrusion by video-taping the rescue in the first instance and the other based on the public disclosure of private facts, i.e., the broadcast. . . .

The trial court granted the media defendants' summary judgment motion, basing its ruling on plaintiffs' admissions that the accident and rescue were matters of public interest and public affairs. Those admissions, in the trial court's view, showed as a matter of law that the broadcast material was news-worthy, thereby vesting the media defendants' conduct with First Amendment protection. The court entered judgment for defendants on all causes of action. . . .

[T]he action for intrusion has two elements: (1) intrusion into a private place, conversation or matter, (2) in a manner highly offensive to a reasonable person. We consider the elements in that order.

We ask first whether defendants "intentionally intrude[d], physically or otherwise, upon the solitude or seclusion of another," that is, into a place or conversation private to Wayne or Ruth. . . .

Cameraman Cooke's mere presence at the accident scene and filming of the events occurring there cannot be deemed either a physical or sensory intrusion on plaintiffs' seclusion. Plaintiffs had no right of ownership or possession of the property where the rescue took place, nor any actual control of the premises. Nor could they have had a reasonable expectation that members of the media would be excluded or prevented from photographing the scene; for journalists to attend and record the scenes of accidents and rescues is in no way unusual or unexpected.

Two aspects of defendants' conduct, however, raise triable issues of intrusion on seclusion. First, a triable issue exists as to whether both plaintiffs had an objectively reasonable expectation of privacy in the interior of the rescue helicopter, which served as an ambulance. Although the attendance of reporters and photographers at the scene of an accident is to be expected, we are aware of no law or custom permitting the press to ride in ambulances or enter hospital rooms during treatment without the patient's consent. Other than the two patients and Cooke, only three people were present in the helicopter, all Mercy Air staff. As the Court of Appeal observed, "[i]t is neither the custom nor the habit of our society that any member of the public at large or its media representatives may hitch a ride in an ambulance and ogle as paramedics care for an injured stranger."

Second, Ruth was entitled to a degree of privacy in her conversations with

Carnahan and other medical rescuers at the accident scene, and in Carnahan's conversations conveying medical information regarding Ruth to the hospital base. Cooke, perhaps, did not intrude into that zone of privacy merely by being present at a place where he could hear such conversations with unaided ears. But by placing a microphone on Carnahan's person, amplifying and recording what she said and heard, defendants may have listened in on conversations the parties could reasonably have expected to be private. . . .

We turn to the second element of the intrusion tort, offensiveness. . . .

On this summary judgment record, we believe a jury could find defendants' recording of Ruth's communications to Carnahan and other rescuers, and filming in the air ambulance, to be "'highly offensive to a reasonable person.'" With regard to the depth of the intrusion, a reasonable jury could find highly offensive the placement of a microphone on a medical rescuer in order to intercept what would otherwise be private conversations with an injured patient. In that setting, as defendants could and should have foreseen, the patient would not know her words were being recorded and would not have occasion to ask about, and object or consent to, recording. Defendants, it could reasonably be said, took calculated advantage of the patient's "vulnerability and confusion." Arguably, the last thing an injured accident victim should have to worry about while being pried from her wrecked car is that a television producer may be recording everything she says to medical personnel for the possible edification and entertainment of casual television viewers.

For much the same reason, a jury could reasonably regard entering and riding in an ambulance — whether on the ground or in the air — with two seriously injured patients to be an egregious intrusion on a place of expected seclusion. Again, the patients, at least in this case, were hardly in a position to keep careful watch on who was riding with them, or to inquire as to everyone's business and consent or object to their presence. A jury could reasonably believe that fundamental respect for human dignity requires the patients' anxious journey be taken only with those whose care is solely for them and out of sight of the prying eyes (or cameras) of others.

Nor can we say as a matter of law that defendants' motive — to gather usable material for a potentially newsworthy story — necessarily privileged their intrusive conduct as a matter of common law tort liability. A reasonable jury could conclude the producers' desire to get footage that would convey the "feel" of the event — the real sights and sounds of a difficult rescue — did not justify either placing a microphone on Nurse Carnahan or filming inside the rescue helicopter. Although defendants' purposes could scarcely be regarded as evil or malicious (in the colloquial sense), their behavior could, even in light of their motives, be thought to show a highly offensive lack of sensitivity and respect for plaintiffs' privacy. A reasonable jury could find that defendants, in placing a microphone on an emergency treatment nurse and recording her conversation with a distressed, disoriented and severely injured patient, without the patient's knowledge or consent, acted with highly offensive disrespect for the patient's personal privacy. . . .

Turning to the question of constitutional protection for newsgathering, one finds the decisional law reflects a general rule of *nonprotection*: the press in its newsgathering activities enjoys no immunity or exemption from generally applicable laws. . . .

As should be apparent from the above discussion, the constitutional protection accorded newsgathering, if any, is far narrower than the protection surrounding the publication of truthful material; consequently, the fact that a reporter may be seeking "newsworthy" material does not in itself privilege the investigatory activity. The reason for the difference is simple: the intrusion tort, unlike that for publication of private facts, does not subject the press to liability for the contents of its publications. Newsworthiness . . . is a complete bar to liability for publication of private facts and is evaluated with a high degree of deference to editorial judgment. The same deference is not due, however, when the issue is not the media's right to publish or broadcast what they choose, but their right to intrude into secluded areas or conversations in pursuit of publishable material. At most, the Constitution may preclude tort liability that would "place an impermissible burden on newsgatherers" by depriving them of their "'indispensable tools'" . . .

NOTES & QUESTIONS

1. *Intrusion in Public Places.* Consider *Sanders v. ABC*, 978 P.2d 67 (Cal. 1999), decided by the same court one year after *Shulman*. In *Sanders*, a reporter obtained a job with a telephone psychics company that gave "readings" to callers for a fee. The psychics worked in a large room with rows of cubicles. The reporter secretly videotaped conversations of the plaintiff, an employee, with others at his cubicle or other cubicles. The plaintiff sued for intrusion upon seclusion. The defendants argued that the employee lacked a reasonable expectation of privacy in his conversations because they could be seen and overheard by co-workers. The court sided with the plaintiff:

> . . . [W]e adhere to the view suggested in *Shulman*: privacy, for purposes of the intrusion tort, is not a binary, all-or-nothing characteristic. There are degrees and nuances to societal recognition of our expectations of privacy: the fact that the privacy one expects in a given setting is not complete or absolute does not render the expectation unreasonable as a matter of law. Although the intrusion tort is often defined in terms of "seclusion" the seclusion referred to need not be absolute. "Like 'privacy,' the concept of 'seclusion' is relative. The mere fact that a person can be seen by someone does not automatically mean that he or she can legally be forced to be subject to being seen by everyone."

2. PAPARAZZI

Paparazzi are aggressive photographers who often harass celebrities to take candid photographs to sell to newspapers, tabloids, and magazines. The word "paparazzi" comes from "paparazzo," a kind of annoying insect. Fueling the behavior of the paparazzi are the exorbitant prices that photographs of celebrities command. For example, a photo of Diana embracing Dodi al-Fayed was sold for over $3 million. Paparazzi have a reputation for being very invasive into the privacy of celebrities. For example, paparazzi flew over Michael J. Fox's wedding in helicopters to take photographs. Disguised photographers took photographs of Paul Reiser's premature baby in the hospital. Paparazzi also camped outside Reiser's backyard taking photographs with telephoto lenses.

Paparazzi chased Arnold Schwarzenegger and Maria Shriver off the road to take the first photos of him leaving the hospital after heart surgery. To what extent does the law of privacy restrict the behavior of paparazzi?

GALELLA V. ONASSIS

487 F.2d 986 (2d Cir. 1973)

SMITH, J. . . . Galella is a free-lance photographer specializing in the making and sale of photographs of well-known persons. Defendant Onassis is the widow of the late President, John F. Kennedy, mother of the two Kennedy children, John and Caroline, and is the wife of Aristotle Onassis, widely known shipping figure and reputed multimillionaire. John Walsh, James Kalafatis and John Connelly are U. S. Secret Service agents assigned to the duty of protecting the Kennedy children under 18 U.S.C. § 3056, which provides for protection of the children of deceased presidents up to the age of 16.

Galella fancies himself as a "paparazzo" (literally a kind of annoying insect, perhaps roughly equivalent to the English "gadfly.") Paparazzi make themselves as visible to the public and obnoxious to their photographic subjects as possible to aid in the advertisement and wide sale of their works.[9]

Some examples of Galella's conduct brought out at trial are illustrative. Galella took pictures of John Kennedy riding his bicycle in Central Park across the way from his home. He jumped out into the boy's path, causing the agents concern for John's safety. The agents' reaction and interrogation of Galella led to Galella's arrest and his action against the agents; Galella on other occasions interrupted Caroline at tennis, and invaded the children's private schools. At one time he came uncomfortably close in a power boat to Mrs. Onassis swimming. He often jumped and postured around while taking pictures of her party notably at a theater opening but also on numerous other occasions. He followed a practice of bribing apartment house, restaurant and nightclub doormen as well as romancing a family servant to keep him advised of the movements of the family.

After detention and arrest following complaint by the Secret Service agents protecting Mrs. Onassis' son and his acquittal in the state court, Galella filed suit in state court against the agents and Mrs. Onassis. Galella claimed that under orders from Mrs. Onassis, the three agents had falsely arrested and maliciously prosecuted him, and that this incident in addition to several others described in the complaint constituted an unlawful interference with his trade.

Mrs. Onassis answered denying any role in the arrest or any part in the claimed interference with his attempts to photograph her, and counterclaimed for damages and injunctive relief, charging that Galella had invaded her privacy, assaulted and battered her, intentionally inflicted emotional distress and engaged in a campaign of harassment. . . .

After a six-week trial the court dismissed Galella's claim and granted relief to both the defendant and the intervenor. Galella was enjoined from (1) keeping the defendant and her children under surveillance or following any of

---

[9]The newspapers report a recent incident in which one Marlon Brando, annoyed by Galella, punched Galella, breaking Galella's jaw and infecting Brando's hand.

them; (2) approaching within 100 yards of the home of defendant or her children, or within 100 yards of either child's school or within 75 yards of either child or 50 yards of defendant; (3) using the name, portrait or picture of defendant or her children for advertising; (4) attempting to communicate with defendant or her children except through her attorney.

We conclude that grant of summary judgment and dismissal of Galella's claim against the Secret Service agents was proper. . . .

Evidence offered by the defense showed that Galella had on occasion intentionally physically touched Mrs. Onassis and her daughter, caused fear of physical contact in his frenzied attempts to get their pictures, followed defendant and her children too closely in an automobile, endangered the safety of the children while they were swimming, water skiing and horseback riding. Galella cannot successfully challenge the court's finding of tortious conduct.

Finding that Galella had "insinuated himself into the very fabric of Mrs. Onassis' life . . ." the court framed its relief in part on the need to prevent further invasion of the defendant's privacy. Whether or not this accords with present New York law, there is no doubt that it is sustainable under New York's proscription of harassment.

Of course legitimate countervailing social needs may warrant some intrusion despite an individual's reasonable expectation of privacy and freedom from harassment. However the interference allowed may be no greater than that necessary to protect the overriding public interest. Mrs. Onassis was properly found to be a public figure and thus subject to news coverage. Nonetheless, Galella's action went far beyond the reasonable bounds of news gathering. When weighed against the de minimis public importance of the daily activities of the defendant, Galella's constant surveillance, his obtrusive and intruding presence, was unwarranted and unreasonable. If there were any doubt in our minds, Galella's inexcusable conduct toward defendant's minor children would resolve it.

Galella does not seriously dispute the court's finding of tortious conduct. Rather, he sets up the First Amendment as a wall of immunity protecting newsmen from any liability for their conduct while gathering news. There is no such scope to the First Amendment right. Crimes and torts committed in news gathering are not protected. There is no threat to a free press in requiring its agents to act within the law. . . .

CALIFORNIA ANTI-PAPARAZZI ACT

Cal. Civ. Code § 1708.8

Princess Diana's death in 1997 precipitated calls for anti-paparazzi legislation in the United States. On the evening of August 30, Princess Diana and Dodi Al-Fayed were being chauffeured in a Mercedes from the Ritz Hotel in Paris. Paparazzi followed the Mercedes on motorcycles and in cars. A chase developed, and according to eyewitnesses, the motorcycles were swarming the Mercedes as it entered a tunnel. The Mercedes crashed in the tunnel, killing both Princess Diana and Dodi Al-Fayed. About 10 to 15 photographers gathered around the Mercedes after the crash and continued to take pictures at the scene of the accident. Seven photographers were arrested by French police at the scene of the accident.

In the United States, anti-paparazzi legislation was introduced in Congress but failed to be passed. California was the first state to adopt anti-paparazzi legislation.

California's Anti-Paparazzi Act does not supplant the state's existing privacy torts. Rather, it provides rights and remedies "in addition to any other rights and remedies provided by law." § 1708.8(h).

The Act recognizes two forms of invasion of privacy. First, it defines liability for "physical invasion of privacy":

> (a) A person is liable for physical invasion of privacy when the defendant knowingly enters onto the land of another without permission or otherwise committed a trespass, in order to physically invade the privacy of the plaintiff with the intent to capture any type of visual image, sound recording, or other physical impression of the plaintiff engaging in a personal or familial activity and the physical invasion occurs in a manner that is offensive to a reasonable person.

"Personal or familial activity" is defined as including, but not limited to: "intimate details of the plaintiff's personal life, interactions with the plaintiff's family or significant others, or other aspects of plaintiff's private affairs or concerns." § 1708.8(k).

Second, the Act defines liability for "constructive invasion of privacy":

> (b) A person is liable for constructive invasion of privacy when the defendant attempts to capture, in a manner that is offensive to a reasonable person, any type of visual image, sound recording, or other physical impression of the plaintiff engaging in a personal or familial activity under circumstances in which the plaintiff had a reasonable expectation of privacy, through the use of a visual or auditory enhancing device, regardless of whether there is a physical trespass, if this image, sound recording, or other physical impression could not have been achieved without a trespass unless the visual or auditory enhancing device was used.

The Act provides for increased damages for the two types of privacy violations defined above:

> (c) A person who commits physical invasion of privacy or constructive invasion of privacy, or both, is liable for up to three times the amount of any general and special damages that are proximately caused by the violation of this section. This person may also be liable for punitive damages, subject to proof according to Section 3294. If the plaintiff proves that the invasion of privacy was committed for a commercial purpose, the defendant shall also be subject to disgorgement to the plaintiff of any proceeds or other consideration obtained as a result of the violation of this section.

Equitable relief is also available. § 1708.8(g).

Further, the Act punishes a person who "directs, solicits, actually induces, or actually causes" a person to violate the law. § 1708.8(d). However, the Act does not punish the sale or dissemination of images or recordings in violation of the Act. § 1708.8(e).

Since the Act is aimed at limiting the intrusive activities of paparazzi, not merely the invasion of privacy caused by having one's photograph taken or voice recorded, the Act applies even if no image or recording is ever captured or sold. § 1708.8(i).

The Act exempts the activities of law enforcement personnel or government employees who "in the course and scope of their employment, and supported by an articulable suspicion, attempt to capture any type of visual image, sound recording, or other physical impression of a person during an investigation, surveillance, or monitoring of any conduct to obtain evidence of suspected illegal activity, the suspected violation of any administrative rule or regulation, a suspected fraudulent insurance claim, or any other suspected fraudulent conduct or activity involving a violation of law or pattern of business practices adversely affecting the public health or safety." § 1708.8(f).

NOTES & QUESTIONS

1. How does California's Anti-Paparazzi Act differ from the ordinary intrusion upon seclusion tort?
2. Is California's Anti-Paparazzi Act constitutional? Rodney Smolla argues that this law is content based because it looks to the perpetrator's intent to sell or transfer communicative material. Smolla also argues that the First Amendment should prohibit liability for intrusion when a plaintiff is in a public place.[10] However, much paparazzi activity occurs in public. Would an anti-paparazzi law be viable if it were limited only to instances where plaintiffs were in private places? Do you agree with Smolla that the Act violates the First Amendment?

Erwin Chemerinsky contends that newsgathering, although currently not protected by the First Amendment, should be protected by interediate scrutiny:

> Speech is protected because it matters in people's lives, and aggressive newsgathering is often crucial to obtaining the information. The very notion of a marketplace of ideas rests on the availability of information. Aggressive newsgathering, such as by undercover reporters, is often the key to gathering the information. People on their own cannot expose unhealthy practices in supermarkets or fraud by telemarketers or unnecessary surgery by doctors. But the media can expose this, if it is allowed the tools to do so, and the public directly benefits from the reporting.[11]

However, Chemerinsky goes on to argue that the California Anti-Paparazzi Act would survive intermediate scrutiny:

> Despite strongly believing in First Amendment protection for newsgathering, I believe that this law is constitutional. The government has an important interest in protecting the privacy of the home. Fourth Amendment cases have recognized the special privacy interests surrounding the home. Additionally, in the First Amendment area, the Court has expressly protected the privacy of the home. In *Frisby v. Schultz*, the Court sustained an ordinance that prohibited picketing "before or about" any residence. Although the law was adopted in response to targeted picketing by antiabortion pro-

---

[10] *See* Rodney A. Smolla, *Privacy and the First Amendment Right to Gather News*, 67 Geo. Wash. L. Rev. 1097, 1113, 1127 (1999).

[11] Erwin Chemerinsky, *Protect the Press: A First Amendment Standard for Safeguarding Aggressive Newsgathering*, 33 U. Rich. L. Rev. 1143, 1159 (2000).

testors of a doctor's home, the Court concluded that the law was permissible because it was content neutral and narrowly tailored to protect people's tranquility and repose in their homes. Justice O'Connor, writing for the Court, said that "[t]he First Amendment permits the government to prohibit offensive speech as intrusive when the 'captive' audience cannot avoid the objectionable speech. The target of the focused picketing banned by the . . . ordinance is just such a 'captive.' The resident is figuratively, and perhaps literally, trapped within the home."

The California Privacy Protection Act says that people, no matter how famous, should be able to shut their door and close out the media and the world. If the image could not have been gained except through a trespass, the media should not be able to obtain it through technological enhancement equipment. Simply put, the law is constitutional because it substantially advances the government's interest in safeguarding privacy in the home.[12]

C. DISCLOSURE OF TRUTHFUL INFORMATION

In certain circumstances, the law provides remedies for individuals who suffer harm as a result of the disclosure of their personal information. One of the primary remedies is the tort of public disclosure of private facts. Other remedies include statutes passed by states and the federal government that restrict the disclosure of specific information. For example, a number of states have laws prohibiting the disclosure of the identities of sexual offense victims. *See, e.g.,* N.Y. Civil Rights L. §50-b; 42 Pa. Comp. Stat. §5988. States have also provided statutory remedies for the disclosure that a person has AIDS. *See, e.g.,* 410 Illinois Comp. Stat. 305/9; Florida Stat. §381.004. Federal wiretap law prohibits the disclosure of a communication that one has reason to know was obtained through an illegal wiretap. *See* 18 U.S.C. §2511(1)(c). This provision of federal wiretap law is the subject of *Bartnicki v. Vopper,* discussed in section 2 below. What types of disclosures of personal information can and should give rise to civil liability? How can liability for the disclosure of true information coexist with the First Amendment's protection of free speech?

1. PUBLIC DISCLOSURE OF PRIVATE FACTS

(a) Introduction

RESTATEMENT (SECOND) OF TORTS §652D:
PUBLICITY GIVEN TO PRIVATE LIFE

One who gives publicity to a matter concerning the private life of another is subject to liability to the other for invasion of his privacy, if the matter publicized is of a kind that

---

[12]*Id.* at 1163–1164.

> (a) would be highly offensive to a reasonable person, and
>
> (b) is not of legitimate concern to the public

NOTES & QUESTIONS

1. ***Publicity.*** "Publicity" is not the same as "publication." According to the Restatement, "publication" includes any communication by the defendant to a third person. "Publicity" means that the matter is communicated to the "public at large" or "to so many persons that the matter must be regarded as substantially certain to become one of public knowledge."

2. ***Highly Offensive.*** The disclosure must be highly offensive. According to the Restatement (comment c):

> Complete privacy does not exist in this world except in a desert, and anyone who is not a hermit must expect and endure the ordinary incidents of the community life of which he is a part. Thus he must expect the more or less casual observation of his neighbors as to what he does, and that his comings and goings and his ordinary daily activities, will be described in the press as a matter of casual interest to others. The ordinary reasonable man does not take offense at a report in a newspaper that he has returned from a visit, gone camping in the woods or given a party at his house for his friends. Even minor and moderate annoyance, as for example through public disclosure of the fact that the plaintiff has clumsily fallen downstairs and broken his ankle, is not sufficient to give him a cause of action under the rule stated in this Section. It is only when the publicity given to him is such that a reasonable person would feel justified in feeling seriously aggrieved by it, that the cause of action arises.

Note the irony. The Restatement commentary suggests that the ordinary person does not take offense of a newspaper report that he has "given a party at his house for his friends." Indeed, it was such a newspaper report that some suggest inspired Samuel Warren to write the law review article that gave rise to this very tort.

3. ***Newsworthiness.*** As stated by Restatement (comment f): "When the subject-matter of the publicity is of legitimate public concern, there is no invasion of privacy." Recall that the first exception to the right to privacy proposed by Brandeis and Warren was for "any publication of matter which is of general public interest."

4. ***Recognition of the Tort by the States.*** Most states recognize the public disclosure tort.[13] There are some states that have not recognized the tort: Nebraska, New York, North Carolina, North Dakota, Rhode Island, Utah, and

---

[13] For more background about the public disclosure tort, see Jonathan B. Mintz, *The Remains of Privacy's Disclosure Tort: An Exploration of the Private Domain*, 55 Md. L. Rev. 425 (1996); Robert C. Post, *The Social Foundations of Privacy: Community and Self in the Common Law Tort*, 77 Cal. L. Rev. 957 (1989); Peter L. Felcher & Edward L. Rubin, *Privacy, Publicity, and the Portrayal of Real People by the Media*, 88 Yale L.J. 1577 (1979); Dorsey D. Ellis, Jr., *Damages and the Privacy Tort: Sketching a "Legal Profile,"* 64 Iowa L. Rev. 1111 (1979); Randall Bezanson, *Public Disclosure as News: Injunctive Relief and Newsworthiness in Privacy Actions Involving the Press*, 64 Iowa L. Rev. 1061 (1979); John W. Wade, *Defamation and the Right to Privacy*, 15 Vand. L. Rev. 1093 (1962).

Virginia.[14] As you read in *Lake v. Wal-Mart*, Minnesota, a long time holdout on recognizing the public disclosure tort, recently recognized the tort.

(b) Private Matters

MELVIN V. REID

297 P. 91 (Cal. 1931)

MARKS, J. Appellant filed her complaint in the court below seeking judgment against defendants for money. The complaint contains four causes of action separately stated. The first is based upon the violation of what has become known as the "right of privacy." . . .

It is alleged that appellant's maiden name was Gabrielle Darley; that a number of years ago she was a prostitute and was tried for murder, the trial resulting in her acquittal; that during the year 1918, and after her acquittal, she abandoned her life of shame and became entirely rehabilitated; that during the year 1919 she married Bernard Melvin and commenced the duties of caring for their home, and thereafter at all times lived an exemplary, virtuous, honorable, and righteous life; that she assumed a place in respectable society, and made many friends who were not aware of the incidents of her earlier life; that during the month of July, 1925, the defendants, without her permission, knowledge, or consent, made, photographed, produced, and released a moving picture film entitled "The Red Kimono," and thereafter exhibited it in moving picture houses in California, Arizona, and throughout many other states; that this moving picture was based upon the true story of the past life of appellant, and that her maiden name, Gabrielle Darley, was used therein; that defendants featured and advertised that the plot of the film was the true story of the unsavory incidents in the life of appellant; that Gabrielle Darley was the true name of the principal character; and that Gabrielle Darley was appellant; that by the production and showing of the picture, friends of appellant learned for the first time of the unsavory incidents of her early life. This caused them to scorn and abandon her, and exposed her to obloquy, contempt, and ridicule, causing her grievous mental and physical suffering to her damage in the sum of $50,000. These allegations were set forth in the first cause of action. . . .

The law of privacy is of recent origin. It was first discussed in an essay published in a law journal in 1890. It did not gain prominence or notice of the bench or bar until an article appeared in 4 Harvard Law Review, p. 193, written by the Honorable Louis D. Brandeis in collaboration with Samuel D. Warren. Since the publication of this article, a number of cases have arisen in various states involving the so-called doctrine of the right of privacy. It is recognized in some jurisdictions, while others have refused to put it into effect. . . .

The right of privacy as recognized in a number of states has been defined as follows: "The right of privacy may be defined as the right to live one's life in seclusion, without being subjected to unwarranted and undesired publicity.

---

[14] *See* Geoff Dendy, Note, *The Newsworthiness Defense to the Public Disclosure Tort*, 85 Ky. L.J. 147, 158 (1997).

In short, it is the right to be let alone. There are times, however, when one, whether willingly or not, becomes an actor in an occurrence of public or general interest. When this takes place, he emerges from his seclusion, and it is not an invasion of his right of privacy to publish his photograph with an account of such occurrence." . . .

. . . [T]he use of the incidents from the life of appellant in the moving picture is in itself not actionable. These incidents appeared in the records of her trial for murder, which is a public record, open to the perusal of all. The very fact that they were contained in a public record is sufficient to negative the idea that their publication was a violation of a right of privacy. When the incidents of a life are so public as to be spread upon a public record, they come within the knowledge and into the possession of the public and cease to be private. Had respondents, in the story of "The Red Kimono," stopped with the use of those incidents from the life of appellant which were spread upon the record of her trial, no right of action would have accrued. They went further, and in the formation of the plot used the true maiden name of appellant. If any right of action exists, it arises from the use of this true name in connection with the true incidents from her life together with their advertisements in which they stated that the story of the picture was taken from true incidents in the life of Gabrielle Darley, who was Gabrielle Darley Melvin. . . .

The right to pursue and obtain happiness is guaranteed to all by the fundamental law of our state. This right by its very nature includes the right to live free from the unwarranted attack of others upon one's liberty, property, and reputation. Any person living a life of rectitude has that right to happiness which includes a freedom from unnecessary attacks on his character, social standing, or reputation.

The use of appellant's true name in connection with the incidents of her former life in the plot and advertisements was unnecessary and indelicate, and a willful and wanton disregard of that charity which should actuate us in our social intercourse, and which should keep us from unnecessarily holding another up to the scorn and contempt of upright members of society.

Upon demurrer, the allegations of the complaint must be taken as true. We must therefore conclude that eight years before the production of "The Red Kimono" appellant had abandoned her life of shame, had rehabilitated herself, and had taken her place as a respected and honored member of society. This change having occurred in her life, she should have been permitted to continue its course without having her reputation and social standing destroyed by the publication of the story of her former depravity with no other excuse than the expectation of private gain by the publishers.

One of the major objectives of society as it is now constituted, and of the administration of our penal system, is the rehabilitation of the fallen and the reformation of the criminal. Under these theories of sociology, it is our object to lift up and sustain the unfortunate rather than tear him down. Where a person has by his own efforts rehabilitated himself, we, as right-thinking members of society, should permit him to continue in the path of rectitude rather than throw him back into a life of shame or crime. Even the thief on the cross was permitted to repent during the hours of his final agony.

We believe that the publication by respondents of the unsavory incidents in the past life of appellant after she had reformed, coupled with her true name, was not justified by any standard of morals or ethics known to us, and was a direct invasion of her inalienable right guaranteed to her by our Constitution, to pursue and obtain happiness. Whether we call this a right of privacy or give it any other name is immaterial, because it is a right guaranteed by our Constitution that must not be ruthlessly and needlessly invaded by others. We are of the opinion that the first cause of action of appellant's complaint states facts sufficient to constitute a cause of action against respondents. . . .

NOTES & QUESTIONS

1. Do you agree that Darley's name is private even though it is available in the public record? Today, it would be easy to pull up a newspaper article about a person's murder trial by searching a computer database such as Westlaw or LEXIS. Would Darley have less of an expectation of privacy in her past life today than in 1931?
2. Suppose that a reporter were to publish the fact that a person had been convicted of hijacking a truck 11 years ago in connection with an article about hijacking in general. Should the Melvin approach apply in this instance? See *Briscoe v. Reader's Digest Assn.* in Chapter 4.

DAILY TIMES DEMOCRAT V. GRAHAM

162 So. 2d 474 (Ala. 1964)

HARWOOD, J. This is an appeal from a judgment in favor of the plaintiff in an action charging an invasion by the defendant of the plaintiff's right of privacy. Damages were assessed by the jury at $4,166.00. . . .

Appellee is a woman 44 years of age who has lived in Cullman County, Alabama her entire life. She is married and has two sons, ages 10 and 8. The family resides in a rural community where her husband is engaged in the business of raising chickens. . . .

On 9 October 1961, the Cullman County Fair was in progress. On that day the appellee took her two children to the Fair. After going on some of the rides, the boys expressed a wish to go through what is called in the record the "Fun House." The boys were afraid to enter alone so the appellee accompanied them. She testified she had never been through a Fun House before and had no knowledge that there was a device that blew jets of air up from the platform of the Fun House upon which one exited therefrom.

The appellee entered the Fun House with her two boys and as she was leaving her dress was blown up by the air jets and her body was exposed from the waist down, with the exception of that portion covered by her "panties."

At this moment the appellant's photographer snapped a picture of the appellee in this situation. This was done without the appellee's knowledge or consent. Four days later the appellant published this picture on the front page of its newspaper.

The appellant publishes about five thousand newspapers daily which are delivered to homes, mailed to subscribers, and displayed on racks in various locations in the city of Cullman and elsewhere.

On the Sunday following the publication of the picture, the appellee went into the city of Cullman. There she saw the appellant's newspaper display with her picture on the front page in one of the appellant's newspaper racks, and she also saw copies of the said newspaper in other places.

While the appellee's back was largely towards the camera in the picture, her two sons are in the picture, and the photograph was recognized as being of her by other people with whom she was acquainted. The matter of her photograph was mentioned to the appellee by others on several occasions. Evidence offered by the appellee during the trial tended to show that the appellee, as a result of the publication of the picture, became embarrassed, self-conscious, upset and was known to cry on occasions. . . .

. . . Counsel contends that as a matter of law the publication of the photograph was a matter of legitimate news of interest to the public; that the publishing of the picture was in connection with a write-up of the Fair, which was a matter of legitimate news. If this be so, then of course the appellant would have been privileged to have published the picture.

Counsel has quoted from an array of cases as to what constitutes news. We see no need to refer to these cases in that their applicability to the facts now before us is negligible. We can see nothing of legitimate news value in the photograph. Certainly it discloses nothing as to which the public is entitled to be informed. . . .

Not only was this photograph embarrassing to one of normal sensibilities, we think it could properly be classified as obscene, in that "obscene" means "offensive to modesty or decency"; or expressing to the mind or view something which delicacy, purity, or decency forbid to be expressed.

The appellant's insistence of error in this aspect is therefore without merit.

Counsel further argues that the court erred in refusal of appellant's requested affirmative charges in that appellee's picture was taken at the time she was a part of a public scene, and the publication of the photograph could not therefore be deemed an invasion of her privacy as a matter of law.

The proposition for which appellant contends is probably best illustrated by the following quotation from *Forster v. Manchester*, 410 Pa. 192, 189 A.2d 147:

> On the public street, or in any other public place, the plaintiff has no right to be alone, and it is no invasion of his privacy to do no more than follow him about. Neither is it such an invasion to take his photograph in such a place, since this amounts to nothing more than making a record, not differing essentially from a full written description of a public sight which anyone present would be free to see.

Admittedly this principle is established by the cases. As well stated in *Hinish v. Meir & Frank Co.*, Inc., 113 P.2d 438:

> When a legal principle is pushed to an absurdity, the principle is not abandoned, but the absurdity avoided.

In other words, a purely mechanical application of legal principles should not be permitted to create an illogical conclusion.

To hold that one who is involuntarily and instantaneously enmeshed in an embarrassing pose forfeits her right of privacy merely because she happened at the moment to be part of a public scene would be illogical, wrong, and unjust.

One who is a part of a public scene may be lawfully photographed as an incidental part of that scene in his ordinary status. Where the status he expects to occupy is changed without his volition to a status embarrassing to an ordinary person of reasonable sensitivity, then he should not be deemed to have forfeited his right to be protected from an indecent and vulgar intrusion of his right of privacy merely because misfortune overtakes him in a public place. . . .

NOTES & QUESTIONS

1. The court holds that although Graham was in public, the exposure of her body was involuntary, and hence a private matter. Does whether a matter is public or private depend upon voluntary or involuntary disclosure or upon one's expectation?
2. Would a change in the focus of the news article change the outcome?
3. *Privacy in Public.* Many courts hold that matters cease to be "private" when occurring in public. Appearing in public "necessarily involves doffing the cloak of privacy which the law protects." *Cefalu v. Globe Newspaper Co.,* 391 N.E.2d 935, 939 (Mass. App. 1979). In *Penwell v. Taft Broadcasting,* 469 N.E.2d 1025 (Ohio App. 1984), a husband and wife were arrested in a bar, handcuffed, and taken to the police station where it was discovered that they had been arrested due to mistaken identity. A television film crew that arrived at the bar with the police filmed the plaintiff's arrest and removal from the bar, and the footage was later broadcast by the television station. The court dismissed the plaintiff's public disclosure action because the arrest was filmed in public and was "left open to the public eye."

   In *Gill v. Hearst Pub. Co.,* 253 P.2d 441 (Cal. 1953), a husband and wife were photographed in an affectionate pose at their business, an ice cream concession in a farmer's market. The court dismissed their public disclosure claim, reasoning:

   > In considering the nature of the picture in question, it is significant that it was not surreptitiously snapped on private grounds, but rather was taken of plaintiffs in a pose voluntarily assumed in a public market place. . . . Here plaintiffs . . . had voluntarily exposed themselves to public gaze in a pose open to the view of any persons who might then be at or near their place of business. By their own voluntary action plaintiffs waived their right of privacy so far as this particular public pose was assumed. . . . Consistent which their own voluntary assumption of this particular pose in a public place, plaintiffs' right to privacy as to this photographed incident ceased and it in effect became a part of the public domain. . . . In short, the photograph did not disclose anything which until then had been private, but rather only extended knowledge of the particular incident to a somewhat larger public then had actually witnessed it at the time of occurrence.

   Consider the dissent of Judge Carter in *Gill*:

   > [T]he discussion in the majority opinion to the effect that plaintiffs consented to the publication because they assumed the pose in a public place is fallacious. But in addition, such a theory is completely at odds with the violation of the right of privacy. By plaintiffs doing what they did in view of a tiny fraction of the public, does not mean that they consented to observa-

tion by the millions of readers of the defendant's magazine. In effect, the majority holding means that anything any one does outside of his own home is with consent to the publication thereof, because, under those circumstances he waives his right of privacy even though there is no news value in the event. If such were the case, the blameless exposure of a portion of the naked body of a man or woman in a public place as the result of inefficient buttons, hooks or other clothes-holding devices could be freely photographed and widely published with complete immunity. . . . There is no basis for the conclusion that the second a person leaves the portals of his home he consents to have his photograph taken under all circumstances thereafter. There being no legitimate public interest, there is no excuse for the publication.

In *McNamara v. Freedom Newspapers, Inc.*, 802 S.W.2d 901 (Tex. Ct. App. 1991), a newspaper published a photo of high school soccer player's inadvertently exposed genitalia while running on the soccer field. The plaintiff, McNamara, relied on *Daily Times Democrat v. Graham*, but the court found *Graham* unpersuasive and concluded:

> The uncontroverted facts in this case establish that the photograph of McNamara was taken by a newspaper photographer for media purposes. The picture accurately depicted a public event and was published as part of a newspaper article describing the game. At the time the photograph was taken, McNamara was voluntarily participating in a spectator sport at a public place. None of the persons involved in the publishing procedure actually noticed that McNamara's genitals were exposed.

4. ***Privacy in Other Places.*** In *Barber v. Time, Inc.*, 159 S.W.2d 291 (Mo. 1942), the plaintiff's photograph taken in a hospital was published in a *Time* magazine article about the plaintiff's unusual disease. The article, "Starving Glutton," described the plaintiff's rare disorder where no matter how much she ate, she continued to lose weight. The photograph showed the plaintiff in her hospital bed. The court held that this constituted a private matter:

> While plaintiff's ailment may have been a matter of some public interest because unusual, certainly the identity of the person who suffered this ailment was not. Whatever the limits of the right of privacy may be, it seems clear that it must include the right to have information given to or gained by a physician in the treatment of an individual's personal ailment kept from publication which would state his name in connection therewith without such person's consent. Likewise, whatever may be the right of the press, tabloids or news reel companies to take and use pictures of persons in public places, certainly any right of privacy ought to protect a person from publication of a picture taken without consent while ill or in bed for treatment and recuperation.

5. ***Privacy and Communication to Other People.*** Generally, a fact widely known about a person is not considered private; however, certain limited disclosures of information do not destroy its private nature. In *Times Mirror Co. v. Superior Court*, 244 Cal. Rptr. 556 (Cal. Ct. App. 1988), the plaintiff (Doe) discovered the murdered body of her roommate lying on the floor of her apartment and saw the perpetrator before fleeing. Doe's identity was

withheld from the public by the police to protect her safety (since the murderer was still at large), but her identity was leaked to a reporter and published in a newspaper article about the incident. Doe sued for public disclosure, and the newspaper argued that the matter was not private because Doe revealed it to certain neighbors, friends, family members, and investigating officials. The court, however, concluded that Doe had not "rendered otherwise private information public by cooperating in the criminal investigation and seeking solace from friends and relatives."

In *Virgil v. Time, Inc.*, 527 F.2d 1122 (9th Cir. 1975), a well-known body surfer was interviewed by *Sports Illustrated* and photographs of the surfer were taken for the story. The surfer revoked his consent to publishing the story when he discovered that the article was not going to be exclusively about his surfing but was also going to discuss some of his personal eccentricities and incidents about his life in order to explain the psychological profile of those who engage in such a dangerous sport. The story was published, and the surfer sued for public disclosure. The court held that the information about the surfer's life was private:

> It is not the manner in which information has been obtained that determines whether it is public or private. Here it is undisputed that the information was obtained without commission of a tort and in a manner wholly unobjectionable. However, that it not determinative as to this particular tort. The offense with which we are here involved is not the intrusion by means of which information is obtained; it is the publicizing of that which is private in character. The question, then, is whether the information disclosed was public rather than private — whether it was generally known and, if not, whether the disclosure by appellant can be said to have been to the public at large.
>
> Talking freely to someone is not in itself . . . making public the substance of the talk. There is an obvious and substantial difference between the disclosure of private facts to an individual — a disclosure that is selective and based on a judgment as to whether knowledge by that person would be felt to be objectionable — and the disclosure of the same facts to the public at large. . . .
>
> Talking freely to a member of the press, knowing the listener to be a member of the press, is not then in itself making public. Such communication can be said to anticipate that what is said will be made public since making public is the function of the press, and accordingly such communication can be construed as a consent to publicize. Thus if publicity results it can be said to have been consented to. However, if consent is withdrawn prior to the act of publicizing, the consequent publicity is without consent. . . .

6. ***Further Dissemination of Previously Disclosed Information.*** Media entities that further disseminate information already disclosed by another media entity are not liable for public disclosure. *Ritzmann v. Weekly World News*, 614 F. Supp. 1336 (N.D. Tex. 1985) (giving further publicity to information contained in news stories already published is not actionable because the information is no longer private); *Heath v. Playboy Enterprises, Inc.*, 732 F. Supp. 1145 (S.D. Fla. 1990) ("Republication of facts already publicized elsewhere cannot provide a basis for an invasion of privacy claim.").

However, when only partial facts are revealed, the disclosure of more information can give rise to a viable action for public disclosure. For example, in *Michaels v. Internet Entertainment Group, Inc.*, 5 F. Supp. 2d 823 (C.D. Cal. 1998), Bret Michaels, the former lead singer for the rock band Poison, and Pamela Anderson Lee, a famous celebrity, sought a preliminary injunction to prevent the defendant from making a videotape of the two having sex available on the Internet. The defendant argued that the plaintiffs lacked a privacy interest in the tape because a part of the tape had already been released by a foreign Internet source. The court, however, concluded that "plaintiffs' privacy interest in the unreleased portions of the Tape is undiminished." Further, another videotape depicting Lee having sex with her husband Tommy Lee had been widely distributed, and the defendant contended that this negated Lee's privacy interest. The court rejected the defendant's argument: "The Court is not prepared to conclude that public exposure of one sexual encounter forever removes a person's privacy interest in all subsequent and previous sexual encounters." The defendant also contended that Lee lacked a privacy interest because she had previously appeared nude in magazines and on video, but the court concluded that the defendant's "contention unreasonably blurs the line between fiction and reality. Lee is a professional actor. She has played roles involving sex and sexual appeal. The fact that she has performed a role involving sex does not, however, make her real sex life open to the public."

(c) Publicity

MILLER V. MOTOROLA, INC.

560 N.E.2d 900 (Ill. App. 1990)

BUCKLEY, J. Joy V. Miller (plaintiff) filed an action in the circuit court of Cook County against her employer, Motorola, Inc. (defendant), seeking recovery for damages resulting from defendant's disclosure of her mastectomy surgery to plaintiff's co-employees. Plaintiff appeals from the circuit court's order dismissing her complaint with prejudice. . . .

Considering first plaintiff's public disclosure claim, this cause of action is defined by the Restatement (Second) of Torts as follows:

> One who gives publicity to a matter concerning the private life of another is subject to liability to the other for invasion of privacy, if the matter publicized is of a kind that (a) would be highly offensive to a reasonable person, and (b) is not of a legitimate concern to the public. . . .

Plaintiff's complaint alleges that she consulted with defendant's resident nurse, Felicia Masters, relative to three leaves of absence taken by plaintiff from 1984 to 1986 to undergo mastectomy and reconstructive surgeries and that Masters advised her during those consultations that her medical information would be confidential. The complaint further alleges that plaintiff, who did not consent to the release of any of her medical information which was maintained at defendant's place of business, was told by a co-employee on or about October 1, 1987, that she had been informed of plaintiff's mastectomy. As a result of defendant's disclosure and plaintiff's belief of the awareness by numerous other employees of her condition, the complaint alleges that plaintiff suffered severe physical, mental and emotional distress and took an early retirement from her 23-year employment with defendant.

Defendant argues that these allegations are insufficient to show that any private facts were publicized because Illinois law requires the disclosure be widespread and that the communication be written. . . .

. . . The Restatement indicates that the required communication must be more than that made to a small group; rather, the communication must be made to the public at large. In acknowledging this general requirement, however, some courts have recognized the need for flexibility in the application of the Restatement's theory to permit recovery for egregious conduct. These courts have realized that in circumstances where a special relationship exists between the plaintiff and the "public" to whom the information has been disclosed, the disclosure may be just as devastating to the person even though the disclosure was made to a limited number of people. The court in *Beaumont* [*v. Brown*, 257 N.W.2d 522 (Mich. 1977)] explained:

> Communication of embarrassing facts about an individual to a public not concerned with that individual and with whom the individual is not concerned obviously is not a "serious interference" with plaintiff's right to privacy, although it might be "unnecessary" or "unreasonable." An invasion of a plaintiff's right to privacy is important if it exposes private facts to a public whose knowledge of those facts would be embarrassing to the plaintiff. Such a public might be the general public, if the person were a public figure, or a particular public such as fellow employees, club members, church members, family, or neighbors, if the person were not a public figure.

We adopt the position of the above authorities that the public disclosure requirement may be satisfied by proof that the plaintiff has a special relationship with the "public" to whom the information is disclosed. Plaintiff's allegation that her medical condition was disclosed to her fellow employees sufficiently satisfies the requirement that publicity be given to the private fact. . . .

NOTES & QUESTIONS

1. Consider the Restatement (comment b):

> Thus it is not an invasion of the right of privacy, within the rule stated in this Section, to communicate a fact concerning the plaintiff's private life to a single person or even to a small group of persons. On the other hand, any publication in a newspaper or a magazine, even of small circulation, or in a handbill distributed to a large number of persons, or any broadcast over the radio, or statement made in an address to a large audience, is sufficient to give publicity within the meaning of the term as it is used in this Section. The distinction, in other words, is one between private and public communication.

Is *Miller v. Motorola* at odds with the commentary of the Restatement?
2. ***The "Publicity" Element and the Extent of the Disclosure.*** Many courts have held that disclosure to a small group of individuals does not constitute publicity. In *Yoder v. Smith*, 112 N.W.2d 862 (Iowa 1962), the court held

that the publicity element was not satisfied when the defendant disclosed the plaintiff's debts to the plaintiff's employer. In *Vogel v. W.T. Grant Co.*, 327 A.2d 133 (Pa. 1974), the court held that the publicity element was not satisfied when the defendant contacted the plaintiff's employer and mother in an attempt to collect a debt owed by the plaintiff because the "notification of two or four third parties is not sufficient to constitute publication" of the debt. Likewise, in *Wells v. Thomas*, 569 F. Supp. 426 (E.D. Pa. 1983), the court held that disclosure to "the community of employees at [hospital] staff meetings and discussions between defendants and other employees" was not sufficient to establish the requisite publicity for a viable public disclosure action.

In contrast, consider *Brents v. Morgan*, 299 S.W. 967 (Ky. 1927), where the court held that there was sufficient publicity when the owner of an automobile garage posted a large sign on a show window of his garage stating that the plaintiff owed him a debt. Also consider *Biederman's of Springfield, Inc. v. Wright*, 322 S.W.2d 892 (Mo. 1959), where the defendant, attempting to collect a debt owed by the plaintiff, made "loud, overbearing, tough, degrading and embarrassing demands that she pay [the debt]" in a café while she was working as a waitress. This occurred in front of numerous customers. The court concluded: "We believe that the oral publication over the three-day period in a public restaurant with numerous customers present satisfies any reasonable requirement as to publicity." How do *Brents* and *Biederman's* differ from *Yoder*, *Vogel*, and *Wells*?

A few courts have applied the publicity requirement in a similar manner as *Miller v. Motorola*. Consider the following statement in *Beaumont v. Brown*, 257 N.W.2d 522 (Mich. 1977):

> To begin with "communication to the general public" is somewhat ambiguous, because a communication rarely, if ever, reaches everyone. . . . Communication of embarrassing facts about an individual to a public not concerned with that individual and with whom the individual is not concerned obviously is not a "serious interference" with plaintiff's right to privacy, although it might be "unnecessary" or "unreasonable." An invasion of a plaintiff's right to privacy is important if it exposes private facts to a public whose knowledge of those facts would be embarrassing to the plaintiff. Such a public might be the general public, if the person were a public figure, or a particular public such as fellow employees, club members, church members, family, or neighbors, if the person were not a public figure.
>
> Here we have developed the criterion of a particular public, whose knowledge of the private facts would be embarrassing to the plaintiff. . . . [W]e do not engage in a numbers game. . . .

3. ***Criticism of the Publicity Requirement.*** As one court observed, the requirement of widespread publicity "singles out the print, film, and broadcast media for legal restraints that will not be applied to gossip-mongers in neighborhood taverns or card-parties, to letter writers or telephone tattlers." *Anderson v. Fisher Broadcasting Co.*, 712 P.2d 803, 805 (Or. 1986). Consider Jonathan Mintz's criticism of the publicity requirement:

> This hair-splitting rationale seems plainly flawed. It facilitates the conservation of judicial resources far more than the dignity interests deemed worthy

of protection by tort law. The difference in the injury to a person's dignity between five persons' and fifty persons' access to a private fact is merely one of degree, not of nature. A person loses some sense of privacy the moment a second person divulges a private fact to a third person, particularly when the third person is a member of the same community as the first person. Thus, the degree of publicity, and the corresponding degree of injury to a person's dignity, is a factor better addressed in damage calculations than in summary judgments or motions to dismiss.[15]

Also consider Robert Post:

We often care more about what those within our "group" think of us than we do about our reputation among the strangers who comprise the general public. Yet the publicity requirement, as defined by the Restatement, would impose sanctions for the disclosure of a husband's marital infidelity to the general public, but not for its disclosure to his wife. . . .[16]

(d) The Newsworthiness Test

SIDIS v. F-R PUBLISHING CORP.

113 F.2d 806 (2d Cir. 1940)

[William James Sidis (1898–1944) was perhaps the most famous child prodigy of his day. At the age of 5, Sidis wrote a treatise on anatomy. When he was 8, Sidis developed a new table of logarithms. At the age of 10, Sidis could speak six languages. Boris Sidis, William's father, published a number of papers in scientific journals describing his boy's achievements. Boris also published a book about his son called *Philistine and Genius*. In 1908, at the age of 10, William Sidis enrolled in Tufts College. In 1909, Sidis was permitted to enroll in Harvard at the age of 11. He made the front pages of newspapers around the nation when, at age 11, he delivered a lecture to about a hundred professors and advanced students in mathematics at Harvard University. The *New York Times* featured Sidis on its front page of October 11, 1909, as "Harvard's Child Prodigy."[17]

When he graduated from Harvard at age 16, he told reporters: "I want to live the perfect life. The only way to live the perfect life is to live it in seclusion. I have always hated crowds." After graduating, Sidis attended Harvard Law School. However, he remained more interested in mathematics and accepted a teaching position at a university in Texas after graduating from law school. Sidis "found himself the centre of an interest that annoyed and dismayed him. He suddenly gave up his position and returned bitterly and quietly to Boston, where he lived obscurely for some months."[18]

---

[15] Jonathan B. Mintz, *The Remains of Privacy's Disclosure Tort: An Exploration of the Private Domain*, 55 Md. L. Rev. 425, 438 (1996).

[16] Robert C. Post, *The Social Foundations of Privacy: Community and Self in the Common Law Tort*, 77 Cal. L. Rev. 957, 992 (1989).

[17] *Harvard's Child Prodigy: All Amazed at Mathematical Grasp of Youngest Matriculate, Aged 13 Years*, N.Y. Times (Oct. 10, 1909), at A1.

[18] *Where Are They Now?: April Fool!*, New Yorker 22 (Aug. 14, 1937).

Decades later, the August 14, 1937, issue of *The New Yorker* contained a brief biographical sketch about Sidis, his life following his graduation from Harvard, and the subsequent decades where he lived in obscurity. The article was part of a regular feature of the magazine called "Where Are They Now?," which provided brief updates on the lives of famous figures of the past. The article was printed under the subtitle *April Fool*, a reference to the fact that Sidis was born on April Fool's day. The article recounted the history of Sidis's life and his current whereabouts: "William James Sidis lives today, at the age of thirty-nine, in a hall bedroom of Boston's shabby south end." Apparently, a young woman succeeded in getting Sidis to let her into his apartment and to interview him. (It is unclear whether Sidis knew that he was being interviewed or that the interview would appear in a national periodical, but based on his desire to remain out of the public eye and his suing the publisher of the magazine, there is good reason to infer that Sidis was unaware of these facts.) The article described Sidis's famous childhood and then recounted his subsequent career as an insignificant clerk: "He seems to get a great and ironic enjoyment out of leading a life of wandering irresponsibility after a childhood of scrupulous regimentation." Sidis never remained at one job for too long because "his employers or fellow-workers [would] soon find out that he is the famous boy wonder, and he can't tolerate a position after that." According to Sidis: "The every sight of a mathematical formula makes me physically ill. . . . All I want to do is run an adding machine, but they won't let me alone." The article also described Sidis's dwelling, a small bedroom in a poor part of Boston and his personal activities, interests, and habits.

Sidis sued F-R Publishing Corporation (the publisher of *The New Yorker*) for, among other things, violating his privacy rights under §§ 50-51 of the N.Y. Civil Rights Law.]

CLARK, C. J. . . . It is not contended that any of the matter printed is untrue. Nor is the manner described as having "a certain childlike charm." But the article is merciless in its dissection of intimate details of its subject's personal life, and this in company with elaborate accounts of Sidis' passion for privacy and the pitiable lengths to which he has gone in order to avoid public scrutiny. The work posseses great reader interest, for it is both amusing and instructive; but it may be fairly described as a ruthless exposure of a once public character, who has since sought and has now been deprived of the seclusion of private life.

The article of December 25, 1937, was a biographical sketch of another former child prodigy, in the course of which William James Sidis and the recent account of him were mentioned. The advertisement published in the New York World-Telegram of August 13, 1937, read: "Out Today. Harvard Prodigy. Biography of the man who astonished Harvard at age 11. Where are they now? by J. L. Manley. Page 22. The New Yorker."

The complaint contains a general allegation, repeated for all the claims, of publication by the defendant of The New Yorker, "a weekly magazine of wide circulation throughout the United States." Then each separate "cause" contains an allegation that the defendant publicly circulated the articles or caused them to be circulated in the particular states upon whose law that cause is assumed to be founded. Circulation of the New York World-Telegram advertisement is, however, alleged only with respect to the second "cause," for asserted violation of New York law.

Under the first "cause of action" we are asked to declare that this exposure transgresses upon plaintiff's right of privacy, as recognized in California, Georgia, Kansas, Kentucky, and Missouri. Each of these states except California grants to the individual a common law right, and California a constitutional right, to be let alone to a certain extent. The decisions have been carefully analyzed by the court below, and we need not examine them further. None of the cited rulings goes so far as to prevent a newspaper or magazine from publishing the truth about a person, however intimate, revealing, or harmful the truth may be. Nor are there any decided cases that confer such a privilege upon the press. . . .

It must be conceded that under the strict standards suggested by [Warren and Brandeis in their article, *The Right to Privacy*] plaintiff's right of privacy has been invaded. Sidis today is neither politician, public administrator, nor statesman. Even if he were, some of the personal details revealed were of the sort that Warren and Brandeis believed "all men alike are entitled to keep from popular curiosity."

But despite eminent opinion to the contrary, we are not yet disposed to afford to all of the intimate details of private life an absolute immunity from the prying of the press. Everyone will agree that at some point the public interest in obtaining information becomes dominant over the individual's desire for privacy. Warren and Brandeis were willing to lift the veil somewhat in the case of public officers. We would go further, though we are not yet prepared to say how far. At least we would permit limited scrutiny of the "private" life of any person who has achieved, or has had thrust upon him, the questionable and indefinable status of a "public figure."

William James Sidis was once a public figure. As a child prodigy, he excited both admiration and curiosity. Of him great deeds were expected. In 1910, he was a person about whom the newspapers might display a legitimate intellectual interest, in the sense meant by Warren and Brandeis, as distinguished from a trivial and unseemly curiosity. But the precise motives of the press we regard as unimportant. And even if Sidis had loathed public attention at that time, we think his uncommon achievements and personality would have made the attention permissible. Since then Sidis has cloaked himself in obscurity, but his subsequent history, containing as it did the answer to the question of whether or not he had fulfilled his early promise, was still a matter of public concern. The article in The New Yorker sketched the life of an unusual personality, and it possessed considerable popular news interest.

We express no comment on whether or not the newsworthiness of the matter printed will always constitute a complete defense. Revelations may be so intimate and so unwarranted in view of the victim's position as to outrage the community's notions of decency. But when focused upon public characters, truthful comments upon dress, speech, habits, and the ordinary aspects of personality will usually not transgress this line. Regrettably or not, the misfortunes and frailties of neighbors and "public figures" are subjects of considerable interest and discussion to the rest of the population. And when such are the mores of the community, it would be unwise for a court to bar their expression in the newspapers, books, and magazines of the day.

Plaintiff in his first "cause of action" charged actual malice in the publication, and now claims that an order of dismissal was improper in the face of such an allegation. We cannot agree. If plaintiff's right of privacy was not invaded by the article, the existence of actual malice in its publication would not change that result. Unless made so by statute, a truthful and therefore non-libelous statement will not become libelous when uttered maliciously. A similar rule should prevail on invasions of the right of privacy. "Personal ill-will is not an ingredient of the offence, any more than in an ordinary case of trespass to person or to property." Warren and Brandeis, supra at page 218. Nor does the malice give rise to an independent wrong based on an intentional invasion of the plaintiff's interest in mental and emotional tranquility.

If the article appearing in the issue of August 14, 1937, does not furnish grounds for action, then it is clear that the brief and incidental reference to it contained in the article of December 25, 1937, is not actionable. . . .

[The court concluded that the second cause of action under N.Y. Civil Rights Law was properly dismissed as well.]

NOTES & QUESTIONS

1. Sidis spent the remainder of his life writing books on unusual topics, such as a treatise on the classification of streetcar transfer slips. After losing his privacy suit, Sidis sued *The New Yorker* for libel for the false information in the story and settled the case out of court for a small amount of money.[19] Sidis died alone at the age of 46.

   The story of William Sidis illustrates a man profoundly disturbed by being thrust by his father into the limelight as a child and by being hounded by the media. It seems that he tried to spend much of his life fleeing from being a public figure. Sidis was involuntarily thrust into the public eye as a very young child. If he were an involuntary public figure in the past, should this affect whether he should be able to retreat from the public eye in the future?

2. The *Sidis* case suggests the principle that once one is a public figure, one is always a public figure. But *Melvin v. Reid* suggests otherwise — that if one has faded from public view for a while, then one is no longer a public figure. How can these cases be reconciled?

3. Consider the Restatement of Torts § 652D (comments h and k):

   > h. Private Facts. Permissible publicity to information concerning either voluntary or involuntary public figures is not limited to the particular events that arouse the interest of the public. That interest, once aroused by the event, may legitimately extend, to some reasonable degree, to further information concerning the individual and to facts about him, which are not public and which, in the case of one who had not become a public figure,

---

[19] *See* Robert Ellis Smith, *Ben Franklin's Website*, at 228.

would be regarded as an invasion of his purely private life. Thus the life history of one accused of murder, together with such heretofore private facts as may throw some light upon what kind of person he is, his possible guilt or innocence, or his reasons for committing the crime, are a matter of legitimate public interest. On the same basis the home life and daily habits of a motion picture actress may be of legitimate and reasonable interest to the public that sees her on the screen. . . .

k. Lapse of Time. The fact that there has been a lapse of time, even of considerable length, since the event that has made the plaintiff a public figure, does not of itself defeat the authority to give him publicity or to renew publicity when it has formerly been given. Past events and activities may still be of legitimate interest to the public, and a narrative reviving recollection of what has happened even many years ago may be both interesting and valuable for purposes of information and education. Such a lapse of time is, however, a factor to be considered, with other facts, in determining whether the publicity goes to unreasonable lengths in revealing facts about one who has resumed the private, lawful and unexciting life led by the great bulk of the community. . . .

Does the Restatement commentary reconcile *Sidis* and *Melvin*? Do you agree with the Restatement approach?

SIPPLE V. CHRONICLE PUBLISHING CO.

201 Cal. Rptr. 665 (Cal. App. 1984)

CALDECOTT, J. On September 22, 1975, Sara Jane Moore attempted to assassinate President Gerald R. Ford while the latter was visiting San Francisco, California. Plaintiff Oliver W. Sipple (hereafter appellant or Sipple) who was in the crowd at Union Square, San Francisco, grabbed or struck Moore's arm as the latter was about to fire the gun and shoot at the President. Although no one can be certain whether or not Sipple actually saved the President's life, the assassination attempt did not succeed and Sipple was considered a hero for his selfless action and was subject to significant publicity throughout the nation following the assassination attempt.

Among the many articles concerning the event was a column, written by Herb Caen and published by the San Francisco Chronicle on September 24, 1975. The article read in part as follows: "One of the heroes of the day, Oliver 'Bill' Sipple, the ex-Marine who grabbed Sara Jane Moore's arm just as her gun was fired and thereby may have saved the President's life, was the center of midnight attention at the Red Lantern, a Golden Gate Ave. bar he favors. The Rev. Ray Broshears, head of Helping Hands, and Gay Politico, Harvey Milk, who claim to be among Sipple's close friends, describe themselves as 'proud — maybe this will help break the stereotype'. Sipple is among the workers in Milk's campaign for Supervisor."

Thereafter, the Los Angeles Times and numerous out-of-state newspapers published articles which referring to the primary source, (i.e., the story published in the San Francisco Chronicle) mentioned both the heroic act shown by Sipple and the fact that he was a prominent member of the San Francisco gay community. Some of those articles speculated that President Ford's failure to promptly thank Sipple for his heroic act was a result of Sipple's sexual orientation.[20]

. . . Sipple filed an action against the [newspapers]. The complaint was predicated upon the theory of invasion of privacy and alleged in essence that defendants without authorization and consent published private facts about plaintiff's life by disclosing that plaintiff was homosexual in his personal and private sexual orientation; that said publications were highly offensive to plaintiff inasmuch as his parents, brothers and sisters learned for the first time of his homosexual orientation; and that as a consequence of disclosure of private facts about his life plaintiff was abandoned by his family, exposed to contempt and ridicule causing him great mental anguish, embarrassment and humiliation. Plaintiff finally alleged that defendants' conduct amounted to malice and oppression calling for both compensatory and punitive damages.

Appellant's principal contention on appeal is that the trial court prejudicially erred in granting summary judgment in favor of respondents. More precisely, appellant argues that the individual elements of the invasion of privacy (i.e., public disclosure of private facts; the offensiveness of the public disclosure; and the newsworthiness of the publication as an exception to tort liability) constituted a factual determination which could not be resolved or adjudicated by way of summary procedure.

Before discussing appellant's contentions on the merit, as an initial matter we set out the legal principles governing the case. It is well settled that there are three elements of a cause of action predicated on tortious invasion of privacy. First, the disclosure of the private facts must be a public disclosure. Second, the facts disclosed must be private facts, and not public ones. Third, the matter made public must be one which would be offensive and objectionable to a reasonable person of ordinary sensibilities. It is likewise recognized, however, that due to the supreme mandate of the constitutional protection of freedom of the press even a tortious invasion of one's privacy is exempt from liability if the publication of private facts is truthful and newsworthy. . . .

When viewed in light of the aforegoing principles, the summary judgment in this case must be upheld on two grounds. First, as appears from the record properly considered for the purposes of summary judgment, the facts disclosed by the articles were not private facts within the meaning of the law. Second, the record likewise reveals on its face that the publications in dispute were newsworthy and thus constituted a protective shield from liability based upon invasion of privacy.

(A) The Facts Published Were Not Private

As pointed out earlier, a crucial ingredient of the tort premised upon invasion of one's privacy is a public disclosure of private facts, that is the unwar-

---

[20]For example, the September 25, 1975, issue of the Los Angeles Times wrote inter alia as follows: "A husky ex-marine who was a hero in the attempted assassination of President Ford emerged Wednesday as a prominent figure in the gay community. And questions were raised in the gay community if Oliver (Bill) Sipple, 32, was being shunned by the White House because of his associations. Sipple, who lunged at Sara Jane Moore and deflected her revolver as she fired at the President, conceded that he is a member of the 'court' of Mike Caringi, who was elected

ranted publication of intimate details of one's private life which are outside the realm of legitimate public interest. In elaborating on the notion, the cases explain that there can be no privacy with respect to a matter which is already public or which has previously become part of the "public domain." Moreover, it is equally underlined that there is no liability when the defendant merely gives further publicity to information about the plaintiff which is already public or when the further publicity relates to matters which the plaintiff leaves open to the public eye.

The case at bench falls within the aforestated rules. The undisputed facts reveal that prior to the publication of the newspaper articles in question appellant's homosexual orientation and participation in gay community activities had been known by hundreds of people in a variety of cities, including New York, Dallas, Houston, San Diego, Los Angeles and San Francisco. Thus, appellant's deposition shows that prior to the assassination attempt appellant spent a lot of time in "Tenderloin" and "Castro," the well-known gay sections of San Francisco; that he frequented gay bars and other homosexual gatherings in both San Francisco and other cities; that he marched in gay parades on several occasions; that he supported the campaign of Mike Caringi for the election of "Emperor"; that he participated in the coronation of the "Emperor" and sat at Caringi's table on that occasion; that his friendship with Harvey Milk, another prominent gay, was well-known and publicized in gay newspapers; and that his homosexual association and name had been reported in gay magazines (such as Data Boy, Pacific Coast Times, Male Express, etc.) several times before the publications in question. In fact, appellant quite candidly conceded that he did not make a secret of his being a homosexual and that if anyone would ask, he would frankly admit that he was gay. In short, since appellant's sexual orientation was already in public domain and since the articles in question did no more than to give further publicity to matters which appellant left open to the eye of the public, a vital element of the tort was missing rendering it vulnerable to summary disposal. . . .

(B) The Publication Was Newsworthy

. . . [O]ur courts have recognized a broad privilege cloaking the truthful publication of all newsworthy matters. . . . [T]he cases and authorities further explain that the paramount test of newsworthiness is whether the matter is of legitimate public interest which in turn must be determined according to the community mores. As pointed out in *Virgil v. Time, Inc.*, "'In determining what is a matter of legitimate public interest, account must be taken of the customs and conventions of the community; and in the last analysis what is proper becomes a matter of the community mores. The line is to be drawn when the publicity ceases to be the giving of information to which the public is entitled, and becomes a morbid and sensational prying into private lives for its own

---

'emperor of San Francisco' by the gay community. A column item in a morning newspaper here strongly implied Wednesday that Sipple is gay. . . . Harvey Milk, a prominent member of this city's large homosexual community and a longtime friend of Sipple, speculated Wednesday that the absence of a phone call or telegram of gratitude from the White House might not be just an oversight."

sake, with which a reasonable member of the public, with decent standards, would say that he had no concern.'"

In the case at bench the publication of appellant's homosexual orientation which had already been widely known by many people in a number of communities was not so offensive even at the time of the publication as to shock the community notions of decency. Moreover, and perhaps even more to the point, the record shows that the publications were not motivated by a morbid and sensational prying into appellant's private life but rather were prompted by legitimate political considerations, i.e., to dispel the false public opinion that gays were timid, weak and unheroic figures and to raise the equally important political question whether the President of the United States entertained a discriminatory attitude or bias against a minority group such as homosexuals. . . .

Appellant's contention that by saving the President's life he did not intend to enter into the limelight and become a public figure, can be easily answered. In elaborating on involuntary public figures, Restatement Second of Torts section 625D, comment f, sets out in part as follows: "There are other individuals who have not sought publicity or consented to it, but through their own conduct or otherwise have become a legitimate subject of public interest. They have, in other words, become 'news.'" . . .

NOTES & QUESTIONS

1. The court rejects Sipple's claim in part because Sipple's homosexuality and participation in the gay community were known by hundreds of people in many cities. But Sipple's argument is that he wanted to keep his homosexuality a secret from certain people — namely his parents and siblings. Can Sipple legitimately claim that something known widely to many people can still remain private?

2. In *Sipple*, the newsworthiness of the story did not just turn on exposing the background of a hero who prevented an assassination. The story also exposed President Ford's possible prejudice against homosexuals. Does this fact alone establish that the story was newsworthy?

3. *Newsworthiness Tests.* There are at least three newsworthiness tests used by courts.[21] First is the "leave it to the press" approach, where courts defer to editorial judgment and do not attempt to distinguish between what is news and what is entertainment. Second, the Restatement looks to the "customs and conventions of the community" and draws a line between the "giving of information to which the public is entitled" and "morbid and sensational prying into private lives for its own sake." A third approach is the "nexus test," which involves the Restatement approach but also requires a "logical nexus (or relationship) . . . between the complaining individual and the matter of legitimate public interest." Which test do you find most appropriate?

---

[21] *See* Geoff Dendy, Note, *The Newsworthiness Defense to the Public Disclosure Tort*, 85 Ky. L.J. 147 (1997).

4. According to First Amendment scholar Rodney Smolla, the newsworthiness test should require that the plaintiff prove that the reporter subjectively did not believe that a story was newsworthy.[22] This creates a form of a malice requirement. Do you think that this newsworthiness test should be adopted by courts?

5. *What Is Newsworthy?* Many of the cases applying the newsworthiness test do so to avoid First Amendment problems. Keep in mind that the newsworthiness test is an element of the tort of public disclosure. Applications of the tort — involving possibly even nonnewsworthy facts — can still be subject to an independent First Amendment challenge. This will be discussed later in this chapter.

How are courts to determine what is newsworthy? According to the Restatement of Torts, adopting language from *Virgil v. Time*, 527 F.2d 1122, 1129 (9th Cir. 1975), courts are to look to the "customs and conventions of the community." According to the Restatement § 652D (comment h),

> The extent of the authority to make public private facts is not, however, unlimited. There may be some intimate details of her life, such as sexual relations, which even the actress is entitled to keep to herself. In determining what is a matter of legitimate public interest, account must be taken of the customs and conventions of the community; and in the last analysis what is proper becomes a matter of the community mores. The line is to be drawn when the publicity ceases to be the giving of information to which the public is entitled, and becomes a morbid and sensational prying into private lives for its own sake, with which a reasonable member of the public, with decent standards, would say that he had no concern. . . .

When is the press ever "prying into private lives for its own sake"? Sensationalistic television and tabloids command a wide audience. Why isn't the private life of an individual newsworthy?

Consider the case of *Diaz v. Oakland Tribune*, 188 Cal. Rptr. 762 (Ct. App. 1983). Diaz was the first woman student body president elected at a community college. The Oakland Tribune published the fact that Diaz was a transsexual. Diaz sued for public disclosure, and the court held that the suit could proceed to the jury, which would determine whether the fact that Diaz was a transsexual was newsworthy. The court noted: "[W]e find little if any connection between the information disclosed and Diaz's fitness for office. The fact that she is a transsexual does not adversely reflect on her honesty or judgment." Eugene Volokh, who opposes the tort of public disclosure altogether, argues:

> Now I agree with the [*Diaz*] court's factual conclusion; people's gender identity strikes me as irrelevant to their fitness for office. But other voters take a different view. Transsexuality, in their opinion, may say various things about politicians (even student body politicians): It may say that they lack attachment to traditional values, that they are morally corrupt, or even just that they have undergone an unnatural procedure and therefore are somehow

---

[22] *See* Rodney A. Smolla, *Privacy and the First Amendment Right to Gather News*, 67 Geo. Wash. L. Rev. 1097, 1134 (1999).

tainted by it. These views may be wrong and even immoral, but surely it is not for government agents — whether judges or jurors — to dictate the relevant criteria for people's political choices, and to use the coercive force of law to keep others from informing them of things that they may consider relevant to those choices. I may disagree with what you base your vote on, but I must defend your right to base your vote on it, and the right of others to tell you about it.[23]

If Volokh is right, then what isn't relevant for fitness for office? Do public figures have any claim to privacy or is everything about them newsworthy?

6. ***The Privacy of Public Figures.*** To what extent can a public figure's life be private? Recall that the Restatement notes that even a public figure is entitled to keep certain matters private, including "intimate details of her life, such as sexual relations." Restatement § 652D (comment h). Are all "intimate details" private? J. M. Balkin argues that by creating media events that show the politician "with his or her family, participating in casual activities or in a seemingly unguarded and intimate moment," politicians have been "willing accomplices in the creation of a new political culture that sees private aspects of a person's life as politically relevant, that collapses older boundaries between public and private."[24]

Who decides what is in the public and private spheres? Balkin argues that these spheres are dynamic, in constant flux, and that the media is actively shaping their contours:

> . . . [B]y making these new forms of knowledge part of democratic decisionmaking, journalists change the contours of public discourse and the definition of a "public issue." Journalists do not simply respect the existing boundaries of the public and the private but actively reshape them: Merely by talking about sexual scandal and encouraging others to do so journalists make these topics part of public discourse and public comment. . . .
>
> Some journalists can even convince themselves that they are empowering the public through these revelations. But instead of empowering their audiences or increasing information, journalists may in fact simply be altering the mix of stories presented to the public; the practical effect may be a contraction of the scope of public discourse. . . .[25]

7. ***The Disclosure of Identifying Information.*** In *Briscoe v. Reader's Digest*, 483 P.2d 34 (Cal. 1971), a magazine article about hijacking discussed the plaintiff's hijacking of a truck 11 years earlier. Since then, the plaintiff had rehabilitated himself and many people did not know of his previous crime. Similar to *Melvin v. Reid* (*see* section B above), the court held that the article was newsworthy, but that the use of the plaintiff's real name had no relevance to the article. (*Briscoe* is covered in more depth in Chapter 4.)

---

[23] Eugene Volokh, *Freedom of Speech and Information Privacy: The Troubling Implications of a Right to Stop People from Speaking About You*, 52 Stan. L. Rev. 1049, 1090 (2000).

[24] J. M. Balkin, *How Mass Media Stimulate Political Transparency*, 3 Cultural Values 393 (1999).

[25] *Id.* For a discussion of when public figures should be entitled to privacy, see Anita L. Allen, *Lying to Protect Privacy*, 44 Vill. L. Rev. 161, 177 (1999); Anita L. Allen, *Privacy and the Public Official: Talking about Sex as a Dilemma for Democracy*, 67 Geo. Wash. L. Rev. 1165 (1999).

In contrast, consider *Haynes v. Alfred A. Knopf, Inc.*, 8 F.3d 1222 (7th Cir. 1993). In 1991, Alfred A. Knopf, Inc. published Nicholas Lemann's best-selling historical book entitled *The Promised Land: The Great Black Migration and How It Changed America*. The book chronicled the migration of five million African-Americans from the rural areas in the South to urban areas in the North from 1940 to 1970. The book focuses centrally around the story of one individual, Ruby Lee Daniels. The book recounts Ruby's troubled marriage to Luther Haynes. Luther had a well-paying factory job, but began to drink too much, waste money, and get into bitter fights with Ruby. The book recounts the couple's financial struggles, Luther's squandering of their money, their spiral into poverty, and their difficulties in providing for their children. When the couple was finally able to buy a home, Luther purchased a new car, and as a result, they couldn't meet their house payments and lost the home. Luther would frequently lose jobs and would often fail to come home. Luther then began to have an affair with their neighbor Dorothy Johnson, which was discovered by the children. Ruby and Luther got a divorce. Subsequently, Luther married Dorothy. He turned his life around and began acting more responsibly. In their new community, nobody knew of Luther's selfish and nasty behavior toward Ruby. Luther and Dorothy sued under the public disclosure tort, claiming that the book threatened to destroy the new life Luther had built. The court, however, rejected their claim:

> The two criteria, offensiveness and newsworthiness, are related. An individual, and more pertinently perhaps the community, is most offended by the publication of intimate personal facts when the community has no interest in them beyond the voyeuristic thrill of penetrating the wall of privacy that surrounds a stranger. The reader of a book about the black migration to the North would have no legitimate interest in the details of Luther Haynes's sex life; but no such details are disclosed. Such a reader does have a legitimate interest in the aspects of Luther's conduct that the book reveals. . . . No detail in the book claimed to invade the Hayneses' privacy is not germane to the story that the author wanted to tell, a story not only of legitimate but of transcendent public interest. . . .
>
> Well, argue the Hayneses, at least Lemann could have changed their names. But the use of pseudonyms would not have gotten Lemann and Knopf off the legal hook. The details of the Hayneses' lives recounted in the book would identify them unmistakably to anyone who has known the Hayneses well for a long time (members of their families, for example), or who knew them before they got married; and no more is required for liability either in defamation law, or in privacy law. Lemann would have had to change some, perhaps many, of the details. But then he would no longer have been writing history. He would have been writing fiction. . . .

Why doesn't the reasoning of *Melvin v. Reid* apply to *Haynes*? Was Luther Haynes's actual name really necessary for the telling of the story?

Also consider *Gilbert v. Medical Economics Co.*, 665 F.2d 305 (10th Cir. 1981). An article describing a doctor's malpractice and arguing that hospitals and other physicians were not adequately self-policing included the doctor's name and photograph and discussed her psychiatric and marital problems. The doctor sued, contending that her photo, name, and personal life "add[ed] nothing to the concededly newsworthy topic of policing failures in the medical profession." The court disagreed, concluding:

> . . . [T]hese truthful representations are substantially relevant to a newsworthy topic because they strengthen the impact and credibility of the article. They obviate any impression that the problems raised in the article are remote or hypothetical, thus providing an aura of immediacy and even urgency that might not exist had plaintiff's name and photograph been suppressed. Similarly, we find the publication of plaintiff's psychiatric and marital problems to be substantially relevant to the newsworthy topic [because] . . . they are connected to the newsworthy topic by the rational inference that plaintiff's personal problems were the underlying cause of the acts of alleged malpractice.

Can you distinguish this case from *Melvin v. Reid*? When is identifying information newsworthy?

8. ***Who Decides What Is Newsworthy?*** Who ought to determine what is the proper subject for news? Courts? Journalists? The market? Juries? In *Neff v. Time, Inc.*, 406 F. Supp. 858 (W.D. Pa. 1976), a *Sports Illustrated* photographer printed a photograph of John W. Neff, a teacher, with the front zipper of his pants open in *Sports Illustrated*. The photograph was used in a story about Pittsburgh Steelers fans, and the article was entitled: "A Strange Kind of Love." The photograph was taken while Neff was with a group of fans at a football game between the Cleveland Browns and Pittsburgh Steelers. The fans were waving Steeler banners, drinking beer, and appeared slightly intoxicated. When the *Sports Illustrated* photographer approached them and the group found out that the photographer was covering the game for *Sports Illustrated*, the group "hammed it up" while the photographer snapped the pictures. Of the 30 pictures of the group that were taken, a committee of five employees at *Sports Illustrated* selected the photograph of Neff with his fly open for inclusion in the issue. According to the court, "[a]lthough Neff's fly was not open to the point of being revealing, the selection was deliberate and surely in utmost bad taste; subjectively, as to Neff, the published picture could have been embarrassing, humiliating and offensive to his sensibilities." According to Neff, the photograph implied "that he is a 'crazy, drunken slob,' and combined with the title of the article, 'a sexual deviate.'" Neff asserted that the article invaded his right to privacy, caused him reputational injury, subjected him to public ridicule, destroyed his peace of mind, and caused him severe emotional distress. The court, however, rejected Neff's claim:

> . . . It seems to us that art directors and editors should hesitate to deliberately publish a picture which most likely would be offensive and cause embarrassment to the subject when many other pictures of the same variety are available. Notwithstanding, "(t)he courts are not concerned with establishing canons of good taste for the press or the public." . . .
>
> The article about Pittsburgh Steeler fans was of legitimate public interest; the football game in Cleveland was of legitimate public interest; Neff's picture was taken in a public place with his knowledge and with his encouragement; he was catapulted into the news by his own actions; nothing was falsified; a photograph taken at a public event which everyone present could see, with the knowledge and implied consent of the subject, is not a matter

concerning a private fact. A factually accurate public disclosure is not tortious when connected with a newsworthy event even though offensive to ordinary sensibilities. The constitutional privilege protects all truthful publications relevant to matters of public interest. . . .

Is the court correct to say that it cannot second-guess the judgment of the press? If this is the case, how are courts to determine newsworthiness? Is anything not newsworthy?

Graham involved a photograph taken of a woman who was in an embarrassing position in public. How does the situation in *Neff* differ from that in *Graham*?

9. In 1998, Joyce Maynard wrote an autobiography that describes her romance with J. D. Salinger in the 1970s. J. D. Salinger, an acclaimed author who wrote *The Catcher in the Rye*, had long ago completely retreated from public life and had lived a highly secluded existence in New Hampshire. In 1999, Maynard auctioned the letters J. D. Salinger wrote to her. Does Salinger have a cause of action for the writing of the book or the disclosure of the letters?

SHULMAN V. GROUP W. PRODUCTIONS, INC.

955 P.2d 469 (Cal. 1998)

[Recall the facts of this case earlier in this chapter. The plaintiffs, Ruth and Wayne Shulman, mother and son, were injured in a car accident. A medical transport and rescue helicopter crew came to their assistance along with a video camera operator, who filmed the plaintiffs' rescue from the car, the flight nurse and medic's medical aid during the rescue, as well as their medical aid in the helicopter on route to the hospital. The flight nurse wore a small microphone that picked up her conversations with Ruth and other rescue workers. The segment was broadcast on a television show called *On Scene: Emergency Response*. Ruth, a paraplegic from the accident, watched the episode in her hospital room in shock. Neither Ruth nor Wyane Shulman consented to the filming or broadcasting. They sued the producers of the show and their complaint included causes of action for public disclosure of private facts and intrusion upon seclusion. The trial court granted the defendants' motion for summary judgment on all causes of action.

On the intrusion claim, the California Supreme Court held that the activities of the defendants in recording the events in the helicopter constituted a valid cause of action for intrusion upon seclusion. The court's decision on the public disclosure claim is excerpted below.]

WERDEGAR, J. . . . [U]nder California common law the dissemination of truthful, newsworthy material is not actionable as a publication of private facts. If the contents of a broadcast or publication are of legitimate public concern, the plaintiff cannot establish a necessary element of the tort action, the lack of newsworthiness. . . .

Although we speak of the lack of newsworthiness as an element of the private facts tort, newsworthiness is at the same time a constitutional defense to, or privilege against, liability for publication of truthful information. . . . Tort liability, obviously, can extend no further than the First Amendment allows; conversely, we see no reason or authority for fashioning the newsworthiness element of the private facts tort to *preclude* liability where the Constitution would allow it. . . .

Newsworthiness — constitutional or common law — is also difficult to define because it may be used as either a descriptive or a normative term. "Is the term 'newsworthy' a descriptive predicate, intended to refer to the fact there is widespread public interest? Or is it a value predicate, intended to indicate that the publication is a meritorious contribution and that the public's interest is praiseworthy?" A position at either extreme has unpalatable consequences. If "newsworthiness" is completely descriptive — if all coverage that sells papers or boosts ratings is deemed newsworthy — it would seem to swallow the publication of private facts tort, for "it would be difficult to suppose that publishers were in the habit of reporting occurrences of little interest." At the other extreme, if newsworthiness is viewed as a purely normative concept, the courts could become to an unacceptable degree editors of the news and self-appointed guardians of public taste. . . .

Courts balancing these interests in cases similar to this have recognized that, when a person is involuntarily involved in a newsworthy incident, not all aspects of the person's life, and not everything the person says or does, is thereby rendered newsworthy. . . . This principle is illustrated in the decisions holding that, while a particular event was newsworthy, identification of the plaintiff as the person involved, or use of the plaintiff's identifiable image, added nothing of significance to the story and was therefore an unnecessary invasion of privacy. (*See Briscoe*, 483 P.2d 34; *Melvin v. Reid*, 297 P. 91) . . .

Consistent with the above, courts have generally protected the privacy of otherwise private individual involved in events of public interest "by requiring that a logical nexus exist between the complaining individual and the matter of legitimate public interest." . . .

Intensely personal or intimate revelations might not, in a given case, be considered newsworthy, especially where they bear only slight relevance to a topic of legitimate public concern. . . .

Turning now to the case at bar, we consider whether the possibly private facts complained of here — broadly speaking, Ruth's appearance and words during the rescue and evacuation — were of legitimate public interest. If so, summary judgment was properly entered. . . .

We agree at the outset with defendants that the subject matter of the broadcast as a whole was of legitimate public concern. Automobile accidents are by their nature of interest to that great portion of the public that travels frequently by automobile. The rescue and medical treatment of accident victims is also of legitimate concern to much of the public, involving as it does a critical service that any member of the public may someday need. The story of Ruth's difficult extrication from the crushed car, the medical attention given her at the scene, and her evacuation by helicopter was of particular interest because it highlighted some of the challenges facing emergency workers dealing with serious accidents.

The more difficult question is whether Ruth's appearance and words as she was extricated from the overturned car, placed in the helicopter and transported to the hospital were of legitimate public concern. Pursuant to the analysis outlined earlier, we conclude the disputed material was newsworthy as a matter of law. One of the dramatic and interesting aspects of the story as a whole is its focus on flight nurse Carnahan, who appears to be in charge of communications with other emergency workers, the hospital base and Ruth, and who leads the medical assistance to Ruth at the scene. Her work is portrayed as demanding and important and as involving a measure of personal risk (e.g., in crawling under the car to aid Ruth despite warnings that gasoline may be dripping from the car). The broadcast segment makes apparent that this type of emergency care requires not only medical knowledge, concentration and courage, but an ability to talk and listen to severely traumatized patients. One of the challenges Carnahan faces in assisting Ruth is the confusion, pain and fear that Ruth understandably feels in the aftermath of the accident. For that reason the broadcast video depicting Ruth's injured physical state (which was not luridly shown) and audio showing her disorientation and despair were substantially relevant to the segment's newsworthy subject matter.

Plaintiffs argue that showing Ruth's "intimate private, medical facts and her suffering was not *necessary* to enable the public to understand the significance of the accident or the rescue as a public event." The standard, however, is not necessity. That the broadcast *could* have been edited to exclude some of Ruth's words and images and still excite a minimum degree of viewer interest is not determinative. Nor is the possibility that the members of this or another court, or a jury, might find a differently edited broadcast more to their taste or even more interesting. The courts do not, and constitutionally could not, sit as superior editors of the press. . . .

BROWN, J. concurring and dissenting. . . . I respectfully dissent . . . from the conclusion that summary judgment was proper as to plaintiff Ruth Shulman's cause of action for publication of private facts. . . .

. . . The private facts broadcast had little, if any, social value. The public has no legitimate interest in witnessing Ruth's disorientation and despair. Nor does it have any legitimate interest in knowing Ruth's personal and innermost thoughts immediately after sustaining injuries that rendered her a paraplegic and left her hospitalized for months — "I just want to die. I don't want to go through this." The depth of the broadcast's intrusion into ostensibly private affairs was substantial. . . . There was nothing voluntary about Ruth's position of public notoriety. She was involuntarily caught up in events of public interest, all the more so because defendants appear to have surreptitiously and unlawfully recorded her private conversations with nurse Laura Carnahan. . . .

NOTES & QUESTIONS

1. Real-life television shows and "caught on film" docudramas frequently capture people in moments of profound trauma and grief. Is it newsworthy to display footage of grieving relatives after a disaster?
2. Is this case consistent with *Graham*?
3. Should autopsy photographs be published by the media? This question arose in a case involving the famous race car driver Dale Earnhardt who

died tragically when his car collided with a barrier. Would it be significant if the photos accompanied an article on auto racing safety? What if they were posted on a web site of "famous dead people"?

(e) First Amendment Limitations

The First Amendment has a complex relationship to privacy. In many instances, the First Amendment and privacy are mutually reinforcing. Privacy is often essential to freedom of assembly. The Supreme Court has noted that there is a "vital relationship between freedom to associate and privacy in one's associations." *NAACP v. Alabama*, 357 U.S. 449 (1958). Privacy is also essential for freedom of speech, as the Supreme Court has recognized the importance of protecting the anonymity of speakers. *See McIntyre v. Ohio Elections Commission*, 514 U.S. 334 (1995). The relationship between privacy and freedom of association and anonymity will be covered in more depth in Chapter 5. Additionally, freedom of speech is in harmony with privacy in the context of protecting encryption technology. See *Junger v. Daley*, 209 F.3d 481 (6th Cir. 2000). This issue will be covered in Chapter 4.

However, privacy can come into conflict with the First Amendment. The privacy torts exist in an uneasy tension with the First Amendment. Indeed, Warren and Brandeis's article was aimed at the excesses of the press. Recall the authors' strong criticism of the press: "The press is overstepping in every direction the obvious bounds of propriety and of decency. Gossip is no longer the resource of the idle and of the vicious, but has become a trade, which is pursued with industry as well as effrontery." [26]

It is interesting to note that as a Supreme Court Justice, Louis Brandeis was one of the champions of free speech. Consider Brandeis's concurrence in *Whitney v. California*, 274 U.S. 357, 375 (1927):

> Those who won our independence believed that the final end of the state was to make men free to develop their faculties, and that in its government the deliberative forces should prevail over the arbitrary. They valued liberty both as an end and as a means. They believed liberty to be the secret of happiness and courage to be the secret of liberty. They believed that freedom to think as you will and to speak as you think are means indispensable to the discovery and spread of political truth; that without free speech and assembly discussion would be futile; that with them, discussion affords ordinarily adequate protection against the dissemination of noxious doctrine; that the greatest menace to freedom is an inert people; that public discussion is a political duty; and that this should be a fundamental principle of the American government. They recognized the risks to which all human institutions are subject. But they knew that order cannot be secured merely through fear of punishment for its infraction; that it is hazardous to discourage thought, hope and imagination; that fear breeds repression; that repression breeds hate; that hate menaces stable government; that the path of safety lies in the opportunity to discuss freely supposed grievances and proposed remedies; and that the fitting remedy for evil counsels is good ones. Believing in the power of reason as applied through

---

[26] Samuel Warren & Louis Brandeis, *The Right to Privacy*, 4 Harv. L. Rev. 193 (1890).

public discussion, they eschewed silence coerced by law — the argument of force in its worst form. Recognizing the occasional tyrannies of governing majorities, they amended the Constitution so that free speech and assembly should be guaranteed.

Although the privacy torts are litigated by private parties, they employ the machinery of the state (its tort law and legal system) to impose costs on the press for gathering, producing, and disseminating news. The danger is that the threat of lawsuits will chill the press from running certain stories. Further, the threat of lawsuits alone might chill the press, because even if the press ultimately prevails in such suits, the lawsuits cost money to defend.

The public disclosure tort raises complicated tensions with the First Amendment, for it permits liability for the publication of truthful information. Built into the tort, however, is the newsworthiness test, which a number of courts have stated is required to square the tort with the First Amendment. The newsworthiness test, however, is a limitation *within* the tort. Does the First Amendment provide any additional limitations upon the tort?[27] Consider the following cases:

Cox Broadcasting Corp. v. Cohn

420 U.S. 469 (1975)

White, J. . . . In August 1971, appellee's 17-year-old daughter was the victim of a rape and did not survive the incident. Six youths were soon indicted for murder and rape. Although there was substantial press coverage of the crime and of subsequent developments, the identity of the victim was not disclosed pending trial, perhaps because of Ga. Code Ann. § 26-9901 (1972),[28] which makes it a misdemeanor to publish or broadcast the name or identity of a rape victim. In April 1972, some eight months later, the six defendants appeared in court. Five pleaded guilty to rape or attempted rape, the charge of murder having been dropped. The guilty pleas were accepted by the court, and the trial of the defendant pleading not guilty was set for a later date.

---

[27] For more background on the First Amendment and the privacy torts, see Peter B. Edelman, *Free Press v. Privacy: Haunted by the Ghost of Justice Black*, 68 Tex. L. Rev. 1195 (1990); Diane Leenheer Zimmerman, *Real People in Fiction: Cautionary Words About Troublesome Old Torts Poured into New Jugs*, 51 Brook. L. Rev. 355 (1985); Thomas I. Emerson, *The Right of Privacy and Freedom of Press*, 14 Harv. CR-CL L. Rev. 329 (1979); Alfred Hill, *Defamation and Privacy Under the First Amendment*, 76 Colum. L. Rev. 1205 (1976); Edward Bloustein, *The First Amendment and Privacy: The Supreme Court Justice and the Philosopher*, 28 Rutgers L. Rev. 41 (1974); Melville B. Nimmer, *The Right to Speak from Times to Time: First Amendment Theory Applied to Libel and Misapplied to Privacy*, 56 Calif. L. Rev. 935 (1968); Harry Kalven, Jr., *Privacy in Tort Law — Were Warren and Brandeis Wrong?*, 31 Law & Contemp. Probs. 326 (1966); Marc A. Franklin, *A Constitutional Problem in Privacy Protection: Legal Inhibitions on Reporting of Fact*, 16 Stan. L. Rev. 107 (1963).

[28] "It shall be unlawful for any news media or any other person to print and publish, broadcast, televise, or disseminate through any other medium of public dissemination or cause to be printed and published, broadcast, televised, or disseminated in any newspaper, magazine, periodical or other publication published in this State or through any radio or television broadcast originating in the State the name or identity or any female who may have been raped or upon whom an assault with intent to commit rape may have been made. Any person or corporation violating the provisions of this section shall, upon conviction, be punished as for a misdemeanor." Three other States have similar statutes. . . .

In the course of the proceedings that day, appellant Wasell, a reporter covering the incident for his employer, learned the name of the victim from an examination of the indictments which were made available for his inspection in the courtroom. That the name of the victim appears in the indictments and that the indictments were public records available for inspection are not disputed. Later that day, Wassell broadcast over the facilities of station WSB-TV, a television station owned by appellant Cox Broadcasting Corp., a news report concerning the court proceedings. The report named the victim of the crime and was repeated the following day.

In May 1972, appellee brought an action for money damages against appellants, relying on §26-9901 and claiming that his right to privacy had been invaded by the television broadcasts giving the name of his deceased daughter. . . .

Georgia stoutly defends both §26-9901 and the State's common-law privacy action challenged here. Its claims are not without force, for powerful arguments can be made, and have been made, that however it may be ultimately defined, there is a zone of privacy surrounding every individual, a zone within which the State may protect him from intrusion by the press, with all its attendant publicity. Indeed, the central thesis of the root article by Warren and Brandeis, *The Right to Privacy*, 4 Harv. L. Rev. 193 (1890), was that the press was overstepping its prerogatives by publishing essentially private information and that there should be a remedy for the alleged abuses.

More compellingly, the century has experienced a strong tide running in favor of the so-called right of privacy. In 1967, we noted that "[it] has been said that a 'right of privacy' has been recognized at common law in 30 States plus the District of Columbia and by statute in four States." *Time, Inc. v. Hill*, 385 U.S. 374, 383 n.7. We there cited the 1964 edition of Prosser's *Law of Torts*. The 1971 edition of that same source states that "[in] one form or another, the right of privacy is by this time recognized and accepted in all but a very few jurisdictions." . . .

These are impressive credentials for a right of privacy, but we should recognize that we do not have at issue here an action for the invasion of privacy involving the appropriation of one's name or photograph, a physical or other tangible intrusion into a private area, or a publication of otherwise private information that is also false although perhaps not defamatory. The version of the privacy tort now before us — termed in Georgia "the tort of public disclosure," — is that in which the plaintiff claims the right to be free from unwanted publicity about his private affairs, which, although wholly true, would be offensive to a person of ordinary sensibilities. Because the gravamen of the claimed injury is the publication of information, whether true or not, the dissemination of which is embarrassing or otherwise painful to an individual, it is here that claims of privacy most directly confront the constitutional freedoms of speech and press. The face-off is apparent, and the appellants urge upon us the broad holding that the press may not be made criminally or civilly liable for publishing information that is neither false nor misleading but absolutely accurate, however damaging it may be to reputation or individual sensibilities. . . .

It is true that in defamation actions, where the protected interest is personal reputation, the prevailing view is that truth is a defense. . . .

The Court has nevertheless carefully left open the question whether the First and Fourteenth Amendments require that truth be recognized as a defense in a defamation action brought by a private person as distinguished from a public official or public figure. . . . In similar fashion, *Time, Inc. v. Hill*, expressly saved the question whether truthful publication of very private matters unrelated to public affairs could be constitutionally proscribed. . . .

Those precedents, as well as other considerations, counsel similar caution here. In this sphere of collision between claims of privacy and those of the free press, the interests on both sides are plainly rooted in the traditions and significant concerns of our society. Rather than address the broader question whether truthful publications may ever be subjected to civil or criminal liability consistently with the First and Fourteenth Amendments, or to put it another way, whether the State may ever define and protect an area of privacy free from unwanted publicity in the press, it is appropriate to focus on the narrower interface between press and privacy that this case presents, namely, whether the State may impose sanctions on the accurate publication of the name of a rape victim obtained from public records — more specifically, from judicial records which are maintained in connection with a public prosecution and which themselves are open to public inspection. We are convinced that the State may not do so.

In the first place, in a society in which each individual has but limited time and resources with which to observe at first hand the operations of his government, he relies necessarily upon the press to bring to him in convenient form the facts of those operations. Great responsibility is accordingly placed upon the news media to report fully and accurately the proceedings of government, and official records and documents open to the public are the basic data of governmental operations. Without the information provided by the press most of us and many of our representatives would be unable to vote intelligently or to register opinions on the administration of government generally. With respect to judicial proceedings in particular, the function of the press serves to guarantee the fairness of trials and to bring to bear the beneficial effects of public scrutiny upon the administration of justice. . . .

. . . By placing the information in the public domain on official court records, the State must be presumed to have concluded that the public interest was thereby being served. Public records by their very nature are of interest to those concerned with the administration of government, and a public benefit is performed by the reporting of the true contents of the records by the media. The freedom of the press to publish that information appears to us to be of critical importance to our type of government in which the citizenry is the final judge of the proper conduct of public business. In preserving that form of government the First and Fourteenth Amendments command nothing less than that the States may not impose sanctions on the publication of truthful information contained in official court records open to public inspection.

We are reluctant to embark on a course that would make public records generally available to the media but forbid their publication if offensive to the sensibilities of the supposed reasonable man. Such a rule would make it very difficult for the media to inform citizens about the public business and yet stay within the law. The rule would invite timidity and self-censorship and very likely lead to the suppression of many items that would otherwise be published and that should be made available to the public. At the very least, the First and Fourteenth Amendments will not allow exposing the press to liability for truthfully publishing information released to the public in official court records. If there are privacy interests to be protected in judicial proceedings, the States must respond by means which avoid public documentation or other exposure of private information. Their political institutions must weigh the interests in privacy with the interests of the public to know and of the press to publish. Once true information is disclosed in public court documents open to public inspection, the press cannot be sanctioned for publishing it. In this instance as in others reliance must rest upon the judgment of those who decide what to publish or broadcast. . . .

NOTES & QUESTIONS

1. There are two potential justifications for the rule in *Cox*. The first is that the information in public records is not private because it is in the public domain, and once that information falls into the public domain, the First Amendment prohibits restrictions on speaking about it. The other justification is that the press must be able to report on public records dealing with the criminal justice system to permit greater accountability and transparency in government. Which justification does the Court's opinion rely upon most heavily? Under the second justification, would the state be permitted to keep rape victims' names confidential?

2. After *Cox*, the Supreme Court held in *Oklahoma Publishing Co. v. Oklahoma County District Court*, 430 U.S. 308 (1977), that a state court violated the First Amendment by prohibiting the media from publishing the name or photograph of an 11-year-old boy in a juvenile proceeding which members of the media attended. A few years later, the Court confronted the issue of whether a state could prohibit the press from publishing the name of a juvenile offender. In *Smith v. Daily Mail Publishing Co.*, 443 U.S. 97 (1979), two newspapers published the name and photograph of a 15 year old who had shot and killed his 14-year-old classmate. The newspapers were indicted with the misdemeanor offense of publishing the name of a juvenile offender without a court order. The Court stated: "At issue is simply the power of a state to punish the truthful publication of an alleged juvenile delinquent's name lawfully obtained by a newspaper. The asserted state interest [to protect the anonymity of juvenile offenders] cannot justify the statute's imposition of criminal sanctions on this type of publication."

THE FLORIDA STAR V. B.J.F.

491 U.S. 524 (1989)

MARSHALL, J. Florida Stat. § 794.03 (1987) makes it unlawful to "print, publish, or broadcast . . . in any instrument of mass communication" the name of the victim of a sexual offense. Pursuant to this statute, appellant The Florida Star was found civilly liable for publishing the name of a rape victim which it had obtained from a publicly released police report. The issue presented here is whether this result comports with the First Amendment. We hold that it does not. . . .

The Florida Star is a weekly newspaper which serves the community of Jacksonville, Florida, and which has an average circulation of approximately 18,000 copies. A regular feature of the newspaper is its "Police Reports" section. That section, typically two to three pages in length, contains brief articles describing local criminal incidents under police investigation.

On October 20, 1983, appellee B.J.F.[29] reported to the Duval County, Florida, Sheriff's Department (Department) that she had been robbed and sexually assaulted by an unknown assailant. The Department prepared a report on the incident which identified B.J.F. by her full name. The Department then placed the report in its pressroom. The Department does not restrict access either to the pressroom or to the reports made available therein.

A Florida Star reporter-trainee sent to the pressroom copied the police report verbatim, including B.J.F.'s full name, on a blank duplicate of the Department's forms. A Florida Star reporter then prepared a one-paragraph article about the crime, derived entirely from the trainee's copy of the police report. The article included B.J.F.'s full name. It appeared in the "Robberies" subsection of the "Police Reports" section on October 29, 1983, one of 54 police blotter stories in that day's edition. . . .

In printing B.J.F.'s full name, The Florida Star violated its internal policy of not publishing the names of sexual offense victims.

On September 26, 1984, B.J.F. filed suit in the Circuit Court of Duval County against the Department and The Florida Star, alleging that these parties negligently violated § 794.03. Before trial, the Department settled with B.J.F. for $2,500. The Florida Star moved to dismiss, claiming, inter alia, that imposing civil sanctions on the newspaper pursuant to § 794.03 violated the First Amendment. The trial judge rejected the motion.

At the ensuing daylong trial, B.J.F. testified that she had suffered emotional distress from the publication of her name. She stated that she had heard about the article from fellow workers and acquaintances; that her mother had received several threatening phone calls from a man who stated that he would rape B.J.F. again; and that these events had forced B.J.F. to change her phone number and residence, to seek police protection, and to obtain mental health counseling. In defense, The Florida Star put forth evidence indicating that the newspaper had learned B.J.F.'s name from the incident report released by the Department, and that the newspaper's violation of its internal rule against publishing the names of sexual offense victims was inadvertent.

At the close of B.J.F.'s case, and again at the close of its defense, The Florida Star moved for a directed verdict. On both occasions, the trial judge denied these motions. He ruled from the bench that § 794.03 was constitutional because it reflected a proper balance between the First Amendment and privacy rights, as it applied only to a narrow set of "rather sensitive . . . criminal offenses." . . . The jury awarded B.J.F. $75,000 in compensatory damages and $25,000 in punitive damages. . . .

---

[29] In filing this lawsuit, appellee used her full name in the caption of the case. On appeal, the Florida District Court of Appeal sua sponte revised the caption, stating that it would refer to the appellee by her initials, "in order to preserve [her] privacy interests." Respecting those interests, we, too, refer to appellee by her initials, both in the caption and in our discussion.

Appellant takes the position that this case is indistinguishable from *Cox Broadcasting*. Alternatively, it urges that our decisions . . . can be distilled to yield a broader First Amendment principle that the press may never be punished, civilly or criminally, for publishing the truth. . . .

We conclude that imposing damages on appellant for publishing B.J.F.'s name violates the First Amendment, although not for either of the reasons appellant urges. Despite the strong resemblance this case bears to *Cox Broadcasting*, that case cannot fairly be read as controlling here. The name of the rape victim in that case was obtained from courthouse records that were open to public inspection. . . . Significantly, one of the reasons we gave in *Cox Broadcasting* for invalidating the challenged damages award was the important role the press plays in subjecting trials to public scrutiny and thereby helping guarantee their fairness. That role is not directly compromised where, as here, the information in question comes from a police report prepared and disseminated at a time at which not only had no adversarial criminal proceedings begun, but no suspect had been identified.

Nor need we accept appellant's invitation to hold broadly that truthful publication may never be punished consistent with the First Amendment. Our cases have carefully eschewed reaching this ultimate question, mindful that the future may bring scenarios which prudence counsels our not resolving anticipatorily. . . . We continue to believe that the sensitivity and significance of the interests presented in clashes between First Amendment and privacy rights counsel relying on limited principles that sweep no more broadly than the appropriate context of the instant case.

In our view, this case is appropriately analyzed with reference to such a limited First Amendment principle. It is the one, in fact, which we articulated in *Daily Mail* in our synthesis of prior cases involving attempts to punish truthful publication: "[I]f a newspaper lawfully obtains truthful information about a matter of public significance then state officials may not constitutionally punish publication of the information, absent a need to further a state interest of the highest order." According the press the ample protection provided by that principle is supported by at least three separate considerations, in addition to, of course, the overarching "'public interest, secured by the Constitution, in the dissemination of truth.'" . . . .

First, because the *Daily Mail* formulation only protects the publication of information which a newspaper has "lawfully obtain[ed]," the government retains ample means of safeguarding significant interests upon which publication may impinge, including protecting a rape victim's anonymity. . . . Where information is entrusted to the government, a less drastic means than punishing truthful publication almost always exists for guarding against the dissemination of private facts.[30]

A second consideration undergirding the *Daily Mail* principle is the fact

---

[30]The *Daily Mail* principle does not settle the issue whether, in cases where information has been acquired unlawfully by a newspaper or by a source, government may ever punish not only the unlawful acquisition, but the ensuing publication as well. This issue was raised but not definitively resolved in *New York Times Co. v. United States*, 403 U.S. 713 (1971), and reserved in *Landmark Communications*, 435 U.S., at 837. We have no occasion to address it here.

that punishing the press for its dissemination of information which is already publicly available is relatively unlikely to advance the interests in the service of which the State seeks to act. . . . [W]here the government has made certain information publicly available, it is highly anomalous to sanction persons other than the source of its release. . . . As *Daily Mail* observed in its summary of Oklahoma Publishing, "once the truthful information was 'publicly revealed' or 'in the public domain' the court could not constitutionally restrain its dissemination."

A third and final consideration is the "timidity and self-censorship" which may result from allowing the media to be punished for publishing certain truthful information. . . . A contrary rule, depriving protection to those who rely on the government's implied representations of the lawfulness of dissemination, would force upon the media the onerous obligation of sifting through government press releases, reports, and pronouncements to prune out material arguably unlawful for publication. . . .

Applied to the instant case, the *Daily Mail* principle clearly commands reversal. The first inquiry is whether the newspaper "lawfully obtain[ed] truthful information about a matter of public significance." It is undisputed that the news article describing the assault on B.J.F. was accurate. In addition, appellant lawfully obtained B.J.F.'s name. Appellee's argument to the contrary is based on the fact that under Florida law, police reports which reveal the identity of the victim of a sexual offense are not among the matters of "public record" which the public, by law, is entitled to inspect. But the fact that state officials are not required to disclose such reports does not make it unlawful for a newspaper to receive them when furnished by the government. . . . It is, clear, furthermore, that the news article concerned "a matter of public significance," in the sense in which the *Daily Mail* synthesis of prior cases used that term. That is, the article generally, as opposed to the specific identity contained within it, involved a matter of paramount public import: the commission, and investigation, of a violent crime which had been reported to authorities.

The second inquiry is whether imposing liability on appellant pursuant to §794.03 serves "a need to further a state interest of the highest order." Appellee argues that a rule punishing publication furthers three closely related interests: the privacy of victims of sexual offenses; the physical safety of such victims, who may be targeted for retaliation if their names become known to their assailants; and the goal of encouraging victims of such crimes to report these offenses without fear of exposure.

At a time in which we are daily reminded of the tragic reality of rape, it is undeniable that these are highly significant interests. . . . For three independent reasons, however, imposing liability for publication under the circumstances of this case is too precipitous a means of advancing these interests to convince us that there is a "need" within the meaning of the *Daily Mail* formulation for Florida to take this extreme step.

First is the manner in which appellant obtained the identifying information in question. As we have noted, where the government itself provides information to the media, it is most appropriate to assume that the government had, but failed to utilize, far more limited means of guarding against dissemination than the extreme step of punishing truthful speech. That assumption is richly borne out in this case. B.J.F.'s identity would never have come to light were it not for the erroneous, if inadvertent, inclusion by the Department of her full name in an incident report made available in a pressroom open to the public. Florida's policy against disclosure of rape victims' identities, reflected in § 794.03, was undercut by the Department's failure to abide by this policy. Where, as here, the government has failed to police itself in disseminating information, it is clear under *Cox Broadcasting, Oklahoma Publishing,* and *Landmark Communications* that the imposition of damages against the press for its subsequent publication can hardly be said to be a narrowly tailored means of safeguarding anonymity. . . .

A second problem with Florida's imposition of liability for publication is the broad sweep of the negligence per se standard applied under the civil cause of action implied from § 794.03. Unlike claims based on the common law tort of invasion of privacy, civil actions based on § 794.03 require no case-by-case findings that the disclosure of a fact about a person's private life was one that a reasonable person would find highly offensive. On the contrary, under the per se theory of negligence adopted by the courts below, liability follows automatically from publication. This is so regardless of whether the identity of the victim is already known throughout the community; whether the victim has voluntarily called public attention to the offense; or whether the identity of the victim has otherwise become a reasonable subject of public concern — because, perhaps, questions have arisen whether the victim fabricated an assault by a particular person. Nor is there a scienter requirement of any kind under § 794.03, engendering the perverse result that truthful publications challenged pursuant to this cause of action are less protected by the First Amendment than even the least protected defamatory falsehoods. . . .

Our holding today is limited. We do not hold that truthful publication is automatically constitutionally protected, or that there is no zone of personal privacy within which the State may protect the individual from intrusion by the press, or even that a State may never punish publication of the name of a victim of a sexual offense. We hold only that where a newspaper publishes truthful information which it has lawfully obtained, punishment may lawfully be imposed, if at all, only when narrowly tailored to a state interest of the highest order, and that no such interest is satisfactorily served by imposing liability under § 794.03 to appellant under the facts of this case. . . .

WHITE, J. joined by REHNQUIST, C. J. and O'CONNOR, J. dissenting. . . . *Cox Broadcasting* reversed a damages award entered against a television station, which had obtained a rape victim's name from public records maintained in connection with the judicial proceedings brought against her assailants. While there are similarities, critical aspects of that case make it wholly distinguishable from this one. First, in *Cox Broadcasting,* the victim's name had been disclosed in the hearing where her assailants pleaded guilty; and, as we recognized, judicial records have always been considered public information in this country. . . . Second, unlike the incident report at issue here, which was meant by state law to be withheld from public release, the judicial proceedings at issue in *Cox Broadcasting* were open as a matter of state law. . . .

Cox Broadcasting stands for the proposition that the State cannot make the press its first line of defense in withholding private information from the public — it cannot ask the press to secrete private facts that the State makes no effort to safeguard in the first place. In this case, however, the State has undertaken "means which avoid [but obviously, not altogether prevent] public documentation or other exposure of private information." . . .

More importantly, at issue in *Daily Mail* was the disclosure of the name of the perpetrator of an infamous murder of a 15-year-old student. Surely the rights of those accused of crimes and those who are their victims must differ with respect to privacy concerns. That is, whatever rights alleged criminals have to maintain their anonymity pending an adjudication of guilt — and after *Daily Mail*, those rights would seem to be minimal — the rights of crime victims to stay shielded from public view must be infinitely more substantial. . . .

Consequently, I cannot agree that *Cox Broadcasting*, or *Oklahoma Publishing*, or *Daily Mail* requires — or even substantially supports — the result reached by the Court today. . . .

We are left, then, to wonder whether the . . . "independent reasons" the Court cites for reversing the judgment for B.J.F. support its result.

The first of these reasons relied on by the Court is the fact "appellant gained access to [B.J.F.'s name] through a government news release." "The government's issuance of such a release, without qualification, can only convey to recipients that the government considered dissemination lawful," the Court suggests. So described, this case begins to look like the situation in *Oklahoma Publishing*, where a judge invited reporters into his courtroom, but then tried to prohibit them from reporting on the proceedings they observed. But this case is profoundly different. Here, the "release" of information provided by the government was not, as the Court says, "without qualification." As the Star's own reporter conceded at trial, the crime incident report that inadvertently included B.J.F.'s name was posted in a room that contained signs making it clear that the names of rape victims were not matters of public record, and were not to be published. The Star's reporter indicated that she understood that she "[was not] allowed to take down that information" (i.e., B.J.F.'s name) and that she "[was] not supposed to take the information from the police department." Thus, by her own admission the posting of the incident report did not convey to the Star's reporter the idea that "the government considered dissemination lawful"; the Court's suggestion to the contrary is inapt. . . .

. . . By amending its public records statute to exempt rape victims names from disclosure, and forbidding its officials to release such information, the State has taken virtually every step imaginable to prevent what happened here. This case presents a far cry, then, from *Cox Broadcasting* or *Oklahoma Publishing*, where the State asked the news media not to publish information it had made generally available to the public: here, the State is not asking the media to do the State's job in the first instance. Unfortunately, as this case illustrates, mistakes happen: even when States take measures to "avoid" disclosure, sometimes rape victims' names are found out. As I see it, it is not too much to ask the press, in instances such as this, to respect simple standards of decency and refrain from publishing a victims' name, address, and/or phone number. . . .

. . . By holding that only "a state interest of the highest order" permits the State to penalize the publication of truthful information, and by holding that protecting a rape victim's right to privacy is not among those state interests of the highest order, the Court accepts appellant's invitation to obliterate one of the most noteworthy legal inventions of the 20th century: the tort of the publication of private facts. Even if the Court's opinion does not say as much today, such obliteration will follow inevitably from the Court's conclusion here. . . .

NOTES & QUESTIONS

1. What more could the state do to protect the information? Florida made it a crime to disseminate the information. The state recognized that in certain cases, the police might make a mistake and accidentally fail to redact a rape victim's name from the report. To protect against this, signs were put up outside the room notifying the press not to record a rape victim's name that was inadvertently left on the report. Is it overreaching for the state to punish the press for disclosing the information under these circumstances?

2. The Court relies in part on the fact that the information was "legally available." If the journalist had stolen a confidential police report and published the information, would the Court's holding have been different? Since the Florida law proscribed both the government dissemination of the information and the press publication of it, was the information "legally available"?

3. *The Future of the Public Disclosure Tort After* **Florida Star.** What effect does *Florida Star* have on the public disclosure tort? Rodney Smolla writes that the public disclosure tort exists "more 'in the books' than in practice."[31] One commentator described the tort as "alive, but on life support."[32] Do you agree with these characterizations?

4. What are the implications of this case for *Melvin v. Reid*? Recall in *Reid* that the court held that although the disclosure of a former prostitute's life story was of public concern, the disclosure of her name was not. If B.J.F.'s name is not of public concern (not newsworthy), then why isn't this a sufficient enough basis to restrict the publication of it by the press?

5. *The First Amendment and Threats to People's Private Lives.* In *Planned Parenthood v. American Coalition of Life Activists*, 290 F.3d 1058 (9th Cir. 2002) (en banc), the American Coalition of Life Activists (ACLA), an antiabortion advocacy group, provided a series of dossiers it assembled on doctors, clinic employees, politicians, judges, and other abortion rights supporters to Neal Horsley, an antiabortion activist, who posted the information on his web site entitled the "Nuremberg Files." The "Nuremberg Files" dossiers included doctors' names, photos, social security numbers, home addresses, descriptions of their cars, and information about their families. The

---

[31] Rodney A. Smolla, *Privacy and the First Amendment Right to Gather News*, 67 Geo. Wash. L. Rev. 1097 (1999).

[32] Richard S. Murphy, *Property Rights in Personal Information: An Economic Defense of Privacy*, 84 Geo. L.J. 2381, 2388 (1996). *But see* John A. Jurata, Jr., *Comment, The Tort That Refuses to Go Away: The Subtle Reemergence of Public Disclosure of Private Facts*, 36 San Diego L. Rev. 489 (1999).

web site marked the names of doctors who had been killed with a black line through them and the names of wounded doctors shaded in gray. The web site did not contain any explicit threats against the doctors. The web site caused the doctors great fear, and several protected themselves by wearing bulletproof vests, closing all the curtains to the windows of their homes, and even asking for the protection of the U.S. Marshals. Some of the doctors sued ACLA alleging a variety of causes of action including the Freedom of Access to Clinic Entrances Act of 1994 (FACE), 18 U.S.C. § 248. A jury awarded the doctors $107 million in actual and punitive damages. The Ninth Circuit, en banc, affirmed the actual damages and reversed on punitive damages. The court held that the "Nuremberg Files" (in combination with "wanted" posters of various doctors) constituted a "true threat" to the doctors' lives under FACE, and such true threats were not protected under the First Amendment. Although speech advocating violence is protected, speech "directed to inciting or producing imminent lawless action" is not. "Violence is not a protected value. Nor is a *true threat* of violence *with intent to intimidate*. . . . ACLA was not staking out a position of debate but of threatened demise." According to a dissent by Judge Kozinski: "The Nuremberg Files website is clearly an expression of a political point of view. . . . [S]peech, including the intimidating message, does not constitute a direct threat because there is no evidence other than the speech itself that the speakers intend to resort to physical violence if their threat is not heeded." Would the doctors have a cause of action for public disclosure of private facts? Would the First Amendment prohibit liability on this basis?

Recently, antiabortion protesters have begun to photograph individuals entering abortion clinics. There is a loose network of activists across the country that photograph women and place the photos on web sites. Sometimes personal information, such as license plate numbers or medical records, are posted next to the photograph. Should these activities be actionable? What does the Restatement suggest? Based on the *American Coalition of Life Activists* case above, would liability for this activity run afoul of the First Amendment?

6. ***The Tension Between Privacy and the First Amendment.*** Diane Zimmerman questions the very existence of the public disclosure tort. She argues that the tort should be "scuttled" as inconsistent with the First Amendment. According to Zimmerman, the "idle gossip" Warren and Brandeis complained about is highly valuable speech, entitled to no less protection than any other form of speech:

> . . . [G]ossip — the exchange of personal information about character, habits and lifestyles — does not merely serve as an instrument of social control. Students of the phenomenon claim that gossip, and the rules governing who participates and who is privy to what information about whom, helps mark out social groupings and establish community ties. By providing people with a way to learn about social groups to which they do not belong, gossip increases intimacy and a sense of community among disparate individuals and groups. Gossip may also foster the development of relationships by giving two strangers the means to bridge a gap of silence when they are thrown together in a casual social situation.

Thus, from the perspective of the anthropologist and sociologist, gossip is a basic form of information exchange that teaches about other lifestyles and attitudes, and through which community values are changed or reinforced. This description is a far cry from that of Warren and Brandeis, which characterized gossip as a trivializing influence that destroys "robustness of thought and delicacy of feeling" and serves the interests primarily of the "prurient" and the "indolent."

Gossip thus appears to be a normal and necessary part of life for all but the rare hermit among us. Perceived in this way, gossip contributes directly to the first amendment "marketplace of ideas," and the comparative weight assigned to an interest in its limitation merits careful consideration. . . .

. . . The distinction between press coverage and gossip may be important to our subjective sense of well-being, but it appears to be a dubious basis for imposing liability only on mass communicators of public facts, especially in light of the serious infringement on the press and free speech that such a limitation engenders. . . .[33]

Do you agree with Zimmerman about the high value of gossip? Does the value of gossip outweigh the harms it causes?

7. **The Value of the Truth.** Frederick Schauer argues that many commentators discussing the tension between free speech and privacy are too quick to assume that "truth is an ultimate, irreducible, and noninstrumental value." According to Schauer, we should be concerned with issues of power, and sometimes truth is outweighed by protecting those who lack power (i.e., private figures) from those who have it (i.e., media entities).[34] Likewise, Anita Allen contends:

Judicial ascription of privacy rights is an allocation of power. Those who have license to say what they please about others without fear of criminal penalty or civil liability enjoy a brand of power. . . . Professor Schauer correctly concludes that the media should not always win: the mere fact that the media is the media and has published the truth should not automatically bar actions for invasion of privacy premised on the publication of private facts. The reason that the media and other defendants should not have legal immunity is that immunity gives them more power than the Constitution requires and fairness permits.[35]

On the other hand, Susan Gilles responds that if Schauer and Allen are correct and some truths have less value, then it "would require empowering the courts to decide what truths are of value to the public." This would embroil courts in making content-based discriminations about speech, and the "power to determine which truths are acceptable has been abused in the past."[36]

---

[33] Diane L. Zimmerman, *Requiem for a Heavyweight: A Farewell to Warren and Brandeis's Privacy Tort*, 68 Cornell L. Rev. 291, 333–334, 340 (1983).

[34] Frederick Schauer, *Reflections on the Value of Truth*, 41 Case W. Res. L. Rev. 699 (1991). For a critique of Schauer's position, see Erwin Chemerinsky, *In Defense of Truth*, 41 Case W. Res. L. Rev. 745 (1991).

[35] Anita L. Allen, *The Power of Private Facts*, 41 Case W. Res. L. Rev. 757 (1991).

[36] Susan M. Gilles, *All Truths Are Equal, But Are Some Truths More Equal Than Others?*, 41 Case W. Res. L. Rev. 725 (1991).

Do we really want speech to be so unfettered that it is subsidized by the harming of people, the destruction of their lives and reputations? The rise of television newsmagazines such as *Dateline, 60 Minutes, 20/20,* and so on create a great demand for human interest stories, which often involve examining the private lives of individuals. These newsmagazines often earn high ratings and make a significant profit for television networks. Volokh argues, in defense of the media, that "[t]he essence of news is precisely the reporting of things done or discovered by others; the essence of the news business is profiting from reporting on things done or discovered by others."[37] Shouldn't the press bear some of the costs for its invasions into private lives?

8. ***The Press and Generally Applicable Laws.*** In *Cohen v. Cowles Media Co.,* 501 U.S. 663 (1991), the Court rejected a journalist's argument that the application of contract law against him violated the First Amendment. The journalist had promised a source confidentiality but nevertheless published the source's name. The source sued and obtained a promissory estoppel damage award. According to the Court, *Florida Star* did not control because "generally applicable laws do not offend the First Amendment simply because their enforcement against the press has incidental effects on its ability to gather and report the news."

2. DISCLOSURE OF ILLEGALLY OBTAINED INFORMATION

Sometimes, the press learns information from people who obtain it illegally. In certain instances, whistleblowers breach their contracts by leaking information or stealing documents. In a number of instances, laws protecting privacy are violated in the course of gathering information. Suppose a journalist gains private information that she knew her source had obtained in violation of the law. Can she still publish that information? Can the government enact laws to prohibit the disclosure of private information obtained illegally? Consider the following case:

BARTNICKI V. VOPPER

532 U.S. 514 (2001)

STEVENS, J. These cases raise an important question concerning what degree of protection, if any, the First Amendment provides to speech that discloses the contents of an illegally intercepted communication. That question is both novel and narrow. Despite the fact that federal law has prohibited such disclosures since 1934, this is the first time that we have confronted such an issue. . . .

During 1992 and most of 1993, the Pennsylvania State Education Association, a union representing the teachers at the Wyoming Valley West High School, engaged in collective-bargaining negotiations with the school board.

---

[37] Eugene Volokh, *Freedom of Speech and Information Privacy: The Troubling Implications of a Right to Stop People from Speaking About You,* 52 Stan. L. Rev. 1049 (2000).

Petitioner Kane, then the president of the local union, testified that the negotiations were "'contentious'" and received "a lot of media attention." In May 1993, petitioner Bartnicki, who was acting as the union's "chief negotiator," used the cellular phone in her car to call Kane and engage in a lengthy conversation about the status of the negotiations. An unidentified person intercepted and recorded that call.

In their conversation, Kane and Bartnicki discussed the timing of a proposed strike, difficulties created by public comment on the negotiations, and the need for a dramatic response to the board's intransigence. At one point, Kane said: "'If they're not gonna move for three percent, we're gonna have to go to their, their homes. . . . To blow off their front porches, we'll have to do some work on some of those guys. (PAUSES). Really, uh, really and truthfully because this is, you know, this is bad news. (UNDECIPHERABLE).'"

In the early fall of 1993, the parties accepted a non-binding arbitration proposal that was generally favorable to the teachers. In connection with news reports about the settlement, respondent Vopper, a radio commentator who had been critical of the union in the past, played a tape of the intercepted conversation on his public affairs talk show. Another station also broadcast the tape, and local newspapers published its contents. After filing suit against Vopper and other representatives of the media, Bartnicki and Kane (hereinafter petitioners) learned through discovery that Vopper had obtained the tape from Jack Yocum, the head of a local taxpayers' organization that had opposed the union's demands throughout the negotiations. Yocum, who was added as a defendant, testified that he had found the tape in his mailbox shortly after the interception and recognized the voices of Bartnicki and Kane. Yocum played the tape for some members of the school board, and later delivered the tape itself to Vopper. . . .

In their amended complaint, petitioners alleged that their telephone conversation had been surreptitiously intercepted by an unknown person using an electronic device, that Yocum had obtained a tape of that conversation, and that he intentionally disclosed it to Vopper, as well as other individuals and media representatives. Thereafter, Vopper and other members of the media repeatedly published the contents of that conversation. The amended complaint alleged that each of the defendants "knew or had reason to know" that the recording of the private telephone conversation had been obtained by means of an illegal interception. Relying on both federal and Pennsylvania statutory provisions, petitioners sought actual damages, statutory damages, punitive damages, and attorney's fees and costs. . . .

[Title 18 U.S.C. §2511(1)(c) provides that any person who "intentionally discloses, or endeavors to disclose, to any other person the contents of any wire, oral, or electronic communication, knowing or having reason to know that the information was obtained through the interception of a wire, oral, or electronic communication in violation of this subsection; . . . shall be punished. . . ." The Pennsylvania Act contains a similar provision.]

. . . [W]e accept respondents' submission on three factual matters that serve to distinguish most of the cases that have arisen under §2511. First, respondents played no part in the illegal interception. Rather, they found out about the interception only after it occurred, and in fact never learned the identity of the person or persons who made the interception. Second, their access to the information on the tapes was obtained lawfully, even though the information itself was intercepted unlawfully by someone else. Third, the subject matter of the conversation was a matter of public concern. If the statements about the labor negotiations had been made in a public arena — during a bargaining session, for example — they would have been newsworthy. This would also be true if a third party had inadvertently overheard Bartnicki making the same statements to Kane when the two thought they were alone. . . .

We agree with petitioners that § 2511(1)(c), as well as its Pennsylvania analog, is in fact a content-neutral law of general applicability. "Deciding whether a particular regulation is content based or content neutral is not always a simple task. . . . As a general rule, laws that by their terms distinguish favored speech from disfavored speech on the basis of the ideas or views expressed are content based." In determining whether a regulation is content based or content neutral, we look to the purpose behind the regulation; typically, "[g]overnment regulation of expressive activity is content neutral so long as it is 'justified without reference to the content of the regulated speech.'"

In this case, the basic purpose of the statute at issue is to "protec[t] the privacy of wire[, electronic,] and oral communications." S. Rep. No. 1097, 90th Cong., 2d Sess., 66 (1968). The statute does not distinguish based on the content of the intercepted conversations, nor is it justified by reference to the content of those conversations. Rather, the communications at issue are singled out by virtue of the fact that they were illegally intercepted — by virtue of the source, rather than the subject matter.

On the other hand, the naked prohibition against disclosures is fairly characterized as a regulation of pure speech. . . .

As a general matter, "state action to punish the publication of truthful information seldom can satisfy constitutional standards." *Smith v. Daily Mail Publishing Co.*, 443 U.S. 97, 102 (1979). More specifically, this Court has repeatedly held that "if a newspaper lawfully obtains truthful information about a matter of public significance then state officials may not constitutionally punish publication of the information, absent a need . . . of the highest order." *Id.*, at 103; *see also Florida Star v. B.J.F.; Landmark Communications, Inc. v. Virginia.* . . .

. . . [T]he issue here is this: "Where the punished publisher of information has obtained the information in question in a manner lawful in itself but from a source who has obtained it unlawfully, may the government punish the ensuing publication of that information based on the defect in a chain?" . . .

The Government identifies two interests served by the statute — first, the interest in removing an incentive for parties to intercept private conversations, and second, the interest in minimizing the harm to persons whose conversations have been illegally intercepted. . . .

The normal method of deterring unlawful conduct is to impose an appropriate punishment on the person who engages in it. If the sanctions that presently attach to a violation of § 2511(1)(a) do not provide sufficient deterrence, perhaps those sanctions should be made more severe. But it would be quite remarkable to hold that speech by a law-abiding possessor of information can be suppressed in order to deter conduct by a non-law-abiding third party. . . .

The Government's second argument, however, is considerably stronger. Privacy of communication is an important interest, and Title III's restrictions are intended to protect that interest, thereby "encouraging the uninhibited exchange of ideas and information among private parties. . . ." Moreover, the fear of public disclosure of private conversations might well have a chilling effect on private speech. . . .

Accordingly, it seems to us that there are important interests to be considered on both sides of the constitutional calculus. . . .

In this case, privacy concerns give way when balanced against the interest in publishing matters of public importance. As Warren and Brandeis stated in their classic law review article: "The right of privacy does not prohibit any publication of matter which is of public or general interest." *The Right to Privacy*, 4 Harv. L. Rev. 193, 214 (1890). One of the costs associated with participation in public affairs is an attendant loss of privacy. . . .

Our opinion in *New York Times Co. v. Sullivan*, 376 U.S. 254 (1964), reviewed many of the decisions that settled the "general proposition that freedom of expression upon public questions is secured by the First Amendment." . . .

We think it clear that parallel reasoning requires the conclusion that a stranger's illegal conduct does not suffice to remove the First Amendment shield from speech about a matter of public concern. The months of negotiations over the proper level of compensation for teachers at the Wyoming Valley West High School were unquestionably a matter of public concern, and respondents were clearly engaged in debate about that concern. . . .

BREYER, J. joined by O'CONNOR, J. concurring. I join the Court's opinion because I agree with its "narrow" holding, limited to the special circumstances present here: (1) the radio broadcasters acted lawfully (up to the time of final public disclosure); and (2) the information publicized involved a matter of unusual public concern, namely a threat of potential physical harm to others. I write separately to explain why, in my view, the Court's holding does not imply a significantly broader constitutional immunity for the media. . . .

The statutory restrictions before us directly enhance private speech. The statutes ensure the privacy of telephone conversations much as a trespass statute ensures privacy within the home. That assurance of privacy helps to overcome our natural reluctance to discuss private matters when we fear that our private conversations may become public. And the statutory restrictions consequently encourage conversations that otherwise might not take place.

At the same time, these statutes restrict public speech directly, deliberately, and of necessity. They include media publication within their scope not simply as a means, say, to deter interception, but also as an end. Media dissemination of an intimate conversation to an entire community will often cause the speakers serious harm over and above the harm caused by an initial disclosure to the person who intercepted the phone call. . . .

As a general matter, despite the statutes' direct restrictions on speech, the Federal Constitution must tolerate laws of this kind because of the importance of these privacy and speech-related objectives. . . .

Nonetheless, looked at more specifically, the statutes, as applied in these circumstances, do not reasonably reconcile the competing constitutional objectives. Rather, they disproportionately interfere with media freedom. For one thing, the broadcasters here engaged in no unlawful activity other than the ultimate publication of the information another had previously obtained. . . .

Further, the speakers themselves, the president of a teacher's union and the union's chief negotiator, were "limited public figures," for they voluntarily engaged in a public controversy. They thereby subjected themselves to somewhat greater public scrutiny and had a lesser interest in privacy than an individual engaged in purely private affairs. . . .

Rehnquist, C. J., joined by Scalia and Thomas, J. J., dissenting. Technology now permits millions of important and confidential conversations to occur through a vast system of electronic networks. These advances, however, raise significant privacy concerns. We are placed in the uncomfortable position of not knowing who might have access to our personal and business e-mails, our medical and financial records, or our cordless and cellular telephone conversations. In an attempt to prevent some of the most egregious violations of privacy, the United States, the District of Columbia, and 40 States have enacted laws prohibiting the intentional interception and knowing disclosure of electronic communications. The Court holds that all of these statutes violate the First Amendment insofar as the illegally intercepted conversation touches upon a matter of "public concern," an amorphous concept that the Court does not even attempt to define. But the Court's decision diminishes, rather than enhances, the purposes of the First Amendment: chilling the speech of the millions of Americans who rely upon electronic technology to communicate each day. . . .

The Court correctly observes that these are "content-neutral law[s] of general applicability" which serve recognized interests of the "highest order": "the interest in individual privacy and . . . in fostering private speech." It nonetheless subjects these laws to the strict scrutiny normally reserved for governmental attempts to censor different viewpoints or ideas. There is scant support, either in precedent or in reason, for the Court's tacit application of strict scrutiny.

A content-neutral regulation will be sustained if

> "'it furthers an important or substantial governmental interest; if the governmental interest is unrelated to the suppression of free expression; and if the incidental restriction on alleged First Amendment freedoms is no greater than is essential to the furtherance of that interest.'" *Turner Broadcasting System, Inc. v. FCC*, 512 U.S. 622, 662 (1994). . . .

The Court's attempt to avoid these precedents by reliance upon the *Daily Mail* string of newspaper cases is unpersuasive. In these cases, we held that statutes prohibiting the media from publishing certain truthful information — the name of a rape victim, *Florida Star v. B. J. F.*; *Cox Broadcasting Corp. v. Cohn*, the confidential proceedings before a state judicial review commission, *Landmark Communications, Inc. v. Virginia*, and the name of a juvenile defendant, *Daily Mail* — violated the First Amendment. In so doing, we stated that "if a newspaper lawfully obtains truthful information about a matter of public significance then state officials may not constitutionally punish publication of the information, absent a need to further a state interest of the highest order." *Daily Mail*. Neither this *Daily Mail* principle nor any other aspect of these cases, however, justifies the Court's imposition of strict scrutiny here. . . .

First, the information published by the newspapers had been lawfully obtained from the government itself. . . . This factor has no relevance in the present cases, where we deal with private conversations that have been intentionally kept out of the public domain.

Second, the information in each case was already "publicly available," and punishing further dissemination would not have advanced the purported government interests of confidentiality. . . . These laws thus do not fall under the axiom that "the interests in privacy fade when the information involved already appears on the public record."

Third, these cases were concerned with "the 'timidity and self-censorship' which may result from allowing the media to be punished for publishing certain truthful information." But fear of "timidity and self-censorship" is a basis for upholding, not striking down, these antidisclosure provisions: They allow private conversations to transpire without inhibition. And unlike the statute at issue in *Florida Star*, which had no scienter requirement, these statutes only address those who knowingly disclose an illegally intercepted conversation. They do not impose a duty to inquire into the source of the information and one could negligently disclose the contents of an illegally intercepted communication without liability.

In sum, it is obvious that the *Daily Mail* cases upon which the Court relies do not address the question presented here. . . .

These laws are content neutral; they only regulate information that was illegally obtained; they do not restrict republication of what is already in the public domain; they impose no special burdens upon the media; they have a scienter requirement to provide fair warning; and they promote the privacy and free speech of those using cellular telephones. It is hard to imagine a more narrowly tailored prohibition of the disclosure of illegally intercepted communications, and it distorts our precedents to review these statutes under the often fatal standard of strict scrutiny. These laws therefore should be upheld if they further a substantial governmental interest unrelated to the suppression of free speech, and they do. . . .

The "dry up the market" theory, which posits that it is possible to deter an illegal act that is difficult to police by preventing the wrongdoer from enjoying the fruits of the crime, is neither novel nor implausible. It is a time-tested theory that undergirds numerous laws, such as the prohibition of the knowing possession of stolen goods. We ourselves adopted the exclusionary rule based upon similar reasoning, believing that it would "deter unreasonable searches," by removing an officer's "incentive to disregard [the Fourth Amendment]."

The same logic applies here and demonstrates that the incidental restriction on alleged First Amendment freedoms is no greater than essential to further the interest of protecting the privacy of individual communications. Were there no prohibition on disclosure, an unlawful eavesdropper who wanted to disclose the conversation could anonymously launder the interception through a third party and thereby avoid detection. Indeed, demand for illegally obtained private information would only increase if it could be disclosed without repercussion. The law against interceptions, which the Court agrees is valid, would be utterly ineffectual without these antidisclosure provisions. . . .

NOTES & QUESTIONS

1. *Privacy and Free Speech.* The concurrence and dissent both recognize that the statutory provisions of federal wiretap law serve to protect, rather than merely infringe, First Amendment values. According to the concurrence, the statutory provisions "directly enhance private speech" and in the words of the dissent, the statutory provisions serve to protect against "chilling the speech of millions of Americans who rely upon electronic technology to communicate each day." How should the Court analyze statutes that restrict some speech in order to promote more speech? Should such statutes be treated like laws that exclusively restrict speech?[38]

2. Consider the following argument by Richard Epstein:

> What sense is there to a regime that allows the imposition of criminal sanctions on those who leak the information, but does not allow the plaintiff to keep the information quiet? Under the current regime, government operations take the form of a kind of Hobbesian struggle where the government's ability to keep its own secrets depends on the happenstance of whether it can snuff out the illegal release of information by threatening government employees with dismissal, fines, and punishment beforehand.[39]

3. *Protections Against the Disclosure of Leaked Information.* In *Landmark Communications v. Virginia*, 435 U.S. 829 (1978), a newspaper was indicted for violating a Virginia law making it a misdemeanor to disclose the identity of a state judge whose conduct was being investigated by the Virginia Judicial Inquiry and Review Commission. The law was designed to ensure that judicial disciplinary proceedings would remain confidential (until such proceedings were concluded) to protect judges from the publication of frivolous and unwarranted complaints. The newspaper did not challenge the requirement of confidentiality, only the prohibition of disclosing the identities of judges if the newspaper happened to find out that a judge was the subject of a disciplinary proceeding. The Supreme Court held that such prohibition violated the First Amendment. Although the interest in confidentiality of disciplinary proceedings was legitimate, it was not sufficient to justify the encroachment on the First Amendment because "[t]he operations of the courts and the judicial conduct of judges are matters of utmost public concern." Further, the statutory scheme could remain effective by restricting the improper leaking of such information rather than criminalizing the disclosure of that information by parties that did not participate in the illegal obtaining of such information.

---

[38] For a discussion of *Bartnicki*, see Paul Gewirtz, *Privacy and Speech*, 2001 Sup. Ct. Rev. 139 (2001).

[39] Richard A. Epstein, *Privacy, Publication, and the First Amendment: The Dangers of First Amendment Exceptionalism*, 52 Stan. L. Rev. 1003 1044–1045 (2000).

4. *Privacy and Intellectual Property: Disparate Treatment?* In *Ford Motor Co. v. Lane*, 67 F. Supp. 2d 745 (E.D. Mich. 1999), the court held that the First Amendment prohibits enjoining a web site from posting copyrighted material. Likewise, in *Oregon ex rel. Sports Management News, Inc. v. Nachtisal*, 921 P.2d 1304 (Or. 1996), the First Amendment prohibits enjoining a newsletter from publishing trade secrets. Should courts treat information obtained in violation of intellectual property law differently from information obtained in violation of privacy laws?

D. DISSEMINATION OF FALSE OR MISLEADING INFORMATION

1. DEFAMATION

(a) Introduction

At the most practical level, an understanding of defamation law is essential to understanding some of the aspects and issues related to the privacy torts. While the privacy torts are a relatively recent invention, a remedy for defamation extends far back in history. Since ancient times, one's reputation and character have been viewed as indispensable to one's ability to engage in public life. Accordingly, the importance of permitting people to protect their reputations has given rise to the law of defamation.[40]

Defamation goes way back to pre-Norman times. "Defamation" (*diffamatus*) was a technical term in church law. It signified a reputation bad enough to be put on trial in ecclesiastical court. Money awards for defamation were a way to prevent people from engaging in duels. Defamation law also served as a popular tool of the monarchy to prosecute its critics.[41]

According to modern defamation law:

> To create liability for defamation there must be:
>
>   (a) a false and defamatory statement concerning another;
>   (b) an unprivileged publication to a third party;
>   (c) fault amounting at least to negligence on the part of the publisher; and
>   (d) either actionability of the statement irrespective of special harm or the existence of special harm caused by the publication. Restatement (Second) of Torts §558.

A "defamatory" statement "tends so to harm the reputation of another as to lower him in the estimation of the community or to deter third persons from associating or dealing with him." Restatement §559.

---

[40] For an excellent discussion of the rationales behind defamation law, see Robert C. Post, *The Social Foundations of Defamation Law: Reputation and the Constitution*, 74 Cal. L. Rev. 691 (1986).

[41] *See generally* Theodore F. T. Plucknett, *A Concise History of the Common Law* 484-487 (5th ed. 1956).

A defamatory statement must also be "false." Therefore, a true statement that harms the reputation of another cannot give rise to liability for defamation.

"Publication" means that a defamatory statement is communicated "intentionally or by a negligent act to one other than the person defamed." Restatement § 577. If a person intentionally and unreasonably fails to remove defamatory matter that she knows is under her control, then that person is subject to liability for its continued publication. See Restatement § 577. Further "one who repeats or otherwise republishes defamatory matter is subject to liability as if he had originally published it." Restatement § 578.

One who distributes, transmits, or broadcasts on television or radio defamatory material is also liable if she knows or would have reason to know of its defamatory character. *See* Restatement § 581.

Libel vs. Slander. There are two forms of defamation: libel, which consists of written defamatory statements, and slander, which consists of spoken defamatory statements. According to the Restatement:

> (1) Libel consists of the publication of defamatory matter by written or printed words, by its embodiment in physical form or by any other form of communication that has the potentially harmful qualities characteristic of written or printed words.

> (2) Slander consists of the publication of defamatory matter by spoken words, transitory gestures or by any form of communication other than those stated in Subsection (1). Restatement § 568.

As is demonstrated by the above definitions, the Restatement takes a rather broad view of what constitutes libel.

The classification of certain types of statements as either libel or slander has proven difficult. One example is a statement made over the radio or on television. According to the Restatement, all broadcasting is libel, see Restatement § 568A, but some states take a contrary view.

The distinction between libel and slander is important for the purposes of proving harm. To establish libel, a plaintiff does not need to show "special harm" (i.e., a particular harm or injury); damages are presumed. In contrast, for slander, a plaintiff must show actual pecuniary harm, with the exception of four types of slander known as "slander per se" for which damages are presumed. Slander per se consists of defamatory statements imputing to another (1) a criminal offense; (2) a loathsome disease; (3) a matter incompatible with one's business, trade, profession, or office; or (4) serious sexual misconduct. *See* Restatement §§ 570-574. The distinction between libel and slander is less important today, since, in the cases you will read below, the Supreme Court curtailed the availability of presumed damages in defamation law.

Why is libel treated more severely than slander? As then Judge Cardozo put it:

> The schism in the law of defamation between the older wrong of slander and the newer one of libel is not the product of mere accident. It has its genesis in evils which the years have not erased. Many things that are defamatory may be said with impunity through the medium of speech. Not so, however, when

speech is caught upon the wing and transmuted into print. What gives the sting to writing is its permanence in form. The spoken word dissolves, but the written one abides and perpetuates the scandal.[42]

Defamation and Privacy. It might strike you that defamation does not have much to do with privacy. After all, defamation involves false information about individuals whereas privacy seems to be about true information. This, however, is a limited view of privacy. Privacy involves more than finding out true things about individuals. If privacy is understood as an individual's ability to have some control over the self-image she projects to society, then the ability to prevent the spread of false information about oneself is essential for this sort of control. Indeed, one of the cornerstone principles of privacy law is the ability to correct errors in one's records.

(b) Defamation and the Internet

The Internet presents interesting problems for the application of defamation law and the privacy torts because the Internet enables the widespread publication of information by any individual. Typically, it was through the news media that defamatory or private information about individuals was communicated. As a result, it would be viable to sue such entities, since they would be able to pay any judgment a plaintiff might obtain. With the Internet, however, suppose an individual posts defamatory information about another person on her web site. Most likely, that individual isn't wealthy enough to be sued. Further, information is sometimes posted anonymously. As a result of this difficulty, plaintiffs have attempted to advance theories upon which Internet Service Providers (ISPs) would be liable.

In defamation law, in addition to the one who makes a libelous statement, other parties who disseminate the libelous statement can also be found liable. Repeating or publishing the libelous statements of others can give rise to "publisher" liability. A newspaper is an example of a publisher because it exercises editorial control over its content. Merely disseminating a libelous statement can give rise to "distributor" liability. In contrast to a publisher, a distributor cannot be found liable unless it is found to be at fault — if it knew or had reason to know about the defamatory statement. Book stores and libraries are examples of distributors. When a person posts a statement on an ISP's electronic bulletin board or other online forum, is the ISP a "publisher," "distributor," or neither?

The first two courts to reach this issue reached contrary conclusions. In *Cubby, Inc. v. CompuServe, Inc.*, 776 F. Supp. 135 (S.D.N.Y. 1991), CompuServe, an Internet Service Provider, offered CompuServe Information Service (CIS), an online general information service giving subscribers access to special interest forums. One publication available in such a forum was Rumorville USA, a newsletter published daily about journalism. CompuServe did not review Rumorville's contents before it was published in CompuServe's forums, available

---

[42]*Ostrowe v. Lee*, 175 N.E. 505, 506 (N.Y. Ct. App. 1931).

to subscribers. The plaintiffs developed Skuttlebut, a competing gossip service to Rumorville. The plaintiffs sued CompuServe, alleging that Rumorville published false and defamatory statements relating to Skuttlebut. CompuServe moved for summary judgment, arguing that even if the statements were defamatory, CompuServe could not be held liable for the statements because it didn't have knowledge or reason to know of the statements. The court held that CompuServe was a distributor rather than a publisher:

> With respect to the Rumorville publication, the undisputed facts are that DFA uploads the text of Rumorville into CompuServe's data banks and makes it available to approved CIS subscribers instantaneously. CompuServe has no more editorial control over such a publication than does a public library, book store, or newsstand, and it would be no more feasible for CompuServe to examine every publication it carries for potentially defamatory statements than it would be for any other distributor to do so. . . .

In *Stratton Oakmont, Inc. v. Prodigy Services Co.*, 23 Media L. Rep. 1794 (N.Y. Sup. 1995), the plaintiff brought a defamation action against Prodigy, the operator of the computer network. An unidentified user posted allegedly defamatory statements on one of Prodigy's electronic bulletin boards. The plaintiffs contended that Prodigy should be considered the "publisher" of the statements. Under Prodigy's stated policy, it was a family oriented computer network:

> We make no apology for pursuing a value system that reflects the culture of the millions of American families we aspire to serve. Certainly no responsible newspaper does less when it chooses the type of advertising it publishes, the letters it prints, the degree of nudity and unsupported gossip its editors tolerate. . . .

Prodigy, relying on *Cubby, Inc. v. CompuServe*, contended that it could not be liable as a publisher. Because of the great volume of messages posted daily on Prodigy bulletin boards — about 60,000 per day — it could not review each one. The court, however, concluded that Prodigy was liable as a publisher:

> The key distinction between CompuServe and Prodigy is two fold. First, Prodigy held itself out to the public and its members as controlling the content of its computer bulletin boards. Second, Prodigy implemented this control through its automatic software screening program, and the Guidelines which Board Leaders are required to enforce. By actively utilizing technology and manpower to delete notes from its computer bulletin boards on the basis of offensiveness and "bad taste," for example, Prodigy is clearly making decisions as to content, and such decisions constitute editorial control. That such control is not complete and is enforced both as early as the notes arrive and as late as a complaint is made, does not minimize or eviscerate the simple fact that Prodigy has uniquely arrogated to itself the role of determining what is proper for its members to post and read on its bulletin boards. Based on the foregoing, this Court is compelled to conclude that for the purposes of Plaintiffs' claims in this action, Prodigy is a publisher rather than a distributor. . . .

In response to these cases, Congress passed § 230 of the Communications Decency Act (CDA) of 1996, which provides in relevant part: "No provider or user of an interactive computer service shall be treated as the publisher or speaker of any information provided by another information content provider." 47 U.S.C. §230(c)(1). Based on this provision, will ISPs that provide forums where defamatory statements are posted be treated as publishers, distributors, or neither?

ZERAN V. AMERICA ONLINE, INC.

129 F.3d 327 (4th Cir. 1997)

WILKINSON, C.J. . . . On April 25, 1995, an unidentified person posted a message on an [America Online (AOL)] bulletin board advertising "Naughty Oklahoma T-Shirts." The posting described the sale of shirts featuring offensive and tasteless slogans related to the April 19, 1995, bombing of the Alfred P. Murrah Federal Building in Oklahoma City. Those interested in purchasing the shirts were instructed to call "Ken" at [Kenneth] Zeran's home phone number in Seattle, Washington. As a result of this anonymously perpetrated prank, Zeran received a high volume of calls, comprised primarily of angry and derogatory messages, but also including death threats. Zeran could not change his phone number because he relied on its availability to the public in running his business out of his home. Later that day, Zeran called AOL and informed a company representative of his predicament. The employee assured Zeran that the posting would be removed from AOL's bulletin board but explained that as a matter of policy AOL would not post a retraction. The parties dispute the date that AOL removed this original posting from its bulletin board.

On April 26, the next day, an unknown person posted another message advertising additional shirts with new tasteless slogans related to the Oklahoma City bombing. Again, interested buyers were told to call Zeran's phone number, to ask for "Ken," and to "please call back if busy" due to high demand. The angry, threatening phone calls intensified. Over the next four days, an unidentified party continued to post messages on AOL's bulletin board, advertising additional items including bumper stickers and key chains with still more offensive slogans. During this time period, Zeran called AOL repeatedly and was told by company representatives that the individual account from which the messages were posted would soon be closed. Zeran also reported his case to Seattle FBI agents. By April 30, Zeran was receiving an abusive phone call approximately every two minutes.

Meanwhile, an announcer for Oklahoma City radio station KRXO received a copy of the first AOL posting. On May 1, the announcer related the message's contents on the air, attributed them to "Ken" at Zeran's phone number, and urged the listening audience to call the number. After this radio broadcast, Zeran was inundated with death threats and other violent calls from Oklahoma City residents. Over the next few days, Zeran talked to both KRXO and AOL representatives. He also spoke to his local police, who subsequently surveilled his home to protect his safety. By May 14, after an Oklahoma City newspaper published a story exposing the shirt advertisements as a hoax and after KRXO made an on-air apology, the number of calls to Zeran's residence finally subsided to fifteen per day.

Zeran first filed suit on January 4, 1996, against radio station KRXO in the United States District Court for the Western District of Oklahoma. On April 23, 1996, he filed this separate suit against AOL in the same court. Zeran did not

bring any action against the party who posted the offensive messages.[43] . . .
AOL answered Zeran's complaint and interposed [the Communications Decency Act,] 47 U.S.C. §230 as an affirmative defense. AOL then moved for
judgment on the pleadings pursuant to Fed. R. Civ. P. 12(c). The district court
granted AOL's motion, and Zeran filed this appeal.

Because §230 was successfully advanced by AOL in the district court as a
defense to Zeran's claims, we shall briefly examine its operation here. Zeran
seeks to hold AOL liable for defamatory speech initiated by a third party. He
argued to the district court that once he notified AOL of the unidentified third
party's hoax, AOL had a duty to remove the defamatory posting promptly, to
notify its subscribers of the message's false nature, and to effectively screen future defamatory material. Section 230 entered this litigation as an affirmative
defense pled by AOL. The company claimed that Congress immunized interactive computer service providers from claims based on information posted by
a third party.

The relevant portion of §230 states: "No provider or user of an interactive
computer service shall be treated as the publisher or speaker of any information provided by another information content provider." 47 U.S.C. §230(c)(1).
By its plain language, §230 creates a federal immunity to any cause of action
that would make service providers liable for information originating with a
third-party user of the service. Specifically, §230 precludes courts from entertaining claims that would place a computer service provider in a publisher's
role. Thus, lawsuits seeking to hold a service provider liable for its exercise
of a publisher's traditional editorial functions — such as deciding whether to
publish, withdraw, postpone or alter content — are barred.

The purpose of this statutory immunity is not difficult to discern. Congress
recognized the threat that tort-based lawsuits pose to freedom of speech in the
new and burgeoning Internet medium. The imposition of tort liability on service providers for the communications of others represented, for Congress,
simply another form of intrusive government regulation of speech. . . .

. . . Interactive computer services have millions of users. The amount of
information communicated via interactive computer services is therefore
staggering. The specter of tort liability in an area of such prolific speech would
have an obvious chilling effect. It would be impossible for service providers to
screen each of their millions of postings for possible problems. Faced with potential liability for each message republished by their services, interactive computer service providers might choose to severely restrict the number and type
of messages posted. Congress considered the weight of the speech interests
implicated and chose to immunize service providers to avoid any such restrictive effect.

Another important purpose of §230 was to encourage service providers to
self-regulate the dissemination of offensive material over their services. In this
respect, §230 responded to a New York state court decision, *Stratton Oakmont,
Inc. v. Prodigy Servs. Co.* . . . .

---

[43]Zeran maintains that AOL made it impossible to identify the original party by failing to
maintain adequate records of its users. The issue of AOL's recordkeeping practices, however, is not
presented by this appeal.

Congress enacted § 230 to remove the disincentives to self-regulation created by the *Stratton Oakmont* decision. Under that court's holding, computer service providers who regulated the dissemination of offensive material on their services risked subjecting themselves to liability, because such regulation cast the service provider in the role of a publisher. Fearing that the specter of liability would therefore deter service providers from blocking and screening offensive material, Congress enacted § 230's broad immunity "to remove disincentives for the development and utilization of blocking and filtering technologies that empower parents to restrict their children's access to objectionable or inappropriate online material." 47 U.S.C. § 230(b)(4). In line with this purpose, § 230 forbids the imposition of publisher liability on a service provider for the exercise of its editorial and self-regulatory functions.

Zeran argues, however, that the § 230 immunity eliminates only publisher liability, leaving distributor liability intact. Publishers can be held liable for defamatory statements contained in their works even absent proof that they had specific knowledge of the statement's inclusion. According to Zeran, interactive computer service providers like AOL are normally considered instead to be distributors, like traditional news vendors or book sellers. Distributors cannot be held liable for defamatory statements contained in the materials they distribute unless it is proven at a minimum that they have actual knowledge of the defamatory statements upon which liability is predicated. Zeran contends that he provided AOL with sufficient notice of the defamatory statements appearing on the company's bulletin board. This notice is significant, says Zeran, because AOL could be held liable as a distributor only if it acquired knowledge of the defamatory statements' existence.

Because of the difference between these two forms of liability, Zeran contends that the term "distributor" carries a legally distinct meaning from the term "publisher." Accordingly, he asserts that Congress' use of only the term "publisher" in § 230 indicates a purpose to immunize service providers only from publisher liability. He argues that distributors are left unprotected by § 230 and, therefore, his suit should be permitted to proceed against AOL. We disagree. Assuming arguendo that Zeran has satisfied the requirements for imposition of distributor liability, this theory of liability is merely a subset, or a species, of publisher liability, and is therefore also foreclosed by § 230. . . .

AOL falls squarely within this traditional definition of a publisher and, therefore, is clearly protected by § 230's immunity. . . .

Zeran simply attaches too much importance to the presence of the distinct notice element in distributor liability. The simple fact of notice surely cannot transform one from an original publisher to a distributor in the eyes of the law. . . .

If computer service providers were subject to distributor liability, they would face potential liability each time they receive notice of a potentially defamatory statement — from any party, concerning any message. Each notification would require a careful yet rapid investigation of the circumstances surrounding the posted information, a legal judgment concerning the information's defamatory character, and an on-the-spot editorial decision whether to risk liability by allowing the continued publication of that information. Although this might be feasible for the traditional print publisher, the sheer number of postings on interactive computer services would create an impossible burden in the Internet context. Because service providers would be subject to liability only for the publication of information, and not for its removal, they would have a natural incentive simply to remove messages upon notification, whether the contents were defamatory or not. Thus, like strict liability, liability upon notice has a chilling effect on the freedom of Internet speech. . . .

More generally, notice-based liability for interactive computer service providers would provide third parties with a no-cost means to create the basis for future lawsuits. Whenever one was displeased with the speech of another party conducted over an interactive computer service, the offended party could simply "notify" the relevant service provider, claiming the information to be legally defamatory. In light of the vast amount of speech communicated through interactive computer services, these notices could produce an impossible burden for service providers, who would be faced with ceaseless choices of suppressing controversial speech or sustaining prohibitive liability. Because the probable effects of distributor liability on the vigor of Internet speech and on service provider self-regulation are directly contrary to §230's statutory purposes, we will not assume that Congress intended to leave liability upon notice intact. . . .

BLUMENTHAL V. DRUDGE (AOL)

992 F. Supp. 44 (D.D.C. 1998)

[A day before Sidney Blumenthal began his employment as an assistant to President Clinton on August 11, 1997, Matt Drudge, the creator of an Internet gossip publication called the Drudge Report, posted a story about Blumenthal having engaged in spousal abuse of his wife, Jacqueline Jordan Blumenthal, who also worked in the White House as director of White House fellowships. In addition to making its stories available on the Internet, the Drudge Report would be e-mailed to a list of regular readers. Since its creation in 1995, the Drudge Report grew from 1,000 e-mail subscribers to 85,000 by 1997. In 1997, Drudge and America Online (AOL), an Internet Service Provider, entered into a license agreement. Pursuant to the agreement, the Drudge Report would be made available to AOL members and Drudge would receive a monthly royalty of $3,000 from AOL. The royalty was Drudge's only source of income. Under the agreement, Drudge would create the content of the Report, and AOL may "remove content that AOL reasonably determine[s] to violate AOL's then standard terms of service." The Blumenthals sued AOL and Drudge, contending that the statement was defamatory. Drudge later retracted the story and publicly apologized to the Blumenthals. AOL filed a motion for summary judgment, arguing that it was immune from suit by the Communications Decency Act.]

FRIEDMAN, J. . . . Section 230(c) of the Communications Decency Act of 1996 provides:

> No provider or user of an interactive computer service shall be treated as the publisher or speaker of any information provided by another information content provider.

47 U.S.C. §230(c)(1). The statute goes on to define the term "information content provider" as "any person or entity that is responsible, in whole or in part, for the creation or development of information provided through the Internet or any other interactive computer service." 47 U.S.C. §230(e)(3). In view of this statutory language, plaintiffs' argument that the Washington Post would be liable if it had done what AOL did here—"publish Drudge's story without doing anything whatsoever to edit, verify, or even read it (despite knowing what Drudge did for a living and how he did it),"—has been rendered irrelevant by Congress. . . .

Plaintiffs [argue] that Section 230 of the Communications Decency Act does not provide immunity to AOL in this case because Drudge was not just an anonymous person who sent a message over the Internet through AOL. He is a person with whom AOL contracted, whom AOL paid $3,000 a month—$36,000 a year, Drudge's sole, consistent source of income—and whom AOL promoted to its subscribers and potential subscribers as a reason to subscribe to AOL. Furthermore, the license agreement between AOL and Drudge by its terms contemplates more than a passive role for AOL. . . .

In addition, shortly after it entered into the licensing agreement with Drudge, AOL issued a press release making clear the kind of material Drudge would provide to AOL subscribers — gossip and rumor — and urged potential subscribers to sign onto AOL in order to get the benefit of the Drudge Report. The press release was captioned: "AOL Hires Runaway Gossip Success Matt Drudge." . . .

If it were writing on a clean slate, this Court would agree with plaintiffs. AOL has certain editorial rights with respect to the content provided by Drudge and disseminated by AOL, including the right to require changes in content and to remove it; and it has affirmatively promoted Drudge as a new source of unverified instant gossip on AOL. Yet it takes no responsibility for any damage he may cause. AOL is not a passive conduit like the telephone company, a common carrier with no control and therefore no responsibility for what is said over the telephone wires. Because it has the right to exercise editorial control over those with whom it contracts and whose words it disseminates, it would seem only fair to hold AOL to the liability standards applied to a publisher or, at least, like a book store owner or library, to the liability standards applied to a distributor. But Congress has made a different policy choice by providing immunity even where the interactive service provider has an active, even aggressive role in making available content prepared by others. In some sort of tacit quid pro quo arrangement with the service provider community, Congress has conferred immunity from tort liability as an incentive to Internet service providers to self-police the Internet for obscenity and other offensive material, even where the self-policing is unsuccessful or not even attempted. . . .

. . . While it appears to this Court that AOL in this case has taken advantage of all the benefits conferred by Congress in the Communications Decency Act, and then some, without accepting any of the burdens that Congress intended, the statutory language is clear: AOL is immune from suit, and the Court therefore must grant its motion for summary judgment.

NOTES & QUESTIONS

1. *The Applicability of the CDA § 230 to the Privacy Torts.* Is § 230 of the CDA applicable to the privacy torts? Suppose an Internet Service Provider maintained a special web site called "GossipVille." The web site permits any individual to anonymously post gossip or photographs about anybody else. People can post intimate information about others such as naked pictures, diaries, and even hidden videos. The web site has a searchable database by name so that people can dig up dirt on their friends, lovers, and enemies. The web site disavows any responsibility for the content of the site; people can post whatever they want. Can the Internet Service Provider be sued under the public disclosure tort based on § 230?
2. What about suing the anonymous individual who posted the information? Should the web site be forced to maintain records of the identities of the individuals who post so that people can sue those individuals?

(c) First Amendment Limitations

NEW YORK TIMES CO. V. SULLIVAN

376 U.S. 254 (1964)

[L.B. Sullivan, one of the three elected Commissioners of Montgomery, Alabama, sued four African-American clergymen and the *New York Times* for libel. Sullivan claimed that a full-page advertisement in the *New York Times* on March 29, 1960, entitled "Heed Their Rising Voices" defamed him. The advertisement discussed the civil rights movement and the wave of terror against the nonviolent protest. It was signed by various clergymen in Southern cities, including the four clergymen named in the lawsuit.

Two paragraphs of the ten in the advertisement were the basis of Sullivan's libel claim.

> . . . In Montgomery, Alabama, after students sang "My Country, 'Tis of Thee" on the State Capitol steps, their leaders were expelled from school, and truckloads of police armed with shotguns and tear-gas ringed the Alabama State College Campus. When the entire student body protested to state authorities by refusing to re-register, their dining hall was padlocked in an attempt to starve them into submission. . . .
>
> Again and again the Southern violators have answered Dr. King's peaceful protests with intimidation and violence. They have bombed his home almost killing his wife and child. They have assaulted his person. They have arrested him seven times — for "speeding," "loitering" and similar "offenses." And now they have charged him with "perjury" — a felony under which they could imprison him for ten years. . . .

Although Sullivan was never mentioned by name, he claimed that the word "police" implicated him because he supervised the police department. Although Sullivan made no effort to prove he suffered actual pecuniary loss as a result of the alleged libel, a Montgomery County jury awarded Sullivan damages of $500,000, the full amount claimed against all the petitioners, and the Supreme Court of Alabama affirmed.]

BRENNAN, J. . . . Under Alabama law as applied in this case, a publication is "libelous per se" if the words "tend to injure a person . . . in his reputation" or to "bring (him) into public contempt"; the trial court stated that the standard was met if the words are such as to "injure him in his public office, or impute misconduct to him in his office, or want of official integrity, or want of fidelity to a public trust. . . ." The jury must find that the words were published "of and concerning" the plaintiff, but where the plaintiff is a public official his place in the governmental hierarchy is sufficient evidence to support a finding that his reputation has been affected by statements that reflect upon the agency of which he is in charge. Once "libel per se" has been established, the defendant has no defense as to stated facts unless he can persuade the jury that they were true in all their particulars. His privilege of "fair comment" for expressions of opinion depends on the truth of the facts upon which the comment is based. Unless he can discharge the burden of proving truth, general damages are presumed, and may be awarded without proof of pecuniary injury. A showing of actual malice is apparently a prerequisite to recovery of punitive damages, and the defendant may in any event forestall a punitive award by a retraction meeting the statutory requirements. Good motives and belief in truth do not negate an inference of malice, but are relevant only in mitigation of punitive damages if the jury chooses to accord them weight.

The question before us is whether this rule of liability, as applied to an action brought by a public official against critics of his official conduct, abridges the freedom of speech and of the press that is guaranteed by the First and Fourteenth Amendments.

Respondent relies heavily, as did the Alabama courts, on statements of this Court to the effect that the Constitution does not protect libelous publications. . . . Like insurrection, contempt, advocacy of unlawful acts, breach of the peace, obscenity, solicitation of legal business, and the various other formulae for the repression of expression that have been challenged in this Court, libel can claim no talismanic immunity from constitutional limitations. It must be measured by standards that satisfy the First Amendment.

The general proposition that freedom of expression upon public questions is secured by the First Amendment has long been settled by our decisions. . . .

. . . [W]e consider this case against the background of a profound national commitment to the principle that debate on public issues should be uninhibited, robust, and wide-open, and that it may well include vehement, caustic, and sometimes unpleasantly sharp attacks on government and public officials. The present advertisement, as an expression of grievance and protest on one of the major public issues of our time, would seem clearly to qualify for the constitutional protection. The question is whether it forfeits that protection by the falsity of some of its factual statements and by its alleged defamation of respondent.

Authoritative interpretations of the First Amendment guarantees have consistently refused to recognize an exception for any test of truth — whether administered by judges, juries, or administrative officials — and especially one that puts the burden of proving truth on the speaker. The constitutional protection does not turn upon "the truth, popularity, or social utility of the ideas and beliefs which are offered." . . .

That erroneous statement is inevitable in free debate, and that it must be protected if the freedoms of expression are to have the "breathing space" that they "need to survive." . . .

A rule compelling the critic of official conduct to guarantee the truth of all his factual assertions — and to do so on pain of libel judgments virtually unlimited in amount — leads to a comparable "self-censorship." . . . Under such a rule, would-be critics of official conduct may be deterred from voicing their criticism, even though it is believed to be true and even though it is in fact true, because of doubt whether it can be proved in court or fear of the expense of having to do so. They tend to make only statements which "steer far wider of the unlawful zone." The rule thus dampens the vigor and limits the variety of public debate. It is inconsistent with the First and Fourteenth Amendments.

The constitutional guarantees require, we think, a federal rule that prohibits a public official from recovering damages for a defamatory falsehood relating to his official conduct unless he proves that the statement was made with "actual malice" — that is, with knowledge that it was false or with reckless disregard of whether it was false or not. . . .

We hold today that the Constitution delimits a State's power to award damages for libel in actions brought by public officials against critics of their official conduct. Since this is such an action, the rule requiring proof of actual malice is applicable. While Alabama law apparently requires proof of actual malice for an award of punitive damages, where general damages are concerned malice is "presumed." Such a presumption is inconsistent with the federal rule. Since the trial judge did not instruct the jury to differentiate between general and punitive damages, it may be that the verdict was wholly an award of one or the other. But it is impossible to know, in view of the general verdict returned. Because of this uncertainty, the judgment must be reversed and the case remanded. . . .

NOTES & QUESTIONS

1. Justices Black, Douglas, and Goldberg would have gone further, eliminating all defamation liability for public officials. In other words, public officials could not sue for defamation even if the defamatory statement were made with actual malice. As Justice Goldberg explained, the right to criticize public officials is unconditional and "should not depend upon a probing by the jury of the motivation of the citizen or press." Does Justice Brennan's logic lead to this result? Why not just bar all libel actions by public officials? Consider Justice Holmes's dissent in *Abrams v. United States*, 250 U.S. 616, 630 (1919):

   But when men have realized that time has upset many fighting faiths, they may come to believe even more than they believe the very foundations of their own conduct that the ultimate good desired is better reached by free trade in ideas — that the best test of truth is the power of the thought to get itself accepted in the competition of the market, and that truth is the only ground upon which their wishes safely can be carried out. That at any rate is the theory of our Constitution.

If Holmes is right, and the marketplace of ideas will result in the truth eventually winning out, then is defamation law even necessary?[44]

2. *New York Times* involved a matter of public concern. Consider a defamatory statement about a public official's private life. Indeed, public officials stand a lot to lose from defamation, as their careers depend heavily upon reputation. In this context, why should the law give a public official less protection against defamation?

3. *Postscript.* Subsequently, the Court extended the approach in *New York Times* to persons who were not public officials but who were "'public figures' and involved in issues in which the public has a justified and important interest." *Curtis Publishing Co. v. Butts*, 388 U.S. 130 (1967).

In *Gertz v. Robert Welch, Inc.*, 418 U.S. 323 (1974), which is excerpted below, the Court turned to the issue of whether the *New York Times* approach should be extended to private figures.

GERTZ v. ROBERT WELCH, INC.

418 U.S. 323 (1974)

[In 1968, Nuccio, a Chicago policeman shot and killed Nelson, a youth. Nuccio was prosecuted and convicted for murder in the second degree. The Nelson family retained petitioner Elmer Gertz, a reputable attorney, to represent them in civil litigation against Nuccio. Robert Welch, Inc. published *American Opinion*, a monthly magazine representing the views of the John Birch Society. The magazine had been warning of a national conspiracy to discredit local police forces and create a national police force as a step toward establishing a Communist dictatorship. In 1969, the magazine published an article about the murder trial of Officer Nuccio, alleging that he was framed as part of the Communist campaign against the police. Among other things, the article portrayed Gertz as the mastermind of the frame-up. It stated that Gertz was a "Leninist" and a "Communist-fronter," that Gertz belonged to Marxist and Socialist organizations, and that Gertz had a criminal record. All of these statements were false. The managing editor made no effort to verify the charges; in fact, he wrote an editorial introduction stating that the author had conducted extensive research. Gertz sued for libel and won a jury verdict of $50,000. The district court, however, decided that the *New York Times* standard should apply and entered judgment for Robert Welch, Inc.]

POWELL, J. . . . The principal issue in this case is whether a newspaper or broadcaster that publishes defamatory falsehoods about an individual who is neither a public official nor a public figure may claim a constitutional privilege against liability for the injury inflicted by those statements. . . .

The legitimate state interest underlying the law of libel is the compensation of individuals for the harm inflicted on them by defamatory falsehood. We would not lightly require the State to abandon this purpose, for, as Mr. Jus-

---

[44] For more background about *New York Times v. Sullivan*, see Anthony Lewis, *Make No Law: The Sullivan Case and the First Amendment* (1991).

tice Stewart has reminded us, the individual's right to the protection of his own good name

> reflects no more than our basic concept of the essential dignity and worth of every human being — a concept at the root of any decent system of ordered liberty. The protection of private personality, like the protection of life itself, is left primarily to the individual States under the Ninth and Tenth Amendments. But this does not mean that the right is entitled to any less recognition by this Court as a basic of our constitutional system. *Rosenblatt v. Baer*, 383 U.S. 75, 92 (1966) (concurring opinion). . . .

. . . [W]e have no difficulty in distinguishing among defamation plaintiffs. The first remedy of any victim of defamation is self-help — using available opportunities to contradict the lie or correct the error and thereby to minimize its adverse impact on reputation. Public officials and public figures usually enjoy significantly greater access to the channels of effective communication and hence have a more realistic opportunity to counteract false statements then private individuals normally enjoy. Private individuals are therefore more vulnerable to injury, and the state interest in protecting them is correspondingly greater.

More important than the likelihood that private individuals will lack effective opportunities for rebuttal, there is a compelling normative consideration underlying the distinction between public and private defamation plaintiffs. An individual who decides to seek governmental office must accept certain necessary consequences of that involvement in public affairs. He runs the risk of closer public scrutiny than might otherwise be the case. And society's interest in the officers of government is not strictly limited to the formal discharge of official duties. As the Court pointed out in *Garrison v. Louisiana*, the public's interest extends to "anything which might touch on an official's fitness for office. . . . Few personal attributes are more germane to fitness for office than dishonesty, malfeasance, or improper motivation, even though these characteristics may also affect the official's private character."

Those classed as public figures stand in a similar position. Hypothetically, it may be possible for someone to become a public figure through no purposeful action of his own, but the instances of truly involuntary public figures must be exceedingly rare. For the most part those who attain this status have assumed roles of especial prominence in the affairs of society. Some occupy positions of such persuasive power and influence that they are deemed public figures for all purposes. More commonly, those classed as public figures have thrust themselves to the forefront of particular public controversies in order to influence the resolution of the issues involved. In either event, they invite attention and comment.

Even if the foregoing generalities do not obtain in every instance, the communications media are entitled to act on the assumption that public officials and public figures have voluntarily exposed themselves to increased risk of injury from defamatory falsehood concerning them. No such assumption is justified with respect to a private individual. He has not accepted public office or assumed an "influential role in ordering society." He has relinquished no part of his interest in the protection of his own good name, and consequently he has a more compelling call on the courts for redress of injury inflicted by defamatory falsehood. Thus, private individuals are not only more vulnerable to injury than public officials and public figures; they are also more deserving of recovery.

For these reasons we conclude that the States should retain substantial latitude in their efforts to enforce a legal remedy for defamatory falsehood injurious to the reputation of a private individual. The extension of the *New York Times* test . . . would abridge this legitimate state interest to a degree that we find unacceptable. And it would occasion the additional difficulty of forcing state and federal judges to decide on an ad hoc basis which publications address issues of "general or public interest" and which do not — to determine, in the words of Mr. Justice Marshall, "what information is relevant to self-government." We doubt the wisdom of committing this task to the conscience of judges. . . .

We hold that, so long as they do not impose liability without fault, the States may define for themselves the appropriate standard of liability for a publisher or broadcaster of defamatory falsehood injurious to a private individual. . . .

. . . Under the traditional rules pertaining to actions for libel, the existence of injury is presumed from the fact of publication. Juries may award substantial sums as compensation for supposed damage to reputation without any proof that such harm actually occurred. The largely uncontrolled discretion of juries to award damages where there is no loss unnecessarily compounds the potential of any system of liability for defamatory falsehood to inhibit the vigorous exercise of First Amendment freedoms. Additionally, the doctrine of presumed damages invites juries to punish unpopular opinion rather than to compensate individuals for injury sustained by the publication of a false fact. More to the point, the States have no substantial interest in securing for plaintiffs such as this petitioner gratuitous awards of money damages far in excess of any actual injury. . . .

. . . It is necessary to restrict defamation plaintiffs who do not prove knowledge of falsity or reckless disregard for the truth to compensation for actual injury. . . . Suffice it to say that actual injury is not limited to out-of-pocket loss. Indeed, the more customary types of actual harm inflicted by defamatory falsehood include impairment of reputation and standing in the community, personal humiliation, and mental anguish and suffering. . . .

We also find no justification for allowing awards of punitive damages against publishers and broadcasters held liable under state-defined standards of liability for defamation. In most jurisdictions jury discretion over the amounts awarded is limited only by the gentle rule that they not be excessive. Consequently, juries assess punitive damages in wholly unpredictable amounts bearing no necessary relation to the actual harm caused. And they remain free to use their discretion selectively to punish expressions of unpopular views. Like the doctrine of presumed damages, jury discretion to award punitive damages unnecessarily exacerbates the danger of media self-censorship, but, unlike the former rule, punitive damages are wholly irrelevant to the state interest that justifies a negligence standard for private defamation actions. They are not compensation for injury. Instead, they are private fines levied by civil juries to punish reprehensible conduct and to deter its future occurrence. In short, the private defamation plaintiff who establishes liability under a less demanding standard than that stated by *New York Times* may recover only such damages as are sufficient to compensate him for actual injury.

Notwithstanding our refusal to extend the New York Times privilege to defamation of private individuals, respondent contends that we should affirm the judgment below on the ground that petitioner is either a public official or a public figure. . . .

. . . In some instances an individual may achieve such pervasive fame or notoriety that he becomes a public figure for all purposes and in all contexts. More commonly, an individual voluntarily injects himself or is drawn into a particular public controversy and thereby becomes a public figure for a limited range of issues. In either case such persons assume special prominence in the resolution of public questions.

Petitioner has long been active in community and professional affairs. He has served as an officer of local civic groups and of various professional organizations, and he has published several books and articles on legal subjects. Although petitioner was consequently well known in some circles, he had achieved no general fame or notoriety in the community. None of the prospective jurors called at the trial had ever heard of petitioner prior to this litigation, and respondent offered no proof that this response was atypical of the local population. We would not lightly assume that a citizen's participation in community and professional affairs rendered him a public figure for all purposes. Absent clear evidence of general fame or notoriety in the community, and pervasive involvement in the affairs of society, an individual should not be deemed a public personality for all aspects of his life. It is preferable to reduce the public-figure question to a more meaningful context by looking to the nature and extent of an individual's participation in the particular controversy giving rise to the defamation.

In this context it is plain that petitioner was not a public figure. He played a minimal role at the coroner's inquest, and his participation related solely to his representation of a private client. He took no part in the criminal prosecution of Officer Nuccio. Moreover, he never discussed either the criminal or civil litigation with the press and was never quoted as having done so. He plainly did not thrust himself into the vortex of this public issue, nor did he engage the public's attention in an attempt to influence its outcome. We are persuaded that the trial court did not err in refusing to characterize petitioner as a public figure for the purpose of this litigation. . . .

WHITE, J. dissenting. . . . I assume these sweeping changes [the curtailment of punitive damages] will be popular with the press, but this is not the road to salvation for a court of law. As I see it, there are wholly insufficient grounds for scuttling the libel laws of the States in such wholesale fashion, to say nothing of deprecating the reputation interest of ordinary citizens and rendering them powerless to protect themselves. . . .

. . . The press today is vigorous and robust. To me, it is quite incredible to suggest that threats of libel suits from private citizens are causing the press to refrain from publishing the truth. I know of no hard facts to support that proposition, and the Court furnishes none.

The communications industry has increasingly become concentrated in a few powerful hands operating very lucrative businesses reaching across the Nation and into almost every home. Neither the industry as a whole nor its individual components are easily intimidated, and we are fortunate that they are not. Requiring them to pay for the occasional damage they do to private reputation will play no substantial part in their future performance or their existence. . . .

NOTES & QUESTIONS

1. Justice Brennan dissented, stating that the *New York Times* standard should govern in this case as well. Do you agree?
2. Subsequent to *Gertz*, a plurality of the Court examined whether the *Gertz* rule would apply when, in contrast to the situation in *Gertz*, the alleged defamatory statements did not involve a matter of public concern. In *Dun & Bradstreet, Inc. v. Greenmoss Builders, Inc.*, 472 U.S. 749 (1985), Dun & Bradstreet, a credit reporting agency, provided an erroneous report about the financial condition of Greenmoss Builders. Upon learning of the defamatory report, the president of Greenmoss called Dun & Bradstreet and asked for a correction and a list of all those to whom Dun & Bradstreet had sent the report. Dun & Bradstreet corrected the report but did not inform Greenmoss of the list of recipients of the report. Greenmoss sued for defamation, winning $50,000 in compensatory or presumed damages and $300,000 in punitive damages. The Court held that this did not involve a matter of public concern and that therefore, the *Gertz* rule should not apply:

   > The First Amendment interest . . . is less important than the one weighed in *Gertz*. We have long recognized that not all speech is of equal First Amendment importance. It is speech on "'matters of public concern'" that is "at the heart of the First Amendment's protection." . . .
   >
   > In contrast, speech on matters of purely private concern is of less First Amendment concern. As a number of state courts, including the court below, have recognized, the role of the Constitution in regulating state libel law is far more limited when the concerns that activated *New York Times* and *Gertz* are absent. . . .
   >
   > While such speech is not totally unprotected by the First Amendment, its protections are less stringent. In *Gertz*, we found that the state interest in awarding presumed and punitive damages was not "substantial" in view of their effect on speech at the core of First Amendment concern. . . . In light of the reduced constitutional value of speech involving no matters of public concern, we hold that the state interest adequately supports awards of presumed and punitive damages — even absent a showing of "actual malice." . . . .

3. ***Public vs. Private Figures.*** What distinguishes a public from a private figure? In *Time, Inc. v. Firestone*, 424 U.S. 448 (1976), Mary Alice Firestone and her husband had a messy divorce. The court issued a judgment granting the divorce, stating that according to the testimony of the husband, the wife's

"extramarital escapades . . . were bizarre and of an amatory nature which would have made Dr. Freud's hair curl. Other testimony . . . would indicate that [the husband] was guilty of bounding from one bedpartner to another with the erotic zest of a satyr. The court is inclined to discount much of this testimony as unreliable." *Time* magazine published the following article in its "Milestones" section the following week:

> DIVORCED. By Russell A. Firestone Jr., 41, heir to the tire fortune: Mary Alice Sullivan Firestone, 32, his third wife; a onetime Palm Beach schoolteacher; on grounds of extreme cruelty and adultery; after six years of marriage, one son; in West Palm Beach, Fla. The 17-month intermittent trial produced enough testimony of extramarital adventures on both sides, said the judge, "to make Dr. Freud's hair curl."

Mary Firestone sued for libel. When the case ended up in the U.S. Supreme Court, the issue was whether Firestone was a public or private figure. According to the Court:

> Petitioner contends that because the Firestone divorce was characterized by the Florida Supreme Court as a "cause celebre," it must have been a public controversy and respondent must be considered a public figure. But in so doing petitioner seeks to equate "public controversy" with all controversies of interest to the public. . . .
>
> Dissolution of a marriage through judicial proceedings is not the sort of "public controversy" referred to in *Gertz*, even though the marital difficulties of extremely wealthy individuals may be of interest to some portion of the reading public. Nor did respondent freely choose to publicize issues as to the propriety of her married life. She was compelled to go to court by the State in order to obtain legal release from the bonds of matrimony. We have said that in such an instance "(r)esort to the judicial process . . . is no more voluntary in a realistic sense than that of the defendant called upon to defend his interests in court." . . . She assumed no "special prominence in the resolution of public questions." *Gertz*, 418 U.S., at 351. We hold respondent was not a "public figure" for the purpose of determining the constitutional protection afforded petitioner's report of the factual and legal basis for her divorce.

In *Wolston v. Readers Digest Assn., Inc.*, 443 U.S. 157 (1979), the plaintiff was summoned to appear before a grand jury in connection with an investigation into his aunt and uncle's spying for the Soviet Union in 1958. Due to mental depression, the plaintiff failed to appear before the grand jury and was held in contempt. In 1984, a book about Soviet agents stated that the plaintiff had been indicted for being such an agent. The district court and court of appeals held that the plaintiff was a limited purpose public figure (regarding Soviet espionage)—those who, under the language of *Gertz*, "thrust themselves to the forefront of particular public controversies in order to influence the resolution of the issues involved." The Supreme Court disagreed:

> . . . [T]he undisputed facts do not justify the conclusion of the District Court and Court of Appeals that petitioner "voluntarily thrust" or "injected" himself into the forefront of the public controversy surrounding the investiga-

tion of Soviet espionage in the United States. It would be more accurate to say that petitioner was dragged unwillingly into the controversy. The Government pursued him in its investigation. Petitioner did fail to respond to a grand jury subpoena, and this failure, as well as his subsequent citation for contempt, did attract media attention. But the mere fact that petitioner voluntarily chose not to appear before the grand jury, knowing that his action might be attended by publicity, is not decisive on the question of public-figure status. . . . It is clear that petitioner played only a minor role in whatever public controversy there may have been concerning the investigation of Soviet espionage. We decline to hold that his mere citation for contempt rendered him a public figure for purposes of comment on the investigation of Soviet espionage.

Petitioner's failure to appear before the grand jury and citation for contempt no doubt were "newsworthy," but the simple fact that these events attracted media attention also is not conclusive of the public-figure issue. A private individual is not automatically transformed into a public figure just by becoming involved in or associated with a matter that attracts public attention. . . . A libel defendant must show more than mere newsworthiness to justify application of the demanding burden of *New York Times*. . . .

If being involved in newsworthy events is not the appropriate test for whether a person is a public figure, then what are the dispositive factors according to the Court?

2. FALSE LIGHT

(a) Introduction

RESTATEMENT (SECOND) OF TORTS § 652E:
PUBLICITY PLACING PERSON IN FALSE LIGHT

One who gives publicity to a matter concerning another that places the other before the public in a false light is subject to liability to the other for invasion of his privacy, if

(a) the false light in which the other was placed would be highly offensive to a reasonable person, and

(b) the actor had knowledge of or acted in reckless disregard as to the falsity of the publicized matter and the false light in which the other would be placed.

NOTES & QUESTIONS

1. *False Light vs. Defamation.* False light is similar in many respects to defamation. Both torts protect against material false statements. However, defamation requires some form of reputational injury (although, once shown, one can collect for emotional distress). False light, on the other hand, can compensate exclusively for emotional distress. According to the Restatement: "It is enough that he is given unreasonable and highly objectionable publicity that attributes to him characteristics, conduct or beliefs that are

false, and so is placed before the public in a false position. When this is the case and the matter attributed to the plaintiff is not defamatory, the rule here stated affords a different remedy, not available in an action for defamation." Comment (b). Since false light does not require reputational harm, a plaintiff can recover for false light that even improves her reputation.[45] While defamation concerns one's status in the community, false light concerns one's peace of mind. As Bryan Lasswell explains, the "false light tort, to the extent distinct from the tort of defamation . . . rests on an awareness that people who are made to seem pathetic or ridiculous may be shunned, and not just people who are thought to be dishonest or incompetent or immoral."[46]

Another difference between false light and defamation is that false light requires a wider communication of the information. False light requires "publicity," which must be made to the public at large. Defamation requires "publication," which means that the communication merely requires communication to another person.

2. Damages for False Light and Defamation. In *Braun v. Flynt*, 726 F.2d 245 (5th Cir. 1984), Jeannie Braun worked at an amusement park and performed a routine with "Ralph the Diving Pig." The pig dove into the pool and was fed by Braun from a milk bottle. One of Larry Flynt's publications, *Chic*, a pornographic magazine, obtained a photograph of Braun's act. The picture appeared in a section of the magazine called "Chic Thrills" implying that something kinky was going on. When Braun saw the photograph, she was mortified. She could not return to work and suffered from depression. She sued Flynt for defamation and false light. A jury awarded her actual and punitive damages for both causes of action. Flynt appealed, arguing among other things that liability was barred by the First Amendment. The court, applying the *Gertz* rule, concluded that Braun was not a public figure and that the First Amendment did not bar her recovery. However, the court concluded that she could not recover damages for both false light and defamation. Accordingly, the case was remanded for a new trial on damages.

3. Critics of the False Light Tort. Consider Diane Zimmerman:

> Most injuries from untruths will, and should, be handled as defamation actions; of those that cannot be, many will either be too trivial to remedy or will not be actionable because the "falsity" complained of will be constitutionally-protected opinion or ideas. . . . Its splendid pedigree notwithstanding, false light has proved in practice to illuminate nothing. From the viewpoint of coherent first amendment theory, it has served instead to deepen the darkness.[47]

Do you agree? A number of courts do. Recall *Lake v. Wal-Mart* from section A of this chapter. There, the court recognized three of the four Warren

---

[45] *See, e.g.,* Nathan E. Ray, *Let There Be False Light: Resisting the Growing Trend Against an Important Tort,* 84 Minn. L. Rev. 713, 735 (2000).

[46] Bryan R. Lasswell, *In Defense of False Light: Why False Light Must Remain a Viable Cause of Action,* 34 S. Tex. L. Rev. 149, 176 (1993).

[47] Diane Leehneer Zimmerman, *False Light Invasion of Privacy: The Light That Failed,* 64 N.Y.U. L. Rev. 364, 452 (1989). For a defense of the false light tort, see Ray, *Let There Be False Light, supra;* Lasswell, *In Defense of False Light, supra;* Gary T. Schwartz, *Explaining and Justifying a Limited Tort of False Light Invasion of Privacy,* 41 Case W. Res. L. Rev. 885 (1991).

and Brandeis privacy torts, declining to recognize false light: "We are concerned that claims under false light are similar to claims of defamation, and to the extent that false light is more expansive than defamation, tension between this tort and the First Amendment is increased." *See also Renwick v. News and Observer Publishing Co.*, 312 S.E.2d 405 (N.C. 1984) (declining to recognize false light tort). Does the false light tort serve a viable purpose?

4. ***Forms of False Light.*** An illustration of the type of misleading statement that can give rise to a false light action is when a mostly true story is somewhat embellished. *See Varnish v. Best Medium Publishing Co.*, 405 F.2d 608 (2d Cir. 1968) (viable false light action for false facts about the relationship between husband and wife who killed herself and their three children). Another example of a false light claim is when one's photograph is used out of context. *See, e.g., Thompson v. Close-up, Inc.*, 98 N.Y.S.2d 300 (1950) (article on drug dealing using the plaintiff's photo); *Holmes v. Curtis Publishing Co.*, 303 F. Supp. 522 (D.S.C. 1969) (use of plaintiff's photo with caption that plaintiff was a high-stakes gambler); *Morrell v. Forbes, Inc.*, 603 F. Supp. 1305 (D. Mass. 1985) (photo used in connection with article about organized crime). In *Wood v. Hustler Magazine*, 736 F.2d 1084 (5th Cir. 1984), a photograph of LaJuan Wood was stolen by another person, who sent it into *Hustler*, a pornographic magazine, along with a forged consent form. *Hustler* sent a mailgram to the address given on the forged consent form asking the sender to call *Hustler*. The sender did, and again lied that there was consent. *Hustler* published LaJuan's photo in its magazine stating: "LaJuan Wood is a 22-year old housewife and mother from Bryan, Texas, whose hobby is collecting arrowheads. Her fantasy is 'to be screwed by two bikers.'" LaJuan sued *Hustler*, and the court held that *Hustler* could be liable for false light because of the "publication of the false and highly offensive fantasy." The court reasoned that the magazine was negligent in making sure that the consent form was valid.

5. ***Obvious Fictions.*** Suppose a story is deliberately designed to be fictional, and is so preposterous that a reasonable person could not possibly believe it to be true. Would there be a viable claim for false light? The answer is no, although the story must be clear that it is pure fiction. In *People's Bank and Trust Co. v. Globe International Publishing, Inc.*, 978 F.2d 1065 (8th Cir. 1992), a tabloid ran a story about a 97-year-old woman who became pregnant. The story used the name of a real person, who sued. The tabloid contended that no reader could reasonably believe that the story was true. The court rejected the contention because the publisher of the tabloid "holds out the publication as factual and true" and it "mingles factual, fictional, and hybrid stories without overtly identifying one from the other."

(b) First Amendment Limitations

TIME, INC. V. HILL

385 U.S. 374 (1967)

[In 1952, the Hill family was held prisoner in their home for 19 hours by three escaped convicts. The family escaped unharmed and were treated courteously by the convicts. The convicts were later killed by police during their apprehension. The story made the front page news. The Hill family tried hard to remain out of the spotlight. Nevertheless, the Hill family's experience was written about in a novel by Joseph Hayes called *The Desperate Hours*. In contrast to the actual events, the book depicted the convicts beating the father and son and making a verbal sexual insult to the daughter. A Broadway play and a movie were made based on the book. In 1955, *Life* magazine published an article entitled: *True Crime Inspires Tense Play*. The article stated that "Americans all over the country read about the desperate ordeal of the James Hill family" and "read about it in Joseph Hayes's novel, *The Desperate Hours*, inspired by the family's experience." The article then stated: "Now they can see the story re-enacted in Hayes's Broadway play based on the book." Pictures accompanying the article displayed scenes from the play depicting the son being beaten and the daughter biting the hand of a convict. The Hills sued under §§ 50-51 of the New York Civil Rights Law contending that the *Life* article gave the false impression that the play accurately depicted the Hills's experience. A jury awarded the Hills $50,000 compensatory and $25,000 punitive damages.]

BRENNAN, J. . . . The question in this case is whether appellant, publisher of Life Magazine, was denied constitutional protections of speech and press by the application by the New York courts of §§ 50–51 of the New York Civil Rights Law to award appellee damages on allegations that Life falsely reported that a new play portrayed an experience suffered by appellee and his family.

. . . In *New York Times Co. v. Sullivan*, we held that the Constitution delimits a State's power to award damages for libel in actions brought by public officials against critics of their official conduct. Factual error, content defamatory of official reputation, or both, are insufficient for an award of damages for false statements unless actual malice — knowledge that the statements are false or in reckless disregard of the truth — is alleged and proved. . . .

. . . We hold that the constitutional protections for speech and press preclude the application of the New York statute to redress false reports of matters of public interest in the absence of proof that the defendant published the report with knowledge of its falsity or in reckless disregard of the truth.

The guarantees for speech and press are not the preserve of political expression or comment upon public affairs, essential as those are to healthy government. One need only pick up any newspaper or magazine to comprehend the vast range of published matter which exposes persons to public view, both private citizens and public officials. Exposure of the self to others in varying degrees is a concomitant of life in a civilized community. The risk of this exposure is an essential incident of life in a society which places a primary value on freedom of speech and of press. "Freedom of discussion, if it would fulfill its historic function in this nation, must embrace all issues about which information is needed or appropriate to enable the members of society to cope with the exigencies of their period." . . . . We have no doubt that the subject of the Life article, the opening of a new play linked to an actual incident, is a matter of public interest. "The line between the informing and the entertaining is too elusive for the protection of . . . (freedom of the press)." Erroneous statement is no less inevitable in such a case than in the case of comment upon public affairs, and in both, if innocent or merely negligent, ". . . it must be protected if the freedoms of expression are to have the 'breathing space' that they 'need . . . to survive' . . . ." *New York Times Co. v. Sullivan*. . . . We create a grave risk of serious impairment of the indispensable service of a free press in a free society if we saddle the press with the impossible burden of verifying to a certainty the facts associated in news articles with a person's name, picture or portrait, particularly as related to nondefamatory matter. Even negligence would be a most elusive standard, especially when the content of the speech itself affords no warning of prospective harm to another through falsity. A negligence test would place on the press the intolerable burden of guessing how a jury might assess the reasonableness of steps taken by it to verify the accuracy of every reference to a name, picture or portrait.

In this context, sanctions against either innocent or negligent misstatement would present a grave hazard of discouraging the press from exercising the constitutional guarantees. Those guarantees are not for the benefit of the press so much as for the benefit of all of us. A broadly defined freedom of the press assures the maintenance of our political system and an open society. Fear of large verdicts in damage suits for innocent or merely negligent misstatement, even fear of the expense involved in their defense, must inevitably cause publishers to "steer . . . wider of the unlawful zone," *New York Times Co. v. Sullivan*, and thus "create the danger that the legitimate utterance will be penalized."

But the constitutional guarantees can tolerate sanctions against calculated falsehood without significant impairment of their essential function. We held in *New York Times* that calculated falsehood enjoyed no immunity in the case of alleged defamation of a public official concerning his official conduct. Similarly, calculated falsehood should enjoy no immunity in the situation here presented us. . . .

. . . Turning to the facts of the present case, the proofs reasonably would support either a jury finding of innocent or merely negligent misstatement by Life, or a finding that Life portrayed the play as a reenactment of the Hill family's experience reckless of the truth or with actual knowledge that the portrayal was false. . . . [The jury instructions were thus defective because they did not instruct the jury that liability could only be found against *Life* if *Life* acted in reckless disregard for the truth or with actual knowledge that the play was false.]

The judgment of the Court of Appeals is set aside and the case is remanded for further proceedings not inconsistent with this opinion. . . .

NOTES & QUESTIONS

1. *Time, Inc. v. Hill* was decided after *New York Times v. Sullivan* but before *Gertz*. Do false light actions involving private figures also have to prove actual malice under *New York Times*? Although the Court never explicitly applied the *Gertz* rule to a false light case, courts are split in cases involving private figures as to whether *Gertz* applies to false light or whether all false light claims must satisfy the more stringent *New York Times* standard. *See, e.g., Braun v. Flynt*, 726 F.2d 245 (5th Cir. 1984) (applying *Gertz*); *Dietz v. Wometco West Michigan TV*, 407 N.W.2d 649 (Mich. App. 1987) (applying

Gertz); *Dodrill v. Arkansas Democrat*, 590 S.W.2d 840 (Ark. 1979) (applying *New York Times*); *Schifano v. Greene County Greyhound Park, Inc.*, 624 So. 2d 178 (Ala. 1993) (applying *New York Times*). Consider Restatement (Second) of Torts §652E comment d:

> If *Time v. Hill* is modified along the lines of *Gertz v. Robert Welch*, then the reckless-disregard rule would apparently apply if the plaintiff is a public official or public figure and the negligence rule will apply to other plaintiffs.

3. INFLICTION OF EMOTIONAL DISTRESS

Another tort remedy for the dissemination of false or misleading information is the tort of infliction of emotional distress. This tort may also serve as a remedy to the disclosure of true information. As defined by the Restatement (Second) of Torts § 46, the tort requires:

> One who by extreme and outrageous conduct intentionally or recklessly causes severe emotional distress to another is subject to liability for such emotional distress, and if bodily harm to the other results from it, for such bodily harm.

The tort has some significant limitations as a remedy for privacy infringements. First, it requires "extreme and outrageous conduct," which is conduct significantly outside the bounds of propriety. This is quite a high bar for a plaintiff to leap over. Second, it requires "severe emotional distress," and many privacy violations may not be viewed by courts as causing such a high level of psychological turmoil. For example, in *DeGregario v. CBS*, 473 N.Y.S.2d 922 (N.Y. Sup. Ct. 1984), a news segment called "Couples in New York" included video of two construction workers, a male and a female, holding hands. Each was married or engaged to another person. After the video was shot, the workers asked the television crew not to include them in the segment, but they were included anyway. The court rejected their infliction of emotional distress claim because "broadcasting a film depicting unnamed couples engaging in romantic conduct on a public street . . . in a news report about romance cannot be said to be unusual conduct transcending the norms tolerated by a decent society."

In a similar fashion to the privacy torts, the tort of infliction of emotional distress is subject to First Amendment restrictions. Consider the following case:

HUSTLER MAGAZINE V. FALWELL

485 U.S. 46 (1988)

[A 1983 issue of *Hustler* magazine featured a parody using nationally known minister Jerry Falwell's name and photo. The parody, entitled "Jerry Falwell Talks About His First Time," was patterned after a series of ads for a brand of liquor which interviewed celebrities about their "first times" trying the liquor (but playing on the sexual double meaning). In a similar layout, *Hustler's* parody interview with Falwell had him drunk and engaging in incest with his mother. In small print, the parody contained the disclaimer, "ad parody — not to be taken seriously." Falwell sued for, among other things, intentional infliction of emotional distress. This issue made it up to the U.S. Supreme Court, where the Court confronted the task of defining whether the First Amendment limitations that applied to defamation and false light also be applied to intentional infliction of emotional distress.]

REHNQUIST, C.J. . . . "Freedoms of expression require 'breathing space.'" This breathing space is provided by a constitutional rule that allows public figures to recover for libel or defamation only when they can prove *both* that the statement was false and that the statement was made with the requisite level of culpability.

Respondent argues, however, that a different standard should apply in this case because here the State seeks to prevent not reputational damage, but the severe emotional distress suffered by the person who is the subject of an offensive publication. *Cf. Zacchini v. Scripps-Howard Broadcasting Co.*, 433 U.S. 562 (ruling that the "actual malice" standard does not apply to the tort of appropriation of a right of publicity). In respondent's view, and in the view of the Court of Appeals, so long as the utterance was intended to inflict emotional distress, was outrageous, and did in fact inflict serious emotional distress, it is of no constitutional import whether the statement was a fact or an opinion, or whether it was true or false. It is the intent to cause injury that is the gravamen of the tort, and the State's interest in preventing emotional harm simply outweighs whatever interest a speaker may have in speech of this type.

Generally speaking the law does not regard the intent to inflict emotional distress as one which should receive much solicitude, and it is quite understandable that most if not all jurisdictions have chosen to make it civilly culpable where the conduct in question is sufficiently "outrageous." But in the world of debate about public affairs, many things done with motives that are less than admirable are protected by the First Amendment. . . .

Thus while such a bad motive may be deemed controlling for purposes of tort liability in other areas of the law, we think the First Amendment prohibits such a result in the area of public debate about public figures. . . .

We conclude that public figures and public officials may not recover for the tort of intentional infliction of emotional distress by reason of publications such as the one here at issue without showing in addition that the publication contains a false statement of fact which was made with "actual malice," *i.e.*, with knowledge that the statement was false or with reckless disregard as to whether or not it was true. This is not merely a "blind application" of the *New York Times* standard, see *Time, Inc. v. Hill*, 385 U.S. 374 (1967), it reflects our considered judgment that such a standard is necessary to give adequate "breathing space" to the freedoms protected by the First Amendment.

Here it is clear that respondent Falwell is a "public figure" for purposes of First Amendment law. The jury found against respondent on his libel claim when it decided that the Hustler ad parody could not "reasonably be understood as describing actual facts about [respondent] or actual events in which [he] participated." The Court of Appeals interpreted the jury's finding to be that the ad parody "was not reasonably believable," and in accordance with our custom we accept this finding. Respondent is thus relegated to his claim for damages awarded by the jury for the intentional infliction of emotional distress by "outrageous" conduct. But for reasons heretofore stated this claim cannot, consistently with the First Amendment, form a basis for the award of damages when the conduct in question is the publication of a caricature such as the ad parody involved here. . . .

E. APPROPRIATION OF NAME OR LIKENESS

1. INTRODUCTION

RESTATEMENT (SECOND) OF TORTS § 652C:
APPROPRIATION OF NAME OR LIKENESS

One who appropriates to his own use or benefit the name or likeness of another is subject to liability to the other for invasion of his privacy.

NOTES & QUESTIONS

1. The tort of appropriation protects "the interest of the individual in the exclusive use of his own identity, in so far as it is represented by his name or likeness, and in so far as the use may be of benefit to him or to others." Restatement § 652C, comment (a). To be liable for appropriation, "the defendant must have appropriated to his own use or benefit the reputation, prestige, social or commercial standing, public interest or other values of the plaintiff's name or likeness." *Id.*, comment (c).

Recall from section A that two of the first cases to address the creation of new causes of action in response to the Warren and Brandeis article — *Roberson* and *Pavesich* — both involved appropriation claims.

One of the most widely discussed state appropriation tort formulations is that of New York. New York's statute, passed in response to *Roberson*, which refused to recognize the tort in the common law, provides criminal and civil remedies for appropriation. Pursuant to N.Y. Civil Rights L. § 50:

> A person, firm or corporation that uses for advertising purposes, or for the purposes of trade, the name, portrait or picture of any living person without having first obtained the written consent of such person, or if a minor of his or her parent or guardian, is guilty of a misdemeanor.

N.Y. Civil Rights L. § 51 provides a civil remedy:

> Any person whose name, portrait, picture or voice is used within this state for advertising purposes or for the purposes of trade without the written consent first obtained . . . may maintain an equitable action in the supreme court of this state against the person, firm or corporation so using his name, portrait, picture or voice, to prevent and restrain the use thereof; and may also sue and recover damages for any injuries sustained by reason of such use. . . .

California has a similar statute, which provides: "Any person who knowingly uses another's name, photograph or likeness, in any manner, for purposes of advertising . . . or for purposes of solicitation of purchases of prod-

ucts . . . without . . . prior consent . . . shall be liable for any damages. . . ."
Cal. Civ. Code §3344. In many states, the tort of appropriation is recognized through the common law and is not statutory in nature.

2. ***Appropriation and the "Right of Publicity."*** The original rationale for the
tort of appropriation was privacy-based, as a protection of one's dignity
against the exploitation of her identity. However, another rationale for the
tort has emerged, one that is property-based. Many courts and commentators refer to this alternative rationale as the "right of publicity."[48] The "right
of publicity" was first referred to as such in *Haelan Laboratories v. Topps
Chewing Gum, Inc.*, 202 F.2d 866 (2d Cir. 1953), where Judge Jerome Frank
held that New York recognized a common law tort of "publicity" distinct
from §§50-51's remedy for appropriation:

> We think that, in addition to and independent of that right of privacy (which
> in New York derives from statute), a man has a right in the publicity value of
> his photograph, i.e., the right to grant the exclusive privilege of publishing
> his picture, and that such a grant may validly be made "in gross," i.e., with-
> out an accompanying transfer of a business or of anything else. Whether it
> be labeled a "property" right is immaterial; for here, as often elsewhere, the
> tag "property" simply symbolizes the fact that courts enforce a claim which
> has pecuniary worth.
>
> This right might be called a "right of publicity." For it is common knowl-
> edge that many prominent persons (especially actors and ball-players), far
> from having their feelings bruised through public exposure of their like-
> nesses, would feel sorely deprived if they no longer received money for au-
> thorizing advertisements, popularizing their countenances, displayed in
> newspapers, magazines, busses, trains and subways.

Subsequently, courts held that the publicity tort was subsumed under §51
and was not a common law cause of action. *See Welch v. Group W. Productions, Inc.*, 525 N.Y.S.2d 466, 468 n.1 (N.Y. Sup. Ct. 1987) ("In New York
State the so-called 'right of publicity' is merely an aspect of the right of privacy and is not an independent common-law right.").

How is the "right of publicity" distinct from the privacy interests involved in appropriation? As one court describes the distinction:

> The privacy-based action is designed for individuals who have not placed
> themselves in the public eye. It shields such people from the embarrassment
> of having their faces plastered on billboards and cereal boxes without their
> permission. The interests protected are dignity and peace of mind, and dam-
> ages are measured in terms of emotional distress. By contrast, a right of pub-
> licity action is designed for individuals who have placed themselves in the
> public eye. It secures for them the exclusive right to exploit the commercial
> value that attaches to their identities by virtue of their celebrity. The right to

---

[48]J. Thomas McCarthy, *The Rights of Publicity and Privacy* (2000); Melville B. Nimmer, *The
Right of Publicity*, 19 Law & Contemp. Probs. 203 (1954); Sheldon Halpern, *The Right of Publicity:
Maturation of an Independent Right Protecting the Associative Value of Personality*, 46 Hastings L.J. 853
(1995); Oliver R. Goodenough, *Go Fish: Evaluating the Restatement's Formulation of the Law of Publicity*, 47 S.C. L. Rev. 709 (1996).

publicity protects that value as property, and its infringement is a commercial, rather than a personal tort. Damages stem not from embarrassment but from the unauthorized use of the plaintiffs' property. *Jim Henson Productions, Inc. v. John T. Brady & Associates, Inc.*, 687 F. Supp. 185, 188-89 (S.D.N.Y. 1994)

Thomas McCarthy articulates the distinction most succinctly: "Simplistically put, while the appropriation branch of the right of privacy is invaded by an injury to the psyche, the right of publicity is infringed by an injury to the pocket book." [49]

There has been considerable confusion as to whether the "right of publicity" is a distinct tort from appropriation, an alternative theory upon which appropriation liability may rest, or the central interest protected by the appropriation tort. Prosser, in his 1960 article describing the torts spawned by Warren and Brandeis's article (*see* section A), did not recognize a distinct tort of publicity; it was merely a part of the appropriation tort. Likewise, the Restatement (Second) of Torts did not recognize a distinct tort of publicity. However, according to the Restatement, it appears that the central interest protected by appropriation is property rather than privacy: "Although the protection of [a person's] personal feelings against mental distress is an important factor leading to a recognition of the [appropriation tort], the right created by it is in the nature of a property right. . . ." Restatement (Second) of Torts § 652C, comment (a). A number of jurisdictions follow this approach. *See Ainsworth v. Century Supply Co.*, 693 N.E.2d 510 (Ill. App. 1998); *Candlebat v. Flanagan*, 487 So. 2d 207 (Miss. 1986).

The Restatement (Third) of the Law of Unfair Competition § 46 provides for a distinct tort of "publicity":

> *Appropriation of the Commercial Value of a Person's Identity: The Right of Publicity.* One who appropriates the commercial value of a person's identity by using without consent the person's name, likeness, or other indicia of identity for purposes of trade is subject to liability for [monetary and injunctive] relief.

The commentary to the Restatement § 46 contrasts the "publicity" right in § 46 with the "appropriation tort" in the Restatement of Torts: "The 'appropriation' tort as described by Prosser and the Restatement, Second, of Torts, subsumes harm to both personal and commercial interests caused by an unauthorized exploitation of the plaintiff's identity." Restatement (Third) of the Law of Unfair Competition § 46 comment (b). A number of jurisdictions recognize a distinct tort of "publicity."

This chapter will treat "publicity" as subsumed under the tort of appropriation. Is privacy or property the central interest of appropriation? Or does the tort adequately redress both interests? As you read the subsequent cases, think about whether the appropriation tort protects a privacy interest or a property interest or both.

---

[49] J. Thomas McCarthy, *The Rights of Publicity and Privacy* § 5:61, at pp. 5-110 (2000). For a discussion of how the right to publicity is impacting the development of the tort of appropriation, see Jonathan Kahn, *Bringing Dignity Back to Light: Publicity Rights and the Eclipse of the Tort of Appropriation of Identity*, 17 Cardozo Arts & Ent. L.J. 213, 250 (1999).

2. NAME OR LIKENESS

Carson v. Here's Johnny Portable Toilets, Inc.

698 F.2d 831 (6th Cir. 1983)

Brown, J. . . . Appellant, John W. Carson (Carson), is the host and star of "The Tonight Show," a well-known television program broadcast five nights a week by the National Broadcasting Company. . . . From the time he began hosting "The Tonight Show" in 1962, he has been introduced [by Ed McMahon] on the show each night with the phrase "Here's Johnny." . . . The phrase "Here's Johnny" is generally associated with Carson by a substantial segment of the television viewing public. In 1967, Carson first authorized use of this phrase by an outside business venture, permitting it to be used by a chain of restaurants called "Here's Johnny Restaurants." . . .

. . . The phrase "Here's Johnny" has never been registered by appellants as a trademark or service mark.

Appellee, Here's Johnny Portable Toilets, Inc., is a Michigan corporation engaged in the business of renting and selling "Here's Johnny" portable toilets. Appellee's founder was aware at the time he formed the corporation that "Here's Johnny" was the introductory slogan for Carson on "The Tonight Show." He indicated that he coupled the phrase with a second one, "The World's Foremost Commodian," to make "a good play on a phrase."

[Carson brought an action for, among other things, invasion of privacy and the right to publicity.] . . . .

We do not believe that Carson's claim that his right of privacy has been invaded is supported by the law or the facts. Apparently, the gist of this claim is that Carson is embarrassed by and considers it odious to be associated with the appellee's product. Clearly, the association does not appeal to Carson's sense of humor. But the facts here presented do not, it appears to us, amount to an invasion of any of the interests protected by the right of privacy. . . .

The right of publicity has developed to protect the commercial interest of celebrities in their identities. The theory of the right is that a celebrity's identity can be valuable in the promotion of products, and the celebrity has an interest that may be protected from the unauthorized commercial exploitation of that identity. . . .

The district court dismissed appellants' claim based on the right of publicity because appellee does not use Carson's name or likeness. . . . We believe that, on the contrary, the district court's conception of the right of publicity is too narrow. The right of publicity, as we have stated, is that a celebrity has a protected pecuniary interest in the commercial exploitation of his identity. If the celebrity's identity is commercially exploited, there has been an invasion of his right whether or not his "name or likeness" is used. Carson's identity may be exploited even if his name, John W. Carson, or his picture is not used. . . .

In this case, Earl Braxton, president and owner of Here's Johnny Portable Toilets, Inc., admitted that he knew that the phrase "Here's Johnny" had been used for years to introduce Carson. Moreover, in the opening statement in the district court, appellee's counsel stated:

Now, we've stipulated in this case that the public tends to associate the words "Johnny Carson," the words "Here's Johnny" with plaintiff, John Carson and, Mr. Braxton, in his deposition, admitted that he knew that and probably absent that identification, he would not have chosen it.

That the "Here's Johnny" name was selected by Braxton because of its identification with Carson was the clear inference from Braxton's testimony irrespective of such admission in the opening statement.

We therefore conclude that, applying the correct legal standards, appellants are entitled to judgment. The proof showed without question that appellee had appropriated Carson's identity in connection with its corporate name and its product. . . .

. . . It is not fatal to appellant's claim that appellee did not use his "name." Indeed, there would have been no violation of his right of publicity even if appellee had used his name, such as "J. William Carson Portable Toilet" or the "John William Carson Portable Toilet" or the "J. W. Carson Portable Toilet." The reason is that, though literally using appellant's "name," the appellee would not have appropriated Carson's identity as a celebrity. Here there was an appropriation of Carson's identity without using his "name.". . .

KENNEDY, J. dissenting. . . . The majority's extension of the right of publicity to include phrases or other things which are merely associated with the individual permits a popular entertainer or public figure, by associating himself or herself with a common phrase, to remove those words from the public domain. . . .

. . . [T]he majority is awarding Johnny Carson a windfall, rather than vindicating his economic interests, by protecting the phrase "Here's Johnny" which is merely associated with him. In *Zacchini*, the Supreme Court stated that a mechanism to vindicate an individual's economic rights is indicated where the appropriated thing is "the product of . . . [the individual's] own talents and energy, the end result of much time, effort and expense." There is nothing in the record to suggest that "Here's Johnny" has any nexus to Johnny Carson other than being the introduction to his personal appearances. The phrase is not part of an identity that he created. In its content "Here's Johnny" is a very simple and common introduction. The content of the phrase neither originated with Johnny Carson nor is it confined to the world of entertainment. The phrase is not said by Johnny Carson, but said of him. Its association with him is derived, in large part, by the context in which it is said — generally by Ed McMahon in a drawn out and distinctive voice after the theme music to "The Tonight Show" is played, and immediately prior to Johnny Carson's own entrance. Appellee's use of the content "Here's Johnny," in light of its value as a double entendre, written on its product and corporate name, and therefore outside of the context in which it is associated with Johnny Carson, does little to rob Johnny Carson of something which is unique to him or a product of his own efforts. . . .

Protection under the right of publicity confers a monopoly on the protected individual that is potentially broader, offers fewer protections and potentially competes with federal statutory monopolies. As an essential part of three federal monopoly rights, copyright, trademark and patents, notice to the public is required in the form of filing with the appropriate governmental office and use of an appropriate mark. This apprises members of the public of the nature and extent of what is being removed from the public domain and subject to claims of infringement. The right of publicity provides limited notice to the public of the extent of the monopoly right to be asserted, if one is to be asserted at all. As the right of privacy is expanded beyond protections of name, likeness and actual performances, which provide relatively objective notice to the public of the extent of an individual's rights, to more subjective attributes such as achievements and identifying characteristics, the public's ability to be on notice of a common law monopoly right, if one is even asserted by a given famous individual, is severely diminished. Protecting phrases and other things merely associated with an individual provides virtually no notice to the public at all of what is claimed to be protected. By ensuring the invocation of the adjudicative process whenever the commercial use of a phrase or other associated thing is considered to have been wrongfully appropriated, the public is left to act at their peril. The result is a chilling effect on commercial innovation and opportunity.

Also unlike the federal statutory monopolies, this common law monopoly right offers no protections against the monopoly existing for an indefinite time or even in perpetuity. . . .

NOTES & QUESTIONS

1. ***Privacy or Property?*** In *Carson*, Johnny Carson made two claims. First, he contended that a privacy interest was violated because his identity was being associated with toilets, which he found quite unflattering. The court appears to reject this claim. Carson's other claim is that a property interest was violated by his valuable identity being stolen and used for the commercial purposes of another. What do you think was the real reason Carson brought this suit? To vindicate his privacy interest, his property interest, or both? Suppose Carson were not famous and his name had little value? Would he be likely to succeed under the reasoning of the court?

2. ***What Constitutes "Name or Likeness"?*** The appropriation tort has been extended far beyond a person's actual name and likeness. Courts have held that the use of well-known nicknames can give rise to an appropriation action. In *Hirsch v. S.C. Johnson & Son, Inc.*, 280 N.W.2d 129 (Wis. 1979), the use of the Elroy Hirsch's (a famous football player) nickname "Crazylegs" was a violation of the appropriation tort because "[a]ll that is required is that the name clearly identify the wronged person."

   Courts have also held that certain drawings depicting one's profession but otherwise with no distinctive facial characteristics can still give rise to an appropriation claim. In *Ali v. Playgirl, Inc.*, 447 F. Supp. 723 (S.D.N.Y. 1978), Muhammad Ali, former heavyweight boxing champion, sued *Playgirl* magazine for appropriation when the magazine published a drawing of a nude African-American male sitting on a stool in a corner of a boxing ring with hands taped. The drawing did not mention Ali's name and was entitled "Mystery Man," but accompanying text identified the man in the drawing as "The Greatest." Because "The Greatest" was Ali's nickname, the picture was sufficiently identifiable as Ali to constitute his likeness.

Appropriation has even been extended to identifying characteristics. In *Motschenbacher v. R. J. Reynolds Tobacco Co.*, 498 F.2d 821 (9th Cir. 1974), a famous race car driver alleged that a photograph of his distinctive racing car, which did not include a likeness of himself or use his name, was nevertheless an appropriation of his name or likeness. The court agreed. The photograph did use a "likeness" of the plaintiff because the "distinctive decorations" on his car "were not only peculiar to the plaintiff's cars but they caused some persons to think the car in question was plaintiff's and to infer that the person driving the car was the plaintiff."

Further, appropriation extends to one's likeness represented as an impersonation. *See Guglielmi v. Spelling-Goldberg Productions*, 603 P.2d 454 (Cal. 1979). Recall that in *Zacchini v. Scripps-Howard Broadcasting Co.*, 433 U.S. 562 (1977), the plaintiff brought an appropriation action for his distinctive performance act.

Courts have extended appropriation to fictitious personas created by an individual. *See Groucho Marx Productions, Inc. v. Day & Night Co.*, 523 F. Supp. 485 (S.D.N.Y. 1981); *Price v. Hal Roach Studios, Inc.*, 400 F. Supp. 836 (S.D.N.Y. 1975) (Laurel & Hardy characters).

Courts have also recognized appropriation liability for the imitation of one's voice. In *Midler v. Ford Motor Co.*, 849 F.2d 460 (9th Cir. 1988), the court held that singer Bette Midler had a viable cause of action for appropriation for the use of a singer to imitate her voice in a commercial.

However, appropriation actions have been rejected for the telling of an individual's life story. *See, e.g., Guglielmi v. Spelling-Goldberg Productions*, 603 P.2d 454 (Cal. 1979).

3. ***Property Rights and Creativity.*** Consider the following argument against the propertization of identity by Judge Kozinski dissenting from the denial of a petition for rehearing en banc in *White v. Samsung Electronics America, Inc.*, 989 F.2d 1512 (9th Cir. 1993):

> . . . Saddam Hussein wants to keep advertisers from using his picture in unflattering contexts. Clint Eastwood doesn't want tabloids to write about him. Rudolf Valentino's heirs want to control his film biography. The Girl Scouts don't want their image soiled by association with certain activities. . . . And scads of copyright holders see purple when their creations are made fun of.
>
> Something very dangerous is going on here. . . .
>
> . . . Overprotecting intellectual property is as harmful as underprotecting it. Creativity is impossible without a rich public domain. . . .
>
> . . . Intellectual property rights aren't free. They're imposed at the expense of future creators and of the public at large. Where would we be if Charles Lindbergh had an exclusive right in the concept of a heroic solo aviator? If Arthur Conan Doyle had gotten a copyright in the idea of the detective story, or Albert Einstein had patented the theory of relativity? If every author and celebrity had been given the right to keep people from mocking them or their work? Surely this would have made the world poorer, not richer, culturally as well as economically. . . .

4. ***Property Rights and the Manufacturing of Identity.*** One of the predominant rationales for the right of publicity is that the celebrity, through
her labor, creates her persona. But, with regard to celebrities, does this rationale always hold true? According to Michael Madow, the identity of
a celebrity is "the product of a complex social process in which the 'labor' of the celebrity is but one ingredient, and not always the main one."[50]
In a similar argument, Rosemary Coombe observes: "Star images are authored by studios, the mass media, public relations agencies, fan clubs, gossip columnists, photographers, hairdressers, body-building coaches, athletic trainers, teachers, screenwriters, ghostwriters, directors, lawyers, and
doctors."[51] Why should we afford celebrities property rights in their names
and likenesses when frequently a celebrity's persona is manufactured by
others?

5. ***Are Privacy and Property Rights Mutually Exclusive?*** According to Robert
Post, the right of publicity views one's personality as "commodified," as an
object separate from oneself that can be valued by the market. Warren and
Brandeis's right to privacy, in contrast, "attaches personality firmly to the
actual identity of a living individual." The right of publicity protects personality as detachable from individuals, as a commodity that can be bought
and sold (and can persist after the death of the individual). The right to privacy, in contrast, protects personality as constitutive of the individual. Post
suggests that perhaps we need both property rights and privacy rights to
protect our personalities: "Personality can so effortlessly be legally embodied by either property or privacy rights precisely because it embraces both
these aspects."[52]

3. CONNECTION TO MATTERS OF PUBLIC INTEREST

Unlike the tort of public disclosure, the lack of newsworthiness is not an
element of the appropriation tort. However, appropriation protects against
the "commercial" exploitation of one's name or likeness, not the use of one's
name or likeness for news, art, literature, parody, satire, history, and biography. Otherwise, a newspaper would have to obtain the consent of every person it wrote about or photographed for use in a story. People could prevent
others from writing their biographies or from criticizing them, making a parody of them, or using their names in a work of literature. In New York, for example, one's name or likeness must be used for "advertising purposes or for the
uses of trade." N.Y. Civ. Rights L. §§ 50-51. Although not employing the same
language, other states adopt a similar approach, requiring that the use of one's

---

[50] Michael T. Madow, *Private Ownership of Public Image: Popular Culture and Publicity Rights,* 81
Cal. L. Rev. 127, 195 (1993).

[51] Rosemary J. Coombe, *The Cultural Life of Intellectual Properties: Authorship, Appropriation, and
the Law* 94 (1998).

[52] Robert C. Post, *Rereading Warren and Brandeis: Privacy, Property, and Appropriation,* 41 Case
W. Res. L. Rev. 647 (1991).

name or likeness be for "commercial" purposes. Some courts refer to this as a "First Amendment privilege" to use one's name or likeness in matters of legitimate public concern.

The quintessential instance where the use of one's name or likeness is newsworthy and not "commercial" is in connection with the reporting of the news. In *Time Inc. v. Sand Creek Partners*, 825 F. Supp. 210 (S.D. Ind. 1993), country singer Lyle Lovett and actress Julia Roberts were photographed together at a Lovett concert immediately prior to their marriage. Roberts was in her wedding gown. A photographer for *People* magazine snapped several rolls of film, but they were confiscated by security. The magazine's publisher sued to get the photos back, but Lovett claimed that they were his, since he had a property interest in his name or likeness. The court sided with the magazine:

> Lovett and Roberts are widely known celebrities and in that sense are public figures and, in addition, their appearance on stage before thousands of people on the day of their highly-publicized but theretofore unannounced and private wedding ceremony, with Roberts still wearing her wedding dress, was a newsworthy event of widespread public interest.

Beyond news, uses that are "commercial" or "for advertising or trade purposes" generally do not encompass works of fiction or nonfiction or artistic expression. In *Rosemont Enterprises, Inc. v. Random House, Inc.*, 294 N.Y.S.2d 122 (1968), the defendants published an unauthorized biography of the reclusive Howard Hughes. The court concluded that the biography "falls within those 'reports of newsworthy people or events'" and is therefore not subject to liability for appropriation. A sculpture of supermodel Cheryl Tiegs was not appropriation because "[w]orks of art, including sculptures, convey ideas, just as do literature, movies or theater." *Simeonov v. Tiegs*, 602 N.Y.S.2d 1014 (Civ. Ct. 1993). The use of a person's identity in a work of fiction generally cannot give rise to an appropriation action. *See, e.g., Maritote v. Desilue Productions, Inc.*, 345 F.2d 418 (7th Cir. 1965); *Loft v. Fuller*, 408 So. 2d 619 (Fla. Ct. App. 1981).

However, in New York and other states, the right of the media to use one's name or likeness for news purposes is not absolute. There must exist a "legitimate connection between the use of plaintiff's name and picture and the matter of public interest sought to be portrayed." *Delan by Delan v. CBS, Inc.*, 458 N.Y.S.2d 608, 613 (N.Y. Ct. App. 1983). As another court articulated the test:

> A picture illustrating an article on a matter of public interest is not considered used for the purpose of trade or advertising within the prohibition of the statute unless it has no real relationship to the article, or unless the article is an advertisement in disguise. It makes no difference whether the article appears in a newspaper; a magazine; a newsreel; on television; in a motion picture; or in a book. The test of permissible use is not the currency of the publication in which the picture appears but whether it is illustrative of a matter of public interest. *Dallesandro v. Henry Holt & Co.*, 106 N.Y.S.2d 805, 806-807 (1957).

This test has become known as the "real relationship" test. *See, e.g., Haskell v. Stauffer Communications, Inc.*, 990 P.2d 163 (Kan. App. 1999); *Lane v. Random House*, 985 F. Supp. 141 (D.D.C. 1995).

Finger v. Omni Publications International, Ltd.

566 N.E.2d 141 (N.Y. Ct. App. 1990)

ALEXANDER, J. Plaintiffs Joseph and Ida Finger commenced this action on behalf of themselves and their six children against defendant Omni Publications International, Ltd. seeking damages for the publication, without their consent, of a photograph of plaintiffs in conjunction with an article in Omni magazine discussing a research project relating to caffeine-aided fertilization. . . .

. . . The June 1988 issue of Omni magazine included in its "Continuum" segment an article entitled "Caffeine and Fast Sperm," in which it was indicated that based on research conducted at the University of Pennsylvania School of Medicine, in vitro fertilization rates may be enhanced by exposing sperm to high concentrations of caffeine.

A photograph of plaintiffs depicting two adults surrounded by six attractive and apparently healthy children accompanied the article. The caption beneath the photograph read "Want a big family? Maybe your sperm needs a cup of Java in the morning. Tests reveal that caffeine-spritzed sperm swim faster, which may increase the chances for in vitro fertilization." Neither the article nor the caption mentioned plaintiffs' names or indicated in any fashion that the adult plaintiffs used caffeine or that the children were produced through in vitro fertilization.

Plaintiffs commenced this action alleging only violations of Civil Rights Law §§ 50 and 51. Defendant moved to dismiss the complaint, arguing that its use of the photograph in conjunction with the article did not violate Civil Rights Law §§ 50 and 51 because the picture was not used for trade or advertising but to illustrate a related news article on fertility. Defendant contended that because fertility is a topic of legitimate public interest, its use of the picture fit within the "newsworthiness exception" to the prohibitions of Civil Rights Law § 50. . . .

Plaintiffs contend that defendant violated Civil Rights Law §§ 50 and 51 by using their photograph without their consent "for advertising purposes or for the purposes of trade."

We have repeatedly observed that the prohibitions of Civil Rights Law §§ 50 and 51 are to be strictly limited to nonconsensual commercial appropriations of the name, portrait or picture of a living person. These statutory provisions prohibit the use of pictures, names or portraits "for advertising purposes or for the purposes of trade" only, and nothing more. . . .

Although the statute does not define "purposes of trade" or "advertising," courts have consistently refused to construe these terms as encompassing publications concerning newsworthy events or matters of public interest. Additionally, it is also well settled that "'[a] picture illustrating an article on a matter of public interest is not considered used for the purpose of trade or advertising within the prohibition of the statute . . . unless it has no real relationship to the article . . . or unless the article is an advertisement in disguise.'"

Plaintiffs do not contest the existence of this "newsworthiness exception" and concede that the discussion of in vitro fertilization and the use of caffeine to enhance sperm velocity and motility are newsworthy topics. They contend, however, that their photograph bears "no real relationship" to the article, that none of plaintiffs' children were conceived by in vitro fertilization or any other artificial means, and that they never participated in the caffeine-enhanced reproductive research conducted at the University of Pennsylvania.

Consequently, according to plaintiffs, there was no "real relationship" between their photograph and the article, and any relationship that may exist is too tenuous to be considered a relationship at all. They argue that there are no "external and objective" criteria, such as were found to exist in *Arrington*, 434 N.E.2d 1319, that would indicate that plaintiffs have any real or legitimate connection with the subject of caffeine-enhanced in vitro fertilization, the subject of the accompanying article and that unlike the plaintiff in *Murray v. New York Mag. Co.*, 267 N.E.2d 256, these plaintiffs had not "voluntarily become part of the spectacle" or "visual[ly] participat[ed] in a public event which invited special attention."

Plaintiffs misperceive the "newsworthy" theme of the article, which is fertility or increased fertility. Indeed, the article, in its opening sentences, observes that caffeine "can increase a man's fertility by boosting the performance of his sperm" and further indicates that "those who are looking for a fertility tonic shouldn't head for the nearest coffee pot" because the concentrations of caffeine used in the experiment "were so high [as to] be toxic."

The theme of fertility is reasonably reflected both in the caption beneath the picture, "Want a big family?", and the images used — six healthy and attractive children with their parents to whom each child bears a striking resemblance. Clearly then, there is a "real relationship" between the fertility theme of the article and the large family depicted in the photograph. That the article also discusses in vitro fertilization as being enhanced by "caffeine-spritzed sperm" does no more than discuss a specific aspect of fertilization and does not detract from the relationship between the photograph and the article.

As we have noted, the "newsworthiness exception" should be liberally applied (see, *Arrington*). The exception applies not only to reports of political happenings and social trends as in *Arrington* . . . but to matters of scientific and biological interest such as enhanced fertility and in vitro fertilization as well. Moreover, questions of "newsworthiness" are better left to reasonable editorial judgment and discretion; judicial intervention should occur only in those instances where there is "'no real relationship'" between a photograph and an article or where the article is an "'advertisement in disguise.'" . . .

NOTES & QUESTIONS

1. Do you agree with the court's approach to the relationship between the photograph and the article? Does the court properly view the topic of the article broadly as about fertility in general? The Fingers' argument, however, is not that the picture has no relation to the subject matter of the article; rather, they contend that they have nothing to do with the article's topic. Is this relevant to the court?

2. What type of interest are the Fingers attempting to protect? Why doesn't the appropriation tort protect that interest?

3. Consider *Arrington v. New York Times*, 434 N.E.2d 1319 (N.Y. Ct. App. 1982). The *New York Times Magazine* published an article called *The Black Middle Class: Making It.* On the cover of the publication was the photograph of the plaintiff Clarence W. Arrington in a suit. The photograph was taken without Arrington's consent or knowledge as he was walking down the street. Arrington, a young African-American financial analyst, strongly disagreed with the views stated in the article, which criticized how the "expanding black middle/professional class in today's society" was growing more removed from its "less fortunate brethren." Arrington, along with many other readers, found the article to be "insulting, degrading, distorting and disparaging." Others, including his friends and acquaintances, thought that he had shared the ideas in the article because his picture was featured as the exemplar of the "black middle class." Arrington sued the publisher, the freelance photographer who took the picture, and the agency that arranged for the photo to be sold to the *Times* for appropriation and false light. With regard to appropriation, the New York law recognized the importance of protecting free speech values:

> . . . [W]e not too long ago reiterated that "'[a] picture illustrating an article on a matter of public interest is not considered used for the purposes of trade or advertising within the prohibition of the statute . . . unless it has no real relationship to the article . . . or unless the article is an advertisement in disguise.'" And this holds true though the dissemination of news and views is carried on for a profit or that illustrations are added for the very purpose of encouraging sales of the publications.

Arrington contended that his picture had no "real relationship" to the article, but the court disagreed:

> Plaintiff's emphasis . . . is on the fact that, as he reads it, the article depicts the "black middle class" as one peopled by "materialistic, status-conscious and frivolous individuals without any sense of moral obligation to those of their race who are economically less fortunate," a conception of the "class" with which he disclaims any "legitimate connection." While the concededly innocuous title of the article is superimposed over part of the picture (as is the title of another on Christmas pleasures), nothing of the ideas with which he wishes to disassociate himself appear at this point. And, though the article itself gives the names and quotes the statements and opinions of persons whom the author interviewed, as indicated earlier, the plaintiff is neither mentioned, nor are any of the ideas or opinions it expresses attributed to him. The asserted lack of a "real relationship" boils down then, to his conviction that his views are not consonant with those of the author. . . . [However,] it would be unwise for us to essay the dangerous task of passing on value judgments based on the subjective happenstance of whether there is agreement with views expressed on a social issue.
>
> No more persuasive is plaintiff's perfectly understandable preference that his photograph not have been employed in this manner and in this connection. However, other than in the purely commercial setting covered by [New York's appropriation tort], an inability to vindicate a personal predilection for greater privacy may be part of the price every person must be prepared to pay for a society in which information and opinion flow freely.

However, as to the photographer and the agency that sold the photo, the court declared that Arrington's action could proceed because the sale of the photo "commercialized" it, and the other defendants were not protected in the same way by the statute as the publisher. Subsequent to *Arrington*, the New York legislature amended §51 to protect photographers and agents.

How would you characterize Arrington's injury? Did it involve the commercial use of his photograph? Or did it involve his being associated with an article that he found distasteful? Should a person have legal recourse from having her image associated, without her consent, with views that she disagrees with?

Arrington also raised a false light claim, but the court rejected it because the use of the photo was not "highly offensive." Do you agree?

4. FIRST AMENDMENT LIMITATIONS

ZACCHINI V. SCRIPPS-HOWARD BROADCASTING CO.

433 U.S. 562 (1977)

WHITE, J. Petitioner, Hugo Zacchini, is an entertainer. He performs a "human cannonball" act in which he is shot from a cannon into a net some 200 feet away. Each performance occupies some 15 seconds. In August and September 1972, petitioner was engaged to perform his act on a regular basis at the Geauga County Fair in Burton, Ohio. He performed in a fenced area, surrounded by grandstands, at the fair grounds. Members of the public attending the fair were not charged a separate admission fee to observe his act.

On August 30, a freelance reporter for Scripps-Howard Broadcasting Co., the operator of a television broadcasting station and respondent in this case, attended the fair. He carried a small movie camera. Petitioner noticed the reporter and asked him not to film the performance. The reporter did not do so on that day; but on the instructions of the producer of respondent's daily newscast, he returned the following day and videotaped the entire act. This film clip approximately 15 seconds in length, was shown on the 11 o'clock news program that night, together with favorable commentary.

Petitioner then brought this action for damages, alleging that he is "engaged in the entertainment business," that the act he performs is one "invented by his father and . . . performed only by his family for the last fifty years," that respondent "showed and commercialized the film of his act without his consent," and that such conduct was an "unlawful appropriation of plaintiff's professional property." Respondent answered and moved for summary judgment, which was granted by the trial court.

[The Ohio Supreme Court held that the broadcast was protected by the First Amendment because the press "must be accorded broad latitude in its choice of how much it presents of each story or incident, and of the emphasis to be given to such presentation." The United States Supreme Court granted certiorari to determine whether the First Amendment immunized the media broadcaster from damages under Ohio's "right of publicity" (appropriation tort)].

. . . The Ohio Supreme Court relied heavily on *Time, Inc. v. Hill*, 385 U.S. 374 (1967), but that case does not mandate a media privilege to televise a performer's entire act without his consent. Involved in *Time, Inc. v. Hill* was a claim under the New York "Right of Privacy" statute that Life Magazine, in the course of reviewing a new play, had connected the play with a long-past incident involving petitioner and his family and had falsely described their experience and conduct at that time. The complaint sought damages for humiliation and suffering flowing from these nondefamatory falsehoods that allegedly invaded Hill's privacy. The Court held, however, that the opening of a new play linked to an actual incident was a matter of public interest and that Hill could not recover without showing that the Life report was knowingly false or was published with reckless disregard for the truth the same rigorous standard that had been applied in *New York Times Co. v. Sullivan*.

Time, Inc. v. Hill, which was hotly contested and decided by a divided Court, involved an entirely different tort from the "right of publicity" recognized by the Ohio Supreme Court. As the opinion reveals in *Time, Inc. v. Hill*, the Court was steeped in the literature of privacy law and was aware of the developing distinctions and nuances in this branch of the law. . . . The Court was aware that it was adjudicating a "false light" privacy case involving a matter of public interest, not a case involving "intrusion," "appropriation" of a name or likeness for the purposes of trade, or "private details" about a non-newsworthy person or event. It is also abundantly clear that *Time, Inc. v. Hill* did not involve a performer, a person with a name having commercial value, or any claim to a "right of publicity." This discrete kind of "appropriation" case was plainly identified in the literature cited by the Court and had been adjudicated in the reported cases.

The differences between these two torts are important. First, the State's interests in providing a cause of action in each instance are different. "The interest protected" in permitting recovery for placing the plaintiff in a false light "is clearly that of reputation, with the same overtones of mental distress as in defamation." By contrast, the State's interest in permitting a "right of publicity" is in protecting the proprietary interest of the individual in his act in part to encourage such entertainment. As we later note, the State's interest is closely analogous to the goals of patent and copyright law, focusing on the right of the individual to reap the reward of his endeavors and having little to do with protecting feelings or reputation. Second, the two torts differ in the degree to which they intrude on dissemination of information to the public. In "false light" cases the only way to protect the interests involved is to attempt to minimize publication of the damaging matter, while in "right of publicity" cases the only question is who gets to do the publishing. An entertainer such as petitioner usually has no objection to the widespread publication of his act as long as the gets the commercial benefit of such publication. Indeed, in the present case petitioner did not seek to enjoin the broadcast of his act; he simply sought compensation for the broadcast in the form of damages. . . .

. . . *Time, Inc. v. Hill*, *New York Times*, *Metromedia*, *Gertz*, and *Firestone* all involved the reporting of events; in none of them was there an attempt to broadcast or publish an entire act for which the performer ordinarily gets paid. It is evident, and there is no claim here to the contrary, that petitioner's state-law right of publicity would not serve to prevent respondent from reporting the newsworthy facts about petitioner's act. Wherever the line in particular situations is to be drawn between media reports that are protected and those that are not, we are quite sure that the First and Fourteenth Amendments do not immunize the media when they broadcast a performer's entire act without his consent. The Constitution no more prevents a State from requiring respondent to compensate petitioner for broadcasting his act on television than it would privilege respondent to film and broadcast a copyrighted dramatic work without liability to the copyright owner, or to film and broadcast a prize fight, or a baseball game, where the promoters or the participants had other plans for publicizing the event. . . .

The broadcast of a film of petitioner's entire act poses a substantial threat to the economic value of that performance. . . . The effect of a public broadcast of the performance is similar to preventing petitioner from charging an admission fee. The rationale for (protecting the right of publicity) is the straightforward one of preventing unjust enrichment by the theft of good will. . . .

There is no doubt that entertainment, as well as news, enjoys First Amendment protection. It is also true that entertainment itself can be important news. But it is important to note that neither the public nor respondent will be deprived of the benefit of petitioner's performance as long as his commercial stake in his act is appropriately recognized. Petitioner does not seek to enjoin the broadcast of his performance; he simply wants to be paid for it. . . .

We conclude that although the State of Ohio may as a matter of its own law privilege the press in the circumstances of this case, the First and Fourteenth Amendments do not require it to do so. . . .

NOTES & QUESTIONS

1. Why does the Court conclude that the First Amendment impacts the tort of appropriation differently than the other privacy torts? Do you agree with the distinction the Court makes?
2. Is Zacchini's cannonball act newsworthy? The media frequently provides news about entertainment, such as sports and movies. If the act is newsworthy, then why shouldn't the First Amendment protect the broadcast of it?

3
HEALTH AND
GENETIC PRIVACY

Health and genetic information is considered by many to be among the most private of information. People desire to keep matters about their health confidential because certain diseases have long been associated with great stigma (e.g., leprosy); other diseases are correlated in other people's minds with certain lifestyles and behaviors (e.g., sexually transmitted diseases); and certain debilitating or fatal illnesses might alter people's perception of the sufferer's capabilities and potentialities. Further, people want to keep illnesses private because they want to prevent others from viewing them differently. Knowledge of a person's health can result in being turned down for a job, being fired, being discriminated against, being rejected for a loan, and so on.

Today's health care system is vast and complex. Medical data is frequently disclosed to doctors and is widely circulated among hospitals, insurers, employers, and government agencies. At hospitals, dozens of nurses and staff have access to a patient's records. Currently, we are undergoing a transformation in medical recordkeeping, as more and more medical records are computerized. The increasing transformation of medical records into digital format will greatly facilitate the flow of health data. This can bring great benefits, as it will enhance the accuracy of people's medical histories as well as the ease with which doctors can learn about important and relevant aspects of their patient's health (e.g., allergies and conditions of the patient that affect the medical decisions a doctor might make). However, the increasing flow of health information raises substantial privacy concerns as well.

This chapter will provide an introduction to the many laws and regulations affecting health and genetic information. Health privacy in the United States is governed by a myriad of different laws and regulations. States have been the primary source for health privacy law. The privacy torts can provide remedies for intrusions into areas where one is receiving health care or public disclosures of private medical information. Recall *Shulman v. Group W. Productions, Inc.* from Chapter 2. Tort law also regulates the confidentiality of the relationship between patients and their physicians or other health caregivers. Additionally, many states have passed a variety of statutes to regulate health privacy. The level of protection, however, varies widely from state to state.

At the federal level, health privacy was unregulated until 1996, when Congress passed the Health Insurance Portability and Accountability Act (HIPAA). The Department of Health and Human Services has promulgated regulations under HIPAA, which provide a minimum level of protection for all states. State regulations more protective of privacy still remain in effect. Health privacy is also protected by the constitutional right to privacy, but this applies only to data maintained by government officials and entities.

A. MEDICAL INFORMATION

1. PRIVACY IN HEALTH CARE

PAUL SCHWARTZ, *PRIVACY AND THE*
ECONOMICS OF HEALTH CARE INFORMATION

76 Tex. L. Rev. 1 (1997)

. . . Enormous changes have taken place in the way medical services are provided in the United States. At one time, a physician's "practice was largely invisible to his peers, . . . and unconstrained by external institutions." As Professor Timothy S. Jost writes of this period, "In ordinary day to day life, . . . the physician answered to no one but himself." Today, information technology renders accessible to external observation the staggering amount of data involved in the diagnosis, treatment, and billing of patients. A tradition of deference to the medical profession and its definition and application of professional standards has been replaced by a model of control through processing and use of personal information. A widening audience of outsiders monitors the behavior of doctors, nurses, and patients. As two physicians have written, "Medicine is increasingly a spectator sport."

The provision, regulation, and financing of health care in the United States and other industrial nations depend on outside access to personal health care data. In addition to allowing this external monitoring of physicians and patients, the sharing of personal medical data plays a fundamental role in the shift to large, integrated systems for providing health care in the United States. Under a single corporate umbrella, an integrated delivery system now provides medical care by coordinating the services of numerous health care professionals located in hospitals, clinics, and outpatient facilities. The computer is essential to this transformation because it permits both the collection of extensive personal health data and the rapid sharing of such information. As an essay in the New England Journal of Medicine notes, the computer is seen "as a device to transform the medical record into a semipublic record used routinely for a wide range of investigations." This aspect of information technology has been heightened by the introduction of computer-based health care records.

When stored within these electronic dossiers and used within networked systems that link different sites, personal data become "multifunctional." The computer changes personal information into a fluid form and allows it to be applied in many different kinds of administration and decisionmaking. Personal health care information is now transmitted electronically among the computers of hospitals, insurers, governmental regulators, and physicians — each of whom may use it for different purposes. Such data-sharing already functions as part of statewide computer networks and soon will be extended on a nationwide and even international basis. . . .

Lawrence O. Gostin, *Health Information Privacy*

80 Cornell L. Rev. 451 (1995)

. . . Thoughtful scholarship in the area of informational privacy sometimes assumes that a significant level of privacy can coexist with the development of a modern health information infrastructure. Some commentators suggest that we can have it both ways: that adequate legal protection of informational privacy will eliminate the need to significantly limit the collection of health data. [However,] there is no such easy resolution of the conflict between the need for information and the need for privacy. Because significant levels of privacy cannot realistically be achieved within the health information infrastructure currently envisaged by policymakers, we confront a hard choice: should we sharply limit the systematic collection of identifiable health care data in order to achieve reasonable levels of informational privacy? The result of that choice would be to reduce considerably the social good that would be achieved from the thoughtful use of health data. Alternatively, we may decide that the value of information collection is so important to the achievement of societal aspirations for health that the law ought not promise absolute or even significant levels of privacy at all, but rather should require that the data be used only for authorized and limited purposes. . . .

Currently, most individual health records are kept manually in voluminous paper files. The General Accounting Office estimates that the 34 million annual hospital admissions and 1.2 billion physician visits could generate the equivalent of 10 billion pages of medical records. These records are fragmented, poorly documented and duplicative; they are often not accurate, complete, timely, or accessible when needed for patient care. "Information about a single episode of care could reside in the records of several different providers — history and symptoms in a physician record, laboratory results and surgical procedures in a hospital record, and rehabilitation in a home care agency record." Further, there are no systematic operational models for the electronic storage of all aspects of health records.

Despite the technical problems and the cost, several governmental and private committees have proposed automation of health data, and such automation is frequently discussed in the computer and health care literature. The federal government specifically cites the need for access to health data as one of the driving forces behind its initiative for a national information superhighway. Three conceptual and technological innovations are likely to accelerate the pace of automation of health records: the development of a patient-based longitudinal health record, the assignment of a unique identifier to every American, and the eventual use of advanced technologies for health identification cards. . . .

Privacy advocates . . . see computerization as a significant threat to privacy. As vastly greater quantities of information are collected and transmitted to an ever increasing number of users in remote locations, the ability of consumers to control the dissemination of personal information is sharply reduced. While electronic records are not qualitatively different than manual records, it is much easier to build a personal dossier using automated, on line, and interconnected systems. . . .

Manual records also pose problems of privacy and security, but these problems are less severe than those in the electronic data context. Manual records are often maintained by the health care provider in secure locations with limited numbers of persons having physical access. The cumbersome nature of manual records makes it an arduous task to acquire, copy, and use them. The relevant data may be held in many different records in diverse locations, making it difficult to combine data from separate sources.

By contrast, computerization makes it easy to enter, transmit, copy, or delete vast amounts of data. The acquisition and dissemination of information is efficient, rapid, and silent. In an electronic, on-line system, the data can be viewed, studied, and downloaded from any location. The viewer of the information has not acquired any physical materials, making any theft virtually undetectable. Moreover, the viewer of electronic data is not restricted to one set of records but can access many records in diverse geographic locations and databases. This linking capacity allows aggregation, comparisons and matching of data to discover much more about the private lives of patients. Thus, even data that have no personal identifiers may be linked to other data that provide a picture of an identifiable person or population. The linking capacity of computers also enables health database organizations to select characteristics of types of individuals, and to determine the probabilities of such individuals engaging in activities or behavior of interest to the organization. This use of "computer profiling" could, for example, be used to identify individuals who pose a risk to themselves or others due to communicable or sexually transmitted diseases or the failure to take medication. . . .

SIMSON GARFINKEL, "NOBODY KNOWS THE MIB"

in Database Nation: The Death of Privacy in the 21st Century (2000)

. . . As part of his Ph.D. thesis at Harvard Business School on privacy policies in corporate America, Jeff Smith surveyed more than a thousand people on a variety of privacy issues, and conducted in-depth interviews with several dozen. One of the key questions he asked as whether people had ever heard of a company called the Medical Information Bureau (MIB). What he found wasn't terribly surprising: they hadn't. . . .

I asked my wife if she knew what the Medical Information Bureau was. She said she didn't. I then showed her a medical insurance application that she had filled out nearly two years before. It included these two paragraphs:

> I AUTHORIZE any physician, medical practitioner, hospital, clinic, other medical or medically-related facility, the Medical Information Bureau, Inc. (MIB,

Inc.), consumer reporting agency, insurance or reinsuring company, or employer having certain information about *me or my dependents* to give John Alden Life Insurance Company or its legal representative any and all such information. The nature of the information to be disclosed includes information about: (1) physical condition(s), (2) health history(ies), (3) avocation(s), (4) age(s), (5) occupation(s), and (6) personal characteristics. This authorization includes information about: (1) drugs, (2) alcoholism, (3) mental illness, or (4) communicable diseases.

I UNDERSTAND the information obtained by use of the Authorization will be used by JOHN ALDEN LIFE INSURANCE COMPANY to determine eligibility for benefits. I ALSO AUTHORIZE JOHN ALDEN LIFE INSURANCE COMPANY to release any information obtained to reinsuring companies, Medical Information Bureau, Inc., or other persons or organizations performing business or legal services in connection with my application, claim, or as may be otherwise lawfully required, or as I may further authorize.

"Is that your signature at the bottom of the form?" I asked her. Yes, it was. She then read the form again. Still, she had no real clue what MIB was, other than that it was probably some kind of clearinghouse for medical information.

In fact, what the Medical Information Bureau keeps in its computers is information about people. Specifically, every time you report a significant medical condition on an insurance application — anything from heart problems to skin cancer — the insurance company can report that condition to MIB. The next time you apply for insurance, your "new" insurance company will pull your MIB file and find out what you previously reported.

In theory, MIB is supposed to prevent people who have significant medical conditions (and have been repeatedly rejected when they apply for insurance) from suddenly omitting their conditions from their applications and then getting health and life insurance with low-cost premiums that are reserved for healthy people. MIB helps "keep the cost of insurance down for insurance companies and for consumers by preventing losses that would occur due to fraud or omissions," says Neil Day, MIB's president.

MIB isn't supposed to be a medical blacklist. Member insurers are officially forbidden from using the information obtained in MIB's files as the basis for denying insurance. Instead, they are only allowed to use the information as the basis for further investigation. At least, those are the rules.

MIB was organized in 1902 as a nonprofit trade organization; today, roughly 750 insurance companies belong. MIB's files don't contain medical records, test results, or X-rays. Instead, each person's file contains one or more codes that stand for a particular medical condition that has been reported for that person. There are codes that signify diabetes, heart problems, and drug use. Some codes are very detailed. For example, Jeff Smith found that MIB had five codes for AIDS. . . .

Not all of the codes at the Medical Information Bureau are medical, Smith noted. For example, MIB has five codes that indicate a dangerous lifestyle, including "adverse driving records, hazardous sports, or aviation activity." These codes map to similar questions on most life insurance forms.

MIB is thus the official insurance agency gossip columnist. MIB helps make sure that if one life insurance company rejects a person on medical grounds, then other life insurance companies will be made aware of the ailment and reject that person as well.

MIB has been the subject of ongoing controversy since the 1970s, when its existence first became generally known. At the root of the controversy is the organization's penchant for secrecy. For many years, insurance agencies consulted MIB without telling applicants about the files. MIB even had an unlisted phone number. Today, the secrecy continues, if to a lesser extent: MIB won't release the list of codes that it uses. . . .

In the past, says *Privacy Journal* publisher Robert Smith, MIB had codes that stood for "sexual deviance" and "sloppy appearance." Day disagrees, but since MIB won't release the list of conditions for which it has created codes, there is really no way to know for sure.

There have also been disagreements over the accuracy of MIB's files. The Fair Credit Reporting Act specifically exempts medical records, but MIB agreed to be voluntarily bound by the rules after a 1983 examination by the Federal Trade Commission. Since then, MIB has received roughly 15,000 requests by individuals each year, says Day. Between 250 and 300 patients per year argue with the content of their report, he says. Overall, "97% of all consumers who received their MIB report [in 1996] found that their MIB record was accurate," reads a company pamphlet.

But if you happen to be one of those 300 patients, you might find yourself without medical or life insurance. In 1990, the Massachusetts Public Interest Research Group (MASSPIRG) did a study on MIB and found numerous cases in which erroneous records in the company's files had prevented people from getting insurance. In one case, says Josh Kratka, a MASSPIRG attorney, a Massachusetts man told his insurance company that he had been an alcoholic but had managed to remain sober for several years and that he regularly attended Alcoholics Anonymous. The insurance company denied him coverage and forwarded a code to MIB: "alcohol abuse; dangerous to health." The next company the man applied to for insurance learned of the "alcohol abuse" through the information bureau and charged the man a 25% higher rate. . . .

2. CONSTITUTIONAL INFORMATION PRIVACY AND MEDICAL INFORMATION

SUBSTANTIVE DUE PROCESS AND THE CONSTITUTIONAL RIGHT TO PRIVACY

Although the United States Constitution does not explicitly mention privacy, in a line of cases commonly referred to as "substantive due process," the Supreme Court has held that there exists a "right to privacy" in the United States Constitution.

As early as 1891, in *Union Pacific Railway v. Botsford*, 141 U.S. 250 (1891), the Court articulated some of the basic reasoning that would later develop into the "right to privacy" as it exists today. There, in holding that a court could not compel a plaintiff in a civil action to submit to a surgical examination, the Court declared:

> No right is held more sacred, or is more carefully guarded by the common law, than the right of every individual to the possession and control of his own person, free from all restraint or interference of others, unless by clear and unquestionable authority of law. As well said by Judge Cooley: "The right to one's person may be said to be a right of complete immunity; to be let alone." . . . The inviolability of the person is as much invaded by a compulsory stripping and exposure as by a blow. To compel any one, and especially a woman, to lay bare the body, or to submit it to the touch of a stranger, without lawful authority, is an indignity, an assault, and a trespass.

Later, in *Pierce v. Society of Sisters*, 268 U.S. 510 (1925), the Court held that parents cannot be compelled to have their children attend public schools because of the "liberty of parents and guardians to direct the upbringing and education of children under their control."

The watershed case for substantive due process privacy was *Griswold v. Connecticut*, 381 U.S. 479 (1965). There, the directors of Planned Parenthood Association challenged a Connecticut law criminalizing contraceptives and counseling about contraceptives to married couples. The Court held that the law was unconstitutional because it infringed upon the "zone of privacy" created by the "penumbras" of the First, Third, Fourth, Fifth, and Ninth Amendments.

The Court reasoned that explicitly guaranteed rights in the Bill of Rights have corollary rights:

> The association of people is not mentioned in the Constitution nor in the Bill of Rights. The right to educate a child in a school of the parents' choice — whether public or private or parochial — is also not mentioned. Nor is the right to study any particular subject or any foreign language. Yet the First Amendment has been construed to include certain of those rights. . . .
>
> . . . The right of freedom of speech and press includes not only the right to utter or to print, but the right to distribute, the right to receive, the right to read and freedom of inquiry, freedom of thought, and freedom to teach — indeed the freedom of the entire university community. Without those peripheral rights the specific rights would be less secure. And so we reaffirm the principle of the Pierce and the Meyer cases.
>
> In *NAACP v. State of Alabama*, we protected the "freedom to associate and privacy in one's associations," noting that freedom of association was a peripheral First Amendment right. Disclosure of membership lists of a constitutionally valid association, we held, was invalid "as entailing the likelihood of a substantial restraint upon the exercise by petitioner's members of their right to freedom of association." In other words, the First Amendment has a penumbra where privacy is protected from governmental intrusion.

The Court reasoned that "specific guarantees in the Bill of Rights have penumbras, formed by emanations from those guarantees that help give them life and substance. Various guarantees create zones of privacy." Applying this discussion to the contraceptive law, the Court held that the law had a "destructive impact" upon the relationship of marriage, a relationship which fell "within the zone of privacy created by several fundamental constitutional guarantees." "Would we allow the police to search the sacred precincts of marital bedrooms for telltale signs of the use of contraceptives? The very idea is repulsive to the notions of privacy surrounding the marriage relationship."

Subsequent to *Griswold*, the Court elaborated upon the right to privacy in *Eisenstadt v. Baird*, 405 U.S. 438 (1972). *Eisenstadt* involved a statute that permitted the use of contraceptives only to married couples. Although *Griswold* rested upon the sanctity of the marital bedroom, the Court held that this law was also unconstitutional because right of privacy "is the right of the individual, married or single, to be free from unwarranted government intrusion into matters so fundamentally affecting a person as the decision whether to bear or beget a child."

The next year, the Court decided one of the most controversial cases in its history—*Roe v. Wade*, 410 U.S. 113 (1973). There, the Court concluded that a Texas statute criminalizing abortion was unconstitutional as "violative of the Due Process Clause of the Fourteenth Amendment." As the Court explained:

> . . . The Constitution does not explicitly mention any right of privacy. In a line of decisions, however, going back perhaps as far as *Union Pacific R. Co. v. Botsford*, the Court has recognized that a right of personal privacy, or a guarantee of certain areas or zones of privacy, does exist under the Constitution. In varying contexts, the Court or individual Justices have, indeed, found at least the roots of that right in the First Amendment; in the Fourth and Fifth Amendments; in the penumbras of the Bill of Rights; or in the concept of liberty guaranteed by the first section of the Fourteenth Amendment. These decisions make it clear that only personal rights that can be deemed "fundamental" or "implicit in the concept of ordered liberty" are included in this guarantee of personal privacy. They also make it clear that the right has some extension to activities relating to marriage; procreation; contraception; family relationships; and child rearing and education.
>
> This right of privacy, whether it be founded in the Fourteenth Amendment's concept of personal liberty and restrictions upon state action, as we feel it is, or, as the District Court determined, in the Ninth Amendment's reservation of rights to the people, is broad enough to encompass a woman's decision whether or not to terminate her pregnancy. The detriment that the State would impose upon the pregnant woman by denying this choice altogether is apparent. Specific and direct harm medically diagnosable even in early pregnancy may be involved. Maternity, or additional offspring, may force upon the woman a distressful life and future. Psychological harm may be imminent. Mental and physical health may be taxed by child care. There is also the distress, for all concerned, associated with the unwanted child, and there is the problem of bringing a child into a family already unable, psychologically and otherwise, to care for it. In other cases, as in this one, the additional difficulties and continuing stigma of unwed motherhood may be involved. All these are factors the woman and her responsible physician necessarily will consider in consultation.

This set the stage for *Whalen v. Roe*, 429 U.S. 589 (1977).

WHALEN v. ROE

429 U.S. 589 (1977)

STEVENS, J. . . . Many drugs have both legitimate and illegitimate uses. In response to a concern that such drugs were being diverted into unlawful channels, in 1970 the New York Legislature created a special commission to evaluate the State's drug-control laws. The commission found the existing laws deficient in several respects. There was no effective way to prevent the use of stolen or revised prescriptions, to prevent unscrupulous pharmacists from repeatedly refilling prescriptions, to prevent users from obtaining prescriptions from more than one doctor, or to prevent doctors from over-prescribing, either by authorizing an excessive amount in one prescription or by giving one patient multiple prescriptions. . . .

The new New York statute classified potentially harmful drugs in five schedules. Drugs, such as heroin, which are highly abused and have no recognized medical use, are in Schedule I; they cannot be prescribed. Schedules II through V include drugs which have a progressively lower potential for abuse but also have a recognized medical use. Our concern is limited to Schedule II which includes the most dangerous of the legitimate drugs.[1]

With an exception for emergencies, the Act requires that all prescriptions for Schedule II drugs be prepared by the physician in triplicate on an official form. The completed form identifies the prescribing physician; the dispensing pharmacy; the drug and dosage; and the name, address, and age of the patient. One copy of the form is retained by the physician, the second by the pharmacist, and the third is forwarded to the New York State Department of Health in Albany. A prescription made on an official form may not exceed a 30-day supply, and may not be refilled.

The District Court found that about 100,000 Schedule II prescription forms are delivered to a receiving room at the Department of Health in Albany each month. They are sorted, coded, and logged and then taken to another room where the data on the forms is recorded on magnetic tapes for processing by a computer. Thereafter, the forms are returned to the receiving room to be retained in a vault for a five-year period and then destroyed as required by the statute.[2] The receiving room is surrounded by a locked wire fence and protected by an alarm system. The computer tapes containing the prescription data are kept in a locked cabinet. When the tapes are used, the computer is run "off-line," which means that no terminal outside of the computer room can read or record any information. Public disclosure of the identity of patients is expressly prohibited by the statute and by a Department of Health regulation. Willful violation of these prohibitions is a crime punishable by up to one year in prison and a $2,000 fine. At the time of trial there were 17 Department of Health employees with access to the files; in addition, there were 24 investigators with authority to investigate cases of overdispensing which might be identified by the computer. Twenty months after the effective date of the Act, the computerized data had only been used in two investigations involving alleged overuse by specific patients.

---

[1] These include opium and opium derivatives, cocaine, methadone, amphetamines, and methaqualone. Pub. Health Law §3306. These drugs have accepted uses in the amelioration of pain and in the treatment of epilepsy, narcolepsy, hyperkinesia, schizo-affective disorders, and migraine headaches.

[2] Pub. Health Law §3370(3), 1974 N.Y.Laws, c. 965, §16. The physician and the pharmacist are required to retain their copies for five years also, but they are not required to destroy them.

A few days before the Act became effective, this litigation was commenced by a group of patients regularly receiving prescriptions for Schedule II drugs, by doctors who prescribe such drugs, and by two associations of physicians. After various preliminary proceedings, a three-judge District Court conducted a one-day trial. Appellees offered evidence tending to prove that persons in need of treatment with Schedule II drugs will from time to time decline such treatment because of their fear that the misuse of the computerized data will cause them to be stigmatized as "drug addicts."[3]

Appellees contend that the statute invades a constitutionally protected "zone of privacy." The cases sometimes characterized as protecting "privacy" have in fact involved at least two different kinds of interests. One is the individual interest in avoiding disclosure of personal matters, and another is the interest in independence in making certain kinds of important decisions. Appellees argue that both of these interests are impaired by this statute. The mere existence in readily available form of the information about patients' use of Schedule II drugs creates a genuine concern that the information will become publicly known and that it will adversely affect their reputations. This concern makes some patients reluctant to use, and some doctors reluctant to prescribe, such drugs even when their use is medically indicated. It follows, they argue, that the making of decisions about matters vital to the care of their health is inevitably affected by the statute. Thus, the statute threatens to impair both their interest in the nondisclosure of private information and also their interest in making important decisions independently.

We are persuaded, however, that the New York program does not, on its face, pose a sufficiently grievous threat to either interest to establish a constitutional violation.

Public disclosure of patient information can come about in three ways. Health Department employees may violate the statute by failing, either deliberately or negligently, to maintain proper security. A patient or a doctor may be accused of a violation and the stored data may be offered in evidence in a judicial proceeding. Or, thirdly, a doctor, a pharmacist, or the patient may voluntarily reveal information on a prescription form.

The third possibility existed under the prior law and is entirely unrelated to the existence of the computerized data bank. Neither of the other two possibilities provides a proper ground for attacking the statute as invalid on its face. There is no support in the record, or in the experience of the two States

---

[3] Two parents testified that they were concerned that their children would be stigmatized by the State's central filing system. One child had been taken off his Schedule II medication because of this concern. Three adult patients testified that they feared disclosure of their names would result from central filing of patient identifications. One of them now obtains his drugs in another State. The other two continue to receive Schedule II prescriptions in New York, but continue to fear disclosure and stigmatization. Four physicians testified that the prescription system entrenches on patients' privacy, and that each had observed a reaction of shock, fear, and concern on the part of their patients whom they had informed of the plan. One doctor refuses to prescribe Schedule II drugs for his patients. On the other hand, over 100,000 patients per month have been receiving Schedule II drug prescriptions without their objections, if any, to central filing having come to the attention of the District Court. The record shows that the provisions of the Act were brought to the attention of the section on psychiatry of the New York State Medical Society, but that body apparently declined to support this suit.

that New York has emulated, for an assumption that the security provisions of the statute will be administered improperly. And the remote possibility that judicial supervision of the evidentiary use of particular items of stored information will provide inadequate protection against unwarranted disclosures is surely not a sufficient reason for invalidating the entire patient-identification program.

Even without public disclosure, it is, of course, true that private information must be disclosed to the authorized employees of the New York Department of Health. Such disclosures, however, are not significantly different from those that were required under the prior law. Nor are they meaningfully distinguishable from a host of other unpleasant invasions of privacy that are associated with many facets of health care. Unquestionably, some individuals' concern for their own privacy may lead them to avoid or to postpone needed medical attention. Nevertheless, disclosures of private medical information to doctors, to hospital personnel, to insurance companies, and to public health agencies are often an essential part of modern medical practice even when the disclosure may reflect unfavorably on the character of the patient. Requiring such disclosures to representatives of the State having responsibility for the health of the community, does not automatically amount to an impermissible invasion of privacy.

Appellees also argue, however, that even if unwarranted disclosures do not actually occur, the knowledge that the information is readily available in a computerized file creates a genuine concern that causes some persons to decline needed medication. The record supports the conclusion that some use of Schedule II drugs has been discouraged by that concern; it also is clear, however, that about 100,000 prescriptions for such drugs were being filled each month prior to the entry of the District Court's injunction. Clearly, therefore, the statute did not deprive the public of access to the drugs. . . .

We hold that neither the immediate nor the threatened impact of the patient-identification requirements in the New York State Controlled Substances Act of 1972 on either the reputation or the independence of patients for whom Schedule II drugs are medically indicated is sufficient to constitute an invasion of any right or liberty protected by the Fourteenth Amendment. . . .

A final word about issues we have not decided. We are not unaware of the threat to privacy implicit in the accumulation of vast amounts of personal information in computerized data banks or other massive government files. The collection of taxes, the distribution of welfare and social security benefits, the supervision of public health, the direction of our Armed Forces, and the enforcement of the criminal laws all require the orderly preservation of great quantities of information, much of which is personal in character and potentially embarrassing or harmful if disclosed. The right to collect and use such data for public purposes is typically accompanied by a concomitant statutory or regulatory duty to avoid unwarranted disclosures. Recognizing that in some circumstances that duty arguably has its roots in the Constitution, nevertheless New York's statutory scheme, and its implementing administrative procedures, evidence a proper concern with, and protection of, the individual's interest in privacy. We therefore need not, and do not, decide any question which might be presented by the unwarranted disclosure of accumulated private data whether intentional or unintentional or by a system that did not contain comparable security provisions. We simply hold that this record does not establish an invasion of any right or liberty protected by the Fourteenth Amendment. . . .

BRENNAN, J. concurring. . . . The information disclosed by the physician under this program is made available only to a small number of public health officials with a legitimate interest in the information. As the record makes clear, New York has long required doctors to make this information available to its officials on request, and that practice is not challenged here. Such limited reporting requirements in the medical field are familiar and are not generally regarded as an invasion of privacy. Broad dissemination by state officials of such information, however, would clearly implicate constitutionally protected privacy rights, and would presumably be justified only by compelling state interests.

What is more troubling about this scheme, however, is the central computer storage of the data thus collected. Obviously, as the State argues, collection and storage of data by the State that is in itself legitimate is not rendered unconstitutional simply because new technology makes the State's operations more efficient. However, as the example of the Fourth Amendment shows the Constitution puts limits not only on the type of information the State may gather, but also on the means it may use to gather it. The central storage and easy accessibility of computerized data vastly increase the potential for abuse of that information, and I am not prepared to say that future developments will not demonstrate the necessity of some curb on such technology. . . .

NOTES & QUESTIONS

1. *The Constitutional Right to Information Privacy.* The Court characterizes the line of substantive due process cases protecting the right to privacy as involving two "different kinds of interests"—(1) "the individual interest in avoiding disclosure of personal matters"; and (2) "the interest in independence in making certain kinds of important decisions." The latter interest is often referred to as decisional privacy because it involves the extent to which the state can become involved with the decisions an individual makes with regard to her body and family. The former interest involves the privacy implications of the collection, use, and disclosure of personal information. This former interest is often referred to as the "constitutional right to information privacy." What is the Court's implicit conception of privacy as manifested by this interest?

2. *Nixon v. Administrator of General Services.* After *Whalen*, the Court affirmed this notion of constitutional protection for information privacy in *Nixon v. Administrator of General Services*, 433 U.S. 425 (1977) concluding that President Nixon had a constitutional privacy interest in records of his private communications with his family but not in records involving his official duties. Although ex-president Nixon had a legitimate expectation of

privacy in private communications with his family, doctor, and minister, it was outweighed by the public interest in Nixon's papers.

3. *The Constitutional Right to Information Privacy After* **Whalen** *and* **Nixon.** After *Whalen* and *Nixon*, the Court did little to develop the right of information privacy. As one court observed, the right "has been infrequently examined; as a result, its contours remain less than clear." *Davis v. Bucher*, 853 F.2d 718, 720 (9th Cir. 1988). Since the constitutional right to information privacy has yet to develop a distinctive identity, courts applying the right often draw from other types of privacy law. At least one court has observed that the constitutional right to information privacy "closely resembles — and may be identical to — the interest protected by the common law prohibition against unreasonable publicity given to one's private life." *Smith v. City of Artesia*, 772 P.2d 373, 376 (N.M. App. 1989). One court has looked to the "reasonable expectations of privacy" test to determine whether information is entitled to protection under the constitutional right to information privacy. *See Fraternal Order of Police, Lodge No. 5, Philadelphia* 812 F.2d 105, 112 (3d Cir. 1987).

Not all courts have accepted the constitutional right to information privacy. In *J.P. v. DeSanti*, 653 F.2d 1080, 1090 (6th Cir. 1981), the Sixth Circuit concluded that "[a]bsent a clear indication from the Supreme Court we will not construe isolated statements in *Whalen* and *Nixon* more broadly than their context allows to recognize a general constitutional right to have disclosure of private information measured against the need for disclosure." *Id.* at 1089; *see also Bloch v. Ribar*, 156 F.3d 673, 684 (6th Cir. 1998) ("[T]he right to informational privacy will be triggered only when the interest at stake relates to those personal rights that can be deemed 'fundamental' or 'implicit in the concept of ordered liberty.'") (quoting *J.P. v. DeSanti*, 653 F.2d 1080, 1090 (6th Cir. 1981)).

At least one other Circuit court has expressed doubts as to whether the constitutional right to information privacy exists at all. In *American Federation of Government Employees, AFL-CIO v. Department of Housing & Urban Development*, 118 F.3d 786 (D.C. Cir. 1997), the court observed:

> We begin our analysis by expressing our grave doubts as to the existence of a constitutional right of privacy in the nondisclosure of personal information. Were we the first to confront the issue we would conclude with little difficulty that such a right does not exist, but we do not, of course, write on a blank slate. The Supreme Court [in *Whalen v. Roe*] has addressed the issue in recurring dicta without, we believe, resolving it. . . .
>
> The Court was equally Delphic in *Nixon v. Administrator of General Services*. . . .

Based upon your reading of *Whalen*, do you conclude: (1) there is a broad constitutional right to information privacy that pertains to a variety of kinds of personal information; (2) there is a narrow constitutional right to information privacy that only pertains to personal information relating to one's health, family, children, and other interests protected by the Court's substantive due process right to privacy decisions; or (3) there is no constitutional right to information privacy and the passage in *Whalen* was mere dicta?

4. ***The* Westinghouse *Test.*** The Third Circuit has developed the most well-known test for deciding constitutional right to information privacy cases. In *United States v. Westinghouse Electric Corp.*, 638 F.2d 570, 578 (3d Cir. 1980), the court articulated seven factors that "should be considered in deciding whether an intrusion into an individual's privacy is justified": (1) "the type of record requested"; (2) "the information it does or might contain"; (3) "the potential for harm in any subsequent nonconsensual disclosure"; (4) "the injury from disclosure to the relationship in which the record was generated"; (5) "the adequacy of safeguards to prevent unauthorized disclosure"; (6) "the degree of need for access"; and (7) "whether there is an express statutory mandate, articulated public policy, or other recognizable public interest militating toward access." In addition to the Third Circuit, the *Westinghouse* test is used by some other circuit courts.

5. ***Substantive Due Process Privacy After* Whalen.** After *Whalen,* the Court's substantive due process line of cases have left a contentious and checkered jurisprudence. In *Bowers v. Hardwick*, 478 U.S. 186 (1986), the Court upheld a Georgia statute criminalizing sodomy because the Constitution does not confer "a fundamental right upon homosexuals to engage in sodomy." In *Cruzan v. Director, Missouri Department of Health*, 497 U.S. 261 (1990), the Court held that a competent person has a liberty interest in refusing unwanted medical treatment but that the state could require proof of "clear and convincing" evidence that an incompetent person would have wanted to discontinue medical treatment. In *Planned Parenthood v. Casey*, 505 U.S. 833 (1992), the Court upheld *Roe*, but limited its reach. In so doing, the Court provided its most elaborate discussion of the conceptual foundations for the constitutional right to privacy:

> These matters, involving the most intimate and personal choices a person makes in a lifetime, choices central to personal dignity and autonomy, are central to the liberty protected by the Fourteenth Amendment. At the heart of liberty is the right to define one's own concept of existence, of meaning, of the universe, and of the mystery of human life. Beliefs about these matters could not define the attributes of personhood were they formed under compulsion of the State.

The Court refused to extend the right to privacy to the so-called right to die. *Washington v. Glucksberg*, 521 U.S. 702 (1997). It is arguable whether the "right to die" is properly phrased as such or is better characterized as encompassed by the right to privacy generally as "involving the most intimate and personal choices a person makes in a lifetime, choices central to personal dignity and autonomy," *Planned Parenthood*, 505 U.S. at 851.

42 U.S.C. § 1983 AND "CONSTITUTIONAL TORTS"

Most cases involving the constitutional right to information privacy are litigated by way of 42 U.S.C. § 1983. This statute was part of the Civil Rights Act of 1871 and was designed to facilitate the enforcement of civil rights protected by the Constitution and federal law. This famous civil rights statute provides:

> Every person who, under color of any statute, ordinance, regulation, custom, or usage, of any state or territory, subjects, or causes to be subjected, any citizen of the United States or other person within the jurisdiction thereof to the deprivation of any rights, privileges, or immunities secured by the Constitution and laws, shall be liable to the party injured in an action at law, suit at equity, or other proper proceeding for redress.

Section 1983 provides a way to remedy constitutional violations in the civil law (as opposed to criminal) context. Section 1983 creates a cause of action against those who, acting under state governmental authority, violate federal law and the federal Constitution. Section 1983 transforms constitutional violations into tort actions and enables plaintiffs to collect damages and obtain injunctive relief.

Section 1983 requires that the wrongful conduct be "under color of state law, custom, or usage." This is often referred to as the "state action" requirement.

The word "person" in §1983 includes government entities and officials. However, state governments are not "persons" and the Eleventh Amendment immunizes states against suits by private citizens. The Eleventh Amendment provides:

> The Judicial power of the United States shall not be construed to extend to any suit in law or equity, commenced or prosecuted against one of the United States by Citizens of another State, or by Citizens or Subjects of any Foreign State.

The Supreme Court has interpreted the Eleventh Amendment not just to bar a citizen of one state from suing another state, but also to bar a citizen from suing his or her own state. *See Hans v. Louisiana*, 134 U.S. 1 (1890). Therefore, instead of suing states directly, plaintiffs sue state officials.

Although states cannot be sued directly, municipalities and local governments can. In *Monell v. New York City Department of Social Services*, 436 U.S. 658 (1978), the Court held that municipalities can be sued as "persons" under §1983. However, municipalities cannot be sued for the acts of their employees. In other words, municipalities are not liable under §1983 on the basis of the *respondeat superior* doctrine. Municipalities are liable "when execution of a government's policy or custom, whether made by its lawmakers or by those whose edicts or acts may fairly represent official policy, inflicts the injury." Of course, *Monell* does not bar a suit against a local official directly.

In short, any state or local official can be sued directly under §1983. State governments cannot be sued. Local governments can be sued, but only when their policy or custom inflicts the injury, not merely because they employ the officials who caused the injury.

What about federal officials? Section 1983 does not authorize suits against federal officials. However, the Supreme Court held that federal officials can be sued for violating constitutional rights. *See Bivens v. Six Unknown Named Agents of Federal Bureau of Narcotics*, 403 U.S. 388 (1971). *Bivens* claims are addressed in a similar way as §1983 claims.

When sued, government officials (both state and local) can raise certain defenses known as "immunities." Certain officials are absolutely immune from liability under § 1983 — they cannot be liable at all if they are acting in their capacities as officials. Such officials include legislators and judges. Executive officials such as police officers only receive a limited immunity defense known as "qualified immunity." They are immune if "their conduct does not violate *clearly established* statutory or constitutional rights of which a reasonable person would have known." *Harlow v. Fitzgerald*, 457 U.S. 800 (1982). Immunities are generally the same for federal officials, with at least one notable exception. Although state governors only receive qualified immunity, *see Scheuer v. Rhodes*, 416 U.S. 232 (1974), the President of the United States receives absolute immunity, *see Nixon v. Fitzgerald*, 457 U.S. 731 (1982).

This introduction is by no means a comprehensive background into § 1983. It is important, however, to understand the basic structure of § 1983 because constitutional right to information privacy cases are often litigated by way of § 1983.

Carter v. Broadlawns Medical Center

667 F. Supp. 1269 (S.D. Iowa 1987)

[The Broadlawns Medical Center (BMC), a public county hospital located in Des Moines, Iowa, decided to employ a full-time chaplain. Its previous reliance on volunteer chaplains proved to be inadequate because it was difficult for volunteer chaplains to visit patients regularly. The Board of Trustees for BMC hired Maggie Alenzo Rogers, a female who was not an ordained minister. Rogers graduated from the University of Dubuque Theological Seminary in 1984 and was "endorsed" by the United Church of Christ. Her job description stated that she would "provide consistent pastoral care throughout the Medical Center, adding spiritual support and counseling to the ongoing healing effort." BMC had a policy of allowing Rogers to have open access to patient medical records. A group of plaintiffs challenged this policy as a violation of the constitutional right to information privacy.]

O'Brien, C. J. . . . The Court also concludes that the policy of chaplains having open access to patient medical records is constitutionally infirm under the Fourteenth Amendment. Patients at BMC have a right of privacy founded on the Fourteenth Amendment's concept of personal liberty. *Whalen v. Roe*, 429 U.S. 589 (1977). One facet of the right of privacy "is the right of an individual not to have his private affairs made public by the government." In *Planned Parenthood v. Danforth*, 428 U.S. 52 (1976), the Supreme Court refused to strike down record-keeping and reporting requirements regarding abortions that were (1) reasonably directed to the preservation of maternal health and which (2) properly respect a patient's confidentiality and privacy. In allowing chaplains free access to medical records, BMC is not properly respecting a patient's confidentiality and privacy. The Court concludes that patient medical records can only be accessed by a chaplain upon prior express approval of the individual patient or his guardian. This will not be so broad as to bar doctors, medical and psychiatric professionals and nurses to provide to the chaplain basic information, not privileged, which would enable the chaplain to understand what the patient's basic problem was, e.g., a suicide attempt. The Court shall enter injunctive relief regarding this violation. . . .

DOE v. BOROUGH OF BARRINGTON

729 F. Supp. 376 (D.N.J. 1990)

BROTMAN, J. . . . On March 25, 1987, Jane Doe, her husband, and their friend James Tarvis were traveling in the Doe's pickup truck through the Borough of Barrington ("Barrington"). At approximately 9:00 A.M., a Barrington police officer stopped the truck and questioned the occupants. As a result of the vehicle stop, Barrington officers arrested Jane Doe's husband and impounded the pickup truck. Barrington officers escorted Jane Doe, her husband, and James Tarvis to the Barrington Police Station.

When he was initially arrested, Jane Doe's husband told the police officers that he had tested HIV positive and that the officers should be careful in searching him because he had "weeping lesions.". . . Barrington police released Jane Doe and James Tarvis from custody, but detained Jane Doe's husband on charges of unlawful possession of a hypodermic needle and a burglary detainer entered by Essex County.

Sometime in the late afternoon of the same day, Jane Doe and James Tarvis drove Tarvis's car to the Doe residence in the Borough of Runnemede ("Runnemede"). The car engine was left running, and the car apparently slipped into gear, rolling down the driveway into a neighbor's fence. The neighbors owning the fence are Michael DiAngelo and defendant Rita DiAngelo. Rita DiAngelo is an employee in the school district in Runnemede.

Two Runnemede police officers, Steven Van Camp and defendant Russell Smith, responded to the radio call about the incident. While they were at the scene, Detective Preen of the Barrington police arrived and, in a private conversation with Van Camp, revealed that Jane Doe's husband had been arrested earlier in the day and had told Barrington police officers that he had AIDS. Van Camp then told defendant Smith.

After Jane Doe and Tarvis left the immediate vicinity, defendant Smith told the DiAngelos that Jane Doe's husband had AIDS and that, to protect herself, Rita DiAngelo should wash with disinfectant. . . . Defendant Rita DiAngelo became upset upon hearing this information. Knowing that the four Doe children attended the Downing School in Runnemede, the school that her own daughter attended, DiAngelo contacted other parents with children in the school. She also contacted the media. The next day, eleven parents removed nineteen children from the Downing School due to a panic over the Doe children's attending the school. The media was present, and the story was covered in the local newspapers and on television. At least one of the reports mentioned the name of the Doe family. Plaintiffs allege that as a result of the disclosure, they have suffered harassment, discrimination, and humiliation. They allege they have been shunned by the community.

Plaintiffs brought this civil rights action against the police officer Smith and the municipalities of Barrington and Runnemede for violations of their federal constitutional rights pursuant to 42 U.S.C. § 1983. The federal constitutional right is their right to privacy under the fourteenth amendment. . . .

AIDS is a viral disease that weakens or destroys the body's immune system. The disease is caused by the presence of the Human Immunodeficiency Virus ("HIV"), which attacks the body's T-lymphocyte cells that are a critical part of the body's immune system. As a result, the body is unable to withstand infections it would normally suppress. These resulting infections, known as "opportunistic diseases," eventually cause permanent disability and death. . . .

HIV is transmitted through contact with contaminated blood, semen, or vaginal fluids. The virus is transmitted through activities such as sexual intercourse, anal sex, use of nonsterile hypodermic needles, and transfusions of contaminated blood or blood products. Additionally, women infected with HIV can transmit the virus to their children before or during birth. Although HIV has been detected in other bodily fluids such as saliva and urine, the virus is much less concentrated, and there are no known cases of transmission of the virus by such means. The Centers for Disease Control ("CDC") terms the risk of infection from such fluids as "extremely low or nonexistent."

In 1986, the Surgeon General announced that HIV is not transmitted through casual contact with an infected person, such as shaking hands, kissing, or contacting an object used by an infected person. . . .

This court finds that the Constitution protects plaintiffs from governmental disclosure of their husband's and father's infection with the AIDS virus. The United States Supreme Court has recognized that the fourteenth amendment protects two types of privacy interests. "One is the individual interest in avoiding disclosure of personal matters, and another is the interest in independence in making certain kinds of important decisions." *Whalen v. Roe*, 429 U.S. 589, 599-600 (1977). Disclosure of a family member's medical condition, especially exposure to or infection with the AIDS virus, is a disclosure of a "personal matter."

The Third Circuit recognizes a privacy right in medical records and medical information. *United States v. Westinghouse*, 638 F.2d 570, 577 (3d Cir. 1980). . . .

Lower courts have held that, once the government has confidential information, it has the obligation to avoid disclosure of the information. In *Carter v. Broadlawns Medical Center*, the court held that a public hospital had violated plaintiffs' constitutional rights by giving chaplains open access to patient medical records without patient authorization. The court noted that, in permitting free access to medical records, the hospital did not properly respect a patient's confidentiality and privacy as recognized in *Whalen v. Roe*. . . . The case demonstrates that, not only is the government restricted from collecting personal medical information, it may be restricted from disclosing such private information it lawfully receives. . . .

. . . The sensitive nature of medical information about AIDS makes a compelling argument for keeping this information confidential. Society's moral judgments about the high-risk activities associated with the disease, including sexual relations and drug use, make the information of the most personal kind. Also, the privacy interest in one's exposure to the AIDS virus is even greater than one's privacy interest in ordinary medical records because of the stigma that attaches with the disease.

The hysteria surrounding AIDS extends beyond those who have the disease. The stigma attaches not only to the AIDS victim, but to those in contact with AIDS patients. Revealing that one's family or household member has AIDS causes the entire family to be ostracized. The right to privacy in this information extends to members of the AIDS patient's immediate family. Those sharing a household with an infected person suffer from disclosure just as the victim does. Family members, therefore, have a substantial interest in keeping this information confidential. Disclosures about AIDS cause a violation of the family's privacy much greater than simply revealing any other aspect of their family medical history.

An individual's privacy interest in medical information and records is not absolute. The court must determine whether the societal interest in disclosure outweighs the privacy interest involved. To avoid a constitutional violation, the government must show a compelling state interest in breaching that privacy.

The government's interest in disclosure here does not outweigh the substantial privacy interest involved. The government has not shown a compelling state interest in breaching the Does' privacy. The government contends that Officer Smith advised the DiAngelos to wash with disinfectant because of his concern for the prevention and avoidance of AIDS, an incurable and contagious disease. While prevention of this deadly disease is clearly an appropriate state objective, this objective was not served by Smith's statement that the DiAngelos should wash with disinfectant. Disclosure of the Does' confidential information did not advance a compelling governmental interest in preventing the spread of the disease because there was no risk that Mr. or Mrs. DiAngelo might be exposed to the HIV virus through casual contact with Jane Doe. The state of medical knowledge at the time of this incident established that AIDS is not transmitted by casual contact. Smith's statement could not prevent the transmission of AIDS because there was no threat of transmission present.

This court concludes that the Does have a constitutional right of privacy in the information disclosed by Smith and the state had no compelling interest in revealing that information. As such, the disclosure violated the Does' constitutional rights. . . .

. . . [Defendant Smith] argues that plaintiffs have no standing to bring this action because Smith's statement violated only the privacy rights of Jane Doe's husband. . . .

Plaintiffs here do not assert the constitutional rights of Jane Doe's husband. Jane Doe sues as guardian for her minor children for the violation of their own rights to privacy. The children have standing to sue for the violation of their right to privacy from governmental disclosure of their father's infection with AIDS. Likewise, Jane Doe individually asserts a violation of her constitutional right to privacy. That the officer did not reveal information about the children's own medical condition is immaterial. A family member's diagnosis with AIDS is a personal matter, as defined in *Whalen v. Roe*, that falls within the protection of the Constitution.

This court rejects the standing argument because Smith's statement communicated private, confidential information about Jane Doe and her children. The stigma of AIDS extends to all family members, whether or not they actually have the disease. Smith's statement also implicitly suggested that Jane Doe herself might somehow transmit the disease to the DiAngelos. Jane Doe clearly has standing to assert a violation of her right to privacy. . . .

. . . [Next, the Defendant] asserts that, because Jane Doe's husband told police that he had AIDS, the husband "published" the information, giving up any right to privacy in the information. . . .

Clearly, an arrestee's disclosure to police that he or she has AIDS is preferable to nondisclosure. Police can take whatever precautions are necessary to prevent transmission of the disease. Police have more than "casual contact" with arrestee, increasing the likelihood that the disease can be transmitted. For example, by frisking an arrested person, police may come into contact with hypodermic needles. Thus, disclosure should be encouraged to protect police officers. Common sense demands that persons with AIDS be able to make such disclosures without fear that police will inform neighbors, employers, or the media. Smith's publication argument, therefore, is rejected as contrary to public policy. . . .

NOTES & QUESTIONS

1. Suppose only private parties had disclosed that Mr. Doe had AIDS. Would there be a cause of action?
2. Suppose Mrs. Doe didn't know that her husband had HIV. Would the police violate Mr. Doe's constitutional right to information privacy by telling her?
3. What if the disease were highly contagious with casual contact? Does that matter for the application of the constitutional right to information privacy? The facts of this case occurred early on in the AIDS epidemic, when information about AIDS was just beginning to dispel some of the myths and hysteria surrounding AIDS. What effect should this have on the liability of the police?

Doe v. Southeastern Pennsylvania
Transportation Authority

---

72 F.3d 1133 (3d Cir. 1995)

Rosenn, J. This appeal requires that we probe the depth and breadth of an employee's conditional right to privacy in his prescription drug records. John Doe, an employee of the Southeastern Pennsylvania Transportation Authority (SEPTA), initiated this action under 42 U.S.C. § 1983 against his self-insured employer, alleging that the defendants violated his right to privacy. Plaintiff claims that, in monitoring the prescription drug program put in place by SEPTA for fraud, drug abuse and excessive costs, the Chief Administrative Officer, Judith Pierce, and the Director of Benefits, Jacob Aufschauer, learned that John Doe had contracted Acquired Immunodeficiency Syndrome (AIDS). This, he alleges, invaded his right to privacy.

A jury found for the plaintiff and awarded him $125,000 in compensatory damages for his emotional distress. The trial court denied defendants' motion under Rule 50 for judgment as a matter of law, or alternatively for a new trial. . . . The defendants timely appealed. We reverse.

We set forth the facts as the jury could have found them in support of its verdict. Accordingly, all evidence and inferences therefrom must be taken in the light most favorable to the verdict winner. In 1990, Judith Pierce became the Chief Administrative Officer for SEPTA. Her responsibilities included containing the costs of SEPTA's self-insured health program. In 1992, a bargaining agreement with Local Union 234 required SEPTA to provide, inter alia, prescription drugs for the employees. SEPTA entered into a contract with Rite-Aid Drug Store to be the sole provider for all of SEPTA's prescription drug programs. As part of this contract, Rite-Aid provided SEPTA with an estimate of the yearly costs of this program. If, at the end of the year, the actual cost to Rite-Aid amounted to over 115% of that estimate, SEPTA would have to pay substantial penalties; however, if the actual cost was 90% or less of that estimate, SEPTA would be entitled to rebates. Pierce was responsible for monitoring those costs.

John Doe is a SEPTA employee. At all times relevant to this appeal, Doe was HIV-positive, and had contracted AIDS by the time of trial. In 1991, Doe began to take Retrovir for his condition. Retrovir is a prescription drug used solely to treat HIV. Before filling his prescription, Doe asked Dr. Richard Press, the head of SEPTA's Medical Department and Doe's direct supervisor, if he or anyone else reviewed employee names in association with the drugs the employees were taking. Doe wished to keep his condition a secret from his co-workers. Dr. Press assured Doe that he had only been asked to review names on prescriptions in cases of suspected narcotics abuse and knew of no other review that included names. After receiving this information, Doe filled his prescription through the employer's health insurance. He continued to do so after SEPTA switched to Rite-Aid; he was never informed that this change might alter his confidentiality status.

In November of 1992, Pierce requested and received utilization reports from Rite-Aid. These reports were part of the contract between Rite-Aid and SEPTA. Pierce did not request the names of SEPTA employees in the reports, and Rite-Aid sent the reports in their standard format. . . . [One report] listed employees who were filling prescriptions at a cost of $100 or more per employee in the past month. Each line of the report included the name of an employee or dependent, a code to identify the prescribing doctor, the dispense date of the prescription, the name of the drug, the number of days supplied, and the total cost. Pierce called Aufschauer into her office, and the two of them reviewed the report. It was immediately apparent to Pierce that the reports would reveal employees' medications; however, she reviewed them in the format as submitted. She did not at that time request Rite-Aid to redesign SEPTA's reports to encode employees' names.

Pierce stated that her purpose in reviewing the reports with Aufschauer was several-fold. First, she wanted to look for signs of fraud and drug abuse. . . . Second, Pierce wanted to determine if Rite-Aid was fulfilling its promise to use generic rather than brand name drugs whenever possible. Third, although they were both covered in the Rite-Aid contract, Pierce wanted to determine the cost to SEPTA of fertility drugs and medications to help employees stop smoking, such as nicotine patches. Finally, Pierce wanted to determine whether the reports were in a summary form and whether they would permit an audit. Her review, however, focused almost entirely on the current report, which included employees' names. . . .

Pierce and Aufschauer scanned the reports. When they came across a drug name neither one recognized, they would look it up in a Physician's Desk Reference (PDR) that Pierce had. Pierce then called Dr. Louis Van de Beek, a SEPTA staff physician, and inquired about the drugs not listed in the PDR. She asked the doctor for what Retrovir was used. When Dr. Van de Beek told her it was used in the treatment of AIDS, she inquired whether there was any other use for it. He told her no. She then asked about the three other medications that Doe was taking, and was informed that they were all AIDS medications as well. Pierce discreetly never mentioned Doe by name; however, Dr. Van de Beek was aware of Doe's condition and Doe's medications because Doe himself had disclosed this information to him. Therefore, Dr. Van de Beek deduced that Pierce was asking about Doe. He told her that if she were trying to diagnose employees' conditions through prescriptions, he felt this was improper and possibly illegal. Pierce immediately ended the conversation and told him not to speak of the conversation to anyone.

Pierce then took the report to Dr. Press. She asked him if he would be able to perform an audit using the information in the report. Press noted that Pierce had highlighted certain lines on the report, including employees' names and the drugs that each of those highlighted employees were taking. Press testified that the drugs highlighted were all HIV or AIDS-related. Pierce asked Press if he knew whether any of the people whose names were highlighted were HIV-positive. Press said that he was aware of Doe's condition. He then told Pierce that he was uncomfortable with the presence of the names on the report. He also told her that he had neither the expertise nor the resources to perform an audit. . . .

Dr. Van de Beek informed Doe of Pierce's questions. He told Doe that Pierce had likely found out that Doe was HIV-positive. Doe claims he became upset at this news. He avers that he became more upset upon discovering from Dr. Press that Pierce had his name highlighted on a list because he didn't know who had access to or had seen this "AIDS list" and only a few SEPTA employees knew of his HIV-status. He had told Press and Van de Beek, as well as his acting supervisor and the administrative assistant of his department that he had AIDS. . . .

After these incidents, Doe remained at SEPTA in his current position. He makes no claim of personal discrimination or of any economic deprivation. He later received a salary upgrade and promotion. However, he testified that he felt as though he were being treated differently. A proposal he had made for an in house employee assistance program met with scant interest; he felt that this was because of his HIV condition. In addition, an administrator who reported to Pierce did not call on Doe to assist in the same way that he had called on Doe earlier. Doe testified that he felt as though there was less social chit-chat, co-workers ate less of the baked goods he brought to the office to share, and that his work space seemed more lonely than before. He also became fearful of Pierce, who never told Doe that she knew of his illness. Doe alleges that he became depressed and requested a prescription for Zoloft, an antidepressant, from his physician. Later, another antidepressant called Elavil was added to the medications Doe was taking. . . .

As a preliminary matter, this court must decide if a person's medical prescription record is within the ambit of information protected by the Constitution. If there is no right to privacy, our inquiry stops. A § 1983 action cannot be maintained unless the underlying act violates a plaintiff's Constitutional rights. . . .

. . . The Supreme Court, in *Whalen v. Roe*, noted that the right to privacy encompasses two separate spheres. One of these is an individual's interest in independence in making certain decisions. The other is an interest in avoiding disclosure of personal information. Medical records fall within the second category. Therefore, the Court held that individuals do have a limited right to privacy in their medical records. . . .

. . . An individual using prescription drugs has a right to expect that such information will customarily remain private. The district court, therefore, committed no error in its holding that there is a constitutional right to privacy in one's prescription records. . . .

. . . As with many individual rights, the right of privacy in one's prescription drug records must be balanced against important competing interests.

Before we can perform this balancing test, we must first assess whether, and to what extent, Pierce disclosed Doe's prescription drug information. . . .

Both Pierce and Aufschauer learned of Doe's illness through the Rite-Aid report. Pierce's initial discovery of the names on the report was inadvertent. . . . However, Pierce then spent some time and effort researching the report with the names on it. She highlighted, for her research purposes, those names on the report whose medications she was unfamiliar with and which were expensive, including Doe's, and called two SEPTA staff physicians to ask about medications she did not recognize. It was through this inquiry that Pierce learned about Doe's condition. She did not know the uses of Retrovir before she did this research.

Aufschauer learned of Doe's condition through his work as Director of Benefits and Pierce's subordinate. Pierce disclosed the information to him in the course of their work. SEPTA argues that this disclosure was necessary, as Aufschauer also had reasons for needing this information. Aufschauer's legitimate need for this information may affect whether the disclosure is an actionable one. It does not alter the existence of disclosure.

Nor can Pierce and Aufschauer be considered as a single unit for the purpose of determining disclosure. A disclosure occurs in the workplace each time private information is communicated to a new person, regardless of the relationship between the co-workers sharing that information. . . . Therefore, we hold that each person who learned of Doe's condition constitutes a separate disclosure for the purposes of Doe's invasion of privacy action.

To hold differently would lead us to a decision that Doe had waived his right to privacy by voluntarily disclosing his medical condition to co-workers at SEPTA. We are not faced with a situation where persons to whom Doe disclosed this information told others. Rather, Pierce and Aufschauer learned his condition completely independently of Doe's disclosures. His decision to give private information to some co-workers does not give carte blanche to other co-workers to invade his privacy.

However, we are not persuaded that the impingement on Doe's privacy by the disclosure to SEPTA's Chief Medical Officer, Dr. Press, amounts to a constitutional violation. Doe himself had already voluntarily informed Dr. Press of his condition. Dr. Press did not learn any new information from Pierce's actions. Plaintiff asserts that Dr. Van de Beek, as well, learned of the information from Pierce. Van de Beek, like Dr. Press, had already heard of Doe's condition from Doe himself. Moreover, Pierce did not disclose Doe's name to Van de Beek. She asked him about medications, and he deduced who she was asking about based on his independent knowledge of Doe's condition. It stretches any theory of liability far too thin to base an invasion of privacy on such conduct. Therefore, there was no disclosure to Dr. Van de Beek. Also, as a matter of law, the cursory disclosure Pierce made to Dr. Press, chief of SEPTA's medical department, a physician, and largely responsible for the health of SEPTA's employees, did not "amount to an impermissible invasion of privacy," because John Doe had already provided him with this information. . . .

As we noted earlier, an individual's privacy interest in his or her prescription records is not an absolute right against disclosure. This interest must be weighed against the interests of the employer in obtaining the information. We apply an intermediate standard of review in making this determination. . . . The intrusion upon Doe's privacy was minimal at worst.

This court has previously enumerated the factors to be weighed in determining whether a given disclosure constitutes an actionable invasion of privacy in *United States v. Westinghouse Electric Corp.*, 638 F.2d 570 (3d Cir. 1980). . . . *Westinghouse* mandates a consideration of seven different factors. They are: (1) the type of record requested; (2) the information it does or might contain; (3) the potential for harm in any subsequent nonconsensual disclosure; (4) the injury from disclosure to the relationship in which the record was generated; (5) the adequacy of safeguards to prevent unauthorized disclosure; (6) the degree of need for access; and (7) whether there is an express statutory mandate, articulated public policy, or other recognizable public interest favoring access. Although some of these factors may be in Doe's favor, overall, we believe the balance weighs on the side of permitting the disclosures present here. There is a strong public interest of the Transportation Authority, and the many thousands of people it serves, in containing its costs and expenses by permitting this sort of research by authorized personnel. This interest outweighs the minimal intrusion, particularly given the lack of any economic loss, discrimination, or harassment actually suffered by plaintiff. . . .

. . . In *Doe v. Borough of Barrington*, a borough police officer, without justification, told the neighbors of a man suffering from AIDS that the entire family had AIDS. The neighbors reacted by organizing a protest, and trying to prevent the man's children from attending public school. In that case, the court quite rightly held such conduct violated the plaintiffs' privacy rights, and there was no competing interest to justify the disclosure.

By contrast, SEPTA had legitimate reasons for obtaining the prescription information from Rite-Aid. Pierce had requested the information in Rite-Aid's standard format; she did not request the names of any employees. She did not disclose the information relating to Doe except to Aufschauer, in connection with their review, and to Dr. Press, for purposes of an audit. Dr. Press, the Chief Medical Officer, already knew of Doe's condition through Doe's voluntary disclosure. Moreover, Pierce destroyed the first report. Under these circumstances, we cannot conclude that Westinghouse factor (3) would impose liability on SEPTA. . . .

Factors six and seven strongly favor the defendants. Pierce had a genuine, legitimate and compelling need for the document she requested. Aufschauer, as Director of Benefits, also had a need for the document. Each had a responsibility and obligation to keep insurance costs down and to detect fraudulent and abusive behavior. The report was intended for that purpose. Employers have a legitimate need for monitoring the costs and uses of their employee benefit programs, especially employers who have fiscal responsibilities, as does SEPTA, to the public. . . .

Employers also have a right to ensure that their health plan is only being used by those who are authorized to be covered. Finally, the employers have a right to contain costs by requiring that employees use generic drugs rather than brand name when an adequate substitute exists. To accomplish these goals, employers must have access to reports from their prescription suppliers, and they must inspect and audit those reports. That is precisely what Pierce and Aufschauer were engaged in, and this was a legitimate function of their positions. They had a legitimate need for access to information from the drug supplier, and they carefully controlled its use. . . .

We hold that a self-insured employer's need for access to employee prescription records under its health insurance plan, when the information disclosed is only for the purpose of monitoring the plans by those with a need to know, outweighs an employee's interest in keeping his prescription drug purchases confidential. Such minimal intrusion, although an impingement on privacy, is insufficient to constitute a constitutional violation. . . . .

NOTES & QUESTIONS

1. What if SEPTA were a private sector employer? Would Doe have a good case under the public disclosure of private facts tort?
2. Should employers be permitted to ask for or receive health information from their employees? Should parents be permitted to ask their babysitter for health information (such as mental health, HIV, and other diseases) as part of the hiring decision?
3. Daniel Solove argues that the court in *Doe v. SEPTA* misconceptualized Doe's claim that his privacy was invaded:

> [The court] missed the nature of Doe's complaint. Regardless of whether he was imagining how his co-workers were treating him, he was indeed suffering a real palpable fear. His real injury was the powerlessness of having no idea who else knew he had HIV, what his employer thought of him, or how the information could be used against him. This feeling of unease changed the way he perceived everything at his place of employment. The privacy problem was not merely the fact that Pierce divulged his secret or that Doe himself had lost control over his information, but rather that the information appeared to be entirely out of anyone's control.[4]

---

[4] Daniel J. Solove, *Privacy and Power: Computer Databases and Metaphors for Information Privacy*, 53 Stan. L. Rev. 1393, 1438-1439 (2001).

Is this a type of injury that the law should recognize? Had the court recognized the injury in this way, how would its analysis have been different?

3. MEDICAL TESTING: CONSTITUTIONAL LIMITATIONS

ANONYMOUS FIREMAN v. CITY OF WILLOUGHBY

779 F. Supp. 402 (N.D. Ohio 1991)

KRENZLER, J. . . . [T]his case requires this Court to decide whether the City of Willoughby, Ohio, can require mandatory testing of its firefighters and paramedics for the AIDS virus as part of its annual physical examination for fitness to serve.

Plaintiff alleges, in substance, that he is a fireman and paramedic who has been an employee of the City of Willoughby for over ten years. . . .

Plaintiff alleges that on the morning of May 10, 1988, without prior notice, he and the rest of his squad were transported to Bio-Path Lab in Willoughby and ordered to submit to a human immunodeficiency virus ("HIV") blood test, that he objected to the test, but that he complied with the directive to take the test, and that his blood was drawn.

He alleges that the City has no medical or other justification for imposing mandatory routine HIV testing on all fire division personnel, including plaintiff. The City has no facts constituting probable cause or reasonable cause or suspicion of HIV positive status as to any divisional personnel, including plaintiff. The City has no procedures for obtaining warrants authorizing the HIV test nor does it plan to obtain warrants. The City had not adopted a policy to deal with division employees who tested positive for HIV. The City's testing policy contains no provision for education or counseling, either before or after testing, and the City did not afford plaintiff such education or counseling upon testing him. The City has not adopted procedures adequate to insure the confidentiality of HIV test data.

The plaintiff prays for a declaratory judgment that the City's testing violates the Fourth, Ninth and Fourteenth Amendments to the United States Constitution and seeks a permanent injunction prohibiting the City from conducting such testing. . . .

In this case, we are dealing with a governmental agency, to wit, the City of Willoughby, which requires mandatory AIDS testing of its firefighters and paramedics as part of an annual physical examination. . . .

The plaintiff contends that the mandatory testing for AIDS is not a necessary part of an annual physical examination for fitness for duty. The plaintiff says HIV testing is not the same as other physical examinations because it is intrusive. The plaintiff contends that the taking of blood for AIDS testing violates the Fourth Amendment as an unreasonable search and seizure. . . .

The defendants contend that the blood is already drawn and, therefore, it is reasonable to use it for AIDS testing and such testing is not a search. . . . The defendants contend that the City wants to protect the firefighters and the public, and that any lacerations or any flowing blood may transmit the HIV virus, and the virus may also be transmitted by mouth-to-mouth resuscitation. The defendants contend that this compelling government interest outweighs any private interest. . . .

The Fourth Amendment states:

> The right of the people to be secure in their persons, houses, papers, and effects, against unreasonable searches and seizures, shall not be violated, and no Warrants shall issue, but upon probable cause, supported by oath or affirmation, and particularly describing the place to be searched, and persons or things to be seized. . . .

Public employers are subject to the constraints of the Fourth Amendment.

The Fourth Amendment is implicated in a case only if the plaintiff can show that the conduct of the defendant has infringed on an expectation of privacy that society is prepared to consider reasonable.

The Fourth Amendment does not prohibit all searches, only those that are unreasonable. The determination of the reasonableness of a search requires balancing the need to search against the invasion which the search entails. On one side of the balance is placed the individual's legitimate expectations of privacy; on the other, the government's need for effective methods to deal with legitimate governmental interests. *Skinner v. Railway Labor Executives' Ass'n*, 489 U.S. 602 (1989). . . .

The constitutional protection against unreasonable searches by the government does not simply disappear because the government has the right to make reasonable intrusions by conducting physical examinations in its capacity as employer. The HIV test requires a separate chemical analysis to obtain new and distinct information from that previously obtained in the blood tests given as part of the annual physical examination. The HIV test is a new search and is subject to a separate analysis under the Fourth Amendment.

HIV testing on blood already drawn from public employees as part of an annual physical examination constitutes an intrusion and a search and seizure within the meaning of the Fourth Amendment. The issue is whether it is reasonable or unreasonable. . . .

The fire and police industries are among the most highly regulated of any industry with respect to the performance of their employees. "[T]he expectations of privacy of covered employees are diminished by reason of their participation in an industry that is regulated pervasively to ensure safety, a goal dependent, in substantial part on the health and fitness of covered employees." *Skinner, supra.* . . .

Because plaintiff's Fourth Amendment interests are implicated by HIV testing, it is incumbent on the City to offer a justification based upon the public interest, and the Court finds the City's evidence does support the City's mandatory HIV testing. . . .

The City's justification for the testing offered here is the pursuit of a safe work environment for its employees and the public. . . .

The protection of the public from the contraction and transmission of AIDS by firefighters and paramedics is a compelling governmental interest. Stopping the spread of the deadly AIDS epidemic is a compelling governmental interest. . . .

Mandatory testing, in and of itself, does not prevent the contraction and/or transmission of AIDS. This Court recognizes that universal precautions are the most accepted method of preventing the contraction and/or transmission of the HIV virus. There is a direct link or nexus between the information conveyed by mandatory HIV test results for high-risk public employees and the prevention of the contraction and/or transmission of the HIV virus and AIDS. For high-risk government employees, mandatory testing and universal and other precautions against transmission of the disease are integrally related. . . .

The medical evidence demonstrates that the risk of HIV transmission in the performance of the duties of firefighter paramedic is high. . . .

State and local authorities have compelling interests in ensuring that its firefighters and paramedics are performing their duties free of having AIDS. Reasonable and particularized suspicion is not necessary as a precondition to mandatory AIDS testing of firefighters and paramedics.

After careful consideration, the Court finds that the City's mandatory HIV blood testing policy for firefighters and paramedics is justified at its inception and is not an unreasonable search and seizure in violation of the Fourth Amendment to the United States Constitution. . . .

NOTES & QUESTIONS

1. A 2001 survey by the American Management Association revealed that 65 percent of major companies require medical examinations of new employees.[5] To what extent should employers be able to require medical testing and the disclosure of medical information for new hires? Should public sector employers be treated differently from private sector employers? We will return to these issues in Chapter 7 when we examine privacy in the workplace.

2. Should employers be permitted to test for genetic predisposition for certain debilitating or fatal conditions? Is genetic testing different from medical testing? We will explore this issue later in section C of this chapter.

FERGUSON V. CITY OF CHARLESTON

532 U.S. 67 (2001)

[A Charleston public hospital operated by the Medical University of South Carolina (MUSC) developed a policy of testing pregnant patients suspected of drug use. The drug testing was done by testing urine samples. Patients testing positive were provided with referrals for education and treatment and were sometimes arrested and prosecuted for drug offenses or child neglect. In rejecting a Fourth Amendment challenge to the testing, the Fourth Circuit concluded that the testing was reasonable under the "special needs" doctrine.]

---

[5] *See Health Privacy Project, Report: Genetics and Privacy: A Patchwork of Protections* 18 (2002).

STEVENS, J. . . . Because MUSC is a state hospital, the members of its staff are government actors, subject to the strictures of the Fourth Amendment. Moreover, the urine tests conducted by those staff members were indisputably searches within the meaning of the Fourth Amendment. Neither the District Court nor the Court of Appeals concluded that any of the nine criteria used to identify the women to be searched provided either probable cause to believe that they were using cocaine, or even the basis for a reasonable suspicion of such use. Rather, the District Court and the Court of Appeals viewed the case as one involving MUSC's right to conduct searches without warrants or probable cause. Furthermore, given the posture in which the case comes to us, we must assume for purposes of our decision that the tests were performed without the informed consent of the patients.

Because the hospital seeks to justify its authority to conduct drug tests and to turn the results over to law enforcement agents without the knowledge or consent of the patients, this case differs from the four previous cases in which we have considered whether comparable drug tests "fit within the closely guarded category of constitutionally permissible suspicionless searches." In three of those cases, we sustained drug tests for railway employees involved in train accidents, *Skinner v. Railway Labor Executives' Assn.*, 489 U.S. 602 (1989), for United States Customs Service employees seeking promotion to certain sensitive positions, *Treasury Employees v. Von Raab*, 489 U.S. 656 (1989), and for high school students participating in interscholastic sports, *Vernonia School Dist. v. Acton*, 515 U.S. 646 (1995). In the fourth case, we struck down such testing for candidates for designated state offices as unreasonable. *Chandler v. Miller*, 520 U.S. 305, 513 (1997).

In each of those cases, we employed a balancing test that weighed the intrusion on the individual's interest in privacy against the "special needs" that supported the program. As an initial matter, we note that the invasion of privacy in this case is far more substantial than in those cases. In the previous four cases, there was no misunderstanding about the purpose of the test or the potential use of the test results, and there were protections against the dissemination of the results to third parties. The use of an adverse test result to disqualify one from eligibility for a particular benefit, such as a promotion or an opportunity to participate in an extracurricular activity, involves a less serious intrusion on privacy than the unauthorized dissemination of such results to third parties. The reasonable expectation of privacy enjoyed by the typical patient undergoing diagnostic tests in a hospital is that the results of those tests will not be shared with nonmedical personnel without her consent. . . .

The critical difference between those four drug-testing cases and this one, however, lies in the nature of the "special need" asserted as justification for the warrantless searches. In each of those earlier cases, the "special need" that was advanced as a justification for the absence of a warrant or individualized suspicion was one divorced from the State's general interest in law enforcement. . . . In this case, however, the central and indispensable feature of the policy from its inception was the use of law enforcement to coerce the patients into substance abuse treatment. This fact distinguishes this case from circumstances in which physicians or psychologists, in the course of ordinary medical procedures aimed at helping the patient herself, come across information that under rules of law or ethics is subject to reporting requirements, which no one has challenged here.

Respondents argue in essence that their ultimate purpose — namely, protecting the health of both mother and child — is a beneficent one. . . . In this case, a review of the M-7 policy plainly reveals that the purpose actually served by the MUSC searches "is ultimately indistinguishable from the general interest in crime control." . . .

. . . [T]hroughout the development and application of the policy, the Charleston prosecutors and police were extensively involved in the day-to-day administration of the policy. . . .

While the ultimate goal of the program may well have been to get the women in question into substance abuse treatment and off of drugs, the immediate objective of the searches was to generate evidence *for law enforcement purposes* in order to reach that goal. . . . Given the primary purpose of the Charleston program, which was to use the threat of arrest and prosecution in order to force women into treatment, and given the extensive involvement of law enforcement officials at every stage of the policy, this case simply does not fit within the closely guarded category of "special needs." . . .

As respondents have repeatedly insisted, their motive was benign rather than punitive. Such a motive, however, cannot justify a departure from Fourth Amendment protections, given the pervasive involvement of law enforcement with the development and application of the MUSC policy. . . . The Fourth Amendment's general prohibition against nonconsensual, warrantless, and suspicionless searches necessarily applies to such a policy. . . .

NOTES & QUESTIONS

1. In light of *Ferguson*, reevaluate *Anonymous Fireman*. Does *Ferguson* affect the reasoning of this case?
2. In *In re J.G.*, 701 A.2d 1260 (N.J. 1997), New Jersey enacted statutes providing for AIDS testing of assailants who were charged with sexual assault at the request of the victim. Three juveniles charged with sexual assault violations and required to submit to AIDS testing challenged the statutes on Fourth Amendment grounds. Experts testifying on behalf of the juveniles stated that the harms of testing would be outweighed by the benefits:

> In the opinion of Dr. James Oleske, testing sexual assailants for HIV would provide no medical benefit in the diagnosis or treatment of victims because the test would not reveal whether transmission, which does not occur in all cases, had in fact occurred, and because testing the assailant might produce a false-negative result due to the three-to six-month latency period. . . .
>
> The experts offered their opinions about whether there was any "psychosocial benefit" to the victim in knowing the HIV status of the assailant. In Dr. Oleske's view, victims may suffer actual harm from knowing their assailants' status. They may wrongly rely on a false-negative result and discontinue medical care and testing, or they may react to a positive result without considering their actual risk of infection or their own status. He acknowledged, however, that for the victim and the victim's family "[t]he question of peace of mind, . . . in lay terms, may be real." . . .

The court, however, concluded that on balance, the alleged offenders' Fourth Amendment rights were outweighed by the benefits of the testing:

> . . . A court must balance the encroachment on an individual's Fourth Amendment interests against the advancement of legitimate state goals. When a search is conducted in furtherance of a criminal investigation, the balance is most often tipped "in favor of the procedures described by the Warrant Clause of the Fourth Amendment," that is, toward a finding that the search "is not reasonable unless it is accomplished pursuant to a judicial warrant issued upon probable cause."
>
> An exception to the Warrant Clause may apply "when 'special needs, beyond the normal need for law enforcement, make the warrant and probable-cause requirement impracticable.'" . . .
>
> Serological testing of sex offenders . . . is not intended to facilitate the criminal prosecution of those offenders. HIV test results are required to be kept confidential (with certain limited exceptions). Notably, the statute does not authorize disclosure to the prosecutor's office. The State has said that the tests are not intended to be used to gain evidence for criminal prosecutions and do not place offenders at risk of a new conviction or longer sentence. We agree, and hold that the results of HIV tests . . . may not be used against an accused sex offender in a criminal prosecution.
>
> Moreover, both the warrant and individualized suspicion requirements are impractical in this context. . . . "HIV infected sexual offenders often have no outward manifestations of infection," which means that probable cause or individualized suspicion that an assailant is infected with the AIDS virus could not be found without testing. Requiring probable cause or individualized suspicion before testing could be conducted would create the proverbial Catch-22 and would "frustrate the governmental purpose behind the search." . . .
>
> Unquestionably, the state has a compelling interest in making information available when it directly affects the physical and mental well-being of survivors of sexual assault. . . .
>
> . . . Survivors of sexual assault, and those close to them, face significant psychological as well as physical trauma. [The statutes] respond to these significant concerns by requiring the testing of offenders at the victim's request, and by establishing counseling, testing, and other support services for victims. . . .
>
> The dissemination of test results . . . is carefully restricted. It is, therefore, reasonable to require assailants to submit to this intrusion upon their privacy. . . .
>
> . . . . [However, only if] . . . a demonstration of a risk that the AIDS virus may have been transmitted from the offender to the victim. . . . is made will the interests of the state in enacting the testing statutes outweigh the privacy interests of the offender. . . .

4. STATE LAW PROTECTIONS

Until the Health Insurance Portability and Accountability Act (HIPAA) of 1996, which mandated federal privacy regulation for medical information, health privacy was a concern of the states. As we have seen, although the constitutional right to information privacy and the Fourth Amendment provide some protection, it is significantly limited. State regulation is more extensive in its protection; however, it is very uneven. The Health Privacy Project at

Georgetown University has prepared a comprehensive overview and analysis of every state's health privacy statutes and regulations.[6] This report is an excellent resource for researching state health privacy law.

    Privacy Torts. The Warren and Brandeis privacy torts protect medical information. Recall *Shulman v. Group W. Productions, Inc.* from Chapter 2, where the court found that a TV show that taped the plaintiff as she was being rescued from a car accident and transported to the hospital via helicopter could give rise to a cause of action for intrusion upon seclusion (but not for public disclosure of private facts). In *Estate of Berthiaume v. Pratt,* 365 A.2d 792 (Me. 1976), a doctor attempted to take photographs of his patient, who was dying of cancer of the larynx. The patient raised a clenched fist and tried to remove his head from the camera's range. The patient died later that day. The court held that the patient had a claim for intrusion upon seclusion because the doctor did not have the right, against the patient's wishes, to complete his photographic record by taking pictures of the patient in his dying hours.

    Many courts have found that the disclosure of medical information can give rise to a claim for public disclosure of private facts. In *Urbaniak v. Newton,* 277 Cal. Rptr. 354 (Cal. App. 1991), the court held that the disclosure of a patient's HIV status was "clearly a 'private fact' of which the disclosure may 'be offensive and objectionable to a reasonable [person] of ordinary sensibilities.'" *See also Susan S. v. Israels,* 67 Cal. Rptr. 2d 42 (Cal. App. 1997) (public disclosure action for disclosure of mental health records). In *Doe v. Mills,* 536 N.W.2d 824 (Mich. App. 1995), a group of abortion protestors held up large signs displaying the names of the plaintiffs outside the abortion clinic where they were getting abortions. The court held that the plaintiffs could bring a claim for public disclosure:

> . . . [A]bortion concerns matters of sexual relations and medical treatment, both of which are regarded as private matters. Furthermore, even though the abortion issue may be regarded as a matter of public interest, the plaintiffs' identities in this case were not matters of legitimate public concern, nor a matter of public record, but, instead, were purely private matters.

Likewise, in *Y.G. & L.G. v. Jewish Hospital of St. Louis,* 795 S.W.2d 488 (Mo. App. 1990), the court held that the plaintiffs had a viable public disclosure claim against a television station that broadcast the plaintiffs' involvement in a hospital's *in vitro* fertilization plan: "The *in vitro* program and its success may well have been matters of public interest, but the identity of the plaintiffs participating in the program was, we conclude, a private matter."

    Tort Law Regulation of Patient-Physician Confidentiality. In addition to the privacy torts, a number of states recognize tort liability for instances where physicians disclose a patient's medical information. In certain circumstances,

---

[6] *See* Joy Pritts, Janlori Goldman, Zoe Hudson, Aimee Berenson, and Elizabeth Hadley, The State of Health Privacy: An Uneven Terrain (A Comprehensive Survey of State Health Privacy Statutes), at <*http://www.healthprivacy.org*>.

physicians can be liable for failing to disclose medical data about a patient. *See* section B below.

Mandatory Reporting Laws. Many states require that medical personnel or institutions report certain health information to state agencies or to others. Examples of information required to be disclosed include communicable diseases and child abuse. *See* section B below.

Research Disclosure Laws. A number of states regulate the use of medical data for research purposes. For example, California generally prohibits nonconsensual disclosure of alcohol and drug abuse data but permits such nonconsensual disclosure for the purpose of conducting research provided that the individual cannot be identified. *See* Cal. Health & Safety Code § 11977.

Medical Confidentiality Laws. Many states have specific statutes providing civil and criminal protection against the disclosure of medical information. Some laws restrict disclosure of medical data by particular entities: government agencies, HMOs, insurance companies, employers, pharmacists, and health data clearinghouses.

Other laws prohibit the disclosure by any entity of particular types of medical data, such as AIDS/HIV, alcohol or drug abuse, mental health, and genetic information. *See, e.g.*, Cal. Health & Safety Code § 199.21 (prohibiting disclosure of HIV test results); N.Y. Pub. Health L. § 17 (prohibiting the nonconsensual disclosure of medical records of minors relating to sexually transmitted diseases and abortion; even the disclosure to parents is prohibited without consent); Pa. Cons. Stat. § 1690.108 (prohibiting the disclosure of all records prepared during alcohol or drug abuse treatment).

Patient Access Laws. The vast majority of states (44) have statutes providing patients with a right to access certain medical records. A few states grant wide access to medical records held by all types of entities. On the other end of the spectrum, some states have no right of access, and others only have a limited right to access mental health records. The remaining states fall somewhere in between, permitting access to records from certain health care providers but not others (e.g., from some but not all of the following entities: hospitals, HMO's, insurers, and pharmacists).[7]

Comprehensive Health Privacy Laws. Most states do not have a comprehensive law governing medical privacy. According to the Health Privacy Project Report, only three states have a comprehensive law: Hawaii, Rhode Island, and Wisconsin. As the Report notes, most states regulate specific entities handling health data:

> The end result of this legislating by entity is that state laws — with a few notable exceptions — do not extend *comprehensive* protections to people's medi-

---

[7] *See id.*

cal records. Thus, a state statute may impose privacy rules on hospitals but not dentists. The state may restrict the use and disclosure of information derived from a genetic test but not information obtained in a routine physical.[8]

5. HEALTH INSURANCE PORTABILITY AND ACCOUNTABILITY ACT OF 1996

In 1996, Congress enacted the Health Insurance Portability and Accountability Act (HIPAA). The primary purpose of HIPAA was to permit employees to change jobs without having their new health plans exclude pre-existing conditions. Congress also mandated a uniform set of transaction codes to process insurance claims more easily. Given the greater ease of data sharing and transmission that uniform codes would enable, Congress was concerned about the privacy and security of medical data. However, Congress did not address the issue of privacy at the time HIPAA was passed. Rather, Congress established a deadline of August 21, 1999, for the enactment of comprehensive legislation to provide for privacy of medical information. The Act provided that if Congress failed to act by that date, then the Department of Health and Human Services (HHS) must promulgate regulations with regard to health privacy. The deadline passed without congressional action. Accordingly, HHS issued regulations, initially in the form of proposed regulations subject to revision. These were published at 64 Fed. Reg. 59,917 (Nov. 3, 1999). HHS received more than 50,000 comment letters on the proposed rule. *See HHS Rule Protecting Health Care Privacy Irks Some Employers, Likely to Affect Many*, 68 U.S.L.W. 2627, 2628 (Apr. 25, 2000).

The final version of the regulations was issued in December 2000 at the end of the Clinton Administration. Due to a procedural error, implementation of the regulations was delayed, and the Bush Administration initially criticized the regulations and vowed to delay and possibly to reconsider them. Later, the Administration changed course and announced that the regulations would go into effect. However, in 2002, the Bush Administration made significant changes in the regulations. *See* 67 Fed. Reg. 53, 182 (Aug. 14, 2002).

The HIPAA regulations are the first comprehensive federal rules on health privacy and are promulgated under 45 C.F.R. parts 160 through 164.

ENTITIES SUBJECT TO THE REGULATIONS

Covered Entities. The regulations do not apply to all people or entities that have access to an individual's health information. Rather, they apply "to health plans, health care clearinghouses, and health care providers." 45 C.F.R. § 160.102. Health care plans, clearinghouses, and providers that are covered by the regulation are called "covered entities."

A "health care provider" is a "provider of medical or health services . . . and any other person or organization who furnishes, bills, or is paid for health care in the normal course of business." § 160.103. Examples of health care providers are physicians, hospitals, and pharmacists.

---

[8] *See id.*

A "health plan" is "an individual or group plan that provides, or pays the cost of, medical care" §160.103. This definition encompasses health insurers and HMOs.

A "health care clearinghouse" is a public or private entity that processes health information into various formats — either into a standard format or into specialized formats for the needs of specific entities. §160.103.

Electronic Processing. There is one other important consideration for determining the applicability of the HIPAA regulations — whether the person or entity processes and transmits health information electronically in a "standard" format as described in the HIPAA statute. The HIPAA statute was passed in order to standardize the format of the way health care information is transmitted, and only those entities using that format are covered under the regulations. As is stated in a report of the Pew Internet and American Life Project:

> If a person or an organization is a "health care provider" under the regulation, the next question to ask is whether it engages in the type of "standard transactions" that will bring it within the scope of the privacy rule. Since the intent of the administrative simplification provisions of HIPAA (including the privacy rule) is to simplify the processing of health insurance claims, the privacy rule applies only to providers who conduct insurance related transactions. Some of the electronic transaction that trigger application of HIPAA to a provider include: submitting health claims or equivalent information related to physician-patient interactions; determining eligibility for a health plan; receiving health care payment and remittance advice; and receiving referral certification and authorization. . . .
>
> In a very general sense, the question can be boiled down to: "Does the provider accept health insurance (including Medicaid) or participate in an HMO?"[9]

Hybrid Entities. Many entities provide a variety of products and services, only some of which pertain to health care. These entities are called "hybrid entities." §164.504. An example of a hybrid entity is an employer that provides health care or a large company that has a division or subsidiary that provides health care or health insurance. Hybrid entities are less stringently regulated than covered entities. With a hybrid entity, the entity as a whole does not have to comply with the regulations — only the component that is actually performing the health care functions must comply. To address the danger that health information will spread beyond the health care component of a hybrid entity, the regulations require that firewalls be erected to protect against improper uses or disclosures within the entity. *See* §164.504(c)(2).

Under the initial rule, only when the entity's primary mission was not health care related could it be deemed a hybrid rather than a covered entity. Under the revised rule proposed by the Bush Administration, any entity that

---

[9] Pew Internet & American Life Project, *Exposed Online: Why the New Federal Health Privacy Regulation Doesn't Offer Much Protection to Internet Users* 13 (Nov. 2001).

provides a mixture of health care and other functions can elect to be a hybrid rather than a covered entity.

TYPE OF INFORMATION AND RECORDS COVERED

Individually Identifiable Health Information. The proposed regulations only applied to electronic records, not paper records. In the final rule, HHS extended the regulations to all individually identifiable health information in any form, electronic or nonelectronic. The information covered by the regulations is called "protected health information" and it generally consists of "individually identifiable health information." Under § 160.103, such information was defined as follows:

> *Individually identifiable health information* is information that is a subset of health information, including demographic information collected from an individual, and:
>> (1) Is created or received by a health care provider, health plan, employer, or health care clearinghouse; and
>> (2) Relates to the past, present, or future physical or mental health or condition of an individual; the provision of health care to an individual; or the past, present, or future payment for the provision of health care to an individual; and
>>> (i) That identifies the individual; or
>>> (ii) With respect to which there is a reasonable basis to believe the information can be used to identify the individual.

De-Identified Information. Under 164.502(d)(2), if health information is "de-identified" then it is not considered to be individually identifiable health information and will not be subject to many of the restrictions of the regulation. De-identification does not need to be permanent, but if information is re-identified, then it becomes subject to the regulations.

Education and Employment Records. The Bush Administration revised the regulation to exclude individually identifiable health information in education records and employment records. Such data is not covered by the regulations. § 164.501.

PRIVACY PROTECTIONS

Consent. Under the original regulations crafted by the Clinton Administration, covered entities had to obtain a general "consent" from the individual in order to use or disclose protected health information about the individual for treatment, payment, and health care operations. The Bush Administration revised the regulations to eliminate the requirement of consent. Entities may voluntarily obtain the individual's consent for the use or disclose protected health information about the individual for treatment, payment, and health care operations—but entities no longer have to do so. § 164.502.

Authorization. Covered health care providers must obtain the permission of the individual (subject to certain exceptions) in order to use or disclose protected health information in certain ways. There are two types of permission under the regulations: (1) "consent" and (2) "authorization." Put simply, the terms of a "consent" are less detailed than an "authorization." An "authorization" requires the following: (1) a "description of the information to be used or disclosed that identifies the information in a specific and meaningful fashion"; (2) who is authorized to make the requested use or disclosure; (3) to whom the use or disclosure will be made; (4) the purpose of the requested use or disclosure; (5) when the authorization will expire; (6) the authorizing individual's signature. § 164.508(c)(1). The authorization must place the individual on notice of: (1) her right to revoke the authorization in writing; (2) the rules regarding the conditioning of treatment on the authorization (discussed below); (3) "[t]he potential for information disclosed pursuant to the authorization to be subject to redisclosure by the recipient and no longer be protected by this rule." § 164.508(c)(2).

Health care providers can refuse services if an individual refuses to consent; providers cannot do so if an individual refuses to authorize. A "covered entity may not condition the provision to an individual of treatment, payment, enrollment in the health plan, or eligibility for benefits on the provision of an authorization." § 164.508(b)(4). There are a number of exceptions to this rule. First, treatment can be conditioned on the provision of research-related disclosure. Second, treatment can be conditioned if authorization is necessary to determine whether the individual is eligible for benefits or enrollment under a health plan, and for underwriting or risk rating determinations (this does not include psychotherapy notes). Third, payment of a claim or benefits can be conditioned upon authorization if the disclosure is necessary to determine a payment and is not for the use or disclosure of psychotherapy notes.

Generally, authorization is required for all uses and disclosures beyond those for treatment, payment, or health care operations. § 164.508(a).

Marketing. Authorization is required for the use and disclosure of health data for the marketing of items and services. If a covered entity wants to provide a person's health data to a third party who wants to use it to peddle goods or services, it must first obtain that person's authorization. Authorization is required even if the marketing is done by the covered entity or one of its divisions. However, the Bush Administration revised the regulations to narrow the definition of what constitutes "marketing." Excluded from the definition of "marketing" is the marketing of health-related services and products provided by the covered entity. § 164.501. In other words, a covered entity can use an individual's health information without authorization to try to sell to her its own different products, treatments, and services — so long as they are health care related. Since these activities are not defined as "marketing," the individual cannot opt out or remove herself from the mailing list.

Other Uses and Disclosures Requiring Authorization. Other uses of data requiring authorization include, among other things, the disclosure to an employer for use in making employment decisions and the use of the information for fund-raising.

Psychotherapy Notes. Authorization is required "for any use or disclosure of psychotherapy notes" even if that use or disclosure is for treatment, payment, and health care operations. § 164.508. According to the regulation commentary, the reason why psychotherapy notes require authorization is because "psychotherapy notes do not include information that covered entities typically need for treatment, payment, or other types of health care operations."

The Right to Request Restrictions. An individual retains the right to request restrictions on the use or disclosure of health information by all covered entities. § 164.502(c). Covered entities must permit individuals to make such requests. § 164.522(a). If an entity agrees to an individual's request, it must adhere to its agreement. However, an entity is not required to agree to a restriction. § 164.522(a).

In emergency treatment situations, an entity can break this agreement, but if it discloses health information to other health care providers, it must request that the provider not further use or disclose the information. § 164.522(a).

Accommodation of Communication Preferences. Under § 164.502(h), individuals have the right to require covered providers to accommodate their requests about how providers communicate with the individual. According to the regulation's commentary,

> [A]n individual who does not want his or her family members to know about a certain treatment may request that the provider communicate with the individual at his or her place of employment, or to send communications to a designated address. Covered providers must accommodate the request unless it is unreasonable.

Minimum Necessary Uses and Disclosures. When using or disclosing protected health information, covered entities must "make reasonable efforts to limit protected health information to the minimum necessary" to accomplish their goal. § 164.502(b)(1). This provision does not apply to disclosures to health care providers for treatment or to disclosures to the individual.

Under § 164.502(e)(1), a covered entity may disclose protected health information to a "business associate" so long as the "covered entity obtains satisfactory assurance that the business associate will appropriately safeguard the information."

Notice of Privacy Practices. Under § 164.520, covered entities must produce a notice of privacy practices.

Right of Access. Individuals have a right to access any protected health information that is used in whole or in part to make decisions about the individual.

EXCEPTIONS

Nonauthorized Uses and Disclosures. The regulation provides for a number of situations where health information can be used or disclosed without either authorization: (1) required by law; (2) for public health activities; (3) regarding victims of abuse, neglect, or domestic violence (under certain circumstances); (4) for health oversight activities; (5) for judicial and administrative proceedings; (6) for law enforcement purposes; (7) to avert a serious threat to health or safety; and (8) for specialized government functions; for workers' compensation. § 164.512.

Disclosure to Law Enforcement Officials. Pursuant to § 164.512(f), health information may be disclosed to law enforcement officials without consent or authorization if required by a court order, warrant, or subpoena. § 164.512(f)(1). However, health information may also be disclosed "in response to a law enforcement official's request for such information for the purpose of identifying or locating a suspect, fugitive, material witness, or missing person." *Id.*

COMPLIANCE AND ENFORCEMENT

Privacy Officials and Contact Persons. Covered entities must designate an individual as the covered entity's privacy official, responsible for the implementation and development of the entity's privacy policies and procedures. A person must be designated as a contact person to receive complaints about privacy and provide information about the matters covered by the entity's notice. The contact person can be the same person as the privacy official.

Enforcement. The regulations provide for criminal penalties for wrongful disclosures and civil damages of up to $25,000. Certain wrongful disclosures of medical data can also result in up to ten years' imprisonment and/or a $250,000 fine. However, the HIPAA regulations do not permit individuals a private cause of action.

EFFECT ON EXISTING LAW

State Law Preemption. HIPAA provides a baseline of protections but still allows states to pass more stringent requirements. § 160.203(b).

NOTES & QUESTIONS

1. *The Application of HIPAA Regulations.* Consider the following argument from Paul Schwartz:

> . . . [O]ne of the most critical aspects of [*Doe v. SEPTA*] . . . concerns something that is absent from it. In this decision, the Third Circuit does not discuss any privacy statute or regulation that SEPTA might or might not have violated when its officials eagerly pored over its workers' prescription records and explored the health implications of these data. A reason exists for this

judicial silence: in the United States, no comprehensive regulation applies to the use of health care information, and no law currently forbids the underlying behavior in SEPTA. This employer acted as if the files developed by the health care plan it sponsored were its property, over which the employer had a complete right of access.

SEPTA is also important for its implications about self-insurance and privacy. Due to this agency's direct payment of its employees' medical bills, SEPTA viewed itself as having a special need to scrutinize patient information. The consequences of self-insurance for health care privacy are even more significant in the private sector because of the Employment Retirement Income Security Act (ERISA), which preempts state regulation of private companies that provide health care benefits through self-insurance. Due to weak federal privacy protection, ERISA has thereby created a considerable loophole for self-insured companies. A private company that opts for self-insurance will be subject neither to constitutional requirements for informational privacy (due to the lack of state action) nor to any existing state regulations (due to ERISA preemption).[10]

Suppose the facts of *Doe v. SEPTA* occurred after the HIPAA regulations were promulgated. Would Doe have a remedy? Do the HIPAA regulations address Paul Schwartz's concern with *Doe v. SEPTA*?

2. *Law Enforcement Access.* Section 164.512(f) has come under significant criticism by commentators in that it too broadly allows law enforcement officials to have access to health information. Do you agree?

3. *HIPAA and Health-Related Web Sites.* A study by the Pew Internet and American Life Project in the year 2000 concluded that over 65 million Americans sought health information on the Internet.[11] A report by the same organization in November 2001 concluded that "a significant portion of activities at health-related Web sites are not covered [by the HIPAA regulations] for several reasons. The major reason is that a great many Web sites are run by organizations that are not 'covered entities.'"[12] The report further stated:

> Most health-related Web sites engage in a number of different activities, from providing general educational health information to allowing patients to review test results online. Only some of these activities will be protected by the privacy regulations. For example, drugstore.com sells both drugs pursuant to a prescription and over-the-counter products. While information related to the prescription drug will be covered by the privacy regulation, information related to the over-the-counter product will not. The privacy rule

---

[10] Paul Schwartz, *Privacy and the Economics of Health Care Information*, 76 Tex. L. Rev. 1, 46-47 (1997). For more background about HIPAA, see Lawrence O. Gostin & James G. Hodge, Jr., *Personal Privacy and Common Goods: A Framework for Balancing Under the National Health Information Privacy Rule*, 86 Minn. L. Rev. 1439 (2002); Peter D. Jacobson, *Medical Records and HIPAA: Is it Too Late to Protect Privacy?*, 86 Minn. L. Rev. 1497 (2002); Peter P. Swire & Lauren B. Steinfeld, *Security and Privacy After September 11: The Health Care Example*, 86 Minn. L. Rev. 1515 (2002); Mike Hatch, *HIPAA: Commercial Interests Win Round Two*, 86 Minn. L. Rev. 1481 (2002).

[11] *The Online Health Care Revolution: How the Web Helps Americans Take Better Care of Themselves*, Pew Internet & American Life Project (Nov. 2000).

[12] Pew Internet & American Life Project, *Exposed Online: Why the New Federal Health Privacy Regulation Doesn't Offer Much Protection to Internet Users* 7 (Nov. 2001).

covers only identifiable information related to "health care." This term does not include selling or distributing non-prescription health care items. . . .

Many Web sites offer a "health assessment" feature where users may enter all sorts of information from height and weight to drug and alcohol use. . . . For example, HealthStatus.com offers free general health assessments as well as disease specific assessments to determine an individual's risk for some of the leading causes of death. . . . [B]ecause HealthStatus.com does not accept any insurance it will not be covered by the privacy rule. . . .[13]

B. PHYSICIAN/PSYCHOTHERAPIST-PATIENT CONFIDENTIALITY

1. PROFESSIONAL ETHICS AND EVIDENTIARY PRIVILEGES

(a) Ethical Rules

OATH AND LAW OF HIPPOCRATES

(circa 400 B.C.)

Whatever, in connection with my professional service, or not in connection with it, I see or hear, in the life of men, which ought not to be spoken of abroad, I will not divulge, as reckoning that all such should be kept secret.

CURRENT OPINIONS OF THE JUDICIAL COUNCIL
OF THE AMERICAN MEDICAL ASSOCIATION CANON 5.05

. . . [T]he information disclosed to a physician during the course of the relationship between physician and patient is confidential to the greatest possible degree. . . . The physician should not reveal confidential communications or information without the express consent of the patient, unless required to do so by law.

(b) Evidentiary Privileges

EVIDENTIARY PRIVILEGES AND THE
PHYSICIAN-PATIENT PRIVILEGE

An evidentiary privilege confers on an individual the right to refuse to testify or reveal facts about certain matters or the right to prevent another from doing so. Evidentiary privileges apply to almost all governmental proceedings, particularly judicial proceedings. Privileges permit the suppression of truthful and relevant evidence. For example, a client may tell her attorney certain confidential inculpatory information. The attorney-client privilege protects the

---

[13]*Id.* at 14, 17.

confidentiality of that communication; the attorney cannot be forced to testify as to that information.

There are a number of recognized privileges. The central privilege is the attorney-client privilege. In *Upjohn Co. v. United States*, 449 U.S. 383 (1981), the Supreme Court explained the rationale behind this privilege:

> The attorney-client privilege is the oldest of the privileges for confidential communications known to the common law. Its purpose is to encourage full and frank communication between attorneys and their clients and thereby promote broader public interests in the observance of law and administration of justice. The privilege recognizes that sound legal advice or advocacy serves public ends and that such advice or advocacy depends upon the lawyer's being fully informed by the client. As we stated last Term in *Trammel v. United States*, "The lawyer-client privilege rests on the need for the advocate and counselor to know all that relates to the client's reasons for seeking representation if the professional mission is to be carried out." And in *Fisher v. United States*, we recognized the purpose of the privilege to be "to encourage clients to make full disclosure to their attorneys."

Privileges protect only certain confidential relationships. Some recognized privileges include the (1) spousal privilege whereby a person can refuse to testify against his or her spouse in a criminal case; (2) spousal privilege in preventing one's spouse or former spouse from disclosing marital communications in criminal or civil cases; (3) accountant-client privilege; (4) priest-penitent privilege, whereby a person can prevent the disclosure of confidential communications made when seeking spiritual advice from his or her clergy member; (5) physician-patient privilege; (6) voter privilege, whereby a person can refuse to testify as to how he or she voted in any political election; (7) journalist privilege where journalists can refuse to divulge information sources; and (8) executive privilege, permitting the President of the United States from divulging secrets necessary to the carrying out of his or her constitutional functions. Not all of these privileges are recognized in every state or in the federal courts. Further, the precise contours of each privilege sometimes vary from state to state.

Not all confidential relationships are protected by privileges. Although spousal privileges are widely recognized, the vast majority of jurisdictions do not recognize a parent-child privilege.

Privileges protect communications by both parties to a confidential relationship. Thus, with regard to the physician-patient privilege, statements made by the holder of the privilege (the patient) as well as by the physician to the patient are privileged.

The holder of the privilege may waive the privilege, but the professional remains bound by the privilege and is not permitted to waive it without the holder's consent. It is well-settled that a voluntary knowing disclosure waives a privilege. *See Gray v. Bicknell*, 86 F.3d 1472, 1482 (8th Cir. 1996). However, courts are split as to whether inadvertent disclosures waive the privilege. *See, e.g., Georgetown Manor, Inc. v. Ethan Allen, Inc.*, 753 F. Supp. 936 (S.D. Fla. 1991) (inadvertent disclosure does not waive the privilege); *In re Sealed Case*, 877 F.2d 976 (D.C. Cir. 1989) (inadvertent disclosure waives the privilege); *Gray v. Bicknell*, 86 F.3d 1472, 1484 (8th Cir. 1996) (inadvertent disclosure sometimes waives the privilege based on application of a five-factor test).

In certain circumstances the privilege does not apply. For example, if a patient sues a physician or a client sues an attorney, the physician or attorney can testify as to confidential matters at issue in the lawsuit. Another limitation is the crime-fraud exception, which provides that if the communication is made in furtherance of a crime, fraud, or other misconduct, then it is not privileged. *See United States v. Zolin*, 491 U.S. 554 (1989).

The physician-patient privilege, unlike certain other privileges such as the attorney-client privilege and priest-penitent privilege, was not recognized at common law. However, a majority of states have established a physician-patient privilege.[14] States make exceptions in the physician-patient privilege for the reporting of certain diseases or injuries that implicate public health and safety.

JAFFEE V. REDMOND

518 U.S. 1 (1996)

STEVENS, J. . . . Petitioner is the administrator of the estate of Ricky Allen. Respondents are Mary Lu Redmond, a former police officer, and the Village of Hoffman Estates, Illinois, her employer during the time that she served on the police force. Petitioner commenced this action against respondents after Redmond shot and killed Allen while on patrol duty.

On June 27, 1991, Redmond was the first officer to respond to a "fight in progress" call at an apartment complex. As she arrived at the scene, two of Allen's sisters ran toward her squad car, waving their arms and shouting that there had been a stabbing in one of the apartments. Redmond testified at trial that she relayed this information to her dispatcher and requested an ambulance. She then exited her car and walked toward the apartment building. Before Redmond reached the building, several men ran out, one waving a pipe. When the men ignored her order to get on the ground, Redmond drew her service revolver. Two other men then burst out of the building, one, Ricky Allen, chasing the other. According to Redmond, Allen was brandishing a butcher knife and disregarded her repeated commands to drop the weapon. Redmond shot Allen when she believed he was about to stab the man he was chasing. Allen died at the scene. Redmond testified that before other officers arrived to provide support, "people came pouring out of the buildings," and a threatening confrontation between her and the crowd ensued.

Petitioner filed suit in Federal District Court alleging that Redmond had violated Allen's constitutional rights by using excessive force during the encounter at the apartment complex. The complaint sought damages under Rev. Stat. § 1979, 42 U.S.C. § 1983, and the Illinois wrongful-death statute. At trial, petitioner presented testimony from members of Allen's family that conflicted with Redmond's version of the incident in several important respects. They testified, for example, that Redmond drew her gun before exiting her squad car and that Allen was unarmed when he emerged from the apartment building.

---

[14] *See* Glen Weissenberger, *Federal Evidence* § 501.8 (1996).

During pretrial discovery petitioner learned that after the shooting Redmond had participated in about 50 counseling sessions with Karen Beyer, a clinical social worker licensed by the State of Illinois and employed at that time by the Village of Hoffman Estates. Petitioner sought access to Beyer's notes concerning the sessions for use in cross-examining Redmond. Respondents vigorously resisted the discovery. They asserted that the contents of the conversations between Beyer and Redmond were protected against involuntary disclosure by a psychotherapist-patient privilege. The district judge rejected this argument. Neither Beyer nor Redmond, however, complied with his order to disclose the contents of Beyer's notes. At depositions and on the witness stand both either refused to answer certain questions or professed an inability to recall details of their conversations.

In his instructions at the end of the trial, the judge advised the jury that the refusal to turn over Beyer's notes had no "legal justification" and that the jury could therefore presume that the contents of the notes would have been unfavorable to respondents. The jury awarded petitioner $45,000 on the federal claim and $500,000 on her state-law claim. . . .

Rule 501 of the Federal Rules of Evidence authorizes federal courts to define new privileges by interpreting "common law principles . . . in the light of reason and experience." The authors of the Rule borrowed this phrase from our opinion in *Wolfle v. United States*, 291 U.S. 7 (1934), which in turn referred to the oft-repeated observation that "the common law is not immutable but flexible, and by its own principles adapts itself to varying conditions." The Senate Report accompanying the 1975 adoption of the Rules indicates that Rule 501 "should be understood as reflecting the view that the recognition of a privilege based on a confidential relationship . . . should be determined on a case-by-case basis." The Rule thus did not freeze the law governing the privileges of witnesses in federal trials at a particular point in our history, but rather directed federal courts to "continue the evolutionary development of testimonial privileges."

The common-law principles underlying the recognition of testimonial privileges can be stated simply. "'For more than three centuries it has now been recognized as a fundamental maxim that the public . . . has a right to every man's evidence. When we come to examine the various claims of exemption, we start with the primary assumption that there is a general duty to give what testimony one is capable of giving, and that any exemptions which may exist are distinctly exceptional, being so many derogations from a positive general rule.'" Exceptions from the general rule disfavoring testimonial privileges may be justified, however, by a "'public good transcending the normally predominant principle of utilizing all rational means for ascertaining truth.'"

Guided by these principles, the question we address today is whether a privilege protecting confidential communications between a psychotherapist and her patient "promotes sufficiently important interests to outweigh the need for probative evidence. . . ." Both "reason and experience" persuade us that it does. . . .

Like the spousal and attorney-client privileges, the psychotherapist-patient privilege is "rooted in the imperative need for confidence and trust." Treatment by a physician for physical ailments can often proceed successfully on the basis of a physical examination, objective information supplied by the patient, and the results of diagnostic tests. Effective psychotherapy, by contrast, depends upon an atmosphere of confidence and trust in which the patient is willing to make a frank and complete disclosure of facts, emotions, memories, and fears. Because of the sensitive nature of the problems for which individuals consult psychotherapists, disclosure of confidential communications made during counseling sessions may cause embarrassment or disgrace. For this reason, the mere possibility of disclosure may impede development of the confidential relationship necessary for successful treatment. . . . By protecting confidential communications between a psychotherapist and her patient from involuntary disclosure, the proposed privilege thus serves important private interests.

Our cases make clear that an asserted privilege must also "serv[e] public ends." Thus, the purpose of the attorney-client privilege is to "encourage full and frank communication between attorneys and their clients and thereby promote broader public interests in the observance of law and administration of justice." And the spousal privilege . . . is justified because it "furthers the important public interest in marital harmony." The psychotherapist privilege serves the public interest by facilitating the provision of appropriate treatment for individuals suffering the effects of a mental or emotional problem. The mental health of our citizenry, no less than its physical health, is a public good of transcendent importance.

In contrast to the significant public and private interests supporting recognition of the privilege, the likely evidentiary benefit that would result from the denial of the privilege is modest. If the privilege were rejected, confidential conversations between psychotherapists and their patients would surely be chilled, particularly when it is obvious that the circumstances that give rise to the need for treatment will probably result in litigation. Without a privilege, much of the desirable evidence to which litigants such as petitioner seek access — for example, admissions against interest by a party — is unlikely to come into being. This unspoken "evidence" will therefore serve no greater truth-seeking function than if it had been spoken and privileged.

That it is appropriate for the federal courts to recognize a psychotherapist privilege under Rule 501 is confirmed by the fact that all 50 States and the District of Columbia have enacted into law some form of psychotherapist privilege. We have previously observed that the policy decisions of the States bear on the question whether federal courts should recognize a new privilege or amend the coverage of an existing one. Because state legislatures are fully aware of the need to protect the integrity of the factfinding functions of their courts, the existence of a consensus among the States indicates that "reason and experience" support recognition of the privilege. In addition, given the importance of the patient's understanding that her communications with her therapist will not be publicly disclosed, any State's promise of confidentiality would have little value if the patient were aware that the privilege would not be honored in a federal court. Denial of the federal privilege therefore would frustrate the purposes of the state legislation that was enacted to foster these confidential communications. . . .

. . . [W]e hold that confidential communications between a licensed psychotherapist and her patients in the course of diagnosis or treatment are protected from compelled disclosure under Rule 501 of the Federal Rules of Evidence. . . .

. . . The reasons for recognizing a privilege for treatment by psychiatrists and psychologists apply with equal force to treatment by a clinical social worker such as Karen Beyer. Today, social workers provide a significant amount of mental health treatment. Their clients often include the poor and those of modest means who could not afford the assistance of a psychiatrist or psychologist, but whose counseling sessions serve the same public goals. Perhaps in recognition of these circumstances, the vast majority of States explicitly extend a testimonial privilege to licensed social workers. We therefore agree with the Court of Appeals that "[d]rawing a distinction between the counseling provided by costly psychotherapists and the counseling provided by more readily accessible social workers serves no discernible public purpose." . . .

SCALIA, J. joined by REHNQUIST, C. J. dissenting. . . . The Court has discussed at some length the benefit that will be purchased by creation of the evidentiary privilege in this case: the encouragement of psychoanalytic counseling. It has not mentioned the purchase price: occasional injustice. That is the cost of every rule which excludes reliable and probative evidence — or at least every one categorical enough to achieve its announced policy objective. . . . For the rule proposed here, the victim is more likely to be some individual who is prevented from proving a valid claim — or (worse still) prevented from establishing a valid defense. The latter is particularly unpalatable for those who love justice, because it causes the courts of law not merely to let stand a wrong, but to become themselves the instruments of wrong. . . .

. . . Effective psychotherapy undoubtedly is beneficial to individuals with mental problems, and surely serves some larger social interest in maintaining a mentally stable society. But merely mentioning these values does not answer the critical question: Are they of such importance, and is the contribution of psychotherapy to them so distinctive, and is the application of normal evidentiary rules so destructive to psychotherapy, as to justify making our federal courts occasional instruments of injustice? On that central question I find the Court's analysis insufficiently convincing to satisfy the high standard we have set for rules that "are in derogation of the search for truth."

When is it, one must wonder, that the psychotherapist came to play such an indispensable role in the maintenance of the citizenry's mental health? For most of history, men and women have worked out their difficulties by talking to, inter alios, parents, siblings, best friends, and bartenders — none of whom was awarded a privilege against testifying in court. Ask the average citizen: Would your mental health be more significantly impaired by preventing you from seeing a psychotherapist, or by preventing you from getting advice from your mom? I have little doubt what the answer would be. Yet there is no mother-child privilege. . . .

Even where it is certain that absence of the psychotherapist privilege will inhibit disclosure of the information, it is not clear to me that that is an unacceptable state of affairs. Let us assume the very worst in the circumstances of the present case: that to be truthful about what was troubling her, the police officer who sought counseling would have to confess that she shot without reason, and wounded an innocent man. . . . [There is no] reason why she should be enabled to deny her guilt in the criminal trial — or in a civil trial for negligence — while yet obtaining the benefits of psychotherapy by confessing guilt to a social worker who cannot testify. It seems to me entirely fair to say that if she wishes the benefits of telling the truth she must also accept the adverse consequences. . . .

The Court confidently asserts that not much truth-finding capacity would be destroyed by the privilege anyway, since "[w]ithout a privilege, much of the desirable evidence to which litigants such as petitioner seek access . . . is unlikely to come into being." If that is so, how come psychotherapy got to be a thriving practice before the "psychotherapist privilege" was invented? Were the patients paying money to lie to their analysts all those years? . . .

. . . The Court's conclusion that a social-worker psychotherapeutic privilege deserves recognition is even less persuasive. . . .

. . . A licensed psychiatrist or psychologist is an expert in psychotherapy — and that may suffice (though I think it not so clear that this Court should make the judgment) to justify the use of extraordinary means to encourage counseling with him, as opposed to counseling with one's rabbi, minister, family, or friends. One must presume that a social worker does not bring this greatly heightened degree of skill to bear, which is alone a reason for not encouraging that consultation as generously. Does a social worker bring to bear at least a significantly heightened degree of skill — more than a minister or rabbi, for example? I have no idea, and neither does the Court. The social worker in the present case, Karen Beyer, was a "licensed clinical social worker" in Illinois, a job title whose training requirements consist of a "master's degree in social work from an approved program," and "3,000 hours of satisfactory, supervised clinical professional experience." Ill. Comp. Stat., ch. 225, § 20/9 (1994). It is not clear that the degree in social work requires any training in psychotherapy. . . .

. . . [A]lthough the Court is technically correct that "the vast majority of States explicitly extend a testimonial privilege to licensed social workers," that uniformity exists only at the most superficial level. No State has adopted the privilege without restriction; the nature of the restrictions varies enormously from jurisdiction to jurisdiction; and 10 States . . . effectively reject the privilege entirely. It is fair to say that there is scant national consensus even as to the propriety of a social-worker psychotherapist privilege, and none whatever as to its appropriate scope. In other words, the state laws to which the Court appeals for support demonstrate most convincingly that adoption of a social-worker psychotherapist privilege is a job for Congress. . . .

NOTES & QUESTIONS

1. Most people are unaware of evidence law when speaking with their therapist or doctor. Are privileges necessary to encourage frank disclosures by patients to therapists?
2. Would Justice Scalia's reasoning apply to the attorney-client privilege?

3. Are there any limits to the privilege? In a footnote the Court indicated that there might be certain limits:

> Although it would be premature to speculate about most future developments in the federal psychotherapist privilege, we do not doubt that there are situations in which the privilege must give way, for example, if a serious threat of harm to the patient or to others can be averted only by means of a disclosure by the therapist.

2. TORT LIABILITY FOR DISCLOSURE OF PATIENT INFORMATION

McCormick v. England

494 S.E.2d 431 (S.C. Ct. App. 1997)

ANDERSON, J. . . . Dr. England was the family physician for McCormick, her former husband, and their children. McCormick and her husband became involved in a divorce action in which custody of the children was at issue. In support of his Motion for Emergency Relief and a Restraining Order, McCormick's husband submitted . . . letters to the family court regarding McCormick's emotional status. . . . [One] letter was prepared by Dr. England and was addressed "To Whom It May Concern." In his letter, Dr. England diagnosed McCormick as suffering from "major depression and alcoholism, acute and chronic." Further, Dr. England stated the children had experienced school difficulties due to the family discord caused by McCormick's drinking. He stated it was his medical opinion that McCormick was "a danger to herself and to her family with her substance abuse and major depressive symptoms," and concluded that she required hospitalization. There is no indication in the record that the letter was prepared under court order. [Among other things, McCormick sued for public disclosure of private facts and breach of confidentiality. The trial court dismissed her breach of confidentiality claim, stating that "It is well known that South Carolina does not recognize the physician-patient privilege at common law." McCormick appeals.] . . .

Whether a separate tort action for a physician's breach of a duty of confidentiality exists under the common law is a novel issue in this state. Dr. England contends South Carolina courts have previously ruled that no duty of confidentiality exists between a physician and patient; therefore, there can be no action for its breach. . . .

"At common law neither the patient nor the physician has the privilege to refuse to *disclose in court* a communication of one to the other, nor does either have a privilege that the communication not be disclosed to a third person." Although many states have statutorily created a "physician-patient testimonial privilege," South Carolina has not enacted a similar statute and does not recognize the physician-patient privilege. However, the absence of a testimonial privilege prohibiting certain in-court disclosures is not determinative of our issue because this evidentiary privilege is distinguishable from a duty of confidentiality. As our Supreme Court recently observed in *South Carolina State Board of Medical Examiners v. Hedgepath,* 480 S.E.2d 724 (S.C. 1997): "The terms 'privilege' and 'confidences' are not synonymous, and a professional's duty to maintain his client's confidences is independent of the issue whether he can be legally compelled to reveal some or all of those confidences, that is, whether those communications are privileged." . . .

A person who lacks medical training usually must disclose much information to his or her physician which may have a bearing upon diagnosis and treatment. Such disclosures are not totally voluntary; therefore, in order to obtain cooperation, it is expected that the physician will keep such information confidential. "Being a fiduciary relationship, mutual trust and confidence are essential."

The belief that physicians should respect the confidences revealed by their patients in the course of treatment is a concept that has its genesis in the Hippocratic Oath, which states in pertinent part: "Whatever, in connection with my professional practice, or not in connection with it, I see or hear, in the life of men, which ought not to be spoken of abroad, I will not divulge as reckoning that all such should be kept secret."

The modern trend recognizes that the confidentiality of the physician-patient relationship is an interest worth protecting. A majority of the jurisdictions faced with the issue have recognized a cause of action against a physician for the unauthorized disclosure of confidential information unless the disclosure is compelled by law or is in the patient's interest or the public interest.

In the absence of express legislation, courts have found the basis for a right of action for wrongful disclosure in four main sources: (1) state physician licensing statutes, (2) evidentiary rules and privileged communication statutes which prohibit a physician from testifying in judicial proceedings, (3) common law principles of trust, and (4) the Hippocratic Oath and principles of medical ethics which proscribe the revelation of patient confidences. The jurisdictions that recognize the duty of confidentiality have relied on various theories for the cause of action, including invasion of privacy, breach of implied contract, medical malpractice, and breach of a fiduciary duty or a duty of confidentiality. . . .

We find the reasoning of the cases from other jurisdictions persuasive on this issue and today we join the majority and hold that an actionable tort lies for a physician's breach of the duty to maintain the confidences of his or her patient in the absence of a compelling public interest or other justification for the disclosure. . . .

[Breach of confidentiality is a distinct tort from the tort of public disclosure of private facts.] Invasion of privacy consists of the public disclosure of private facts about the plaintiff, and the gravamen of the tort is publicity as opposed to mere publication. The defendant must intentionally reveal facts which are of no legitimate public interest, as there is no right of privacy in public matters. In addition, the disclosure must be such as would be highly offensive and likely to cause serious mental injury to a person of ordinary sensibilities.

Thus, an invasion of privacy claim narrowly proscribes the conduct to that which is "highly offensive" and "likely to cause serious mental injury." This standard is not consistent with the duty attaching to a confidential relationship because it focuses on the *content,* rather than the *source* of the information. The unauthorized revelation of confidential medical information should be protected without regard to the degree of its offensiveness. The privacy standard would not protect information that happens to be very distressing to a particular patient, even though the individual would likely not have revealed it without the expectation of confidentiality.

Further, the requirement of "publicity" is a limitation which would preclude many cases involving a breach of confidentiality. Publicity involves disclosure to the public, not just an individual or a small group. However, where the information disclosed is received in confidence, "one can imagine many cases where the greatest injury results from disclosure to a single person, such as a spouse, or to a small group, such as an insurance company resisting a claim. A confidential relationship is breached if unauthorized disclosure is made to only one person not a party to the confidence, but the right of privacy does not cover such a case." . . .

NOTES & QUESTIONS

1. *The Limits of the Breach of Confidentiality Tort.* In *Simonsen v. Swenson,* 177 N.W. 831 (Neb. 1920), a physician disclosed that the plaintiff was suffering from syphilis to the proprietor of the hotel where he was residing. Although syphilis is curable today, at the time of *Simonsen,* syphilis was viewed as a dangerous epidemic. Without treatment, the disease progresses to the nervous system, causing mental disorders. Death can result from buildup of tumor-like masses in bodily organs. The use of penicillin to treat syphilis began in the United States after World War II. This brought the epidemic under control.[15] The court, although recognizing tort liability for breach of physician confidentiality, held that the physician's disclosure was appropriate:

> No patient can expect that if his malady is found to be of a dangerously contagious nature he can still require it to be kept secret from those to whom, if there was no disclosure, such disease would be transmitted. The information given to a physician by his patient, though confidential, must, it seems to us, be given and received subject to the qualification that if the patient's disease is found to be of a dangerous and so highly contagious or infectious a nature that it will necessarily be transmitted to others unless the danger of contagion is disclosed to them, then the physician should, in that event, if no other means of protection is possible, be privileged to make so much of a disclosure to such persons as is necessary to prevent the spread of the disease. A disclosure in such case would, it follows, not be a betrayal of the confidence of the patient, since the patient must know, when he imparts the information or subjects himself to the examination, that, in the exception stated, his disease may be disclosed. . . .

---

[15] *See* Lawrence O. Gostin & James G. Hodge, Jr., *Piercing the Veil of Secrecy in HIV/AIDS and Other Sexually Transmitted Diseases: Theories of Privacy and Disclosure in Partner Notification,* 5 Duke J. of Gender L. & Pol'y 9, 16-23 (1998).

Like *Simonsen,* most courts recognizing the tort of breach of confidentiality hold that the tort is not absolute and does not apply when disclosure is required to protect the public health or when disclosure is required by statute.

2. Recall *Doe v. Borough of Barrington* (Section A, *supra*). Do doctors have greater or lesser duties to maintain the confidentiality of medical information than public officials?

HAMMONDS V. AETNA CASUALTY & SURETY CO.

243 F. Supp. 793 (D. Ohio 1965)

CONNELL, C.J. Plaintiff has complained that the defendant insurance company, without just cause, had persuaded the plaintiff's treating physician to discontinue that relationship, and, further, that the defendant induced the doctor to divulge confidential information gained through the physician-patient relationship. In particular, it is alleged that the defendant, at the behest of a prominent defense attorney, persuaded Dr. Alexander Ling, the plaintiff's treating physician, to surrender certain undisclosed confidential information for use in pending litigation against the plaintiff on the false pretext that the plaintiff was contemplating a malpractice suit against Dr. Ling. . . .

In all medical jurisprudence there are few problems which have deserved and received more concentrated attention than the protection of the personal information which a patient remits to his physician. This relationship "is one of trust and confidence. It is submitted that the best interest of the patient is served in trusting his welfare to the skill and industry of his physician." To foster the best interest of the patient and to insure a climate most favorable to a complete recovery, men of medicine have urged that patients be totally frank in their discussions with their physicians. To encourage the desired candor, men of law have formulated a strong policy of confidentiality to assure patients that only they themselves may unlock the doctor's silence in regard to those private disclosures. . . .

The defendant generously concedes that the Hippocratic Oath embodies some restriction on a doctor's right to discuss the condition of, and communications from, his patient. The Oath of Hippocrates, in so far as here pertinent, provides:

> Whatever in connection with my professional practice or not in connection with it I see or hear in the life of men which ought not to be spoken abroad I will not divulge as recommending that all such should be kept secret.

We agree with the defendant that there are some situations[16] where divulgence will insure to the benefit of the public at large or even to the patient himself, but we have no such situation before us. The plaintiff here was

---

[16] For example, where a doctor discovers that his patient is afflicted with a communicable disease, he must report that fact to proper health authorities. In Ohio he is specifically absolved by statute from any liability for such disclosure. Ohio Rev. Code § 3701.26.1. When a doctor discovers that one of the parties to a contemplated marriage has contracted a venereal disease, he may, without fear of legal ramifications, make that fact known to certain specified persons. Ohio Rev. Code § 4731.22. Some jurisdictions require that doctors report all wounds inflicted by bullet, knife, or other weapon.

engaged in litigation for an injury (which Dr. Ling was treating) allegedly sustained at the negligent hand of the Euclid-Glenville Hospital, which was represented by an attorney for whom the defendant here allegedly secured confidential information from Dr. Ling. In this adversary judicial system, with its intensity heightened by the continuing friction between insurance companies and claimants, is there no impropriety in a doctor discussing the case of his patient-plaintiff with the lawyer for the defending insurance company? Who would dare say so? . . .

It cannot be questioned that part of a doctor's duty of total care requires him to offer his medical testimony on behalf of his patient if the patient becomes involved in litigation over the injury or illness which the doctor treated. Thus, during the course of such litigation, in addition to the duty of secrecy, there arises the duty of undivided loyalty. Should a doctor breach either of these two duties, the law must afford the patient some legal recourse against such perfidy. We should not suffer a wrong without a remedy, especially when the wrong complained of involves the abuse of a fiduciary position. . . .

. . . We conclude, therefore, that ordinarily a physician receives information relating to a patient's health in a confidential capacity and should not disclose such information without the patient's consent, except where the public interest or the private interest of the patient so demands. . . .

Any time a doctor undertakes the treatment of a patient, and the consensual relationship of physician and patient is established, two jural obligations (of significance here) are simultaneously assumed by the doctor. Doctor and patient enter into a simple contract, the patient hoping that he will be cured and the doctor optimistically assuming that he will be compensated. As an implied condition of that contract, this Court is of the opinion that the doctor warrants that any confidential information gained through the relationship will not be released without the patient's permission. Almost every member of the public is aware of the promise of discretion contained in the Hippocratic Oath, and every patient has a right to rely upon this warranty of silence. The promise of secrecy is as much an express warranty as the advertisement of a commercial entrepreneur. Consequently, when a doctor breaches his duty of secrecy, he is in violation of part of his obligations under the contract.

When a patient seeks out a doctor and retains him, he must admit him to the most private part of the material domain of man. Nothing material is more important or more intimate to man than the health of his mind and body. Since the layman is unfamiliar with the road to recovery, he cannot sift the circumstances of his life and habits to determine what is information pertinent to his health. As a consequence, he must disclose all information in his consultations with his doctor—even that which is embarrassing, disgraceful or incriminating. To promote full disclosure, the medical profession extends the promise of secrecy referred to above. The candor which this promise elicits is necessary to the effective pursuit of health; there can be no reticence, no reservation, no reluctance when patients discuss their problems with their doctors. But the disclosure is certainly intended to be private. If a doctor should reveal any of these confidences, he surely effects an invasion of the privacy of his patient. We are of the opinion that the preservation of the patient's privacy is no mere ethical duty upon the part of the doctor; there is a legal duty as well. The unauthorized revelation of medical secrets, or any confidential communication given in the course of treatment, is tortious conduct which may be the basis for an action in damages. . . .

However, we are not critically concerned here solely with an alleged disclosure by a doctor since the complaint accuses Dr. Ling only of a misfeasance predicated upon misinformation and directs its plea for redress not against the doctor but against the defendant insurance company which allegedly supplied this inaccurate information. . . . As we have noted above, the patient necessarily reposes a great deal of trust not only in the skill of the physician but in his discretion as well. The introduction into the relationship of this aura of trust, and the expectation of confidentiality which results therefrom, imposes the fiduciary obligations upon the doctor. As a consequence, all reported cases dealing with this point hold that the relationship of physician and patient is a fiduciary one.

If the analogy expressed in the Court's earlier opinion (comparing the relationship of physician and patient to that of trustee and principal and comparing the confidences exchanged between doctor and patient to a trust res) is offensive to the defendant, it comes as no surprise to the medical profession. The Code of Medical Ethics itself recommends the following attitude:

> The confidences . . . should be held as a trust and should never be revealed except when imperatively required by the laws of the state. Principles of Medical Ethics of A.M.A. Ch. II, § 1 (1943).

Nor does the imposition of a trustee's duties upon a physician as a fiduciary fashion any new doctrine in American jurisprudence. By its very definition, the term "fiduciary relationship" imports the notion that "if a wrong arises, the same remedy exists against the wrongdoer on behalf of the principal as would exist against a trustee on behalf of the cestui que trust." Therefore it is readily apparent that the legal obligations of a trustee are imposed upon any person operating in a fiduciary capacity and the same principles of law participation in breaches of trust must applicable to all fiduciaries.

It also follows that the same principles of law governing third party participation in breaches of trust must also apply to one who participates in or induces the breach of any fiduciary duty. The law is settled in Ohio and elsewhere participation in breaches of trust must also apply to one who participates in or induces the breach of any fiduciary duty. The law is settled in Ohio and elsewhere that a third party who induces a breach of a trustee's duty of loyalty, or participates in such a breach, or knowingly accepts any benefit from such a breach, becomes directly liable to the aggrieved party. . . . [W]hen one induces a doctor to divulge confidential information in violation of that doctor's legal responsibility to his patient, the third party may also be held liable in damages to the patient.

NOTES & QUESTIONS

1. Upon what theory does the court locate the duty not to disclose in this case?

2. Recall the following statement in the court's opinion: "The law is settled in Ohio and elsewhere that a third party who induces a breach of a trustee's duty of loyalty, or participates in such a breach, or knowingly accepts any benefit from such a breach, becomes directly liable to the aggrieved party." Suppose a person's physician were to disclose, without the patient's consent, the patient's medical file to a journalist. The journalist, knowing that the medical file was disclosed in breach of the doctor's fiduciary duty to the patient, accepted it anyway and published details about the patient's medical condition in the newspaper. Would the patient have a cause of action against the journalist in addition to the doctor? Would your conclusion be different in light of *Bartnicki v. Vopper* (Chapter 2)?

3. In *Biddle v. Warren General Hospital*, 715 N.E.2d 518 (Ohio 1999), a law firm decided to earn extra money by making a deal to assist a hospital in determining whether unpaid patient bills could be submitted to the Social Security Administration (SSA) for payment. Under the plan, the hospital released its patient registration forms to the law firm, which would evaluate which patients could qualify for Social Security benefits and then contact those patients and urge them to apply for benefits. In this way, the hospital would be paid by the SSA for these patients. However, the hospital released the patient data to the firm without obtaining the consent of the patients. The patients brought a class action against the hospital and the firm. The court held that not only was there a viable breach of confidentiality claim against the hospital, but also the firm could be liable for inducing such a breach:

> We hold that a third party can be held liable for inducing the unauthorized, unprivileged disclosure of nonpublic medical information that a physician or hospital has learned within a physician-patient relationship. To establish liability the plaintiff must prove that: (1) the defendant knew or reasonably should have known of the existence of the physician-patient relationship; (2) the defendant intended to induce the physician to disclose information about the patient or the defendant reasonably should have anticipated that his actions would induce the physician to disclose such information; and (3) the defendant did not reasonably believe that the physician could disclose that information to the defendant without violating the duty of confidentiality that the physician owed the patient.

4. Are tort actions protecting the confidentiality of medical data sufficient to protect privacy? Consider Lawrence Gostin:

> . . . The rule of confidentiality is widely respected in law and medicine, and rightfully so. Indeed, in the past, confidentiality has worked reasonably well in safeguarding privacy. Much, if not all, of the intimate knowledge of the patient was generated within the physician-patient relationship, which was often meaningful and enduring. The patient's health record contained information primarily obtained during sessions between the physician and patient, so that the entire record was regarded as confidential. The record keepers, moreover, were the physicians themselves who took primary responsibility for the security of medical records.
>
> The rule of confidentiality does not work nearly as well in a modern information society. Health data today, in an era of electronic information gathering, is based only in small part on the physician-patient relationship.

Many therapeutic encounters in a managed care context are not with a primary care physician. Patients may see many different physicians, nonphysician specialists, nurse practitioners and other ancillary health care professionals within and outside of the health care plan. The information obtained in these encounters has uncertain protection under traditional rules of confidentiality. Focusing legal protection on a single therapeutic relationship within this information environment is an anachronistic vestige of an earlier and simpler time in medicine. The health record, moreover, contains a substantial amount of information gathered from numerous primary and secondary sources: laboratories, pharmacies, schools, public health officials, researchers, insurers, and other individuals and institutions. The health records of patients are kept not only in the office of a private physician or in a health plan, but also may be kept by government agencies, regional health database organizations, or information brokers. Databases maintained in each of these settings will be collected and transmitted electronically, reconfigured, and linked.

Rules enforcing informational privacy in health care place a duty on the entity that possesses the information. Thus, the keeper of the record — whether it is in a private physician's office, a hospital, or an HMO — holds the primary duty to maintain the confidentiality of the data. The development of electronic health care networks permitting standardized patient-based information to flow nationwide, and perhaps worldwide, means that the current privacy protection system, which focuses on requiring the institution to protect its records, needs to be reconsidered. Our past thinking assumed a paper or automated record created and protected by the provider. We must now envision a patient-based record that anyone in the system can call up on a screen. Because location has less meaning in an electronic world, protecting privacy requires attaching protection to the health record itself, rather than to the institution that generates it. . . .[17]

In contrast, Peter Winn argues that the breach of confidentiality tort might be strengthened with the new HIPAA regulations and may prove to be quite effective in providing a remedy against privacy invasions:

[A]lthough the HIPAA Privacy Rules create no federal cause of action, an analysis of the case law suggests that the Rules may well be adopted by common law courts to establish a national minimum standard for liability for breach of confidentiality under state law. . . .

With respect to the second perceived weakness of the Rules, because the breach of confidentiality tort traditionally requires that the patient be in a professional or contractual relationship with the person responsible for the wrongful disclosure, and because many harmful disclosures take place by entities such as Business Associates who are not in such a relationship, the breach of confidentiality tort has been viewed as unable to address the problems caused by the widespread dissemination of electronic health information among "downstream" users not in a relationship of confidentiality with the injured person. . . . [U]nder the developing case law, such federally required agreements with Business Associates, while ostensibly creating no liability other than between the contracting parties, are likely to facilitate the establishment of claims for breach of confidentiality against Business Asso-

---

[17] Lawrence O. Gostin, *Health Information Privacy*, 80 Cornell L. Rev. 451 (1995).

ciates by patients for misuse of their personal information in spite of the lack of a professional or contractual relationship. . . .[18]

3. TORT LIABILITY FOR FAILURE TO DISCLOSE PATIENT INFORMATION

TARASOFF V. REGENTS OF UNIVERSITY OF CALIFORNIA

551 P.2d 334 (Cal. 1976)

TOBRINER, J. On October 27, 1969, Prosenjit Poddar killed Tatiana Tarasoff. Plaintiffs, Tatiana's parents, allege that two months earlier Poddar confided his intention to kill Tatiana to Dr. Lawrence Moore, a psychologist employed by the Cowell Memorial Hospital at the University of California at Berkeley. They allege that on Moore's request, the campus police briefly detained Poddar, but released him when he appeared rational. They further claim that Dr. Harvey Powelson, Moore's superior, then directed that no further action be taken to detain Poddar. No one warned plaintiffs of Tatiana's peril.

Plaintiffs' complaints predicate liability on . . . defendants' failure to warn plaintiffs of the impending danger. . . . Defendants, in turn, assert that they owed no duty of reasonable care to Tatiana. . . .

We shall explain that defendant therapists cannot escape liability merely because Tatiana herself was not their patient. When a therapist determines, or pursuant to the standards of his profession should determine, that his patient presents a serious danger of violence to another, he incurs an obligation to use reasonable care to protect the intended victim against such danger. The discharge of this duty may require the therapist to take one or more of various steps, depending upon the nature of the case. Thus it may call for him to warn the intended victim or others likely to apprise the victim of the danger, to notify the police, or to take whatever other steps are reasonably necessary under the circumstances. . . .

. . . [O]n August 20, 1969, Poddar was a voluntary outpatient receiving therapy at Cowell Memorial Hospital. Poddar informed Moore, his therapist, that he was going to kill an unnamed girl, readily identifiable as Tatiana, when she returned home from spending the summer in Brazil. Moore, with the concurrence of Dr. Gold, who had initially examined Poddar, and Dr. Yandell, Assistant to the director of the department of psychiatry, decided that Poddar should be committed for observation in a mental hospital. Moore orally notified Officers Atkinson and Teel of the campus police that he would request commitment. He then sent a letter to Police Chief William Beall requesting the assistance of the police department in securing Poddar's confinement.

Officers Atkinson, Brownrigg, and Halleran took Poddar into custody, but, satisfied that Poddar was rational, released him on his promise to stay away from Tatiana. Powelson, director of the department of psychiatry at Cowell Memorial Hospital, then asked the police to return Moore's letter, directed that

---

[18]Peter A. Winn, *Confidentiality in Cyberspace: The HIPAA Privacy Rules and the Common Law*, 33 Rutgers L.J. 617 (2002).

all copies of the letter and notes that Moore had taken as therapist be destroyed, and "ordered no action to place Prosenjit Poddar in 72-hour treatment and evaluation facility." . . . .

. . . Poddar persuaded Tatiana's brother to share an apartment with him near Tatiana's residence; shortly after her return from Brazil, Poddar went to her residence and killed her.

Plaintiffs contend that [the defendants were negligent in not notifying them of Poddar's intent to kill Tatiana]. Defendants, however, contend that in the circumstances of the present case they owed no duty of care to Tatiana or her parents and that, in the absence of such duty, they were free to act in careless disregard of Tatiana's life and safety. . . .

. . . As a general principle, a "defendant owes a duty of care to all persons who are foreseeably endangered by his conduct, with respect to all risks which make the conduct unreasonably dangerous." As we shall explain, however, when the avoidance of foreseeable harm requires a defendant to control the conduct of another person, or to warn of such conduct, the common law has traditionally imposed liability only if the defendant bears some special relationship to the dangerous person or to the potential victim. Since the relationship between a therapist and his patient satisfies this requirement, we need not here decide whether foreseeability alone is sufficient to create a duty to exercise reasonable care to protect a potential victim of another's conduct.

Although, as we have stated above, under the common law, as a general rule, one person owed no duty to control the conduct of another, nor to warn those endangered by such conduct, the courts have carved out an exception to this rule in cases in which the defendant stands in some special relationship to either the person whose conduct needs to be controlled or in a relationship to the foreseeable victim of that conduct. Applying this exception to the present case, we note that a relationship of defendant therapists to either Tatiana or Poddar will suffice to establish a duty of care; as explained in section 315 of the Restatement Second of Torts, a duty of care may arise from either "(a) a special relation . . . between the actor and the third person which imposes a duty upon the actor to control the third person's conduct, or (b) a special relation . . . between the actor and the other which gives to the other a right of protection."

Although plaintiffs' pleadings assert no special relation between Tatiana and defendant therapists, they establish as between Poddar and defendant therapists the special relation that arises between a patient and his doctor or psychotherapist. Such a relationship may support affirmative duties for the benefit of third persons. Thus, for example, a hospital must exercise reasonable care to control the behavior of a patient which may endanger other persons. A doctor must also warn a patient if the patient's condition or medication renders certain conduct, such as driving a car, dangerous to others. . . .

. . . Decisions of other jurisdictions hold that the single relationship of a doctor to his patient is sufficient to support the duty to exercise reasonable care to protect others against dangers emanating from the patient's illness. The courts hold that a doctor is liable to persons infected by his patient if he negligently fails to diagnose a contagious disease or, having diagnosed the illness, fails to warn members of the patient's family. . . .

". . . [T]here now seems to be sufficient authority to support the conclusion that by entering into a doctor-patient relationship the therapist becomes sufficiently involved to assume some responsibility for the safety, not only of the patient himself, but also of any third person whom the doctor knows to be threatened by the patient." (Fleming & Maximov, The Patient or His Victim: The Therapist's Dilemma (1974) 62 Cal. L. Rev. 1025, 1030.)

Defendants contend, however, that imposition of a duty to exercise reasonable care to protect third persons is unworkable because therapists cannot accurately predict whether or not a patient will resort to violence. In support of this argument amicus representing the American Psychiatric Association and other professional societies cites numerous articles which indicate that therapists, in the present state of the art, are unable reliably to predict violent acts; their forecasts, amicus claims, tend consistently to overpredict violence, and indeed are more often wrong than right. Since predictions of violence are often erroneous, amicus concludes, the courts should not render rulings that predicate the liability of therapists upon the validity of such predictions.

The role of the psychiatrist, who is indeed a practitioner of medicine, and that of the psychologist who performs an allied function, are like that of the physician who must conform to the standards of the profession and who must often make diagnoses and predictions based upon such evaluations. Thus the judgment of the therapist in diagnosing emotional disorders and in predicting whether a patient presents a serious danger of violence is comparable to the judgment which doctors and professionals must regularly render under accepted rules of responsibility.

We recognize the difficulty that a therapist encounters in attempting to forecast whether a patient presents a serious danger of violence. Obviously we do not require that the therapist, in making that determination, render a perfect performance; the therapist need only exercise "that reasonable degree of skill, knowledge, and care ordinarily possessed and exercised by members of (that professional specialty) under similar circumstances." Within the broad range of reasonable practice and treatment in which professional opinion and judgment may differ, the therapist is free to exercise his or her own best judgment without liability; proof, aided by hindsight, that he or she judged wrongly is insufficient to establish negligence.

In the instant case, however, the pleadings do not raise any question as to failure of defendant therapists to predict that Poddar presented a serious danger of violence. On the contrary, the present complaints allege that defendant therapists did in fact predict that Poddar would kill, but were negligent in failing to warn. . . .

The risk that unnecessary warnings may be given is a reasonable price to pay for the lives of possible victims that may be saved. We would hesitate to hold that the therapist who is aware that his patient expects to attempt to assassinate the President of the United States would not be obligated to warn the authorities because the therapist cannot predict with accuracy that his patient will commit the crime.

Defendants further argue that free and open communication is essential to psychotherapy; that "Unless a patient . . . is assured that . . . information (revealed by him) can and will be held in utmost confidence, he will be reluctant to make the full disclosure upon which diagnosis and treatment . . . depends." The giving of a warning, defendants contend, constitutes a breach of trust which entails the revelation of confidential communications.

We recognize the public interest in supporting effective treatment of mental illness and in protecting the rights of patients to privacy, and the consequent public importance of safeguarding the confidential character of psychotherapeutic communication. Against this interest, however, we must weigh the public interest in safety from violent assault. The Legislature has undertaken the difficult task of balancing the countervailing concerns. In Evidence Code section 1014, it established a broad rule of privilege to protect confidential communications between patient and psychotherapist. In Evidence Code section 1024, the Legislature created a specific and limited exception to the psychotherapist-patient privilege: "There is no privilege . . . if the psychotherapist has reasonable cause to believe that the patient is in such mental or emotional condition as to be dangerous to himself or to the person or property of another and that disclosure of the communication is necessary to prevent the threatened danger."

We realize that the open and confidential character of psychotherapeutic dialogue encourages patients to express threats of violence, few of which are ever executed. Certainly a therapist should not be encouraged routinely to reveal such threats; such disclosures could seriously disrupt the patient's relationship with his therapist and with the persons threatened. To the contrary, the therapist's obligations to his patient require that he not disclose a confidence unless such disclosure is necessary to avert danger to others, and even then that he do so discreetly, and in a fashion that would preserve the privacy of his patient to the fullest extent compatible with the prevention of the threatened danger.

The revelation of a communication under the above circumstances is not a breach of trust or a violation of professional ethics; as stated in the Principles of Medical Ethics of the American Medical Association (1957), section 9: "A physician may not reveal the confidence entrusted to him in the course of medical attendance . . . unless he is required to do so by law or unless it becomes necessary in order to protect the welfare of the individual or of the community." We conclude that the public policy favoring protection of the confidential character of patient-psychotherapist communications must yield to the extent to which disclosure is essential to avert danger to others. The protective privilege ends where the public peril begins.

Our current crowded and computerized society compels the interdependence of its members. In this risk-infested society we can hardly tolerate the further exposure to danger that would result from a concealed knowledge of the therapist that his patient was lethal. If the exercise of reasonable care to protect the threatened victim requires the therapist to warn the endangered party or those who can reasonably be expected to notify him, we see no sufficient societal interest that would protect and justify concealment. The containment of such risks lies in the public interest. For the foregoing reasons, we find that plaintiffs [can state a cause of action against the defendants]. . . .

CLARK, J. dissenting. . . . Overwhelming policy considerations weigh against imposing a duty on psychotherapists to warn a potential victim against harm. While offering virtually no benefit to society, such a duty will frustrate psychiatric treatment, invade fundamental patient rights and increase violence.

The importance of psychiatric treatment and its need for confidentiality have been recognized by this court. "It is clearly recognized that the very practice of psychiatry vitally depends upon the reputation in the community that the psychiatrist will not tell."

Assurance of confidentiality is important for three reasons.

First, without substantial assurance of confidentiality, those requiring treatment will be deterred from seeking assistance. It remains an unfortunate fact in our society that people seeking psychiatric guidance tend to become stigmatized. Apprehension of such stigma — apparently increased by the propensity of people considering treatment to see themselves in the worst possible light — creates a well-recognized reluctance to seek aid. This reluctance is alleviated by the psychiatrist's assurance of confidentiality.

Second, the guarantee of confidentiality is essential in eliciting the full disclosure necessary for effective treatment. The psychiatric patient approaches treatment with conscious and unconscious inhibitions against revealing his innermost thoughts. "Every person, however well-motivated, has to overcome resistances to therapeutic exploration. These resistances seek support from every possible source and the possibility of disclosure would easily be employed in the service of resistance." Until a patient can trust his psychiatrist not to violate their confidential relationship, "the unconscious psychological control mechanism of repression will prevent the recall of past experiences."

Third, even if the patient fully discloses his thoughts, assurance that the confidential relationship will not be breached is necessary to maintain his trust in his psychiatrist — the very means by which treatment is effected. "(T)he essence of much psychotherapy is the contribution of trust in the external world and ultimately in the self, modeled upon the trusting relationship established during therapy." Patients will be helped only if they can form a trusting relationship with the psychiatrist. All authorities appear to agree that if the trust relationship cannot be developed because of collusive communication between the psychiatrist and others, treatment will be frustrated.

Given the importance of confidentiality to the practice of psychiatry, it becomes clear the duty to warn imposed by the majority will cripple the use and effectiveness of psychiatry. Many people, potentially violent — yet susceptible to treatment — will be deterred from seeking it; those seeking it will be inhibited from making revelations necessary to effective treatment; and, forcing the psychiatrist to violate the patient's trust will destroy the interpersonal relationship by which treatment is effected.

By imposing a duty to warn, the majority contributes to the danger to society of violence by the mentally ill and greatly increases the risk of civil commitment — the total deprivation of liberty — of those who should not be confined.[19] The impairment of treatment and risk of improper commitment resulting from the new duty to warn will not be limited to a few patients but

---

[19]The burden placed by the majority on psychiatrists may also result in the improper deprivation of two other constitutionally protected rights. First, the patient's constitutional right of privacy is obviously encroached upon by requiring the psychotherapist to disclose confidential communications. Secondly, because confidentiality is essential to effective treatment, the majority's decision also threatens the constitutionally recognized right to receive treatment.

will extend to a large number of the mentally ill. Although under existing psychiatric procedures only a relatively few receiving treatment will ever present a risk of violence, the number making threats is huge, and it is the latter group — not just the former — whose treatment will be impaired and whose risk of commitment will be increased.

Both the legal and psychiatric communities recognize that the process of determining potential violence in a patient is far from exact, being fraught with complexity and uncertainty. In fact precision has not even been attained in predicting who of those having already committed violent acts will again become violent, a task recognized to be of much simpler proportions.

This predictive uncertainty means that the number of disclosures will necessarily be large. As noted above, psychiatric patients are encouraged to discuss all thoughts of violence, and they often express such thoughts. However, unlike this court, the psychiatrist does not enjoy the benefit of overwhelming hindsight in seeing which few, if any, of his patients will ultimately become violent. Now, confronted by the majority's new duty, the psychiatrist must instantaneously calculate potential violence from each patient on each visit. The difficulties researchers have encountered in accurately predicting violence will be heightened for the practicing psychiatrist dealing for brief periods in his office with heretofore nonviolent patients. And, given the decision not to warn or commit must always be made at the psychiatrist's civil peril, one can expect most doubts will be resolved in favor of the psychiatrist protecting himself.

Neither alternative open to the psychiatrist seeking to protect himself is in the public interest. The warning itself is an impairment of the psychiatrist's ability to treat, depriving many patients of adequate treatment. It is to be expected that after disclosing their threats, a significant number of patients, who would not become violent if treated according to existing practices, will engage in violent conduct as a result of unsuccessful treatment. In short, the majority's duty to warn will not only impair treatment of many who would never become violent but worse, will result in a net increase in violence.

The second alternative open to the psychiatrist is to commit his patient rather than to warn. Even in the absence of threat of civil liability, the doubts of psychiatrists as to the seriousness of patient threats have led psychiatrists to overcommit to mental institutions. This overcommitment has been authoritatively documented in both legal and psychiatric studies. This practice is so prevalent that it has been estimated that "as many as twenty harmless persons are incarcerated for every one who will commit a violent act." (Steadman & Cocozza, Stimulus/Response: We Can't Predict Who Is Dangerous (Jan. 1975) 8 Psych. Today 32, 35.) . . .

NOTES & QUESTIONS

1. Today, a majority of jurisdictions have adopted the *Tarasoff* rule. Given the *Tarasoff* rule, should psychotherapists have an ethical duty to warn patients that they may have to disclose to others when a patient makes a threat? In a study after *Tarasoff*, only 26 percent of psychotherapists informed pa-

tients of the possibility of disclosure at the outset of therapy; 51 percent informed patients when the patient threatened violence.[20]

2. In a footnote in his dissent, Justice Clark argues:

> However compassionate, the psychiatrist hearing the threat remains faced with potential crushing civil liability for a mistaken evaluation of his patient and will be forced to resolve even the slightest doubt in favor of disclosure or commitment.

Will the result in *Tarasoff* lead to too many disclosures by psychotherapists?

3. *Tarasoff*, although it involved a psychotherapist, would seemingly apply to physicians, nurses, and social workers. Could it apply even more broadly — to marriage counselors or any professional having knowledge of a person's dangerous propensities?

4. The psychiatric community was up in arms over *Tarasoff*. Ironically, however, even before *Tarasoff*, almost 80 percent of therapists believed they had an ethical duty to warn under circumstances akin to those in *Tarasoff*. In a 1987 study, almost all therapists had warned a potential victim and most believed their duty to warn was based on an ethical obligation regardless of the law.[21] Does it matter whether this is a legal duty or merely an ethical one? What if the option to disclose were simply left to the conscience of medical professionals?

5. Under the ABA Model Rule 1.6(b)(1), an attorney *may* reveal a client's intention to commit future crimes that are likely to cause imminent death or substantial bodily harm. This rule differs among the states, although the majority agree with this rule. About one-fifth of the states provide that an attorney *must* disclose under such circumstances. Suppose an attorney were in a similar position to the therapist in *Tarasoff*. Although the ethical obligations of each state suggest that the attorney may disclose, the attorney does not. Would the attorney be liable under a *Tarasoff* theory?

6. **Tarasoff *and the Psychotherapist-Patient Privilege.*** In *Menendez v. Superior Court*, 834 P.2d 786 (Cal. 1992), law enforcement officials sought audio tape recordings and written notes of psychotherapy sessions of Erik and Lyle Menendez, two brothers who had murdered their parents. The case of the Menendezes garnered great publicity. Their psychotherapist was Dr. Leon Oziel, and the tapes contained information related to the killings. The tapes also involved threats made by Erik and Lyle to Dr. Oziel. The threats were aimed at him alone, but Dr. Oziel believed that his wife (Laurel Oziel) as well as his lover (Judalon Smyth) could also be endangered, so he warned them. Neither Lyle nor Erik attempted any harm to Dr. Oziel, Laurel, or Smyth. Both Laurel Oziel and Smyth were employed in Dr. Oziel's psychotherapy practice. The police served a search warrant on Dr. Oziel for the recordings and/or notes for three therapy sessions. The Menendezes claimed

---

[20] *See* D.L. Rosenhan, Terri Wolff Teitelbaum, Kathi Weiss Teitelbaum, & Martin Davidson, *Warning Third Parties: The Ripple Effects of Tarasoff*, 24 Pac. L.J. 1165, 1208 (1993).

[21] *See* Fillmore Buckner & Marvin Firestone, *"Where the Public Peril Begins" 25 Years After Tarasoff*, 21 J. Legal Med. 187, 219 (2000).

psychotherapist-patient privilege. The government argued that Evidence Code § 1024 provided that there is no privilege if "the psychotherapist has reasonable cause to believe that the patient is in such mental or emotional condition as to be dangerous to himself or to the person or property of another and that disclosure of the communication is necessary to prevent the threatened danger." The case went up to the Supreme Court of California, which concluded that one of the sessions was not privileged, but that the other two were. First, the court held that even though the Menendezes' communications were publicly disclosed to Smyth, the Menendezes did not lose their privilege. "[T]he privilege can cover a communication that has lost its 'confidential' status." Second, the court held that all of the sessions should not be considered one communication; each therapy session should be treated separately. Third, the court concluded that if the conditions for a valid *Tarasoff* warning exist, a communication is not privileged, regardless of whether the therapist actually gave a *Tarasoff* warning or not. The exception to the privilege is "not keyed to . . . disclosure or warning, but to the existence of the specified factual predicate, viz., reasonable cause for belief in the dangerousness of the patient and the necessity of disclosure." Thus, the one session where the Menendezes made the threat to Dr. Oziel, which gave him reason to believe his wife and lover could be in danger, was not privileged.

MCINTOSH V. MILANO

403 A.2d 500 (N.J. Super. 1979)

PETRELLA, J. Defendant [Michael Milano, M.D., a board-certified psychiatrist] first met Lee Morgenstein, then age 15, and began his treatment on May 5, 1973, after the latter's school psychologist had given Morgenstein's parents defendant's name and that of certain other therapists, partially because of Morgenstein's involvement with drugs. His treatment was on a weekly basis for what was initially diagnosed as "an adjustment reaction of adolescence." Initially it also included family therapy. During the course of therapy over the approximate two-year period, Morgenstein related many "fantasies" to defendant on various subjects, including fantasies of fear of other people, being a hero or an important villain, and using a knife to threaten people who might intimidate or frighten him.

Morgenstein also related certain alleged experiences and emotional involvements with decedent, who in 1973 was about 20 years old and at that time lived with her parents next door to the Morgensteins. Decedent's father was a doctor who from time to time had treated Lee Morgenstein for minor ailments. Defendant considered all such "fantasies" referred to above as just that, but he came to accept, after initial reservations, that the experiences related to him by Morgenstein as to his eventual victim represented truth and not fantasy. Dr. Milano stated he was somewhat "nonplussed" initially about the revelations of Morgenstein concerning Miss [Kimberly] McIntosh and alleged sexual experiences because of the five-year age difference. However, he said that he came to believe it because the way Morgenstein responded emotionally fit with what he told him, and Milano claimed he never had any reason to doubt Morgenstein. The doctor testified at Morgenstein's criminal trial that "(h)e (Morgenstein) didn't spend a lot of time describing in detail what he and Kim did, but that also sort of fit, if anything, his character in that he thought that nobody would believe him." Defendant did indicate in his deposition that he advised Morgenstein to break off the relationship.

Morgenstein had possessive feelings towards Kimberly, according to the doctor, and was "overwhelmed" by the relationship. Although Morgenstein is said to have repeatedly expressed anxiety to defendant over his relationship with Miss McIntosh, defendant asserts she was not the dominant theme of the therapy.

It is undisputed, and Dr. Milano admits, that Morgenstein had confided that he had fired a B.B. gun at what he recalled to be a car (Miss McIntosh's or her boyfriend's) on one occasion when he was upset because she was going on a date with her boyfriend. There is evidence proffered by plaintiff that other windows in the McIntosh house and another vehicle had been shot at and damaged by a B.B. or some other gun, and a factfinder might infer that these were actions of Morgenstein. It is also undisputed that Dr. Milano had been told by Morgenstein that he had purchased and carried a knife to show to people to scare them away if they should attempt to frighten or intimidate him, and brought it to a therapy session to show the doctor.

Although Dr. Milano said that Morgenstein wished Miss McIntosh would "suffer" as he did and had expressed jealousy and a very possessive attitude towards her, was jealous of other men and hateful towards her boyfriends, had difficulty convincing himself that fights or things were really over or finished, he denied that Morgenstein ever indicated or exhibited any feelings of violence toward decedent or said that he intended to kill her or inflict bodily harm. Morgenstein was also very angry that he had not been able to obtain Miss McIntosh's phone number when she moved from the family home. He may not even have known where she lived in 1975. Plaintiff proffered testimony that Miss McIntosh had told her family of Morgenstein's drug problems, felt sorry for him, and hoped he could get help.

Following an incident in which Morgenstein fell off a bicycle and injured his face the day before the July 8, 1975 therapy session, and after an incident during the course of that day's therapy (apparently when Dr. Milano briefly left the room), he stole a prescription form from the doctor's desk. Later that day he attempted to obtain 30 Seconal tablets from a pharmacist with the stolen form. The pharmacist apparently became suspicious and called Dr. Milano, who instructed him to retain the unauthorized prescription form, not to fill it, and to send Morgenstein home. He later tried to reach Morgenstein at home, but between then and the early evening hours Morgenstein was involved in the tragedy which took Miss McIntosh's life. Whatever exactly transpired thereafter, it would appear that Morgenstein left the pharmacy upset and at some point either late that afternoon or early evening obtained a pistol which he had kept hidden at his home, and knowing Miss McIntosh was expected to visit her parents, waited for her and either got her to go with him, wittingly or unwittingly, to a local park area where he fatally shot her in the back.

Dr. Milano had indicated in his testimony at the criminal trial that sometimes he inquired further when he felt that a patient was in some ways endangering himself or someone else, and in those instances he would contact his patient's parents, school, or people like that. In his deposition in this civil case Dr. Milano said he had spoken to Morgenstein's parents about a problem with a car accident and this resulted in their withholding certain privileges from their son. He also indicated he spoke to a school teacher about one of Morgenstein's problems. Apparently this was usually with Morgenstein's consent. Dr. Milano had said he would "look into it" if he felt the patient was endangering himself or someone else. He apparently talked to Morgenstein's parents in some fashion about the relationship between their son and Miss McIntosh a number of times in late 1974 and in 1975, but never attempted to contact decedent or her parents. Despite Morgenstein's fantasies and the incidents previously recited, and wishes for her suffering, he felt that Morgenstein had never expressed a desire for retaliation or "fantasies" of retaliation. Dr. Milano had said at the criminal trial that Morgenstein had fantasies of magical power and violence, which meant that if somebody said he was a scrawny little runt and wouldn't dare fight back, that he would be able to pull out a gun and shoot them. But he denied that Morgenstein ever had fantasies of pulling out a gun, and claimed that his fantasies apparently related to pulling out a knife and scaring people off. Morgenstein, nevertheless, was quoted as saying that if he had a gun, that would scare men and then nobody would dare threaten him. . . .

Plaintiff [McIntosh's mother] instituted this wrongful death action based in large part on the trial testimony of Dr. Milano. She relies also on a report of a psychiatrist retained as an expert witness expressing the opinion that defendant had a duty to warn Kimberly McIntosh, her parents or appropriate authorities that Morgenstein posed a physical threat or danger to decedent. Plaintiff asserts defendant breached that duty. . . .

The argument in this case is whether principles analogous to those expressed in *Tarasoff* [*v. Regents of University of California*] apply or should be applied in New Jersey.

Plaintiff in the instant case asserts that a duty of a therapist towards third parties or potential victims is appropriate under the law of this State and forms a basis for a claim of actionable negligence analogous to that in *Tarasoff*. Defendant asserts such a duty is unworkable. . . .

It may be true that there cannot be 100% accurate prediction of dangerousness in all cases. However, a therapist does have a basis for giving an opinion and a prognosis based on the history of the patient and the course of treatment. Where reasonable men might differ and a fact issue exists, the therapist is only held to the standard for a therapist in the particular field in the particular community. Unless therapists clearly state when called upon to treat patients or to testify that they have no ability to predict or even determine whether their treatment will be efficacious or may even be necessary with any degree of certainty, there is no basis for a legal conclusion negating any and all duty with respect to a particular class of professionals. This is not to say that isolated or vague threats will of necessity give rise in all circumstances and cases to a duty. . . .

The *Tarasoff* duty has received criticism from some, but not all authors, mostly those in the medical professions. However, the concept of legal duties for the medical profession is not new. A doctor-patient relationship in some circumstances admittedly places a duty to warn others of contagious diseases. New Jersey recognizes the general rule that a person who negligently exposes another to a contagious disease, which the other contracts, is liable in damages. Specifically, a physician has the duty to warn third persons against possible exposure to contagious or infectious diseases, e.g., tuberculosis, venereal diseases, and so forth. That duty extends to instances where the physician should have known of the infectious disease.

Physicians also must report tuberculosis, venereal disease and various other contagious diseases, see, e.g., N.J.S.A. 26:4-15, as well as certain other conditions. There is, to be sure, a relative certainty and uniformity present in a diagnosis of most physical illnesses, conditions and injuries as opposed to a psychiatric prediction of dangerousness based on symptoms and historical performance. Nevertheless, psychiatrists diagnose, treat and give opinions based on medical probabilities, particularly relying on a patient's history, without any clear indication of an inability to predict that is here asserted.

As a further illustration of types of duties imposed by statutes, N.J.S.A. 2A:97-2 provides that any person who has knowledge of actual commission of high misdemeanors and certain other crimes, but fails to report or disclose same, is himself guilty of a misdemeanor. No exception is set forth therein for a physician. To threaten to take the life of another person is also a crime. . . . Disclosure is, therefore, required in numerous situations. . . . [E]ven the Principles of Medical Ethics recognize that confidentiality gives way where "it becomes necessary in order to protect the welfare of the individual or of the community." . . .

. . . [T]his court holds that a psychiatrist or therapist may have a duty to take whatever steps are reasonably necessary to protect an intended or potential victim of his patient when he determines, or should determine, in the appropriate factual setting and in accordance with the standards of his profession established at trial, that the patient is or may present a probability of danger to that person. The relationship giving rise to that duty may be found either in that existing between the therapist and the patient, as was alluded to in *Tarasoff,* or in the more broadly based obligation a practitioner may have to protect the welfare of the community, which is analogous to the obligation a physician has to warn third persons of infectious or contagious disease. . . .

NOTES & QUESTIONS

1. Does it seem foreseeable for Dr. Milano to know that Morgenstein would harm McIntosh? Even if Dr. Milano prevails in court, there still is a strong incentive for him to disclose — to avoid a very costly litigation. Does the fear of a long court battle make therapists more likely to err on the side of disclosure? If Dr. Milano did disclose, would Morgenstein have a tort action for breach of confidentiality?

2. *McIntosh* recognizes a broader source for the legal duty to disclose than does *Tarasoff.* Consider the following passage at the conclusion of *McIntosh*:

   The relationship giving rise to that duty may be found either in that existing between the therapist and the patient, as was alluded to in *Tarasoff,* or in the more broadly based obligation a practitioner may have to protect the welfare of the community, which is analogous to the obligation a physician has to warn third persons of infectious or contagious disease.

If the duty arises in this "more broadly based obligation" to protect the public welfare, does this suggest that the duty itself may be broader than that in *Tarasoff*? Do therapists and medical personnel have a duty to warn the public at large if they believe a patient is generally dangerous and the patient has not made any threats to specific individuals?

3. *The Duty to Warn About Relatives' Genetic Conditions.* In *Pate v. Threlkel*, 661 So. 2d 278 (Fla. 1995), plaintiff Heidi Pate's mother received treatment for medullary thyroid carcinoma, a disorder that was genetically transferable. When Pate learned that she also had the disease, she sued the doctors who treated her mother, alleging that the doctors were under a duty to warn Pate's mother that her children should be tested for the disease. Pate alleged that had she been tested, she would have taken preventative action that might have made her condition curable. The physicians argued that they lacked a duty of care to Pate. The court held that Pate had a valid claim:

> . . . [T]o whom does the alleged duty to warn [the patient] of the nature of her disease run? The duty obviously runs to the patient who is in privity with the physician. In the past, courts have held that in order to maintain a cause of action against a physician, privity must exist between the plaintiff and the physician. In other professional relationships, however, we have recognized the rights of identified third party beneficiaries to recover from a professional because that party was the intended beneficiary of the prevailing standard of care. . . .
>
> Here, the alleged prevailing standard of care was obviously developed for the benefit of the patient's children as well as the patient. We conclude that when the prevailing standard of care creates a duty that is obviously for the benefit of certain identified third parties and the physician knows of the existence of those third parties, then the physician's duty runs to those third parties. . . .
>
> . . . If there is a duty to warn, to whom must the physician convey the warning? Our holding should not be read to require the physician to warn the patient's children of the disease. In most instances the physician is prohibited from disclosing the patient's medical condition to others except with the patient's permission. Moreover, the patient ordinarily can be expected to pass on the warning. To require the physician to seek out and warn various members of the patient's family would often be difficult or impractical and would place too heavy a burden upon the physician. Thus, we emphasize that in any circumstances in which the physician has a duty to warn of a genetically transferable disease, that duty will be satisfied by warning the patient. . . .

Compare *Pate* to *Safer v. Estate of Pack*, 677 A.2d 1188 (N.J. Super. 1996). The plaintiff, Donna Safer, sued the estate of the deceased physician (Dr. Pack) who treated her father for colon cancer and multiple polyposis. After seven years of treatment, Safer's father died of cancer. Safer was ten years old at the time. About 25 years later, when Safer was 36 years old and newly married, she was diagnosed with colon cancer and multiple polyposis. She had a complete colectomy and one of her ovaries had to be removed. Safer contended that multiple polyposis is a hereditary condition which if untreated leads to colorectal cancer. Since the hereditary nature of the disease was known at the time Dr. Pack was treating Safer's father, Dr. Pack had a duty to warn Safer's father, and perhaps Safer herself. The court agreed with Safer:

> . . . We see no impediment, legal or otherwise, to recognizing a physician's duty to warn those known to be at risk of avoidable harm from a genetically transmissible condition. In terms of foreseeability especially, there is no essential difference between the type of genetic threat at issue here and the menace of infection, contagion or a threat of physical harm. *See generally, e.g., McIntosh v. Milano; Tarasoff v. Regents of Univ. of Cal.* . . . The individual or group at risk is easily identified, and substantial future harm may be averted or minimized by a timely and effective warning. . . .
>
> Although an overly broad and general application of the physician's duty to warn might lead to confusion, conflict or unfairness in many types of circumstances, we are confident that the duty to warn of avertable risk from genetic causes, by definition a matter of familial concern, is sufficiently narrow to serve the interests of justice. Further, it is appropriate, for reasons already expressed by our Supreme Court, that the duty be seen as owed not only to the patient himself but that it also "extend[s] beyond the interests of a patient to members of the immediate family of the patient who may be adversely affected by a breach of that duty." We need not decide, in the present posture of this case, how, precisely, that duty is to be discharged, especially with respect to young children who may be at risk, except to require that reasonable steps be taken to assure that the information reaches those likely to be affected or is made available for their benefit. . . .
>
> We decline to hold as the Florida Supreme Court did in *Pate v. Threlkel*, that, in all circumstances, the duty to warn will be satisfied by informing the patient. It may be necessary, at some stage, to resolve a conflict between the physician's broader duty to warn and his fidelity to an expressed preference of the patient that nothing be said to family members about the details of the disease. . . .

How does the holding in *Pate* differ from that in *Safer*? Are these holdings a logical extension of *Tarasoff* and *McIntosh*? What are the potential privacy risks created by these holdings? Do the potential benefits of the rules established in *Pate* and *Safer* outweigh these privacy risks?

4. STATUTORY REPORTING REQUIREMENTS

New York Public Health Law § 2130: Control of Acute Communicable Diseases—HIV

New York, along with many other states, has enacted a partner notification law when people are diagnosed with HIV. According to N.Y. Pub. Health L. § 2130:

> 1. Every physician or other person authorized by law to order diagnostic tests or make a medical diagnosis, or any laboratory performing such tests shall im-

mediately (a) upon initial determination that a person is infected with human immunodeficiency virus (HIV), or (b) upon initial diagnosis that a person is afflicted with the disease known as acquired immune deficiency syndrome (AIDS), or (c) upon initial diagnosis that a person is afflicted with HIV related illness, report such case to the commissioner.

2. The commissioner shall promptly forward such report to the health commissioner of the municipality where such disease, illness or infection occurred. When cases of such disease, illness or infection occur in a municipality not having a health commissioner, such reports shall be forwarded directly to the district health officer.

3. Such report shall contain such information concerning the case as shall be required by the commissioner. Such report shall include information identifying the protected individual as well as the names, if available, of any contacts of the protected individual, as defined in subdivision ten of section twenty-seven hundred eighty of this chapter, known to the physician or provided to the physician by the infected person.

After the information is collected, any "contacts" of the individual may be notified by public health officials. *See* § 2133. "In notifying any contact identified in the course of any investigation conducted pursuant to this section, the physician or public health officer shall not disclose the identity of the protected individual or the identity of any other contact." § 2133(3).

A "contact" means "an identified spouse or sex partner of the protected individual, a person identified as having shared hypodermic needles or syringes with the protected individual or a person who the protected individual may have exposed to HIV under circumstances that present a risk of transmission of HIV, as determined by the commissioner." § 2180(10).

Pursuant to § 2136(3): "No criminal or civil liability shall arise against any protected individual solely due to his or her failure to cooperate in contact tracing conducted pursuant to section twenty-one hundred thirty-three of this title."

NOTES & QUESTIONS

1. Thirty-three states have partner notification laws. Thirty-one states collect HIV names. In support of the laws is the fact that many infected people have difficulty telling others of infection. In one study, 40 percent didn't disclose their HIV status to their partners. According to the Centers for Disease Control, 70 percent of partners are not informed. The argument against such disclosure laws is that they might deter people from getting tested. Further, HIV positive women experience violence when their partners find out they have HIV. Almost half fear violence. Twenty-five percent were actually assaulted. Finally, it remains unclear whether such notification laws are effective.[22]

---

[22] *See* Sonia Bhatnager, Note, *HIV Name Reporting and Partner Notification in New York State*, 26 Fordham Urb. L.J. 1457, 1458 (1999).

2. Would the New York law survive a challenge under the constitutional right to information privacy?

3. Tort and criminal law requires people to inform others of HIV before engaging in activities likely to transmit the virus, such as sexual intercourse. For example, Indiana Code § 16-41-7-1(d) provides that carriers who know they have a dangerous communicable disease (including AIDS) have a duty to warn a third party at risk. In contrast, the New York law aims for disclosure to partners regardless of when or whether the patient will engage with his or her partner in such activities.

4. Consider Robert Gellman's conclusion about the preferability of legislation rather than existing case law and ethical principles to define the responsibilities of physicians with respect to patient privacy:

> Existing legal and ethical principles that guide physicians with respect to their obligations to protect the confidentiality of medical records are generally out of date and are not comprehensive. Physicians faced with requests or demands for patient information will find little in law or ethics to define their responsibilities with any precision. Yet the physician frequently is the only one who is in a position to take action to protect the confidentiality of his records and the privacy of his patients.
>
> This problem has always existed, but was not as serious in the past because medical records were only occasionally used outside the medical treatment process. Confidentiality increasingly is taking second place to a growing list of competing interests, however, and the expanded use of medical records for nontreatment purposes is exacerbating the shortcomings in existing confidentiality principles.
>
> There are several major consequences of these developments. First, as demand for medical records increases, the physician is being called upon to play a more central role in the protection of confidentiality. But the role that a physician should play is undefined because the physician's responsibilities are unclear. The result may be increased litigation over medical confidentiality issues and the obligations of physicians.
>
> Second, the widespread dissemination and use of medical records ultimately may give rise to the general belief that information provided "in confidence" to a physician is no longer confidential. If this occurs, the consequences for the practice of medicine are uncertain. If confidentiality is important to the practice of medicine, it may become necessary to require physicians to protect patient confidentiality or to permit patients to protect their own interests in confidentiality.
>
> Third, because of the magnitude and complexity of privacy issues today, the courts cannot be expected to develop appropriate solutions in a timely fashion. . . .
>
> . . . Therefore, the only practical way to develop suitable guidance defining the responsibilities of physicians, the right of patients, and the proper protection for medical information is through legislation.[23]

5. Consider the following argument by Richard Turkington about HIV notification:

---

[23] Robert M. Gellman, *Prescribing Privacy: The Uncertain Role of the Physician in the Protection of Patient Privacy*, 62 N.C. L. Rev. 255 (1984).

. . . Are cases involving notification of HIV-related information sufficiently different from infectious disease notification cases and *Tarasoff* to consider adopting policies other than mandatory notification? There is a strong case for treating notification of HIV status differently. Disclosure without consent constitutes a serious invasion of privacy and involves risks of adverse consequences to the patient, such as discrimination or violence, through further publication by the sexual partner. Mandatory disclosure may also exacerbate psychiatric disorders caused by infection. Unless the patient is informed by the professional that HIV status would be disclosed to known current contacts at risk, disclosure threatens the trust necessary for free communication and the integrity of the professional-patient relationship. If the patient is informed of contact notification, he or she may be deterred from being tested. Third-party notification might save some lives in the short run but, in the long run, if it damages the trust between professional and client, and deters persons from voluntary testing, more transmission and deaths may result.

Also, unlike the *Tarasoff* situation, the health professional is not the only potential source of notification to the third party. The infected person and the health department are both in the position to notify third parties, and the infected person is arguably in a better position to do so. Only the subject knows who is at risk. The physician may only know that a spouse is at risk. Imposing a duty upon the physician to discover those that may be sexually involved with the patient requires the physician to undertake a police-type activity that many are reluctant to perform and that ought not to be imposed. . . .

The possibility of significant tort damage awards for disclosure under breach of confidentiality theories and the lack of clarity in the existing law on the duty to disclose to contacts leave the health care professional between a rock and a hard place. . . .

Many states have not addressed the question of notification of at-risk contacts. In such states, because precedent on disclosure of other health care information may not be controlling, health professionals are at risk of significant liability even if they take action consistent with their professional ethics and judgment as to what is medically and therapeutically correct for their patient. This is an unacceptable situation. . . .[24]

6. *Other Disclosure Requirements.* Many states have statutory requirements for physicians to disclose health information for certain types of diseases or injuries. Recall from earlier in this chapter the New York statute upheld in *Whalen v. Roe,* which required the disclosure to the state of information about patients using certain prescription medications. Similar to the statute in *Whalen,* many state statutes require the collection of medical data for state registries. For example, New Jersey maintains a registry of birth defects, *see* N.J. Stat. 26:8-40.21; blindness, *see* N.J. Stat. 30:6-1.2; and cancer, *see* N.J. Stat. 26:2-106.

Other statutes require the reporting of certain conditions to various state agencies and officials. Ohio mandates the disclosure to appropriate government officials of occupational diseases (R.C. 3701.25 and 4123.71); diseases

---

[24]Richard C. Turkington, *Confidentiality Policy for HIV-Related Information: An Analytical Framework for Sorting Out Hard and Easy Cases,* 34 Vill. L. Rev. 871 (1989).

that are infectious, contagious, or dangerous to public health (R.C. 3701.24, 3701.52, 3707.06); health injuries indicative of child abuse or neglect (R.C. 2151.421), and injuries indicative of criminal conduct (R.C. 2921.22). Other states have similar reporting requirements. As discussed above, some states require, or provide for, disclosure of a person's medical condition to other individuals, such as partners and spouses.

A number of states place statutory bars on liability for the disclosure of certain conditions. For example, South Carolina has eliminated the "[t]he privileged quality of [patient-physician] communication" regarding the abuse or neglect of children. *See* S.C. Code Ann. § 20-7-550. Further, in South Carolina, "[a] physician or state agency identifying and notifying a spouse or known contact of a person having . . . (HIV) infection or . . . (AIDS) is not liable for damages resulting from the disclosure." S.C. Code Ann. § 44-29-146.

7. ***The Constitutionality of Disclosure and Reporting Requirements.*** Recall *Whalen*, which upheld the constitutionality of New York's prescription drug user reporting statute under the constitutional right to information privacy. In *Planned Parenthood of Central Missouri v. Danforth*, 428 U.S. 52 (1976), Missouri required that physicians report abortions to the state, which would keep the data confidential, except that the data can "be inspected and health data acquired by local, state, or national public health officers." The records must also be retained for seven years in the permanent files of the health facility where the abortion was performed. The reporting requirements were challenged "on the ground that they . . . impose an extra layer and burden of regulation" on a woman's right to seek an abortion. The Court held that the regulations were constitutional: "Recordkeeping and reporting requirements that are reasonably directed to the preservation of maternal health and that properly respect a patient's confidentiality and privacy are permissible."

C. GENETIC INFORMATION

1. BACKGROUND: GENETIC PRIVACY

Deoxyribonucleic acid, otherwise known as DNA, is present in all cellular organisms and contains the information an organism needs to live and to transfer genetic material. The DNA molecule's structure consists of two strands coiled around one another forming a double helix. Each strand of DNA is comprised of different sequences of four chemical compounds. The chemical compounds are adenine, guanine, thymine, and cytosine, denoted with A, G, T, and C, respectively. A "nucleotide" is a subunit of a DNA strand that contains one of these four chemical compounds. Nucleotides, each containing A, G, T, or C, are arranged in sequences along each strand of DNA. The nucleotides in one strand of DNA are paired with the nucleotides in the other DNA strand. Each pair of nucleotides is known as a base pair. The base pairs are joined to each other by chemical bonds called "hydrogen bonds." There are about 3 billion base pairs in the human genome.

DNA contains the recipe for the creation of proteins. A protein consists of smaller molecules known as amino acids. The structure of each protein is determined by the sequence of its amino acids. The sequence of base pairs of nucleotides in DNA determines the sequence of amino acids.

A "gene" is a sequence of nucleotides that codes for the production of a particular protein. Genes are responsible for transmitting inherited traits. Genes are located inside chromosomes, which are contained in the nucleus of each cell.[25] Humans have 23 pairs of chromosomes. It had been previously estimated that there are about 100,000 genes in the 23 chromosomes, but recent research suggests that the number is between 30,000 and 40,000.

Every cell in the human body, which is comprised of about 100 trillion cells, contains DNA (except red blood cells). DNA can be isolated from white blood cells, sperm cells, cells in saliva, nasal secretions, sweat, and the cells surrounding the roots of hair.

An individual's complete genetic makeup is known as a "genome." With the exception of identical twins, no two humans have an identical genome. However, only a small portion of DNA differs among individuals. About 99 percent of the 3 billion base pairs of nucleotides are the same in all humans. The 1 percent that is different enables DNA forensic analysis.

The Human Genome Project, the first draft of which was completed in 2000, has mapped out all of the genes in the human chromosomes. With further study, the Human Genome Project will enable the identification of the particular genes that cause certain diseases.

Along with these developments comes a new threat to privacy. Once genes and gene mutations are better understood, and are linked to particular diseases and traits, one's genetic information can reveal one's medical history and even the future of one's health. Further, one's genetic information can reveal information about one's family members. As Anita Allen explains:

> According to legal doctrine, to appropriate a person's name or likeness is a way of invading his or her privacy. Privacy, it appears, has something to do with controlling one's identity. . . .
>
> The question whether our genes comprise our identities is a difficult one. Proprietary genetic privacy is suggested by the idea that the human DNA is a repository of valuable human personality. Proprietary genetic privacy is further suggested by the related notion that human DNA is owned by the persons from whom it is taken, as a species of private property.
>
> If DNA is the human essence — that is, the thing that makes individuals special and perhaps unique — it arguably ought to belong to the individual from whom it was ultimately derived. If DNA "belongs" to individual sources, it might belong to them exclusively and inalienably. Or DNA could qualify as alienable property that others can acquire both lawfully through voluntary private transactions and wrongfully through nonconsensual appropriation. . . .[26]

---

[25] Some cells, such as red blood cells, do not contain a nucleus and do not have nuclear DNA (but they may have mitochondrial DNA).

[26] Anita L. Allen, *Genetic Privacy: Emerging Concepts and Values*, in *Genetic Secrets: Protecting Privacy and Confidentiality in the Genetic Era* (Mark A. Rothstein, ed. 1997).

2. PROPERTY RIGHTS IN BODY PARTS AND DNA

MOORE V. REGENTS OF THE UNIVERSITY OF CALIFORNIA

793 P.2d 479 (Cal. 1990)

PANELLI, J. . . . The plaintiff is John Moore (Moore), who underwent treatment for hairy-cell leukemia at the Medical Center of the University of California at Los Angeles (UCLA Medical Center). The five defendants are: (1) Dr. David W. Golde (Golde), a physician who attended Moore at UCLA Medical Center; (2) the Regents of the University of California (Regents), who own and operate the university; (3) Shirley G. Quan, a researcher employed by the Regents; (4) Genetics Institute, Inc. (Genetics Institute); and (5) Sandoz Pharmaceuticals Corporation and related entities (collectively Sandoz).

Moore first visited UCLA Medical Center on October 5, 1976, shortly after he learned that he had hairy-cell leukemia. After hospitalizing Moore and "withdr[awing] extensive amounts of blood, bone marrow aspirate, and other bodily substances," Golde confirmed that diagnosis. At this time all defendants, including Golde, were aware that "certain blood products and blood components were of great value in a number of commercial and scientific efforts" and that access to a patient whose blood contained these substances would provide "competitive, commercial, and scientific advantages."

On October 8, 1976, Golde recommended that Moore's spleen be removed. Golde informed Moore "that he had reason to fear for his life, and that the proposed splenectomy operation . . . was necessary to slow down the progress of his disease." Based upon Golde's representations, Moore signed a written consent form authorizing the splenectomy.

Before the operation, Golde and Quan "formed the intent and made arrangements to obtain portions of [Moore's] spleen following its removal" and to take them to a separate research unit. Golde gave written instructions to this effect on October 18 and 19, 1976. These research activities "were not intended to have . . . any relation to [Moore's] medical . . . care." However, neither Golde nor Quan informed Moore of their plans to conduct this research or requested his permission. Surgeons at UCLA Medical Center, whom the complaint does not name as defendants, removed Moore's spleen on October 20, 1976.

Moore returned to the UCLA Medical Center several times between November 1976 and September 1983. He did so at Golde's direction and based upon representations "that such visits were necessary and required for his health and well-being, and based upon the trust inherent in and by virtue of the physician-patient relationship. . . ." On each of these visits Golde withdrew additional samples of "blood, blood serum, skin, bone marrow aspirate, and sperm." On each occasion Moore traveled to the UCLA Medical Center from his home in Seattle because he had been told that the procedures were to be performed only there and only under Golde's direction.

"In fact, [however,] throughout the period of time that [Moore] was under [Golde's] care and treatment, . . . the defendants were actively involved in a number of activities which they concealed from [Moore]. . . ." Specifically, defendants were conducting research on Moore's cells and planned to "benefit financially and competitively . . . [by exploiting the cells] and [their] exclusive access to [the cells] by virtue of [Golde's] on-going physician-patient relationship. . . ."

Sometime before August 1979, Golde established a cell line from Moore's T-lymphocytes.[27] [In 1984, the Regents had the cell line patented. The potential market value for products derived from the cell line was estimated to be in the billions of dollars.] . . . .

. . . Moore attempted to state 13 causes of action, [which included among them a cause of action for conversion, for breach of fiduciary duty, and for lack of informed consent]. . . .

A. Breach of Fiduciary Duty and Lack of Informed Consent

Moore repeatedly alleges that Golde failed to disclose the extent of his research and economic interests in Moore's cells before obtaining consent to the medical procedures by which the cells were extracted. These allegations, in our view, state a cause of action against Golde for invading a legally protected interest of his patient. This cause of action can properly be characterized either as the breach of a fiduciary duty to disclose facts material to the patient's consent or, alternatively, as the performance of medical procedures without first having obtained the patient's informed consent.

Our analysis begins with three well-established principles. First, "a person of adult years and in sound mind has the right, in the exercise of control over his own body, to determine whether or not to submit to lawful medical treatment." Second, "the patient's consent to treatment, to be effective, must be an informed consent." Third, in soliciting the patient's consent, a physician has a fiduciary duty to disclose all information material to the patient's decision.

These principles lead to the following conclusions: (1) a physician must disclose personal interests unrelated to the patient's health, whether research or economic, that may affect the physician's professional judgment; and (2) a physician's failure to disclose such interests may give rise to a cause of action for performing medical procedures without informed consent or breach of fiduciary duty.

To be sure, questions about the validity of a patient's consent to a procedure typically arise when the patient alleges that the physician failed to disclose medical risks, as in malpractice cases, and not when the patient alleges that the physician had a personal interest, as in this case. The concept of informed consent, however, is broad enough to encompass the latter. "The

---

[27] A T-lymphocyte is a type of white blood cell. T-lymphocytes produce lymphokines, or proteins that regulate the immune system. Some lymphokines have potential therapeutic value. If the genetic material responsible for producing a particular lymphokine can be identified, it can sometimes be used to manufacture large quantities of the lymphokine through the techniques of recombinant DNA. . . . While the genetic code for lymphokines does not vary from individual to individual, it can nevertheless be quite difficult to locate the gene responsible for a particular lymphokine. Because T-lymphocytes produce many different lymphokines, the relevant gene is often like a needle in a haystack. Moore's T-lymphocytes were interesting to the defendants because they overproduced certain lymphokines, thus making the corresponding genetic material easier to identify.

scope of the physician's communication to the patient . . . must be measured by the patient's need, and that need is whatever information is material to the decision."

Indeed, the law already recognizes that a reasonable patient would want to know whether a physician has an economic interest that might affect the physician's professional judgment. As the Court of Appeal has said, "[c]ertainly a sick patient deserves to be free of any reasonable suspicion that his doctor's judgment is influenced by a profit motive." . . .

. . . A physician who adds his own research interests to this balance may be tempted to order a scientifically useful procedure or test that offers marginal, or no, benefits to the patient. The possibility that an interest extraneous to the patient's health has affected the physician's judgment is something that a reasonable patient would want to know in deciding whether to consent to a proposed course of treatment. It is material to the patient's decision and, thus, a prerequisite to informed consent. . . .

B. Conversion

Moore also attempts to characterize the invasion of his rights as a conversion — a tort that protects against interference with possessory and ownership interests in personal property. He theorizes that he continued to own his cells following their removal from his body, at least for the purpose of directing their use, and that he never consented to their use in potentially lucrative medical research. Thus, to complete Moore's argument, defendants' unauthorized use of his cells constitutes a conversion. As a result of the alleged conversion, Moore claims a proprietary interest in each of the products that any of the defendants might ever create from his cells or the patented cell line. . . .

1. Moore's Claim Under Existing Law

"To establish a conversion, plaintiff must establish an actual interference with his ownership or right of possession. . . . Where plaintiff neither has title to the property alleged to have been converted, nor possession thereof, he cannot maintain an action for conversion."

Since Moore clearly did not expect to retain possession of his cells following their removal, to sue for their conversion he must have retained an ownership interest in them. But there are several reasons to doubt that he did retain any such interest. First, no reported judicial decision supports Moore's claim, either directly or by close analogy. Second, California statutory law drastically limits any continuing interest of a patient in excised cells. Third, the subject matters of the Regents' patent — the patented cell line and the products derived from it — cannot be Moore's property. . . .

Lacking direct authority for importing the law of conversion into this context, Moore relies, as did the Court of Appeal, primarily on decisions addressing privacy rights. One line of cases involves unwanted publicity. These opinions hold that every person has a proprietary interest in his own likeness and that unauthorized, business use of a likeness is redressible as a tort. But in neither opinion did the authoring court expressly base its holding on property law. Each court stated, following Prosser, that it was "pointless" to debate the proper characterization of the proprietary interest in a likeness. For purposes of determining whether the tort of conversion lies, however, the characterization of the right in question is far from pointless. Only property can be converted.

Not only are the wrongful-publicity cases irrelevant to the issue of conversion, but the analogy to them seriously misconceives the nature of the genetic materials and research involved in this case. Moore, adopting the analogy originally advanced by the Court of Appeal, argues that "[i]f the courts have found a sufficient proprietary interest in one's persona, how could one not have a right in one's own genetic material, something far more profoundly the essence of one's human uniqueness than a name or a face?" However, as the defendants' patent makes clear — and the complaint, too, if read with an understanding of the scientific terms which it has borrowed from the patent — the goal and result of defendants' efforts has been to manufacture lymphokines. Lymphokines, unlike a name or a face, have the same molecular structure in every human being and the same, important functions in every human being's immune system. Moreover, the particular genetic material which is responsible for the natural production of lymphokines, and which defendants use to manufacture lymphokines in the laboratory, is also the same in every person; it is no more unique to Moore than the number of vertebrae in the spine or the chemical formula of hemoglobin.[28]

Another privacy case offered by analogy to support Moore's claim establishes only that patients have a right to refuse medical treatment. In this context the court in *Bouvia* wrote that "'[e]very human being of adult years and sound mind has a right to determine what shall be done with his own body. . . .'" Relying on this language to support the proposition that a patient has a continuing right to control the use of excised cells, the Court of Appeal in this case concluded that "[a] patient must have the ultimate power to control what becomes of his or her tissues. To hold otherwise would open the door to a massive invasion of human privacy and dignity in the name of medical progress." Yet one may earnestly wish to protect privacy and dignity without accepting the extremely problematic conclusion that interference with those interests amounts to a conversion of personal property. Nor is it necessary to force the round pegs of "privacy" and "dignity" into the square hole of "property" in order to protect the patient, since the fiduciary-duty and informed-consent theories protect these interests directly by requiring full disclosure.

The next consideration that makes Moore's claim of ownership problematic is California statutory law, which drastically limits a patient's control over excised cells. Pursuant to Health and Safety Code section 7054.4, "[n]otwith-

---

[28] By definition, a gene responsible for producing a protein found in more than one individual will be the same in each. It is precisely because everyone needs the same basic proteins that proteins produced by one person's cells may have therapeutic value for another person. (See generally OTA Rep., supra, at pp. 38-40.) Thus, the proteins that defendants hope to manufacture — lymphokines such as interferon — are in no way a "likeness" of Moore. Because all normal persons possess the genes responsible for production of lymphokines, it is sometimes possible to make normal cells into overproducers. According to a research paper to which defendants contributed, Moore's cells overproduced lymphokines because they were infected by a virus, HTLV-II (human T-cell leukemia virus type II). The same virus has been shown to transform normal T-lymphocytes into overproducers like Moore's.

standing any other provision of law, recognizable anatomical parts, human tissues, anatomical human remains, or infectious waste following conclusion of scientific use shall be disposed of by interment, incineration, or any other method determined by the state department [of health services] to protect the public health and safety." Clearly the Legislature did not specifically intend this statute to resolve the question of whether a patient is entitled to compensation for the nonconsensual use of excised cells. A primary object of the statute is to ensure the safe handling of potentially hazardous biological waste materials. Yet one cannot escape the conclusion that the statute's practical effect is to limit, drastically, a patient's control over excised cells. By restricting how excised cells may be used and requiring their eventual destruction, the statute eliminates so many of the rights ordinarily attached to property that one cannot simply assume that what is left amounts to "property" or "ownership" for purposes of conversion law. . . .

Finally, the subject matter of the Regents' patent — the patented cell line and the products derived from it — cannot be Moore's property. This is because the patented cell line is both factually and legally distinct from the cells taken from Moore's body. Federal law permits the patenting of organisms that represent the product of "human ingenuity," but not naturally occurring organisms. Human cell lines are patentable because "[l]ong-term adaptation and growth of human tissues and cells in culture is difficult — often considered an art . . . ," and the probability of success is low. It is this inventive effort that patent law rewards, not the discovery of naturally occurring raw materials. . . .

2. Should Conversion Liability Be Extended?

As we have discussed, Moore's novel claim to own the biological materials at issue in this case is problematic, at best. Accordingly, his attempt to apply the theory of conversion within this context must frankly be recognized as a request to extend that theory. . . .

There are three reasons why it is inappropriate to impose liability for conversion based upon the allegations of Moore's complaint. First, a fair balancing of the relevant policy considerations counsels against extending the tort. Second, problems in this area are better suited to legislative resolution. Third, the tort of conversion is not necessary to protect patients' rights. For these reasons, we conclude that the use of excised human cells in medical research does not amount to a conversion.

Of the relevant policy considerations, two are of overriding importance. The first is protection of a competent patient's right to make autonomous medical decisions. That right, as already discussed, is grounded in well-recognized and long-standing principles of fiduciary duty and informed consent. This policy weighs in favor of providing a remedy to patients when physicians act with undisclosed motives that may affect their professional judgment. The second important policy consideration is that we not threaten with disabling civil liability innocent parties who are engaged in socially useful activities, such as researchers who have no reason to believe that their use of a particular cell sample is, or may be, against a donor's wishes. . . .

. . . Liability based upon existing disclosure obligations, rather than an unprecedented extension of the conversion theory, protects patients' rights of privacy and autonomy without unnecessarily hindering research. . . .

Research on human cells plays a critical role in medical research. This is so because researchers are increasingly able to isolate naturally occurring, medically useful biological substances and to produce useful quantities of such substances through genetic engineering. . . .

The extension of conversion law into this area will hinder research by restricting access to the necessary raw materials. . . . At present, human cell lines are routinely copied and distributed to other researchers for experimental purposes, usually free of charge. This exchange of scientific materials, which still is relatively free and efficient, will surely be compromised if each cell sample becomes the potential subject matter of a lawsuit. . . .

. . . [T]he theory of liability that Moore urges us to endorse threatens to destroy the economic incentive to conduct important medical research. If the use of cells in research is a conversion, then with every cell sample a researcher purchases a ticket in a litigation lottery. Because liability for conversion is predicated on a continuing ownership interest, "companies are unlikely to invest heavily in developing, manufacturing, or marketing a product when uncertainty about clear title exists." . . .

BROUSSARD, J. concurring and dissenting. [Justice Broussard concurred in the majority's holding that the complaint states a cause of action for breach of fiduciary duty.]

With respect to the conversion cause of action, I dissent from the majority's conclusion that the facts alleged in this case do not state a cause of action for conversion. . . .

. . . Because plaintiff alleges that defendants wrongfully interfered with his right to determine, prior to the removal of his body parts, how those parts would be used after removal, I conclude that the complaint states a cause of action under traditional, common law conversion principles. . . .

. . . Although the majority opinion, at several points, appears to suggest that a removed body part, by its nature, may never constitute "property" for purposes of a conversion action, there is no reason to think that the majority opinion actually intends to embrace such a broad or dubious proposition. If, for example, another medical center or drug company had stolen all of the cells in question from the UCLA Medical Center laboratory and had used them for its own benefit, there would be no question but that a cause of action for conversion would properly lie against the thief, and the majority opinion does not suggest otherwise. Thus, the majority's analysis cannot rest on the broad proposition that a removed body part is not property, but rather rests on the proposition that a patient retains no ownership interest in a body part once the body part has been removed from his or her body.

The majority opinion fails to recognize, however, that, in light of the allegations of the present complaint, the pertinent inquiry is not whether a patient generally retains an ownership interest in a body part after its removal from his body, but rather whether a patient has a right to determine, before a body part is removed, the use to which the part will be put after removal. Although the majority opinion suggests that there are "reasons to doubt" that a patient retains "any" ownership interest in his organs or cells after removal, the opinion fails to identify any statutory provision or common law authority that indicates that a patient does not generally have the right, before a body part is removed, to choose among the permissible uses to which the part may be put after removal. On the contrary, the most closely related statutory scheme — the Uniform Anatomical Gift Act (Health & Saf. Code, §7150 et seq.) — makes it quite clear that a patient does have this right.

The Uniform Anatomical Gift Act is a comprehensive statutory scheme that was initially adopted in California in 1970 and most recently revised in 1988. . . . [T]he act clearly recognizes that it is the donor of the body part, rather than the hospital or physician who receives the part, who has the authority to designate, within the parameters of the statutorily authorized uses, the particular use to which the part may be put.

Although, as noted, the Uniform Anatomical Gift Act applies only to anatomical gifts that take effect on or after the death of the donor, the general principle of "donor control" which the act embodies is clearly not limited to that setting. In the transplantation context, for example, it is common for a living donor to designate the specific donee — often a relative — who is to receive a donated organ. If a hospital, after removing an organ from such a donor, decided on its own to give the organ to a different donee, no one would deny that the hospital had violated the legal right of the donor by its unauthorized use of the donated organ. Accordingly, it is clear under California law that a patient has the right, prior to the removal of an organ, to control the use to which the organ will be put after removal.

It is also clear, under traditional common law principles, that this right of a patient to control the future use of his organ is protected by the law of conversion. As a general matter, the tort of conversion protects an individual not only against improper interference with the right of possession of his property but also against unauthorized use of his property or improper interference with his right to control the use of his property. . . . California cases have also long recognized that "unauthorized use" of property can give rise to a conversion action.

The application of these principles to the present case is evident. If defendants had informed plaintiff, prior to removal, of the possible uses to which his body part could be put and plaintiff had authorized one particular use, it is clear under the foregoing authorities that defendants would be liable for conversion if they disregarded plaintiff's decision and used the body part in an unauthorized manner for their own economic benefit. Although in this case defendants did not disregard a specific directive from plaintiff with regard to the future use of his body part, the complaint alleges that, before the body part was removed, defendants intentionally withheld material information that they were under an obligation to disclose to plaintiff and that was necessary for his exercise of control over the body part; the complaint also alleges that defendants withheld such information in order to appropriate the control over the future use of such body part for their own economic benefit. If these allegations are true, defendants clearly improperly interfered with plaintiff's right in his body part at a time when he had the authority to determine the future use of such part, thereby misappropriating plaintiff's right of control for their own advantage. Under these circumstances, the complaint fully satisfies the established requirements of a conversion cause of action. . . .

Finally, the majority maintains that plaintiff's conversion action is not viable because "the subject matter of the Regents' patent — the patented cell line and the products derived from it — cannot be Moore's property." Even if this is an accurate statement of federal patent law, it does not explain why plaintiff may not maintain a conversion action for defendants' unauthorized use of his own body parts, blood, blood serum, bone marrow, and sperm. Although the damages which plaintiff may recover in a conversion action may not include the value of the patent and the derivative products, the fact that plaintiff may not be entitled to all of the damages which his complaint seeks does not justify denying his right to maintain any conversion action at all. . . .

Mosk, J. dissenting. . . . The majority claim that a conversion cause of action threatens to "destroy the economic incentive" to conduct the type of research here in issue. . . .

In any event, in my view whatever merit the majority's single policy consideration may have is outweighed by two contrary considerations, i.e., policies that are promoted by recognizing that every individual has a legally protectible property interest in his own body and its products. First, our society acknowledges a profound ethical imperative to respect the human body as the physical and temporal expression of the unique human persona. One manifestation of that respect is our prohibition against direct abuse of the body by torture or other forms of cruel or unusual punishment. Another is our prohibition against indirect abuse of the body by its economic exploitation for the sole benefit of another person. The most abhorrent form of such exploitation, of course, was the institution of slavery. Lesser forms, such as indentured servitude or even debtor's prison, have also disappeared. Yet their specter haunts the laboratories and boardrooms of today's biotechnological research-industrial complex. It arises wherever scientists or industrialists claim, as defendants claim here, the right to appropriate and exploit a patient's tissue for their sole economic benefit — the right, in other words, to freely mine or harvest valuable physical properties of the patient's body: "Research with human cells that results in significant economic gain for the researcher and no gain for the patient offends the traditional mores of our society in a manner impossible to quantify. Such research tends to treat the human body as a commodity — a means to a profitable end. The dignity and sanctity with which we regard the human whole, body as well as mind and soul, are absent when we allow researchers to further their own interests without the patient's participation by using a patient's cells as the basis for a marketable product." (Danforth, *supra*.) . . . .

The majority's final reason for refusing to recognize a conversion cause of action on these facts is that "there is no pressing need" to do so because the complaint also states another cause of action that is assuredly adequate to the task; that cause of action is "the breach of a fiduciary duty to disclose facts material to the patient's consent or, alternatively, . . . the performance of medical procedures without first having obtained the patient's informed consent" . . . I disagree . . . with the majority's further conclusion that in the present context a nondisclosure cause of action is an adequate — in fact, a superior — substitute for a conversion cause of action. . . .

The remedy is largely illusory. . . . There are two barriers to recovery. First, "the patient must show that if he or she had been informed of all pertinent information, he or she would have declined to consent to the procedure in question." . . . .

The second barrier to recovery is still higher, and is erected on the first: it is not even enough for the plaintiff to prove that he personally would have refused consent to the proposed treatment if he had been fully informed; he must also prove that in the same circumstances no reasonably prudent person would have given such consent. . . .

. . . [I]t may be difficult for a plaintiff to prove that no reasonably prudent person would have consented to the proposed treatment if the doctor had disclosed the particular risk of physical harm that ultimately caused the injury. This is because in many cases the potential benefits of the treatment to the plaintiff clearly outweigh the undisclosed risk of harm. . . . Few if any judges or juries are likely to believe that disclosure of such a possibility of research or development would dissuade a reasonably prudent person from consenting to the treatment. For example, in the case at bar no trier of fact is likely to believe that if defendants had disclosed their plans for using Moore's cells, no reasonably prudent person in Moore's position — i.e., a leukemia patient suffering from a grossly enlarged spleen — would have consented to the routine operation that saved or at least prolonged his life. . . .

The second reason why the nondisclosure cause of action is inadequate for the task that the majority assign to it is that it fails to solve half the problem before us: it gives the patient only the right to refuse consent, i.e., the right to prohibit the commercialization of his tissue; it does not give him the right to grant consent to that commercialization on the condition that he share in its proceeds. "Even though good reasons exist to support informed consent with tissue commercialization, a disclosure requirement is only the first step toward full recognition of a patient's right to participate fully. Informed consent to commercialization, absent a right to share in the profits from such commercial development, would only give patients a veto over their own exploitation. But recognition that the patient[s] [have] an ownership interest in their own tissues would give patients an affirmative right of participation. Then patients would be able to assume the role of equal partners with their physicians in commercial biotechnology research." . . .

Third, the nondisclosure cause of action fails to reach a major class of potential defendants: all those who are outside the strict physician-patient relationship with the plaintiff. . . . [T]he nondisclosure cause of action will thus be inadequate to reach a number of parties to the commercial exploitation of his tissue. Such parties include, for example, any physician-researcher who is not personally treating the patient, any other researcher who is not a physician, any employer of the foregoing (or even of the treating physician), and any person or corporation thereafter participating in the commercial exploitation of the tissue. Yet some or all of those parties may well have participated more in, and profited more from, such exploitation than the particular physician with whom the plaintiff happened to have a formal doctor-patient relationship at the time. . . .

NOTES & QUESTIONS

1. The *Moore* case asks us to examine whether we can own our body parts (specifically, a spleen) once they are removed from our bodies. This suggests a broader question: Do we own our genetic information? To what extent can we control this information?

2. The majority concludes that the interests of privacy and dignity can adequately be protected with a fiduciary duty; therefore, it is unnecessary to resort to property rights. Is a fiduciary duty sufficient to protect Moore's privacy interest?

3. Moore certainly had a property right in his spleen when it was in his body. Why does he lose that right when the spleen is removed?

4. Compare Broussard's view of Moore's claim of harm to that of the majority. Is the real harm to Moore, as Broussard argues, that he lost control over his body parts rather than, as the majority characterizes Moore's claim, that his property was taken? Is Broussard's view not one of property but of privacy? Is ownership of the spleen the same as control over it?

   Suppose Moore had a privacy interest in his cells — a right to control future use. Moore would be entitled to damages for his loss of privacy (i.e., for the emotional harm of knowing his cells were used without his consent). Are these damages likely to deter the doctors considering the billions of dollars that the cell line was worth?

5. If Moore has a privacy interest in his genetic information, how would you characterize it? According to James Boyle, it is difficult to view genetic information alone as implicating privacy. Only when genetic information is deciphered (to reveal certain traits or diseases) will it yield the type of information we consider to be private:

   > [O]ur intuitive notions of privacy are constructed around the notion of preventing disclosure of intimate, embarrassing, or simply "personal" *socially constructed facts* about ourselves to others like ourselves. I could stare at my genetic code all day and not even know it was mine. . . .
   >
   > The difficulty with Moore's case is, first, that no one would think worse of him for having a genetic make-up that could be mined for a socially valuable drug and, second, that specialized knowledge would be necessary to make the connection between the "facts revealed" and the "inner life." . . .
   >
   > If Moore's claim is not to the protection of his "privacy" . . . but rather to the protection of his ability to commodify the genetic information derived from his cells, then the inquiry shifts from privacy to [property], from the home and the secret to the market and the commodity. . . .[29]

6. How should genetic privacy be protected? With a property right that gives people complete ownership of their genetic information? With a fiduciary duty that remedies duplicitous actions to take one's genetic information or the unlawful disclosure of one's genetic information? With tort damages for the loss of a privacy right in one's genetic information (i.e., for the loss of control over one's genetic information)? With a limited right to con-

---

[29] James Boyle, *Shamans, Software, and Spleens: Law and the Construction of the Information Society* 105-106 (1996).

trol one's genetic information short of complete ownership? Or with a rule that genetic information is in the public domain and belongs to society as a whole?

7. Consider Radhika Rao:

> . . . If the body is considered property, it can be carved up into its component parts, and either body parts themselves or discrete "sticks" in the bundle of rights may be separated from the original owner and transferred to others. Thus, property permits fragmentation, while bodily fragmentation in turn begets the possibility of alienation of rights to others. In fact, property traditionally implies alienability — the power to transfer rights to others. Although many categories of inalienable property exist, alienability is the norm for property. The law views limits upon alienability as exceptions, justifiable only in response to market failure or other externalities. Consequently, inalienable property is an inherently unstable and precarious category, destined to be the target of sustained assault.
>
> Privacy, on the other hand, does not carry the same connotations. Personal privacy encompasses the right to possess one's own body and the right to exclude others, but does not embrace the power to give, sell, or otherwise transfer body rights to other individuals. And relational privacy safeguards intimate and consensual relationships, but affords little shelter to commercial transactions. Accordingly, we should adopt the language of privacy rather than that of property when we seek to protect self-ownership without suggesting that rights in the human body can be conveyed to others and when we wish to distinguish gifts of the body to family members from sales to strangers.
>
> The principal feature of bodily property may be this power to transfer rights to others, whether by sale, gift, or disposition after death. By contrast, the right of personal privacy can be curtailed or relinquished altogether, but it cannot be conveyed to another. . . .
>
> As a result, the lines that courts draw in many of these decisions precisely track the parameters of privacy jurisprudence. Common law cadaver cases, for example, grant the right to control disposition of a dead body to decedents and their close relatives, but repeatedly deny the right to treat the corpse as an article of commerce. Similarly, *Moore v. Regents of the University of California* affirms the patient's autonomy over his own body but rejects his claim to receive a share of the profits reaped from the valuable cell line derived from his spleen cells. In addition, *Hecht v. Superior Court* ultimately held that a man may bestow his sperm upon a lover, but the recipient may not trade the sperm to others. These decisions differentiate between self-ownership and sale of the body to others, while separating the rights of intimate relatives from the interests of strangers. Although such subtle distinctions are alien to property law, they are entirely consistent with the right of privacy. . . .[30]

NEW JERSEY GENETIC PRIVACY ACT

N.J.S.A. § 10:5-43 et seq.

In 1996, New Jersey passed the Genetic Privacy Act, one of the broadest state protections of genetic privacy. The Act prohibits discrimination based on genetic information:

---

[30] Radhika Rao, *Property, Privacy, and the Human Body*, 80 B.U. L. Rev. 359 (2000).

Section 3:
. . . No person shall make or permit any unfair discrimination against an individual in the application of the results of a genetic test or genetic information in the underwriting of or determining insurability for insurance, withholding, extension or renewal of a policy of life insurance, including credit life insurance, an annuity, disability income insurance contract or credit accident insurance overage. . . .

Section 5:
It shall be an unlawful employment practice, or, as the case may be, an unlawful discrimination:
    a. For an employer because of the race, creed, color, national origin, ancestry, age, marital status, affectational or sexual orientation, genetic information, sex or atypical hereditary cellular or blood trait of any individual . . . or because of the refusal to submit to a genetic test or make available the results of a genetic test to an employer, to refuse to hire or employ or to bar or to discharge or require to retire, unless justified by lawful considerations other than age, from employment such individual or to discriminate against such individual in compensation or in terms, conditions, or privileges of employment. . . .

The Act further limits the collection, retention, or disclosure of genetic information about an individual without first obtaining the individual's informed consent. *See* Sections 6, 7, and 8, respectively. Exceptions include the use of genetic information by law enforcement for the purposes of establishing the identity of a person in the course of a criminal investigation, to determine paternity, to determine the identity of deceased individuals, and a number of other exceptions.

Section 7 declares: "An individual's genetic information is the property of the individual." Among exceptions to the retention restriction, Section 7 provides for retention if it "is for anonymous research where the identity of the subject will not be released."

With regard to disclosure, Section 8 provides, subject to certain exceptions, that "[r]egardless of the manner of receipt or the source of genetic information, including information received from an individual, a person may not disclose or be compelled, by subpoena or other means, to disclose the identity of an individual upon whom a genetic test has been performed or to disclose genetic information about the individual in a manner that permits identification of the individual." The exceptions allow for disclosure if authorized by court order or if "for the purpose of furnishing genetic information relating to a decedent for medical diagnosis of blood relatives of the decedent."

NOTES & QUESTIONS

1. At least 18 states have passed statutes protecting the privacy of genetic information.[31]

---

[31] *See* Joy Pritts, Janlori Goldman, Zoe Hudson, Aimee Berenson, and Elizabeth Hadley, *The State of Health Privacy: An Uneven Terrain (A Comprehensive Survey of State Health Privacy Statutes)* (1999), <*http://www.georgetown.edu/research/ihcrp/privacy/statereport.pdf*>.

2. How does the New Jersey Act deal with the trade-off in *Moore* between property rights and research?

3. How does the Act affect the case of *Safer v. Estate of Pack,* where the court held that a duty of care may require a doctor to disclose genetic information about a parent to a child?

4. ***Genetic Information vs. Other Medical Information.*** Should genetic information be treated any differently than other medical information? Consider George Annas, who contends that genetic information constitutes a "future diary" about individuals:

> First, let us examine the nature of privacy and why genetic information is private. The first thing that must be understood is that all your genetic information is contained in the nucleus of each of your cells. All that a geneticist needs is one cell from you to read your genetic code. It could be a blood cell — most genetic testing is done with blood cells. It could also be hair cells or even saliva. Once someone has a drop of your blood, or, perhaps, hair or saliva, they have your DNA from which your genetic code can be extracted.
>
> Therefore, we have to think of one drop of blood as a medical record. It is in code, it is a code that has not been broken yet, and it will require sophisticated codebreakers to break it. But the fact remains that it is a complete record of your DNA. You do not have to agree with many boosters of the Genome Project who think it is the Book of Life, that your DNA is going to tell the story of your life. I would not get that carried away, but it does contain an enormous amount of information about you and your probable medical future.[32]

Contrast Annas's view with Judge Douglas Ginsburg:

> I believe it was Dr. Annas who coined the term "future diary" to describe the information in our genes. The metaphor derives its power from the jealousy with which people guard the secrets in their written diaries and therefore implicitly supports genetic exceptionalism. Upon analysis, however, the metaphor breaks down. First, our future diaries are much less diverse than our written ones: "while a child is 99.95 percent the same as its genetic mother at the level of the DNA molecule, it is also 99.90 percent the same as any randomly chosen person on the planet earth." Second, unlike the past thoughts and actions contained in our written diaries, the secrets that our future diaries are supposed to hold, like our family histories, speak only to probabilities. . . .
>
> The sober, unexciting realization that genetic information is but the latest iteration of our evolving medical knowledge yields one final suggestion: areas in which changes in degree are endemic are not well suited to statutory solutions. Courts, following in the common law tradition, can address the issues that genetic information raises as the extension of an existing phenomenon. Recognizing that genetic information is not qualitatively different from other types of medical information allows courts to draw upon past experience and to adapt that experience to meet new challenges. Engrafting a unique statutory solution for genetic information onto this common law landscape will simply create two divergent legal regimes for what is essentially a single problem.[33]

---

[32] George J. Annas, *Genetic Privacy: There Ought to Be a Law,* 4 Tex. Rev. L. & Pol. 9 (1999).

[33] Douglas H. Ginsburg, *Genetics and Privacy,* 4 Tex. Rev. L. & Pol. 17 (1999).

3. GENETIC TESTING AND DISCRIMINATION

A genetic disorder occurs as a result of a particular genetic mutation. Sometimes, a mutation of a single gene alone can cause the disorder. Sometimes, disorders are caused by many mutated genes and environmental factors. Genetic testing can give people the opportunity to find out if they have a high risk of contracting certain genetic disorders — such as cystic fibrosis, muscular dystrophy, Huntington's disease, and some rare forms of breast and colon cancer. Often, genetic testing does not predict with 100 percent accuracy whether a person will come down with a particular disorder. But it can predict that the risks will be very high for contracting certain disorders.

The information that a person has a high risk to contract a disorder that is disabling or fatal is not merely of use to that person, but also is of great interest to one's spouse, fiancée, or partner. Additionally, such information is useful to one's health or life insurer, since having the disorder dramatically affects the potential risk the insurer expects as well as the level of insurance payments it demands. It may be of interest to one's creditors, as one who has a high risk of contracting a fatal disorder may not be worth the risk of lending money to. Further, it may be of interest to one's employer, who may not want to spend the time, resources, and money training a worker who may have to retire earlier than expected. Employers that self-insure may also be interested in the information, as the potential employee will affect the employer's financial condition.

Currently, most companies do not require genetic testing, but 20 percent require data about the medical history of employees' families, which can serve as a source for genetic information.[34] In 2001, Burlington Northern Santa Fe Railroad secretly tested employees suffering from carpal tunnel syndrome to see if they were genetically predisposed to coming down with the condition. When the testing came to light, and the company was sued by the EEOC and a workers' union, the company settled, agreeing to halt the testing. Twenty-eight states have statutes restricting employers from gathering, using, and/or disclosing employee genetic data.[35]

RICHARD A. EPSTEIN, *THE LEGAL REGULATION OF GENETIC DISCRIMINATION: OLD RESPONSES TO NEW TECHNOLOGY*

74 B.U. L. Rev. 1 (1994)

. . . Must the person disclose the information [learned from a genetic test] to other parties? I think that in the case of Huntington's disease it is immoral for a person to marry (or even take a job) and conceal the condition from the potential spouse or employer. This conclusion is valid in commercial settings as well as in marital ones so long as the concealment results in selective knowledge to one side that is denied to the other. When an individual has knowledge that he is at risk of incapacitation, perhaps from family history, then full

---

[34] *See Health Privacy Project, Report: Genetics and Privacy: A Patchwork of Protections* 19 (2002).
[35] National Conference of State Legislatures, <*www.ncsl.org/programs/health/genetics/ndiscrim.htm*>.

disclosure should be the norm. When the individual knows to a certainty that he is a carrier of the trait, from a reliable genetic test, the same is true. The principle does not change; all that changes is the information that must be disclosed. . . .

At this point it is critical to note that the plea for privacy is often a plea for the right to misrepresent one's self to the rest of the world. In and of itself that may not be a bad thing. We are certainly not obligated to disclose all of our embarrassing past to persons in ordinary social conversations; and it is certainly acceptable to use long sleeves to cover an ugly scar. White lies are part of the glue that makes human interaction possible without shame and loss of face. Strictly speaking, people may be deceived, but they are rarely hurt, and they may even be relieved to be spared an awkward encounter. However, when a major change in personal or financial status is contemplated by another party, the white lies that make human interaction possible turn into frauds of a somewhat deeper dye. In order to see why this is the case, recall that the traditional tort of misrepresentation stressed the usual five fingers: a false statement, known to be false, material to the listener, and relied on, to the listener's detriment. There is little question, whether we deal with marriage or with business, that concealment of relevant genetic information satisfies each element. The only question, therefore, is whether one can justify what is a prima facie wrong.

I am hard pressed to see what that justification might be. No doubt the individual who engages in this type of deception has much to gain. But equally there can be no doubt that this gain exists in all garden variety cases of fraud as well. To show the advantage of the fraud to the party who commits it is hardly to excuse or to justify it, for the same can be said of all cases of successful wrongs. On the other side of the transaction, there is a pronounced loss from not knowing the information when key decisions have to be made. . . .

False statements about or deliberate concealment of genetic information is as much a fraud as false statements about or concealment of any other issue. The only possible justification for concealment, therefore, would be that it is unfair for the person with the pending disorder to deal alone with the suffering and financial loss. Yet, that loss is not sustained because of the wrong of another. Could the victim of a natural catastrophe keep it secret, and single out one other person to bear some substantial fraction of the loss? If not, then why give that same privilege to the victim of a genetic defect? Today, it is easy to find strong support for socializing losses. But why should a person laboring under a genetic defect be entitled to pick the person or group that has to pay the subsidy? . . .

PAUL SCHWARTZ, *PRIVACY AND THE*
ECONOMICS OF HEALTH CARE INFORMATION

76 Tex. L. Rev. 1 (1997)

. . . Most people who receive health benefits in this country obtain it at their place of employment. In the United States approximately 140 million people, or nearly two-thirds of the population under sixty-five, receive medical benefits through their job. Because these benefits are an increasingly costly part of the overall package of compensation, employers have a great incentive to weed out workers with expensive health care needs. Despite any amount of soothing statements about the rationality of employers, the actual use of genetic information and health records in employment decisions is far from efficient. . . .

The argument against [Richard Epstein's] position is greatly strengthened by the generally poor societal record in this area; a considerable historical pattern exists of misapplication of [genetic] information. This story begins with the eugenics movement, whose misunderstanding and deformation of genetic science encouraged public policies that included the sterilization of "inferior" members of society. As for the recent era of modern genetics, the United States has far from a perfect record. Genetic discrimination already takes place in the United States. Studies by scientists at Stanford and Harvard have documented numerous instances of genetic discrimination in the public and private sectors. Another study found a high rate of discrimination in obtaining insurance and employment for people who have a genetic condition or for their family members. Many of these individuals will never suffer from any genetic illness; yet, the testing process itself creates a category of individuals now deemed to be genetically unfit. . . .

Like genetic information, health care data are also being used to make employment decisions. According to one empirical study of privacy in the workplace, over one-third of Fortune 500 companies surveyed in 1995 admitted to using the medical records of their personnel in employment-related decisions. In previous years, this survey found that as many as one-half of these companies admitted to engaging in such behavior. Evidence also indicates that some of this reliance on employees' health data is leading to economically inefficient employment decisions. According to a recent nationwide survey, for example, cancer patients currently lose their jobs at over five times the rate of those who do not have the disease. Considerable ignorance has also been found regarding the workplace implications of this disease; another survey found common overestimation by supervisors of the actual experience of cancer patients regarding fatigue, infections, and nausea during treatment. To consider another socially charged illness, one can point to evidence that greater insurance discrimination is faced by those who are HIV-positive than individuals who suffer from equally serious illnesses with similar costs. Discrimination between employees with different health conditions can be based on social stigma and misunderstandings rather than the relative costs of different workers' medical conditions. . . .

. . . The individual to whom these data refer faces a high price when attempting to explain the significance or insignificance of the information, and these explanatory costs can exceed the value of unrestricted disclosure to society. Indeed, many parties, including employers, believe that they are not ignorant about the full dimensions or implications of certain personal data, and will continue to (mis)apply genetic personal information based simply on their popular beliefs. Thus, achieving economic efficiency necessitates placing certain kinds of limits on access to personal information because of the excessive social costs of placing such data in the proper context under a policy of unrestricted access. . . .

An excessive disclosure norm for certain kinds of information will distort or eliminate the kinds of personal information that health care consumers share in future transactions with physicians. . . . Inadequate safeguards for protecting medical data will make the encounters that take place between physicians and patients less effective because of the likelihood that patients will withhold important information. . . .

Open access to health care or genetic information has a final negative effect on individual behavior. It ties individuals to current jobs out of the fear that they will be denied new employment or health insurance. . . . These workers were afraid that their health history or that of family members would lead a new insurer to reject or limit their coverage. As this Article has indicated, such fears are far from baseless. The resulting phenomenon, which has been termed "job lock," introduces significant distortions in the labor market. As health care economist Victor Fuchs notes, "[L]abor market efficiency suffers" when health insurance considerations affect workers' choices of jobs and decisions about job change. . . .

. . . To summarize our argument thus far, employers are not making purely rational use of medical and genetic data. Rather, this information provides an excuse for the exercise of social stigma and misunderstandings of science. Open access to these data also distorts individual behavior by encouraging patients to share incomplete data with physicians and by causing employees to be locked in jobs that they would otherwise leave. Moreover, open disclosure permits certain workers to be cast off into an increasingly strained public insurance market. This process has contributed to an increase in aggregate health care costs. . . .

NOTES & QUESTIONS

1. On February 8, 2000, President Clinton issued Executive Order 13145: To Prohibit Discrimination in Federal Employment Based on Genetic Information. It applies to all Executive departments and agencies with regard to all employees covered by § 717 of Title VII of the Civil Rights Act of 1964. The Order protects "protected genetic information," which is defined as "information about an individual's genetic tests," "information about the genetic tests of an individual's family members," or "information about the occurrence of a disease, or medical condition or disorder in family members of the individual." Pursuant to the Order:

> (a) The employing department or agency shall not discharge, fail or refuse to hire, or otherwise discriminate against any employee with respect to the compensation, terms, conditions, or privileges of employment of that employee, because of protected genetic information with respect to the employee, or because of information about a request for or the receipt of genetic services by such employee.
>
> (b) The employing department or agency shall not limit, segregate, or classify employees in any way that would deprive or tend to deprive any employee of employment opportunities or otherwise adversely affect that employee's status, because of protected genetic information with respect to the employee or because of information about a request for or the receipt of genetic services by such employee.

(c) The employing department or agency shall not request, require, collect, or purchase protected genetic information with respect to an employee, or information about a request for or the receipt of genetic services by such employee.

2. As of 2002, thirty states have laws prohibiting employment discrimination based on genetic information.[36] Thirty-four states have statutes barring the use of genetic data by insurers for risk classification.[37]
3. Recall from Chapter 1 Judge Posner's view that privacy is a desire to misrepresent oneself, a type of fraud. How does this compare to Epstein's view of privacy? Suppose a person has diabetes, heart disease, or cancer. In an application for health or life insurance, that person would have to disclose all pre-existing conditions. Otherwise, the individual would be committing a fraud if she deliberately left out health conditions that she was aware of. Why not view the knowledge of genetic predisposition the same way? What is the difference between the nondisclosure of regular medical information versus genetic information?

4. DNA DATABASES

One current use of DNA is known as DNA fingerprinting or DNA typing.[38] This involves the comparison of DNA from two samples. At a crime scene, most often with violent crimes, the criminal might have unwittingly deposited genetic material. A pulled-out hair, a drop of blood, a scratched-off skin cell, semen, and so on can enable forensic scientists to extract DNA. The entire genome is not used; only particular portions or fragments of DNA that are known to contain differences among individuals. An early method of analyzing DNA was restriction fragment length polymorphism (RFLP). DNA was extracted from samples using special enzymes and cut into fragments and organized by size. These fragments were then exposed on X-ray film, where they formed a pattern of dark bands, which are unique to each type of DNA. Today, a newer technology called short tandem repeat (STR) analysis is the most common method of DNA typing. STR analysis examines length polymorphisms known as short tandem repeats.[39]

The fact that a suspect's DNA matches that found at a crime scene does not indicate with certainty that the suspect is likely to be the culprit or even is likely to have been at the crime scene. Statistically, a portion of the population will match the DNA found at a crime scene. What DNA evidence can determine with near certainty is that certain individuals do not match the DNA at the scene. In other words, DNA evidence can more accurately exclude individuals as suspects than include them.

---

[36] National Conference of State Legislatures, <*www.ncsl.org/programs/health/genetics/ndiscrim.htm*>.

[37] National Conference of State Legislatures, <*www.ncsl.org/programs/health/genetics/ndishlth.htm*>.

[38] For a legal discussion of DNA fingerprinting, see Dan L. Burk & Jennifer A. Hess, *Genetic Privacy: Constitutional Considerations in Forensic DNA Testing*, 5 Geo. Mason U. Civ. Rts. L.J. 1 (1994).

[39] *See* William C. Thompson, *DNA Testing*, in 2 *Encyclopedia of Crime and Punishment* 537 (David Levinson, ed. 2002).

Since DNA has proven to be a very useful tool for forensic scientists in solving crimes, the states and the FBI are assembling DNA databases of felons. All states permit DNA to be taken from sex offenders and other violent criminals. There is currently a push to expand DNA collection to all arrestees. The FBI maintains a national DNA database known as the Combined DNA Indexing System (CODIS).[40] These DNA databases do not contain a person's entire genetic code, just fragments useful for identification. Currently, in the United States, the collection of DNA is limited to those convicted or accused of a crime. There are some notable exceptions, one of which is the United States' military, which maintains a DNA database for identification of the remains of soldiers in combat. For the most part, however, the government does not collect DNA from ordinary citizens to help solve crimes.

In contrast, Britain more widely collects DNA from its citizens. In 1987, British authorities collected DNA samples from every male citizen in Leicestershire after two young women were raped. This technique has been dubbed a "DNA dragnet," and this case was explored in depth in Joseph Wambaugh's *The Blooding* (1989).[41] Since 1995, British authorities have been collecting DNA from everybody taken into police custody. The British government has plans to expand its DNA database to allow the retention of the DNA of individuals later found to be innocent. In many other countries, such DNA profiles are destroyed.

DNA databases can be used for other purposes than crime solving. As scientists better understand the human genome, other uses for genetic information will arise.

The following case involves a Fourth Amendment challenge to a state's creation of a DNA database. The Fourth Amendment will be covered in greater depth in Chapter 4. For the purposes of understanding this case, the Fourth Amendment requires that searches (looking around for evidence) and seizures (taking of items and evidence) be "reasonable" and generally be authorized by a warrant supported by probable cause. The warrant requirement ensures that a neutral judge or magistrate approves of the search and that the police have a good justification for a search. This typically means "individualized suspicion"—that there is a good reason to suspect that a particular individual has engaged in a crime. This requirement prevents searches that are "fishing expeditions." However, there are exceptions to the warrant requirement, as indicated by the case below.

RISE V. OREGON

59 F.3d 1556 (9th Cir. 1995)

FLETCHER, C.J. The plaintiffs in this 42 U.S.C. § 1983 suit appeal the district court's summary judgment dismissing their claims. We have jurisdiction and affirm.

---

[40] *See id.*
[41] *See id.*

Chapter 669, Oregon Laws 1991, O.R.S. §§ 137.076, 161.325(4), 181.085, 419.507(11), and 419.800(4)(k), requires persons convicted of murder, a sexual offense,[42] or conspiracy or attempt to commit a sexual offense to submit a blood sample to the Oregon Department of Corrections ("DOC"). DOC uses the blood that is submitted to create a deoxyribonucleic acid (DNA) data bank. Plaintiffs Erik Rise, David Durham, and Jeffery Rhodes were convicted before the enactment of Chapter 669 of one or more of the offenses to which the Chapter applies. Plaintiff Michael Milligan was convicted of attempted murder, which is not a predicate offense under Chapter 669.

The plaintiffs allege that Chapter 669 violates the Fourth Amendment's prohibition against unreasonable searches and seizures. . . .

Non-consensual extraction of blood implicates Fourth Amendment privacy rights. *Skinner v. Railway Labor Executives' Ass'n*, 489 U.S. 602, 616 (1989) ("this physical intrusion, penetrating beneath the skin, infringes [a reasonable] expectation of privacy"); *Schmerber v. California*, 384 U.S. 757, 767 (1966) (compulsory blood test "plainly involves the broadly conceived reach of a search and seizure under the Fourth Amendment"). To hold that the Fourth Amendment applies to the blood sampling authorized by Chapter 669, however, is only the start of our inquiry, "[f]or the Fourth Amendment does not proscribe all searches and seizures, but only those that are unreasonable." A search's reasonableness under the Fourth Amendment generally depends on whether the search was made pursuant to a warrant issued upon probable cause. The plaintiffs maintain that because Chapter 669 requires them to submit blood samples without warrants and without probable cause to believe that they have committed any unsolved criminal offenses, it violates the Fourth Amendment's prohibition against unreasonable searches and seizures. We do not agree. . . .

Even in the law enforcement context, the State may interfere with an individual's Fourth Amendment interests with less than probable cause and without a warrant if the intrusion is only minimal and is justified by law enforcement purposes. To determine whether the intrusions authorized by Chapter 669 are minimal, we examine separately the privacy interests implicated by the state's derivation and retention of identifying DNA information from a convicted felon's blood, and the interest in bodily integrity implicated by the physical intrusion necessary to obtain the blood sample.

The gathering of genetic information for identification purposes from a convicted murderer's or sexual offender's blood once the blood has been drawn does not constitute more than a minimal intrusion upon the plaintiffs' Fourth Amendment interests. The information derived from the blood sample is substantially the same as that derived from fingerprinting — an identifying marker unique to the individual from whom the information is derived. The gathering of fingerprint evidence from "free persons" consti-

---

[42] Chapter 669 includes as predicate offenses the following sex-related crimes: rape, sodomy, unlawful sexual penetration, sexual abuse, public indecency, incest, using a child in a display of sexually explicit conduct, and promoting or compelling prostitution. O.R.S. § 137.076(1). We refer to them collectively as "sexual offenses."

tutes a sufficiently significant interference with individual expectations of privacy that law enforcement officials are required to demonstrate that they have probable cause, or at least an articulable suspicion, to believe that the person committed a criminal offense and that the fingerprinting will establish or negate the person's connection to the offense. Nevertheless, everyday "booking" procedures routinely require even the merely accused to provide fingerprint identification, regardless of whether investigation of the crime involves fingerprint evidence. See *Smith v. United States*, 324 F.2d 879, 882 (D.C.Cir. 1963) (Burger, J.) ("it is elementary that a person in lawful custody may be required to submit to . . . fingerprinting . . . as part of the routine identification processes"); *Napolitano v. United States*, 340 F.2d 313, 314 (1st Cir. 1965) ("Taking fingerprints [prior to bail] is universally standard procedure, and no violation of constitutional rights."). Thus, in the fingerprinting context, there exists a constitutionally significant distinction between the gathering of fingerprints from free persons to determine their guilt of an unsolved criminal offense and the gathering of fingerprints for identification purposes from persons within the lawful custody of the state.

A similar, but even more compelling, distinction is applicable here. Although the drawing of blood from free persons generally requires a warrant supported by probable cause to believe that a person has committed a criminal offense and that his blood will reveal evidence relevant to that offense, the absence of such a warrant does not a fortiori establish a violation of the plaintiffs' Fourth Amendment rights. Chapter 669 authorizes DOC to acquire blood samples not from free persons or even mere arrestees, but only from certain classes of convicted felons in order to create a record for possible use for identification in the future. These persons do not have the same expectations of privacy in their identifying genetic information that "free persons" have. Once a person is convicted of one of the felonies included as predicate offenses under Chapter 669, his identity has become a matter of state interest and he has lost any legitimate expectation of privacy in the identifying information derived from the blood sampling.

That the gathering of DNA information requires the drawing of blood rather than inking and rolling a person's fingertips does not elevate the intrusion upon the plaintiffs' Fourth Amendment interests to a level beyond minimal.[43] The Supreme Court has noted repeatedly that the drawing of blood constitutes only a minimally intrusive search.

---

[43] The dissent suggests that our comparison to traditional fingerprinting is inapt because fingerprints "are personal attributes that are routinely exposed to the public at large in daily life" and, accordingly, the gathering of fingerprints, unlike the drawing of blood, implicates "a categorically different and lesser expectation of privacy." However, the fingerprints gathered by law enforcement officials and included in fingerprint identification data banks are not ones that have been left behind voluntarily on doorknobs and water glasses. They are the ones gathered by holding the person's hand firmly and taking the prints. Much like the process of providing a blood sample, providing one's fingerprints can be quick and simple if one submits voluntarily, but has the potential for the use of force if resisted. It is for this reason that, outside the "booking" process to which we analogize, courts do generally require some level of individualized suspicion to support the seizure necessary to gather a person's fingerprints.

Because Chapter 669 authorizes only a minimal intrusion into the plaintiffs' Fourth Amendment interests, determining its constitutionality requires us to balance the gravity of the public interest served by the creation of a DNA data bank, the degree to which the data bank would advance the public interest, and the severity of the resulting interference with individual liberty. . . .

. . . The defendants produced uncontroverted evidence documenting the high rates of recidivism among certain types of murderers and sexual offenders. Moreover, investigations of murders and sexual offenses are more likely to yield the types of evidence from which DNA information can be derived, such as blood, semen, saliva, and hair evidence, than property crimes or other offenses committed without substantial personal contact. Taken together, these two facts suggest that a data bank of DNA information derived from the blood of convicted murderers and sexual offenders will help the state to identify and prosecute the perpetrators of future offenses. The creation of a DNA data bank also advances the overwhelming public interest in prosecuting crimes accurately — DNA evidence can exculpate an accused just as effectively as it can inculpate him.

Chapter 669 applies only to persons actually convicted of murder or a sexual offense and requires no more than one blood extraction from an individual in his lifetime. Blood samples can be taken only in a medically acceptable manner by appropriately trained medical personnel, and a convicted person is not required to submit a blood sample if doing so would present a substantial and unreasonable risk to his health.

Chapter 669 also limits the State's use of blood samples taken pursuant to the Chapter. Only district attorneys, courts, grand juries, certain law enforcement officers, and parties to a criminal prosecution may be privy to the information derived from the blood sample, and the State may not analyze the samples to discover genetic predispositions to physical or mental conditions. . . .

Taking into account all of the factors discussed above . . . we conclude that Chapter 669 is reasonable and therefore constitutional under the Fourth Amendment. . . .

D. W. NELSON, J. dissenting. The majority fails to find a Fourth Amendment violation arising from the nonconsensual DNA genetic pattern analysis of persons convicted for murder or various sexual offenses (including such nonviolent crimes as public indecency or pimping, or attempts at any of the included sexual offenses). Ostensibly applying a traditional balancing test that weighs the severity of the intrusion on personal prsivacy interests against the importance of the public interest served, the majority upholds extraction and analysis of blood samples, without any showing of probable cause or even individualized suspicion, solely for the ordinary law enforcement purpose of facilitating investigation of crimes that may be committed in the future. . . .

Focusing on the Supreme Court's discussion of the routine and commonplace manner of the blood extraction process, the majority minimizes the import of *Schmerber v. California*, 384 U.S. 757 (1966), erroneously concluding that the scope of the search is a de minimis concern. The *Schmerber* Court, however, considered such an intrusion into bodily integrity to be so significant that it normally would require a warrant supported by probable cause.

Except in certain narrowly limited cases, the Court repeatedly has stated its "insist[ence] upon probable cause as a minimum requirement for a reasonable search permitted by the Constitution." Because "[t]he integrity of an individual's person is a cherished value in our society," searches that invade bodily integrity cannot be executed as mere fishing expeditions to acquire useful evidence: "The interests in human dignity and privacy which the Fourth Amendment protects forbid any such intrusions on the mere chance that desired evidence might be obtained."

Only when law enforcement faces an exigent circumstance, such as a need to preserve evanescent blood alcohol evidence, and has probable cause to link the sought-after information to a crime under investigation is it constitutional to conduct non-consensual blood testing without a warrant. Therefore, forced extraction of blood not only "implicates the Fourth Amendment," as the majority notes, but also falls squarely within the area of privacy interests for which the traditional probable cause requirement determines reasonableness in the law enforcement context. Forced blood extraction intrudes on the private personal sphere and infringes upon an individual's "most personal and deep-rooted expectations of privacy." *Winston v. Lee*, 470 U.S. 753, 760 (1985). . . .

The majority cannot distinguish *Schmerber* on this basis, because furthering the public's interest in prosecuting criminals was also the purpose for the blood test in *Schmerber*. In addition, the rational relationship to the goal of prosecuting perpetrators of potential future crimes is certainly more attenuated than the direct relationship of the blood testing in *Schmerber* to the goal of finding evidence of blood alcohol content for use in the prosecution of a drunk driver who has already violated the law. . . . The majority's approach stands Fourth Amendment jurisprudence on its head by suggesting that statistical probabilities of future conduct can suffice in lieu of the probable cause requirement in the traditional law enforcement context. . . .

. . . [Next, t]he majority suggests that a person's status as a convict is sufficient to allow nonconsensual extraction of blood unrelated to securing evidence for use in the prosecution of the individual for the crime for which he or she was convicted, just as status as an arrestee is sufficient to allow fingerprinting. Nonetheless, routine searches that intrude into prisoners' bodies without probable cause may be upheld only when the search is undertaken pursuant to a valid prison regulation that is reasonably related to a legitimate penological objective. . . . The creation of the data bank has nothing to do with prison administration. . . .

Felons enjoy those constitutional rights that are not subject to attenuation because of the security concerns of the prison context. *Bell v. Wolfish*, 441 U.S. 520, 545 (1979) ("convicted prisoners do not forfeit all constitutional protections by reason of their conviction"). Those retained rights include the protection from unjustified invasions of bodily integrity, including a right not to have blood drawn if there is no evidence of a legitimate penological objective for the search. The *Wolfish* Court upheld certain body cavity searches of inmates only "in light of the central objective of prison administration, safeguarding institutional security." Consequently, we have rejected any extension of *Wolfish* beyond the prison security rationale to ordinary criminal investigatory searches of inmates. . . .

The majority's rationale ultimately rests on a fourth indefensible premise that, even in the absence of prison regulations to achieve penological objectives, the protections of the Fourth Amendment do not apply to this particular use of forced blood extraction of convicted offenders for creation of a criminal identification data bank. Relying on the glib linguistic ease with which various commentators categorize DNA genetic pattern analysis as a kind of genetic "fingerprinting," the majority simply asserts that the purpose of identifying future criminal perpetrators makes it possible constitutionally to equate a forced blood extraction with a forced fingerprinting.

This premise fails, because the Supreme Court and this circuit have consistently recognized a distinction of constitutional significance between a forced invasion of bodily integrity and fingerprinting. Blood samples for DNA genetic pattern analysis must be extracted by puncturing the skin and withdrawing body fluids. *Schmerber* clearly requires a warrant for that forced blood extraction, unless probable cause combines with exigent circumstances such as the dissipation of blood alcohol evidence. In addition, DNA genetic pattern analysis is even more intrusive than the blood alcohol test, discussed in *Schmerber* and *Skinner*, which revealed only the current blood levels of alcohol and other behavior-altering substances. DNA genetic pattern analysis catalogs uniquely private genetic facts about the individual that should be subject to rigorous confidentiality requirements even broader than the protection of an individual's medical records. *See Whalen v. Roe*, 429 U.S. 589, 599 (1977) (recognizing the individual's "interest in avoiding disclosure of personal matters").

Conversely, individuals have a categorically different and lesser expectation of privacy in their fingerprints, visual images, or voice prints — even when their production is compelled — because they are personal attributes that are routinely exposed to the public at large in daily life. *Katz v. United States*, 389 U.S. 347, 351 (1967) (finding a lesser expectation of privacy in personal effects that "a person knowingly exposes to the public, even in his own home or office").

> [T]he Fourth Amendment provides no protection for what "a person knowingly exposes to the public" . . . Like a man's facial characteristics, or handwriting, his voice is repeatedly produced for others to hear. No person can have a reasonable expectation that others will not know the sound of his voice, any more than he can reasonably expect that his face will be a mystery to the world. . . .
>
> The required disclosure of a person's voice is thus immeasurably further removed from the Fourth Amendment protection than was the intrusion into the body effected by the blood extraction in *Schmerber*. . . .

United States v. Dionisio, 410 U.S. 1, 14-15 (1973). "Fingerprinting"— like the compelled production of other aspects of an individual's identification that are routinely exposed to and superficially observable by the public at large, such as voice prints, handwriting exemplars, and photographs — simply belongs to a different category of search that "represents a much less serious intrusion upon personal security than other types of searches and detentions." The majority's analysis obliterates this critical constitutional distinction between coerced fingerprinting and blood extraction for DNA genetic pattern analysis. . . .

NOTES & QUESTIONS

1. What is the privacy injury with regard to DNA databases? Is it the physical invasion of the body to remove the blood? Or is it the fact that DNA can include significant information about a person? Currently, DNA identification only involves a small portion of one's DNA. The entire genome is not mapped out. Sequencing is done for certain known sites where particular genes show a significant variability, as much of our DNA is identical. DNA databases do not contain the entire DNA of an individual but only samples of certain genes. Should this fact alleviate any concern over DNA databases? What if one's entire genome were included in the database?

2. What is wrong with the government having a DNA database of convicts and doing searches to identify the perpetrators of crimes? Would your opinion change if the database contained the DNA of everybody, not just those who were convicted of a crime? Would a national DNA database consisting of DNA for every citizen collected through a mandatory collection program be constitutional? Suppose that the DNA were obtained without requiring a physical intrusion into the body. Would this affect your view of the constitutionality of the national DNA database?

3. Does the existence of the DNA databases mean that for offenders in the database, they will always be investigated (by a search in the database) every time there is a sexual or violent crime? Is this any different from what is already done through the use of fingerprints and mug shots?[44]

4. In 2000, in a small rural Australian village, police used a mass DNA screening investigation technique to locate the man who raped a 91-year-old woman. Villagers were free to refuse the DNA test, but critics said that the DNA testing was not really voluntary because a person who refuses will appear guilty in the eyes of the rest of the village. Suppose this occurred in a small town in the United States. What legal challenges could be raised?

---

[44]Thus far, courts have typically agreed with the rationale of *Rise v. Oregon* and have sustained DNA databases against Fourth Amendment challenges. *See, e.g., Jones v. Murray*, 962 F.2d 302 (4th Cir. 1992); *Boling v. Romer*, 101 F.3d 1336 (10th Cir. 1996); *Shaffer v. Saffle*, 148 F.3d 1180 (10th Cir. 1998); *Roe v. Marcotte*, 193 F.3d 72 (2d Cir. 1999).

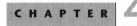

CHAPTER 4

PRIVACY AND LAW ENFORCEMENT

A. THE FOURTH AMENDMENT AND EMERGING TECHNOLOGY

1. INTRODUCTION

(a) Privacy and Security

One of the central tensions in information privacy law is between privacy and security. Security involves society's interest in protecting itself from physical and monetary threats and crimes. One way that government promotes security is by investigating and punishing crimes. To do this, law enforcement officials must gather information about suspected individuals. Monitoring and information gathering pose substantial threats to privacy. Throughout the twentieth century, technology provided the government significantly greater ability to probe into the private lives of individuals.

The prevailing metaphor for the threat to privacy caused by law enforcement surveillance techniques is George Orwell's novel, *Nineteen Eighty-Four*. Written in 1949, the novel depicted an all-powerful and omniscient government called "Big Brother" that monitored and controlled every facet of individuals' lives:

> Outside, even through the shut window-pane, the world looked cold. Down in the street little eddies of wind were whirling dust and torn paper into spirals, and though the sun was shining and the sky a harsh blue, there seemed to be no colour in anything, except the posters that were plastered everywhere. The blackmoustachio'd face gazed down from every commanding corner. There was one on the house-front immediately opposite. BIG BROTHER IS WATCHING YOU, the caption said, while the dark eyes looked deep into Winston's own. Down at streetlevel another poster, torn at one corner, flapped fitfully in the wind, alternately covering and uncovering the single word INGSOC. In the far distance a helicopter skimmed down between the roofs, hovered for an instant like a bluebottle, and darted away again with a curving flight. It was the police patrol, snooping into people's windows. The patrols did not matter, however. Only the Thought Police mattered.

Behind Winston's back the voice from the telescreen was still babbling away about pig-iron and the overfulfilment of the Ninth Three-Year Plan. The tele-screen received and transmitted simultaneously. Any sound that Winston made, above the level of a very low whisper, would be picked up by it, more-over, so long as he remained within the field of vision which the metal plaque commanded, he could be seen as well as heard. There was of course no way of knowing whether you were being watched at any given moment. How often, or on what system, the Thought Police plugged in on any individual wire was guesswork. It was even conceivable that they watched everybody all the time. But at any rate they could plug in your wire whenever they wanted to. You had to live — did live, from habit that became instinct — in the assumption that every sound you made was overheard, and, except in darkness, every move-ment scrutinized. . . .[1]

Orwell's harrowing portrait of a police state illustrates the importance of limiting the power of the government to monitor its citizens.

(b) The Fourth and Fifth Amendments

In the United States, policing is predominantly carried out by local gov-ernments. The Constitution, however, provides a national regulatory regime for police conduct. The Fourth and Fifth Amendments significantly limit the government's power to gather information. The Fourth Amendment provides:

The right of the people to be secure in their persons, houses, papers, and ef-fects, against unreasonable searches and seizures, shall not be violated, and no warrants shall issue, but upon probable cause, supported by oath or affirma-tion, and particularly describing the place to be searched, and the persons or things to be seized.

As the Supreme Court has recognized, "[t]he overriding function of the Fourth Amendment is to protect personal privacy and dignity against unwar-ranted intrusion by the State." *Schmerber v. California*, 384 U.S. 757, 767 (1966).

The Fifth Amendment guarantees that: "No person . . . shall be compelled in any criminal case to be a witness against himself. . . ." The Fifth Amendment establishes a "privilege against self-incrimination," and it prohibits the gov-ernment from compelling individuals to disclose inculpatory information about themselves.

In *Boyd v. United States*, 116 U.S. 616 (1886), one of the foundational cases defining the meaning of the Fourth and Fifth Amendments, the government issued a subpoena to compel Boyd, a merchant, to produce invoices on cases of imported glass for use in a civil forfeiture proceeding. The Court held that the subpoena violated the Fourth and Fifth Amendments:

. . . [B]y the proceeding now under consideration, the court attempts to extort from the party his private books and papers to make him liable for a penalty or to forfeit his property. . . .

. . . It is not the breaking of his doors, and the rummaging of his drawers, that constitutes the essence of the offence; but it is the invasion of his inde-

---

[1] George Orwell, *Nineteen Eighty-Four* 3-4 (1949).

feasible right to personal security, personal liberty and private property, where the right has never been forfeited by his conviction of some public offence. . . . Breaking into a house and opening boxes and drawers are circumstances of aggravation; but any forcible and compulsory extortion of a man's own testimony or of his private papers to be used as evidence to convict him of crime or to forfeit his goods, is within the condemnation of that judgment. In this regard the Fourth and Fifth Amendments run almost into each other.

In *Gouled v. United States*, 255 U.S. 298 (1921), the Court held that law enforcement officials could not use search warrants to search a person's "house or office or papers" to obtain evidence to use against her in a criminal proceeding. The holdings of *Boyd* and *Gouled* became known as the "mere evidence" rule — the government could only seize papers if they were instrumentalities of a crime, fruits of a crime, or illegal contraband.

The holding in *Boyd* has been significantly cut back. In *Warden v. Hayden*, 387 U.S. 294 (1967), the Court abolished the mere evidence rule. As the Court currently interprets the Fifth Amendment, the government can require a person to produce papers and records. *See Shapiro v. United States*, 335 U.S. 1 (1948). The Fifth Amendment also does not protect against subpoenas for a person's records and papers held by third parties. In *Couch v. United States*, 409 U.S. 322 (1973), the Court upheld a subpoena to a person's accountant for documents because "the Fifth Amendment privilege is a personal privilege: it adheres basically to the person, not to information that may incriminate him." The Fifth Amendment, the Court reasoned, only prevents "[i]nquisitorial pressure or coercion against a potentially accused person, compelling her, against her will, to utter self-condemning words or produce incriminating documents." Similarly, in *Fisher v. United States*, 425 U.S. 391 (1976), the Court upheld a subpoena to a person's attorney for documents pertaining to that person. The Fifth Amendment is not a "general protector of privacy" but protects against the "compelled self-incrimination."

Therefore, the Fifth Amendment protects against compelled testimonial incrimination. The Fifth Amendment does not apply to all incriminating statements, but to information that is compelled. Further, the information must be "testimonial" in nature, and the Court has held that the Fifth Amendment does not apply to fingerprinting, photographing, taking measurements, writing or speaking for identification purposes, and having blood or bodily fluids drawn and tested. *See Schmerber v. California*, 384 U.S. 757 (1966). Finally, the information must be incriminating. The Fifth Amendment does not protect broadly against prying into private secrets; it is limited to information that is incriminating.[2]

---

[2] For more background about the Fifth Amendment, see R. Kent Greenawalt, *Silence as a Moral and Constitutional Right*, 23 Wm. & Mary L. Rev. 15 (1981); Stephen J. Schulhofer, *Some Kind Words for the Privilege Against Self-Incrimination*, 26 Val. U. L. Rev. 311 (1991); William J. Stuntz, *Self-Incrimination and Excuse*, 99 Colum. L. Rev. 1227 (1988); David Donlinko, *Is There a Rationale for the Privilege Against Self-Incrimination?*, 33 UCLA L. Rev. 1063 (1986); Donald A. Dripps, *Self-Incrimination and Self-Preservation: A Skeptical View*, 1991 U. Ill. L. Rev. 329; Michael Dann, *The Fifth Amendment Privilege Against Self-Incrimination: Extorting Evidence from a Suspect*, 43 S. Cal. L. Rev. 597 (1970). For background into the history and origins of the Fifth Amendment, see Leonard W. Levy, *The Origins of the Fifth Amendment: The Right Against Self-Incrimination* (Ivan R. Dee, 1999);

(c) The Applicability of the Fourth Amendment

The Fourth Amendment governs the investigatory power of government officials. It applies every time a government official (not just police) conducts a "search" or the "seizure" of an object or document. Some examples of "searches" include peeking into one's pockets or searching one's person; entering into and looking around one's house, apartment, office, hotel room, or private property; and opening up and examining the contents of one's luggage or parcels. A "seizure" is a taking away of items by the police. A seizure can be of physical things or of persons (arrests). There must be a search or seizure to invoke the protection of the Fourth Amendment.

The Fourth Amendment does not apply simply when the police happen to observe something in "plain view." Whatever law enforcement officials see in plain view is not covered by the protection of the Fourth Amendment. Thus, the first issue in Fourth Amendment analysis is whether the Amendment applies in the first place. This issue is the subject of the cases in sections 2 and 3, below.[3]

(d) Reasonable Searches and Seizures

If the Fourth Amendment applies, then it requires that the search be "reasonable." Generally, a search is reasonable if the police have obtained a valid search warrant. To obtain a warrant, the police must go before a judge or magistrate and demonstrate that they have "probable cause" to conduct a search or seizure. Probable cause requires that government officials have "reasonably trustworthy information" that is sufficient to "warrant a man of reasonable caution in the belief that an offense has been or is being committed" or that evidence will be found in the place to be searched. *Brinegar v. United States*, 338 U.S. 160, 175–176 (1949). Probable cause is more than "bare suspicion." Probable cause must be measured on a case-by-case basis, via the facts of particular cases. *See Wong Sun v. United States*, 371 U.S. 471 (1963). The purpose of a warrant is to have an independent party (judges) ensure that police really do have probable cause to conduct a search.

A search is valid if the warrant is supported by probable cause and the search is within the scope of the warrant. A warrantless search is generally considered to be per se unreasonable; however, there are a number of exceptions to this rule. Under these exceptions, a search is valid even if a warrant was not obtained as long as there was probable cause. For example, a search is not un-

---

R. H. Hemholtz et al. *The Privilege Against Self-Incrimination: Its Origins and Development* (1997); Eben Moglen, *Taking The Fifth: Reconsidering the Origins of the Constitutional Privilege Against Self-Incrimination*, 92 Mich. L. Rev. 1086 (1994); John H. Langbein, *The Historical Origins of the Privilege Against Self-Incrimination at Common Law*, 92 Mich. L. Rev. 1047 (1994).

[3] There have been extensive writings about the Fourth Amendment's function of protecting privacy. For some background, see Christopher Slobogin, *The World Without a Fourth Amendment*, 39 UCLA L. Rev. 1 (1991); Silas J. Wasserstrom & Louis Michael Seidman, *The Fourth Amendment as Constitutional Theory*, 77 Geo. L.J. 19, 34 (1988); William J. Stuntz, *Privacy's Problem and the Law of Criminal Procedure*, 93 Mich. L. Rev. 1016 (1995); Scott E. Sundby, *"Everyman's" Fourth Amendment: Privacy or Mutual Trust Between Government and Citizen?*, 94 Colum. L. Rev. 1751 (1994); John Kent Walker, Jr., Note, *Covert Searches*, 39 Stan. L. Rev. 545 (1987).

reasonable if consent is obtained. When exigent circumstances make obtaining a warrant impractical, certain warrantless searches are reasonable.

Another exception is what has become known as the "special needs" doctrine. Searches and seizures are reasonable without a warrant or probable cause if "special needs, beyond the normal need for law enforcement, make the warrant and probable-cause requirement impracticable." *Griffin v. Wisconsin*, 483 U.S. 868, 872 (1987). The reasonableness of a search is conducted by balancing the individual's interest in privacy against the government's need to search. Searches by government employers do not require a warrant or probable cause; they only need to be judged by the standard of "reasonableness . . . under all the circumstances." *O'Connor v. Ortega*, 480 U.S. 709, 726 (1987).

Generally, inspecting homes for health and safety violations is outweighed by the individual's privacy interest. *See Camara v. Municipal Court*, 387 U.S. 523 (1967) (holding that warrantless inspections of residences for housing code violations were unreasonable); *See v. City of Seattle*, 387 U.S. 541 (1967) (holding that search of a warehouse for fire code violations was unreasonable).

The police cannot randomly stop cars to check license and registration. *See Delaware v. Prouse*, 440 U.S. 648 (1979). However, fixed sobriety checkpoints are constitutional. *See Michigan Department of State Police v. Sitz*, 496 U.S. 444 (1990). Such a checkpoint search does not require "particularized suspicion." On the other hand, in *Indianapolis v. Edmonds*, 531 U.S. 32, 41–42 (2000), the Court held that checkpoints established to investigate possible drug violations were indistinguishable from a general purpose crime control search and were therefore unconstitutional:

> We have never approved a checkpoint program whose primary purpose was to detect evidence of ordinary criminal wrongdoing. Rather, our checkpoint cases have recognized only limited exceptions to the general rule that a seizure must be accompanied by some measure of individualized suspicion. We suggested in *Prouse* that we would not credit the "general interest in crime control" as justification for a regime of suspicionless stops. Consistent with this suggestion, each of the checkpoint programs that we have approved was designed primarily to serve purposes closely related to the problems of policing the border or the necessity of ensuring roadway safety. Because the primary purpose of the Indianapolis narcotics checkpoint program is to uncover evidence of ordinary criminal wrongdoing, the program contravenes the Fourth Amendment. . . .

Even with a warrant, certain searches are unreasonable. For example, in *Winston v. Lee*, 470 U.S. 753 (1985), the removal of a bullet lodged deep in the accused's chest was deemed unreasonable. However, the Court concluded that the taking of blood from a suspect constituted a reasonable search. *See Schmerber v. California*, 384 U.S. 757 (1966).[4]

---

[4]For more background about the Fourth Amendment's requirement of "reasonableness," see Sherry F. Colb, *The Qualitative Dimension of Fourth Amendment "Reasonableness,"* 98 Colum. L. Rev. 1642 (1998); Tracey Maclin, *Constructing Fourth Amendment Principles from the Government Perspective: Whose Amendment Is It, Anyway?*, 25 Am. Crim. L. Rev. 669 (1988).

(e) The Enforcement of the Fourth Amendment

When law enforcement officials violate an individual's Fourth Amendment rights, the individual can seek at least two forms of redress. First, if the individual is a defendant in a criminal trial, she can move to have the evidence obtained in violation of the Fourth Amendment suppressed. This is known as the "exclusionary rule." In *Weeks v. United States*, 232 U.S. 383 (1914), the Court established the exclusionary rule as the way to enforce the Fourth Amendment on federal officials. Later, in *Mapp v. Ohio*, 367 U.S. 643 (1961), the Court held that the exclusionary rule applies to all government searches, whether state or federal. The purpose of the exclusionary rule is to deter law enforcement officials from violating the Constitution.

If the police illegally search or seize evidence in violation of the Constitution, not only is that evidence suppressed but all other evidence derived from the illegally obtained evidence is also suppressed. This is known as the "fruit of the poisonous tree" doctrine. For example, suppose the police illegally search a person's luggage and find evidence that the person is a drug trafficker. Armed with that evidence, the police obtain a warrant to search the person's home, where they uncover new evidence of drug-trafficking along with a weapon used in a murder. The person is charged with drug trafficking and murder. Under the Fourth Amendment, the evidence found in the person's luggage will be suppressed. Additionally, since the search warrant could not have been obtained but for the evidence turned up in the illegal search, the evidence found at the house, including the additional drug trafficking evidence as well as the murder evidence, will be suppressed. However, if the police obtained a warrant or located evidence by an "independent source," then the fruit of the poisonous tree doctrine does not apply. *See Silverthorne Lumber Co. v. United States*, 251 U.S. 385 (1920). Returning to the example above, if the police had evidence supplied from the person's cohort that the person was engaged in drug trafficking out of his home and had murdered somebody, this evidence may suffice to give the police probable cause to have a warrant issued to search the person's house. This evidence is independent from the illegal search, and it is admissible. Further, any evidence that was obtained by this nontainted evidence can also be admitted in a court proceeding.[5]

The second form of redress for a violation of the Fourth Amendment is a civil remedy. A person, whether a criminal defendant or anybody else, can obtain civil damages for a Fourth Amendment violation by way of 42 U.S.C. § 1983.

2. WIRETAPPING, BUGGING, AND BEYOND

At common law, eavesdropping was considered a nuisance. "Eavesdropping" as William Blackstone defined it, meant to "listen under walls or window,

---

[5] The exclusionary rule has received significant scholarly attention. A number of scholars question its efficacy and advocate that the Fourth Amendment be enforced through other mechanisms such as civil sanctions. *See* Akhil Reed Amar, *The Constitution and Criminal Procedure* 28 (1997); Christopher Slobogin, *Why Liberals Should Chuck the Exclusionary Rule*, 1999 U. Ill. L. Rev. 363, 400-401 (1999). Other commentators contend that civil sanctions will be ineffective. *See* Arnold H. Loewy, *The Fourth Amendment as a Device for Protecting the Innocent*, 81 Mich. L. Rev.

or the eaves of a house, to hearken after discourse, and thereupon to frame slanderous and mischievous tales."[6] Before the advent of electronic communication, people could easily avoid eavesdroppers by ensuring that nobody else was around during their conversations.

The invention of the telegraph in 1844 followed by the telephone in 1876 substantially altered the way people communicated with each other. Today, the telephone has become an essential part of everyday communications.

The advent of electronic communications was soon followed by the invention of recording and transmitting devices that enabled new and more sophisticated forms of eavesdropping than overhearing a conversation with the naked ear. One feature of electronic surveillance is that unlike the unsealing of letters, the interception of communications is undetectable. Some of the current forms of electronic surveillance technology include wiretaps, bugs, and parabolic microphones.

A "wiretap" is a device used to intercept telephone (or telegraph) communications. Wiretapping began before the invention of the telephone. Wiretapping was used to intercept telegraph communications during the Civil War and became very prevalent after the invention of the telephone. The first police wiretap occurred in the early 1890s. In the first half of the twentieth century, wiretaps proliferated due to law enforcement attempts to monitor protests over bad industrial working conditions, social unrest caused by World War I, and the smuggling of alcohol during the Prohibition Years.[7]

A "bug" is a device, often quite miniature in size, that can be hidden on a person or in a place that can transmit conversations in a room to a remote receiving device, where the conversation can be listened to.

A "parabolic microphone" can pick up a conversation from a distance.

Electronic surveillance devices were not in existence at the time that the Fourth Amendment was drafted. How, then, should the Fourth Amendment regulate these devices? In 1928, the Supreme Court attempted to answer this question in *Olmstead v. United States,* the first electronic surveillance case to come before the Court.

OLMSTEAD v. UNITED STATES

277 U.S. 438 (1928)

TAFT, C. J. The petitioners were convicted in the District Court for the Western District of Washington of a conspiracy to violate the National Prohibition

---

1229, 1266 (1983); Tracey Maclin, *When the Cure for the Fourth Amendment Is Worse Than the Disease,* 68 S. Cal. L. Rev. 1, 62 (1994).

   [6] 4 Blackstone, *Commentaries* 168 (1769).

   [7] For more background on the history of wiretapping, see generally Robert Ellis Smith, *Ben Franklin's Web Site: Privacy and Curiosity from Plymouth Rock to the Internet* (2000); Priscilla M. Regan, *Legislating Privacy: Technology, Social Values, and Public Policy* (1995); Samuel Dash, Richard Schwartz, & Robert Knowlton, *The Eavesdroppers* (1959); James G. Carr, *The Law of Electronic Surveillance* (1994); Whitfield Diffie & Susan Landau, *Privacy on the Line: The Politics of Wiretapping and Encryption* (1998); Jeremiah Courtney, *Electronic Eavesdropping, Wiretapping and Your Right to Privacy,* 26 Fed. Comm. B.J. 1 (1973); Herbert Brownell, Jr., *The Public Security and Wire Tapping,* 39 Cornell L.Q. 195 (1954).

Act by unlawfully possessing, transporting and importing intoxicating liquors and maintaining nuisances, and by selling intoxicating liquors. Seventy-two others, in addition to the petitioners, were indicted. Some were not apprehended, some were acquitted, and others pleaded guilty. . . .

The information which led to the discovery of the conspiracy and its nature and extent was largely obtained by intercepting messages on the telephones of the conspirators by four federal prohibition officers. Small wires were inserted along the ordinary telephone wires from the residences of four of the petitioners and those leading from the chief office. The insertions were made without trespass upon any property of the defendants. They were made in the basement of the large office building. The taps from house lines were made in the streets near the houses. . . .

The well-known historical purpose of the Fourth Amendment, directed against general warrants and writs of assistance, was to prevent the use of governmental force to search a man's house, his person, his papers, and his effects, and to prevent their seizure against his will. This phase of the misuse of governmental power of compulsion is the emphasis of the opinion of the court in the *Boyd* Case. . . .

. . . The Fourth Amendment may have proper application to a sealed letter in the mail, because of the constitutional provision for the Postoffice Department and the relations between the government and those who pay to secure protection of their sealed letters. . . . It is plainly within the words of the amendment to say that the unlawful rifling by a government agent of a sealed letter is a search and seizure of the sender's papers or effects. The letter is a paper, an effect, and in the custody of a government that forbids carriage, except under its protection.

The United States takes no such care of telegraph or telephone messages as of mailed sealed letters. The amendment does not forbid what was done here. There was no searching. There was no seizure. The evidence was secured by the use of the sense of hearing and that only. There was no entry of the houses or offices of the defendants.

By the invention of the telephone 50 years ago, and its application for the purpose of extending communications, one can talk with another at a far distant place.

The language of the amendment cannot be extended and expanded to include telephone wires, reaching to the whole world from the defendant's house or office. The intervening wires are not part of his house or office, any more than are the highways along which they are stretched. . . .

Congress may, of course, protect the secrecy of telephone messages by making them, when intercepted, inadmissible in evidence in federal criminal trials, by direct legislation, and thus depart from the common law of evidence. But the courts may not adopt such a policy by attributing an enlarged and unusual meaning to the Fourth Amendment. The reasonable view is that one who installs in his house a telephone instrument with connecting wires intends to project his voice to those quite outside, and that the wires beyond his house, and messages while passing over them, are not within the protection of the Fourth Amendment. Here those who intercepted the projected voices were not in the house of either party to the conversation. . . .

BRANDEIS, J. dissenting. The government makes no attempt to defend the methods employed by its officers. Indeed, it concedes that, if wire tapping can be deemed a search and seizure within the Fourth Amendment, such wire tapping as was practiced in the case at bar was an unreasonable search and seizure, and that the evidence thus obtained was inadmissible. But it relies on the language of the amendment, and it claims that the protection given thereby cannot properly be held to include a telephone conversation.

"We must never forget," said Mr. Chief Justice Marshall in *McCulloch v. Maryland*, "that it is a Constitution we are expounding." Since then this court has repeatedly sustained the exercise of power by Congress, under various clauses of that instrument, over objects of which the fathers could not have dreamed. We have likewise held that general limitations on the powers of government, like those embodied in the due process clauses of the Fifth and Fourteenth Amendments, do not forbid the United States or the states from meeting modern conditions by regulations which "a century ago, or even half a century ago, probably would have been rejected as arbitrary and oppressive." Clauses guaranteeing to the individual protection against specific abuses of power, must have a similar capacity of adaptation to a changing world. It was with reference to such a clause that this court said in *Weems v. United States*, 217 U.S. 349, 373:

> Legislation, both statutory and constitutional, is enacted, it is true, from an experience of evils, but its general language should not, therefore, be necessarily confined to the form that evil had theretofore taken. Time works changes, brings into existence new conditions and purposes. Therefore a principle to be vital must be capable of wider application than the mischief which gave it birth. This is peculiarly true of Constitutions. They are not ephemeral enactments, designed to meet passing occasions. They are, to use the words of Chief Justice Marshall, "designed to approach immortality as nearly as human institutions can approach it." The future is their care and provision for events of good and bad tendencies of which no prophecy can be made. In the application of a Constitution, therefore, our contemplation cannot be only of what has been but of what may be. Under any other rule a Constitution would indeed be as easy of application as it would be deficient in efficacy and power. Its general principles would have little value and be converted by precedent into impotent and lifeless formulas. Rights declared in words might be lost in reality.

When the Fourth and Fifth Amendments were adopted, "the form that evil had theretofore taken" had been necessarily simple. Force and violence were then the only means known to man by which a government could directly effect self-incrimination. It could compel the individual to testify — a compulsion effected, if need be, by torture. It could secure possession of his papers and other articles incident to his private life — a seizure effected, if need be, by breaking and entry. Protection against such invasion of "the sanctities of a man's home and the privacies of life" was provided in the Fourth and Fifth Amendments by specific language. *Boyd v. United States*, 116 U.S. 616 (1886). But "time works changes, brings into existence new conditions and purposes." Subtler and more far-reaching means of invading privacy have become available to the government. Discovery and invention have made it possible for the government, by means far more effective than stretching upon the rack, to obtain disclosure in court of what is whispered in the closet.

Moreover, "in the application of a Constitution, our contemplation cannot be only of what has been, but of what may be." The progress of science in furnishing the government with means of espionage is not likely to stop with wire tapping. Ways may some day be developed by which the government, without removing papers from secret drawers, can reproduce them in court, and by which it will be enabled to expose to a jury the most intimate occurrences of the home. Advances in the psychic and related sciences may bring means of exploring unexpressed beliefs, thoughts and emotions. "That places the liberty of every man in the hands of every petty officer" was said by James Otis of much lesser intrusions than these. To Lord Camden a far slighter intrusion seemed "subversive of all the comforts of society." Can it be that the Constitution affords no protection against such invasions of individual security?

A sufficient answer is found in *Boyd v. United States*, 116 U.S. 616 (1886), a case that will be remembered as long as civil liberty lives in the United States. . . .

In *Ex parte Jackson*, 96 U.S. 727 (1877), it was held that a sealed letter entrusted to the mail is protected by the amendments. The mail is a public service furnished by the government. The telephone is a public service furnished by its authority. There is, in essence, no difference between the sealed letter and the private telephone message. . . .

The evil incident to invasion of the privacy of the telephone is far greater than that involved in tampering with the mails. Whenever a telephone line is tapped, the privacy of the persons at both ends of the line is invaded, and all conversations between them upon any subject, and although proper, confidential, and privileged, may be overheard. Moreover, the tapping of one man's telephone line involves the tapping of the telephone of every other person whom he may call, or who may call him. As a means of espionage, writs of assistance and general warrants are but puny instruments of tyranny and oppression when compared with wire tapping.

Time and again this court, in giving effect to the principle underlying the Fourth Amendment, has refused to place an unduly literal construction upon it. . . .

The protection guaranteed by the amendments is much broader in scope. The makers of our Constitution undertook to secure conditions favorable to the pursuit of happiness. They recognized the significance of man's spiritual nature, of his feelings and of his intellect. They knew that only a part of the pain, pleasure and satisfactions of life are to be found in material things. They sought to protect Americans in their beliefs, their thoughts, their emotions and their sensations. They conferred, as against the government, the right to be let alone — the most comprehensive of rights and the right most valued by civilized men. To protect that right, every unjustifiable intrusion by the government upon the privacy of the individual, whatever the means employed, must be deemed a violation of the Fourth Amendment. And the use, as evidence in a criminal proceeding, of facts ascertained by such intrusion must be deemed a violation of the Fifth.

Applying to the Fourth and Fifth Amendments the established rule of construction, the defendants' objections to the evidence obtained by wire tapping must, in my opinion, be sustained. It is, of course, immaterial where the physical connection with the telephone wires leading into the defendants' premises was made. And it is also immaterial that the intrusion was in aid of law enforcement. Experience should teach us to be most on our guard to protect liberty when the government's purposes are beneficent. Men born to freedom are naturally alert to repel invasion of their liberty by evil-minded rulers. The greatest dangers to liberty lurk in insidious encroachment by men of zeal, well-meaning but without understanding. . . .

NOTES & QUESTIONS

1. Justice Brandeis's dissent is one of the most famous dissents in Supreme Court history. Note the similarities between Brandeis's 1890 article, *The Right to Privacy*, and his dissent nearly 40 years later in *Olmstead*. What themes are repeated? Recall that *The Right to Privacy* concerned locating common law roots for privacy protection. What is Brandeis saying about the roots of constitutional protection of privacy?

2. Brandeis contends that the Constitution should keep pace with changing technology. But given the rapid pace of technological change and the fact that the Constitution must serve as the stable foundation for our society, can the Constitution keep pace? How adaptable should the Constitution be? Should new technology be regulated by statutory law?

3. Brandeis contends that wiretapping is more insidious than tampering with the mail. Why? Do you agree?

4. **State Wiretapping Law.** In the state of Washington, where the wiretapping in *Olmstead* took place, wiretapping was a criminal act, and the officers had thus violated the law. In a separate dissenting opinion, Justice Holmes noted that:

> . . . [A]part from the Constitution the government ought not to use evidence obtained and only obtainable by a criminal act. . . . It is desirable that criminals should be detected, and to that end that all available evidence should be used. It also is desirable that the government should not itself foster and pay for other crimes, when they are the means by which the evidence is to be obtained. If it pays its officers for having got evidence by crime I do not see why it may not as well pay them for getting it in the same way, and I can attach no importance to protestations of disapproval if it knowingly accepts and pays and announces that in future it will pay for the fruits. We have to choose, and for my part I think it a less evil that some criminals should escape than that the government should play an ignoble part.

5. **The Birth of Federal Wiretap Law.** The *Olmstead* decision was not well-received by the public. In fact, in 1934, Congress responded to *Olmstead* by enacting §605 of the Federal Communications Act, making wiretapping a federal crime. Congress enacted a comprehensive federal statute for wiretapping in 1968, which was amended in 1986 and again in 1994. Federal wiretap law will be discussed later in this chapter.

6. ***Secret Agents and Misplaced Trust.*** In *Hoffa v. United States,* 385 U.S. 293 (1966), an undercover informant, Edward Partin, befriended James Hoffa and elicited statements from him about his plans to bribe jurors in a criminal trial in which Hoffa was a defendant. According to the Court:

> In the present case . . . it is evident that no interest legitimately protected by the Fourth Amendment is involved. It is obvious that the petitioner was not relying on the security of his hotel suite when he made the incriminating statements to Partin or in Partin's presence. Partin did not enter the suite by force or by stealth. He was not a surreptitious eavesdropper. Partin was in the suite by invitation, and every conversation which he heard was either directed to him or knowingly carried on in his presence. The petitioner, in a word, was not relying on the security of the hotel room; he was relying upon his misplaced confidence that Partin would not reveal his wrongdoing.

Likewise, in *Lewis v. United States*, 385 U.S. 206 (1966), the defendant sold drugs to an undercover agent in his house. The Court held:

> In the instant case . . . the petitioner invited the undercover agent to his home for the specific purpose of executing a felonious sale of narcotics. Petitioner's only concern was whether the agent was a willing purchaser who could pay the agreed price. . . During neither of his visits to petitioner's home did the agent see, hear, or take anything that was not contemplated, and in fact intended, by petitioner as a necessary part of his illegal business. Were we to hold the deceptions of the agent in this case constitutionally prohibited, we would come near to a rule that the use of undercover agents in any manner is virtually unconstitutional per se. Such a rule would, for example, severely hamper the Government in ferreting out those organized criminal activities that are characterized by covert dealings with victims who either cannot or do not protest. A prime example is provided by the narcotics traffic. . . .

Hoffa and *Lewis* establish that a person does not have a privacy interest in the loyalty of her friends. The government may deceive a person by sending in secret agents to befriend her. Is it problematic that government is permitted to use spies and deception as a law enforcement technique? Consider the following observation by Anthony Amsterdam:

> I can see no significant difference between police spies . . . and electronic surveillance, either in their uses or abuses. Both have long been asserted by law enforcement officers to be indispensable tools in investigating crime, particularly victimless and political crime, precisely because they both search out privacies that government could not otherwise invade. Both tend to repress crime in the same way, by making people distrustful and unwilling to talk to one another. The only difference is that under electronic surveillance you are afraid to talk to anybody in your office or over the phone, while under a spy system you are afraid to talk to anybody at all.[8]

7. ***Bugs, Transmitters, and Recording Devices.*** In *Goldman v. United States*, 316 U.S. 129 (1942), the police placed a device called a "detectaphone" next

---

[8] Anthony G. Amsterdam, *Perspectives on the Fourth Amendment*, 58 Minn. L. Rev. 349, 407 (1974). For a detailed analysis of undercover agents, see Gary T. Marx, Under Cover: Police Surveillance in America (1988).

to wall adjacent to a person's office. The device enabled the police to listen in on conversations inside the office. The Court concluded that since there was no trespass, there was no Fourth Amendment violation.

In *On Lee v. United States*, 343 U.S. 747 (1952), Chin Poy, a government informant with a concealed transmitter, engaged On Lee in conversation for the purpose of eliciting that On Lee was a drug dealer. The conversation was transmitted to a law enforcement agent, who later testified at trial about the content of the conversation. The Court held that the Fourth Amendment did not apply:

> Petitioner was talking confidentially and indiscreetly with one he trusted, and he was overheard. This was due to aid from a transmitter and receiver, to be sure, but with the same effect on his privacy as if agent Lee had been eavesdropping outside an open window. The use of bifocals, field glasses or the telescope to magnify the object of a witness' vision is not a forbidden search or seizure, even if they focus without his knowledge or consent upon what one supposes to be private indiscretions. It would be a dubious service to the genuine liberties protected by the Fourth Amendment to make them bedfellows with spurious liberties improvised by farfetched analogies which would liken eavesdropping on a conversation, with the connivance of one of the parties, to an unreasonable search or seizure. We find no violation of the Fourth Amendment here.

Does the use of electronic devices distinguish *On Lee* from *Hoffa* and *Lewis* in a material way?

8. *"Spike Mikes."* In *Silverman v. United States*, 365 U.S. 505 (1961), the police used a device called a "spike mike" to listen in from a vacant row house to conversations in an adjoining row house. The device consisted of a microphone with a spike of about a foot in length attached to it. The spike was inserted into a baseboard of the vacant row house on the wall adjoining the row house next door. The spike hit the heating duct serving the next door row house, which transformed the heating system into a sound conductor. The Court held that the use of the "spike mike" violated the Fourth Amendment because it constituted an "unauthorized physical encroachment" into the adjoining row house. The Court distinguished *Olmstead* and *Goldman* because those cases did not involve any "physical invasion" or "trespass" onto the defendant's property whereas the "spike mike" "usurp[ed] part of the [defendants'] house or office." Do you agree with the Court's distinction between *Goldman/Olmstead* and *Silverman* — between surveillance involving physical intrusion (however slight) and surveillance not involving any trespassing on the premises?

LOPEZ V. UNITED STATES

373 U.S. 427 (1963)

[The petitioner, German S. Lopez, was tried in a federal court on a four-count indictment charging him with attempted bribery of an Internal Revenue Agent, Roger S. Davis. The evidence against him had been obtained by a series of meetings between him and Davis. The last meeting was recorded by Davis with a pocket wire recorder. Prior to trial, Davis moved to suppress the recorded conversation.]

HARLAN, J. . . . [Petitioner's] argument is primarily addressed to the recording of the conversation, which he claims was obtained in violation of his rights under the Fourth Amendment. Recognizing the weakness of this position if Davis was properly permitted to testify about the same conversation, petitioner now challenges that testimony as well, although he failed to do so at the trial. . . .

Once it is plain that Davis could properly testify about his conversation with Lopez, the constitutional claim relating to the recording of that conversation emerges in proper perspective. The Court has in the past sustained instances of "electronic eavesdropping" against constitutional challenge, when devices have been used to enable government agents to overhear conversations which would have been beyond the reach of the human ear. *See, e.g., Olmstead v. United States.* It has been insisted only that the electronic device not be planted by an unlawful physical invasion of a constitutionally protected area. . . . Indeed this case involves no "eavesdropping" whatever in any proper sense of that term. The Government did not use an electronic device to listen in on conversations it could not otherwise have heard. Instead, the device was used only to obtain the most reliable evidence possible of a conversation in which the Government's own agent was a participant and which that agent was fully entitled to disclose. And the device was not planted by means of an unlawful physical invasion of petitioner's premises under circumstances which would violate the Fourth Amendment. It was carried in and out by an agent who was there with petitioner's assent, and it neither saw nor heard more than the agent himself. . . .

Stripped to its essentials, petitioner's argument amounts to saying that he has a constitutional right to rely on possible flaws in the agent's memory, or to challenge the agent's credibility without being beset by corroborating evidence that is not susceptible of impeachment. For no other argument can justify excluding an accurate version of a conversation that the agent could testify to from memory. We think the risk that petitioner took in offering a bribe to Davis fairly included the risk that the offer would be accurately reproduced in court, whether by faultless memory or mechanical recording. . . .

WARREN, C. J. concurring. I also share the opinion of Mr. Justice Brennan that the fantastic advances in the field of electronic communication constitute a great danger to the privacy of the individual; that indiscriminate use of such devices in law enforcement raises grave constitutional questions under the Fourth and Fifth Amendments; and that these considerations impose a heavier responsibility on this Court in its supervision of the fairness of procedures in the federal court system. However, I do not believe that, as a result, all uses of such devices should be proscribed either as unconstitutional or as unfair law enforcement methods. One of the lines I would draw would be between this case and *On Lee.* . . .

The use and purpose of the transmitter in *On Lee* was substantially different from the use of the recorder here. Its advantage was not to corroborate the testimony of Chin Poy, but rather, to obviate the need to put him on the stand. The Court in *On Lee* itself stated:

> We can only speculate on the reasons why Chin Poy was not called. It seems a not unlikely assumption that the very defects of character and blemishes of record which made On Lee trust him with confidences would make a jury distrust his testimony. Chin Poy was close enough to the underworld to serve as bait, near enough the criminal design so that petitioner would embrace him as a confidante, but too close to it for the Government to vouch for him as a witness. Instead, the Government called agent Lee.

However, there were further advantages in not using Chin Poy. Had Chin Poy been available for cross-examination, counsel for On Lee could have explored the nature of Chin Poy's friendship with On Lee, the possibility of other unmonitored conversations and appeals to friendship, the possibility of entrapments, police pressure brought to bear to persuade Chin Poy to turn informer, and Chin Poy's own recollection of the contents of the conversation. . . .

Thus while I join the Court in permitting the use of electronic devices to corroborate an agent under the particular facts of this case, I cannot sanction by implication the use of these same devices to radically shift the pattern of presentation of evidence in the criminal trial, a shift that may be used to conceal substantial factual and legal issues concerning the rights of the accused and the administration of criminal justice.

Brennan, J. joined by Douglas and Goldberg, J. J. dissenting. . . . [T]he Government's argument is that Lopez surrendered his right of privacy when he communicated his "secret thoughts" to Agent Davis. The assumption, manifestly untenable, is that the Fourth Amendment is only designed to protect secrecy. If a person commits his secret thoughts to paper, that is no license for the police to seize the paper; if a person communicates his secret thoughts verbally to another, that is no license for the police to record the words. *On Lee* certainly rested on no such theory of waiver. The right of privacy would mean little if it were limited to a person's solitary thoughts, and so fostered secretiveness. It must embrace a concept of the liberty of one's communications, and historically it has. "The common law secures to each individual the right of determining, ordinarily, to what extent his thoughts, sentiments, and emotions shall be communicated to others . . . and even if he has chosen to give them expression, he generally retains the power to fix the limits of the publicity which shall be given them." Warren and Brandeis, *The Right to Privacy*, 4 Harv. L. Rev. 193, 198 (1890).

That is not to say that all communications are privileged. On Lee assumed the risk that his acquaintance would divulge their conversation; Lopez assumed the same risk vis-à-vis Davis. The risk inheres in all communications which are not in the sight of the law privileged. It is not an undue risk to ask persons to assume, for it does no more than compel them to use discretion in choosing their auditors, to make damaging disclosures only to persons whose character and motives may be trusted. But the risk which both *On Lee* and today's decision impose is of a different order. It is the risk that third parties, whether mechanical auditors like the Minifon or human transcribers of mechanical transmissions as in *On Lee*—third parties who cannot be shut out of a conversation as conventional eavesdroppers can be, merely by a lowering of voices, or withdrawing to a private place — may give independent evidence of any conversation. There is only one way to guard against such a risk, and that is to keep one's mouth shut on all occasions. . . .

. . . The risk of being overheard by an eavesdropper or betrayed by an informer or deceived as to the identity of one with whom one deals is probably inherent in the conditions of human society. It is the kind of risk we necessarily assume whenever we speak. But as soon as electronic surveillance comes into play, the risk changes crucially. There is no security from that kind of eavesdropping, no way of mitigating the risk, and so not even a residuum of true privacy. . . .

. . . Electronic aids add a wholly new dimension to eavesdropping. They make it more penetrating, more indiscriminate, more truly obnoxious to a free society. Electronic surveillance, in fact, makes the police omniscient; and police omniscience is one of the most effective tools of tyranny. . . .

. . . Electronic surveillance strikes deeper than at the ancient feeling that a man's home is his castle; it strikes at freedom of communication, a postulate of our kind of society. Lopez's words to Agent Davis captured by the Minifon were not constitutionally privileged by force of the First Amendment. But freedom of speech is undermined where people fear to speak unconstrainedly in what they suppose to be the privacy of home and office. If electronic surveillance by government becomes sufficiently widespread, and there is little in prospect for checking it, the hazard that as a people we may become hagridden and furtive is not fantasy. . . .

. . . Electronic surveillance destroys all anonymity and all privacy; it makes government privy to everything that goes on. . . .

NOTES & QUESTIONS

1. Should electronic surveillance be treated similarly or differently than regular eavesdropping? Is it consistent to agree that Davis could testify as to what Lopez said via his memory but cannot introduce a recording of what Lopez said?

KATZ v. UNITED STATES

389 U.S. 347 (1967)

STEWART, J. The petitioner was convicted in the District Court for the Southern District of California under an eight-count indictment charging him with transmitting wagering information by telephone from Los Angeles to Miami and Boston in violation of a federal statute. At trial the Government was permitted, over the petitioner's objection, to introduce evidence of the petitioner's end of telephone conversations, overheard by FBI agents who had attached an electronic listening and recording device to the outside of the public telephone booth from which he had placed his calls. In affirming his conviction, the Court of Appeals rejected the contention that the recordings had been obtained in violation of the Fourth Amendment, because "[t]here was no physical entrance into the area occupied by, (the petitioner)." We granted certiorari in order to consider the constitutional questions thus presented.

The petitioner had phrased those questions as follows:

A. Whether a public telephone booth is a constitutionally protected area so that evidence obtained by attaching an electronic listening recording device to the top of such a booth is obtained in violation of the right to privacy of the user of the booth.

B. Whether physical penetration of a constitutionally protected area is necessary before a search and seizure can be said to be violative of the Fourth Amendment to the United States Constitution.

We decline to adopt this formulation of the issues. In the first place the correct solution of Fourth Amendment problems is not necessarily promoted by incantation of the phrase "constitutionally protected area." Secondly, the Fourth Amendment cannot be translated into a general constitutional "right to privacy." That Amendment protects individual privacy against certain kinds of governmental intrusion, but its protections go further, and often have nothing to do with privacy at all. Other provisions of the Constitution protect personal privacy from other forms of governmental invasion. But the protection of a person's general right to privacy — his right to be let alone by other people — is, like the protection of his property and of his very life, left largely to the law of the individual States.   *4th protects*

Because of the misleading way the issues have been formulated, the parties have attached great significance to the characterization of the telephone booth from which the petitioner placed his calls. The petitioner has strenuously argued that the booth was a "constitutionally protected area." The Government has maintained with equal vigor that it was not. But this effort to decide whether or not a given "area," viewed in the abstract, is "constitutionally protected" deflects attention from the problem presented by this case. For the Fourth Amendment protects people, not places. What a person knowingly exposes to the public, even in his own home or office, is not a subject of Fourth Amendment protection. But what he seeks to preserve as private, even in an area accessible to the public, may be constitutionally protected.

The Government stresses the fact that the telephone booth from which the petitioner made his calls was constructed partly of glass, so that he was as visible after he entered it as he would have been if he had remained outside. But what he sought to exclude when he entered the booth was not the intruding eye — it was the uninvited ear. He did not shed his right to do so simply because he made his calls from a place where he might be seen. No less than an individual in a business office, in a friend's apartment, or in a taxicab, a person in a telephone booth may rely upon the protection of the Fourth Amendment. One who occupies it, shuts the door behind him, and pays the toll that permits him to place a call is surely entitled to assume that the words he utters into the mouthpiece will not be broadcast to the world. To read the Constitution more narrowly is to ignore the vital role that the public telephone has come to play in private communication.

The Government contends, however, that the activities of its agents in this case should not be tested by Fourth Amendment requirements, for the surveillance technique they employed involved no physical penetration of the telephone booth from which the petitioner placed his calls. It is true that the absence of such penetration was at one time thought to foreclose further Fourth Amendment inquiry, *Olmstead v. United States*, *Goldman v. United States*, for that Amendment was thought to limit only searches and seizures of tangible property. But "[t]he premise that property interests control the right of the Government to search and seize has been discredited." . . . [O]nce this much is acknowledged, and once it is recognized that the Fourth Amendment protects people — and not simply "areas" — against unreasonable searches and seizures it becomes clear that the reach of that Amendment cannot turn upon the presence or absence of a physical intrusion into any given enclosure.

We conclude that the underpinnings of *Olmstead* and *Goldman* have been so eroded by our subsequent decisions that the "trespass" doctrine there enunciated can no longer be regarded as controlling. . . .

The question remaining for decision, then, is whether the search and seizure conducted in this case complied with constitutional standards. In that regard, the Government's position is that its agents acted in an entirely defensible manner: They did not begin their electronic surveillance until investigation of the petitioner's activities had established a strong probability that he was using the telephone in question to transmit gambling information to persons in other States, in violation of federal law. Moreover, the surveillance was limited, both in scope and in duration, to the specific purpose of establishing the contents of the petitioner's unlawful telephonic communications. The agents confined their surveillance to the brief periods during which he used the telephone booth, and they took great care to overhear only the conversations of the petitioner himself. . . .

. . . It is apparent that the agents in this case acted with restraint. Yet the inescapable fact is that this restraint was imposed by the agents themselves, not by a judicial officer. They were not required, before commencing the search, to present their estimate of probable cause for detached scrutiny by a neutral magistrate. They were not compelled, during the conduct of the search itself, to observe precise limits established in advance by a specific court order. Nor were they directed, after the search had been completed, to notify the authorizing magistrate in detail of all that had been seized. In the absence of such safeguards, this Court has never sustained a search upon the sole ground that officers reasonably expected to find evidence of a particular crime and voluntarily confined their activities to the least intrusive means consistent with that end. Searches conducted without warrants have been held unlawful "notwithstanding facts unquestionably showing probable cause," . . . "Over and again this Court has emphasized that the mandate of the [Fourth] Amendment requires adherence to judicial processes," and that searches conducted outside the judicial process, without prior approval by judge or magistrate, are per se unreasonable under the Fourth Amendment — subject only to a few specifically established and well-delineated exceptions. . . .

BLACK, J. dissenting. . . My basic objection is twofold: (1) I do not believe that the words of the Amendment will bear the meaning given them by today's decision, and (2) I do not believe that it is the proper role of this Court to rewrite the Amendment in order "to bring it into harmony with the times" and thus reach a result that many people believe to be desirable.

While I realize that an argument based on the meaning of words lacks the scope, and no doubt the appeal, of broad policy discussions and philosophical discourses on such nebulous subjects as privacy, for me the language of the Amendment is the crucial place to look in construing a written document such as our Constitution. The Fourth Amendment says that

> The right of the people to be secure in their persons, houses, papers, and effects, against unreasonable searches and seizures, shall not be violated, and no Warrants shall issue, but upon probable cause, supported by Oath or affirmation, and particularly describing the place to be searched, and the persons or things to be seized.

The first clause protects "persons, houses, papers, and effects, against unreasonable searches and seizures . . . ." These words connote the idea of tangible things with size, form, and weight, things capable of being searched, seized, or both. The second clause of the Amendment still further establishes its Framers' purpose to limit its protection to tangible things by providing that no warrants shall issue but those "particularly describing the place to be searched, and the persons or things to be seized." A conversation overheard by eavesdropping, whether by plain snooping or wiretapping, is not tangible and, under the normally accepted meanings of the words, can neither be searched nor seized. . . .

NOTES & QUESTIONS

1. *The Reasonable Expectation of Privacy Test.* The *Katz* decision established a widely cited test for whether the Fourth Amendment is applicable in a given situation. That test was articulated not in the majority opinion but in a concurring opinion by Justice Harlan:

> As the Court's opinion states, "the Fourth Amendment protects people, not places." The question, however, is what protection it affords to those people. Generally, as here, the answer to that question requires reference to a "place." My understanding of the rule that has emerged from prior decisions is that there is a twofold requirement, first that a person have exhibited an actual (subjective) expectation of privacy and, second, that the expectation be one that society is prepared to recognize as "reasonable." Thus a man's home is, for most purposes, a place where he expects privacy, but objects, activities, or statements that he exposes to the "plain view" of outsiders are not "protected" because no intention to keep them to himself has been exhibited. On the other hand, conversations in the open would not be protected against being overheard, for the expectation of privacy under the circumstances would be unreasonable.

The rule as articulated in Justice Harlan's concurrence has become known as the "reasonable expectation of privacy test." Under the test, (1) a person must exhibit an "actual (subjective) expectation of privacy"; and (2) "the expectation [must] be one that society is prepared to recognize as 'reasonable.'"

2. What if the door to the telephone booth in *Katz* had been open? Would the Court still have concluded that the Fourth Amendment applied? What if the cop stood outside the booth, and Katz spoke loud enough for the cop to hear? Suppose the police placed a sound recording device outside the phone booth, and the device could pick up Katz's voice, which would be inaudible to the naked ear outside the phone booth. Would this be a violation of the Fourth Amendment?

3. Before *Katz*, police frequently tapped phones. A person might expect that wiretapping would be likely. Consider the following observation by the Court in *Smith v. Maryland*, 442 U.S. 735, 741 n.5 (1979):

> Situations can be imagined, of course, in which Katz' two-pronged inquiry would provide an inadequate index of Fourth Amendment protection. For example, if the Government were suddenly to announce on nationwide television that all homes henceforth would be subject to warrantless entry, individuals thereafter might not in fact entertain any actual expectation or privacy regarding their homes, papers, and effects. Similarly, if a refugee from a totalitarian country, unaware of this Nation's traditions, erroneously assumed that police were continuously monitoring his telephone conversations, a subjective expectation of privacy regarding the contents of his calls might be lacking as well. In such circumstances, where an individual's subjective expectations had been "conditioned" by influences alien to well-recognized Fourth Amendment freedoms, those subjective expectations obviously could play no meaningful role in ascertaining what the scope of Fourth Amendment protection was. In determining whether a "legitimate expectation of privacy" existed in such cases, a normative inquiry would be proper.

4. ***Wiretapping and Warrants.*** In *Berger v. New York*, 388 U.S. 41 (1967), the Court struck down portions of New York's eavesdropping statute as violating the Fourth Amendment. The New York law authorized the installation of electronic surveillance devices for 60 days and it allowed the surveillance to be extended beyond the 60 days without a showing of present probable cause to continue the eavesdrop. The Court held:

> . . . The Fourth Amendment commands that a warrant issue not only upon probable cause supported by oath or affirmation, but also "particularly describing the place to be searched, and the persons or things to be seized." New York's statute lacks this particularization. It merely says that a warrant may issue on reasonable ground to believe that evidence of crime may be obtained by the eavesdrop. It lays down no requirement for particularity in the warrant as to what specific crime has been or is being committed, nor "the place to be searched," or "the persons or things to be seized" as specifically required by the Fourth Amendment. The need for particularity and evidence of reliability in the showing required when judicial authorization of a search is sought is especially great in the case of eavesdropping. By its very nature eavesdropping involves an intrusion on privacy that is broad in scope. . . .
> . . . New York's statute . . . lays down no . . . "precise and discriminate" requirements. . . . New York's broadside authorization rather than being "carefully circumscribed" so as to prevent unauthorized invasions of privacy actually permits general searches by electronic devices, the truly offensive character of which was first condemned in *Entick v. Carrington*, 19 How. St. Tr. 1029, and which were then known as "general warrants." The use of the

latter was a motivating factor behind the Declaration of Independence. In view of the many cases commenting on the practice it is sufficient here to point out that under these "general warrants" customs officials were given blanket authority to conduct general searches for goods imported to the Colonies in violation of the tax laws of the Crown. The Fourth Amendment's requirement that a warrant "particularly describ(e) the place to be searched, and the persons or things to be seized," repudiated these general warrants and "makes general searches . . . impossible and prevents the seizure of one thing under a warrant describing another. As to what is to be taken, nothing is left to the discretion of the officer executing the warrant."

We believe the statute here is equally offensive. First, as we have mentioned, eavesdropping is authorized without requiring belief that any particular offense has been or is being committed; nor that the "property" sought, the conversations, be particularly described. The purpose of the probable cause requirement of the Fourth Amendment, to keep the state out of constitutionally protected areas until it has reason to believe that a specific crime has been or is being committed, is thereby wholly aborted. Likewise the statute's failure to describe with particularity the conversations sought gives the officer a roving commission to "seize" any and all conversations. . . . As with general warrants this leaves too much to the discretion of the officer executing the order. Secondly, authorization of eavesdropping for a two-month period is the equivalent of a series of intrusions, searches, and seizures pursuant to a single showing of probable cause. Prompt execution is also avoided. During such a long and continuous (24 hours a day) period the conversations of any and all persons coming into the area covered by the device will be seized indiscriminately and without regard to their connection with the crime under investigation. Moreover, the statute permits, and there were authorized here, extensions of the original two-month period — presumably for two months each — on a mere showing that such extension is "in the public interest." Apparently the original grounds on which the eavesdrop order was initially issued also form the basis of the renewal. This we believe insufficient without a showing of present probable cause for the continuance of the eavesdrop. Third, the statute places no termination date on the eavesdrop once the conversation sought is seized. This is left entirely in the discretion of the officer. Finally, the statute's procedure, necessarily because its success depends on secrecy, has no requirement for notice as do conventional warrants, nor does it overcome this defect by requiring some showing of special facts. On the contrary, it permits uncontested entry without any showing of exigent circumstances. . . . In short, the statute's blanket grant of permission to eavesdrop is without adequate judicial supervision or protective procedures. . . .

In a concurring opinion, Justice Douglas observed:

. . . A discreet selective wiretap or electronic "bugging" is of course not rummaging around, collecting everything in the particular time and space zone. But even though it is limited in time, it is the greatest of all invasions of privacy. It places a government agent in the bedroom, in the business conference, in the social hour, in the lawyer's office — everywhere and anywhere a "bug" can be placed.

If a statute were to authorize placing a policeman in every home or office where it was shown that there was probable cause to believe that evidence of crime would be obtained, there is little doubt that it would be struck down as a bald invasion of privacy, far worse than the general warrants prohibited by the Fourth Amendment. I can see no difference between such a statute and one authorizing electronic surveillance, which, in effect, places an invisible policeman in the home. If anything, the latter is more offensive because the homeowner is completely unaware of the invasion of privacy. . . .

5. *An Exception for National Security?* In a footnote to *Katz*, the Court stated:

> Whether safeguards other than prior authorization by a magistrate would satisfy the Fourth Amendment in a situation involving the national security is a question not presented by this case.

Justice White, in a concurring opinion, declared:

> In joining the Court's opinion, I note the Court's acknowledgment that there are circumstance in which it is reasonable to search without a warrant. In this connection . . . the Court points out that today's decision does not reach national security cases. Wiretapping to protect the security of the Nation has been authorized by successive Presidents. The present Administration would apparently save national security cases from restrictions against wiretapping. We should not require the warrant procedure and the magistrate's judgment if the President of the United States or his chief legal officer, the Attorney General, has considered the requirements of national security and authorized electronic surveillance as reasonable.

Justices Douglas and Brennan, in another concurring opinion, took issue with Justice White:

> . . . Neither the President nor the Attorney General is a magistrate. In matters where they believe national security may be involved they are not detached, disinterested, and neutral as a court or magistrate must be. . . .
>
> There is, so far as I understand constitutional history, no distinction under the Fourth Amendment between types of crimes. Article III, § 3, gives "treason" a very narrow definition and puts restrictions on its proof. But the Fourth Amendment draws no lines between various substantive offenses. The arrests on cases of "hot pursuit" and the arrests on visible or other evidence of probable cause cut across the board and are not peculiar to any kind of crime.
>
> I would respect the present lines of distinction and not improvise because a particular crime seems particularly heinous. When the Framers took that step, as they did with treason, the worst crime of all, they made their purpose manifest.

In 1978, Congress enacted the Foreign Intelligence Surveillance Act (FISA). FISA established a statutory standard for electronic surveillance in cases involving agents of a foreign power. *See infra* Part B.5.

UNITED STATES v. WHITE

401 U.S. 745 (1971)

WHITE, J. In 1966, respondent James A. White was tried and convicted under two consolidated indictments charging various illegal transactions in narcotics. . . . He was fined and sentenced as a second offender to 25-year con-current sentences. The issue before us is whether the Fourth Amendment bars from evidence the testimony of governmental agents who related certain conversations which had occurred between defendant White and a government informant, Harvey Jackson, and which the agents overheard by monitoring the frequency of a radio transmitter carried by Jackson and concealed on his person. On four occasions the conversations took place in Jackson's home; each of these conversations was overheard by an agent concealed in a kitchen closet with Jackson's consent and by a second agent outside the house using a radio receiver. Four other conversations — one in respondent's home, one in a restaurant, and two in Jackson's car — were overheard by the use of radio equipment. The prosecution was unable to locate and produce Jackson at the trial and the trial court overruled objections to the testimony of the agents who conducted the electronic surveillance. The jury returned a guilty verdict and defendant appealed. . . .

Until *Katz v. United States*, neither wiretapping nor electronic eavesdropping violated a defendant's Fourth Amendment rights "unless there has been an official search and seizure of his person, or such a seizure of his papers or his tangible material effects, or an actual physical invasion of his house 'or curtilage' for the purpose of making a seizure." *Olmstead v. United States*. But where "eavesdropping was accomplished by means of an unauthorized physical penetration into the premises occupied" by the defendant, although falling short of a "technical trespass under the local property law," the Fourth Amendment was violated and any evidence of what was seen and heard, as well as tangible objects seized, was considered the inadmissible fruit of an unlawful invasion. *Silverman v. United States*, 365 U.S. 505, 509 (1961).

Katz v. United States, however, finally swept away doctrines that electronic eavesdropping is permissible under the Fourth Amendment unless physical invasion of a constitutionally protected area produced the challenged evidence. . . . [T]he Court overruled *Olmstead* and *Goldman* and held that the absence of physical intrusion into the telephone booth did not justify using electronic devices in listening to and recording Katz' words, thereby violating the privacy on which he justifiably relied while using the telephone in those circumstances.

The Court of Appeals understood *Katz* to render inadmissible against White the agents' testimony concerning conversations that Jackson broadcast to them. We cannot agree. *Katz* involved no revelation to the Government by a party to conversations with the defendant nor did the Court indicate in any way that a defendant has a justifiable and constitutionally protected expectation that a person with whom he is conversing will not then or later reveal the conversation to the police.

Hoffa v. United States, 385 U.S. 293 (1966), which was left undisturbed by *Katz*, held that however strongly a defendant may trust an apparent colleague, his expectations in this respect are not protected by the Fourth Amendment when it turns out that the colleague is a government agent regularly communicating with the authorities. In these circumstances, "no interest legitimately protected by the Fourth Amendment is involved," for that amendment affords no protection to "a wrongdoer's misplaced belief that a person to whom he voluntarily confides his wrongdoing will not reveal it." No warrant to "search and seize" is required in such circumstances, nor is it when the Government sends to defendant's home a secret agent who conceals his identity and makes a purchase of narcotics from the accused, *Lewis v. United States*, 385 U.S. 206 (1966), or when the same agent, unbeknown to the defendant, carries electronic equipment to record the defendant's words and the evidence so gathered is later offered in evidence. *Lopez v. United States*, 373 U.S. 427 (1963).

Conceding that *Hoffa*, *Lewis*, and *Lopez* remained unaffected by *Katz*, the Court of Appeals nevertheless read both *Katz* and the Fourth Amendment to require a different result if the agent not only records his conversations with the defendant but instantaneously transmits them electronically to other agents equipped with radio receivers. Where this occurs, the Court of Appeals held, the Fourth Amendment is violated and the testimony of the listening agents must be excluded from evidence.

To reach this result it was necessary for the Court of Appeals to hold that *On Lee v. United States* was no longer good law. . . . We see no indication in *Katz* that the Court meant to disturb that understanding of the Fourth Amendment or to disturb the result reached in the *On Lee* case, nor are we now inclined to overturn this view of the Fourth Amendment.

Concededly a police agent who conceals his police connections may write down for official use his conversations with a defendant and testify concerning them, without a warrant authorizing his encounters with the defendant and without otherwise violating the latter's Fourth Amendment rights. For constitutional purposes, no different result is required if the agent instead of immediately reporting and transcribing his conversations with defendant, either (1) simultaneously records them with electronic equipment which he is carrying on his person, *Lopez v. United States*; (2) or carries radio equipment which simultaneously transmits the conversations either to recording equipment located elsewhere or to other agents monitoring the transmitting frequency. *On Lee v. United States*. If the conduct and revelations of an agent operating without electronic equipment do not invade the defendant's constitutionally justifiable expectations of privacy, neither does a simultaneous recording of the same conversations made by the agent or by others from transmissions received from the agent to whom the defendant is talking and whose trustworthiness the defendant necessarily risks.

Our problem is not what the privacy expectations of particular defendants in particular situations may be or the extent to which they may in fact have relied on the discretion of their companions. Very probably, individual defendants neither know nor suspect that their colleagues have gone or will go to the police or are carrying recorders or transmitters. Otherwise, conversation would cease and our problem with these encounters would be nonexistent or far different from those now before us. Our problem, in terms of the principles announced in *Katz*, is what expectations of privacy are constitutionally "justifiable" — what expectations the Fourth Amendment will protect in the absence of a warrant. So far, the law permits the frustration of actual expectations of privacy by permitting authorities to use the testimony of those associates who for one reason or another have determined to turn to the police, as well as by authorizing the use of informants in the manner exemplified by *Hoffa* and *Lewis*. If the law gives no protection to the wrongdoer whose trusted accomplice is or becomes a police agent, neither should it protect him when that same agent has recorded or transmitted the conversations which are later offered in evidence to prove the State's case.

Inescapably, one contemplating illegal activities must realize and risk that his companions may be reporting to the police. If he sufficiently doubts their trustworthiness, the association will very probably end or never materialize. But if he has no doubts, or allays them, or risks what doubt he has, the risk is his. In terms of what his course will be, what he will or will not do or say, we are unpersuaded that he would distinguish between probably informers on the one hand and probable informers with transmitters on the other. . . .

Nor should we be too ready to erect constitutional barriers to relevant and probative evidence which is also accurate and reliable. An electronic recording will many times produce a more reliable rendition of what a defendant has said than will the unaided memory of a police agent. It may also be that with the recording in existence it is less likely that the informant will change his mind, less chance that threat or injury will suppress unfavorable evidence and less chance that cross-examination will confound the testimony. Considerations like these obviously do not favor the defendant, but we are not prepared to hold that a defendant who has no constitutional right to exclude the informer's unaided testimony nevertheless has a Fourth Amendment privilege against a more accurate version of the events in question. . . .

DOUGLAS, J. dissenting. . . . *On Lee* and *Lopez* are of a vintage opposed to *Berger* and *Katz*. However they may be explained, they are products of the old common-law notions of trespass. *Katz*, on the other hand, emphasized that with few exceptions "searches conducted outside the judicial process, without prior approval by judge or magistrate, are per se unreasonable under the Fourth Amendment." . . .

The threads of thought running through our recent decisions are that these extensive intrusions into privacy made by electronic surveillance make self-restraint by law enforcement officials an inadequate protection, that the requirement of warrants under the Fourth Amendment is essential to a free society.

Monitoring, if prevalent, certainly kills free discourse and spontaneous utterances. Free discourse — a First Amendment value — may be frivolous or serious, humble or defiant, reactionary or revolutionary, profane or in good taste; but it is not free if there is surveillance. Free discourse liberates the spirit, though it may produce only froth. The individual must keep some facts concerning his thoughts within a small zone of people. At the same time he must be free to pour out his woes or inspirations or dreams to others. He remains the sole judge as to what must be said and what must remain unspoken. This is the essence of the idea of privacy implicit in the First and Fifth Amendments as well as in the Fourth. . . .

Now that the discredited decisions in *On Lee* and *Lopez* are resuscitated and revived, must everyone live in fear that every word he speaks may be transmitted or recorded and later repeated to the entire world? I can imagine nothing that has a more chilling effect on people speaking their minds and expressing their views on important matters. The advocates of that regime should spend some time in totalitarian countries and learn firsthand the kind of regime they are creating here. . . .

NOTES & QUESTIONS

1. Is this case more akin to the bugging in *On Lee* and *Lopez* rather than the wiretapping of *Katz*? Does it matter whether the police heard the conversation simultaneously? Suppose the conversation had been recorded by a hidden recorder and then handed over later to the police.
2. Do we have a reasonable expectation that our friends aren't government agents in disguise?
3. Justice Douglas contends that electronic surveillance impinges upon and chills freedom of expression for all individuals in society. Is electronic surveillance without a warrant consistent with the First Amendment?

3. THE REASONABLE EXPECTATION OF PRIVACY TEST AND EMERGING TECHNOLOGY

(a) Applying the Reasonable Expectation of Privacy Test

SMITH V. MARYLAND   ·

442 U.S. 735 (1979)

BLACKMUN, J. This case presents the question whether the installation and use of a pen register[9] constitutes a "search" within the meaning of the Fourth Amendment, made applicable to the States through the Fourteenth Amendment.

On March 5, 1976, in Baltimore, Md., Patricia McDonough was robbed. She gave the police a description of the robber and of a 1975 Monte Carlo automobile she had observed near the scene of the crime. After the robbery, McDonough began receiving threatening and obscene phone calls from a man identifying himself as the robber. On one occasion, the caller asked that she step out on her front porch; she did so, and saw the 1975 Monte Carlo she had earlier described to police moving slowly past her home. On March 16, police spotted a man who met McDonough's description driving a 1975 Monte Carlo in her neighborhood. By tracing the license plate number, police learned that the car was registered in the name of petitioner, Michael Lee Smith.

The next day, the telephone company, at police request, installed a pen register at its central offices to record the numbers dialed from the telephone at petitioner's home. The police did not get a warrant or court order before

---

[9] "A pen register is a mechanical device that records the numbers dialed on a telephone by monitoring the electrical impulses caused when the dial on the telephone is released. It does not overhear oral communications and does not indicate whether calls are actually completed." A pen register is "usually installed at a central telephone facility [and] records on a paper tape all numbers dialed from [the] line" to which it is attached.

having the pen register installed. The register revealed that on March 17 a call was placed from petitioner's home to McDonough's phone. On the basis of this and other evidence, the police obtained a warrant to search petitioner's residence. [A search of Smith's home revealed more evidence that Smith was the robber. Smith moved to suppress all evidence obtained from (and derived from) the pen register. The trial court denied his motion, and Smith was convicted and sentenced to six years imprisonment.] . . .

The Fourth Amendment guarantees "[t]he right of the people to be secure in their persons, houses, papers, and effects, against unreasonable searches and seizures." In determining whether a particular form of government-initiated electronic surveillance is a "search" within the meaning of the Fourth Amendment,[10] our lodestar is *Katz v. United States*, 389 U.S. 347 (1967). . . .

Consistently with *Katz*, this Court uniformly has held that the application of the Fourth Amendment depends on whether the person invoking its protection can claim a "justifiable," a "reasonable," or a "legitimate expectation of privacy" that has been invaded by government action. This inquiry, as Mr. Justice Harlan aptly noted in his *Katz* concurrence, normally embraces two discrete questions. The first is whether the individual, by his conduct, has "exhibited an actual (subjective) expectation of privacy,"—whether, in the words of the *Katz* majority, the individual has shown that "he seeks to preserve [something] as private." The second question is whether the individual's subjective expectation of privacy is "one that society is prepared to recognize as 'reasonable,'"—whether, in the words of the *Katz* majority, the individual's expectation, viewed objectively, is "justifiable" under the circumstances.[11]

In applying the *Katz* analysis to this case, it is important to begin by specifying precisely the nature of the state activity that is challenged. The activity here took the form of installing and using a pen register. Since the pen register was installed on telephone company property at the telephone company's central offices, petitioner obviously cannot claim that his "property" was invaded or that police intruded into a "constitutionally protected area." Petitioner's claim, rather, is that, notwithstanding the absence of a trespass, the State, as did the Government in *Katz*, infringed a "legitimate expectation of privacy" that petitioner held. Yet a pen register differs significantly from the listening

---

[10] In this case, the pen register was installed, and the numbers dialed were recorded, by the telephone company. The telephone company, however, acted at police request. In view of this, respondent appears to concede that the company is to be deemed an "agent" of the police for purposes of this case, so as to render the installation and use of the pen register "state action" under the Fourth and Fourteenth Amendments. We may assume that "state action" was present here.

[11] Situations can be imagined, of course, in which Katz' two-pronged inquiry would provide an inadequate index of Fourth Amendment protection. For example, if the Government were suddenly to announce on nationwide television that all homes henceforth would be subject to warrantless entry, individuals thereafter might not in fact entertain any actual expectation of privacy regarding their homes, papers, and effects. Similarly, if a refugee from a totalitarian country, unaware of this Nation's traditions, erroneously assumed that police were continuously monitoring his telephone conversations, a subjective expectation of privacy regarding the contents of his calls might be lacking as well. In such circumstances, where an individual's subjective expectations had been "conditioned" by influences alien to well-recognized Fourth Amendment freedoms, those subjective expectations obviously could play no meaningful role in ascertaining what the scope of Fourth Amendment protection was. In determining whether a "legitimate expectation of privacy" existed in such cases, a normative inquiry would be proper.

device employed in *Katz*, for pen registers do not acquire the contents of communications. This Court recently noted:

> Indeed, a law enforcement official could not even determine from the use of a pen register whether a communication existed. These devices do not hear sound. They disclose only the telephone numbers that have been dialed — a means of establishing communication. Neither the purport of any communication between the caller and the recipient of the call, their identities, nor whether the call was even completed is disclosed by pen registers. *United States v. New York Tel. Co.*, 434 U.S. 159, 167 (1977).

Given a pen register's limited capabilities, therefore, petitioner's argument that its installation and use constituted a "search" necessarily rests upon a claim that he had a "legitimate expectation of privacy" regarding the numbers he dialed on his phone.

This claim must be rejected. First, we doubt that people in general entertain any actual expectation of privacy in the numbers they dial. All telephone users realize that they must "convey" phone numbers to the telephone company, since it is through telephone company switching equipment that their calls are completed. All subscribers realize, moreover, that the phone company has facilities for making permanent records of the numbers they dial, for they see a list of their long-distance (toll) calls on their monthly bills. In fact, pen registers and similar devices are routinely used by telephone companies "for the purposes of checking billing operations, detecting fraud and preventing violations of law." Electronic equipment is used not only to keep billing records of toll calls, but also "to keep a record of all calls dialed from a telephone which is subject to a special rate structure." Pen registers are regularly employed "to determine whether a home phone is being used to conduct a business, to check for a defective dial, or to check for overbilling." Although most people may be oblivious to a pen register's esoteric functions, they presumably have some awareness of one common use: to aid in the identification of persons making annoying or obscene calls. Most phone books tell subscribers, on a page entitled "Consumer Information," that the company "can frequently help in identifying to the authorities the origin of unwelcome and troublesome calls." Telephone users, in sum, typically know that they must convey numerical information to the phone company; that the phone company has facilities for recording this information; and that the phone company does in fact record this information for a variety of legitimate business purposes. Although subjective expectations cannot be scientifically gauged, it is too much to believe that telephone subscribers, under these circumstances, harbor any general expectation that the numbers they dial will remain secret. . . .

. . . [E]ven if petitioner did harbor some subjective expectation that the phone numbers he dialed would remain private, this expectation is not "one that society is prepared to recognize as 'reasonable.'" This Court consistently has held that a person has no legitimate expectation of privacy in information he voluntarily turns over to third parties. In [*United States v.*] *Miller*, for example, the Court held that a bank depositor has no "legitimate 'expectation of privacy'" in financial information "voluntarily conveyed to . . . banks and exposed to their employees in the ordinary course of business." The Court explained:

> The depositor takes the risk, in revealing his affairs to another, that the information will be conveyed by that person to the Government. . . . This Court has held repeatedly that the Fourth Amendment does not prohibit the obtaining of information revealed to a third party and conveyed by him to Government authorities, even if the information is revealed on the assumption that it will be used only for a limited purpose and the confidence placed in the third party will not be betrayed.

Because the depositor "assumed the risk" of disclosure, the Court held that it would be unreasonable for him to expect his financial records to remain private.

This analysis dictates that petitioner can claim no legitimate expectation of privacy here. When he used his phone, petitioner voluntarily conveyed numerical information to the telephone company and "exposed" that information to its equipment in the ordinary course of business. In so doing, petitioner assumed the risk that the company would reveal to police the numbers he dialed. The switching equipment that processed those numbers is merely the modern counterpart of the operator who, in an earlier day, personally completed calls for the subscriber. Petitioner concedes that if he had placed his calls through an operator, he could claim no legitimate expectation of privacy. We are not inclined to hold that a different constitutional result is required because the telephone company has decided to automate.

Petitioner argues, however, that automatic switching equipment differs from a live operator in one pertinent respect. An operator, in theory at least, is capable of remembering every number that is conveyed to him by callers. Electronic equipment, by contrast can "remember" only those numbers it is programmed to record, and telephone companies, in view of their present billing practices, usually do not record local calls. Since petitioner, in calling McDonough, was making a local call, his expectation of privacy as to her number, on this theory, would be "legitimate."

This argument does not withstand scrutiny. The fortuity of whether or not the phone company in fact elects to make a quasi-permanent record of a particular number dialed does not in our view, make any constitutional difference. Regardless of the phone company's election, petitioner voluntarily conveyed to it information that it had facilities for recording and that it was free to record. In these circumstances, petitioner assumed the risk that the information would be divulged to police. . . .

STEWART, J. joined by BRENNAN, J. dissenting. . . The numbers dialed from a private telephone — although certainly more prosaic than the conversation itself — are not without "content." Most private telephone subscribers may have their own numbers listed in a publicly distributed directory, but I doubt there are any who would be happy to have broadcast to the world a list of the local or long distance numbers they have called. This is not because such a list might in some sense be incriminating, but because it easily could reveal the identities of the persons and the places called, and thus reveal the most intimate details of a person's life.

MARSHALL J. joined by BRENNAN, J. dissenting . . Privacy is not a discrete commodity, possessed absolutely or not at all. Those who disclose certain facts to a bank or phone company for a limited business purpose need not assume that this information will be released to other persons for other purposes.

The crux of the Court's holding, however, is that whatever expectation of privacy petitioner may in fact have entertained regarding his calls, it is not one "society is prepared to recognize as 'reasonable.'" In so ruling, the Court determines that individuals who convey information to third parties have "assumed the risk" of disclosure to the government. This analysis is misconceived in two critical respects.

Implicit in the concept of assumption of risk is some notion of choice. At least in the third-party consensual surveillance cases, which first incorporated risk analysis into Fourth Amendment doctrine, the defendant presumably had exercised some discretion in deciding who should enjoy his confidential communications. By contrast here, unless a person is prepared to forgo use of what for many has become a personal or professional necessity, he cannot help but accept the risk of surveillance. It is idle to speak of "assuming" risks in contexts where, as a practical matter, individuals have no realistic alternative.

More fundamentally, to make risk analysis dispositive in assessing the reasonableness of privacy expectations would allow the government to define the scope of Fourth Amendment protections. For example, law enforcement officials, simply by announcing their intent to monitor the content of random samples of first-class mail or private phone conversations, could put the public on notice of the risks they would thereafter assume in such communications. . . .

In my view, whether privacy expectations are legitimate within the meaning of *Katz* depends not on the risks an individual can be presumed to accept when imparting information to third parties, but on the risks he should be forced to assume in a free and open society. . . .

The use of pen registers, I believe, constitutes such an extensive intrusion. To hold otherwise ignores the vital role telephonic communication plays in our personal and professional relationships, as well as the First and Fourth Amendment interests implicated by unfettered official surveillance. Privacy in placing calls is of value not only to those engaged in criminal activity. The prospect of unregulated governmental monitoring will undoubtedly prove disturbing even to those with nothing illicit to hide. Many individuals, including members of unpopular political organizations or journalists with confidential sources, may legitimately wish to avoid disclosure of their personal contacts. Permitting governmental access to telephone records on less than probable cause may thus impede certain forms of political affiliation and journalistic endeavor that are the hallmark of a truly free society. Particularly given the Government's previous reliance on warrantless telephonic surveillance to trace reporters' sources and monitor protected political activity, I am unwilling to insulate use of pen registers from independent judicial review. . . .

NOTES & QUESTIONS

1. *Pen Registers and Trap and Trace Devices.* A pen register records outgoing telephone calls. Another device, known as a trap and trace device, records all incoming calls. Why aren't pen registers and trap and trace devices a form of wiretap akin to that in *Katz*?

2. Consider the following observation by Laurence Tribe about *Smith*:

> The "assumption of risk"—more aptly, "assumption of broadcast"—notion underling the holding in *Smith* . . . reveals alarming tendencies in the Supreme Court's understanding of what privacy means and ought to mean. The Court treats privacy almost as if it were "a discrete commodity, possessed absolutely or not at all." [quoting Justice Marshall's dissent]. Yet what could be more commonplace than the idea that it is up to the *individual to measure out information* about herself *selectively*—to whomever she chooses?[12]

3. *State Constitutional Law.* Some states have rejected the *Smith* holding under their constitutions. For example, in *State v. Hunt,* 450 A.2d 952 (N.J. 1982), the New Jersey Supreme Court rejected *Smith* and held that under the New Jersey Constitution, there is a reasonable expectation of privacy in telephone records:

> The telephone has become an essential instrument in carrying on our personal affairs. It has become part and parcel of the home. When a telephone call is made, it is as if two people are having a private conversation in the sanctity of their living room. . . .
>
> The telephone caller is . . . entitled to assume that the numbers he dials in the privacy of his home will be recorded solely for the telephone company's business purposes. From the viewpoint of the customer, all the information which he furnishes with respect to a particular call is private. The numbers dialed are private. . . .
>
> It is unrealistic to say that the cloak of privacy has been shed because the telephone company and some of its employees are aware of this information. Telephone calls cannot be made except through the telephone company's property and without payment to it for the service. This disclosure has been necessitated because of the nature of the instrumentality, but more significantly the disclosure has been made for a limited business purpose and not for release to other persons for other reasons. . . .

4. *Federal Statutory Law.* As is sometimes the case when the Court fails to find a right of privacy in the collection of personal information, Congress will enact legislation to create such a right by statutory means. That happened with pen registers after *Smith*, though it took until 1986 with the Electronic Communications Privacy Act. *See* 18 U.S.C. §§ 3121-3127 (Part B.3). In 2001, the USA-PATRIOT Act changed the definition of pen registers and trap and trace devices to include not only telephone numbers, but all "dialing, routing, addressing, or signaling information." USA-PATRIOT Act § 216. Thus, the definition of pen registers and trap and trace devices now encompasses Internet addresses and e-mail addressing information. *See* Part B.6.

UNITED STATES V. PLACE

462 U.S. 696 (1983)

O'CONNOR, J. The Fourth Amendment "protects people from unreasonable government intrusions into their legitimate expectations of privacy." We have

---

[12] Laurence Tribe, *American Constitutional Law* 1391 (2d ed. 1988). For another critique of *Smith v. Maryland*, see Daniel J. Solove, *Digital Dossiers and the Dissipation*, 75 S. Cal. L. Rev. 1083 (2002).

affirmed that a person possesses a privacy interest in the contents of personal luggage that is protected by the Fourth Amendment. A "canine sniff" by a well-trained narcotics detection dog, however, does not require opening the luggage. It does not expose noncontraband items that otherwise would remain hidden from public view, as does, for example, an officer's rummaging through the contents of the luggage. Thus, the manner in which information is obtained through this investigative technique is much less intrusive than a typical search. Moreover, the sniff discloses only the presence or absence of narcotics, a contraband item. Thus, despite the fact that the sniff tells the authorities something about the contents of the luggage, the information obtained is limited. This limited disclosure also ensures that the owner of the property is not subjected to the embarrassment and inconvenience entailed in less discriminate and more intrusive investigative methods.

In these respects, the canine sniff is *sui generis*. We are aware of no other investigative procedure that is so limited both in the manner in which the information is obtained and in the content of the information revealed by the procedure. Therefore, we conclude that the particular course of investigation that the agents intended to pursue here — exposure of respondent's luggage, which was located in a public place, to a trained canine — did not constitute a "search" within the meaning of the Fourth Amendment. . . .

NOTES & QUESTIONS

1. Suppose the police had used a special x-ray machine to examine the contents of the bag. Would this be a Fourth Amendment violation under *Place*? Why or why not?

2. Currently, judges decide whether a defendant has a reasonable expectation of privacy in a particular activity. Is this question appropriate for judges to decide? Or should juries decide it? In all of the cases so far, observe the sources that the Court cites to for support that there is no reasonable expectation of privacy. How is a reasonable expectation of privacy to be measured? Is it an empirical question about what most people in society would generally consider to be private? If so, why aren't polls taken? If you're an attorney arguing that there is a reasonable expectation of privacy in something, what do you cite to? How should courts measure what society as a whole thinks is private?

3. Consider the following observation by Anthony Amsterdam:

> [Should the Fourth Amendment] be viewed as a collection of protections of atomistic spheres of interest of individual citizens or as a regulation of governmental conduct[?] Does it safeguard *my* person and *your* house and *her* papers and *his* effects against unreasonable searches and seizures; or is it essentially a regulatory canon requiring government to order its law enforcement procedures in a fashion that keeps us collectively secure in our persons, houses, papers, and effects, against unreasonable searches and seizures?[13]

---

[13]Anthony G. Amsterdam, *Perspectives on the Fourth Amendment*, 58 Minn. L. Rev. 349, 367 (1974).

Under what view does the Supreme Court seem to be operating? Which view do you think is the most appropriate?

4. Amsterdam also argues that one's privacy may be violated by being observed by the police but may not be violated by the very same observation from others:

> [I]f you live in a cheap hotel or in a ghetto flat, your neighbors can hear you breathing quietly even in temperate weather when it is possible to keep the windows and doors closed. For the tenement dweller, the difference between observation by neighbors and visitors who ordinarily use the common hallways and observation by policemen who come into hallways to "check up" or "look around" is the difference between all the privacy that his condition allows and none. Is that small difference too unimportant to claim fourth amendment protection?[14]

Do you agree that our expectations of privacy turn on who is watching rather than simply whether we are being watched? Should the "reasonable expectation of privacy" test be changed to the "reasonable expectation of what the police can observe or search" test?

CALIFORNIA v. GREENWOOD

486 U.S. 35 (1988)

[Police investigators searched the plastic garbage bags that Greenwood left on the curb in front of his house to be picked up by the trash collector. The officers found indications of drug use from the search of Greenwood's trash and obtained a warrant to search the house, where they uncovered more evidence of drug trafficking. Greenwood was arrested.]

WHITE, J. . . . The warrantless search and seizure of the garbage bags left at the curb outside the Greenwood house would violate the Fourth Amendment only if respondents manifested a subjective expectation of privacy in their garbage that society accepts as objectively reasonable.

. . . [The Greenwoods] assert . . . that they had, and exhibited, an expectation of privacy with respect to the trash that was searched by the police: The trash, which was placed on the street for collection at a fixed time, was contained in opaque plastic bags, which the garbage collector was expected to pick up, mingle with the trash of others, and deposit at the garbage dump. The trash was only temporarily on the street, and there was little likelihood that it would be inspected by anyone.

It may well be that respondents did not expect that the contents of their garbage bags would become known to the police or other members of the public. An expectation of privacy does not give rise to Fourth Amendment protection, however, unless society is prepared to accept that expectation as objectively reasonable.

---

[14]*Id.* at 404.

Here, we conclude that respondents exposed their garbage to the public sufficiently to defeat their claim to Fourth Amendment protection. It is common knowledge that plastic garbage bags left on or at the side of a public street are readily accessible to animals, children, scavengers, snoops, and other members of the public. Moreover, respondents placed their refuse at the curb for the express purpose of conveying it to a third party, the trash collector, who might himself have sorted through respondents' trash or permitted others, such as the police, to do so. Accordingly, having deposited their garbage "in an area particularly suited for public inspection and, in a manner of speaking, public consumption, for the express purpose of having strangers take it," respondents could have had no reasonable expectation of privacy in the inculpatory items that they discarded. . . .

BRENNAN, J. joined by MARSHALL, J. dissenting, . . . Scrutiny of another's trash is contrary to commonly accepted notions of civilized behavior. I suspect, therefore, that members of our society will be shocked to learn that the Court, the ultimate guarantor of liberty, deems unreasonable our expectation that the aspects of our private lives that are concealed safely in a trash bag will not become public.

"A container which can support a reasonable expectation of privacy may not be searched, even on probable cause, without a warrant." *United States v. Jacobsen*, 466 U.S. 109, 120, n. 17 (1984) (citations omitted). Thus, as the Court observes, if Greenwood had a reasonable expectation that the contents of the bags that he placed on the curb would remain private, the warrantless search of those bags violated the Fourth Amendment. . . .

Our precedent, therefore, leaves no room to doubt that had respondents been carrying their personal effects in opaque, sealed plastic bags — identical to the ones they placed on the curb — their privacy would have been protected from warrantless police intrusion. . . .

Respondents deserve no less protection just because Greenwood used the bags to discard rather than to transport his personal effects. Their contents are not inherently any less private, and Greenwood's decision to discard them, at least in the manner in which he did, does not diminish his expectation of privacy.

A trash bag, like any of the above-mentioned containers, "is a common repository for one's personal effects" and, even more than many of them, is "therefore . . . inevitably associated with the expectation of privacy." "[A]lmost every human activity ultimately manifests itself in waste products. . . ." *Smith v. State*, 510 P.2d 793, 798 (Alaska 1973). A single bag of trash testifies eloquently to the eating, reading, and recreational habits of the person who produced it. A search of trash, like a search of the bedroom, can relate intimate details about sexual practices, health, and personal hygiene. Like rifling through desk drawers or intercepting phone calls, rummaging through trash can divulge the target's financial and professional status, political affiliations and inclinations, private thoughts, personal relationships, and romantic interests. It cannot be doubted that a sealed trash bag harbors telling evidence of the "intimate activity associated with the 'sanctity of a man's home and the privacies of life,'" which the Fourth Amendment is designed to protect. . . .

. . . Most of us, I believe, would be incensed to discover a meddler — whether a neighbor, a reporter, or a detective — scrutinizing our sealed trash containers to discover some detail of our personal lives. . . .

The mere possibility that unwelcome meddlers might open and rummage through the containers does not negate the expectation of privacy in their contents any more than the possibility of a burglary negates an expectation of privacy in the home; or the possibility of a private intrusion negates an expectation of privacy in an unopened package; or the possibility that an operator will listen in on a telephone conversation negates an expectation of privacy in the words spoken on the telephone. "What a person . . . seeks to preserve as private, even in an area accessible to the public, may be constitutionally protected." *Katz*, 389 U.S. at 351–52. . . .

NOTES & QUESTIONS

1. Do you agree with the Court's argument in *Greenwood* that there is no reasonable expectation of privacy in garbage because it is accessible to the public?
2. In addition to searching through Greenwood's trash, the police were staking out his home, watching who came and went from his house. Does the Fourth Amendment protect against such surveillance? Imagine that for one year, the police were to stake out a person's home and follow the person wherever he or she went throughout the day. The person would be under 24-hour surveillance. However, no intrusions would be made into the home and no wiretaps would be used. The police would simply observe the person anytime she were in public. Is this more invasive to privacy than a one-time search of particular items, such as one's luggage? Does the Fourth Amendment provide any limitation on the police activities described above?
3. ***State Constitutional Law.*** The federal Constitution is not the only protection against certain law enforcement tactics. Each state's constitution also contains protections similar to the U.S. Constitution's Fourth Amendment. Certain state constitutions have been interpreted as being more protective than the federal constitution. Therefore, the federal Constitution is the floor, the minimum threshold. States can be more protective if they desire. For example, some state courts have interpreted their constitution to prohibit the search of garbage without a warrant. *See, e.g., State v. Hempele*, 120 N.J. 182 (1990).

PLAIN VIEW, OPEN FIELDS, AND CURTILAGE

"[I]t has long been settled that objects falling in the plain view of an officer who has a right to be in the position to have that view are subject to seizure and may be introduced in evidence." *Harris v. United States*, 390 U.S. 234, 236 (1968). This has become known as the "plain view" doctrine. If it is possible for something to be seen or heard from a public vantage point, there can be no reasonable expectation of privacy.

An extension of the plain view doctrine is the "open fields" doctrine. An individual does not have a reasonable expectation of privacy in the open fields that she owns. In *Oliver v. United States*, 466 U.S. 170 (1984), the defendant placed "No Trespassing" signs throughout his farm and maintained a locked gate around the farm's entrance. The fields could not be seen from any public vantage point. The police trespassed onto the fields and found marijuana. The Court held, however, that there is no reasonable expectation of privacy in open fields, and the defendant's attempt to keep them secluded and shielded from public view was irrelevant.

An exception to the open fields doctrine is the "curtilage" doctrine. Under this doctrine, parts of one's property immediately outside one's home do not fall within the open fields doctrine. This does not mean that the curtilage is automatically afforded Fourth Amendment protection; a reasonable expectation of privacy analysis still must be performed. The question of whether an area constitutes a curtilage "depends upon 'whether the area in question is so intimately tied to the home itself that it should be placed within the home's 'umbrella' of Fourth Amendment protection.'" *United States v. Dunn*, 480 U.S. 294, 301 (1987).

FLORIDA V. RILEY

488 U.S. 445 (1989)

WHITE, J. . . . Respondent Riley lived in a mobile home located on five acres of rural property. A greenhouse was located 10 to 20 feet behind the mobile home. Two sides of the greenhouse were enclosed. The other two sides were not enclosed but the contents of the greenhouse were obscured from view from surrounding property by trees, shrubs, and the mobile home. The greenhouse was covered by corrugated roofing panels, some translucent and some opaque. At the time relevant to this case, two of the panels, amounting to approximately 10% of the roof area, were missing. A wire fence surrounded the mobile home and the greenhouse, and the property was posted with a "DO NOT ENTER" sign.

This case originated with an anonymous tip to the Pasco County Sheriff's office that marijuana was being grown on respondent's property. When an investigating officer discovered that he could not see the contents of the greenhouse from the road, he circled twice over respondent's property in a helicopter at the height of 400 feet. With his naked eye, he was able to see through the openings in the roof and one or more of the open sides of the greenhouse and to identify what he thought was marijuana growing in the structure. A warrant was obtained based on these observations, and the ensuing search revealed marijuana growing in the greenhouse. Respondent was charged with possession of marijuana under Florida law. . . .

We agree with the State's submission that our decision in *California v. Ciraolo*, 476 U.S. 207 (1986), controls this case. There, acting on a tip, the police inspected the back-yard of a particular house while flying in a fixed-wing aircraft at 1,000 feet. With the naked eye the officers saw what they concluded was marijuana growing in the yard. A search warrant was obtained on the strength of this airborne inspection, and marijuana plants were found. The trial court refused to suppress this evidence, but a state appellate court held that the inspection violated the Fourth and Fourteenth Amendments to the United States Constitution, and that the warrant was therefore invalid. We in turn reversed, holding that the inspection was not a search subject to the Fourth Amendment. We recognized that the yard was within the curtilage of the house, that a fence shielded the yard from observation from the street, and that the occupant had a subjective expectation of privacy. We held, however, that such an expectation was not reasonable and not one "that society is prepared to honor." Our reasoning was that the home and its curtilage are not necessarily protected from inspection that involves no physical invasion. "'What a person knowingly exposes to the public, even in his own home or office, is not a subject of Fourth Amendment protection.'" As a general proposition, the police may see what may be seen "from a public vantage point where [they have] a right to be." Thus the police, like the public, would have been free to inspect the backyard garden from the street if their view had been unobstructed. They were likewise free to inspect the yard from the vantage point of an aircraft flying in the navigable airspace as this plane was. "In an age where private and commercial flight in the public airways is routine, it is unreasonable for respondent to expect that his marijuana plants were constitutionally protected from being observed with the naked eye from an altitude of 1,000 feet. The Fourth Amendment simply does not require the police traveling in the public airways at this altitude to obtain a warrant in order to observe what is visible to the naked eye."

We arrive at the same conclusion in the present case. In this case, as in *Ciraolo*, the property surveyed was within the curtilage of respondent's home. Riley no doubt intended and expected that his greenhouse would not be open to public inspection, and the precautions he took protected against ground-level observation. Because the sides and roof of his greenhouse were left partially open, however, what was growing in the greenhouse was subject to viewing from the air. Under the holding in *Ciraolo*, Riley could not reasonably have expected the contents of his greenhouse to be immune from examination by an officer seated in a fixed-wing aircraft flying in navigable airspace at an altitude of 1,000 feet or, as the Florida Supreme Court seemed to recognize, at an altitude of 500 feet, the lower limit of the navigable airspace for such an aircraft. Here, the inspection was made from a helicopter, but as is the case with fixed-wing planes, "private and commercial flight [by helicopter] in the public airways is routine" in this country, and there is no indication that such flights are unheard of in Pasco County, Florida. Riley could not reasonably have expected that his greenhouse was protected from public or official observation from a helicopter had it been flying within the navigable airspace for fixed-wing aircraft.

Nor on the facts before us, does it make a difference for Fourth Amendment purposes that the helicopter was flying at 400 feet when the officer saw what was growing in the greenhouse through the partially open roof and sides of the structure. We would have a different case if flying at that altitude had been contrary to law or regulation. But helicopters are not bound by the lower limits of the navigable airspace allowed to other aircraft. Any member of the public could legally have been flying over Riley's property in a helicopter at the altitude of 400 feet and could have observed Riley's greenhouse. The police officer did no more. . . . As far as this record reveals, no intimate details connected with the use of the home or curtilage were observed, and there was no undue noise, and no wind, dust, or threat of injury. In these circumstances, there was no violation of the Fourth Amendment.

BRENNAN, J. joined by MARSHALL and STEVENS, J. J. dissenting. Under the plurality's exceedingly grudging Fourth Amendment theory, the expectation of privacy is defeated if a single member of the public could conceivably position herself to see into the area in question without doing anything illegal. It is defeated whatever the difficulty a person would have in so positioning herself, and however infrequently anyone would in fact do so. In taking this view the plurality ignores the very essence of *Katz*. The reason why there is no reasonable expectation of privacy in an area that is exposed to the public is that little diminution in "the amount of privacy and freedom remaining to citizens" will result from police surveillance of something that any passerby readily sees. To pretend, as the plurality opinion does, that the same is true when the police use a helicopter to peer over high fences is, at best, disingenuous. . . .

The police officer positioned 400 feet above Riley's backyard was not, however, standing on a public road. The vantage point he enjoyed was not one any citizen could readily share. His ability to see over Riley's fence depended on his use of a very expensive and sophisticated piece of machinery to which few ordinary citizens have access. In such circumstances it makes no more sense to rely on the legality of the officer's position in the skies than it would to judge the constitutionality of the wiretap in *Katz* by the legality of the officer's position outside the telephone booth. The simple inquiry whether the police officer had the legal right to be in the position from which he made his observations cannot suffice, for we cannot assume that Riley's curtilage was so open to the observations of passersby in the skies that he retained little privacy or personal security to be lost to police surveillance. The question before us must be not whether the police were where they had a right to be, but whether public observation of Riley's curtilage was so commonplace that Riley's expectation of privacy in his backyard could not be considered reasonable. . . .

. . . The Fourth Amendment demands that we temper our efforts to apprehend criminals with a concern for the impact on our fundamental liberties of the methods we use. I hope it will be a matter of concern to my colleagues that the police surveillance methods they would sanction were among those described 40 years ago in George Orwell's dread vision of life in the 1980's:

> The black-mustachio'd face gazed down from every commanding corner. There was one on the house front immediately opposite. BIG BROTHER IS WATCHING YOU, the caption said. . . . In the far distance a helicopter skimmed down between the roofs, hovered for an instant like a bluebottle, and darted away again with a curving flight. It was the Police Patrol, snooping into people's windows.[15]

Who can read this passage without a shudder, and without the instinctive reaction that it depicts life in some country other than ours? I respectfully dissent.

---

[15] George Orwell, *Nineteen Eighty-Four* 4 (1949).

NOTES & QUESTIONS

1. *Privacy in Public.* The court quotes from *Katz v. United States* that "[w]hat a person knowingly exposes to the public . . . is not a subject of Fourth Amendment protection." How far does this principle extend? Can there be situations where a person might have a reasonable expectation of privacy even when exposed in public? Recall the public disclosure tort cases in Chapter 2, which indicate that sometimes a person does have a privacy interest even in the event of public exposure or being in a public place.

2. *Surveillance Cameras.* The use of surveillance cameras is increasing. Since 1994, in response to terrorist bombings, Britain has been watching city streets through a system of surveillance cameras monitored by closed circuit television (CCTV).[16] In 2002, the National Park Service announced plans to set up a surveillance system at all major monuments on the National Mall in Washington, D.C. Given the frequent use of surveillance cameras, do we still have an expectation of privacy not to be filmed in our day-to-day activities?

3. *Face Recognition Systems.* In Tampa, a computer software program called "FaceIt" linked to 36 cameras attempts to scan the faces of individuals on public streets to match them against mug shots of wanted fugitives. A similar system was used to scan faces at Super Bowl XXXV in January 2001. The Tampa Police Department argues that FaceIt is analogous to a police officer standing on a street holding a mug shot. Do you agree? Philip Agre contends that face recognition systems are different:

   > A human being who spots me in the park has the accountability that some-one can spot them as well. Cameras are much more anonymous and easy to hide. More important is the question of scale. Most people understand the moral difference between a single chance observation in a park and an investigator who follows you everywhere you go.[17]

   Further, contends Agre, the information used and collected by face recognition systems could fall into the wrong hands and be potentially abused by the government to exercise social control. Additionally, such systems can have errors, resulting in the tracking and potential arrest of innocent persons. As a policy matter, do the costs of facial recognition systems outweigh the benefits? Given the information privacy law you have learned so far, assess the legality and constitutionality of facial recognition systems.

4. *Video Surveillance in Other Countries.* The question of whether video surveillance is lawful has been raised in a number of other countries. In Canada, for example, Article 8 of the Canadian Charter of Rights and Freedoms, which is similar to the U.S. Fourth Amendment, states simply: "Everyone has the right to be secure against unreasonable search or seizure." Both the Canadian Privacy Commissioner and a former Justice of the High Court be-

---

[16] For more background about CCTV, see Clive Norris & Gary Armstrong, *The Maximum Surveillance Society: The Rise of CCTV* (1999); Jeffrey Rosen, *A Cautionary Tale for a New Age of Surveillance*, N.Y. Times Magazine (Oct. 7, 2001).

[17] Philip E. Agre, *Your Face Is Not a Bar Code: Arguments Against Automatic Face Recognition in Public Places* (Sept. 9, 2001), available at *<http://dlis.gseis.ucla.edu/people/pagre/bar-code.html>*.

lieve that this prevents the use of surveillance cameras in public places by the police.[18]

(b) Sensory Enhancement Technology

DOW CHEMICAL CO. v. UNITED STATES

476 U.S. 227 (1986)

BURGER, C. J. . . . Petitioner Dow Chemical Co. operates a 2,000-acre facility manufacturing chemicals at Midland, Michigan. The facility consists of numerous covered buildings, with manufacturing equipment and piping conduits located between the various buildings exposed to visual observation from the air. At all times, Dow has maintained elaborate security around the perimeter of the complex barring ground-level public views of these areas. It also investigates any low-level flights by aircraft over the facility. Dow has not undertaken, however, to conceal all manufacturing equipment within the complex from aerial views. Dow maintains that the cost of covering its exposed equipment would be prohibitive.

In early 1978, enforcement officials of EPA, with Dow's consent, made an on-site inspection of two powerplants in this complex. A subsequent EPA request for a second inspection, however, was denied, and EPA did not thereafter seek an administrative search warrant. Instead, EPA employed a commercial aerial photographer, using a standard floor-mounted, precision aerial mapping camera, to take photographs of the facility from altitudes of 12,000, 3,000, and 1,200 feet. At all times the aircraft was lawfully within navigable airspace.

EPA did not inform Dow of this aerial photography, but when Dow became aware of it, Dow brought suit in the District Court alleging that EPA's action violated the Fourth Amendment and was beyond EPA's statutory investigative authority. The District Court granted Dow's motion for summary judgment on the ground that EPA had no authority to take aerial photographs and that doing so was a search violating the Fourth Amendment. EPA was permanently enjoined from taking aerial photographs of Dow's premises and from disseminating, releasing, or copying the photographs already taken. . . .

The photographs at issue in this case are essentially like those commonly used in mapmaking. Any person with an airplane and an aerial camera could readily duplicate them. In common with much else, the technology of photography has changed in this century. These developments have enhanced industrial processes, and indeed all areas of life; they have also enhanced law enforcement techniques. . . .

. . . Dow claims EPA's use of aerial photography was a "search" of an area that, notwithstanding the large size of the plant, was within an "industrial curtilage" rather than an "open field," and that it had a reasonable expectation of privacy from such photography protected by the Fourth Amendment. . . .

. . . Dow concedes that a simple flyover with naked-eye observation, or

---

[18] *See generally* Electronic Privacy Information Center & Privacy International, *Privacy and Human Rights: An International Survey of Privacy Laws and Developments* 59–62 (2001).

the taking of a photograph from a nearby hillside overlooking such a facility, would give rise to no Fourth Amendment problem.

In *California v. Ciraolo*, 476 U.S. 207 (1986), decided today, we hold that naked-eye aerial observation from an altitude of 1,000 feet of a backyard within the curtilage of a home does not constitute a search under the Fourth Amendment.

In the instant case, two additional Fourth Amendment claims are presented: whether the common-law "curtilage" doctrine encompasses a large industrial complex such as Dow's, and whether photography employing an aerial mapping camera is permissible in this context. Dow argues that an industrial plant, even one occupying 2,000 acres, does not fall within the "open fields" doctrine of *Oliver v. United States* but rather is an "industrial curtilage" having constitutional protection equivalent to that of the curtilage of a private home. Dow further contends that any aerial photography of this "industrial curtilage" intrudes upon its reasonable expectations of privacy. Plainly a business establishment or an industrial or commercial facility enjoys certain protections under the Fourth Amendment. . . .

. . . The curtilage area immediately surrounding a private house has long been given protection as a place where the occupants have a reasonable and legitimate expectation of privacy that society is prepared to accept. . . .

Dow plainly has a reasonable, legitimate, and objective expectation of privacy within the interior of its covered buildings, and it is equally clear that expectation is one society is prepared to observe. Moreover, it could hardly be expected that Dow would erect a huge cover over a 2,000-acre tract. In contending that its entire enclosed plant complex is an "industrial curtilage," Dow argues that its exposed manufacturing facilities are analogous to the curtilage surrounding a home because it has taken every possible step to bar access from ground level. . . .

. . . The intimate activities associated with family privacy and the home and its curtilage simply do not reach the outdoor areas or spaces between structures and buildings of a manufacturing plant. . . .

Oliver recognized that in the open field context, "the public and police lawfully may survey lands from the air." Here, EPA was not employing some unique sensory device that, for example, could penetrate the walls of buildings and record conversations in Dow's plants, offices, or laboratories, but rather a conventional, albeit precise, commercial camera commonly used in mapmaking. The Government asserts it has not yet enlarged the photographs to any significant degree, but Dow points out that simple magnification permits identification of objects such as wires as small as ½-inch in diameter.

It may well be, as the Government concedes, that surveillance of private property by using highly sophisticated surveillance equipment not generally available to the public, such as satellite technology, might be constitutionally proscribed absent a warrant. But the photographs here are not so revealing of intimate details as to raise constitutional concerns. Although they undoubtedly give EPA more detailed information than naked-eye views, they remain limited to an outline of the facility's buildings and equipment. The mere fact that human vision is enhanced somewhat, at least to the degree here, does not give rise to constitutional problems. An electronic device to penetrate walls or windows so as to hear and record confidential discussions of chemical formulae or other trade secrets would raise very different and far more serious questions; other protections such as trade secret laws are available to protect commercial activities from private surveillance by competitors. . . .

We hold that the taking of aerial photographs of an industrial plant complex from navigable airspace is not a search prohibited by the Fourth Amendment. . . .

POWELL, J. joined by BRENNAN, MARSHALL, and BLACKMUN, J. J. concurring in part and dissenting in part. The Fourth Amendment protects private citizens from arbitrary surveillance by their Government. For nearly 20 years, this Court has adhered to a standard that ensured that Fourth Amendment rights would retain their vitality as technology expanded the Government's capacity to commit unsuspected intrusions into private areas and activities. Today, in the context of administrative aerial photography of commercial premises, the Court retreats from that standard. It holds that the photography was not a Fourth Amendment "search" because it was not accompanied by a physical trespass and because the equipment used was not the most highly sophisticated form of technology available to the Government. Under this holding, the existence of an asserted privacy interest apparently will be decided solely by reference to the manner of surveillance used to intrude on that interest. Such an inquiry will not protect Fourth Amendment rights, but rather will permit their gradual decay as technology advances. . . .

NOTES & QUESTIONS

1. One of the rationales of *Dow Chemical* is that the device could have been acquired by a member of the general public. Does the case turn on this point? Suppose the police used a special camera that was developed exclusively for law enforcement purposes?

2. The use of a flashlight "to illuminate a darkened area simply does not constitute a search, and thus triggers no Fourth Amendment protection." *Texas v. Brown*, 460 U.S. 730 (1983). If this conclusion seems rather evident, how is a flashlight different from other devices that enhance human senses? Is any device that enhances the human senses merely an extension of ordinary sense? In the absence of an absolute rule one way or the other as to whether sense-enhancement devices are permissible under the Fourth Amendment, where should the line be drawn or what factors should the Court consider?

3. *Beepers.* In *United States v. Knotts*, 460 U.S. 276 (1983), the police placed a beeper in a five-gallon drum of chloroform purchased by the defendants and placed in their car. The beeper transmitted signals that enabled the police to track the location of the defendants' vehicle. The Court held that the Fourth Amendment did not apply to the use of this device because a "person traveling in an automobile on public thoroughfares has no reasonable expectation of privacy in his movements from one place to another." Therefore, "[t]he governmental surveillance conducted by means of the beeper in this case amounted principally to the following of an automobile on public streets and highways." In *United States v. Karo*, 468 U.S. 705 (1984), law enforcement officials planted a beeper in a can of ether that the de-

fendant bought from an informant. The officials tracked the movements of the can of ether through a variety of places, including within a residence. While the movements in *Knotts* were in public, the movements within the residence were not, and this amounted to an impermissible search of the residence:

> The monitoring of an electronic device such as a beeper is, of course, less intrusive than a full-scale search, but it does reveal a critical fact about the interior of the premises that the Government is extremely interested in knowing and that it could not have otherwise obtained without a warrant. The case is thus not like *Knotts*, for there the beeper told the authorities nothing about the interior of Knotts' cabin. The information obtained in *Knotts* was "voluntarily conveyed to anyone who wanted to look. . . ."

4. *Video Surveillance Technology.* In *The Right to Privacy*, Warren and Brandeis complained of the new ability to take candid photographs of individuals. Before the invention of the snap camera, people did not expect to be photographed without their consent. Clearly today we expect that our picture might be taken in public. Today, there are video cameras, night-vision cameras, powerful zoom-lenses and magnification techniques. Are these new technologies eroding our reasonable expectation of privacy?[19]

KYLLO v. UNITED STATES

533 U.S. 27 (2001)

SCALIA, J. In 1991 Agent William Elliott of the United States Department of the Interior came to suspect that marijuana was being grown in the home belonging to petitioner Danny Kyllo, part of a triplex on Rhododendron Drive in Florence, Oregon. Indoor marijuana growth typically requires high-intensity lamps. In order to determine whether an amount of heat was emanating from petitioner's home consistent with the use of such lamps, at 3:20 A.M. on January 16, 1992, Agent Elliott and Dan Haas used an Agema Thermovision 210 thermal imager to scan the triplex. Thermal imagers detect infrared radiation, which virtually all objects emit but which is not visible to the naked eye. The imager converts radiation into images based on relative warmth—black is cool, white is hot, shades of gray connote relative differences; in that respect, it operates somewhat like a video camera showing heat images. The scan of Kyllo's home took only a few minutes and was performed from the passenger seat of Agent Elliott's vehicle across the street from the front of the house and also from the street in back of the house. The scan showed that the roof over the garage and a side wall of petitioner's home were relatively hot compared to the rest of the home and substantially warmer than neighboring homes in the triplex. Agent Elliott concluded that petitioner was using halide lights to grow marijuana in his house, which indeed he was. Based on tips from informants, utility bills, and the thermal imaging, a Federal Magistrate Judge issued

---

[19]For an argument that people do have reasonable expectations of privacy in public, see Helen Nissenbaum, *Protecting Privacy in an Information Age: The Problem of Privacy in Public*, 17 Law & Philosophy 559 (1998).

a warrant authorizing a search of petitioner's home, and the agents found an indoor growing operation involving more than 100 plants. Petitioner was indicted on one count of manufacturing marijuana, in violation of 21 U.S.C. §841(a)(1). He unsuccessfully moved to suppress the evidence seized from his home and then entered a conditional guilty plea. . . .

. . . "At the very core" of the Fourth Amendment "stands the right of a man to retreat into his own home and there be free from unreasonable governmental intrusion." With few exceptions, the question whether a warrantless search of a home is reasonable and hence constitutional must be answered no.

On the other hand, the antecedent question of whether or not a Fourth Amendment "search" has occurred is not so simple under our precedent. The permissibility of ordinary visual surveillance of a home used to be clear because, well into the 20th century, our Fourth Amendment jurisprudence was tied to common-law trespass. Visual surveillance was unquestionably lawful because "the eye cannot by the laws of England be guilty of a trespass." We have since decoupled violation of a person's Fourth Amendment rights from trespassory violation of his property, but the lawfulness of warrantless visual surveillance of a home has still been preserved. As we observed in *California v. Ciraolo*, 476 U.S. 207, (1986), "[t]he Fourth Amendment protection of the home has never been extended to require law enforcement officers to shield their eyes when passing by a home on public thoroughfares." . . .

The present case involves officers on a public street engaged in more than naked-eye surveillance of a home. We have previously reserved judgment as to how much technological enhancement of ordinary perception from such a vantage point, if any, is too much. While we upheld enhanced aerial photography of an industrial complex in *Dow Chemical*, we noted that we found "it important that this is not an area immediately adjacent to a private home, where privacy expectations are most heightened."

It would be foolish to contend that the degree of privacy secured to citizens by the Fourth Amendment has been entirely unaffected by the advance of technology. For example, as the cases discussed above make clear, the technology enabling human flight has exposed to public view (and hence, we have said, to official observation) uncovered portions of the house and its curtilage that once were private. The question we confront today is what limits there are upon this power of technology to shrink the realm of guaranteed privacy. . . .

. . . [I]n the case of the search of the interior of homes — the prototypical and hence most commonly litigated area of protected privacy — there is a ready criterion, with roots deep in the common law, of the minimal expectation of privacy that exists, and that is acknowledged to be reasonable. To withdraw protection of this minimum expectation would be to permit police technology to erode the privacy guaranteed by the Fourth Amendment. We think that obtaining by sense-enhancing technology any information regarding the interior of the home that could not otherwise have been obtained without physical "intrusion into a constitutionally protected area," *Silverman*, 365 U.S., at 512, constitutes a search — at least where (as here) the technology in question is not in general public use. This assures preservation of that degree of privacy against government that existed when the Fourth Amendment was adopted. On the basis of this criterion, the information obtained by the thermal imager in this case was the product of a search.[20]

The Government maintains, however, that the thermal imaging must be upheld because it detected "only heat radiating from the external surface of the house." The dissent makes this its leading point, contending that there is a fundamental difference between what it calls "off-the-wall" observations and "through-the-wall surveillance." But just as a thermal imager captures only heat emanating from a house, so also a powerful directional microphone picks up only sound emanating from a house — and a satellite capable of scanning from many miles away would pick up only visible light emanating from a house. We rejected such a mechanical interpretation of the Fourth Amendment in *Katz*, where the eavesdropping device picked up only sound waves that reached the exterior of the phone booth. Reversing that approach would leave the homeowner at the mercy of advancing technology — including imaging technology that could discern all human activity in the home. While the technology used in the present case was relatively crude, the rule we adopt must take account of more sophisticated systems that are already in use or in development. The dissent's reliance on the distinction between "off-the-wall" and "through-the-wall" observation is entirely incompatible with the dissent's belief, which we discuss below, that thermal-imaging observations of the intimate details of a home are impermissible. The most sophisticated thermal imaging devices continue to measure heat "off-the-wall" rather than "through-the-wall"; the dissent's disapproval of those more sophisticated thermal-imaging devices, is an acknowledgement that there is no substance to this distinction. As for the dissent's extraordinary assertion that anything learned through "an inference" cannot be a search, that would validate even the "through-the-wall" technologies that the dissent purports to disapprove. Surely the dissent does not believe that the through-the-wall radar or ultrasound technology produces an 8-by-10 Kodak glossy that needs no analysis (i.e., the making of inferences). And, of course, the novel proposition that inference insulates a search is blatantly contrary to *United States v. Karo*, 468 U.S. 705 (1984), where the police "inferred" from the activation of a beeper that a certain can of ether was in the home. The police activity was held to be a search, and the search was held unlawful.

The Government also contends that the thermal imaging was constitutional because it did not "detect private activities occurring in private areas." . . .

---

[20]The dissent's repeated assertion that the thermal imaging did not obtain information regarding the interior of the home is simply inaccurate. A thermal imager reveals the relative heat of various rooms in the home. The dissent may not find that information particularly private or important, but there is no basis for saying it is not information regarding the interior of the home. The dissent's comparison of the thermal imaging to various circumstances in which outside observers might be able to perceive, without technology, the heat of the home — for example, by observing snowmelt on the roof — is quite irrelevant. The fact that equivalent information could sometimes be obtained by other means does not make lawful the use of means that violate the Fourth Amendment. The police might, for example, learn how many people are in a particular house by setting up year-round surveillance; but that does not make breaking and entering to find out the same information lawful. In any event, on the night of January 16, 1992, no outside observer could have discerned the relative heat of Kyllo's home without thermal imaging.

The Fourth Amendment's protection of the home has never been tied to measurement of the quality or quantity of information obtained. In *Silverman*, for example, we made clear that any physical invasion of the structure of the home, "by even a fraction of an inch," was too much, and there is certainly no exception to the warrant requirement for the officer who barely cracks open the front door and sees nothing but the nonintimate rug on the vestibule floor. . . .

We have said that the Fourth Amendment draws "a firm line at the entrance to the house." That line, we think, must be not only firm but also bright—which requires clear specification of those methods of surveillance that require a warrant. While it is certainly possible to conclude from the videotape of the thermal imaging that occurred in this case that no "significant" compromise of the homeowner's privacy has occurred, we must take the long view, from the original meaning of the Fourth Amendment forward. . . .

Where, as here, the Government uses a device that is not in general public use, to explore details of the home that would previously have been unknowable without physical intrusion, the surveillance is a "search" and is presumptively unreasonable without a warrant. . . .

STEVENS, J. joined by REHNQUIST, C. J. and O'CONNOR and KENNEDY, J. dissenting. . . . [S]earches and seizures of property in plain view are presumptively reasonable. Whether that property is residential or commercial, the basic principle is the same: "What a person knowingly exposes to the public, even in his own home or office, is not a subject of Fourth Amendment protection." That is the principle implicated here.

While the Court "take[s] the long view" and decides this case based largely on the potential of yet-to-be-developed technology that might allow "through-the-wall surveillance," this case involves nothing more than off-the-wall surveillance by law enforcement officers to gather information exposed to the general public from the outside of petitioner's home. All that the infrared camera did in this case was passively measure heat emitted from the exterior surfaces of petitioner's home; all that those measurements showed were relative differences in emission levels, vaguely indicating that some areas of the roof and outside walls were warmer than others. As still images from the infrared scans show, no details regarding the interior of petitioner's home were revealed. Unlike an x-ray scan, or other possible "through-the-wall" techniques, the detection of infrared radiation emanating from the home did not accomplish "an unauthorized physical penetration into the premises," *Silverman v. United States*, 365 U.S. 505, 509 (1961), nor did it "obtain information that it could not have obtained by observation from outside the curtilage of the house." . . .

. . . Heat waves, like aromas that are generated in a kitchen, or in a laboratory or opium den, enter the public domain if and when they leave a building. A subjective expectation that they would remain private is not only implausible but also surely not "one that society is prepared to recognize as 'reasonable.'" . . .

Despite the Court's attempt to draw a line that is "not only firm but also bright," the contours of its new rule are uncertain because its protection apparently dissipates as soon as the relevant technology is "in general public use." Yet how much use is general public use is not even hinted at by the

Court's opinion, which makes the somewhat doubtful assumption that the thermal imager used in this case does not satisfy that criterion. In any event, putting aside its lack of clarity, this criterion is somewhat perverse because it seems likely that the threat to privacy will grow, rather than recede, as the use of intrusive equipment becomes more readily available. . . .

The application of the Court's new rule to "any information regarding the interior of the home," is also unnecessarily broad. If it takes sensitive equipment to detect an odor that identifies criminal conduct and nothing else, the fact that the odor emanates from the interior of a home should not provide it with constitutional protection. The criterion, moreover, is too sweeping in that information "regarding" the interior of a home apparently is not just information obtained through its walls, but also information concerning the outside of the building that could lead to (however many) inferences "regarding" what might be inside. . . .

Because the new rule applies to information regarding the "interior" of the home, it is too narrow as well as too broad. Clearly, a rule that is designed to protect individuals from the overly intrusive use of sense-enhancing equipment should not be limited to a home. If such equipment did provide its user with the functional equivalent of access to a private place — such as, for example, the telephone booth involved in *Katz*, or an office building — then the rule should apply to such an area as well as to a home. . . .

NOTES & QUESTIONS

1. How does the Court distinguish the thermal imager in *Kyllo* from the camera in *Dow Chemical* and the dog-sniff in *Place*? Does this distinction make sense?
2. The Court notes that there must be some limits on sense enhancement technology. What is the limiting principle according to the Court? Do you think this is the appropriate limiting principle?[21]
3. Justice Stevens argues that "a rule that is designed to protect individuals from the overly intrusive use of sense-enhancing equipment should not be limited to a home." Do you agree? Given the reasoning of the majority, would the Court reach the same result if the thermal imager had been used outside a person's office rather than her home?
4. *The Fourth Amendment and Separation of Powers.* Raymond Ku contends that the Fourth Amendment must be understood as an aspect of separation of powers. In other words, the Fourth Amendment serves as a fundamental limitation on the power of the Executive Branch: "The absence of Fourth Amendment safeguards raises very serious separation of powers concerns given that executive branch decisions to adopt and implement new surveillance technologies are often made without express legislative or constitutional authorization."

---

[21]For background into sensory enhancement technology, see Christopher Slobogin, *Technologically-Assisted Physican Surveillance: The American Bar Association's Tentative Draft Standards*, 10 Harv. J. L. & Tech. 383 (1997); ABA Standards for Criminal Justice, Electronic Surveillance §B (3d ed. 1999) (technologically assisted physical surveillance), available at <*http://abanet.org/ crimjust/standards/taps_toc.html*>.

The Supreme Court's recent decision in *Kyllo v. United States* may be a step in the right direction. . . . In deciding that the government's use of thermal imaging equipment without a warrant was unlawful, Justice Scalia concludes that when a technology is "not in general public use," the Court should "assure[ ] preservation of that degree of privacy against government that existed when the Fourth Amendment was adopted." In other words, instead of asking whether the Founders would have considered the act in question a search, the Court should ask whether the Founders enjoyed this level of security from government surveillance and harassment. By grounding the analysis in the privacy enjoyed by the Founders, *Kyllo* has the potential to return the Fourth Amendment to its proper role, not because its definition of privacy is superior, but because it would subject all searches assisted by new technologies to the amendment's restraints. Taken to its logical conclusion *Kyllo* suggests that government use of new technologies should always be subject to the warrant requirement unless they are in general public use. . . .

. . . [Prior to *Kyllo*, through the reasonable expectation of privacy test], the Court presumed that the government could employ new surveillance technologies unless the surveillance invaded interests the Justices subjectively considered private. The people's only role in the process was to respond to government and the courts after the fact. They were relegated to enacting legislation to limit government use of technology or amending the Constitution. . . . [In contrast,] *Kyllo* creates an opportunity to return the people to their rightful position as the primary source and arbiter of governmental power. . . .[22]

B. FEDERAL WIRETAP LAW

1. SECTION 605 OF THE FEDERAL COMMUNICATIONS ACT OF 1934

Recall that in 1928, the Court in *Olmstead* declared that wiretapping did not constitute a Fourth Amendment violation. By the time *Olmstead* was decided, more than 25 states had made wiretapping a crime.

Six years later, responding to significant criticism of the *Olmstead* decision, Congress enacted the Federal Communications Act of 1934. Section 605 of the Act provided that "no person not being authorized by the sender shall intercept any communication and divulge or publish the existence, contents, substance, purport, effect, or meaning of such intercepted communications to any person." Although §605 did not expressly provide for an exclusionary rule, the Court in *Nardone v. United States*, 302 U.S. 379 (1937), held that federal officers could not introduce evidence obtained by illegal wiretapping in federal court.

---

[22] Raymond Shih Ray Ku, *The Founders' Privacy: The Fourth Amendment and the Power of Technological Surveillance*, 86 Minn. L. Rev. 1325 (2002). For other perspectives on *Kyllo*, see Richard H. Seamon, *Kyllo v. United States and the Partial Ascendance of Justice Scalia's Fourth Amendment*, 79 Wash. U. L.Q. 1013 (2001); Susan Bandes, *Power, Privacy, and Thermal Imaging*, 86 Minn. L. Rev. 1379 (2002); Christopher Slobogin, *Peeping Techno-Toms and the Fourth Amendment: Seeing Through* Kyllo's *Rules Governing Technological Surveillance*, 86 Minn. L. Rev. 1393 (2002).

Section 605 had significant limitations. The statute did not preempt state law, so states could still use evidence in violation of § 605 in state prosecutions. Further, § 605 only applied to wire communications and wiretapping, not to eavesdropping on nonwire communications. Thus, bugging was not covered.

For a brief period around 1940, United States Attorney General Robert Jackson ordered a complete stop of FBI wiretapping. The FBI manual characterized wiretapping as an "unethical tactic." However, the ban was short-lived, because during World War II, J. Edgar Hoover, the director of the FBI, successfully urged President Franklin Roosevelt to allow FBI wiretapping to investigate subversive activities and threats to national security. During the Truman Administration, the justification for electronic surveillance expanded to include domestic security as well. In the 1950s, fear of Communism led to a significant increase in electronic surveillance by the FBI. This broad electronic surveillance included members of the Socialist Party, leaders of the Civil Rights Movement, and even Supreme Court Justices. One of the most monitored individuals was Martin Luther King, Jr., whom Hoover disliked and believed was a Communist. No evidence that King was a Communist was ever uncovered. When the FBI's electronic surveillance of King's hotel room revealed King's rowdy partying, the FBI sent the tapes to King's wife and played them to President Lyndon Johnson.[23]

During this time, state police also conducted wiretapping. This wiretapping was regulated only at the state level, since § 605 did not apply to the states. An influential study by Samuel Dash, Richard Schwartz, and Robert Knowlton revealed that regulation of wiretapping by the states was often ineffective, resulting in numerous unauthorized wiretaps and few checks against abuses.[24]

2. TITLE III OF THE OMNIBUS CRIME CONTROL ACT OF 1968

In 1968, in response to *Katz v. United States* and *Berger v. New York*, Congress enacted Title III of the Omnibus Crime Control and Safe Streets Act of 1968, Pub. L. No. 90-351, codified at 18 U.S.C. §§ 2510-20. This Act is commonly referred to as "Title III" or "The Federal Wiretap Act." Title III extended far beyond § 605; it applied to wiretaps by federal and state officials as well as by private parties. Title III required federal agents to apply for a warrant before wiretapping. The Act criminalized private wiretaps. However, if any party to the conversation consented to the tapping, then there was no violation of Title III.

Title III authorized the Attorney General to apply to a federal judge for an order authorizing the interception of a "wire or oral communication." A judge could not issue court order unless there was probable cause. Many other procedural safeguards were established.

Title III excluded wiretaps for national security purposes from any restrictions at all. President Nixon frequently used the national security exception to place internal dissidents and radicals under surveillance. However, in *United*

---

[23] *See generally* Priscilla M. Regan, *Legislating Privacy: Technology, Social Values, and Public Policy* (1995); Whitfield Diffie & Susan Landau, *Privacy on the Line: The Politics of Wiretapping and Encryption* (1998).

[24] *See* Samuel Dash, Richard Schwartz & Robert Knowlton, *The Eavesdroppers* (1959).

States v. United States District Court, 407 U.S. 297 (1972), the Court unanimously rejected Nixon's approach, stating that Title III's national security exception does not apply to internal threats but only to foreign threats.

Another limitation of Title III was that it only applied to "aural" communications (heard by ear). It did not apply to visual surveillance or to other kinds of electronic communication.

3. THE ELECTRONIC COMMUNICATIONS PRIVACY ACT (ECPA) OF 1986

(a) Statutory Structure

In 1986, Congress modernized federal wiretap law by passing the Electronic Communications Privacy Act (ECPA). The ECPA amended Title III and restructured it. There are three titles under the ECPA — Titles I, II, and III. The previous "Title III" is now Title I of federal wiretap law after the ECPA.

This book will use the "ECPA" and "federal wiretap law" interchangeably to refer to modern federal wiretap law as amended by the ECPA.

Many of the provisions of federal wiretap law apply not only to government officials, but to private individuals and entities as well. In particular, cases involving the violation of federal wiretap law by private parties often occur in the employment context when employers desire to use forms of electronic surveillance on their employees. This will be discussed in Chapter 7 when we examine privacy in the workplace.

TITLE I

Interceptions. Title I, codified at 18 U.S.C. §§ 2510–2522, governs the interception of communications and is commonly referred to as the "Wiretap Act." In particular, Title I § 2511 provides that:

(1) Except as otherwise specifically provided in this chapter any person who —
    (a) intentionally intercepts, endeavors to intercept, or procures any other person to intercept or endeavor to intercept, any wire, oral, or electronic communication;
    (b) intentionally uses, endeavors to use, or procures any other person to use or endeavor to use any electronic, mechanical, or other device to intercept any oral communication when —
        (i) such device is affixed to, or otherwise transmits a signal through, a wire, cable, or other like connection used in wire communication; or
        (ii) such device transmits communications by radio, or interferes with the transmission of such communication; or
        (iii) such person knows, or has reason to know, that such device or any component thereof has been sent through the mail or transported in interstate or foreign commerce . . . .
    (c) intentionally discloses, or endeavors to disclose, to any other person the contents of any wire, oral, or electronic communication, knowing or having reason to know that the information was obtained through the interception of a wire, oral, or electronic communication in violation of this subsection;
    (d) intentionally uses, or endeavors to use, the contents of any wire, oral, or electronic communication, knowing or having reason to know that the informa-

tion was obtained through the interception of a wire, oral, or electronic communication in violation of this subsection. . . .

Title I applies to intentional interceptions. To "intercept" a communications means to acquire its contents through the use of any electronic, mechanical, or other device. §2510(4). Title I applies when communications are intercepted while in flight (while being transmitted). Once the communication is completed and stored, then Title I no longer applies.

Recently, §2511(1)(c) was struck down as unconstitutional as applied to matters of public concern. *See Bartnicki v. Vopper*, 532 U.S. 514 (2001).

Exclusionary Rule. Under Title I, "any aggrieved person . . . may move to suppress the contents of any wire or oral communication intercepted pursuant to this chapter, or evidence derived therefrom." §2518 (10)(a).

Penalties. Violations of Title I can result in fines of a minimum of $10,000 per violation as well as up to five years' imprisonment. *See* §§2511(4)(a); 2520(c)(2)(B).

Court Orders. Pursuant to §2518, an application for a court wiretapping or electronic surveillance order must be made under oath and contain a variety of information including details to justify the agent's belief that a crime has been, is being, or will be committed; specific description of place where communications will be intercepted; description of the type of communication; and period of time of interception. The judge may require the applicant to furnish additional testimony or documentary evidence in support of the application. The judge must find probable cause and that the particular communications concerning that offense will be obtained through the interception. Further, the court must find that alternatives to wiretapping were attempted and failed; or reasonably appear to be unlikely to succeed or to be too dangerous. The order can last for up to 30 days and can be renewed. *See* §2518.

Under Title I, only certain government officials are able to apply to a court for a wiretapping order — for federal officials, the attorney general or a deputy or assistant attorney general; for state officials, the principal prosecuting attorney of a state or a local government or any government attorney. In other words, the police themselves cannot attempt to obtain a wiretap order alone. Title I also provides an exclusive list of crimes for which a wiretap order can be issued. The list is broad and includes most felonies. A wiretap order cannot be obtained to investigate a misdemeanor.

Minimization. Title I requires that interception must be minimized to avoid sweeping in communications beyond the purpose for which the order was sought. Pursuant to §2518(6): "Every order and extension thereof shall contain a provision that the authorization to intercept shall be executed as soon as practicable, shall be conducted in such a way as to minimize the interception of communications not otherwise subject to interception under this chapter, and must terminate upon attainment of the authorized objective." For example, if law enforcement officials are wiretapping the home phone line of a person suspected of running an illegal gambling operation and the person's daughter is talking on the line to a friend about going to the movies, the officials should stop listening to the conversation.

Notice. After the surveillance is over, copies of the recorded conversations must be turned over to the court issuing the order. The court must notify the party that surveillance was undertaken within 90 days after the denial of a surveillance order or after the completion of the surveillance authorized by a granted surveillance order. § 2518(8)(d).

Exceptions. There are two notable exceptions under Title I. First, Title I does not apply if one of the parties to the communication consents. § 2511(2)(c). For example, a person can secretly tap and record a communication to which that person is a party. Thus, secretly recording one's own phone conversations is not illegal under federal wiretap law. If they participate in the conversation, government agents and informants can record others without their knowledge. An exception to the consent exception is when an interception is carried out for the purpose of committing any criminal or tortious act. In that case, even when a party has consented, interception is illegal. § 2511(2)(d).

Second, a service provider is exempt from federal wiretap law. Under Title I, § 2511(2)(a)(i):

> It shall not be unlawful under this chapter for an operator of a switchboard, or on officer, employee, or agent of a provider of wire or electronic communication service, whose facilities are used in the transmission of a wire or electronic communication, to intercept, disclose, or use that communication in the normal course of his employment while engaged in any activity which is a necessary incident to the rendition of his service or to the protection of the rights or property of the provider of that service, except that a provider of wire communication service to the public shall not utilize service observing or random monitoring except for mechanical or service quality control checks.

TITLE II

Stored Communications. Title II, codified at 18 U.S.C. §§ 2701-2711, applies to stored communications and is commonly referred to as the "Stored Communications Act." With many forms of modern communication, such as Internet service, communications and subscriber records are often maintained in storage by the electronic communications service provider. Pursuant to § 2701:

> (a) Offense.— Except as provided in subsection (c) of this section whoever—
> (1) intentionally accesses without authorization a facility through which an electronic communication service is provided; or
> (2) intentionally exceeds an authorization to access that facility; and thereby obtains, alters, or prevents authorized access to a wire or electronic communication while it is in electronic storage in such system shall be punished as provided in subsection (b) of this section.

The definition of "electronic storage" in Title I also applies to the term as used in Title II. Under Title I, "electronic storage" means:

(A) any temporary, intermediate storage of a wire or electronic communication incidental to the electronic transmission thereof; and

(B) any storage of such communication by an electronic communications service for purposes of backup protection of such communication. § 2510(17).

Section 2701(a) does not apply to "the person or entity providing a wire or electronic communications service" (such as Internet Service Providers) or to "a user of that service with respect to a communication of or intended for that user." § 2701(c).

Title II also forbids the disclosure of the contents of stored communications by communications service providers. *See* § 2702(a). There are a number of exceptions, including disclosures to the intended recipient of the communication, disclosures with the consent of the creator or recipient of the communication, disclosures that are "necessarily incident to the rendition of the service or to the protection of the rights or property of the provider of that service," and disclosures to a law enforcement agency under certain circumstances. *See* § 2702(b).

Penalties. Title II has less severe criminal penalties and civil liability than Title I. Under § 2701(b), violations can result in fines of a minimum of $1,000 per violation and up to six months' imprisonment. If the wiretap is done for commercial advantage or gain, then a violation can result in up to one year of imprisonment.

Exclusionary Rule. Title II does not provide for an exclusionary rule.

Judicial Authority for Obtaining Stored Communications. Under Title II, the judicial process required for obtaining permission to access stored communications held by electronic communications service providers is much less rigorous than under Title I. If the government seeks access to the contents of a communication that has been in storage for 180 days or less, then it must first obtain a warrant supported by probable cause. § 2703(a). If the government wants to access a communication that has been in storage for more than 180 days, the government must provide prior notice to the subscriber and obtain an administrative subpoena, a grand jury subpoena, a trial subpoena, or a court order. § 2703(b). The court order does not require probable cause, only "specific and articulable facts showing that there are reasonable grounds" to believe communications are relevant to the criminal investigation 18 U.S.C. § 2703(d). However, if the government seeks to access a communication that has been in storage for more than 180 days and does not want to provide prior notice to the subscriber, it must obtain a warrant. § 2703(b). Notice to the subscriber that the government obtained her communications can be delayed for up to 90 days. § 2705.

Court Orders to Obtain Subscriber Records. According to § 2703(c)(1)(B), communication service providers must disclose subscriber information (i.e., identifying information, address, phone number, etc.) to the government under certain circumstances:

(B) A provider of electronic communication service or remote computing service shall disclose a record or other information pertaining to a subscriber to or customer of such service (not including the contents of communications covered by subsection (a) or (b) of this section) to a governmental entity only when the governmental entity —

(i) obtains a warrant issued under the Federal Rules of Criminal Procedure or equivalent State warrant;

(ii) obtains a court order for such disclosure under subsection (d) of this section;

(iii) has the consent of the subscriber or customer to such disclosure. . . .

Communications service providers who disclose stored communications in accordance with any of the above orders or subpoenas cannot be held liable for that disclosure. *See* § 2703(e).

Exceptions. Similar to Title I, Title II also has a consent exception, *see* § 2702(b), and a service provider exception, *see* § 2701(c)(1).

TITLE I VERSUS TITLE II

The differences between Title I and Title II are important in federal wiretap law, especially since certain accessing of communications can be viewed as falling within either Title I (intercepting communications) or Title II (accessing stored communications). Title I has significantly stronger protections than Title II. Title I has an exclusionary rule, but Title II does not. Title I has greater civil penalties than Title II as well as greater terms of imprisonment. Further, Title I imposes stricter restrictions on court wiretap orders than Title II.

TITLE III

Title III, codified at 18 U.S.C. §§ 3121-3127, governs pen registers and trap and trace devices, and is referred to as the "Pen Register Act." Recall *Smith v. Maryland* earlier in this chapter, where the Court held that pen register information was not protected by the Fourth Amendment. Title III provides some limited protection for such information. Subject to certain exceptions, "no person may install or use a pen register or a trap and trace device without first obtaining a court order." § 3121(a). A pen register is a device that records the telephone numbers dialed from a particular telephone line (phone numbers of outgoing calls). A trap and trace device records the telephone numbers where incoming calls originate.

Court Orders. If the government certifies that "the information likely to be obtained by such installation and use is relevant to an ongoing investigation," § 3123(a), then courts "shall authorize the installation and use of a pen register or a trap and trace device for a period not to exceed sixty days." § 3123(c).

Enforcement. There is no exclusionary rule for violations of Title III. Rather, Title III provides: "Whoever knowingly violates subsection (a) shall be fined under this title or imprisoned not more than one year, or both." § 3121(d).

Changes by the USA-PATRIOT Act. The USA-PATRIOT Act of 2001 changes the definition of pen register and trap and trace devices. This will be discussed below in Section B.6.

TYPES OF COMMUNICATIONS

In addition to knowing the protections of Titles I, II, and III, an understanding of federal wiretap law requires an understanding of the three types of communications it applies to. These three types of communications are defined in Title I, and they apply throughout all of federal wiretap law. The three types of communications are: (1) "wire communications"; (2) "oral communications"; and (3) "electronic communications." To apply federal wiretap law, one must first distinguish what type of communication is involved, as each type is protected differently, with wire communications receiving the most protection.

Wire Communications. A "wire communication," defined in §2510(1), involves all "aural transfers" that travel through a wire or a similar medium:

> (1) "wire communication" means any aural transfer made in whole or in part through the use of facilities for the transmission of communications by the aid of wire, cable, or other like connection between the point of origin and the point of reception (including the use of such connection in a switching station) furnished or operated by any person engaged in providing or operating such facilities for the transmission of interstate or foreign communications or communications affecting interstate or foreign commerce.

An "aural transfer" is a communication containing the human voice at any point. §2510(18). The human voice need only be a minor part of the communication. Further, the human voice need not always be present throughout the journey of the communication. Therefore, a communication that once consisted of the human voice that has been translated into code or tones still qualifies as an "aural transfer."

The aural transfer must travel through wire (i.e., telephone wires or cable wires) or a similar medium. The entire journey from origin to destination need not take place through wire, as many communications travel through a host of different mediums — wire, radio, satellite, and so on. Only part of the communication's journey must be through a wire.

The interception must take place through an "electronic, mechanical, or other device."

Oral Communications. The second type of communication under federal wiretap law are "oral communications." Pursuant to §2510(2), an "oral communication" is a communication "uttered by a person exhibiting an expectation that such communication is not subject to interception under circumstances justifying such expectation." Oral communications are typically intercepted through bugs and other recording or transmitting devices.

Electronic Communications. The final type of communication is an "electronic communication." Under §2510(12), an electronic communication consists of all nonwire and nonoral communications:

> (12) "electronic communication" means any transfer of signs, signals, writing, images, sounds, data, or intelligence of any nature transmitted in whole or in part by a wire, radio, electromagnetic, photoelectronic or photooptical system that affects interstate or foreign commerce, but does not include —
> (A) any wire or oral communication;

In other words, an electronic communication consists of all communications that do not constitute wire or oral communications. An electronic communication encompasses a wide range of mediums of transmission (not just wire or the like). Electronic communications are not as stringently protected as wire or oral communications. An example of an electronic communication is an e-mail that does not consist of the human voice.

Unlike wire and oral communications, the acquisition of electronic communications in temporary storage cannot constitute an intercept. Therefore, any time that an electronic communication is accessed in storage — however temporary that storage may be — it falls within Title II, not Title I.

Although electronic communications are protected under Title I as well as Title II, they are treated differently than wire and oral communications. The most notable difference is that the exclusionary rule in Title I does not apply to electronic communications. Therefore, wire or oral communications that fall within Title I are protected by the exclusionary rule, but not when they fall within Title II (which has no exclusionary rule). Electronic communications are not protected by the exclusionary rule in Titles I or II.

FEDERAL WIRETAP LAW AND THE FOURTH AMENDMENT

Federal wiretap law operates independently of the Fourth Amendment. Even if a search is reasonable under the Fourth Amendment, federal wiretap law may bar the evidence. Even if a search is authorized by a judge under federal wiretap law, the Fourth Amendment could still prohibit the wiretap.

Procedures for obtaining a court order under Title I are more stringent than those for obtaining a search warrant under the Fourth Amendment. Under the Fourth Amendment, any law enforcement official can apply for a warrant. Under Title I, only certain officials (prosecuting attorneys) can apply.

In at least one significant way, federal wiretap law is more broad than the Fourth Amendment. Under the Fourth Amendment, search warrants generally authorize a single entry and prompt search. Warrants must be narrowly circumscribed. They are not a license for unlimited and continued investigation. However, under federal wiretap law, courts can authorize continuing surveillance — 24 hours a day for a 30-day period, which can be extended.

THE INSTALLATION OF ELECTRONIC SURVEILLANCE DEVICES

The Supreme Court has held that the government can secretly enter one's residence or private property to install electronic surveillance devices, such as bugs. *See Dalia v. United States*, 441 U.S. 238 (1979). First, examining whether covert entry into a home violated the Fourth Amendment, the Court concluded:

> [W]e find no basis for a constitutional rule proscribing all covert entries. It is well established that law officers constitutionally may break and enter to exe-

cute a search warrant where such entry is the only means by which the warrant effectively may be executed. Petitioner nonetheless argues that covert entries are unconstitutional for their lack of notice. This argument is frivolous, as was indicated in *Katz v. United States*, where the Court stated that "officers need not announce their purpose before conducting an otherwise [duly] authorized search if such an announcement would provoke the escape of the suspect or the destruction of critical evidence." In *United States v. Donovan*, we held that Title III provided a constitutionally adequate substitute for advance notice by requiring that once the surveillance operation is completed the authorizing judge must cause notice to be served on those subjected to surveillance. See 18 U.S.C. § 2518(8)(d). There is no reason why the same notice is not equally sufficient with respect to electronic surveillances requiring covert entry. We make explicit, therefore, what has long been implicit in our decisions dealing with this subject: The Fourth Amendment does not prohibit *per se* a covert entry performed for the purpose of installing otherwise legal electronic bugging equipment.

Moreover, the Court concluded that the Fourth Amendment does not require that an electronic surveillance order include a specific authorization to enter covertly the premises described in the order. In other words, the police need not request permission to make a covert entry when applying for an electronic surveillance order; and the order authorizing the use of electronic surveillance need not make any reference to a covert entry.

The defendant also argued that federal wiretap law did not provide for covert entry. However, the Court reasoned:

> . . . Title III does not refer explicitly to covert entry. The language, structure, and history of the statute, however, demonstrate that Congress meant to authorize courts — in certain specified circumstances — to approve electronic surveillance without limitation on the means necessary to its accomplishment, so long as they are reasonable under the circumstances. Title III provides a comprehensive scheme for the regulation of electronic surveillance, prohibiting all secret interception of communications except as authorized by certain state and federal judges in response to applications from specified federal and state law enforcement officials. Although Congress was fully aware of the distinction between bugging and wiretapping, Title III by its terms deals with each form of surveillance in essentially the same manner. . . .
>
> The plain effect of the detailed restrictions of § 2518 is to guarantee that wiretapping or bugging occurs only when there is a genuine need for it and only to the extent that it is needed. Once this need has been demonstrated in accord with the requirements of § 2518, the courts have broad authority to "approv[e] interception of wire or oral communications," 18 U.S.C. §§ 2516(1), (2), subject of course to constitutional limitations. Nowhere in Title III is there any indication that the authority of courts under § 2518 is to be limited to approving those methods of interception that do not require covert entry for installation of the intercepting equipment. . . .
>
> . . . [O]ne simply cannot assume that Congress, aware that most bugging requires covert entry, nonetheless wished to except surveillance requiring such entries from the broad authorization of Title III, and that it resolved to do so by remaining silent on the subject. On the contrary, the language and history of Title III convey quite a different explanation for Congress' failure to distinguish between surveillance that requires covert entry and that which does not:

Those considering the surveillance legislation understood that, by authorizing electronic interception of oral communications in addition to wire communications, they were necessarily authorizing surreptitious entries.

Justice Stevens dissented:

> . . . [O]ne simply cannot assume that Congress wished to erect various procedural barriers against poor judgment on the part of the Attorney General and his subordinates in seeking, and on the part of federal district judges in issuing, eavesdropping orders only to commit their execution, even through illegal means, entirely to "the judgment and moderation of officers whose own interests and records are often at stake in the search." The detailed timing and minimization restrictions on the executing officer, as well as the 1970 amendment to Title III concerning "unobtrusive" execution, lead inescapably to the conclusion that Congress withheld authority to trespass on private property except through the limited means expressly dealt with in the statute. . . .
>
> Only one relevant conclusion can be drawn from a review of the entire legislative history of Title III. The legislators never even considered the possibility that they were passing a statute that would authorize federal agents to break into private premises without any finding of necessity by a neutral and detached magistrate.

ELECTRONIC SURVEILLANCE ORDERS

The number of electronic surveillance orders issued under federal wiretap law has greatly expanded. In 1968, there were a total of 174 orders approved. In 1980, there were 564 approved; in 1990, 872 orders were approved; and in 1999, the number of approved orders was 1,350. In 2001, federal and state courts authorized 1,491 wiretap applications.[25] Most wiretap authorizations involved drug offenses (1,167). The remainder concerned gambling (82), racketeering (70), and homicide/assault (52).[26] The majority of orders are approved by state judges, although the number by federal judges is increasing.[27]

The vast majority of requests for electronic surveillance orders have been granted. From 1968 to 1996, about 20,000 requests for electronic surveillance orders have been made, and only 28 have been denied.[28]

(b) Video Surveillance

Prior to the ECPA, in *United States v. Torres*, 751 F.2d 875 (7th Cir. 1984), Judge Posner recognized the invasiveness to privacy caused by video surveillance, but noted that it was not encompassed within the language of Title III:

> . . . Television surveillance is identical in its indiscriminate character to wiretapping and bugging. It is even more invasive of privacy, just as a strip search

---

[25] *See 2001 Wiretap Report, A Report of the Director of the Administrative Office of the U.S. Courts on Application Orders Authorizing or Approving the Interception of Wire, Oral, or Electronic Communications*, available at <*www.uscourts.gov/wiretap.html*>.

[26] *See id.*

[27] *See* Title III Electronic Surveillance 1968-1999 <*http://www.epic.org/privacy/wiretap/stats/wiretap_stats.html*>.

[28] *See* <*http://www.epic.org/privacy/wiretap/stats/taps_denied.html*>.

is more invasive than a pat-down search, but it is not more indiscriminate: the microphone is as "dumb" as the television camera; both devices pick up anything within their electronic reach, however irrelevant to the investigation. . . .

. . . Congress said in language that could not be clearer that Title III is about the interception of wire and oral communications and that interception means aural acquisition. There is no way in which these words can be read to include silent television surveillance; and the legislative history quoted earlier indicates that the exclusion from the scope of the statute of other methods of surveillance besides those defined in the statute was deliberate. Statutory language, to be stretchable, should be elastic. This statutory language is not. To read the words of this statute — intercept, aural, communication — as if they encompassed silent visual surveillance would be to say to Congress that there is no form of words that it can use to mark off the limits of a statute that will prevent aggressive, imaginative judges from disregarding those limits. And we naturally shrink from saying any such thing. . . .

The court went on to state: "We would think it a very good thing if Congress responded to the issues discussed in this opinion by amending Title III to bring television surveillance within its scope."

When it amended federal wiretap law in 1986 with the ECPA, Congress again failed to address video surveillance. Of course, if the government intercepts a *communication* consisting of video images, then Title I applies. If the government accesses an individual's stored video image, then Title II applies. However, video *surveillance* does not involve an interception or an accessing of stored images. The video surveillance must be silent video surveillance, or else it could be an "oral" communication subject to either Title I or II. Therefore, silent video surveillance is not covered under federal wiretap law.[29]

In *United States v. Mesa-Rincon*, 911 F.2d 1433 (10th Cir. 1990), the court observed that although federal wiretap law did not apply to video surveillance, the Fourth Amendment did:

. . . Unfortunately, Congress has not yet specifically defined the constitutional requirements for video surveillance. Nevertheless, the general fourth amendment requirements are still applicable to video surveillance; and suppression is required when the government fails to follow these requirements.

Title III establishes elaborate warrant requirements for wiretapping and bugging. Unfortunately, Title III does not discuss television surveillance in any way. Thus, its requirements are not binding on this court in the context of video surveillance. However, the fact that Title III does not discuss television surveillance is no authority for the proposition that Congress meant to outlaw the practice. . . .

The court held that under the Fourth Amendment, federal wiretap law's requirements should be applied as guiding factors in determining whether a warrant for video surveillance should be issued:

Despite Congress' silence concerning video surveillance, we believe that Title III's provisions provide strong guidance for establishing video surveillance

---

[29] *See, e.g., United States v. Biasuci*, 786 F.2d 504 (2d Cir. 1986); *United States v. Koyomejian*, 970 F.2d 536 (9th Cir. 1992); *United States v. Falls*, 34 F.3d 674 (8th Cir. 1994).

requirements. For example, Title III provides requirements for the surreptitious interception of oral communications within a private or business dwelling. We believe that the interception of oral communications provides a strong analogy to video surveillance even though video surveillance can be vastly more intrusive, as demonstrated by the surveillance in this case that recorded a person masturbating before the hidden camera.

(c) E-Mail

STEVE JACKSON GAMES, INC. v. UNITED STATES SECRET SERVICE

36 F.3d 457 (5th Cir. 1994)

BARKSDALE, J. Appellant Steve Jackson Games, Incorporated (SJG), publishes books, magazines, role-playing games, and related products. Starting in the mid-1980s, SJG operated an electronic bulletin board system, called "Illuminati" (BBS), from one of its computers. SJG used the BBS to post public information about its business, games, publications, and the role-playing hobby; to facilitate play-testing of games being developed; and to communicate with its customers and free-lance writers by electronic mail (E-mail).

Central to the issue before us, the BBS also offered customers the ability to send and receive private E-mail. Private E-mail was stored on the BBS computer's hard disk drive temporarily, until the addressees "called" the BBS (using their computers and modems) and read their mail. After reading their E-mail, the recipients could choose to either store it on the BBS computer's hard drive or delete it. In February 1990, there were 365 BBS users. Among other uses, appellants Steve Jackson, Elizabeth McCoy, William Milliken, and Steffan O'Sullivan used the BBS for communication by private E-mail. . . .

On February 28, 1990, [Secret Service] Agent Foley applied for a warrant to search SJG's premises and Blankenship's residence for evidence of violations of 18 U.S.C. §§ 1030 (proscribes interstate transportation of computer access information) and 2314 (proscribes interstate transportation of stolen property). A search warrant for SJG was issued that same day, authorizing the seizure of [computer hardware, software, and computer data.]

The next day, March 1, the warrant was executed by the Secret Service, including Agents Foley and Golden. Among the items seized was the computer which operated the BBS. At the time of the seizure, 162 items of unread, private E-mail were stored on the BBS, including items addressed to the individual appellants. . . .

Appellants filed suit in May 1991 against, among others, the Secret Service and the United States, claiming [among other things, a violation of] the Federal Wiretap Act, as amended by Title I of the Electronic Communications Privacy Act (ECPA), 18 U.S.C. §§ 2510-2521; and Title II of the ECPA, 18 U.S.C. §§ 2701-2711. . . .

As stated, the sole issue is a very narrow one: whether the seizure of a computer on which is stored private E-mail that has been sent to an electronic bulletin board, but not yet read (retrieved) by the recipients, constitutes an "intercept" proscribed by 18 U.S.C. § 2511(1)(a).

Section 2511 was enacted in 1968 as part of Title III of the Omnibus Crime Control and Safe Streets Act of 1968, often referred to as the Federal Wiretap

Act. Prior to the 1986 amendment by Title I of the ECPA, it covered only wire and oral communications. Title I of the ECPA extended that coverage to electronic communications. In relevant part, §2511(1)(a) proscribes "intentionally intercept[ing] . . . any wire, oral, or electronic communication," unless the intercept is authorized by court order or by other exceptions not relevant here. Section 2520 authorizes, *inter alia*, persons whose electronic communications are intercepted in violation of §2511 to bring a civil action against the interceptor for actual damages, or for statutory damages of $10,000 per violation or $100 per day of the violation, whichever is greater. 18 U.S.C. §2520.

The Act defines "intercept" as "the aural or other acquisition of the contents of any wire, electronic, or oral communication through the use of any electronic, mechanical, or other device." 18 U.S.C. §2510(4). . . .

Webster's Third New International Dictionary (1986) defines "aural" as "of or relating to the ear" or "of or relating to the sense of hearing." And, the Act defines "aural transfer" as "a transfer containing the human voice at any point between and including the point of origin and the point of reception." 18 U.S.C. §2510(18). This definition is extremely important for purposes of understanding the definition of a "wire communication," which is defined by the Act as

> any aural transfer made in whole or in part through the use of facilities for the transmission of communications by the aid of wire, cable, or other like connection between the point of origin and the point of reception (including the use of such connection in a switching station) . . . *and such term includes any electronic storage of such communication.*

18 U.S.C. §2510(1) (emphasis added). In contrast, as noted, an "electronic communication" is defined as "any *transfer* of signs, signals, writing, images, sounds, data, or intelligence of any nature transmitted in whole or in part by a wire, radio, electromagnetic, photoelectronic or photooptical system . . . but does not include . . . any wire or oral communication. . . ." 18 U.S.C. §2510(12) (emphasis added).

Critical to the issue before us is the fact that, unlike the definition of "wire communication," *the definition of "electronic communication" does not include electronic storage of such communications. See* 18 U.S.C. §2510(12). "Electronic storage" is defined as

> (A) any *temporary*, intermediate *storage* of a wire or *electronic communication incidental to the electronic transmission thereof;* and
> (B) any storage of such communication by an electronic communication service for purposes of backup protection of such communication. . . .

18 U.S.C. §2510(17) (emphasis added). The E-mail in issue was in "electronic storage." Congress' use of the word "transfer" in the definition of "electronic communication," and its omission in that definition of the phrase "any electronic storage of such communication" (part of the definition of "wire communication") reflects that Congress did not intend for "intercept" to apply to "electronic communications" when those communications are in "electronic storage." . . .

Title II generally proscribes unauthorized access to stored wire or electronic communications. Section 2701(a) provides:

Except as provided in subsection (c) of this section whoever —
(1) intentionally accesses without authorization a facility through which an electronic communication service is provided; or
(2) intentionally exceeds an authorization to access that facility; and thereby obtains, alters, or prevents authorized access to a wire or electronic communication *while it is in electronic storage in such system* shall be punished. . . .

18 U.S.C. § 2701(a) (emphasis added).

As stated, the district court found that the Secret Service violated § 2701 when it

> intentionally accesse[d] without authorization a facility [the computer] through which an electronic communication service [the BBS] is provided . . . and thereby obtain[ed] [and] prevent[ed] authorized access [by appellants] to a[n] . . . electronic communication while it is in electronic storage in such system.

18 U.S.C. § 2701(a). (The Secret Service does not challenge this ruling.) We find no indication in either the Act or its legislative history that Congress intended for conduct that is clearly prohibited by Title II to furnish the basis for a civil remedy under Title I as well. . . .

NOTES & QUESTIONS

1. Is unread e-mail in storage because it is sitting on a hard drive at the ISP? Or is it in transmission because the recipient hasn't read it yet? Is the court applying an overly formalistic and strict reading of "interception"?[30]
2. We will return to the ECPA and e-mail in Chapter 7, when we explore the monitoring of e-mail in the workplace.

(d) State Wiretap Law

A number of states have enacted their own versions of wiretap law, some of which are more protective than federal wiretap law. For example, several states require the consent of all parties to a conversation for a legal wiretap rather than just one as required by federal wiretap law. One prominent example was the indictment on July 30, 1999, of Linda Tripp on two counts of violating Maryland's wiretapping law. At the request of the Office of the Independent Counsel, Linda Tripp secretly taped a phone conversation she had with Monica Lewinsky about Lewinsky's affair with President Clinton and disclosed the contents of that conversation to a news magazine. Possible penalties included up to ten years' imprisonment and a $20,000 fine. Maryland's wiretapping law, in contrast to federal wiretap law, requires the consent of the other party to a communication. Tripp was indicted by a Maryland grand jury. Although Tripp was protected by a federal grant of immunity from prosecution, Maryland was not part of the immunity agreement and could prosecute

---

[30] *See generally* Thomas R. Greenberg, Comment, *E-Mail and Voice Mail: Employee Privacy and the Federal Wiretap Statute*, 44 Am. U. L. Rev. 219 (1994).

Tripp. After a judicial ruling suppressing certain evidence, the case against Tripp was dropped.

4. THE COMMUNICATIONS ASSISTANCE FOR LAW ENFORCEMENT ACT

In *United States v. New York Telephone*, 434 U.S. 159 (1977), the Supreme Court held that 18 U.S.C. § 2518(4) required telecommunications providers to furnish "any assistance necessary to accomplish an electronic interception." However, the issue of whether a provider had to create and design its technology to facilitate authorized electronic surveillance remained an open question.

In the 1980s, new communications technology was developed to enable more wireless communications — cellular telephones, microwave, and satellite communications. As a result of fears that these new technologies would be harder to monitor, the law enforcement community successfully convinced Congress to force telecommunications providers to ensure that the government could continue to monitor electronic communications.[31]

The Communications Assistance for Law Enforcement Act (CALEA) of 1994, Pub. L. No. 103-414, (also known as the "Digital Telephony Act") requires telecommunication providers to help facilitate the government in executing legally authorized surveillance. The Act was passed against strong opposition from some civil liberties organizations. Congress appropriated federal funding of $500 million to telephone companies to make the proposed changes.

The CALEA requires all telecommunications providers to be able to isolate and intercept electronic communications and be able to deliver them to law enforcement personnel. If carriers provide an encryption service to users, then they must decrypt the communications. The CALEA permits the telecommunications industry to develop the technology. Under a "safe harbor" provision, carriers that comply with accepted industry standards are in compliance with CALEA. 47 U.S.C. § 1006(a)(2).

The CALEA contains some important limits. Carriers must "facilitat[e] authorized communications interceptions and access to call-identifying information . . . in a manner that protects . . . the privacy and security of communications and call-identifying information not authorized to be intercepted." § 1002(a)(4)(A). Further, CALEA is designed to provide "law enforcement no more and no less access to information than it had in the past." H.R. Rep. No. 103-827, pt. 1, at 22. Additionally, the CALEA does not apply to "information services" such as e-mail and Internet access. §§ 1001(8)(C)(i), 1002(b)(2)(A).

In *United States Telecom Association v. FCC*, 227 F.3d 450 (D.C. Cir. 2000), the limits of CALEA were elucidated. In 1995, the telecommunications industry started to develop a safe harbor standard, which was adopted by the industry in December 1997. The standard is known as the Interim Standard/Trial Use Standard J-STD-025 (the "J-Standard"). The J-Standard sets forth the

---

[31] For a detailed analysis of CALEA, see Susan Freiwald, *Uncertain Privacy: Communication Attributes After the Digital Telephony Act*, 69 S. Cal. L. Rev. 949 (1996).

standards by which carriers can make communications and call-identifying information available to law enforcement officials. The U.S. Telephone Association and privacy organizations challenged the J-Standard by petitioning the Federal Communications Commission (FCC) to remove provisions that the organizations argued extended beyond CALEA's authorization.

One item was "post-cut-through dialed digit extraction," a list of the digits a person dials after a call has been connected. The court concluded that this item failed to comply with CALEA's requirement to "protect the privacy and security of communications not authorized to be intercepted," 47 U.S.C. § 1006(b)(2) because the information collected by post-cut-through extraction goes beyond the information involved in pen registers (telephone numbers only):

> Post-cut-through dialed digits can also represent call content. For example, subjects calling automated banking services enter account numbers. When calling voicemail systems, they enter passwords. When calling pagers, they dial digits that convey actual messages. And when calling pharmacies to renew prescriptions, they enter prescription numbers.

Another item was a requirement that carriers inform law enforcement officials of the nearest antenna tower to a mobile telephone user, giving officials the ability to track the location of mobile telephones. The court held that the requirement was valid under CALEA:

> Not only did the Commission elucidate the textual basis for interpreting "call-identifying information" to include location information, but it also explained how that result comports with CALEA's goal of preserving the same surveillance capabilities that law enforcement agencies had in POTS (plain old telephone service). "[I]n the wireline environment," the Commission explained, law enforcement agencies "have generally been able to obtain location information routinely from the telephone number because the telephone number usually corresponds with location." In the wireless environment, "the equivalent location information" is "the location of the cell sites to which the mobile terminal or handset is connected at the beginning and at the termination of the call." Accordingly, the Commission concluded, "[p]rovision of this particular location information does not appear to expand or diminish law enforcement's surveillance authority under prior law applicable to the wireline environment.". . .

5. THE FOREIGN INTELLIGENCE SURVEILLANCE ACT

The Foreign Intelligence Surveillance Act (FISA) of 1978, Pub. L. No. 95-511, codified at 50 U.S.C. §§ 1801–1811, establishes standards and procedures for use of electronic surveillance to collect "foreign intelligence" within the United States. § 1804(a)(7)(B). The FISA creates a different regime than the legal regime that governs regular government surveillance (federal wiretap law). The regime created by FISA is designed primarily for intelligence gathering agencies to regulate how they gain general intelligence about foreign powers within the borders of the United States. In contrast, the regime of federal wiretap law is designed for domestic law enforcement to govern the gathering of information for criminal investigations involving people in United States.

Applicability of FISA. When does FISA govern rather than regular federal wiretap law? FISA applies when foreign intelligence gathering is "a significant purpose" of the investigation. 50 U.S.C. § 1804(a)(7)(B) and 1823(a)(7)(B). The language of "a significant purpose" comes from the USA-PATRIOT Act of 2001. Prior to the USA-PATRIOT Act, FISA required that the collection of foreign intelligence be the primary purpose for surveillance. After the USA-PATRIOT Act, foreign intelligence gathering need no longer be the primary purpose.

FISA permits electronic surveillance, covert searches, pen register and trap and trace orders, and the obtaining of certain records.

Court Orders. Requests for FISA orders are reviewed by a special court of seven federal district court judges. § 1803. The proceedings are ex parte, with the Department of Justice (DOJ) making the applications to the court on behalf of the CIA and other agencies. Surveillance is permitted under FISA not based upon whether there is probable cause that the monitored party is involved in criminal activity; rather, the court must find probable cause that the monitored party is a "foreign power" or "an agent of a foreign power." § 1801. Therefore, unlike federal wiretap law or the Fourth Amendment, FISA surveillance is not tied to any required showing of a connection to criminal activity. However, if the monitored party is a "United States person" (a citizen or permanent resident alien), then the government must establish probable cause that the party's activities "may" or "are about to" involve a criminal violation. § 1801(b)(2)(A).

From 1979 to 1999, the number of FISA electronic surveillance orders has expanded from 199 orders in 1979 to 886 orders in 1999.[32] In 2001, the FISA court approved 934 applications for electronic surveillance orders. None were denied.[33]

Surveillance Without Court Orders. In certain circumstances, FISA authorizes surveillance without having to first obtain a court order. § 1802. In particular, the surveillance must be "solely directed at" obtaining intelligence exclusively from "foreign powers." § 1802(a). There must be "no substantial likelihood that the surveillance will acquire the contents of any communications to which a United States person is a party." § 1802(a)(1)(B). Electronic surveillance without a court order requires the authorization of the President, through the Attorney General, in writing under oath. § 1802(a)(1).

Use of Information Obtained Through FISA Orders. Although FISA surveillance need not be conducted to detect or investigate criminal activity, information obtained via FISA can be used in criminal trials.

Video Surveillance. Unlike federal wiretap law, FISA explicitly regulates video surveillance. In order to have court approval for video surveillance, the

---

[32] Foreign Intelligence Surveillance Act Orders 1979–1999, <*http://www.epic.org/privacy/wiretap/stats/fisa_stats.html*>.

[33] Office of Attorney General, 2001 Annual FISA Report to Congress, available at <*www.usdoj.gov/o4foia/readingrooms/2001annualfisareporttocongress.htm*>.

FISA requires the government to submit, among other things, "a detailed description of the nature of the information sought and the type of communications or activities to be subjected to the surveillance," § 1804(a)(6); "a certification . . . that such information cannot reasonably be obtained by normal investigative techniques," § 1804(a)(7); and "a statement of the period of time for which the electronic surveillance is required to be maintained," § 1804(a)(10). Video surveillance orders can last for 90 days.

Surveillance Outside of the United States. FISA does not apply to surveillance outside of the United States. Law enforcement officials can conduct electronic surveillance without judicial oversight.

Minimization. FISA requires that procedures be implemented to minimize the collection, retention, and dissemination of information about United States persons. § 1801(h)(1). Minimization procedures are designed to prevent the broad power of "foreign intelligence gathering" from being used for routine criminal investigations. In a number of instances, however, there are overlaps between foreign intelligence gathering and criminal investigations. One common minimization procedure is what is known as an "information screening wall." These "walls" require an official not involved in the criminal investigation to review the raw materials gathered by FISA surveillance and only pass on information that might be relevant evidence. In 2002, the Attorney General submitted to the FISA court new procedures for minimization, which significantly curtailed the walls. The procedures were reviewed by the FISA court in *In re All Matters Submitted to the Foreign Intelligence Surveillance Court* (May 17, 2002). The court expressed concern over the new procedures in light of the fact that in September 2000, the government had confessed error in about 75 FISA applications, including false statements that the targets of FISA surveillance were not under criminal investigations, that intelligence and criminal investigations were separate, and that information was not shared with FBI criminal investigators and assistant U.S. attorneys. The FISA court rejected the proposed procedures because they would allow criminal prosecutors to advise on FISA information gathering activities.

The FISA court of review (composed of three judges from the D.C. Circuit) reversed. This was the first appeal from the FISA court since the passage of the FISA. In *In re Sealed Case No. 02-001*, the court of review concluded that the walls were not required by the language of the FISA. "[W]e think that the FISA as passed by Congress in 1978 clearly did *not* preclude or limit the government's use or proposed use of foreign intelligence information, which included evidence of certain kinds of criminal activity, in a criminal prosecution." Further, the court declared:

> [T]he Patriot Act amendment, by using the word "significant," eliminated any justification for the FISA court to balance the relative weight the government places on criminal prosecution as compared to other counterintelligence responses. If the certification of the application's purpose articulates a broader objective than criminal prosecution — such as stopping an ongoing conspiracy — and includes other potential non-prosecutorial responses, the government meets the statutory test. Of course, if the court concluded that the government's sole objective was merely to gain evidence of past criminal conduct —

even foreign intelligence crimes — to punish the agent rather than halt ongoing espionage or terrorist activity, the application should be denied.

6. THE USA-PATRIOT ACT

On September 11, 2001, terrorists hijacked four planes and crashed three of them into the World Trade Center and the Pentagon, killing thousands of people. The nation was awakened into a world filled with new frightening dangers, and shortly after the September 11 attacks, letters laced with the deadly bacteria Anthrax were sent in the mails to several prominent individuals in the news media and in politics. Acting with great haste, Congress passed a sweeping new law expanding the government's electronic surveillance powers in many significant ways. Called the "Uniting and Strengthening America By Providing Appropriate Tools Required To Intercept and Obstruct Terrorism Act" (USA-PATRIOT Act), the Act made a number of substantial changes to federal wiretap law, FISA, FERPA, immigration law, and money laundering statutes. The discussion below will focus on the changes that pertain to information privacy law, with particular emphasis on federal wiretap law and FISA.[34]

Definition of Terrorism. Section 802 of the USA-PATRIOT Act added to 18 U.S.C. § 2331 a new definition of "domestic terrorism." According to the Act, domestic terrorism involves "acts dangerous to human life that are a violation of the criminal laws of the United States or of any State" that "appear to be intended: (i) to intimidate or coerce a civilian population; (ii) to influence the policy of a government by intimidation or coercion; or (iii) to affect the conduct of a government by mass destruction, assassination, or kidnapping; and . . . occur primarily within the territorial jurisdiction of the United States." According to many proponents of civil liberties, this definition is very broad and could potentially encompass many forms of civil disobedience, which, although consisting of criminal conduct (minor violence, threats, property damage), includes conduct that has historically been present in many political protests and has never been considered to be terrorism.

Delayed Notice of Search Warrants. Under the Fourth Amendment, the government must obtain a warrant and provide notice to a person before conducting a search or seizure. Case law provided for certain limited exceptions. Section 213 of the USA-PATRIOT Act adds a provision to 18 U.S.C. § 3103a, enabling the government to delay notice if the court concludes that there is "reasonable cause" that immediate notice will create an "adverse result" such as physical danger, the destruction of evidence, delayed trial, flight from prosecution, and other circumstances. § 3103a(b). This provision does not sunset. Warrants enabling a covert search with delayed notice are often referred to as "sneak and peek" warrants. Civil libertarians consider "sneak and peek" warrants dan-

---

[34]For more background about the USA-PATRIOT Act, see Steven A. Osher, *Privacy, Computers, and the Patriot Act: The Fourth Amendment Isn't Dead, But No One Will Insure It*, 54 Fla. L. Rev. 521 (2002); Sharon H. Rackow, Comment, *How the USA PATRIOT Act Will Permit Governmental Infringement upon the Privacy of Americans in the Name of "Intelligence" Investigations*, 150 U. Pa. L. Rev. 1651 (2002).

gerous because in a covert search, the individual cannot safeguard her rights and there is little supervision of the government's carrying out of the search.

Shifting Stored Wire Communications from Title I to Title II. Under Title I of federal wiretap law, the definition of wire communications consisted of the temporary storage of such communications. As a result, obtaining access to certain stored wire communications, such as voicemail, was considered an "intercept" under Title I rather than accessing stored communications under Title II. *See United States v. Smith*, 155 F.3d 1051 (9th Cir. 1986) (holding that the retrieval of a voicemail message was an interception governed by Title I). Likewise, if a stored e-mail had a voice attachment, Title I's strict court order requirements applied rather than Title II's more relaxed requirements. The USA-PATRIOT Act (§ 209) deleted "electronic storage" from the definition of wire communications, making stored wire communications fall under Title II. This provision will sunset on December 31, 2005.

Increased Number of Subscriber Records Obtainable Under Title II. Under Title II of federal wiretap law, § 2703(c), the government could obtain only certain subscriber records from a communications service provider: name, address, length of service, means of payment, and so on. Section 210 of the USA-PATRIOT Act adds new records to this list, including "records of session times and durations," "any temporarily assigned network address," and "any credit card or bank account number" used for payment. § 2703(c)(2).

New Definition of Pen Registers and Trap and Trace Devices. Under Title III of the ECPA, § 3121 *et seq.*, the definitions of pen registers and trap and trace devices focus primarily on telephone numbers. Thus, a pen register is defined under 18 U.S.C. § 3127(3) as:

> a device which records or decodes electronic or other impulses which identify the numbers dialed or otherwise transmitted on the telephone line to which such device is attached. . . .

Section 216 of the USA-PATRIOT Act changed the definition to read:

> a device *or process* which records or decodes *dialing, routing, addressing, or signaling information transmitted by an instrument or facility from which a wire or electronic communication is transmitted, provided, however, that such information shall not include the contents of any communication* is attached. . . (changes emphasized).

These changes alter the definition of a pen register from applying not only to telephone numbers but also to Internet addresses, e-mail addressing information (the "to" and "from" lines on e-mail), and the routing information of a wide spectrum of communications. The inclusion of "or process" after "device" enlarges the means by which such routing information can be intercepted beyond the use of a physical device. The definition of a trap and trace device was changed in a similar way. These provisions do not sunset.

Recall that under Title III, a court order to obtain such information does not require probable cause, but merely certification that "the information likely to be obtained by such installation and use is relevant to an ongoing criminal investigation." 18 U.S.C. § 3123. The person whose communications are subject to this order need not even be a criminal suspect; all that the government needs to certify is relevance to an investigation.

Recall *Smith v. Maryland* earlier in this chapter where the Court held that pen registers were not protected under the Fourth Amendment. Does the new definition of pen register and trap and trace device under the USA-PATRIOT Act go beyond *Smith v. Maryland*? Are Internet addresses and e-mail addressing information analogous to pen registers? Or are they different? Note that Internet addresses reveal how a person navigates the Internet. Based on *Smith v. Maryland*, does the Fourth Amendment apply to such information? If the government were to obtain e-mail header information or Internet addresses through a Title III order, is such information properly obtained under the Fourth Amendment?

Nationwide Scope of Pen Register/Trap and Trace Orders. Originally, pen register/trap and trace orders were only valid within the jurisdiction of the court issuing the order. The USA-PATRIOT Act, § 216, permits the court having jurisdiction over the crime under investigation to issue pen register/trap and trace orders that are valid throughout the nation. This provision applies to all crimes, not just terrorism, and may place a significant burden on smaller ISPs to challenge in court the scope and duration of the order.

Nationwide Scope of Search Warrants for E-Mail. For warrants to obtain stored e-mail less than 180 days old under Title II of the ECPA, § 2703(a), § 220 of the USA-PATRIOT Act permitted the court having jurisdiction over a crime to issue a warrant applying beyond the court's jurisdiction to anywhere in the nation. This provision will sunset on December 31, 2005.

Expansion of Application of FISA. Prior to the USA-PATRIOT Act, FISA applied when foreign intelligence gathering was "the purpose" of the investigation. The USA-PATRIOT Act (§ 204) changed this language to make the FISA applicable when foreign intelligence gathering is "a significant purpose" of the investigation. § 50 U.S.C. 1804(a)(7)(B) and 1823(a)(7)(B).

Sharing of Foreign Intelligence Information. Section 203 of the USA-PATRIOT Act permits extensive sharing of foreign intelligence information among various law enforcement entities and intelligence agencies. The purposes for which the information can be shared are defined very broadly: "to assist the official who is to receive that information in the performance of his official duties."

Roving Wiretaps Under FISA. Section 206 of the USA-PATRIOT Act amended the FISA to allow the interception of communications beyond "specified person[s]." Previously, the FISA, 50 U.S.C. § 1805(c)(2)(B) provided that an order approving electronic surveillance shall direct

> that, upon the request of the applicant, a specified communication or other common carrier, landlord, custodian, or other specified person furnish the applicant forthwith all information, facilities, or technical assistance necessary to accomplish the electronic surveillance in such a manner as will protect its secrecy and produce a minimum of interference with the services that such

carrier, landlord, custodian, or other person is providing that target of electronic surveillance.

As amended by the USA-PATRIOT Act, the provision reads:

that, upon the request of the applicant, a specified communication or other common carrier, landlord, custodian, or other specified person *or in circumstances where the Court finds that the actions of the target of the application may have the effect of thwarting the identification of a specified person, such other persons*, furnish the applicant forthwith all information, facilities, or technical assistance necessary to accomplish the electronic surveillance in such a manner as will protect its secrecy and produce a minimum of interference with the services that such carrier, landlord, custodian, or other person is providing that target of electronic surveillance (changes emphasized).

Private Right of Action for Government Disclosures. The USA-PATRIOT Act adds a provision to Title II of federal wiretap law which provides for civil actions against the United States for any "willful" violations. 18 U.S.C. § 2712. The court may assess actual damages or $10,000 (whichever is greater) and litigation costs. Such an action must first be presented before the "appropriate department or agency under the procedures of the Federal Tort Claims Act."

Changes to FERPA and the Cable Act. These changes will be discussed later on in Chapter 6, when these Acts are discussed.

C. ENCRYPTION

Encryption includes the ability to keep communications secure by concealing the contents of a message. With encryption, even if a communication is intercepted, it still remains secure. Encryption works by translating a message into a code of letters or numbers called "cypher text." The parties to the communication hold a *key*, which consists of the information necessary to translate the code back to the original message, or "plain text." Since ancient times, code-makers have devised cryptographic systems to encode messages. But along with the code-makers arose code-breakers, who were able to figure out the keys to cryptographic systems by, for example, examining the patterns in the encoded messages and comparing them to patterns in a particular language and the frequency of use of certain letters in that language. Today, computers have vastly increased the complexity of encryption.

Encryption presents a difficult trade-off between privacy and security. It is an essential device to protect the privacy of electronic communications in an age where such communications can so easily be intercepted and monitored. On the other hand, it enables individuals to disguise their communications from detection by law enforcement officials.[35] As Whitfield Diffie and Susan Landau observe:

---

[35] For more background on encryption, see Simon Singh, *The Code: The Evolution of Secrecy from Mary, Queen of Scots to Quantum Cryptography* (1999); Steven Levy, *Crypto: How the Code Rebels Beat the Government — Saving Privacy in the Digital Age* (2002); A. Michael Froomkin, *The Met-*

The explosion in cryptography and the US government's attempts to control it have given rise to a debate between those who hail the new technology's contribution to privacy, business, and security and those who fear both its interference with the work of police and its adverse effect on the collection of intelligence. Positions have often been extreme. The advocates for unfettered cryptography maintain that a free society depends on privacy to protect freedom of association, artistic creativity, and political discussion. The advocates of control hold that there will be no freedom at all unless we can protect ourselves from criminals, terrorists, and foreign threats. Many have tried to present themselves as seeking to maintain or restore the status quo. For the police, the status quo is the continued ability to wiretap. For civil libertarians, it is the ready availability of conversational privacy that prevailed at the time of the country's founding. . . .[36]

The U.S. government has become increasingly concerned that the growing sophistication of encryption would make it virtually impossible for the government to decrypt. In 1994, the government proposed implementing the "Clipper Chip," a federal encryption standard in which the government would retain a copy of the key in a system called "key escrow." By holding a "spare key," the government could readily decrypt encrypted communications if it desired. The Clipper Chip was strongly criticized, and the government's encryption standard has not been widely used.

BERNSTEIN V. UNITED STATES DEPARTMENT OF JUSTICE

176 F.3d 1132 (9th Cir. 1999) (withdrawn pending rehearing en banc)

B. FLETCHER, J. The government defendants appeal the grant of summary judgment to the plaintiff, Professor Daniel J. Bernstein ("Bernstein"), enjoining the enforcement of certain Export Administration Regulations ("EAR") that limit Bernstein's ability to distribute encryption software. . . .

Bernstein is currently a professor in the Department of Mathematics, Statistics, and Computer Science at the University of Illinois at Chicago. As a doctoral candidate at the University of California, Berkeley, he developed an encryption method — "a zero-delay private-key stream encryptor based upon a one-way hash function"[37] — that he dubbed "Snuffle." Bernstein described his method in two ways: in a paper containing analysis and mathematical equations (the "Paper") and in two computer programs written in "C," a high-level

---

aphor Is the Key: Cryptography, the Clipper Chip, and the Constitution, 143 U. Pa. L. Rev. 709 (1995); Robert C. Post, *Encryption Source Code and the First Amendment*, 15 Berkeley Tech. L.J. 713 (2000); A. Michael Froomkin, *The Constitution and Encryption Regulation: Do We Need a "New Privacy"?*, 3 N.Y.U. J. Legis. & Pub. Pol'y 25 (1999).

[36] Whitfield Diffie & Susan Landau, *Privacy on the Line: The Politics of Wiretapping and Encryption* (1998).

[37] The term "hash function" describes a function that transforms an input into a unique output of fixed (and usually smaller) size that is dependent on the input. For some purposes (e.g., error checking, digital signatures), it is desirable that it be impossible to derive the input data given only the hash function's output — this type of function is known as a "one-way hash function." Hash functions have many uses in cryptography and computer science, and numerous one-way hash functions are widely known. "Zero-delay" means that Snuffle can be used for interactive communications because it encrypts and decrypts on a character-by-character basis — the users need not complete an entire message before encrypting and sending.

computer programming language ("Source Code"). Bernstein later wrote a set of instructions in English (the "Instructions") explaining how to program a computer to encrypt and decrypt data utilizing a one-way hash function, essentially translating verbatim his Source Code into prose form.

Seeking to present his work on Snuffle within the academic and scientific communities, Bernstein asked the State Department whether he needed a license to publish Snuffle in any of its various forms. The State Department responded that Snuffle was a munition under the International Traffic in Arms Regulations ("ITAR"), and that Bernstein would need a license to "export" the Paper, the Source Code, or the Instructions. There followed a protracted and unproductive series of letter communications between Bernstein and the government, wherein Bernstein unsuccessfully attempted to determine the scope and application of the export regulations to Snuffle. . . .

Cryptography is the science of secret writing, a science that has roots stretching back hundreds, and perhaps thousands, of years. For much of its history, cryptography has been the jealously guarded province of governments and militaries. In the past twenty years, however, the science has blossomed in the civilian sphere, driven on the one hand by dramatic theoretical innovations within the field, and on the other by the needs of modern communication and information technologies. As a result, cryptography has become a dynamic academic discipline within applied mathematics. It is the cryptographer's primary task to find secure methods to encrypt messages, making them unintelligible to all except the intended recipients. . . .

The interception and deciphering of foreign communications has long played an important part in our nation's national security efforts. In the words of a high-ranking State Department official:

> Policies concerning the export control of cryptographic products are based on the fact that the proliferation of such products will make it easier for foreign intelligence targets to deny the United States Government access to information vital to national security interests. Cryptographic products and software have military and intelligence applications. As demonstrated throughout history, encryption has been used to conceal foreign military communications, on the battlefield, aboard ships and submarines, or in other military settings. Encryption is also used to conceal other foreign communications that have foreign policy and national security significance for the United States. For example, encryption can be used to conceal communications of terrorists, drug smugglers, or others intent on taking hostile action against U.S. facilities, personnel, or security interests.

As increasingly sophisticated and secure encryption methods are developed, the government's interest in halting or slowing the proliferation of such methods has grown keen. The EAR regulations at issue in this appeal evidence this interest. . . .

The EAR contain specific regulations to control the export of encryption software, expressly including computer source code. . . .

If encryption software falls within the ambit of the relevant EAR provisions, the "export" of such software requires a prepublication license. When a prepublication license is requested, the relevant agencies undertake a "case-by-case" analysis to determine if the export is "consistent with U.S. national security and foreign policy interests." 15 C.F.R. §742.15(b). All applications must be "resolved or referred to the President no later than 90 days" from the date an application is entered into the BXA's electronic license processing system. There is no time limit, however, that applies once an application is referred to the President. Although the regulations do provide for an internal administrative appeal procedure, such appeals are governed only by the exhortation that they be completed "within a reasonable time." Final administrative decisions are not subject to judicial review. . . .

The parties and amici urge a number of theories on us. We limit our attention here, for the most part, to only one: whether the EAR restrictions on the export of encryption software in source code form constitute a prior restraint in violation of the First Amendment. . . .

It is axiomatic that "prior restraints on speech and publication are the most serious and least tolerable infringement on First Amendment rights." Indeed, the Supreme Court has opined that "it is the chief purpose of the [First Amendment] guaranty to prevent previous restraints upon publication." Accordingly, "[a]ny prior restraint on expression comes . . . with a 'heavy presumption' against its constitutional validity." . . .

The Supreme Court has treated licensing schemes that act as prior restraints on speech with suspicion because such restraints run the twin risks of encouraging self-censorship and concealing illegitimate abuses of censorial power. As a result, "even if the government may constitutionally impose content-neutral prohibitions on a particular manner of speech, it may not condition that speech on obtaining a license or permit from a government official in that official's boundless discretion." . . .

A licensing regime is always subject to facial challenge as a prior restraint where it "gives a government official or agency substantial power to discriminate based on the content or viewpoint of speech by suppressing disfavored speech or disliked speakers," and has "a close enough nexus to expression, or to conduct commonly associated with expression, to pose a real and substantial threat of . . . censorship risks."

The EAR regulations at issue plainly satisfy the first requirement — "the determination of who may speak and who may not is left to the unbridled discretion of a government official." BXA administrators are empowered to deny licenses whenever export might be inconsistent with "U.S. national security and foreign policy interests." No more specific guidance is provided. Obviously, this constraint on official discretion is little better than no constraint at all. . . .

The more difficult issue arises in relation to the second requirement — that the challenged regulations exhibit "a close enough nexus to expression." We are called on to determine whether encryption source code is expression for First Amendment purposes.

We begin by explaining what source code is. "Source code," at least as currently understood by computer programmers, refers to the text of a program written in a "high-level" programming language, such as "PASCAL" or "C." The distinguishing feature of source code is that it is meant to be read and understood by humans and that it can be used to express an idea or a method. A computer, in fact, can make no direct use of source code until it has been translated ("compiled") into a "low-level" or "machine" language, resulting in computer-executable "object code." That source code is meant for human eyes and understanding, however, does not mean that an untutored layperson can understand it. Because source code is destined for the maw of an automated, ruthlessly literal translator — the compiler — a programmer must follow stringent grammatical, syntactical, formatting, and punctuation conventions. As a result, only those trained in programming can easily understand source code.[38]

Also important for our purposes is an understanding of how source code is used in the field of cryptography. Bernstein has submitted numerous declarations from cryptographers and computer programmers explaining that cryptographic ideas and algorithms are conveniently expressed in source code. That this should be so is, on reflection, not surprising. As noted earlier, the chief task for cryptographers is the development of secure methods of encryption. While the articulation of such a system in layman's English or in general mathematical terms may be useful, the devil is, at least for cryptographers, often in the algorithmic details. By utilizing source code, a cryptographer can express algorithmic ideas with precision and methodological rigor that is otherwise difficult to achieve. . . .

Thus, cryptographers use source code to express their scientific ideas in much the same way that mathematicians use equations or economists use graphs. . . .

In light of these considerations, we conclude that encryption software, in its source code form and as employed by those in the field of cryptography, must be viewed as expressive for First Amendment purposes, and thus is entitled to the protections of the prior restraint doctrine. If the government required that mathematicians obtain a prepublication license prior to publishing material that included mathematical equations, we have no doubt that such a regime would be subject to scrutiny as a prior restraint. . . .

Because the prepublication licensing scheme challenged here vests unbridled discretion in government officials, and because it directly jeopardizes scientific expression, we are satisfied that Bernstein may properly bring a facial challenge against the regulations. . . .

"[T]he protection even as to previous restraint is not absolutely unlimited." The Supreme Court has suggested that the "heavy presumption" against prior restraints may be overcome where official discretion is bounded by stringent procedural safeguards. As our analysis above suggests, the challenged reg-

---

[38] It must be emphasized, however, that source code is merely text, albeit text that conforms to stringent formatting and punctuation requirements. For example, the following is an excerpt from Bernstein's Snuffle source code:

```
for (; ;)
(
uch = gtchr( );
if (!(n & 31)) (
for (i = 0; i64; i++)
l[ ctr[i] ] = k[i] + h[n — 64 + i]
Hash512 (wm, wl, level, 8);
)
```

As source code goes, Snuffle is quite compact; the entirety of the Snuffle source code occupies fewer than four printed pages.

ulations do not qualify for this First Amendment safe harbor. In *Freedman v. Maryland*, the Supreme Court set out three factors for determining the validity of licensing schemes that impose a prior restraint on speech: (1) any restraint must be for a specified brief period of time; (2) there must be expeditious judicial review; and (3) the censor must bear the burden of going to court to suppress the speech in question and must bear the burden of proof. . . .

Although the regulations require that license applications be resolved or referred to the President within 90 days, there is no time limit once an application is referred to the President. Thus, the 90-day limit can be rendered meaningless by referral. Moreover, if the license application is denied, no firm time limit governs the internal appeals process. Accordingly, the EAR regulations do not satisfy the first Freedman requirement that a licensing decision be made within a reasonably short, specified period of time. The EAR regulatory regime further offends *Freedman's* procedural requirements insofar as it denies a disappointed applicant the opportunity for judicial review.

We conclude that the challenged regulations allow the government to restrain speech indefinitely with no clear criteria for review. As a result, Bernstein and other scientists have been effectively chilled from engaging in valuable scientific expression. . . .

. . . [W]e note that the government's efforts to regulate and control the spread of knowledge relating to encryption may implicate more than the First Amendment rights of cryptographers. In this increasingly electronic age, we are all required in our everyday lives to rely on modern technology to communicate with one another. This reliance on electronic communication, however, has brought with it a dramatic diminution in our ability to communicate privately. Cellular phones are subject to monitoring, email is easily intercepted, and transactions over the internet are often less than secure. Something as commonplace as furnishing our credit card number, social security number, or bank account number puts each of us at risk. Moreover, when we employ electronic methods of communication, we often leave electronic "fingerprints" behind, fingerprints that can be traced back to us. Whether we are surveilled by our government, by criminals, or by our neighbors, it is fair to say that never has our ability to shield our affairs from prying eyes been at such a low ebb. The availability and use of secure encryption may offer an opportunity to reclaim some portion of the privacy we have lost. Government efforts to control encryption thus may well implicate not only the First Amendment rights of cryptographers intent on pushing the boundaries of their science, but also the constitutional rights of each of us as potential recipients of encryption's bounty. Viewed from this perspective, the government's efforts to retard progress in cryptography may implicate the Fourth Amendment, as well as the right to speak anonymously, see *McIntyre v. Ohio Elections Comm'n*, 514 U.S. 334 (1995), the right against compelled speech, see *Wooley v. Maynard*, 430 U.S. 705 (1977), and the right to informational privacy, see *Whalen v. Roe*, 429 U.S. 589 (1977). While we leave for another day the resolution of these difficult issues, it is important to point out that Bernstein's is a suit not merely concerning a small group of scientists laboring in an esoteric field, but also touches on the public interest broadly defined. . . .

T. G. NELSON, J. dissenting. . . . [E]ncryption source code is more like conduct than speech. Encryption source code is a building tool. Academics and computer programmers can convey this source code to each other in order to reveal the encryption machine they have built. But, the ultimate purpose of encryption code is, as its name suggests, to perform the function of encrypting messages. Thus, while encryption source code may occasionally be used in an expressive manner, it is inherently a functional device. . . .

. . . Export of encryption source code is not conduct commonly associated with expression. Rather, it is conduct that is normally associated with providing other persons with the means to make their computer messages secret. The overwhelming majority of people do not want to talk about the source code and are not interested in any recondite message that may be contained in encryption source code. Only a few people can actually understand what a line of source code would direct a computer to do. Most people simply want to use the encryption source code to protect their computer communications. Export of encryption source code simply does not fall within the bounds of conduct commonly associated with expression such as picketing or handbilling. . . .

NOTES & QUESTIONS

1. The Ninth Circuit voted to rehear *Bernstein* en banc and withdrew the panel's opinion. *See* 192 F.3d 1308 (9th Cir. 1999). The en banc decision is still pending in the Ninth Circuit. In *Junger v. Daley*, 209 F.3d 481 (6th Cir. 2000), the Sixth Circuit agreed with the *Bernstein* court:

   Much like a mathematical or scientific formula, one can describe the function and design of encryption software by a prose explanation; however, for individuals fluent in a computer programming language, source code is the most efficient and precise means by which to communicate ideas about cryptography.

   Consider *Karn v. United States Department of State*, 925 F. Supp. 1 (D.D.C. 1996), where the court came to the contrary conclusion:

   . . . The government regulation at issue here is clearly content-neutral. . . . The defendants are not regulating the export of the diskette because of the expressive content of the comments and or source code, but instead are regulating because of the belief that the combination of encryption source code on machine readable media will make it easier for foreign intelligence sources to encode their communications. . . .

   . . . [A] content-neutral regulation is justified . . . if it is within the constitutional power of the government, it "furthers an important or substantial governmental interest," and "the incidental restriction on alleged First Amendment freedoms is no greater than is essential to the furtherance of that interest." . . .

   . . . By placing cryptographic products on the ITAR, the President has determined that the proliferation of cryptographic products will harm the United States. . . .

   . . . [T]he plaintiff has not advanced any argument that the regulation is "substantially broader than necessary" to prevent the proliferation of cryptographic products. Nor has the plaintiff articulated any present barrier to the spreading of information on cryptography "by any other means" other than those containing encryption source code on machine-readable media. Therefore, the Court holds that the regulation of the plaintiff's diskette is narrowly tailored to the goal of limiting the proliferation of cryptographic products and that the regulation is justified. . . .

2. ***Encryption and the Fourth Amendment.*** Suppose law enforcement officials legally obtain an encrypted communication. Does the Fourth Amendment require a warrant before the government can decrypt an encrypted communication? Consider the following argument by Orin Kerr:

> Encryption is often explained as a lock-and-key system, in which a "key" is used to "lock" plaintext by turning it into ciphertext, and then a "key" is used to "unlock" the ciphertext by turning it into plaintext. We know that locking a container is a common way to create a reasonable expectation of privacy in its contents: the government ordinarily cannot break the lock and search a closed container without a warrant. . . .
>
> When we use a "lock" and "unlock" in the metaphorical sense to denote understanding, however, a lock cannot trigger the rights-based Fourth Amendment. If I tell you a riddle, I do not have a right to stop you from figuring it out. Although figuring out the secret of an inscrutable communication may "unlock" its meaning, the Fourth Amendment cannot regulate such a cognitive discovery. . . .[39]

Do you agree?

3. ***Encryption and the Fifth Amendment.*** Can the government compel the production of a private key if it is stored on a personal computer? What if the key is known only to the individual and not stored or recorded?

D. GOVERNMENT COMPUTER SEARCHES

Today, the computer has become a central medium of communication. Instead of writing letters or making a telephone call, people e-mail each other or talk in Internet chat rooms. In addition, people use the Internet to obtain information and purchase products and services. The computer also enables the storage of information and greatly facilitates the searching of information. The computer enables people to save an extensive record of their e-mail communications — all of their incoming as well as outgoing messages. Computers also store information about what web sites people have visited. This consists of one's "cookies" (files that are deployed into a user's computer by a web site in order to identify visitors), which are stored together in a registry in one's computer. How do the Fourth Amendment and federal wiretap law regulate the government's ability to search and monitor communications made through this new medium? This section will explore how courts are beginning to answer this question.

---

[39] Orin S. Kerr, *The Fourth Amendment in Cyberspace: Can Encryption Create a "Reasonable Expectation of Privacy?,"* 33 Conn. L. Rev. 503 520–521, 522 (2001).

1. FOURTH AMENDMENT LIMITATIONS

UNITED STATES V. CHARBONNEAU

979 F. Supp. 1177 (S.D. Ohio 1997)

KINNEARY, J. Early in 1994, federal law enforcement agents began an investigation into child pornography on the Internet. The investigators included D. Douglas Rehman of the Florida Department of Law Enforcement assigned to an FBI task force in Orlando, Florida. Agent Rehman would "go on-line," using the America OnLine Internet service, and pose as a pedophile. Using the screen or user name of "Mikey1L," Agent Rehman would enter private AOL chat rooms and observe the on-line conversations between users. Agent Rehman operated primarily in the private chat rooms, "BOYS" and "PRETEEN." Both private chat rooms (maintained by private users and not by AOL) contained many users interested in trading graphic files with pictures of child pornography.

After entering a chat room, Agent Rehman would "record" the "conversations" as they occurred in the private room. . . . Agent Rehman was not active in these conversations but passively "sat" in the rooms as an observer. In the course of his investigation, Agent Rehman observed the transmission of numerous graphic pictures containing child pornography.

The child pornography was distributed by one user using a "list." A user generally would create the list by identifying all users in a private room; the user then would enter the screen names of the identified users onto an "e-mail" message and create a list of recipients. The sender of the pornographic pictures would next send an e-mail to the recipients identified on the list. The e-mail often would contain a brief message and an attached graphic file containing child pornography. Recipients frequently recycled the list so that every user on a list could trade graphic files with each other. Because Agent Rehman was present in the private chat rooms, users would include his screen name on such lists. Agent Rehman then would receive the same pornographic pictures of children as the other recipients on the list.

One of the users that Agent Rehman observed sending child pornography was a user identified as "Charbyq." Through the use of a search warrant, the FBI in Virginia identified this user as Defendant. Consequently, the FBI learned that Defendant lived in the Columbus area and referred the investigation to its Columbus office. [The agents procured a search warrant to search Charbonneau's home and seized his computer. During this time, Charbonneau was out of town, and when he returned, the agents met him at the airport and showed him a picture of child pornography allegedly taken from his computer. Charbonneau confessed to possessing child pornography.] . . .

. . . [Among other things,] Defendant moves to suppress [under the Fourth Amendment] any statements made by Defendant while on the Internet using the AOL computer service. . . .

. . . A person challenging the validity of a search or seizure may only assert a "reasonable" "subjective expectation of privacy." As another court addressing a very similar issue found, this Court finds that Defendant possessed a limited reasonable expectation of privacy in the e-mail messages he sent and/or received on AOL. *Cf. United States v. Maxwell*, 45 M.J. 406, 417 (Armed Forces 1996). E-mail is almost equivalent to sending a letter via the mails. When an individual sends or mails letters, messages, or other information on the computer, that Fourth Amendment expectation of privacy diminishes incrementally. Furthermore, the openness of the "chat room" diminishes Defendant's reasonable expectation of privacy.

As the *Maxwell* court noted:

> . . . E-mail transmissions are not unlike other forms of modern communication. We can draw parallels from these other mediums. For example, if a sender of first-class mail seals an envelope and addresses it to another person, the sender can reasonably expect the contents to remain private and free from the eyes of the police absent a search warrant founded upon probable cause. However, once the letter is received and opened, the destiny of the letter then lies in the control of the recipient of the letter, not the sender, absent some legal privilege.
>
> Similarly, the maker of a telephone call has a reasonable expectation that police officials will not intercept and listen to the conversation; however, the conversation itself is held with the risk that one of the participants may reveal what is said to others.
>
> Drawing from these parallels, we can say that the transmitter of an e-mail message enjoys a reasonable expectation that police officials will not intercept the transmission without probable cause and a search warrant. However, once the transmissions are received by another person, the transmitter no longer controls its destiny.

Thus an e-mail message, like a letter, cannot be afforded a reasonable expectation of privacy once that message is received.

Moreover, a sender of e-mail runs the risk that he is sending the message to an undercover agent. In *Hoffa v. United States*, 385 U.S. 293 (1966), the Supreme Court . . . found that no Fourth Amendment rights exist where "a wrongdoer's misplaced belief that a person to whom he voluntarily confides his wrongdoing will not reveal it." Indeed, "The risk of being overheard by an eavesdropper . . . or deceived as to the identity of one with whom one deals is probably inherent in the conditions of human society. It is the kind of risk we necessarily assume whenever we speak."

The expectations of privacy in e-mail transmissions depend in large part on both the type of e-mail sent and recipient of the e-mail. E-mail messages sent to an addressee who later forwards the e-mail to a third party do not enjoy the same reasonable expectations of privacy once they have been forwarded. Similarly, "Messages sent to the public at large in the 'chat room' or e-mail that is 'forwarded' from correspondent to correspondent lose any semblance of privacy."

In this case, Defendant wishes to suppress all of the statements made in AOL chat rooms. All of the evidence gathered by the FBI from the chat rooms resulted from the presence of undercover agents in the rooms. Clearly, when Defendant engaged in chat room conversations, he ran the risk of speaking to an undercover agent. Furthermore, Defendant could not have a reasonable expectation of privacy in the chat rooms. Accordingly, the e-mail sent by

Defendant to others in a "chat room" is not afforded any semblance of privacy; the government may present the evidence at trial. In addition, all e-mail sent or forwarded to the undercover agents is not protected by the Fourth Amendment. . . .

NOTES & QUESTIONS

1. Do you agree with the court's conclusion that there is no reasonable expectation of privacy in an Internet chat room? Is a chat room like meeting in a person's home? Or is it like talking in public?
2. Is there any part of the Internet that is a private place?

UNITED STATES V. LACY

119 F.3d 742 (9th Cir. 1997)

BROWNING, J. The United States Customs Service was informed that child pornography from a Danish computer bulletin board system called BAMSE was being brought into the United States by computer. BAMSE's records indicated several people, including a caller from Seattle who identified himself as "Jim Bakker," had received material from BAMSE by telephone. "Bakker" had called BAMSE sixteen times and had downloaded six picture files containing computerized visual depictions known as GIFs. Customs agents traced the caller's phone number to an apartment occupied by a computer analyst named Scott Lacy. Telephone records reflected calls made from Lacy's telephone to BAMSE on the dates shown in BAMSE's records.

A warrant was issued authorizing the search of Lacy's apartment and seizure of computer equipment and records, and documents relating to BAMSE. Customs agents seized Lacy's computer, more than 100 computer disks, and various documents. The computer hard drive and disks contained GIF files depicting minors engaged in sexually explicit activity.

Lacy was indicted for possessing child pornography. Lacy's motion to suppress was denied, [and he was tried and convicted. Lacy appeals the suppression ruling]. . . .

Lacy argues the affidavit supporting the application for the warrant was insufficient to establish probable cause because it rested on stale information and demonstrated only that he "might have attempted to order" obscene pictures.

Evidence the defendant has ordered child pornography is insufficient to establish probable cause to believe the defendant possesses such pornography. However, the affidavit stated Lacy downloaded at least two GIFs depicting minors engaged in sexual activity from BAMSE, providing sufficient evidence Lacy actually received computerized visual depictions of child pornography. . . .

Lacy also argues the warrant was too general because it authorized the seizure of his entire computer system.[40] Lacy relies primarily upon *United States*

---

[40] A warrant must describe the specific place to be searched and person or things to be seized "with particularity sufficient to prevent 'a general, exploratory rummaging in a person's belongings.'" The warrant need only be "reasonably specific, rather than elaborately detailed, and

v. Kow, 58 F.3d 423 (9th Cir.1995), in which we invalidated a warrant authorizing seizure of all the defendant's computer hardware and software, as well as "essentially all" of its "records . . . files, ledgers, and invoices." Unlike the affidavit in *Kow*, the affidavit in this case established probable cause to believe Lacy's entire computer system was "likely to evidence criminal activity." And while the warrant in *Kow* "contained no limits on which documents within each category could be seized or suggested how they related to specific criminal activity," the Lacy warrant contained objective limits to help officers determine which items they could seize — allowing seizure only of documents linked to BAMSE, for example.

Both warrants described the computer equipment itself in generic terms and subjected it to blanket seizure. However, this type of generic classification is acceptable "when a more precise description is not possible," and in this case no more specific description of the computer equipment sought was possible. The government knew Lacy had downloaded computerized visual depictions of child pornography, but did not know whether the images were stored on the hard drive or on one or more of his many computer disks. In the affidavit supporting the search warrant application, a Customs agent explained there was no way to specify what hardware and software had to be seized to retrieve the images accurately.

We conclude that Lacy's challenge to the district court's suppression ruling is without merit. . . .

NOTES & QUESTIONS

1. *The Scope of Computer Searches.* Several other courts have followed a similar approach as in *Lacy*, upholding generic warrants. In *United States v. Upham*, 168 F.3d 532 (1st Cir. 1999), the court reasoned: "A sufficient chance of finding some needles in the computer haystack was established by the probable-cause showing in the warrant application; and a search of a computer and co-located disks is not inherently more intrusive than the physical search of an entire house for a weapon or drugs." *See also United States v. Hay*, 231 F.3d 630 (9th Cir. 2000) (following *Lacy* and upholding a "generic" warrant application).[41]

   However, there are limits to the scope of a search of a computer. In *United States v. Carey*, 172 F.3d 1268 (10th Cir. 1999), an officer obtained a warrant to search a computer for records about illegal drug distribution. When the officer stumbled upon a pornographic file, he began to search for similar files. The court concluded that these actions amounted to an expansion of the scope of the search and would require the obtaining of a second warrant.

   In *United States v. Campos*, 221 F.3d 1143 (10th Cir. 2000), the defendant e-mailed two images of child pornography to a person he talked to in a

---

the required specificity varies depending on the circumstances of the case and the type of items involved." . . .

   [41] For more about computer searches, see Raphael Winnick, *Searches and Seizures of Computers and Computer Data*, 88 Harv. J.L. & Tech. 75 (1994).

chat room. The person informed the FBI, and the FBI obtained a warrant to search the defendant's home and computer. The agents seized the defendant's computer and a search revealed the two images of child pornography as well as six other images on child pornography. The defendant challenged the search as beyond the scope of the warrant because the agents "had grounds to search only for the two images that had been sent." However, the court rejected the defendant's contention, quoting from the FBI's explanation why it is not feasible to search only for particular computer files in one's home:

> . . . Computer storage devices . . . can store the equivalent of thousands of pages of information. Especially when the user wants to conceal criminal evidence, he often stores it in random order with deceptive file names. This requires searching authorities to examine all the stored data to determine whether it is included in the warrant. This sorting process can take weeks or months, depending on the volume of data stored, and it would be impractical to attempt this kind of data search on site. . . .
>
> Searching computer systems for criminal evidence is a highly technical process requiring expert skill and a properly controlled environment. The wide variety of computer hardware and software available requires even computer experts to specialize in some systems and applications, so it is difficult to know before a search which expert should analyze the system and its data. . . . Since computer evidence is extremely vulnerable to tampering or destruction (both from external sources or from destructive code embedded into the system as "booby trap"), the controlled environment of a laboratory is essential to its complete analysis. . . .

2. In *State v. Schroeder*, 613 N.W.2d 911 (Wis. App. 2000), a person called the police complaining that her name and telephone number had been posted on the Internet along with sexually suggestive comments. The police obtained a court order directing the Internet Service Provider to identify the individual who posted the information, and then obtained a warrant to enter the defendant's residence to seize his computer and gather evidence for crimes of online harassment and disorderly conduct. While executing the warrant, the officers discovered a CD-ROM that appeared to contain pornography, and an officer asked the defendant whether pornography would be on his computer. The defendant replied in the affirmative. The officer then asked whether child pornography would be on the computer and the defendant again said that there would be. The computer was sent to a state laboratory to search for evidence about online harassment. The officer informed the lab personnel that there might be child pornography on the computer, and that if such material were found, they should halt their search and contact the officer. The lab personnel did indeed find child pornography and contacted the officer. A court issued a second warrant authorizing the search for child pornography. This search resulted in the discovery of additional images of child pornography. The defendant contended that the government was actively looking for child pornography despite the fact that the warrant only permitted the search for evidence of harassment and disorderly conduct. The court held, however, that the computer search required that the lab personnel "systematically [go] through and

[open] user-created files, regardless of their names." Because the initial discovery of child pornography occurred during the course of systematically opening files, the evidence was in "plain view":

> [H]is initial discovery of child pornography was when he opened a file and saw a nude picture of a child pop up on the screen. It was in plain view. This was no different than an investigator opening a drawer while searching for drugs and seeing a nude picture of a child on top of a pile of socks.

3. ***Shared Computers.*** In *Trulock v. Freeh*, 275 F.3d 391 (4th Cir. 2001), Notra Trulock and Linda Conrad shared a computer but maintained separate files protected by passwords. They did not know each other's password and could not access each other's files. When FBI officials, without a warrant, asked to search and seize the computer, Conrad consented. The court held that the FBI could not search Trulock's files since Trulock had not consented:

> Consent to search in the absence of a warrant may, in some circumstances, be given by a person other than the target of the search. Two criteria must be met in order for third party consent to be effective. First, the third party must have authority to consent to the search. Second, the third party's consent must be voluntary. . . .
>
> We conclude that, based on the facts in the complaint, Conrad lacked authority to consent to the search of Trulock's files. Conrad and Trulock both used a computer located in Conrad's bedroom and each had joint access to the hard drive. Conrad and Trulock, however, protected their personal files with passwords; Conrad did not have access to Trulock's passwords. Although Conrad had authority to consent to a general search of the computer, her authority did not extend to Trulock's password-protected files.

UNITED STATES V. HAMBRICK

55 F. Supp. 2d 504 (W.D. Va. 1999)

MICHAEL, J. Defendant Scott M. Hambrick seeks the suppression of all evidence obtained from his Internet Service Provider ("ISP"), MindSpring, and seeks the suppression of all evidence seized from his home pursuant to a warrant issued by this court. For the reasons discussed below, the court denies the defendant's motion.

On March 14, 1998, J. L. McLaughlin, a police officer with the Keene, New Hampshire Police Department, connected to the Internet and entered a chat room called "Gay dads 4 sex." McLaughlin's screen name was "Rory14." In this chat room, Detective McLaughlin encountered someone using the screen name "Blowuinva." Based on a series of online conversations between "Rory14" (Det. McLaughlin) and "Blowuinva," McLaughlin concluded that "Blowuinva" sought to entice a fourteen-year-old boy to leave New Hampshire and live with "Blowuinva." Because of the anonymity of the Internet, Detective McLaughlin did not know the true identity of the person with whom he was communicating nor did he know where "Blowuinva" lived. "Blowuinva" had only identified himself as "Brad."

To determine Blowuinva's identity and location, McLaughlin obtained a New Hampshire state subpoena that he served on Blowuinva's Internet Service Provider, MindSpring, located in Atlanta, Georgia. The New Hampshire state subpoena requested that MindSpring produce "any records pertaining to the billing and/or user records documenting the subject using your services on March 14th, 1998 at 1210HRS (EST) using Internet Protocol Number 207.69.169.92." MindSpring complied with the subpoena. On March 20, 1998, MindSpring supplied McLaughlin with defendant's name, address, credit card number, e-mail address, home and work telephone numbers, fax number, and the fact that the Defendant's account was connected to the Internet at the Internet Protocol (IP) address.

A justice of the peace, Richard R. Richards, signed the New Hampshire state subpoena. Mr. Richards is not only a New Hampshire justice of the peace, but he is also a detective in the Keene Police Department, Investigation Division. Mr. Richards did not issue the subpoena pursuant to a matter pending before himself, any other judicial officer, or a grand jury. At the hearing on the defendant's motion, the government conceded the invalidity of the warrant. The question before this court, therefore, is whether the court must suppress the information obtained from MindSpring, and all that flowed from it, because the government failed to obtain a proper subpoena. . . .

. . . [Under *Katz v. United States*,] the Fourth Amendment applies only where: (1) the citizen has manifested a subjective expectation of privacy, and (2) the expectation is one that society accepts as "objectively reasonable." . . . Applying the first part of the *Katz* analysis, Mr. Hambrick asserts that he had a subjective expectation of privacy in the information that MindSpring gave to the government. However, resolution of this matter hinges on whether Mr. Hambrick's expectation is one that society accepts as "objectively reasonable."

The objective reasonableness prong of the privacy test is ultimately a value judgment and a determination of how much privacy we should have as a society. In making this constitutional determination, this court must employ a sort of risk analysis, asking whether the individual affected should have expected the material at issue to remain private. The defendant asserts that the Electronic Communications Privacy Act ("ECPA") "legislatively resolves" this question. . . .

. . . The information obtained through the use of the government's invalid subpoena consisted of the defendant's name, address, social security number, credit card number, and certification that the defendant was connected to the Internet on March 14, 1998. Thus, this information falls within the provisions of Title II of the ECPA.

The government may require that an ISP provide stored communications and transactional records only if (1) it obtains a warrant issued under the Federal Rules of Criminal Procedure or state equivalent, or (2) it gives prior notice to the online subscriber and then issues a subpoena or receives a court order authorizing disclosure of the information in question. *See* 18 U.S.C. §2703(a)(c)(1)(B). When an ISP discloses stored communications or transactional records to a government entity without the requisite authority, the aggrieved customer's sole remedy is damages.

Although Congress is willing to recognize that individuals have some degree of privacy in the stored data and transactional records that their ISPs retain, the ECPA is hardly a legislative determination that this expectation of privacy is one that rises to the level of "reasonably objective" for Fourth Amendment purposes. Despite its concern for privacy, Congress did not provide for suppression where a party obtains stored data or transactional records in violation of the Act. Additionally, the ECPA's concern for privacy extends only to government invasions of privacy. ISPs are free to turn stored data and transactional records over to nongovernmental entities. See 18 U.S.C. § 2703(c)(1)(A) ("[A] provider of electronic communication service or remote computing service may disclose a record or other information pertaining to a subscriber to or customer of such service . . . to any person other than a governmental entity."). For Fourth Amendment purposes, this court does not find that the ECPA has legislatively determined that an individual has a reasonable expectation of privacy in his name, address, social security number, credit card number, and proof of Internet connection. The fact that the ECPA does not proscribe turning over such information to private entities buttresses the conclusion that the ECPA does not create a reasonable expectation of privacy in that information. This, however, does not end the court's inquiry. This court must determine, within the constitutional framework that the Supreme Court has established, whether Mr. Hambrick's subjective expectation of privacy is one that society is willing to recognize.

To have any interest in privacy, there must be some exclusion of others. To have a reasonable expectation of privacy under the Supreme Court's risk-analysis approach to the Fourth Amendment, two conditions must be met: (1) the data must not be knowingly exposed to others, and (2) the Internet service provider's ability to access the data must not constitute a disclosure. In *Katz*, the Supreme Court expressly held that "what a person knowingly exposes to the public, even in his home or office, is not a subject of Fourth Amendment protection." Further, the Court "consistently has held that a person has no legitimate expectation of privacy in information he voluntarily turns over to third parties." *Smith v. Maryland*, 442 U.S. 735, 743-44 (1979). . . .

When Scott Hambrick surfed the Internet using the screen name "Blowuinva," he was not a completely anonymous actor. It is true that an average member of the public could not easily determine the true identity of "Blowuinva." Nevertheless, when Mr. Hambrick entered into an agreement to obtain Internet access from MindSpring, he knowingly revealed his name, address, credit card number, and telephone number to MindSpring and its employees. Mr. Hambrick also selected the screen name "Blowuinva." When the defendant selected his screen name it became tied to his true identity in all MindSpring records. MindSpring employees had ready access to these records in the normal course of MindSpring's business, for example, in the keeping of its records for billing purposes, and nothing prevented MindSpring from revealing this information to nongovernmental actors.[42] Also, there is nothing in the record to suggest that there was a restrictive agreement between the defendant and MindSpring that would limit the right of MindSpring to reveal

---

[42] It is apparently common for ISPs to provide certain information that Mr. Hambrick alleges to be private to marketing firms and other organizations interested in soliciting business from Internet users.

the defendant's personal information to nongovernmental entities. Where such dissemination of information to nongovernment entities is not prohibited, there can be no reasonable expectation of privacy in that information.

Although not dispositive to the outcome of this motion, it is important to note that the court's decision does not leave members of cybersociety without privacy protection. Under the ECPA, Internet Service Providers are civilly liable when they reveal subscriber information or the contents of stored communications to the government without first requiring a warrant, court order, or subpoena. Here, nothing suggests that MindSpring had any knowledge that the facially valid subpoena submitted to it was in fact an invalid subpoena. Had MindSpring revealed the information at issue in this case to the government without first requiring a subpoena, apparently valid on its face, Mr. Hambrick could have sued MindSpring. This is a powerful deterrent protecting privacy in the online world and should not be taken lightly. . . .

NOTES & QUESTIONS

1. Note that this is not a federal wiretap law case. Hambrick makes a very interesting argument. He argues that under the *Katz* reasonable expectation of privacy test, the ECPA "legislatively resolves" that there is a reasonable expectation of privacy in information that Mindspring gave to the government. To what extent should federal wiretap law form the basis for whether there is a reasonable expectation of privacy under the Fourth Amendment?
2. Mindspring couldn't release information to the government without a warrant or subpoena or else it would face civil liability. However, in this case, the government presented Mindspring with a subpoena that Mindspring had no knowledge was invalid. Therefore, it is unlikely that Mindspring would be liable. If the court is correct in its conclusion that 18 U.S.C. § 2703(a)(c)(1)(B) of the ECPA only applies to the conduct of Internet Service Providers, then is there any remedy against Officer Richards's blatantly false subpoena? Could a police officer obtain a person's Internet subscriber information by falsifying a subpoena and escape without any civil liability or exclusionary rule?

UNITED STATES v. KENNEDY

81 F. Supp. 2d 1103 (D. Kan. 2000)

BELOT, J. . . . On July 2, 1999, Steven Idelman was working as a customer support specialist for Road Runner, a high speed Internet service provider. At approximately 9:00 P.M., Idelman received an anonymous phone call from a still-unidentified male ("the caller"). The caller told Idelman that he was at a friend's house, scanning other computers through the Internet and had viewed images of child pornography on a computer the caller believed to be serviced by Road Runner. The caller told Idelman the IP address of the computer from which the images were viewed, 24.94.200.54,[43] and the directory

---

[43]The IP, or Internet Protocol, address is unique to a specific computer. Only one computer would be assigned a particular IP address.

and file names in which the images were located.[44] The caller did not say that he was a law enforcement officer or that he was directed to view the computer's files by any law enforcement officer. The caller did not ask Idelman to call the police.

Shortly after the anonymous call, Idelman went to a computer and accessed the IP address given to him by the caller. His purpose was to determine if what the caller told him was correct. He located the computer with the IP address 24.94.200.54 and the directory tree and files mentioned by the caller. Idelman viewed two images located within those files. One of the images depicted two boys, whom Idelman estimated to be approximately eight or nine years old, posed in a sexual nature. Idelman then sent an e-mail to his supervisor, Anna Madden, describing the anonymous phone call and the results of his search of the computer with IP address 24.94.200.54.

On July 6, 1999, Kerry Jones, a network engineer for Road Runner, received an e-mail from Anna Madden asking him to research the owner of the Road Runner account connecting to the computer with the IP address 24.94.200.54. Jones was able to determine that the account was assigned to Rosemary D. Kennedy. Mr. Jones was able to determine that the account was assigned to the same IP address on July 2, 1999. Believing that the customer service agreement between Road Runner and the account holder authorized him to search a computer's files for offensive material, Jones then viewed the files on the computer's hard drive. The files depicted images of boys, whom Jones estimated to be approximately 10 to 13 years old, engaged in sexual activity. Jones then printed out an image of the computer's directory tree in which the files with offensive material were located.

That same day, after consulting with Road Runner's corporate attorney, Scott Petrie, the manager of Road Runner, made the decision to contact law enforcement authorities. Kerry Jones contacted the Exploited Children's Unit of the Wichita Police Department, but his phone call was not returned. Road Runner then contacted Special Agent Leslie Earl of the FBI. Special Agent Earl was informed by Road Runner that the FBI would need to obtain a court order for it to be able to supply the FBI with any subscriber information.

The United States Attorney's Office then applied to a United States magistrate judge for an order directing Road Runner to disclose subscriber information related to IP address 24.94.200.54. . . .

The magistrate judge issued an order, which was presented to Road Runner personnel, who provided the FBI with the following information:

> The subscriber whose computer used I.P. address 24.94.200.54 on July 2, 1999, at 11:49 P.M. was Rosemay (sic) D. Kennedy of 9120 Harvest Court, Wichita, Kansas, telephone 316-722-6593. Two users were listed for that account: RKENNEDY@KSCable.COM and KENNEDYM@KSCable.Com. The account had been active since June 7, 1999.

Special Agent Earl next went to the house located at 9120 Harvest Court in Wichita, Kansas. He observed a Chrysler Sebring parked in the driveway. A

---

[44]The caller was able to view the computer's files because the computer with IP address 24.94.200.54 had its print and file sharing mechanism turned on, allowing other computers to view its files over the Internet.

records check with the Kansas Department of Motor Vehicles revealed that the car was registered to Michael R. Kennedy. Special Agent Earl then called the phone number given to the government by Road Runner. A person identifying himself as Michael Kennedy answered the phone.

In initiating the phone call, Special Agent Earl asked Kennedy if he was satisfied with his Road Runner cable modem Internet service. [Kennedy confirmed his address and stated he was the primary user of his Internet service. The agents went to Kennedy's home to execute the search warrant and interviewed him. The Defendant confessed to possessing child pornography, and the Defendant was subsequently indicted and convicted for receipt of child pornography.] . . .

Defendant first argues the subscriber information the FBI received from Road Runner should be suppressed. Defendant argues that the information was received in violation of the Electronic Communications Privacy Act and the Cable Communications Policy Act. Defendant further argues that all evidence obtained as a result of the illegal attainment of defendant's subscriber information should be suppressed as fruit of the poisonous tree. Although the court finds that the ECPA was violated, suppression of the evidence is not a remedy for such a violation. Because suppression is likewise not a remedy provided for under the CCPA, the court need not determine whether or not that statute was implicated.

18 U.S.C. §§ 2701 et seq. regulates the disclosure of electronic communications and subscriber information. Section 2703(c)(1)(B) states that "[a] provider of electronic communication service . . . shall disclose a record or other information pertaining to a subscriber to or customer of such service . . . to a governmental entity only when the governmental entity . . . (ii) obtains a court order for such disclosure under subsection (d) of this section." Subsection (d) sets forth the requirements of such a court order:

> (d) Requirements for court order. — A court order for disclosure under subsection (b) or (c) . . . shall issue only if the governmental entity offers specific and articulable facts showing that there are reasonable grounds to believe that the contents of a wire or electronic communication, or the records or other information sought, are relevant and material to an ongoing criminal investigation.

Defendant argues the government's application did not state specific and articulable facts, but mere conclusions. The government responds that at the time of the application, it did not know the identity of the subscriber, whether the subscriber was the person using the computer to store illegal material and how much child pornography was held by the computer. The government argues that the information it had at the time was minimal and the purpose of obtaining the order was to investigate the subscriber information completely. . . .

. . . The government's application merely listed that the subscriber information connected to IP address 24.94.200.54 would possibly relate to an on-going criminal investigation. In accordance with 18 U.S.C. § 2703(d), the government should have articulated more specific facts such as how the government obtained the information it did have at the time and how this information lead the agents to believe that the attainment of the subscriber information of this particular IP address would assist in the investigation. The government's application for a section 2703(d) order did not meet the requirements of the statute.

Nonetheless, the government correctly points out that even if Road Runner divulged defendant's subscriber information pursuant to a court order based on an inadequate government application, suppression is not a remedy contemplated under the ECPA. The statute specifically allows for civil damages and criminal punishment for violations of the ECPA, see 18 U.S.C. §§ 2707, 2701(b), but speaks nothing about the suppression of information in a court proceeding. Instead, Congress clearly intended for suppression not to be an option for a defendant whose electronic communications have been intercepted in violation of the ECPA. The statute specifically states that "[t]he remedies and sanctions described in this chapter are the only judicial remedies and sanctions for nonconstitutional violations of this chapter." 18 U.S.C. § 2708.

Defendant's constitutional rights were not violated when Road Runner divulged his subscriber information to the government. Defendant has not demonstrated an objectively reasonable legitimate expectation of privacy in his subscriber information. On the contrary, the evidence is that defendant's computer had its sharing mechanism turned on. The only reasonable inference is that defendant had done so. "[W]hat a person knowingly exposes to the public, even in his home or office, is not a subject of Fourth Amendment protection." *Katz v. United States*, 389 U.S. 347, 351 (1967). "[A] person has no legitimate expectation of privacy in information he voluntarily turns over to third parties." *Smith v. Maryland*, 442 U.S. 735, 743-44 (1979). When defendant entered into an agreement with Road Runner for Internet service, he knowing revealed all information connected to the IP address 24.94.200.54. He cannot now claim to have a Fourth Amendment privacy interest in his subscriber information. . . .

Defendant argues that the initial warrantless searches of his computer files were done by government actors and were therefore in violation of his Fourth Amendment rights. The searches he refers to are those performed by the anonymous caller and Road Runner personnel. He asks this court to suppress all evidence as fruit of this poisonous tree. Because the court finds that these searches were done entirely by private individuals, the searches were not within the purview of the Fourth Amendment.

The Fourth Amendment's protection against unreasonable searches and seizures "proscribe[es] only governmental action; it is wholly inapplicable 'to a search or seizure, even an unreasonable one, effected by a private individual not acting as an agent of the Government or with the participation or knowledge of any governmental official.'" The Tenth Circuit applies a two part test in determining when a search by a private individual becomes government action: "1) whether the government knew of and acquiesced in the intrusive conduct, and 2) whether the party performing the search intended to assist law enforcement efforts or to further his own ends." *Pleasant v. Lovell*, 876 F.2d 787, 797 (10th Cir. 1989). Both inquiries must be answered in the affirmative before an otherwise private search will be deemed governmental for Fourth Amendment purposes.

In this case, the first requirement is not met. There is no evidence to support defendant's allegation that the government either knew of or acquiesced in either the caller's or the Road Runner personnel's search of defendant's computer. . . .

CARNIVORE

Since 1998, the FBI has been using a hardware and software mechanism called "Carnivore" to intercept people's e-mail and instant messaging information from their Internet Service Providers (ISPs). The existence of Carnivore came to the attention of the public in a *Wall Street Journal* article in 2000. After obtaining judicial authorization, the FBI installs Carnivore by connecting a computer directly to the ISP's server and initiating the program. Carnivore's software is a "packet sniffer" program. When an e-mail is sent over the Internet, it is broken into separate "packets" of data. Each packet is labeled with codes that identify the sender and the recipient. When the packets arrive at their destination, they are reassembled. After locating the packets pertaining to a particular suspect, Carnivore can then scan them for content, effectively searching through the suspect's e-mail.

Carnivore is capable of analyzing the entire traffic of an ISP, although the FBI maintains it is only used to search for the e-mails of a suspect. The program filters out the e-mail messages of ISP subscribers who are not the subject of the investigation, but to do so, it must scan the e-mail headers that identify the senders and recipients. The FBI likens e-mail headers to the information captured by a pen register, a device that registers the phone numbers a person dials. Recall that in *Smith v. Maryland*, 442 U.S. 735 (1979), the Court held that the Fourth Amendment does not apply to searches of pen registers because an individual does not have a reasonable expectation of privacy in the numbers she dials from her telephone.

However, Carnivore can be programmed to search through the entire text of all e-mails, to capture e-mails with certain key words. In this way, Carnivore resembles a wiretap. Recall that under federal wiretap law, judicial approval for obtaining pen register information only requires a certification that "the information likely to be obtained by such installation and use is relevant to an ongoing investigation." 18 U.S.C. §3123. In contrast, judicial approval of a wiretap requires a full panoply of requirements under Title I, including a showing of probable cause.

Carnivore raises at least two significant privacy concerns. First, in order to obtain information about a particular suspect, Carnivore must access certain information (sender/recipient) about all other individuals. In this way, Carnivore is akin to the FBI stationing an agent in a post office to examine the addresses on each envelope and picking out the ones addressed to the suspect. However, according to the FBI, Carnivore scans through e-mail in nanoseconds, and no agent reads or examines any e-mail. Second, the FBI has a significant amount of power to abuse Carnivore, since it can be programmed to scan through everybody's e-mail.

In August 2000, the Electronic Privacy Information Center (EPIC) filed a Freedom of Information Act request seeking documents pertaining to Carnivore. Documents obtained by EPIC revealed that in fact Carnivore "could reliably capture and archive all unfiltered traffic."[45] Responding to public displeasure about Carnivore and the secretive way it had been used, the Justice Department asked a review team from the Illinois Institute of Technology Research Institute (IITRI) to examine whether Carnivore sufficiently protected the privacy of nontargets of an investigation.

To eliminate the negative associations with the term "Carnivore," the device was renamed "DCS1000." Many members of Congress viewed Carnivore with great suspicion. Congress held hearings over the summer of 2000 pertaining to Carnivore and several bills have been proposed to halt or limit the use of Carnivore.

The anti-Carnivore sentiment abruptly ended after the September 11, 2001, World Trade Center and Pentagon terrorist attacks. Section 216 of the USA-PATRIOT Act of 2001, in anticipation of the use of Carnivore, required reports on the use of Carnivore to be filed with a court. These reports, filed under seal, require: (1) the names of the officers using the device; (2) when the device was installed, used, and removed; (3) the configuration of the device; and (4) the information collected by the device. 18 U.S.C. § 3133(a)(3).

Does Carnivore comport with the Fourth Amendment?[46] Do individuals have a reasonable expectation of privacy in their e-mail addresses? Do individuals have a reasonable expectation of privacy in the contents of their e-mails, which are often stored on the server of one's Internet Service Provider?

Consider E. Judson Jennnigs:

> . . . Carnivore is a mere prototype, and could very easily evolve with great speed into a system with enormous capacities for data monitoring. It is disturbing that the IITRI study, with its focus on technical issues, did not consider the strong likelihood that it was looking at the cub rather than the fully mature creature. . . .
>
> The FBI claims that Carnivore can satisfy the specificity requirements [of the Fourth Amendment] through a combination of measures. First, the warrant itself will limit the scope of the intercept. Second, Carnivore minimizes the seizure by immediately filtering out and ignoring all data packets that don't meet the specified criteria for sender, recipient, or content. Third, intercepted documents that do not satisfy the search warrant criteria are deleted by the case agent. However, Carnivore does not actually behave in the way the FBI claims it does. It is true that the search warrant can specify an Internet address or addresses that may be collected. However, the intercept can extend to any transmission either from or to the target address, so that, for example, the several thousand members of a discussion group will have their messages intercepted just because they are written to or from a group member who is also a target. Moreover, IITRI has documented that whenever a Carnivore operation attempts to combine addresses with content criteria (i.e., text string searches),

---

[45] EPIC Carnivore FOIA Documents, available at *http://www.epic.org/privacy/carnivore/foia_documents.html.*

[46] For a discussion of the applicability of the Fourth Amendment to a search of the entire Internet, see Michael Adler, Note, *Cyberspace, General Searches, and Digital Contraband: The Fourth Amendment and the Net-Wide Search,* 105 Yale L.J. 1093 (1996).

the string search criteria is ignored and all documents are kept. The only remedy for this drastic over-inclusion is the *case agent*, who, under current FBI procedures, has sole access to the information which is kept and stored to the Zip disks, and who will remove those Zip disks from the Carnivore computer, and then "immediately" review their contents and delete the information that does not fit the requirements of the warrant. Unless the courts treat Carnivore searches as *sui generis*, it is difficult to reconcile these described procedures with the decisions that have analyzed the specificity requirements in more traditional contexts.[47]

UNITED STATES V. SCARFO

180 F. Supp. 2d 572 (D.N.J. 2001)

POLITAN, J. . . . Acting pursuant to federal search warrants, the F.B.I. on January 15, 1999, entered Scarfo and Paolercio's business office, Merchant Services of Essex County, to search for evidence of an illegal gambling and loansharking operation. During their search of Merchant Services, the F.B.I. came across a personal computer and attempted to access its various files. They were unable to gain entry to an encrypted file named "Factors."

Suspecting the "Factors" file contained evidence of an illegal gambling and loansharking operation, the F.B.I. returned to the location and, pursuant to two search warrants, installed what is known as a "Key Logger System" ("KLS") on the computer and/or computer keyboard in order to decipher the passphrase to the encrypted file, thereby gaining entry to the file. The KLS records the keystrokes an individual enters on a personal computer's keyboard. The government utilized the KLS in order to "catch" Scarfo's passphrases to the encrypted file while he was entering them onto his keyboard. Scarfo's personal computer features a modem for communication over telephone lines and he possesses an America Online account. The F.B.I. obtained the passphrase to the "Factors" file and retrieved what is alleged to be incriminating evidence.

On June 21, 2000, a federal grand jury returned a three count indictment against the Defendants charging them with gambling and loansharking. The Defendant Scarfo then filed his motion for discovery and to suppress the evidence recovered from his computer. After oral argument was heard on July 30, 2001, the Court ordered additional briefing by the parties. In an August 7, 2001, Letter Opinion and Order, this Court expressed serious concerns over whether the government violated the wiretap statute in utilizing the KLS on Scarfo's computer. Specifically, the Court expressed concern over whether the KLS may have operated during periods when Scarfo (or any other user of his personal computer) was communicating via modem over telephone lines, thereby un-

---

[47] E. Judson Jennings, *Carnivore: U.S. Government Surveillance of Internet Transmissions*, 6 Va. J. L. & Tech. 10, 49, 96 (2001). For more background about Carnivore, see Thomas R. McCarthy, *Don't Fear Carnivore: It Won't Devour Individual Privacy*, 66 Mo. L. Rev. 827 (2001); Manton M. Grier, Jr., *The Software Formerly Known as "Carnivore": When Does E-Mail Surveillance Encroach upon a Reasonable Expectation of Privacy?*, 52 S.C. L. Rev. 875 (2001); Maricela Segura, Note, *Is Carnivore Devouring Your Privacy?*, 75 S. Cal. L. Rev. 231 (2001).

lawfully intercepting wire communications without having applied for a wiretap pursuant to Title III, 18 U.S.C. §2510.

As a result of these concerns, on August 7, 2001, this Court ordered the United States to file with the Court a report explaining fully how the KLS device functions and describing the KLS technology and how it works vis-à-vis the computer modem, Internet communications, e-mail and all other uses of a computer. In light of the government's grave concern over the national security implications such a revelation might raise, the Court permitted the United States to submit any additional evidence which would provide particular and specific reasons how and why disclosure of the KLS would jeopardize both ongoing and future domestic criminal investigations and national security interests.

The United States responded by filing a request for modification of this Court's August 7, 2001, Letter Opinion and Order so as to comply with the procedures set forth in the Classified Information Procedures Act, Title 18, United States Code, Appendix III, § 1 *et seq.* ("CIPA"). [The FBI contended that a detailed disclosure of how the KLS worked would negatively affect national security and that this information was classified. After in in camera, ex parte hearing with several officials from the Attorney General's office and the FBI, the court granted the government's request not to release the details of how KLS functioned. Instead, the government would provide Scarfo and his attorneys with an unclassified summary about how KLS worked. Based on that summary, Scarfo contended that the KLS violated the Fourth Amendment because the KLS had the capability of collecting data on all of his keystrokes, not merely those of his passphrase.]

. . . Where a search warrant is obtained, the Fourth Amendment requires a certain modicum of particularity in the language of the warrant with respect to the area and items to be searched and/or seized. The particularity requirement exists so that law enforcement officers are constrained from undertaking a boundless and exploratory rummaging through one's personal property. . . .

That the KLS certainly recorded keystrokes typed into Scarfo's keyboard *other* than the searched-for passphrase is of no consequence. This does not, as Scarfo argues, convert the limited search for the passphrase into a general exploratory search. During many lawful searches, police officers may not know the exact nature of the incriminating evidence sought until they stumble upon it. Just like searches for incriminating documents in a closet or filing cabinet, it is true that during a search for a passphrase "some innocuous [items] will be at least cursorily perused in order to determine whether they are among those [items] to be seized."

Hence, "no tenet of the Fourth Amendment prohibits a search merely because it cannot be performed with surgical precision." Where proof of wrongdoing depends upon documents or computer passphrases whose precise nature cannot be known in advance, law enforcement officers must be afforded the leeway to wade through a potential morass of information in the target location to find the particular evidence which is properly specified in the warrant. . . . Accordingly, Scarfo's claim that the warrants were written and executed as general warrants is rejected. . . .

The principal mystery surrounding this case was whether the KLS intercepted a wire communication in violation of the wiretap statute by recording keystrokes of e-mail or other communications made over a telephone or cable line while the modem operated. These are the only conceivable wire communications which might emanate from Scarfo's computer and potentially fall under the wiretap statute. . . .

The KLS, which is the exclusive property of the F.B.I., was devised by F.B.I. engineers using previously developed techniques in order to obtain a target's key and key-related information. As part of the investigation into Scarfo's computer, the F.B.I. "did not install and operate any component which would search for and record data entering or exiting the computer from the transmission pathway through the modem attached to the computer." Neither did the F.B.I. "install or operate any KLS component which would search for or record any fixed data stored within the computer."

Recognizing that Scarfo's computer had a modem and thus was capable of transmitting electronic communications via the modem, the F.B.I. configured the KLS to avoid intercepting electronic communications typed on the keyboard and simultaneously transmitted in real time via the communication ports. . . . Hence, when the modem was operating, the KLS did not record keystrokes. It was designed to prohibit the capture of keyboard keystrokes whenever the modem operated. Since Scarfo's computer possessed no other means of communicating with another computer save for the modem, the KLS did not intercept any wire communications. Accordingly, the Defendants' motion to suppress evidence for violation of Title III is denied. . . .

NOTES & QUESTIONS

1. Consider the following argument by Raymond Ku:

> . . . By monitoring what an individual enters into her computer as she enters it, the government has the ability to monitor thought itself. Keystroke-recording devices allow the government to record formless thoughts and ideas an individual never intended to share with anyone, never intended to save on the hard drive and never intended to preserve for future reference in any form. The devices also allow the government to record thoughts and ideas the individual may have rejected the moment they were typed. . . .
>
> Similarly, before authorizing such an intrusive form of surveillance, the government should demonstrate that it is not technologically feasible to limit the surveillance. Why was the keystroke-recording device not programmed to record only after Scarfo launched his encryption program, thus minimizing what was recorded? Technology is not fixed, and bugs can be made into many shapes and sizes. When possible, technology should be adapted to conform to society's values, and not the other way around. . . .
>
> . . . [T]he techniques used in the Scarfo case bring us closer to a world in which the only privacy we are guaranteed is the privacy found in the confines of our own minds. While there will almost certainly be those who would accept even greater intrusions on privacy (including the permanent installation of government-monitored cameras within their homes if it

helped fight crime), I believe that the accompanying loss of freedom and privacy exemplified by this case is far too precious a price to pay.[48]

2. Do you agree with the court that the fact that the warrant comprehensively lists all of the types of items to be searched satisfies the Fourth Amendment's particularity requirement?

3. *Old Technologies in New Bottles?* A common defense of new technological surveillance devices is that they are analogous to existing technologies. Carnivore can be likened to pen registers; the keystroke monitor in the Scarfo case can be analogized to a bug. To what extent are these analogies apt? Are new surveillance technologies simply old forms of surveillance in new bottles? Or is there something different involved? If so, what is new with these technologies and how ought they be regulated?

4. *Magic Lantern.* The FBI has developed technology through which a keystroke logging device can be installed into a person's computer through a computer virus that is e-mailed to the suspect's computer. The virus keeps track of keystrokes and secretly transmits the information to the government. Thus, the government can install a keystroke logging device without ever having to physically enter one's office or home. Recall your Fourth Amendment analysis of Carnivore. How does Magic Lantern differ with respect to its Fourth Amendment implications? How does your Fourth Amendment analysis of Magic Lantern differ from that of the keystroke logging device in *Scarfo*?

2. STATUTORY LIMITATIONS

McVEIGH v. COHEN

983 F. Supp. 215 (D.D.C. 1998)

SPORKIN, J. . . . Plaintiff Timothy R. McVeigh, who bears no relation to the Oklahoma City bombing defendant, seeks to enjoin the United States Navy from discharging him under the statutory policy colloquially known as "Don't Ask, Don't Tell, Don't Pursue." See 10 U.S.C. § 654 ("new policy"). In the course of investigating his sexual orientation, the Plaintiff contends that the Defendants violated his rights under the Electronic Communications Privacy Act ("ECPA"), 18 U.S.C. § 2701 et seq., the Administrative Procedure Act ("APA") 5 U.S.C. § 706, the Department's own policy, and the Fourth and Fifth Amendments of the U.S. Constitution. Absent an injunction, the Plaintiff avers that he will suffer irreparable injury from the discharge, even if he were ultimately to prevail on the merits of his claims.

The Plaintiff, Senior Chief Timothy R. McVeigh, is a highly decorated seventeen-year veteran of the United States Navy who has served honorably and continuously since he was nineteen years old. At the time of the Navy's decision to discharge him, he was the senior-most enlisted man aboard the United States nuclear submarine U.S.S. Chicago.

---

[48] Raymond Ku, *Think Twice Before You Type*, 163 N.J.L.J. 747 (Feb. 19, 2001).

On September 2, 1997, Ms. Helen Hajne, a civilian Navy volunteer, received an electronic mail ("email") message through the America Online Service ("AOL") regarding the toy-drive that she was coordinating for the Chicago crew members' children. The message box stated that it came from the alias "boysrch," but the text of the email was signed by a "Tim." Through an option available to AOL subscribers, the volunteer searched through the "member profile directory" to find the member profile for this sender. The directory specified that "boysrch" was an AOL subscriber named Tim who lived in Honolulu, Hawaii, worked in the military, and identified his marital status as "gay." Although the profile included some telling interests such as "collecting pics of other young studs" and "boy watching," it did not include any further identifying information such as full name, address, or phone number. . . .

Ms. Hajne proceeded to forward the email and directory profile to her husband, who, like Plaintiff, was also a noncommissioned officer aboard the U.S.S. Chicago. The material eventually found its way to Commander John Mickey, the captain of the ship and Plaintiff's commanding officer. In turn, Lieutenant Karin S. Morean, the ship's principal legal adviser and a member of the Judge Advocate General's ("JAG") Corps was called in to investigate the matter. By this point, the Navy suspected the "Tim" who authored the email might be Senior Chief Timothy McVeigh. Before she spoke to the Plaintiff and without a warrant or court order, Lieutenant Morean requested a Navy paralegal on her staff, Legalman First Class Joseph M. Kaiser, to contact AOL and obtain information from the service that could "connect" the screen name "boysrch" and accompanying user profile to McVeigh. Legalman Kaiser called AOL's toll-free customer service number and talked to a representative at technical services. Legalman Kaiser did not identify himself as a Naval serviceman. According to his testimony at the administrative hearing, he stated that he was "a third party in receipt of a fax sheet and wanted to confirm the profile sheet, [and] who it belonged to." The AOL representative affirmatively identified Timothy R. McVeigh as the customer in question.

Upon verification from AOL, Lieutenant Morean notified Senior Chief McVeigh that the Navy had obtained "some indication[ ] that he made a statement of homosexuality" in violation of § 654(b)(2) of "Don't Ask, Don't Tell." In light of the Uniform Code of Military Justice prohibition of sodomy and indecent acts, she then advised him of his right to remain silent. Shortly thereafter, in a memorandum dated September 22, 1997, the Navy advised Plaintiff that it was commencing an administrative discharge proceeding (termed by the Navy as an "administrative separation") against him. The reason stated was for "homosexual conduct, as evidenced by your statement that you are a homosexual."

On November 7, 1997, the Navy conducted an administrative discharge hearing before a three-member board. . . . At the conclusion of the administrative hearing, the board held that the government had sufficiently shown by a preponderance of the evidence that Senior Chief McVeigh had engaged in "homosexual conduct," a dischargeable offense. . . .

. . . Plaintiff is now scheduled to be discharged barring relief from this Court. . . .

... At its core, the Plaintiff's complaint is with the Navy's compliance, or lack thereof, with its new regulations under the "Don't Ask, Don't Tell, Don't Pursue" policy. Plaintiff contends that he did not "tell," as prescribed by the statute, but that nonetheless, the Navy impermissibly "asked" and zealously "pursued."

In short, this case raises the central issue of whether there is really a place for gay officers in the military under the new policy, "Don't Ask, Don't Tell, Don't Pursue." [This policy was adopted in 1993, and it prohibits the military from investigating sexual orientation unless there is "credible information" that a gay serviceman or servicewoman has the "propensity or intent to engage in homosexual acts."] ...

The facts as stated above clearly demonstrate that the Plaintiff did not openly express his homosexuality in a way that compromised this "Don't Ask, Don't Tell" policy. Suggestions of sexual orientation in a private, anonymous email account did not give the Navy a sufficient reason to investigate to determine whether to commence discharge proceedings. In its actions, the Navy violated its own regulations. An investigation into sexual orientation may be initiated "only when [a commander] has received credible information that there is a basis for discharge," such as when an officer "has said that he or she is a homosexual or bisexual, or made some other statement that indicates a propensity or intent to engage in homosexual acts." Yet in this case, there was no such credible information that Senior Chief McVeigh had made such a statement. Under the Guidelines, "credible information" requires more than "just a belief or suspicion" that a Service member has engaged in homosexual conduct. In the examples provided, the Guidelines state that "credible information" would exist in this case only if "a reliable person" stated that he or she directly observed or heard a Service member make an oral or written statement that "a reasonable person would believe was intended to convey the fact that he or she engages in or has a propensity or intent to engage in homosexual acts."

Clearly, the facts as stated above in this case demonstrate that there was no such "credible information." All that the Navy had was an email message and user profile that it suspected was authored by Plaintiff. Under the military regulation, that information alone should not have triggered any sort of investigation. When the Navy affirmatively took steps to confirm the identity of the email respondent, it violated the very essence of "Don't Ask, Don't Pursue" by launching a search and destroy mission. Even if the Navy had a factual basis to believe that the email message and profile were written by Plaintiff, it was unreasonable to infer that they were necessarily intended to convey a propensity or intent to engage in homosexual conduct. Particularly in the context of cyberspace, a medium of "virtual reality" that invites fantasy and affords anonymity, the comments attributed to McVeigh do not by definition amount to a declaration of homosexuality. At most, they express "an abstract preference or desire to engage in homosexual acts." Yet the regulations specify that a statement professing homosexuality so as to warrant investigation must declare "more than an abstract preference or desire"; they must indicate a likelihood actually to carry out homosexual acts.

The subsequent steps taken by the Navy in its "pursuit" of the Plaintiff were not only unauthorized under its policy, but likely illegal under the Electronic Communications Privacy Act of 1986 ("ECPA"). The ECPA, enacted by Congress to address privacy concerns on the Internet, allows the government to obtain information from an online service provider — as the Navy did in this instance from AOL — but only if a) it obtains a warrant issued under the Federal Rules of Criminal Procedure or state equivalent; or b) it gives prior notice to the online subscriber and then issues a subpoena or receives a court order authorizing disclosure of the information in question. See 18 U.S.C. § 2703(b)(1)(A)-(B), (c)(1)(B).

In soliciting and obtaining over the phone personal information about the Plaintiff from AOL, his private on-line service provider, the government in this case invoked neither of these provisions and thus failed to comply with the ECPA. From the record, it is undisputed that the Navy directly solicited by phone information from AOL. Lieutenant Karin S. Morean, the ship's principal legal counsel and a member of the JAG corp, personally requested Legalman Kaiser to contact AOL and obtain the identity of the subscriber. Without this information, Plaintiff credibly contends that the Navy could not have made the necessary connection between him and the user profile which was the sole basis on which to commence discharge proceedings.

The government, in its defense, contends that the Plaintiff cannot succeed on his ECPA claim. It argues that the substantive provision of the statute that Plaintiff cites, 18 U.S.C. § 2703(c)(1)(B), puts the obligation on the online service provider to withhold information from the government, and not vice versa. In support of its position, Defendants cite to the Fourth Circuit opinion in *Tucker v. Waddell*, 83 F.3d 688 (4th Cir. 1996), which held that § 2703(c)(1)(B) only prohibits the actions of online providers, not the government. Accordingly, Defendants allege that Plaintiff has no cause of action against the government on the basis of the ECPA. . . .

. . . [However,] Section 2703(c)(1)(B) must be read in the context of the statute as a whole. In comparison, § 2703(a) and (b) imposes on the government a reciprocal obligation to obtain a warrant or the like before requiring disclosure. It appears from the face of the statute that all of the subsections of § 2703 were intended to work in tandem to protect consumer privacy. Even if, however, the government ultimately proves to be right in its assessment of § 2703(c)(1)(B), the Plaintiff has plead § 2703(a) and (b) as alternative grounds for relief. In his claim that the government, at the least, solicited a violation of the ECPA by AOL, the Court finds that there is likely success on the merits with regard to this issue. The government knew, or should have known, that by turning over the information without a warrant, AOL was breaking the law. Yet the Navy, in this case, directly solicited the information anyway. What is most telling is that the Naval investigator did not identify himself when he made his request. While the government makes much of the fact that § 2703(c)(1)(B) does not provide a cause of action against the government, it is elementary that information obtained improperly can be suppressed where an individual's rights have been violated. In these days of "big brother," where through technology and otherwise the privacy interests of individuals from all walks of life are being ignored or marginalized, it is imperative that statutes explicitly protecting these rights be strictly observed. . . .

. . . With literally the entire world on the world-wide web, enforcement of the ECPA is of great concern to those who bare the most personal information about their lives in private accounts through the Internet. . . .

. . . Although Officer McVeigh did not publicly announce his sexual orientation, the Navy nonetheless impermissibly embarked on a search and "outing" mission.

NOTES & QUESTIONS

1. Recall the following statement in *McVeigh*: "The government knew, or should have known, that by turning over the information without a warrant, AOL was breaking the law. . . . While the government makes much of the fact that § 2703(c)(1)(B) does not provide a cause of action against the government, it is elementary that information obtained improperly can be suppressed where an individual's rights have been violated." Is this last statement correct? Title II does not have a suppression remedy; the court is creating a suppression remedy for Title II. Is this appropriate? Without a suppression remedy for the conduct of the government in this case, what would deter the government from violating Title II?
2. Is this case consistent with *Hambrick*? Does McVeigh have a reasonable expectation of privacy in his subscriber information maintained by AOL?

E. RECORDS OF INNOCENT PARTIES

Under the Fourth Amendment, a search warrant may be issued if there is probable cause to believe that there is incriminating evidence in the place to be searched. This is not limited to places owned or occupied by the criminal suspect. In certain instances, incriminating documents or things may be possessed by an innocent party. What if that innocent party is a journalist or news entity, and the search implicates First Amendment rights? Consider the following case:

ZURCHER V. THE STANFORD DAILY

436 U.S. 547 (1978)

[A demonstration at the Stanford University Hospital turned violent when police tried to force demonstrators to leave. A group of demonstrators attacked and injured nine police officers. The officers were able to identify only two of the assailants. The *Stanford Daily*, a student newspaper, published articles and photographs about the incident. The District Attorney obtained a search warrant to search the *Daily*'s offices for negatives, film, and pictures about the incident. After the search, the *Daily* brought suit under 42 U.S.C. § 1983, alleging that the search was unconstitutional.]

WHITE, J. . . . The issue here is how the Fourth Amendment is to be construed and applied to the "third party" search, the recurring situation where state authorities have probable cause to believe that fruits, instrumentalities, or other evidence of crime is located on identified property but do not then have probable cause to believe that the owner or possessor of the property is himself implicated in the crime that has occurred or is occurring. . . .

Under existing law, valid warrants may be issued to search *any* property, whether or not occupied by a third party, at which there is probable cause to believe that fruits, instrumentalities, or evidence of a crime will be found. Nothing on the face of the Amendment suggests that a third-party search warrant should not normally issue. . . .

As the Fourth Amendment has been construed and applied by this Court, "when the State's reason to believe incriminating evidence will be found becomes sufficiently great, the invasion of privacy becomes justified and a warrant to search and seize will issue." . . .

As we understand the structure and language of the Fourth Amendment and our cases expounding it, valid warrants to search property may be issued when it is satisfactorily demonstrated to the magistrate that fruits, instrumentalities, or evidence of crime is located on the premises. The Fourth Amendment has itself struck the balance between privacy and public need, and there is no occasion or justification for a court to revise the Amendment and strike a new balance by denying the search warrant in the circumstances present here and by insisting that the investigation proceed by subpoena *duces tecum*, whether on the theory that the latter is a less intrusive alternative or otherwise. . . .

[The *Daily* argues] that searches of newspaper offices for evidence of crime reasonably believed to be on the premises will seriously threaten the ability of the press to gather, analyze, and disseminate news. This is said to be true for several reasons: First, searches will be physically disruptive to such an extent that timely publication will be impeded. Second, confidential sources of information will dry up, and the press will also lose opportunities to cover various events because of fears of the participants that press files will be readily available to the authorities. Third, reporters will be deterred from recording and preserving their recollections for future use if such information is subject to seizure. Fourth, the processing of news and its dissemination will be chilled by the prospects that searches will disclose internal editorial deliberations. Fifth, the press will resort to self-censorship to conceal its possession of information of potential interest to the police.

It is true that the struggle from which the Fourth Amendment emerged "is largely a history of conflict between the Crown and the press," and that in issuing warrants and determining the reasonableness of a search, state and federal magistrates should be aware that "unrestricted power of search and seizure could also be an instrument for stifling liberty of expression." Where the materials sought to be seized may be protected by the First Amendment, the requirements of the Fourth Amendment must be applied with "scrupulous exactitude." . . . Where presumptively protected materials are sought to be seized, the warrant requirement should be administered to leave as little as possible to the discretion or whim of the officer in the field. . . .

Aware of the long struggle between Crown and press and desiring to curb unjustified official intrusions, the Framers took the enormously important step of subjecting searches to the test of reasonableness and to the general rule requiring search warrants issued by neutral magistrates. They nevertheless did not forbid warrants where the press was involved, did not require special showings that subpoenas would be impractical, and did not insist that the owner of the place to be searched, if connected with the press, must be shown to be implicated in the offense being investigated. Further, the prior cases do no more than insist that the courts apply the warrant requirements with particular exactitude when First Amendment interests would be endangered by the search. As we see it, no more than this is required where the warrant requested is for the seizure of criminal evidence reasonably believed to be on the premises occupied by a newspaper. Properly administered, the preconditions for a warrant — probable cause, specificity with respect to the place to be searched and the things to be seized, and overall reasonableness — should afford sufficient protection against the harms that are assertedly threatened by warrants for searching newspaper offices. . . .

STEWART, J. joined by MARSHALL, J. dissenting. It seems to me self-evident that police searches of newspaper offices burden the freedom of the press. The most immediate and obvious First Amendment injury caused by such a visitation by the police is physical disruption of the operation of the newspaper. Policemen occupying a newsroom and searching it thoroughly for what may be an extended period of time will inevitably interrupt its normal operations, and thus impair or even temporarily prevent the processes of newsgathering, writing, editing, and publishing. By contrast, a subpoena would afford the newspaper itself an opportunity to locate whatever material might be requested and produce it.

But there is another and more serious burden on a free press imposed by an unannounced police search of a newspaper office: the possibility of disclosure of information received from confidential sources, or of the identity of the sources themselves. . . .

It requires no blind leap of faith to understand that a person who gives information to a journalist only on condition that his identity will not be revealed will be less likely to give that information if he knows that, despite the journalist's assurance his identity may in fact be disclosed. And it cannot be denied that confidential information may be exposed to the eyes of police officers who execute a search warrant by rummaging through the files, cabinets, desks, and wastebaskets of a newsroom. Since the indisputable effect of such searches will thus be to prevent a newsman from being able to promise confidentiality to his potential sources, it seems obvious to me that a journalist's access to information, and thus the public's will thereby be impaired.

PRIVACY PROTECTION ACT

42 U.S.C. § 2000aa

In 1980, Congress responded to *Zurcher* by passing the Privacy Protection Act (PPA), Pub. L. No. 96-440, 94 Stat. 1879, codified at 42 U.S.C. § 2000aa.

Work Product. Pursuant to the PPA:

> Notwithstanding any other law, it shall be unlawful for a government officer or employee, in connection with the investigation or prosecution of a criminal offense, to search for or seize any work product materials possessed by a person reasonably believed to have a purpose to disseminate to the public a newspaper, book, broadcast, or other similar form of public communication, in or affecting interstate or foreign commerce. . . . § 2000aa(a).

However, if "there is probable cause to believe that the person possessing such materials has committed or is committing the criminal offense to which the materials relate," then such materials may be searched or seized. The "criminal offense" cannot consist of the mere receipt, possession, or communication of the materials (except if it involves national defense data, classified information, or child pornography). § 2000aa(a)(1). The materials may be searched or seized if "there is reason to believe that the immediate seizure of such materials is necessary to prevent the death of, or serious bodily injury to, a human being," § 2000aa(a)(2).

Other Documents. The PPA also restricts the search or seizure of "documentary materials, other than work product materials, possessed by a person in connection with a purpose to disseminate to the public a newspaper, book, broadcast, or other similar form of public communication." § 2000aa(b). This provision has the same exceptions as the work product provision, with additional exceptions permitting search or seizure when there is reason to believe that the documents will be destroyed or concealed.

Subpoenas. The effect of the PPA is to require law enforcement officials to obtain a subpoena in order to obtain such information. Unlike search warrants, subpoenas permit the party subject to them to challenge them in court before having to comply. Further, instead of law enforcement officials searching through offices or records, the person(s) served with the subpoena produce the documents themselves.

NOTES & QUESTIONS

1. ***Searches Implicating the First Amendment.*** In certain circumstances, a search may implicate the First Amendment, as it did in *Zurcher*. Suppose the police desire to search a bookstore's records to determine who purchased a particular book. The police obtain a valid warrant. However, First Amendment rights may be implicated, as such searches might chill people's ability to read. Would the government have to, in addition to securing a warrant, satisfy First Amendment scrutiny? For one court's answer, see *Tattered Cover v. City of Thornton* in Chapter 5.
2. ***Subpoenas Versus Warrants.*** In certain ways, subpoenas can be more protective of privacy than warrants. The person served with the subpoena can produce the requested documents herself rather than having government officials physically enter the person's office or dwelling to conduct the search. Further, the person can challenge the subpoena in court prior to

complying; with a search warrant, judicial authorization is granted ex parte, and the warrant is most often challenged only after it is executed. On the other hand, subpoenas can be obtained without any requirement of particularized suspicion or probable cause. The role for judicial oversight is rather minimal.

F. POLICE RECORDS

1. CONSTITUTIONAL PROTECTIONS FROM PUBLIC DISCLOSURE

PAUL v. DAVIS

424 U.S. 693 (1976)

REHNQUIST, J. . . . Petitioner Paul is the Chief of Police of the Louisville, Ky., Division of Police, while petitioner McDaniel occupies the same position in the Jefferson County, Ky., Division of Police. In late 1972 they agreed to combine their efforts for the purpose of alerting local area merchants to possible shoplifters who might be operating during the Christmas season. In early December petitioners distributed to approximately 800 merchants in the Louisville metropolitan area a "flyer," which began as follows:

TO: BUSINESS MEN IN THE METROPOLITAN AREA

The Chiefs of The Jefferson County and City of Louisville Police Departments, in an effort to keep their officers advised on shoplifting activity, have approved the attached alphabetically arranged flyer of subjects known to be active in this criminal field.

This flyer is being distributed to you, the business man, so that you may inform your security personnel to watch for these subjects. These persons have been arrested during 1971 and 1972 or have been active in various criminal fields in high density shopping areas.

Only the photograph and name of the subject is shown on this flyer, if additional information is desired, please forward a request in writing. . . .

The flyer consisted of five pages of "mug shot" photos, arranged alphabetically. [Each page had the heading: "ACTIVE SHOPLIFTERS."]

In approximately the center of page 2 there appeared photos and the name of the respondent, Edward Charles Davis III.

Respondent appeared on the flyer because on June 14, 1971, he had been arrested in Louisville on a charge of shoplifting. He had been arraigned on this charge in September 1971, and, upon his plea of not guilty, the charge had been "filed away with leave (to reinstate)," a disposition which left the charge outstanding. Thus, at the time petitioners caused the flyer to be prepared and circulated respondent had been charged with shoplifting but his guilt or innocence of that offense had never been resolved. Shortly after circulation of the flyer the charge against respondent was finally dismissed by a judge of the Louisville Police Court.

At the time the flyer was circulated respondent was employed as a photographer by the Louisville Courier-Journal and Times. The flyer, and respondent's inclusion therein, soon came to the attention of respondent's supervisor, the executive director of photography for the two newspapers. This individual called respondent in to hear his version of the events leading to his appearing in the flyer. Following this discussion, the supervisor informed respondent that although he would not be fired, he "had best not find himself in a similar situation" in the future.

Respondent thereupon brought this §1983 action in the District Court for the Western District of Kentucky, seeking redress for the alleged violation of rights guaranteed to him by the Constitution of the United States. . . .

Respondent's due process claim is grounded upon his assertion that the flyer, and in particular the phrase "Active Shoplifters" appearing at the head of the page upon which his name and photograph appear, impermissibly deprived him of some "liberty" protected by the Fourteenth Amendment. His complaint asserted that the "active shoplifter" designation would inhibit him from entering business establishments for fear of being suspected of shoplifting and possibly apprehended, and would seriously impair his future employment opportunities. Accepting that such consequences may flow from the flyer in question, respondent's complaint would appear to state a classical claim for defamation actionable in the courts of virtually every State. Imputing criminal behavior to an individual is generally considered defamatory per se, and actionable without proof of special damages.

Respondent brought his action, however, not in the state courts of Kentucky, but in a United States District Court for that State. He asserted not a claim for defamation under the laws of Kentucky, but a claim that he had been deprived of rights secured to him by the Fourteenth Amendment of the United States Constitution. Concededly if the same allegations had been made about respondent by a private individual, he would have nothing more than a claim for defamation under state law. But, he contends, since petitioners are respectively an official of city and of county government, his action is thereby transmuted into one for deprivation by the State of rights secured under the Fourteenth Amendment. . . .

If respondent's view is to prevail, a person arrested by law enforcement officers who announce that they believe such person to be responsible for a particular crime in order to calm the fears of an aroused populace, presumably obtains a claim against such officers under § 1983. And since it is surely far more clear from the language of the Fourteenth Amendment that "life" is protected against state deprivation than it is that reputation is protected against state injury, it would be difficult to see why the survivors of an innocent bystander mistakenly shot by a policeman or negligently killed by a sheriff driving a government vehicle, would not have claims equally cognizable under § 1983.

It is hard to perceive any logical stopping place to such a line of reasoning. Respondent's construction would seem almost necessarily to result in every legally cognizable injury which may have been inflicted by a state official acting under "color of law" establishing a violation of the Fourteenth Amendment. We think it would come as a great surprise to those who drafted and shepherded the adoption of that Amendment to learn that it worked such a result, and a study of our decisions convinces us they do not support the construction urged by respondent. . . .

The second premise upon which the result reached by the Court of Appeals could be rested that the infliction by state officials of a "stigma" to one's reputation is somehow different in kind from infliction by a state official of harm to other interests protected by state law is equally untenable. The words "liberty" and "property" as used in the Fourteenth Amendment do not in terms single out reputation as a candidate for special protection over and above other interests that may be protected by state law. While we have in a number of our prior cases pointed out the frequently drastic effect of the "stigma" which may result from defamation by the government in a variety of contexts, this line of cases does not establish the proposition that reputation alone, apart from some more tangible interests such as employment, is either "liberty" or "property" by itself sufficient to invoke the procedural protection of the Due Process Clause. . . .

Respondent's complaint also alleged a violation of a "right to privacy guaranteed by the First, Fourth, Fifth, Ninth, and Fourteenth Amendments." . . .

While there is no "right of privacy" found in any specific guarantee of the Constitution, the Court has recognized that "zones of privacy" may be created by more specific constitutional guarantees and thereby impose limits upon government power. *See Roe v. Wade*, 410 U.S. 113, 152-153 (1973). Respondent's case, however, comes within none of these areas. He does not seek to suppress evidence seized in the course of an unreasonable search. *See Katz v. United States*, 389 U.S. 347, 351 (1967). And our other "right of privacy" cases, while defying categorical description, deal generally with substantive aspects of the Fourteenth Amendment. In *Roe* the Court pointed out that the personal rights found in this guarantee of personal privacy must be limited to those which are "fundamental" or "implicit in the concept of ordered liberty" as described in *Palko v. Connecticut*, 302 U.S. 319, 325 (1937). The activities detailed as being within this definition were ones very different from that for which respondent claims constitutional protection matters relating to marriage, procreation, contraception, family relationships, and child rearing and education. In these areas it has been held that there are limitations on the States' power to substantively regulate conduct.

Respondent's claim is far afield from this line of decisions. He claims constitutional protection against the disclosure of the fact of his arrest on a shoplifting charge. His claim is based, not upon any challenge to the State's ability to restrict his freedom of action in a sphere contended to be "private," but instead on a claim that the State may not publicize a record of an official act such as an arrest. None of our substantive privacy decisions hold this or anything like this, and we decline to enlarge them in this manner. . . .

NOTES & QUESTIONS

1. Five years prior to *Paul*, the Court was more receptive to constitutional protection for reputational harms in *Wisconsin v. Constantineau*, 400 U.S. 433 (1971). There, the Court struck down a law authorizing the posting of names

of people who had been designated excessive drinkers in retail liquor outlets. Alcohol was not to be sold to these individuals. The Court reasoned:

> Where a person's good name, reputation, honor, or integrity is at stake because of what the government is doing to him, notice and an opportunity to be heard are essential. "Posting" under the Wisconsin Act may to some be merely the mark of illness, to others it is a stigma, an official branding of a person. The label is a degrading one. Under the Wisconsin Act, a resident of Hartford is given no process at all. This appellee was not afforded a chance to defend herself. She may have been the victim of an official's caprice. Only when the whole proceedings leading to the pinning of an unsavory label on a person are aired can oppressive results be prevented.

Is *Paul* consistent with this case?

2. *Paul v. Davis* was decided one year prior to *Whalen v. Roe* (Chapter 3). How does *Paul* square with *Whalen*? Does *Whalen* implicitly overrule *Paul* by recognizing a constitutional right to avoid disclosure of certain information? How can these cases be reconciled?

CLINE V. ROGERS

87 F.3d 176 (6th Cir. 1996)

BATCHELDER, J. . . . The plaintiff-appellant, Jackie Ray Cline ("Cline"), alleges that in 1992, a private citizen contacted the Sheriff's Department of McMinn County, Tennessee ("the County"), and asked Sheriff George Rogers to check Cline's arrest record. According to Cline, Rogers searched state and local records and requested a computer search of National Crime Information Center ("NCIC") records of the Federal Bureau of Investigation ("FBI"). Cline alleges that Rogers disclosed to the private citizen the information Rogers obtained regarding Cline's criminal history, in violation of both Tennessee and federal law.

Cline filed this lawsuit against Rogers, individually and in his official capacity as sheriff. Cline also named the County as a defendant, alleging that improper searches of criminal records is "a routine and customary practice in McMinn County," that the County "lacks adequate controls to ensure that access to criminal records is for authorized purposes only," that the County did not have in place an adequate system to detect misuse of criminal records, that the County had provided inadequate training to prevent such abuse, and that the County had "been indifferent to the civil rights of private citizens by allowing such abuses to continue."

Cline's complaint sought damages under 42 U.S.C. § 1983 for violation of his federal civil rights. . . . [The district court dismissed Cline's complaint and Cline appealed.]

There is no violation of the United States Constitution in this case because there is no constitutional right to privacy in one's criminal record. Nondisclosure of one's criminal record is not one of those personal rights that is "fundamental" or "implicit in the concept of ordered liberty." *See Whalen v. Roe.* In *Whalen*, the Supreme Court distinguished fundamental privacy interests in "matters relating to marriage, procreation, contraception, family relationships, and child rearing and education" and "individual interest in avoiding disclosure of personal matters."

Moreover, one's criminal history is arguably not a private "personal matter" at all, since arrest and conviction information are matters of public record. *See Paul v. Davis* (rejecting a similar claim based on facts more egregious than those alleged here). Although there may be a dispute among the circuit courts regarding the existence and extent of an individual privacy right to nondisclosure of "personal matters," see *Slayton v. Willingham*, 726 F.2d 631 (10th Cir. 1984); *Fadjo v. Coon*, 633 F.2d 1172, 1176 (5th Cir. Unit B 1981) (both opining that *Paul* has been at least partially overruled by the Supreme Court's decisions in *Whalen* and *Nixon*), this circuit does not recognize a constitutional privacy interest in avoiding disclosure of, e.g., one's criminal record. See *DeSanti*, 653 F.2d at 1090 (regarding disclosure of juvenile delinquents' "social histories"); see also *Doe v. Wigginton*, 21 F.3d 733 (6th Cir. 1994) (disclosure of inmate's HIV infection did not violate constitutional right of privacy).

Because there is no privacy interest in one's criminal record that is protected by the United States Constitution, Cline could prove no set of facts that would entitle him to relief; therefore, the district court correctly dismissed this claim. . . .

SCHEETZ V. THE MORNING CALL, INC.

946 F.2d 202 (3d Cir. 1991)

NYGAARD, J. . . . Kenneth Scheetz is a police officer in the City of Allentown. Rosann Scheetz is his wife. In the course of an argument between them in their home in January of 1988, Kenneth struck Rosann. Rosann left the house, but returned approximately a half an hour later. The argument resumed, and Kenneth again struck Rosann.

Rosann called the Allentown police. Two officers responded and prepared a standard "offense/incident" report, consisting of a face sheet and supplemental reports. The "face sheet" of this report[49] stated that Rosann Scheetz had reported a domestic disturbance, that two police cars had responded, and that Rosann had left the home.

In the meantime, Rosann had driven to the Allentown police station, apparently with the intention of filing a Pennsylvania Protection From Abuse Petition. The officers who interviewed Rosann prepared two "supplemental reports" and made them part of the file. They reveal that Rosann stated that her husband had beaten her before and had refused counseling. The police gave Rosann three options: file criminal charges, request a protection from abuse order, or initiate department disciplinary action against Kenneth. These supplements also note that Rosann had visible physical injuries, that Rosann did not want to return home and that she was permitted to spend the night in the shift commander's office.

---

[49] The "face sheet" is a public document similar to a police blotter. The parties agree that this document is a public record. The parties dispute whether the "supplemental reports" are public records available under Pennsylvania's Right to Know Law. There is some evidence that these reports were generally available, subject to the approval of a police supervisor.

Chief Wayne Stephens filed a third supplement to the report. He had spoken to Kenneth about the incident, and the third supplement memorialized this fact, as well as Kenneth's statement to the Chief that he and his wife were scheduled to speak with a marriage counselor. None of the supplements indicated that the Chief took any disciplinary action against Kenneth.

Shortly after the incident, Kenneth Scheetz was named "Officer of the Year" by Chief Stephens. Several months later, as part of "Respect for Law Week," press releases and photos of Kenneth were released. A dinner and official ceremony were held in Kenneth's honor. The Morning Call ("The Call"), a local newspaper, published a story and photo on this honor.

Terry Mutchler, a reporter for The Call, became interested in investigating the prior incident involving Kenneth and Rosann. Another reporter from the paper had tried to get the police report from the police, who refused to release it. Mutchler's request for a copy of the report from the department was also formally refused. Mutchler nonetheless managed to get a copy of the report.

Mutchler then interviewed Chief Stephens about the incident. Chief Stephens initially denied the incident, but when confronted with Mutchler's information, he claimed that the report was stolen and refused further comment. Chief Stephens did, however, offer his insights into the subject of spousal abuse, stating "people fake it" and "women . . . tear their dresses and rip up their bras and say they were raped." Mutchler also interviewed Deputy Chief Monaghan, who offered assorted rationalizations for why no follow-up had been done on the Scheetz incident. The Scheetzes refused comment on the incident.

The Call published an article by Mutchler titled "Police didn't investigate assault complaint against officer." Eight paragraphs of the article were comprised of quotes from the police report of the beating incident which detailed the injuries Rosann received. The bulk of the article, however, focused on the lack of investigation and follow-up by the police department. Chief Stephens was quoted as saying that the incident had not been investigated. The article also quoted the comments Chief Stephens had made to Mutchler about domestic abuse, as well as Deputy Chief Monaghan's explanations for why no charges were pressed. The last two columns of the article consisted of quotes from Kenneth's superiors praising his work. . . .

. . . Kenneth and Rosann then sued Mutchler, The Call, and "John or Jane Doe." The complaint alleged that Mutchler and The Call had conspired with an unknown state actor (the Doe defendant) to deprive the Scheetzes of their constitutional right to privacy in violation of 42 U.S.C. § 1983. The complaint also raised several pendent state law claims. . . .

The district court granted the defendants' motion for summary judgment in part, denied it in part, granted judgment to the defendants on the § 1983 claim, dismissed the pendent state claims, dismissed the Doe defendant and dismissed all remaining motions as moot. The Scheetzes appeal. . . .

. . . Because we conclude that the Scheetzes have not alleged a violation of a constitutionally protected privacy interest, we will affirm.

The defendants rely on dicta in *Paul v. Davis* to support their argument that "garden variety" invasion of privacy claims are not actionable under section 1983. . . . The Supreme Court rejected the proposition that reputation alone was a liberty or property interest within the meaning of the due process clause. In dicta, the Court went on to consider the alternative argument that the police chiefs' action constituted a violation of the plaintiff's right to privacy. After first noting that privacy decisions had been limited in the past to family and procreative matters, the Court concluded that publication by the state of an official act such as an arrest could not constitute invasion of the constitutional right to privacy.

The very next year, however, the Court held in *Whalen v. Roe*, that the right to privacy extends to both "the individual interest in avoiding disclosure of personal matters, and . . . the interest in independence in making certain kinds of important decisions." *Whalen* recognized that the information contained in medical records is constitutionally protected under the confidentiality branch of the privacy right.

Thus, some confidential information is protected under the confidentiality branch of the right to privacy, the dicta in *Paul* notwithstanding.[50] Accordingly, the Scheetzes in this case contend that the information contained in the police incident report is similarly protected by the federal right.

Although cases exploring the autonomy branch of the right of privacy are legion, the contours of the confidentiality branch are murky. We have recognized that some confidential information, such as medical records, is constitutionally protected under the confidentiality branch of the federal privacy right. Other courts have similarly recognized that § 1983 may be used to redress violations of a constitutional confidentiality right.

Concluding that violations of the confidentiality right of privacy may be actionable under § 1983 does not, however, end our inquiry. Although defendants are wrong in arguing that *Paul* prohibits any privacy § 1983 action, we conclude that they correctly argue that the Scheetzes did not have a constitutionally protected privacy interest in the information they divulged in a police report. . . .

Although the outlines of the confidentiality right are not definite, the information that has been protected in other cases was information that the disclosing person reasonably expected to remain private. In reporting this potential crime to the police, Rosann Scheetz could not reasonably expect the information to remain secret. The police could have brought charges without her concurrence, at which point all the information would have wound up on the public record, where it would have been non-confidential. *See Cox Broadcasting Corp. v. Cohn*, 420 U.S. 469 (1975) (privacy interest fades when information is in the public record). This information is not like medical or financial records (which have been accorded some constitutional protection by this court) where there is a reasonable expectation that privacy will be preserved. When police are called, a private disturbance loses much of its private character. We conclude that the information Rosann Scheetz disclosed in the police reports is not constitutionally protected. . . .

MANSMANN, J. dissenting. . . . I agree that some of the information contained in the police report, specifically that information contained in the "Of-

---

[50] *Paul* can be reconciled with *Whalen* since the information at issue in *Paul* (the fact of plaintiff's arrest for shoplifting) is not the kind of information entitled to constitutional protection.

fense/Incident Report," is not protected under a constitutional privacy interest. Because the "Offense/Incident Report" is classified as a public document under the police department's policy, that information was not treated as confidential. . . .

Some of the information reported by The Call, however, was contained only in confidential portions of the police report entitled "Investigative Supplements" and was not discernable from the public portion of the report. That information detailed the private facts of the Scheetzes' marital counseling and precise details of their marital disturbance, including a description of Rosann's injuries and her statements. Since this information is clearly confidential, I would then examine the nature of the Scheetzes' privacy interest in keeping it confidential. . . .

. . . The majority suggests that because the information could have been publicly disclosed, the Scheetzes had no privacy interest. While it is true that criminal charges could have been brought without Rosann's concurrence, it does not necessarily follow that in spite of the fact that she declined to press charges or take alternative legal action, and no legal action ensued, Rosann Scheetz could have reasonably expected public disclosure of the confidential information that had remained quietly dormant in confidential police department reports.

This is especially true where the public disclosure occurred 16 months after the incident. *See, e.g., Briscoe v. Reader's Digest Ass'n,* 483 P.2d 34 (Cal. 1971) (common law right to privacy infringed by publication of truck hijacking conviction of 11 years ago); *Melvin v. Reid,* 297 P. 91 (Cal. 1931) (liability for common law invasion of privacy imposed upon producers of movie that revealed prior life of prostitution and crime of woman who had long since taken a new name and established a respectable life). . . .

. . . Because this confidential information had lain undisclosed in the confidential police department files for over a year and Rosann Scheetz had not pursued any legal action, the Scheetzes could reasonably have expected that the confidential information would never be publicly disclosed. In light of this delay, I cannot agree with the majority's otherwise appropriate assertion that "[w]hen police are called, a private disturbance loses much of its private character." Information that has remained confidential over a period of time, absent any legal action, can reasonably be expected to recede from public notice. . . .

NOTES & QUESTIONS

1. Recall *Doe v. Barrington* in Chapter 3, where the police disclosed that a person had HIV to his neighbors, and the court found a valid action for violation of the constitutional right to information privacy. Suppose the police decided to make the person's HIV status part of a publicly disclosed police report. Would the person still be able to claim a privacy interest in the information? Are there limits to what information the police can include in a public police report?
2. The information about the police department's treatment of Ken Scheetz's abuse of his wife is highly newsworthy. The information reveals a police

department that praised rather than disciplined Ken Scheetz and virtually ignored his wife's complaints of abuse. Is privacy being used to cover up the scandalous way the police department reacted to Rosann Scheetz's complaint?

3. Would routine disclosure of complaints of spousal abuse inhibit victims such as Rosann Scheetz from coming forward? Keep in mind that it is Rosann Scheetz, in addition to her husband, who is suing for a violation of her privacy.

4. Consider *Sterling v. Borough of Minersville*, 232 F.3d. 190 (3d Cir. 2000). Marcus Wayman, who was 18 years old, along with a 17-year-old male friend were in a car parked in a lot adjacent to a beer distributor. F. Scott Wilinsky, a police officer, observed the vehicle and became suspicious that the youths might be attempting to burglarize the beer distributor. Wilinsky called for backup. After investigating, the officers determined that there had not been a break-in at the beer distributor, but that the youths had been drinking. Wilinsky searched the vehicle and discovered two condoms and asked about the boys' sexual orientation. The boys said that they were homosexuals and that they were in the lot to engage in consensual sex. The boys were arrested for underage drinking and taken to the police station, where Wilinsky lectured them that homosexual activity was contrary to the dictates of the Bible. Wilinsky then told Wayman that he must inform his grandfather about his homosexuality or else Wilinsky himself would inform Wayman's grandfather. When he was released from custody, Wayman committed suicide. Wayman's mother filed a § 1983 suit against the Borough of Minersville, Wilinksy, and other officers and officials alleging, among other things, a violation of the constitutional right to information privacy. The court reasoned:

> . . . We first ask whether Wayman had a protected privacy right concerning Wilinsky's threat to disclose his suspected sexual orientation. . . .
>
> We recognize that the Supreme Court has not definitively extended the right to privacy to the confidentiality of one's sexual orientation. Indeed, a later case gives us pause. In *Bowers v. Hardwick*, 478 U.S. 186 (1986), the Supreme Court overturned a decision of the Court of Appeals of the Eleventh Circuit that had invalidated a Georgia statute that made consensual homosexual sodomy a criminal offense. The majority rejected the claim that the Constitution confers a "fundamental right to homosexuals to engage in consensual sodomy."
>
> While *Bowers* indicates that the Court is resistant to bestowing the protection of the Constitution on some sexual behavior, its ruling focused on the practice of homosexual sodomy and is not determinative of whether the right to privacy protects an individual from being forced to disclose his sexual orientation. In other words, the decision did not purport to punish homosexual status. Such a determination would in fact be contrary to the Court's holding in *Robinson v. California*, 370 U.S. 660 (1962), that the Eighth and Fourteenth Amendments forbid punishment of status as opposed to conduct. We do not read *Bowers* as placing a limit on privacy protection for the intensely personal decision of sexual preference.
>
> Our jurisprudence takes an encompassing view of information entitled to a protected right to privacy. . . .

. . . It is difficult to imagine a more private matter than one's sexuality and a less likely probability that the government would have a legitimate interest in disclosure of sexual identity.

We can, therefore, readily conclude that Wayman's sexual orientation was an intimate aspect of his personality entitled to privacy protection under *Whalen*. The Supreme Court, despite the *Bowers* decision, and our court have clearly spoken that matters of personal intimacy are safeguarded against unwarranted disclosure. . . .

Before we can definitely conclude that a constitutional tort has occurred, however, we must further ask whether Wilinsky's threat of disclosure, rather than actual disclosure, constituted a violation of Wayman's right to privacy. . . .

. . . The threat to breach some confidential aspect of one's life . . . is tantamount to a violation of the privacy right because the security of one's privacy has been compromised by the threat of disclosure. Thus, Wilinsky's threat to disclose Wayman's suspected homosexuality suffices as a violation of Wayman's constitutionally protected privacy interest. . . .

2. TORT LIABILITY FOR DISCLOSURE OF PRIOR CRIMINAL HISTORY

BRISCOE V. READER'S DIGEST ASSOCIATION

483 P.2d 34 (Cal. 1971)

PETERS, J. On December 15, 1956, plaintiff [Marvin Briscoe] and another man hijacked a truck in Danville, Kenucky. [After this incident, Briscoe reformed his ways and made many friends who were unaware of his earlier misconduct.]

"The Big Business of Hijacking," published by defendant [Readers Digest Magazine] 11 years after the hijacking incident, commences with a picture whose caption reads, "Today's highwaymen are looting trucks at a rate of more than $100 million a year. But the truckers have now declared all-out war." The article describes various truck thefts and the efforts being made to stop such thefts. Dates ranging from 1965 to the time of publication are mentioned throughout the article, but none of the described thefts is itself dated.

One sentence in the article refers to plaintiff: "Typical of many beginners, Marvin Briscoe and (another man) stole a 'valuable-looking' truck in Danville, Ky., and then fought a gun battle with the local police, only to learn that they had hijacked four bowling-pin spotters." There is nothing in the article to indicate that the hijacking occurred in 1956.

As the result of defendant's publication, plaintiff's 11-year-old daughter, as well as his friends, for the first time learned of this incident. They thereafter scorned and abandoned him.

Conceding the truth of the facts published in defendant's article, plaintiff claims that the public disclosure of these private facts has humiliated him and exposed him to contempt and ridicule. Conceding that the subject of the article may have been "newsworthy," he contends that the use of his name was not, and that the defendant has thus invaded his right to privacy. . . .

Acceptance of the right to privacy has grown with the increasing capability of the mass media and electronic devices with their capacity to destroy an individual's anonymity, intrude upon his most intimate activities, and expose his most personal characteristics to public gaze.

In a society in which multiple, often conflicting role performances are demanded of each individual, the original etymological meaning of the word "person"—mask—has taken on new meaning. Men fear exposure not only to those closest to them; much of the outrage underlying the asserted right to privacy is a reaction to exposure to persons known only through business or other secondary relationships. The claim is not so much one of total secrecy as it is of the right to define one's circle of intimacy—to choose who shall see beneath the quotidian mask. Loss of control over which "face" one puts on may result in literal loss of self-identity, and is humiliating beneath the gaze of those whose curiosity treats a human being as an object.

A common law right to privacy, based on Warren and Brandeis' article, is now recognized in at least 36 states. . . . California has recognized the right to privacy for 40 years. . . .

There can be no doubt that reports of current criminal activities are the legitimate province of a free press. The circumstances under which crimes occur, the techniques used by those outside the law, the tragedy that may befall the victims — these are vital bits of information for people coping with the exigencies of modern life. Reports of these events may also promote the values served by the constitutional guarantee of a public trial. Although a case is not to be "tried in the papers," reports regarding a crime or criminal proceedings may encourage unknown witnesses to come forward with useful testimony and friends or relatives to come to the aid of the victim.

It is also generally in the social interest to identify adults currently charged with the commission of a crime. While such an identification may not presume guilt, it may legitimately put others on notice that the named individual is suspected of having committed a crime. Naming the suspect may also persuade eye witnesses and character witnesses to testify. For these reasons, while the suspect or offender obviously does not consent to public exposure, his right to privacy must give way to the overriding social interest.

In general, therefore, truthful reports of recent crimes and the names of suspects or offenders will be deemed protected by the First Amendment.

The instant case, however, compels us to consider whether reports of the facts of *past* crimes and the identification of *past* offenders serve these same public-interest functions.

We have no doubt that reports of the facts of past crimes are newsworthy. Media publication of the circumstances under which crimes were committed in the past may prove educational in the same way that reports of current crimes do. The public has a strong interest in enforcing the law, and this interest is served by accumulating and disseminating data cataloguing the reasons men commit crimes, the methods they use, and the ways in which they are apprehended. Thus in an article on truck hijackings, Reader's Digest certainly had the right to report the facts of plaintiff's criminal act.

However, identification of the Actor in reports of long past crimes usually serves little independent public purpose. Once legal proceedings have terminated, and a suspect or offender has been released, identification of the individual will not usually aid the administration of justice. Identification will no longer serve to bring forth witnesses or obtain succor for victims. Unless the individual has reattracted the public eye to himself in some independent fashion, the only public "interest" that would usually be served is that of curiosity.

There may be times, of course, when an event involving private citizens may be so unique as to capture the imagination of all. In such cases — e.g., the behavior of the passengers on the sinking Titanic, the heroism of Nathan Hale, the horror of the Saint Valentine's Day Massacre — purely private individuals may by an accident of history lose their privacy regarding that incident for all time. There need be no "reattraction" of the public eye because the public interest never wavered. An individual whose name is fixed in the public's memory, such as that of the political assassin, never becomes an anonymous member of the community again. But in each case it is for the trier of fact to determine whether the individual's infamy is such that he has never left the public arena; we cannot do so as a matter of law. . . .

Another factor militating in favor of protecting the individual's privacy here is the state's interest in the integrity of the rehabilitative process. Our courts recognized this issue four decades ago in *Melvin v. Reid*, 297 P. 91. . . .

One of the premises of the rehabilitative process is that the rehabilitated offender can rejoin that great bulk of the community from which he has been ostracized for his anti-social acts. In return for becoming a "new man," he is allowed to melt into the shadows of obscurity. . . .

Plaintiff is a man whose last offense took place 11 years before, who has paid his debt to society, who has friends and an 11-year-old daughter who were unaware of his early life — a man who assumed a position in "respectable" society. Ideally, his neighbors should recognize his present worth and forget his past life of shame. But men are not so divine as to forgive the past trespasses of others, and plaintiff therefore endeavored to reveal as little as possible of his past life. Yet, as if in some bizarre canyon of echoes, petitioner's past life pursues him through the pages of Reader's Digest, now published in 13 languages and distributed in 100 nations, with a circulation in California alone of almost 2,000,000 copies. . . .

On the assumed set of facts before us we are convinced that a jury could reasonably find that plaintiff's identity as a former hijacker was not newsworthy. First, as discussed above, a jury could find that publication of plaintiff's identity in connection with incidents of his past life was in this case of minimal social value. There was no independent reason whatsoever for focusing public attention on Mr. Briscoe as an individual at this time. A jury could certainly find that Mr. Briscoe had once again become an anonymous member of the community. . . .

Second, a jury might find that revealing one's criminal past for all to see is grossly offensive to most people in America. Certainly a criminal background is kept even more hidden from others than a humiliating disease or the existence of business debts. The consequences of revelation in this case — ostracism, isolation, and the alienation of one's family — make all too clear just how deeply offensive to most persons a prior crime is and thus how hidden the former offender must keep the knowledge of his prior indiscretion.

Third, in no way can plaintiff be said to have voluntarily consented to the publicity accorded him here. He committed a crime. He was punished. He was rehabilitated. And he became, for 11 years, an obscure and law-abiding citizen. His every effort was to forget and have others forget that he had once hijacked a truck.

Finally, the interests at stake here are not merely those of publication and privacy alone, for the state has a compelling interest in the efficacy of penal systems in rehabilitating criminals and returning them as productive and law-abiding citizens to the society whence they came. A jury might well find that a continuing threat that the rehabilitated offender's old identity will be resurrected by the media is counter-productive to the goals of this correctional process. . . .

NOTES & QUESTIONS

1. ***Rehabilitation.*** Consider Eugene Volokh's criticism of the *Briscoe* case:

> . . . Judges are of course entitled to have their own views about which things "right-thinking members of society" should "recognize" and which they should forget; but it seems to me that under the First Amendment members of society have a constitutional right to think things through in their own ways. And some people do take a view that differs from that of the *Briscoe* judges: While criminals can change their character, this view asserts, they often don't. Someone who was willing to fight a gun battle with the police eleven years ago may be more willing than the average person to do something bad today, even if he has led a blameless life since then (something that no court can assure us of, since it may be that he has continued acting violently on occasion, but just hasn't yet been caught).
>
> Under this ideology, it's perfectly proper to keep this possibility in mind in one's dealings with the supposedly "reformed" felon. While the government may want to give him a second chance by releasing him from prison, restoring his right to vote and possess firearms, and even erasing its publicly accessible records related to the conviction, his friends, acquaintances, and business associates are entitled to adopt a different attitude. Most presumably wouldn't treat him as a total pariah, but they might use extra caution in dealing with him, especially when it comes to trusting their business welfare or even their physical safety (or that of their children) to his care. . . .[51]

According to Richard Posner, the *Briscoe* case improperly assumes that people will behave irrationally toward rehabilitated people:

> Remote past criminal activity is less relevant to a prediction of future misconduct than recent — and those who learn of it will discount it accordingly — but such information is hardly irrelevant to people considering whether to enter into or continue social or business relations with the individual; if it were irrelevant, publicizing it would not injure the individual. People conceal past criminal acts not out of bashfulness but because poten-

---

[51] Eugene Volokh, *Freedom of Speech and Information Privacy: The Troubling Implications of a Right to Stop People from Speaking About You*, 52 Stan. L. Rev. 1049, 1091–1092 (2000). For another critique, see T. Markus Funk, *The Dangers of Hiding Criminal Pasts*, 66 Tenn. L. Rev. 287 (1998).

tial acquaintances quite sensibly regard a criminal past as negative evidence of the value of associating with a person.[52]

Do you agree?

2. Few courts have followed *Briscoe*, and *Briscoe* is practically confined to its facts. For example, in *Roshto v. Herbert*, 439 So. 2d 428 (La. 1983), the court rejected a public disclosure action for the random republication of a 25-year-old article concerning the plaintiff's past criminal convictions in a local newspaper. The court rejected the plaintiff's reliance on *Briscoe* because the article was part of a "randomly selected front page, which contained a number of articles," and that although the defendants "were arguably insensitive and careless in reproducing a former front page for publication without checking for information that might be currently offensive to some members of the community. . . . more than insensitivity or simple carelessness is required for the imposition of liability for damages when the publication is truthful, accurate, and non-malicious."[53]

3. Recall *Cox Broadcasting Corp. v. Cohn, Smith v. Daily Mail*, and *Florida Star v. B.J.F.* from Chapter 2. As the *Cox* Court stated: "[o]nce true information is disclosed in public court documents open to public inspection, the press cannot be sanctioned for publishing it." Consider *Rawlins v. Hutchinson Publishing Co.*, 543 P.2d 988, 993 (Kan. 1975):

> *Cox*, as we read it, would surely dictate a different result in both *Melvin* and *Briscoe*. In both of these cases, the name of the plaintiff, like the name in *Cox*, could be found in the public records. Liability for publishing the names would be, as we see it, prohibited by the First and Fourteenth Amendments. *Cox* strikes us as more sound than *Melvin* or *Briscoe*. The purpose of the tort is to protect an individual against unwarranted publication of private facts. Once facts become public the right to privacy ceases. We do not see how public facts, once fully exposed to the public view, can ever become private again.[54]

Do the *Cox* line of cases make *Briscoe* invalid? Is there any way that *Briscoe* can survive the *Cox* line of cases?

4. Under the constitutional right to information privacy, there is no privacy interest in police records. *See Cline v. Rogers*. But under the public disclosure tort, there can be. Even though these cases occur in different contexts, are they coherent?

5. *Access Restrictions.* Some states have restricted access to certain information in law enforcement records. For example, California prohibited access to the addresses of arrestees and crime victims for those seeking to use the information to sell products and services. *See* Cal. Govt. Code § 6254(f)(3). Are such restrictions constitutional under the First Amendment? For the

---

[52] Richard A. Posner, *The Economics of Justice* 260–261 (1983).

[53] *See also Forsher v. Bugliosi*, 608 P.2d 716, 726 (Cal. 1980); *Beruan v. French*, 128 Cal. Rptr. 869 (Cal. 1976); *Baker v. Burlington Northern, Inc.*, 587 P.2d 829 (Idaho 1978); *Johnson v. Harcourt Brace Jovanovich*, 188 Cal. Rptr. 370 (Cal. 1975).

[54] *See also Montesano v. Donrey Media Group*, 668 P.2d 1081 (Nev. 1983); *Romaine v. Kallinger*, 537 A.2d 284 (N.J. 1988).

Court's answer, see *Los Angeles Police Department v. United Reporting Publishing Co.*, 528 U.S. 32 (1999) (Chapter 6).

6. Recall *Scheetz v. The Morning Call, Inc.* Could Ken and Rosann Scheetz prevail on a suit against the newspaper for public disclosure of private facts under a *Briscoe* theory?

7. Today, many newspaper articles are readily archived and available over the Internet or in Westlaw or LEXIS/NEXIS. Does a reformed criminal still have an expectation of privacy when articles about her past crimes can readily be accessed over the Internet?

3. MEGAN'S LAW

In 1994, in New Jersey, a seven-year-old girl, Megan Kanka, was brutally raped and murdered by her neighbor, Jesse Timmendequas, who had two earlier sexual assault convictions. Nobody in Megan's family knew about Timmendequas's prior criminal record. Seventeen days after Megan's death, New Jersey Assembly Speaker Chuck Haytaian declared a legislative emergency. A law was proposed, called "Megan's Law," to establish a system for people to learn of the whereabouts of sexual offenders who were released from prison. The statute passed without committee hearings and without supportive research. Within three months of Megan's death, the law was signed by Governor Christie Whitman and became law. Similar laws appeared in other states. These laws, commonly called "Megan's Laws," set up databases of personal information about sexual offenders so that people can learn their identities and where they live.

In 1996, Congress passed a federal Megan's Law restricting states from receiving federal anticrime funds unless they agreed to "release relevant information that is necessary to protect the public" from released sex offenders. *See* Pub. L. No. 104-145, codified at 42 U.S.C. 14071(d)(2). Today, all 50 states have passed a version of Megan's Law. Sex offender registries under Megan's Law often contain information such as the sex offender's Social Security number, photograph, address, prior convictions, and places of employment.

States differ in how they disseminate sexual offender information. In California, booths are set up at county fairs so that individuals can browse through the registry. Some states have 1-800 or 1-900 numbers where people can call in and ask if particular people are sex offenders. At least 16 states have made their registries available on the Internet.

PAUL P. V. VERNIERO

170 F.3d 396 (3d Cir. 1999)

SLOVITER, J. Plaintiff Paul P. sues on his behalf and on behalf of a class of persons who, having been convicted of specified sex crimes, are required to comply with N.J. Stat. Ann. § 2c:7-1 et seq., known as "Megan's Law," which provides for a system of registration and community notification. . . .

In a related action, *E.B. v. Verniero*, 119 F.3d 1077 (3d Cir. 1997), this court rejected the claims of comparably situated persons that the community notification requirements violate the Double Jeopardy Clause or the Ex Post Facto

Clause of the United States Constitution. That holding of *E.B.* was predicated on the conclusion that the notification required by Megan's Law does not constitute punishment. . . .

In this case, plaintiffs raise a challenge to Megan's Law that they claim is different from that considered in *E.B.* They argue that the statutory requirement that the class members provide extensive information to local law enforcement personnel, including each registrant's current biographical data, physical description, home address, place of employment, schooling, and a description and license plate number of the registrant's vehicle, and the subsequent community notification is a violation of their constitutionally protected right to privacy.

The statutory scheme is described in detail in *E.B.*, and we refer only briefly to the salient details. We explained the registration requirements as follows:

> The registrant must provide the following information to the chief law enforcement officer of the municipality in which he resides: name, social security number, age, race, sex, date of birth, height, weight, hair and eye color, address of legal residence, address of any current temporary legal residence, and date and place of employment. N.J.S.A. 2C:7-4b(1). He must confirm his address every ninety days, notify the municipal law enforcement agency if he moves, and re-register with the law enforcement agency of any new municipality. N.J.S.A. 2C:7-2d to e.

The information provided by the registrant is put into a central registry, open to other law enforcement personnel but not to public inspection. Law enforcement officials then use the data provided to apply a "Risk Assessment Scale," a numerical scoring system, to determine the registrant's "risk of offense" and the tier in which the registrant should be classified. In the case of Tier 1 registrants, notification is given only to law enforcement agents "likely to encounter" the registrant. Tier 2, or "moderate risk," notification is given to law enforcement agents, schools, and community organizations "likely to encounter" the registrant. Tier 3, or "high risk," notification goes to all members of the public "likely to encounter" the registrant. Notifications generally contain a warning that the information is confidential and should not be disseminated to others, as well as an admonition that actions taken against the registrant, such as assaults, are illegal.

The prosecutor must provide the registrant with notice of the proposed notification. A pre-notification judicial review process is available for any registrant who wishes to challenge his or her classification.

The plaintiffs are Tier 2 and Tier 3 registrants who have been certified as a class and whose offenses were committed after the enactment of Megan's Law. . . .

The legal foundation for plaintiffs' claim is the Supreme Court's recognition that there is "a right of personal privacy, or a guarantee of certain areas or zones of privacy," protected by the United States Constitution. *Roe v. Wade*, 410 U.S. 113, 152 (1973). This "guarantee of personal privacy" covers "only personal rights that can be deemed 'fundamental' or 'implicit in the concept of ordered liberty.'" This privacy right "has some extension to activities relating to marriage, procreation, contraception, family relationships, and child rearing and education."

Plaintiffs argue that Megan's Law infringes upon their constitutionally protected privacy interests in two ways. One is by the dissemination of information about them, most particularly by disseminating both their home addresses and a "compilation of information which would otherwise remain 'scattered' or 'wholly forgotten.'" Their other claim is that the community notification infringes upon their "privacy interests in their most intimate relationships — those with their spouses, children, parents, and other family members."

Plaintiffs thus seek to invoke the two categories of privacy interests identified by the Supreme Court in *Whalen v. Roe*. . . .

The parties dispute the extent to which our decision in *E.B.* is dispositive of the privacy issue before us in this case. Plaintiffs contend that no privacy issue was raised, briefed, or argued in *E.B.* and that the discussion in *E.B.* relating to cases on which they rely is dictum. The State defendants, on the other hand, regard "[t]he portions of the *E.B.* decision holding that community notification does not implicate a fundamental privacy interest and the finding of a compelling state interest in protecting the public from recidivist sex offenders," as "control[ling] the decision in this case." We thus turn to examine the *E.B.* decision.

The privacy issue arose in *E.B.* during our analysis of whether community notification mandated by Megan's Law constitutes punishment for purposes of the Ex Post Facto and Double Jeopardy Clauses. In that context, we stated that the "primary sting from Megan's law notification comes by way of injury to what is denoted . . . as reputational interests. This includes . . . the myriad of . . . ways in which one is treated differently by virtue of being known as a potentially dangerous sex offender." *E.B.*, 119 F.3d at 1102. We then referred to the Supreme Court's holding in *Paul v. Davis*, stating:

> Just as Davis sought constitutional protection from the consequences of state disclosure of the fact of his shoplifting arrest and law enforcement's assessment that he was a continuing risk, so registrants seek protection from what may follow disclosure of facts related to their sex offense convictions and the resulting judgment of the state that they are a continuing risk. It follows that, just as the officers' publication of the official act of Davis' arrest did not violate any fundamental privacy right of Davis', neither does New Jersey's publication (through notification) of registrants' convictions and findings of dangerousness implicate any interest of fundamental constitutional magnitude.

We rejected the contention that dissemination of information about criminal activity beyond law enforcement personnel is analogous to historical punishments, such as the stocks, cages, and scarlet letters. We found instead that the dissemination is more like the dissemination of "rap sheet" information to regulatory agencies, bar associations, prospective employers, and interested members of the public that public indictment, public trial, and public imposition of sentence necessarily entail. We noted that although the Supreme Court later recognized in *United States Department of Justice v. Reporters Committee for Freedom of the Press*, 489 U.S. 749 (1989), that the dissemination of "rap sheets" implicates a privacy interest, the Court there was determining whether a "rap sheet" fell under the "privacy interest" protected by an exemption to the Freedom of Information Act ("FOIA"), not that protected by the Constitution. We pointed out that the Supreme Court itself made the distinction between the two types of privacy interest, and we quoted its statement in *Reporters Committee*, that "[t]he question of the statutory meaning of privacy under the FOIA is, of course, not the same as the question . . . whether an individual's interest in privacy is protected by the Constitution." . . .

. . . Finally, we concluded in *E.B.* that even if a "fundamental right" were implicated, "the state's interest here would suffice to justify the deprivation." . . .

The District Court here concluded that there was no privacy interest in the plaintiffs' home addresses, stating that "[b]ecause such information is public, plaintiffs' privacy interests are not implicated." As to the argument based on the "compilation" of various information, the court held that "[i]t is of little consequence whether this public information is disclosed piecemeal or whether it is disclosed in compilation."

To the extent that plaintiffs' alleged injury stems from the disclosure of their sex offender status, alone or in conjunction with other information, the District Court's opinion is in line with other cases in this court and elsewhere holding specifically that arrest records and related information are not protected by a right to privacy. See *Fraternal Order of Police*, 812 F.2d at 117 (holding that "arrest records are not entitled to privacy protection" because they are public); *Cline v. Rogers*, 87 F.3d 176, 179 (6th Cir.) (holding that "there is no constitutional right to privacy in one's criminal record" because "arrest and conviction information are matters of public record"). . . .

We are not insensitive to the argument that notification implicates plaintiffs' privacy interest by disclosing their home addresses. The compilation of home addresses in widely available telephone directories might suggest a consensus that these addresses are not considered private were it not for the fact that a significant number of persons, ranging from public officials and performers to just ordinary folk, choose to list their telephones privately, because they regard their home addresses to be private information. Indeed, their view is supported by decisions holding that home addresses are entitled to privacy under FOIA, which exempts from disclosure personal files "the disclosure of which would constitute a clearly unwarranted invasion of personal privacy." 5 U.S.C. § 552(b)(6). . . .

Although these cases are not dispositive, they reflect the general understanding that home addresses are entitled to some privacy protection, whether or not so required by a statute. We are therefore unwilling to hold that absent a statute, a person's home address is never entitled to privacy protection. . . .

Accepting therefore the claim by the plaintiffs that there is some nontrivial interest in one's home address by persons who do not wish it disclosed, we must engage in the balancing inquiry repeatedly held appropriate in privacy cases. . . .

The nature and significance of the state interest served by Megan's Law was considered in *E.B.* There, we stated that the state interest, which we characterized as compelling, "would suffice to justify the deprivation even if a fundamental right of the registrant's were implicated." We find no reason to disagree. The public interest in knowing where prior sex offenders live so that susceptible individuals can be appropriately cautioned does not differ whether the issue is the registrant's claim under the Double Jeopardy or Ex Post Facto Clauses, or is the registrant's claim to privacy. . . .

The other argument raised by plaintiffs as part of their privacy claim is that community notification infringes upon their fundamental interest in family relationships. . . . In *E.B.*, we recognized that Megan's Law "impose[s] no restrictions on a registrant's ability to live and work in a community," but that plaintiffs complain of the law's "indirect effects: Actions that members of the community may take as a result of learning of the registrant's past, his potential danger, and his presence in the community." Even if we concede, as the District Court did, that "being subject to Megan's Law community notification places a constitutionally cognizable strain upon familial relationships," these indirect effects which follow from plaintiffs' commission of a crime are too substantially different from the government actions at issue in the prior cases to fall within the penumbra of constitutional privacy protection. Megan's Law does not restrict plaintiffs' freedom of action with respect to their families and therefore does not intrude upon the aspect of the right to privacy that protects an individual's independence in making certain types of important decisions. . . .

During the pendency of this appeal, appellants filed a series of motions under seal, six in all, seeking to supplement the record with evidence of recent incidents which have caused serious adverse consequences to them and their families. . . .

. . . [T]his court has previously held that "[t]he fact that protected information must be disclosed to a party who has a particular need for it . . . does not strip the information of its protection against disclosure to those who have no similar need," and we have required the government to implement adequate safeguards against unnecessary disclosure. Because these motions were filed in this court in the first instance, the District Court has not had the opportunity to consider the information contained therein and to determine whether any action is appropriate in light of our precedent.

[We] will remand this matter so that the District Court can consider whether plaintiffs' interest in assuring that information is disclosed only to those who have a particular need for it has been accorded adequate protection in light of the information set forth in the motions. . . .

NOTES & QUESTIONS

1. In *Russell v. Gregoire*, 124 F.3d 1079 (9th Cir. 1997), the court considered a similar challenge under the constitutional right to information privacy to Washington's version of Megan's Law. The law required a sex offender released from custody to provide his or her name, address, date and place of birth, place of employment, crime convicted of, Social Security number, and other information. A photograph and fingerprints are also collected. Wash. Rev. Code §9A.44.130(1). If there is "some evidence of an offender's future dangerousness, likelihood of reoffense, or threat to the community," some of the information the offender supplied may be disseminated to the public. The public notification includes the offender's photo, name, age, birth date, other identifying information, and a summary of his or her crime. It includes the general vicinity of his or her residence, but not the exact ad-

dress. It does not include data about employment. The court held that the statute did not run afoul of the constitutional right to information privacy:

> In this case, the collection and dissemination of information is carefully designed and narrowly limited. Even if *Whalen* and *Nixon* had established a broad right to privacy in data compilations, the Act does not unduly disseminate private information about Russell and Stearns.
>
> Moreover, any such right to privacy, to the extent it exists at all, would protect only personal information. The information collected and disseminated by the Washington statute is already fully available to the public and is not constitutionally protected, with the exception of the general vicinity of the offender's residence (which is published) and the offender's employer (which is collected but not released to the public). Neither of these two items are generally considered "private."
>
> Likewise, the Supreme Court in *Paul v. Davis*, held that damage to one's reputation by a state actor does not violate a liberty or property interest "apart from some more tangible interests such as employment." The collection and dissemination of information under the Washington law does not violate any protected privacy interest, and does not amount to a deprivation of liberty or property.

2. ***The Privacy Interest.*** Recall that in *Paul P.*, the court held that the reasoning of *United States Department of Justice v. Reporters Committee for Freedom of the Press*, 489 U.S. 749 (1989), was inapplicable to the constitutional right to information privacy. In *Reporters Committee*, reporters sought disclosure of FBI "rap sheets" (compilations of a person's arrests, charges, and convictions) under the Freedom of Information Act (FOIA), which mandates that government agencies disclose their records and documents unless one of FOIA's exceptions applies. Under one exception, the government can refuse to release records if they will constitute an invasion of a person's privacy. Although the reporters claimed that the events summarized in the rap sheet had previously been publicly disclosed, the Court held:

> In an organized society, there are few facts that are not at one time or another divulged to another. Thus, the extent of the protection accorded a privacy right at common law rested in part on the degree of dissemination of the allegedly private fact and the extent to which the passage of time rendered it private. . . . Recognition of this attribute of a privacy interest supports the distinction, in terms of personal privacy, between scattered disclosure of the bits of information contained in a rap sheet and revelation of the rap sheet as a whole.

This case will be discussed in greater depth when FOIA is covered in Chapter 6. The reasoning of this case suggests that sexual offenders have a privacy interest in their prior convictions. Should the reasoning of *Reporters Committee* apply to the constitutional right to information privacy?

Prior to *Paul P.*, the New Jersey Supreme Court had upheld New Jersey's Megan's Law in *Doe v. Poritz*, 662 A.2d 367 (N.J. 1995). There, the court, relying on *Reporters Committee*, recognized a privacy interest in some of the information divulged by New Jersey's Megan's Law:

> . . . We find . . . that considering the totality of the information disclosed to the public, the Notification Law implicates a privacy interest. That the information disseminated under the Notification Law may be available to the

public, in some form or other, does not mean that plaintiff has no interest in limiting its dissemination. As the Court recognized in *United States Department of Justice v. Reporters Committee for Freedom of the Press*, 489 U.S. 749, 763 (1989), privacy "encompass[es] the individual's control of information concerning his or her person." . . .

. . . [T]he Court recognized a "distinction . . . between scattered disclosure of the bits of information contained in a rap sheet and revelation of the rap sheet as a whole." . . . The Court noted, furthermore, that there was a "privacy interest inherent in the nondisclosure of certain information even when the information may have been at one time public." . . .

The distinction between merely providing access to information and compiling and disclosing that information is evident in this case. Government dissemination of information to which the public merely has access through various sources eliminates the costs, in time, effort, and expense, that members of the public would incur in assembling the information themselves. Those costs, however, may severely limit the extent to which the information becomes a matter of public knowledge. The Notification Law therefore exposes various bits of information that, although accessible to the public, may remain obscure. Indeed, as in *Reporters Committee*, if the information disclosed under the Notification Law were, in fact, freely available, there would be no need for the law.

In exposing those various bits of information to the public, the Notification Law links various bits of information — name, appearance, address, and crime — that otherwise might remain unconnected. However public any of those individual pieces of information may be, were it not for the Notification Law, those connections might never be made. We believe a privacy interest is implicated when the government assembles those diverse pieces of information into a single package and disseminates that package to the public, thereby ensuring that a person cannot assume anonymity — in this case, preventing a person's criminal history from fading into obscurity and being wholly forgotten. Those convicted of crime may have no cognizable privacy interest in the fact of their conviction, but the Notification Law, given the compilation and dissemination of information, nonetheless implicates a privacy interest. The interests in privacy may fade when the information is a matter of public record, but they are not non-existent. . . .

The court, however, concluded that the state interest outweighed the sexual offender's privacy interest:

> . . . We find . . . that the state interest in public disclosure substantially outweighs plaintiff's interest in privacy. First, the information requested is not deserving of a particularly high degree of protection. We are not dealing with thoughts and feelings revealed in the course of psychiatric treatment, medical information in general, or medical information regarding HIV status. Plaintiff, therefore, can claim only a most limited expectation of privacy in the information to be disseminated. Second, because of the public nature of the information, we cannot speak of harm either from non-consensual disclosure or damage to the relationship in which the records were generated. We neither risk exposing intimate details of plaintiff's life, like those laid bare to a psychiatrist, nor do we risk damaging a relationship like that between patient and doctor by releasing plaintiff's name, address or description.
>
> Counterbalanced against plaintiff's diminished privacy interest is a strong state interest in public disclosure. There is an express public policy militat-

ing toward disclosure: the danger of recidivism posed by sex offenders. The state interest in protecting the safety of members of the public from sex offenders is clear and compelling. The Legislature has determined that there is a substantial danger of recidivism by sex offenders, and public notification clearly advances the purpose of protecting the public from that danger. . . .

Compare the treatment of *Reporter's Committee* in *Paul P.* and *Poritz.* How do the cases differ in the way they deal with the import of *Reporter's Committee?* [55]

3. Do Megan's Laws strike the appropriate balance between community safety and privacy? [56]

4. *Postscript to* **Paul P.** Following the Third Circuit's decision in *Paul P.*, the district court on remand held that the Megan's Law regulations in New Jersey did not sufficiently protect against unauthorized disclosures. The plaintiffs had cited to 45 instances where information had been released to unauthorized persons, with one disclosure resulting in the offender's name and address being printed in an article on the front page of a newspaper. Although noting that zero leakage is unattainable, the court stated that the government must avoid "unreasonably impinging on the 'nontrivial' privacy interests" of the plaintiffs and that the current Megan's Law regulations failed to meet this standard. *Paul P. v. Farmer*, 80 F. Supp. 2d 320 (D.N.J. 2000). The state attorney general promulgated new guidelines which were approved by the district court and affirmed on appeal. *See Paul P. v. Farmer*, 227 F.3d 98 (3d Cir. 2000). Under the new guidelines, there are two forms of notice. An "unredacted notice" contains all information. A "redacted notice" omits the specific home address of the offender as well as the name and address of the employer. To receive an unredacted notice, the recipient must sign a form agreeing to be bound by court order and submitting to the jurisdiction of the court. The recipient must agree to share information only with her household and those caring for her children. If the person refuses to sign the receipt, then she can only receive the redacted notice.

In 2000, New Jersey amended its Constitution by a referendum which provided that nothing in the New Jersey Constitution shall prohibit the disclosure of Megan's Law information over the Internet. New Jersey subsequently posted its sexual offender data on a web site, excluding the offenders' current home addresses. Based on the Third Circuit in *Paul P.*, would this be upheld under the federal Constitution?

5. *The Breadth of Megan's Laws.* Megan's Law does not merely involve offenses against children. It encompasses a wide range of sex offenses, which

---

[55] *See also Cutshall v. Sundquist*, 193 F.3d 466 (6th Cir. 1999) (rejecting reliance on *Reporters Committee* and concluding that constitutional right to information privacy is not implicated by Megan's Law).

[56] For more on the privacy implications of Megan's Laws, see Caroline Louise Lewis, *The Jacob Wetterling Crimes Against Children and Sexually Violent Offender Registration Act: An Unconstitutional Deprivation of the Right to Privacy and Substantive Due Process*, 31 Harv. C.R.-C.L. L. Rev. 89 (1996); Symposium, *Critical Perspectives on Megan's Law: Protection vs. Privacy*, 13 N.Y.L. Sch. J. Hum. Rts. 1 (1996).

can range from sodomy, prostitution, consensual homosexual acts, masturbation in public places, flashing, and statutory rape. In some states, the disclosure does not indicate what particular sexual offense the offender committed. Is such a listing appropriate? Is Megan's Law justified under the constitutional right to information privacy for every offense that a state classifies as a sexual offense? Or does the balance weigh in favor of Megan's Law only for specific offenses? If so, how should such offenses be distinguished from ones in which the balance does not weigh in favor of Megan's Law?

6. ***Recidivism Rates.*** One of the justifications for Megan's Law is that sexual offenders have a high recidivism rate and, hence, pose a threat to the community. But sexual offenders have a lower recidivism rate than other forms of violent crime, such as robberies. In one study of offenders re-arrested within three years for any crime, previously convicted murderers had approximately a 42 percent re-arrest rate; rapists had a 51.5 percent re-arrest rate; other sexual offenders had a 48 percent re-arrest rate; and robbers had a 66 percent re-arrest rate. However, re-arrest rates, without more information, are misleading. Of the 51.5 percent of rapists who were re-arrested within three years after being released, only 7.7 percent were re-arrested for a sex crime. Further, different types of sexual offenders have different recidivism rates.[57]

7. ***Family Stigma.*** The majority of sexual offenses against children are committed by family members or close friends of the family (estimated at about 92 percent).[58] When a child's parent is released and is listed in the sex offender registry, the child's privacy is also compromised because the entire family is under the stigma of harboring a sexual offender.

8. ***Shaming Punishments.*** In colonial America, marking criminals with branding, mutilation, or letter-wearing (such as the scarlet letter) was common. Marks would be burned into the convict's hand or forehead. This was often done because there was no way of imprisoning people. This was the sort of punishment used against Hester Prynne in Nathaniel Hawthorne's *The Scarlet Letter*, where Prynne was made to stitch a red letter "A" to her clothing to punish her for adultery. Does Megan's Law amount to a shaming punishment? Is this form of punishment appropriate?

Today, shaming punishments are making a comeback. In a move more broad than Megan's Law, some localities are publicizing the names of certain arrestees. For example, in 1997, Kansas City created "John TV," broadcasting on television the names, photographs, addresses, and ages of people who had been arrested for soliciting prostitutes. Similar programs have been started in other cities. Is this more or less problematic to you than Megan's Law?

---

[57] *See* Jane A. Small, *Who Are the People in Your Neighborhood? Due Process, Public Protection, and Sex Offender Notification Laws*, 74 N.Y.U. L. Rev. 1451 (1999). For a contrary view regarding recidivism rates for sex offenders, see Daniel L. Feldman, *The "Scarlet Letter Laws" of the 1990s: A Response to Critics*, 60 Alb. L. Rev. 1081 (1997).

[58.] Michele L. Earl-Hubbard, Comment, *The Child Sex Offender Registration Laws: The Punishment, Liberty Deprivation, and Unintended Results Associated with the Scarlet Letter Laws of the 1990s*, 90 Nw. U. L. Rev. 788, 851–852 (1996).

9. A growing number of states are furnishing online databases of all of their current inmates and parolees. Do these databases serve the statutory purpose of protecting the community? Should registries of felons stop at sexual offenders? Why not all people convicted of a crime?

10. In May 2001, Judge J. Manuel Banales of Texas ordered 21 convicted sex offenders to post signs in their front yards stating: "Danger! Registered Sex Offender Lives Here." Additionally, the offenders must place bumper stickers on their cars stating: "Danger! Registered Sex Offender in Vehicle." Other offenders were ordered to send letters to all the people who lived within three blocks of their homes. Compliance is monitored by the probation department. "The whole idea is that everybody is looking at you," Judge Banales said to the offenders. "You have no one else to blame but yourself." Under the reasoning of either *Russell* and *Paul P.*, is this a violation of the constitutional right to information privacy?

11. Does Megan's Law thwart rehabilitation? Recall the reasoning in *Briscoe* that privacy is essential to the ability of a person to become reintegrated into the community. There have been a number of instances of sexual offenders being harassed, threatened, assaulted, and driven out of their homes by angry citizens and neighbors. Perhaps exposing sexual offenders to these reactions will thwart their ability to rehabilitate and will make them more likely to commit crimes or sexual offenses in the future.

    Is Megan's Law consistent with the reasoning of *Briscoe*? Suppose a state repealed its Megan's Law, but a private organization decided to construct its own sexual offender database with public record data and make it available on the Internet. Could a sexual offender bring a successful suit for public disclosure of private facts?

12. Suppose that instead of enacting Megan's Laws, society just decided to extend the sentences for sexual offenses and lock up sexual offenders for life. Perhaps if states could not enact Megan's Law, they would resort to more life sentences for sexual offenders. Most likely, many offenders would choose a regime where they would be released from prison and subject to Megan's Law to a regime where they would spend the rest of their lives in prison. What do you think about this potential trade-off?

5

PRIVACY OF ASSOCIATIONS, ANONYMITY, AND IDENTIFICATION

Privacy is deeply related to the development of individual identity. This chapter focuses on the relationship between privacy and identity in three principal areas: (1) group associations; (2) anonymous communication; and (3) identification systems. Although these three areas are very different, they all implicate privacy interests. We construct our identities based on our families, our activities, reading and reacting to ideas, discourse with others, and associations with other people and various groups and organizations.

This chapter begins with group association because the Court's freedom of association cases have significantly influenced the Court's view of anonymity. The groups we belong to form an important component of who we are as individuals. As Oscar Gandy observes:

> It is important to note that individual identities are formed in interaction with others. The characteristics of those interactions help to determine the salience, as well as the level of comfort with which different aspects of one's identity co-exist. Self-esteem, or how an individual feels about herself is determined, in part, by the ways in which her relevant reference groups are evaluated by others. . . .[1]

Consider as well the following argument of Edward Bloustein:

> Group privacy is an extension of individual privacy. The interest protected by group privacy is the desire and need of people to come together, to exchange information, share feelings, make plans and act in concert to attain their objectives. This requires that people reveal themselves to one another — breach their individual privacy — and rely on those with whom they associate to keep within the group what was revealed.[2]

Identification as a member of an unpopular group may result in severe social and financial repercussions. For example, identification as being a mem-

---

[1] Oscar H. Gandy, Jr., *Exploring Identity and Identification in Cyberspace*, 14 Notre Dame J.L. Ethics & Pub. Pol'y 1085 (2000).

[2] Edward J. Bloustein, *Individual and Group Privacy* 125 (1978).

ber of the Communist Party, especially during the McCarthy era in the 1950s, often resulted in the loss of one's job and being blacklisted from future employment. People may also belong to groups that they do not want other people (their parents, employers, or certain friends) to know about. Privacy is essential to preserving people's ability to form bonds and associate with others having similar beliefs and views. The First Amendment recognizes the importance of preserving the freedom to associate: "Congress shall make no law . . . abridging . . . the right of the people peacefully to assemble." Additionally, group association is often central to political expression, implicating the First Amendment's protection of speech. Without privacy, people will be deterred from engaging in these important identity forming and expressive activities.

In a similar way, the ability to communicate anonymously helps to promote freedom of expression. People often express, listen to, and read unpopular ideas. The identification of a speaker or reader can severely chill these activities. As Gary Marx notes, anonymity can "facilitate the flow of information and communication on public issues" and "encourage experimentation and risk taking without facing large consequences, risk of failure or embarrassment since one's identity is protected."[3] Consider the following argument by A. Michael Froomkin:

> . . . Not everyone is so courageous as to wish to be known for everything they say, and some timorous speech deserves encouragement. Corporate whistle-blowers, even junior professors, may fear losing their jobs. People criticizing a religious cult or other movement from which they might fear retaliation may fear losing their lives. In some countries, even this one in some times and places, it is unsafe to be heard to criticize the government. Persons who wish to criticize a repressive government or foment a revolution against it may find anonymity invaluable. Indeed, given the ability to broadcast messages widely using the Internet, anonymous e-mail may become the modern replacement of the anonymous handbill.
>
> Communicative anonymity encourages people to post requests for information to public bulletin boards about matters they may find too personal to discuss if there were any chance that the message might be traced back to its origin. In addition to the obvious psychological benefits to people who thus find themselves enabled to communicate, there may be external benefits to the entire community. . . .[4]

This chapter also explores identification by way of various identification systems (such as numbers assigned to individuals, identification cards, biometric identifiers, and so on). This form of systematic social identification has profound implications for the type of society we wish to create. Identification systems have both social benefits and costs. Identification is increasingly important for a society as large and sophisticated as ours, where transactions are made impersonally among strangers. Further, proponents of identification systems have contended that they will promote security. However, such sys-

---

[3] Gary T. Marx, *Identity and Anonymity: Some Conceptual Distinctions and Issues for Research*, in Jane Caplan & John Torpey, *Documenting Individual Identity* 311, 316, 318 (2001).

[4] A. Michael Froomkin, *Flood Control on the Information Ocean: Living with Anonymity, Digital Cash, and Distributed Databases*, 15 J.L. & Comm. 395, 408 (1996).

tems have been criticized because they can impede one's ability to travel freely in society. Such systems can also threaten the individual's freedom to define her own identity by imposing on her a government mandated identity that reduces her to a mere number and associated data in a database. Further, such systems may facilitate dangerous forms of social control and subject individuals to a variety of bureaucratic abuses.

A. PRIVACY OF GROUP ASSOCIATIONS

1. COMPELLED DISCLOSURE OF GROUP MEMBERSHIP LISTS

NATIONAL ASSOCIATION FOR THE ADVANCEMENT OF COLORED PEOPLE v. STATE OF ALABAMA

357 U.S. 449 (1958)

HARLAN, J. . . . Alabama has a statute similar to those of many other States which requires a foreign corporation, except as exempted, to qualify before doing business by filing its corporate charter with the Secretary of State and designating a place of business and an agent to receive service of process. The statute imposes a fine on a corporation transacting intrastate business before qualifying and provides for criminal prosecution of officers of such a corporation. The National Association for the Advancement of Colored People is a nonprofit membership corporation organized under the laws of New York. . . . [Although operating an office in Alabama, the] Association has never complied with the qualification statute, from which it considered itself exempt.

In 1956 the Attorney General of Alabama brought an equity suit in the State Circuit Court, Montgomery County, to enjoin the Association from conducting further activities within, and to oust it from, the State. . . . The bill [in equity] recited that the Association, by continuing to do business in Alabama without complying with the qualification statute, was ". . . causing irreparable injury to the property and civil rights of the residents and citizens of the State of Alabama. . . ." On the day the complaint was filed, the Circuit Court issued ex parte an order restraining the Association, pendente lite, from engaging in further activities within the State and forbidding it to take any steps to qualify itself to do business therein.

Petitioner demurred to the allegations of the bill and moved to dissolve the restraining order. . . . Before the date set for a hearing on this motion, the State moved for the production of a large number of the Association's records and papers, including bank statements, leases, deeds, and records containing the names and addresses of all Alabama "members" and "agents" of the Association. It alleged that all such documents were necessary for adequate preparation for the hearing, in view of petitioner's denial of the conduct of intrastate business within the meaning of the qualification statute. Over petitioner's objections, the court ordered the production of a substantial part of the requested records, including the membership lists, and postponed the hearing on the restraining order to a date later than the time ordered for production. . . .

Petitioner argues that in view of the facts and circumstances shown in the record, the effect of compelled disclosure of the membership lists will be to abridge the rights of its rank-and-file members to engage in lawful association in support of their common beliefs. It contends that governmental action which, although not directly suppressing association, nevertheless carries this consequence, can be justified only upon some overriding valid interest of the State.

Effective advocacy of both public and private points of view, particularly controversial ones, is undeniably enhanced by group association, as this Court has more than once recognized by remarking upon the close nexus between the freedoms of speech and assembly. It is beyond debate that freedom to engage in association for the advancement of beliefs and ideas is an inseparable aspect of the "liberty" assured by the Due Process Clause of the Fourteenth Amendment, which embraces freedom of speech. Of course, it is immaterial whether the beliefs sought to be advanced by association pertain to political, economic, religious or cultural matters, and state action which may have the effect of curtailing the freedom to associate is subject to the closest scrutiny.

The fact that Alabama, so far as is relevant to the validity of the contempt judgment presently under review, has taken no direct action to restrict the right of petitioner's members to associate freely, does not end inquiry into the effect of the production order. In the domain of these indispensable liberties, whether of speech, press, or association, the decisions of this Court recognize that abridgement of such rights, even though unintended, may inevitably follow from varied forms of governmental action. . . .

It is hardly a novel perception that compelled disclosure of affiliation with groups engaged in advocacy may constitute as effective a restraint on freedom of association as the forms of governmental action in the cases above were thought likely to produce upon the particular constitutional rights there involved. This Court has recognized the vital relationship between freedom to associate and privacy in one's associations. When referring to the varied forms of governmental action which might interfere with freedom of assembly, it said in *American Communications Ass'n v. Douds*: "A requirement that adherents of particular religious faiths or political parties wear identifying arm-bands, for example, is obviously of this nature." Compelled disclosure of membership in an organization engaged in advocacy of particular beliefs is of the same order. Inviolability of privacy in group association may in many circumstances be indispensable to preservation of freedom of association, particularly where a group espouses dissident beliefs.

We think that the production order, in the respects here drawn in question, must be regarded as entailing the likelihood of a substantial restraint upon the exercise by petitioner's members of their right to freedom of association. Petitioner has made an uncontroverted showing that on past occasions revelation of the identity of its rank-and-file members has exposed these members to economic reprisal, loss of employment, threat of physical coercion, and other manifestations of public hostility. Under these circumstances, we think it apparent that compelled disclosure of petitioner's Alabama membership is likely to affect adversely the ability of petitioner and its members to pursue their collective effort to foster beliefs which they admittedly have the right to advocate, in that it may induce members to withdraw from the Association and dissuade others from joining it because of fear of exposure of their beliefs shown through their associations and of the consequences of this exposure.

It is not sufficient to answer, as the State does here, that whatever repressive effect compulsory disclosure of names of petitioner's members may have upon participation by Alabama citizens in petitioner's activities follows not from state action but from private community pressures. The crucial factor is the interplay of governmental and private action, for it is only after the initial exertion of state power represented by the production order that private action takes hold.

We turn to the final question whether Alabama has demonstrated an interest in obtaining the disclosures it seeks from petitioner which is sufficient to justify the deterrent effect which we have concluded these disclosures may well have on the free exercise by petitioner's members of their constitutionally protected right of association. Such a ". . . subordinating interest of the State must be compelling." . . .

Whether there was "justification" in this instance turns solely on the substantiality of Alabama's interest in obtaining the membership lists. . . . The issues in the litigation commenced by Alabama by its bill in equity were whether the character of petitioner and its activities in Alabama had been such as to make petitioner subject to the registration statute, and whether the extent of petitioner's activities without qualifying suggested its permanent ouster from the State. Without intimating the slightest view upon the merits of these issues, we are unable to perceive that the disclosure of the names of petitioner's rank-and-file members has a substantial bearing on either of them. . . .

NOTES & QUESTIONS

1. In *Bates v. City of Little Rock*, 361 U.S. 516 (1960), the Court struck down a Little Rock, Arkansas, ordinance requiring the disclosure of the NAACP's members and contributors:

   > On this record it sufficiently appears that compulsory disclosure of the membership lists of the local branches of the National Association for the Advancement of Colored People would work a significant interference with the freedom of association of their members. There was substantial uncontroverted evidence that public identification of persons in the community as members of the organizations had been followed by harassment and threats of bodily harm. There was also evidence that fear of community hostility and economic reprisals that would follow public disclosure of the membership lists had discouraged new members from joining the organizations and induced former members to withdraw. This repressive effect, while in part the result of private attitudes and pressures, was brought to bear only after the exercise of governmental power had threatened to force disclosure of the members' names.

2. Would campaign finance regulation requiring disclosure of information about one's contributions to political candidates and parties violate one's right to free association? That was the question at issue in *Buckley v. Valeo*, 424 U.S. 1 (1976):

We long have recognized that significant encroachments on First Amendment rights of the sort that compelled disclosure imposes cannot be justified by a mere showing of some legitimate governmental interest. Since *NAACP v. Alabama* we have required that the subordinating interests of the State must survive exacting scrutiny. . . .

The strict test established by *NAACP v. Alabama* is necessary because compelled disclosure has the potential for substantially infringing the exercise of First Amendment rights. But we have acknowledged that there are governmental interests sufficiently important to outweigh the possibility of infringement, particularly when the "free functioning of our national institutions" is involved. *Communist Party v. Subversive Activities Control Bd.*, 367 U.S. 1 (1961).

The governmental interests sought to be vindicated by the disclosure requirements are of this magnitude. They fall into three categories. First, disclosure provides the electorate with information "as to where political campaign money comes from and how it is spent by the candidate" in order to aid the voters in evaluating those who seek federal office. It allows voters to place each candidate in the political spectrum more precisely than is often possible solely on the basis of party labels and campaign speeches. The sources of a candidate's financial support also alert the voter to the interests to which a candidate is most likely to be responsive and thus facilitate predictions of future performance in office.

Second, disclosure requirements deter actual corruption and avoid the appearance of corruption by exposing large contributions and expenditures to the light of publicity. This exposure may discourage those who would use money for improper purposes either before or after the election. A public armed with information about a candidate's most generous supporters is better able to detect any post-election special favors that may be given in return. . . .

Third, and not least significant, recordkeeping, reporting, and disclosure requirements are an essential means of gathering the data necessary to detect violations of the contribution limitations described above.

2. INTERROGATION ABOUT GROUP ASSOCIATIONS

BARENBLATT V. UNITED STATES

360 U.S. 109 (1959)

[In 1954, a Subcommittee of the House Un-American Activities Committee summoned Lloyd Barenblatt, a 31-year-old teacher of psychology at Vassar College, to testify. The House Un-American Activities Committee was a long-standing Committee that investigated Communist activities by forcing suspected Communist Party members to disclose that they were Party members and reveal the names of other members. Before Barenblatt appeared, his contract with Vassar expired and was not renewed. The Committee wanted to question Barenblatt because another witness had stated that when Barenblatt was a graduate student, he had been associated with a small group of Communists. When called before the Committee, Barenblatt refused to answer questions pertaining to his current and past membership in the Communist Party. He was found in contempt, tried in federal district court, and sentenced to six months in prison.]

HARLAN, J. . . . The precise constitutional issue confronting us is whether the Subcommittee's inquiry into petitioner's past or present membership in the Communist Party transgressed the provisions of the First Amendment, which of course reach and limit congressional investigations.

. . . Undeniably, the First Amendment in some circumstances protects an individual from being compelled to disclose his associational relationships. However, the protections of the First Amendment, unlike a proper claim of the privilege against self-incrimination under the Fifth Amendment, do not afford a witness the right to resist inquiry in all circumstances. Where First Amendment rights are asserted to bar governmental interrogation reso- lution of the issue always involves a balancing by the courts of the competing private and public interests at stake in the particular circumstances shown. These principles were recognized in *Watkins* [*v. United States*, 354 U.S. 178], where, in speaking of the First Amendment in relation to congressional in- quiries, we said: "It is manifest that despite the adverse effects which follow upon compelled disclosure of private matters, not all such inquiries are barred. . . . The critical element is the existence of, and the weight to be as- cribed to, the interest of the Congress in demanding disclosures from an un- willing witness." . . .

The first question is whether this investigation was related to a valid leg- islative purpose, for Congress may not constitutionally require an individual to disclose his political relationships or other private affairs except in relation to such a purpose.

That Congress has wide power to legislate in the field of Communist activity in this Country, and to conduct appropriate investigations in aid thereof, is hardly debatable. . . . Justification for its exercise in turn rests on the long and widely accepted view that the tenets of the Communist Party include the ultimate overthrow of the Government of the United States by force and violence, a view which has been given formal expression by the Congress. . . .

. . . [T]he record is barren of other factors which in themselves might some- times lead to the conclusion that the individual interests at stake were not subordinate to those of the state. There is no indication in this record that the Subcommittee was attempting to pillory witnesses. Nor did petitioner's ap- pearance as a witness follow from indiscriminate dragnet procedures, lacking in probable cause for belief that he possessed information which might be helpful to the Subcommittee. And the relevancy of the questions put to him by the Subcommittee is not open to doubt.

We conclude that the balance between the individual and the govern- mental interests here at stake must be struck in favor of the latter, and that therefore the provisions of the First Amendment have not been offended. . . .

BLACK, J. joined by WARREN, C. J. and DOUGLAS, J. dissenting. . . . The First Amendment says in no equivocal language that Congress shall pass no law abridging freedom of speech, press, assembly or petition. The activities of this Committee, authorized by Congress, do precisely that, through exposure, ob- loquy and public scorn. . . .

I do not agree that laws directly abridging First Amendment freedoms can be justified by a congressional or judicial balancing process. . . .

But even assuming what I cannot assume, that some balancing is proper in this case, I feel that the Court after stating the test ignores it completely. At most it balances the right of the Government to preserve itself, against Barenblatt's right to refrain from revealing Communist affiliations. Such a balance, however, mistakes the factors to be weighed. In the first place, it completely leaves out the real interest in Barenblatt's silence, the interest of the people as a whole in being able to join organizations, advocate causes and make political "mistakes" without later being subjected to governmental penalties for having dared to think for themselves. . . .

The fact is that once we allow any group which has some political aims or ideas to be driven from the ballot and from the battle for men's minds because some of its members are bad and some of its tenets are illegal, no group is safe. Today we deal with Communists or suspected Communists. In 1920, instead, the New York Assembly suspended duly elected legislators on the ground that, being Socialists, they were disloyal to the country's principles. In the 1830's the Masons were hunted as outlaws and subversives, and abolitionists were considered revolutionaries of the most dangerous kind in both North and South. Earlier still, at the time of the universally unlamented alien and sedition laws, Thomas Jefferson's party was attacked and its members were derisively called "Jacobins." Fisher Ames described the party as a "French faction" guilty of "subversion" and "officered, regimented and formed to subordination." Its members, he claimed, intended to "take arms against the laws as soon as they dare." History should teach us then, that in times of high emotional excitement minority parties and groups which advocate extremely unpopular social or governmental innovations will always be typed as criminal gangs and attempts will always be made to drive them out. It was knowledge of this fact, and of its great dangers, that caused the Founders of our land to enact the First Amendment as a guarantee that neither Congress nor the people would do anything to hinder or destroy the capacity of individuals and groups to seek converts and votes for any cause, however radical or unpalatable their principles might seem under the accepted notions of the time. . . .

Finally, I think Barenblatt's conviction violates the Constitution because the chief aim, purpose and practice of the House Un-American Activities Committee, as disclosed by its many reports, is to try witnesses and punish them because they are or have been Communists or because they refuse to admit or deny Communist affiliations. The punishment imposed is generally punishment by humiliation and public shame. There is nothing strange or novel about this kind of punishment. It is in fact one of the oldest forms of governmental punishment known to mankind; branding, the pillory, ostracism and subjection to public hatred being but a few examples of it. . . .

. . . [T]he Committee has called witnesses who are suspected of Communist affiliation, has subjected them to severe questioning and has insisted that each tell the name of every person he has ever known at any time to have been a Communist, and, if possible, to give the addresses and occupations of the people named. These names are then indexed, published, and reported to Congress, and often to the press. The same technique is employed to cripple the job opportunities of those who strongly criticize the Committee or take other actions it deems undesirable. . . .

NOTES & QUESTIONS

1. In *Shelton v. Tucker*, 364 U.S. 479 (1960), the Court struck down a law requiring teachers to list the organizations they belonged or contributed to within the past five years. The Court held that "the statute's comprehensive interference with associational freedom goes far beyond what might be justified in the exercise of the State's legitimate inquiry into the fitness and competency of its teachers."

   > The scope of the inquiry required by [the statute] is completely unlimited. The statute requires a teacher to reveal the church to which he belongs, or to which he has given financial support. It requires him to disclose his political party, and every political organization to which he may have contributed over a five-year period. It requires him to list, without number, every conceivable kind of associational tie — social, professional, political, vocational, or religious. Many such relationships could have no possible bearing upon the teacher's occupational competence or fitness.

   Can you reconcile the Court's decision in *Barenblatt* with *Shelton v. Tucker* and *NAACP v. Alabama*?

2. ***Communist Party Membership.*** Cases involving privacy of group associations have frequently arisen when various legislative committees or licensing boards questioned individuals about their membership in Communist organizations. Many cases, like *Barenblatt*, involved questioning before the House Un-American Activities Committee (HUAC). In *Wilkinson v. United States*, 365 U.S. 399 (1961), an individual refused to answer a question by the Committee about membership in the Communist Party. The individual contended that the reason he was being questioned was because he had voiced public criticism of the Committee. The Court, however, concluded that *Barenblatt* still controlled, and that the Committee had "reasonable ground to suppose that the petitioner was an active Communist Party member." Dissenting, Justices Black and Douglas, and Chief Justice Warren argued that "this case involves nothing more nor less than an attempt by the Un-American Activities Committee to use the contempt power of the House of Representatives as a weapon against those who dare to criticize it." *See also Braden v. United States*, 365 U.S. 431 (1961).

   A number of cases involved challenges to questions asked by state bar committees. In *Konigsberg v. State Bar of California*, 366 U.S. 36 (1961), an applicant for membership in the California Bar refused to answer questions about his membership in the Communist Party. The committee refused to certify him. The Court held that the applicant's First Amendment rights were not violated because "[t]here is here no likelihood that deterrence of association may result from foreseeable private action, for bar committee interrogations such as this are conducted in private." *See also In re Anastalpo*, 366 U.S. 82 (1961) (questioning of applicant by Illinois Bar about his Communist Party membership was proper under the First Amendment).

   Can these cases be reconciled with *NAACP v. Alabama*? If so, how?

3. ***Prior Versus Current Communist Party Membership.*** In *DeGregory v. Attorney General*, 383 U.S. 825 (1966), an individual was jailed for contempt for refusing to answer questions by the New Hampshire Attorney

General about his past (rather than current) membership in the Communist Party. The individual feared that "the details of his political associations to which he might testify would be reported in a pamphlet purporting to describe the nature of subversion in New Hampshire." The court held that the First Amendment prohibited the inquiry into the individual's prior group activities:

> There is no showing of "overriding and compelling state interest" that would warrant intrusion into the realm of political and associational privacy protected by the First Amendment. The information being sought was historical, not current. Lawmaking at the investigatory stage may properly probe historic events for any light that may be thrown on present conditions and problems. But the First Amendment prevents use of the power to investigate enforced by the contempt power to probe at will and without relation to existing need. The present record is devoid of any evidence that there is any Communist movement in New Hampshire.

4. **The Scope of the Inquiry.** In *Baird v. State Bar*, 401 U.S. 1 (1971), an applicant before the Arizona Bar Committee refused to answer whether she was a member of the Communist Party or any organization "that advocates overthrow of the United States Government by force or violence." As a result, the applicant was denied admission to the bar. The Court held that the questioning was improper because the government cannot attempt to conduct "[b]road and sweeping state inquiries" into people's political views or group associations. "In effect this young lady was asked by the State to make a guess as to whether any organization to which she ever belonged 'advocates overthrow of the United States Government by force or violence.'" The Court reasoned:

> The First Amendment's protection of association prohibits a State from excluding a person from a profession or punishing him solely because he is a member of a particular political organization or because he holds certain beliefs. Similarly, when a State attempts to make inquiries about a person's beliefs or associations, its power is limited by the First Amendment. Broad and sweeping state inquiries into these protected areas, as Arizona has engaged in here, discourage citizens from exercising rights protected by the Constitution.
>
> When a State seeks to inquire about an individual's beliefs and associations a heavy burden lies upon it to show that the inquiry is necessary to protect a legitimate state interest. Of course Arizona has a legitimate interest in determining whether petitioner has the qualities of character and the professional competence requisite to the practice of law. But here petitioner has already supplied the Committee with extensive personal and professional information to assist its determination. By her answers to questions other than No. 25, and her listing of former employers, law school professors, and other references, she has made available to the Committee the information relevant to her fitness to practice law. And whatever justification may be offered, a State may not inquire about a man's views or associations solely for the purpose of withholding a right or benefit because of what he believes.

Can you distinguish *Baird* from *Barenblatt*, *Konigsberg*, and the other Communist Party membership cases?

3. SURVEILLANCE OF GROUP ACTIVITIES

LAIRD V. TATUM

408 U.S. 1 (1972)

BURGER, C.J. . . . The President is authorized by 10 U.S.C. § 331 to make use of the armed forces to quell insurrection and other domestic violence if and when the conditions described in that section obtain within one of the States. Pursuant to those provisions, President Johnson ordered federal troops to assist local authorities at the time of the civil disorders in Detroit, Michigan, in the summer of 1967 and during the disturbances that followed the assassination of Dr. Martin Luther King. Prior to the Detroit disorders, the Army had a general contingency plan for providing such assistance to local authorities, but the 1967 experience led Army authorities to believe that more attention should be given to such preparatory planning. The data-gathering system here involved is said to have been established in connection with the development of more detailed and specific contingency planning designed to permit the Army, when called upon to assist local authorities, to be able to respond effectively with a minimum of force. . . .

The system put into operation as a result of the Army's 1967 experience consisted essentially of the collection of information about public activities that were thought to have at least some potential for civil disorder, the reporting of that information to Army Intelligence headquarters at Fort Holabird, Maryland, the dissemination of these reports from headquarters to major Army posts around the country, and the storage of the reported information in a computer data bank located at Fort Holabird. The information itself was collected by a variety of means, but it is significant that the principal sources of information were the news media and publications in general circulation. Some of the information came from Army Intelligence agents who attended meetings that were open to the public and who wrote field reports describing the meetings, giving such data as the name of the sponsoring organization, the identity of speakers, the approximate number of persons in attendance, and an indication of whether any disorder occurred. And still other information was provided to the Army by civilian law enforcement agencies. . . .

By early 1970 Congress became concerned with the scope of the Army's domestic surveillance system; hearings on the matter were held before the Subcommittee on Constitutional Rights of the Senate Committee on the Judiciary. Meanwhile, the Army, in the course of a review of the system, ordered a significant reduction in its scope. For example, information referred to in the complaint as the "blacklist" and the records in the computer data bank at Fort Holabird were found unnecessary and were destroyed, along with other related records. One copy of all the material relevant to the instant suit was retained, however, because of the pendency of this litigation. The review leading to the destruction of these records was said at the time the District Court ruled on petitioners' motion to dismiss to be a "continuing" one, and the Army's policies at that time were represented as follows in a letter from the Under Secretary of the Army to Senator Sam J. Ervin, Chairman of the Senate Subcommittee on Constitutional Rights:

[R]eports concerning civil disturbances will be limited to matters of immediate concern to the Army — that is, reports concerning outbreaks of violence or incidents with a high potential for violence beyond the capability of state and local police and the National Guard to control. These reports will be collected by liaison with other Government agencies and reported by teletype to the Intelligence Command. They will not be placed in a computer. . . . These reports are destroyed 60 days after publication or 60 days after the end of the disturbance. This limited reporting system will ensure that the Army is prepared to respond to whatever directions the President may issue in civil disturbance situations and without "watching" the lawful activities of civilians. . . .

In recent years this Court has found in a number of cases that constitutional violations may arise from the deterrent, or "chilling," effect of governmental regulations that fall short of a direct prohibition against the exercise of First Amendment rights. In none of these cases, however, did the chilling effect arise merely from the individual's knowledge that a governmental agency was engaged in certain activities or from the individual's concomitant fear that, armed with the fruits of those activities, the agency might in the future take some other and additional action detrimental to that individual. Rather, in each of these cases, the challenged exercise of governmental power was regulatory, proscriptive, or compulsory in nature, and the complainant was either presently or prospectively subject to the regulations, proscriptions, or compulsions that he was challenging.

For example, the petitioner in *Baird v. State Bar of Arizona* had been denied admission to the bar solely because of her refusal to answer a question regarding the organizations with which she had been associated in the past. In announcing the judgment of the Court, Mr. Justice Black said that "a State may not inquire about a man's views or associations solely for the purpose of withholding a right or benefit because of what he believes." Some of the teachers who were the complainants in *Keyishian v. Board of Regents* had been discharged from employment by the State, and the others were threatened with such discharge, because of their political acts or associations. The Court concluded that the State's "complicated and intricate scheme" of laws and regulations relating to teacher loyalty could not withstand constitutional scrutiny. . . .

The decisions in these cases fully recognize that governmental action may be subject to constitutional challenge even though it has only an indirect effect on the exercise of First Amendment rights. At the same time, however, these decisions have in no way eroded the

established principle that to entitle a private individual to invoke the judicial power to determine the validity of executive or legislative action he must show that he has sustained, or is immediately in danger of sustaining, a direct injury as the result of that action. . . . *Ex parte Levitt*, 302 U.S. 633 (1937).

The respondents do not meet this test; their claim, simply stated, is that they disagree with the judgments made by the Executive Branch with respect to the type and amount of information the Army needs and that the very existence of the Army's data-gathering system produces a constitutionally impermissible chilling effect upon the exercise of their First Amendment rights. That alleged "chilling" effect may perhaps be seen as arising from respondents' very perception of the system as inappropriate to the Army's role under our form of government, or as arising from respondents' beliefs that it is inherently dangerous for the military to be concerned with activities in the civilian sector, or as arising from respondents' less generalized yet speculative apprehensiveness that the Army may at some future date misuse the information in some way that would cause direct harm to respondents. Allegations of a subjective "chill" are not an adequate substitute for a claim of specific present objective harm or a threat of specific future harm; "the federal courts established pursuant to Article III of the Constitution do not render advisory opinions." . . .

DOUGLAS, J. joined by MARSHALL, J. dissenting. . . . If Congress had passed a law authorizing the armed services to establish surveillance over the civilian population, a most serious constitutional problem would be presented. There is, however, no law authorizing surveillance over civilians, which in this case the Pentagon concededly had undertaken. The question is whether such authority may be implied. One can search the Constitution in vain for any such authority. . . .

 . . . [T]he Armed Services — as distinguished from the "militia" — are not regulatory agencies or bureaus that may be created as Congress desires and granted such powers as seem necessary and proper. The authority to provide rules "governing" the Armed Services means the grant of authority to the Armed Services to govern themselves, not the authority to govern civilians. Even when "martial law" is declared, as it often has been, its appropriateness is subject to judicial review. . . .

Our tradition reflects a desire for civilian supremacy and subordination of military power. The tradition goes back to the Declaration of Independence, in which it was recited that the King "has affected to render the Military independent of and superior to the Civil power." . . .

The action in turning the "armies" loose on surveillance of civilians was a gross repudiation of our traditions. The military, though important to us, is subservient and restricted purely to military missions. . . .

The claim that respondents have no standing to challenge the Army's surveillance of them and the other members of the class they seek to represent is too transparent for serious argument. The surveillance of the Army over the civilian sector — a part of society hitherto immune from its control — is a serious charge. It is alleged that the Army maintains files on the membership, ideology, programs, and practices of virtually every activist political group in the country, including groups such as the Southern Christian Leadership Conference, Clergy and Laymen United Against the War in Vietnam, the American Civil Liberties Union, Women's Strike for Peace, and the National Association for the Advancement of Colored People. The Army uses undercover agents to infiltrate these civilian groups and to reach into confidential files of students and other groups. The Army moves as a secret group among civilian audiences, using cameras and electronic ears for surveillance. The data it collects are distributed to civilian officials in state, federal, and local governments and to each military intelligence unit and troop command under the Army's jurisdiction (both here and abroad); and these data are stored in one or more data banks.

Those are the allegations; and the charge is that the purpose and effect of the system of surveillance is to harass and intimidate the respondents and to deter them from exercising their rights of political expression, protest, and dissent "by invading their privacy, damaging their reputations, adversely affecting their employment and their opportunities for employment, and in other ways." Their fear is that "permanent reports of their activities will be maintained in the Army's data bank, and their 'profiles' will appear in the so-called 'Blacklist' and that all of this information will be released to numerous federal and state agencies upon request." . . .

One need not wait to sue until he loses his job or until his reputation is defamed. To withhold standing to sue until that time arrives would in practical effect immunize from judicial scrutiny all surveillance activities, regardless of their misuse and their deterrent effect. . . .

This case involves a cancer in our body politic. It is a measure of the disease which afflicts us. Army surveillance, like Army regimentation, is at war with the principles of the First Amendment. Those who already walk submissively will say there is no cause for alarm. But submissiveness is not our heritage. The First Amendment was designed to allow rebellion to remain as our heritage. The Constitution was designed to keep government off the backs of the people. The Bill of Rights was added to keep the precincts of belief and expression, of the press, of political and social activities free from surveillance. The Bill of Rights was designed to keep agents of government and official eavesdroppers away from assemblies of people. The aim was to allow men to be free and independent and to assert their rights against government. There can be no influence more paralyzing of that objective than Army surveillance. When an intelligence officer looks over every nonconformist's shoulder in the library, or walks invisibly by his side in a picket line, or infiltrates his club, the America once extolled as the voice of liberty heard around the world no longer is cast in the image which Jefferson and Madison designed, but more in the Russian image. . . .

NOTES & QUESTIONS

1. Why doesn't surveillance create a cognizable injury under the First Amendment? Being watched inhibits one's ability to be free and candid in one's expression. If *Laird* had been decided in the plaintiffs' favor, could individuals challenge wiretapping and other forms of police surveillance as a violation of the First Amendment? Such a holding could have far-reaching implications because many forms of police monitoring and investigation would be subject not only to Fourth Amendment limitations but to First Amendment ones as well. Where should the line be drawn?

2. Justice Douglas's dissent expresses great alarm that the Army is engaging in surveillance. Does the fact that the Army is doing the surveillance make it more problematic than if the FBI were doing it?

3. How significant was the creation of the database for the outcome in *Laird*? What measures were taken to protect privacy?

PHILADELPHIA YEARLY MEETING OF
THE RELIGIOUS SOCIETY OF FRIENDS V. TATE

519 F.2d 1335 (3d Cir. 1975)

SEITZ, C. J. Plaintiffs, two organizations and six individuals, appeal an order of the district court dismissing their complaint for failure to state a claim. Defendants are the former Mayor of Philadelphia, the Managing Director and certain police officers of the City of Philadelphia. . . .

Plaintiffs allege that at many public assemblies or demonstrations attended by citizen groups whose general political or social views conflict with those of government officials and/or the Philadelphia Police Department, members of the Philadelphia Police Department, under the command of some of the defendants, are present, photograph many of those in attendance, and make a record of the event, regardless of whether or not such demonstrations are peaceful or lawful.

Plaintiffs further allege that the Philadelphia Police Department, through its Political Disobedience Unit, has compiled intelligence files on numerous individuals and groups. These files, about 18,000 in number, are separate from police interrogation and investigation records. They contain basic information plus information concerning the individual subject's political views, associations and personal life and habits. The files are allegedly kept indefinitely and sometimes without the knowledge of the subjects of the files.

Plaintiffs allege, on information and belief, that no safeguards exist as to the disposition of or access to the political and personal information contained in the files; that such information is available to other law enforcement agencies and, on information and belief, to private employers, to governmental agencies for purposes of considering employment, promotion, granting of licenses, passports, etc., to private political organizations which seek to suppress "subversive" or dissident political activity or views, and to the press.

It is also charged that Philadelphia Police Department has improperly and unlawfully publicized its political intelligence gathering system by the unauthorized public disclosure of information concerning certain named individuals and groups who are the subject of police intelligence files. On June 2, 1970, in a network television broadcast the above named defendants and their agents publicly discussed their system and disclosed the names of certain groups and individuals on whom such files were kept, without the approval of such groups and individuals, including plaintiff organizations and four individual plaintiffs.

After the foregoing factual allegations the plaintiffs allege that such facts resulted in violations of their rights under the First and Fourteenth Amendments. . . .

Plaintiffs sought declaratory, injunctive and other relief under 42 U.S.C. §§ 1983 and 1985 and 28 U.S.C. § 2201. This appeal followed the dismissal of the complaint for failure to state a claim upon which relief could be granted. . . .

In [*Laird v.*] *Tatum*, the Supreme Court was confronted by the claims of a plaintiff who alleged "that the exercise of his First Amendment rights is being chilled by the mere existence, without more, of a governmental investigative and data-gathering activity that is alleged to be broader in scope than is reasonably necessary for the accomplishment of a valid government purpose." The Court held that the jurisdiction of a federal court could not be invoked in such circumstances, where there was no immediate threat to the individual's constitutional rights and any chilling effect was subjective. . . .

We think it is clear that *Tatum* supports the action of the district court here to the extent the complaint alleges a constitutional violation on the basis of mere police photographing and data gathering at public meetings. We say this because such activity by law enforcement authorities, without more, is legally unobjectionable and creates at best a so-called subjective chill which the Supreme Court has said is not a substitute for a claim of specific present harm or a threat of specific future harm.

Nor does the sharing of this information with other agencies of government having a legitimate law enforcement function give rise to a constitutional violation. We cannot see where the traditional exchange of information with other law enforcement agencies results in any more objective harm than the original collation of such information. Although plaintiffs would distinguish their case from *Tatum* on the ground that they are direct targets of the intelligence system and their dossiers contain information about their individual political views, etc., we think that this is not sufficient to distinguish *Tatum* insofar as plaintiffs rely on the mere existence of police intelligence gathering and the sharing of information with other enforcement agencies. . . .

. . . [Next, we consider] plaintiffs' allegation that no safeguards exist on the disposition of or access to the political and personal information and conclusions contained in the dossiers and lists which defendants maintain and that such information is actually or potentially available, *inter alia*, to a wide spectrum of individuals, governmental agencies, private political organizations and the press.

It is not apparent how making information concerning the lawful activities of plaintiffs available to non-police groups or individuals could be considered within the proper ambit of law enforcement activity, particularly since it is alleged that plaintiffs are subject to surveillance only because their political views deviate from those of the "establishment." We think these allegations, at a minimum, show immediately threatened injury to plaintiffs by way of a chilling of their rights of freedom of speech and associational privacy. Some examples of immediately threatened harm come readily to mind. The general availability of such materials and lists could interfere with the job opportunities, careers or travel rights of the individual plaintiffs and such practical consequences may ensue without any specific awareness on plaintiffs' part. The mere anticipation of the practical consequences of joining or remaining with plaintiff organizations may well dissuade some individuals from becoming members, or may persuade others to resign their membership. We therefore conclude that, except for the allegation concerning the availability of the material to other law enforcement agencies, the allegations of paragraph 3 above state a claim sufficient to withstand a motion to dismiss. . . .

In paragraph 4 above, it is alleged that the Philadelphia Police Department described their political intelligence gathering system in a nationwide television show and specifically identified the plaintiff organizations and four of the individual plaintiffs as being the subjects of police dossiers.

The district court held that the allegations summarized in paragraph 4 amounted to no more than a subjective complaint of a chilling effect based on the "mere existence" of governmental information gathering activities. The court indicated that in order to create a justiciable controversy, plaintiffs were required to allege tangible consequences, such as a contempt citation, a criminal prosecution, exclusion from a profession, a threat of conscription and the like. However, we cannot believe that the *Tatum* opinion was meant to find non-justiciable a case such as the one before us where the alleged threatened injury, although not concrete, is nonetheless strikingly apparent. It cannot be doubted that disclosure on nationwide television that certain named persons or organizations are subjects of police intelligence files has a potential for a substantial adverse impact on such persons and organizations even though tangible evidence of the impact may be difficult, if not impossible, to obtain. . . .

. . . If plaintiffs' allegations are true, this type of activity strikes at the heart of a free society. We therefore conclude that the allegations of paragraph 4 as well as the improper dispersal claims of paragraph 3 set forth justiciable claims.

NOTES & QUESTIONS

1. Does *Tate* adequately distinguish *Laird*? Is public disclosure always a more injurious privacy violation than government surveillance and information collection?
2. Is the result of *Tate* also supported by the constitutional right to information privacy in *Whalen*? Recall that under several constitutional right to information privacy cases, information in public records is not private and therefore cannot give rise to a claim for a violation of the constitutional right to information privacy. *See Cline v. Rogers* (Chapter 4). Suppose that in *Tate*, the police made their dossiers available as public records. Would the plaintiffs still have a viable claim under the constitutional right to information privacy? Would the plaintiffs have any other constitutional claims? A tort claim for a violation of the public disclosure tort?
3. The police can gather all sorts of public information about *individuals* while investigating them. Why should the police be prohibited or restricted in gathering data about *group* activities? In other words, why should group activities be given more protection than individual activities?
4. New technology has made it easier for the police today to monitor public protests and create photographic and video records of protesters. Does this strengthen or weaken group privacy claims?

B. ANONYMITY

1. ANONYMOUS SPEECH

TALLEY v. STATE OF CALIFORNIA

362 U.S. 60 (1960)

BLACK, J. The question presented here is whether the provisions of a Los Angeles City ordinance restricting the distribution of handbills "abridge the freedom of speech and of the press secured against state invasion by the Fourteenth Amendment of the Constitution." The ordinance, § 28.06 of the Municipal Code of the City of Los Angeles, provides:

> No person shall distribute any hand-bill in any place under any circumstances, which does not have printed on the cover, or the face thereof, the name and address of the following:
>
> (a) The person who printed, wrote, compiled or manufactured the same.
>
> (b) The person who caused the same to be distributed; provided, however, that in the case of a fictitious person or club, in addition to such fictitious name, the true names and addresses of the owners, managers or agents of the person sponsoring said hand-bill shall also appear thereon.

The petitioner was arrested and tried in a Los Angeles Municipal Court for violating this ordinance. . . .

In *Lovell v. City of Griffin*, 303 U.S. 444, we held void on its face an ordinance that comprehensively forbade any distribution of literature at any time or place in Griffin, Georgia, without a license. Pamphlets and leaflets it was pointed out, "have been historic weapons in the defense of liberty" and enforcement of the Griffin ordinance "would restore the system of license and censorship in its baldest form." . . .

The broad ordinance now before us, barring distribution of "any handbill in any place under any circumstances," falls precisely under the ban of our prior cases unless this ordinance is saved by the qualification that handbills can be distributed if they have printed on them the names and addresses of the persons who prepared, distributed or sponsored them. For, as in *Griffin*, the ordinance here is not limited to handbills whose content is "obscene or offensive to public morals or that advocates unlawful conduct." Counsel has urged that this ordinance is aimed at providing a way to identify those responsible for fraud, false advertising and libel. Yet the ordinance is in no manner so limited, nor have we been referred to any legislative history indicating such a purpose. Therefore we do not pass on the validity of an ordinance limited to prevent these or any other supposed evils. This ordinance simply bars all handbills under all circumstances anywhere that do not have the names and addresses printed on them in the place the ordinance requires.

There can be no doubt that such an identification requirement would tend to restrict freedom to distribute information and thereby freedom of expression. "Liberty of circulating is as essential to that freedom as liberty of publishing; indeed, without the circulation, the publication would be of little value."

Anonymous pamphlets, leaflets, brochures and even books have played an important role in the progress of mankind. Persecuted groups and sects from time to time throughout history have been able to criticize oppressive practices and laws either anonymously or not at all. The obnoxious press licensing law of England, which was also enforced on the Colonies was due in part to the knowledge that exposure of the names of printers, writers and distributors would lessen the circulation of literature critical of the government. The old seditious libel cases in England show the lengths to which government had to go to find out who was responsible for books that were obnoxious to the rulers. John Lilburne was whipped, pilloried and fined for refusing to answer questions designed to get evidence to convict him or someone else for the secret distribution of books in England. Two Puritan Ministers, John Penry and John Udal, were sentenced to death on charges that they were responsible for writing, printing or publishing books. Before the Revolutionary War colonial patriots frequently had to conceal their authorship or distribution of literature that easily could have brought down on them prosecutions by English-controlled courts. Along about that time the Letters of Junius were written and the identity of their author is unknown to this day. Even the Federalist Papers, written in favor of the adoption of our Constitution, were published under fictitious names. It is plain that anonymity has sometimes been assumed for the most constructive purposes.

We have recently had occasion to hold in two cases that there are times and circumstances when States may not compel members of groups engaged in the dissemination of ideas to be publicly identified. *Bates v. City of Little Rock*, 361 U.S. 516; *N.A.A.C.P. v. State of Alabama*, 357 U.S. 449. The reason for those holdings was that identification and fear of reprisal might deter perfectly peaceful discussions of public matters of importance. This broad Los Angeles ordinance is subject to the same infirmity. We hold that it, like the Griffin, Georgia, ordinance, is void on its face. . . .

McINTYRE V. OHIO ELECTIONS COMMISSION

514 U.S. 334 (1995)

STEVENS, J. . . . On April 27, 1988, Margaret McIntyre distributed leaflets to persons attending a public meeting at the Blendon Middle School in Westerville, Ohio. At this meeting, the superintendent of schools planned to discuss an imminent referendum on a proposed school tax levy. The leaflets expressed Mrs. McIntyre's opposition to the levy. There is no suggestion that the text of her message was false, misleading, or libelous. She had composed and printed it on her home computer and had paid a professional printer to make additional copies. Some of the handbills identified her as the author; others merely purported to express the views of "CONCERNED PARENTS AND TAX PAYERS." Except for the help provided by her son and a friend, who placed some of the leaflets on car windshields in the school parking lot, Mrs. McIntyre acted independently.

While Mrs. McIntyre distributed her handbills, an official of the school district, who supported the tax proposal, advised her that the unsigned leaflets did not conform to the Ohio election laws. Undeterred, Mrs. McIntyre appeared at another meeting on the next evening and handed out more of the handbills.

The proposed school levy was defeated at the next two elections, but it finally passed on its third try in November 1988. Five months later, the same school official filed a complaint with the Ohio Elections Commission charging that Mrs. McIntyre's distribution of unsigned leaflets violated § 3599.09(A) of the Ohio Code [which prohibited the distribution of political literature without the name and address of the person or organization responsible for the distribution]. The commission agreed and imposed a fine of $100. . . .

Mrs. McIntyre passed away during the pendency of this litigation. Even though the amount in controversy is only $100, petitioner, as the executor of her estate, has pursued her claim in this Court. Our grant of certiorari reflects our agreement with his appraisal of the importance of the question presented. . . .

Ohio maintains that the statute under review is a reasonable regulation of the electoral process. . . .

"Anonymous pamphlets, leaflets, brochures and even books have played an important role in the progress of mankind." *Talley v. California.* Great works of literature have frequently been produced by authors writing under assumed names.[5] Despite readers' curiosity and the public's interest in identifying the creator of a work of art, an author generally is free to decide whether or not to disclose his or her true identity. The decision in favor of anonymity may be motivated by fear of economic or official retaliation, by concern about social ostracism, or merely by a desire to preserve as much of one's privacy as possible. Whatever the motivation may be, at least in the field of literary endeavor, the interest in having anonymous works enter the marketplace of ideas unquestionably outweighs any public interest in requiring disclosure as a condition of entry. Accordingly, an author's decision to remain anonymous, like other decisions concerning omissions or additions to the content of a publication, is an aspect of the freedom of speech protected by the First Amendment.

. . . On occasion, quite apart from any threat of persecution, an advocate may believe her ideas will be more persuasive if her readers are unaware of her identity. Anonymity thereby provides a way for a writer who may be personally unpopular to ensure that readers will not prejudge her message simply because they do not like its proponent. Thus, even in the field of political rhetoric, where "the identity of the speaker is an important component of many attempts to persuade," the most effective advocates have sometimes opted for

---

[5] American names such as Mark Twain (Samuel Langhorne Clemens) and O. Henry (William Sydney Porter) come readily to mind. Benjamin Franklin employed numerous different pseudonyms. Distinguished French authors such as Voltaire (Francois Marie Arouet) and George Sand (Amandine Aurore Lucie Dupin), and British authors such as George Eliot (Mary Ann Evans), Charles Lamb (sometimes wrote as "Elia"), and Charles Dickens (sometimes wrote as "Boz"), also published under assumed names. Indeed, some believe the works of Shakespeare were actually written by the Earl of Oxford rather than by William Shakespeare of Stratford-on-Avon. . . .

anonymity. The specific holding in *Talley* related to advocacy of an economic boycott, but the Court's reasoning embraced a respected tradition of anonymity in the advocacy of political causes.[6] This tradition is perhaps best exemplified by the secret ballot, the hard-won right to vote one's conscience without fear of retaliation. . . .

California had defended the Los Angeles ordinance at issue in *Talley* as a law "aimed at providing a way to identify those responsible for fraud, false advertising and libel." We rejected that argument because nothing in the text or legislative history of the ordinance limited its application to those evils. We then made clear that we did "not pass on the validity of an ordinance limited to prevent these or any other supposed evils." The Ohio statute likewise contains no language limiting its application to fraudulent, false, or libelous statements; to the extent, therefore, that Ohio seeks to justify § 3599.09(A) as a means to prevent the dissemination of untruths, its defense must fail for the same reason given in *Talley*. As the facts of this case demonstrate, the ordinance plainly applies even when there is no hint of falsity or libel. . . .

. . . § 3599.09(A) of the Ohio Code does not control the mechanics of the electoral process. It is a regulation of pure speech. Moreover, even though this provision applies evenhandedly to advocates of differing viewpoints, it is a direct regulation of the content of speech. Every written document covered by the statute must contain "the name and residence or business address of the chairman, treasurer, or secretary of the organization issuing the same, or the person who issues, makes, or is responsible therefor." Furthermore, the category of covered documents is defined by their content — only those publications containing speech designed to influence the voters in an election need bear the required markings. Consequently, we are not faced with an ordinary election restriction; this case "involves a limitation on political expression subject to exacting scrutiny." . . .

When a law burdens core political speech, we apply "exacting scrutiny," and we uphold the restriction only if it is narrowly tailored to serve an overriding state interest. . . .

Nevertheless, the State argues that, even under the strictest standard of review, the disclosure requirement in § 3599.09(A) is justified by two important and legitimate state interests. Ohio judges its interest in preventing fraudulent and libelous statements and its interest in providing the electorate with relevant information to be sufficiently compelling to justify the anonymous speech ban. These two interests necessarily overlap to some extent, but it is useful to discuss them separately.

Insofar as the interest in informing the electorate means nothing more than the provision of additional information that may either buttress or undermine the argument in a document, we think the identity of the speaker is no different from other components of the document's content that the author is free to include or exclude. . . . The simple interest in providing voters

---

[6] That tradition is most famously embodied in the Federalist Papers, authored by James Madison, Alexander Hamilton, and John Jay, but signed "Publius." Publius' opponents, the Anti-Federalists, also tended to publish under pseudonyms. . . .

with additional relevant information does not justify a state requirement that a writer make statements or disclosures she would otherwise omit. Moreover, in the case of a handbill written by a private citizen who is not known to the recipient, the name and address of the author add little, if anything, to the reader's ability to evaluate the document's message. . . .

The state interest in preventing fraud and libel stands on a different footing. We agree with Ohio's submission that this interest carries special weight during election campaigns when false statements, if credited, may have serious adverse consequences for the public at large. Ohio does not, however, rely solely on § 3599.09(A) to protect that interest. Its Election Code includes detailed and specific prohibitions against making or disseminating false statements during political campaigns. These regulations apply both to candidate elections and to issue-driven ballot measures. Thus, Ohio's prohibition of anonymous leaflets plainly is not its principal weapon against fraud. Rather, it serves as an aid to enforcement of the specific prohibitions and as a deterrent to the making of false statements by unscrupulous prevaricators. Although these ancillary benefits are assuredly legitimate, we are not persuaded that they justify § 3599.09(A)'s extremely broad prohibition. . . .

Under our Constitution, anonymous pamphleteering is not a pernicious, fraudulent practice, but an honorable tradition of advocacy and of dissent. Anonymity is a shield from the tyranny of the majority. It thus exemplifies the purpose behind the Bill of Rights, and of the First Amendment in particular: to protect unpopular individuals from retaliation — and their ideas from suppression — at the hand of an intolerant society. . . .

THOMAS, J. concurring. . . . I agree with the majority's conclusion that Ohio's election law . . . is inconsistent with the First Amendment. I would apply, however, a different methodology to this case. Instead of asking whether "an honorable tradition" of anonymous speech has existed throughout American history, or what the "value" of anonymous speech might be, we should determine whether the phrase "freedom of speech, or of the press," as originally understood, protected anonymous political leafleting. I believe that it did. . . .

Unfortunately, we have no record of discussions of anonymous political expression either in the First Congress, which drafted the Bill of Rights, or in the state ratifying conventions. Thus, our analysis must focus on the practices and beliefs held by the Founders concerning anonymous political articles and pamphlets. . . .

There is little doubt that the Framers engaged in anonymous political writing. The essays in the *Federalist Papers*, published under the pseudonym of "Publius," are only the most famous example of the outpouring of anonymous political writing that occurred during the ratification of the Constitution. . . .

The large quantity of newspapers and pamphlets the Framers produced during the various crises of their generation show the remarkable extent to which the Framers relied upon anonymity. During the break with Great Britain, the revolutionaries employed pseudonyms both to conceal their identity from Crown authorities and to impart a message. Often, writers would choose names to signal their point of view or to invoke specific classical and modern "crusaders in an agelong struggle against tyranny." Thus, leaders of the struggle for independence would adopt descriptive names such as "Common Sense," a "Farmer," or "A True Patriot," or historical ones such as "Cato" (a name used by many to refer to the Roman Cato and to Cato's letters), or "Mucius Scaevola." The practice was even more prevalent during the great outpouring of political argument and commentary that accompanied the ratification of the Constitution. Besides "Publius," prominent Federalists signed their articles and pamphlets with names such as "An American Citizen," "Marcus," "A Landholder," "Americanus"; Anti-Federalists replied with the pseudonyms "Cato," "Centinel," "Brutus," the "Federal Farmer," and "The Impartial Examiner." The practice of publishing one's thoughts anonymously or under pseudonym was so widespread that only two major Federalist or Anti-Federalist pieces appear to have been signed by their true authors, and they may have had special reasons to do so. . . .

I cannot join the majority's analysis because it deviates from our settled approach to interpreting the Constitution and because it superimposes its modern theories concerning expression upon the constitutional text. Whether "great works of literature"—by Voltaire or George Eliot have been published anonymously should be irrelevant to our analysis, because it sheds no light on what the phrases "free speech" or "free press" meant to the people who drafted and ratified the First Amendment. Similarly, whether certain types of expression have "value" today has little significance; what is important is whether the Framers in 1791 believed anonymous speech sufficiently valuable to deserve the protection of the Bill of Rights. . . .

Because the majority has adopted an analysis that is largely unconnected to the Constitution's text and history, I concur only in the judgment.

SCALIA, J. joined by REHNQUIST, C. J. dissenting. . . . The Court's unprecedented protection for anonymous speech does not even have the virtue of establishing a clear (albeit erroneous) rule of law. . . . It may take decades to work out the shape of this newly expanded right-to-speak-incognito, even in the elections field. And in other areas, of course, a whole new boutique of wonderful First Amendment litigation opens its doors. Must a parade permit, for example, be issued to a group that refuses to provide its identity, or that agrees to do so only under assurance that the identity will not be made public? Must a municipally owned theater that is leased for private productions book anonymously sponsored presentations? Must a government periodical that has a "letters to the editor" column disavow the policy that most newspapers have against the publication of anonymous letters? Must a public university that makes its facilities available for a speech by Louis Farrakhan or David Duke refuse to disclose the on-campus or off-campus group that has sponsored or paid for the speech? Must a municipal "public-access" cable channel permit anonymous (and masked) performers? The silliness that follows upon a generalized right to anonymous speech has no end. . . .

The Court says that the State has not explained "why it can more easily enforce the direct bans on disseminating false documents against anonymous authors and distributors than against wrongdoers who might use false names and addresses in an attempt to avoid detection." I am not sure what this complicated comparison means. I am sure, however, that (1) a person who is required to put his name to a document is much less likely to lie than one who can lie anonymously, and (2) the distributor of a leaflet which is unlawful because it is anonymous runs much more risk of immediate detection and punishment than the distributor of a leaflet which is unlawful because it is false. Thus, people will be more likely to observe a signing requirement than a naked "no falsity" requirement; and, having observed that requirement, will then be significantly less likely to lie in what they have signed.

But the usefulness of a signing requirement lies not only in promoting observance of the law against campaign falsehoods (though that alone is enough to sustain it). It lies also in promoting a civil and dignified level of campaign debate—which the State has no power to command, but ample power to encourage by such undemanding measures as a signature requirement. Observers of the past few national elections have expressed concern about the increase of character assassination—"mudslinging" is the colloquial term—engaged in by political candidates and their supporters to the detriment of the democratic process. Not all of this, in fact not much of it, consists of actionable untruth; most is innuendo, or demeaning characterization, or mere disclosure of items of personal life that have no bearing upon suitability for office. Imagine how much all of this would increase if it could be done anonymously. The principal impediment against it is the reluctance of most individuals and organizations to be publicly associated with uncharitable and uncivil expression. Consider, moreover, the increased potential for "dirty tricks." It is not unheard-of for campaign operatives to circulate material over the name of their opponents or their opponents' supporters (a violation of election laws) in order to attract or alienate certain interest groups. How much easier—and sanction free!—it would be to circulate anonymous material (for example, a really tasteless, though not actionably false, attack upon one's own candidate) with the hope and expectation that it will be attributed to, and held against, the other side. . . .

I do not know where the Court derives its perception that "anonymous pamphleteering is not a pernicious, fraudulent practice, but an honorable tradition of advocacy and of dissent." I can imagine no reason why an anonymous leaflet is any more honorable, as a general matter, than an anonymous phone call or an anonymous letter. It facilitates wrong by eliminating accountability, which is ordinarily the very purpose of the anonymity. . . .

NOTES & QUESTIONS

1. *Talley* and *McIntyre* conclude that anonymous speech is protected under the First Amendment based on different rationales. What are those rationales? Which rationale seems most persuasive to you?
2. In *Buckley v. ACLF*, 525 U.S. 182 (1999), the Court struck down part of a Colorado statute requiring individuals handing out petitions to wear name-tags. The Court reasoned:

> [T]he name badge requirement forces circulators to reveal their identities at the same time they deliver their political message, it operates when reaction to the circulator's message is immediate and may be the most intense, emo-

tional, and unreasoned. . . . The injury to speech is heightened for the petition circulator because the badge requirement compels personal name identification at the precise moment when the circulator's interest in anonymity is the greatest.

WATCHTOWER BIBLE & TRACT SOCIETY V. VILLAGE OF STRATTON

122 S. Ct. 2080 (2002)

[A local ordinance required all solicitors of private residences to obtain a permit, which required that the individuals supply data about their cause as well as their name, home addresses, and employers or affiliated organizations. The Sixth Circuit upheld the ordinance, distinguishing *McIntyre* because "individuals going door-to-door to engage in political speech are not anonymous by virtue of the fact that they reveal a portion of their identities — their physical identities — to the residents they canvass." Therefore, the court reasoned, the right to speak anonymously did not apply. *See* 240 F.3d 553 (6th Cir. 2001). The Supreme Court granted certiorari and reversed the Sixth Circuit.]

STEVENS, J. . . . The Village argues that three interests are served by its ordinance: the prevention of fraud, the prevention of crime, and the protection of residents' privacy. . . . We have no difficulty concluding, in light of our precedent, that these are important interests that the Village may seek to safeguard through some form of regulation of solicitation activity. We must also look, however, to the amount of speech covered by the ordinance and whether there is an appropriate balance between the affected speech and the governmental interests that the ordinance purports to serve.

The text of the Village's ordinance prohibits "canvassers" from going on private property for the purpose of explaining or promoting any "cause," unless they receive a permit and the residents visited have not opted for a "no solicitation" sign. Had this provision been construed to apply only to commercial activities and the solicitation of funds, arguably the ordinance would have been tailored to the Village's interest in protecting the privacy of its residents and preventing fraud. Yet, even though the Village has explained that the ordinance was adopted to serve those interests, it has never contended that it should be so narrowly interpreted. To the contrary, the Village's administration of its ordinance unquestionably demonstrates that the provisions apply to a significant number of noncommercial "canvassers" promoting a wide variety of "causes." Indeed, on the "No Solicitation Forms" provided to the residents, the canvassers include "Camp Fire Girls," "Jehovah's Witnesses," "Political Candidates," "Trick or Treaters during Halloween Season," and "Persons Affiliated with Stratton Church." The ordinance unquestionably applies, not only to religious causes, but to political activity as well. It would seem to extend to "residents casually soliciting the votes of neighbors," or ringing doorbells to enlist support for employing a more efficient garbage collector.

The mere fact that the ordinance covers so much speech raises constitutional concerns. It is offensive — not only to the values protected by the First Amendment, but to the very notion of a free society — that in the context of everyday public discourse a citizen must first inform the government of her desire to speak to her neighbors and then obtain a permit to do so. Even if the issuance of permits by the mayor's office is a ministerial task that is performed promptly and at no cost to the applicant, a law requiring a permit to engage in such speech constitutes a dramatic departure from our national heritage and constitutional tradition. . . .

First, as our cases involving distribution of unsigned handbills demonstrate, there are a significant number of persons who support causes anonymously. "The decision to favor anonymity may be motivated by fear of economic or official retaliation, by concern about social ostracism, or merely by a desire to preserve as much of one's privacy as possible." *McIntyre v. Ohio Elections Comm'n.* The requirement that a canvasser must be identified in a permit application filed in the mayor's office and available for public inspection necessarily results in a surrender of that anonymity. Although it is true, as the Court of Appeals suggested, that persons who are known to the resident reveal their allegiance to a group or cause when they present themselves at the front door to advocate an issue or to deliver a handbill, the Court of Appeals erred in concluding that the ordinance does not implicate anonymity interests. The Sixth Circuit's reasoning is undermined by our decision in *Buckley v. American Constitutional Law Foundation, Inc.*, 525 U.S. 182 (1999). The badge requirement that we invalidated in *Buckley* applied to petition circulators seeking signatures in face-to-face interactions. The fact that circulators revealed their physical identities did not foreclose our consideration of the circulators' interest in maintaining their anonymity. In the Village, strangers to the resident certainly maintain their anonymity, and the ordinance may preclude such persons from canvassing for unpopular causes. Such preclusion may well be justified in some situations—for example, by the special state interest in protecting the integrity of a ballot-initiative process, or by the interest in preventing fraudulent commercial transactions. The Village ordinance, however, sweeps more broadly, covering unpopular causes unrelated to commercial transactions or to any special interest in protecting the electoral process. . . .

The breadth and unprecedented nature of this regulation does not alone render the ordinance invalid. Also central to our conclusion that the ordinance does not pass First Amendment scrutiny is that it is not tailored to the Village's stated interests. Even if the interest in preventing fraud could adequately support the ordinance insofar as it applies to commercial transactions and the solicitation of funds, that interest provides no support for its application to petitioners, to political campaigns, or to enlisting support for unpopular causes. The Village, however, argues that the ordinance is nonetheless valid because it serves the two additional interests of protecting the privacy of the resident and the prevention of crime.

With respect to the former, it seems clear that § 107 of the ordinance, which provides for the posting of "No Solicitation" signs and which is not challenged in this case, coupled with the resident's unquestioned right to refuse to engage in conversation with unwelcome visitors, provides ample protection for the unwilling listener. The annoyance caused by an uninvited knock on the front door is the same whether or not the visitor is armed with a permit.

With respect to the latter, it seems unlikely that the absence of a permit would preclude criminals from knocking on doors and engaging in conversations not covered by the ordinance. They might, for example, ask for directions or permission to use the telephone, or pose as surveyers or census takers. Or they might register under a false name with impunity because the ordinance contains no provision for verifying an applicant's identity or organizational credentials. Moreover, the Village did not assert an interest in crime prevention below, and there is an absence of any evidence of a special crime problem related to door-to-door solicitation in the record before us. . . .

2. ANONYMITY IN CYBERSPACE

E-mail and the Internet enable people to communicate anonymously with ease. People can send e-mail or post messages to electronic bulletin boards under pseudonyms. However, this anonymity is quite fragile, and in some cases illusory. First, many people expect that their web surfing is anonymous — in other words, that when they visit various web sites, their identities are not known to the operators of those sites unless they choose to disclose who they are. However, the use of "cookies" — small text files that are downloaded into the user's computer when a user visits a web site — means that web surfing is far from an anonymous activity. With cookies, users are tagged with an identification number, which can be used to look up a variety of information collected about them, often including their identity.

Second, an individual's Internet Service Provider (ISP) has information linking one's screen name (the pseudonym one writes under) to one's actual identity. As was illustrated in *McVeigh v. Cohen* in Chapter 4, the security of this information depends upon the policies and carefulness of one's ISP. Recall that in *McVeigh*, an AOL representative improperly divulged to a Navy official that the AOL user under the alias "boysrch" was the plaintiff. Under federal wiretap law, an ISP must disclose information identifying a particular user to the government pursuant to a subpoena. However, no subpoena is required for private parties. An ISP "may disclose a record or other information pertaining to a subscriber . . . to any person other than a governmental entity." 18 U.S.C. §2703(c)(1)(A).

As David Sobel observes:

> Since 1998, scores of civil lawsuits have been filed against "John Doe" defendants by plaintiffs allegedly harmed by anonymous Internet postings. The underlying causes of action vary, ranging from defamation to unauthorized disclosure of proprietary information.
>
> The common denominator in these suits is that they all raise novel yet fundamental questions of fairness and due process. Upon the filing of civil complaints, plaintiffs' counsel serve subpoenas on message board operators and Internet service providers seeking the identities of anonymous posters. Some service providers, including America Online, notify subscribers when civil subpoenas are received and allow them a period of time to challenge the process. But many online services — most notably Yahoo! — comply with such subpoenas as a matter of course, without notice to their users. As a result, "John Doe" defendants frequently have no opportunity to quash subpoenas and the

courts have no role in evaluating the propriety of requests for identifying information.[7]

Anonymity creates dangers of potential fraud and abuse. For example, "cybersmearers" anonymously post false information about a company to manipulate stock prices. How should one's interest in anonymity be reconciled with the interests of preventing fraud and permitting people to sue for defamatory statements? Consider the following cases:

ACLU v. MILLER

977 F. Supp. 1228 (N.D. Ga. 1997)

SHOOB, J. This action is before the Court on plaintiffs' motion for preliminary injunction and defendants' motion to dismiss. . . .

Plaintiffs bring this action for declaratory and injunctive relief challenging the constitutionality of Act No. 1029, Ga. Laws 1996, p. 1505, codified at O.C.G.A. §16-9-93.1 ("act" or "statute"). The act makes it a crime for

> any person . . . knowingly to transmit any data through a computer network . . . for the purpose of setting up, maintaining, operating, or exchanging data with an electronic mailbox, home page, or any other electronic information storage bank or point of access to electronic information if such data uses any individual name . . . to falsely identify the person . . .

and for

> any person . . . knowingly to transmit any data through a computer network . . . if such data uses any . . . trade name, registered trademark, logo, legal or official seal, or copyrighted symbol . . . which would falsely state or imply that such person . . . has permission or is legally authorized to use [it] for such purpose when such permission or authorization has not been obtained.

. . . Plaintiffs, a group of individuals and organization members who communicate over the internet, interpret it as imposing unconstitutional content-based restrictions on their right to communicate anonymously and pseudonymously over the internet, as well as on their right to use trade names, logos, and other graphics in a manner held to be constitutional in other contexts.

Plaintiffs argue that the act has tremendous implications for internet users, many of whom "falsely identify" themselves on a regular basis for the purpose of communicating about sensitive topics without subjecting themselves to ostracism or embarrassment. Plaintiffs further contend that the trade name and logo restriction frustrates one of the internet's unique features — the "links" that connect web pages on the World Wide Web and enable users

---

[7] David L. Sobel, *The Process That "John Doe" Is Due: Addressing the Legal Challenge to Internet Anonymity*, 5 Va. J.L. & Tech. 3 (2000). For more background, see generally Lyrissa Barnett Lidsky, *Silencing John Doe: Defamation and Discourse in Cyberspace*, 49 Duke L.J. 855 (2000); Philip Giordano, *Invoking Law as a Basis for Identity in Cyberspace*, 1998 Stan. Tech. L. Rev. 1.

to browse easily from topic to topic through the computer network system. Plaintiffs claim that the act's broad language is further damaging in that it allows for selective prosecution of persons communicating about controversial topics.

Defendants contend that the act prohibits a much narrower class of communications. They interpret it as forbidding only fraudulent transmissions or the appropriation of the identity of another person or entity for some improper purpose. . . .

. . . It appears from the record that plaintiffs are likely to prove that the statute imposes content-based restrictions which are not narrowly tailored to achieve the state's purported compelling interest. Furthermore, plaintiffs are likely to show that the statute is overbroad and void for vagueness.

First, because "the identity of the speaker is no different from other components of [a] document's contents that the author is free to include or exclude," *McIntyre v. Ohio Elections Comm'n*, 514 U.S. 334 (1995), the statute's prohibition of internet transmissions which "falsely identify" the sender constitutes a presumptively invalid content-based restriction. The state may impose content-based restrictions only to promote a "compelling state interest" and only through use of "the least restrictive means to further the articulated interest." Thus, in order to overcome the presumption of invalidity, defendants must demonstrate that the statute furthers a compelling state interest and is narrowly tailored to achieve it.

Defendants allege that the statute's purpose is fraud prevention, which the Court agrees is a compelling state interest. However, the statute is not narrowly tailored to achieve that end and instead sweeps innocent, protected speech within its scope. Specifically, by its plain language the criminal prohibition applies regardless of whether a speaker has any intent to deceive or whether deception actually occurs. Therefore, it could apply to a wide range of transmissions which "falsely identify" the sender, but are not "fraudulent" within the specific meaning of the criminal code. . . .

For similar reasons, plaintiffs are likely to succeed on their overbreadth claim because the statute "sweeps protected activity within its proscription." In the first amendment context, the overbreadth doctrine, which invalidates overbroad statutes even when some of their applications are valid, is based on the recognition that "the very existence of some broadly written laws has the potential to chill the expressive activity of others not before the Court."

The Court concludes that the statute was not drafted with the precision necessary for laws regulating speech. On its face, the act prohibits such protected speech as the use of false identification to avoid social ostracism, to prevent discrimination and harassment, and to protect privacy, as well as the use of trade names or logos in non-commercial educational speech, news, and commentary — a prohibition with well-recognized first amendment problems. Therefore, even if the statute could constitutionally be used to prosecute persons who intentionally "falsely identify" themselves in order to deceive or defraud the public, or to persons whose commercial use of trade names and logos creates a substantial likelihood of confusion or the dilution of a famous mark, the statute is nevertheless overbroad because it operates unconstitutionally for a substantial category of the speakers it covers. . . .

NOTES & QUESTIONS

1. *Privacy Enhancing Technologies.* Given the fragile state of privacy on the Internet, individuals can resort to certain technological devices to help preserve their anonymity. An "anonymous remailer" is a computer service that enables people to send e-mail anonymously. A person sends a message through a remailer, which removes a person's actual name and e-mail address, substitutes it with a pseudonym, and sends it on its way. Certain remailers maintain accounts with individuals, and as a result, the individual's identifying information is known to the remailer and can be obtained by getting a court order to force the remailer to divulge the identity. Other remailers operate in such a way that even the remailer does not know the identities of its clients. There are a number of remailer services on the World Wide Web. However, remailers do not offer foolproof anonymity. One's e-mail messages to a remailer can be intercepted by the government, by one's employer, by one's Internet Service Provider, or by others.[8]

Consider A. Michael Froomkin:

> Remailer operators already have come under various forms of attack, most recently lawsuits or subpoenas instigated by officials of the Church of Scientology who sought to identify the person they allege used remailers to disseminate copyrighted and secret Church teachings. As a result, operating a remailer is not a risk-free activity today. Indeed, one can imagine a number of creative lawsuits that might reasonably be launched at the operator of a remailer. Examples include a new tort of concealment of identity, a claim of conspiracy with the wrong-doer, and a RICO claim. A remailer operator whose remailer was used to harass someone might face a common law tort claim of harassment. . . . Although it is far from obvious that any of these legal theories would or should succeed, some raise non-frivolous issues and thus would be expensive to defend.[9]

Also consider Marc Rotenberg:

> The search for an architecture of privacy has prompted a useful discussion of the various privacy techniques. One of the key questions of course is what constitutes an architecture of privacy. When the U.S. government first proposed the Clipper encryption scheme it said that it would protect privacy by enabling the government to apprehend criminals who break into computer systems and violate privacy interests. Even the recent computer security announcement from the White House, which called for expanded government monitoring of computer networks, echoed the theme that greater surveillance would promote greater privacy protection. It is necessary to develop analytic tools that make it possible to speak coher-

---

[8] For further information on anonymous remailers, see Andre Bacard, Anonymous Remailer FAQ, <http://www.andrebacard.com/remail.html>.

[9] A. Michael Froomkin, *Flood Control on the Information Ocean: Living with Anonymity, Digital Cash, and Distributed Databases*, 15 J.L. & Comm. 395, 425-426 (1996).

ently about what constitutes an architecture of privacy. Herbert Burkert did this in part in an article entitled *Privacy Enhancing Technologies: Typology, Critique, Vision.* Burkert provides a useful taxonomy of Privacy Enhancing Technologies (also known as Privacy Enhancing Techniques or "PETs") concepts and various strategies for implementation. Burkert notes that PETs are a "technological innovation that attempt to solve a set of socio-economic problems."

The concept of PETs has resonated in the privacy world. Governments have undertaken studies to explore how Privacy Enhancing Techniques, oftentimes based on pseudonyms, could be implemented in the world of the Internet and e-commerce. PETs typically seek to implement Fair Information Practices and where possible to minimize or eliminate the collection of personally identifiable information. To understand the concept of PETs in more detail it is useful to have a contrasting notion. Elsewhere, I had proposed the term "privacy extracting techniques" as the appropriate counterpart to Privacy Enhancing Techniques, but here I will follow Roger Clarke's phrase "Privacy Intrusive Techniques" ("PITs"), which provides the useful pairing of PETs and PITs. It is fairly obvious that techniques that covertly collect personally identifiable information might be considered intrusive. Techniques that coerce the collection of personal information might also be considered intrusive. The interesting comparison arises from the voluntary disclosure of personal information. Here the distinctions between PETs and PITs are most apparent. The key point in this example is that PETs will typically limit or eliminate the collection of personally identifiable information whereas PITs would facilitate it. . . .[10]

2. In *ACLU v. Miller*, suppose that instead of passing the law that it did, Georgia passed a narrower law that provided:

    > Any anonymous remailer service or Internet Service Provider must retain identifying information for all communications it transmits or helps to transmit. This identifying information must be provided pursuant to a search warrant, court order, or subpoena.

    Would such a law be constitutional?

3. ***The WHOIS Database.*** Currently, the Internet Corporation for Assigned Names and Numbers (ICANN) Registrar Accreditation Agreement (RAA) requires that the identity and addresses of domain name holders be publicly disclosed as well as the identities, addresses, e-mail addresses, and telephone numbers for technical and administrative contacts. Domain names are the names assigned to particular web sites (e.g., *www.yahoo.com, www.cnn.com*). In other words, an individual who wants to create her own web site must publicly disclose personal information and cannot remain anonymous. The registration scheme includes both commercial services and publishers of political newsletters. Is the WHOIS database constitutional?

---

[10] Marc Rotenberg, *Fair Information Practices and the Architecture of Privacy (What Larry Doesn't Get)*, 2001 Stan. Tech. L. Rev. 1.

COLUMBIA INSURANCE CO. V. SEESCANDY.COM

185 F.R.D. 573 (N.D. Cal. 1999)

[The plaintiff brought an action for trademark infringement against anonymous parties who registered Internet domain names "seescandy.com" and "seescandys.com." The plaintiff sought discovery of the identities of the parties.]

JENSEN, J. . . . In such cases the traditional reluctance for permitting filings against John Doe defendants or fictitious names and the traditional enforcement of strict compliance with service requirements should be tempered by the need to provide injured parties with an forum in which they may seek redress for grievances. However, this need must be balanced against the legitimate and valuable right to participate in online forums anonymously or pseudonymously. People are permitted to interact pseudonymously and anonymously with each other so long as those acts are not in violation of the law. This ability to speak one's mind without the burden of the other party knowing all the facts about one's identity can foster open communication and robust debate. Furthermore, it permits persons to obtain information relevant to a sensitive or intimate condition without fear of embarrassment. People who have committed no wrong should be able to participate online without fear that someone who wishes to harass or embarrass them can file a frivolous lawsuit and thereby gain the power of the court's order to discover their identity.

Thus some limiting principals should apply to the determination of whether discovery to uncover the identity of a defendant is warranted. The following safeguards will ensure that this unusual procedure will only be employed in cases where the plaintiff has in good faith exhausted traditional avenues for identifying a civil defendant pre-service, and will prevent use of this method to harass or intimidate.

First, the plaintiff should identify the missing party with sufficient specificity such that the Court can determine that defendant is a real person or entity who could be sued in federal court. This requirement is necessary to ensure that federal requirements of jurisdiction and justiciability can be satisfied. . . .

Second, the party should identify all previous steps taken to locate the elusive defendant. This element is aimed at ensuring that plaintiffs make a good faith effort to comply with the requirements of service of process and specifically identifying defendants. . . .

Third, plaintiff should establish to the Court's satisfaction that plaintiff's suit against defendant could withstand a motion to dismiss. . . . Pre-service discovery is akin to the process used during criminal investigations to obtain warrants. The requirement that the government show probable cause is, in part, a protection against the misuse of ex parte procedures to invade the privacy of one who has done no wrong. A similar requirement is necessary here to prevent abuse of this extraordinary application of the discovery process and to ensure that plaintiff has standing to pursue an action against defendant. Thus, plaintiff must make some showing that an act giving rise to civil liability actually occurred and that the discovery is aimed at revealing specific identifying features of the person or entity who committed that act. . . .

Lastly, the plaintiff should file a request for discovery with the Court, along with a statement of reasons justifying the specific discovery requested as well as identification of a limited number of persons or entities on whom discovery process might be served and for which there is a reasonable likelihood that the discovery process will lead to identifying information about defendant that would make service of process possible. . . .

Doe v. 2TheMart.com, Inc.

140 F. Supp. 2d 1088 (W.D. Wash. 2001)

ZILLY, J. This matter comes before the Court on the motion of J. Doe (Doe) to proceed under a pseudonym and to quash a subpoena issued by 2TheMart.com (TMRT) to a local internet service provider, Silicon Investor/InfoSpace, Inc. (InfoSpace). . . .

There is a federal court lawsuit pending in the Central District of California in which the shareholders of TMRT have brought a shareholder derivative class action against the company and its officers and directors alleging fraud on the market. In that litigation, the defendants have asserted as an affirmative defense that no act or omission by the defendants caused the plaintiffs' injury. By subpoena, TMRT seeks to obtain the identity of twenty-three speakers who have participated anonymously on Internet message boards operated by InfoSpace. That subpoena is the subject of the present motion to quash.

InfoSpace is a Seattle based Internet company that operates a website called "Silicon Investor." The Silicon Investor site contains a series of electronic bulletin boards, and some of these bulletin boards are devoted to specific publicly traded companies. InfoSpace users can freely post and exchange messages on these boards. Many do so using Internet pseudonyms, the often fanciful names that people choose for themselves when interacting on the Internet. By using a pseudonym, a person who posts or responds to a message on an Internet bulletin board maintains anonymity.

One of the Internet bulletin boards on the Silicon Investor website is specifically devoted to TMRT. . . .

Some of the messages posted on the TMRT site have been less than flattering to the company. In fact, some have been downright nasty. For example, a user calling himself "Truthseeker" posted a message stating "TMRT is a Ponzi scam that Charles Ponzi would be proud of. . . . The company's CEO, Magliarditi, has defrauded employees in the past. The company's other large shareholder, Rebeil, defrauded customers in the past." Another poster named "Cuemaster" indicated that "they were dumped by their accountants . . . these guys are friggin liars . . . why haven't they told the public this yet? ? ? Liars and criminals!!!!!" Another user, not identified in the exhibits, wrote "Lying, cheating, thieving, stealing, lowlife criminals!!!!" . . .

TMRT, the defendant in the California lawsuit, issued the present subpoena to InfoSpace pursuant to Fed. R. Civ. P. 45(a)(2). The subpoena seeks, among other things, "[a]ll identifying information and documents, including, but not limited to, computerized or computer stored records and logs, electronic mail (E-mail), and postings on your online message boards," concerning a list of twenty-three InfoSpace users, including Truthseeker, Cuemaster, and the current J. Doe, who used the pseudonym NoGuano. These users have posted messages on the TMRT bulletin board or have communicated via the Internet with users who have posted such messages. The subpoena would require InfoSpace to disclose the subscriber information for these twenty-three users, thereby stripping them of their Internet anonymity.

InfoSpace notified these users by e-mail that it had received the subpoena, and gave them time to file a motion to quash. One such user who used the Internet pseudonym NoGuano now seeks to quash the subpoena.[11]

NoGuano alleges that enforcement of the subpoena would violate his or her First Amendment right to speak anonymously. . . .

A component of the First Amendment is the right to speak with anonymity. This component of free speech is well established. *See, e.g., Buckley v. American Constitutional Law Found.*, 525 U.S. 182 (1999) (invalidating, on First Amendment grounds, a Colorado statute that required initiative petition circulators to wear identification badges); *McIntyre v. Ohio Elections Comm'n*, 514 U.S. 334 (1995) (overturning an Ohio law that prohibited the distribution of campaign literature that did not contain the name and address of the person issuing the literature. . . .); *Talley v. California*, 362 U.S. 60 (1960) (invalidating a California statute prohibiting the distribution of "any handbill in any place under any circumstances" that did not contain the name and address of the person who prepared it, holding that identification and fear of reprisal might deter "perfectly peaceful discussions of public matters of importance."). . . .

The right to speak anonymously extends to speech via the Internet. Internet anonymity facilitates the rich, diverse, and far ranging exchange of ideas. The "ability to speak one's mind" on the Internet "without the burden of the other party knowing all the facts about one's identity can foster open communication and robust debate." People who have committed no wrongdoing should be free to participate in online forums without fear that their identity will be exposed under the authority of the court. [The speech in this case is entitled to strict scrutiny protection.] . . .

In support of its subpoena request, TMRT argues that the right to speak anonymously does not create any corresponding right to remain anonymous after speech. In support of this contention, TMRT cites only to *Buckley*. TMRT argues that in *Buckley*, while the Court struck down a requirement that petition circulators wear identification badges when soliciting signatures, the Court upheld a provision of the same statute that required circulators to execute an identifying affidavit when they submitted the collected signatures to the state for counting. However, the Court's reasoning in *Buckley* does not support the contention that there is no First Amendment right to remain anonymous. It merely establishes that in the context of the submission of initiative petitions to the State, the State's enforcement interest outweighs the circulator's First Amendment protections. The right to speak anonymously is there-

---

[11] NoGuano has moved anonymously to quash the subpoena. At oral argument, counsel for all parties agreed that NoGuano was entitled to appear before this Court anonymously on the motion to quash. When an individual wishes to protect their First Amendment right to speak anonymously, he or she must be entitled to vindicate that right without disclosing their identity. Accordingly, this Court grants NoGuano's request to proceed under a pseudonym for the purposes of this motion. . . .

fore not absolute. However, this right would be of little practical value if, as TMRT urges, there was no concomitant right to remain anonymous after the speech is concluded. . . .

The free exchange of ideas on the Internet is driven in large part by the ability of Internet users to communicate anonymously. If Internet users could be stripped of that anonymity by a civil subpoena enforced under the liberal rules of civil discovery, this would have a significant chilling effect on Internet communications and thus on basic First Amendment rights. Therefore, discovery requests seeking to identify anonymous Internet users must be subjected to careful scrutiny by the courts.

As InfoSpace has urged, "[u]nmeritorious attempts to unmask the identities of online speakers . . . have a chilling effect on" Internet speech. The "potential chilling effect imposed by the unmasking of anonymous speakers would diminish if litigants first were required to make a showing in court of their need for the identifying information." "[R]equiring litigants to make such a showing would allow [the Internet] to thrive as a forum for speakers to express their views on topics of public concern." . . .

In the context of a civil subpoena issued pursuant to Fed. R. Civ. P. 45, this Court must determine when and under what circumstances a civil litigant will be permitted to obtain the identity of persons who have exercised their First Amendment right to speak anonymously. There is little in the way of persuasive authority to assist this Court. However, courts that have addressed related issues have used balancing tests to decide when to protect an individual's First Amendment rights. . . .

The standard for disclosing the identity of a non-party *witness* must be higher than that articulated in *Seescandy.Com.* . . . When the anonymous Internet user is not a party to the case, the litigation can go forward without the disclosure of their identity. Therefore, non-party disclosure is only appropriate in the exceptional case where the compelling need for the discovery sought outweighs the First Amendment rights of the anonymous speaker.

Accordingly, this Court adopts the following standard for evaluating a civil subpoena that seeks the identity of an anonymous Internet user who is not a party to the underlying litigation. The Court will consider four factors in determining whether the subpoena should issue. These are whether: (1) the subpoena seeking the information was issued in good faith and not for any improper purpose, (2) the information sought relates to a core claim or defense, (3) the identifying information is directly and materially relevant to that claim or defense, and (4) information sufficient to establish or to disprove that claim or defense is unavailable from any other source.[12] . . .

This Court does not conclude that this subpoena was brought in bad faith or for an improper purpose. TMRT and its officers and directors are defend-

---

[12]This Court is aware that many civil subpoenas seeking the identifying information of Internet users may be complied with, and the identifying information disclosed, without notice to the Internet users themselves. This is because some Internet service providers do not notify their users when such a civil subpoena is received. The standard set forth in this Order may guide Internet service providers in determining whether to challenge a specific subpoena on behalf of their users. However, this will provide little solace to Internet users whose Internet service company does not provide them notice when a subpoena is received.

ing against a shareholder derivative class action lawsuit. They have asserted numerous affirmative defenses, one of which alleges that the defendants did not cause the drop in TMRT's stock value. TMRT could reasonably believe that the posted messages are relevant to this defense. . . .

Only when the identifying information is needed to advance core claims or defenses can it be sufficiently material to compromise First Amendment rights. If the information relates only to a secondary claim or to one of numerous affirmative defenses, then the primary substance of the case can go forward without disturbing the First Amendment rights of the anonymous Internet users.

The information sought by TMRT does not relate to a core defense. Here, the information relates to only one of twenty-seven affirmative defenses raised by the defendant, the defense that "no act or omission of any of the Defendants was the cause in fact or the proximate cause of any injury or damage to the plaintiffs." This is a generalized assertion of the lack of causation. Defendants have asserted numerous other affirmative defenses that go more "to the heart of the matter," such as the lack of material misstatements by the defendants, actual disclosure of material facts by the defendants, and the business judgment defense. Therefore, this factor also weighs in favor of quashing the subpoena.

Even when the claim or defense for which the information is sought is deemed core to the case, the identity of the Internet users must also be materially relevant to that claim or defense. Under the Federal Rules of Civil Procedure discovery is normally very broad, requiring disclosure of any relevant information that "appears reasonably calculated to lead to the discovery of admissible evidence." Fed. R. Civ. P. 26(b)(1). But when First Amendment rights are at stake, a higher threshold of relevancy must be imposed. Only when the information sought is directly and materially relevant to a core claim or defense can the need for the information outweigh the First Amendment right to speak anonymously.

TMRT has failed to demonstrate that the identity of the Internet users is directly and materially relevant to a core defense. These Internet users are not parties to the case and have not been named as defendants as to any claim, cross-claim or third-party claim. Therefore, unlike in *Seescandy.Com* . . . , their identity is not needed to allow the litigation to proceed. . . .

. . . TMRT argues that the Internet postings caused a drop in TMRT's stock price. However, what was said in these postings is a matter of public record, and the identity of the anonymous posters had no effect on investors. If these messages did influence the stock price, they did so without anyone knowing the identity of the speakers. . . .

NOTES & QUESTIONS

1. How does the situation in *Seescandy* differ from that in *2TheMart*? How do the approaches toward anonymity differ in these two cases? Should the approach in *Seescandy* be applied to the situation in *2TheMart* or vice versa?[13]

---

[13]See also *Dendrite International, Inc. v. John Doe No. 3*, 775 A.2d 756 (N.J. Super. A.D. 2001) (following *Seescandy* approach).

2. Anonymity presents a unique and difficult privacy problem on the Internet. Anonymity can impede law enforcement of fraud, child molestation, hacking, harassment, and other crimes on the Internet. On the other hand, anonymity is essential for privacy. In cases involving libel over the Internet, a person cannot successfully recover damages from the poster of defamatory comments without first knowing who to sue. We see in libel lawsuits subpoenas served on ISPs to reveal the identity of the poster of a message. Should ISPs be required to (1) keep records of people's identities so that such information can be recovered; and (2) disclose such information if there is a libel suit?

3. Anonymity can also pose a threat to privacy. Anonymity permits people to get away with defamation, public disclosure of private facts, intrusion, and other privacy torts. For example, a person can anonymously post gossip about a person or post a candid photograph of a person in the nude. Without being able to discover the identity of the poster, the victim has little legal recourse against the poster. Should a victim be able to obtain the name of an anonymous poster from an ISP? How could this authority be misused?

3. ANONYMOUS READING AND RECEIVING OF IDEAS

TATTERED COVER, INC. V. CITY OF THORNTON

44 P.3d 1044 (Colo. 2002)

[Law enforcement officials (local City of Thornton police and a federal DEA agent) suspected that a methamphetamine lab was being operated out of a trailer home. On searching through some garbage from the trailer, an officer discovered evidence of drug operations and a mailing envelope from the Tattered Cover bookstore addressed to one of the suspects (Suspect A). There was an invoice and order number corresponding to the books shipped in the envelope, but no evidence about what those books were. Subsequently, a search warrant was obtained for the trailer home. In the bedroom, the police discovered a methamphetamine laboratory and drugs. Although there were a number of suspects, the police believed that Suspect A occupied the bedroom. Among the items seized from the bedroom were two books: *Advanced Techniques of Clandestine Psychedelic and Amphetamine Manufacture*, by Uncle Fester, and *The Construction and Operation of Clandestine Drug Laboratories*, by Jack B. Nimble. The officers believed that these books were the ones mailed to Suspect A in the mailing envelope from the Tattered Cover found in the trash. The officers served the Tattered Cover with a DEA administrative subpoena. The subpoena requested the title of the books corresponding to the order and invoice numbers of the mailer, as well as information about all other book orders Suspect A had made. Joyce Meskis, the owner of the Tattered Cover, refused to comply with the subpoena, citing concern for its customers' privacy and First Amendment rights. The officers then approached prosecutors from the Adams County District Attorney's office to obtain a search warrant for the Tattered Cover. The prosecutors believed that the warrant sought was too broad and refused to sign off on it. The officers then went to the Denver DA's office, which approved the warrant. A Denver county court judge authorized the warrant. The Tattered Cover sued to enjoin the officers from executing the warrant.]

BENDER, J. . . . The First Amendment to the United States Constitution protects more than simply the right to speak freely. It is well established that it safeguards a wide spectrum of activities, including the right to distribute and sell expressive materials, the right to associate with others, and, most importantly to this case, the right to receive information and ideas. . . .

Without the right to receive information and ideas, the protection of speech under the United States and Colorado Constitutions would be meaningless. It makes no difference that one can voice whatever view one wishes to express if others are not free to listen to these thoughts. The converse also holds true. Everyone must be permitted to discover and consider the full range of expression and ideas available in our "marketplace of ideas." As Justice Brandeis so eloquently stated, "[Our founders] believed that freedom to think as you will and to speak as you think are means indispensable to the discovery and spread of political truth.". . .

Bookstores are places where a citizen can explore ideas, receive information, and discover myriad perspectives on every topic imaginable. When a person buys a book at a bookstore, he engages in activity protected by the First Amendment because he is exercising his right to read and receive ideas and information. Any governmental action that interferes with the willingness of customers to purchase books, or booksellers to sell books, thus implicates First Amendment concerns.

Anonymity is often essential to the successful and uninhibited exercise of First Amendment rights, precisely because of the chilling effects that can result from disclosure of identity. The Supreme Court has recognized this principle numerous times in various contexts. For instance, in *McIntyre v. Ohio Elections Commission*, the Court stated, "Anonymity is a shield from the tyranny of the majority. It thus exemplifies the purpose behind the Bill of Rights, and of the First Amendment in particular: to protect unpopular individuals from retaliation — and their ideas from suppression — at the hand of an intolerant society." . . .

The need to protect anonymity in the context of the First Amendment has particular applicability to book-buying activity. . . . The right to engage in expressive activities anonymously, without government intrusion or observation, is critical to the protection of the First Amendment rights of book buyers and sellers, precisely because of the chilling effects of such disclosures. Search warrants directed to bookstores, demanding information about the reading history of customers, intrude upon the First Amendment rights of customers and bookstores because compelled disclosure of book-buying records threatens to destroy the anonymity upon which many customers depend. . . .

Like the Federal Constitution, our Colorado Constitution protects speech rights. Specifically, Article II, Section 10, entitled "Freedom of speech and press," provides that:

> No law shall be passed impairing the freedom of speech; every person shall be free to speak, write or publish whatever he will on any subject, being responsible for all abuse of that liberty. . . .

The United States Supreme Court has repeatedly acknowledged that its interpretation of the Federal Constitution defines the minimum level of protections that must be afforded, through the Fourteenth Amendment, by the states. However, the Supreme Court has also recognized that a state may, if it so chooses, afford its residents a greater level of protection under its state constitution than that bestowed by the Federal Constitution.

With respect to expressive freedoms, this court has recognized that the Colorado Constitution provides broader free speech protections than the Federal Constitution. . . .

Having defined the right at issue in this case, we next address the collision between the exercise of this right and the investigative efforts of law enforcement officials. We consider the legal test that applies to determine when law enforcement officials may use a search warrant to obtain customer book purchase records from an innocent, third-party bookstore, and the circumstances that trigger application of that test. . . .

Search warrants are the mechanism used to protect against unjustified police intrusions that would otherwise violate the dictates of the Fourth Amendment and Article II, Section 7. In order to obtain a search warrant, law enforcement officials must demonstrate, prior to any search, that probable cause exists to believe that the legitimate object of such a search is located in a specific place. The warrant itself must describe with particularity the place to be searched and the objects that may be seized. . . .

Conflicts between First Amendment and Fourth Amendment rights are inevitable when law enforcement officials attempt to use search warrants to obtain expressive materials. . . .

. . . [T]he Supreme Court has made clear that, when expressive rights are implicated, a search warrant must comply with the particularity requirements of the Fourth Amendment with "scrupulous exactitude." *Zurcher v. Stanford Daily*, 436 U.S. 547, 564 (1978); *Stanford v. Texas*, 379 U.S. 476, 485 (1965). . . .

. . . [In *Zurcher*, the Court held] that First Amendment concerns can never entirely preclude the execution of a search warrant that complies with the Fourth Amendment: "Properly administered, the preconditions for a warrant — probable cause, specificity with respect to the place to be searched and the things to be seized, and overall reasonableness — should afford sufficient protection against the harms that are assertedly threatened by warrants for searching newspaper offices."

The Supreme Court's pronouncements in *Zurcher* can be read to mean that, beyond the "scrupulous exactitude" requirement, the First Amendment places no special limitation on the ability of the government to seize expressive materials under the Fourth Amendment. We acknowledge that this is arguably the import of *Zurcher*. Thus, we ground the holding in this case in our Colorado Constitution. . . .

. . . [W]e find the protections afforded to fundamental expressive rights by federal law, under the above interpretation of *Zurcher*, to be inadequate. We turn to our Colorado Constitution, which we now hold requires a more substantial justification from the government than is required by the Fourth Amendment of the United States Constitution when law enforcement officials attempt to use a search warrant to obtain an innocent, third-party bookstore's customer purchase records.

Our basic rationale for this holding is that, before law enforcement officials are permitted to take actions that are likely to chill people's willingness to read a full panoply of books and be exposed to diverse ideas, law enforcement officials must make a heightened showing of their need for the innocent bookstore's customer purchase records. We emphasize that a bookstore's customer purchase records are not absolutely protected from discovery and that this question must be decided on the particular facts of each case. . . .

. . . [C]ourts have recognized that a very high level of review, referred to as "strict scrutiny" or "exacting scrutiny" is to be undertaken when government action collides with First Amendment rights. This heightened standard is necessary because governmental action that burdens the exercise of First Amendment rights compromises the core principles of an open, democratic society. . . .

We hold that law enforcement officials must demonstrate a sufficiently compelling need for the specific customer purchase record sought from the innocent, third-party bookstore. . . .

. . . [T]he court must engage in a more specific inquiry as to whether law enforcement officials have a compelling need *for the precise and specific information sought.* . . .

. . . [W]e [also] hold that an innocent, third-party bookstore must be afforded an opportunity for a hearing prior to the execution of any search warrant that seeks to obtain its customers' book-purchasing records. At the hearing, the court will apply the balancing test described above to determine whether law enforcement officials have a sufficiently compelling need for the book purchase record that outweighs the harms associated with enforcement of the search warrant. . . .

. . . [Turning to the case at bar,] the City describes three reasons that it is important for it to know whether Suspect A purchased the two "how to" books found at the scene of the crime. First, the City states that this will help them to prove the mens rea of the crime, that Suspect A "intentionally or knowingly" operated the methamphetamine lab. Second, the City contends that proof that Suspect A purchased the "how to" books will help them to prove that Suspect A occupied the master bedroom, the place where the books and methamphetamine lab were found. Finally, the City asserts that the Tattered Cover invoice "connects" Suspect A to the crime. . . .

With respect to the argument that evidence that Suspect A purchased the books will help prove that he knowingly or intentionally operated a methamphetamine lab, we note that the City's search of the bedroom revealed a fully operational and functional methamphetamine lab as well as a small quantity of the manufactured drug. The two "how to" books were found in the immediate vicinity of the lab. The physical presence of the lab itself, and of these books, goes a long way towards proving that the operator of the lab did not accidentally manufacture methamphetamines. These facts leave no doubt that the person or persons who operated this lab did so intentionally. . . .

Thus, we turn to the City's second justification, that the invoice will help them to demonstrate that Suspect A occupied the master bedroom and, hence, must have operated the methamphetamine lab. In essence, the City wishes to use the purchasing record to place Suspect A at the scene of the crime. . . .

If the City needs evidence of who occupied the master bedroom, as indirect evidence of who must have operated the lab, the record reveals a number of alternative ways in which this information could have been ascertained. . . . Clothes and shoes could have been examined to see if the sizes matched Suspect A. Objects could have been fingerprinted. The bed and flooring could have been examined for hair or other DNA samples. Beyond this physical evidence, there are numerous witnesses that the City likely could have interviewed without compromising the integrity of their criminal investigation. . . .

The City's final justification is that proof that Suspect A bought the two books will "connect" him to the crime. The City's argument is somewhat amorphous because it never elaborates on the specific reason as to why the connection exists. At its core, however, the argument rests on the premise that if Suspect A bought the "how to" books, he must have operated the lab. The rationale for this argument is thus directly tied to the contents of the books Suspect A may have purchased. This is precisely the reason that this search warrant is likely to have chilling effects on the willingness of the general public to purchase books about controversial topics.

The dangers, both to Suspect A and to the book-buying public, of permitting the government to access the information it seeks, and to use this proof of purchase as evidence of Suspect A's guilt, are grave. Assuming that Suspect A purchased the books in question, he may have done so for any of a number of reasons, many of which are in no way linked to his commission of any crime. He might have bought them for a friend or roommate, unaware that they would subsequently be placed in the vicinity of an illegal drug lab. He might have been curious about the process of making drugs, without having any intention to act on what he read. It may be that none of these scenarios is as likely as that suggested by the City, that Suspect A bought the books intending to use them to help him make an illegal drug. Nonetheless, Colorado's long tradition of protecting expressive freedoms cautions against permitting the City to seize the Tattered Cover's book purchase record.

We acknowledge that the Tattered Cover invoice helps the City to connect Suspect A to the crime and constitutes "a piece of the evidentiary puzzle." However, because of the strength of other evidence at the City's disposal and because of the substantial chilling effects that are likely to result from execution of the warrant, we hold that the City has failed to demonstrate that its need for this evidence is sufficiently compelling to outweigh the harmful effects of the search warrant. . . .

NOTES & QUESTIONS

1. Do you agree with the decision in *Tattered Cover* that in addition to the right to speak anonymously there is also a right to read anonymously? Does such a right follow logically from the Court's freedom of association and anonymity cases?

2. How far can the rationale of *Tattered Cover* be extended? Suppose the police obtained a search warrant for one's home and sought to seize a person's diary? Would such a seizure be subject to strict scrutiny? What about the search of one's computer, which can reveal anonymous speech as well as

one's online reading activities? Isn't the government's questioning of various witnesses to whom a person spoke also likely to interfere with that person's expressive activities? Why are books different (or are they)?

3. ***The Right to Read Anonymously.*** Consider the following argument by Julie Cohen:

> For the most part, First Amendment jurisprudence has defined readers' rights only incidentally. Historically, both courts and commentators have been more concerned with protecting speakers than with protecting readers. . . .
>
> As a matter of both historical and current practice, the distinction between "active" expression and "passive" receipt is less clear than one might suppose. From a historical perspective, the strict demarcation between speaking and reading is a relatively recent one. For much of human history, everything from stories to important business matters was transmitted orally. Even after the advent of written manuscripts, the words they contained were first "read" by speaking them aloud. We have come a long way from the days of medieval scribes and public readings of texts and missives. However, with the advent of electronic networks and hypertext links, expression and receipt of information are blurring once again. Electronic text is dynamic; rather than following a single, linear progression, the reader is free to choose his or her own path through a network of linked material. Through this process, the reader participates in the construction of the author's message. While it may be premature to speak of the demise of the author, the creation of at least some "speech" in cyberspace thus reflects the combined efforts of both "authors" and "readers." . . .
>
> . . . All speech responds to prior speech of some sort. The person who expresses vigorous disapproval of Hillary Clinton after months of reading electronic bulletins on "femi-nazis" from Rush Limbaugh and subscribing to anti-feminist Usenet newsgroups is no different in this regard than the person who reads a judicious mixture of New York Times op-ed pieces and scholarly literature on feminism before venturing to express an opinion regarding Mrs. Clinton's conduct. When the two readers choose to express their own views, the First Amendment protects both speakers equally. Logically, that zone of protection should encompass the entire series of intellectual transactions through which they formed the opinions they ultimately chose to express. Any less protection would chill inquiry, and as a result, public discourse, concerning politically and socially controversial issues — precisely those areas where vigorous public debate is most needed, and most sacrosanct. . . .
>
> The freedom to read anonymously is just as much a part of our tradition, and the choice of reading materials just as expressive of identity, as the decision to use or withhold one's name. Indeed, based purely on tradition, the freedom to read anonymously may be even more fundamental than the freedom to engage in anonymous political speech. Anonymous advocacy has always been controversial. Anonymous reading, in contrast, is something that is taken for granted. The material conditions for non-anonymous reading — the technologies that enable content providers to monitor readers' activities and choices — have only recently come to exist. With them has come the realization that the act of reading communicates, and that our tradition of anonymous exploration and inquiry is threatened. Reader profiles are valuable to marketers precisely because they disclose information about the

reader's tastes, preferences, interests, and beliefs. That information is content that the reader should have a constitutionally protected interest in refusing to share. . . .[14]

Cohen argues that the government should recognize and pass legislation to protect one's right to read anonymously. If there were such a right to read anonymously, then under Cohen's reasoning, should the government enact a law to restrict the use of cookies on public web sites?

4. In *Lamont v. Postmaster General of the United States*, 381 U.S. 301 (1965), a 1962 federal statute required that all mail (except sealed letters) that originates or is prepared in a foreign country and is determined by the Secretary of the Treasury to be "communist political propaganda" be detained at the post office. The addressee would be notified of the matter and the mail would be delivered to the addressee only upon her request. The Court struck down the statute on First Amendment grounds:

> We rest on the narrow ground that the addressee in order to receive his mail must request in writing that it be delivered. This amounts in our judgment to an unconstitutional abridgment of the addressee's First Amendment rights. The addressee carries an affirmative obligation which we do not think the Government may impose on him. This requirement is almost certain to have a deterrent effect, especially as respects those who have sensitive positions. Their livelihood may be dependent on a security clearance. Public officials like schoolteachers who have no tenure, might think they would invite disaster if they read what the Federal Government says contains the seeds of treason. Apart from them, any addressee is likely to feel some inhibition in sending for literature which federal officials have condemned as "communist political propaganda." The regime of this Act is at war with the "uninhibited, robust, and wide-open debate and discussion" that are contemplated by the First Amendment.

5. ***The First Amendment and Government Searches.*** Recall in Chapter 4 that based on *Smith v. Maryland*, a person does not have a reasonable expectation of privacy in records held by third parties. Also recall that under the ECPA Title II, the government can obtain identifying information (as well as other personal information) from one's Internet Service Provider with a court order. 18 U.S.C. §2703(c)(1)(B). This is how the government obtains the identities of people engaging in illegal activity who use screen names. *See United States v. Charbonneau; United States v. Hambrick; United States v. Kennedy* (Chapter 4). However, based on the cases you have read in this chapter about the right to anonymity, does the First Amendment have a role to play in these situations? Consider the following argument by Daniel Solove:

> Extensive government information gathering from third party records also implicates the right to speak anonymously. . . . With government information gathering from third parties, namely ISPs, the government can readily obtain an anonymous or pseudonymous speaker's identity. Only computer-savvy users can speak with more secure anonymity. When private

---

[14]Julie E. Cohen, *A Right to Read Anonymously: A Closer Look at "Copyright Management" in Cyberspace*, 28 Conn. L. Rev. 981 (1996).

parties attempt to obtain the identifying information, courts have held that subpoenas for this information must contain heightened standards. However, no such heightened standards apply when the *government* seeks to obtain the information.

Further, beyond typical anonymity is the ability to receive information anonymously. As Julie Cohen persuasively contends: "The freedom to read anonymously is just as much a part of our tradition, and the choice of reading materials just as expressive of identity, as the decision to use or withhold one's name." The lack of sufficient controls on the government obtaining the extensive records about how a person surfs the web, what books and magazines they read, and what videos or television channels they listen to can implicate this interest.[15]

Recall *Columbia Insurance Co. v. Seescandy.com* and *Doe v. 2TheMart.com* from the previous section. If private parties must satisfy heightened scrutiny under the First Amendment to obtain information relating to an anonymous speaker on the Internet, shouldn't the government also have to satisfy such scrutiny as well? Recall from Chapter 4 that generally, if the government obtains a search warrant supported by probable cause and issued by a neutral judge or magistrate, then the search is valid under the Fourth Amendment. Does having to satisfy heightened scrutiny, in addition to meeting the requirements of the Fourth Amendment, place too great a burden on law enforcement officials before conducting a search?

C. IDENTIFICATION

1. IDENTIFICATION DEVICES

How do we know whether a person is who she says she is? For many economic transactions, this is a fundamental question. A person visits her bank to make a withdrawal. A teller who has never seen or met that person must find some way to verify that she is the true owner of the bank account. A person calls her school to obtain a copy of her transcript. The registrar needs to be able to verify that the caller is who she claims to be. Roger Clarke defines identification as "the association of data with a particular human being."[16] "Identity authentication is the process whereby evidence of identity is assessed in order to establish a sufficient degree of confidence that data is being associated with the correct human being."[17] What system should we adopt to identify people? Different devices to authenticate identity differ in effectiveness, potential for error and abuse, and social benefits and costs.

---

[15] Daniel J. Solove, *Digital Dossiers and the Dissipation of Fourth Amendment Privacy*, 75 S. Cal. L. Rev. 1083 (2002).

[16] Roger Clarke, *Human Identification and Identity Authentication* (1998), available at *http://www .anu.edu.au/people/Roger.Clarke/DV/SCTISK3.html*. As Roger Clarke observes: "In the context of information systems, the purpose of identification is more concrete: it is used to link a stream of data with a person." Roger Clarke, Human Identification in *Information Systems: Management Challenges and Public Policy Issues*, 7 Information Tech. & People; People 6 (1994), available at *http://www .anu.edu.au/people/Roger.Clarke/DV/ HumanID.html*.

[17] Clarke, *Human Identification and Identity Authentication, supra.*

Identification Cards. One type of identification system is for people to carry cards. Cards can contain a variety of information — typically, one's photograph, name, date of birth, address, and physical characteristics. Modern identification cards often not only have information printed on the card, but have data encoded in a magnetic strip on the card. Data can either be stored on the card or consist of a number that corresponds to a record of information in a database. In the United States, drivers' licenses have been used as identification cards.

Passwords and Secret Codes. Another way to verify identity is through the use of passwords and secret codes. These devices require the person to memorize a password or code. Examples include a combination to open a lock, a personal identification number (PIN) to use with a bank card, or a password to log onto a computer network or e-mail server.

Biometric Identification. Biometric identification and authentication use unique and time-invariant biological or behavioral characteristics. Fingerprints are a long-standing form of biometric identification. Modern technology has enabled sophisticated devices to detect hand prints, voice patterns, iris and retina patterns, facial appearance, and gait.

Computer Chip Implants. A new form of identification under development is a computer chip implanted beneath one's skin. In the past, chips have been implanted into animals to track them. In December 2001, a Florida company announced that it had developed a small chip (about the size of a grain of rice) that could be surgically implanted in humans. The chip, called VeriChip, can transmit a signal that can be detected several feet away by a scanner. The chip can either directly contain personal data or transmit a number that corresponds to personal data in a database.

The Costs and Benefits of Identification. The ability to authenticate identity has important social benefits. It enables greater accountability and efficiency in economic transactions. Quickly and accurately linking people to data can also be useful when others need to learn information about them (e.g., when doctors need to obtain a person's medical history). According to Lynn LoPucki, the crime of identity theft is caused by difficulties in identification. Identity theft occurs where the thief impersonates the victim and gains access to the victim's records and accounts as well as opens up new accounts and conducts business by pretending to be the victim. LoPucki contends: "The problem is not that thieves have access to personal information, but that creditors and credit-reporting agencies often lack both the means and the incentives to correctly identify the persons who seek credit from them or on whom they report."[18] Further, identification systems can promote security by enabling the better screening and detection of criminals and terrorists.

---

[18] Lynn M. LoPucki, *Human Identification Theory and the Identity Theft Problem*, 80 Tex. L. Rev. 89 (2001).

However, greater identification makes anonymity more difficult, and in many instances, impossible. Further, identification can alter the type of society we are building, curtailing freedom and subjecting people to the ills of bureaucracy. As Roger Clarke observes:

> The need to identify oneself may be intrinsically distasteful to some people. For example, they may regard it as demeaning, or implicit recognition that the organisation with whom they are dealing exercises power over them. Many people accept that, at least in particular contexts, an organisation with which they are dealing needs to have their name. Some, however, feel it is an insult to human dignity to require them to use a number or code instead of a name. Some feel demeaned by demands, as part of the identification process, that they reveal information about themselves or their family, or embarrassed at having to memorize a password or PIN.
>
> Some people are unwilling to submit to the regimen of carrying tokens, or unprepared to produce them, on the grounds that this reeks of a totalitarian regime, reflects and perpetuates a power relationship that they despise (such as the South African pass laws during the period of apartheid), or carries with it the seeds of discrimination (as reflected by the content of the token).
>
> Another factor which forces compromise between the interests of accountability and law and order on the one hand, and civil liberties on the other, is the importance of multiple identities as a means of avoiding physical harm and death at the hands of violent opponents.[19]

For what purposes should we require identification? Identification may be necessary for certain purposes but not others. The remainder of this chapter explores identification in the United States.

It is also important to consider that a particular identity need not be linked to actual identity. Cards can grant admission to clubs; passwords can be used to access special accounts; and tokens can be employed to select services. Systems of identification that do not require actual identity are sometimes described as Privacy Enhancing Technologies.

2. IDENTIFICATION AND THE CONSTITUTION

In *Kolender v. Lawson*, 461 U.S. 352 (1983), the Court considered a facial challenge to a California law that required any person who "loiters or wanders . . . without apparent reason or business" to "identify himself and to account for his presence when requested by any peace officer to do so." The Court struck down the statute as unconstitutionally vague:

> . . . [The statute] as presently drafted and construed by the state courts, contains no standard for determining what a suspect has to do in order to satisfy the requirement to provide a "credible and reliable" identification. As such, the statute vests virtually complete discretion in the hands of the police to determine whether the suspect has satisfied the statute and must be permitted to go on his way in the absence of probable cause to arrest. An individual, whom

---

[19] Roger Clarke, *Human Identification in Information Systems: Management Challenges and Public Policy Issues*, 7 Information Tech. & People 6 (1994), available at *http://www.anu.edu.au/people/ Roger.Clarke/DV/HumanID.html.*

police may think is suspicious but do not have probable cause to believe has committed a crime, is entitled to continue to walk the public streets "only at the whim of any police officer" who happens to stop that individual under §647(e). Our concern here is based upon the potential for arbitrarily suppressing First Amendment liberties. In addition, [the statute] implicates consideration of the constitutional right to freedom of movement.

Justice Brennan concurred, arguing that the statute also violated the Fourth Amendment:

> . . . [U]nder the Fourth Amendment, police officers with reasonable suspicion that an individual has committed or is about to commit a crime may detain that individual, using some force if necessary, for the purpose of asking investigative questions. They may ask their questions in a way calculated to obtain an answer. But they may not compel an answer, and they must allow the person to leave after a reasonably brief period of time unless the information they have acquired during the encounter has given them probable cause sufficient to justify an arrest.

In *Carey v. Nevada Gaming Control Board*, 279 F.3d 873 (9th Cir. 2002), James Carey was detained by an official of the Nevada Gaming Control Board on suspicion of cheating while gambling. When asked to identify himself verbally or through identification documents, Carey refused. Although the official determined that there was no probable cause that Carey violated gaming laws, the official arrested Carey for refusing to identify himself. The official cited two statutes that required individuals detained by officials to identify themselves or else face criminal sanctions. Carey spent the evening in prison. No charges were brought against him. Carey sued under §1983 alleging a violation of, among other things, his Fourth Amendment rights. The court agreed with Carey:

> [S]uch [identification] statutes violate the Fourth Amendment because as a result of the demand for identification, the statutes bootstrap the authority to arrest on less than probable cause and because the serious intrusion on personal security outweighs the mere possibility that identification might provide a link leading to arrest. . . . [The official] was able to arrest Carey even though there was no probable cause to believe that Carey had violated the gaming laws, and even though Carey's name was not relevant to determining whether Carey had cheated. An arrest under such circumstances is unreasonable. We therefore hold that Carey's arrest violated the Fourth Amendment.

3. SOCIAL SECURITY NUMBERS

The closest thing that the United States has to a national identifier is the Social Security number (SSN). The SSN, a nine-digit identifier, was created in 1936 as part of the Social Security System. Because Social Security benefits would not be paid until a worker's retirement or death, a unique number was necessary to identify his or her account. Over time, various federal agencies began to use the SSN for other purposes. In 1961, for example, the IRS was authorized by Congress to use SSNs as taxpayer identification numbers. Subsequently, throughout the 1960s and 1970s, the SSN began to be used for military personnel, legally admitted aliens, anyone receiving or applying for federal benefits, food stamps, school lunch program eligibility, draft registration, and federal loans. State and local governments, as well as private sector entities such as schools and banks, began to use SSNs as well — for driver's licenses, birth certificates, blood donation, jury selection, worker's compensation, occupational licenses, and marriage licenses. In 1996, Congress required driver's licenses to display a SSN.[20]

In the early 1970s, the early spurt in the growing uses of the SSN raised serious concerns that the SSN would become a de facto universal identifier. In 1973, the Department of Health, Education, and Welfare issued a major report on privacy, stating:

> We take the position that a standard universal identifier (SUI) should not be established in the United States now or in the foreseeable future. By our definition, the Social Security Number (SSN) cannot fully qualify as an SUI; it only approximates one. However, there is an increasing tendency for the Social Security number to be used as if it were an SUI.[21]

In the Privacy Act of 1974, Congress partially responded to these concerns by prohibiting any governmental agency from denying any right, benefit, or privilege merely because an individual refused to disclose his or her SSN. Pursuant to § 7 of the Privacy Act:

> (a)(1) It shall be unlawful for any federal, state or local government agency to deny to any individual any right, benefit, or privilege provided by law because of such individual's refusal to disclose his Social Security account number.
>
> (2) The provisions of paragraph (1) of this subsection shall not apply with respect to —
>
> (A) Any disclosure which is required by federal statute, or
>
> (B) The disclosure of a social security number to any federal, state, or local agency maintaining a system of records in existence and operating before January 1, 1975, if such disclosure was required under statute or regulation adopted prior to such date to verity the identity of an individual.
>
> (b) Any federal state or local government agency which requests an individual disclose his social security account number shall inform that individual whether that disclosure is mandatory or voluntary, by what statutory or other authority such number is solicited, and what uses will be made of it. 5 U.S.C. § 552a note.

The Privacy Act was passed to "curtail the expanding use of social security numbers by federal and local agencies and, by so doing, to eliminate the threat to individual privacy and confidentiality of information posed by common numerical identifiers." *Doyle v. Wilson*, 529 F. Supp. 1343, 1348 (D. Del. 1982).

---

[20] For a chart of the increasing uses of the SSN, see Simson Garfinkel, *Database Nation: The Death of Privacy in the 21st Century* 33-34 (2000). *See also* Social Security Administration, *Social Security: Your Number* (1998) <http://www.ssa.gov/pubs/10002.html>.

[21] U.S. Department of Health, Education, and Welfare, *Report of the Secretary's Advisory Committee on Automated Personal Data Systems: Records, Computers, and the Rights of Citizens* xxxii (1973).

Nevertheless, the use of the SSN continued to escalate after the Privacy Act. A 1999 study by the United States General Accounting Office documented the current widespread use of SSNs.[22]

SSNs are collected by private-sector database firms from a number of public and nonpublic sources, such as court records or credit reports. It is currently legal for private firms to sell or disclose SSNs.

As one commentator has observed:

> . . . [W]ith respect to collecting SSNs from individuals (1) federal law does not bar private actors from requesting SSNs or refusing to do business with someone if they refuse; and (2) state laws, although reaching a few private actors, contain no general prohibitions against SSN use or collection. . . . [G]overnmental use of SSNs is forbidden by Section 7 of the Privacy Act unless an exception applies, but . . . over the years Congress has made so many exceptions, that the collection of SSNs in government is quite widespread. This is the case for two reasons: Congress has passed many mandates of SSN use, and where states or private actors are left to decide whether or not to require the SSN, these entities generally choose to use it.
>
> With respect to using and disseminating SSNs, the law is somewhat more unprotective of privacy rights, but is still quite unsatisfying to privacy advocates. While federal statutes like FERPA or some states' informational privacy laws contain restrictions on information dissemination, the fact remains that governmental dissemination of personal identifying numbers is still widespread, and limits on private actors are also virtually nonexistent.[23]

GREIDINGER V. DAVIS

---

988 F.2d 1344 (4th Cir. 1993)

HAMILTON, J. The Constitution of Virginia requires all citizens otherwise qualified to vote and possessing a [Social Security number ("SSN")] (registering after July 1, 1971) to provide their SSN on their Virginia Voter Registration Application (Application) in order to become registered to vote. Va. Const. art. II, § 2. If an individual otherwise qualified to vote does not possess a SSN, a "dummy" number will be provided. The scheme also provides that any registered voter may inspect the voter registration books in the Office of the General Registrar. In practice, these books contain the registration application of a registered voter.

The scheme further provides that Statewide Voter Registration lists containing the SSNs of voters can be obtained by: (a) candidates for election to further their candidacy, (b) political party committees for political purposes only, (c) incumbent office holders to report to their constituents, and (d) nonprofit organizations which promote voter participation and registration for that purpose only.

---

[22] See United States General Accounting Office, Report to the Chairman, Subcomm. on Social Security, Comm. On Ways and Means, House of Representatives: *Social Security: Government and Commercial Use of the Social Security Number Is Widespread* (Feb. 1999).

[23] Flavio L. Komuves, *We've Got Your Number: An Overview of Legislation and Decisions to Control the Use of Social Security Numbers as Personal Identifiers*, 16 J. Marshall J. Computer & Info. L. 529, 569 (1998).

On July 24, 1991, appellant, Marc Alan Greidinger, filled out an Application, but refused to disclose his SSN. Because of this omission, Greidinger received a Denial of Application for Virginia Voter Registration from the General Registrar of Stafford County. Consequently, the Virginia State Board of Elections (the Board) prevented Greidinger from voting in the November 5, 1991, general election. The Application completed by Greidinger did not state whether disclosure of his SSN was mandatory or voluntary, by what statutory or other authority the SSN was requested, what uses would be made of the SSN, or that the SSN might be disseminated to registered voters or political parties. [Greidinger sued] . . .

Greidinger argues that the "public disclosure" accompanying Virginia's requirement that he provide his SSN on his voter registration application unconstitutionally burdens his right to vote as protected by the First and Fourteenth Amendments. In making this argument, Greidinger attacks two components of Virginia's voter registration scheme. He objects to Virginia's permitting registered voters to obtain another registered voter's SSN via § 24.1-56, which provides that all registration books, containing all of the registration forms, "shall be opened to the inspection of any qualified voter." He also objects to § 24.1-23(8) which allows dissemination of a registered voter's SSN to a candidate for election or political party nomination, political party committee or official, incumbent office holder, and nonprofit organization which promotes voter participation and registration.

Notably, Greidinger does not challenge Virginia's receipt and internal use of his SSN. He challenges only the dissemination of the SSN to the public pursuant to § 24.1-23(8) (candidates, political parties and officials, incumbents, and nonprofit organizations which promote voter participation and voter registration) and § 24.1-56 (general public). In addition, Greidinger does not assert any constitutional right to privacy in his SSN. Rather, he argues that the privacy interest in his SSN is sufficiently strong that his right to vote cannot be predicated on the disclosure of his SSN to the public or political entities.

It is axiomatic that "[n]o right is more precious in a free country than that of having a voice in the election of those who make the laws under which, as good citizens, we must live. Other rights, even the most basic, are illusory if the right to vote is undermined." Despite the fundamental nature of the right to vote, states may nevertheless impose certain qualifications on and regulate access to the franchise. . . .

However, the state's broad power to regulate the franchise "does not extinguish the State's responsibility to observe the limits established by the First Amendment rights of the State's citizens." . . .

. . . If a substantial burden exists [on the right to vote, the restriction] on the right to vote must serve a compelling state interest and be narrowly tailored to serve that state interest. . . .

Before we begin examining the burden on Greidinger's right to vote, we note that the Virginia statutes at issue, for all practical purposes, condition Greidinger's right to vote on the public disclosure of his SSN. Admittedly, at first glance, the disclosure of a SSN to the general public is a rather subtle price to pay to exercise the right to vote. Nevertheless, it is nothing short of a condition on the exercise of that right. To be sure, by definition, the fact that the SSN may be potentially disseminated to any registered voter or political party with the attendant possibility of a serious invasion of one's privacy is demonstrably more restrictive than predicating the right to vote on the simple receipt and internal use of the SSN. By allowing the SSN to be disseminated to registered voters or political parties upon request, Virginia's voter registration scheme conditions the right to vote on the consent to the public disclosure of a would-be voter's SSN.

Because Virginia's voter registration scheme conditions Greidinger's right to vote on the public disclosure of his SSN, we must examine whether this condition imposes a substantial burden. . . .

In response to growing concerns over the accumulation of massive amounts of personal information, Congress passed the Privacy Act of 1974. This Act makes it unlawful for a governmental agency to deny a right, benefit, or privilege merely because the individual refuses to disclose his SSN. In addition, Section 7 of the Privacy Act further provides that any agency requesting an individual to disclose his SSN must "inform that individual whether that disclosure is mandatory or voluntary, by what statutory authority such number is solicited, and what uses will be made of it." At the time of its enactment, Congress recognized the dangers of widespread use of SSNs as universal identifiers. In its report supporting the adoption of this provision, the Senate Committee stated that the widespread use of SSNs as universal identifiers in the public and private sectors is "one of the most serious manifestations of privacy concerns in the Nation." In subsequent decisions, the Supreme Court took notice of the serious threats to privacy interests by the mass accumulation of information in computer data banks. For example, in *Whalen v. Roe*, 429 U.S. 589 (1977), in rejecting a privacy challenge to a New York statute that: (1) required doctors to disclose to the state information about prescriptions for certain drugs with a high potential for abuse and (2) provided for the storage of that information in a centralized computerized file, the Court observed:

> We are not unaware of the threat to privacy implicit in the accumulation of vast amounts of personal information in computerized data banks or other massive government files. The collection of taxes, the distribution of welfare and social security benefits, the supervision of public health, the direction of our Armed Forces, and the enforcement of all criminal laws all require the orderly preservation of great quantities of information, much of which is personal in character and potentially embarrassing or harmful if disclosed. The right to collect and use such data is typically accompanied by a concomitant statutory or regulatory duty to avoid unwarranted disclosures.

Since the passage of the Privacy Act, an individual's concern over his SSN's confidentiality and misuse has become significantly more compelling. For example, armed with one's SSN, an unscrupulous individual could obtain a person's welfare benefits or Social Security benefits, order new checks at a new address on that person's checking account, obtain credit cards, or even obtain the person's paycheck. Succinctly stated, the harm that can be inflicted from the disclosure of a SSN to an unscrupulous individual is alarming and potentially financially ruinous. These are just examples, and our review is by no means exhaustive; we highlight a few to elucidate the egregiousness of the harm.

The degree of the burden on Greidinger's right to vote can also be seen through the case law's uniform recognition that SSNs are exempt from disclosure under Exemption 6 of the Freedom of Information Act (FOIA), 5 U.S.C.

§ 552(b)(6), because their disclosure would "constitute a clearly unwarranted invasion of privacy." Further Congressional recognition of the privacy concerns is evident from § 7 of the Privacy Act which prohibits the denial of any right, benefit, or privilege by a governmental agency because of an individual's refusal to disclose his SSN.

The statutes at issue compel a would-be voter in Virginia to consent to the possibility of a profound invasion of privacy when exercising the fundamental right to vote. As illustrated by the examples of the potential harm that the dissemination of an individual's SSN can inflict, Greidinger's decision not to provide his SSN is eminently reasonable. In other words, Greidinger's fundamental right to vote is substantially burdened to the extent the statutes at issue permit the public disclosure of his SSN.

Having identified that Greidinger's right to vote is substantially burdened by the public disclosure of his SSN, we must next determine whether Virginia has advanced a compelling state interest that justifies the disclosure and dissemination of his SSN. If Virginia advances a compelling state interest, we must determine whether disclosure of the SSN is narrowly tailored to fulfill that state interest.

. . . Virginia argues that the disclosure of SSNs is a safeguard against voter fraud. With respect to § 24.1-23(8), in addition to preventing voter fraud, Virginia argues that the statute furthers Virginia's interest in promoting "participation in the electoral process." Unquestionably, Virginia has a compelling state interest in preventing voter fraud and promoting voter participation. However, the inquiry does not end here. We must determine whether the disclosure of the SSN under § 24.1-23(8) and/or § 24.1-56 is narrowly tailored to fulfill that state interest. We conclude that it is not.

Virginia's voter registration form requires a registrant to supply, among other things, his name, address, SSN, age, place of birth, and county of previous registration. Virginia's interest in preventing voter fraud and voter participation could easily be met without the disclosure of the SSN and the attendant possibility of a serious invasion of privacy that would result from that disclosure. . . . Most assuredly, an address or date of birth would sufficiently distinguish among voters that shared a common name. Moreover, the same state interest could be achieved through the use of a voter registration number as opposed to a SSN. Following this tack, Virginia would derive the same benefits as the disclosure of a SSN. Thus, to the extent § 24.1-23(8) and § 24.1-56 allow Virginia's voter registration scheme to "sweep [ ] broader than necessary to advance electoral order," it creates an intolerable burden on Greidinger's fundamental right to vote.

In summary, we hold to the extent that § 24.1-23(8) and/or § 24.1-56 permit the public disclosure of Greidinger's SSN as a condition of his right to vote, it creates an intolerable burden on that right as protected by the First and Fourteenth Amendments. . . .

NOTES & QUESTIONS

1. *Greidinger* does not explore whether the disclosure would violate the constitutional right to information privacy. Under the cases you studied so far,

would Virginia's disclosure of SSNs violate the constitutional right to information privacy?

2. Consider *Beacon Journal v. City of Akron*, 70 Ohio St. 3d 605 (Ohio 1994). There, private parties requested that a city provide them with public employees' personnel records containing employees' names, addresses, telephone numbers, birth dates, education, employment status, and SSNs. The city provided the records with the SSNs deleted. The private parties sued to obtain the SSNs. The court concluded that the SSNs were not "public records" for the purposes of Ohio's Public Records Act:

> . . . R.C. 149.43(A) expressly excludes the release of records which would violate state or federal law. Because we find that the disclosure of the SSNs would violate the federal constitutional right to privacy, we find them to be excluded from mandatory disclosure.
>
> "The cases sometimes characterized as protecting 'privacy' have in fact involved at least two different kinds of interests. One is the individual interest in avoiding disclosure of personal matters, and another is the interest in independence in making certain kinds of important decisions." *Whalen v. Roe.* The first interest is relevant to the matter before us.
>
> The right to avoid disclosure of personal matters is so broad in scope that it applies to the most public of our public figures. Even the President of the United States possesses this right. *Nixon v. Admr. of Gen. Serv.* (1977), 433 U.S. 425. . . .
>
> . . . [A]ccording to the *Nixon* case, there is a federal right to privacy which protects against governmental disclosure of the private details of one's life. . . . We must determine whether the city employees have a legitimate expectation of privacy in their SSNs and then whether their privacy interests outweigh those interests benefited by disclosure of the numbers. . . .
>
> Due to the federal legislative scheme involving the use of SSNs, city employees have a legitimate expectation of privacy in their SSNs. [The court quoted § 7 of the Privacy Act of 1974.] . . .
>
> Congress when enacting the Privacy Act of 1974 was codifying the societal perception that SSNs should not to be available to all. This legislative scheme is sufficient to create an expectation of privacy in the minds of city employees concerning the use and disclosure of their SSNs. . . .
>
> The city's refusal to release its employees' SSNs does not significantly interfere with the public's right to monitor governmental conduct. The numbers by themselves reveal little information about the city's employees. The city provided appellees with enormous amounts of other information about each city employee; only the SSNs numbers were deleted. Employees' addresses, telephone numbers, salaries, level of education, and birth dates, among other things, were all provided. The data supplied by the city provides far more enlightening information about the composition of the city's workforce than would SSNs.
>
> While the release of all city employees' SSNs would provide inquirers with little useful information about the organization of their government, the release of the numbers could allow an inquirer to discover the intimate, personal details of each city employee's life, which are completely irrelevant to the operations of government. As the *Greidinger* court warned, a person's SSN is a device which can quickly be used by the unscrupulous to acquire a tremendous amount of information about a person. . . .

Thanks to the abundance of data bases in the private sector that include the SSNs of persons listed in their files, an intruder using an SSN can quietly discover the intimate details of a victim's personal life without the victim ever knowing of the intrusion.

We find today that the high potential for fraud and victimization caused by the unchecked release of city employee SSNs outweighs the minimal information about governmental processes gained through the release of the SSNs. . . .

How does the legal theory in *Beacon* differ from that in *Greidinger*?

3. *Disclosure of Social Security Numbers and the First Amendment.* In *City of Kirkland v. Sheehan*, 29 Media L. Rep. 2367 (Wash. Sup. Ct. 2001), a group of law enforcement personnel sued the operators of a web site critical of the police that listed the names, addresses, dates of birth, phone numbers, Social Security numbers, and other personal data. Although the court held that the disclosure of most of the personal data was protected under the First Amendment, the disclosure of Social Security numbers was different:

In this case, as in numerous others, in the absence of a credible specific threat of harm, the publication of lawfully obtained addresses and telephone numbers, while certainly unwelcome to those who had desired a greater degree of anonymity, is traditionally viewed as having the ability to promote political speech. Publication may arguably expose wrongdoers and/or facilitate peaceful picketing of homes or worksites and render other communication possible.

However, Social Security numbers are different from addresses and telephone numbers. The blanket identification of the Social Security numbers of a group of people, without more, does not provide a similar opportunity for or otherwise facilitate or promote substantive communication. It cannot reasonably be disputed that at its core the SSN is simply a government-originated identifying number. It is a key or a tool, created by the government and unique for each individual. Access to an individual's SSN enables a new holder to obtain access to and to control, manipulate or alter other personal information. In effect, access to an SSN allows a person, agency or company to more efficiently and effectively search for and seize information and assets of another, a power originally available only to the government and one which was subject to direct Constitutional restraint. . . .

On its face, the SSN is a tag or an identifier which at best has only a distant possibility of a substantive communicative purpose. Keeping Social Security numbers private is a compelling interest for the government and citizens alike. . . .

4. The next section discusses national identification systems. As you read the material in that section, think about whether such systems would be constitutional in light of the cases you read in this and the previous sections.

4. NATIONAL IDENTIFICATION SYSTEMS

A national identification system is a nationwide system for identifying individuals. It consists of linking a database of information about individuals to an identifier, so that individuals can be readily connected to a stream of data about them.

More than 100 countries have some form of national identification card. These countries include most nations in Europe (including Germany, France, Spain, Greece, Finland, and others), Malaysia, Singapore, Thailand, and many others. However, Americans have repeatedly eschewed such systems. Throughout the latter half of the twentieth century, government officials have entertained the idea of creating a national identification system on a number of occasions, but each time, the idea has been rejected.

Proponents of national identification systems point to greater efficiencies, ease of use, prevention of fraud, and greater capacity to screen for terrorists and criminals. Critics contend that having one single identification card can vastly increase the dangers if the card is lost or stolen. Such a system of national identification could magnify the effects of fraud. To the extent that the card would bring added efficiency in terms of cardholders having to undergo less stringent security checks, the possessors of forged or stolen cards could better avoid such screenings. Cards could impede free movement throughout the country. Errors in the bureaucratic system administering the cards and linking the cardholders to information in a database could have a severe impact on people's lives. Further, national identifiers would be used by the private sector to link together data about individuals.

RICHARD SOBEL, *THE DEGRADATION OF POLITICAL IDENTITY UNDER A NATIONAL IDENTIFICATION SYSTEM*

8 B.U. J. Sci. & Tech. L. 37 (2002)

America is moving toward a system of national identification numbers, databanks, and identity cards that contradicts the constitutional and philosophical bases of democratic government and undermines the moral economy of political and personal identity. Because the kinds of problems that a national identification system ("NIDS") is supposed to solve tend to occur in relatively closed societies, the troubles a NIDS creates as a bureaucratic scheme may soon foreclose options and opportunities central to a free society. . . . The growing impact of NIDS on due process, burden of proof, freedom from search, free expression, freedom of travel, the right to employment, and federalism makes this issue particularly appropriate for contemporary ethical and policy analysis. . . .

The ongoing developments toward a NIDS, as privacy advocate Robert Ellis Smith notes, fundamentally contradict what it means to be an American. In an open democratic society, the government derives its powers from the consent of the governed, constitutions are developed to circumscribe state power, and activities such as work, travel, and medical care are readily available and treated in ways respectful of privacy. In contrast, the government in authoritarian societies bestows, or denies, identities and opportunities through identification numbers or documents, intruding into individuals' lives. In addition, especially because the government has the power to coerce individuals and to control their lives, people confront force when they must follow, or if they disobey, the government's directions. . . .

A formal NIDS would require an identity number, databank, and ID card. The system would begin by assigning each American resident a unique national identity number. Each citizen and identifiable immigrant would be uniquely identified by a numeral. Resident enumeration and data collection would begin at birth, defining each newborn as a data point to be tracked from cradle to grave through a government-issued number. Such a process has already begun with the relatively recent practice of issuing Social Security numbers at birth and requiring them to obtain marriage licenses and tax deductions for one's children of any age. . . .

For the existence and implementation of a NIDS, particularly a national identity card, there must also be a national computer databank organized by ID numbers. An individual would have to be entered into the databank to exist in a legal sense or to have a bureaucratic existence. Receiving an ID card would require meeting the criteria for being registered in the databank. ID numbers would be used for multiple purposes, and computer databanks would collect disparate pieces of information. For reasons of proposed efficiency, such a computer system would centralize and interconnect with educational, employment, social security, tax, and medical information. These data would paint a detailed portrait of each individual's habits and preference even though such collections would not be fully accurate or secure. One would not, moreover, have a political identity or be able to exercise political rights without proper ID. Inclusion in the databank would create a paper, plastic, or electronic person. . . .

Citizens or residents might be required to carry their national ID at all times or produce it when entering school, applying for a job or government benefits, and traveling away from home. . . .

Identity systems and documents have a long history of uses and abuses for social control and discrimination. Through the Civil War, slaves were required to carry passes in order to travel outside of plantations. . . .

A system of identification cards was used to isolate and round up Jews in Germany and other Nazi-occupied territories prior to World War II and in the occupied countries once the war began. All German Jews were required to apply for such cards by December 31, 1938. . . .

Even before the Japanese attack on Pearl Harbor, however, President Franklin Delano Roosevelt . . . ordered the Census Bureau to collect all information on "foreign-born and American-born Japanese" from the Census data lists. Within days, information from the 1930 and 1940 censuses on all Japanese Americans was gathered and distributed to the Federal Bureau of Investigation, the governors, and the top military officials in western states. Its use facilitated the internment of Japanese Americans on the West Coast. . . .[24]

NOTES & QUESTIONS

1. As a policy matter, do you agree with Richard Sobel that efforts to collect and combine information should be blocked or perhaps undone? Consider the contrary view of Amitai Etzioni:

---

[24] For a discussion of national identification systems in light of September 11, 2001, see Richard Sobel, *The Demeaning of Identity and Personhood in National Identification Systems*, 15 Harv. J. L. & Tech. 319 (2002).

American society incurs high costs — social, economic, and other kinds — because of its inability to identify many hundreds of thousands of violent criminals, white-collar criminals, welfare and credit card cheats, parents who do not pay child support, and illegal immigrants. If individuals could be properly identified, public safety would be significantly enhanced and social and economic costs would be reduced significantly. . . .

In response to the claim that universal identifiers will cause a police state or totalitarian regime to arise, it should be noted that ID cards are quite common in European democracies and have been in place for quite some time without undermining these democracies. . . .

If a totalitarian regime were to arise, and no universal identification system was in place, the new secret police would have only to consolidate existing private databases and add existing public ones (those maintained by the IRS, INS, FBI, and SSA, among others) to have a very elaborate description of most Americans. . . .[25]

2. What are the benefits of a national identification system? What are the costs? What privacy interests could a national identification card in the United States implicate?

3. Consider the cases on anonymity. What would be the impact of a national identification system on First Amendment values?

---

[25] Amitai Etzioni, *The Limits of Privacy* 103-104, 126, 130 (1999).

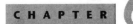
PRIVACY, RECORDS, AND COMPUTER DATABASES

A. PUBLIC SECTOR RECORDS AND COMPUTER DATABASES

1. INTRODUCTION

In the United States, government records about citizens became widely used after the rise of the administrative state in the early part of the twentieth century. The administrative state's extensive and complex systems of regulation, licensing, and entitlements demanded the collection of a significant amount of personal information. For example, the Social Security System, created in 1935, required that records be kept about every employed individual's earnings. To better identify records with particular individuals, each individual under the Social Security System was assigned a unique nine-digit number known as a Social Security number (SSN). *See* Chapter 5 for a more extensive discussion about SSNs.

One of the greatest catalysts for the creation of government records has been technology — namely, the computer. The invention of the mainframe computer in 1946 sparked a revolution in recordkeeping. By the 1960s, computers provided a fast, efficient, and inexpensive way to store, analyze, and transfer information. Federal and state agencies began to computerize their records, often using SSNs as identifiers for these records.[1]

Today, federal agencies maintain thousands of databases. States also maintain a panoply of public records, pertaining to births, marriages, divorces, property ownership, licensing, voter registration, and sex offenders. State public records will be covered later in this chapter.

---

[1] *See* Alan F. Westin & Michael A. Baker, *Databanks in a Free Society: Computers, Record-Keeping and Privacy* 229 (1972); Priscilla Regan, *Legislating Privacy* 69 (1995); Daniel J. Solove, *Privacy and Power: Computer Databases and Metaphors for Information Privacy*, 53 Stan. L. Rev. 1393, 1400-1403 (2001).

The vast stores of personal information spread throughout government databases have given rise to significant fears that one day this information might be combined to create a file on each citizen. In his influential book on privacy, Arthur Miller warned of the "possibility of constructing a sophisticated data center capable of generating a comprehensive womb-to-tomb dossier on every individual and transmitting it to a wide range of data users over a national network."[2] At least three times, the federal government has seriously considered the idea of creating a national database of personal information. In the 1960s, the Johnson Administration proposed a National Data Center that would combine data held by various federal agencies into one large computer database. However, the plan was abandoned after a public outcry. In the 1970s, the Ford Administration proposed linking up all of the federal government's computer databases, but again, the plan was halted by a public outcry.[3] Following the events of September 11, there was a new effort to build a national database based on records contained in state motor vehicle agencies. Unlike the earlier proposal that envisioned a centralized system of records management, the new system would be based on standardized record formats and data linkages to enable information sharing among federal and state agencies. Such an arrangement might be appropriately described as a national identification system.

DANIEL J. SOLOVE, *ACCESS AND AGGREGATION:*
PUBLIC RECORDS, PRIVACY, AND THE CONSTITUTION

---

86 Minn. L. Rev. 1137 (2002)

. . . For decades, federal, state, and local governments have been keeping records about their citizens. States maintain records spanning an individual's life from birth to death, including records of births, marriages, divorces, professional licenses, voting information, worker's compensation, personnel files (for public employees), property ownership, arrests, victims of crime, criminal and civil court proceedings, and scores of other information. Federal agencies maintain records pertaining to immigration, bankruptcy, social security, military personnel, an so on. These records contain personal information including a person's physical description (age, photograph, height, weight, eye color); race, nationality, and gender; family life (children, marital history, divorces, and even intimate details about one's marital relationship); residence, location, and contact information (address, telephone number, value and type of property owned, description of one's home); political activity (political party affiliation, contributions to political groups, frequency of voting); financial condition (bankruptcies, financial information, salary, debts); employment (place of employment, job position salary, sick leave); criminal history (arrests, convictions, traffic citations); health and medical condition (doctor's reports, psychiatrist's notes, drug prescriptions, diseases and other disorders); and iden-

---

[2] Arthur Miller, *Assault on Privacy* 39 (1971).
[3] *See generally* Charles J. Sykes, *The End of Privacy: Personal Rights in the Surveillance Society* 44 (1999); Robert Ellis Smith, *Ben Franklin's Web Site: Privacy and Curiosity from Plymouth Rock to the Internet* (2000); Note, *Privacy and Efficient Government: Proposals for a National Data Center*, 82 Harv. L. Rev. 400 (1968).

tifying information (mother's maiden name, Social Security number). This list is far from complete. Many of these records are open for public inspection.

Until recently, public records were difficult to access. For a long time, public records were only available locally. Finding information about a person often involved a treasure hunt around the country to a series of local offices to dig up records. But with the Internet revolution, public records can be easily obtained and searched from anywhere. Once scattered about the country, now public records are consolidated by private sector entities into gigantic databases. Recently, the federal court system has proposed to make court records available electronically, sparking a considerable debate over privacy because highly sensitive information such as one's Social Security number, medical and psychological records, financial information, and even details about one's marital relationship are sometimes lodged in court records.

A complicated web of state and federal regulation governs the accessibility of these records. This regulation was formulated to balance two important, yet sometimes conflicting, interests. One of these interests is transparency, the need to expose government bureaucracy to public scrutiny. The Federal Freedom of Information Act is an attempt to promote such transparency. Access to court records, in the words of Justice Holmes, ensures "that those who administer justice should always act under the sense of public responsibility, and that every citizen should be able to satisfy himself with his own eyes as to the mode in which a public duty is performed."

The other interest is privacy. Increasingly, as more personal information is collected, stored, and consolidated in government databases, the threat to privacy becomes more paramount. Federal, state, and local governments have been one of the principal suppliers of personal information to the private sector. There are a growing number of large corporations that assemble dossiers on practically every individual by combining information in public records with information collected in the private sector such as one's purchases, spending habits, magazine subscriptions, web surfing activity, and credit history. Increasingly, this dossier of fortified public record information is sold back to government agencies for use in investigating people. . . .

Public records contribute to this privacy problem because they enable the creation of a dossier of personal information about individuals. . . . [P]ublic records are often a principal source of information for the private sector in the construction of their databases. The personal information in public records is often supplied involuntarily and typically for a purpose linked to the reason why particular records are kept. The problem is that, often without the individual's knowledge or consent, the information is then used for a host of different purposes by both the government and businesses. . . . [M]arketers stock their databases with public record information, and the uses to which these databases are put are manifold and potentially limitless. . . .

2. THE FREEDOM OF INFORMATION ACT

Until the second half of the twentieth century, only a few states had created a statutory right of public access to government records. The federal government had no such statute until the passage in 1966 of the Freedom of Information Act (FOIA). President Lyndon Johnson, in signing the FOIA into law, stated:

> This legislation springs from one of our most essential principles: A democracy works best when the people have all the information that the security of the Nation permits. No one should be able to pull curtains of secrecy around decisions which can be revealed without injury to the public interest.[4]

Significant amendments to the FOIA in 1974 strengthened the Act. *See* P.L. No. 93-502. Key provisions established administrative deadlines, reduced fees, imposed sanctions for arbitrary and capricious withholding of agency records, and provided for attorneys' fees and costs.

Right to Access. The FOIA grants all persons the right to inspect and copy records and documents maintained by any federal agency, federal corporation, or federal department. Certain documents must be disclosed automatically — without anybody explicitly requesting them. The FOIA requires disclosure in the Federal Register of descriptions of agency functions, procedures, rules, and policies. 5 U.S.C. § 552(a)(1). The FOIA also requires that opinions, orders, administrative staff manuals, and other materials be automatically released into the public domain. § 552(a)(2).

According to the central provision of the FOIA, § 552(a)(3):

> . . . [E]ach agency, upon any request for records which (i) reasonably describes such records and (ii) is made in accordance with published rules stating the time, place, fees (if any), and procedures to be followed, shall make the records promptly available to any person.

If the agency refuses to provide the records, a person can go to court to force the agency to reveal the information. § 552(a)(4). The court determines de novo whether the agency has properly withheld the documents. In making this determination, the court may review the records in camera.

Exemptions to Protect Privacy. The FOIA contains nine enumerated exemptions to disclosure. *See* § 552(b). Among other things, the exemptions include documents that may be withheld for national security purposes; documents related solely to the internal personnel rules and practices of an agency; and trade secrets and confidential commercial or financial information.[5]

Two of the exemptions involve privacy concerns. Exemption (6) exempts from disclosure "personnel and medical files and similar files the disclosure of which would constitute a clearly unwarranted invasion of personal privacy." § 552(b)(6). Exemption (7)(C) exempts from disclosure "records or information compiled for law enforcement purposes . . . which could reasonably be expected to constitute an unwarranted invasion of personal privacy." § 552(b)(7)(C). Further, FOIA provides that "[t]o the extent required to prevent a clearly unwarranted invasion of personal privacy, an agency may delete identifying de-

---

[4] 2 *Public Papers of the Presidents of the United States: Lyndon B. Johnson* 699 (1967), quoted in H.R. Rep. 104-795 (104th Cong. 2d Sess), at 8 (1996).

[5] *See generally* Harry A. Hammitt, David L. Sobel, & Mark S. Zaid, eds., *Litigation Under the Federal Open Government Laws* (EPIC 2002).

tails when it makes available or publishes an opinion, statement of policy, interpretation, or staff manual or instruction." § 552(a)(2).

The exemptions are permissive; that is, agencies are not required to apply the exemptions. A memo from the Attorney General indicates the government's position as to whether agencies should favor disclosure. *See, e.g.,* Ashcroft memo, Oct. 12, 2001.[6]

Only the government agency can raise Exemptions 6 and 7(C). The individual to whom the information pertains has no right to litigate the issue if the agency does not choose to; nor does the individual have a right to be given notice that her personal information falls within a FOIA request.[7]

Fees. The fees that a requester pays for location, review, and copying by the agency depends upon the requester's status. Media requesters typically have all fees waived. Commercial requesters may be required to pay search, review, and duplication costs for the processing of a FOIA request.

E-FOIA. In 1996, Congress amended FOIA by passing the Electronic Freedom of Information Amendments (E-FOIA), Pub. L. No. 104-231, which aimed to treat public access to electronic documents the same as public access to regular paper documents. Documents that agencies anticipate will be widely requested must be placed in "electronic reading rooms" for people to read them online.

State FOIAs. Since the passage of the FOIA in 1966, a number of states enacted their own open records statutes. Today, every state has an open records law, most of which are patterned after the federal FOIA. These statutes are often referred to as "freedom of information," "open access," "right to know," or "sunshine" laws.

UNITED STATES DEPARTMENT OF JUSTICE V. REPORTERS COMMITTEE FOR FREEDOM OF THE PRESS

489 U.S. 749 (1989)

STEVENS, J. The Federal Bureau of Investigation (FBI) has accumulated and maintains criminal identification records, sometimes referred to as "rap sheets," on over 24 million persons. The question presented by this case is whether the disclosure of the contents of such a file to a third party "could reasonably be expected to constitute an unwarranted invasion of personal privacy" within the meaning of the Freedom of Information Act (FOIA), 5 U.S.C. § 552(b)(7)(C). . . .

In 1924 Congress appropriated funds to enable the Department of Justice (Department) to establish a program to collect and preserve fingerprints and

---

[6] Available at <*http://www.usdoj.gov/oip/foiapost/2001foiapost19.htm*>.

[7] For more background about FOIA's privacy exceptions, see James T. O'Reilly, *Expanding the Purpose of Federal Records Access: New Private Entitlement or New Threat to Privacy?*, 50 Admin. L. Rev. 371 (1998); Patricia M. Wald, *The Freedom of Information Act: A Short Case Study in the Perils and Paybacks of Legislating Democratic Values*, 33 Emory L.J. 649 (1984); Anthony T. Kronman, *The Privacy Exemption to the Freedom of Information Act*, 9 J. Legal Stud. 727 (1980).

other criminal identification records. That statute authorized the Department to exchange such information with "officials of States, cities and other institutions." Six years later Congress created the FBI's identification division, and gave it responsibility for "acquiring, collecting, classifying, and preserving criminal identification and other crime records and the exchanging of said criminal identification records with the duly authorized officials of governmental agencies, of States, cities, and penal institutions." Rap sheets compiled pursuant to such authority contain certain descriptive information, such as date of birth and physical characteristics, as well as a history of arrests, charges, convictions, and incarcerations of the subject. Normally a rap sheet is preserved until its subject attains age 80. . . .

. . . As a matter of executive policy, the Department has generally treated rap sheets as confidential and, with certain exceptions, has restricted their use to governmental purposes. . . .

Although much rap-sheet information is a matter of public record, the availability and dissemination of the actual rap sheet to the public is limited. Arrests, indictments, convictions, and sentences are public events that are usually documented in court records. In addition, if a person's entire criminal history transpired in a single jurisdiction, all of the contents of his or her rap sheet may be available upon request in that jurisdiction. That possibility, however, is present in only three States. All of the other 47 States place substantial restrictions on the availability of criminal-history summaries even though individual events in those summaries are matters of public record. Moreover, even in Florida, Wisconsin, and Oklahoma, the publicly available summaries may not include information about out-of-state arrests or convictions. . . .

The statute known as the FOIA is actually a part of the Administrative Procedure Act (APA). Section 3 of the APA as enacted in 1946 gave agencies broad discretion concerning the publication of governmental records. In 1966 Congress amended that section to implement "'a general philosophy of full agency disclosure.'" . . . The amendment . . . requires every agency "upon any request for records which . . . reasonably describes such records" to make such records "promptly available to any person." If an agency improperly withholds any documents, the district court has jurisdiction to order their production. Unlike the review of other agency action that must be upheld if supported by substantial evidence and not arbitrary or capricious, the FOIA expressly places the burden "on the agency to sustain its action" and directs the district courts to "determine the matter de novo."

Congress exempted nine categories of documents from the FOIA's broad disclosure requirements. Three of those exemptions are arguably relevant to this case. Exemption 3 applies to documents that are specifically exempted from disclosure by another statute. § 552(b)(3). Exemption 6 protects "personnel and medical files and similar files the disclosure of which would constitute a clearly unwarranted invasion of personal privacy." § 552(b)(6). Exemption 7(C) excludes records or information compiled for law enforcement purposes, "but only to the extent that the production of such [materials] . . . could reasonably be expected to constitute an unwarranted invasion of personal privacy." § 552(b)(7)(C). . . .

This case arises out of requests made by a CBS news correspondent and the Reporters Committee for Freedom of the Press (respondents) for information concerning the criminal records of four members of the Medico family. The Pennsylvania Crime Commission had identified the family's company, Medico Industries, as a legitimate business dominated by organized crime figures. Moreover, the company allegedly had obtained a number of defense contracts as a result of an improper arrangement with a corrupt Congressman.

The FOIA requests sought disclosure of any arrests, indictments, acquittals, convictions, and sentences of any of the four Medicos. Although the FBI originally denied the requests, it provided the requested data concerning three of the Medicos after their deaths. In their complaint in the District Court, respondents sought the rap sheet for the fourth, Charles Medico (Medico), insofar as it contained "matters of public record." . . .

Exemption 7(C) requires us to balance the privacy interest in maintaining, as the Government puts it, the "practical obscurity" of the rap sheets against the public interest in their release.

The preliminary question is whether Medico's interest in the nondisclosure of any rap sheet the FBI might have on him is the sort of "personal privacy" interest that Congress intended Exemption 7(C) to protect. . . . Because events summarized in a rap sheet have been previously disclosed to the public, respondents contend that Medico's privacy interest in avoiding disclosure of a federal compilation of these events approaches zero. We reject respondents' cramped notion of personal privacy.

To begin with, both the common law and the literal understandings of privacy encompass the individual's control of information concerning his or her person. In an organized society, there are few facts that are not at one time or another divulged to another. Thus the extent of the protection accorded a privacy right at common law rested in part on the degree of dissemination of the allegedly private fact and the extent to which the passage of time rendered it private. According to Webster's initial definition, information may be classified as "private" if it is "intended for or restricted to the use of a particular person or group or class of persons: not freely available to the public." Recognition of this attribute of a privacy interest supports the distinction, in terms of personal privacy, between scattered disclosure of the bits of information contained in a rap sheet and revelation of the rap sheet as a whole. The very fact that federal funds have been spent to prepare, index, and maintain these criminal-history files demonstrates that the individual items of information in the summaries would not otherwise be "freely available" either to the officials who have access to the underlying files or to the general public. Indeed, if the summaries were "freely available," there would be no reason to invoke the FOIA to obtain access to the information they contain. Granted, in many contexts the fact that information is not freely available is no reason to exempt that information from a statute generally requiring its dissemination. But the issue here is whether the compilation of otherwise hard-to-obtain information alters the privacy interest implicated by disclosure of that information. Plainly there is a vast difference between the public records that might be found after a diligent search of courthouse files, county archives, and local police stations throughout the country and a computerized summary located in a single clearinghouse of information. . . .

We have also recognized the privacy interest in keeping personal facts away from the public eye. In *Whalen v. Roe*, 429 U.S. 589 (1977), we held that "the State of New York may record, in a centralized computer file, the names and addresses of all persons who have obtained, pursuant to a doctor's prescription, certain drugs for which there is both a lawful and an unlawful market." In holding only that the Federal Constitution does not prohibit such a compilation, we recognized that such a centralized computer file posed a "threat to privacy":

> We are not unaware of the threat to privacy implicit in the accumulation of vast amounts of personal information in computerized data banks or other massive government files. The collection of taxes, the distribution of welfare and social security benefits, the supervision of public health, the direction of our Armed Forces, and the enforcement of the criminal laws all require the orderly preservation of great quantities of information, much of which is personal in character and potentially embarrassing or harmful if disclosed. The right to collect and use such data for public purposes is typically accompanied by a concomitant statutory or regulatory duty to avoid unwarranted disclosures. Recognizing that in some circumstances that duty arguably has its roots in the Constitution, nevertheless New York's statutory scheme, and its implementing administrative procedures, evidence a proper concern with, and protection of, the individual's interest in privacy.

In sum, the fact that "an event is not wholly 'private' does not mean that an individual has no interest in limiting disclosure or dissemination of the information." The privacy interest in a rap sheet is substantial. The substantial character of that interest is affected by the fact that in today's society the computer can accumulate and store information that would otherwise have surely been forgotten long before a person attains age 80, when the FBI's rap sheets are discarded. . . .

Exemption 7(C), by its terms, permits an agency to withhold a document only when revelation "could reasonably be expected to constitute an unwarranted invasion of personal privacy." We must next address what factors might warrant an invasion of the interest described [above].

Our previous decisions establish that whether an invasion of privacy is warranted cannot turn on the purposes for which the request for information is made. Except for cases in which the objection to disclosure is based on a claim of privilege and the person requesting disclosure is the party protected by the privilege, the identity of the requesting party has no bearing on the merits of his or her FOIA request. . . . As we have repeatedly stated, Congress "clearly intended" the FOIA "to give any member of the public as much right to disclosure as one with a special interest [in a particular document]."

Thus whether disclosure of a private document under Exemption 7(C) is warranted must turn on the nature of the requested document and its relationship to "the basic purpose of the Freedom of Information Act 'to open agency action to the light of public scrutiny,'" rather than on the particular purpose for which the document is being requested. . . .

This basic policy of "'full agency disclosure unless information is exempted under clearly delineated statutory language,'" indeed focuses on the citizens' right to be informed about "what their government is up to." Official information that sheds light on an agency's performance of its statutory duties falls squarely within that statutory purpose. That purpose, however, is not fostered by disclosure of information about private citizens that is accumulated in various governmental files but that reveals little or nothing about an agency's own conduct. In this case — and presumably in the typical case in which one private citizen is seeking information about another — the requester does not intend to discover anything about the conduct of the agency that has possession of the requested records. Indeed, response to this request would not shed any light on the conduct of any Government agency or official. . . .

Respondents argue that there is a two-fold public interest in learning about Medico's past arrests or convictions: He allegedly had improper dealings with a corrupt Congressman, and he is an officer of a corporation with defense contracts. But if Medico has, in fact, been arrested or convicted of certain crimes, that information would neither aggravate nor mitigate his allegedly improper relationship with the Congressman; more specifically, it would tell us nothing directly about the character of the Congressman's behavior. Nor would it tell us anything about the conduct of the Department of Defense (DOD) in awarding one or more contracts to the Medico Company. . . . Conceivably Medico's rap sheet would provide details to include in a news story, but, in itself, this is not the kind of public interest for which Congress enacted the FOIA. In other words, although there is undoubtedly some public interest in anyone's criminal history, especially if the history is in some way related to the subject's dealing with a public official or agency, the FOIA's central purpose is to ensure that the Government's activities be opened to the sharp eye of public scrutiny, not that information about private citizens that happens to be in the warehouse of the Government be so disclosed. . . .

. . . The privacy interest in maintaining the practical obscurity of rap-sheet information will always be high. When the subject of such a rap sheet is a private citizen and when the information is in the Government's control as a compilation, rather than as a record of "what the Government is up to," the privacy interest protected by Exemption 7(C) is in fact at its apex while the FOIA-based public interest in disclosure is at its nadir. Such a disparity on the scales of justice holds for a class of cases without regard to individual circumstances; the standard virtues of bright-line rules are thus present, and the difficulties attendant to ad hoc adjudication may be avoided. Accordingly, we hold as a categorical matter that a third party's request for law enforcement records or information about a private citizen can reasonably be expected to invade that citizen's privacy, and that when the request seeks no "official information" about a Government agency, but merely records that the Government happens to be storing, the invasion of privacy is "unwarranted." . . .

Blackmun J., joined by Brennan, J. concurring in the judgment: I concur in the result the Court reaches in this case, but I cannot follow the route the Court takes to reach that result. In other words, the Court's use of "categorical balancing" under Exemption 7(C), I think, is not basically sound. Such a bright-line rule obviously has its appeal, but I wonder whether it would not run aground on occasion, such as in a situation where a rap sheet discloses a congressional candidate's conviction of tax fraud five years before. Surely, the FBI's disclosure of that information could not "reasonably be expected" to constitute an invasion of personal privacy, much less an unwarranted invasion, inasmuch as the candidate relinquished any interest in preventing the dissemination of this information when he chose to run for Congress. In short, I do not believe that Exemption 7(C)'s language and its legislative history, or the case law, support interpreting that provision as exempting all rap-sheet information from the FOIA's disclosure requirements.

NOTES & QUESTIONS

1. Does the reasoning of this case square with the reasoning of the constitutional right to information privacy cases involving law enforcement records (e.g., *Scheetz* and *Cline* in Chapter 4)?

2. In a footnote, the Court stated that the reasoning of this case is confined to the FOIA context. Suppose there were no privacy exemptions to FOIA and the FBI disclosed the rap sheets. The Medicos sue, claiming a violation of their constitutional right to information privacy. What result? Can the Court coherently claim that people have a privacy interest in their rap sheet information under FOIA but not in the context of the constitutional right to information privacy?

3. *Exemption 6.* The *Reporters Committee* case concerned Exemption 7(C). Exemption 6 provides that FOIA's disclosure provisions do not apply to "*personnel and medical files and similar files* the disclosure of which would constitute a clearly unwarranted invasion of personal privacy." § 552(b)(6) (emphasis added). Does Exemption 6 only apply to "personnel and medical files"? What does "similar files" mean?

   The Supreme Court answered these questions in *United States Department of State v. Washington Post Co.*, 456 U.S. 595 (1982). There, the *Washington Post* requested documents indicating whether two Iranian nationals were holding valid United States passports. According to the Department of State, the two individuals were prominent figures in Iran's Revolutionary Government; several Iranian revolutionary leaders had been strongly criticized in Iran for ties to the United States; and the two could be subject to violence if United States ties, such as passports, were disclosed. The *Washington Post* contended that the language of Exemption 6 simply did not cover these types of documents. The Court disagreed:

   > The language of Exemption 6 sheds little light on what Congress meant by "similar files." Fortunately, the legislative history is somewhat more illuminating. The House and Senate Reports, although not defining the phrase "similar files," suggest that Congress' primary purpose in enacting Exemption 6 was to protect individuals from the injury and embarrassment that can result from the unnecessary disclosure of personal information. . . .
   >   . . . Congress' statements that it was creating a "general exemption" for information contained in "great quantities of files," suggest that the phrase

"similar files" was to have a broad, rather than a narrow, meaning. This impression is confirmed by the frequent characterization of the "clearly unwarranted invasion of personal privacy" language as a "limitation" which holds Exemption 6 "within bounds." Had the words "similar files" been intended to be only a narrow addition to "personnel and medical files," there would seem to be no reason for concern about the exemption's being "held within bounds," and there surely would be clear suggestions in the legislative history that such a narrow meaning was intended. We have found none.

A proper analysis of the exemption must also take into account the fact that "personnel and medical files," the two benchmarks for measuring the term "similar files," are likely to contain much information about a particular individual that is not intimate. Information such as place of birth, date of birth, date of marriage, employment history, and comparable data is not normally regarded as highly personal, and yet respondent does not disagree that such information, if contained in a "personnel" or "medical" file, would be exempt from any disclosure that would constitute a clearly unwarranted invasion of personal privacy. . . .

. . . "[T]he protection of an individual's right of privacy" which Congress sought to achieve by preventing "the disclosure of [information] which might harm the individual," surely was not intended to turn upon the label of the file which contains the damaging information. . . .

In sum, we do not think that Congress meant to limit Exemption 6 to a narrow class of files containing only a discrete kind of personal information. Rather, "[t]he exemption [was] intended to cover detailed Government records on an individual which can be identified as applying to that individual." When disclosure of information which applies to a particular individual is sought from Government records, courts must determine whether release of the information would constitute a clearly unwarranted invasion of that person's privacy. . . .

4. *Definition of Agency.* The FOIA requires only that "agencies" respond to requesters. Congress is not a federal agency, and is therefore not subject to the Act. Nor is the President or his advisors, whose "sole function" is to "advise and assist" the President. For similar reasons, the National Security Council is not an agency. *Armstrong v. Executive Office of the President*, 90 F.3d 556 (D.C. Cir. 1996). But what about the recently created Office of Homeland Security? Is OHS an agency that should be subject to the FOIA? That issue is raised in *Electronic Privacy Information Center v. Office of Homeland Security* (D.D.C. filed Apr. 2, 2002).

3. FAIR INFORMATION PRACTICES

In the 1960s, the increasing use of computers gave rise to a significant public debate about privacy.[8] In particular, commentators expressed opposition to the increasing amount of personal information collected by government agencies and stored in computer databases.

---

[8] *See, e.g.*, Vance Packard, *The Naked Society* (1965). *See also* Alan F. Westin & Michael A. Baker, *Databanks in a Free Society: Computers, Record-Keeping and Privacy* 229 (1972); Regan, *Legislating Privacy, supra* note 1, at 69.

In 1973, the Department of Housing, Education, and Welfare (HEW) issued a highly influential report about government records maintained in computer databases.[9] The HEW Report characterized the growing concern over privacy:

> . . . It is no wonder that people have come to distrust computer-based record-keeping operations. Even in non-governmental settings, an individual's control over the personal information that he gives to an organization or that an organization obtains about him, is lessening as the relationship between the giver and receiver of personal data grows more attenuated, impersonal, and diffused. There was a time when information about an individual tended to be elicited in face-to-face contacts involving personal trust and a certain symmetry, or balance, between giver and receiver. Nowadays, an individual must increasingly give information about himself to large and relatively faceless institutions, for handling and use by strangers — unknown, unseen, and, all too frequently, unresponsive. Sometimes the individual does not even know that an organization maintains a record about him. Often he may not see it, much less contest its accuracy, control its dissemination, or challenge its use by others. . . .
>
> . . . The poet, the novelist, and the social scientist tell us, each in his own way, that the life of a small-town man, woman, or family is an open book compared to the more anonymous existence of urban dwellers. Yet the individual in a small town can retain his confidence because he can be more sure of retaining control. He lives in a face-to-face world, in a social system where irresponsible behavior can be identified and called to account. By contrast, the impersonal data system, and faceless users of the information it contains, tend to be accountable only in the formal sense of the word. In practice they are for the most part immune to whatever sanctions the individual can invoke. . . .[10]

To remedy these growing concerns over the accumulation and use of personal information by the government, the HEW Report recommended that a Code of Fair Information Practices be established:

> Safeguards for personal privacy based on our concept of mutuality in record-keeping would require adherence by record-keeping organizations to certain fundamental principles of fair information practice.
>
> - There must be no personal-data record-keeping systems whose very existence is secret.
> - There must be a way for an individual to find out what information about him is in a record and how it is used.
> - There must be a way for an individual to prevent information about him obtained for one purpose from being used or made available for other purposes without his consent.
> - There must be a way for an individual to correct or amend a record of identifiable information about him.

---

[9] *See* U.S. Dep't of Health, Educ. & Welfare, *Records, Computers, and the Rights of Citizens: Report of the Secretary's Advisory Comm. on Automated Personal Data Systems* (1973) ("*HEW Report*"); *see also* Philippa Strum, *Privacy: The Debate in the United States Since 1945*, at 46 (1998) (describing HEW report's condemnation of Social Security numbers as identifiers); Regan, *Legislating Privacy*, *supra* note 1, at 76 (describing HEW report's code of fair information practices).

[10] *HEW Report*, at 29-30.

- Any organization creating, maintaining, using, or disseminating records of identifiable personal data must assure the reliability of the data for their intended use and must take reasonable precautions to prevent misuse of the data.

These principles should govern the conduct of all personal-data record-keeping systems. Deviations from them should be permitted only if it is clear that some significant interest of the individual data subject will be served or if some paramount societal interest can be clearly demonstrated; no deviation should be permitted except as specifically provided by law.[11]

Fair Information Practices can be understood most simply as the rights and responsibilities that are associated with the transfer and use of personal information. Since the intent is to correct information asymmetries that result from the transfer of personal data from an individual to an organization, Fair Information Practices typically assign rights to individuals and responsibilities to organizations.

MARC ROTENBERG, *FAIR INFORMATION PRACTICES AND THE ARCHITECTURE OF PRIVACY (WHAT LARRY DOESN'T GET)*

2001 Stan. Tech. L. Rev. 1 (2001)

. . . Not only have Fair Information Practices played a significant role in framing privacy laws in the United States, these basic principles have also contributed to the development of privacy laws around the world and even to the development of important international guidelines for privacy protection. The most well known of these international guidelines are the Organization for Economic Cooperation and Development's Recommendations Concerning and Guidelines Governing the Protection of Privacy and Transborder Flows of Personal Data ("OECD Guidelines"). The OECD Guidelines set out eight principles for data protection that are still the benchmark for assessing privacy policy and legislation: Collection Limitation; Data Quality; Purpose Specification; Use Limitation; Security Safeguards; Openness; Individual Participation; and Accountability. The principles articulate in only a couple of pages a set of rules that have guided the development of national law and increasingly the design of information systems.

It is generally understood that the challenge of privacy protection in the information age is the application and enforcement of Fair Information Practices and the OECD Guidelines. While some recommendations for improvement have been made, the level of consensus, at least outside of the United States, about the viability of Fair Information Practices as a general solution to the problem of privacy protection is remarkable. As recently as 1998 the OECD reaffirmed support for the 1980 guidelines, and countries that are adopting privacy legislation have generally done so in the tradition of Fair Information Practices.

---

[11] *HEW Report*, at 41-42.

While some commentators have made recommendations for updating or expanding the principles, there is general agreement that the concept of Fair Information Practices and the specific standards set out in the OECD Guidelines continue to provide a useful and effective framework for privacy protection in information systems.

Commentators have also noted a remarkable convergence of privacy policies. Countries around the world, with very distinct cultural backgrounds and systems of governance, nonetheless have adopted roughly similar approaches to privacy protection. Perhaps this is not so surprising. The original OECD Guidelines were drafted by representatives from North America, Europe, and Asia. The OECD Guidelines reflect a broad consensus about how to safeguard the control and use of personal information in a world where data can flow freely across national borders. Just as it does today on the Internet. . . .

Viewed against this background, the problem of privacy protection in the United States in the early 1990s was fairly well understood. The coverage of U.S. law was uneven: Fair Information Practices were in force in some sectors and not others. There was inadequate enforcement and oversight. Technology continued to outpace the law. And the failure to adopt a comprehensive legal framework to safeguard privacy rights could jeopardize transborder data flows with Europe and other regions. These factors should all have played a significant role in coding a solution to the privacy problem. . . .

4. THE PRIVACY ACT

Influenced by the HEW Report's Fair Information Practices and inspired by the Watergate scandal, Congress enacted the Privacy Act of 1974 four months after President Nixon resigned from office. In passing the Privacy Act, Congress found that:

(1) the privacy of an individual is directly affected by the collection, maintenance, use, and dissemination of personal information by Federal agencies;

(2) the increasing use of computers and sophisticated information technology, while essential to the efficient operations of the Government, has greatly magnified the harm to individual privacy that can occur from any collection, maintenance, use, or dissemination of personal information;

(3) the opportunities for an individual to secure employment, insurance, and credit, and his right to due process, and other legal protections are endangered by the misuse of certain information systems;

(4) the right to privacy is a personal and fundamental right protected by the Constitution of the United States; and

(5) in order to protect the privacy of individuals identified in information systems maintained by Federal agencies, it is necessary and proper for the Congress to regulate the collection, maintenance, use, and dissemination of information by such agencies.

Purposes of the Privacy Act. The Privacy Act sets forth an extensive discussion of its purposes:

The purpose of this Act is to provide certain safeguards for an individual against an invasion of personal privacy by requiring Federal agencies, except as otherwise provided by law, to —

(1) permit an individual to determine what records pertaining to him are collected, maintained, used, or disseminated by such agencies;

(2) permit an individual to prevent records pertaining to him obtained by such agencies for a particular purpose from being used or made available for another purpose without his consent;

(3) permit an individual to gain access to information pertaining to him in Federal agency records, to have a copy made of all or any portion thereof, and to correct or amend such records;

(4) collect, maintain, use, or disseminate any record of identifiable personal information in a manner that assures that such action is for a necessary and lawful purpose, that the information is current and accurate for its intended use, and that adequate safeguards are provided to prevent misuse of such information;

(5) permit exemptions from the requirements with respect to records provided in this Act only in those cases where there is an important public policy need for such exemption as has been determined by specific statutory authority; and

(6) be subject to civil suit for any damages which occur as a result of willful or intentional action which violates any individual's rights under this Act.

Limits on Disclosure. Pursuant to the Privacy Act:

No agency shall disclose any record which is contained in a system of records by any means of communication to any person, or to another agency, except pursuant to a written request by, or with prior written consent of, the individual to whom the record pertains. 5 U.S.C. § 552a(b).

Responsibilities for Recordkeeping. The Privacy Act establishes restrictions and responsibilities for agencies maintaining records about individuals. Pursuant to § 552a(e):

(e) Agency requirements.—Each agency that maintains a system of records shall—

(1) maintain in its records only such information about an individual as is relevant and necessary to accomplish a purpose of the agency required to be accomplished by statute or by executive order of the President;

(2) collect information to the greatest extent practicable directly from the subject individual when the information may result in adverse determinations about an individual's rights, benefits, and privileges under Federal programs;

(3) inform each individual whom it asks to supply information, on the form which it uses to collect the information or on a separate form that can be retained by the individual—

(A) the authority (whether granted by statute, or by executive order of the President) which authorizes the solicitation of the information and whether disclosure of such information is mandatory or voluntary;

(B) the principal purpose or purposes for which the information is intended to be used;

(C) the routine uses which may be made of the information . . . ; and

(D) the effects on him, if any, of not providing all or any part of the requested information;

(4) . . . publish in the Federal Register upon establishment or revision a notice of the existence and character of the system of records. . . .

(5) maintain all records which are used by the agency in making any determination about any individual with such accuracy, relevance, timeliness, and completeness as is reasonably necessary to assure fairness to the individual in the determination;

(6) prior to disseminating any record about an individual to any person other than an agency . . . make reasonable efforts to assure that such records are accurate, complete, timely, and relevant for agency purposes;

(7) maintain no record describing how any individual exercises rights guaranteed by the First Amendment unless expressly authorized by statute or by the individual about whom the record is maintained or unless pertinent to and within the scope of an authorized law enforcement activity;

(8) make reasonable efforts to serve notice on an individual when any record on such individual is made available to any person under compulsory legal process when such process becomes a matter of public record;

(9) establish rules of conduct for persons involved in the design, development, operation, or maintenance of any system of records, or in maintaining any record, and instruct each such person with respect to such rules and the requirements of this section, including any other rules and procedures adopted pursuant to this section and the penalties for noncompliance;

(10) establish appropriate administrative, technical, and physical safeguards to insure the security and confidentiality of records and to protect against any anticipated threats or hazards to their security or integrity which could result in substantial harm, embarrassment, inconvenience, or unfairness to any individual on whom information is maintained. . . .

State Privacy Acts. Although every state has a statute comparable to the federal FOIA, requiring public access to government records, most states do not have a statute comparable to the federal Privacy Act. Only about a third of states have adopted such a statute.

Right to Access and Correct Records. Pursuant to the federal Privacy Act, upon request, individuals can review their records and can ask that the agency correct any inaccuracies in their records. § 552a(d).

Enforcement. If an agency fails to comply with any provision of the Privacy Act, or refuses to comply with an individual's request to obtain access to her records or correct her records, individuals can bring a civil action in federal court. § 552a(g)(1). The court can enjoin the agency from withholding access of records. § 552a(g)(3). In limited circumstances, monetary damages may be awarded:

(4) In any suit brought under the provisions of subsection (g)(1)(C) or (D) of this section in which the court determines that the agency acted in a man-

ner which was intentional or willful, the United States shall be liable to the individual in an amount equal to the sum of —

> (A) actual damages sustained by the individual as a result of the refusal or failure, but in no case shall a person entitled to recovery receive less than the sum of $1,000; and
> (B) the costs of the action together with reasonable attorney fees as determined by the court. § 552a(g)(4).

Limitations and Exceptions. However, the Privacy Act has a number of notable limitations. When FOIA requires that information be released, the Privacy Act does not apply. § 552a(b)(3). The Privacy Act is limited to the public sector. The Act applies only to federal, not state and local, agencies.

Further, the Act contains about a dozen exceptions. The broadest exception under the Privacy Act is that information may be disclosed for any "routine use" if disclosure is "compatible" with the purpose for which the agency collected the information. § 552a(b)(3).

In order to establish a violation of the Privacy Act, a plaintiff must prove several things:

First, the plaintiff must prove that the agency violated its obligations under the Act (most often, that the agency improperly disclosed information).

Second, the information disclosed must be a "record" contained within a "system of records." A "record" must be identifiable to an individual (contain her name or other identifying information) and must contain information about the individual. The record must be kept as part of a "system of records," which is "a group of any records under the control of any agency from which information is retrieved by the name of the individual or by some identifying number, symbol, or other identifying particular assigned to the individual."

Third, to collect damages, the plaintiff must show that an adverse impact resulted from the Privacy Act violation and that the violation was "willful or intentional."

ROBERT GELLMAN, *DOES PRIVACY LAW WORK?*

in *Technology and Privacy: The New Landscape*
(Philip E. Agre & Marc Rotenberg eds. 1997)

. . . In some ways, the Privacy Act was a tremendously influential piece of legislation. It was the world's first attempt to apply the principles of fair information practices. The notion of fair information practices came directly from the work of the HEW advisory committee. The articulation of principles of fair information practices may be the computer age's most significant policy development with respect to privacy.

This does not mean that the Privacy Act was a success at home. There is a big difference between adopting good policies and implementing them well. A review of the act under the framework of fair information practices illustrates the statutory and administrative shortcomings.

The first principle of fair information practices is openness or transparency: there should be no secret record-keeping systems. The Privacy Act succeeded (at least initially) in meeting this objective by requiring that descriptions of record systems containing personal information be published. Before the various agencies prepared this inventory, few had any idea what data they maintained. Openness was a positive exercise in good administration and good records management. There were redundant and unnecessary systems throughout the government, and many were eliminated.

Between 1975 and 1990, the number of personal-record systems shrank from almost 7000 to under 5000. On the surface this seems an improvement, and it may be. It is difficult to determine whether the reduction really increases privacy protection. Some reductions resulted from mergers of existing systems. . . .

The initial burst of file cleaning that took place when the Privacy Act took effect in 1975 has long since dissipated. Strong evidence suggests that agencies grew sloppy and lost interest in keeping up with their obligations to publish accurate descriptions of their record systems. The absence of an effective oversight mechanism to keep pressure on agencies may be one reason for this.

The second principle of fair information practices is individual participation. The subject of a record should be able to see and correct the record. The Privacy Act's procedures for access and correction appear to work adequately for US citizens and resident aliens, who have rights under the Privacy Act. Foreigners have no access rights or correction rights. . . .

The third principle of fair information practices is that there should be limits on the collection of personal information. The fourth principle is that personal data should be relevant to the purposes for which they are to be used and should be accurate, complete, and timely. The Privacy Act's implementation of these two principles is just as vague and general as the principles themselves, and it is difficult to measure the actual impact of the act. Anecdotal evidence suggests that agencies rely on these requirements mostly when they provide excuses for avoiding an unwanted task.

There is, however, no specific enforcement or oversight of these information-collection principles. . . .

The fifth principle of fair information practices requires limits on the internal use of personal data by the record keeper. This is where the major shortcomings of the Privacy Act begin to become clearer. The act limits use of personal data to those officers and employees of the agency maintaining the data who have a need for the data in the performance their duties. This vague standard is not a significant barrier to the sharing of personal information within agencies. . . . No administrative process exists to control or limit internal agency uses. Suits have been brought by individuals who objected to specific uses, but most uses have been upheld.

The sixth principle prohibits external disclosure without the consent of the subject or other legal authority. This is almost certainly the biggest failure of the Privacy Act. A standard rendition of the policy goal is that records should be used or disclosed only for the purpose for which they were collected. . . . The legislation left most decisions about external uses to the agencies, and this created the biggest loophole in the law.

An agency can establish a "routine use" if it determines that a disclosure is compatible with the purpose for which the record was collected. This vague formula has not created much of a substantive barrier to external disclosure of personal information. . . . Later legislation, political pressures, and bureaucratic convenience tended to overwhelm the law's weak limitations. Without any effective restriction on disclosure, the Privacy Act lost much of its vitality and became more procedural and more symbolic. . . .

The seventh principle of fair information practices calls for a reasonable level of security. The Privacy Act includes a general requirement for appropriate administrative, technical, and physical safeguards to protect information against anticipated threats. It is difficult to assess general compliance with this statutory standard. The adequacy of computer security for classified national-security information and for government computers in general has been repeatedly called into question, and there are almost certainly equivalent deficiencies for Privacy Act security. There is no effective oversight of the security requirement.

The final principle of fair information practices requires that record keepers be accountable for compliance with the other principles. The Privacy Act contains civil and criminal penalties for violations, but it is far from clear that the enforcement methods are useful. . . . In more than 20 years, federal prosecutors have brought no more than a handful of criminal cases, and perhaps only one, under the Privacy Act.

The basic method for enforcing the Privacy Act is the individual lawsuit. Aggrieved individuals can sue the government for violations. . . . The former General Counsel to the Privacy Protection Study Commission testified that the act was "to a large extent, unenforceable by individuals." The main reasons are that it is difficult to recover damages and that limited injunctive relief is available under the law. Individual enforcement does not offer any significant incentive for agencies to comply more carefully with the Privacy Act's provisions. . . .

ANDREWS v. VETERANS ADMINISTRATION

838 F.2d 418 (10th Cir. 1988)

ANDERSON, J. The Veterans Administration of the United States of America ("VA") appeals from a judgment of the United States District Court for the District of Wyoming finding that the VA's disclosure of certain personnel records violated the Privacy Act rights of plaintiffs, registered nurses employed at a VA Medical Center ("Medical Center") in Cheyenne, Wyoming. We reverse. . . .

On June 4, 1984, Ms. Pat Sanchez, president of the union local which was the exclusive bargaining representative for nurses employed at the Medical Center, made a written request to Ms. Hazel Gilligan, the Chief of Personnel Service at the Medical Center, seeking copies of proficiency reports (essentially job performance evaluations) for all registered nurses at the Medical Center for the years 1982-84. The request acknowledged that such reports would have to be "sanitized" by deleting all information that might tend to identify the subjects of the reports prior to disclosure. Pursuant to a written inquiry from Ms. Gilligan, Ms. Sanchez stated that the proficiency reports were needed in connection with a grievance the union would possibly file and to facilitate preparation for upcoming labor-management negotiations. Certain of the plaintiff nurses, upon learning of the request for the reports, asked both orally and in writing that the records not be released.

Ms. Gilligan sought the advice of VA personnel in Washington, D.C. in determining how to respond to the request.[12] The Labor Relations Department of the VA advised her that the Federal Service Labor-Management Relations Act, 5 U.S.C. § 7101-7135, ("FSLRA") required disclosure of the reports, but that they should be sanitized prior to disclosure to preserve the anonymity of the subjects of the reports. Accordingly, Ms. Gilligan attempted to sanitize the reports by deleting with a black felt-tip pen any information which she felt would identify the subjects of the reports. . . . She then asked her assistant to further sanitize the reports. Finally, Ms. Gilligan asked the head nurse at the Medical Center to review the reports and make any other deletions she felt necessary to protect the identities of the nurses. On June 19, she released the sanitized reports to Ms. Sanchez. Ms. Sanchez and two other nurses reviewed the records but no other people obtained access to them. . . .

As it turned out, the reports released were never in fact used in connection with any grievance or other union activity. The district court concluded that "Mrs. Sanchez was on a general fishing expedition, which may have been motivated by spite or anger resulting from her own failure to obtain a requested promotion."

The plaintiffs, registered nurses employed at the Medical Center, brought this action, seeking to enjoin the VA and the Medical Center from releasing the personnel records of the plaintiffs and others similarly situated "in an unsanitized or improperly sanitized condition" and seeking damages for the release of the records which, they alleged, was an intentional and willful violation of the Privacy Act of 1974, 5 U.S.C. § 552a. They alleged that the disclosure of the reports resulted in "injury and damages including, but not limited to, mental distress and embarrassment" and they sought damages of $1,000 for each plaintiff as well as attorneys' fees. . . .

. . . After a two day trial, the district court entered its findings of fact and conclusions of law. It found that the record established that third parties acquainted with ten of the plaintiffs could and did recognize their identity from information released in the reports. . . .

The district court [held] that each plaintiff "suffered some degree of anguish, embarrassment, or other mental trauma" from the release of the reports, but that "none suffered any pecuniary loss." Finally, the court found that the release of the reports adversely affected the Medical Center's entire proficiency reporting system "due to fear that the information contained in the reports may later be disclosed to third persons," and harmed the working environment at the Center, causing increased "tensions and antagonism."

In assessing the culpability of the VA, the district court found that Ms. Gilligan "acted conscientiously, in good faith, though inadvertently negligently,

---

[12]The district court, in its findings of fact, stated that "Ms. Gilligan had received some training concerning her duties under the Privacy Act, and was supplied with a Federal Personnel Manual which contains guidelines for responses to requests for information contained in personnel files." However, as the district court further found, Ms. Gilligan had never before received a "blanket request" such as was made in this case, nor had she ever received a request for disclosure "without the consent of the individual to which the file pertained."

in releasing the proficiency reports in an inadequately sanitized condition." She failed to balance the privacy interests of the nurses against the interests of the union in having the reports, "which interests were ambiguous and virtually undefined." The court further held that the VA personnel in Washington were "grossly negligent" in failing to adequately train or guide Ms. Gilligan regarding the release of information subject to the Privacy Act and in directing her in this case that release was required by FSLRA. It found that the gross negligence of the Washington VA personnel was a willful or intentional violation of the Privacy Act. . . .

[The district court] found the violation of the nurses' privacy interests was "substantial" and that the union's interest in obtaining the documents was "minimal." It therefore concluded that the disclosure of inadequately sanitized reports to Ms. Sanchez "constituted a clearly unwarranted invasion of the privacy interests of the subjects" in violation of the Privacy Act. The court denied plaintiffs' request for injunctive relief but awarded them $1,000 per plaintiff, finding that emotional trauma, even without pecuniary loss, was sufficient to sustain such an award. Finally, the court awarded plaintiffs, as prevailing parties, attorneys' fees of $5,000.

The VA appeals, alleging that the plaintiffs failed to show that the VA committed a willful or intentional violation of the Privacy Act. It essentially argues that it was faced with the difficult task of reconciling the pro-disclosure mandates of FSLRA and the Freedom of Information Act, 5 U.S.C. § 552 ("FOIA") with the anti-disclosure mandate of the Privacy Act. While it concededly may have been negligent, the VA argues it did not act in an intentional or willful manner. . . .

The Privacy Act, 5 U.S.C. § 552a was enacted "'to protect the privacy of individuals identified in information systems maintained by Federal agencies' by preventing the 'misuse' of that information." . . .

Thus, in this case, without the consent of the nurses who were the subjects of the proficiency reports, the VA was prohibited from disclosing the reports unless disclosure was required by FOIA.

The Privacy Act further provides:

(g)(1) Civil remedies — *Whenever any agency.* . . .

> (D) *fails to comply with any other provision of this section,* or any rule promulgated thereunder, *in such a way as to have an adverse effect on an individual, the individual may bring a civil action against the agency.* . . .
>
> (4) *In any suit brought under the provisions of subsection (g)(1)(C) or (D) of this section in which the court determines that the agency acted in a manner which was intentional or willful,* the United States shall be liable to the individual in an amount equal to the sum of —
>
> > (A) actual damages sustained by the individual as a result of the refusal or failure, but in no case shall a person entitled to recovery receive less than the sum of $1,000; and
> >
> > (B) the costs of the action together with reasonable attorney fees as determined by the court.

5 U.S.C. § 552a(g)(1) (emphasis added). Accordingly, if release of the reports was not required by FOIA and had an "adverse effect" upon the nurses, and if

the VA's action amounted to an "intentional or willful" violation of the Privacy Act, the nurses are entitled to damages and attorneys' fees. . . .

FOIA generally provides for public disclosure of information contained in agency files, with specified exceptions. . . [FOIA Exception 6 applies in this case]. As the district court acknowledged, an agency must attempt to segregate sensitive from nonsensitive material, if a document contains both, and release the nonsensitive information. "If the exempt materials are inextricably intertwined with the non-exempt materials, the entire document is exempt from mandatory disclosure under the Freedom of Information Act."

In this case, if the disclosure of the personnel files at issue "would constitute a clearly unwarranted invasion of personal privacy" such files are not subject to mandatory disclosure under FOIA; as such, they are protected from disclosure under the Privacy Act. . . .

As the foregoing discussion of the relevant statutes indicates, if the reports in this case were "personnel . . . files the disclosure of which would constitute a clearly unwarranted invasion of personal privacy" under 5 U.S.C. § 552(a) of FOIA, the Privacy Act prohibited their disclosure absent the consent of the nurses. And if the Privacy Act thus prohibited disclosure in this case, they could not be disclosed to Ms. Sanchez pursuant to FSLRA. . . .

As previously indicated, even if the Privacy Act is violated, no punishment may be imposed unless the agency acted in a manner which was intentional or willful. In this case the district court equated "intentional or willful" with gross negligence. The district court founded the VA's gross negligence, and therefore its willful or intentional violation of the Privacy Act, on its failure to adequately train or guide Ms. Gilligan on the Privacy Act and in directing her that FSLRA mandated release in this case. We hold that the district court erred as a matter of law when it equated gross negligence with a willful or intentional violation of the Privacy Act. . . .

. . . [T]he term "willful or intentional" clearly requires conduct amounting to more than gross negligence. We are persuaded by the District of Columbia Circuit's definitions of willful or intentional that contemplate action "so 'patently egregious and unlawful' that anyone undertaking the conduct should have known it 'unlawful,'" or conduct committed "without grounds for believing it to be lawful" or action "flagrantly disregarding others' rights under the Act," and we adopt those definitions, and add the view . . . that the conduct must amount to, at the very least, reckless behavior. Those, and similar definitions, describe conduct more extreme than gross negligence.

Applying that standard to this case, our review of the record convinces us that the VA's conduct falls far short of a "willful or intentional" violation of the Privacy Act. Indeed, we find that it falls short of even the gross negligence standard applied by the district court to that conduct. . . .

NOTES & QUESTIONS

1. The most common form of improper disclosure of records is due to carelessness rather than willful behavior. Does the requirement that disclosure be done "willfully and intentionally" make damages under the Privacy Act virtually impossible to collect? As Paul Schwartz observes, "individuals who

seek to enforce their rights under the Privacy Act face numerous statutory hurdles, limited damages, and scant chance to effect an agency's overall behavior."[13] Do you agree?

2. What if the standard for collecting damages were negligence? Would agencies that must handle millions of records and respond to thousands of FOIA requests be exposed to too great a risk of liability?

3. *The Interaction Between the Privacy Act and FOIA.* The Privacy Act does not apply to information that must be disclosed pursuant to the FOIA. § 552a(k)(1). However, if one of FOIA's privacy exceptions applies, then the Privacy Act would require that the government refrain from disclosing certain information. The interaction of the Privacy Act and FOIA is best illustrated in *United States Department of Defense v. Federal Labor Relations Authority*, 510 U.S. 487 (1994). There, two local unions requested the names and home addresses of employees in federal agencies. The agencies disclosed the employees' names and work stations to the unions, but refused to release their home addresses. The unions filed unfair labor practice charges with the Federal Labor Relations Authority (FLRA) arguing that federal labor law required the agencies to disclose the addresses. Pursuant to the Federal Service Labor-Management Relations Statute, 5 U.S.C. §§ 7101-7135, agencies must, "to the extent not prohibited by law," furnish unions with data necessary for collective-bargaining purposes. § 7114(b)(4). The agencies argued that disclosure of the home addresses was prohibited by the Privacy Act. The Court agreed with the agencies:

> The employee addresses sought by the unions are "records" covered by the broad terms of the Privacy Act. Therefore, unless FOIA would require release of the addresses, their disclosure is "prohibited by law," and the agencies may not reveal them to the unions.
>
> We turn, then, to FOIA. . . . The exemption potentially applicable to employee addresses is Exemption 6, which provides that FOIA's disclosure requirements do not apply to "personnel and medical files and similar files the disclosure of which would constitute a clearly unwarranted invasion of personal privacy." 5 U.S.C. § 552(b)(6).
>
> Thus, although this case requires us to follow a somewhat convoluted path of statutory cross-references, its proper resolution depends upon a discrete inquiry: whether disclosure of the home addresses "would constitute a clearly unwarranted invasion of [the] personal privacy" of bargaining unit employees within the meaning of FOIA. . . .
>
> We must weigh the privacy interest of bargaining unit employees in nondisclosure of their addresses against the only relevant public interest in the FOIA balancing analysis — the extent to which disclosure of the information sought would "she[d] light on an agency's performance of its statutory duties" or otherwise let citizens know "what their government is up to."
>
> The relevant public interest supporting disclosure in this case is negligible, at best. Disclosure of the addresses might allow the unions to communicate more effectively with employees, but it would not appreciably further

---

[13] Paul M. Schwartz, *Privacy and Participation: Personal Information and Public Sector Regulation in the United States*, 80 Iowa L. Rev. 553, 596 (1995).

"the citizens' right to be informed about what their government is up to." Indeed, such disclosure would reveal little or nothing about the employing agencies or their activities. . . .

Against the virtually nonexistent FOIA-related public interest in disclosure, we weigh the interest of bargaining unit employees in nondisclosure of their home addresses. Because a very slight privacy interest would suffice to outweigh the relevant public interest, we need not be exact in our quantification of the privacy interest. It is enough for present purposes to observe that the employees' interest in nondisclosure is not insubstantial.

It is true that home addresses often are publicly available through sources such as telephone directories and voter registration lists, but "[i]n an organized society, there are few facts that are not at one time or another divulged to another." *Reporters Comm.* The privacy interest protected by Exemption 6 "encompass[es] the individual's control of information concerning his or her person." An individual's interest in controlling the dissemination of information regarding personal matters does not dissolve simply because that information may be available to the public in some form. Here, for the most part, the unions seek to obtain the addresses of nonunion employees who have decided not to reveal their addresses to their exclusive representative. . . . Whatever the reason that these employees have chosen not to become members of the union or to provide the union with their addresses, however, it is clear that they have *some* nontrivial privacy interest in nondisclosure, and in avoiding the influx of union-related mail, and, perhaps, union-related telephone calls or visits, that would follow disclosure.

Many people simply do not want to be disturbed at home by work-related matters. . . . Moreover, when we consider that other parties, such as commercial advertisers and solicitors, must have the same access under FOIA as the unions to the employee address lists sought in this case, it is clear that the individual privacy interest that would be protected by nondisclosure is far from insignificant.

Because the privacy interest of bargaining unit employees in nondisclosure of their home addresses substantially outweighs the negligible FOIA-related public interest in disclosure, we conclude that disclosure would constitute a "clearly unwarranted invasion of personal privacy." 5 U.S.C. § 552(b)(6). FOIA, thus, does not require the agencies to divulge the addresses, and the Privacy Act, therefore, prohibits their release to the unions. . . .

Suppose the agencies opted not to litigate and disclosed the addresses of their employees. Would an employee have a cause of action under the Privacy Act for the disclosure of her address? Would that employee likely prevail in such an action? What type of remedy could the employee obtain?

4. *The Complementary Values of the Privacy Act and FOIA.* Although the Privacy Act restricts disclosures and the FOIA promotes disclosures, Marc Rotenberg contends that these statutes promote "complementary values." He observes:

> In enacting both the Privacy Act of 1974 and adopting the amendments that same year which significantly strengthened the Freedom of Information Act, Congress sought to ensure that personal information collected and maintained by federal agencies would be properly protected while also seeking to ensure that public information in the possession of federal agencies would be widely available to the public. The complementary goals of safeguarding

individual liberty and ensuring government accountability were enabled by legislation that protected privacy on the one hand and promoted government oversight on the other.[14]

THE COMPUTER MATCHING AND PRIVACY PROTECTION ACT

Justifying it under the routine use exception, in 1977 the federal government initiated Project Match, a program where it compared computer employee records to records of people receiving benefits through Aid to Families with Dependent Children to detect fraud. According to Priscilla Regan:

> . . . The scope of computer matches . . . raises Fourth Amendment questions. Computer matches are generalized electronic searches of millions of records. Under the Fourth Amendment, the Supreme Court has determined that searches must not be overly inclusive; no "fishing expeditions" or "dragnet investigations" are allowed. Yet in computer matches, many people who have not engaged in fraud or are not actually suspected of criminal activity are subject to the computer search. This raises questions about the presumption of innocence, as reflected in Fourth and Fifth Amendment case law. If matches are considered a Fourth Amendment search, then some limitations on the breadth of the match and/or justifications for a match are necessary. For example, a government agency could be required to show that a less intrusive means of carrying out the search was not available and that procedural safeguards limiting the dangers of abuse and agency discretion were applied. Additionally, procedural safeguards are required under due process protections. A final constitutional issue is whether matching conflicts with the equal protection clause because categories of people, not individual suspects, are subject to computer matches. Two groups — federal employees and welfare recipients — are most often the subjects of computer matching.
>
> Despite these arguments about the constitutionality of computer matches, the courts have generally not upheld individual privacy claims in cases challenging computer-matching programs. Moreover, there has been little litigation in this area for two reasons. First, the damage requirements of the Privacy Act are so difficult to prove that they serve as a deterrent to its use. . . . Secondly, in large-scale computer matching, single individuals are rarely sufficiently harmed to litigate claims and most individuals are not even aware of the match. . . . [15]

In 1988, Congress passed the Computer Matching and Privacy Protection Act (CMPPA), Pub. L. No. 100-503, to regulate the practice of computer matching. The CMPPA establishes Data Integrity Boards within each agency to oversee matching, requires agencies to perform a cost-benefit analysis of proposed matching endeavors, and requires agencies to notify individuals of the termination of benefits due to computer matching and permit them an opportunity to refute the termination.

Are computer matchings a violation of the Fourth Amendment? If you believe that matchings contravene the Fourth Amendment, are the

---

[14]Marc Rotenberg, *Privacy and Secrecy After September 11*, 86 Minn. L. Rev. 1115, 1129 (2002).
[15]Priscilla Regan, *Legislating Privacy* 89-90 (1995).

due process rights provided by the CMPPA sufficient to cure the constitutional deficiencies?[16]

5. PUBLIC RECORDS

States maintain a panoply of records about individuals, many available to the public, including vital records pertaining to births, deaths, marriages, and divorces. These records contain varying bits of information. Birth records often disclose one's name, date of birth, place of birth, name and ages of one's parents, and mother's maiden name. States maintain driver's license records as well as accident reports. Voting records, which can disclose one's political party affiliation, date of birth, e-mail address, home address, and telephone number, are publicly available in many states. Several types of professions require state licensing, such as doctors, attorneys, engineers, nurses, police, and teachers. Property ownership records contain a physical description of one's property, including the number and size of rooms as well as the value of the property. Police records, such as records of arrests, are also frequently made publicly available.

Court records are public in all states, though settlements are sometimes sealed. A significant amount of personal data can find its way into court records. In a civil case, for example, medical and financial information often is entered into evidence. The names, addresses, and occupations of jurors become part of the court record, as well as the jurors' answers to voir dire questions. In some states, family court proceedings are public.

For information in court records, privacy is protected by way of protective orders, which are issued at the discretion of trial court judges. Courts also have the discretion to seal certain court proceedings or portions of court proceedings from the public as well as permit parties to proceed anonymously under special circumstances.

Privacy in records maintained by state agencies is protected under each state's freedom of information law. Most states have some form of exemption for privacy, often patterned after the federal FOIA's privacy exceptions. Not all states interpret their privacy exemptions as broadly as the Supreme Court has interpreted FOIA's, however. Further, certain state FOIAs do not have privacy exemptions.

Are there limitations on what information state governments can release to the public under an FOI law if there is no exemption for privacy? Consider the case below:

KALLSTROM v. CITY OF COLUMBUS

136 F.3d 1055 (6th Cir. 1998)

MOORE, J. . . . The three plaintiffs, Melissa Kallstrom, Thomas Coelho, and Gary Householder, are undercover officers employed by the Columbus Police Department. All three were actively involved in the drug conspiracy investiga-

---

[16] For an interesting account of the psychological effects and other harms caused by endeavors such as computer matching on welfare recipients, see John Gilliom, *Overseers of the Poor: Surveillance, Resistance, and the Limits of Privacy* (2001).

tion of the Short North Posse, a violent gang in the Short North area of Columbus, Ohio. In *United States v. Derrick Russell, et al.,* No. CR-2 95-044, (S.D. Ohio), forty-one members of the Short North Posse were prosecuted on drug conspiracy charges. Plaintiffs testified at the trial of eight of the *Russell* defendants.

During the *Russell* criminal trial, defense counsel requested and obtained from the City Kallstrom's personnel and pre-employment file, which defense counsel appears to have passed on to several of the *Russell* defendants. Officers Coelho and Householder also suspect that copies of their personnel and pre-employment files were obtained by the same defense attorney. The City additionally released Officer Coelho's file to the Police Officers for Equal Rights organization following its request for the file in the fall of 1995 in order to investigate possible discriminatory hiring and promotion practices by the City. The officers' personnel files include the officers' addresses and phone numbers; the names, addresses, and phone numbers of immediate family members; the names and addresses of personal references; the officers' banking institutions and corresponding account information, including account balances; their social security numbers; responses to questions regarding their personal life asked during the course of polygraph examinations; and copies of their drivers' licenses, including pictures and home addresses. The district court found that in light of the Short North Posse's propensity for violence and intimidation, the release of these personnel files created a serious risk to the personal safety of the plaintiffs and those relatives named in the files.

Prior to accepting employment with the City, the plaintiffs were assured by the City that personal information contained in their files would be held in strict confidence. Despite its earlier promise of confidentiality, however, the City believed Ohio's Public Records Act, Ohio Rev. Code Ann. § 149.43, required it to release the officers' files upon request from any member of the public.

The officers brought suit under 42 U.S.C. §§ 1983 and 1988 against the City, claiming that the dissemination of personal information contained in their personnel files violates their right to privacy as guaranteed by the Due Process Clause of the Fourteenth Amendment. . . . In addition to seeking compensatory damages, the officers request an injunction restraining the City from releasing personal information regarding them. . . .

Section 1983 imposes civil liability on a person acting under color of state law who deprives another of the "rights, privileges, or immunities secured by the Constitution and laws." 42 U.S.C. § 1983. The threshold question, therefore, is whether the City deprived the officers of a right "secured by the Constitution and laws." . . .

In *Whalen v. Roe,* the Supreme Court declared that the constitutional right to privacy grounded in the Fourteenth Amendment respects not only individual autonomy in intimate matters, but also the individual's interest in avoiding divulgence of highly personal information. The court echoed these sentiments in *Nixon v. Administrator of Gen. Servs.,* 433 U.S. 425 (1977), acknowledging that "[o]ne element of privacy has been characterized as 'the individual interest in avoiding disclosure of personal matters.'" Although *Whalen* and *Nixon* appear to recognize constitutional protection for an individual's interest in safeguarding personal matters from public view, in both cases the Court found that public interests outweighed the individuals' privacy interests.

This circuit has read *Whalen* and *Nixon* narrowly, and will only balance an individual's interest in nondisclosure of informational privacy against the public's interest in and need for the invasion of privacy where the individual privacy interest is of constitutional dimension. . . . We hold that the officers' privacy interests do indeed implicate a fundamental liberty interest, specifically their interest in preserving their lives and the lives of their family members, as well as preserving their personal security and bodily integrity. . . .

In light of the Short North Posse's propensity for violence and intimidation, the district court found that the City's release of the plaintiffs-appellants' addresses, phone numbers, and driver's licenses to defense counsel in the *Russell* case, as well as their family members' names, addresses, and phone numbers, created a serious risk to the personal safety of the plaintiffs and those relatives named in the files. We see no reason to doubt that where disclosure of this personal information may fall into the hands of persons likely to seek revenge upon the officers for their involvement in the *Russell* case, the City created a very real threat to the officers' and their family members' personal security and bodily integrity, and possibly their lives. Accordingly, we hold that the City's disclosure of this private information about the officers to defense counsel in the *Russell* case rises to constitutional dimensions, thereby requiring us . . . to balance the officers' interests against those of the City.

The district court found that although there was no indication that the Police Officers for Equal Rights organization posed any threat to the officers and their family members, disclosure even to that group of the officers' phone numbers, addresses, and driver's licenses, and their family members' names, addresses and phone numbers "increases the risk that the information will fall into the wrong hands." . . . Since the district court did not indicate its view of the severity of risks inherent in disclosure of information to the Police Officers for Equal Rights organization, we remand to the district court for reconsideration in light of this opinion of issues regarding disclosure of personal information to that organization.

In finding that the City's release of private information concerning the officers to defense counsel in the *Russell* case rises to constitutional dimensions by threatening the personal security and bodily integrity of the officers and their family members, we do not mean to imply that every governmental act which intrudes upon or threatens to intrude upon an individual's body invokes the Fourteenth Amendment. But where the release of private information places an individual at substantial risk of serious bodily harm, possibly even death, from a perceived likely threat, the "magnitude of the liberty deprivation . . . strips the very essence of personhood." . . .

Where state action infringes upon a fundamental right, such action will be upheld under the substantive due process component of the Fourteenth Amendment only where the governmental action furthers a compelling state interest, and is narrowly drawn to further that state interest. Having found that the officers have a fundamental constitutional interest in preventing the release of personal information contained in their personnel files where such disclosure creates a substantial risk of serious bodily harm, we must now turn to whether the City's actions narrowly serve a compelling public purpose.

The City believed Ohio's Public Records Act, Ohio Rev. Code Ann. § 149.43, required it to disclose the personal information contained in the officers' records. Ohio's Public Records Act requires the state to make available all public records to any person, unless the record falls within one of the statute's enumerated exceptions. The State mandates release of state agency records in order to shed light on the state government's performance, thereby enabling Ohio citizens to understand better the operations of their government. In the judicial setting, courts have long recognized the importance of permitting public access to judicial records so that citizens may understand and exercise oversight over the judicial system. We see no reason why public access to government agency records should be considered any less important. For purposes of this case, we assume that the interests served by allowing public access to agency records rises to the level of a compelling state interest. Nevertheless, the City's release to the criminal defense counsel of the officers' and their family members' home addresses and phone numbers, as well as the family members' names and the officers' driver's licenses, does not narrowly serve these interests.

While there may be situations in which the release of the this type of personal information might further the public's understanding of the workings of its law enforcement agencies, the facts as presented here do not support such a conclusion. The City released the information at issue to defense counsel in a large drug conspiracy case, who is asserted to have passed the information onto his clients. We simply fail to see how placing this personal information into the hands of the *Russell* defendants in any way increases public understanding of the City's law enforcement agency where the *Russell* defendants and their attorney make no claim that they sought this personal information about the officers in order to shed light on the internal workings of the Columbus Police Department. We therefore cannot conclude that the disclosure narrowly serves the state's interest in ensuring accountable governance. Accordingly, we hold that the City's actions in automatically disclosing this information to any member of the public requesting it are not narrowly tailored to serve this important public interest. . . .

NOTES & QUESTIONS

1. Suppose the information released would not subject the officers to physical danger but would simply reveal embarrassing family secrets. Under the rationale of *Kallstrom*, would the constitutional right to information privacy still apply?

2. Consider the operation of the privacy exemption based in statute, as in the federal FOIA under *Reporters Committee*, and based on the constitutional right to information privacy, as in *Kallstrom*. Which is preferable? Could a constitutional right to information privacy claim be asserted where a statutory exemption exists?

3. In *Moak v. Philadelphia Newspapers, Inc.*, 336 A.2d 920 (Pa. 1975), the court held that the employee records of a police department, which contained the name, gender, date of birth, salary, and other personal information about the employees, did not fall within the privacy exemption to Pennsylvania's Right to Know Law because the records would not "operate to the prejudice or impairment of a person's reputation or personal security." Should the privacy of personal information turn on whether it will harm a person's reputation or security?

THE DRIVER'S PRIVACY PROTECTION ACT

For decades, many states had been selling to private sector companies their motor vehicle records. Motor vehicle records contain information such as one's name, address, phone number, Social Security number, medical information, height, weight, gender, eye color, photograph, and date of birth. This information was highly desired by marketers, who paid states millions of dollars to obtain these records. In 1994, Congress passed the Driver's Privacy Protection Act (DPPA), 18 U.S.C. §§ 2721-2725, to halt this practice.

Restriction on Disclosure. Pursuant to DPPA:

> [A] State department of motor vehicles . . . shall not knowingly disclose or otherwise make available to any person or entity personal information about any individual obtained by the department in connection with a motor vehicle record. 18 U.S.C. § 2721(a).

"Personal information" is defined as data "that identifies an individual, including an individual's photograph, social security number, driver identification number, name, address (but not the 5-digit zip code), telephone number, and medical or disability information." § 2725(3). The definition of "personal information" specifically excludes "information on vehicular accidents, driving violations, and driver's status." § 2725(3).

DPPA applies to state DMVs and their officials and employees. Further, DPPA only applies to motor vehicle records.

Consent. State DMVs can disclose personal information in motor vehicle records if the individual consents. In order to disclose a driver's personal information for marketing or other restricted uses, the driver must affirmatively indicate her consent (opt-in). § 2721(b) and (d).

Exceptions. The DPPA contains a number of exceptions. Personal information can be disclosed for purposes of law enforcement, recalls, legal proceedings, and insurance claims investigations. § 2721(b). Additionally, DPPA permits disclosure to licensed private investigative agencies. § 2721(b). Ironically, the event that motivated Congress to pass the DPPA was the murder of actress Rebecca Shaeffer. Her murderer ascertained her address from a private detective, who had received it from the DMV.[17]

Restrictions on Further Dissemination. If private entities obtain motor vehicle record information, they cannot resell or further disseminate that information. 18 U.S.C. § 2721(c). However, if the driver consents to the disclosure of her data, then information may be disseminated for any purpose.

Enforcement. The DPPA establishes criminal fines for any "person" who knowingly obtains or discloses motor vehicle record data in ways prohibited by

---

[17] *See* Charles J. Sykes, *The End of Privacy: Personal Rights in the Surveillance Society* 30-31 (1999).

the DPPA. §2722, §2723(a), §2725(2). The driver may also bring a civil action for those who violate the DPPA knowingly. §2724. States and state agencies are generally excluded from the DPPA, but the U.S. Attorney General may impose a civil penalty of up to $5,000 per day for state agencies that maintain a "policy or practice of substantial noncompliance" with the DPPA. §2723(b).

RENO V. CONDON

528 U.S. 141 (2000)

REHNQUIST, C. J. . . . South Carolina law conflicts with the DPPA's provisions. Under that law, the information contained in the State's DMV records is available to any person or entity that fills out a form listing the requester's name and address and stating that the information will not be used for telephone solicitation. S.C. Code Ann. §§56-3-510 to 56-3-540. South Carolina's DMV retains a copy of all requests for information from the State's motor vehicle records, and it is required to release copies of all requests relating to a person upon that person's written petition. State law authorizes the South Carolina DMV to charge a fee for releasing motor vehicle information, and it requires the DMV to allow drivers to prohibit the use of their motor vehicle information for certain commercial activities.

Following the DPPA's enactment, South Carolina and its Attorney General, respondent Condon, filed suit in the United States District Court for the District of South Carolina, alleging that the DPPA violates the Tenth and Eleventh Amendments to the United States Constitution. The District Court concluded that the Act is incompatible with the principles of federalism inherent in the Constitution's division of power between the States and the Federal Government. The court accordingly granted summary judgment for the State and permanently enjoined the Act's enforcement against the State and its officers. The Court of Appeals for the Fourth Circuit affirmed, concluding that the Act violates constitutional principles of federalism. We granted certiorari, and now reverse. . . .

The United States asserts that the DPPA is a proper exercise of Congress' authority to regulate interstate commerce under the Commerce Clause, U.S. Const., Art. I, §8, cl. 3. The United States bases its Commerce Clause argument on the fact that the personal, identifying information that the DPPA regulates is a "thin[g] in interstate commerce," and that the sale or release of that information in interstate commerce is therefore a proper subject of congressional regulation. We agree with the United States' contention. The motor vehicle information which the States have historically sold is used by insurers, manufacturers, direct marketers, and others engaged in interstate commerce to contact drivers with customized solicitations. The information is also used in the stream of interstate commerce by various public and private entities for matters related to interstate motoring. Because drivers' information is, in this context, an article of commerce, its sale or release into the interstate stream of business is sufficient to support congressional regulation. We therefore need not address the Government's alternative argument that the States' individual, intrastate activities in gathering, maintaining, and distributing drivers' personal information has a sufficiently substantial impact on interstate commerce to create a constitutional base for federal legislation.

But the fact that drivers' personal information is, in the context of this case, an article in interstate commerce does not conclusively resolve the constitutionality of the DPPA. In *New York* and *Printz*, we held federal statutes invalid, not because Congress lacked legislative authority over the subject matter, but because those statutes violated the principles of federalism contained in the Tenth Amendment. In *New York*, Congress commandeered the state legislative process by requiring a state legislature to enact a particular kind of law. We said:

> While Congress has substantial powers to govern the Nation directly, including in areas of intimate concern to the States, the Constitution has never been understood to confer upon Congress the ability to the require the States to govern according to Congress' instructions.

In *Printz*, we invalidated a provision of the Brady Act which commanded "state and local enforcement officers to conduct background check on prospective handgun purchasers." We said:

> We held in New York that Congress cannot compel the States to enact or enforce a federal regulatory program. Today we hold that Congress cannot circumvent that prohibition by conscripting the States' officers directly. The Federal Government may neither issue directives requiring the States to address particular problems, nor command the States' officers, or those of their political subdivisions, to administer or enforce a federal regulatory program.

South Carolina contends that the DPPA violates the Tenth Amendment because it "thrusts upon the States all of the day-to-day responsibility for administering its complex provisions," and thereby makes "state officials the unwilling implementers of federal policy." South Carolina emphasizes that the DPPA requires the State's employees to learn and apply the Act's substantive restrictions, which are summarized above, and notes that these activities will consume the employees' time and thus the State's resources. South Carolina further notes that the DPPA's penalty provisions hang over the States as a potential punishment should they fail to comply with the Act.

We agree with South Carolina's assertion that the DPPA's provisions will require time and effort on the part of state employees, but reject the State's argument that the DPPA violates the principles laid down in either *New York* or *Printz*. . . .

. . . [T]he DPPA does not require the States in their sovereign capacity to regulate their own citizens. The DPPA regulates the States as the owners of databases. It does not require the South Carolina Legislature to enact any laws or regulations, and it does not require state officials to assist in the enforcement of federal statutes regulating private individuals. We accordingly conclude that the DPPA is consistent with the constitutional principles enunciated in *New York* and *Printz*. . . .

NOTES & QUESTIONS

1. In *Lamont v. Commissioner of Motor Vehicles*, 269 F. Supp. 880 (S.D.N.Y. 1967), a famous early case involving the disclosure of motor vehicle information, a plaintiff sued the New York Commissioner of Motor Vehicles al-

leging that the practice of selling motor vehicle information to the highest bidder was unconstitutional. The plaintiff contended that the sale of this information increased the amount of unwanted marketing mail and tele-marketing calls he received. The court concluded that the plaintiff had failed to allege an injury of constitutional magnitude:

> The mail box, however noxious its advertising contents often seem to judges as well as other people, is hardly the kind of enclave that requires con-stitutional defense to protect "the privacies of life." The short, though regu-lar, journey from mail box to trash can — for the contents of which the State chooses to pay the freight when it facilitates the distribution of trash — is an acceptable burden, at least so far as the Constitution is concerned. And the bells at the door and on the telephone, though their ring is a more im-perious nuisance than the mailman's tidings, accomplish more peripheral as-saults than the blare of an inescapable radio.
>
> The information sold by the Commissioner is not vital or intimate. It is, moreover, in the category of "public records," available to anyone upon de-mand. . . . What the State has done in practical effect is to tap a small source of much needed revenue by offering a convenient "packaging" service. . . .

Note that this case was decided prior to *Whalen v. Roe* (Chapter 2), which recognized the constitutional right to information privacy — the "interest in avoiding disclosure of personal matters." Would this case be decided dif-ferently after *Whalen*?

2. Based on *Reno v. Condon*, what is the extent of Congress's power to regu-late information maintained by the states? Suppose Congress amended the Privacy Act to apply not just to federal agencies but to all state and local governments as well. Would such an extension of the Privacy Act be constitutional?

3. To what extent does the DPPA anticipate privacy issues that may arise from new technologies? For example, following September 11, proposals have been put forward to incorporate a biometric identifier, such as a fingerprint or an iris scan, in the state drivers license. Does the DPPA address this issue? What about data sharing among state and federal agencies that might re-sult from standardized record formats?

B. PRIVATE SECTOR RECORDS AND COMPUTER DATABASES

1. PRIVATE SECTOR COLLECTION AND USE OF PERSONAL INFORMATION

(a) Profiling and Cookies

The computer has revolutionized the ability of the private sector to col-lect and analyze personal information. In our day-to-day transactions with private sector businesses and services, we release a significant amount of per-sonal information — about our purchases, our finances, and even our health.

Marketers use personal information to conduct "targeted" or "direct" marketing, which consists of directly sending individuals advertisements or contacting them by telephone. The goal of targeted marketing is to identify consumers likely to purchase one's product. Personal information about consumers is essential to achieving this goal. An entire industry has arisen devoted to the creation of gigantic databases of personal information that can be analyzed based on purchasing habits, income levels, race, lifestyle, age, and hobbies and interests. This industry is rapidly growing and has annual revenues in the billions of dollars. Today, targeted marketing through the use of databases is called "database marketing" and is currently the fastest growing field of marketing.

Companies that maintain databases of personal information on consumers "rent" their databases to marketers at a few cents to a dollar per name. These companies obtain personal information from public records, from buying and selling it to each other, from merging with other database companies, and from directly soliciting it from consumers. An example of direct solicitation of personal information is a warranty registration card. These cards often misleadingly imply that they must be mailed in for a warranty on a product to be effective. The cards often contain a detailed questionnaire, asking a host of questions about one's income, education, occupation, and lifestyle. The return address on the cards is not that of the manufacturer of the product but of National Demographics and Lifestyles Company at a Denver post office box. This company compiles the information in the surveys on the warranty cards.

Another example of information solicitation is the use of frequent shopper programs and discount cards. The consumer fills out a questionnaire and then carries a special card that provides discounts. This enables the scanner data to be matched to data about individual consumers. This technique involves offering savings in return for personal information and the ability to track a person's grocery purchases.[18]

The Internet is rapidly becoming the hub of the personal information market. The Internet provides an enhanced ability to access information. For example, public record information is much more widely available since the advent of the Internet because a number of companies have gathered public records from around the country and have combined them into searchable online databases.

The Internet also enables new forms of targeted marketing. Unlike a page in a magazine or a newspaper, where one advertisement gets placed and read by all, a web page enables a different advertisement to be displayed for each user. This is a cheap and effective way to deliver advertisements to the consumers most likely to respond to them. The key to making this work is collecting personal information about users to better target the advertisements. Al-

---

[18] *See* Erik Larson, *The Naked Consumer: How Our Private Lives Become Public Commodities* (1992) (discussing various techniques of consumer profiling). For other accounts of the rise of profiling, see David Lyon, *Surveillance Society: Monitoring Everyday Life* (2001); Reg Whitaker, *The End of Privacy: How Total Surveillance Is Becoming a Reality* (2000); Oscar H. Gandy, Jr., *The Panoptic Sort: A Political Economy of Personal Information* (1993); David Burnham, *The Rise of the Computer State* (1983); James B. Rule, *Private Lives and Public Surveillance: Social Control in the Computer Age* (1974).

ternatively, web-based advertising could be based on the editorial content of a web site. For example, a site that provides sports news and reports could offer advertising for sports equipment. This is the traditional advertising model of many publications.

A company can use two general methods to collect personal information. First, it can collect it directly from users by requesting users to log in to access parts of a web site. It also collects information whenever a user purchases merchandise from a web site. Second, web sites can secretly track a user's web surfing. When a person interacts with a web site, the site can record certain information about the person, such as what parts of the web site the user visited, what the user clicked on, and how long the user spent reading different parts of the web site. This information is called "clickstream data."

Web sites use "cookies" to identify particular users. A cookie is a small text file that is downloaded into the user's computer when a user accesses a web page. The text in a cookie, which is often encoded, usually includes an identification number and several other data elements, such as the web site and the expiration date. The cookie lets a web site know that a particular user has returned. The web site can then access any information it collected about that individual on her previous visits to the web site. Cookies can also be used to track users as they visit multiple web sites.[19]

The case below illustrates the ways in which cookies are used to build profiles of individuals:

In Re DoubleClick Inc. Privacy Litigation

154 F. Supp. 2d 497 (S.D.N.Y. 2001)

Buchwald, J. Plaintiffs bring this class action on behalf of themselves and all others similarly situated against defendant DoubleClick, Inc. seeking injunctive and monetary relief for injuries they have suffered as a result of DoubleClick's purported illegal conduct. [Among other things, the plaintiffs sued under federal wiretap law, Titles I and II.] . . .

Now pending is DoubleClick's motion, pursuant to Fed. R. Civ. P. 12(b)(6), to dismiss Claims I, II and III of the Amended Complaint for failure to state a claim on which relief can be granted. For the reasons discussed below, Double-Click's motion is granted and the Amended Complaint is dismissed with prejudice. . . .

DoubleClick, a Delaware corporation, is the largest provider of Internet advertising products and services in the world. Its Internet-based advertising network of over 11,000 Web publishers has enabled DoubleClick to become the

---

[19] For more information about computer databases and information collection in cyberspace, see Simson Garfinkel, *Database Nation* (2000); *Technology and Privacy: The New Landscape* (Philip E. Agre & Marc Rotenberg eds., 1997); *Computers, Surveillance, and Privacy* (David Lyon & Elia Zuriek eds. 1996); David Lyon, *The Electronic Eye: The Rise of Surveillance Society* (1994); Susan E. Gindin, *Lost and Found in Cyberspace: Informational Privacy in the Age of the Internet*, 34 San Diego L. Rev. 1153 (1997); Dorothy Glancy, *At the Intersection of Visible and Invisible Worlds: United States Privacy Law and the Internet*, 16 Santa Clara Computer & High Tech. L.J. 357 (2000); Ann Bartow, *Our Data, Ourselves: Privacy, Propertization, and Gender*, 34 U.S.F. L. Rev. 633 (2000); Anita L. Allen, *Gender and Privacy in Cyberspace*, 52 Stan. L. Rev. 1175 (2000); Symposium, *Cyberspace and Privacy — A New Legal Paradigm?*, 52 Stan. L. Rev. 987 (2000).

market leader in delivering online advertising. DoubleClick specializes in collecting, compiling and analyzing information about Internet users through proprietary technologies and techniques, and using it to target online advertising. DoubleClick has placed billions of advertisements on its clients' behalf and its services reach the majority of Internet users in the United States. . . .

The World Wide Web is often mistakenly referred to as the Internet. However, the two are quite different. The Internet is the physical infrastructure of the online world: the servers, computers, fiber-optic cables and routers through which data is shared online. The Web is data: a vast collection of documents containing text, visual images, audio clips and other information media that is accessed through the Internet. Computers known as "servers" store these documents and make them available over the Internet through "TCP/IP" (Transmission Control Protocol/Internet Protocol), a set of standard operating and transmission protocols that structure the Web's operation. Every document has a unique "URL" (Universal Resource Locator) that identifies its physical location in the Internet's infrastructure. Users access documents by sending request messages to the servers that store the documents. When a server receives a user's request (for example, for Lycos.com's home page), it prepares the document and then transmits the information back to the user.

The Internet utilizes a technology called "packet switching" to carry data. Packet switching works as follows. The computer wishing to send a document ("originating computer"), such as a music file or digital image, cuts the document up into many small "packets" of information. Each packet contains the Internet Protocol ("IP") address of the destination Web site, a small portion of data from the original document, and an indication of the data's place in the original document. The originating computer then sends all of the packets through its local network to an external "router." A router is a device that contains continuously-updated directories of Internet addresses called "routing tables." The router takes each packet from the original document and sends it to the next available router in the direction of the destination Web site. Because each router is connected to many other routers and because the connection between any two given routers may be congested with traffic at a given moment, packets from the same document are often sent to different routers. Each of these routers, in turn, repeats this process, forwarding each packet it receives to the next available router in the direction of the destination Web site. Collectively, this process is called "dynamic routing."

The result is that packets of information from the originating computer may take entirely different routes over the Internet (i.e., traveling over different routers and cables) to their ultimate destination. Obviously, the packets arrive out of their original order because some have been forced to take much longer or slower routes between the originating and destination computers. However, because each packet contains code that identifies its place in the original document, the destination computer is able to reassemble the original document from the disorganized packets. At that point, the destination computer sends a message back to the originating computer either reporting that it received the full message, or requesting that the originating computer re-send any packets that never arrived. This entire process typically occurs in a matter of seconds. Packet-switching technology and dynamic routing have helped to give the Internet's infrastructure its extraordinary efficiency and resiliency. . . .

DoubleClick provides the Internet's largest advertising service. Commercial Web sites often rent-out online advertising "space" to other Web sites. In the simplest type of arrangement, the host Web site (e.g., Lycos.com) rents space on its webpages to another Web site (e.g., TheGlobe.com) to place a "hotlink" banner advertisement ("banner advertisement"). When a user on the host Web site "clicks" on the banner advertisement, he is automatically connected to the advertiser's designated Web site.

DoubleClick acts as an intermediary between host Web sites and Web sites seeking to place banner advertisements. It promises client Web sites that it will place their banner advertisements in front of viewers who match their demographic target. For example, DoubleClick might try to place banner advertisements for a Web site that sells golf clubs in front of high-income people who follow golf and have a track record of making expensive online purchases. DoubleClick creates value for its customers in large part by building detailed profiles of Internet users and using them to target clients' advertisements.

DoubleClick compiles user profiles utilizing its proprietary technologies and analyses in cooperation with its affiliated Web sites. DoubleClick is affiliated with over 11,000 Web sites for which and on which it provides targeted banner advertisements. A select group of over 1,500 of these Web sites form the "DoubleClick Network" and are among "the most highly trafficked and branded sites on the Web." In addition, DoubleClick owns and operates two Web sites through which it also collects user data: (1) the Internet Address Finder ("IAF"); and (2) NetDeals.com.

When users visit any of these DoubleClick-affiliated Web sites, a "cookie" is placed on their hard drives. Cookies are computer programs commonly used by Web sites to store useful information such as usernames, passwords, and preferences, making it easier for users to access Web pages in an efficient manner. However, Plaintiffs allege that DoubleClick's cookies collect "information that Web users, including plaintiffs and the Class, consider to be personal and private, such as names, e-mail addresses, home and business addresses, telephone numbers, searches performed on the Internet, Web pages or sites visited on the Internet and other communications and information that users would not ordinarily expect advertisers to be able to collect." DoubleClick's cookies store this personal information on users' hard drives until DoubleClick electronically accesses the cookies and uploads the data. . . .

DoubleClick's advertising targeting process involves three participants and four steps. The three participants are: (1) the user; (2) the DoubleClick-affiliated Web site; (3) the DoubleClick server. For the purposes of this discussion, we assume that a DoubleClick cookie already sits on the user's computer with the identification number "# 0001."

In Step One, a user seeks to access a DoubleClick-affiliated Web site such as Lycos.com. The user's browser sends a communication to Lycos.com (technically, to Lycos.com's server) saying, in essence, "Send me your homepage." This communication may contain data submitted as part of the request, such as a query string or field information.

In Step Two, Lycos.com receives the request, processes it, and returns a communication to the user saying "Here is the Web page you requested." The communication has two parts. The first part is a copy of the Lycos.com homepage, essentially the collection article summaries, pictures and hotlinks a user sees on his screen when Lycos.com appears. The only objects missing are the banner advertisements; in their places lie blank spaces. The second part of the communication is an IP-address link to the DoubleClick server. This link instructs the user's computer to send a communication automatically to Double-Click's server.

In Step Three, as per the IP-address instruction, the user's computer sends a communication to the DoubleClick server saying "I am cookie # 0001, send me banner advertisements to fill the blank spaces in the Lycos.com Web page." This communication contains information including the cookie identification number, the name of the DoubleClick-affiliated Web site the user requested, and the user's browser-type.

Finally, in Step Four, the DoubleClick server identifies the user's profile by the cookie identification number and runs a complex set of algorithms based, in part, on the user's profile, to determine which advertisements it will present to the user. It then sends a communication to the user with banner advertisements saying "Here are the targeted banner advertisements for the Lycos.com homepage." Meanwhile, it also updates the user's profile with the information from the request.

DoubleClick's targeted advertising process is invisible to the user. His experience consists simply of requesting the Lycos.com homepage and, several moments later, receiving it complete with banner advertisements. . . .

DoubleClick's cookies only collect information from one step of the above process: Step One. The cookies capture certain parts of the communications that users send to DoubleClick-affiliated Web sites. They collect this information in three ways: (1) "GET" submissions, (2) "POST" submissions, and (3) "GIF" submissions.

GET information is submitted as part of a Web site's address or "URL," in what is known as a "query string." For example, a request for a hypothetical online record store's selection of Bon Jovi albums might read: *http://recordstore .hypothetical.com/search? terms=bonjovi*. The URL query string begins with the "?" character meaning the cookie would record that the user requested information about Bon Jovi.

Users submit POST information when they fill-in multiple blank fields on a webpage. For example, if a user signed-up for an online discussion group, he might have to fill-in fields with his name, address, email address, phone number and discussion group alias. The cookie would capture this submitted POST information.

Finally, DoubleClick places GIF tags on its affiliated Web sites. GIF tags are the size of a single pixel and are invisible to users. Unseen, they record the users' movements throughout the affiliated Web site, enabling DoubleClick to learn what information the user sought and viewed. . . .

Once DoubleClick collects information from the cookies on users' hard drives, it aggregates and compiles the information to build demographic profiles of users. Plaintiffs allege that DoubleClick has more than 100 million user profiles in its database. Exploiting its proprietary Dynamic Advertising Reporting & Targeting ("DART") technology, DoubleClick and its licensees target banner advertisements using these demographic profiles. . . .

Defendants move to dismiss plaintiffs' claims, pursuant to Fed. R. Civ. P. 12(b)(6), for failure to state a claim upon which relief may be granted. . . .

Claim I. Title II of the ECPA

Title II ("Title II") of the Electronic Communications Privacy Act ("ECPA"), 18 U.S.C. §2701 et. seq., aims to prevent hackers from obtaining, altering or destroying certain stored electronic communications. It creates both criminal sanctions and a civil right of action against persons who gain unauthorized access to communications facilities and thereby access electronic communications stored incident to their transmission. Title II specifically defines the relevant prohibited conduct as follows:

> (a) Offense. Except as provided in subsection (c) of this section whoever (1) intentionally accesses without authorization a facility through which an electronic information service is provided; or (2) intentionally exceeds an authorization to access that facility; and thereby obtains . . . access to a wire or electronic communication while it is in electronic storage in such system shall be punished. . . .

Plaintiffs contend that DoubleClick's placement of cookies on plaintiffs' hard drives constitutes unauthorized access and, as a result, DoubleClick's collection of information from the cookies violates Title II. However, Title II contains an exception to its general prohibition.

> (c) Exceptions.—Subsection (a) of this section does not apply with respect to conduct authorized . . . (2) by a user of that [wire or electronic communications] service with respect to a communication of or intended for that user;

DoubleClick argues that its conduct falls under this exception. It contends that the DoubleClick-affiliated Web sites are "users" of the Internet and that all of plaintiffs' communications accessed by DoubleClick's cookies have been "of or intended for" these Web sites. Therefore, it asserts, the Web sites' authorization excepts DoubleClick's access from §2701(a)'s general prohibition. . . .

Assuming that the communications are considered to be in "electronic storage," it appears that plaintiffs have adequately pled that DoubleClick's conduct constitutes an offense under §2701(a), absent the exception under §2701(c)(2). Therefore, the issue is whether DoubleClick's conduct falls under §2701(c)(2)'s exception. This issue has three parts: (1) what is the relevant electronic communications service?; (2) were DoubleClick-affiliated Web sites "users" of this service?; and (3) did the DoubleClick-affiliated Web sites give DoubleClick sufficient authorization to access plaintiffs' stored communications "intended for" those Web sites?

A. "Internet Access" Is the Relevant Electronic Communications Service

Obviously, in a broad sense, the "Internet" is the relevant communications service. However, for the purposes of this motion, it is important that we define Internet service with somewhat greater care and precision. Plaintiff, at turns, argues that the electronic communications service is "Internet access" and "the ISP [Internet Service Provider]." The difference is important. An ISP is *an entity* that provides access to the Internet; examples include America Online, UUNET and Juno. Access to the Internet is *the service* an ISP provides. Therefore, the "service which provides to users thereof the ability to send or receive wire or electronic communications" is "Internet access."

B. *Web Sites Are "Users" Under the ECPA*

The ECPA defines a "user" as "any person or entity who (A) uses an electronic communication service; and (B) is duly authorized by the provider of such service to engage in such use." 18 U.S.C. § 2510(13). On first reading, the DoubleClick-affiliated Web sites appear to be users — they are (1) "entities" that (2) use Internet access and (3) are authorized to use Internet access by the ISPs to which they subscribe. However, plaintiffs make two arguments that Web sites nevertheless are not users. Both are unpersuasive.

First, plaintiffs argue that "[t]he most natural reading of 'user' is the person who has signed up for Internet access, which means the individual plaintiffs and Class members — *not* the Web servers." Insofar as this argument implies that the statute meant to differentiate between human and non-human users, it is clearly contradicted by the statute's language that defines a "user" as "any person *or entity* . . ." (emphasis added). Furthermore, it rests on the erroneous assumption that only human users "sign[ ] up for Internet access," not Web sites or servers. . . . Although the vast majority of people who sign-up for Internet access from consumer-focused ISPs such as America Online and Juno are individuals, every Web site, company, university, and government agency that utilizes Internet access also subscribes to an ISP or is one. These larger entities generally purchase "Internet access" in bulk from ISPs, often with value-added services and technologically advanced hardware. Nevertheless, they purchase the same underlying Internet access as individual users. . . .

Second, plaintiffs argue that "[t]he individual plaintiff ('user') owns the personal computer ('facility'), while the Web sites she visits do not. [And that] [u]nder basic property and privacy notions, therefore, only she can authorize access to her own messages stored on that facility." Again, plaintiffs seem to ignore the statute's plain language. The general rule under § 2701(a) embodies plaintiffs' position that only those authorized to use a "facility" may consent to its access. Nevertheless, Congress explicitly chose to make § 2701(a)'s general rule subject to § 2701(c)(2)'s exception for access authorized by authors and intended recipients of electronic communications. Thus, plaintiffs' argument is essentially that this Court should ignore § 2701(c)(2) because Congress failed to take adequate account of "basic property and privacy notions." However, it is not this Court's role to revisit Congress' legislative judgments. . . .

C. *All of the Communications DoubleClick Has Accessed Through Its Cookies Have Been Authorized or Have Fallen Outside of Title II's Scope*

Because plaintiffs only allege that DoubleClick accessed communications from plaintiffs to DoubleClick-affiliated Web sites, the issue becomes whether the Web sites gave DoubleClick adequate authorization under § 2701(c)(2) to access those communications. This issue, in turn, has two parts: (1) have the DoubleClick-affiliated Web sites authorized DoubleClick to access plaintiffs' communications to them?; and (2) is that authorization sufficient under § 2701(c)(2)? . . . .

Examining DoubleClick's technological and commercial relationships with its affiliated Web sites, we find it implausible to infer that the Web sites have not authorized DoubleClick's access. In a practical sense, the very reason clients hire DoubleClick is to target advertisements based on users' demographic profiles. . . . Therefore, we find that the DoubleClick-affiliated Web sites consented to DoubleClick's access of plaintiffs' communications to them. . . .

Plaintiffs' GET, POST and GIF submissions to DoubleClick-affiliated Web sites are all "intended for" those Web sites. In the case of the GET and POST submissions, users voluntarily type-in information they wish to submit to the Web sites, information such as queries, commercial orders, and personal information. GIF information is generated and collected when users use their computer "mouse" or other instruments to navigate through Web pages and access information. Although the users' requests for data come through clicks, not keystrokes, they nonetheless are voluntary and purposeful. Therefore, because plaintiffs' GET, POST and GIF submissions to DoubleClick-affiliated Web sites are all "intended for" those Web sites, the Web sites' authorization is sufficient to except DoubleClick's access under § 2701(c)(2). . . .

Plaintiffs argue that even if DoubleClick's access to plaintiffs' GET, POST and GIF submissions is properly authorized under § 2701(c)(2), the cookie identification numbers that accompany these submissions are not because they are never sent to, or through, the Web sites. However, this argument too is unavailing. . . .

Putting aside the issue of whether the cookie identification numbers are electronic communications at all, DoubleClick does not need anyone's authority to access them. The cookies' long-term residence on plaintiffs' hard drives places them outside of § 2510(17)'s definition of "electronic storage" and, hence, Title II's protection. Section 2510(17) defines "electronic storage" as:

> (A) any *temporary, intermediate storage* of a wire or electronic communication incidental to the electronic transmission thereof; and
> (B) any storage of such communication *by an electronic communication service* for the purpose of backup protection of such communication." (emphasis added).

Clearly, the cookies' residence on plaintiffs' computers does not fall into § 2510(17)(B) because plaintiffs are not "electronic communication service" providers. . . .

. . . Title II only protects electronic communications stored "for a limited time" in the "middle" of a transmission, i.e. when an electronic communication service temporarily stores a communication while waiting to deliver it. . . .

Turning to the facts of this case, it is clear that DoubleClick's cookies fall outside § 2510(17)'s definition of electronic storage and, hence, § 2701's scope. Plaintiffs plead that in contrast to most cookies' ephemeral existence, DoubleClick cookies remain on plaintiffs' computers "for a virtually indefinite time period," and that their indefinite existence is critical to their function. In plain language, "indefinite" existence is the opposite of "temporary," and the DoubleClick cookies's residence on plaintiffs' hard drives is certainly not an "intermediate" step in their transmission to another addressee. This plain language controls in the absence of any legislative history suggesting that Congress intended it to cover conduct like DoubleClick's. Indeed, if § 2510(17) were interpreted in the manner plaintiffs advocate, Web sites would commit federal felonies every time they accessed cookies on users' hard drives, regardless of whether those cookies contained any sensitive information. This expansive reading of a criminal statute runs contrary to the canons of statutory interpretation and Congress' evident intent. Thus, because the cookies and their identification numbers are never in "electronic storage" under the ECPA, they are not protected by Title II and DoubleClick cannot be held liable for obtaining them. . . .

Even if we were to assume that cookies and their identification numbers were "electronic communication[s] . . . in electronic storage," DoubleClick's access is still authorized. Section 2701(c)(2) excepts from Title II's prohibition access, authorized by a "user," to communications (1) "of" (2) "or intended for" that user. In every practical sense, the cookies' identification numbers are internal DoubleClick communications — both "of" and "intended for" Double-Click. DoubleClick creates the cookies, assigns them identification numbers, and places them on plaintiffs' hard drives. The cookies and their identification numbers are vital to DoubleClick and meaningless to anyone else. In contrast, virtually all plaintiffs are unaware that the cookies exist, that these cookies have identification numbers, that DoubleClick accesses these identification numbers and that these numbers are critical to DoubleClick's operations.

In this sense, cookie identification numbers are much akin to computer bar-codes or identification numbers placed on "business reply cards" found in magazines. These bar-codes and identification numbers are meaningless to consumers, but are valuable to companies in compiling data on consumer responses (e.g., from which magazine did the consumer get the card?). Although consumers fill-out business reply cards and return them to companies by mail, the bar-codes and identification numbers that appear on the cards are purely internal administrative data for the companies. The cookie identification numbers are every bit as internal to DoubleClick as the bar-codes and identification numbers are to business reply mailers. Therefore, it seems both sensible to consider the identification numbers to be "of or intended for" DoubleClick and bizarre to describe them as "of or intended for" plaintiffs. Accordingly, because the identification numbers are "of or intended for" DoubleClick, it does not violate Title II for DoubleClick to obtain them from plaintiffs' electronic storage. . . .

In light of the above findings, we rule that all of plaintiffs' communications accessed by DoubleClick fall under §2701(c)(2)'s exception or outside Title II and, accordingly, are not actionable. Therefore, plaintiffs' claim under the Title II (Claim I) is dismissed.

Claim II. Wiretap Act

Plaintiffs' second claim is that DoubleClick violated the Federal Wiretap Act ("Wiretap Act"), 18 U.S.C. §2510, et. seq. The Wiretap Act provides for criminal punishment and a private right of action against:

> any person who—(a) intentionally intercepts, endeavors to intercept, or procures any other person to intercept or endeavor to intercept any wire, oral, or electronic communication [except as provided in the statute]. 18 U.S.C. §2511.

For the purposes of this motion, DoubleClick concedes that its conduct, as pled, violates this prohibition. However, DoubleClick claims that its actions fall under an explicit statutory exception:

> It shall not be unlawful under this chapter for a person not acting under color of law to intercept a wire, oral, or electronic communication where such person is a party to the communication or where one of the parties to the communication has given prior consent to such interception *unless such communication is intercepted for the purpose of committing any criminal or tortious act in violation of the Constitution or laws of the United States or any State.* 18 U.S.C. § 2511(2)(d) ("§ 2511(2)(d)") (emphasis added).

DoubleClick argues once again that the DoubleClick-affiliated Web sites have consented to its interceptions and, accordingly, that its conduct is exempted from the Wiretap Act's general prohibition as it was from the Title II's. Plaintiffs deny that the Web sites have consented and argue that even if the Web sites do consent, the exception does not apply because DoubleClick's purpose is to commit "criminal or tortious act[s]."

As a preliminary matter, we find that the DoubleClick-affiliated Web sites are "parties to the communication[s]" from plaintiffs and have given sufficient consent to DoubleClick to intercept them. . . . Therefore, the issue before us is: assuming that DoubleClick committed every act alleged in the Amended Complaint, could this evince a "criminal or tortious" purpose on Double-Click's part?

In light of the DoubleClick-affiliated Web sites' consent, plaintiffs must allege "either (1) that the primary motivation, or (2) that a determinative factor in the actor's [DoubleClick's] motivation for intercepting the conversation was to commit a criminal [or] tortious . . . act." *United States v. Dale,* 991 F.2d 819, 841–42 (D.C. Cir. 1993). . . .

Section 2511(2)(d)'s legislative history and caselaw make clear that the "criminal" or "tortious" purpose requirement is to be construed narrowly, covering only acts accompanied by a specific contemporary intention to commit a crime or tort. The Wiretap Act originally exempted from its prohibition any interception of a wire or oral communication where one of the parties to the communication consented. However, Senator Phillip Hart objected that the exemption was too permissive because it conceivably allowed a party to intercept a communication for the purpose of breaking the law and injuring others. He feared that parties would use secret recordings for "insidious purposes such as blackmail, stealing business secrets, or other criminal or tortious acts in violation of Federal or State laws." Senators Hart and McClellan proposed an amendment to narrow the exemption to acts with "criminal, tortious or injurious" purposes, part of which was enacted as § 2511(2)(d). The key distinction Senator Hart suggested should distinguish permissible from impermissible one-party consent recordings by private citizens was whether the defendant's *intent* in recording was to injure another party. Thus, the legislative record suggests that the element of "tortious" or "criminal" *mens rea* is required to establish a prohibited purpose under § 2511(2)(d).

Plaintiffs attempt to meet §2511(2)(d)'s "purpose" requirement by arguing that their six non-Wiretap Act claims against DoubleClick "plead conduct that has underlying it a tortious purpose and/or that translates into tortious acts." In other words, by virtue of its tortious acts, DoubleClick must have had a tortious purpose.

Courts applying §2511(2)(d) have consistently ruled that a plaintiff cannot establish that a defendant acted with a "criminal or tortious" purpose simply by proving that the defendant committed any tort or crime. . . .

. . . [P]laintiffs overreach when they argue that Congress and the courts created a general rule that "tortious purpose" exists wherever an intentional action is later determined to have constituted a tort, save when journalism is involved. Although Congress deleted "injurious" purpose from §2511(2)(d) partly out of concern for press freedom, it in no way indicated that the press enjoyed special standing under the remaining terms of §2511(2)(d). Had Congress wished to confer special protection on the press, it could have done so explicitly. Courts interpreting §2511(2)(d) have drawn no distinction between media defendants and the general public. In cases involving media defendants, they have consistently grounded their demand for specific contemporary tortious or criminal purpose in §2511(2)(d)'s general language and legislative history, not in an exception for the media. And in suits not involving journalism, courts have demanded evidence of the same tortious or criminal purpose.

In the instant case, plaintiffs clearly allege that DoubleClick has committed a number of torts. However, nowhere have they alleged that DoubleClick's "primary motivation" or a "determining factor" in its actions has been to injure plaintiffs tortiously. The Amended Complaint does not articulate any facts that could support an inference that DoubleClick accessed plaintiffs' electronic communications with the "insidious" intent to harm plaintiffs or others. In fact, everything in the Amended Complaint suggests that DoubleClick has been consciously and purposefully executing a highly-publicized market-financed business model in pursuit of commercial gain — a goal courts have found permissible under §2511(2)(d). Its technology and business strategy have been described, and indeed promoted, in the company's Security and Exchange Commission ("SEC") filings and have been the focus of numerous articles in prominent periodicals and newspapers. Indeed, the intricate details of each proprietary technology challenged by plaintiffs are public record in DoubleClick's patents. DoubleClick's purpose has plainly not been to perpetuate torts on millions of Internet users, but to make money by providing a valued service to commercial Web sites. If any of its practices ultimately prove tortious, then DoubleClick may be held liable for the resulting damage. However, a culpable mind does not accompany every tortious act. In light of the abundant evidence that DoubleClick's motivations have been licit and commercial and the utter lack of evidence that its intent has been tortious, we find as a matter of law that plaintiffs have failed to allege that DoubleClick has acted with a "tortious" purpose.

To summarize, we find that the DoubleClick-affiliated Web sites are "parties" to plaintiffs' intercepted communications under the Wiretap Act and that they consent to DoubleClick's interceptions. Furthermore, we find that plaintiffs have failed to allege that DoubleClick has intercepted plaintiffs' communications for a "criminal or tortious" purpose. Accordingly, we find that DoubleClick's actions are exempted from liability under the Wiretap Act by § 2511(2)(d) and, thus, we dismiss Claim II. . . .

NOTES & QUESTIONS

1. Do you agree with the court that federal wiretap law permits a company to place an identifying tag on a private computer?
2. ***The Computer Fraud and Abuse Act.*** Another issue in the *DoubleClick* case involved the Computer Fraud and Abuse Act, 18 U.S.C. § 1030. The Act provides criminal penalties when a person or entity "intentionally accesses a computer without authorization or exceeds authorized access, and thereby obtains . . . information from any protected computer." § 1030(a)(2)(c). Additionally, the Act applies to a person or entity who "causes damage" by knowingly transmitting information or code to a protected computer or by accessing a protected computer. § 1030(a)(5). A "protected computer" is any computer used in interstate commerce or communication. "Any person who suffers damage or loss by reason of a violation of this section may maintain a civil action against the violator to obtain compensatory damages or injunctive relief or other equitable relief." § 1030(g). "Damage" must cause a "loss aggregating at least $5,000 in value during any 1-year period to one or more individuals." § 1030(e).

   In *DoubleClick,* the court held that the plaintiffs failed to allege that they met the $5,000 damages threshold. The plaintiffs contended that collectively they suffered more than $5,000 in damages, but the court held that the $5,000 only could be aggregated from different victims "for a single act" against "a particular computer."
3. In November 1999, DoubleClick purchased Abacus Direct Corporation, a direct marketing company that maintained a database of personal information on about 90 percent of American households. DoubleClick amended its privacy policy to eliminate its promise that information gathered online would not be associated with other personally identifiable data about users. Privacy advocates alleged that DoubleClick was planning to combine their database of online profiles with Abacus' database of off-line profiles and that this was contrary to DoubleClick's representations that it would not collect personally identifiable information. The Federal Trade Commission (FTC) launched an investigation into whether DoubleClick was engaging in unfair and deceptive trade practices in violation of the FTC Act. In March 2000, DoubleClick stated that it would not merge the databases until it reached an agreement with the U.S. government about the privacy concerns. On January 22, 2001, the FTC closed its investigation after DoubleClick and other Internet advertisers agreed to establish privacy policies for Internet advertisers.
4. ***Perspectives on Computer Profiling.*** What is wrong with companies such as DoubleClick amassing profiles about consumers? Is it a problem when private sector companies collect information about consumers and use it to market products to them?

Julie Cohen argues that profiling is a form of shaping of individuals, with important ramifications for social structure:

> . . . Data processing practices are predicated on a belief that individuals are reducible to the sum of their transactions, genetic markers, and other measurable attributes, and that these attributes are good predictors of risk and reward in future dealings. Plainly, this belief is not entirely wrong; there is much about individual behavior that is predictable on this basis. Yet there also is much about individual behavior that is not. Some relevant information is inherently incapable of measurement or prediction. Human motivation is internal, partly emotional, and often adventitious. The question is whether systematically ignoring this dimension of human behavior, and human potential, produces policy consequences that we would rather avoid. . . .
>
> . . . [T]he data privacy debate is not only about whether prediction is possible, or about how much predictability we require, but also (with apologies to Marx) about who controls the modes of prediction — in other words, about power over knowledge. It follows that mechanisms for accountability (a watchword for data privacy advocates) should concern at least this much. If categorization determines eligibility for rewards or opportunities, then we may have an interest in the algorithms used to categorize. More fundamentally, if preferences are subject to shaping and reshaping over time, then we may have an interest in the sorts of shaping that are permitted. . . .[20]

According to Jerry Kang, the problem with data collection and compiling is that it is a form of surveillance that inhibits individual freedom and choice:

> . . . Information collection presupposes observation of the individual. I concur with Stanley Benn that observation, when nonconsensual and extensive, is in tension with human dignity. As Benn argues, human beings have dignity because they are moral persons — entities capable of self-determination. In other words, they have the capacity to reflect upon and choose personal and political projects and how best to further them. Extensive, undesired observation — what may be called "surveillance" — interferes with this exercise of choice because knowledge of observation "brings one to a new consciousness of oneself, as something seen through another's eyes." Simply put, surveillance leads to self-censorship. This is true even when the observable information would not be otherwise misused or disclosed. . . .
>
> . . . [I]information collection in cyberspace is more like surveillance than like casual observation. . . . [D]ata collection in cyberspace produces data that are detailed, computer-processable, indexed to the individual, and permanent. . . .[21]

Daniel Solove contends that the problem of computer databases does not stem from surveillance. He argues that numerous theorists describe the problem in terms of the metaphor of Big Brother, the ruthless totalitarian government in George Orwell's *Nineteen Eighty-Four,* which constantly

---

[20]Julie E. Cohen, *Examined Lives: Informational Privacy and the Subject as Object,* 52 Stan. L. Rev. 1373, 1405-1407 (2000).

[21]Jerry Kang, *Information Privacy in Cyberspace Transactions,* 50 Stan. L. Rev. 1193 (1998).

monitors its citizens. Solove contends that the Big Brother metaphor fails to adequately conceptualize the problem:

> The most insidious aspect of the surveillance of Big Brother is missing in the context of databases: human judgment about the activities being observed (or the fear of that judgment). Surveillance leads to conformity, inhibition, and self-censorship in situations where it is likely to involve human judgment. Being observed by an insect on the wall is not invasive for privacy; rather, privacy is threatened by being subject to *human* observation, which involves judgments that can affect one's life and reputation. Since marketers generally are interested in aggregate data, they do not care about snooping into particular people's private lives. Much personal information is amassed and processed by computers; we are being watched not by other humans, but by machines, which gather information, compute profiles, and generate lists for mailing, emailing, or calling. This impersonality makes the surveillance less invasive. . . .
>
> Although the effects of surveillance are certainly a part of the database problem, the heavy focus on surveillance miscomprehends the most central and pernicious effects of databases. Understanding the problem as surveillance fails to account for the majority of our activities in the world and web. A large portion of our personal information involves facts that we are not embarrassed about: our financial information, race, marital status, hobbies, occupation, and the like. Most people surf the web without wandering into its dark corners. The vast majority of the information collected about us concerns relatively innocuous details. The surveillance model does not explain why the recording of this non-taboo information poses a problem. The focus of the surveillance model is on the fringes — and often involves behaviors we may indeed want to inhibit such as cult activity, terrorism, and child pornography. . . .[22]

In contrast, Solove proposes that data collection and processing is most aptly captured by Franz Kafka's *The Trial*, where the protagonist (Joseph K.) is arrested by officials from a clandestine court system but is not informed of the reason for his arrest. From what little he manages to learn about the court system, which operates largely in secret, Joseph K. discovers that a vast bureaucratic court has examined his life and assembled a dossier on him. His records, however, are "inaccessible," and K.'s life gradually becomes taken over by his frustrating quest for answers:

> *The Trial* captures the sense of helplessness, frustration, and vulnerability one experiences when a large bureaucratic organization has control over a vast dossier of details about one's life. At any time, something could happen to Joseph K.; decisions are made based on his data, and Joseph K. has no say, no knowledge, and no ability to fight back. He is completely at the mercy of the bureaucratic process. . . .
>
> The problem with databases emerges from subjecting personal information to the bureaucratic process with little intelligent control or limitation, resulting in a lack of meaningful participation in decisions about our infor-

---

[22] Daniel J. Solove, *Privacy and Power: Computer Databases and Metaphors for Information Privacy*, 53 Stan. L. Rev. 1393 (2001).

mation. Bureaucratic decisionmaking processes are being exercised ever more frequently over a greater sphere of our lives, and we have little power or say within such a system, which tends to structure our participation along standardized ways that fail to enable us to achieve our goals, wants, and needs. . . .

What is more discernible than any motive on the part of the Court or any overt exercise of power are the social effects of the power relationship between the bureaucracy and Joseph K. . . . What *The Trial* illustrates is that power is not merely exercised in totalitarian forms, and that relationships to bureaucracies which are unbalanced in power can have debilitating effects upon individuals — regardless of the bureaucracies' purposes (which may, in fact, turn out to be quite benign).

Under this view, the problem with databases and the practices currently associated with them is that they disempower people. They make people vulnerable by stripping them of control over their personal information. There is no diabolical motive or secret plan for domination; rather, there is a web of thoughtless decisions made by low-level bureaucrats, standardized policies, rigid routines, and a way of relating to individuals and their information that often becomes indifferent to their welfare. . . .[23]

Oscar Gandy views profiling as an "inherently conservative" technology that reinforces existing stereotypes and behaviors:

. . . The computer profile is a discriminatory technology. It is a resource used to differentiate between persons and groups. We are concerned about these distinctions because they nearly always involve evaluation.

While the popular perception of a profile is linked to a dossier that contains exquisite detail about an individual, a cyberspace profile is something different. A profile is primarily a list of categories that have been determined to be relevant to some administrative decision that must be made by an organization with regard to an individual, a group, or a class. Individual categories or variables are the dimensions along which an entity may be evaluated. Subsets of categories may be combined into an index score. The fundamental purpose of a profile is the assignment of an individual into a class or category that represents a decision. This is a process of identification with a consequence. . . .

The use of predictive models based on historical data is inherently conservative. Their use tends to reproduce and reinforce assessments and decisions made in the past. . . .[24]

Similarly, Julie Cohen contends:

. . . Better profiling enables discrimination in the broad sense, on any ground deemed reasonable, desirable, and not illegal. And even "benign" discrimination — say, a decision to market only to those subsets of consumers who are statistically more likely to buy — operates to categorize at least some individuals on a basis other than the one they would wish.[25]

---

[23] *Id.*

[24] Oscar H. Gandy, Jr., *Exploring Identity and Identification in Cyberspace*, 14 Notre Dame J.L. Ethics & Pub. Pol'y 1085 (2000).

[25] Julie E. Cohen, *Examined Lives: Informational Privacy and the Subject as Object*, 52 Stan. L. Rev. 1373 (2000).

According to Joel Reidenberg, profiling can threaten anonymity and democratic activities:

> The combination of current technology and existing targeted standards erode protective anonymity. "Information traces" destroy anonymity. Individuals perceive transactions in public places, such as the purchase of groceries at the supermarket or books at the bookstore, as anonymous activities, yet information records collected and maintained by store computer systems enable these activities to be personalized. Stores and other third parties can link specific transactions to individuals. Citizens no longer have the freedom to choose the terms of personal information disclosure and consequently have lost the capacity to participate in decisions about societal information flows.[26]

5. ***Profiling and Transparency.*** Should profiling techniques be made public? Article 12(1) of the European Union Data Protection Directive gives every data subject the right to obtain "knowledge of the logic involved in any automatic processing of data" that produces legal effects or is intended to evaluate personal aspects, such as work performance, credit-worthiness, reliability, and conduct. In the United States, the credit scoring algorithm used to determine eligibility for home loans was kept secret for many years. What about profiling in the context of law enforcement? Should this information be disclosed?

6. ***Privacy Today Versus Privacy in the Past.*** Janna Malamud Smith makes the following observation: "Control over private behavior, previously in the hands of the family, the community or neighborhood, and the church, is now redistributed, with more power granted on the one hand to individuals, and on the other, at a greater distance, to the bureaucracies and institutions that attempt to keep track of vast numbers of mobile people."[27] The small town used to exercise great control over individuals' lives. This was often oppressive for individuals who did not subscribe to the same morality and norms as their neighbors. Today, a majority of Americans live in urban areas. To some extent, people today are more free of the influence of community norms and the gossip of small towns. Does this mean that people generally have more privacy today? Which form of social control is more problematic—that of the small community or that of big bureaucracies?

7. ***Is Privacy Still Possible?*** Is privacy still possible in an Information Age? Scott McNealy, CEO of Sun Microsystems, Inc. once remarked: "You already have zero privacy. Get over it." Should we eulogize the death of privacy and move on? Or is it possible to protect privacy in modern times?

Consider David Brin:

> . . . [I]t is already far too late to prevent the invasion of cameras and databases. The *djinn* cannot be crammed back into its bottle. No matter how many laws are passed, it will prove quite impossible to legislate away the new surveillance tools and databases. They are here to stay.

---

[26]Joel R. Reidenberg, *Setting Standards for Fair Information Practice in the U.S. Private Sector*, 80 Iowa L. Rev. 497 (1995).

[27]Janna Malamud Smith, *Private Matters: In Defense of the Personal Life* 65 (1997).

Light *is* going to shine into nearly every corner of our lives. . . .

If neo-Western civilization has one great trick in its repertoire, a technique more responsible than any other for its success, that trick is *accountability*. Especially the knack—which no other culture ever mastered—of making accountability apply to the mighty. . . .

Kevin Kelly, executive editor of *Wired* magazine, expressed the same idea with the gritty clarity of information-age journalism: "The answer to the whole privacy question is more knowledge. More knowledge about who's watching you. More knowledge about the information that flows between us—particularly the meta-information about who knows what and where it's going."

In other words, we may not be able to eliminate the intrusive glare shining on citizens of the next century, but the glare just might be rendered harmless through the application of more light aimed in the other direction.[28]

8. *Market Solutions: Contractual Default Rules and Property Rights.* A number of commentators propose that privacy can be protected by restructuring property rights in personal information as well as contractual default rules. Proponents of industry self-regulation argue that the market is already functioning properly.[29] People willingly relinquish their personal information to receive certain benefits, such as access to web sites as well as goods and services. Companies have good incentives to keep personal information confidential, because if they do not, they will experience a backlash from the public, who will stop conducting business with them.

In contrast to the self-regulatory approach, in which personal information belongs to whatever entity happens to obtain it, Jerry Kang argues that a default rule that individuals retain control over information they surrender during Internet transactions is more efficient than a default rule where companies can use the data as they see fit. According to Kang, the latter default rule would create two inefficiencies for individuals in attempting to bargain around the rule:

. . . First, [the individual] would face substantial research costs to determine what information is being collected and how it is being used. That is because individuals today are largely clueless about how personal information is processed through cyberspace. Transacting parties and transaction facilitators do not generally provide adequate, relevant notice about what information will be collected and how it will be used. What is worse, consumer ignorance is sometimes fostered by deceptive practices.

Second, the individual would run into a collective action problem. Realistically, the information collector—the "firm"—would not entertain one person's idiosyncratic request to purchase back personal information because the costs of administering such an individually tailored program would be prohibitive. This explains the popular use of form contracts, even in cyberspace, that cannot be varied much, if at all. Therefore, to make it worth the firm's while, the individual would have to band together with like-minded individuals to renegotiate the privacy terms of the underlying transaction.

---

[28] David Brin, *The Transparent Society* 8-23 (1998).
[29] *See* Fred H. Cate, *Privacy in the Information Age* (1997); Fred H. Cate, *Privacy in Perspective* (2001).

These individuals would suffer the collective action costs of locating each other, coming to some mutual agreement and strategy, proposing an offer to the information collector and negotiating with it — all the while discouraging free riders. . . .

Therefore, Kang argues, the appropriate default is to give control of information to the individual:

With this default, if the firm valued personal data more than the individual, then the firm would have to buy permission to process the data in functionally unnecessary ways. Note, however, two critical differences in contracting around this default. First, unlike the individual who had to find out what information is being collected and how it is being used, the collector need not bear such research costs since it already knows what its information practices are. Second, the collector does not confront collective action problems. It need not seek out other like-minded firms and reach consensus before coming to the individual with a request. This is because an individual would gladly entertain an individualized, even idiosyncratic, offer to purchase personal information. In addition, there will be no general "holdout" problem because one individual's refusal to sell personal information to the collector will not generally destroy the value of personal information purchased from others.[30]

Richard Murphy agrees with Kang that contractual default rules should favor the individual to whom the information pertains rather than the companies that collect the information. According to Murphy, personal information "like all information, is property." He goes on to conclude:

. . . [I]n many instances, privacy rules are in fact implied contractual terms. To the extent that information is generated through a voluntary transaction, imposing nondisclosure obligations on the recipient of the information may be the best approach for certain categories of information. The value that information has ex post is of secondary importance; the primary question is what is the efficient contractual rule. Common-law courts are increasingly willing to impose an implied contractual rule of nondisclosure for many categories of transactions, including those with attorneys, medical providers, bankers, and accountants. Many statutes can also be seen in this light — that is, as default rules of privacy. And an argument can be made for the efficiency of a privacy default rule in the generic transaction between a merchant and a consumer.[31]

Lawrence Lessig also contends that privacy should be protected with property rights:

A property regime is fundamentally different from what we have now. Privacy now is protected through liability rules — if you invade someone's pri-

---

[30] Jerry Kang, *Information Privacy in Cyberspace Transactions*, 50 Stan. L. Rev. 1193, 1253-1254, 1257 (1998).

[31] Richard S. Murphy, *Property Rights in Personal Information: An Economic Defense of Privacy*, 84 Geo. L.J. 2381, 2416-2417 (1996). For more examples of commentators who speak of privacy in terms of property rights, see Richard A. Posner, *The Economics of Justice* (1981); Richard A. Posner, *The Right of Privacy*, 12 Ga. L. Rev. 393 (1978); Alan Westin, *Privacy and Freedom* 324 (1967).

vacy, they can sue you and you must then pay. There are two important differences between liability rules and property rules.

The first difference is that a property regime requires negotiation before taking; a liability regime allows a taking, and payment later. The key to a property regime is to give control, and power, to the person holding the property right; the key in a liability regime is to protect the right but facilitate the transfer of some asset from one person to another. There can be holdouts (people who will not agree to transfer) with a property regime; there can be no holdouts in a liability regime. Their is individual control or autonomy with a property regime, but not with a liability regime. Property protects choice; liability protects transfer.

The second difference follows directly from the first. With a liability rule, a court, jury, or statute determines how valuable certain privacy is to you. Ordinarily, you are compensated only for what a reasonable person would have suffered. It is like a regime for buying and selling cars in which, rather than negotiating up front, people simply take other people's cars and a court later determines what they must pay.

Property regimes work very differently. When you have a property right, before someone takes your property they must negotiate with you about how much it is worth. If you have a sentimental attachment to your 1974 Nova, there is little the buyer can do about it. The car's market value might be $200, but if you will not sell it for less than $1,000, the buyer is stuck. You cannot be forced to give up your Nova unless you get your minimum price.

A property regime thus protects both those who value their privacy more than others and those who value it less, by requiring that someone who wants to take a given resource must ask. Such a regime gives us confidence that if a trade occurs, it will be at a price that makes neither party worse off. . . .[32]

Other commentators critique the translation of privacy into a form of property right that can be bartered and sold. For example, Katrin Schatz Byford argues:

> . . . An approach that treats private information as the equivalent of private property has the effect of territorializing the networld and thus of rendering it a conceptual version of physical space, organized according to lines of ownership, with legal boundaries protecting personal property. This economic view of privacy as an item of trade, however, offers an unsatisfactory resolution to the cyberspace privacy dilemma because it proves to be overly reductionistic and disregards the underlying moral and social value of privacy. In effect, the trade theory of privacy presupposes an atomistic vision of privacy's role that values privacy only to the extent it is considered to be of personal worth by the individual who claims it. Hence, a person's decision to release information for the right price is presumed to have no significant impact on anyone other than the seller and purchaser of the information.
>
> Such a perspective plainly conflicts with the notion that privacy is a collective value and that privacy intrusions at the individual level necessarily have broader social implications because they affect access to social power and stifle public participation. Thus, Regan notes that any theory that considers privacy interests as economic goods is counterproductive, since it ren-

---

[32] Lawrence Lessig, *Code and Other Laws of Cyberspace* (1999).

ders privacy protection dependent upon individual wealth and leads to strat-ification by dividing those who can afford privacy from those who cannot. The weakness of the economic privacy model, however, ultimately stems from an even more fundamental misconception. Since the model treats pri-vacy as a quasi-material possession external to the individual, it cannot take account of privacy's function as an inalienable precondition of personal identity and social existence. As a consequence, the model is incapable of ex-plaining what it is that imbues privacy with value and renders it a desirable item of trade in the first place. Because it regards privacy as an alienable pos-session, the trade theory cannot account for privacy's presumed value as a marketplace commodity.[33]

Consider Pamela Samuelson's argument as to why property rights are in-adequate to protect privacy:

> . . . Achieving information privacy goals through a property rights system may be difficult for reasons other than market complexities. Chief among them is the difficulty with alienability of personal information. It is a com-mon, if not ubiquitous, characteristic of property rights systems that when the owner of a property right sells her interest to another person, that buyer can freely transfer to third parties whatever interest the buyer acquired from her initial seller. Free alienability works very well in the market for automo-biles and land, but it is far from clear that it will work well for information privacy. . . . Collectors of data may prefer a default rule allowing them to freely transfer personal data to whomever they wish on whatever terms they can negotiate with their future buyers. However, individuals concerned with information privacy will generally want a default rule prohibiting retransfer of the data unless separate permission is negotiated. They will also want any future recipient to bind itself to the same constraints that the initial pur-chaser of the data may have agreed to as a condition of sale. Information pri-vacy goals may not be achievable unless the default rule of the new property rights regime limits transferability. . . .
>   . . . From a civil liberties perspective, propertizing personal information las a way of achieving information privacy goals may seem an anathema. Not only might it be viewed as an unnecessary and possibly dangerous way to achieve information privacy goals, it might be considered morally ob-noxious. If information privacy is a civil liberty, it may make no more sense to propertize personal data than to commodify voting rights. . . .[34]

Solove also counsels against protecting privacy as a form of property right:

> A market approach has difficulty assigning the proper value to personal information. It is difficult for the individual to adequately value specific pieces of personal information. . . . Because this value is linked to uncertain future uses, it is difficult, if not impossible, for an individual to adequately value her information. Since the ownership model involves individuals re-

---

[33] Katrin Schatz Byford, *Privacy in Cyberspace: Constructing A Model of Privacy for the Electronic Communications Environment*, 24 Rutgers Computer & Tech. L.J. 1 (1998). For an argument about the problems of commodifying certain goods and of viewing all human conduct in light of the market metaphor, see Margaret Jane Radin, *Contested Commodities* (1996).

[34] Pamela Samuelson, *Privacy as Intellectual Property?*, 52 Stan. L. Rev. 1125, 1137-1147 (2000).

linquishing full title to the information, they have little idea how such information will be used when in the hands of others.

Furthermore, the aggregation problem severely complicates the valuation process. An individual may give out bits of information in different contexts, each transfer appearing innocuous. However, the information can be aggregated and could prove to be invasive of the private life when combined with other information. It is the totality of information about a person and how it is used that poses the greatest threat to privacy. As Julie Cohen notes, "[a] comprehensive collection of data about an individual is vastly more than the sum of its parts." From the standpoint of each particular information transaction, individuals will not have enough facts to make a truly informed decision. The potential future uses of that information are too vast and unknown to enable individuals to make the appropriate valuation. . . .

It is not merely sufficient to allow people to sell their information, relinquish all title to it and allow companies to use it as they see fit. This provides people with an all-or-nothing type of exchange, which they are likely to take when they are unaware of how information can or might be used in the future. . . . [Property rights] cannot work effectively in a situation where the power relationship and information distribution between individuals and public and private bureaucracies is so greatly unbalanced. In other words, the problem with market solutions is not merely that it is difficult to commodify information (which it is), but also that a regime of default rules alone (consisting of property rights in information and contractual defaults) will not enable fair and equitable market transactions in personal information. . . .[35]

Consider what Warren and Brandeis said about privacy as a property claim:

The aim of [copyright] statutes is to secure to the author, composer, or artist the entire profits arising from publication; but the common-law protection enables him to control absolutely the act of publication, and in the exercise of his own discretion, to decide whether there shall be any publication at all. . . .

But where the value of the production is found not in the right to take the profits arising from publication, but in the peace of mind or the relief afforded by the ability to prevent any publication at all, it is difficult to regard the right as one of property, in the common acceptation of that term. . . .[36]

How do their views compare with the views of the other scholars excerpted above?

9. *Technological Solutions—Privacy Enhancing Technologies.* Privacy on the Internet can be protected by another form of regulatory mechanism — technology. According to Joel Reidenberg, "law and government regulation are not the only source of rule-making. Technological capabilities and system design choices impose rules on participants."[37] Reidenberg calls such forms of technological governance "Lex Informatica."

---

[35] Daniel J. Solove, *Privacy and Power: Computer Databases and Metaphors for Information Privacy*, 53 Stan. L. Rev. 1393 (2001).

[36] Samuel Warren & Louis Brandeis, *The Right to Privacy*, 4 Harv. L. Rev. 193 (1890).

[37] Joel Reidenberg, *Lex Informatica: The Formulation of Information Policy Rules Through Technology*, 76 Tex. L. Rev. 553 (1998).

Herbert Burkhert describes Privacy Enhancing Technologies (PETs) as "technical and organizational concepts that aim at protecting personal identity. These concepts usually involve encryption in the form digital signatures, blind signature or digital pseudonyms." Burkhert goes on to suggest that anonymity may be a critical form of PETs:

> It has been made clear from the beginning by those advocating PETs that the first question to be asked in PET design is whether personal information is needed at all. The availability of PETs creates a burden of legitimization on those who want to have personal information in their information system.
>
> A further achievement of PETs it that they take pressure off the consent principle. Too often, designers of systems intended to handle personal information have sought to avoid problems caused by handling such information by seeking the consent of the subjects. Rather than put effort into avoiding the use of personal information or into adjusting the system to specific legal requirements, they simply seek to get the subject's consent for whatever they wish to do with personal information.[38]

10. ***Technological Solutions—P3P.*** Lawrence Lessig argues that privacy can be protected via computer code. He contends that an "electronic butler" can enable people's computers to negotiate privacy preferences with the web sites they visit. This "butler" is a computer program called P3P.[39]

Is P3P a Privacy Enhancing Technology? Consider Marc Rotenberg:

> The problems with P3P have now been widely reported. Technical experts have noted that the protocols are complex, difficult to implement, and unlikely to enable consumer to protect privacy. Privacy experts have emphasized that the standard is intended to enable collection of personal information rather than the protection of personal information. Industry analysts have also found shortcomings in the P3P proposal. . . .
>
> Still, the argument over P3P is not simply a debate over the pros and cons of a particular approach to the privacy problem. It is rather a battle over public code versus private code, an argument about whether the designers of the communications infrastructure should be accountable to the views of lawyers, policymakers and especially citizens, or whether they should be free to pursue whatever architecture provides private advantage. P3P is a form of private code, much like the Windows operating system, that reflect a particular institution's views of how choices and behavior should be constrained in cyberspace. It elevates notice and choice as a preferred method for privacy protection and downplays the role and history of Fair Information Practices. It maps nicely to the anti-regulatory views espoused by industry but not at all to the well-established tradition of privacy protection in law. P3P is in the end an invitation to reject privacy as a political value that can be protected in law and to ask individuals to now bargain with those in possession of their secrets over how much privacy they can afford. . . .[40]

---

[38] Herbert Burkert, *Privacy-Enhancing Technologies: Typology, Critique, Vision*, in Technology and Privacy: The New Landscape 123, 125, 128 (Philip E. Agre & Marc Rotenberg, eds., 1997).

[39] Lawrence Lessig, *Code and Other Laws of Cyberspace* (1999).

[40] Marc Rotenberg, *Fair Information Practices and the Architecture of Privacy (What Larry Doesn't Get)*, 2001 Stan. Tech. L. Rev. 1, 72-89.

(b) Spam

Spam is a term to describe unsolicited commercial e-mail sent to individuals to advertise products and services.[41] Companies that send unsolicited e-mail are referred to as spammers. Spam is often mailed out in bulk to large lists of e-mail addresses. A recent practice has been to insert hidden HTML tags (also known as "pixel tags") into spam. This enables the sender of the e-mail to detect whether the e-mail was opened. It can also inform the sender about whether the e-mail message was forwarded, to what e-mail address it was forwarded, and sometimes, even comments added by a user when forwarding the e-mail. This only works if the recipient has an HTML-enabled e-mail reader rather than a text-only reader. HTML e-mail is e-mail that contains pictures and images rather than simply plain text. The practice has become known as a "web bug."

Is spam a form of speech, protected by the First Amendment? In *Cyber Promotions, Inc. v. America Online, Inc.*, 948 F. Supp. 436 (E.D. Pa. 1996), Cyber Promotions, Inc. sought a declaratory judgment that America OnLine (AOL) was prohibited under the First Amendment from denying it the ability to send AOL customers unsolicited e-mail. The court rejected Cyber Promotion's argument because of a lack of state action: "AOL is a private online company that is not owned in whole or part by the government." Today, the Internet is increasingly becoming a major medium of communication. Prior to modern communications media, individuals could express their views in traditional "public fora" — parks and street corners. These public fora are no longer the central place for public discourse. Perhaps the Internet is the modern public forum, the place where individuals come to speak and express their views. If this is the case, is it preferable for access to the Internet to be controlled by private entities?

At least 20 states have anti-spam statutes. For example, Cal. Bus. & Professions Code §17538.4 mandates that senders of spam include in the text of their e-mails a way through which recipients can request to receive no further e-mails. The sender must remove the person from its list. A provider of an e-mail service located within the state of California can request that spammers stop sending spam through its equipment. If the spammer continues to send e-mail, it can be liable for $50 per message up to a maximum of $25,000 per day. *See* §17538.45.

(c) Cyberstalking and Identity Theft

The ready availability of information about individuals over the Internet provides a fertile source of data for criminals. In a number of recent stalking cases, stalkers have obtained information about their victims over the Internet. Additionally, the glut of personal identifying information available over the Internet has enabled identity thieves to more easily obtain the necessary information to steal the identity of unsuspecting victims.

---

[41] For more information on spam, see David E. Sorkin, *Technical and Legal Approaches to Unsolicited Electronic Mail*, 35 U.S.F. L. Rev. 325, 336 (2001).

According to Lynn LoPucki the problem of identity theft is not caused by the ready availability of personal information but by the frequent use of SSNs and other personal information as an identifier:

> The problem is not that thieves have access to personal information, but that creditors and credit-reporting agencies often lack both the means and the incentives to correctly identify the persons who seek credit from them or on whom they report.[42]

Identity theft is one of the most rapidly growing forms of crime. Identity theft occurs when a criminal obtains an individual's personal information and uses it to open new bank accounts, acquire credit cards, and obtain loans in that individual's name. It has been estimated that a victim of identity theft must spend up to two years to repair the damage done to her credit.

Congress responded to the growth of identity theft by passing the Identity Theft and Identity Theft and Assumption Deterrence Act in 1998. The Act makes it a federal crime to "knowingly transfer or use, without lawful authority, a means of identification of another person with the intent to commit, or to aid or abet, any unlawful activity that constitutes a violation of Federal law, or that constitutes a felony under any applicable State or local law." 18 U.S.C. § 1028. Before the passage of the Act, federal law only dealt with the creation, use, or transfer of identification documents, not the theft of personal information. The vast majority of states now have statutes concerning identity theft.

2. TORT LAW AND PRIVATE SECTOR DATABASES

DWYER V. AMERICAN EXPRESS CO.

652 N.E.2d 1351 (Ill. App. 1995)

BUCKLEY, J. Plaintiffs, American Express cardholders, appeal the circuit court's dismissal of their claims for invasion of privacy and consumer fraud against defendants, American Express Company, American Express Credit Corporation, and American Express Travel Related Services Company, for their practice of renting information regarding cardholder spending habits.

On May 13, 1992, the New York Attorney General released a press statement describing an agreement it had entered into with defendants. The following day, newspapers reported defendants' actions which gave rise to this agreement. According to the news articles, defendants categorize and rank their cardholders into six tiers based on spending habits and then rent this information to participating merchants as part of a targeted joint-marketing and sales program. For example, a cardholder may be characterized as "Rodeo Drive Chic" or "Value Oriented." In order to characterize its cardholders, defendants analyze where they shop and how much they spend, and also con-

---

[42] Lynn M. LoPucki, *Human Identification Theory and the Identity Theft Problem*, 80 Tex. L. Rev. 89, 94 (2001).

sider behavioral characteristics and spending histories. Defendants then offer to create a list of cardholders who would most likely shop in a particular store and rent that list to the merchant.

Defendants also offer to create lists which target cardholders who purchase specific types of items, such as fine jewelry. The merchants using the defendants' service can also target shoppers in categories such as mail-order apparel buyers, home-improvement shoppers, electronics shoppers, luxury lodgers, card members with children, skiers, frequent business travelers, resort users, Asian/European travelers, luxury European car owners, or recent movers. Finally, defendants offer joint-marketing ventures to merchants who generate substantial sales through the American Express card. Defendants mail special promotions devised by the merchants to its cardholders and share the profits generated by these advertisements.

On May 14, 1992, Patrick E. Dwyer filed a class action against defendants. His complaint alleges that defendants intruded into their cardholders' seclusion, commercially appropriated their cardholders' personal spending habits, and violated the Illinois consumer fraud statute and consumer fraud statutes in other jurisdictions. Maria Teresa Rojas later filed a class action containing the same claims. The circuit court consolidated the two actions. Plaintiffs moved to certify the class, add parties, and file an amended, consolidated complaint. Defendants moved to dismiss the claims. . . .

Plaintiffs have alleged that defendants' practices constitute an invasion of their privacy [in particular, a violation of the intrusion upon seclusion tort]. . . .

. . . [There are] four elements [to intrusion upon seclusion] which must be alleged in order to state a cause of action: (1) an unauthorized intrusion or prying into the plaintiff's seclusion; (2) an intrusion which is offensive or objectionable to a reasonable man; (3) the matter upon which the intrusion occurs is private; and (4) the intrusion causes anguish and suffering. . . .

Plaintiffs' allegations fail to satisfy the first element, an unauthorized intrusion or prying into the plaintiffs' seclusion. The alleged wrongful actions involve the defendants' practice of renting lists that they have compiled from information contained in their own records. By using the American Express card, a cardholder is voluntarily, and necessarily, giving information to defendants that, if analyzed, will reveal a cardholder's spending habits and shopping preferences. We cannot hold that a defendant has committed an unauthorized intrusion by compiling the information voluntarily given to it and then renting its compilation.

Plaintiffs claim that because defendants rented lists based on this compiled information, this case involves the disclosure of private financial information and most closely resembles cases involving intrusion into private financial dealings, such as bank account transactions. Plaintiffs cite several cases in which courts have recognized the right to privacy surrounding financial transactions.

However, we find that this case more closely resembles the sale of magazine subscription lists, which was at issue in *Shibley v. Time, Inc.* In *Shibley*, the plaintiffs claimed that the defendant's practice of selling and renting magazine subscription lists without the subscribers' prior consent "constitut[ed] an invasion of privacy because it amount[ed] to a sale of individual 'personality profiles,' which subjects the subscribers to solicitations from direct mail advertisers." The plaintiffs also claimed that the lists amounted to a tortious appropriation of their names and "personality profiles." . . .

The *Shibley* court found that an Ohio statute, which permitted the sale of names and addresses of registrants of motor vehicles, indicated that the defendant's activity was not an invasion of privacy. . . .

Defendants rent names and addresses after they create a list of cardholders who have certain shopping tendencies; they are not disclosing financial information about particular cardholders. These lists are being used solely for the purpose of determining what type of advertising should be sent to whom. We also note that the Illinois Vehicle Code authorizes the Secretary of State to sell lists of names and addresses of licensed drivers and registered motor-vehicle owners. Thus, we hold that the alleged actions here do not constitute an unreasonable intrusion into the seclusion of another. We so hold without expressing a view as to the appellate court conflict regarding the recognition of this cause of action.

Considering plaintiffs' appropriation claim, the elements of the tort are: an appropriation, without consent, of one's name or likeness for another's use or benefit. This branch of the privacy doctrine is designed to protect a person from having his name or image used for commercial purposes without consent. According to the Restatement, the purpose of this tort is to protect the "interest of the individual in the exclusive use of his own identity, in so far as it is represented by his name or likeness." Illustrations of this tort provided by the Restatement include the publication of a person's photograph without consent in an advertisement; operating a corporation named after a prominent public figure without the person's consent; impersonating a man to obtain information regarding the affairs of the man's wife; and filing a lawsuit in the name of another without the other's consent.

Plaintiffs claim that defendants appropriate information about cardholders' personalities, including their names and perceived lifestyles, without their consent. Defendants argue that their practice does not adversely affect the interest of a cardholder in the "exclusive use of his own identity," using the language of the Restatement. Defendants also argue that the cardholders' names lack value and that the lists that defendants create are valuable because "they identify a useful aggregate of potential customers to whom offers may be sent.". . .

To counter defendants' argument, plaintiffs point out that the tort of appropriation is not limited to strictly commercial situations.

Nonetheless, we again follow the reasoning in *Shibley* and find that plaintiffs have not stated a claim for tortious appropriation because they have failed to allege the first element. Undeniably, each cardholder's name is valuable to defendants. The more names included on a list, the more that list will be worth. However, a single, random cardholder's name has little or no intrinsic value to defendants (or a merchant). Rather, an individual name has value only when it is associated with one of defendants' lists. Defendants create value by categorizing and aggregating these names. Furthermore, defendants' practices do not deprive any of the cardholders of any value their individual names may possess. . . .

NOTES & QUESTIONS

1. In *Shibley v. Time, Inc.* 341 N.E.2d 337 (Ohio Ct. App. 1975), the plaintiff sued the publishers of a number of magazines for selling subscription lists to direct mail advertising businesses. The plaintiff sued under the public disclosure tort and the appropriation tort. The court dismissed the plaintiff's public disclosure action, because despite the fact that the purchasers of the lists can learn about the plaintiff's lifestyle from the data, it did not "cause mental suffering, shame or humiliation to a person of ordinary sensibilities." The court also rejected the plaintiff's argument that by selling the lists, the defendants were appropriating his name and likeness because the tort of appropriation is available only in those "situations where the plaintiff's name or likeness is displayed to the public to indicate that the plaintiff indorses the defendant's product or business."

   According to *Shibley* and *Dwyer*, why does the public disclosure tort fail to provide a remedy for the disclosure of personal information to other companies? Why does the tort of intrusion upon seclusion fail? Why does the tort of appropriation fail?

   Recall from Chapter 2 the extensive case law concerning these torts. Based on what you learned in Chapter 2, do *Shibley* and *Dwyer* seem adequately reasoned?

2. Can tort law adequately remedy the privacy problems created by profiling and databases?[43]

3. FINANCIAL INFORMATION

PETER P. SWIRE, *FINANCIAL PRIVACY AND THE*
THEORY OF HIGH-TECH GOVERNMENT SURVEILLANCE

77 Wash. U. L.Q. 461 (1999)

The shift from cash to checks to credit and debit cards shows an evolution toward creating records, placing the records automatically in databases, and potentially linking the databases to reveal extremely detailed information about an individual's purchasing history. In considering the effects of this evolution on financial privacy, the next issue is the extent to which people will adopt the more traceable means of payment. . . .

If all of an individual's financial transactions can be traced and are accessible by others, one can envision many possible harms. . . .

The first example is identity theft, or the assumption of an individual's name for financial gain. As more personal information becomes available over networks, it becomes easier for criminals to get hold of previously-private information. For instance, public birth records (now available from database companies) often reveal a mother's maiden name. State drivers license records,

---

[43] For an interesting argument about how the tort of breach of trust might provide a weak but potential solution to the problem, see Jessica Litman, *Information Privacy/Information Property*, 52 Stan. L Rev. 1283 (2000).

available for law enforcement and marketing purposes, often reveal an individual's Social Security Number. Armed with this information, a criminal can impersonate an individual, get a credit card, and run up large bills under the stolen name. Trans Union, a major credit bureau, reported 350,000 cases of identity fraud in 1997. In the same year, at least 10,000 people were arrested for participating in organized identity theft rings. According to the Secret Service, losses from identity theft soared from about $440 million in 1995 to more than $740 million in 1997. As financial records become more traceable by more people, criminals have greater opportunities to access the records and use them to impersonate innocent victims.

A second problem to consider is government and private-sector access to each book and web page that an individual has accessed. A good deal of public concern accompanied special prosecutor Kenneth Starr's subpoena of the bookstore records of Monica Lewinsky's purchases. To many observers, this subpoena seemed to be a worse invasion of privacy than a subpoena of other sorts of financial records. The concerns are likely linked to what Professor Julie Cohen has called "the right to read anonymously," the idea that surveillance of reading threatens First Amendment and related free speech values.

That right to read anonymously becomes even more threatened if records are kept for every web site that a user visits. As web browsing becomes a more pervasive aspect of daily life, records of each page visited may provide a startlingly detailed profile of an individual's interests and activities. Depending on how individual users configure their web browsers, personal computers already keep extensive records of what web sites have been visited. Users today have the ability to tell their browser not to retain these sorts of history files. By contrast, users in the future may have less choice about whether to leave traces of their web browsing. Some sites today charge to download desirable content. For instance, USA Today allows free access to same-day articles. Articles from the archive, however, cost $1.00 each, payable by credit card. In coming years, as "micropayment" systems develop that can charge pennies or fractions of pennies per page, such pay-for-content services may become far more common. Unless privacy protections are built in, these payment systems may be fully traceable, allowing after-the-fact access to each web page visited.

The third problem, perhaps even more troubling, is how an authoritarian or totalitarian government might use and abuse information about citizens' financial transactions. Payment technologies developed in the United States are likely to spread to many countries around the world. Some of those countries lack the democratic history and judicial oversight that exist in the United States. Dictators and other officials in these countries might be able to track the financial transactions of ordinary citizens and political opponents. Surveillance technology that we might find acceptable in the United States, due to a well-functioning system of checks and balances, may be unacceptable in other countries. . . .

THE FAIR CREDIT REPORTING ACT

Increasingly, sales have been made based on credit in the United States. Since 1980, almost all homes and most new cars are purchased on credit. Well over half of retail items are purchased on credit as well.[44] As a result, credit reporting agencies have taken on an ever-greater role in economic transactions. Credit reporting agencies prepare credit reports about people's credit history for use by creditors seeking to loan people money. Credit reports contain financial information such as bankruptcy filings, judgments and liens, mortgage foreclosures, and checking account data. Some companies also prepare investigative consumer reports, which supplement the credit report with information about an individual's character and lifestyle. Creditors depend upon credit reports to determine whether or not to offer a person a loan as well as what interest rate to charge that person. Employers use credit reports to make hiring and promotion decisions. Credit reports are also reviewed by some landlords before renting out an apartment.

There are three major national credit reporting agencies: Experian, Equifax, and Trans Union. Each of these three companies has information on virtually every adult American citizen, and they routinely prepare credit reports about individuals.

In 1970, Congress passed the Fair Credit Reporting Act (FCRA), Pub. L. No. 90-321, to regulate credit reporting agencies. The Act was inspired by allegations of abuse and lack of responsiveness of credit agencies to consumer complaints. In its statement of purpose, the FCRA states: "There is a need to insure that consumer reporting agencies exercise their grave responsibilities with fairness, impartiality, and a respect for the consumer's right to privacy." 15 U.S.C. § 1681. The FCRA requires credit reporting companies to provide an individual access to her records, establishes procedures for correcting information, and sets limitations on disclosure.

Permissible Uses of Credit Reports.   The FCRA, 15 U.S.C. § 1681b, defines the permissible uses of credit reports. These uses include, among other things: (1) credit review; (2) insurance underwriting; (3) licensing; (4) employment; (5) "legitimate business need" when engaging in "a business transaction involving the consumer." § 1681b(3).

Credit Reports for Employment Purposes.   When an employer or potential employer seeks a credit report for employment purposes, she must first disclose in writing to the consumer that a credit report may be obtained and the consumer must authorize in writing that the report can be obtained. The person seeking the report from a credit reporting agency must certify that she obtained the consent of the individual and that she will not use the information in violation of any equal employment opportunity law or regulation. § 1681b(b). If the person who obtained the report takes adverse action based in any way on the report, she must provide the consumer a copy of the report and a description of the consumer's rights under the FCRA. § 1681b(b).

Pursuant to § 1681b(g):

---

[44] *See generally* Robert Ellis Smith, *Ben Franklin's Web Site: Privacy and Curiosity from Plymouth Rock to the Internet* 313-325 (2000); Steven L. Nock, *The Costs of Privacy: Surveillance and Reputation in America* (1993).

A consumer reporting agency shall not furnish for employment purposes, or in connection with a credit or insurance transaction or a direct marketing transaction, a consumer report that contains medical information about a consumer, unless the consumer consents to the furnishing of the report.

Unauthorized Disclosures of Credit Reports. A credit reporting agency can furnish a credit report, without the consumer's authorization, if:

(i) the transaction consists of a firm offer of credit or insurance;
(ii) the consumer reporting agency has complied with subsection (e); and
(iii) there is not in effect the election by the consumer, made in accordance with subsection (e), to have the consumer's name and address excluded from lists of names provided by the agency pursuant to this paragraph. § 1681b(c).

Subsection (e) of § 1681b provides the consumer with a right to opt out of such unauthorized disclosures. If the consumer notifies the credit reporting agency by phone, the opt out shall last for two years and then expire. If the consumer notifies the credit reporting agency by submitting a signed opt out form, then the opt out remains effective until the consumer notifies the agency otherwise. § 1681b(e)

Limitations on Information Contained in Credit Reports. Credit reporting agencies are excluded from providing certain information in credit reports, such as bankruptcy proceedings more than ten years old, suits and judgments more than seven years old, paid tax liens more than seven years old, and records of arrest, indictment, or conviction of a crime more than seven years old. § 1681c(a). However, these limitations do not apply when preparing a credit report used in connection with a credit transaction over $150,000, the underwriting of life insurance over $150,000, or the employment of an individual with an annual salary over $75,000. § 1681c(b).

Limitations on Investigative Consumer Reports. The FCRA provides limitations on investigative consumer reports. These reports cannot be prepared unless "it is clearly and accurately disclosed to the consumer that an investigative consumer report including information as to his character, general reputation, personal characteristics and mode of living, whichever are applicable, may be made." § 1681d(a)(1). The consumer, if she requests, can require disclosure "of the nature and scope of the investigation requested." § 1681d(b). Further, if the report contains any adverse information about a person gleaned from interviews with neighbors, friends, or associates, the agency must take reasonable steps to corroborate that information "from an additional source that has independent and direct knowledge of the information" or ensure that "the person interviewed is the best possible source of the information." § 1681d(d).

Accuracy. "Whenever a consumer reporting agency prepares a consumer report it shall follow reasonable procedures to assure maximum possible accuracy of the information concerning the individual about whom the report relates." § 1681e(b).

Disclosures to the Consumer. The FCRA requires that credit reporting agencies, upon request of the consumer, disclose, among other things:

> (1) All information in the consumer's file at the time of the request, except . . . any information concerning credit scores or any other risk scores or predictors relating to the consumer.
> (2) The sources of the information. . . .
> (3) Identification of each person . . . that procured a consumer report [within two years for employment purposes; within one year for all other purposes] . . . .
> (4) The dates, original payees, and amounts of any checks upon which is based any adverse characterization of the consumer, included in the file at the time of disclosure. . . . § 1681g.

Responsiveness to Consumer Complaints. National credit reporting agencies must provide consumers who request disclosures under the FCRA with a toll-free telephone number at which personnel are accessible to respond to consumer inquiries during normal business hours. § 1681g(c).

Procedures in Case of Disputed Accuracy. Pursuant to § 1681i(a)(1):

> If the completeness or accuracy of any item of information contained in a consumer's file at a consumer reporting agency is disputed by the consumer and the consumer notifies the agency directly of such dispute, the agency shall reinvestigate free of charge and record the current status of the disputed information or delete the item from the file. . . .

The consumer reporting agency must provide written notice to a consumer of the results of an reinvestigation within five business days after completing the investigation. § 1681i.

If the information is found to be inaccurate or incomplete or cannot be verified, the consumer reporting agency must promptly delete it from the file. § 1681i. At the request of the consumer, the credit reporting agency must furnish notification that the item has been deleted to "any person specifically designated by the consumer who has within two years prior thereto received a consumer report for employment purposes, or within six months prior thereto received a consumer report for any other purpose." § 1681i(d).

"If the reinvestigation does not resolve the dispute, the consumer may file a brief statement setting forth the nature of the dispute. The consumer reporting agency may limit such statements to not more than one hundred words if it provides the consumer with assistance in writing a clear summary of the dispute." § 1681i(b).

In any subsequent credit report, the agency must clearly note that the information in question is disputed by the consumer and provide the consumer's statement. § 1681i(c).

Public Record Information for Employment Purposes. If a credit reporting agency furnishes a credit report for employment purposes containing information obtained in public records that is likely to have an adverse effect on the consumer, it must either notify the consumer of the fact that public record information is being reported along with the name and address of the person to whom the information is being reported or "maintain strict procedures designed to insure that whenever public record information which is likely to have an adverse effect on a consumer's ability to obtain employment is reported it is complete and up to date." § 1681k.

Requirements on Users of Consumer Reports. If a user of a credit report takes any adverse action on a consumer based in any way on the report, the user shall provide notice of the adverse action to the consumer, information for the consumer to contact the credit reporting agency that prepared the report, and notice of the consumer's right to obtain a free copy of the report and to dispute the accuracy of the report. § 1681m(a). Whenever credit is denied based on information obtained through sources other than a credit report, upon the consumer's written request, the person or entity denying credit shall disclose the nature of that information. § 1681m(b).

Civil Liability. A person who "willfully fails to comply with any requirement" of the FCRA is liable to the consumer for actual damages or damages between $100 and $1,000, as well as punitive damages and attorneys' fees and costs. § 1681n. Negligent failure to comply with any requirement of the FCRA results in liability to the consumer for actual damages as well as attorneys' fees and costs. § 1681n. The FTC also has the power to enforce the FCRA.

The FCRA states that an action to enforce liability under the Act must be brought within two years "from the date on which the liability arises." § 1681p. However, when the defendant has "willfully misrepresented any information required under [the FCRA] to be disclosed and the information . . . is material to [a claim under the FCRA], the actions may be brought at a time within two years after [the plaintiff's] discovery of the misrepresentation." § 1681p.

In *TRW, Inc. v. Andrews*, 534 U.S. 19 (2001), an imposter attempted on several occasions to open credit accounts using the plaintiff's Social Security number and her last name and address. TRW, a credit reporting agency, provided the plaintiff's credit history to the potential creditors. The plaintiff did not learn about these disclosures until almost a year after the first attempt when she wanted to refinance her home mortgage. Her damaged credit report hindered her refinancing. She filed suit about a year later. The plaintiff argued that TRW's disclosures violated the FCRA because TRW disclosed even though the birth date, address, and first name supplied to TRW when the requests were made did not match her profile. The plaintiff contended that TRW's failure to verify the request for credit reports before disclosing violated § 1681e(a) of the FCRA which required "reasonable procedures" to avoid improper disclosures. The Court concluded that the statute of limitations had run out. With the exception of willful misrepresentation of information to the plaintiff, this two-year statute of limitations period does not begin to run when the plaintiff discovers that the FCRA has been violated. Instead, the limitations period begins to run when the violations occurred, even if the plaintiff does not find out.

Credit Headers. In a much criticized exception to the FCRA, the FTC permitted credit reporting agencies to sell "credit headers" to other companies. A credit header is the information at the top of a credit report, and it often includes a person's name, address, phone number (whether listed or unlisted), mother's maiden name, and Social Security number.

An Assessment of the FCRA. Consider the following critique of the FCRA by Joel Reidenberg:

> . . . The FCRA primarily regulates disclosures of personal information and does not generally address the collection of personal information. . . . The FCRA ignores the acquisition of unnecessary information. In fact, the expansive categories of regulated personal information ranging from credit worthiness to personal characteristics reflect that excessive personal information may be collected by credit reporting agencies.
>
> The accuracy of personal information is, nevertheless, treated by the FCRA. Credit reporting agencies must follow reasonable procedures to assure accuracy of personal information, though agencies are not held strictly liable for errors. The FCRA also requires that a dispute process be implemented to investigate and correct errors. To promote fairness and accuracy, individuals have a right to be informed of the contents of personal information files and of the names of recipients of credit reports. In practice, however, this right may be extremely difficult to enforce because there is no requirement that credit reporting agencies notify individuals of the existence of files containing personal information or of the procedures to learn of the contents and uses of those files. And, despite these obligations, recent reports have found that forty-three percent of all personal information files held by the three major credit reporting agencies contain false or misleading information.
>
> A credit reporting agency has substantial latitude to disseminate regulated personal information without an individual's consent. The FCRA generally permits the disclosure of personal information by a credit reporting agency for statutorily specified purposes, namely establishing the individual's eligibility for credit, employment, insurance, or any other legitimate business need. The statutory authority for disclosures related to "legitimate business needs" offers a credit reporting agency broad permission to disseminate personal information. Anyone seeking to obtain a credit report must certify to the credit reporting agency that the use of the personal information is permitted by the FCRA. Disclosures by a credit reporting agency for other uses require the written consent of the individual whose data is involved. As long as there is a statutorily permitted use or consensual disclosure of a credit report, a recipient is not restricted from making associated or secondary uses of the personal information without the individual's consent, including subsequent disseminations. If an adverse decision on credit, insurance or employment is based on a consumer report, the decision-maker must inform the consumer of the use of the report and identify the source of the report. The user of a credit report need not inform the consumer of any other adverse decision based on the report.
>
> Although the FCRA does not generally restrict the scope of personal information which may be stored or the duration of storage, it does prohibit the dissemination of certain types of obsolete information, such as bankruptcy adjudications more than ten years prior to the report, suits and judgments older than seven years, paid tax liens older than seven years, records of arrests and convictions older than seven years and any other adverse information older than seven years. A significant exception, however, provides that even obsolete information may be disseminated if requested in connection with an em-

ployment application for a position with a salary over $20,000, a credit transaction over $50,000 or the underwriting of life insurance over $50,000. In today's economy, this exception can broadly permit the use and disclosure of obsolete information.[45]

THE BANK SECRECY ACT

The Bank Secrecy Act, Pub. L. No. 91-508, was enacted by Congress in 1970. The Act requires the retention of bank records and creation of reports that would be useful in criminal, tax, or regulatory investigations or proceedings. The Bank Secrecy Act was passed because of worry that shifting from paper to computer records would make white collar law enforcement more complicated.[46] The Act requires that federally insured banks record the identities of account holders as well as copies of each check, draft, or other financial instrument. Not all records and financial instruments must be maintained; only those that the Secretary of the Treasury designates as having a "high degree of usefulness." 12 U.S.C. § 1829b. Further, the Act authorizes the Secretary of the Treasury to promulgate regulations for the reporting of domestic financial transactions. 31 U.S.C. § 1081. The regulations require that a report be made for every deposit, withdrawal, or other transfer of currency exceeding $10,000. *See* 31 C.F.R. § 103.22. For transactions exceeding $5,000 into or out of the United States, the amount, the date of receipt, the form of financial instrument, and the person who received it must be reported. *See* 31 C.F.R. §§ 103.23, 103.25.

In *California Bankers Association v. Shultz*, 416 U.S. 21 (1974), the Court held that the Act did not violate the Fourth Amendment. First, the Court held that the bankers did not possess Fourth Amendment rights in the information because "corporations can claim no equality with individuals in the enjoyment of a right to privacy." Second, as to the Fourth Amendment rights of the individual depositors, the Court concluded that they lacked standing to pursue their claims:

> The complaint filed in the District Court by the ACLU and the depositors contains no allegation by any of the individual depositors that they were engaged in the type of $10,000 domestic currency transaction which would necessitate that their bank report it to the Government. . . . [W]e simply cannot assume that the mere fact that one is a depositor in a bank means that he has engaged or will engage in a transaction involving more than $10,000 in currency, which is the only type of domestic transaction which the Secretary's regulations require that the banks report. That being so, the depositor plaintiffs lack standing to challenge the domestic reporting regulations, since they do not show that their transactions are required to be reported. . . .
>
> We therefore hold that the Fourth Amendment claims of the depositor plaintiffs may not be considered on the record before us. Nor do we think that the California Bankers Association or the Security National Bank can vicariously assert such Fourth Amendment claims on behalf of bank customers in general. . . .

---

[45] Joel R. Reidenberg, *Privacy in the Information Economy: A Fortress or Frontier for Individual Rights?*, 44 Fed. Comm. L.J. 195 (1992).

[46] H. Jeff Smith, *Managing Privacy* 24 (1994).

The Court also rejected a Fifth Amendment challenge to the Act as well as a First Amendment challenge. With regard to the First Amendment challenge, the Court concluded that the "threat to any First Amendment rights of the ACLU or its members from the mere existence of the records in the hands of the bank is a good deal more remote than the threat assertedly posed by the Army's system of compilation and distribution of information which we declined to adjudicate in *Laird v. Tatum*, 408 U.S. 1 (1972)."

Justice Douglas dissented:

> One's reading habits furnish telltale clues to those who are bent on bending us to one point of view. What one buys at the hardware and retail stores may furnish clues to potential uses of wires, soap powders, and the like used by criminals. A mandatory recording of all telephone conversations would be better than the recording of checks under the Bank Secrecy Act, if Big Brother is to have his way. The records of checks — now available to the investigators — are highly useful. In a sense a person is defined by the checks he writes. By examining them the agents get to know his doctors, lawyers, creditors, political allies, social connections, religious affiliation, educational interests, the papers and magazines he reads, and so on ad infinitum. These are all tied to one's social security number; and now that we have the data banks, these other items will enrich that storehouse and make it possible for a bureaucrat — by pushing one button — to get in an instant the names of the 190 million Americans who are subversives or potential and likely candidates.
>
> It is, I submit, sheer nonsense to agree with the Secretary that all bank records of every citizen "have a high degree of usefulness in criminal, tax, or regulatory investigations or proceedings." That is unadulterated nonsense unless we are to assume that every citizen is a crook, an assumption I cannot make.
>
> Since the banking transactions of an individual give a fairly accurate account of his religion, ideology, opinions, and interests, a regulation impounding them and making them automatically available to all federal investigative agencies is a sledge-hammer approach to a problem that only a delicate scalpel can manage. Where fundamental personal rights are involved — as is true when as here the Government gets large access to one's beliefs, ideas, politics, religion, cultural concerns, and the like — the Act should be "narrowly drawn" to meet the precise evil. Bank accounts at times harbor criminal plans. But we only rush with the crowd when we vent on our banks and their customers the devastating and leveling requirements of the present Act. I am not yet ready to agree that America is so possessed with evil that we must level all constitutional barriers to give our civil authorities the tools to catch criminals. . . .

UNITED STATES V. MILLER

425 U.S. 435 (1976)

POWELL, J. . . . [A]gents from the Treasury Department's Alcohol, Tobacco and Firearms Bureau presented grand jury subpoenas issued in blank by the clerk of the District Court, and completed by the United States Attorney's office, to the presidents of the Citizens & Southern National Bank of Warner Robins and the Bank of Byron, where respondent maintained accounts. The subpoenas required the two presidents to appear on January 24, 1973, and to produce [all records of loans as well as of savings and checking accounts in the name of Mitch Miller]. . . .

The banks did not advise respondent that the subpoenas had been served but ordered their employees to make the records available and to provide copies of any documents the agents desired. . . .

The grand jury met on February 12, 1973, 19 days after the return date on the subpoenas. Respondent and four others were indicted. . . . The record does not indicate whether any of the bank records were in fact presented to the grand jury. They were used in the investigation and provided "one or two" investigatory leads. Copies of the checks also were introduced at trial to establish the overt acts [in a conspiracy in which the defendants were charged].

In his motion to suppress, denied by the District Court, respondent contended that the bank documents were illegally seized. It was urged that the subpoenas were defective because they were issued by the United States Attorney rather than a court, no return was made to a court, and the subpoenas were returnable on a date when the grand jury was not in session. The Court of Appeals reversed. Citing the prohibition in *Boyd v. United States*, 116 U.S. 616, 622 (1886), against "compulsory production of a man's private papers to establish a criminal charge against him," the court held that the Government had improperly circumvented *Boyd*'s protections of respondent's Fourth Amendment right against "unreasonable searches and seizures" by "first requiring a third party bank to copy all of its depositors' personal checks and then, with an improper invocation of legal process, calling upon the bank to allow inspection and reproduction of those copies." . . . The subpoenas issued here were found not to constitute adequate "legal process." The fact that the bank officers cooperated voluntarily was found to be irrelevant, for "he whose rights are threatened by the improper disclosure here was a bank depositor, not a bank official." . . .

We find that there was no intrusion into any area in which respondent had a protected Fourth Amendment interest and that the District Court therefore correctly denied respondent's motion to suppress. . . .

On their face, the documents subpoenaed here are not respondent's "private papers." Unlike the claimant in *Boyd* [*v. United States*], respondent can assert neither ownership nor possession. Instead, these are the business records of the banks. Respondent argues, however, that the Bank Secrecy Act introduces a factor that makes the subpoena in this case the functional equivalent of a search and seizure of the depositor's "private papers." We have held, in *California Bankers Assn. v. Shultz*, that the mere maintenance of records pursuant to the requirements of the Act "invade(s) no Fourth Amendment right of any depositor." But respondent contends that the combination of the recordkeeping requirements of the Act and the issuance of a subpoena to obtain those records permits the Government to circumvent the requirements of the Fourth Amendment by allowing it to obtain a depositor's private records without complying with the legal requirements that would be applicable had it proceeded against him directly. Therefore, we must address the question whether the compulsion embodied in the Bank Secrecy Act as exercised in this case creates a Fourth Amendment interest in the depositor where none existed before. This question was expressly reserved in *California Bankers Assn.*

Respondent urges that he has a Fourth Amendment interest in the records kept by the banks because they are merely copies of personal records that were made available to the banks for a limited purpose and in which he has a reasonable expectation of privacy. He relies on this Court's statement in *Katz v. United States*, 389 U.S. 347, 353 (1967), that "we have . . . departed from the narrow view" that "'property interests control the right of the Government to search and seize,'" and that a "search and seizure" become unreasonable when the Government's activities violate "the privacy upon which (a person) justifiably relie(s)." But in *Katz* the Court also stressed that "(w)hat a person knowingly exposes to the public . . . is not a subject of Fourth Amendment protection." We must examine the nature of the particular documents sought to be protected in order to determine whether there is a legitimate "expectation of privacy" concerning their contents.

Even if we direct our attention to the original checks and deposit slips, rather than to the microfilm copies actually viewed and obtained by means of the subpoena, we perceive no legitimate "expectation of privacy" in their contents. The checks are not confidential communications but negotiable instruments to be used in commercial transactions. All of the documents obtained, including financial statements and deposit slips, contain only information voluntarily conveyed to the banks and exposed to their employees in the ordinary course of business. The lack of any legitimate expectation of privacy concerning the information kept in bank records was assumed by Congress in enacting the Bank Secrecy Act, the expressed purpose of which is to require records to be maintained because they "have a high degree of usefulness in criminal tax, and regulatory investigations and proceedings." 12 U.S.C. § 1829b(a)(1).

The depositor takes the risk, in revealing his affairs to another, that the information will be conveyed by that person to the Government. This Court has held repeatedly that the Fourth Amendment does not prohibit the obtaining of information revealed to a third party and conveyed by him to Government authorities, even if the information is revealed on the assumption that it will be used only for a limited purpose and the confidence placed in the third party will not be betrayed.

This analysis is not changed by the mandate of the Bank Secrecy Act that records of depositors' transactions be maintained by banks. In *California Bankers Assn. v. Shultz*, we rejected the contention that banks, when keeping records of their depositors' transactions pursuant to the Act, are acting solely as agents of the Government. But, even if the banks could be said to have been acting solely as Government agents in transcribing the necessary information and complying without protest with the requirements of the subpoenas, there would be no intrusion upon the depositors' Fourth Amendment rights. . . .

Since no Fourth Amendment interests of the depositor are implicated here, this case is governed by the general rule that the issuance of a subpoena to a third party to obtain the records of that party does not violate the rights of a defendant, even if a criminal prosecution is contemplated at the time of the subpoena is issued. Under these principles, it was firmly settled, before the passage of the Bank Secrecy Act, that an Internal Revenue Service summons directed to a third-party bank does not violate the Fourth Amendment rights of a depositor under investigation.

Many banks traditionally kept permanent records of their depositors' accounts, although not all banks did so and the practice was declining in recent years. By requiring that such records be kept by all banks, the Bank Secrecy Act is not a novel means designed to circumvent established Fourth Amendment rights. It is merely an attempt to facilitate the use of a proper and long-standing law enforcement technique by insuring that records are available when they are needed.

We hold that the District Court correctly denied respondent's motion to suppress, since he possessed no Fourth Amendment interest that could be vindicated by a challenge to the subpoenas. . . .

BRENNAN, J. dissenting. . . . The pertinent phrasing of the Fourth Amendment "The right of the people to be secure in their persons, houses, papers, and effects, against unreasonable searches and seizures, shall not be violated" is virtually in haec verba as Art. I, § 19, of the California Constitution "The right of the people to be secure in their persons, houses, papers, and effects, against unreasonable seizures and searches, shall not be violated." The California Supreme Court has reached a conclusion under Art. I, § 13, in the same factual situation, contrary to that reached by the Court today under the Fourth Amendment. I dissent because in my view the California Supreme Court correctly interpreted the relevant constitutional language. . . .

Addressing the threshold question whether the accused's right of privacy was invaded, and relying on part on the decision of the Court of Appeals in this case, Mr. Justice Mosk stated in his excellent opinion for a unanimous court:

> It cannot be gainsaid that the customer of a bank expects that the documents, such as checks, which he transmits to the bank in the course of his business operations, will remain private, and that such an expectation is reasonable. The prosecution concedes as much, although it asserts that this expectation is not constitutionally cognizable. Representatives of several banks testified at the suppression hearing that information in their possession regarding a customer's account is deemed by them to be confidential.
>
> In the present case, although the record establishes that copies of petitioner's bank statements rather than of his checks were provided to the officer, the distinction is not significant with relation to petitioner's expectation of privacy. That the bank alters the form in which it records the information transmitted to it by the depositor to show the receipt and disbursement of money on a bank statement does not diminish the depositor's anticipation of privacy in the matters which he confides to the bank. A bank customer's reasonable expectation is that, absent compulsion by legal process, the matters he reveals to the bank will be utilized by the bank only for internal banking purposes. Thus, we hold petitioner had a reasonable expectation that the bank would maintain the confidentiality of those papers which originated with him in check form and of the bank statements into which a record of those same checks had been transformed pursuant to internal bank practice. . . .

The underlying dilemma in this and related cases is that the bank, a detached and disinterested entity, relinquished the records voluntarily. But that circumstance should not be crucial. For all practical purposes, the disclosure by individuals or business firms of their financial affairs to a bank is not entirely volitional, since it is impossible to participate in the economic life of contemporary society without maintaining a bank account. In the course of such dealings, a depositor reveals many aspects of his personal affairs, opinions, habits and associations. Indeed, the totality of bank records provides a virtual current biography. While we are concerned in the present case only with bank statements, the logical extension of the contention that the bank's ownership of records permits free access to them by any police officer extends far beyond such statements to checks, savings, bonds, loan applications, loan guarantees, and all papers which the customer has supplied to the bank to facilitate the conduct of his financial affairs upon the reasonable assumption that the information would remain confidential. To permit a police officer access to these records merely upon his request, without any judicial control as to relevancy or other traditional requirements of legal process, and to allow the evidence to be used in any subsequent criminal prosecution against a defendant, opens the door to a vast and unlimited range of very real abuses of police power.

Cases are legion that condemn violent searches and invasions of an individual's right to the privacy of his dwelling. The imposition upon privacy, although perhaps not so dramatic, may be equally devastating when other methods are employed. Development of photocopying machines, electronic computers and other sophisticated instruments have accelerated the ability of government to intrude into areas which a person normally chooses to exclude from prying eyes and inquisitive minds. Consequently judicial interpretations of the reach of the constitutional protection of individual privacy must keep pace with the perils created by these new devices. . . .

NOTES & QUESTIONS

1. *The Right to Financial Privacy Act.* Two years after *Miller*, in 1978, Congress passed the Right to Financial Privacy Act (RFPA), Pub. L. No. 95-630, which partially filled the void left by *Miller*. The RFPA prevents banks and other financial institutions from disclosing a person's financial information to the government unless the records are disclosed pursuant to subpoena or search warrant. *See* 29 U.S.C. §§ 3401-3422.[47]

2. Recall the Court's reasoning in *Smith v. Maryland* (Chapter 4), where the Court held that the Fourth Amendment was inapplicable to pen registers of phone numbers. How does the Court's rationale in *Smith* compare to that in *Miller*?

3. Daniel Solove contends that *Miller* and *Smith* pose a substantial threat to privacy in the modern world given the dramatic extent to which third parties hold personal information:

> In the Information Age, an increasing amount of personal information is contained in records maintained by private sector entities, Internet Service Providers, phone companies, cable companies, merchants, bookstores, web-

---

[47] For more information on the RFPA, see George B. Trubow & Dennis L. Hudson, *The Right to Financial Privacy Act of 1978: New Protection from Federal Intrusion*, 12 John Marshall J. Prac. & Proc. 487 (1979).

sites, hotels, landlords and employers. Many private sector entities are beginning to aggregate the information in these records to create extensive digital dossiers.

The data in these digital dossiers increasingly flows from the private sector to the government, particularly for law enforcement use. Law enforcement agencies have long sought personal information about individuals from various third parties to investigate fraud, white collar crime, drug trafficking, computer crime, child pornography, and other types of criminal activity. In the aftermath of the terrorist attacks of September 11, 2001, the impetus for the government to gather personal information has greatly increased, as such data can be useful to track down terrorists and to profile those airline passengers to be more thoroughly searched. Detailed records of an individual's reading materials, purchases, magazines, diseases and ailments, and website activity, enable the government to assemble a profile of an individual's finances, health, psychology, beliefs, politics, interests, and lifestyle. This data can unveil a person's anonymous speech, groups and personal associations.

The increasing amount of personal information flowing to the government poses significant problems with far-reaching social effects. Inadequately constrained government information gathering can lead to at least three types of harms. First, it can result in the slow creep toward a totalitarian state. Second, it can chill democratic activities and interfere with individual self-determination. Third, it can lead to the danger of harms arising in bureaucratic settings. Individuals, especially in times of crisis, are vulnerable to abuse from government misuse of personal information. Once government entities have collected personal information, there are few regulations in how it can be used and how long it can be kept. The bureaucratic nature of modern law enforcement institutions can enable sweeping searches, the misuse of personal data, improper exercises of discretion, unjustified interrogation, arrests, roundups of disfavored individuals, and discriminatory profiling. . . .

The transfer of personal information from the private sector to the government thus requires some form of regulatory control, a way to balance privacy with effective law enforcement. The first source for protecting privacy against infringement by law enforcement agencies is the Fourth Amendment, which prohibits unreasonable searches and seizures and requires that the government first obtain judicial authorization before conducting a search or seizure. . . . The Court, however, has held that there is no reasonable expectation of privacy in records maintained by third parties. In the void left by the absence of the Fourth Amendment protection, a series of statutes provide some limited restraints on government access to third party records. The protections of the statutory regime are far less exacting than those of the Fourth Amendment; information can be obtained through mere subpoenas and court orders, which have relatively few constraints and little meaningful judicial oversight. Further, numerous classes of records are not covered at all. Thus, there is a profoundly inadequate legal response to the emerging problem of government access to aggregations of data, digital dossiers that are increasingly becoming digital biographies.[48]

---

[48] Daniel J. Solove, *Digital Dossiers and the Dissipation of Fourth Amendment Privacy*, 75 S. Cal. L. Rev. 1083, 1084-1086 (2002).

Miller and *Smith* were decided in the 1970s. Should they be reconsidered in light of the extensive computerized records maintained today? What would be the consequences of overruling *Miller* and *Smith*?

4. ***Financial Privacy of Public Officials.*** In *Plante v. Gonzalez*, 575 F.2d 1119 (5th Cir. 1978), Florida enacted a statute that required local officers, state officers, "specified employees," and candidates for state and local elective office to make certain public financial disclosures. These disclosures consisted of a listing of each asset and liability in excess of $1,000 and either a copy of the person's most recent tax return or a sworn statement identifying each separate source and amount of income exceeding $1,000. Five senators filed suit, seeking declaratory relief that the statute violated the constitutional right to information privacy under *Whalen v. Roe*. The court, applying a form of intermediate scrutiny, concluded that the disclosure requirements passed constitutional muster:

> The district court found that four important state concerns are significantly advanced by the Amendment: the public's "right to know" an official's interests, deterrence of corruption and conflicting interests, creation of public confidence in Florida's officials, and assistance in detecting and prosecuting officials who have violated the law. The importance of these goals cannot be denied. The question is whether the Sunshine Amendment significantly promotes them.
>
> What the district court called the public's "right to know" is promoted by the Amendment. This phrase, however, is misleading. Disclosure is helpful not because it fulfills an independent "right," but because it makes voters better able to judge their elected officials and candidates for those positions. All of the officials covered by the Amendment are elected. It is relevant to the voters to know what financial interests the candidates have. . . .
>
> The senators contend that the Amendment will not stop corruption. They make the reasonable point that few officials are likely to make a public disclosure of illegal income. Yet, the existence of the reporting requirement will discourage corruption. Sunshine will make detection more likely. The interest in an honest administration is so strong that even small advances are important. . . .
>
> Ranged against these important interests are the senators' interests in financial privacy. Their interest is substantial. For better or for worse, money too makes the world go round. Financial privacy is important not only for the reasons the California Supreme Court accepted: the threat of kidnapping, the irritation of solicitations, the embarrassment of poverty. When a legitimate expectation of privacy exists, violation of privacy is harmful without any concrete consequential damages. Privacy of personal matters is an interest in and of itself, protected constitutionally, as discussed above, and at common law.
>
> The extent of the interest is not independent of the circumstances. Plaintiffs in this case are not ordinary citizens, but state senators, people who have chosen to run for office. That does not strip them of all constitutional protection. It does put some limits on the privacy they may reasonably expect. The first amendment puts much greater restrictions on libel and slander actions by public officials or public figures than similar actions by private parties. *New York Times v. Sullivan* established that public official must show "actual malice" to recover for libel. . . . By comparison, private parties need

only show fault of some kind to recover actual damages. Even in financial matters, public officials usually have less privacy than their private counterparts. The salaries of most officials, including federal judges, are matters of public record.

Financial privacy is a matter of serious concern, deserving strong protection. The public interests supporting public disclosure for these elected officials are even stronger. We join the majority of courts considering the matter and conclude that mandatory financial disclosure for elected officials is constitutional. . . .

In *Barry v. City of New York*, 712 F.3d 1554 (2d Cir. 1983), New York passed a financial disclosure law requiring yearly reports from most elected and appointed officials, candidates for city offices, and all civil service employees with an annual salary equal to or greater than $30,000 to disclose a significant amount of financial information. Employees of the fire and police departments filed class action suits contesting the constitutionality of the law under the constitutional right to information privacy. Applying intermediate scrutiny, the court concluded:

> We do not think that the right to privacy protects public employees from the release of financial information that is related to their employment or indicative of a possible conflict of interest. Nor do we think the release of information that is not "highly personal" rises to the level of a constitutional violation. . . .
>
> In any event, we think the City's interest in public disclosure outweighs the possible infringement of plaintiffs' privacy interests. Plaintiffs argue that the City's efforts to deter corruption and conflicts of interest would be as well served by disclosure to the City only as by public disclosure. We disagree.
>
> In the City's view, public disclosure will significantly bolster its efforts to deter official malfeasance. The City cites the example of the 1972 Knapp Commission investigation, which uncovered extensive corruption in the Police Department, and determined that despite charges of corruption, no serious official investigation was made until the press publicized the allegations. According to the City, public disclosure of financial reports will spur City agencies and officials to be aggressive in their efforts to police corruption, if only for fear that evidence of misconduct might be found in a financial report and publicized by the press, a public interest group, or a vigilant citizen. In addition, the City contends that public disclosure will enhance public confidence in the integrity of City government if only because the reports will demonstrate that most City officials and employees are honest and not subject to conflicts of interest in the performance of their duties. . . .

Note than in both cases, the types of public officials encompassed by the statutes are quite broad. Should the disclosure requirements be the same for low-level officials or civil service employees as for politicians?

THE GRAMM-LEACH-BLILEY ACT

In 1999, Congress passed the Financial Services Modernization Act, more commonly known as the Gramm-Leach-Bliley (GLB) Act, Pub. L. No. 106-102, codified at 15 U.S.C. §§ 6801-6809. The purpose of the GLB Act is "to enhance competition in the financial services industry by providing a prudential framework for the affiliation of banks, securities firms, insurance companies, and other financial service providers. . . ."[49] The GLB Act was designed to restructure financial service industries, which had long been regulated under the Glass-Steagall Act of 1933. The Glass-Steagall Act, passed in response to the Great Depression, prevented different types of financial institutions (e.g., banks, brokerage houses, insurers) from affiliating with each other. The GLB Act enables the creation of financial conglomerates that provide a host of different forms of financial services.

The law authorizes widespread sharing of personal information by financial institutions such as banks, insurers, and investment companies. The law permits sharing of personal information between companies that are joined together or affiliated with each other as well as sharing of information between unaffiliated companies. To protect privacy, the Act requires a variety of agencies (FTC, Comptroller of Currency, SEC, and a number of others) to establish "appropriate standards for the financial institutions subject to their jurisdiction" to "insure security and confidentiality of customer records and information" and "protect against unauthorized access" to the records. 15 U.S.C. § 6801.

Nonpublic Personal Information. The privacy provisions of the GLB Act only apply to "nonpublic personal information" that consists of "personally identifiable financial information." § 6809(4). Thus, the law only protects *financial* information that is *not public.*

Sharing of Information with Affiliated Companies. The GLB Act permits financial institutions that are joined together to share the "nonpublic personal information" that each affiliate possesses. For example, suppose an affiliate has access to a person's medical information. This could be shared with an affiliate bank that could then turn down a person for a loan. Affiliates must tell customers that they are sharing this information. § 6802(a). The disclosure can be in the form of a general disclosure in a privacy policy. § 6803(a). There is no way for individuals to block this sharing of information.

Sharing of Information with Nonaffiliated Companies. Financial institutions can share personal information with nonaffiliated companies if they first provide individuals with the ability to opt out of the disclosure. § 6802(b). However, people cannot opt out if the financial institution provides personal data to nonaffiliated third parties "to perform services for or functions on behalf of the financial institution, including marketing of the financial institution's own products and services, or financial products or services offered pursuant to joint agreements between two or more financial institutions." § 6802(b)(2). However, the financial institution must disclose the information sharing and must have a contract with the third party requiring the third party to maintain the confidentiality of the information. § 6802(b)(2). Third parties receiving personal data from a financial institution cannot reuse that informa-

---

[49] H.R. Rep. 106-434, at 245 (1999), *reprinted in* 1999 U.S.C.C.A.N. 245, 245.

tion. § 6802(c). These provisions do not apply to disclosures to credit reporting agencies.

Limits on Disclosure. Financial institutions cannot disclose (other than to credit reporting agencies) account numbers or credit card numbers for use in direct marketing (telemarketing, e-mail, or mail). § 6802(d).

Privacy Notices. The GLB Act requires that financial institutions inform customers of their privacy policies. In particular, customers must be informed about policies concerning the disclosure of personal information to affiliates and other companies and categories of information that are disclosed and the security of personal data. § 6803(a). Full compliance with the Act was required by July 1, 2001, and prior to that date, financial institutions mailed privacy policies and opt-out forms to their customers. Many individuals, who conducted business with multiple financial institutions, received a number of such mailings.

Security. The GLBA requires the FTC and other agencies to establish security standards for nonpublic personal information. *See* 15 U.S.C. §§ 6801(b); 6805(b)(2). The FTC issued its final regulations on May 23, 2002. According to the regulations, financial institutions "shall develop, implement, and maintain a comprehensive information security program" that is appropriate to the "size and complexity" of the institution, the "nature and scope" of the institution's activities, and the "sensitivity of any customer information at issue." 16 C.F.R. § 314.3(a). An "information security program" is defined as "the administrative, technical, or physical safeguards [an institution uses] to access, collect, distribute, process, store, use, transmit, dispose of, or otherwise handle customer information." § 314.2(b). A security program should achieve three objectives:

(1) Insure the security and confidentiality of customer information;
(2) Protect against any anticipated threats or hazards to the security or integrity of such information; and
(3) Protect against unauthorized access to or use of such information that could result in substantial harm or inconvenience to any customer. § 314.3(b).

Preemption. The GLB Act does not preempt state laws that provide greater protection to privacy. § 6807(b).

Constitutional Challenge. The GLB Act and the regulations promulgated thereunder were upheld against a First Amendment challenge in *Individual Reference Services Group v. FTC*, 145 F. Supp. 2d 6 (D.D.C. 2001). This case will be discussed later in this chapter in the section dealing with the First Amendment and statutory protections of privacy.

Critics and Supporters. Consider the following critique by Paul Schwartz and Ted Janger:

The GLB Act has managed to disappoint both industry leaders and privacy advocates alike. Why are so many observers frustrated with the GLB Act? We have already noted the complaint of financial services companies regarding the expense of privacy notices. These organizations also argue that there have been scant pay-off from the costly mailings — and strong evidence backs up this claim. For example, a survey from the American Banker's Association found that 22% of banking customers said that they received a privacy notice but did not read it, and 41% could not even recall receiving a notice. The survey also found only 0.5% of banking customers had exercised their opt-out rights. . . .

Not only are privacy notices difficult to understand, but they are written in a fashion that makes it hard to exercise the opt-out rights that GLB Act mandates. For example, opt-out provisions are sometimes buried in privacy notices. As the Public Citizen Litigation Group has found, "Explanations of how to opt-out invariably appear at the end of the notices. Thus, before they learn how to opt-out, consumers must trudge through up to ten pages of fine print. . . ." Public Citizen also identified many passages regarding opt-out that "are obviously designed to discourage consumers from exercising their rights under the statute." For example, some financial institutions include an opt-out box only "in a thicket of misleading statements.". . . A final tactic of GLB Act privacy notices is to state that consumers who opt-out may fail to receive "valuable offers." . . .

The GLB Act merely contains an opt-out requirement; as a result, information can be disclosed to non-affiliated entities unless individuals take affirmative action, namely, informing the financial entity that they refuse this sharing of their personal data. By setting its default as an opt-out, the GLB Act fails to create any penalty on the party with superior knowledge, the financial entity, should negotiations fail to occur. In other words, the GLB leaves the burden of bargaining on the less informed party, the individual consumer. These doubts about the efficacy of opt-out are supported, at least indirectly, by the evidence concerning sometimes confusing, sometimes misleading privacy notices. . . . An opt-out default creates incentives for privacy notices that lead to *inaction* by the consumer.[50]

In contrast, Peter Swire argues that the GLB Act "works surprisingly well as privacy legislation":

Recognizing the criticisms to date, and the limits of the available evidence, I would like to make the case for a decidedly more optimistic view of the effect of the GLB notices. Even in their current flawed form and even if not a single consumer exercised the opt-out right, I contend that a principal effect of the notices has been to require financial institutions to inspect their own practices. In this respect, the detail and complexity of the GLB notices is actually a virtue. In order to draft the notice, many financial institutions undertook an extensive process, often for the first time, to learn just how data is and is not shared between different parts of the organization and with third parties. Based on my extensive discussions with people in the industry, I believe that many institutions discovered practices that they decided, upon deliberation, to change. One public example of this was the decision of Bank of America no longer to share its customers' data with third parties, even subject to opt-out.

---

[50] Ted Janger & Paul M. Schwartz, *The Gramm-Leach-Bliley Act, Information Privacy, and the Limits of Default Rules*, 86 Minn. L. Rev. 1219, 1230-1232, 1241 (2002).

The detailed and complex notice, in short, created a more detailed roadmap for privacy compliance.[51]

4. PRIVACY POLICIES: PRIVATE VS. PUBLIC ENFORCEMENT

(a) Privacy Policies

Privacy policies are statements made by companies about their practices regarding personal information. Increasingly, companies on the Internet are posting privacy policies, and statutes such as the Gramm-Leach-Bliley Act require certain types of companies (financial institutions, insurance companies, and brokerage companies) to maintain privacy policies.

One of the common provisions of many privacy policies is an "opt-out" provision. An opt-out provision establishes a default rule that the company can use or disclose personal information in the ways it desires so long as the consumer does not indicate otherwise. The consumer must take affirmative steps, such as checking a box, calling the company, or writing a letter, to express her desire to opt out of a particular information use or disclosure. In contrast, an "opt-in" provision establishes a default rule that the company cannot use or disclose personal information without first obtaining the express consent of the individual. Consider the following opt-out provision from Chase Manhattan Bank:

> We may share information about you and/or outside the Chase family of companies. You have the Opt-Out Choices listed below to direct us not to share information. We also give you the choices not to get direct mail or telephone offers of products or services. If you want to choose any or all of these options, please have your Chase account number and contact us as indicated below. . . .
>
> By telephone: call us at [phone number].
>
> By mail: mail this Opt-Out notice, completing the appropriate sections that follow to us at [address].
>
> Your request may take up to four to six weeks to be processed. . . .

Do you think that the opt-out policy above is the best way to safeguard the consumer's interest in privacy?

Consider the following statements in Citibank's privacy policy regarding data security:

> We will safeguard, according to strict standards of security and confidentiality, any information our customers share with us. . . .
> We will permit only authorized employees, who are trained in the proper handling of customer information, to have access to that information. Employees who violate our Privacy Promise will be subject to our normal disciplinary process. . . .

What does this policy tell the consumer about the measures taken to keep information secure? Is this adequate to keep the consumer well informed? Is the

---

[51] Peter P. Swire, *The Surprising Virtues of the New Financial Privacy Law*, 86 Minn. L. Rev.1263, 1315-1316 (2002).

policy specific enough? Suppose a Citibank employee were to carelessly disclose a customer's bank account balance on the Internet for all to see. Would the customer have a good case for breach of contract?

JEFF SOVERN, *OPTING IN, OPTING OUT, OR NO OPTIONS AT ALL: THE FIGHT FOR CONTROL OF PERSONAL INFORMATION*

74 Wash. L. Rev. 1033 (1999)

. . . [F]ew consumers understand how much of their personal information is for sale, although they may have a general idea that there is a trade in personal data and that the specifics about that trade are kept from them. . . .

. . . [C]onsumers cannot protect their personal information when they are unaware of how it is being used by others. . . .

The second reason consumers have not acted to protect their privacy, notwithstanding surveys that suggest considerable consumer concern with confidentiality, has to do with how difficult it is to opt out. . . .

. . . Even if consumers can obtain the information needed to opt out, the cost in time and money of communicating and negotiating with all the relevant information gatherers may be substantial. . . .

Companies may not be eager to offer opt-outs because they may rationally conclude that they will incur costs when consumers opt out, while receiving few offsetting benefits. When consumers exercise the option of having their names deleted, mailing lists shrink and presumably become less valuable. . . .

Because of these added costs, companies might decide that while they must offer an opt-out plan, they do not want consumers to take advantage of it. . . . [C]ompanies that offer opt-outs have an incentive to increase the transaction costs incurred by consumers who opt out. . . .

Companies can increase consumers' transaction costs in opting out in a number of ways. A brochure titled "Privacy Notice," which my local cable company included with its bill, provides an example. This Privacy Notice discussed, among other things, how cable subscribers could write to the company to ask that the company not sell their names and other information to third parties. There are at least four reasons why this particular notice may not be effective in eliciting a response from consumers troubled by the sale of their names to others.

First, the Privacy Notice may be obscured by other information included in the mailing. . . .

The second reason why consumers may not respond to the Privacy Notice is its length. The brochure is four pages long and contains 17 paragraphs, 36 sentences, and 1062 words. . . .

Some companies have gone in the other direction, providing so little information in such vague terms that consumers are unable to discern what they are being told. . . .

A third reason why the Privacy Notice may not be effective stems from its prose. Notwithstanding the Plain Language Law in my home state, computer analysis of the text found it extremely difficult, requiring more than a college education for comprehension. By comparison, a similar analysis of this Article found that it required a lower reading level than that of the Privacy Notice.

Fourth, the Privacy Notice may be ineffective because it does not provide an easy or convenient mechanism for opting out. For example, the Privacy Notice invites consumers who object to the sale of their personal information to write to the cable company in a separate letter. By contrast, cable subscribers desiring to add a new premium channel can do so over the telephone, speaking either to a person or tapping buttons on their telephone, depending on their preference. The more difficult the opt-out process, the less likely consumers are to avail themselves of it. . . .

A third explanation for the failure of consumers to opt out as often as their survey answers might suggest is the consumers themselves. Extensive literature on consumer complaint behavior makes clear that many consumers who are distressed by merchant conduct cannot bring themselves to tell the merchant about it. This inability to communicate might translate into failure by consumers to add their names to opt-out lists. . . .

[Sovern suggests that an opt-in system would be more preferable than an opt-out system.]

One benefit of an opt-in system is that it minimizes transaction costs. While some transaction costs are inevitable in any system in which consumers can opt out or opt in, strategic-behavior transaction costs, at least, can be avoided by using a system which discourages parties from generating such costs. The current system encourages businesses to inflate strategic-behavior costs to increase their own gains, albeit at the expense of consumers and the total surplus from exchange. An opt-in system would encourage businesses to reduce strategic-behavior costs without giving consumers an incentive to increase these costs. Instead of an opt-out situation in which merchants are obligated to provide a message they do not wish consumers to receive, an opt-in regime would harness merchants' efforts in providing a message they want the consumer to receive. . . .

An opt-in system thus increases the likelihood that consumers will choose according to their preferences rather than choosing according to the default. . . .

An opt-in system also increases the prospect that direct mailing would be tailored to what consumers wish to receive, thus benefiting consumers who want to receive some, but not all, solicitations. . . .

The sale of information is troublesome in part because it creates externalities, or costs borne by others. Externalities are created when a person engages in an activity that imposes costs on others but is not required to take those costs into account when deciding whether to pursue the activity. The feelings experienced by consumers whose information is sold and used against their wishes constitute just such externalities. An opt-in system — or an opt-out system in which consumers who object to the trade in their personal information have a genuine opportunity to opt out — can shift costs and thereby "internalize" this externality. To put it another way, consumers could bar the sale of their information unless businesses paid them an amount they deemed adequate, thereby requiring businesses selling personal information to incur a cost otherwise borne by consumers. . . .

A regulated opt-out system is less likely than an opt-in system to solve the problem. Opt-out systems do not give businesses the incentive to minimize consumer transaction costs. Consequently, firms might respond to such regulation by generating formal, legalistic notices that consumers would likely ignore. An opt-out system might thus create only the illusion of a cure.

Accordingly, an opt-in system is preferable, chiefly because it eliminates the incentive firms have to engage in strategic behavior and thus inflate consumer transaction costs. An opt-in system would permit consumers who wish to protect their privacy to do so without incurring transaction costs. Consumers who permit the use of their personal information should also be able to realize their wish easily. Indeed, because firms profit from the use of consumer information, firms would have an incentive to make it as easy as possible for consumers to consent to the use of their personal information. . . . An opt-in system, therefore, seems to offer the best hope of accommodating consumer preferences while minimizing transaction costs. . . .

NOTES & QUESTIONS

1. Do you agree with Sovern that an opt-in policy is more efficient than an opt-out policy? Do you think that an opt-in policy is feasible? Do you think it should be required by law?
2. Would a law requiring an opt-in present First Amendment problems? We will explore this issue later in this Chapter in *US West v. FCC* and *Trans Union Corp. v. FTC* (*see* section B.6).

(b) Private Enforcement: Contract Remedies

A privacy policy can be thought of as a type of contract, though the terms are typically dictated by the company and are non-negotiable. Consider the following advice of Scott Killingsworth to the drafters of web site privacy policies:

> . . . Considering enforcement leads to the question: what is the legal effect of a privacy policy? As between the website and the user, a privacy policy bears all of the earmarks of a contract, but perhaps one enforceable only at the option of the user. It is no stretch to regard the policy as an offer to treat information in specified ways, inviting the user's acceptance, evidenced by using the site or submitting the information. The website's promise and the user's use of the site and submission of personal data are each sufficient consideration to support a contractual obligation. Under this analysis, users would have the right to sue and seek all available remedies for breach of the privacy policy, without the need for private rights of action under such regulatory statutes as the FTC Act.
>
> But for the website, this contract may be a net full of holes, one that the website may get caught in but the user may easily slip through. Many popular websites use contractual concepts by making statements such as, "By using this site you agree to our privacy policy," or even riskier, "We may change our policy at any time, so check back here frequently; your continued use following the posting of a policy change constitutes consent to the new policy." These statements are sometimes contained in a privacy policy accessible only through a tiny link at the bottom of the home page that can be found only by actively scrolling down the page. Any website that relies on the binding effect of such a "contract," for example, by expanding its third-party disclosure of pre-existing customer data, is treading on dangerous ground. In such a case there is no independent evidence that the user assented to this "contract."

In contrast, if the user wishes to enforce the contract, she has only to affirm that, in fact, she did read and accept the website's offer to protect her information and relied on its assurances when she entrusted the site with her personal information.

Of course, in order to claim the benefits of this contract, the user would have to acknowledge having accepted it, and this gives the website an opportunity to turn contractual obligation to its advantage by including protective provisions. But relying on acknowledgment by the consumer as a condition precedent to a contract claim does not solve the amendment problem mentioned above (where the contract assented to was the original one), nor does it afford protection against tort liability or generate a legally reliable consent when one is required by law. . . .[52]

Privacy policies can also be viewed simply as notices that warn consumers about the use of their personal information. Assuming that these notices are subject to change as business practices evolve, how effective are privacy policies as a means to protect privacy?

(c) Public Enforcement: The Role of the FTC

In 1995, Congress and privacy experts[53] asked the Federal Trade Commission (FTC) to become involved with consumer privacy issues. Since 1998, the FTC has maintained the position that the use or dissemination of personal information in a manner contrary to a posted privacy policy is a deceptive practice under the FTC Act, 15 U.S.C. § 45. The Act prohibits "unfair or deceptive acts or practices in or affecting commerce." An "unfair or deceptive" act or practice is one that "causes or is likely to cause substantial injury to consumers which is not reasonably avoidable by consumers themselves and not outweighed by countervailing benefits to consumers or to competition." § 45(n). The FTC does not have jurisdiction over all companies. Exempt from the FTC's jurisdiction are many types of financial institutions, airlines, telecommunications carriers, and other types of entities. § 45(a)(2). The Act authorizes the FTC to bring civil actions for penalties up to $10,000 for a knowing violation of the Act. § 45(m)(1)(A). Further, the FTC can obtain injunctive remedies. § 53. The Act does not provide for private causes of action; only the FTC can enforce the Act. Since it began enforcing the Act for breaches of privacy policies in 1998, the FTC has brought a number of actions, most of which have settled. Consider the following cases:

IN RE GEOCITIES

1999 FTC LEXIS 17 (Feb. 5, 1999)

In its first online privacy enforcement action, the FTC filed a complaint against GeoCities in 1998. At that time, GeoCities was one of the busiest web-

---

[52] Scott Killingsworth, *Minding Your Own Business: Privacy Policies in Principle and in Practice*, 7 J. Intell. Prop. L. 57, 91-92 (1999).

[53] Letter from EPIC Director Marc Rotenberg to FTC Commissioner Christine Varney, Dec. 14, 1995.

sites on the Internet, having over 2 million members. GeoCities was a virtual community consisting of people's home pages that were categorized into a number of different types of "neighborhoods." GeoCities provided free e-mail, children's clubs, and contests. GeoCities collected from its users, including children, mandatory information (names, email addresses, gender, date of birth) and optional information (education level, income, marital status, occupation, and interests). In its privacy policy, GeoCities stated in regard to the optional information: "The following section is completely optional. We will not share this information with anyone without your permission, but will use it to gain a better understanding of who is visiting GeoCities." Further, Geocities stated:

> When [consumers] apply to GeoCities we ask if they would like to receive information on a variety of topics. . . . Before we send anything out, we deliver an orientation e-mail to explain the program, to ensure that only those people who requested topically-oriented mail receive it and to protect your privacy. . . . We assure you this is a free service provided only to GeoCitizens who request this information, and we will NEVER give your information to anyone without your permission.

Additionally, the website declared: "We assure you that we will NEVER give your personal information to anyone without your permission."

In its complaint against GeoCities, the FTC alleged:

> . . . In truth and in fact, the personal identifying information collected through respondent's New Member Application form is not used only for the purpose of providing to members the specific e-mail advertising offers and other products or services they request. Respondent has also sold, rented, or otherwise marketed or disclosed this information, including information collected from children, to third parties who have used this information for purposes other than those for which members have given permission. For example, third parties have targeted unrequested e-mail advertising offers to individual members based on their chosen GeoCities neighborhoods. . . .
>
> In truth and in fact, respondent has disclosed the "optional" information it collects through the New Member Application form to third parties without the consumer's permission, and for purposes other than to gain a better understanding of who is visiting GeoCities. Respondent has disclosed this information, including information collected from children, to third parties who have used this information to target advertising to GeoCities' members. . . .

In 1999, the FTC reached a settlement with GeoCities, requiring GeoCities to post a privacy notice on its website informing users about the information it collects and how it is used. GeoCities also agreed to refrain from gathering information from children ages 12 and under without parental approval. No fines or other punishment were imposed.

NOTES & QUESTIONS

1. Do you think that the settlement terms in *GeoCities* were appropriate?
2. In *In re Liberty Financial Companies,* No. 9823522, 1999 FTC LEXIS 99 (May 6, 1999), the FTC charged the operator of a web site for child and teen investors with falsely promising that the personal information it collected in a

survey would be kept anonymous. The web site gathered data about the child and family's finances, but instead of being anonymously maintained, it was kept in an identifiable form. Liberty Financial settled with the FTC, agreeing to refrain from making future misrepresentations, to post a privacy notice on its web site, and to obtain parental consent prior to gathering personal data from children. FTC commissioners approved the settlement 4-0.

3. In *FTC v. ReverseAuction.com, Inc.*, No. 00-CV-32 (D.D.C. Jan. 6, 2000), the FTC charged ReverseAuction.com with improperly obtaining personal information from eBay customers. ReverseAuction then used the information to spam eBay customers promoting its own auction web site. The message falsely stated to the recipients that their eBay user IDs would expire soon. The FTC charged that ReverseAuction's practice was both unfair and deceptive.

ReverseAuction settled, agreeing to be barred from making future misrepresentations. Further, ReverseAuction had to notify the consumers who received its spam and inform them that its eBay user IDs will not expire and that eBay did not authorize ReverseAuction's spam. Consumers also can delete their personal information from ReverseAuction's database. ReverseAuction must also display its own privacy policy on its web site. FTC commissioners voted 5-0 to approve the settlement. However, two commissioners, agreeing that ReverseAuction acted deceptively, disagreed that ReverseAuction acted unfairly:

> We do not, however, support the unfairness theory in Count One. The Commission has no authority to declare an act or practice unfair unless it "causes or is likely to cause *substantial injury* to consumers which is not reasonably avoidable by consumers themselves and not outweighed by countervailing benefits to consumers or to competition." 15 U.S.C. § 45(n) (emphasis added). . . .
>
> We do not say that privacy concerns can never support an unfairness claim. In this case, however, ReverseAuction's use of eBay members' information to send them e-mail did not cause substantial enough injury to meet the statutory standard. . . .
>
> The injury in this case was caused by deception: that is, by ReverseAuction's failure to honor its express commitments. It is not necessary or appropriate to plead a less precise theory.
>
> . . . The unfairness theory . . . posits substantial injury stemming from ReverseAuction's use of information readily available to millions of eBay members to send commercial e-mail. This standard for substantial injury overstates the appropriate level of government-enforced privacy protection on the Internet, and provides no rationale for when unsolicited commercial e-mail is unfair and when it is not.

One commissioner issued a separate statement to justify the unfairness theory:

> I believe that ReverseAuction's behavior caused substantial injury to members of the eBay community, that the injury could not have been avoided by those members, and it was not outweighed by countervailing benefits. I believe the harm caused in this case is especially significant because it not only

breached the privacy expectation of each and every eBay member, it also undermined consumer confidence in eBay and diminishes the electronic marketplace for all its participants. This injury is exacerbated because consumer concern about privacy and confidence in the electronic marketplace are such critical issues at this time.

4. In *FTC v. Eli Lilly*, No. 012-3214,[54] the FTC charged Eli Lilly, a pharmaceutical company, with disclosing people's health data that it collected through its Prozac.com web site. Prozac is a drug used for treating depression. Lilly offered customers an e-mail service that would send them e-mail messages to remind them to take or refill their medication. In June 2001, the company sent e-mail messages to all 669 users of the reminder service announcing that the service was terminated. However, this message contained the e-mail addresses of all subscribers in the "To" line of the message. The FTC alleged that the company's privacy policy promising confidentiality was deceptive because the company failed to establish adequate security protections for its consumers' data. Specifically, the FTC complaint alleged that Eli Lilly failed to

> provide appropriate training for its employees regarding consumer privacy and information security; provide appropriate oversight and assistance for the employee who sent out the e-mail, who had no prior experience in creating, testing, or implementing the computer program used; and implement appropriate checks and controls on the process, such as reviewing the computer program with experienced personnel and pretesting the program internally before sending out the e-mail.

Eli Lilly settled, agreeing to establish a new security program. The settlement requires Eli Lilly to designate personnel to oversee the program, identify and address various security risks, and conduct an annual review of the security program. FTC Commissioners voted 5-0 to approve the settlement.

Consider the settlements in the cases described above. Do you think that these settlements are adequate to redress the rights of the individuals affected?

5. *Fair Information Practices.* The FTC's ability to pursue privacy complaints is based on its authority to investigate "unfair or deceptive trade practices." Most privacy statutes incorporate responsibilities typically described as "Fair Information Practices." How do these two regimes compare? If the FTC had authority to enforce Fair Information Practices what additional steps could it take?

6. *The FTC Investigation of Microsoft Passport.* Microsoft .NET Passport is one of a growing number of an online identification and authentication services. Internet users submit personal information, such as e-mail addresses, gender, age, photographs, hobbies, and favorite books. Passport then allows consumers to use a single username and password to access multiple web sites. The goal of Passport is to serve as a universal sign-on service, eliminating the need to sign-on to each web site separately. A related service,

---

[54] Available at <*http://www.ftc.gov/opa/2002/01/elililly.htm*>.

Wallet, permits users to submit credit card and billing information in order to make purchases at multiple web sites without having to reenter the information on each web site. The FTC initiated an investigation of the Passport services following a July 2001 complaint from a coalition of consumer groups led by the Electronic Privacy Information Center. The groups alleged that representations made by Microsoft regarding Passport and associated services violated §5 of the FTC Act. In its privacy policy, Microsoft had promised that ".NET Passport is protected by powerful online security technology and a strict privacy policy." Further, Microsoft stated: "Your .NET Passport information is stored on secure .NET Passport servers that are protected in controlled facilities." Microsoft also stated that the personally identifiable information it gathered about users would be limited to the types of information listed in its privacy policy. In the petition to the FTC, the privacy groups raised questions about the collection, use, and disclosure of personal information that Passport would make possible, and asserted that Microsoft's representations about the security of the system were both unfair and deceptive.

On August 8, 2002, the FTC found that Microsoft had violated §5 of the FTC Act and announced a proposed settlement with the company. *See In the Matter of Microsoft Corp.,* No. 012-3240. The Commission found that Microsoft falsely represented that (1) it employs reasonable and appropriate measures under the circumstances to maintain and protect the privacy and confidentiality of consumers' personal information collected through its Passport and Wallet services; (2) purchases made with Passport Wallet are generally safer or more secure than purchases made at the same site without Passport Wallet when, in fact, most consumers received identical security at those sites regardless of whether they used Passport Wallet to complete their transactions; (3) Passport did not collect any personally identifiable information other than that described in its privacy policy when, in fact, Passport collected and held, for a limited time, a personally identifiable sign-in history for each user; and (4) the Kids Passport program provided parents control over what information participating web sites could collect from their children.

Under the terms of the proposed consent order, Microsoft may not make any misrepresentations, expressly or by implication, of any of its information practices. Microsoft is further obligated to establish a "comprehensive information security program," and conduct an annual audit to assess the security practices. Microsoft is also required to make available to the FTC for a period of five years all documents relating to security practices as well as compliance with the orders. The order remains in place for twenty years.

In commenting on the proposed settlement, EPIC and the other privacy organizations said that further steps may be necessary. They suggested that the FTC (1) modify the order to require Microsoft to make its biannual report available to the public, provide Passport account holders with their entire profile, and notify consumers of Microsoft XP or other Microsoft products that Passport isn't needed to enter the Internet; (2) take a look at other authentication systems in development and set a minimum standard for privacy protection for deployed and developed systems; (3) ensure Microsoft is complying with the EU-U.S. safe harbor arrangement; and (4) strengthen the security program by requiring Microsoft to limit the Passport system, accept anonymous authentication, regularly destroy data, and notify the agency whenever a security breach caused an unauthorized transfer of personal information.

The FTC Order adopts a broad definition of "personally identifiable information" that includes not only name, address, e-mail address, phone number, and Social Security, but also a persistent identifier, such as a "cookie," as well as any information that is combined with any of the previous categories. What types of business practices would such a definition of personally identifiable information regulate?

7. ***The FTC as an Enforcer of Privacy: An Assessment.*** Consider Paul Schwartz on the effectiveness of the FTC as an enforcer of privacy policies:

> . . . The FTC's action against GeoCities is a good indication of the limited nature of the present legal regime. The first of the two deceptive practices alleged by the FTC against GeoCities was GeoCities's misrepresentation of a limited use of the data that it collected. Despite its promise, GeoCities engaged in an all-too-classic case of unrestricted utilization of personal data without an individual's knowledge or permission.
>
> The second deceptive practice GeoCities engaged in was to allow third parties on its Web site to maintain and utilize personal data collected from children, despite its promises otherwise. This threat to the privacy of a discrete group, children, raises a separate set of issues. GeoCities turned over potentially sensitive information about children to private individuals whom it had not screened in any meaningful fashion and without any effective restrictions on their use of these data. This practice largely mirrors the first deceptive practice, but extends it to a group that is especially vulnerable.
>
> Due in part to the timing of its initial public offering, GeoCities was willing to settle with the FTC and promised to make significant changes in its privacy practices. Nevertheless, similar behavior elsewhere on the Web is unaffected by this government action. Indeed, the FTC's ability to engage in these kinds of investigations is itself limited. This agency was able to obtain jurisdiction in this case only because GeoCities' false representations regarding its privacy practices constituted "deceptive acts or practices" under the Federal Trade Commission Act. Web sites that make no promises about privacy, therefore, are not only unaffected by the GeoCities consent order, but also are likely to fall outside the FTC's jurisdiction.
>
> Another statutory limit exists on the FTC's jurisdiction. The FTC's enabling act restricts its powers to situations where an unfair act or practice "causes or is likely to cause substantial injury to consumers which is not reasonably avoidable by consumers themselves and not outweighed by countervailing benefits to consumers or to competition." As this statutory language indicates, the FTC may be open to challenges to its power to stop activities that it claims to be unfair or deceptive trade practices. Due to the difficulty in monetizing many privacy violations and other problems in fulfilling this jurisdictional calculus, the FTC may face objections should it take an aggressive role in policing information privacy in cyberspace with no more authorization than the general grant found in its enabling statute. It also faces serious resource constraints because Internet pri-

vacy policy work is only a small part of its overall activities, even concerning cyberspace. The FTC's privacy protection activities already are dwarfed by its more aggressive investigations of fraud and deceptive marketing practices on the Internet. . . .[55]

Consider Steven Hetcher's explanation of the FTC's behavior:

. . . [P]rivacy policies have been the FTC's primary response to the problem of invasion of informational privacy by websites. . . . [T]he Agency has been relatively successful in its effort to bring an increase in the percentage of sites that offer privacy policies. One might expect that privacy advocates would have been cheering the FTC along in its efforts. However, this has not been the case. Instead, privacy advocates have criticized the FTC for focusing too much attention on privacy policies. Leading privacy advocates have instead advocated for a statute that would function to strictly control entities that collect and use data, as does the European Union's Privacy Directive.

By the Agency's lights, its promotion of the fair practice principles should satisfy privacy advocates, as the fair information practice principles are derived from pre-existing norms of the advocacy community. Public interest advocates contend to the contrary, however, that privacy policies ill serve their aspirational privacy norms. They argue that privacy policies are typically not read by website users. They are written in legalese such that even if people read them, they will not understand them. Hence, they do not provide notice and thus cannot lead to consent. In addition, there is evidence that many sites do not adhere to their own policies. The policies are subject to change when companies merge, such that one company's policy is likely to go unheeded. Finally, very few privacy policies guarantee security or enforcement. Thus, the provision of a privacy policy by a website does not automatically promote the fair practice principles.

Despite these problems, the FTC has strongly endorsed privacy policies. This raises a puzzle as to why the Agency should do so, given the severe criticism privacy policies have received. Why, for instance, is the FTC not coming out in support of the creation of a new agency to oversee privacy protection? . . .

There is a public choice answer as to why the Agency has promoted privacy policies, despite their problems (and despite the fact that they do not appear to promote the interests of any industry groups whose favor the FTC might be seeking). It is through privacy policies that the FTC is gaining jurisdiction over the commercial Internet. Jurisdiction is power. In other words, the FTC acts as if it has a plan to migrate its activities to the Internet, and privacy policies have been at the core of this plan. Following is the reason why the FTC has been able to obtain a more secure jurisdictional foothold by means of privacy policies. . . .[56]

---

[55] Paul M. Schwartz, *Privacy and Democracy in Cyberspace*, 52 Vand. L. Rev. 1609, 1637-1638 (1999). For a discussion of the developing privacy jurisprudence under the FTC Act, see Jeff Sovern, *Protecting Privacy with Deceptive Trade Practices Legislation*, 69 Fordham L. Rev. 1305 (2001).

[56] Steven Hetcher, *The FTC as Internet Privacy Norm Entrepreneur*, 53 Vand. L. Rev. 2041 (2000). *See also* Steven Hetcher, *Changing the Social Meaning of Privacy in Cyberspace*, 15 Harv. J. L. & Tech. 149 (2001); Steven A. Hetcher, *Norm Proselytizers Create a Privacy Entitlement in Cyberspace*, 16 Berkeley Tech. L.J. 877 (2001).

In Re Toysmart.com, LLC

(Bankr. D. Mass. 2000)

[Toysmart.com, an Internet toy retailer, was one of the victims of the rash of dot-com bankruptcies in 2000. One of Toysmart's largest assets was its database of personal information—a customer list of over 200,000 individuals with addresses, names and ages of children, purchasing information, and a toy wish list. Toysmart was a member of TRUSTe, an e-commerce industry privacy protection organization that establishes guidelines for privacy policies in return for the right to display TRUSTe's privacy seal. Toysmart agreed to TRUSTe's guidelines and displayed the TRUSTe seal.

In its privacy policy, Toysmart promised:

> At toysmart.com, we take great pride in our relationships with our customers and pledge to maintain your privacy while visiting our site. Personal information voluntarily submitted by visitors to our site, such as name, address, billing information and shopping preferences, is never shared with a third party. All information obtained by toysmart.com is used only to personalize your experience online. This information is received via the following areas of our site: My toysmart and the Gift Center. When you place additional orders, our site will update your order history, which you can view in My toysmart. If you sign up for the gift registry, information you submit will be added to your personal profile. Other than these two instances, the information that you provide us is not supplemented in any way.

To pay back creditors, Toysmart attempted to sell its database of personal information. The FTC filed a complaint, stating:

> 16. Section 5(a) of the FTC Act, 15 U.S.C. §45(a), prohibits "unfair or deceptive acts or practices in or affecting commerce."
>
> 17. From at least September 1999 to the present, defendant Toysmart, directly or through its employees and agents, in connection with its collection of personal consumer information, expressly and/or by implication, represented that it would "never" disclose, sell, or offer for sale customers' or registered members' personal information to third parties.
>
> 18. In truth and in fact, Toysmart has disclosed, sold, or offered for sale its customer lists and profiles. Therefore, the representation set forth in Paragraph 17 was, and is, a deceptive practice. . . .
>
> 19. Since at least May 1, 2000, through its dinosaur trivia contest, which was directed to children, Toysmart collected personal information from children that, in addition, it actually knew to be under the age of 13, without providing notice to parents or obtaining verifiable parental consent prior to the collection of such personal information. The information collected included name, email address, and age.
>
> 20. The practice set forth in Paragraph 19 did not fall within the exception to prior parental consent of 16 C.F.R. §312.5(c)(2) and therefore was, and is, a violation of the Children's Online Privacy Protection Act, 15 U.S.C. §6503 and 16 C.F.R. §§312.3-312.5. . . .
>
> 21. Toysmart's conduct, as set forth in Paragraphs 6-21 will injure consumers throughout the United States by invading their privacy.
>
> 22. Absent injunctive relief by this Court, the defendant is likely to injure consumers and harm the public interest. . . .

The FTC proposed a settlement, restricting how Toysmart could sell its database. The FTC's commissioners approved the settlement 3-2. The settlement is excerpted below, along with one dissent.]

Stipulation and Order Establishing Conditions
on Sale of Customer Information

This Stipulation is entered into this twentieth day of July, 2000, by and between, Toysmart.com, LLC, debtor and debtor-in-possession ("Debtor" or "Toysmart"), and the Federal Trade Commission ("FTC"). . . .

WHEREAS, from at least September 1999 to July 2000, the Debtor's Web site included a privacy statement ("Privacy Statement") stating that (1) "Personal information voluntarily submitted by visitors to our site, such as name, address, billing information and shopping preferences, is never shared with a third party. All information obtained by toysmart.com is used only to personalize your experience online," and (2) "When you register with toysmart.com, you can rest assured that your information will never be shared with a third party;"

WHEREAS, on or about May 22, 2000, the Debtor announced that it had ceased operations and began to offer for sale customer information through advertisements appearing in the Wall Street Journal and the Boston Globe and through its Web site. . . .

NOW THEREFORE, in an effort to resolve this matter without further cost or delay, the parties hereby agree, subject only to the approval of this Court, as follows:

For the purposes of this Agreement, the following definitions shall apply:

"Qualified Buyer" shall mean an entity that (1) concentrates its business in the family commerce market, involving the areas of education, toys, learning, home and/or instruction, including commerce, content, product and services, and (2) expressly agrees to be Toysmart's successor-in-interest as to the Customer Information, and expressly agrees to the obligations set forth in Paragraphs 2, 3 and 4, below. Nothing herein, however, shall create any liability for such Qualified Buyer as a result of any actions or omissions by the Debtor, as the Customer Information is to be sold free and clear of all liens, claims and encumbrances, except for the Qualified Buyer's obligations under the Privacy Statement.

"Customer Information" shall mean information of or relating to consumers collected by the Debtor, including, but not limited to, name, address, billing information, shopping preferences, order history, gift registry selection, family profile information about consumers' children, such as name, gender, birthday, and toy interests.

"Third Party" shall mean any individual, firm, or organization other than the Qualified Buyer and its successors, except to the extent that disclosure of Customer Information to such an individual, firm, or organization is necessary to maintain the technical functioning of the Toysmart Web site or customer databases, or to fulfill a consumer's request. "Third Party" includes any affiliates of the Qualified Buyer. . . .

The Debtor shall only assign or sell its Customer Information as part of the sale of its Goodwill and only to a Qualified Buyer approved by the Bankruptcy

Court. In the process of approving any sale of the Customer Information, the Bankruptcy Court shall require that the Qualified Buyer agree to and comply with the terms of this Stipulation.

The Qualified Buyer shall treat Customer Information in accordance with the terms of the Privacy Statement and shall be responsible for any violation by it following the date of purchase. Among other things, the Qualified Buyer shall use Customer Information only to fulfill customer orders and to personalize customers' experience on the Web site, and shall not disclose, sell or transfer Customer Information to any Third Party.

If the Qualified Buyer materially changes the Privacy Statement, prior notice will be posted on the Web site. Any such material change in policy shall apply only to information collected following the change in policy. The Customer Information shall be governed by the Privacy Statement, unless the consumer provides affirmative consent ("opt-in") to the previously collected information being governed by the new policy.

In the event that an order is not entered on or before July 31, 2001, approving the sale of the Customer Information to a Qualified Buyer or approving a plan of reorganization, the Debtor shall, on or before August 31, 2001, delete or destroy all Customer Information in its possession, custody or control, and provide written confirmation to the FTC, sworn to under penalty of perjury, that all such Customer Information has been deleted or destroyed. Pending approval of any sale of the Customer Information to a Qualified Buyer or of a plan of reorganization, the Debtor shall handle Customer Information in accordance with the Privacy Statement.

This Stipulation and Order, after approval by the Bankruptcy Court, shall be attached to and incorporated in full into the terms of any plan of liquidation or reorganization that is ultimately approved in this bankruptcy case. . . .

Dissenting Statement of Commissioner Orson Swindle

Defendant Toysmart.com, Inc. ("Toysmart") represented that it would never disclose, sell, or offer to sell the personal information of its customers to a third party. When faced with severe financial difficulties, however, Toysmart solicited bids for its customer lists, which include or reflect the personal information of its customers. During the bidding process, Toysmart's creditors filed a petition for involuntary bankruptcy. Toysmart has completed the bidding process but not yet sold its customer lists.

The Commission filed a Section 13(b) complaint alleging that Toysmart's representation that it would never disclose, sell, or offer to sell the personal information of its customers was false because it had solicited bids for its customer lists. The Commission sought an injunction against the sale of the customer lists and a declaration that "Toysmart's transfer of [its customer lists] to any third party [would] be a violation of the FTC Act."

To resolve the allegations in the complaint, the Commission has agreed to allow Toysmart's customer lists to be sold to a third party, essentially so long as the buyer is in a similar line of business and agrees to abide by Toysmart's privacy policies.

I agree that a sale to a third party under the terms of the Bankruptcy Order would be a substantial improvement over the sale that likely would have occurred without Commission action. Nevertheless, I do not think that the Commission should allow the sale. If we really believe that consumers attach great value to the privacy of their personal information and that consumers should be able to limit access to such information through private agreements with businesses, we should compel businesses to honor the promises they make to consumers to gain access to this information. Toysmart promised its customers that their personal information would *never* be sold to a third party, but the Bankruptcy Order in fact would allow a sale to a third party. In my view, such a sale should not be permitted because "never" really means never.[57]

I dissent.

NOTES & QUESTIONS

1. Is this settlement adequate to resolve the problems raised by the FTC in its complaint?
2. *Postscript.* The settlement attracted the support of Toysmart's creditors, since it would allow the sale of the database to certain purchasers, and hence could be used to pay back the creditors. However, in August 2000, Judge Carol Kenner of the U.S. Bankruptcy Court rejected the settlement because there were currently no offers on the table to buy the database and it would hurt the creditors to restrict the sale to certain types of purchasers without first having a potential buyer. In February 2001, Judge Kenner agreed to let Toysmart sell its customer database to Disney, the primary shareholder, for $50,000. Disney agreed, as part of the deal, to destroy the list.
3. *Bankruptcy and Privacy.* When dot-coms file for bankruptcy, one of their greatest assets is their personal information database.[58] The Toysmart bankruptcy led Amazon.com, the Interent's largest retailer, to change its privacy policy.

   Amazon.com collects a significant amount of personal information from its customers. Among other things, it has records of all the books, videos, CDs, electronics, and other merchandise a customer has purchased. Prior to the Toysmart case, Amazon's privacy policy provided:

   > Amazon.com does not sell, trade, or rent your personal information to others. We may choose to do so in the future with trustworthy third parties, but you can tell us not to by sending a blank e-mail message to never@amazon.com. . . .

   In its new policy, Amazon.com states:

---

[57] If Toysmart had obtained the consent of its customers to a sale of the customer lists to a buyer that met the specific conditions spelled out in the Bankruptcy Order, I would have had no objection to the sale.

[58] For more information about the legal implications of dot-com bankruptcies and the selling of consumer databases, see Andrew B. Buxbaum, Louis A. Curcio, Note, *When You Can't Sell to Your Customers, Try Selling Your Customers (But Not Under the Bankruptcy Code)*, 8 Am. Bankr. Inst. L. Rev. 395 (2000); Richard A. Beckmann, Comment, *Privacy Policies and Empty Promises: Closing the "Toysmart Loophole,"* 62 U. Pitt. L. Rev. 765 (2001).

> Information about our customers is an important part of our business, and we are not in the business of selling it to others. We share customer information only with the subsidiaries Amazon.com, Inc., controls and as described below. . . .
>
> As we continue to develop our business, we might sell or buy stores or assets. In such transactions, customer information generally is one of the transferred business assets. Also, in the unlikely event that Amazon.com, Inc., or substantially all of its assets are acquired, customer information will of course be one of the transferred assets. . . .

As a result of Amazon.com's change in policy, the Electronic Privacy Information Center (EPIC) and other privacy organizations withdrew their affiliations with Amazon.com. One of the criticisms of the new policy was that it did not provide even an opt-out right.

Suppose Amazon.com went bankrupt and decided to sell all of its customer data. Can it sell data supplied by consumers under the old policy? Can the new policy apply retroactively?

4. ***Bankruptcy: Property Rights Versus Contract Rights.*** Edward Janger proposes that a property rights regime (as opposed to the contractual rights of a privacy policy) will best protect the privacy of personal data when companies possessing such data go bankrupt:

> Property rules are viewed as reflecting undivided entitlements. They allocate, as Carol Rose puts it, the "whole meatball" to the "owner." Liability rules, by contrast are viewed as dividing an entitlement between two parties. One party holds the right, but the other party is given the option to take the right and compensate the right holder for the deprivation (to breach and pay damages). . . .
>
> Propertization has some crucial benefits, but it also has some serious costs. Both the bankruptcy and non-bankruptcy treatment of privacy policies turn on whether a privacy policy creates a right enforceable only through civil damages, or a right with the status of property. If bankruptcy courts treat privacy policies solely as contract obligations [liability rule], the debtor will be free to breach (or reject) the contract in bankruptcy. Any damage claim will be treated as a prepetition claim, paid, if at all, at a significant discount. Consumer expectations (contractual or otherwise) of privacy are likely to be defeated. By contrast, if personal information is deemed property subject to an encumbrance, then the property interest must be respected, or to use the bankruptcy term, "adequately protected."[59]

In other words, Janger contends that giving individuals property rights in their personal data will provide more protection than giving individuals contract rights in the event a company goes bankrupt. Janger further argues that property rights alone will not be sufficient. Property rights must be "muddy" rather than "crystalline":

> . . . A crystalline rule places all of the relevant rights firmly in the hand of the entitlement holder or "owner." A muddier standard leaves the right subject to challenge by a competing claimant. Crystalline rules situate de-

---

[59] Edward J. Janger, *Muddy Property: Generating and Protecting Information Privacy Norms in Bankruptcy*, 44 William & Mary L. Rev. (forthcoming 2002).

cisionmaking and norm-generating authority in either the legislature or the market. Muddy rules lead to decisions made and legal norms articulated by judges. . . .

. . . [M]uddy standards force parties ex ante to recognize that they might have to justify their contractual terms and negotiating behavior ex post. This attribute of muddy rules operates to enforce behavioral norms in ways that crystalline rules do not. Efforts to resolve norm-based disputes force disclosure of information related to the norm. This norm-based information forcing effect has both public and private implications. Muddy rules may improve the contracting behavior of parties, but muddy rules also serve a more public purpose. Muddy rules force information into the legal system about transactions. They allow judges, and the judiciary, to develop rules incrementally, through common law reasoning, and inform legislative decisionmaking by placing disputes on the record. But muddiness alone is not enough. The benefits of the muddy liability rule may evaporate entirely when a debtor goes bankrupt. These behavior regulating and information forcing effects of muddy rules are maximized only when the muddy rule is given the status of property.[60]

5. ***State Deceptive Trade Practices Acts.*** In addition to the FTC Act, which is enforced exclusively by the FTC, every state has some form of deceptive trade practices act of its own. Many of these statutes not only enable a state attorney general to bring actions but also provide a private cause of action to consumers. Several of these laws have provisions for statutory minimum damages, punitive damages, and attorneys' fees. *See, e.g.,* Cal. Civ. Code § 1780(a)(4) (punitive damages); Conn. Gen. Stat. § 42-110g(a) (punitive damages); Mich. Comp. Laws § 445.911(2) (minimum damages); N.Y. Gen. Bus. Law § 349(h) (minimum damages). In interpreting these state laws, many state courts have been heavily influenced by FTC Act jurisprudence. However, as Jeff Sovern notes, many states "have been more generous to consumers than has the FTC" and "even if the FTC concludes that practices pass muster under the FTC Act, it is still at least theoretically possible for a state to find the practices deceptive under their own legislation." Thus, Sovern concludes, "information practices that are currently in widespread use may indeed violate state little FTC Acts. Marketers should think carefully about whether they wish to alter their practices."[61]

5. STATUTORY REGULATION OF PRIVATE SECTOR RECORDS

In a series of statutes, Congress has regulated certain forms of private sector recordkeeping. Congress's approach is best described as sectoral, as each statute is narrowly tailored to particular types of businesses and services. These statutes embody the Fair Information Practices originally developed by HEW and incorporated into the Privacy Act. However, not all statutes embody all of the Fair Information Practices. As you study each statute, examine which of the Fair Information Practices are required by each statute and which are not.[62]

---

[60] *Id.*

[61] Jeff Sovern, *Protecting Privacy with Deceptive Trade Practices Legislation,* 69 Fordham L. Rev. 1305, 1352-1353, 1357 (2001).

[62] *See generally* Marc Rotenberg, *The Privacy Law Sourcebook* (EPIC 2002).

(a) Video Privacy Protection Act

Incensed when a reporter obtained Supreme Court Justice Nominee Robert Bork's video cassette rental data, Congress passed the Video Privacy Protection Act (VPPA) of 1988, Pub. L. No. 100-618, which has become known as the "Bork Bill."

Restrictions on Disclosure. The VPPA prohibits video tape service providers from knowingly disclosing personal information, such as titles of video cassettes rented or purchased, without the individual's written consent. The VPPA creates a private cause of action when a video tape service provider "knowingly discloses . . . personally identifiable information concerning any consumer of such provider." 18 U.S.C §2710(b)(1).

Destruction of Records. The VPPA requires that records of personal information be destroyed as soon as practicable. §2710(e).

Exceptions. The VPPA contains several exceptions, permitting video tape providers to disclose "to any person if the disclosure is incident to the ordinary course of business of the video tape service provider." §2710(b)(2)(E).

The statute provides that "the subject matter of such materials may be disclosed if the disclosure is for the exclusive use of marketing goods and services directly to the consumer." §2710(b)(2)(D)(ii). Video tape service providers can disclose the names and addresses of consumers if the consumer has been given the right to opt out, and the disclosure does not identify information about the videos the consumer rents. §2710(b)(2)(D).

The statute also permits disclosure to the consumer, §2710(b)(2)(A); disclosure with the informed written consent of the consumer, §2710(b)(2)(B); disclosure to a law enforcement agency pursuant to a warrant or subpoena, §2710(b)(2)(C); and disclosure for civil discovery if there is notice and an opportunity to object, §2710(b)(2).

Preemption. VPPA does not preempt state law claims. §2710(f).

Enforcement. The VPPA's private right of action permits recovery of actual damages and provides for liquidated damages in the amount of $2,500. The Act also authorizes recovery for punitive damages, attorneys' fees, and enables equitable and injunctive relief. §2710(c). The VPPA also includes a statutory exclusionary rule that prevents the admission into evidence of any information obtained in violation of the statute. §2710(d).

DIRKES V. BOROUGH OF RUNNEMEDE

936 F. Supp. 235 (D.N.J. 1996)

BROTMAN, J. Presently before this Court is a motion for summary judgment brought by the Borough of Runnemede, the Borough of Runnemede Police Department, and Lieutenant Emil Busko. . . .

The present action arises from the investigation of and disciplinary action taken against Plaintiff Chester Dirkes, formerly an officer with the Department. On May 24, 1990, in the course of an investigation into a citizen's death, Plaintiff Dirkes allegedly removed pornographic magazines and videotapes from the decedent's apartment. Based on this allegation, the Camden County Grand Jury returned a one count indictment for misconduct in office against him on May 29, 1991. As a result of the indictment, on May 30, 1991, the Department issued a disciplinary notice to Plaintiff Dirkes and suspended him without pay and benefits. Plaintiff Dirkes' trial commenced on April 20, 1992 and on May 5, 1992, he was acquitted of the sole charge against him.

Following the acquittal, the Borough retained special counsel and resumed its internal affairs investigation against Plaintiff Dirkes. The Department assigned Lt. Busko to investigate the matter. On or about May 7, 1992, Lt. Busko obtained the names and rental dates of certain pornographic videotapes previously rented by Plaintiff Dirkes and his wife, co-plaintiff Marie Dirkes. Lt. Busko received this information from an employee of Videos To Go, the store from which Plaintiffs apparently regularly rent or buy video tapes for their private use. In seeking to obtain this information, Lt. Busko failed to secure a warrant, a subpoena or a court order. He simply requested and received the information from an employee of Videos To Go without question.

The internal affairs memorandum listing the video tape rental information was distributed to the Borough's special counsel, who in turn distributed it in connection with Plaintiff Dirkes' disciplinary hearing and in a proceeding before the Superior Court of New Jersey, Camden County.

On or about March 19, 1993, Plaintiffs filed their complaint with this Court alleging that Defendants violated the provisions of the Videotape Privacy Protection Act of 1988, as codified at 18 U.S.C. § 2710 (the "Act"), as well as Plaintiffs' common law privacy rights. . . . Subsequently, the video information was received into evidence at Plaintiff Dirkes' disciplinary hearing. As a result of that hearing, the Department terminated Plaintiff Dirkes from his employment. . . .

Defendants have moved for summary judgment on Count I of Plaintiffs' complaint, which asserts a violation of the Videotape Privacy Protection Act. *See* 18 U.S.C. § 2710. Congress enacted the Videotape Privacy Protection Act "to protect [certain personal information of an individual who rents video materials] from disclosure." S. Rep. No. 100-599, 100th Cong., 2d Sess. at 16 (1988). The impetus for enacting the measure arose as a result of Judge Robert Bork's 1987 Supreme Court nomination battle, during which a Washington, D.C. newspaper obtained a list of 146 video tapes the Bork family had previously rented from their neighborhood store. Members of the Senate Judiciary Committee were outraged by the invasion into the Bork family's privacy. Both houses of Congress acted quickly to outlaw certain disclosures of such clearly private information, resulting in the Videotape Privacy Protection Act. . . .

To address the merits of the Defendants' summary judgment motion, the Court must make two inquiries. Initially, the Court must determine whether the Plaintiffs are entitled to bring an action under the Act. If the Plaintiffs are so entitled, the Court must then determine whether the Plaintiffs have brought suit against the correct defendants.

Section 2710(c) of the Act provides broadly that "[a]ny person aggrieved by any act of a person in violation of [§2710] may bring a civil action" in an appropriate U.S. District Court. The Act can be violated in one or all of three ways. First, a "video tape service provider" violates §2710(b) of the Act by disclosing "personally identifiable information" regarding a customer unless the person to whom the disclosure is made or the disclosure itself falls into one of six categories. 18 U.S.C. §2710(b). Second, §2710(d) of the Act is violated when personally identifiable information obtained in any manner other than as narrowly provided by the Act is "received in evidence" in almost any adversarial proceeding. 18 U.S.C. §2710(d). Third, a person subject to the Act violates §2710(e) by failing to timely destroy a customer's personally identifiable information. 18 U.S.C. §2710(e). Upon finding any of these violations, a court may, but need not, award a range of relief including actual damages, punitive damages, attorneys' fees, or "such other . . . equitable relief as the Court may determine to be appropriate." 18 U.S.C. §2710(c).

Because it is undisputed that subsections (b) and (d) have been violated in the instant matter, §2710(c) authorizes the Plaintiffs to bring a suit. Videos to Go, the video tape service provider in this matter, violated subsection (b) of the Act by disclosing Plaintiffs' video rental information to Lt. Busko. It is undisputed that this disclosure does not fall into one of the six permissible disclosure exceptions delineated in subsection (b)(2) of the Act. A second violation of the Act occurred when Plaintiffs' personally identifiable information was received into evidence at Plaintiff Dirkes' disciplinary hearing. 18 U.S.C. §2710(d).

Having found that there have been two violations of the Act, the Court must now determine whether Lt. Busko, the Department, or the Borough are proper defendants. As noted earlier, subsection (c) provides that "[a]ny person aggrieved by any act of a person in violation of [§2710] may bring a civil action." 18 U.S.C. §2710(c). While it broadly provides relief for violations of §2710, this subsection does not delineate those parties against whom an action may be instituted. 18 U.S.C. §2710(c). In support of its current summary judgment motion, the Defendants argue collectively that they can not be held liable under the Act because their actions did not violate the Act. For example, only the actions of a video tape service provider can cause a violation of §2710(b). Because the Defendants are not video tape service providers as that term is defined under the Act, they argue that they can not be held responsible under the Act.

This Court must reject the Defendants' narrow reading of the statute. Again, the plain language of the Act does not delineate those parties against whom an action under this Act may be maintained. Taking the Defendants' argument to its logical extension, this omission would prevent plaintiffs from bringing a cause of action against anyone. Such an absurd result must be rejected. The clear intent of the Act is to prevent the disclosure of private information. As established by its legislative history, the Act enables consumers "to maintain control over personal information divulged and generated in exchange for receiving services from video tape service providers." S. Rep. No. 100-599, at 8 (1988). This purpose is furthered by allowing parties, like these Plaintiffs, to bring suit against those individuals who have come to possess (and who could disseminate) the private information in flagrant violation of the purposes of the Act. While it need not identify all potential categories of defendants in this opinion, the Court finds that those parties who are in possession of personally identifiable information as a direct result of an improper release of such information are subject to suit under the Act. Because it is undisputed that Lt. Busko, the Department, and the Borough all possess the information as a direct result of a violation of the Act, each is a proper defendant.

Furthermore, the Supreme Court in *Local 28 of Sheet Metal Workers v. E.E.O.C.*, 478 U.S. 421 (1986), reinforced the principle that remedial statutes should be construed broadly. *Local 28* involved a violation of Title VII, a statute designed to address employment discrimination. Upon examining the legislative history of Title VII, the Court determined that "Congress reaffirmed the breadth of the [district] court's remedial powers under §706(g) by adding language authorizing courts to order 'any other equitable relief as the court deems appropriate.' " This added language is identical to that used in subsection (c)(2)(D) of the Videotape Privacy Protection Act. 18 U.S.C. §2710(c). It is evident throughout the *Local 28* opinion that the Supreme Court intended to give effect to the legislators' intent to provide as broad remedial powers as possible to the district courts to eliminate the effects of illegal discrimination. This Court will exercise the same broad powers to give effect to the intent of Videotape Privacy Protection Act's U.S. Senate sponsors. The importance of maintaining the privacy of an individual's personally identifiable information mandates that people who obtain such information from a violation of the Act be held as proper defendants to prevent the further disclosure of the information. . . .

For the reasons set forth above, the Court will deny Defendants' motion for summary judgment. . . .

NOTES & QUESTIONS

1. In *Video Software Dealers Association v. Oklahoma City*, 1998 U.S. Dist. LEXIS 22095 (W.D. Okla. Dec. 18, 1998), the Oklahoma City police department sought to remove the award-winning movie, *The Tin Drum*, from public access because of its view that it constituted child pornography under a state statute. The police requested from Blockbuster Video and Southwest Video employees the names and addresses of customers who had rented *The Tin Drum*. As discussed above, the VPPA states that information from video tape service providers may be disclosed to the government only pursuant to a "warrant . . . an equivalent state warrant, a grand jury subpoena, or a court order." 18 U.S.C. §2710(b)(2)(C). The police officers were unaware of the VPPA, never received training about the VPPA, and therefore, no warrant or court order was issued to the video stores. The plaintiffs contended that the police violated the VPPA. Nevertheless, the police contended that they were not liable under VPPA because they did not disclose information and that the VPPA prohibits disclosures by video tape service providers, not the employees of such providers. The Court, following *Dirkes*, rejected the argument of the police department:

The primary concern of the Act is safeguarding the confidentiality of customers. That it is applicable to law enforcement personnel is apparent from the Act's inclusion of specific prerequisites which must be satisfied before confidential information can be furnished to such personnel. The court agrees with the decision of the court in *Dirkes* as well as the underlying rationale. The Act's requirements were not followed in this case, and defendants are proper parties....

(b) Cable Communications Policy Act

In 1984, Congress passed the Cable Communications Policy Act (CCPA or "Cable Act"), Pub. L. No. 98-549. The Act applies to cable operators and service providers. 47 U.S.C. § 551(a)(1).

Notice. The Cable Act requires cable service providers to notify subscribers (in a written privacy policy) of the nature of personal information collected, the uses of the information, how long the information will be maintained, what types of disclosures will be made, the types of persons to whom the disclosure may be made, and how people can access this information about themselves. § 551(a)(1). The notice must occur when the cable subscriber enters into an agreement with the cable operator and at least once every year afterwards.

Limitations on Data Collection. Cable operators "shall not use the cable system to collect personally identifiable information concerning any subscriber without the prior written or electronic consent of the subscriber concerned." § 551(b)(1).

Limitations on Data Disclosure. Cable operators cannot disclose personally identifiable information about any subscriber without the subscriber's consent:

> [A] cable operator shall not disclose personally identifiable information concerning any subscriber without the prior written or electronic consent of the subscriber concerned and shall take such actions as are necessary to prevent unauthorized access to such information by a person other than the subscriber or cable operator. § 551(c)(1).

However, cable operators can disclose personal data under certain circumstances:

> (2) A cable operator may disclose such information if the disclosure is—
>
> > (A) necessary to render, or conduct a legitimate business activity related to, a cable service or other service provided by the cable operator to the subscriber;
> > (B) subject to subsection (h) of this section, made pursuant to a court order authorizing such disclosure, if the subscriber is notified of such order by the person to whom the order is directed; or
> > (C) a disclosure of the names and addresses of subscribers to any cable service or other service, if—
> > > (i) the cable operator has provided the subscriber the opportunity to prohibit or limit such disclosure, and

(ii) the disclosure does not reveal, directly or indirectly, the —
(I) extent of any viewing or other use by the subscriber of a cable service or other service provided by the cable operator, or
(II) the nature of any transaction made by the subscriber over the cable system of the cable operator. § 551(c)(2).

Access. Subscribers must have access to their personal data that is collected by cable operators:

A cable subscriber shall be provided access to all personally identifiable information regarding that subscriber which is collected and maintained by a cable operator. Such information shall be made available to the subscriber at reasonable times and at a convenient place designated by such cable operator. A cable subscriber shall be provided reasonable opportunity to correct any error in such information. § 551(d).

Data Destruction. Cable operators must destroy personal data if the information is no longer necessary for the purpose for which it was collected. § 551(e).

Government Access to Cable Information. Pursuant to § 551(h):

A governmental entity may obtain personally identifiable information concerning a cable subscriber pursuant to a court order only if, in the court proceeding relevant to such court order —

(1) such entity offers clear and convincing evidence that the subject of the information is reasonably suspected of engaging in criminal activity and that the information sought would be material evidence in the case; and
(2) the subject of the information is afforded the opportunity to appear and contest such entity's claim.

Note that a court order to obtain cable records requires "clear and convincing evidence," a standard higher than probable cause. There is no exclusionary rule for information obtained in violation of the Cable Act.

Enforcement. The Cable Act provides for a private cause of action and actual damages, with a minimum of $1,000 or $100 for each day of the violation, whichever is higher. The plaintiff can collect any actual damages that are more than the statutory minimum. Further, the Cable Act provides for punitive damages and attorneys' fees. § 551(f).

Cable Internet Service. Section 211 of the Patriot Act amends the Cable Act, 47 U.S.C. § 551(c)(2)(D), to provide disclosure to a government entity under federal wiretap law when the government seeks information from cable companies except that "such disclosure shall not include records revealing cable subscriber selection of video programming from a cable operator." This provision of the Patriot Act will not sunset.

(c) Telephone Consumer Protection Act

The Telephone Consumer Protections Act of 1991, Pub. L. No. 102-243, 47 U.S.C. § 227, permits individuals to sue a telemarketer in small claims court for actual loss or up to $500 (whichever is greater), for each call received after requesting to be placed on its "don't call" list:

> A person who has received more than one telephone call within any 12-month period by or on behalf of the same entity in violation of the regulations prescribed under this subsection may, if otherwise permitted by the laws or rules of a court of a State bring in an appropriate court of that State [an action for an injunction and to recover actual damages or $500 for each violation]. § 227(c)(5).

Telemarketers can offer as an affirmative defense that they established "reasonable practices and procedures to effectively prevent telephone solicitations in violation of the regulations prescribed under this subsection." § 227(c)(5). If telemarketer has acted "willfully or knowingly" then damages are trebled. § 227(c)(5).

The TCPA prohibits telemarketers from calling residences and using prerecorded messages without the consent of the called party. 47 U.S.C. § 227(b)(1)(B). The TCPA prohibits the use of a fax, computer, or other device to send an unsolicited advertisement to a fax machine. § 227(b)(1)(C). The Act also requires the FCC to promulgate rules to "protect residential telephone subscribers' privacy rights and to avoid receiving telephone solicitations to which they object." § 227(c)(1). In addition, the FCC is authorized to require that a "single national database" be established of a "list of telephone numbers of residential subscribers who object to receiving telephone solicitations." § 227(c)(3). It is within the discretion of the FCC to determine whether such a database is necessary or feasible.

States may initiate actions against telemarketers "engaging in a pattern or practice of telephone calls or other transmissions to residents of that State" in violation of the TCPA. § 227(f)(1).

In *Destination Ventures, Ltd. v. FCC*, 46 F.3d 54 (9th Cir. 1995), Destination Ventures challenged a provision of the TCPA banning unsolicited faxes that contained advertisements on First Amendment grounds. The ban on faxed advertisements was designed to prevent shifting advertising costs to consumers, who would be forced to undertake added costs of toner and paper to receive the ads. Destination Ventures contended that the ban was not a reasonable means of restricting cost-shifting:

> . . . Destination does not contest the government's substantial interest in preventing the shifting of advertising costs to consumers. Instead, Destination argues that the FCC failed to sustain its burden of demonstrating a "reasonable fit" between this interest and the ban on fax advertisements. Specifically, it contends that the government has not shown that faxes containing advertising are any more costly to consumers than other unsolicited faxes such as those containing political or "prank" messages. According to Destination, Congress may not single out advertisements for regulation when other types of unsolicited faxes produce the same cost-shifting.

We disagree. Because Congress's goal was to prevent the shifting of advertising costs, limiting its regulation to faxes containing advertising was justified. The ban is evenhanded, in that it applies to commercial solicitation by any organization, be it a multinational corporation or the Girl Scouts. . . .

Destination also argues that further proceedings are necessary to examine whether the government's solution is excessive in light of what it asserts is minimal cost-shifting caused by unsolicited advertising faxes. It acknowledges that recipients of faxes incur at least some costs. However, it suggests that such costs may be de minimis, and that computer technology is rendering these costs, as well as the problem of tying up fax machines, obsolete. . . .

Viewing the facts in the light most favorable to Destination, we conclude that Destination's own figures do not rebut the admitted facts that unsolicited fax advertisements shift significant advertising costs to consumers. The possibility of future technological advances allowing simultaneous transmission and eliminating the need for paper does not alter this conclusion. We look at the problem as it existed when Congress enacted the statute, rather than speculate upon what solutions may turn up in the future. Therefore, we hold that the ban on unsolicited fax advertisements meets the *Central Hudson* and *Fox* test for restrictions on commercial speech.

(d) Children's Online Privacy Protection Act

Passed in 1998, the Children's Online Privacy Protection Act (COPPA), Pub. L. No. 106-170, 15 U.S.C. §§ 6501-6506, regulates the collection and use of children's information by Internet web sites. The COPPA applies to "an operator of a website or online service directed to children, or any operator that has actual knowledge that it is collecting personal information from a child." 15 U.S.C. § 6502(a)(1). COPPA only applies to web sites that collect personal information from children under 13. § 6502(1).

Notice. Children's web sites must post privacy policies, describing "what information is collected from children by the operator, how the operator uses such information, and the operator's disclosure practices for such information." § 6502(b)(1)(A)(i).

Consent. Children's web sites must "obtain verifiable parental consent for the collection, use or disclosure of personal information from children." § 6502(b)(1)(A)(ii). Web sites cannot condition child's participation in a game or receipt of a prize on the disclosure of more personal information than is necessary to participate in that activity. § 6502(b)(1)(C). When information is not maintained in retrievable form, then consent is not required. § 6502(b)(2).

Right to Restrict Uses of Information. If parent requests it, the operator must provide to the parent a description of the "specific types of personal information collected," the right to "refuse to permit the operator's further use or maintenance in retrievable form, or future online collection, of personal information from that child," and the right to "obtain any personal information collected from the child." § 6502(b)(1)(B).

Enforcement. Violations of the COPPA are "treated as a violation of a rule defining an unfair or deceptive act or practice" under 15 U.S.C. § 57a(a)(1)(B). Thus, the FTC enforces the law and can impose fines. There is no private cause of action for violations of the COPPA.

States can bring civil actions for violations of the COPPA in the interests of its citizens to obtain injunctions and damages. § 6504.

Preemption. The COPPA preempts state law. § 6502(d).

Safe Harbor. If an operator follows self-regulatory guidelines issued by marketing or online industry groups that are approved by the FTC, then the COPPA requirements will be deemed satisfied. § 6503.

Should the COPPA be extended to apply to everyone, not just children? Should there be a private cause of action under the COPPA? Note that the COPPA only applies when a web site has "actual knowledge" that a user is under 13 or operates a web site specifically targeted to children. Is this too limiting? Would a rule dispensing with the "actual knowledge" requirement be feasible?[63]

Consider the following critique of the COPPA by Anita Allen:

> . . . The picture of parental involvement with children online post-COPPA is murky. It is unclear how COPPA has affected parents' and children's online behavior. Not all parents welcome the veto power COPPA confers. New power has meant new responsibility. The statute forces parents who would otherwise be content to give their children free rein over their computers to get involved in children's use of Internet sites that are geared toward children and collect personal information.
>
> COPPA is least onerous for parents whose children prefer non-commercial sites that do not collect personal information. COPPA is only moderately onerous for parents whose children are content to frequent the same one or two sites for periods of weeks or months at a time. The statute is most onerous for parents whose children are especially fond of children's sites and enjoy constantly exploring the Web to discover new sites. Dynamic young Web-surfers, who enjoy visiting numerous new sites, could easily aggravate parents with repeated requests that they provide "verifiable parental consent." . . .
>
> Parents may want their children to have free access to the World Wide Web because they believe the risks are minimal, or because they do not have the time or interest to deal with their children's Web activities. It is worth observing, though, that some parents may want their children to have free access to the Internet for moral or political reasons. They may believe children should have unfettered access to the Web and the public library equally, as a matter of free speech, free expression, and the right to know. They may want their children to develop judgment and taste by exposure to the best and worst of civilization in the relatively safe and private terrain of books and the Internet. COPPA's requirements are not specifically designed to deny children access to content, but, as civil libertarians observe, that is one of their effects. . . .

---

[63] For more information about COPPA, see Dorothy A. Hertzel, Note, *Don't Talk to Strangers: An Analysis of Government and Industry Efforts to Protect Child's Privacy Online*, 52 Fed. Comm. L.J. 429 (2000).

The Video Privacy Act does not prohibit anyone from authorizing release to third parties the titles of one's own prior video rentals. HIPAA does not prohibit anyone from telling someone else his or her medical history. . . . The Privacy Act does not prohibit one from revealing the criminal history contained on his or her own "rap sheet." . . . COPPA does, however, block voluntary disclosures of personal data. Prohibiting voluntary disclosures by children lacking parental consent in situations in which they and their parents may be indifferent to privacy losses and resentful of government intervention, COPPA is among the most paternalistic and authoritarian of the federal privacy statutes thus far. . . .

Privacy advocates are not so sure about COPPA, despite the characterization of its passage as a consumer privacy victory. On June 9, 2000, in testimony before the Commission on Child Online Protection, a body created by Congress in the COPPA, Electronic Privacy Information Center ("EPIC") general counsel, David L. Sobel, urged the rejection of age verification requirements as a condition of access to the Internet. Instead of blocking access, efforts should be made to help young people learn to safely and responsibly navigate the Internet. Mr. Sobel argued that a new regime for the collection of personal data in the name of "child online protection" would impose additional burdens on Internet users. At present, I am inclined to agree. Privacy protections that barely protect privacy, that seem morally arbitrary, that aggravate parents, frustrate children, and block access to information and communication may come at too high a cost. . . .[64]

(e) Federal Privacy Legislation: An Assessment

Consider the privacy statutes you have studied so far, such as federal wiretap law (including the ECPA), the Health Insurance Portability and Accountability Act, and the Right to Financial Privacy Act; the statutes governing public sector record systems, such as the Freedom of Information Act, the Privacy Act, the Computer Matching and Privacy Protection Act, and the Driver's Privacy Protection Act; and the statutes governing private sector record systems, such as the Video Privacy Protection Act, the Cable Communications Policy Act, the Telephone Consumer Protection Act, and the Children's Online Privacy Protection Act. Notice the sectoral approach — each statute addresses a particular industry or type of record or problem. Think about these laws together as a system of regulation for privacy. Do these laws adequately carry out the vision of the HEW Report's Code of Fair Information Practices? What, if anything, is missing from this system of regulation? What areas are not covered and should be?

Priscilla Regan contends that Congress has been slow to respond to privacy issues. According to Regan, those interests opposed to privacy protections (law enforcement entities, private industry, employers) were able to delay, block, and weaken Congress's statutory responses to privacy problems. Regan offers an explanation for this phenomenon:

---

[64] Anita L. Allen, *Minor Distractions: Children, Privacy and E-Commerce*, 38 Houston L. Rev. 751, 752-753, 768-769, 775-776 (2001).

. . . Generally, the importance of privacy is rooted in traditional liberal thinking — privacy inheres in the individual as an individual and is important to the individual for self-development or for the establishment of intimate or human relationships. Given that the philosophical justification for privacy rests largely on its importance to the individual as an individual, policy discussions about protecting privacy focus on the goal of protecting an individual value or interest. The result has been an emphasis on an atomistic individual and the legal protection of his or her rights.

But as illustrated in congressional attempts to protect privacy, defining privacy primarily in terms of its importance to the individual and in terms of an individual right has served as a weak basis for public policy. . . .

[P]rivacy's importance does not stop with the individual and . . . a recognition of the social importance of privacy will clear a path for more serious policy discourse about privacy and for the formulation of more effective public policy. . . .[65]

Also consider Paul Schwartz's assessment of privacy law:

. . . At present, however, no successful standards, legal or otherwise, exist for limiting the collection and utilization of personal data in cyberspace. The lack of appropriate and enforceable privacy norms poses a significant threat to democracy in the emerging Information Age. Indeed, information privacy concerns are the leading reason why individuals not on the Internet are choosing to stay off.

The stakes are enormous; the norms that we develop for personal data use on the Internet will play an essential role in shaping democracy in the Information Age. . . .

. . . [T]he traditional American legal approach to information privacy law emphasizes regulation of government use of personal data rather than private sector activities. From the earliest days of the Republic, American law has viewed the government as the entity whose data use raises the greatest threat to individual liberty. For example, federal and state constitutional protections seek to assure freedom from governmental interference for communications and for the press. This approach means that treatment of personal information in the private sector is often unaccompanied by the presence of basic legal protections. Yet, private enterprises now control more powerful resources of information technology than ever before. These organizations' information processing contributes to their power over our lives. As the Internet becomes more central to life in the United States, the weaknesses and illogic of this existing legal model for information privacy are heightened. . . .[66]

Joel Reidenberg critiques the ad hoc approach the United States has taken toward the protection of privacy:

The American legal system does not contain a comprehensive set of privacy rights or principles that collectively address the acquisition, storage, transmission, use and disclosure of personal information within the business community. The federal Constitution does not address privacy for information transactions wholly within the private sector and state constitutional provisions

---

[65] Priscilla M. Regan, *Legislating Privacy: Technology, Social Values, and Public Policy* (1995).
[66] Paul M. Schwartz, *Privacy and Democracy in Cyberspace*, 52 Vand. L. Rev. 1609, 1611, 1633-1634 (1999).

similarly do not afford rights for private transactions. Instead, legal protection is accorded exclusively through privacy rights created on an ad hoc basis by federal or state legislation or state common law rules. In addition, self-regulatory schemes have been adopted by some industries and by various companies. Although these schemes may offer privacy protection, they do not provide enforceable legal rights and do not seem to have permeated the vast majority of information processing entities.

In general, the aggregation of the federal and state rights provides targeted protection for individuals in answer to defined problems. This mosaic approach derives from the traditional American fear of government intervention in private activities and the reluctance to broadly regulate industry. The result of the mosaic is a rather haphazard and unsatisfactory response to each of the privacy concerns.[67]

Reidenberg notes that other countries, especially those in the European Union, have taken a more comprehensive approach toward protecting privacy. We will discuss the approaches of other countries further in Chapter 8.

Marc Rotenberg has a more positive outlook on United States privacy law. Rotenberg contends that Congress has been responsive to emerging privacy concerns by passing privacy laws in response to new challenges. He asserts that the privacy statutes have incorporated many of the Fair Information Practices, which continue to guide and shape privacy law in the United States. However, Rotenberg argues that privacy laws could be better enforced and the problem of agency capture could be better addressed:

> . . . From the articulation of a legal theory for a right of privacy in the nineteenth century through the adoption of comprehensive privacy legislation in 1974 and the privacy laws of the 1980s that targeted new technologies, there has been an ongoing effort to bring technological design within the control of the public and to safeguard the right of privacy. But something happened in the 1990s that set the United States on a strange course. At roughly the same point in time that Europe and other governments were developing new legal regimes to protect privacy, the United States was pursuing legal and technical measures to enable surveillance. While Europe faced the challenge of ensuring compliance by all the member states with the requirements of the Data Directive, the U.S. took on the challenge of trying to enforce compliance with the FBI's technical scheme to enable wire surveillance. And when consumers called for privacy safeguards to address the growing problems with the Internet, the United States government turned to the private sector for self-regulatory measures that offered little in the way of actual privacy protection.
>
> Today industry groups continue to press on with self-regulation, P3P, and other market-based approaches to the privacy issue that shift burdens back to consumers and reject the use of public institutions to resolve problems of common concern. Meanwhile, consumer organizations call on their governments to establish safeguards in law for the emerging digital economy and to extend the approaches that have been established in the past to the technologies of the future.

---

[67] Joel R. Reidenberg, *Privacy in the Information Economy: A Fortress or Frontier for Individual Rights?*, 44 Fed. Comm. L.J. 195 (1992).

> One cannot escape the conclusion that privacy policy in the United States today reflects what industry is prepared to do rather than what the public wants done. . . .[68]

6. FIRST AMENDMENT LIMITATIONS ON DATABASE STATUTORY PROTECTIONS

LOS ANGELES POLICE DEPARTMENT V. UNITED REPORTING PUBLISHING CORP.

528 U.S. 32 (1999)

REHNQUIST, C. J. California Government Code § 6254(f)(3) places two conditions on public access to arrestees' addresses — that the person requesting an address declare that the request is being made for one of five prescribed purposes, and that the requestor also declare that the address will not be used directly or indirectly to sell a product or service.

The District Court permanently enjoined enforcement of the statute, and the Court of Appeals affirmed, holding that the statute was facially invalid because it unduly burdens commercial speech. We hold that the statutory section in question was not subject to a "facial" challenge.

Petitioner, the Los Angeles Police Department, maintains records relating to arrestees. Respondent, United Reporting Publishing Corporation, is a private publishing service that provides the names and addresses of recently arrested individuals to its customers, who include attorneys, insurance companies, drug and alcohol counselors, and driving schools.

Before July 1, 1996, respondent received arrestees' names and addresses under the old version of § 6254, which generally required state and local law enforcement agencies to make public the name, address, and occupation of every individual arrested by the agency. Cal. Govt. Code § 6254(f). Effective July 1, 1996, the state legislature amended § 6254(f) to limit the public's access to arrestees' and victims' current addresses. The amended statute provides that state and local law enforcement agencies shall make public:

> [T]he current address of every individual arrested by the agency and the current address of the victim of a crime, where the requester declares under penalty of perjury that the request is made for a scholarly, journalistic, political, or governmental purpose, or that the request is made for investigation purposes by a licensed private investigator . . . except that the address of the victim of [certain crimes] shall remain confidential. Address information obtained pursuant to this paragraph shall not be used directly or indirectly to sell a product or service to any individual or group of individuals, and the requester shall execute a declaration to that effect under penalty of perjury. Cal. Govt. Code § 6254(f)(3) (West Supp. 1999).

---

[68] Marc Rotenberg, *Fair Information Practices and the Architecture of Privacy (What Larry Doesn't Get)*, 2001 Stan. Tech. L. Rev. 1, 117-119.

Sections 6254(f)(1) and (2) require that state and local law enforcement agencies make public, inter alia, the name, occupation, and physical description, including date of birth, of every individual arrested by the agency, as well as the circumstances of the arrest. Thus, amended § 6254(f) limits access only to the arrestees' addresses.

Before the effective date of the amendment, respondent sought declaratory and injunctive relief pursuant to 42 U.S.C. § 1983 to hold the amendment unconstitutional under the First and Fourteenth Amendments to the United States Constitution. On the effective date of the statute, petitioner and other law enforcement agencies denied respondent access to the address information because, according to respondent, "[respondent's] employees could not sign section 6254(f)(3) declarations." Respondent did not allege, and nothing in the record before this Court indicates, that it ever "declar[ed] under penalty of perjury" that it was requesting information for one of the prescribed purposes and that it would not use the address information to "directly or indirectly . . . sell a product or service," as would have been required by the statute. See § 6254(f)(3).

Respondent then amended its complaint and sought a temporary restraining order. The District Court issued a temporary restraining order, and, a few days later, issued a preliminary injunction. Respondent then filed a motion for summary judgment, which was granted. In granting the motion, the District Court construed respondent's claim as presenting a facial challenge to amended § 6254(f). The court held that the statute was facially invalid under the First Amendment.

The Court of Appeals affirmed the District Court's facial invalidation. The court concluded that the statute restricted commercial speech, and, as such, was entitled to "'a limited measure of protection, commensurate with its subordinate position in the scale of First Amendment values.'" The court applied the test set out in *Central Hudson Gas & Elec. Corp. v. Public Serv. Comm'n of N.Y.*, 447 U.S. 557, 566 (1980), and found that the asserted governmental interest in protecting arrestees' privacy was substantial. But, the court held that "the numerous exceptions to § 6254(f)(3) for journalistic, scholarly, political, governmental, and investigative purposes render the statute unconstitutional under the First Amendment." The court noted that "[h]aving one's name, crime, and address printed in the local paper is a far greater affront to privacy than receiving a letter from an attorney, substance abuse counselor, or driving school eager to help one overcome his present difficulties (for a fee, naturally)," and thus that the exceptions "undermine and counteract" the asserted governmental interest in preserving arrestees' privacy. Thus, the Court of Appeals affirmed the District Court's grant of summary judgment in favor of respondent and upheld the injunction against enforcement of § 6254(f)(3). We granted certiorari.

We hold that respondent was not, under our cases, entitled to prevail on a "facial attack" on § 6254(f)(3).

Respondent's primary argument in the District Court and the Court of Appeals was that § 6254(f)(3) was invalid on its face, and respondent maintains that position here. But we believe that our cases hold otherwise.

The traditional rule is that "a person to whom a statute may constitutionally be applied may not challenge that statute on the ground that it may conceivably be applied unconstitutionally to others in situations not before the Court."

Prototypical exceptions to this traditional rule are First Amendment challenges to statutes based on First Amendment overbreadth. "At least when statutes regulate or proscribe speech . . . the transcendent value to all society of constitutionally protected expression is deemed to justify allowing 'attacks on overly broad statutes with no requirement that the person making the attack demonstrate that his own conduct could not be regulated by a statute drawn with the requisite narrow specificity.'" "This is deemed necessary because persons whose expression is constitutionally protected may well refrain from exercising their right for fear of criminal sanctions provided by a statute susceptible of application to protected expression." . . .

Even though the challenge be based on the First Amendment, the overbreadth doctrine is not casually employed. "Because of the wide-reaching effects of striking down a statute on its face at the request of one whose own conduct may be punished despite the First Amendment, we have recognized that the overbreadth doctrine is 'strong medicine' and have employed it with hesitation, and then 'only as a last resort.'" . . .

The Court of Appeals held that § 6254(f)(3) was facially invalid under the First Amendment. Petitioner contends that the section in question is not an abridgment of anyone's right to engage in speech, be it commercial or otherwise, but simply a law regulating access to information in the hands of the police department.

We believe that, at least for purposes of facial invalidation, petitioner's view is correct. This is not a case in which the government is prohibiting a speaker from conveying information that the speaker already possesses. The California statute in question merely requires that if respondent wishes to obtain the addresses of arrestees it must qualify under the statute to do so. Respondent did not attempt to qualify and was therefore denied access to the addresses. For purposes of assessing the propriety of a facial invalidation, what we have before us is nothing more than a governmental denial of access to information in its possession. California could decide not to give out arrestee information at all without violating the First Amendment.

To the extent that respondent's "facial challenge" seeks to rely on the effect of the statute on parties not before the Court — its potential customers, for example — its claim does not fit within the case law allowing courts to entertain facial challenges. No threat of prosecution, for example, or cutoff of funds hangs over their heads. They may seek access under the statute on their own just as respondent did, without incurring any burden other than the prospect that their request will be denied. Resort to a facial challenge here is not warranted because there is "no possibility that protected speech will be muted." . . .

GINSBURG, J. joined by O'CONNOR, SOUTER, and BREYER, J. J. concurring. I join the Court's opinion, which recognizes that California Government Code § 6254(f)(3) is properly analyzed as a restriction on access to government information, not as a restriction on protected speech. That is sufficient reason to reverse the Ninth Circuit's judgment.

As the Court observes, the statute at issue does not restrict speakers from conveying information they already possess. Anyone who comes upon arrestee address information in the public domain is free to use that information as she sees fit. It is true, as Justice Scalia suggests, that the information could be provided to and published by journalists, and § 6254(f)(3) would indeed be a speech restriction if it then prohibited people from using that published information to speak to or about arrestees. But the statute contains no such prohibition. Once address information is in the public domain, the statute does not restrict its use in any way.

California could, as the Court notes, constitutionally decide not to give out arrestee address information at all. It does not appear that the selective disclosure of address information that California has chosen instead impermissibly burdens speech. To be sure, the provision of address information is a kind of subsidy to people who wish to speak to or about arrestees, and once a State decides to make such a benefit available to the public, there are no doubt limits to its freedom to decide how that benefit will be distributed. California could not, for example, release address information only to those whose political views were in line with the party in power. But if the award of the subsidy is not based on an illegitimate criterion such as viewpoint, California is free to support some speech without supporting other speech.

Throughout its argument, respondent assumes that § 6254(f)(3)'s regime of selective disclosure burdens speech in the sense of reducing the total flow of information. Whether that is correct is far from clear and depends on the point of comparison. If California were to publish the names and addresses of arrestees for everyone to use freely, it would indeed be easier to speak to and about arrestees than it is under the present system. But if States were required to choose between keeping proprietary information to themselves and making it available without limits, States might well choose the former option. In that event, disallowing selective disclosure would lead not to more speech overall but to more secrecy and less speech. As noted above, this consideration could not justify limited disclosures that discriminated on the basis of viewpoint or some other proscribed criterion. But it does suggest that society's interest in the free flow of information might argue for upholding laws like the one at issue in this case rather than imposing an all-or-nothing regime under which "nothing" could be a State's easiest response.

STEVENS, J. joined by KENNEDY, J. dissenting. . . . To determine whether the Amendment is valid as applied to respondent, it is similarly not necessary to invoke the overbreadth doctrine. That doctrine is only relevant if the challenger needs to rely on the possibility of invalid applications to third parties. In this case, it is the application of the Amendment to respondent itself that is at issue. Nor, in my opinion, is it necessary to do the four-step *Central Hudson* dance, because I agree with the majority that the Amendment is really a restriction on access to government information rather than a direct restriction on protected speech. For this reason, the majority is surely correct in observing that "California could decide not to give out arrestee information at all without violating the First Amendment." Moreover, I think it equally clear that California could release the information on a selective basis to a limited group of users who have a special, and legitimate, need for the information.

A different, and more difficult, question is presented when the State makes information generally available, but denies access to a small disfavored class. In this case, the State is making the information available to scholars, news media, politicians, and others, while denying access to a narrow category of persons solely because they intend to use the information for a constitutionally protected purpose. As Justice Ginsburg points out, if the State identified the disfavored persons based on their viewpoint, or political affiliation, for example, the discrimination would clearly be invalid.

What the State did here, in my opinion, is comparable to that obviously unconstitutional discrimination. In this case, the denial of access is based on the fact that respondent plans to publish the information to others who, in turn, intend to use it for a commercial speech purpose that the State finds objectionable. Respondent's proposed publication of the information is indisputably lawful — petitioner concedes that if respondent independently acquires the data, the First Amendment protects its right to communicate it to others. Similarly, the First Amendment supports the third parties' use of it for commercial speech purposes. Thus, because the State's discrimination is based on its desire to prevent the information from being used for constitutionally protected purposes, I think it must assume the burden of justifying its conduct.

The only justification advanced by the State is an asserted interest in protecting the privacy of victims and arrestees. Although that interest would explain a total ban on access, or a statute narrowly limiting access, it is insufficient when the data can be published in the news media and obtained by private investigators or others who meet the Amendment's vague criteria. . . . By allowing such widespread access to the information, the State has eviscerated any rational basis for believing that the Amendment will truly protect the privacy of these persons.

That the State might simply withhold the information from all persons does not insulate its actions from constitutional scrutiny. For even though government may withhold a particular benefit entirely, it "may not deny a benefit to a person on a basis that infringes his constitutionally protected interests —especially his interest in freedom of speech." A contrary view would impermissibly allow the government to "'produce a result which [it] could not command directly.'" It is perfectly clear that California could not directly censor the use of this information or the resulting speech. It follows, I believe, that the State's discriminatory ban on access to information — in an attempt to prohibit persons from exercising their constitutional rights to publish it in a truthful and accurate manner — is equally invalid.

Accordingly, I respectfully dissent.

NOTES & QUESTIONS

1. Consider the following argument by Daniel Solove:

> How can the tension between transparency and privacy be reconciled? Must access to public records be sacrificed at the altar of privacy? Or must privacy be compromised as the price for a government disinfected by sunlight?

It is my thesis that both transparency and privacy can be balanced through limitations on the access and use of personal information in public records. . . . Government is not doing enough to protect against the uses of the information that it routinely pumps into the public domain. If we abandon the notion that privacy is an exclusive status, and recognize that information in public records can still remain private even if there is limited access to it, then a workable compromise for the tension between transparency and privacy emerges. We can make information accessible for certain purposes only. When government discloses information, it can limit how it discloses that information by preventing it from being amassed by companies for commercial purposes, to be sold to others, or to be combined with other information and sold back to the government. . . .[69]

2. What if the California statute limited disclosure of the information to anybody who would use a form of mass communication or widespread publicity to disclose that information? In other words, what if it excluded journalists and the media from access?

3. Does the law impermissibly single out certain types of speakers?

4. Is this case consistent with *Florida Star* and *Cox Broadcasting* (Chapter 2)? Recall the following language in *Florida Star*: "[W]here a newspaper publishes truthful information which it has lawfully obtained, punishment may lawfully be imposed, if at all, only when narrowly tailored to a state interest of the highest order." Recall that in *Florida Star*, the Court struck down a Florida law that prohibited the press from publishing a rape victim's name that inadvertently appeared in a public record. Suppose that in *Florida Star*, Florida passed a law stating that its police reports would be disclosed only on the condition that rape victims' names not be disclosed by means of mass communication. Would this law be constitutional?

5. The Court's conclusion in *United Reporting* received significant criticism, as many contend that access and use restrictions on public record information violate the First Amendment because they restrict access based upon the particular type of message that one seeks to use the information for (e.g., commercial solicitation). Solove argues that access and use restrictions pass constitutional muster:

> [T]he Court's jurisprudence in the contexts of free association and the constitutional right to information privacy suggests that the Constitution does not merely mandate public access to information but also obligates the government to refrain from disclosing personal information. . . .
> [T]he government retains significant discretion in how it chooses to distribute its largesse. Public record information is part of this largesse, and the most recently decided unconstitutional condition cases suggest that the government can impose certain conditions on how this information is used before it grants access.
> The Court's jurisprudence thus creates a distinction between pre-access conditions on obtaining information and post-access restrictions on the use or disclosure of the information. If the government is not obligated to provide access to certain information by the First Amendment, it can amend its

---

[69] Daniel J. Solove, *Access and Aggregation: Public Records, Privacy, and the Constitution*, 86 Minn. L. Rev. 1137 (2002).

sunshine laws to establish pre-access conditions, restricting access for certain kinds of uses. Governments can make a public record available *on the condition that* certain information is not disclosed or used in a certain manner. However, governments cannot establish post-access restrictions on the disclosure or use of information that is publicly available. Once the information is made available to the public, the *Florida Star* cases prohibit a state from restricting use. . . .

Without a distinction between post- versus pre-access conditions, the government would be forced into an all-or-nothing tradeoff between transparency and privacy. The government could make records public, allowing all uses of the personal information contained therein, or the government could simply make records unavailable to the public for any purpose. However, by making access conditional on accepting certain responsibilities when using data — such as using it for specific purposes, not disclosing it to others, and so on, certain functions of transparency can be preserved at the same time privacy is protected. . . .

[C]ommercial access restrictions are not being applied because of disagreement with the message that commercial users wish to send. Nor do they favor a particular speaker or specific ideas. Although particular categories of use (i.e., commercial) are being singled out, avoiding viewpoint discrimination does not entail avoiding all attempts to categorize or limit uses of information. Indeed, the First Amendment constitutional regime depends upon categorizing speech. Obscene speech and fighting words are not protected, false speech about public figures is protected in a limited way, and commercial speech is protected by intermediate scrutiny. Although there is no bright line that distinguishes when certain categories map onto particular viewpoints to such a degree as to constitute discrimination based on viewpoint, the category of commercial speech is broad enough to encompass a multitude of viewpoints and is a category that forms part of the architecture of the current constitutional regime. . . .[70]

Do you agree?

U.S. WEST, INC. V. FEDERAL COMMUNICATIONS COMMISSION

182 F.3d 1224 (10th Cir. 1999)

TACHA, J. . . . U.S. West, Inc. petitions for review of a Federal Communication Commission ("FCC") order restricting the use and disclosure of and access to customer proprietary network information ("CPNI"). *See* 63 Fed. Reg. 20,326 (1998) ("CPNI Order"). [U.S. West argues that FCC regulations, implementing 47 U.S.C. §222, among other things, violate the First Amendment. These regulations require telecommunications companies to ask consumers for approval (to "opt-in") before they can use a customer's personal information for marketing purposes.] . . .

The dispute in this case involves regulations the FCC promulgated to implement provisions of 47 U.S.C. §222, which was enacted as part of the Telecommunications Act of 1996. Section 222, entitled "Privacy of customer

---

[70]*Id.*

information," states generally that "[e]very telecommunications carrier has a duty to protect the confidentiality of proprietary information of, and relating to . . . customers." To effectuate that duty, §222 places restrictions on the use, disclosure of, and access to certain customer information. At issue here are the FCC's regulations clarifying the privacy requirements for CPNI. The central provision of §222 dealing with CPNI is §222(c)(1), which states:

> Except as required by law or with the approval of the customer, a telecommunications carrier that receives or obtains customer proprietary network information by virtue of its provision of a telecommunications service shall only use, disclose, or permit access to individually identifiable customer proprietary network information in its provision of (A) the telecommunication service from which such information is derived, or (B) services necessary to, or used in, the provision of such telecommunications service, including the publishing of directories.

Section 222(d) provides three additional exceptions to the CPNI privacy requirements. [These exceptions permit the companies to use and disclose CPNI for billing purposes, to prevent fraud, and to provide services to the consumer if the consumer approves of the use of such information to provide the service. Any other uses or disclosures of CPNI not specifically permitted by §222 require the consumer's consent. The regulations adopted by the CPNI Order implementing §22 divides telecommunications services into three categories: (1) local; (2) long-distance; and (3) mobile or cellular. A telecommunications carrier can use or disclose CPNI to market products within one of these service categories if the customer already subscribes to that category of service. Carriers can't use or disclose CPNI to market categories of service to which the customer does not subscribe unless first obtaining the customer's consent. The regulations also prohibit using CPNI without consent to market other services such as voice mail or Internet access, to track customers that call competitors; or to try to regain the business of customers that switch carriers.] . . .

The regulations also describe the means by which a carrier must obtain customer approval. Section 222(c)(1) did not elaborate as to what form that approval should take. The FCC decided to require an "opt-in" approach, in which a carrier must obtain prior express approval from a customer through written, oral, or electronic means before using the customer's CPNI. The government acknowledged that the means of approval could have taken numerous other forms, including an "opt-out" approach, in which approval would be inferred from the customer-carrier relationship unless the customer specifically requested that his or her CPNI be restricted. . . .

Petitioner argues that the CPNI regulations interpreting 47 U.S.C. §222 violate the First Amendment. . . .

As a threshold requirement for the application of the First Amendment, the government action must abridge or restrict protected speech. The government argues that the FCC's CPNI regulations do not violate or even infringe upon petitioner's First Amendment rights because they only prohibit it from using CPNI to target customers and do not prevent petitioner from communicating with its customers or limit anything that it might say to them. This view is fundamentally flawed. Effective speech has two components: a speaker and an audience. A restriction on either of these components is a restriction on speech. In other words, a restriction on speech tailored to a particular audience, "targeted speech," cannot be cured simply by the fact that a speaker can speak to a larger indiscriminate audience, "broadcast speech." . . .

Because petitioner's targeted speech to its customers is for the purpose of soliciting those customers to purchase more or different telecommunications services, it "does no more than propose a commercial transaction." Consequently, the targeted speech in this case fits soundly within the definition of commercial speech. It is well established that nonmisleading commercial speech regarding a lawful activity is a form of protected speech under the First Amendment, although it is generally afforded less protection than noncommercial speech. The parties do not dispute that the commercial speech based on CPNI is truthful and nonmisleading. Therefore, the CPNI regulations implicate the First Amendment by restricting protected commercial speech. . . .

We analyze whether a government restriction on commercial speech violates the First Amendment under the four-part framework set forth in *Central Hudson* [*Gas & Elec. Corp. v. Public Serv. Comm'n of N.Y.,* 477 U.S. 557 (1980)]. First, we must conduct a threshold inquiry regarding whether the commercial speech concerns lawful activity and is not misleading. If these requirements are not met, the government may freely regulate the speech. If this threshold requirement is met, the government may restrict the speech only if it proves: "(1) it has a substantial state interest in regulating the speech, (2) the regulation directly and materially advances that interest, and (3) the regulation is no more extensive than necessary to serve the interest." As noted above, no one disputes that the commercial speech based on CPNI is truthful and nonmisleading. We therefore proceed directly to whether the government has satisfied its burden under the remaining three prongs of the *Central Hudson* test. . . .

The respondents argue that the FCC's CPNI regulations advance two substantial state interests: protecting customer privacy and promoting competition. While, in the abstract, these may constitute legitimate and substantial interests, we have concerns about the proffered justifications in the context of this case. . . .

. . . Although we agree that privacy may rise to the level of a substantial state interest, the government cannot satisfy the second prong of the *Central Hudson* test by merely asserting a broad interest in privacy. It must specify the particular notion of privacy and interest served. Moreover, privacy is not an absolute good because it imposes real costs on society. Therefore, the specific privacy interest must be substantial, demonstrating that the state has considered the proper balancing of the benefits and harms of privacy. In sum, privacy may only constitute a substantial state interest if the government specifically articulates and properly justifies it.

In the context of a speech restriction imposed to protect privacy by keeping certain information confidential, the government must show that the dissemination of the information desired to be kept private would inflict specific and significant harm on individuals, such as undue embarrassment or ridicule, intimidation or harassment, or misappropriation of sensitive personal information for the purposes of assuming another's identity. Although we may feel uncomfortable knowing that our personal information is circulating in the world, we live in an open society where information may usually pass freely. A general level of discomfort from knowing that people can readily access information about us does not necessarily rise to the level of a substantial state interest under *Central Hudson* for it is not based on an identified harm.

Neither Congress nor the FCC explicitly stated what "privacy" harm § 222 seeks to protect against. The CPNI Order notes that "CPNI includes information that is extremely personal to customers . . . such as to whom, where, and when a customer places a call, as well as the types of service offerings to which the customer subscribes," and it summarily finds "call destinations and other details about a call . . . may be equally or more sensitive [than the content of the calls]." The government never states it directly, but we infer from this thin justification that disclosure of CPNI information could prove embarrassing to some and that the government seeks to combat this potential harm.

We have some doubts about whether this interest, as presented, rises to the level of "substantial." We would prefer to see a more empirical explanation and justification for the government's asserted interest. . . . [W]e recognize the government may have a legitimate interest in helping protect certain information. Therefore, notwithstanding our reservations, we assume for the sake of this appeal that the government has asserted a substantial state interest in protecting people from the disclosure of sensitive and potentially embarrassing personal information. . . .

Under the next prong of *Central Hudson,* the government must "demonstrate that the harms it recites are real and that its restriction will in fact alleviate them to a material degree." . . . On the record before us, the government fails to meet its burden.

The government presents no evidence showing the harm to either privacy or competition is real. Instead, the government relies on speculation that harm to privacy and competition for new services will result if carriers use CPNI. . . . While protecting against disclosure of sensitive and potentially embarrassing personal information may be important in the abstract, we have no indication of how it may occur in reality with respect to CPNI. Indeed, we do not even have indication that the disclosure might actually occur. The government presents no evidence regarding how and to whom carriers would disclose CPNI. . . . [T]he government has not explained how or why a carrier would disclose CPNI to outside parties, especially when the government claims CPNI is information that would give one firm a competitive advantage over another. This leaves us unsure exactly who would potentially receive the sensitive information. . . .

Even assuming, arguendo, that the state interests in privacy and competition are substantial and that the regulations directly and materially advance those interests, we do not find, on this record, the FCC rules regarding customer approval properly tailored. . . . In order for a regulation to satisfy this final *Central Hudson* prong, there must be a fit between the legislature's means and its desired objective — "a fit that is not necessarily perfect, but reasonable; that represents not necessarily the single best disposition but one whose scope is in proportion to the interest served." While clearly the government need not employ the least restrictive means to accomplish its goal, it must utilize a means that is "narrowly tailored" to its desired objective. . . .

576 Chapter 6 Privacy, Records, and Computer Databases

. . . [O]n this record, the FCC's failure to adequately consider an obvious and substantially less restrictive alternative, an opt-out strategy, indicates that it did not narrowly tailor the CPNI regulations regarding customer approval. . . .

The respondents merely speculate that there are a substantial number of individuals who feel strongly about their privacy, yet would not bother to opt-out if given notice and the opportunity to do so. Such speculation hardly reflects the careful calculation of costs and benefits that our commercial speech jurisprudence requires. . . .

In sum, even assuming that respondents met the prior two prongs of *Central Hudson,* we conclude that based on the record before us, the agency has failed to satisfy its burden of showing that the customer approval regulations restrict no more speech than necessary to serve the asserted state interests. Consequently, we find that the CPNI regulations interpreting the customer approval requirement of 47 U.S.C. § 222(c) violate the First Amendment.

BRISCOE, J. dissenting. . . After reviewing the CPNI Order and the administrative record, I am convinced the FCC's interpretation of § 222, more specifically its selection of the opt-in method for obtaining customer approval, is entirely reasonable. Indeed, the CPNI Order makes a strong case that, of the two options seriously considered by the FCC, the opt-in method is the only one that legitimately forwards Congress' goal of ensuring that customers give informed consent for use of their individually identifiable CPNI. . . .

. . . U.S. West suggests the CPNI Order unduly limits its ability to engage in commercial speech with its existing customers regarding new products and services it may offer. . . .

The problem with U.S. West's arguments is they are more appropriately aimed at the restrictions and requirements outlined in § 222 rather than the approval method adopted in the CPNI Order. As outlined above, it is the statute, not the CPNI Order, that prohibits a carrier from using, disclosing, or permitting access to individually identifiable CPNI without first obtaining informed consent from its customers. Yet U.S. West has not challenged the constitutionality of § 222, and this is not the proper forum for addressing such a challenge even if it was raised. . . .

The majority, focusing at this point on the CPNI Order rather than the statute, concludes the FCC failed to adequately consider the opt-out method, which the majority characterizes as "an obvious and substantially less restrictive alternative" than the opt-in method. Notably, however, the majority fails to explain why, in its view, the opt-out method is substantially less restrictive. Presumably, the majority is relying on the fact that the opt-out method typically results in a higher "approval" rate than the opt-in method. Were mere "approval" percentages the only factor relevant to our discussion, the majority would perhaps be correct. As the FCC persuasively concluded in the CPNI Order, however, the opt-out method simply does not comply with § 222's requirement of informed consent. In particular, the opt-out method, unlike the opt-in method, does not guarantee that a customer will make an informed decision about usage of his or her individually identifiable CPNI. To the contrary, the opt-out method creates the very real possibility of "uninformed" customer approval. In the end, I reiterate my point that the opt-in method selected by the FCC is the only method of obtaining approval that serves the governmental interests at issue while simultaneously complying with the express requirement of the statute (i.e., obtaining informed customer consent). . . .

In conclusion, I view U.S. West's petition for review as little more than a run-of-the-mill attack on an agency order "clothed by ingenious argument in the garb" of First Amendment issues. . . .

NOTES & QUESTIONS

1. Consider the following critique of *U.S. West* by Julie Cohen:

> . . . The *U.S. West* majority's lack of interest in the record bespeaks prejudgment — not only about speech, but also about ownership, choice, and the value of transactional information. The court presumed a world in which data processors own their customers' personally-identified information unless the customers say otherwise, and in which "choice" is assessed in the abstract, without considering whether there is enough information to make the choice a real one. And although it did not decide the question, it expressed skepticism that a broad, general interest in "privacy" could ever be weighty enough to support greater restrictions on the flow of "true information." . . .
>
> The law affords numerous instances of regulation of the exchange of information as property or product. Securities markets, which operate entirely by means of information exchange, are subject to extensive regulation, and hardly anybody thinks that securities laws and regulations should be subjected to heightened or strict First Amendment scrutiny. Laws prohibiting patent, copyright, and trademark infringement, and forbidding the misappropriation of trade secrets, have as their fundamental purpose (and their undisputed effect) the restriction of information flows. The securities and intellectual property laws, moreover, are expressly content-based, and thus illustrate that (as several leading First Amendment scholars acknowledge) this characterization doesn't always matter. Finally, federal computer crime laws punish certain uses of information for reasons entirely unrelated to their communicative aspects. . . .
>
> The accumulation, use, and market exchange of personally-identified data don't fit neatly into any recognized category of "commercial speech" . . . because in the ways that matter, these activities aren't really "speech" at all. Although regulation directed at these acts may impose some indirect burden on direct-to-consumer communication, that isn't the primary objective of data privacy regulation. This suggests that, at most, data privacy regulation should be subject to the intermediate scrutiny applied to indirect speech regulation. . . .
>
> . . . [D]ata privacy opponents ignore the implications of their own freedom-of-contract paradigm for arguments from freedom of speech. Courts routinely enforce private, contractual restrictions on expression. It is hard to see why contractual restrictions on the use and exchange of personally-identified data should be presumptively unenforceable. . . .[71]

---

[71] Julie E. Cohen, *Examined Lives: Informational Privacy and the Subject as Object*, 52 Stan. L. Rev. 1373, 1416-1418, 1421 (2000).

2. In *Rowan v. United States Post Office Department,* 397 U.S. 728 (1970), a federal statute permitted individuals to require that entities sending unwanted mailings remove the individuals' names from their mailing lists and cease to send future mailings. A group of organizations challenged the statute on First Amendment grounds. The Court held that the statute did not run afoul of the First Amendment:

> The essence of appellants' argument is that the statute violates their constitutional right to communicate. . . . Without doubt the public postal system is an indispensable adjunct of every civilized society and communication is imperative to a healthy social order. But the right of every person "to be let alone" must be placed in the scales with the right of others to communicate.
>
> In today's complex society we are inescapably captive audiences for many purposes, but a sufficient measure of individual autonomy must survive to permit every householder to exercise control over unwanted mail. To make the householder the exclusive and final judge of what will cross his threshold undoubtedly has the effect of impeding the flow of ideas, information, and arguments that, ideally, he should receive and consider. Today's merchandising methods, the plethora of mass mailings subsidized by low postal rates, and the growth of the sale of large mailing lists as an industry in itself have changed the mailman from a carrier of primarily private communications, as he was in a more leisurely day, and have made him an adjunct of the mass mailer who sends unsolicited and often unwanted mail into every home. It places no strain on the doctrine of judicial notice to observe that whether measured by pieces or pounds, Everyman's mail today is made up overwhelmingly of material he did not seek from persons he does not know. And all too often it is matter he finds offensive. . . .
>
> The Court has traditionally respected the right of a householder to bar, by order or notice, solicitors, hawkers, and peddlers from his property. In this case the mailer's right to communicate is circumscribed only by an affirmative act of the addressee giving notice that he wishes no further mailings from that mailer.
>
> To hold less would tend to license a form of trespass and would make hardly more sense than to say that a radio or television viewer may not twist the dial to cut off an offensive or boring communication and thus bar its entering his home. Nothing in the Constitution compels us to listen to or view any unwanted communication, whatever its merit; we see no basis for according the printed word or pictures a different or more preferred status because they are sent by mail. The ancient concept that "a man's home is his castle" into which "not even the king may enter" has lost none of its vitality, and none of the recognized exceptions includes any right to communicate offensively with another. . . .
>
> If this prohibition operates to impede the flow of even valid ideas, the answer is that no one has a right to press even "good" ideas on an unwilling recipient. That we are often "captives" outside the sanctuary of the home and subject to objectionable speech and other sound does not mean we must be captives everywhere. The asserted right of a mailer, we repeat, stops at the outer boundary of every person's domain. . . .

Is the law in *Rowan* an opt-in or opt-out approach? Would the Court's conclusion be different if the law took the other approach?

TRANS UNION CORP. V. FEDERAL TRADE COMMISSION

245 F.3d 809 (D.C. Cir. 2001)

TATEL, J. . . . Petitioner Trans Union sells two types of products. First, as a credit reporting agency, it compiles credit reports about individual consumers from credit information it collects from banks, credit card companies, and other lenders. It then sells these credit reports to lenders, employers, and insurance companies. Trans Union receives credit information from lenders in the form of "tradelines." A tradeline typically includes a customer's name, address, date of birth, telephone number, Social Security number, account type, opening date of account, credit limit, account status, and payment history. Trans Union receives 1.4 to 1.6 billion records per month. The company's credit database contains information on 190 million adults.

Trans Union's second set of products — those at issue in this case — are known as target marketing products. These consist of lists of names and addresses of individuals who meet specific criteria such as possession of an auto loan, a department store credit card, or two or more mortgages. Marketers purchase these lists, then contact the individuals by mail or telephone to offer them goods and services. To create its target marketing lists, Trans Union maintains a database known as MasterFile, a subset of its consumer credit database. MasterFile consists of information about every consumer in the company's credit database who has (A) at least two tradelines with activity during the previous six months, or (B) one tradeline with activity during the previous six months plus an address confirmed by an outside source. The company compiles target marketing lists by extracting from MasterFile the names and addresses of individuals with characteristics chosen by list purchasers. For example, a department store might buy a list of all individuals in a particular area code who have both a mortgage and a credit card with a $10,000 limit. Although target marketing lists contain only names and addresses, purchasers know that every person on a list has the characteristics they requested because Trans Union uses those characteristics as criteria for culling individual files from its database. Purchasers also know that every individual on a target marketing list satisfies the criteria for inclusion in MasterFile.

The Fair Credit Reporting Act of 1970 ("FCRA"), 15 U.S.C. §§ 1681, 1681a-1681u, regulates consumer reporting agencies like Trans Union, imposing various obligations to protect the privacy and accuracy of credit information. The Federal Trade Commission, acting pursuant to its authority to enforce the FCRA, *see* 15 U.S.C. § 1681s(a), determined that Trans Union's target marketing lists were "consumer reports" subject to the Act's limitations. The FCRA defines "consumer report" as:

> [A]ny written, oral, or other communication of any information by a consumer reporting agency bearing on a consumer's credit worthiness, credit standing, credit capacity, character, general reputation, personal characteristics, or mode of living which is used or expected to be used or collected in whole or in part for the purpose of serving as a factor in establishing the consumer's eligibility for —
>
>   (A) credit or insurance to be used primarily for personal, family, or household purposes;

>(B) employment purposes; or
>(C) any other purpose authorized under section 1681b of this title.

15 U.S.C. §1681a(d)(1). Finding that the information Trans Union sold was "collected in whole or in part by [Trans Union] with the expectation that it would be used by credit grantors for the purpose of serving as a factor in establishing the consumer's eligibility for one of the transactions set forth in the FCRA," and concluding that target marketing is not an authorized use of consumer reports under section 1681b, *In re Trans Union Corp.,* 118 F.T.C. 821, 891 (1994), the Commission ordered Trans Union to stop selling target marketing lists. . . .

. . . [Trans Union challenges the FTC's application of the FCRA as violative of the First Amendment.] Banning the sale of target marketing lists, the company says, amounts to a restriction on its speech subject to strict scrutiny. Again, Trans Union misunderstands our standard of review. In *Dun & Bradstreet, Inc. v. Greenmoss Builders, Inc.,* 472 U.S. 749 (1985), the Supreme Court held that a consumer reporting agency's credit report warranted reduced constitutional protection because it concerned "no public issue." "The protection to be accorded a particular credit report," the Court explained, "depends on whether the report's 'content, form, and context' indicate that it concerns a public matter." Like the credit report in *Dun & Bradstreet,* which the Supreme Court found "was speech solely in the interest of the speaker and its specific business audience," the information about individual consumers and their credit performance communicated by Trans Union target marketing lists is solely of interest to the company and its business customers and relates to no matter of public concern. Trans Union target marketing lists thus warrant "reduced constitutional protection."

We turn then to the specifics of Trans Union's First Amendment argument. The company first claims that neither the FCRA nor the Commission's Order advances a substantial government interest. The "Congressional findings and statement of purpose" at the beginning of the FCRA state: "There is a need to insure that consumer reporting agencies exercise their grave responsibilities with . . . respect for the consumer's right to privacy." 15 U.S.C. §1681 (a)(4). Contrary to the company's assertions, we have no doubt that this interest — protecting the privacy of consumer credit information — is substantial.

Trans Union next argues that Congress should have chosen a "less burdensome alternative," i.e., allowing consumer reporting agencies to sell credit information as long as they notify consumers and give them the ability to "opt out." Because the FCRA is not subject to strict First Amendment scrutiny, however, Congress had no obligation to choose the least restrictive means of accomplishing its goal.

Finally, Trans Union argues that the FCRA is underinclusive because it applies only to consumer reporting agencies and not to other companies that sell consumer information. But given consumer reporting agencies' unique "access to a broad range of continually-updated, detailed information about millions of consumers' personal credit histories," we think it not at all inappropriate for Congress to have singled out consumer reporting agencies for regulation. As we explained in *Blount v. SEC,* "a regulation is not fatally underinclusive simply because an alternative regulation, which would restrict *more* speech or the speech of *more* people, could be more effective." The primary purpose of underinclusiveness analysis is to "ensure that the proffered state interest actually underlies the law, [so] a rule is struck for *under* inclusiveness only if it cannot fairly be said to advance any genuinely substantial governmental interest because it provides only ineffective or remote support for the asserted goals, or limited incremental support." To survive a First Amendment underinclusiveness challenge, therefore, "neither a perfect nor even the best available fit between means and ends is required." The FCRA easily satisfies this standard. . . .

NOTES & QUESTIONS

1. Compare *U.S. West* with *Trans Union*. Are these cases consistent with each other? Which case's reasoning strikes you as more persuasive?
2. In *Trans Union v. FCC*, 295 F.3d 42 (D.C. Cir. 2002) (*Trans Union II*), Trans Union sued to enjoin regulations promulgated pursuant to the Gramm-Leach-Bliley Act, alleging, among other things, they violated the First Amendment. Specifically, the plaintiffs challenged the regulations which defined "nonpublic personal information" and "personally identifiable financial information" under the GLB Act to include all information a consumer provides (or a financial company obtains) in connection with the furnishing of a financial product or service. Trans Union argued that these regulations, along with the restrictions of the GLB Act, would prevent credit reporting agencies from selling credit headers, which they had long been permitted to do under the Fair Credit Reporting Act (FCRA). As discussed earlier in this chapter, credit headers consist of a consumer's name, address, Social Security number, and phone number and are routinely sold by credit reporting agencies to other companies without the consent of the consumer. Trans Union contended that the dissemination of credit header information is commercial speech and that the regulations which would restrict the disclosure of this information violate the First Amendment. The court concluded that Trans Union's First Amendment arguments were "foreclosed" by its earlier opinion in *Trans Union v. FTC*:

> Trans Union first contends the regulations do not advance a substantial state interest [under *Central Hudson*]. This argument as well is precluded by *Trans Union I* which expressly recognized that the governmental interest in "protecting the privacy of consumer credit information" "is substantial." Trans Union also contends the FTC did not satisfy its burden of identifying a harm that the regulation alleviates to a material degree. On rehearing in *Trans Union I*, however, the court concluded that "the government cannot promote its interest (protection of personal financial data) except by regulating speech because the speech itself (dissemination of financial data) causes the very harm the government seeks to prevent." The same is true here. Finally, Trans Union asserts the regulations are overbroad. Trans Union has not proposed any specific means by which "the Government could achieve its interests in a manner that does not restrict speech, or that restricts less speech." The only alternative Trans Union suggests — allowing CRAs to use a notice and opt-out mechanism as other financial institutions do — is not significantly narrower than the regulations' present restrictions under which a

consumer is already provided notice and opportunity to opt out by the financial institution with which he conducts the transaction in the first instance. There is no reason to believe a consumer would be more eager to relinquish his privacy right to a CRA that subsequently obtains his NPI than he was to the financial institution with which he initially dealt.

3. *Free Speech and the Fair Information Practices.* Recall the discussion of the Fair Information Practices from earlier in this chapter (section A.3). The Fair Information Practices provide certain limitations on the uses and disclosure of personal information. Eugene Volokh contends:

> . . . I am especially worried about the normative power of the notion that the government has a compelling interest in creating "codes of fair information practices" restricting true statements made by nongovernmental speakers. The protection of free speech generally rests on an assumption that it's not for the government to decide which speech is "fair" and which isn't; the unfairnesses, excesses, and bad taste of speakers are something that current First Amendment principles generally require us to tolerate. Once people grow to accept and even like government restrictions on one kind of supposedly "unfair" communication of facts, it may become much easier for people to accept "codes of fair reporting," "codes of fair debate," "codes of fair filmmaking," "codes of fair political criticism," and the like. . . .[72]

Consider Paul Schwartz, who contends that free discourse is promoted by the protection of privacy:

> When the government requires fair information practices for the private sector, has it created a right to stop people from speaking about you? As an initial point, I emphasize that the majority of the core fair information practices do not involve the government preventing disclosure of personal information. To return to the schema in the preceding paragraph, fair information practices one, two, and four regulate the business practices of private entities without silencing their speech. No prevention of speech about anyone takes place, for example, when the Fair Credit Reporting Act of 1970 requires that certain information be given to a consumer when an "investigative consumer report" is prepared about her.
>
> These nonsilencing fair information practices are akin to a broad range of other measures that regulate information use in the private sector and do not abridge the freedom of speech under any interpretation of the First Amendment. The First Amendment does not prevent the government from requiring product labels on food products or the use of "plain English" by publicly traded companies in reports sent to their investors or Form 10-Ks filed with the Securities and Exchange Commission. Nor does the First Amendment forbid privacy laws such as the Children's Online Privacy Protection Act, which assigns parents a right of access to their children's online data profiles. The ultimate merit of these laws depends on their specific context and precise details, but such experimentation by the State should be viewed as noncontroversial on free speech grounds.

---

[72] Eugene Volokh, *Freedom of Speech and Information Privacy: The Troubling Implications of a Right to Stop People from Speaking About You,* 52 Stan. L. Rev. 1049, 1090 (2000).

Nevertheless, one subset of fair information practices does correspond to Volokh's idea of information privacy as the right to stop people from speaking about you. . . . [S]o long as [laws protecting personal information disclosure] are viewpoint neutral, these laws are a necessary element of safeguarding free communication in our democratic society. Volokh's reading of the First Amendment seeks to radically and permanently enshrine public discourse as the predominant sphere of communication. By shielding existing and possible future portals to this domain from almost all legal restrictions, Volokh furthers a process by which any topic or record can become the source of public scrutiny and debate. Yet, no less than public discourse, a democratic society depends on other realms of communication. . . .

. . . [A] democratic order depends on both an underlying personal capacity for self-governance and the participation of individuals in community and democratic self-rule. Privacy law thus has an important role in protecting individual self-determination and democratic deliberation. By providing access to one's personal data, information about how it will be processed, and other fair information practices, the law seeks to structure the terms on which individuals confront the information demands of the community, private bureaucratic entities, and the State. Attention to these issues by the legal order is essential to the health of a democracy, which ultimately depends on individual communicative competence. . . .[73]

Recall *Bartnicki v. Vopper,* 532 U.S. 514 (2001) from Chapter 2, a case concerning the publication of an unlawfully intercepted telephone communication. The concurring and dissenting opinions both noted, consistent with Professor Schwartz's viewpoint, that federal wiretap law furthers the First Amendment interests of parties to communications.

---

[73] Paul M. Schwartz, *Free Speech vs. Information Privacy: Eugene Volokh's First Amendment Jurisprudence,* 52 Stan. L. Rev. 1559 (2000).

7

PRIVACY AND PLACE

In *Katz v. United States*, 389 U.S. 347 (1967), the Court declared that the Fourth Amendment "protects people, not places." Nevertheless, in Fourth Amendment jurisprudence — as well as other forms of privacy law — different places receive vastly different privacy protection. This chapter explores privacy in three of the most central places of our lives: home, school, and work.

A. PRIVACY AT HOME

The home has long enjoyed significant protection as a private place. The maxim that the home is one's "castle" appeared as early as 1499.[1] *Semayne's Case*, 77 Eng. Rep. 194, 195 (K.B. 1604) was the first recorded case in which the sanctity of the home was mentioned: "[T]he house of every one is to him as his castle and fortress." According to William Blackstone, the law has "so particular and tender a regard to the immunity of a man's house that it stiles it his castle, and will never suffer it to be violated with impunity."[2] William Pitt once remarked: "The poorest man may in his cottage bid defiance to the Crown. It may be frail — its roof may shake — the wind may enter — the rain may enter — but the King of England cannot enter — all his force dares not cross the threshold of the ruined tenement!"[3]

In the United States, the importance of privacy in the home has long been recognized. The Supreme Court recognized in 1886 the importance of protecting "the sanctity of a man's home" in *Boyd v. United States*, 116 U.S. 616 (1886). As the Court later observed in *Payton v. New York*, 445 U.S. 573, 589 (1980): "In none is the zone of privacy more clearly defined when bounded by the unambiguous physical dimensions of an individual's home." "At the very core [of the Fourth Amendment] stands the right of a man to retreat into his own home and there be free from unreasonable governmental intrusion." *Silverman v. United States*, 365 U.S. 505, 511 (1961).

---

[1] *See* Note, *The Right to Privacy in Nineteenth Century America*, 94 Harv. L. Rev. 1892, 1894 (1981).

[2] 4 William Blackstone, *Commentaries on the Laws of England* 223 (1769).

[3] Charles J. Sykes, *The End of Privacy* 83 (1999).

STANLEY V. GEORGIA

394 U.S. 557 (1969)

MARSHALL, J. . . . An investigation of appellant's alleged bookmaking activities led to the issuance of a search warrant for appellant's home. Under authority of this warrant, federal and state agents secured entrance. They found very little evidence of bookmaking activity, but while looking through a desk drawer in an upstairs bedroom, one of the federal agents, accompanied by a state officer, found three reels of eight-millimeter film. Using a projector and screen found in an upstairs living room, they viewed the films. The state officer concluded that they were obscene and seized them. Since a further examination of the bedroom indicated that appellant occupied it, he was charged with possession of obscene matter and placed under arrest. He was later indicted for "knowingly hav(ing) possession of . . . obscene matter" in violation of Georgia law. Appellant was tried before a jury and convicted. . . .

Appellant raises several challenges to the validity of his conviction. We find it necessary to consider only one. Appellant argues here, and argued below, that the Georgia obscenity statute, insofar as it punishes mere private possession of obscene matter, violates the First Amendment, as made applicable to the States by the Fourteenth Amendment. For reasons set forth below, we agree that the mere private possession of obscene matter cannot constitutionally be made a crime. . . .

It is true that *Roth* does declare, seemingly without qualification, that obscenity is not protected by the First Amendment. That statement has been repeated in various forms in subsequent cases. However, neither *Roth* nor any subsequent decision of this Court dealt with the precise problem involved in the present case. Roth was convicted of mailing obscene circulars and advertising, and an obscene book, in violation of a federal obscenity statute. . . . None of the statements cited by the Court in *Roth* for the proposition that "this Court has always assumed that obscenity is not protected by the freedoms of speech and press" were made in the context of a statute punishing mere private possession of obscene material; the cases cited deal for the most part with use of the mails to distribute objectionable material or with some form of public distribution or dissemination. Moreover, none of this Court's decisions subsequent to *Roth* involved prosecution for private possession of obscene materials. Those cases dealt with the power of the State and Federal Governments to prohibit or regulate certain public actions taken or intended to be taken with respect to obscene matter. . . .

In this context, we do not believe that this case can be decided simply by citing *Roth*. *Roth* and its progeny certainly do mean that the First and Fourteenth Amendments recognize a valid governmental interest in dealing with the problem of obscenity. But the assertion of that interest cannot, in every context, be insulated from all constitutional protections. Neither *Roth* nor any other decision of this Court reaches that far. . . . *Roth* and the cases following it discerned such an "important interest" in the regulation of commercial distribution of obscene material. That holding cannot foreclose an examination of the constitutional implications of a statute forbidding mere private possession of such material.

It is now well established that the Constitution protects the right to receive information and ideas. "This freedom (of speech and press) . . . necessarily protects the right to receive. . . ." This right to receive information and ideas, regardless of their social worth, is fundamental to our free society. Moreover, in the context of this case — a prosecution for mere possession of printed or filmed matter in the privacy of a person's own home — that right takes on an added dimension. For also fundamental is the right to be free, except in very limited circumstances, from unwanted governmental intrusions into one's privacy.

> The makers of our Constitution undertook to secure conditions favorable to the pursuit of happiness. They recognized the significance of man's spiritual nature, of his feelings and of his intellect. They knew that only a part of the pain, pleasure and satisfactions of life are to be found in material things. They sought to protect Americans in their beliefs, their thoughts, their emotions and their sensations. They conferred, as against the government, the right to be let alone — the most comprehensive of rights and the right most valued by civilized man. *Olmstead v. United States,* 277 U.S. 438, 478 (1928) (Brandeis, J., dissenting).

These are the rights that appellant is asserting in the case before us. He is asserting the right to read or observe what he pleases — the right to satisfy his intellectual and emotional needs in the privacy of his own home. He is asserting the right to be free from state inquiry into the contents of his library. Georgia contends that appellant does not have these rights, that there are certain types of materials that the individual may not read or even possess. Georgia justifies this assertion by arguing that the films in the present case are obscene. But we think that mere categorization of these films as "obscene" is insufficient justification for such a drastic invasion of personal liberties guaranteed by the First and Fourteenth Amendments. Whatever may be the justifications for other statutes regulating obscenity, we do not think they reach into the privacy of one's own home. If the First Amendment means anything, it means that a State has no business telling a man, sitting alone in his own house, what books he may read or what films he may watch. Our whole constitutional heritage rebels at the thought of giving government the power to control men's minds.

And yet, in the face of these traditional notions of individual liberty, Georgia asserts the right to protect the individual's mind from the effects of obscenity. We are not certain that this argument amounts to anything more than the assertion that the State has the right to control the moral content of a person's thoughts. To some, this may be a noble purpose, but it is wholly inconsistent with the philosophy of the First Amendment. As the Court said in *Kingsley International Pictures Corp. v. Regents,* 360 U.S. 684 (1959), "[t]his argument misconceives what it is that the Constitution protects. Its guarantee is not confined to the expression of ideas that are conventional or shared by a majority. . . . And in the realm of ideas it protects expression which is eloquent no less than that which is unconvincing." Nor is it relevant that obscene materials in general, or the particular films before the Court, are arguably devoid of any ideological content. The line between the transmission of ideas and mere entertainment is much too elusive for this Court to draw, if indeed such a line can be drawn at all. Whatever the power of the state to control public dissemination of ideas inimical to the public morality, it cannot constitutionally premise legislation on the desirability of controlling a person's private thoughts.

Perhaps recognizing this, Georgia asserts that exposure to obscene materials may lead to deviant sexual behavior or crimes of sexual violence. There appears to be little empirical basis for that assertion. But more important, if the State is only concerned about printed or filmed materials inducing antisocial conduct, we believe that in the context of private consumption of ideas and information we should adhere to the view that "(a)mong free men, the deterrents ordinarily to be applied to prevent crime are education and punishment for violations of the law. . . ." Given the present state of knowledge, the State may no more prohibit mere possession of obscene matter on the ground that it may lead to antisocial conduct than it may prohibit possession of chemistry books on the ground that they may lead to the manufacture of homemade spirits.

It is true that in *Roth* this Court rejected the necessity of proving that exposure to obscene material would create a clear and present danger of antisocial conduct or would probably induce its recipients to such conduct. But that case dealt with public distribution of obscene materials and such distribution is subject to different objections. For example, there is always the danger that obscene material might fall into the hands of children, or that it might intrude upon the sensibilities or privacy of the general public. No such dangers are present in this case. . . .

We hold that the First and Fourteenth Amendments prohibit making mere private possession of obscene material a crime. *Roth* and the cases following that decision are not impaired by today's holding. As we have said, the States retain broad power to regulate obscenity; that power simply does not extend to mere possession by the individual in the privacy of his own home. Accordingly, the judgment of the court below is reversed and the case is remanded for proceedings not inconsistent with this opinion.

NOTES & QUESTIONS

1. *Possession of Obscenity Outside of the Home.* Stanley possessed obscene material that could constitutionally be outlawed by Georgia because obscenity is not protected by the First Amendment. According to the Court, states can ban obscene films outside the home. If Stanley were to step outside the door with his films, he could be arrested. Should being in the home make any difference? Suppose Stanley possessed and used drugs in his home. Does the state have any business telling a person, sitting alone in her home, what substances she may or may not ingest?

2. **Bowers v. Hardwick.** Consider *Bowers v. Hardwick*, 478 U.S. 186 (1986), where the Court held that a state could criminalize consensual homosexual sodomy that occurred inside a home. Is this case distinguishable from *Stanley?*

3. *The Limits of* **Stanley.** In *New York v. Ferber*, 458 U.S. 747 (1982), the Court concluded that the distribution of child pornography was not entitled to First Amendment protection. Consider the viability of *Stanley* after read-

ing the following case involving the possession of child pornography in the home.

OSBORNE v. OHIO

_____

495 U.S. 103 (1990)

WHITE, J. . . . The threshold question in this case is whether Ohio may constitutionally proscribe the possession and viewing of child pornography or whether, as Osborne argues, our decision in _Stanley v. Georgia,_ 394 U.S. 557 (1969), compels the contrary result. In _Stanley,_ we struck down a Georgia law outlawing the private possession of obscene material. We recognized that the statute impinged upon Stanley's right to receive information in the privacy of his home, and we found Georgia's justifications for its law inadequate.

Stanley should not be read too broadly. We have previously noted that _Stanley_ was a narrow holding, and, since the decision in that case, the value of permitting child pornography has been characterized as "exceedingly modest, if not _de minimis._" But assuming, for the sake of argument, that Osborne has a First Amendment interest in viewing and possessing child pornography, we nonetheless find this case distinct from _Stanley_ because the interests underlying child pornography prohibitions far exceed the interests justifying the Georgia law at issue in _Stanley._ . . .

In _Stanley,_ Georgia primarily sought to proscribe the private possession of obscenity because it was concerned that obscenity would poison the minds of its viewers. We responded that "[w]hatever the power of the state to control public dissemination of ideas inimical to the public morality, it cannot constitutionally premise legislation on the desirability of controlling a person's private thoughts." The difference here is obvious: The State does not rely on a paternalistic interest in regulating Osborne's mind. Rather, Ohio has enacted § 2907.323(A)(3) in order to protect the victims of child pornography; it hopes to destroy a market for the exploitative use of children.

"It is evident beyond the need for elaboration that a State's interest in 'safeguarding the physical and psychological well-being of a minor' is 'compelling.' . . . The legislative judgment, as well as the judgment found in relevant literature, is that the use of children as subjects of pornographic materials is harmful to the physiological, emotional, and mental health of the child. That judgment, we think, easily passes muster under the First Amendment." _Ferber,_ 458 U.S., at 756-758. It is also surely reasonable for the State to conclude that it will decrease the production of child pornography if it penalizes those who possess and view the product, thereby decreasing demand. In _Ferber,_ where we upheld a New York statute outlawing the distribution of child pornography, we found a similar argument persuasive: "[T]he advertising and selling of child pornography provide an economic motive for and are thus an integral part of the production of such materials, an activity illegal throughout the Nation. 'It rarely has been suggested that the constitutional freedom for speech and press extends its immunity to speech or writing used as an integral part of conduct in violation of a valid criminal statute.'"

Osborne contends that the State should use other measures, besides penalizing possession, to dry up the child pornography market. Osborne points out that in *Stanley* we rejected Georgia's argument that its prohibition on obscenity possession was a necessary incident to its proscription on obscenity distribution. This holding, however, must be viewed in light of the weak interests asserted by the State in that case. *Stanley* itself emphasized that we did not "mean to express any opinion on statutes making criminal possession of other types of printed, filmed, or recorded materials. . . . In such cases, compelling reasons may exist for overriding the right of the individual to possess those materials."

Given the importance of the State's interest in protecting the victims of child pornography, we cannot fault Ohio for attempting to stamp out this vice at all levels in the distribution chain. According to the State, since the time of our decision in *Ferber,* much of the child pornography market has been driven underground; as a result, it is now difficult, if not impossible, to solve the child pornography problem by only attacking production and distribution. Indeed, 19 States have found it necessary to proscribe the possession of this material.

Other interests also support the Ohio law. First, as *Ferber* recognized, the materials produced by child pornographers permanently record the victim's abuse. The pornography's continued existence causes the child victims continuing harm by haunting the children in years to come. The State's ban on possession and viewing encourages the possessors of these materials to destroy them. Second, encouraging the destruction of these materials is also desirable because evidence suggests that pedophiles use child pornography to seduce other children into sexual activity.

Given the gravity of the State's interests in this context, we find that Ohio may constitutionally proscribe the possession and viewing of child pornography. . . .

BRENNAN, J. joined by MARSHALL and STEVENS, J.J. dissenting. . . . [T]he Court's focus on *Ferber* rather than *Stanley* is misplaced. *Ferber* held only that child pornography is "a category of material the *production* and *distribution* of which is not entitled to First Amendment protection"; our decision did not extend to private *possession.* The authority of a State to regulate the production and distribution of such materials is not dispositive of its power to penalize possession. Indeed, in *Stanley* we assumed that the films at issue were obscene and that their production, sale, and distribution thus could have been prohibited under our decisions. Nevertheless, we reasoned that although the States "retain broad power to regulate obscenity" — and child pornography as well — "that power simply does not extend to mere possession by the individual in the privacy of his own home." *Ferber* did nothing more than place child pornography on the same level of First Amendment protection as *obscene* adult pornography, meaning that its production and distribution could be proscribed. The distinction established in *Stanley* between *what* materials may be regulated and *how* they may be regulated still stands. . . .

The Court today finds *Stanley* inapposite on the ground that "the interests underlying child pornography prohibitions far exceed the interests justifying the Georgia law at issue in *Stanley.*" . . . While the sexual exploitation of children is undoubtedly a serious problem, Ohio may employ other weapons to combat it. Indeed, the State already has enacted a panoply of laws prohibiting the creation, sale, and distribution of child pornography and obscenity involving minors. Ohio has not demonstrated why these laws are inadequate and why the State must forbid mere possession as well. . . .

NOTES & QUESTIONS

1. To what extent does *Osborne* limit the rule in *Stanley?*
2. ***The Fourth Amendment and the Home.*** Although *Katz* declared that "the Fourth Amendment protects people, not places," *Katz v. United States,* 389 U.S. 347, 351 (1967), the Court has afforded the home the strongest protection under the Fourth Amendment. For example, automobiles can generally be searched without warrants while homes rarely can be searched without warrants (except under exigent circumstances). Compare *Chambers v. Maroney,* 399 U.S. 42 (1970) with *Mincey v. Arizona,* 437 U.S. 385 (1978). Arrests can be made without warrants outside the home; but within the home, warrantless arrests are generally not permissible. Compare *United States v. Watson,* 423 U.S. 411 (1976) with *Payton v. New York,* 445 U.S. 573 (1980). In *Payton v. New York,* the Court struck down New York statutes that permitted the police to enter a home without a warrant in order to make a routine felony arrest:

> The Fourth Amendment protects the individual's privacy in a variety of settings. In none is the zone of privacy more clearly defined than when bounded by the unambiguous physical dimensions of an individual's home — a zone that finds its roots in clear and specific constitutional terms: "The right of the people to be secure in their . . . houses . . . shall not be violated." That language unequivocally establishes the proposition that "[a]t the very core [of the Fourth Amendment] stands the right of a man to retreat into his own home and there be free from unreasonable governmental intrusion." *Silverman v. United States,* 365 U.S. 505, 511. In terms that apply equally to seizures of property and to seizures of persons, the Fourth Amendment has drawn a firm line at the entrance to the house. Absent exigent circumstances, that threshold may not reasonably be crossed without a warrant.

3. ***The Scope of the Fourth Amendment Protection of the Home.*** In *Chapman v. United States,* 365 U.S. 610 (1961), the Court held that the Fourth Amendment protection of the home extends to apartment tenants, even though they do not own the apartment. Further, in *Bumper v. North Carolina,* 391 U.S. 543 (1968), the Court held that a person living in the home of another was entitled to the same Fourth Amendment protection as if it were her own home. Later, in *Minnesota v. Olson,* 495 U.S. 91 (1990), the Court extended the Fourth Amendment protection of the home to overnight guests in another's home or apartment:

> To hold that an overnight guest has a legitimate expectation of privacy in his host's home merely recognizes the every day expectations of privacy that we all share. Staying overnight in another's home is a long-standing social custom that serves functions recognized as valuable by society. We stay in others' homes when we travel to a strange city for business or pleasure, we visit our parents, children, or more distant relatives out of town, when we are in between jobs, or homes, or when we house-sit for a friend. . . .

From the overnight guest's perspective, he seeks shelter in another's home precisely because it provides him with privacy, a place where he and his possessions will not be disturbed by anyone but his host and those his host allows inside. We are at our most vulnerable when we are asleep because we cannot monitor our own safety or the security of our belongings. It is for this reason that, although we may spend all day in public places, when we cannot sleep in our own home we seek out another private place to sleep, whether it be a hotel room, or the home of a friend.

However, in *Minnesota v. Carter,* 525 U.S. 83 (1998), the Court held that a visitor who was in a friend's apartment for a short duration (not overnight) had no reasonable expectation of privacy in that apartment:

> . . . The text of the [Fourth] Amendment suggests that its protections extend only to people in "their" houses. But we have held that in some circumstances a person may have a legitimate expectation of privacy in the house of someone else. . . .
>
> . . . But whereas it is plausible to regard a person's overnight lodging as at least his "temporary" residence, it is entirely impossible to give that characterization to an apartment that he uses to package cocaine. Respondents here were not searched in "their . . . hous[e]" under any interpretation of the phrase that bears the remotest relationship to the well understood meaning of the Fourth Amendment.

Justices Ginsburg, Souter, and Stevens dissented:

> A homedweller places her own privacy at risk, the Court's approach indicates, when she opens her home to others. . . . Human frailty suggests that today's decision will tempt police to pry into private dwellings without warrant, to find evidence incriminating guests who do not rest there through the night. As I see it, people are not genuinely "secure in their . . . houses . . . against unreasonable searches and seizures," U.S. Const., Amdt. 4, if their invitations to others increase the risk of unwarranted governmental peering and prying into their dwelling places.
>
> Through the host's invitation, the guest gains a reasonable expectation of privacy in the home. *Minnesota v. Olson* so held with respect to an overnight guest. The logic of that decision extends to shorter term guests as well. One need not remain overnight to anticipate privacy in another's home. . . .

WILSON V. LAYNE

526 U.S. 603 (1999)

REHNQUIST, J. One of the dangerous fugitives identified as a target of "Operation Gunsmoke" [a national program where U.S. Marshals worked with state and local police to apprehend dangerous fugitives] was Dominic Wilson, the son of petitioners Charles and Geraldine Wilson. Dominic Wilson had violated his probation on previous felony charges of robbery, theft, and assault with intent to rob, and the police computer listed "caution indicators" that he was likely to be armed, to resist arrest, and to "assaul[t] police." The computer also listed his address as 909 North StoneStreet Avenue in Rockville, Maryland. Unknown to the police, this was actually the home of petitioners, Dominic Wilson's parents. Thus, in April 1992, the Circuit Court for Montgomery

County issued three arrest warrants for Dominic Wilson, one for each of his probation violations. The warrants were each addressed to "any duly authorized peace officer," and commanded such officers to arrest him and bring him "immediately" before the Circuit Court to answer an indictment as to his probation violation. The warrants made no mention of media presence or assistance.

In the early morning hours of April 16, 1992, a Gunsmoke team of Deputy United States Marshals and Montgomery County Police officers assembled to execute the Dominic Wilson warrants. The team was accompanied by a reporter and a photographer from the Washington Post, who had been invited by the Marshals to accompany them on their mission as part of a Marshal's Service ride-along policy.

At around 6:45 A.M., the officers, with media representatives in tow, entered the dwelling at 909 North StoneStreet Avenue in the Lincoln Park neighborhood of Rockville. Petitioners Charles and Geraldine Wilson were still in bed when they heard the officers enter the home. Petitioner Charles Wilson, dressed only in a pair of briefs, ran into the living room to investigate. Discovering at least five men in street clothes with guns in his living room, he angrily demanded that they state their business, and repeatedly cursed the officers. Believing him to be an angry Dominic Wilson, the officers quickly subdued him on the floor. Geraldine Wilson next entered the living room to investigate, wearing only a nightgown. She observed her husband being restrained by the armed officers.

When their protective sweep was completed, the officers learned that Dominic Wilson was not in the house, and they departed. During the time that the officers were in the home, the Washington Post photographer took numerous pictures. The print reporter was also apparently in the living room observing the confrontation between the police and Charles Wilson. At no time, however, were the reporters involved in the execution of the arrest warrant. The Washington Post never published its photographs of the incident.

Petitioners sued the law enforcement officials in their personal capacities for money damages under *Bivens v. Six Unknown Fed. Narcotics Agents*, 403 U.S. 388 (1971) (the U.S. Marshals Service respondents) and 42 U.S.C. § 1983 (the Montgomery County Sheriff's Department respondents). They contended that the officers' actions in bringing members of the media to observe and record the attempted execution of the arrest warrant violated their Fourth Amendment rights. The District Court denied respondents' motion for summary judgment on the basis of qualified immunity. . . .

In *Payton v. New York*, 445 U.S. 573 (1980), we noted that although clear in its protection of the home, the common-law tradition at the time of the drafting of the Fourth Amendment was ambivalent on the question of whether police could enter a home without a warrant. We were ultimately persuaded that the "overriding respect for the sanctity of the home that has been embedded in our traditions since the origins of the Republic" meant that absent a warrant or exigent circumstances, police could not enter a home to make an arrest. . . .

Here, of course, the officers had such a warrant, and they were undoubtedly entitled to enter the Wilson home in order to execute the arrest warrant for Dominic Wilson. But it does not necessarily follow that they were entitled to bring a newspaper reporter and a photographer with them. In *Horton v.*

California, 496 U.S. 128 (1990), we held "[i]f the scope of the search exceeds that permitted by the terms of a validly issued warrant or the character of the relevant exception from the warrant requirement, the subsequent seizure is unconstitutional without more." While this does not mean that every police action while inside a home must be explicitly authorized by the text of the warrant, the Fourth Amendment does require that police actions in execution of a warrant be related to the objectives of the authorized intrusion.

Certainly the presence of reporters inside the home was not related to the objectives of the authorized intrusion. Respondents concede that the reporters did not engage in the execution of the warrant, and did not assist the police in their task. The reporters therefore were not present for any reason related to the justification for police entry into the home—the apprehension of Dominic Wilson.

This is not a case in which the presence of the third parties directly aided in the execution of the warrant. Where the police enter a home under the authority of a warrant to search for stolen property, the presence of third parties for the purpose of identifying the stolen property has long been approved by this Court and our common-law tradition.

Respondents argue that the presence of the Washington Post reporters in the Wilsons' home nonetheless served a number of legitimate law enforcement purposes. They first assert that officers should be able to exercise reasonable discretion about when it would "further their law enforcement mission to permit members of the news media to accompany them in executing a warrant." But this claim ignores the importance of the right of residential privacy at the core of the Fourth Amendment. It may well be that media ride-alongs further the law enforcement objectives of the police in a general sense, but that is not the same as furthering the purposes of the search. Were such generalized "law enforcement objectives" themselves sufficient to trump the Fourth Amendment, the protections guaranteed by that Amendment's text would be significantly watered down.

Respondents next argue that the presence of third parties could serve the law enforcement purpose of publicizing the government's efforts to combat crime, and facilitate accurate reporting on law enforcement activities. There is certainly language in our opinions interpreting the First Amendment which points to the importance of "the press" in informing the general public about the administration of criminal justice. . . . But the Fourth Amendment also protects a very important right, and in the present case it is in terms of that right that the media ride-alongs must be judged.

Surely the possibility of good public relations for the police is simply not enough, standing alone, to justify the ride-along intrusion into a private home. And even the need for accurate reporting on police issues in general bears no direct relation to the constitutional justification for the police intrusion into a home in order to execute a felony arrest warrant.

Finally, respondents argue that the presence of third parties could serve in some situations to minimize police abuses and protect suspects, and also to protect the safety of the officers. While it might be reasonable for police officers to themselves videotape home entries as part of a "quality control" effort to ensure that the rights of homeowners are being respected, or even to preserve evidence, such a situation is significantly different from the media presence in this case. The Washington Post reporters in the Wilsons' home were working on a story for their own purposes. They were not present for the purpose of protecting the officers, much less the Wilsons. A private photographer was acting for private purposes, as evidenced in part by the fact that the newspaper and not the police retained the photographs. Thus, although the presence of third parties during the execution of a warrant may in some circumstances be constitutionally permissible, the presence of *these* third parties was not.

The reasons advanced by respondents, taken in their entirety, fall short of justifying the presence of media inside a home. We hold that it is a violation of the Fourth Amendment for police to bring members of the media or other third parties into a home during the execution of a warrant when the presence of the third parties in the home was not in aid of the execution of the warrant. . . .

Since the police action in this case violated the petitioners' Fourth Amendment right, we now must decide whether this right was clearly established at the time of the search. . . . [G]overnment officials performing discretionary functions generally are granted a qualified immunity and are "shielded from liability for civil damages insofar as their conduct does not violate clearly established statutory or constitutional rights of which a reasonable person would have known." *Harlow v. Fitzgerald,* 457 U.S., at 818. . . .

. . . "Clearly established" for purposes of qualified immunity means that "[t]he contours of the right must be sufficiently clear that a reasonable official would understand that what he is doing violates that right. This is not to say that an official action is protected by qualified immunity unless the very action in question has previously been held unlawful, but it is to say that in the light of pre-existing law the unlawfulness must be apparent." . . .

We hold that it was not unreasonable for a police officer in April 1992 to have believed that bringing media observers along during the execution of an arrest warrant (even in a home) was lawful. . . .

Given such an undeveloped state of the law, the officers in this case cannot have been "expected to predict the future course of constitutional law." . . .

STEVENS, J. concurring in part and dissenting in part. . . . I share the Court's opinion that it violates the Fourth Amendment for police to bring members of the media or other third parties into a private dwelling during the execution of a warrant unless the homeowner has consented or the presence of the third parties is in aid of the execution of the warrant. . . .

In my view, however, the homeowner's right to protection against this type of trespass was clearly established long before April 16, 1992. . . . The clarity of the constitutional rule, a federal statute (18 U.S.C. § 3105), common-law decisions, and the testimony of the senior law enforcement officer all support my position that it has long been clearly established that officers may not bring third parties into private homes to witness the execution of a warrant. . . .

In its decision today the Court has not announced a new rule of constitutional law. Rather, it has refused to recognize an entirely unprecedented request for an exception to a well-established principle. Police action in the execution of a warrant must be strictly limited to the objectives of the authorized intrusion. That principle, like the broader protection provided by the Fourth Amendment itself, represents the confluence of two important sources: our English forefathers' traditional respect for the sanctity of the private home and the American colonists' hatred of the general warrant.

NOTES & QUESTIONS

1. What cause(s) of action would the Wilsons have against the news reporters? Would they likely be successful in bringing these causes of action?

2. Suppose the police brought in their own video camera and one of the officers filmed the arrest. The police then gave the videotape to the press. Would they violate the Fourth Amendment under *Wilson?*

3. Suppose the police left the door to the Wilsons' house open, and a press camera person filmed the arrest through the open door without entering into the Wilson abode. Would this be unconstitutional under *Wilson?*

4. One could argue that one of the central purposes of the Fourth Amendment is to keep police power in check. The practice of filming the police during arrests serves the purposes of the Fourth Amendment by providing a significant check on police abuses. Do you agree?

5. *The Application of* **Wilson** *Outside the Home: "Perp Walks."* In *Lauro v. Charles,* 219 F.3d 202 (2d Cir. 2000), the court applied *Wilson* to a widespread police practice in New York City known as a "perp walk," in which an arrestee (often in handcuffs and guided by police officers) is walked in front of the press to be photographed or filmed. Although sometimes the arrestee is filmed during the regular course of being transferred from one location to another, the police and the press often cooperate in staging the perp walk. In a perp walk, the police bring the arrestee outside the police station and lead her back inside for no other purpose than to allow the press to photograph her. In *Lauro,* the court held, relying on *Wilson,* that the staged perp walk violated an arrestee's Fourth Amendment rights:

> . . . In the instant case, Lauro was physically restrained, by handcuffs and by the grip of Detective Charles on his arm. In that humiliating position, he was made to walk outside the precinct house, was driven around the block, and was then forced to walk back into the precinct house, in front of television cameras. The fact that Lauro was lawfully under arrest when these events occurred does not mean that no Fourth Amendment interest of Lauro's was implicated. . . .

> Despite its adverse effects on Lauro's dignity and privacy, the perp walk might nevertheless have been reasonable under the Fourth Amendment, had it been sufficiently closely related to a legitimate governmental objective. In this respect, Charles argues that "the importance of the press in informing the general public about the administration of criminal justice has long been recognized by the Supreme Court," and that this interest suffices to justify the perp walk before us.

> The Supreme Court, however, in *Wilson* explicitly rejected an identical argument when it was proffered in support of the media ride-along in that case. . . .

> . . . The interests of the press, and of the public who might want to view perp walks, are far from negligible. In this case, however, the press and the public were not viewing the actual event of Lauro being brought to the police station, but rather, were offered a staged recreation of that event. Even assuming that there is a legitimate state interest in accurate reporting of police activity, that interest is not well served by an inherently fictional dramatization of an event that transpired hours earlier. . . .

6. Recall *Kyllo v. United States* (Chapter 4), the thermal imaging case. How significant was the location of the search to the court's holding? If *Wilson* applies outside the home, could *Kyllo* as well?

7. ***Tranquility of the Home.*** In addition to the Court affording the home greater protection under the Fourth Amendment than other places, the Court has also sustained state regulation protecting the tranquility of the home from First Amendment challenges. In *Kovacs v. Cooper*, 336 U.S. 77 (1949), the Court upheld an ordinance prohibiting the use of sound trucks or other devices to amplify sound used in public streets:

> The right of free speech is guaranteed every citizen that he may reach the minds of willing listeners and to do so there must be opportunity to win their attention. This is the phase of freedom of speech that is involved here. We do not think the Trenton ordinance abridges that freedom. It is an extravagant extension of due process to say that because of it a city cannot forbid talking on the streets through a loud speaker in a loud and raucous tone. . . . The preferred position of freedom of speech in a society that cherishes liberty for all does not require legislators to be insensible to claims by citizens to comfort and convenience. To enforce freedom of speech in disregard of the rights of others would be harsh and arbitrary in itself. That more people may be more easily and cheaply reached by sound trucks, perhaps borrowed without cost from some zealous supporter, is not enough to call forth constitutional protection for what those charged with public welfare reasonably think is a nuisance when easy means of publicity are open. . . . We think that the need for reasonable protection in the homes or business houses from the distracting noises of vehicles equipped with such sound amplifying devices justifies the ordinance.

In *Kovacs*, the Court distinguished an earlier case, *Martin v. City of Struthers*, 319 U.S. 141 (1943), where it struck down an ordinance prohibiting people from going door-to-door to distribute pamphlets:

> We do not think that the *Struthers* case requires us to expand this interdiction of legislation to include ordinance against obtaining an audience for the broadcaster's ideas by way of sound trucks with loud and raucous noises on city streets. The unwilling listener is not like the passer-by who may be offered a pamphlet in the street but cannot be made to take it. In his home or on the street he is practically helpless to escape this interference with his privacy by loud speakers except through the protection of the municipality.

In *Frisby v. Schultz*, 487 U.S. 474 (1988), the Court upheld an ordinance completely banning picketing near any residence. The plaintiffs were a group of pro-life advocates who desired to picket an abortion doctor's residence. The Court concluded that the ordinance was a content neutral restriction on speech (it applied to all residential picketing regardless of the content of the expression) and satisfied the test accorded content neutral restrictions because it was narrowly tailored to serve a significant governmental interest (protecting privacy of the home) and it left open alternative channels for communications. As the Court reasoned:

> . . . "The State's interest in protecting the well-being, tranquility, and privacy of the home is certainly of the highest order in a free and civilized society." Our prior decisions have often remarked on the unique nature of the

home, "the last citadel of the tired, the weary, and the sick," and have recognized that "[p]reserving the sanctity of the home, the one retreat to which men and women can repair to escape from the tribulations of their daily pursuits, is surely an important value."

One important aspect of residential privacy is protection of the unwilling listener. Although in many locations, we expect individuals simply to avoid speech they do not want to hear, the home is different. "That we are often 'captives' outside the sanctuary of the home and subject to objectionable speech . . . does not mean we must be captives everywhere." *Rowan v. Post Office Dept.*, 397 U.S. 728, 738 (1970). Instead, a special benefit of the privacy all citizens enjoy within their own walls, which the State may legislate to protect, is an ability to avoid intrusions. Thus, we have repeatedly held that individuals are not required to welcome unwanted speech into their own homes and that the government may protect this freedom. See, e.g., *FCC v. Pacifica Foundation*, 438 U.S. 726 (1978) (offensive radio broadcasts); *Rowan* (offensive mailings); *Kovacs v. Cooper*, 336 U.S. 77 (1949) (sound trucks). . . .

There simply is no right to force speech into the home of an unwilling listener.

It remains to be considered, however, whether the Brookfield ordinance is narrowly tailored to protect only unwilling recipients of the communications. A statute is narrowly tailored if it targets and eliminates no more than the exact source of the "evil" it seeks to remedy. A complete ban can be narrowly tailored, but only if each activity within the proscription's scope is an appropriately targeted evil. . . .

. . . The type of focused picketing prohibited by the Brookfield ordinance is fundamentally different from more generally directed means of communication that may not be completely banned in residential areas. Here, in contrast, the picketing is narrowly directed at the household, not the public. The type of picketers banned by the Brookfield ordinance generally do not seek to disseminate a message to the general public, but to intrude upon the targeted resident, and to do so in an especially offensive way. Moreover, even if some such picketers have a broader communicative purpose, their activity nonetheless inherently and offensively intrudes on residential privacy. The devastating effect of targeted picketing on the quiet enjoyment of the home is beyond doubt:

> To those inside . . . the home becomes something less than a home when and while the picketing . . . continue[s]. . . . [The] tensions and pressures may be psychological, not physical, but they are not, for that reason, less inimical to family privacy and truly domestic tranquility. *Carey*, 447 U.S., at 478 (Rehnquist, J., dissenting). . . .

B. PRIVACY AT SCHOOL

1. SCHOOL SEARCHES AND SURVEILLANCE

NEW JERSEY V. T.L.O.

469 U.S. 325 (1984)

WHITE, J. . . . On March 7, 1980, a teacher at Piscataway High School in Middlesex County, N.J., discovered two girls smoking in a lavatory. One of the two girls was the respondent T.L.O., who at that time was a 14-year-old high school freshman. Because smoking in the lavatory was a violation of a school rule, the teacher took the two girls to the Principal's office, where they met with Assistant Vice Principal Theodore Choplick. In response to questioning by Mr. Choplick, T.L.O.'s companion admitted that she had violated the rule. T.L.O., however, denied that she had been smoking in the lavatory and claimed that she did not smoke at all.

Mr. Choplick asked T.L.O. to come into his private office and demanded to see her purse. Opening the purse, he found a pack of cigarettes, which he removed from the purse and held before T.L.O. as he accused her of having lied to him. As he reached into the purse for the cigarettes, Mr. Choplick also noticed a package of cigarette rolling papers. In his experience, possession of rolling papers by high school students was closely associated with the use of marihuana. Suspecting that a closer examination of the purse might yield further evidence of drug use, Mr. Choplick proceeded to search the purse thoroughly. The search revealed a small amount of marihuana, a pipe, a number of empty plastic bags, a substantial quantity of money in one-dollar bills, an index card that appeared to be a list of students who owed T.L.O. money, and two letters that implicated T.L.O. in marihuana dealing.

Mr. Choplick notified T.L.O.'s mother and the police, and turned the evidence of drug dealing over to the police. At the request of the police, T.L.O.'s mother took her daughter to police headquarters, where T.L.O. confessed that she had been selling marihuana at the high school. On the basis of the confession and the evidence seized by Mr. Choplick, the State brought delinquency charges against T.L.O. in the Juvenile and Domestic Relations Court of Middlesex County. Contending that Mr. Choplick's search of her purse violated the Fourth Amendment, T.L.O. moved to suppress the evidence found in her purse as well as her confession, which, she argued, was tainted by the allegedly unlawful search. . . .

In determining whether the search at issue in this case violated the Fourth Amendment, we are faced initially with the question whether that Amendment's prohibition on unreasonable searches and seizures applies to searches conducted by public school officials. We hold that it does. . . .

. . . . [T]he State of New Jersey has argued that the history of the Fourth Amendment indicates that the Amendment was intended to regulate only searches and seizures carried out by law enforcement officers; accordingly, although public school officials are concededly state agents for purposes of the Fourteenth Amendment, the Fourth Amendment creates no rights enforceable against them.

It may well be true that the evil toward which the Fourth Amendment was primarily directed was the resurrection of the pre-Revolutionary practice of using general warrants or "writs of assistance" to authorize searches for contraband by officers of the Crown. But this Court has never limited the Amendment's prohibition on unreasonable searches and seizures to operations conducted by the police. Rather, the Court has long spoken of the Fourth Amendment's strictures as restraints imposed upon "governmental action" — that is, "upon the activities of sovereign authority." Accordingly, we have held the Fourth Amendment applicable to the activities of civil as well as criminal authorities: building inspectors, Occupational Safety and Health Act inspectors, and even firemen entering privately owned premises to battle a fire, are all subject to the restraints imposed by the Fourth Amendment. As we observed in *Camara v. Municipal Court,* "[t]he basic purpose of this Amendment, as recognized in countless decisions of this Court, is to safeguard the privacy and security of individuals against arbitrary invasions by governmental officials." . . .

To hold that the Fourth Amendment applies to searches conducted by school authorities is only to begin the inquiry into the standards governing such searches. Although the underlying command of the Fourth Amendment is always that searches and seizures be reasonable, what is reasonable depends on the context within which a search takes place. The determination of the standard of reasonableness governing any specific class of searches requires "balancing the need to search against the invasion which the search entails." On one side of the balance are arrayed the individual's legitimate expectations of privacy and personal security; on the other, the government's need for effective methods to deal with breaches of public order.

We have recognized that even a limited search of the person is a substantial invasion of privacy. We have also recognized that searches of closed items of personal luggage are intrusions on protected privacy interests, for "the Fourth Amendment provides protection to the owner of every container that conceals its contents from plain view." A search of a child's person or of a closed purse or other bag carried on her person, no less than a similar search carried out on an adult, is undoubtedly a severe violation of subjective expectations of privacy.

. . . To receive the protection of the Fourth Amendment, an expectation of privacy must be one that society is "prepared to recognize as legitimate." The State of New Jersey has argued that because of the pervasive supervision to which children in the schools are necessarily subject, a child has virtually no legitimate expectation of privacy in articles of personal property "unnecessarily" carried into a school. This argument has two factual premises: (1) the fundamental incompatibility of expectations of privacy with the maintenance of a sound educational environment; and (2) the minimal interest of the child in bringing any items of personal property into the school. Both premises are severely flawed.

Although this Court may take notice of the difficulty of maintaining discipline in the public schools today, the situation is not so dire that students in the schools may claim no legitimate expectations of privacy. . . .

Nor does the State's suggestion that children have no legitimate need to bring personal property into the schools seem well anchored in reality. Students at a minimum must bring to school not only the supplies needed for their studies, but also keys, money, and the necessaries of personal hygiene and grooming. In addition, students may carry on their persons or in purses or wallets such nondisruptive yet highly personal items as photographs, letters, and diaries. Finally, students may have perfectly legitimate reasons to carry with them articles of property needed in connection with extracurricular or recreational activities. In short, schoolchildren may find it necessary to carry with them a variety of legitimate, noncontraband items, and there is no reason to conclude that they have necessarily waived all rights to privacy in such items merely by bringing them onto school grounds.

Against the child's interest in privacy must be set the substantial interest of teachers and administrators in maintaining discipline in the classroom and on school grounds. Maintaining order in the classroom has never been easy, but in recent years, school disorder has often taken particularly ugly forms: drug use and violent crime in the schools have become major social problems. . . . "Events calling for discipline are frequent occurrences and sometimes require immediate, effective action." Accordingly, we have recognized that maintaining security and order in the schools requires a certain degree of flexibility in school disciplinary procedures, and we have respected the value of preserving the informality of the student-teacher relationship.

How, then, should we strike the balance between the schoolchild's legitimate expectations of privacy and the school's equally legitimate need to maintain an environment in which learning can take place? It is evident that the school setting requires some easing of the restrictions to which searches by public authorities are ordinarily subject. The warrant requirement, in particular, is unsuited to the school environment: requiring a teacher to obtain a warrant before searching a child suspected of an infraction of school rules (or of the criminal law) would unduly interfere with the maintenance of the swift and informal disciplinary procedures needed in the schools. Just as we have in other cases dispensed with the warrant requirement when "the burden of obtaining a warrant is likely to frustrate the governmental purpose behind the search," we hold today that school officials need not obtain a warrant before searching a student who is under their authority.

The school setting also requires some modification of the level of suspicion of illicit activity needed to justify a search. Ordinarily, a search — even one that may permissibly be carried out without a warrant — must be based upon "probable cause" to believe that a violation of the law has occurred. However, "probable cause" is not an irreducible requirement of a valid search. The fundamental command of the Fourth Amendment is that searches and seizures be reasonable, and although "both the concept of probable cause and the requirement of a warrant bear on the reasonableness of a search, . . . in certain limited circumstances neither is required." Thus, we have in a number of cases recognized the legality of searches and seizures based on suspicions that, although "reasonable," do not rise to the level of probable cause. Where a careful balancing of governmental and private interests suggests that the public interest is best served by a Fourth Amendment standard of reasonableness that stops short of probable cause, we have not hesitated to adopt such a standard.

. . . [T]he legality of a search of a student should depend simply on the reasonableness, under all the circumstances, of the search. Determining the reasonableness of any search involves a twofold inquiry: first, one must consider "whether the . . . action was justified at its inception"; second, one must determine whether the search as actually conducted "was reasonably related in scope to the circumstances which justified the interference in the first place." Under ordinary circumstances, a search of a student by a teacher or other school official will be "justified at its inception" when there are reasonable grounds for suspecting that the search will turn up evidence that the student has violated or is violating either the law or the rules of the school. Such a search will be permissible in its scope when the measures adopted are reasonably related to the objectives of the search and not excessively intrusive in light of the age and sex of the student and the nature of the infraction.

This standard will, we trust, neither unduly burden the efforts of school authorities to maintain order in their schools nor authorize unrestrained intrusions upon the privacy of schoolchildren. By focusing attention on the question of reasonableness, the standard will spare teachers and school administrators the necessity of schooling themselves in the niceties of probable cause and permit them to regulate their conduct according to the dictates of reason and common sense. At the same time, the reasonableness standard should ensure that the interests of students will be invaded no more than is necessary to achieve the legitimate end of preserving order in the schools. . . .

There remains the question of the legality of the search in this case. . . . Our review of the facts surrounding the search leads us to conclude that the search was in no sense unreasonable for Fourth Amendment purposes. . . .

T.L.O. had been accused of smoking, and had denied the accusation in the strongest possible terms when she stated that she did not smoke at all. Surely it cannot be said that under these circumstances, T.L.O.'s possession of cigarettes would be irrelevant to the charges against her or to her response to those charges. T.L.O.'s possession of cigarettes, once it was discovered, would both corroborate the report that she had been smoking and undermine the credibility of her defense to the charge of smoking. . . . The relevance of T.L.O.'s possession of cigarettes to the question whether she had been smoking and to the credibility of her denial that she smoked supplied the necessary "nexus" between the item searched for and the infraction under investigation. Thus, if Mr. Choplick in fact had a reasonable suspicion that T.L.O. had cigarettes in her purse, the search was justified despite the fact that the cigarettes, if found, would constitute "mere evidence" of a violation. . . .

This conclusion is puzzling. A teacher had reported that T.L.O. was smoking in the lavatory. Certainly this report gave Mr. Choplick reason to suspect that T.L.O. was carrying cigarettes with her; and if she did have cigarettes, her purse was the obvious place in which to find them. Mr. Choplick's suspicion that there were cigarettes in the purse was not an "inchoate and unparticularized suspicion or 'hunch,'"; rather, it was the sort of "common-sense conclusio[n] about human behavior" upon which "practical people"—including government officials—are entitled to rely. . . .

STEVENS, J. joined by MARSHALL J. (and partially by BRENNAN, J.) concurring in part and dissenting in part. . . . Justice Brandeis was both a great student and a great teacher. It was he who wrote:

> Our Government is the potent, the omnipresent teacher. For good or for ill, it teaches the whole people by its example. Crime is contagious. If the Government becomes a lawbreaker, it breeds contempt for law; it invites every man to become a law unto himself; it invites anarchy. *Olmstead v. United States,* 277 U.S. 438, 485 (1928) (dissenting opinion).

Those of us who revere the flag and the ideals for which it stands believe in the power of symbols. We cannot ignore that rules of law also have a symbolic power that may vastly exceed their utility.

Schools are places where we inculcate the values essential to the meaningful exercise of rights and responsibilities by a self-governing citizenry. If the Nation's students can be convicted through the use of arbitrary methods destructive of personal liberty, they cannot help but feel that they have been dealt with unfairly. The application of the exclusionary rule in criminal proceedings arising from illegal school searches makes an important statement to young people that "our society attaches serious consequences to a violation of constitutional rights," and that this is a principle of "liberty and justice for all.". . . .

. . . . The majority holds that "a search of a student by a teacher or other school official will be 'justified at its inception' when there are reasonable grounds for suspecting that the search will turn up evidence that the student has violated or is violating either the law or the rules of the school." This standard will permit teachers and school administrators to search students when they suspect that the search will reveal evidence of even the most trivial school regulation or precatory guideline for student behavior. The Court's standard for deciding whether a search is justified "at its inception" treats all violations of the rules of the school as though they were fungible. For the Court, a search for curlers and sunglasses in order to enforce the school dress code is apparently just as important as a search for evidence of heroin addiction or violent gang activity. . . .

In this case, Mr. Choplick overreacted to what appeared to be nothing more than a minor infraction — a rule prohibiting smoking in the bathroom of the freshmen's and sophomores' building. . . . Because this conduct was neither unlawful nor significantly disruptive of school order or the educational process, the invasion of privacy associated with the forcible opening of T.L.O.'s purse was entirely unjustified at its inception. . . .

BRENNAN, J. joined by MARSHALL, J. concurring in part and dissenting in part. . . . I emphatically disagree with the Court's decision to cast aside the constitutional probable-cause standard when assessing the constitutional validity of a schoolhouse search. The Court's decision jettisons the probable-cause standard — the only standard that finds support in the text of the Fourth Amendment — on the basis of its Rohrschach-like "balancing test." Use of such a "balancing test" to determine the standard for evaluating the validity of a full-scale search represents a sizable innovation in Fourth Amendment analysis. This innovation finds support neither in precedent nor policy and portends a dangerous weakening of the purpose of the Fourth Amendment to protect the privacy and security of our citizens. Moreover, even if this Court's historic understanding of the Fourth Amendment were mistaken and a balancing test of some kind were appropriate, any such test that gave adequate weight to the privacy and security interests protected by the Fourth Amendment would not reach the preordained result the Court's conclusory analysis reaches today. Therefore, because I believe that the balancing test used by the Court today is flawed both in its inception and in its execution, I respectfully dissent.

NOTES & QUESTIONS

1. *After Columbine: The Privacy Implications.* On April 20, 1999, two high school students entered their school (Columbine High School) in Littleton, Colorado, armed with firearms and explosives. In a brutal rampage, they killed twelve students and one teacher and injured twenty-three others before killing themselves. As a result of the Columbine massacre and other shootings and violent threats in high schools across the country, school administrators began to adopt stricter safety measures to prevent violence. Such measures include the installation of metal detectors, surveillance cameras, routine backpack and locker searches by police officers, and requirements that students carry identification cards at all times while on school grounds. Are such measures good policy? Some critics argue that adopting these measures will teach students that the only way to be secure is to live in a police state. Supporters contend that the loss of privacy is justified by additional security and protection. Under *T.L.O.*, are the new measures described above constitutional?

2. DRUG TESTING

VERNONIA SCHOOL DISTRICT V. ACTON

515 U.S. 646 (1995)

SCALIA, J. . . . Petitioner Vernonia School District 47J (District) operates one high school and three grade schools in the logging community of Vernonia, Oregon. As elsewhere in small-town America, school sports play a prominent role in the town's life, and student athletes are admired in their schools and in the community.

Drugs had not been a major problem in Vernonia schools. In the mid-to-late 1980's, however, teachers and administrators observed a sharp increase in drug use. Students began to speak out about their attraction to the drug culture, and to boast that there was nothing the school could do about it. Along with more drugs came more disciplinary problems. . . .

Not only were student athletes included among the drug users but, as the District Court found, athletes were the leaders of the drug culture. This caused the District's administrators particular concern, since drug use increases the risk of sports-related injury. Expert testimony at the trial confirmed the deleterious effects of drugs on motivation, memory, judgment, reaction, coordination, and performance. The high school football and wrestling coach witnessed a severe sternum injury suffered by a wrestler, and various omissions of safety procedures and misexecutions by football players, all attributable in his belief to the effects of drug use.

Initially, the District responded to the drug problem by offering special classes, speakers, and presentations designed to deter drug use. It even brought in a specially trained dog to detect drugs, but the drug problem persisted. . . .

At that point, District officials began considering a drug-testing program. They held a parent "input night" to discuss the proposed Student Athlete

Drug Policy (Policy), and the parents in attendance gave their unanimous approval. The school board approved the Policy for implementation in the fall of 1989. Its expressed purpose is to prevent student athletes from using drugs, to protect their health and safety, and to provide drug users with assistance programs. . . .

The Policy applies to all students participating in interscholastic athletics. Students wishing to play sports must sign a form consenting to the testing and must obtain the written consent of their parents. Athletes are tested at the beginning of the season for their sport. In addition, once each week of the season the names of the athletes are placed in a "pool" from which a student, with the supervision of two adults, blindly draws the names of 10% of the athletes for random testing. Those selected are notified and tested that same day, if possible.

The student to be tested completes a specimen control form which bears an assigned number. Prescription medications that the student is taking must be identified by providing a copy of the prescription or a doctor's authorization. The student then enters an empty locker room accompanied by an adult monitor of the same sex. Each boy selected produces a sample at a urinal, remaining fully clothed with his back to the monitor, who stands approximately 12 to 15 feet behind the student. Monitors may (though do not always) watch the student while he produces the sample, and they listen for normal sounds of urination. Girls produce samples in an enclosed bathroom stall, so that they can be heard but not observed. After the sample is produced, it is given to the monitor, who checks it for temperature and tampering and then transfers it to a vial.

The samples are sent to an independent laboratory, which routinely tests them for amphetamines, cocaine, and marijuana. Other drugs, such as LSD, may be screened at the request of the District, but the identity of a particular student does not determine which drugs will be tested. The laboratory's procedures are 99.94% accurate. . . . Only the superintendent, principals, vice-principals, and athletic directors have access to test results, and the results are not kept for more than one year.

If a sample tests positive, a second test is administered as soon as possible to confirm the result. If the second test is negative, no further action is taken. If the second test is positive, the athlete's parents are notified, and the school principal convenes a meeting with the student and his parents, at which the student is given the option of (1) participating for six weeks in an assistance program that includes weekly urinalysis, or (2) suffering suspension from athletics for the remainder of the current season and the next athletic season. The student is then retested prior to the start of the next athletic season for which he or she is eligible. The Policy states that a second offense results in automatic imposition of option (2); a third offense in suspension for the remainder of the current season and the next two athletic seasons. . . .

In the fall of 1991, respondent James Acton, then a seventh grader, signed up to play football at one of the District's grade schools. He was denied participation, however, because he and his parents refused to sign the testing consent forms. The Actons filed suit, seeking declaratory and injunctive relief from enforcement of the Policy on the grounds that it violated the Fourth and

Fourteenth Amendments to the United States Constitution and Article I, §9, of the Oregon Constitution. . . .

. . . In *Skinner v. Railway Labor Executives' Assn.,* 489 U.S. 602, 617 (1989), we held that state-compelled collection and testing of urine, such as that required by the Policy, constitutes a "search" subject to the demands of the Fourth Amendment.

As the text of the Fourth Amendment indicates, the ultimate measure of the constitutionality of a governmental search is "reasonableness." . . . Where a search is undertaken by law enforcement officials to discover evidence of criminal wrongdoing, this Court has said that reasonableness generally requires the obtaining of a judicial warrant. Warrants cannot be issued, of course, without the showing of probable cause required by the Warrant Clause. But a warrant is not required to establish the reasonableness of *all* government searches; and when a warrant is not required (and the Warrant Clause therefore not applicable), probable cause is not invariably required either. A search unsupported by probable cause can be constitutional, we have said, "when special needs, beyond the normal need for law enforcement, make the warrant and probable-cause requirement impracticable."

We have found such "special needs" to exist in the public school context. There, the warrant requirement "would unduly interfere with the maintenance of the swift and informal disciplinary procedures [that are] needed," and "strict adherence to the requirement that searches be based upon probable cause" would undercut "the substantial need of teachers and administrators for freedom to maintain order in the schools." *T.L.O.,* 469 U.S., at 340. The school search we approved in *T.L.O.,* while not based on probable cause, *was* based on individualized *suspicion* of wrongdoing. . . .

The first factor to be considered is the nature of the privacy interest upon which the search here at issue intrudes. The Fourth Amendment does not protect all subjective expectations of privacy, but only those that society recognizes as "legitimate." What expectations are legitimate varies, of course, with context, depending, for example, upon whether the individual asserting the privacy interest is at home, at work, in a car, or in a public park. . . .

. . . [W]hile children assuredly do not "shed their constitutional rights . . . at the schoolhouse gate," the nature of those rights is what is appropriate for children in school.

Fourth Amendment rights, no less than First and Fourteenth Amendment rights, are different in public schools than elsewhere; the "reasonableness" inquiry cannot disregard the schools' custodial and tutelary responsibility for children. For their own good and that of their classmates, public school children are routinely required to submit to various physical examinations, and to be vaccinated against various diseases. . . . Particularly with regard to medical examinations and procedures, therefore, "students within the school environment have a lesser expectation of privacy than members of the population generally."

Legitimate privacy expectations are even less with regard to student athletes. School sports are not for the bashful. They require "suiting up" before each practice or event, and showering and changing afterwards. Public school locker rooms, the usual sites for these activities, are not notable for the privacy they afford. The locker rooms in Vernonia are typical: No individual dressing rooms are provided; shower heads are lined up along a wall, unseparated by any sort of partition or curtain; not even all the toilet stalls have doors. . . . [T]here is "an element of 'communal undress' inherent in athletic participation."

There is an additional respect in which school athletes have a reduced expectation of privacy. By choosing to "go out for the team," they voluntarily subject themselves to a degree of regulation even higher than that imposed on students generally. In Vernonia's public schools, they must submit to a preseason physical exam (James testified that his included the giving of a urine sample), they must acquire adequate insurance coverage or sign an insurance waiver, maintain a minimum grade point average, and comply with any "rules of conduct, dress, training hours and related matters as may be established for each sport by the head coach and athletic director with the principal's approval." Somewhat like adults who choose to participate in a "closely regulated industry," students who voluntarily participate in school athletics have reason to expect intrusions upon normal rights and privileges, including privacy. . . .

Having considered the scope of the legitimate expectation of privacy at issue here, we turn next to the character of the intrusion that is complained of. . . . Under the District's Policy, male students produce samples at a urinal along a wall. They remain fully clothed and are only observed from behind, if at all. Female students produce samples in an enclosed stall, with a female monitor standing outside listening only for sounds of tampering. These conditions are nearly identical to those typically encountered in public restrooms, which men, women, and especially schoolchildren use daily. Under such conditions, the privacy interests compromised by the process of obtaining the urine sample are in our view negligible.

The other privacy-invasive aspect of urinalysis is, of course, the information it discloses concerning the state of the subject's body, and the materials he has ingested. In this regard it is significant that the tests at issue here look only for drugs, and not for whether the student is, for example, epileptic, pregnant, or diabetic. Moreover, the drugs for which the samples are screened are standard, and do not vary according to the identity of the student. And finally, the results of the tests are disclosed only to a limited class of school personnel who have a need to know; and they are not turned over to law enforcement authorities or used for any internal disciplinary function.

Respondents argue, however, that the District's Policy is in fact more intrusive than this suggests, because it requires the students, if they are to avoid sanctions for a falsely positive test, to identify *in advance* prescription medications they are taking. We agree that this raises some cause for concern. . . . Nothing in the Policy [states that the school would not keep the information confidential], and when respondents choose, in effect, to challenge the Policy on its face, we will not assume the worst. Accordingly . . . the invasion of privacy was not significant. . . .

Finally, we turn to consider the nature and immediacy of the governmental concern at issue here, and the efficacy of this means for meeting it. . . . Is there a compelling state interest here? . . . .

That the nature of the concern is important — indeed, perhaps com-pelling — can hardly be doubted. Deterring drug use by our Nation's school-children is at least as important as enhancing efficient enforcement of the Na-tion's laws against the importation of drugs. . . . [T]he effects of a drug-infested school are visited not just upon the users, but upon the entire student body and faculty, as the educational process is disrupted. . . .

As to the efficacy of this means for addressing the problem: It seems to us self-evident that a drug problem largely fueled by the "role model" effect of athletes' drug use, and of particular danger to athletes, is effectively addressed by making sure that athletes do not use drugs. Respondents argue that a "less intrusive means to the same end" was available, namely, "drug testing on suspicion of drug use." We have repeatedly refused to declare that only the "least intrusive" search practicable can be reasonable under the Fourth Amendment. Respondents' alternative entails substantial difficulties — if it is indeed practicable at all. It may be impracticable, for one thing, simply be-cause the parents who are willing to accept random drug testing for athletes are not willing to accept accusatory drug testing for all students, which trans-forms the process into a badge of shame. Respondents' proposal brings the risk that teachers will impose testing arbitrarily upon troublesome but not drug-likely students. It generates the expense of defending lawsuits that charge such arbitrary imposition, or that simply demand greater process before accusatory drug testing is imposed. And not least of all, it adds to the ever-expanding di-versionary duties of schoolteachers the new function of spotting and bringing to account drug abuse, a task for which they are ill prepared, and which is not readily compatible with their vocation. In many respects, we think, testing based on "suspicion" of drug use would not be better, but worse. . . .

Taking into account all the factors we have considered above — the de-creased expectation of privacy, the relative unobtrusiveness of the search, and the severity of the need met by the search — we conclude Vernonia's Policy is reasonable and hence constitutional. . . .

O'CONNOR, J. joined by STEVENS and SOUTER, J.J. dissenting. . . . The popu-lation of our Nation's public schools, grades 7 through 12, numbers around 18 million. By the reasoning of today's decision, the millions of these students who participate in interscholastic sports, an overwhelming majority of whom have given school officials no reason whatsoever to suspect they use drugs at school, are open to an intrusive bodily search.

. . . Blanket searches, because they can involve "thousands or millions" of searches, "pos[e] a greater threat to liberty" than do suspicion-based ones, which "affec[t] one person at a time." Searches based on individualized suspi-cion also afford potential targets considerable control over whether they will, in fact, be searched because a person can avoid such a search by not acting in an objectively suspicious way. And given that the surest way to avoid acting suspiciously is to avoid the underlying wrongdoing, the costs of such a regime, one would think, are minimal.

But whether a blanket search is "better" than a regime based on individu-alized suspicion is not a debate in which we should engage. In my view, it is not open to judges or government officials to decide on policy grounds which is better and which is worse. For most of our constitutional history, mass, suspicionless searches have been generally considered *per se* unreasonable within the meaning of the Fourth Amendment. And we have allowed exceptions in recent years only where it has been clear that a suspicion-based regime would be ineffectual. Because that is not the case here, I dissent. . . .

. . . [I]ntrusive, blanket searches of schoolchildren, most of whom are innocent, for evidence of serious wrongdoing are not part of any traditional school function of which I am aware. Indeed, many schools, like many parents, prefer to trust their children unless given reason to do otherwise. As James Acton's father said on the witness stand, "[suspicionless testing] sends a message to children that are trying to be responsible citizens . . . that they have to prove that they're innocent . . ., and I think that kind of sets a bad tone for citizenship." . . .

BOARD OF EDUCATION V. EARLS

122 S. Ct. 2559 (2002)

THOMAS, J. . . . The city of Tecumseh, Oklahoma, is a rural community located approximately 40 miles southeast of Oklahoma City. The School District administers all Tecumseh public schools. In the fall of 1998, the School District adopted the Student Activities Drug Testing Policy (Policy), which requires all middle and high school students to consent to drug testing in order to participate in any extracurricular activity. In practice, the Policy has been applied only to competitive extracurricular activities sanctioned by the Oklahoma Secondary Schools Activities Association, such as the Academic Team, Future Farmers of America, Future Homemakers of America, band, choir, pom pon, cheerleading, and athletics. Under the Policy, students are required to take a drug test before participating in an extracurricular activity, must submit to random drug testing while participating in that activity, and must agree to be tested at any time upon reasonable suspicion. The urinalysis tests are designed to detect only the use of illegal drugs, including amphetamines, marijuana, cocaine, opiates, and barbituates, not medical conditions or the presence of authorized prescription medications. . . .

In *Vernonia*, this Court held that the suspicionless drug testing of athletes was constitutional. The Court, however, did not simply authorize all school drug testing, but rather conducted a fact-specific balancing of the intrusion on the children's Fourth Amendment rights against the promotion of legitimate governmental interests. Applying the principles of *Vernonia* to the somewhat different facts of this case, we conclude that Tecumseh's Policy is also constitutional. . . .

We first consider the nature of the privacy interest allegedly compromised by the drug testing. . . . A student's privacy interest is limited in a public school environment where the State is responsible for maintaining discipline, health, and safety. Schoolchildren are routinely required to submit to physical examinations and vaccinations against disease. Securing order in the school environment sometimes requires that students be subjected to greater controls than those appropriate for adults.

Respondents argue that because children participating in nonathletic extracurricular activities are not subject to regular physicals and communal undress, they have a stronger expectation of privacy than the athletes tested in *Vernonia*. This distinction, however, was not essential to our decision in *Vernonia*, which depended primarily upon the school's custodial responsibility and authority.

In any event, students who participate in competitive extracurricular activities voluntarily subject themselves to many of the same intrusions on their privacy as do athletes. Some of these clubs and activities require occasional off-campus travel and communal undress. All of them have their own rules and requirements for participating students that do not apply to the student body as a whole. . . . We therefore conclude that the students affected by this Policy have a limited expectation of privacy. . . .

Next, we consider the character of the intrusion imposed by the Policy. Urination is "an excretory function traditionally shielded by great privacy." . . .

Under the Policy, a faculty monitor waits outside the closed restroom stall for the student to produce a sample and must "listen for the normal sounds of urination in order to guard against tampered specimens and to insure an accurate chain of custody." The monitor then pours the sample into two bottles that are sealed and placed into a mailing pouch along with a consent form signed by the student. This procedure is virtually identical to that reviewed in *Vernonia*, except that it additionally protects privacy by allowing male students to produce their samples behind a closed stall. Given that we considered the method of collection in *Vernonia* a "negligible" intrusion, the method here is even less problematic.

In addition, the Policy clearly requires that the test results be kept in confidential files separate from a student's other educational records and released to school personnel only on a "need to know" basis. Respondents nonetheless contend that the intrusion on students' privacy is significant because the Policy fails to protect effectively against the disclosure of confidential information and, specifically, that the school "has been careless in protecting that information: for example, the Choir teacher looked at students' prescription drug lists and left them where other students could see them." But the choir teacher is someone with a "need to know," because during off-campus trips she needs to know what medications are taken by her students. Even before the Policy was enacted the choir teacher had access to this information. In any event, there is no allegation that any other student did see such information. This one example of alleged carelessness hardly increases the character of the intrusion.

Moreover, the test results are not turned over to any law enforcement authority. Nor do the test results here lead to the imposition of discipline or have any academic consequences. Rather, the only consequence of a failed drug test is to limit the student's privilege of participating in extracurricular activities. Indeed, a student may test positive for drugs twice and still be allowed to participate in extracurricular activities. After the first positive test, the school contacts the student's parent or guardian for a meeting. The student may continue to participate in the activity if within five days of the meeting the student shows proof of receiving drug counseling and submits to a second drug test in two weeks. For the second positive test, the student is suspended from participation in all extracurricular activities for 14 days, must complete four hours of substance abuse counseling, and must submit to monthly drug tests. Only after a third positive test will the student be suspended from participating in any extracurricular activity for the remainder of the school year, or 88 school days, whichever is longer.

Given the minimally intrusive nature of the sample collection and the limited uses to which the test results are put, we conclude that the invasion of students' privacy is not significant.

Finally, this Court must consider the nature and immediacy of the government's concerns and the efficacy of the Policy in meeting them. . . . The drug abuse problem among our Nation's youth has hardly abated since *Vernonia* was decided in 1995. In fact, evidence suggests that it has only grown worse. . . . The health and safety risks identified in *Vernonia* apply with equal force to Tecumseh's children. Indeed, the nationwide drug epidemic makes the war against drugs a pressing concern in every school.

Additionally, the School District in this case has presented specific evidence of drug use at Tecumseh schools. Teachers testified that they had seen students who appeared to be under the influence of drugs and that they had heard students speaking openly about using drugs. A drug dog found marijuana cigarettes near the school parking lot. Police officers once found drugs or drug paraphernalia in a car driven by a Future Farmers of America member. And the school board president reported that people in the community were calling the board to discuss the "drug situation." . . .

Finally, we find that testing students who participate in extracurricular activities is a reasonably effective means of addressing the School District's legitimate concerns in preventing, deterring, and detecting drug use. While in *Vernonia* there might have been a closer fit between the testing of athletes and the trial court's finding that the drug problem was "fueled by the 'role model' effect of athletes' drug use," such a finding was not essential to the holding. . . .

GINSBURG, J. joined by STEVENS, O'CONNOR, and SOUTER, J.J. dissenting. . . . The particular testing program upheld today is not reasonable, it is capricious, even perverse: Petitioners' policy targets for testing a student population least likely to be at risk from illicit drugs and their damaging effects. . . .

Vernonia cannot be read to endorse invasive and suspicionless drug testing of all students upon any evidence of drug use, solely because drugs jeopardize the life and health of those who use them. Many children, like many adults, engage in dangerous activities on their own time; that the children are enrolled in school scarcely allows government to monitor all such activities. If a student has a reasonable subjective expectation of privacy in the personal items she brings to school, see *T.L.O.*, surely she has a similar expectation regarding the chemical composition of her urine. Had the *Vernonia* Court agreed that public school attendance, in and of itself, permitted the State to test each student's blood or urine for drugs, the opinion in *Vernonia* could have saved many words.

The second commonality to which the Court points is the voluntary character of both interscholastic athletics and other competitive extracurricular activities. . . .

The comparison is enlightening. While extracurricular activities are "voluntary" in the sense that they are not required for graduation, they are part of the school's educational program. . . . Participation in such activities is a key component of school life, essential in reality for students applying to college, and, for all participants, a significant contributor to the breadth and quality of the educational experience. Students "volunteer" for extracurricular pursuits in the same way they might volunteer for honors classes: They subject themselves to additional requirements, but they do so in order to take full advantage of the education offered them.

Voluntary participation in athletics has a distinctly different dimension: Schools regulate student athletes discretely because competitive school sports by their nature require communal undress and, more important, expose students to physical risks that schools have a duty to mitigate. For the very reason that schools cannot offer a program of competitive athletics without intimately affecting the privacy of students, *Vernonia* reasonably analogized school athletes to "adults who choose to participate in a closely regulated industry." Interscholastic athletics similarly require close safety and health regulation; a school's choir, band, and academic team do not. . . .

After describing school athletes' reduced expectation of privacy, the *Vernonia* Court turned to "the character of the intrusion . . . complained of." Observing that students produce urine samples in a bathroom stall with a coach or teacher outside, *Vernonia* typed the privacy interests compromised by the process of obtaining samples "negligible." . . .

In this case, however, Lindsay Earls and her parents allege that the School District handled personal information collected under the policy carelessly, with little regard for its confidentiality. Information about students' prescription drug use, they assert, was routinely viewed by Lindsay's choir teacher, who left files containing the information unlocked and unsealed, where others, including students, could see them; and test results were given out to all activity sponsors whether or not they had a clear "need to know." . . .

The School District cites the dangers faced by members of the band, who must "perform extremely precise routines with heavy equipment and instruments in close proximity to other students," and by Future Farmers of America, who "are required to individually control and restrain animals as large as 1500 pounds." . . . Notwithstanding nightmarish images of out-of-control flatware, livestock run amok, and colliding tubas disturbing the peace and quiet of Tecumseh, the great majority of students the School District seeks to test in truth are engaged in activities that are not safety sensitive to an unusual degree. There is a difference between imperfect tailoring and no tailoring at all.

Even if students might be deterred from drug use in order to preserve their extracurricular eligibility, it is at least as likely that other students might forgo their extracurricular involvement in order to avoid detection of their drug use. Tecumseh's policy thus falls short doubly if deterrence is its aim: It invades the privacy of students who need deterrence least, and risks steering students at greatest risk for substance abuse away from extracurricular involvement that potentially may palliate drug problems.

NOTES & QUESTIONS

1. Do you agree with the Court's conclusion that the holding in this case flows logically from *Vernonia*? Why or why not?
2. Suppose a school district decides to implement mandatory drug testing for all students. Based on the Court's reasoning, would this be constitutional? In other words, is the fact that the students tested are voluntarily engaged in extracurricular activities an essential element of the Court's holding?
3. Suppose, in response to concerns over violence and guns in school, a school district decides to engage in routine searches of the bags and backpacks of all students engaging in extracurricular activities. Based on *T.L.O., Vernonia,* and *Earls,* would this policy be constitutional?
4. *Searches and Symbolism.* Consider the Court's holding in *Chandler v. Miller,* 520 U.S. 305 (1997), a case in which the Court struck down a drug testing requirement for candidates for public office. Writing for the Court, Justice Ginsburg said:

   > What is left, after close review of Georgia's scheme, is the image the State seeks to project. By requiring candidates for public office to submit to drug testing, Georgia displays its commitment to the struggle against drug abuse. . . . But Georgia asserts no evidence of a drug problem among the State's elected officials, those officials typically do not perform high-risk, safety-sensitive tasks, and the required certification immediately aids no interdiction effort. The need revealed, in short, is symbolic, not "special," as that term draws meaning from our case law. . . .

   At what point does drug testing of students become symbolic? Can *Earls* be reconciled with *Chandler?* We will consider *Chandler* in more detail in Part C of this chapter.
5. *State Constitutional Law.* Many states have their own versions of the Fourth Amendment in their constitutions. Accordingly, the constitutions of some states may provide more privacy protection to students than the federal Constitution. In addition to provisions that resemble the Fourth Amendment, some state constitutions also contain an explicit right to privacy. One of these states is California, and its constitution states:

   > All people are by nature free and independent and have inalienable rights. Among these are enjoying and defending life and liberty, acquiring, possessing, and protecting property, and pursuing and obtaining safety, happiness, and privacy. Cal. Const. Art I, § 1.

   In *Hill v. National Collegiate Athletic Association,* 865 P.2d 633 (Cal. 1994), the National Collegiate Athletic Association (NCAA) randomly selected college athletes competing in postseason football games to provide urine samples to be tested for drugs. Student athletes attending Stanford University sued, contending that the NCAA drug testing violated their right to privacy. The court rejected the challenge:

   > By its nature, sports competition demands highly disciplined physical activity conducted in accordance with a special set of social norms. Unlike the general population, student athletes undergo frequent physical examinations, reveal their bodily and medical conditions to coaches and trainers,

and often dress and undress in same-sex locker rooms. In so doing, they normally and reasonably forgo a measure of their privacy in exchange for the personal and professional benefits of extracurricular athletics.

A student athlete's already diminished expectation of privacy is outweighed by the NCAA's legitimate regulatory objectives in conducting testing for proscribed drugs. As a sponsor and regulator of sporting events, the NCAA has self-evident interests in ensuring fair and vigorous competition, as well as protecting the health and safety of student athletes. These interests justify a set of drug testing rules reasonably calculated to achieve drug-free athletic competition. The NCAA's rules contain elements designed to accomplish this purpose, including: (1) advance notice to athletes of testing procedures and written consent to testing; (2) random selection of athletes actually engaged in competition; (3) monitored collection of a sample of a selected athlete's urine in order to avoid substitution or contamination; and (4) chain of custody, limited disclosure, and other procedures designed to safeguard the confidentiality of the testing process and its outcome. As formulated, the NCAA's regulations do not offend the legitimate privacy interests of student athletes.

3. SCHOOL RECORDS

THE FAMILY EDUCATION RIGHTS AND PRIVACY ACT

The Family Educational Rights and Privacy Act (FERPA) of 1974, Pub. L. No. 93-380, commonly known as the "Buckley Amendment," prohibits schools from releasing student records (transcripts, recommendations, financial information) without the authorization of the student or parent. Schools may release names, addresses, dates of attendance, degrees earned, and activities unless the parent or student expressly indicates in writing that he or she wants it to remain confidential. FERPA covers only education records. Thus, information known to school authorities that is not part of a record is not covered.[4]

Educational Records. "Educational records" are "those records, files, documents, and other materials which contain information directly related to a student." 20 U.S.C. § 1232g(a)(4)(A). Law enforcement records and health and psychological records maintained by school officials do not constitute educational records. § 1232g(a)(4)(B). Courts have held that records of a school's disciplinary proceedings against students do not constitute "educational records."[5]

Notice. Schools must inform students and parents of their rights under FERPA. *See* 34 C.F.R. § 99.7.

Access and Ability to Correct Errors. Schools must provide students and parents with access to their school records—a chance to review their records

---

[4] *See Frasca v. Andrews,* 463 F. Supp. 1043, 1050 (E.D.N.Y. 1979) ("Congress could not have constitutionally prohibited comment on, or discussion of, facts about a student which were learned independently of his school records.").

[5] *Red & Black Publishing Co., Inc. v. Board of Regents,* 427 S.E.2d 257 (Ga. 1993); *The Miami Student v. Miami University,* 680 N.E.2d 956 (Ohio 1997).

upon request. §1232g(a)(1)(A). Schools must provide the student with an opportunity for a hearing "to challenge the content of such student's education records, in order to insure that the records are not inaccurate, misleading, or otherwise in violation of the privacy or other rights of students, and to provide an opportunity for the correction or deletion of any inaccurate, misleading, or otherwise inappropriate data contained therein. . . ." §1232g(a)(2).

Limits on Disclosure. Pursuant to §1232g(b), schools cannot disclose a student's educational records without written consent. Certain disclosures are exempted from this rule. For example, the school can disclose records to educational institutions and officials with a "legitimate educational interest," to appropriate persons in order to protect health or safety of the student or others, as well as a number of other entities and officials. §1232g(b)(1).

If the student does not opt out, a school may release to the public the student's name, address, telephone numbers, birth date, major, activities and sports, dates of attendance, and degrees and awards received. §1232g(b)(5).

Enforcement. The FERPA authorizes the Secretary of Education to end all federal funding if a school fails to comply with the FERPA. §1232g(f). The Department of Education's Family Policy Compliance Office oversees the enforcement of FERPA. *See* 34 C.F.R. §99.60(b). Before the Compliance Office takes action, an individual must file a complaint against a school. The Compliance Office then investigates and if the school is found in violation of the FERPA, the Compliance Office recommends specific steps that the institution must take to comply. *See* 34 C.F.R. §99.66. If the school fails to comply, then funding is stopped.

The Law Enforcement Exception. Prior to a number of amendments in the 1990s, campus law enforcement records could only be disclosed to law enforcement officials, not to the public at large. In *Student Press Law Center v. Alexander,* 778 F. Supp. 1227 (D.D.C. 1991), college newspapers and journalists claimed that their college police departments, which had routinely provided campus crime reports to student reporters, had ceased to do so after the Department of Education wrote a "technical assistance" letter to 14 universities to stop disclosing personally identifiable information in crime reports. The court concluded that:

> There is no legitimate privacy interest in arrest records, *Paul v. Davis,* 424 U.S. 693 (1976), and therefore the potential harm to third-parties is not legally cognizable. . . . [Further, the interest of the public in greater access to information] is at its highest in matters that bear on personal safety and the prevention of crime.

In 1990, FERPA was amended to permit schools to inform violent crime victims of the results of school disciplinary proceedings.[6] Pursuant to §1232g(b)(6):

> Nothing in this section shall be construed to prohibit an institution of postsecondary education from disclosing, to an alleged victim of any crime of

---

[6] *See* Student Right-to-Know, Crime Awareness, and Campus Security Act, Pub. L. No. 101-542, §204, 104 Stat. 2381, 2385-2387 (1990) (codified at 20 U.S.C. §1092).

violence . . . the results of any disciplinary proceeding conducted by such institution against the alleged perpetrator of such crime with respect to such crime.[7]

OWASSO INDEPENDENT SCHOOL DISTRICT V. FALVO

534 U.S. 426 (2002)

KENNEDY, J. Teachers sometimes ask students to score each other's tests, papers, and assignments as the teacher explains the correct answers to the entire class. Respondent contends this practice, which the parties refer to as peer grading, violates the Family Educational Rights and Privacy Act of 1974 (FERPA or Act), 88 Stat. 571, 20 U.S.C. § 1232g. We took this case to resolve the issue. . . .

Respondent claimed the peer grading embarrassed her children. She asked the school district to adopt a uniform policy banning peer grading and requiring teachers either to grade assignments themselves or at least to forbid students from grading papers other than their own. The school district declined to do so, and respondent brought a class action pursuant to 42 U.S.C. § 1983. Respondent alleged the school district's grading policy violated FERPA and other laws not relevant here. . . .

Petitioners, supported by the United States as amicus curiae, contend the definition covers only institutional records — namely, those materials retained in a permanent file as a matter of course. They argue that records "maintained by an educational agency or institution" generally would include final course grades, student grade point averages, standardized test scores, attendance records, counseling records, and records of disciplinary actions — but not student homework or classroom work. . . .

Two statutory indicators tell us that the Court of Appeals erred in concluding that an assignment satisfies the definition of education records as soon as it is graded by another student. First, the student papers are not, at that stage, "maintained" within the meaning of § 1232g(a)(4)(A). The ordinary meaning of the word "maintain" is "to keep in existence or continuance; preserve; retain." Random House Dictionary of the English Language 1160 (2d ed. 1987). Even assuming the teacher's grade book is an education record — a point the parties contest and one we do not decide here — the score on a student-graded assignment is not "contained therein," § 1232g(b)(1), until the teacher records it. The teacher does not maintain the grade while students correct their peers' assignments or call out their own marks. Nor do the student graders maintain the grades within the meaning of § 1232g(a)(4)(A). The word "maintain" suggests FERPA records will be kept in a filing cabinet in a records room at the school or on a permanent secure database, perhaps even after the student is no longer enrolled. The student graders only handle assignments for

---

[7]For more background on FERPA, see Nicholas Trott Long, *Privacy in the World of Education: What Hath James Buckley Wrought?*, 46 Rhode Island B.J. 9 (Feb. 1998); Maureen P. Rada, Note, *The Buckley Conspiracy: How Congress Authorized the Cover-Up of Campus Crime and How It Can Be Undone*, 59 Ohio St. L.J. 1799 (1998); Sandra L. Macklin, *Students' Rights in Indiana: Wrongful Distribution of Student Records and Potential Remedies*, 74 Ind. L.J. 1321 (1999).

a few moments as the teacher calls out the answers. It is fanciful to say they maintain the papers in the same way the registrar maintains a student's folder in a permanent file. . . .

Respondent's construction of the term "education records" to cover student homework or classroom work would impose substantial burdens on teachers across the country. It would force all instructors to take time, which otherwise could be spent teaching and in preparation, to correct an assortment of daily student assignments. . . . At argument, counsel for respondent seemed to agree that if a teacher in any of the thousands of covered classrooms in the Nation puts a happy face, a gold star, or a disapproving remark on a classroom assignment, federal law does not allow other students to see it.

We doubt Congress meant to intervene in this drastic fashion with traditional state functions. Under the Court of Appeals' interpretation of FERPA, the federal power would exercise minute control over specific teaching methods and instructional dynamics in classrooms throughout the country. The Congress is not likely to have mandated this result, and we do not interpret the statute to require it. . . .

NOTES & QUESTIONS

1. ***The Enforcement of FERPA.*** In *Owasso,* the individual plaintiffs used § 1983 to challenge the grading policy as an infringement of their FERPA rights. Recall from Chapter 3 that 42 U.S.C. § 1983 authorizes individuals to sue state officials for violations of federal law and the Constitution. Recall that FERPA does not directly provide for a private cause of action; it is enforced by the Secretary of Education. The Court did not reach the issue of whether § 1983 was an appropriate vehicle for private parties to seek redress for violations of FERPA. Instead, the Court addressed the issue in a case decided later in the same term. In *Gonzaga University v. Doe,* 122 S. Ct. 2268 (2002), a student at Gonzaga University was attempting to become a public elementary school teacher upon graduation. Gonzaga was currently investigating Doe for allegations of sexual misconduct. Gonzaga contacted the state agency for teacher certification and disclosed to the agency the allegations. The victim of the alleged sexual misconduct later denied the allegations and stated that Gonzaga officials had blown things out of proportion and were wrong in their assessment of her relationship with Doe. Doe sued Gonzaga under § 1983 alleging a violation of FERPA. Doe contended that FERPA conferred to him a right not to have his education records disclosed to unauthorized persons without his consent. A jury awarded him $1,155,000, including compensatory and punitive damages. The Court held that FERPA could not be enforced by a private right of action under § 1983. "[A] plaintiff must assert the violation of a federal *right*, not merely a violation of federal *law*." A federal statute must provide for an "unambiguously conferred right to support a cause of action brought under § 1983."

   > [I]f Congress wishes to create new rights enforceable under § 1983, it must do so in clear and unambiguous terms — no less and no more than what is

required for Congress to create new rights enforceable under an implied private right of action. FERPA's nondisclosure provisions contain no rights-creating language, they have an aggregate, not individual, focus, and they serve primarily to direct the Secretary of Education's distribution of public funds to educational institutions. They therefore create no rights enforceable under § 1983.

Justices Stevens and Ginsburg dissented, contending that FERPA contains numerous references to rights, including the title of the statute. "The entire statutory scheme was designed to protect such rights." Recall the other federal privacy statutes you studied that do not explicitly create a private right of action such as the HIPAA regulations and COPPA. What are the implications of this case for private causes of action under § 1983 to enforce these other privacy laws?

C. PRIVACY AT WORK

1. INTRODUCTION

Privacy in the workplace is a difficult and complex issue that continues to grow in importance as technology enables new forms of testing and monitoring of workers. Employer monitoring of workers is not new. For decades, employers have sought to keep close tabs on their employees. For example, in the early twentieth century, Ford Motor Company had its "Sociological Department" scrutinize employees to determine whether they gambled, drank, or conducted other frowned-upon activities to determine if they were worthy of receiving bonuses. Today, however, modern technology has enabled vastly more sophisticated forms of surveillance of workers. Employers routinely engage in a number of forms of investigation and monitoring of employees, such as conducting drug tests, obtaining credit reports and medical records, hiring private investigators to investigate employees, conducting psychological tests, administering polygraph examinations, requiring employees to fill out questionnaires containing detailed information about their personal lives, listening to telephone calls and voicemail, reading e-mail, monitoring computer use, searching offices and other employee work spaces, monitoring the number of keystrokes that an employee types, installing video surveillance devices to monitor workers, and even using electronic devices to track the location of workers.

Workplace monitoring is rapidly increasing. According to a 2000 survey by the American Management Association (AMA), 73.5 percent of major United States firms monitor employee communications and activities. This figure has doubled since 1997. Regarding particular forms of monitoring, 11.5 percent record and review telephone conversations; 30.9 percent store and review computer files; 38.1 percent store and review e-mail messages; 54.2 percent monitor Internet use; 14.6 percent engage in video surveillance of workers.

Employers believe that they have good reason to engage in employee surveillance and testing. First, employers desire to hire competent workers who are not likely to cause workplace disruptions or be careless and reckless on the job, possibly exposing the employer to liability. Employers want workers who are not likely to have problems in their personal life or health that will cause absences from work or will decrease productivity. In certain professions, if an employee's troubled past comes to light, it could place the employer in a bad light (e.g., employees of politicians). In other professions, such as child care, there is strong pressure for employers to scrutinize their employees' pasts and other aspects of their private lives to minimize the risk that the employee will engage in misconduct. Employers can be directly liable for negligent hiring.

Second, employers desire to monitor workers to force increased productivity and to curtail employee misconduct. Liability for sexual harassment has made employers more likely to investigate and monitor their employees to ensure that the workplace is free from harassment. The trend in the law is to make employers more responsible for training and monitoring their workers and for ensuring that their workers are competent to perform their jobs, especially when their jobs impact the safety of others (e.g., truck drivers, train operators, pilots, mechanics, and so on). Employers can be vicariously liable if their employees commit a tort on the job. Employers can also be directly liable for inadequate supervision.

Third, employers may desire to search workers to investigate particular incidents of misconduct in the workplace. If items are being stolen or important secrets or documents are being leaked, the employer may want to engage in searches and surveillance to catch the offenders.

Although there are several reasons why employers may want to monitor their workers, there are also many reasons why privacy in the workplace is an important value. Today, people are spending increasingly more time at work, often well over a third of the day and over half of their time while awake. Also, more workers are "telecommuting" from home.

A wide spectrum of law governs the privacy of employees. To understand how this law applies, it is important to distinguish between public and private sector employees.

Public Sector Employees. The federal government is the largest employer in the United States. There are approximately 2.75 million federal civilian employees and 1.4 million employed in the armed forces. State and local governments employ millions of employees as well. Public sector employees are protected by a number of laws. The Fourth Amendment applies not just to the police, but to all government officials, including government employers. Public sector employees are thus protected by the Fourth Amendment, although, as you will see, in a rather limited way. The constitutional right to information privacy (*Whalen v. Roe*) can protect against employer disclosures of information. Recall *Doe v. SEPTA* from Chapter 3. In many states, state constitutions also protect the privacy of public employees. Federal wiretap law applies to government employers and restricts their ability to conduct certain forms of electronic surveillance. State wiretap law may also provide additional protection. The Americans with Disabilities Act (ADA) prohibits employers from asking certain questions about employees. The federal Privacy Act protects against disclosures by government entities and could apply to disclosures of government employee information in certain circumstances. Employees can also sue employers for privacy invasions under the privacy torts — particularly for intrusion upon seclusion, public disclosure of private facts, and false light.

Depending upon the type of employment contract, employees may have additional contractual remedies. Pursuant to some types of employment contracts, employees can only be terminated for certain reasons, such as inadequate performance, unprofessional conduct, or disciplinary violations. If an employee is terminated and the reason is invalid, the employee can sue for wrongful termination and breach of contract. Many employees are "at-will" employees and may be dismissed at the whim of the employer. Generally, an at-will employee cannot bring a wrongful termination action. However, in many jurisdictions, there is an exception to this rule when the employee was fired for a reason that violates public policy (e.g., when the reason is discriminatory or the employee is fired for refusing to commit a criminal act). Employees who are terminated because of a refusal to comply with privacy-invasive testing, questioning, or monitoring or who are terminated because of the facts revealed by such activities can sometimes sue for wrongful termination in violation of public policy.

Private Sector Employees. Private sector employees enjoy some of the same protections as public sector employees, although the Fourth Amendment and most state constitutions do not apply to these employees. As you will see later in this chapter, however, in some states, federal and state constitutions can serve as a source of public policy for suits for wrongful termination in violation of public policy. Federal wiretap law applies not only to government employers but to private sector actors as well, including private sector employers. Additionally, the ADA, breach of contract, and privacy torts serve to protect the privacy of private sector employees.[8]

2. WORKPLACE SEARCHES

O'CONNOR v. ORTEGA

480 U.S. 709 (1987)

O'CONNOR, J. (plurality opinion). This suit under 42 U.S.C. § 1983 presents two issues concerning the Fourth Amendment rights of public employees. First, we must determine whether the respondent, a public employee, had a reasonable expectation of privacy in his office, desk, and file cabinets at his place of work. Second, we must address the appropriate Fourth Amendment standard for a search conducted by a public employer in areas in which a public employee is found to have a reasonable expectation of privacy. . . .

Dr. Magno Ortega, a physician and psychiatrist, held the position of Chief of Professional Education at Napa State Hospital (Hospital) for 17 years, until

---

[8] For more background about privacy in the workplace, see Sharona Hoffman, *Preplacement Examinations and Job-Relatedness: How to Enhance Privacy and Diminish Discrimination in the Workplace,* 49 U. Kan. L. Rev. 517 (2001).

his dismissal from that position in 1981. As Chief of Professional Education, Dr. Ortega had primary responsibility for training young physicians in psychiatric residency programs.

In July 1981, Hospital officials, including Dr. Dennis O'Connor, the Executive Director of the Hospital, became concerned about possible improprieties in Dr. Ortega's management of the residency program. In particular, the Hospital officials were concerned with Dr. Ortega's acquisition of an Apple II computer for use in the residency program. The officials thought that Dr. Ortega may have misled Dr. O'Connor into believing that the computer had been donated, when in fact the computer had been financed by the possibly coerced contributions of residents. Additionally, the Hospital officials were concerned with charges that Dr. Ortega had sexually harassed two female Hospital employees, and had taken inappropriate disciplinary action against a resident.

On July 30, 1981, Dr. O'Connor requested that Dr. Ortega take paid administrative leave during an investigation of these charges. . . . Dr. Ortega remained on administrative leave until the Hospital terminated his employment on September 22, 1981.

Dr. O'Connor selected several Hospital personnel to conduct the investigation, including an accountant, a physician, and a Hospital security officer. Richard Friday, the Hospital Administrator, led this "investigative team." At some point during the investigation, Mr. Friday made the decision to enter Dr. Ortega's office. The specific reason for the entry into Dr. Ortega's office is unclear from the record. . . .

The resulting search of Dr. Ortega's office was quite thorough. The investigators entered the office a number of times and seized several items from Dr. Ortega's desk and file cabinets, including a Valentine's Day card, a photograph, and a book of poetry all sent to Dr. Ortega by a former resident physician. These items were later used in a proceeding before a hearing officer of the California State Personnel Board to impeach the credibility of the former resident, who testified on Dr. Ortega's behalf. The investigators also seized billing documentation of one of Dr. Ortega's private patients under the California Medicaid program. . . .

Dr. Ortega commenced this action against petitioners in Federal District Court under 42 U.S.C. § 1983, alleging that the search of his office violated the Fourth Amendment. . . .

The strictures of the Fourth Amendment, applied to the States through the Fourteenth Amendment, have been applied to the conduct of governmental officials in various civil activities. *New Jersey v. T.L.O.,* 469 U.S. 325, 334-335 (1985). Thus, we have held in the past that the Fourth Amendment governs the conduct of school officials, building inspectors, and Occupational Safety and Health Act inspectors. . . . Searches and seizures by government employers or supervisors of the private property of their employees, therefore, are subject to the restraints of the Fourth Amendment.

. . . Our cases establish that Dr. Ortega's Fourth Amendment rights are implicated only if the conduct of the Hospital officials at issue in this case infringed "an expectation of privacy that society is prepared to consider reasonable." We have no talisman that determines in all cases those privacy expectations that society is prepared to accept as reasonable. Instead, "the

Court has given weight to such factors as the intention of the Framers of the Fourth Amendment, the uses to which the individual has put a location, and our societal understanding that certain areas deserve the most scrupulous protection from government invasion." *Oliver v. United States,* 466 U.S. 170, 178 (1984).

Because the reasonableness of an expectation of privacy, as well as the appropriate standard for a search, is understood to differ according to context, it is essential first to delineate the boundaries of the workplace context. The workplace includes those areas and items that are related to work and are generally within the employer's control. At a hospital, for example, the hallways, cafeteria, offices, desks, and file cabinets, among other areas, are all part of the workplace. These areas remain part of the workplace context even if the employee has placed personal items in them, such as a photograph placed in a desk or a letter posted on an employee bulletin board.

Not everything that passes through the confines of the business address can be considered part of the workplace context, however. An employee may bring closed luggage to the office prior to leaving on a trip, or a handbag or briefcase each workday. While whatever expectation of privacy the employee has in the existence and the outward appearance of the luggage is affected by its presence in the workplace, the employee's expectation of privacy in the *contents* of the luggage is not affected in the same way. The appropriate standard for a workplace search does not necessarily apply to a piece of closed personal luggage, a handbag or a briefcase that happens to be within the employer's business address.

Within the workplace context, this Court has recognized that employees may have a reasonable expectation of privacy against intrusions by police. . . .

Individuals do not lose Fourth Amendment rights merely because they work for the government instead of a private employer. The operational realities of the workplace, however, may make *some* employees' expectations of privacy unreasonable when an intrusion is by a supervisor rather than a law enforcement official. Public employees' expectations of privacy in their offices, desks, and file cabinets, like similar expectations of employees in the private sector, may be reduced by virtue of actual office practices and procedures, or by legitimate regulation. . . . The employee's expectation of privacy must be assessed in the context of the employment relation. An office is seldom a private enclave free from entry by supervisors, other employees, and business and personal invitees. Instead, in many cases offices are continually entered by fellow employees and other visitors during the workday for conferences, consultations, and other work-related visits. Simply put, it is the nature of government offices that others—such as fellow employees, supervisors, consensual visitors, and the general public—may have frequent access to an individual's office. . . . Given the great variety of work environments in the public sector, the question whether an employee has a reasonable expectation of privacy must be addressed on a case-by-case basis. . . .

. . . [W]e recognize that the undisputed evidence suggests that Dr. Ortega had a reasonable expectation of privacy in his desk and file cabinets. The undisputed evidence discloses that Dr. Ortega did not share his desk or file cabinets with any other employees. Dr. Ortega had occupied the office for 17 years and he kept materials in his office, which included personal correspondence, medical files, correspondence from private patients unconnected to the Hospital, personal financial records, teaching aids and notes, and personal gifts and mementos. The files on physicians in residency training were kept outside Dr. Ortega's office. . . .

. . . [A]s we have stated in *T.L.O.*, "[t]o hold that the Fourth Amendment applies to searches conducted by [public employers] is only to begin the inquiry into the standards governing such searches. . . . [W]hat is reasonable depends on the context within which a search takes place." Thus, we must determine the appropriate standard of reasonableness applicable to the search. A determination of the standard of reasonableness applicable to a particular class of searches requires "balanc[ing] the nature and quality of the intrusion on the individual's Fourth Amendment interests against the importance of the governmental interests alleged to justify the intrusion." In the case of searches conducted by a public employer, we must balance the invasion of the employees' legitimate expectations of privacy against the government's need for supervision, control, and the efficient operation of the workplace.

"[I]t is settled . . . that 'except in certain carefully defined classes of cases, a search of private property without proper consent is "unreasonable" unless it has been authorized by a valid search warrant.'" There are some circumstances, however, in which we have recognized that a warrant requirement is unsuitable. . . . [A]s Justice Blackmun stated in *T.L.O.*, "[o]nly in those exceptional circumstances in which special needs, beyond the normal need for law enforcement, make the warrant and probable-cause requirement impracticable." . . .

The legitimate privacy interests of public employees in the private objects they bring to the workplace may be substantial. Against these privacy interests, however, must be balanced the realities of the workplace, which strongly suggest that a warrant requirement would be unworkable. While police, and even administrative enforcement personnel, conduct searches for the primary purpose of obtaining evidence for use in criminal or other enforcement proceedings, employers most frequently need to enter the offices and desks of their employees for legitimate work-related reasons wholly unrelated to illegal conduct. Employers and supervisors are focused primarily on the need to complete the government agency's work in a prompt and efficient manner. An employer may have need for correspondence, or a file or report available only in an employee's office while the employee is away from the office. Or, as is alleged to have been the case here, employers may need to safeguard or identify state property or records in an office in connection with a pending investigation into suspected employee misfeasance.

In our view, requiring an employer to obtain a warrant whenever the employer wished to enter an employee's office, desk, or file cabinets for a work-related purpose would seriously disrupt the routine conduct of business and would be unduly burdensome. Imposing unwieldy warrant procedures in such cases upon supervisors, who would otherwise have no reason to be familiar with such procedures, is simply unreasonable. In contrast to other circumstances in which we have required warrants, supervisors in offices such as at the Hospital are hardly in the business of investigating the violation of criminal laws. Rather, work-related searches are merely incident to the primary business of the agency. Under these circumstances, the imposition of a warrant requirement would conflict with "the common-sense realization that government offices could not function if every employment decision became a constitutional matter."

Whether probable cause is an inappropriate standard for public employer searches of their employees' offices presents a more difficult issue. . . .

The governmental interest justifying work-related intrusions by public employers is the efficient and proper operation of the workplace. Government agencies provide myriad services to the public, and the work of these agencies would suffer if employers were required to have probable cause before they entered an employee's desk for the purpose of finding a file or piece of office correspondence. Indeed, it is difficult to give the concept of probable cause, rooted as it is in the criminal investigatory context, much meaning when the purpose of a search is to retrieve a file for work-related reasons. Similarly, the concept of probable cause has little meaning for a routine inventory conducted by public employers for the purpose of securing state property. To ensure the efficient and proper operation of the agency, therefore, public employers must be given wide latitude to enter employee offices for work-related, noninvestigatory reasons.

We come to a similar conclusion for searches conducted pursuant to an investigation of work-related employee misconduct. Even when employers conduct an investigation, they have an interest substantially different from "the normal need for law enforcement." Public employers have an interest in ensuring that their agencies operate in an effective and efficient manner, and the work of these agencies inevitably suffers from the inefficiency, incompetence, mismanagement, or other work-related misfeasance of its employees. Indeed, in many cases, public employees are entrusted with tremendous responsibility, and the consequences of their misconduct or incompetence to both the agency and the public interest can be severe. . . . In our view, therefore, a probable cause requirement for searches of the type at issue here would impose intolerable burdens on public employers. . . . It is simply unrealistic to expect supervisors in most government agencies to learn the subtleties of the probable cause standard. . . . [W]e conclude that a reasonableness standard will permit regulation of the employer's conduct "according to the dictates of reason and common sense." . . .

. . . We hold, therefore, that public employer intrusions on the constitutionally protected privacy interests of government employees for noninvestigatory, work-related purposes, as well as for investigations of work-related misconduct, should be judged by the standard of reasonableness under all the circumstances. . . .

On remand . . . the District Court must determine the justification for the search and seizure, and evaluate the reasonableness of both the inception of the search and its scope. . . .

BLACKMUN, joined by BRENNAN, MARSHALL, and STEVENS, J.J. dissenting. . . . [T]he reality of work in modern time, whether done by public or private employees, reveals why a public employee's expectation of privacy in the workplace should be carefully safeguarded and not lightly set aside. It is, unfortunately, all too true that the workplace has become another home for most working Americans. Many employees spend the better part of their days and much of their evenings at work. Consequently, an employee's private life must intersect with the workplace, for example, when the employee takes advantage of work or lunch breaks to make personal telephone calls, to attend to personal business, or to receive personal visitors in the office. As a result, the tidy distinctions (to which the plurality alludes) between the workplace and professional affairs, on the one hand, and personal possessions and private activities, on the other, do not exist in reality. Not all of an employee's private possessions will stay in his or her briefcase or handbag. . . .

Although the plurality mentions the "special need" step, it turns immediately to a balancing test to formulate its standard of reasonableness. This error is significant because, given the facts of this case, no "special need" exists here to justify dispensing with the warrant and probable-cause requirements. As observed above, the facts suggest that this was an investigatory search undertaken to obtain evidence of charges of mismanagement at a time when Dr. Ortega was on administrative leave and not permitted to enter the Hospital's grounds. There was no special practical need that might have justified dispensing with the warrant and probable-cause requirements. Without sacrificing their ultimate goal of maintaining an effective institution devoted to training and healing, to which the disciplining of Hospital employees contributed, petitioners could have taken any evidence of Dr. Ortega's alleged improprieties to a magistrate in order to obtain a warrant. . . .

Furthermore, this seems to be exactly the kind of situation where a neutral magistrate's involvement would have been helpful in curtailing the infringement upon Dr. Ortega's privacy. Petitioners would have been forced to articulate their exact reasons for the search and to specify the items in Dr. Ortega's office they sought, which would have prevented the general rummaging through the doctor's office, desk, and file cabinets. . . .

NOTES & QUESTIONS

1. Why does the Court conclude that people's expectation of privacy is diminished in the workplace? Recall in *Katz* that the Court declared that privacy "protects people, not places." Is this still true after *O'Connor v. Ortega?*
2. William Stuntz contends that the result in *Ortega* was paradoxically protective of privacy:

> . . . [I]f the law were to forbid these ordinary work-related entries, employers would have a substantial incentive to restructure the work environment to recover their ability to retrieve information. There are a number of ways of doing this. File cabinets can be moved from closed offices to open secretarial pools to make access easy; more records can be kept in the accounting department and fewer in individual employees' files; computer space can be arranged so that private (and secure) recordkeeping by individual employees is difficult.
>
> In short, the employer . . . has a fair degree of substantive power to reshape the rules of the workplace, in order to accomplish indirectly what he

cannot do directly. If information cannot be taken from offices, offices can be turned into places where little information is stored. . . .

Given this kind of authority, it is easy to imagine that employees might prefer a regime that gives their superiors broad discretion to enter presumptively private work areas. Such authority reduces the likelihood that sanctions (such as the failure to get a desired promotion or job assignment) will be imposed based on unverifiable, and possibly false, suspicions. More importantly, broad search authority vastly reduces the cost to government employers of creating private spaces for their employees. The Fourth Amendment issue is thus turned upside down: the rule that probably maximizes privacy (and thus the rule that search targets would probably want) is the rule that permits searches of work areas for any authentically work-related reason. That is the rule *Ortega* adopts.[9]

3. ***Workplace Computer Searches.*** In *Leventhal v. Knapek,* 266 F.3d 64 (2d Cir. 2001), plaintiff Gary Leventhal worked in the Accounting Bureau of the New York Department of Transportation (DOT). An anonymous letter to Leventhal's superiors complained of various employees who were late or abusing their time at work. The letter spoke of a "grade 27 employee" who was spending most of his time on personal calls or "talking to other personnel about personal computers." Although the letter did not name Leventhal, his supervisors concluded the letter was referring to Leventhal since he was the only grade 27 employee in the office. DOT investigators entered Leventhal's office after business hours one evening and searched the files on his computer's hard drive. To do this, investigators used a special bootdisk to circumvent certain password-protections on his computer. Upon review of Leventhal's files, investigators discovered that he had installed tax software to fill out his personal tax forms. Leventhal was brought up on disciplinary charges and denied a raise. Leventhal brought a §1983 action against DOT and his supervisors alleging a violation of his Fourth Amendment rights. The court rejected Leventhal's suit:

> . . . We hold, based on the particular facts of this case, that Leventhal had a reasonable expectation of privacy in the contents of his office computer. . . .
>
> Leventhal occupied a private office with a door. He had exclusive use of the desk, filing cabinet, and computer in his office. Leventhal did not share use of his computer with other employees in the Accounting Bureau nor was there evidence that visitors or the public had access to his computer. . . .
>
> . . . [W]e do not find that the DOT either had a general practice of routinely conducting searches of office computers or had placed Leventhal on notice that he should have no expectation of privacy in the contents of his office computer. *Cf. United States v. Simons,* 206 F.3d 392 (4th Cir. 2000) (finding no legitimate expectation of privacy in Internet use when employer's known policy allowed monitoring of "all file transfers, all websites visited, and all e-mail messages"). . . .
>
> Even though Leventhal had some expectation of privacy in the contents of his office computer, the investigatory searches by the DOT did not violate

---

[9] William J. Stuntz, *Implicit Bargains, Government Power, and the Fourth Amendment,* 44 Stan. L. Rev. 553, 579 (1992).

his Fourth Amendment rights. An investigatory search for evidence of suspected work-related employee misfeasance will be constitutionally "reasonable" if it is "justified at its inception" and of appropriate scope. . . .

The initial consideration of the search's justification examines whether "there are reasonable grounds for suspecting that the search will turn up evidence that the employee is guilty of work-related misconduct." *O'Connor,* 480 U.S. at 726. Here, there were reasonable grounds to believe that the searches would uncover evidence of misconduct. The specific allegations against the grade 27 employee, who was reasonably assumed to be Leventhal, were that (1) he was "late everyday"; (2) he spent "[t]he majority of his time . . . on non-DOT business related phone calls or talking to other personnel about personal computers"; and that (3) "[h]e is only in the office half the time[; the other half] he is either sick or on vacation." . . .

The scope of a search will be appropriate if "reasonably related to the objectives of the search and not excessively intrusive in light of the nature of the misconduct." . . . Although the anonymous letter did not allege that the grade 27 employee was misusing DOT office computers, it did allege that the grade 27 employee was not attentive to his duties and spent a significant amount of work time discussing personal computers with other employees. . . . In view of the allegations of the misuse of DOT computers among other employees in the Accounting Bureau, Leventhal's alleged penchant for discussing personal computers during work hours, and Leventhal's general inattention to his duties which included, we presume, supervision of the computer use of others, we find that the searches of his computer were "reasonably related" to the DOT investigation of allegations of Leventhal's workplace misconduct. . . .

4. *Waiver of Fourth Amendment Rights.* Can government employers require that their employees undergo unreasonable searches under the Fourth Amendment as a condition of employment? The answer is no. *See Pickering v. Board of Education,* 391 U.S. 563 (1968). However, if an employee voluntarily consents to the search, then such searches can be conducted. *See McDonell v. Hunter,* 809 F.2d 1302 (8th Cir. 1987).

K-MART CORP. V. TROTTI

677 S.W.2d 632 (Tex. Ct. App. 1984)

BULLOCK, J. K-Mart Corporation appeals from a judgment awarding the appellee, Trotti, $8,000.00 in actual damages and $100,000.00 in exemplary damages for [intrusion upon seclusion]. . . .

The appellee was an employee in the hosiery department at the appellants' store number 7441. Her supervisors had never indicated any dissatisfaction with her work nor any suspicion of her honesty.

The appellants provided their employees with lockers for the storage of personal effects during working hours. There was no assignment of any given locker to any individual employee. . . . The appellee, with appellants' knowledge, used one of these lockers and provided her own combination lock.

On October 31, 1981, the appellee placed her purse in her locker when she arrived for work. She testified that she snapped the lock closed and then pulled on it to make sure it was locked. When she returned to her locker during her afternoon break, she discovered the lock hanging open. Searching through her locker, the appellee further discovered her personal items in her purse in considerable disorder. Nothing was missing from either the locker or the purse. The store manager testified that, in the company of three junior administrators at the store, he had that afternoon searched the lockers because of a suspicion raised by the appellants' security personnel that an unidentified employee, not the appellee, had stolen a watch. The manager and his assistants were also searching for missing price-marking guns. The appellee further testified that, as she left the employee's locker area after discovering her locker open, she heard the manager suggest to his assistants, "Let's get busy again." The manager testified that none of the parties searched through employees' personal effects. . . .

The manager testified that during the initial hiring interviews, all prospective employees received verbal notification from personnel supervisors that it was the appellants' policy to conduct ingress-egress searches of employees and also to conduct unannounced searches of lockers. A personnel supervisor and an assistant manager, however, testified that, although locker searches did regularly occur, the personnel supervisors did not apprise prospective employees of this policy. . . .

We hold that the weight of the evidence indicates that the appellants' employees came upon a locker with a lock provided by an employee, disregarded the appellee's demonstration of her expectation of privacy, opened and searched the locker, and probably opened and searched her purse as well; and, in so holding, we consider it is immaterial whether the appellee actually securely locked her locker or not. It is sufficient that an employee in this situation, by having placed a lock on the locker at the employee's own expense and with the appellants' consent, has demonstrated a legitimate expectation to a right of privacy in both the locker itself and those personal effects within it. . . .

NOTES & QUESTIONS

1. In *O'Connor v. Ortega,* suppose that Dr. Ortega sued his employer for intrusion upon seclusion. Assess his chances of successfully pursuing such a suit.
2. ***State Statutory Law.*** A number of states have restricted workplace surveillance. For example, pursuant to Conn. Gen. Stat. § 31-48b(b):

   > No employer or agent or representative of an employer shall operate any electronic surveillance device or system, including but not limited to the recording of sound or voice or a closed circuit television system, or any combination thereof, for the purpose of recording or monitoring the activities of his employees in areas designed for the health or personal comfort of the employees or for safeguarding of their possessions, such as rest rooms, locker rooms or lounges.

   Violations are punishable by fines; repeat violations (third and subsequent violations) are punishable by imprisonment for 30 days.
3. ***Public Disclosure and the Workplace.*** Employers can be liable for public disclosure of private facts for revealing confidential information about their employees. Recall *Miller v. Motorola, Inc.* from Chapter 2. In *Levias v. United*

Airlines, 500 N.E.2d 370 (Ohio Ct. App. 1985), the court held that a flight attendant had a viable public disclosure action when her employer disclosed medical information from her gynecologist to her supervisors and her husband.

The disclosure of personal information by public sector employers can give rise to a §1983 action under the constitutional right to information privacy. Recall *Doe v. SEPTA* from Chapter 3.

3. WORKPLACE SURVEILLANCE

Thompson v. Johnson County Community College

930 F. Supp. 501 (D. Kan. 1996)

[The plaintiffs, a group of community college security personnel, sued the college for conducting video surveillance of their locker area. Among other things, the plaintiffs alleged that the surveillance violated federal wiretap law and the Fourth Amendment.]

Van Bebber, J. . . . Plaintiffs first claim that defendants violated Title I by conducting video surveillance in the workplace. Under Title I, "any person whose wire or oral communications is intercepted, disclosed or used in violation of [the Act] may in a civil action recover from the person or entity which engage in that violation such relief as may be appropriate." 18 U.S.C. §2520. . . .

Virtually every circuit that has addressed the issue of silent video surveillance has held that Title I does not prohibit its use. . . .

On the other hand, the above cited cases implicitly imply that video surveillance that includes the capability to record audio conversations would violate Title I. In that situation, the video image captured by the surveillance camera is not what violates Title I. Rather, it is the interception of an oral communication that subjects the interceptor to liability.

In their current motion, defendants argue that they installed a silent video surveillance camera in the security personnel locker area. Defendants contend that, as a matter of law, they are entitled to summary judgment on this issue because silent video surveillance does not fall within the protection of Title I. The court agrees. . . .

In Count II, plaintiffs have brought a claim pursuant to 42 U.S.C. § 1983. They contend that defendants' warrantless video surveillance searches of the security personnel locker area violated their Fourth Amendment rights. The court disagrees.

Domestic silent video surveillance is subject to Fourth Amendment prohibitions against unreasonable searches. However, this does not mean that defendants' use of video surveillance automatically violated plaintiffs' Fourth Amendment rights. Rather, the court first must determine whether plaintiffs had a reasonable expectation of privacy in their locker area. If plaintiffs had no reasonable expectation of privacy in this area, there is "no fourth amendment violation regardless of the nature of the search." . . .

. . . [D]efendants assert that the security personnel locker area is similar to hallway lockers in a school. The security personnel locker area was part of a storage room that also housed the College's heating and air-conditioning equipment. Additionally, the College did not limit access to this storage room. Security personnel and other college employees, including maintenance and service personnel, had unfettered access to this storage room. Consequently, defendants argue that the open, public nature of the security personnel locker area defeats any reasonable expectation of privacy in this area. The court agrees.

. . . [V]ideo surveillance "in public places, such as banks, does not violate the fourth amendment; the police may record what they normally may view with the naked eye." In the employment context, the Supreme Court has held that "some government offices may be so open to fellow employees or the public that no expectation of privacy is reasonable." *O'Connor v. Ortega*, 480 U.S. 709 (1987). . . .

In the instant action, viewing the facts in a light most favorable to plaintiffs, the court finds that they did not have a reasonable expectation of privacy in the security personnel locker area. This area was not enclosed. Plaintiffs' activities could be viewed by anyone walking into or through the storage room/security personnel locker area. Additionally, plaintiffs cannot maintain that the security personnel locker area was reserved for their exclusive use considering that other college personnel also had regular access to this area. The court concludes that plaintiffs' lack of a reasonable expectation of privacy in the security personnel locker area defeats their claim that defendants violated their Fourth Amendment right to privacy.

NOTES & QUESTIONS

1. *Intrusion upon Seclusion and Surveillance in the Workplace.* In *Speer v. Ohio Department of Rehabilitation and Correction*, 624 N.E.2d 251 (Ohio Ct. App. 1993), rumors reached Leroy Payton, the supervisor of plaintiff Theresa Speer (a prison official) that Speer was being "too friendly" with two inmates. Payton launched an investigation and surveillance of Speer. In one instance, Payton hid in the ceiling of a co-ed staff rest room for over seven hours to spy on Speer. The trial court held that Payton's surveillance was pursuant to a broad policy of decision-making and refused to second-guess Payton's choice of surveillance tactic. The court of appeals reversed, concluding that Payton's tactics were unreasonable and not defensible as a policy matter.

2. *Intrusion upon Seclusion and Surveillance Outside the Workplace.* In *Saldana v. Kelsey-Hayes*, 443 N.W.2d 382 (Mich. Ct. App. 1981), the plaintiff injured his back and arm from falling off a bicycle on the property of his employer, defendant Kelsey-Hayes Company. The defendant's property was comprised of different buildings, and plaintiff used his bicycle to travel from building to building. The plaintiff's employer suspected that the plaintiff was malingering and hired a private investigating firm to determine the extent of the plaintiff's injuries. The investigator observed the plaintiff's home from a parked car near his house, telephoned the plaintiff to determine whether he was home, walked passed the plaintiff's house and observed the plaintiff through an open window, used a powerful zoom lens

to observe the plaintiff through the windows to his house, and posed as a process server in order to gain entry to the plaintiff's home and look around. According to the investigator, the plaintiff was able to move around freely. The plaintiff brought an action against his employer for intrusion upon seclusion. The court, however, concluded that the plaintiff's action should be dismissed:

> . . . [P]laintiff can show an intrusion. First, agents of defendants entered plaintiff's home under false pretenses. Also, agents of defendants observed plaintiff through the windows of his home by the naked eye and with a powerful camera lens. Other jurisdictions have held that "window-peeping" is actionable. Whether the intrusion is objectionable to a reasonable person is a factual question best determined by a jury. It may not be objectionable to peer through an open window where the curtains are not drawn, but the use of a powerful lens to observe the interior of a home or of a subterfuge to enter a home could be found objectionable to a reasonable person.
>
> However, even if we find that looking into plaintiff's window with the naked eye and with a powerful camera lens is an intrusion which would be objectionable to a reasonable person, plaintiff still cannot prevail. Plaintiff does not allege facts that show the intrusions were into matters which plaintiff had a right to keep private. . . . The defendants' duty to refrain from intrusion into another's private affairs is not absolute in nature, but rather is limited by those rights which arise from social conditions, *including the business relationship of the parties*. Defendants' surveillance of plaintiff at his home involved matters which defendants had a legitimate right to investigate. . . . Plaintiff's privacy was subject to the legitimate interest of his employer in investigating suspicions that plaintiff's work-related disability was a pretext. We conclude that plaintiff does not meet the second requirement of the intrusion into seclusion test. Defendant also has a right to investigate matters that are potential sources of legal liability.

The *Saldana* court apparently treated the surveillance of the plaintiff outside of the workplace as equivalent to surveillance inside the workplace. Should an employer be permitted to spy on its employees when they are not at work?

3. Some states have enacted laws prohibiting surveillance cameras in certain areas of the workplace, such as rest rooms. Some of these prohibitions have criminal penalties. Can employees consent to video surveillance in such areas? Recall from note 4 following *O'Connor v. Ortega* in Section B.1 that employees can consent to searches that would ordinarily be unreasonable under the Fourth Amendment. But what about consenting to violations of criminal statutes? For an answer, see *Cramer v. Consolidated Freightways, Inc.* below (note 3 following *Baggs v. Eagle-Pitcher Industries, Inc.* in Section B.4).

4. DRUG TESTING

NATIONAL TREASURY EMPLOYEES UNION V. VON RAAB

489 U.S. 656 (1989)

KENNEDY, J. . . . The United States Customs Service, a bureau of the Department of the Treasury, is the federal agency responsible for processing persons, carriers, cargo, and mail into the United States, collecting revenue from imports, and enforcing customs and related laws. An important responsibility of the Service is the interdiction and seizure of contraband, including illegal drugs. . . . In the routine discharge of their duties, many Customs employees have direct contact with those who traffic in drugs for profit. Drug import operations, often directed by sophisticated criminal syndicates, may be effected by violence or its threat. As a necessary response, many Customs operatives carry and use firearms in connection with their official duties.

In December 1985, respondent, the Commissioner of Customs . . . announced his intention to require drug tests of employees who applied for, or occupied, certain positions within the Service. . . .

In May 1986, the Commissioner announced implementation of the drug-testing program. Drug tests were made a condition of placement or employment for positions that meet one or more of three criteria. The first is direct involvement in drug interdiction or enforcement of related laws, an activity the Commissioner deemed fraught with obvious dangers to the mission of the agency and the lives of Customs agents. The second criterion is a requirement that the incumbent carry firearms, as the Commissioner concluded that "[p]ublic safety demands that employees who carry deadly arms and are prepared to make instant life or death decisions be drug free." The third criterion is a requirement for the incumbent to handle "classified" material, which the Commissioner determined might fall into the hands of smugglers if accessible to employees who, by reason of their own illegal drug use, are susceptible to bribery or blackmail.

After an employee qualifies for a position covered by the Customs testing program, the Service advises him by letter that his final selection is contingent upon successful completion of drug screening. An independent contractor contacts the employee to fix the time and place for collecting the sample. On reporting for the test, the employee must produce photographic identification and remove any outer garments, such as a coat or a jacket, and personal belongings. The employee may produce the sample behind a partition, or in the privacy of a bathroom stall if he so chooses. To ensure against adulteration of the specimen, or substitution of a sample from another person, a monitor of the same sex as the employee remains close at hand to listen for the normal sounds of urination. Dye is added to the toilet water to prevent the employee from using the water to adulterate the sample. . . .

The laboratory tests the sample for the presence of marijuana, cocaine, opiates, amphetamines, and phencyclidine. . . .

Customs employees who test positive for drugs and who can offer no satisfactory explanation are subject to dismissal from the Service. Test results may not, however, be turned over to any other agency, including criminal prosecutors, without the employee's written consent. . . .

Petitioners, a union of federal employees and a union official, commenced this suit . . . on behalf of current Customs Service employees who seek covered positions. Petitioners alleged that the Custom Service drug-testing program violated, inter alia, the Fourth Amendment. . . .

It is clear that the Customs Service's drug-testing program is not designed to serve the ordinary needs of law enforcement. Test results may not be used in a criminal prosecution of the employee without the employee's consent. The purposes of the program are to deter drug use among those eligible for promotion to sensitive positions within the Service and to prevent the promotion of drug users to those positions. These substantial interests . . . present a special need that may justify departure from the ordinary warrant and probable-cause requirements. . . .

. . . [A] warrant would provide little or nothing in the way of additional protection of personal privacy. A warrant serves primarily to advise the citizen that an intrusion is authorized by law and limited in its permissible scope and to interpose a neutral magistrate between the citizen and the law enforcement officer "engaged in the often competitive enterprise of ferreting out crime." . . . A covered employee is simply not subject "to the discretion of the official in the field." The process becomes automatic when the employee elects to apply for, and thereafter pursue, a covered position. Because the Service does not make a discretionary determination to search based on a judgment that certain conditions are present, there are simply "no special facts for a neutral magistrate to evaluate." . . .

Even where it is reasonable to dispense with the warrant requirement in the particular circumstances, a search ordinarily must be based on probable cause. Our cases teach, however, that the probable-cause standard "'is peculiarly related to criminal investigations.'" In particular, the traditional probable-cause standard may be unhelpful in analyzing the reasonableness of routine administrative functions, especially where the Government seeks to prevent the development of hazardous conditions or to detect violations that rarely generate articulable grounds for searching any particular place or person. Our precedents have settled that, in certain limited circumstances, the Government's need to discover such latent or hidden conditions, or to prevent their development, is sufficiently compelling to justify the intrusion on privacy entailed by conducting such searches without any measure of individualized suspicion. We think the Government's need to conduct the suspicionless searches required by the Customs program outweighs the privacy interests of employees engaged directly in drug interdiction, and of those who otherwise are required to carry firearms.

The Customs Service is our Nation's first line of defense against one of the greatest problems affecting the health and welfare of our population. We have adverted before to "the veritable national crisis in law enforcement caused by smuggling of illicit narcotics." . . . [D]rug smugglers do not hesitate to use violence to protect their lucrative trade and avoid apprehension.

Many of the Service's employees are often exposed to this criminal element and to the controlled substances it seeks to smuggle into the country. The physical safety of these employees may be threatened, and many may be tempted not only by bribes from the traffickers with whom they deal, but also by their own access to vast sources of valuable contraband seized and controlled by the Service. . . .

The public interest likewise demands effective measures to prevent the promotion of drug users to positions that require the incumbent to carry a firearm, even if the incumbent is not engaged directly in the interdiction of drugs. Customs employees who may use deadly force plainly "discharge duties fraught with such risks of injury to others that even a momentary lapse of attention can have disastrous consequences." We agree with the Government that the public should not bear the risk that employees who may suffer from impaired perception and judgment will be promoted to positions where they may need to employ deadly force. . . .

Against these valid public interests we must weigh the interference with individual liberty that results from requiring these classes of employees to undergo a urine test. The interference with individual privacy that results from the collection of a urine sample for subsequent chemical analysis could be substantial in some circumstances. . . .

We think Customs employees who are directly involved in the interdiction of illegal drugs or who are required to carry firearms in the line of duty likewise have a diminished expectation of privacy in respect to the intrusions occasioned by a urine test. Unlike most private citizens or government employees in general, employees involved in drug interdiction reasonably should expect effective inquiry into their fitness and probity. Much the same is true of employees who are required to carry firearms. Because successful performance of their duties depends uniquely on their judgment and dexterity, these employees cannot reasonably expect to keep from the Service personal information that bears directly on their fitness. While reasonable tests designed to elicit this information doubtless infringe some privacy expectations, we do not believe these expectations outweigh the Government's compelling interests in safety and in the integrity of our borders.

. . . [P]etitioners argue that the program is unjustified because it is not based on a belief that testing will reveal any drug use by covered employees. In pressing this argument, petitioners point out that the Service's testing scheme was not implemented in response to any perceived drug problem among Customs employees, and that the program actually has not led to the discovery of a significant number of drug users. Counsel for petitioners informed us at oral argument that no more than 5 employees out of 3,600 have tested positive for drugs. Second, petitioners contend that the Service's scheme is not a "sufficiently productive mechanism to justify [its] intrusion upon Fourth Amendment interests," because illegal drug users can avoid detection with ease by temporary abstinence or by surreptitious adulteration of their urine specimens. These contentions are unpersuasive.

Petitioners' first contention evinces an unduly narrow view of the context in which the Service's testing program was implemented. Petitioners do not dispute, nor can there be doubt, that drug abuse is one of the most serious problems confronting our society today. There is little reason to believe that American workplaces are immune from this pervasive social problem. . . .

We are unable, on the present record, to assess the reasonableness of the Government's testing program insofar as it covers employees who are required "to handle classified material." We readily agree that the Government has a compelling interest in protecting truly sensitive information from those who, "under compulsion of circumstances or for other reasons, . . . might compromise [such] information." We also agree that employees who seek promotions to positions where they would handle sensitive information can be required to submit to a urine test under the Service's screening program, especially if the positions covered under this category require background investigations, medical examinations, or other intrusions that may be expected to diminish their expectations of privacy in respect of a urinalysis test.

It is not clear, however, whether the category defined by the Service's testing directive encompasses only those Customs employees likely to gain access to sensitive information. Employees who are tested under the Service's scheme include those holding such diverse positions as "Accountant," "Accounting Technician," "Animal Caretaker," "Attorney (All)," "Baggage Clerk," "Co-op Student (All)," "Electric Equipment Repairer," "Mail Clerk/Assistant," and "Messenger." . . . [I]t is not evident that those occupying these positions are likely to gain access to sensitive information, and this apparent discrepancy raises in our minds the question whether the Service has defined this category of employees more broadly than is necessary to meet the purposes of the Commissioner's directive.

We cannot resolve this ambiguity on the basis of the record before us, and we think it is appropriate to remand the case to the Court of Appeals for such proceedings as may be necessary to clarify the scope of this category of employees subject to testing. Upon remand the Court of Appeals should examine the criteria used by the Service in determining what materials are classified and in deciding whom to test under this rubric. . . .

SCALIA, J. joined by STEVENS, J. dissenting. . . Until today this Court had upheld a bodily search separate from arrest and without individualized suspicion of wrongdoing only with respect to prison inmates, relying upon the uniquely dangerous nature of that environment. . . .

The Court's opinion in the present case . . . will be searched in vain for real evidence of a real problem that will be solved by urine testing of Customs Service employees. . . . The only pertinent points, it seems to me, are supported by nothing but speculation, and not very plausible speculation at that. It is not apparent to me that a Customs Service employee who uses drugs is significantly more likely to be bribed by a drug smuggler, any more than a Customs Service employee who wears diamonds is significantly more likely to be bribed by a diamond smuggler — unless, perhaps, the addiction to drugs is so severe, and requires so much money to maintain, that it would be detectable even without benefit of a urine test. Nor is it apparent to me that Customs officers who use drugs will be appreciably less "sympathetic" to their drug-interdiction mission, any more than police officers who exceed the speed limit in their private cars are appreciably less sympathetic to their mission of enforcing the traffic laws. . . . Nor, finally, is it apparent to me that urine tests will be even marginally more effective in preventing gun-carrying agents from risking "impaired perception and judgment" than is their current knowledge that, if impaired, they may be shot dead in unequal combat with unimpaired smugglers — unless, again, their addiction is so severe that no urine test is needed for detection.

What is absent in the Government's justifications — notably absent, revealingly absent, and as far as I am concerned dispositively absent — is the recitation of even a single instance in which any of the speculated horribles actually occurred: an instance, that is, in which the cause of bribe-taking, or of poor aim, or of unsympathetic law enforcement, or of compromise of classified information, was drug use. Although the Court points out that several employees have in the past been removed from the Service for accepting bribes and other integrity violations, and that at least nine officers have died in the line of duty since 1974, there is no indication whatever that these incidents were related to drug use by Service employees. . . .

Today's decision would be wrong, but at least of more limited effect, if its approval of drug testing were confined to that category of employees assigned specifically to drug interdiction duties. Relatively few public employees fit that description. But in extending approval of drug testing to that category consisting of employees who carry firearms, the Court exposes vast numbers of public employees to this needless indignity. Logically, of course, if those who carry guns can be treated in this fashion, so can all others whose work, if performed under the influence of drugs, may endanger others — automobile drivers, operators of other potentially dangerous equipment, construction workers, school crossing guards. A similarly broad scope attaches to the Court's approval of drug testing for those with access to "sensitive information." Since this category is not limited to Service employees with drug interdiction duties, nor to "sensitive information" specifically relating to drug traffic, today's holding apparently approves drug testing for all federal employees with security clearances — or, indeed, for all federal employees with valuable confidential information to impart. Since drug use is not a particular problem in the Customs Service, employees throughout the Government are no less likely to violate the public trust by taking bribes to feed their drug habit, or by yielding to blackmail. Moreover, there is no reason why this super-protection against harms arising from drug use must be limited to public employees; a law requiring similar testing of private citizens who use dangerous instruments such as guns or cars, or who have access to classified information, would also be constitutional. . . .

NOTES & QUESTIONS

1. In *Skinner v. Railway Labor Executives' Assn.*, 489 U.S. 602 (1989), decided on the same day as *Von Raab*, the Court upheld regulations mandating blood and urine tests of railroad employees who were involved in certain train accidents:

   > The Government's interest in regulating the conduct of railroad employees to ensure safety, like its supervision of probationers or regulated industries, or its operation of a government office, school, or prison, "likewise presents 'special needs' beyond normal law enforcement that may justify departures from the usual warrant and probable-cause requirements." . . .
   >
   > An essential purpose of a warrant requirement is to protect privacy interests by assuring citizens subject to a search or seizure that such intrusions are not the random or arbitrary acts of government agents. A warrant assures the citizen that the intrusion is authorized by law, and that it is narrowly limited in its objectives and scope. A warrant also provides the detached scrutiny of a neutral magistrate, and thus ensures an objective determination whether an intrusion is justified in any given case. In the present context, however,

a warrant would do little to further these aims. Both the circumstances justifying toxicological testing and the permissible limits of such intrusions are defined narrowly and specifically in the regulations that authorize them, and doubtless are well known to covered employees. Indeed, in light of the standardized nature of the tests and the minimal discretion vested in those charged with administering the program, there are virtually no facts for a neutral magistrate to evaluate. . . .

By contrast, the Government interest in testing without a showing of individualized suspicion is compelling. Employees subject to the tests discharge duties fraught with such risks of injury to others that even a momentary lapse of attention can have disastrous consequences. Much like persons who have routine access to dangerous nuclear power facilities, employees who are subject to testing under the FRA regulations can cause great human loss before any signs of impairment become noticeable to supervisors or others. . . .

A requirement of particularized suspicion of drug or alcohol use would seriously impede an employer's ability to obtain this information, despite its obvious importance. Experience confirms the FRA's judgment that the scene of a serious rail accident is chaotic. Investigators who arrive at the scene shortly after a major accident has occurred may find it difficult to determine which members of a train crew contributed to its occurrence. Obtaining evidence that might give rise to the suspicion that a particular employee is impaired, a difficult endeavor in the best of circumstances, is most impracticable in the aftermath of a serious accident. . . .

Justice Scalia was in the majority in *Skinner.* Is this consistent with his dissent in *Von Raab*? Consider Scalia's explanation:

> Today, in *Skinner,* we allow a less intrusive bodily search of railroad employees involved in train accidents. I joined the Court's opinion there because the demonstrated frequency of drug and alcohol use by the targeted class of employees, and the demonstrated connection between such use and grave harm, rendered the search a reasonable means of protecting society. I decline to join the Court's opinion in the present case because neither frequency of use nor connection to harm is demonstrated or even likely. In my view the Customs Service rules are a kind of immolation of privacy and human dignity in symbolic opposition to drug use.

2. Recall Justice Scalia's opinion for the majority in *Vernonia School District,* where the Court held that suspicionless drug testing of student athletes passed constitutional muster. Can his majority opinion in *Vernonia School District* be reconciled with his dissent in *Von Raab*?

3. *Drug Testing.* Drug tests often do not merely test for current drug impairment on the job; they can detect the presence of drug use in urine even if the person is not currently under the influence of drugs. Indeed, drugs can be detected in urine several weeks after use. As one court has observed: "[U]rine testing — unaided by blood or breath testing — is a blunt instrument. A single positive urine test is silent as to when and how much of the drug was taken, the pattern of the employee's drug use, or whether the employee was intoxicated when the test was given." *National Federation of Federal Employees v. Cheney,* 884 F.2d 603 (D.C. Cir. 1989) (sustaining U.S. Army's drug testing program based on *Von Raab* and *Skinner*). Imagine a

worker who uses marijuana while at home and never on the job. What is the justification for forcing that worker to be tested for drugs? An assumption behind drug testing programs is that a drug user will more likely be impaired at work. Is this assumption warranted? For the purposes of ensuring workers are not likely to be impaired on the job, is there any difference between the recreational pot smoker and the social drinker?[10]

4. Consider the observation of John Craig on the Court's decisions on workplace privacy:

> A common element in the Court's constitutional workplace jurisprudence is the view that employment is a separate and unique context in which the Constitution operates less rigorously to restrain the state. The Court has clearly been concerned that imposing strict constitutional limitations on privacy-invasive practices will hamper the day-to-day operations of the public sector workplace, and thereby create inefficiencies.[11]

CHANDLER V. MILLER

520 U.S. 305 (1997)

GINSBURG, J. [The State of Georgia required candidates for certain state offices to take a drug test in order to qualify for election.]

Our precedents establish that the proffered special need for drug testing must be substantial — important enough to override the individual's acknowledged privacy interest, sufficiently vital to suppress the Fourth Amendment's normal requirement of individualized suspicion. Georgia has failed to show, in justification of §21-2-140, a special need of that kind.

Respondents' defense of the statute rests primarily on the incompatibility of unlawful drug use with holding high state office. The statute is justified, respondents contend, because the use of illegal drugs draws into question an official's judgment and integrity; jeopardizes the discharge of public functions, including antidrug law enforcement efforts; and undermines public confidence and trust in elected officials. The statute, according to respondents, serves to deter unlawful drug users from becoming candidates and thus stops them from attaining high state office. Notably lacking in respondents' presentation is any indication of a concrete danger demanding departure from the Fourth Amendment's main rule.

Nothing in the record hints that the hazards respondents broadly describe are real and not simply hypothetical for Georgia's polity. . . .

In contrast to the effective testing regimes upheld in *Skinner, Von Raab,* and *Vernonia,* Georgia's certification requirement is not well designed to identify

---

[10]For more background about drug testing in the workplace, see John Gilliom, *Surveillance, Privacy, and the Law: Employee Drug Testing and the Politics of Social Control* (1994); John B. Wefing, *Employer Drug Testing: Disparate Judicial and Legislative Responses,* 63 Albany L. Rev. 799 (2000); Stephen M. Fogel et al., *Survey of the Law on Employee Drug Testing,* 42 U. Miami L. Rev. 553 (1988); Edward M. Chen, Pauline T. Kim, & John M. True, *Common Law Privacy: A Limit on an Employer's Power to Test for Drugs,* 12 Geo. Mason U. L. Rev. 651 (1990).

[11]John D.R. Craig, *Privacy and Employment Law* 64-65 (1999).

candidates who violate antidrug laws. Nor is the scheme a credible means to deter illicit drug users from seeking election to state office. The test date — to be scheduled by the candidate anytime within 30 days prior to qualifying for a place on the ballot — is no secret. As counsel for respondents acknowledged at oral argument, users of illegal drugs, save for those prohibitively addicted, could abstain for a pretest period sufficient to avoid detection. . . . Moreover, respondents have offered no reason why ordinary law enforcement methods would not suffice to apprehend such addicted individuals, should they appear in the limelight of a public stage. Section 21-2-140, in short, is not needed and cannot work to ferret out lawbreakers, and respondents barely attempt to support the statute on that ground.

Respondents and the United States as *amicus curiae* rely most heavily on our decision in *Von Raab,* which sustained a drug-testing program for Customs Service officers prior to promotion or transfer to certain high-risk positions, despite the absence of any documented drug abuse problem among Service employees. . . .

Hardly a decision opening broad vistas for suspicionless searches, *Von Raab* must be read in its unique context. As the Customs Service reported in announcing the testing program: "Customs employees, more than any other Federal workers, are routinely exposed to the vast network of organized crime that is inextricably tied to illegal drug use." . . .

Respondents overlook a telling difference between *Von Raab* and Georgia's candidate drug-testing program. In *Von Raab* it was "not feasible to subject employees [required to carry firearms or concerned with interdiction of controlled substances] and their work product to the kind of day-to-day scrutiny that is the norm in more traditional office environments." Candidates for public office, in contrast, are subject to relentless scrutiny — by their peers, the public, and the press. Their day-to-day conduct attracts attention notably beyond the norm in ordinary work environments.

What is left, after close review of Georgia's scheme, is the image the State seeks to project. By requiring candidates for public office to submit to drug testing, Georgia displays its commitment to the struggle against drug abuse. . . . But Georgia asserts no evidence of a drug problem among the State's elected officials, those officials typically do not perform high-risk, safety-sensitive tasks, and the required certification immediately aids no interdiction effort. The need revealed, in short, is symbolic, not "special," as that term draws meaning from our case law. . . .

BORSE v. PIECE GOODS SHOP

963 F.2d 611 (3d Cir. 1992)

BECKER, C.J. Plaintiff Sarah Borse brought suit against her former employer, Piece Goods Shop, Inc., in the district court for the Eastern District of Pennsylvania. She claimed that, by dismissing her when she refused to submit to urinalysis screening and personal property searches (conducted by her employer at the workplace pursuant to its drug and alcohol policy), the Shop violated a public policy that precludes employers from engaging in activities that violate their employees' rights to privacy and to freedom from unreasonable searches. Pursuant to Federal Rule of Civil Procedure 12(b)(6), the district court dismissed her complaint for failure to state a claim on which relief could be granted. This appeal requires us to decide whether an at-will employee who is discharged for refusing to consent to urinalysis screening for drug use and to searches of her personal property states a claim for wrongful discharge under Pennsylvania law. . . .

Borse was employed as a sales clerk by the Piece Goods Shop for almost fifteen years. In January 1990, the Shop adopted a drug and alcohol policy which required its employees to sign a form giving their consent to urinalysis screening for drug use and to searches of their personal property located on the Shop's premises.

Borse refused to sign the consent form. On more than one occasion, she asserted that the drug and alcohol policy violated her right to privacy and her right to be free from unreasonable searches and seizures as guaranteed by the United States Constitution. The Shop continued to insist that she sign the form and threatened to discharge her unless she did. On February 9, 1990, the Shop terminated Borse's employment.

The complaint alleges that Borse was discharged in retaliation for her refusal to sign the consent form and for protesting the Shop's drug and alcohol policy. It asserts that her discharge violated a public policy, embodied in the First and Fourth Amendments to the United States Constitution, which precludes employers from engaging in activities that violate their employees' rights to privacy and to freedom from unreasonable searches of their persons and property. Plaintiff seeks compensatory damages for emotional distress, injury to reputation, loss of earnings, and diminished earning capacity. She also alleges that the discharge was willful and malicious and, accordingly, seeks punitive damages. . . .

Ordinarily, Pennsylvania law does not provide a common-law cause of action for the wrongful discharge of an at-will employee. Rather, an employer "may discharge an employee with or without cause, at pleasure, unless restrained by some contract."

In *Geary v. United States Steel Corp.,* 319 A.2d 174 (Pa. 1974), however, the Pennsylvania Supreme Court recognized the possibility that an action for wrongful discharge might lie when the firing of an at-will employee violates public policy. Geary, a salesperson, complained to his immediate superiors about the safety of his employer's product. After being told to "follow directions," Geary took his complaints to the vice-president in charge of the product. As a result, the company withdrew the product from the market, but discharged Geary.

Geary argued that an exception to the at-will doctrine was warranted in his case because his dismissal was contrary to public policy. The Pennsylvania Supreme Court disagreed, relying upon two factors to decide that Geary's case did not merit an exception. First, the court observed that Geary was not responsible for monitoring product safety and that he did not possess expertise in that area. Second, the court noted that Geary had violated the internal chain of command by pressing his concerns before the vice-president.

Summarizing its decision, the court stated:

> It may be granted that there are areas of an employee's life in which his employer has no legitimate interest. An intrusion into one of these areas by virtue of the employer's power of discharge might plausibly give rise to a cause of action, particularly where some recognized facet of public policy is threatened. . . . [However, w]e hold only that where the complaint itself discloses a plausible and legitimate reason for terminating an at-will employment relationship and no clear mandate of public policy is violated thereby, an employee at will has no right of action against his employer for wrongful discharge.

Courts construing Pennsylvania law have interpreted this language as implicitly recognizing that a cause of action for wrongful discharge exists in appropriate circumstances, even though the court refused to uphold such an action on the facts in *Geary*. . . .

In order to evaluate Borse's claim, we must attempt to "discern whether any public policy is threatened" by her discharge. As evidence of a public policy that precludes employers from discharging employees who refuse to consent to the practices at issue, Borse primarily relies upon the First and Fourth Amendments to the United States Constitution and the right to privacy included in the Pennsylvania Constitution. As will be seen, we reject her reliance on these constitutional provisions, concluding instead that, to the extent that her discharge implicates public policy, the source of that policy lies in Pennsylvania common law. . . .

In light of the narrowness of the public policy exception and of the Pennsylvania courts' continuing insistence upon the state action requirement, we predict that if faced with the issue, the Pennsylvania Supreme Court would not look to the First and Fourth Amendments as sources of public policy when there is no state action. . . .

Although we have rejected Borse's reliance upon constitutional provisions as evidence of a public policy allegedly violated by the Piece Goods Shop's drug and alcohol program, our review of Pennsylvania law reveals other evidence of a public policy that may, under certain circumstances, give rise to a wrongful discharge action related to urinalysis or to personal property searches. Specifically, we refer to the Pennsylvania common law regarding tortious invasion of privacy.

Pennsylvania recognizes a cause of action for tortious "intrusion upon seclusion." *Marks v. Bell Telephone Co.*, 331 A.2d 424 (Pa. 1975). The Restatement defines the tort as follows:

> One who intentionally intrudes, physically or otherwise, upon the solitude or seclusion of another or his private affairs or concerns, is subject to liability to the other for invasion of his privacy, if the intrusion would be highly offensive to a reasonable person.

Restatement (Second) of Torts § 652B. . . .

We can envision at least two ways in which an employer's urinalysis program might intrude upon an employee's seclusion. First, the particular manner in which the program is conducted might constitute an intrusion upon seclusion as defined by Pennsylvania law. The process of collecting the urine sample to be tested clearly implicates "expectations of privacy that society has long recognized as reasonable." In addition, many urinalysis programs monitor the collection of the urine specimen to ensure that the employee does not adulterate it or substitute a sample from another person. Monitoring collection of the urine sample appears to fall within the definition of an intrusion upon seclusion because it involves the use of one's senses to oversee the private activities of another.

As the United States Supreme Court has observed:

> There are few activities in our society more personal or private than the passing of urine. Most people describe it by euphemisms if they talk about it at all. It is a function traditionally performed without public observation; indeed, its performance in public is generally prohibited by law as well as social custom.

Skinner, 109 S. Ct. at 1413. If the method used to collect the urine sample fails to give due regard to the employees' privacy, it could constitute a substantial and highly offensive intrusion upon seclusion.

Second, urinalysis "can reveal a host of private medical facts about an employee, including whether she is epileptic, pregnant, or diabetic." *Skinner,* 109 S. Ct. at 1413. A reasonable person might well conclude that submitting urine samples to tests designed to ascertain these types of information constitutes a substantial and highly offensive intrusion upon seclusion.

The same principles apply to an employer's search of an employee's personal property. If the search is not conducted in a discreet manner or if it is done in such a way as to reveal personal matters unrelated to the workplace, the search might well constitute a tortious invasion of the employee's privacy. See, for example, *K-Mart Corp. v. Trotti,* 677 S.W.2d 632 (Tex. App. 1984) (search of employee's locker). . . .

. . . [W]e believe that when an employee alleges that his or her discharge was related to an employer's invasion of his or her privacy, the Pennsylvania Supreme Court would examine the facts and circumstances surrounding the alleged invasion of privacy. If the court determined that the discharge was related to a substantial and highly offensive invasion of the employee's privacy, we believe that it would conclude that the discharge violated public policy. . . .

Only a handful of other jurisdictions have considered urinalysis programs implemented by private employers. The majority of these decisions balance the employee's privacy interest against the employer's interests in order to determine whether to uphold the programs. . . .

In view of the foregoing analysis, we predict that the Pennsylvania Supreme Court would apply a balancing test to determine whether the Shop's drug and alcohol program (consisting of urinalysis and personal property searches) invaded Borse's privacy. . . . The test we believe that Pennsylvania would adopt balances the employee's privacy interest against the employer's interest in maintaining a drug-free workplace in order to determine whether a reasonable person would find the employer's program highly offensive. . . .

In sum, based on our prediction of Pennsylvania law, we hold that dismissing an employee who refused to consent to urinalysis testing and to personal property searches would violate public policy if the testing tortiously invaded the employee's privacy. . . .

NOTES & QUESTIONS

1. *Sources of Public Policy.* Do you agree with the reasoning of *Borse*'s distinction between constitutional law and tort law as sources of public policy in suits for wrongful termination in violation of public policy against private sector employers? For a contrasting view with regard to constitutional law, consider *Hennessey v. Coastal Eagle Point Oil Co.,* 609 A.2d 11 (N.J. 1992), where the New Jersey Supreme Court held that state constitutional law could be a source of public policy as applied in wrongful termination suits against private sector employers (for random urine testing). The court concluded:

> . . . [P]ersuasive precedent supports finding a clear mandate of public policy in privacy rights from several sources. Although one of those sources is the State Constitution, we emphasize that we are *not* finding in this opinion a constitutional right to privacy that governs the conduct of private actors. Rather, we find only that existing constitutional privacy protections may form the basis for a clear mandate of public policy supporting a wrongful-discharge claim. . . .
>
> In ascertaining whether an employee's individual rights constitute a "clear mandate of public policy," we must balance the public interest against the employee's right. If the employee's duties are so fraught with hazard that his or her attempts to perform them while in a state of drug impairment would pose a threat to co-workers, to the workplace, or to the public at large, then the employer must prevail.[12]

What other forms of information privacy law might serve as sources of public policy?

2. *Direct Constitutional Liability for Private Sector Employers.* In most states, and under the federal Constitution, constitutional provisions do not apply directly to private sector employers. As you have seen, however, state and federal constitutional law can serve in some jurisdictions as the source of public policy in a wrongful termination claim. However, in California, the California Constitution applies directly to private sector employers. The California Supreme Court has held that the right to privacy in Article I, § 1 of the California Constitution "creates a right of action against private as well as government entities." *Hill v. NCAA,* 865 P.2d 633 (Cal. 1994).

3. Consider the following argument by Pauline Kim:

> . . . [T]he public-policy exception is now widely recognized to apply in at least three types of situations: when an employee is discharged for refusing to commit an illegal act, for asserting an established job-related right (for

---

[12] For other states that follow a similar approach to *Hennessey,* see *Palmateer v. International Harvester Co.,* 421 N.E.2d 876 (Ill. 1981); *Cort v. Bristol-Myers Co.,* 431 N.E.2d 908 (Mass. Ct. App. 1982); *Twigg v. Hercules Corp.,* 406 S.E.2d 52 (W. Va. Ct. App. 1990); *Luedtke v. Nabors Alaska Drilling, Inc.,* 768 P.2d 1123 (Alaska 1989).

example, by filing for workers' compensation benefits), or for fulfilling a public obligation (such as serving on jury duty). . . .

The common law privacy tort, by prohibiting unreasonable intrusions on the private concerns of another, also imposes a socially defined duty independent of any contractual relationship between the parties. Like participation in the jury system, respect for personal privacy is high on the scale of values in this society. And, as in the case of workers' compensation benefits, an employee's common law right of privacy is socially established independent of the terms of the employment relationship and should not be subject to waiver under threat of discharge. Because the interests it protects are at least as fundamental as others already found to warrant an exception to the at-will rule, the common law tort of invasion of privacy should be recognized as a public policy limiting an employer's authority to discharge. . . .[13]

BAGGS V. EAGLE-PICHER INDUSTRIES, INC.

750 F. Supp. 264 (W.D. Mich. 1990)

BELL, J. . . . This case arises out of surprise drug test conducted by defendant in August 1989. Defendant is an Ohio corporation with a division located in Kalkaska, Michigan. The Kalkaska plant is defendant's Trim Division which makes parts such as headliners and door panels for the automotive industry. Employees at defendant's plant work in teams in the assembly process. Some of the activities conducted by the teams are potentially hazardous such as hydraulic and electronic presses, forklifts and hot glue and adhesive.

Defendant employs approximately 230 people at its Kalkaska plant. [The employees were at-will employees and could be terminated without cause]. . .

In 1988 and 1989, defendant's management became aware of a drug problem at its Kalkaska plant. . . . In response to this information, defendant posted a drug free workplace policy in April 1989. This policy prohibited employees from possessing, using or being under the influence of drugs while at work and provided that employees could be tested for drug use. Defendant also required all new applicants to submit to drug testing as a prerequisite to being hired.

In April 1989, defendant consulted with the Grand Traverse Narcotics Team and the Kalkaska County Sheriff and placed an undercover officer in the plant as an employee. . . . After the undercover officer finished his undercover work, he reported to defendant's management that he estimated that as many as 60% of defendant's employees used drugs at home, at work or both. . . .

On July 17, 1989 a new drug free workplace policy was posted. That policy stated:

> It is the policy of this Company to provide a workplace free of alcohol and drugs, and to ensure that employee alcohol or drug use does not jeopardize the success of its operations, or otherwise affect the Company, its employees or its customers.
>
> The use, sale, attempted sale, manufacture, purchase, attempted purchase, possession or transfer of alcohol or an illegal drug while on Company property

---

[13] Pauline T. Kim, *Privacy Rights, Public Policy, and the Employment Relationship*, 57 Ohio St. L.J. 671, 722, 724 (1996).

or reported to work with alcohol, illegal or illicit drugs in the employee's system is a violation of Company rules and will result in disciplinary action, up to and including discharge. . . .

In order to protect the well-being of our employees, our facilities and the community in which we live, each employee, as a condition of employment will be required, upon request of Company supervisory personnel, to submit to blood and/or urine tests for determining use of alcohol and/or illegal or illicit drugs. . . .

On August 10 and 11, 1989, defendant announced that it was going to conduct drug testing on those days. Only three people in management knew about the tests ahead of time. The men and women employees were asked to go into the men and women's bathrooms respectively and produce urine samples. There was a nurse present in each bathroom (a male nurse in the men's bathroom and a female nurse in the women's). Employees were told that, if they did not want to take the test, they could leave the plant and they would be considered a voluntary quit. Some employees who are plaintiffs in this suit did leave and were considered as voluntary quits as of that date. . . . A number of the plaintiffs tested positive for marijuana, one tested positive for cocaine and one for propoxyphene. . . .

Count I of plaintiffs' third amended complaint alleges breach of contract for the failure of defendant to follow the progressive disciplinary stages set forth in the employee handbook in the drug testing and termination of employees. . . .

Defendant argues that Count I of plaintiffs' third amended complaint should be dismissed because defendant did not breach any contract with plaintiffs. Defendants argue that plaintiffs' employment was an at-will employment and that defendant was under no obligation to use the progressive disciplinary procedures set out in the handbook in this situation. . . .

. . . [T]he employees in the present case signed employment applications which contained language making their employment at-will and the handbook did not contain any language stating that employment with defendant would terminate only upon a showing of just cause. [Therefore, the defendant's motion for summary judgment as to Count I is granted]. . . .

Count III of plaintiffs' third amended complaint alleges invasion of privacy under the United States and Michigan constitutions. Defendant argues that plaintiffs have no cause of action for a constitutional violation because defendant is a private not a government actor. . . .

The Fourth Amendment to the United States Constitution does not protect against a search or seizure by a private party on its own initiative, even if the search or seizure is an arbitrary action. The Court knows of no such protection under the Michigan Constitution and plaintiffs have provided no support for such protection. Plaintiffs are, therefore, left to their claims of the tort of [intrusion upon seclusion]. . . .

Plaintiffs in this case are divided into two classes. One class consists of plaintiffs who refused to participate in the testing and the other consists of those who tested positive for drugs. Those who did not participate cannot succeed on this count because there was no intrusion. Therefore, Count III will be dismissed as to those plaintiffs.

As to the remaining plaintiffs, the Court finds that the taking of urine samples is an intrusion in an area in which plaintiffs may have an expectation of privacy. However, in this case, the Court finds that plaintiffs had no expectation of privacy with regard to drug testing since they had been on notice since July 17, 1989 that they might be subjected to drug testing as a condition of employment. . . . [E]mployers have a right to investigate into areas which would normally be private if the investigation springs from the business relationship. In this case, the employer was concerned about the safety of its workers and the productivity of the plant. This was a justifiable concern since the work at defendant's plant included activity which could be hazardous to someone who was not in total control of his faculties. Defendant has stated that there were several activities at its plant which gave rise to concern. The combination of the notice and the business concerns leads this Court to find that plaintiffs did not have an expectation of privacy with regard to urinalysis under the law of Michigan.

The final element of the tort is that the intrusion be offensive to a reasonable person. The Court finds that plaintiffs cannot prove this third element. The testing was carried on in the bathroom with a nurse present and the nurse was of the appropriate gender. In addition, anyone who wanted the additional privacy of a stall in which to give the sample had just to ask. . . .

In conclusion, the Court finds that all of plaintiffs' claims are without merit and grants defendant's motion for summary judgment as to all counts of plaintiffs' third amended complaint. Plaintiffs' third amended complaint will be dismissed.

NOTES & QUESTIONS

1. *The Effect of Consent on Employer Liability for Privacy Torts.* In *Baggs*, do you agree that providing notice to employees that they will be subjected to drug testing eliminates their expectations of privacy? In a number of cases, courts have held that employers requiring employees to consent to drug testing (or to surveillance or monitoring) shield themselves from liability under the intrusion upon seclusion tort because the employees consented to the intrusion. For example, in *Jennings v. Minco Technology Labs,* 765 S.W.2d 497 (Tex. Ct. App. 1989), Minco Technology Labs initiated a random drug testing program requiring employees to consent before testing about 16 months after plaintiff Brenda Jennings had begun to work for the defendant. An at-will employee, Jennings was unwilling to accept the new terms of employment and sued for intrusion upon seclusion, arguing that she was permitted to continue her employment without agreeing to the drug tests. The Court concluded:

> Jennings's employer threatens no *unlawful* invasion of any employee's privacy interest; therefore it threatens no act contrary to the public policy underlying the common-law right of privacy. The company's plan contemplates, rather, that an employee's urine will be taken and tested only if he consents. The plan therefore assumes, respects, and depends upon the central element of the right of privacy and its attendant public policy: the individual's exclusive right to determine the occasion, extent, and conditions

under which he will disclose his private affairs to others. This consensual predicate to any test reduces Jennings's argument to her remaining contention.

Jennings contends finally that she is poor and needs her salary to maintain herself and her family. Consequently, any "consent" she may give, in submitting to urinalysis, will be illusory and not real. For that practical reason, she argues, the company's plan *does* threaten a non-consensual, and therefore unlawful, invasion of her privacy. We disagree with the theory. A competent person's legal rights and obligations, under the common law governing the making, interpretation, and enforcement of contracts, cannot vary according to his economic circumstances. There cannot be one law of contracts for the rich and another for the poor. We cannot imagine a theory more at war with the basic assumptions held by society and its law. Nothing would introduce greater disorder into both. Because Jennings may not be denied the legal rights others have under the common law of contracts, she may not be given greater rights than they. The law views her economic circumstances as neutral and irrelevant facts insofar as her contracts are concerned.

2. ***The Limits of Consent.*** What does "consent" mean? Given the disparate power relationship between employers and employees, are many employment conditions really consensual? If you view consent narrowly to exist only when power relationships are close to equal, then what is the effect on the ability for employers and employees to make contracts?

Consider *Feminist Women's Health Center v. Superior Court,* 61 Cal. Rptr. 2d 187 (Cal. Ct. App. 1997). The Feminist Women's Health Center hired the plaintiff for the position of "feminist health worker." One of the responsibilities in the job description was to demonstrate a cervical self-examination to other women. In front of a group of other women, the plaintiff was to insert a plastic speculum into her vagina. According to the Health Center, the reason for the demonstration "is to demystify and redefine the normal functions of a woman's body. Our unique and effective, although not strictly necessary tool to accomplish this is for women to visualize their own cervixes and vaginas, which are not usually seen with the naked eye without the use of a vaginal speculum." After being hired, the plaintiff refused to demonstrate the cervical self-examination, and she was terminated by the Health Center. She sued for wrongful termination in violation of public policy, as embodied in the California Constitution, Art. I, § 1, which provides: "All people are by nature free and independent and have inalienable rights. Among these are enjoying and defending life and liberty, acquiring, possessing, and protecting property, and pursuing and obtaining safety, happiness, and privacy." The court held:

> . . . [W]e agree with plaintiff that the observation of the insertion of a speculum into plaintiff's vagina by fellow employees and female clients of the Center infringes a legally protected privacy interest. This invasion is at least as serious as observing urination, and we do not question plaintiff's assertions that it was contrary to her religious and cultural beliefs. . .
>
> The real issue is whether this type of cervical self-examination may reasonably be required of the Center's employees. In other words, the seriousness of the privacy invasion leads us to the third part of the *Hill*

test: consideration of the Center's countervailing interests and the feasibility of the alternatives proposed by plaintiff.

. . . [C]ervical self-examination is important in advancing the Center's fundamental goal of educating women about the function and health of their reproductive systems. . . .

The Center also could reasonably conclude that the alternative methods of self-examination proposed by plaintiff would have stifled such candor. These alternatives, such as the use of mannequins, or the private use of the speculum followed by discussion, are pale imitations of uninhibited group cervical self-examination. . . .

In balancing these competing interests, we return to plaintiff's consent to demonstrate cervical self-examination as part of her employment agreement with the Center. The Center was not obligated to hire plaintiff, and consent remains a viable defense even in cases of serious privacy invasions. Therefore, we believe the facts as disclosed in the trial court give rise to the following inferences only: the requirement that health workers perform cervical self-examinations in front of other females is a reasonable condition of employment and does not violate the health worker's right to privacy where the plaintiff's written employment agreement evidences her knowledge of this condition and agreement to be bound by it. Where the employee thereafter refuses to abide by the agreement, the employee's wrongful termination claim based on a violation of the right to privacy is rendered infirm. Such is the case under the facts presented, and the superior court should have granted summary adjudication of this claim.

There are many laws that restrict an employee's freedom to contract. For example, an employee may not agree to work for below minimum wage, be exposed to certain toxic materials, or commit an illegal act. Upon what basis should legislatures and courts distinguish between those things that people can and cannot consent to?

3. *Consenting to Violations of Privacy Law.* Should the law prohibit employers from bargaining with employees over certain privacy rights? Consider *Cramer v. Consolidated Freightways, Inc.,* 255 F.3d 683 (9th Cir. 2001) (en banc). Consolidated Freightways, a large trucking company, installed concealed video cameras and audio listening devices behind two-way mirrors in its rest rooms in order to discover and prevent drug use by its drivers. Employees discovered the cameras when a mirror fell off the rest room wall. Consolidated employees brought several suits seeking damages for invasion of privacy and infliction of emotional distress. They also sought an injunction to stop the surveillance. These cases were consolidated into one action.

The employees' union had a collective bargaining agreement (CBA) with Consolidated. One of the central issues in the case turned on whether § 301 of the Labor Management Relations Act (LMRA), 29 U.S.C. § 185 preempted the plaintiffs' claims, an issue that turned on whether the CBA's provisions could be interpreted as addressing the issue of surreptitious videotaping. The court concluded that it did not. The court also concluded that

> Even if the CBA did expressly contemplate the use of two-way mirrors to facilitate detection of drug users, such a provision would be illegal under California law, and it is well established in California that illegal provisions

of a contract are void and unenforceable. Section 653n of the California Penal Code makes the installation and maintenance of two-way mirrors permitting the observation of restrooms illegal without reference to the reasonable expectations of those so viewed. Determination of guilt under the statute is not dependent on context or subjective factors; use of the mirrors is a per se violation of the penal code, and an assumption that the mirrors will not be used is per se reasonable.

Under settled Supreme Court precedent, "§ 301 does not grant the parties to a collective-bargaining agreement the ability to contract for what is illegal under state law." Consolidated was therefore required to abide by the provisions of California penal law, and its employees had a right to assume their employer would obey the law. This assumption is inherently reasonable. Indeed, any contrary assumption would be irrational, because illegal behavior is unreasonable. Even if the CBA purported to reduce or limit this expectation in some way, that reduction would be illegal and therefore unenforceable. Because installation of two-way mirrors is immutably illegal, and freedom from the illegality is a "nonnegotiable state-law right[ ]," a court reviewing plaintiffs' claims that their privacy rights were violated need not interpret the CBA to arrive at its conclusion. By definition, therefore, plaintiffs in this action were reasonable in expecting to be free of the two-way mirrors and hidden video cameras installed in the restrooms.

Under California Penal Code § 653n, "[a]ny person who installs or who maintains . . . any two-way mirror permitting observation of any restroom, toilet, bathroom, washroom, shower, locker room, fitting room, motel room, or hotel room, is guilty of a misdemeanor." Do you agree with the court that this law cannot be bargained around? Would your conclusion be different if the law were tort law rather than criminal law?

Under *Cramer,* even if the employees desired to sacrifice their privacy in return for higher wages or other benefits, they could not make this bargain under the reasoning of the court. Does this prevent employees from having the freedom to contract? Would a default rule that such surveillance is improper, but which could be bargained around, be preferable? Or if the law could be bargained around, would this too easily enable employers to circumvent the law by forcing employees to agree to the privacy invasion?

4. Many employers are now providing privacy policies to their employees informing them of the types of workplace monitoring. Does providing notice and consent protect privacy in the workplace? Consider the following argument by Pauline Kim:

> Clearly, the right to fire at will is not absolute. It has come into conflict with fundamental public concerns before, and yielded. Almost all the states recognize an exception to the at-will rule based on public policy. Even the staunchest defenders of employment at will acknowledge some legitimate exceptions to the rule, as when the performance of a public duty or the protection of a public right is threatened. . . .
>
> . . . [E]mployment is not an all-encompassing relationship. Although some territorial boundaries are necessarily breached to make employment possible, this implicit waiver of territorial claims does not automatically

extend to those areas recognized to be at the core of personal privacy. Because employer and employee enter into the relationship for a specific, limited purpose, any implied waiver only extends as far as necessary to achieve that purpose. To conclude otherwise would set the employment relationship apart among social relationships, for the individual who could expect — and enforce — limits on unjustified intrusions by the government or third parties on core areas of privacy would have no such expectation vis-à-vis her employer. Given that the interests at stake are the same regardless of the source of the intrusion, it would be anomalous to treat the employer's actions as uniquely privileged. When core areas of privacy — those central to the self — are threatened, employer intrusions should not be permitted unless essential to meet some business need. . . .[14]

Suppose an employer wanted to film its employees all hours of the day. Should employees be permitted to consent to such monitoring? Isn't this what the "Big Brother" television show did? This television show placed individuals in a house that had cameras in every room, including the bathrooms. The show was filmed in California. Suppose a contestant sued for intrusion upon seclusion. Under the reasoning of *Cramer*, would the contestant be able to sue for intrusion?

5. ***The Limits of Consenting to Privacy Protection.*** In *Giannecchini v. Hospital of St. Raphael*, 780 A.2d 1006 (Conn. Super. 2000), the plaintiff, a nurse, was fired by the defendant hospital (Hospital of St. Raphael) for making serious medication errors and demonstrating below average ability and industry. With the help of an attorney, the plaintiff negotiated an agreement with the hospital that all references in the nurse's file to an involuntary termination of employment would be expunged and that in response to any inquires or reference requests by prospective employers, the hospital would not disclose any information except the plaintiff's dates of service, title, position, and salary information. The plaintiff later applied for a position as a registered nurse with another hospital, which sent St. Raphael a letter requesting information about the plaintiff. St. Raphael responded by stating that the nurse had been discharged, had below average ability and industry, and made several serious medication errors. Among other things, the plaintiff sued for breach of contract. St. Raphael argued that the confidentiality agreement that it entered into with the nurse violated public policy because it did not account for the interest of third parties (namely, the safety of the patients in the hospital planning to hire the nurse). The court concluded that public policy was against disclosure, and therefore, the agreement was valid and St. Raphael had breached. Should public policy prohibit confidentiality agreements that restrict the disclosure of information that might be relevant to the health and safety of third parties? Compare this case to *Tarasoff v. Regents of the University of California* and *McIntosh v. Milano* (Chapter 3).

---

[14] Pauline T. Kim, *Privacy Rights, Public Policy, and the Employment Relationship,* 57 Ohio St. L.J. 671, 682, 703 (1996).

5. MEDICAL TESTING, QUESTIONNAIRES, AND POLYGRAPHS

Norman-Bloodsaw v. Lawrence Berkeley Laboratory

135 F.3d 1260 (9th Cir. 1998)

REINHARDT, J. . . . Plaintiffs . . . are current and former administrative and clerical employees of defendant Lawrence Berkeley Laboratory, a research facility. . . .

. . . [E]ach of the plaintiffs received written offers of employment expressly conditioned upon a "medical examination," "medical approval," or "health evaluation." All accepted these offers and underwent preplacement examinations, and Randolph and Smith underwent subsequent examinations as well. In the course of these examinations, plaintiffs completed medical history questionnaires and provided blood and urine samples. The questionnaires asked, *inter alia,* whether the patient had ever had any of sixty-one medical conditions, including "[s]ickle cell anemia," "[v]enereal disease," and, in the case of women, "[m]enstrual disorders."

The blood and urine samples given by all employees during their preplacement examinations were tested for syphilis; in addition, certain samples were tested for sickle cell trait; and certain samples were tested for pregnancy. . . .

. . . Plaintiffs allege that the testing of their blood and urine samples for syphilis, sickle cell trait, and pregnancy occurred without their knowledge or consent, and without any subsequent notification that the tests had been conducted. They also allege that only black employees were tested for sickle cell trait and assert the obvious fact that only female employees were tested for pregnancy. Finally, they allege that Lawrence failed to provide safeguards to prevent the dissemination of the test results. They contend that they did not discover that the disputed tests had been conducted until approximately January 1995, and specifically deny that they observed any signs indicating that such tests would be performed. Plaintiffs do not allege that the defendants took any subsequent employment-related action on the basis of their test results, or that their test results have been disclosed to third parties. . . .

[Among other claims, including an American with Disabilities Act claim and a Title VII claim, the plaintiffs] contend that the defendants violated the federal constitutional right to privacy by conducting the testing at issue, collecting and maintaining the results of the testing, and failing to provide adequate safeguards against disclosure of the results. Third, they contend that the testing violated their right to privacy under Article I, § 1 of the California Constitution. . . .

The state defendants moved for judgment on the pleadings or, in the alternative, for summary judgment. . . .

. . . We first examine [the district court's] ruling with respect to the claim for violation of the federal constitutional right to privacy. While acknowledging that the government had failed to identify any "undisputed legitimate governmental purpose" for the three tests, the district court concluded that no violation of plaintiffs' right to privacy could have occurred because any intrusions arising from the testing were de minimis in light of (1) the "large overlap" between the subjects covered by the medical questionnaire and the three tests and (2) the "overall intrusiveness" of "a full-scale physical examination." We hold that the district court erred.

The constitutionally protected privacy interest in avoiding disclosure of personal matters clearly encompasses medical information and its confidentiality. Although cases defining the privacy interest in medical information have typically involved its disclosure to "third" parties, rather than the collection of information by illicit means, it goes without saying that the *most basic* violation possible involves the performance of unauthorized tests — that is, the non-consensual retrieval of previously unrevealed medical information that may be unknown even to plaintiffs. These tests may also be viewed as searches in violation of Fourth Amendment rights that require Fourth Amendment scrutiny. The tests at issue in this case thus implicate rights protected under both the Fourth Amendment and the Due Process Clause of the Fifth or Fourteenth Amendments.

Because it would not make sense to examine the collection of medical information under two different approaches, we generally "analyze [ ] [medical tests and examinations] under the rubric of [the Fourth] Amendment." Accordingly, we must balance the government's interest in conducting these particular tests against the plaintiffs' expectations of privacy. Furthermore, "application of the balancing test requires not only considering the degree of intrusiveness and the state's interests in requiring that intrusion, but also 'the efficacy of this [the state's] means for meeting' its needs." . . .

One can think of few subject areas more personal and more likely to implicate privacy interests than that of one's health or genetic make-up. Furthermore, the facts revealed by the tests are highly sensitive, even relative to other medical information. With respect to the testing of plaintiffs for syphilis and pregnancy, it is well established in this circuit "that the Constitution prohibits unregulated, unrestrained employer inquiries into personal sexual matters that have no bearing on job performance." The fact that one has syphilis is an intimate matter that pertains to one's sexual history and may invite tremendous amounts of social stigma. Pregnancy is likewise, for many, an intensely private matter, which also may pertain to one's sexual history and often carries far-reaching societal implications. Finally, the carrying of sickle cell trait can pertain to sensitive information about family history and reproductive decisionmaking. Thus, the conditions tested for were aspects of one's health in which one enjoys the highest expectations of privacy.

As discussed above, with respect to the question of the statute of limitations, there was little, if any, "overlap" between what plaintiffs consented to and the testing at issue here. Nor was the additional invasion only incremental. In some instances, the tests related to entirely different conditions. In all, the information obtained as the result of the testing was qualitatively different from the information that plaintiffs provided in their answers to the questions, and was highly invasive. That one has consented to a general medical examination does not abolish one's privacy right not to be tested for intimate, personal matters involving one's health — nor does consenting to giving blood or urine samples, or filling out a questionnaire. As we have made clear, revealing one's personal knowledge as to whether one has a particular medical condition has *nothing* to do with one's expectations about actually being tested for that condition. Thus, the intrusion was by no means *de minimis*. Rather, if unauthorized, the testing constituted a significant invasion of a right that is of great importance, and labeling it minimal cannot and does not make it so.

Lawrence further contends that the tests in question, even if their intrusiveness is not de minimis, would be justified by an employer's interest in performing a general physical examination. This argument fails because issues of fact exist with respect to whether the testing at issue is normally part of a general physical examination. There would of course be no violation if the testing were authorized, or if the plaintiffs reasonably should have known that the blood and urine samples they provided would be used for the disputed testing and failed to object. However . . . material issues of fact exist as to those questions. Summary judgment . . . was therefore incorrect. . . .

NOTES & QUESTIONS

1. Recall in *Whalen v. Roe* (Chapter 3) that the constitutional right to information privacy generally protects "the individual interest in avoiding disclosure of personal matters." This case involved the collection of information. Do you agree with the court's conclusion that the constitutional right to information privacy applies in this case?
2. ***Employer Questionnaires.*** In *American Federation of Government Employees v. HUD,* 118 F.3d 786 (D.C. Cir. 1997), the Department of Housing and Urban Development required employees holding positions of public trust to fill out a questionnaire requesting personal information, such as prior drug use and financial history. The Department of Defense required employees to fill out a questionnaire for positions requiring a security clearance requesting information about drug and alcohol history, financial history, criminal history, and mental health history. These questionnaires were challenged as a violation of the constitutional right to information privacy. The court concluded:

> To begin with, we hold that the individual interest in protecting the privacy of the information sought by the government is significantly less important where the information is collected by the government but not disseminated publicly. In fact, the employees could cite no case in which a court has found a violation of the constitutional right to privacy where the government has collected, but not disseminated, the information. . . .
>
> Here, as [in *Whalen v. Roe*], there are measures designed to protect the confidentiality of the employees' responses to questionnaires. The Privacy Act, 5 U.S.C. § 552a(b), states that no agency shall disclose any record, except where it has written consent from the individual or under certain limited exceptions, none of which would permit public dissemination of the information obtained here. In addition, the records are maintained under secure conditions. Those charged with maintaining the records are, themselves, subject to background checks. These measures, designed to protect the confidentiality of the information, substantially reduce the employees' privacy interests. Security precautions are never fool-proof, but where the government has enacted reasonable devices to secure the confidentiality of

records we cannot, without grounds, assume that the devices will prove insufficient.

Given the employees' diminished interest in resisting disclosure in cases in which disclosure is not likely to lead to public dissemination, we conclude that the agencies have presented sufficiently important justifications for each item on the questionnaires. . . . [HUD] has presented evidence that an employee using illegal drugs is more likely to compromise the integrity of the computer database by making a negligent error. HUD has also determined that employees with a substance abuse history or a history of financial indiscretion are more likely to embezzle funds. . . . When presented with a reasonable determination we are reluctant to second-guess the agencies' conclusions regarding the dangers associated with drug use or financial trouble among employees in public trust positions. . . . We hold that HUD may constitutionally require employees to disclose prior drug use and financial history. . . .

. . . The drug use and financial history questions posed by DOD are slightly more intrusive than those asked by HUD, but the questions are the same in their material particulars. The release form is substantially identical. As the questions could constitutionally be required to protect the integrity of a computer database they are, *a fortiori*, constitutional when used in the interests of national security. DOD employees also challenged questions regarding the employees' mental health and expunged criminal history. No constitutional right of privacy is violated even by the disclosure "of an official act such as an arrest." *Paul v. Davis*, 424 U.S. 693, 713 (1976). Questions concerning an employees' mental health, on the other hand, may solicit highly personal information. Nevertheless, we uphold the requirement consistent with our traditional reluctance to intrude on Executive decision-making in the area of national defense. . . .

In *Walls v. City of Petersburg*, 895 F.2d 188 (4th Cir. 1990), the plaintiff Walls was hired as the administrator of the city's program to provide alternative sentencing for nonviolent offenders. About six months after Walls was hired, the program was transferred to the city's Bureau of Police. Her supervisor requested that she fill out a questionnaire as part of the background check that all police department employees go through. Walls refused to answer four questions:

> Question 12: Has any member of your immediate family (father, mother, brother, sister, husband, wife, father-in-law, mother-in-law) ever been arrested and/or convicted of a felony, misdemeanor, or other violation other than a minor traffic violation?
>
> Question 30: List all marriages you have had and the present status thereof: If divorced, annulled or separated, give details of date, offending party as decreed by law, and the reason therefore [sic] on a separate sheet of paper. . . . List every child born to you.
>
> Question 40: Have you ever had sexual relations with a person of the same sex?
>
> Question 43: Debts: List all outstanding debts or judgments against you or your spouse or for which you are the co-maker?

When she refused to comply with answering the questions, Walls was fired. Among other things, Walls brought a § 1983 claim alleging a violation of the constitutional right to information privacy. The court held that her claim should be dismissed. With regard to Question 30 (marital history), the court concluded:

> . . . [T]o the extent that this information is freely available in public records, the police should be able to require Walls to disclose the information in this background questionnaire. However, any details that are not part of the public record concerning a divorce, separation, annulment, or the birth of children are private and thus protected. The City's interests in discovering possible alternative names used by employees and identifying potential conflicts of interests can be satisfied by the information in the public records.
>
> We interpret Question 30 to be asking only for information that is available from public records, and therefore hold that it also can be an appropriate part of a background check.

As for Question 12 (criminal history), the court held:

> The analysis here is exactly the same as for Question 30. Walls has no reasonable expectation of privacy in this information because it is already part of the public records. Because she would have access in her position to criminal records, this information would be relevant and could be requested in a questionnaire.

Regarding Question 43 (financial information), the court reasoned that awareness of "Walls' financial position" was necessary to guard against potential corruption, and this interest outweighed her privacy interests.

With regard to Question 40 (homosexuality), the court reasoned:

> In *Bowers v. Hardwick,* 478 U.S. 186 (1986), the Supreme Court "register[ed] [its] disagreement . . . that the Court's prior cases have construed the Constitution to confer a right of privacy that extends to homosexual sodomy. . . ." The Court explicitly rejected "the proposition that any kind of private sexual conduct between consenting adults is constitutionally insulated from state proscription." The relevance of this type of question to Walls' employment is uncertain, but because the *Bowers* decision is controlling, we hold that Question 40 does not ask for information that Walls has a right to keep private.

Do you agree with the reasoning of the court on this question? Recall *Sterling v. Borough of Minersville* in Chapter 3 (in the notes after *Scheetz v. The Morning Call*). Compare the reasoning of the impact of *Bowers* in *Sterling* and *Walls*. Which case do you find more persuasive?

In *Fraternal Order of Police, Lodge No. 5 v. City of Philadelphia,* 812 F.2d 105 (3d Cir. 1987), a police union challenged the constitutionality of a questionnaire used by the police department to select candidates for a special investigations unit. Among other things, the questionnaire contained questions dealing with physical and mental conditions, behavior, and financial information. The court held that the questions about physical and mental conditions were necessary to determine the officer's fitness for their positions in the special investigations unit. The financial information was relevant because of the assumption that officers with large debts would be more susceptible to the temptations of corruption in narcotics investigations. Likewise, the behavior information (gambling and alcohol use) was relevant for this purpose. However, the court held that the city's safeguards against unnecessary disclosure of the information were inadequate.

> Safeguards against disclosure of private material have been held to be adequate when there exists a statutory penalty for unauthorized disclosures; when there exist security provisions to prevent mishandling of files coupled with an express regulatory policy prohibiting disclosure; and in a unique situation when, even absent an explicit statutory or regulatory policy, the record supported the conclusion that those officials with private information would not disclose it.
>
> In contrast, we find a complete absence of comparable protection of the confidential information to be disclosed in response to the SIU questionnaire. There is no directive limiting access to the responses to specific persons or specifying the handling and storage of the responses. . . . Apparently, there is no statute or regulation that penalizes officials with confidential information from disclosing it. . . .

Finally, the court held that a question requiring each applicant to disclose all the positions she or a member of her family held in any entity or association was unconstitutional as a violation of freedom of association.[15]

3. *The Americans with Disabilities Act.* The Americans with Disabilities Act (ADA), 42 U.S.C. § 12112 et seq., restricts the ability of employers to conduct medical examinations of job applicants. The ADA protects the rights of those with disabilities. A "disability" is defined as "a physical or mental impairment that substantially limits one or more of the major life activities of such individual." § 12102.

The ADA treats pre-employment and post-employment examinations and inquiries differently. Pursuant to § 12112(d):

(2) Preemployment.

> (A) Prohibited examination or inquiry. Except as provided in paragraph (3), a covered entity shall not conduct a medical examination or make inquiries of a job applicant as to whether such applicant is an individual with a disability or as to the nature and severity of such disability.
>
> (B) Acceptable injury. A covered entity may make preemployment inquiries into the ability of an applicant to perform job-related functions.

(3) Employment entrance examination. A covered entity may require a medical examination after an offer of employment has been made to a job applicant and prior to the commencement of the employment duties of such applicant, and may condition an offer of employment on the results of such examination, if —

> (A) all entering employees are subjected to such an examination regardless of disability. . . .

---

[15] For more background on workplace testing and questionnaires, see Chai Feldblum, *Medical Examinations and Inquiries Under the Americans with Disabilities Act: A View from the Inside,* 64 Temp. L. Rev. 521 (1991); Mark A. Rothstein, *The Law of Medical and Genetic Privacy in the Workplace,* in *Genetic Secrets: Protecting Privacy and Confidentiality in the Genetic Era* 281-298 (Mark A. Rothstein ed., 1997).

Employers are more restricted in testing and making inquiries of employees once they are hired. Pursuant to § 12112(d)(4):

(4) Examination and inquiry

(A) Prohibited examinations and inquiries. A covered entity shall not require a medical examination and shall not make inquiries of an employee as to whether such employee is an individual with a disability or as to the nature and severity of the disability, unless such examination or inquiry is shown to be job-related and consistent with business necessity.

(B) Acceptable examinations and inquiries. A covered entity may conduct voluntary medical examinations, including voluntary medical histories, which are part of an employee health program available to employees at the work site. A covered entity may make inquiries into the ability of an employee to perform job-related functions.

Drug testing is not considered a "medical examination" under the ADA. § 12114(d).

4. *Genetic Testing.* For a discussion of genetic testing by employers, see Chapter 3, section C.

5. *State Statutory Law.* Many states restrict certain forms of employment testing and questionnaires. For example, Wisconsin prohibits employers from requiring employees or applicants to undergo HIV testing:

. . . [N]o employer or agent of an employer may directly or indirectly. . . . [s]olicit or require as a condition of employment of any employee or prospective employee a test for the presence of HIV, antigen or nonantigenic products of HIV or an antibody to HIV. Wisc. Stat. Ann. § 103.15(2).

Massachusetts prohibits employers from asking prospective employees about arrests not leading to conviction, misdemeanor convictions, or any prior commitment to medical treatment facilities. *See* Mass. Gen. Laws ch. 151B § 4(9). Maryland restricts questions about disability or handicap unless it bears a direct and material relationship to the applicant's fitness for the job. *See* Md. Lab. & Empl. Code § 3-701. A number of states restrict genetic testing. *See, e.g.,* Cal Govt. Code § 12940(o); Conn. Gen. Stat. Ann. § 46a-60(11)(A); Del. Code Ann. tit. 19 § 711(e); N.Y. Exec. Law § 296.19 (a)(1).

ANDERSON V. CITY OF PHILADELPHIA

845 F.2d 1216 (3d Cir. 1988)

STAPLETON, J. . . . As permitted by state law, the police and prison departments of the City of Philadelphia have chosen to make polygraph testing an element of their hiring procedures. The plaintiffs in this case are unsuccessful applicants for employment as City police officers or correctional officers. The reason for the plaintiffs' lack of success in obtaining the employment they sought is their disqualification from consideration for such employment upon their failure to pass the polygraph test.

. . . [The] tests required by the police and prison departments include a medical examination, a psychiatric examination, a background investigation, and, usually last in the process, a polygraph test.

The background investigation includes completion of a Personal Data Questionnaire (PDQ), which contains questions about family and financial status, driving record, educational and employment history, criminal record, use of alcoholic beverages, and use, sale, and possession of illicit drugs. . . .

According to Police Commissioner Tucker, an applicant must pass the polygraph test in order to be hired by the Philadelphia Police Department. . . . In no case has an applicant who failed to pass a polygraph test been hired by either of the departments. The results of the tests are not made public, but are used only within the departments for evaluating the suitability of the applicant for employment.

There is considerable controversy about the validity and reliability of polygraph testing. The polygraph measures stress or anxiety, which in many cases may not correlate very well with deception. In 1983, Congress' Office of Technology Assessment put out a Technical Memorandum on polygraph testing, which read in part as follows:

> There are two major reasons why an overall measure of validity is not possible. First, the polygraph test is, in reality, a very complex process that is much more than the instrument. Although the instrument is essentially the same for all applications, the types of individuals tested, training of the examiner, purpose of the test, and types of questions asked, among other factors, can differ substantially. A polygraph test requires that the examiner infer deception or truthfulness based on a comparison of the person's physiological responses to various questions. . . . Second, the research on polygraph validity varies widely in terms of not only results, but also in the quality of research design and methodology. Thus, conclusions about scientific validity can be made only in the context of specific applications and even then must be tempered by the limitations of available research evidence. . . .
>
> OTA concluded that the available research evidence does not establish the scientific validity of the polygraph test for personnel security screening. . . .
>
> [D]espite many decades of judicial, legislative, and scientific discussion, no consensus has emerged about the accuracy of polygraph tests. . . .

When polygraphs are used for pre-employment screening, the risk of false positive results is generally thought to be higher than that of false negative results.

The City's law enforcement departments consider polygraph tests reliable and valid. An additional advantage of using the polygraph test, in the departments' view, is that it encourages applicants to be candid in responding to questions on the PDQ. The departments do not believe that this secondary advantage can be separated from the trustworthiness that they consider to be the main advantage of the polygraph. Both advantages, the departments believe, enable them to acquire necessary information about potential employees.

The departments do admit that polygraph testing is not perfect. While they recognize the impossibility of conducting error-free polygraph testing, however, they correctly point out that there is no evidence establishing that the polygraph is not valid. Moreover, they point out that there must be some method of acquiring the information necessary to make choices among applicants and stress that the decision to utilize a polygraph examination must be evaluated in light of the available alternatives. . . .

The plaintiffs claim that use of the polygraph test results to deny them employment deprives them of their constitutional rights to procedural and substantive due process and equal protection of law. After a bench trial, the district court held in favor of the plaintiffs.

On appeal, the defendants contend that no protected property or liberty interest of the plaintiffs was at stake, and thus the plaintiffs cannot maintain a procedural due process claim. They also argue that the use of the polygraph by the departments has a rational basis, and so passes muster under the applicable standards of equal protection and substantive due process analysis. . . .

In *Board of Regents v. Roth,* the Supreme Court made it clear that "[t]he requirements of procedural due process apply only to the deprivation of interests encompassed by the Fourteenth Amendment's protection of liberty and property." 408 U.S. 564, 569 (1972). According to the Court, "to determine whether due process requirements apply in the first place, we must look . . . to the *nature* of the interest at stake." In this case, the plaintiffs have alleged that they have been deprived of both property and liberty interests by the City departments' use of the polygraph test to disqualify them from employment. . . .

In *Roth,* the Court explained that

> [t]he Fourteenth Amendment's procedural protection of property is a safeguard of the security of interests that a person has already acquired in specific benefits. . . . [T]o have a property interest in a benefit, a person clearly must have more than an abstract need or desire for it. He must have more than a unilateral expectation of it. He must, instead, have a legitimate claim of entitlement to it. . . .

To demonstrate a property interest, therefore, these plaintiffs must show that under Pennsylvania law they had a legitimate claim of entitlement to employment as City police or prison officers.

The plaintiffs here were never more than applicants for employment by the City. Although the plaintiffs occupied high positions on the civil service eligibility lists for the type of employment they sought, occupancy of these positions entitled the plaintiffs to nothing more than consideration for employment when openings occurred.

While the departments were bound to consider the plaintiffs for employment, they were by no means bound to hire the plaintiffs. The plaintiffs can cite to no section of the Pennsylvania statutes which sets an objective standard for the hiring or rejection of applicants from the eligibility lists, and which might thereby create a legitimate claim of entitlement to employment. On the contrary, under the state law applicable here, agencies such as the defendant departments may and do exercise broad discretion in hiring. Under these circumstances, there can be no tenable claim of entitlement to employment. . . .

We therefore conclude that the plaintiffs' interest in the civil service positions they sought did not rise to the level of a property interest protected by the Constitution. . . .

On the subject of liberty interests in employment, this court has stated that

> [a]n employment action implicates a fourteenth amendment liberty interest only if it (1) is based on a "charge against [the individual] that might seriously damage his standing and associations in the community . . . for example, [by

implying] that he had been guilty of dishonesty, or immorality," or (2) "impose[s] on him a stigma of other disability that forecloses his freedom to take advantage of other employment opportunities." . . .

In this case, plaintiffs assert that they have been "branded as liars" on account of their failure to pass the polygraph examination. While the polygraph results might conceivably be viewed as stigmatizing the plaintiffs or damaging their reputations, the plaintiffs have not alleged that any of their polygraph test results were made public. Rather, the departments' assertion that the polygraph results are kept confidential and undisclosed stands unchallenged. Given that, we find untenable the plaintiffs' claim that they have been deprived of a liberty interest. . . .

We next address the plaintiffs' argument that they have been denied equal protection of the law. The plaintiffs rightly refrain from contending that their equal protection claim is entitled to strict or heightened scrutiny; accordingly, we will apply the "general rule . . . that legislation is presumed to be valid and will be sustained if the classification drawn by the statute is rationally related to a legitimate state interest." *City of Cleburne v. Cleburne Living Center, Inc.*, 473 U.S. 432 (1985). The plaintiffs bear the burden of proof on this issue, and so must show that the requirements imposed by law or regulation "so lack rationality that they constitute a constitutionally impermissible denial of equal protection." . . .

. . . [W]e think it rational for the departments to believe that the polygraph requirement results in fuller, more candid disclosures on the PDQ and thus provides additional information that is helpful in selecting qualified law enforcement officers. . . .

Accordingly, we conclude that in the absence of a scientific consensus, reasonable law enforcement administrators may choose to include a polygraph requirement in their hiring process without offending the equal protection clause. . . .

NOTES & QUESTIONS

1. *Polygraphs.* The first lie detector was invented by William Marston around 1917. Marston claimed that his device could detect deception by measuring increases in systolic blood pressure. In *Frye v. United States,* 293 F. 1013 (D.C. Cir. 1923), a famous case in evidence law, a defendant wanted to offer evidence about his successful lie detector test, but the trial court refused to admit the evidence. The court of appeals concluded that "the systolic blood pressure deception test has not yet gained such standing and scientific recognition among physiological and psychological authorities as would justify the courts in admitting expert testimony deduced from the discovery, development, and experiments thus far made." In the 1930s, the prototype of the modern polygraph machine was developed. The modern polygraph device is a portable machine that uses moving paper and three styluses to record three physiological responses: galvanic skin response, relative blood pressure, and respiration. These responses are recorded by placing devices on the person's chest, abdomen, fingers, and arm. The reli-

ability of polygraphs is still subject to significant dispute, so much so that courts continue to exclude polygraph evidence. A recent report from the National Research Council concluded that polygraph testing was too flawed for security screening. "Polygraph testing now rests on weak scientific underpinnings despite nearly a century of study," the report said. "And much of the available evidence for judging its validity lacks scientific rigor."[16]

Polygraphs merely detect physiological responses to emotional arousal; they cannot detect thoughts or feelings directly. Are polygraphs more invasive to privacy than drug tests or written psychological exams?

2. In *Long Beach City Employees Association v. City of Long Beach*, 719 P.2d 660 (Cal. 1986), the court reached the opposite conclusion from *Anderson*, holding that the California Constitution's right to privacy prohibits use of polygraphs to test public employees. Since private employees were excluded, polygraph testing failed equal protection clause strict scrutiny. Under the Equal Protection Clause, what type of scrutiny is appropriate for these cases? Strict scrutiny or minimal scrutiny?

3. In *States Employees Union v. Department of Mental Health*, 746 S.W.2d 203 (Tex. 1987), the Texas State Employees Union and several employees sued the Texas Department of Mental Health and Mental Retardation to invalidate the department's mandatory polygraph policy. Under the policy, employees were subject to "adverse personnel action" if they refused to submit to a polygraph examination to investigate patient abuse, theft, criminal activity, or health or safety threats. The court concluded:

> We hold that the Texas Constitution protects personal privacy from unreasonable intrusion. This right to privacy should yield only when the government can demonstrate that an intrusion is reasonably warranted for the achievement of a compelling governmental objective that can be achieved by no less intrusive, more reasonable means. . . .
>
> As justification for its polygraph policy, the Department asserts its interest in maintaining a safe environment for Department patients. This interest is in many respects compelling. The Department is not concerned solely with the smooth operation of its agency. It has been charged by the legislature with a unique responsibility towards its patients. . . . In its effort to achieve these goals, the Department must minimize incidents of employee misconduct. . . .
>
> . . . The Department's objectives, important as they are, are not adequately compelling to warrant an intrusion into the privacy rights of the employees.
>
> The polygraph policy itself undoubtedly implicates the privacy rights of the employees. The trial court found that "[The Department's] polygraph's intrusion is highly offensive to a regular person." Further, the trial court found that in light of its unreliability, a polygraph test was not a reasonable means of identifying miscreant employees.
>
> We do not doubt that the Department is entitled to require employees to answer questions that are narrowly and specifically related to the performance of their job duties. The use of a lie detector, however, presents

---

[16]National Research Council, The Polygraph and Lie Detection (2002), available at *http://www.nap.edu/books/0309084369/html/*.

a qualitatively different question. The Department's asserted interests are inadequate to overcome the privacy interests impinged upon by the polygraph testing. We hold that the Department's polygraph policies impermissibly violate privacy rights protected by the Texas Constitution.

4. *Polygraphs and the Fourth Amendment.* Can a public sector employer force its employees to engage in a polygraph examination as part of an investigation of employee misconduct? Under the Fourth Amendment, is a polygraph examination a "reasonable" search based on *O'Connor v. Ortega*?

Recall *Kyllo v. United States* from Chapter 4. In the circuit court opinion, *United States v. Kyllo*, 190 F. 3d 1041 (9th Cir. 1999), Judge Noonan wrote in dissent, and the Supreme Court ultimately agreed, that the government should be required to obtain a warrant before it may make use of a thermal imaging device to detect the presence of marijuana grow lamps in the interior of a home. One of the issues raised by Judge Noonan concerned the accuracy of the technique. He wrote:

> The Agema 210 is a crude instrument. It reveals only two things: Heatcausing activity within a home and the rooms or area where the heat is being generated. For the majority these limited capacities let the Agema 210 pass muster: The "crucial inquiry" for the majority is whether the Agema 210 reveals "intimate details." Because what it reveals is not sensitive or personal or a specific activity, no unconstitutional search is being performed. It is as though if your home was searched by a blind policeman you would have suffered no constitutional deprivation. . . .
>
> The defense of the machine that it does not see very well hurts the government by underscoring the unreliability of the Agema 210. This defense amounts to saying that if a constable makes a blundering search, it should not really count as a search. The argument is the opposite of that which justified the examination[] in *United States v. Place* . . . — [it] revealed only contraband and nothing else. The machine as blind or blundering constable does not pass the criteria of the Fourth Amendment.

Do you agree with Judge Noonan that an imprecise investigative technique raises Fourth Amendment concerns? Are the Fourth Amendment concerns greater when the technique works well or works poorly? What if a new polygraph technique were developed that was extremely accurate? Would it raise greater or lesser Fourth Amendment concerns?

THE EMPLOYEE POLYGRAPH PROTECTION ACT

In 1988, Congress passed the Employee Polygraph Protection Act (EPPA), Pub. L. No. 100-618, codified at 29 U.S.C. §§ 2001-2009. The EPPA applies only to private sector employers. It specifically exempts "the United States Government, any State or local government, or any political subdivision of a State or local government." § 2006(a).

Limitations on Polygraph Testing. Pursuant to 29 U.S.C. § 2002, it is unlawful for private sector employers:

> (1) directly or indirectly, to require, request, suggest, or cause any employee or prospective employee to take or submit to any lie detector test;

(2) to use, accept, refer to, or inquire concerning the results of any lie detector test of any employee or prospective employee;

(3) to discharge, discipline, discriminate against in any manner, or deny employment or promotion to, or threaten to take any such action against

(A) any employee or prospective employee who refuses, declines, or fails to take or submit to any lie detector test, or

(B) any employee or prospective employee on the basis of the results of any lie detector test; or . . .

Exception for Ongoing Investigations. However, there are certain exceptions where employers may use polygraphs:

(1) the test is administered in connection with an ongoing investigation involving economic loss or injury to the employer's business, such as theft, embezzlement, misappropriation, or an act of unlawful industrial espionage or sabotage;

(2) the employee had access to the property that is the subject of the investigation;

(3) the employer has a reasonable suspicion that the employee was involved in the incident or activity under investigation; and

(4) the employer executes a statement, provided to the examinee before the test, that [among other things, describes the particular incident being investigated and describes the basis of the employer's reasonable suspicion of the employee's involvement in the incident]. § 2006(d).

Exception for Security Services. Certain employers who engage in security services (e.g., armored car services, security alarm services, security personnel) are exempt. These security services must protect government interests such as nuclear power, water supply facilities, toxic waste disposal, and public transportation; or the services must protect "currency, negotiable securities, precious commodities or instruments, or proprietary information." § 2006(e).

When polygraphs are used under these exceptions, the test or the refusal to take the test cannot be the sole basis of any adverse employment action. § 2007(a). Further, the EPPA provides certain procedures, responsibilities, and restrictions on the use of polygraphs. For example, polygraph examiners cannot ask questions concerning beliefs regarding religion, racial matters, politics, sexual behavior, or union activities. § 2007(b). The EPPA limits the disclosure of polygraph information to people authorized by the examinee, the employer, or pursuant to a court order. § 2008.

Enforcement. Violations will result in a civil penalty of up to $10,000. The Secretary of Labor may bring an action to obtain restraining orders and injunctions to require compliance with the EPPA. Employers who violate the EPPA are liable to employees or prospective employees for legal and equitable relief including reinstatement, promotion, and payment of lost wages and benefits. § 2005.

Preemption. The EPPA does not preempt state law. About half the states regulate the use of polygraphs by statute.

Suppose an employer were to ask an employee to waive her rights under the EPPA. Could the employer do so?

6. EMPLOYER MONITORING OF THE TELEPHONE

Recall that federal wiretap law (Chapter 4) applies not only to government and law enforcement officials but also to private parties as well. Thus, employers are subject to the restrictions of federal wiretap law. However, three notable exceptions to federal wiretap law are relevant to the employment context. First, federal wiretap law does not apply when one party to a communication consents to the interception. *See* 18 U.S.C. §2511(2)(d). Second, the providers of wire or electronic communications services are exempt from Title II's restrictions on accessing stored communications. *See* 18 U.S.C. §2701(c)(1). Under Title I, providers of wire or electronic communication services whose facilities are used in the transmission of such communications are permitted to intercept, disclose, or use that communication as a necessary incident to render the service or to protect the rights or property of the service. *See* 18 U.S.C. §2511(2). The service provider exception is relevant in the employment context because many employers serve as the providers of certain communications services, such as Internet connections. The third exception is known as the "ordinary course of business" exception. Federal wiretap law does not apply when an employer uses certain intercepting devices "in the ordinary course of [the employer's] business." §2510(5). The device must be furnished to the employer by the provider of the wire or electronic communication service. §2510(5)(a)(i).

WATKINS V. L.M. BERRY & CO.

704 F.2d 577 (11th Cir. 1983)

SMITH, J. In this case appellant Watkins sued her employer, L.M. Berry & Company, and others, alleging violation of the federal wiretapping statute, title III of the Omnibus Crime Control and Safe Streets Act of 1968, 18 U.S.C. §§2510-2520. The district court granted summary judgment on the merits against Watkins, and she now appeals. . . .

. . . Carmie Watkins was employed as a sales representative by L.M. Berry & Company (Berry Co.). Watkins' immediate supervisor was Martha Little, and Little's supervisor was Diane Wright. Berry Co. was under contract with South Central Bell to solicit Yellow Pages advertising from South Central Bell's present and prospective Yellow Pages advertisers. Much of this solicitation was done by telephone and Watkins was hired and trained to make those calls.

Berry Co. has an established policy, of which all employees are informed, of monitoring solicitation calls as part of its regular training program. The monitored calls are reviewed with employees to improve sales techniques. This monitoring is accomplished with a standard extension telephone, located in the supervisor's office, which shares lines with the telephones in the employees' offices. Employees are permitted to make personal calls on company telephones, and they are told that personal calls will not be monitored except to the extent necessary to determine whether a particular call is of a personal or business nature.

In April or May 1980, during her lunch hour, Watkins received a call in her office from a friend. At or near the beginning of the call (there are conflicting indications), the friend asked Watkins about an employment interview Watkins had had with another company (Lipton) the evening before. Watkins responded that the interview had gone well and expressed a strong interest in taking the Lipton job. Unbeknownst to Watkins, Little was monitoring the call from her office and heard the discussion of the interview.

After hearing the conversation (how much is unclear), Little told Wright about it. Later that afternoon Watkins was called into Wright's office and was told that the company did not want her to leave. Watkins responded by asking whether she was being fired. Upon discovering that her supervisors' questions were prompted by Little's interception of her call, Watkins became upset and tempers flared. The upshot was that Wright did fire Watkins the next day. However, Watkins complained to Wright's supervisor and was reinstated with apologies from Wright and Little. Within a week Watkins left Berry Co. to work for Lipton. . . .

Title III forbids the interception, without judicial authorization, of the contents of telephone calls. . . .

It is not disputed that Little's conduct violates section 2511(1)(b) unless it comes within an exemption "specifically provided in" title III (18 U.S.C. §2511(1)). Appellees claim the applicability of two such exemptions. The first is the consent exemption set out in section 2511(2)(d):

> It shall not be unlawful under this chapter for a person not acting under color of law to intercept a wire or oral communication . . . where one of the parties to the communication has given prior consent to such interception. . . .

Appellees argue that, by using Berry Co.'s telephones and knowing that monitoring was possible, Watkins consented to the monitoring. The second is the business extension exemption in section 2510(5)(a)(i):

> "electronic, mechanical, or other device" [in §2511(1)(b)] means any device or apparatus which can be used to intercept a wire or oral communication other than —
>
> > (a) any telephone or telegraph instrument, equipment or facility, or any component thereof, (i) furnished to the subscriber or user by a communications common carrier in the ordinary course of its business and being used by the subscriber or user *in the ordinary course of its business;* * * * [emphasis supplied].

"[E]quipment . . . furnished to the subscriber or user by a communications common carrier in the ordinary course of its business" means in this case simply a standard extension telephone. *See Briggs v. American Air Filter Co.*, 630 F.2d 414 (5th Cir. 1980). The issue is therefore whether the monitoring of this call was in the ordinary course of Berry Co.'s business. Appellees contend that it was and hence that the extension telephone was not a "device" within the statutory meaning (section 2511(1)(b)) of "interception."

Briggs v. American Air Filter Co., decided by the Fifth Circuit in 1980, provides the framework for interpreting these exemptions. The consent and business extension exemptions are analytically separate. Consent may be obtained for any interceptions, and the business or personal nature of the call is entirely irrelevant. Conversely, the business extension exemption operates without regard to consent. So long as the requisite business connection is demonstrated, the business extension exemption represents the "circumstances under which non-consensual interception" is not violative of section 2511(1)(b). Accordingly, in analyzing the present case we will first consider the scope of Watkins' consent to the monitoring of this call and then move to the question whether the interception was justified as being in the ordinary course of Berry Co.'s business, notwithstanding the absence of consent. . . .

Appellees argue that Watkins' acceptance of employment with Berry Co. with knowledge of the monitoring policy constituted her consent to the interception of this call. This is erroneous with respect to both Watkins' actual and implied consent.

It is clear, to start with, that Watkins did not actually consent to interception of *this* particular call. Furthermore, she did not consent to a *policy* of general monitoring. She consented to a policy of monitoring sales calls but not personal calls. This consent included the inadvertent interception of a personal call, but only for as long as necessary to determine the nature of the call. So, if Little's interception went beyond the point necessary to determine the nature of the call, it went beyond the scope of Watkins' actual consent.

Consent under title III is not to be cavalierly implied. Title III expresses a strong purpose to protect individual privacy by strictly limiting the occasions on which interception may lawfully take place. Stiff penalties are provided for its violation. It would thwart this policy if consent could routinely be implied from circumstances. Thus, knowledge of the *capability* of monitoring alone cannot be considered implied consent. . . .

If, as appears from the undisputed facts, there was no consent to interception of the call beyond what was initially required to determine its nature, appellees must rely on the business extension exemption to shield them from liability for any listening beyond that point. To prevail, they must show that the interception of the call beyond the initial period was in the ordinary course of business. It is not enough for Berry Co. to claim that its general policy is justifiable as part of the ordinary course of business. We have no doubt that it is. The question before us, rather, is whether the interception of *this* call was in the ordinary course of business.

Under *Briggs,* the general rule seems to be that if the intercepted call was a business call, then Berry Co.'s monitoring of it was in the ordinary course of business. If it was a personal call, the monitoring was probably, but not certainly, *not* in the ordinary course of business. The undisputed evidence strongly suggests that the intercepted call here was not a business call. Watkins received the call and so could not have been soliciting advertising; the caller was a personal friend; and the topics discussed were mainly social. To that extent this was certainly a personal call.

Appellees argue, however, that the signal topic was Watkins' interview with another employer. This was obviously of interest and concern to Berry Co., so, appellees argue, it was in the ordinary course of business to listen. . . .

The phrase "in the ordinary course of business" cannot be expanded to mean anything that interests a company. Such a broad reading "flouts the words of the statute and establishes an exemption that is without basis in the legislative history" of title III. Berry Co. might have been curious about Watkins' plans, but it had no legal interest in them. Watkins was at liberty to resign at will and so at liberty to interview with other companies. Her interview was thus a personal matter, neither in pursuit nor to the legal detriment of Berry Co.'s business. To expand the business extension exemption as broadly as appellees suggest would permit monitoring of obviously personal and very private calls on the ground, for example, that the company was interested in whether Watkins' friends were "nice" or not. We therefore conclude that the subject call was personal. . . .

We hold that a personal call may not be intercepted in the ordinary course of business under the exemption in section 2510(5)(a)(i), except to the extent necessary to guard against unauthorized use of the telephone or to determine whether a call is personal or not. In other words, a personal call may be intercepted in the ordinary course of business to determine its nature but never its contents. The limit of the exemption for Berry Co.'s business was the policy that Berry Co. in fact instituted. It thus appears that Little was justified in listening to that portion of the call which indicated that it was not a business call; beyond that, she was not. Determination of the relevant points in the call is for the trier of fact. . . .

A final issue remains with respect to both exemptions. *If* it turns out that Little was justified in listening to the beginning of the conversation, either to determine its nature or with consent, and *if* it turns out that during that portion of the conversation the interview was discussed, then we must decide whether Little was obliged to hang up or, having entered the conversation legally, could remain on the line indefinitely. We think that the conclusion is inescapable that these exemptions do not automatically justify interception of an entire call. The expectation of privacy in a conversation is not lost entirely because the privacy of part of it is violated. Under title III a law enforcement officer executing a wiretap order must minimize his intrusion to the extent possible. 18 U.S.C. §2518(5). Therefore, Little was obliged to cease listening as soon as she had determined that the call was personal, regardless of the contents of the legitimately heard conversation.

The violation of section 2511(1)(b) is the intercepting itself, not the interception of particular material. It is not necessary to recovery of damages that the violator hear anything in particular; she need do no more than listen. Thus, the reinstatement of Watkins and her subsequent departure, while they may affect the amount of actual damages, do not moot or render *de minimis* her claim. Watkins' right to recover at least the minimum statutory damages flows from the interception, not from the actual damage caused. It is for the trier of fact to determine at what point the telephone should have been hung up. . . .

We hold that this case was not properly disposed of by summary judgment, as genuinely disputed issues of material fact remain. A detailed factual inquiry into the interception is necessary if the standards set forth above are to be adequately addressed. Among the factual questions that should be considered are: What was the monitoring policy to which Watkins consented? Did Little know that Watkins had received the call and if so did that necessarily indicate a personal call? How long was the call? When was the interview discussed? Were other subjects discussed? For how long did Little listen? How long does it take to discover that a call is personal, for example, is there an immediately recognizable pattern to a sales call? This list of questions is not exhaustive, but it is hoped that it points out the directions in which further inquiries should be pursued. . . .

DEAL V. SPEARS

980 F.2d 1153 (8th Cir. 1992)

BOWMAN, J. . . . Newell and Juanita Spears have owned and operated the White Oak Package Store near Camden, Arkansas, for about twenty years. The Spearses live in a mobile home adjacent to the store. The telephone in the store has an extension in the home, and is the only phone line into either location. The same phone line thus is used for both the residential and the business phones.

Sibbie Deal was an employee at the store from December 1988 until she was fired in August 1990. The store was burglarized in April 1990 and approximately $16,000 was stolen. The Spearses believed that it was an inside job and suspected that Deal was involved. Hoping to catch the suspect in an unguarded admission, Newell Spears purchased and installed a recording device on the extension phone in the mobile home. When turned on, the machine would automatically record all conversations made or received on either phone, with no indication to the parties using the phone that their conversation was being recorded. Before purchasing the recorder, Newell Spears told a sheriff's department investigator that he was considering this surreptitious monitoring and the investigator told Spears that he did not "see anything wrong with that."

Calls were taped from June 27, 1990, through August 13, 1990. During that period, Sibbie Deal, who was married to Mike Deal at the time, was having an extramarital affair with Calvin Lucas, then married to Pam Lucas. Deal and Lucas spoke on the telephone at the store frequently and for long periods of time while Deal was at work. (Lucas was on 100% disability so he was at home all day.) Based on the trial testimony, the District Court concluded that much of the conversation between the two was "sexually provocative." Deal also made or received numerous other personal telephone calls during her workday. Even before Newell Spears purchased the recorder, Deal was asked by her employers to cut down on her use of the phone for personal calls, and the Spearses told her they might resort to monitoring calls or installing a pay phone in order to curtail the abuse.

Newell Spears listened to virtually all twenty-two hours of the tapes he recorded, regardless of the nature of the calls or the content of the conversations, and Juanita Spears listened to some of them. Although there was nothing in the record to indicate that they learned anything about the burglary, they did learn, among other things, that Deal sold Lucas a keg of beer at cost, in violation of store policy. On August 13, 1990, when Deal came in to work the evening shift, Newell Spears played a few seconds of the incriminating tape for Deal and then fired her. Deal and Lucas filed this action on August 29, 1990 [alleging that the Spearses violated Federal Wiretap Law. The district court found the Spearses liable and assessed damages at a total of $40,000 — $10,000 to Deal and Lucas respectively assessed against Newell Spears and $10,000 to Deal and Lucas respectively assessed against Juanita Spears]. . . .

The Spearses challenge the court's finding of liability. They admit the taping but contend that the facts here bring their actions under two statutory exceptions to civil liability. Further, Juanita Spears alleges that she did not disclose information learned from the tapes, thus the statutory damages assessed against her on that ground were improper. For their part Deal and Lucas challenge the court's failure to award them punitive damages as permitted by statute.

The elements of a violation of the wire and electronic communications interception provisions (Title III) of the Omnibus Crime Control and Safe Streets Act of 1968 are set forth in the section that makes such interceptions a criminal offense. 18 U.S.C. §2511 (1988). Under the relevant provisions of the statute, criminal liability attaches and a federal civil cause of action arises when a person intentionally intercepts a wire or electronic communication or intentionally discloses the contents of the interception. The successful civil plaintiff may recover actual damages plus any profits made by the violator. If statutory damages will result in a larger recovery than actual damages, the violator must pay the plaintiff "the greater of $100 a day for each day of violation or $10,000." Further, punitive damages, attorney fees, and "other litigation costs reasonably incurred" are allowed.

The Spearses first claim they are exempt from civil liability because Sibbie Deal consented to the interception of calls that she made from and received at the store. Under the statute, it is not unlawful "to intercept a wire, oral, or electronic communication . . . where one of the parties to the communication has given prior consent to such interception," 18 U.S.C. §2511(2)(d), and thus no civil liability is incurred. The Spearses contend that Deal's consent may be implied because Newell Spears had mentioned that he might be forced to monitor calls or restrict telephone privileges if abuse of the store's telephone for personal calls continued. They further argue that the extension in their home gave actual notice to Deal that her calls could be overheard, and that this notice resulted in her implied consent to interception. We find these arguments unpersuasive. . . .

We do not believe that Deal's consent may be implied from the circumstances relied upon in the Spearses' arguments. The Spearses did not inform Deal that they were monitoring the phone, but only told her they might do so in order to cut down on personal calls. Moreover, it seems clear that the couple anticipated Deal would not suspect that they were intercepting her calls, since they hoped to catch her making an admission about the burglary, an outcome they would not expect if she knew her calls were being recorded. . . .

Given these circumstances, we hold as a matter of law that the Spearses have failed to show Deal's consent to the interception and recording of her conversations.

The Spearses also argue that they are immune from liability under what has become known as an exemption for business use of a telephone extension. The exception is actually a restrictive definition. Under Title III, a party becomes criminally and civilly liable when he or she "intercepts" wire communications. "'[I]ntercept' means the aural or other acquisition of the contents of any wire, electronic, or oral communication through the use of any electronic, mechanical, or other device[.]" Such a device is "any device or apparatus which can be used to intercept a wire, oral, or electronic communication" except when that device is a

> telephone . . . instrument, equipment or facility, or any component thereof, (i) furnished to the subscriber or user by a provider of wire or electronic communication service in the ordinary course of its business and being used by the subscriber or user in the ordinary course of its business or furnished by such subscriber or user for connection to the facilities of such service and used in the ordinary course of its business[.]

Thus there are two essential elements that must be proved before this becomes a viable defense: the intercepting equipment must be furnished to the user by the phone company or connected to the phone line, and it must be used in the ordinary course of business. The Spearses argue that the extension in their residence, to which the recorder was connected, meets the equipment requirement, and the listening-in was done in the ordinary course of business. We disagree. . . .

We hold that the recording device, and not the extension phone, intercepted the calls. But even if the extension phone intercepted the calls, we do not agree that the interception was in the ordinary course of business.

We do not quarrel with the contention that the Spearses had a legitimate business reason for listening in: they suspected Deal's involvement in a burglary of the store and hoped she would incriminate herself in a conversation on the phone. Moreover, Deal was abusing her privileges by using the phone for numerous personal calls even, by her own admission, when there were customers in the store. The Spearses might legitimately have monitored Deal's calls to the extent necessary to determine that the calls were personal and made or received in violation of store policy.

But the Spearses recorded twenty-two hours of calls, and Newell Spears listened to all of them without regard to their relation to his business interests. Granted, Deal might have mentioned the burglary at any time during the conversations, but we do not believe that the Spearses' suspicions justified the extent of the intrusion. We conclude that the scope of the interception in this case takes us well beyond the boundaries of the ordinary course of business.

For the reasons we have indicated, the Spearses cannot avail themselves of the telephone extension/business use exemption of Title III. . . .

Finally, Deal and Lucas cross-appeal the District Court's failure to award punitive damages. *See id.* § 2520(b)(2). Punitive damages are unwarranted under Title III unless Deal and Lucas can prove "a wanton, reckless or malicious violation." It is difficult to conceive of a case less appropriate for punitive damages than this one.

The Spearses had lost $16,000 by theft in what must have been a serious blow to their business, and installed the recorder in hopes that they would be able to recover their loss, or at least catch the thief. They suspected an inside job and naturally they were anxious to find out whether the burglar was one of their employees. Further, despite warnings about abuse of the phone, the Spearses were paying a salary to an employee for the hours she spent on personal calls, including (as it turned out) her conversations with her lover. She sometimes carried on these conversations in the presence of the store's customers and apparently not infrequently used salacious language. The Spearses were not taping to get "dirt" on Lucas and Deal, but believed their business interests justified the recording. Moreover, before installing the recorder, Newell Spears inquired of a law enforcement officer and was told that the officer saw nothing wrong with Spears tapping his own phone. While the Spearses' reliance on the officer's statement does not absolve them of liability, it clearly demonstrates that the taping was neither wanton nor reckless. As for the disclosures, Sibbie Deal was the only person for whom any of the tapes were played. . . .

We agree with the District Court that defendants' conduct does not warrant the imposition of punitive damages. . . .

NOTES & QUESTIONS

1. Suppose the Spearses had a policy that all calls, regardless of whether they were personal or business related, would be recorded and monitored? Would the Spearses still be liable under federal wiretap law?
2. Would it be likely that Deal would speak about the burglary on a business-related call? If the Spearses could not listen to Deal's private calls, their investigation might be significantly limited. If you were the Spearses' attorney and they came to you, explained that they suspected Deal of the burglary, and wanted your advice about how they could legally investigate, how would you advise them?

7. EMPLOYER MONITORING OF MAIL, E-MAIL, AND INTERNET USE

(a) Regular Mail

EX PARTE JACKSON

96 U.S. 727 (1877)

FIELD, J. . . . The power possessed by Congress embraces the regulation of the entire postal system of the country. The right to designate what shall be carried necessarily involves the right to determine what shall be excluded. The difficulty attending the subject arises, not from the want of power in Congress to prescribe regulations as to what shall constitute mail matter, but from the necessity of enforcing them consistently with rights reserved to the people, of far greater importance than the transportation of the mail. In their enforcement, a distinction is to be made between different kinds of mail matter,—between what is intended to be kept free from inspection, such as letters, and sealed packages subject to letter postage; and what is open to inspection, such as newspapers, magazines, pamphlets, and other printed matter, purposely left in a condition to be examined. Letters and sealed packages of this kind in the mail are as fully guarded from examination and inspection, except as to their outward form and weight, as if they were retained by the parties forwarding them in their own domiciles. The constitutional guaranty of the right of the people to be secure in their papers against unreasonable searches and seizures extends to their papers, thus closed against inspection, wherever they may be. Whilst in the mail, they can only be opened and examined under like warrant, issued upon similar oath or affirmation, particularly describing the thing to be seized, as is required when papers are subjected to search in one's own household. No law of Congress can place in the hands of officials connected with the postal service any authority to invade the secrecy of letters and such sealed packages in the mail; and all regulations adopted as to mail matter of this kind must be in subordination to the great principle embodied in the fourth amendment of the Constitution. . . .

Whilst regulations excluding matter from the mail cannot be enforced in a way which would require or permit an examination into letters, or sealed packages subject to letter postage, without warrant, issued upon oath or affirmation, in the search for prohibited matter, they may be enforced upon competent evidence of their violation obtained in other ways; as from the parties receiving the letters or packages, or from agents depositing them in the post-office, or others cognizant of the facts. And as to objectionable printed matter, which is open to examination, the regulations may be enforced in a similar way, by the imposition of penalties for their violation through the courts, and, in some cases, by the direct action of the officers of the postal service. . . .

NOTES & QUESTIONS

1. *Privacy of the Mail.* Privacy of the mail is rarely questioned today. Before the American Revolution, however, British officials frequently opened mail. Mail would often be left at a tavern or other place of congregation for strangers to take to its destination. It was common for the deliverer of the letter to read it and even to add his or her own thoughts. Since letters were not secure, people would try to seal them with sealing wax, use pen names, or encrypt their words.

   Privacy of the mail is the product of both law and technology. In the 1730s, Ben Franklin was put in charge of the colonial mails, and he continued in this capacity until the Revolutionary War. In 1753, Ben Franklin promulgated a regulation requiring his employees to swear "not to open or suffer to be opened any Mail or Bag of Letters." However, still the mail was not very secure. Thomas Jefferson, Alexander Hamilton, and George Washington all lamented the lack of privacy in the mail. Jefferson at times encrypted his private communications.

In 1782, Congress passed a law that mail should not be opened. In 1825, Congress passed a law criminalizing the unauthorized opening of mail. In the mid-nineteenth century, adhesive envelopes were invented, greatly enhancing the privacy of the mail. Today, pursuant to 18 U.S.C. § 1702:

> Whoever takes any letter, postal card, or package out of any post office or any authorized depository for mail matter, or from any letter or mail carrier, or which has been in any post office or authorized depository, or in the custody of any letter or mail carrier, before it has been delivered to the person to whom it was directed, with design to obstruct the correspondence, or to pry into the business or secrets of another, or opens, secretes, embezzles, or destroys the same, shall be fined under this title or imprisoned not more than five years, or both.[17]

2. *Mail and the Fourth Amendment.* As indicated by *Ex Parte Jackson,* the Fourth Amendment prohibits the government from opening a person's mail without a valid warrant. The Court held that although New York's Comstock laws (which banned the mailing of materials relating to gambling, abortion, birth control, and sex) were constitutional, the government could not open up people's mail as a way to enforce these laws. Today, federal law also restricts the government's ability to search people's mail. Pursuant to 39 U.S.C. § 3623(d):

> No letter of such a class of domestic origin shall be opened except under authority of a search warrant authorized by law, or by an officer or employee of the Postal Service for the sole purpose of determining an address at which the letter can be delivered, or pursuant to the authorization of the addressee.

However, the government can search letters sent from abroad. *See United States v. Various Articles of Obscene Merchandise, Schedule No. 1213,* 395 F. Supp. 791 (S.D.N.Y. 1975), *affirmed,* 538 F.2d 317.

VERNARS V. YOUNG

539 F.2d 966 (3d Cir. 1976)

SEITZ, C.J. This is an appeal from an order of the district court dismissing plaintiff's complaint for failure to state claims upon which relief can be granted. Plaintiff is a 27% shareholder, an officer and one of three directors of Young Galvanizing, Inc. (corporation). The second board member is the defendant Young, a 50% shareholder and principal officer of the corporation. . . .

We come finally to plaintiff's attack on the district court's dismissal of Count IV which asserted a claim for invasion of plaintiff's right to privacy. In this count plaintiff alleged that the defendant Young opened and read without her consent mail which was delivered to the corporation's office but was addressed to her and marked personal. . . .

---

[17] For a history of the privacy of letters, see Robert Ellis Smith, *Ben Franklin's Website* (2000); Priscilla Regan, *Legislating Privacy* (1995); David Flaherty, *Privacy in Colonial New England* (1972); David J. Seipp, *The Right to Privacy in American History* (1978).

We note at the outset that the instant case involves the "Intrusion Upon Seclusion" provision of § 652B of the Restatement (Second) of Torts. Since the *Grant* case dealt with the "Publicity Given to Private Life" provision of § 652D, the district court's reliance thereon was misplaced. *Marks v. Bell Telephone,* however, is instructive. That case involved an invasion of privacy by wire-tapping. The Pennsylvania Court said that, in the absence of an intentional overhearing of a private conversation by an unauthorized party, which it did not find, the tort of invasion of privacy had not been committed. Although the court was clearly dealing with the "Intrusion Upon Seclusion" provision of § 652B herein involved, we do not think the *Bell* case supports the dismissal of Count IV.

The Court found against plaintiff in the *Bell* case on his right of privacy claim because the wire-tap did not result in any private conversation being intentionally overheard by an unauthorized person. In the present case the defendant is accused of opening plaintiff's private mail and reading it without authority. If proved, we believe this would constitute just as much of an intrusion as the intentional overhearing by an unauthorized person adverted to by the court in *Bell.* Just as private individuals have a right to expect that their telephonic communications will not be monitored, they also have a reasonable expectation that their personal mail will not be opened and read by unauthorized persons. Recognition of a cause of action for violation of that expectation seems particularly fitting under the right of privacy doctrine.

NOTES & QUESTIONS

1. Suppose an employer adopted a policy that all employees' mail will be opened and read. The employer provided notice to the employees a few months in advance of the policy so employees could take steps to ensure that letters containing intimate secrets were not mailed to them at work. What legal recourse would employees objecting to this policy have?

(b) E-Mail

E-mail presents an interesting privacy problem in the workplace. Unlike regular mail, e-mail is less secure from prying eyes. Because e-mail travels through numerous computers to reach its final destination, it can be intercepted and copied at many points. E-mail goes through the employer's computer network. It may be stored by the employer as part of the routine system backup. E-mail is often stored on the employee's computer even after it is received and read. Employers can easily scan e-mail for certain words. At the same time, encryption techniques may enable employees to send messages so that at least the content is not easily accessible to employers. Given the nature of e-mail — especially e-mail correspondence at the workplace — how should we assess whether individuals have a reasonable expectation of privacy in e-mail? [18]

---

[18] For more background about e-mail and the workplace, see Michael S. Leib, *E-Mail and the Wiretap Laws: Why Congress Should Add Electronic Communications to Title II's Statutory Exclusionary Rule and Expressly Reject a "Good Faith" Exception,* 34 Harv. J. Legis. 393 (1997); Kevin P. Kopp, *Electronic Communications in the Workplace: E-Mail Monitoring and the Right of Privacy,* 8 Seton Hall Const. L.J. 861 (1998); Alexander L. Rodriguez, Comment, *All Bark, No Byte: Employee E-Mail*

The answer to this question depends in part on how we analogize e-mail. Some view e-mail as akin to a letter—just one in electronic form rather than on paper. Should e-mail deserve the same legal protection and privacy expectations as regular letters? Others argue that without any encryption, e-mail is quite insecure and is more akin to a postcard than a letter. Another analogy is that e-mail should be understood as similar to a telephone call. E-mail often travels across phone lines and e-mail correspondence is often conducted fairly rapidly with frequent responses and replies. Should e-mail be given the same legal protection and privacy expectations as telephone conversations? One might argue that given how insecure e-mail is from being intercepted by unauthorized individuals, it is more akin to a radio communication. The following cases examine the privacy of e-mail in the workplace:

SMYTH V. PILLSBURY CO.

914 F. Supp. 97 (E.D. Pa. 1996)

WEINER, J. In this diversity action, plaintiff, an at-will employee, claims he was wrongfully discharged from his position as a regional operations manager by the defendant. Presently before the court is the motion of the defendant to dismiss pursuant to Rule 12(b)(6) of the Federal Rules of Civil Procedure. For the reasons which follow, the motion is granted.

A claim may be dismissed under Fed. R. Civ. P. 12(b)(6) only if the plaintiff can prove no set of facts in support of the claim that would entitle him to relief. The reviewing court must consider only those facts alleged in the Complaint and accept all of the allegations as true. Applying this standard, we find that plaintiff has failed to state a claim upon which relief can be granted.

Defendant maintained an electronic mail communication system ("e-mail") in order to promote internal corporate communications between its employees. Defendant repeatedly assured its employees, including plaintiff, that all e-mail communications would remain confidential and privileged. Defendant further assured its employees, including plaintiff, that e-mail communications could not be intercepted and used by defendant against its employees as grounds for termination or reprimand.

In October 1994, plaintiff received certain e-mail communications from his supervisor over defendant's e-mail system on his computer at home. In reliance on defendant's assurances regarding defendant's e-mail system, plaintiff responded and exchanged e-mails with his supervisor. At some later date, contrary to the assurances of confidentiality made by defendant, defendant, acting through its agents, servants and employees, intercepted plaintiff's private e-mail messages made in October 1994. On January 17, 1995, defendant notified plaintiff that it was terminating his employment effective February 1,

Privacy Rights in the Private Sector Workplace, 47 Emory L.J. 1439 (1998); Kevin J. Baum, Comment, *E-Mail in the Workplace and the Right to Privacy,* 42 Vill. L. Rev. 1011 (1997); Scott A. Sundstrom, *You've Got Mail (and the Government Knows It): Applying the Fourth Amendment to Workplace E-Mail Monitoring,* 73 N.Y.U. L. Rev. 2064 (1998).

1995, for transmitting what it deemed to be inappropriate and unprofessional comments[19] over defendant's e-mail system in October, 1994.

As a general rule, Pennsylvania law does not provide a common law cause of action for the wrongful discharge of an at-will employee such as plaintiff. . . . However, in the most limited of circumstances, exceptions have been recognized where discharge of an at-will employee threatens or violates a clear mandate of public policy. . . .

Plaintiff claims that his termination was in violation of "public policy which precludes an employer from terminating an employee in violation of the employee's right to privacy as embodied in Pennsylvania common law." . . . [O]ur Court of Appeals stated "our review of Pennsylvania law reveals other evidence of a public policy that may, under certain circumstances, give rise to a wrongful discharge action related to urinalysis or to personal property searches. Specifically, we refer to the Pennsylvania common law regarding tortious invasion of privacy."

The Court of Appeals . . . observed that one of the torts which Pennsylvania recognizes as encompassing an action for invasion of privacy is the tort of "intrusion upon seclusion." As noted by the Court of Appeals, the Restatement (Second) of Torts defines the tort as follows:

> One who intentionally intrudes, physically or otherwise, upon the solitude or seclusion of another or his private affairs or concerns, is subject to liability to the other for invasion of his privacy, if the intrusion would be highly offensive to a reasonable person.

Restatement (Second) of Torts § 652B.

Applying the Restatement definition of the tort of intrusion upon seclusion to the facts and circumstances of the case sub judice, we find that plaintiff has failed to state a claim upon which relief can be granted. In the first instance, unlike urinalysis and personal property searches, we do not find a reasonable expectation of privacy in e-mail communications voluntarily made by an employee to his supervisor over the company e-mail system notwithstanding any assurances that such communications would not be intercepted by management. Once plaintiff communicated the alleged unprofessional comments to a second person (his supervisor) over an e-mail system which was apparently utilized by the entire company, any reasonable expectation of privacy was lost. Significantly, the defendant did not require plaintiff, as in the case of an urinalysis or personal property search to disclose any personal information about himself. Rather, plaintiff voluntarily communicated the alleged unprofessional comments over the company e-mail system. We find no privacy interests in such communications.

In the second instance, even if we found that an employee had a reasonable expectation of privacy in the contents of his e-mail communications over the company e-mail system, we do not find that a reasonable person would

---

[19]Defendant alleges in its motion to dismiss that the e-mails concerned sales management and contained threats to "kill the backstabbing bastards" and referred to the planned holiday party as the "Jim Jones Koolaid affair."

consider the defendant's interception of these communications to be a substantial and highly offensive invasion of his privacy. Again, we note that by intercepting such communications, the company is not, as in the case of urinalysis or personal property searches, requiring the employee to disclose any personal information about himself or invading the employee's person or personal effects. Moreover, the company's interest in preventing inappropriate and unprofessional comments or even illegal activity over its e-mail system outweighs any privacy interest the employee may have in those comments.

In sum, we find that the defendant's actions did not tortiously invade the plaintiff's privacy and, therefore, did not violate public policy. As a result, the motion to dismiss is granted.

NOTES & QUESTIONS

1. Employers contend that e-mail monitoring is important because the use of e-mail (and the Internet) can bring in viruses that can harm the employer's computer system. Employers are liable for defamation, copyright violations, and sexual harassment, which can take place over e-mail. Chevron Corporation was sued for hostile work environment when some employees sent around via e-mail a joke list called: "why beer is better than women." The case settled out of court for $2.2 million. Should employers be permitted to monitor e-mail? How would you balance the employees' interest in privacy against the employers' interests in monitoring?[20]

2. The employees' privacy rights are not the only rights implicated here. The rights of third parties who mail employees or chat with them over the Internet are also implicated. Would a third party who e-mailed a private document to an employee, which was subsequently opened and inspected by that employee's employer, have an action for intrusion upon seclusion? Are there other theories or remedies, including self-help, available in this situation?

3. One of the troubling aspects of this case is that the employer promised that the e-mail would remain confidential. Suppose that the employer had an e-mail privacy policy that stated: "The employer's e-mail system is the property of the employer. The employer reserves the right to monitor all e-mail communications over its e-mail system." First, should the employer be permitted to have such a blanket policy without a legitimate reason? Under such a policy, would the employee have a reasonable expectation of privacy in a private e-mail?

   Suppose that the e-mail policy stated: "The employer's e-mail system shall be used exclusively for business-related purposes. The use of e-mail for an employee's own private purposes is prohibited." Would such a policy eliminate any reasonable expectation of privacy in e-mail?

---

[20] For a proposal of how to balance employer and employee interests, see Jay P. Kesan, *Cyber-Working or Cyber-Shirking?: A First Principles Examination of Electronic Privacy in the Workplace*, 54 Fla. L. Rev. 289 (2002). For a discussion of how sexual harassment law inappropriately threatens employee privacy, see Jeffrey Rosen, *The Unwanted Gaze: The Destruction of Privacy in America* (2000). For a critique of Rosen's view, see Anita L. Allen, *The Wanted Gaze: Accountability for Interpersonal Conduct at Work*, 89 Geo. L.J. 2013 (2001).

4. Suppose you were counsel to a company that wanted to establish an e-mail privacy policy. What elements would you include in the policy and why?

5. Private letters mailed to a workplace are monitored much less frequently than e-mail. Recall that federal law makes it a crime to read others' mail. Under the reasoning of *Cramer v. Consolidated Freightways,* could an employer require employees to consent to permitting them to inspect their mail?

6. Some might argue for a laissez-faire approach. Workers will choose to work for employers providing greater privacy. In this way, the market will decide the appropriate level of workplace privacy. Do you agree that the market is properly functioning to reach the appropriate level of workplace privacy? If not, for what reasons is the market failing?

7. Consider *United States v. Maxwell,* 45 M.J. 406 (U.S. Ct. App. Armed Forces 1996):

> E-mail transmissions are not unlike other forms of modern communication. We can draw parallels from these other mediums. For example, if a sender of first-class mail seals an envelope and addresses it to another person, the sender can reasonably expect the contents to remain private and free from the eyes of the police absent a search warrant founded upon probable cause. However, once the letter is received and opened, the destiny of the letter then lies in the control of the recipient of the letter, not the sender, absent some legal privilege.
>
> Similarly, the maker of a telephone call has a reasonable expectation that police officials will not intercept and listen to the conversation; however, the conversation itself is held with the risk that one of the participants may reveal what is said to others.
>
> Drawing from these parallels, we can say that the transmitter of an e-mail message enjoys a reasonable expectation that police officials will not intercept the transmission without probable cause and a search warrant. However, once the transmissions are received by another person, the transmitter no longer controls its destiny. In a sense, e-mail is like a letter. It is sent and lies sealed in the computer until the recipient opens his or her computer and retrieves the transmission. The sender enjoys a reasonable expectation that the initial transmission will not be intercepted by the police. The fact that an unauthorized "hacker" might intercept an e-mail message does not diminish the legitimate expectation of privacy in any way.
>
> There is, however, one major difference between an e-mail message which has been transmitted via a network such as AOL and a direct computer "real time" transmission. The former transmission is stored in a centralized computer until the recipient opens his or her network and retrieves the e-mail, while the latter is lost forever, unless one of the communicators chooses to download the conversation to a disk. This latter action would be much like clandestinely recording one's telephone conversation. Thus, while a user of an e-mail network may enjoy a reasonable expectation that his or her e-mail will not be revealed to police, there is the risk that an employee or other person with direct access to the network service will access the e-mail, despite any company promises to the contrary. One always bears the risk that a recipient of an e-mail message will redistribute the e-mail or an employee of the company will read e-mail against company policy. However, this is not the same as the police commanding an individual to intercept the message.

Also, in another context, the relationship of a computer network subscriber to the network is similar to that of a bank customer to a bank. So far as the company's records are concerned, there is no reasonable expectation that the records are private, and the customer has no control whatsoever over which employees may see the records.

The Government has argued that appellant forfeited any expectation of privacy in his e-mail messages through the e-mail forwarding process. If we accept this premise, any information forwarded would not be subject to Fourth Amendment protections. This argument parallels the rationale used by the Supreme Court in *Hoffa v. United States*. In *Hoffa*, the Court decided that notorious labor leader, James "Jimmy" Hoffa, had no Fourth Amendment protection for a conversation overheard by a government informant who had been invited to be present. The Court reasoned that there is no protection under the Fourth Amendment for "a wrongdoer's misplaced belief that a person to whom he voluntarily confides his wrongdoing will not reveal it." Justice Stewart went on to say: "The risk of being overheard by an eavesdropper or betrayed by an informer or deceived as to the identity of one with whom one deals is probably inherent in the conditions of human society. It is the kind of risk we necessarily assume whenever we speak."

We agree to a limited extent with the Government. Expectations of privacy in e-mail transmissions depend in large part on the type of e-mail involved and the intended recipient. Messages sent to the public at large in the "chat room" or e-mail that is "forwarded" from correspondent to correspondent lose any semblance of privacy. Once these transmissions are sent out to more and more subscribers, the subsequent expectation of privacy incrementally diminishes. This loss of an expectation of privacy, however, only goes to these specific pieces of mail for which privacy interests were lessened and ultimately abandoned. . . .

Compare *Maxwell* to *Pillsbury*. How do the courts differ as to their view about whether there is a reasonable expectation of privacy in e-mail?

BOHACH V. CITY OF RENO

932 F. Supp. 1232 (D. Nev. 1996)

REED, J. Mr. Bohach and Mr. Catalano are officers of the Reno Police Department. In early 1996, they sent messages to one another, and to another member of the Department, over the Department's "Alphapage" message system. Faced with an internal affairs investigation based on the contents of those messages, they filed this lawsuit, claiming that both the storage of the messages by the Department's computer network, and their subsequent retrieval from the computer's files, were violations of the federal wiretapping statutes and of their constitutional right to privacy. They sought to stop the investigation and to bar any disclosure of the contents of the messages. . . .

. . . "Alphapage" is a software program, installed on the Reno Police Department's Local Area Network ("LAN") computer system, which allows the transmission of brief alphanumeric messages to visual display pagers. . . .

. . . All the messages at issue in this case were alphanumeric (no human voice was involved). And all, it seems, were sent to the recipient's pager from a computer terminal, rather than by telephone or "stand-alone" keyboard. . . .

Officers Bohach and Catalano can succeed on their § 1983 fourth amendment claim only if, at a minimum, they demonstrate that they had a reasonable expectation of privacy in their use of the Alphapage system. We assume that they did indeed have a subjective expectation of privacy, if only because we cannot believe that, had they thought otherwise, they would ever have sent over the system the sorts of messages they did send. The question is whether their expectation was objectively reasonable. Based on the evidence now available, we think that is most unlikely.

To begin with, all messages are recorded and stored not because anyone is "tapping" the system, but simply because that's how the system works. It is an integral part of the technology, and in this respect Alphapage is like most pager systems, which store messages in a central computer until they are retrieved by, or sent to, the intended recipient. Moreover, while one phase of an Alphapage transmission (from the pager company to the recipient pager) may involve a radio broadcast, the earlier phase at issue here (from the user's keyboard to the computer) is essentially electronic mail — and e-mail messages are, by definition, stored in a routing computer.

That only a diminished expectation of privacy would be reasonable in this case is also suggested by then-Chief of Police Kirkland's order, issued when Alphapage was first installed and long before the messages in this case were sent, notifying all users that their messages would be "logged on the network" and that certain types of messages (e.g., those violating the Department's antidiscrimination policy) were banned from the system. Now, that is not the same thing as saying that the contents of all messages will be recorded and retained, but it suggests that one should expect less privacy on Alphapage than on, say, a private telephone line. We note, also, that Alphapage is accessible to anyone with access to, and a working knowledge of, the Department's computer system. No special password or clearance is needed. The current Chief of the Reno Police Department, James Weston, testified that the Department's janitor, if he had general access to the computer system, could roam at will through Alphapage. . . .

. . . [W]hile officers Bohach and Catalano attempt liken their communications to private telephone calls, we think that some aspects of the system (its primary though not exclusive purpose, the restrictions placed on the contents of messages, the limited number of persons with whom one can communicate using it, and the fact that police departments routinely and properly record their communications with the public) suggest that one should expect, when using it, less privacy than one might expect when, say, making a private telephone call, even from a police station. . . .

Section 2511(1)(a) [of the ECPA] forbids, among other things, the interception of electronic communications. An "interception" is the "acquisition of the contents of any . . . electronic . . . communication through the use of any electronic, mechanical or other device." § 2510(4). One might ask how any "interception," as the word is usually understood, could be thought to have occurred here. After all, no computer or phone lines have been tapped, no conversations picked up by hidden microphones, no duplicate pager "cloned" to tap into messages intended for another recipient. . . .

Indeed, we do not understand the plaintiffs to object to the mere passage of their messages through the computer. Their complaint, as we understand it, is that the computer stored (or recorded, or downloaded) the contents of those messages. And that, we think, is where their argument breaks down. The computer's storage of an electronic communication, whether that storage was "temporary" and "intermediate" and "incidental to" its impending "electronic transmission," or more permanent storage for backup purposes, was "electronic storage." An "electronic communication," by definition, cannot be "intercepted" when it is in "electronic storage," because only "communications" can be "intercepted," and, as the Fifth Circuit held in *Steve Jackson Games,* the "electronic storage" of an "electronic communication" is by definition not part of the communication. The treatment of messages in "electronic storage" is governed by §§ 2701-11, not by the restrictions on "interception" set out at §§ 2501-22.

This leads us to the plaintiffs' claim that the City acted unlawfully when, months after the messages were sent, it accessed and retrieved them from storage in the computer. The problem with the claim is simple. The City is the "provider" of the "electronic communications service" at issue here: the Reno Police Department's terminals, computer and software, and the pagers it issues to its personnel, are, after all, what provide those users with "the ability to send or receive" electronic communications. But § 2701(c)(1) allows service providers to do as they wish when it comes to accessing communications in electronic storage. Because the City is the provider of the "service," neither it nor its employees can be liable under § 2701. . . .

NOTES & QUESTIONS

1. Under federal wiretap law, service providers (who provide e-mail service) are exempt under Title I, 18 U.S.C. § 2511(2)(a)(i), "while engaged in any activity which is necessary to provide the service, or to protect the rights or property of the provider." In many workplaces — such as government workplaces, universities, and large corporations — the employers are the service providers. Therefore, they would be exempt from intercepting e-mail under Title I. Additionally, employers can have employees sign consent forms to the monitoring, and consent is an exception to federal wiretap law.
2. Consider the availability of encryption techniques to protect e-mail from observation by third parties. Should the use of encryption alter the privacy analysis? If so, what about the failure to encrypt private messages?

(c) Internet Use

UNITED STATES V. SIMONS

206 F.3d 392 (4th Cir. 2000)

WILKINS, J. Mark L. Simons appeals his convictions for receiving and possessing materials constituting or containing child pornography, see 18 U.S.C.A.

§ 2252A(a)(2)(A), (a)(5)(B). Simons, who received the unlawful materials at his government workplace via the Internet, argues that the district court erred in denying his motion to suppress. We affirm in part and remand in part. . . .

Simons was employed as an electronic engineer at the Foreign Bureau of Information Services (FBIS), a division of the Central Intelligence Agency (CIA). FBIS provided Simons with an office, which he did not share with anyone, and a computer with Internet access.

In June 1998, FBIS instituted a policy regarding Internet usage by employees. The policy stated that employees were to use the Internet for official government business only. Accessing unlawful material was specifically prohibited. The policy explained that FBIS would conduct electronic audits to ensure compliance:

> Audits. Electronic auditing shall be implemented within all FBIS unclassified networks that connect to the Internet or other publicly accessible networks to support identification, termination, and prosecution of unauthorized activity. . . .

The policy also stated that "[u]sers shall . . . [u]nderstand FBIS will periodically audit, inspect, and/or monitor the user's Internet access as deemed appropriate."

FBIS contracted with Science Applications International Corporation (SAIC) for the management of FBIS's computer network, including monitoring for any inappropriate use of computer resources. On July 17, 1998, Clifford Mauck, a manager at SAIC, began exploring the capabilities of a firewall recently acquired by SAIC, because Mauck believed that SAIC needed to become more familiar with the firewall to service the FBIS contract properly.[21] Mauck entered the keyword "sex" into the firewall database for July 14 and 17, 1998, and found a large number of Internet "hits" originating from Simons's computer. It was obvious to Mauck from the names of the sites that they were not visited for official FBIS purposes.

Mauck reported this discovery to his contact at FBIS, Katherine Camer. Camer then worked with another SAIC employee, Robert Harper, to further investigate the apparently unauthorized activity. Camer instructed Harper to view one of the websites that Simons had visited. Harper complied and found that the site contained pictures of nude women.

At Camer's direction and from his own workstation, Harper examined Simons's computer to determine whether Simons had downloaded any picture files from the Internet; Harper found over 1,000 such files. Again from his own workstation, Harper viewed several of the pictures and observed that they were pornographic in nature. . . .

[Among the pictures were images of child pornography. Criminal investigators then became involved. Harper entered Simons's office and swapped his hard drive with a copy. FBI Agent John Mesisca found over 50 images of child

---

[21] A firewall is like a funnel through which all Internet access flows and is registered; the firewall collects data and may be searched as a database.

pornography on Simons's hard drive. Simons was indicted on one count of knowingly receiving child pornography and one count of knowingly possessing material containing images of child pornography. Simons moved to suppress the evidence, arguing that the searches of his office and computer violated the Fourth Amendment. The district court denied his motion. Simons was convicted and sentenced to 18 months imprisonment.]

The Fourth Amendment prohibits "unreasonable searches and seizures" by government agents, including government employers or supervisors. To establish a violation of his rights under the Fourth Amendment, Simons must first prove that he had a legitimate expectation of privacy in the place searched or the item seized. And, in order to prove a legitimate expectation of privacy, Simons must show that his subjective expectation of privacy is one that society is prepared to accept as objectively reasonable.

Government employees may have a legitimate expectation of privacy in their offices or in parts of their offices such as their desks or file cabinets. *See O'Connor [v. Ortega]*. However, office practices, procedures, or regulations may reduce legitimate privacy expectations. *See O'Connor*. . . .

We first consider Simons's challenge to the warrantless searches of his computer and office by FBIS. We conclude that the remote searches of Simons's computer did not violate his Fourth Amendment rights because, in light of the Internet policy, Simons lacked a legitimate expectation of privacy in the files downloaded from the Internet. Additionally, we conclude that Simons's Fourth Amendment rights were not violated by FBIS' retrieval of Simons's hard drive from his office.

Simons did not have a legitimate expectation of privacy with regard to the record or fruits of his Internet use in light of the FBIS Internet policy. The policy clearly stated that FBIS would "audit, inspect, and/or monitor" employees' use of the Internet, including all file transfers, all websites visited, and all e-mail messages, "as deemed appropriate." This policy placed employees on notice that they could not reasonably expect that their Internet activity would be private. Therefore, regardless of whether Simons subjectively believed that the files he transferred from the Internet were private, such a belief was not objectively reasonable after FBIS notified him that it would be overseeing his Internet use. Accordingly, FBIS's actions in remotely searching and seizing the computer files Simons downloaded from the Internet did not violate the Fourth Amendment.

We next consider whether Harper's warrantless entry into Simons's office to retrieve his hard drive violated the Fourth Amendment. The district court did not separately address this search; rather, it evaluated all of the warrantless searches together. Although we agree with the district court that Simons lacked a legitimate expectation of privacy in his Internet use, and thus in the hard drive itself, Harper's entry into Simons's office to retrieve the hard drive presents a distinct question.

The burden is on Simons to prove that he had a legitimate expectation of privacy in his office. Here, Simons has shown that he had an office that he did not share. As noted above, the operational realities of Simons's workplace may have diminished his legitimate privacy expectations. However, there is no evidence in the record of any workplace practices, procedures, or regulations that had such an effect.[22] We therefore conclude that, on this record, Simons possessed a legitimate expectation of privacy in his office.

Consequently, we must determine whether FBIS's warrantless entry into Simons's office to retrieve the hard drive was reasonable under the Fourth Amendment. A search conducted without a warrant issued by a judge or magistrate upon a showing of probable cause is "per se unreasonable" unless it falls within one of the "specifically established and well-delineated exceptions" to the warrant requirement. One exception to the warrant requirement arises when the requirement is rendered impracticable by "special needs, beyond the normal need for law enforcement." In *O'Connor,* the Supreme Court held that a government employer's interest in "the efficient and proper operation of the workplace" may justify warrantless work-related searches. In particular, the *O'Connor* Court held that when a government employer conducts a search pursuant to an investigation of work-related misconduct, the Fourth Amendment will be satisfied if the search is reasonable in its inception and its scope. A search normally will be reasonable at its inception "when there are reasonable grounds for suspecting that the search will turn up evidence that the employee is guilty of work-related misconduct." "The search will be permissible in its scope when 'the measures adopted are reasonably related to the objectives of the search and not excessively intrusive in light of . . . the nature of the [misconduct].'"

The question thus becomes whether the search of Simons's office falls within the ambit of the *O'Connor* exception to the warrant requirement, i.e., whether the search was carried out for the purpose of obtaining "evidence of suspected work-related employee misfeasance." The district court found that all of the warrantless searches, and thus the office search, were work-related. The court reasoned that FBIS had an interest in fully investigating Simons's misconduct, even if the misconduct was criminal. We agree. . . .

. . . FBIS did not lose its special need for "the efficient and proper operation of the workplace," id., merely because the evidence obtained was evidence of a crime. Simons's violation of FBIS's Internet policy happened also to be a violation of criminal law; this does not mean that FBIS lost the capacity and interests of an employer.

We have little trouble concluding that the warrantless entry of Simons's office was reasonable under the Fourth Amendment standard announced in *O'Connor.* At the inception of the search FBIS had "reasonable grounds for suspecting" that the hard drive would yield evidence of misconduct because FBIS was already aware that Simons had misused his Internet access to download over a thousand pornographic images, some of which involved minors. The search was also permissible in scope. The measure adopted, entering Simons's office, was reasonably related to the objective of the search, retrieval of the hard drive. And, the search was not excessively intrusive. Indeed, there has

---

[22]The Internet policy did not render Simons's expectation of privacy in his office unreasonable. The policy does not mention employees' offices, and although it does not prohibit FBIS from carrying out its "audit[ing], inspect[ing], and/or monitor[ing]" activities at employees' individual workstations, this fact alone is insufficient to render unreasonable an employee's subjective expectation of privacy in his office.

been no suggestion that Harper searched Simons's desk or any other items in the office; rather, Harper simply crossed the floor of Simons's office, switched hard drives, and exited. . . .

NOTES & QUESTIONS

1. In its analysis under *O'Connor v. Ortega,* the Court notes that "the dominant purpose of the warrantless search of Simons's office was to acquire evidence of criminal activity." If this is so, then is *Simons* a correct application of *O'Connor?*
2. *Telecommuting.* Consider an employee working from home. What factors should be considered if a dispute arises concerning e-mail or use of the Internet? Would it matter if the computer or the e-mail service were provided by the employer? What if the computer is also for personal use? Is this an issue that should be considered in an e-mail privacy policy?

CHAPTER 8

INTERNATIONAL PRIVACY LAW

The study of information privacy provides an opportunity to understand the development of privacy law in various countries around the world. The purpose of this chapter is to explore the European Union Data Protection Directive, important European privacy case law, and other international privacy materials that may have an impact in the United States. We have also selected texts that provide the opportunity for a comparative analysis on the U.S. and European privacy regimes.

While the development of privacy law in the United States is typically described as "sectoral," a reference to the fact that privacy legislation in the United States focuses on specific sectors of the economy, European privacy law tends to sweep more broadly. Privacy principles are generally applied to all entities that collect personally identifiable information without regard to the nature of the business or the technology involved. In this respect, European privacy law is often characterized as "omnibus." Consider the following observation by Joel Reidenberg:

> Despite the growth of the Information Society, the United States has resisted all calls for omnibus or comprehensive legal rules for fair information practice in the private sector. Legal rules have developed on an ad hoc, targeted basis, while industry has elaborated voluntary norms and practices for particular problems. Over the years, there has been an almost zealous adherence to this ideal of narrowly targeted standards. In other countries, the response to the Information Age has been quite different. Foreign nations have enacted broad, sweeping "data protection" laws to establish fair information practices in both public and private sectors.[1]

Outside of Europe, other countries from around the world are moving toward adopting comprehensive privacy legislation. According to David Banisar and Simon Davies:

> There are three major reasons for the movement towards comprehensive privacy and data protection laws. Many countries are adopting these laws for one or more of the following reasons:

---

[1] Joel R. Reidenberg, *Setting Standards for Fair Information Practice in the U.S. Private Sector*, 80 Iowa L. Rev. 497, 500 (1995).

To remedy past injustices. Many countries, especially in Central Europe, South America and South Africa, are adopting laws to remedy privacy violations that occurred under previous authoritarian regimes.

To promote electronic commerce. Many countries, especially in Asia, but also Canada, have developed or are currently developing laws in an effort to promote electronic commerce. These countries recognize consumers are uneasy with their personal information being sent worldwide. Privacy laws are being introduced as part of a package of laws intended to facilitate electronic commerce by setting up uniform rules.

To ensure laws are consistent with Pan-European laws. Most countries in Central and Eastern Europe are adopting new laws based on the Council of Europe Convention and the European Union Data Protection Directive. Many of these countries hope to join the European Union in the near future. Countries in other regions, such as Canada, are adopting new laws to ensure that trade will not be affected by the requirements of the E.U. Directive.[2]

In Europe, privacy law is shaped by the traditional role of the Council of Europe and the emerging role of the European Union. It was Article 8 of the Council of Europe Convention of 1950 that firmly established privacy protection as a critical human rights claim in postwar Europe. The provision in Article 8 has been given effect both by the decisions of the European Court of Human Rights and also by the Convention on Data Protection established by the Council of Europe in 1980.

But the central focus of European privacy law for almost a decade is the Data Directive of the European Union, which established a basic legislative framework for the processing of personal information in the European Union. The EU Data Directive has had a profound effect on the development of privacy law, not only in Europe but also around the world.

It is worth noting that the phrase "data processing" is frequently used to describe privacy protection in the European context. This is a reflection of the modern concept of privacy protection that emerged in the 1970s as computer systems were increasingly used to process information on citizens. Still, the concept of privacy, or more generally *la vie privée*, continues to play an important role in the European conception of information privacy.

Beyond Europe, important international and regional agreements have helped shape the structure of national privacy law and influenced the development of privacy as a legal claim in particular countries. The Privacy Guidelines of the Organization for Economic Cooperation and Development (OECD), adopted in 1980, represent a consensus position of countries from North America, Europe, and East Asia as to the basic structure of privacy law.

Other privacy laws follow from Article 12 of the Universal Declaration of Human Rights, adopted by the United Nations in 1948, which states that: "No one shall be subjected to arbitrary interference with his privacy, family, home or correspondence, nor to attacks upon his honour and reputation. Everyone has the right to the protection of the law against such interference or attacks."

---

[2] David Banisar & Simon Davies, *Global Trends in Privacy Protection: An International Survey of Privacy, Data Protection, and Surveillance Laws and Developments*, 18 J. Marshall J. Computer & Info. L. 1, 11-12 (1999).

A. THE PROTECTION OF PRIVACY IN EUROPE

1. INTRODUCTION

COLIN J. BENNETT, *CONVERGENCE REVISITED: TOWARD A GLOBAL POLICY FOR THE PROTECTION OF PERSONAL DATA?*

In *Technology and Privacy: The New Landscape* 99 (Philip E. Agre & Marc Rotenberg eds. 1997)

. . . Much has already been written about the European Union's Data Protection Directive. Its provisions are complicated and reflect a lengthy process of bargaining in which a multitude of national and sectoral interests exerted influence. There are many derogations, qualifications, and alternatives available to member states, which may reduce important aspects of data protection to the "lowest common denominator."

The importance of this instrument stems from its status as a legally binding instrument. It therefore differs from both the "guidelines" of the OECD and the "convention" of the Council of Europe. Directives are designed to harmonize public policy throughout the European Union by expressing an agreed set of goals and principles, while granting member states some latitude (or subsidiary) in deciding the actual ways in which those aims might be met. Thus, the goals of the Data Protection Directive are to "ensure a high level of protection for the privacy of individuals in all member states . . . and also to help ensure the free flow of information society services in the Single Market by fostering consumer confidence and minimizing differences between the Member States' rules." This directive is one of several instruments that have been, or are being, debated, in the EU and which are designed to ensure that the free flow of capital and labor will be complemented by the free flow of information.

As European governments have until 1998 to bring their laws up to this new European standard, it is too early to predict the extent to which data-protection legislation will further be harmonized. Nevertheless, certain features of the Data Protection Directive suggest that the process of policy convergence begun in the 1970s will continue. Certainly the familiar set of "fair information principles" find further reinforcement. Beyond this, however, I would hypothesize a potential convergence of public policy in three further areas.

First, distinctions between "public" and "private" organizations were almost completely removed from the Data Protection Directive. Earlier drafts differentiated between the sectors in regard to the fair obtaining and processing of personal data, placing a greater onus on the private sector than on the public. The final version largely avoids this distinction, perhaps reflecting the increasing difficulty of determining where the public sector ends and the private begins.

Second, many battles were fought over the question of the inclusion of "manual" data within the directive's scope. The British, whose 1984 Data Protection Act regulates only "automated" data processing, wee strongly opposed to the regulation of non-automatically-stored personal data, arguing that the efficiency of storage and communication of personal data, which raised the data-protection issue in the first place, should continue to be the primary target of regulation. The final version reflects the opposite position — that "the scope of this protection must not in effect depend on the techniques used, otherwise this would create a serious risk of circumvention." The directive covers, therefore, "structured manual filing systems" that form part of a "filing system." The British were given some extra time, beyond 1998, to bring manual filing systems under their law. This issue was central to the decision of the British to abstain from the final vote in the Council of Ministers.

Third, the directive makes some strides in trying to harmonize the policy instruments through which data-protection principles are implemented. Article 18 [1], for instance, deals with the obligation of the data controller "to notify the supervisory authority . . . before carrying out any wholly or partly automatic processing operation or set of such operations." Moreover, "Member States shall provide that a register of processing operation notified in accordance with Article 18 shall be kept by the supervisory authority" (Article 21 [2]). This register is to include a range of information, including the identity of the controller, the purpose of the processing, the recipients of the data, and any proposed transfers to third countries. "Notification" seems to contemplate a form of registration similar to that within the UK Data Protection Act of 1984, with exemptions for more routine personal data and optional registration for manual records. It seems that the principle of "notification" can be seriously translated into practice only by means of a system of registration that many experts have regarded as excessively burdensome and expensive.

The Data Protection Directive also specifies the nature and function of a member state's "supervisory authority." Each country must assign one or more public authorities responsibility for monitoring the application of the national provisions adopted pursuant to the directive (Article 28 [1]). These authorities must act with "complete independence" and must be endowed with investigative powers, effective powers of intervention (especially before processing operations begin), powers to engage in legal proceedings, and powers to "hear claims" concerning the protection of rights and freedoms and regarding the "lawfulness of data processing" under the directive. In addition, member states are to consult the supervisory authorities when developing administrative measures with privacy implications. In total, these provisions require a greater range of powers and responsibilities than exist within most European data-protection regimes.

Thus, for the first time in an international agreement, we see an attempt to extend the process of policy convergence to the policy instruments. While there is much margin for maneuver, the Data Protection Directive begins the process of codifying a consensus on the most effective ways to implement data-protection law. This was anticipated in Regulating Privacy in the observation that "data protection officials will learn more and more about the approaches of their colleagues overseas and will try to draw lessons about the most effective responses to these common challenges." The directive, however, signifies that the functions and powers of data-protection authorities will not simply be something that states can choose to fulfill in response to the emulation of overseas experience. Rather the policy instruments have become a matter for policy harmonization, and an obligation under European law. . . .

NOTES & QUESTIONS

1. Colin Bennett's article provides a useful starting point for the exploration of international privacy law. What does Bennett mean by "policy convergence"? Which factors support this view? Elsewhere, Bennett discusses "American exceptionalism" to characterize the situation in the United States. What does Bennett mean by this?

2. An annual survey on privacy practices around the world is published by the Electronic Privacy Information Center and Privacy International. A similar survey is conducted by the United States Department of State. In constructing such a survey, what factors would you consider? For example, is compliance with the OECD Privacy Guidelines a possible way to measure privacy protection in a particular country? What about compliance with the EU Data Directive? What other approaches would you consider?

3. As you go through the materials in this chapter, consider whether privacy claims vary in different parts of the world, and more generally which factors contribute to the structuring of privacy norms. For example, is the concept of privacy determined by cultural traditions, trade requirements, legal developments, or technological influences?

2. COUNCIL OF EUROPE CONVENTION FOR THE PROTECTION OF HUMAN RIGHTS AND FUNDAMENTAL FREEDOMS (ECHR)

The Council of Europe Convention for the Protection of Human Rights and Fundamental Freedoms (ECHR),[3] an international convention covering a wide range of civil and political rights, was adopted in 1950, shortly after the Universal Declaration of Human Rights of the United Nations. It was drafted under the auspices of the Council of Europe, an international organization composed today of 43 European states, which was formed in 1949 as a result of a strong political willingness to unify European countries, to consolidate and stabilize its democracies after World War II, to prevent any future outrageous violations of human rights such as those that had taken place during the Nazi regime, and to establish a bulwark against Communism. The European Convention was intended to bring violations of human rights to the attention of the international community. As some commentators have observed:

> In practice, this function of the ECHR, which imagines large-scale violations of human rights, has largely remained dormant. The ECHR has instead been used primarily to raise questions of isolated weaknesses in legal systems that basically conform to its requirements and which are representative of the "common heritage of political traditions, ideals, freedom and the rule of law" to which the Preamble to the ECHR refers.[4]

---

[3] *<http://conventions.coe.int/Treaty/EN/CadreListeTraites.htm>* and *<http://conventions.coe.int/treaty/en/Treaties/Word/005.doc>*.
[4] S.H. Bailey, D.J. Harris, B.L. Jones, *Civil Liberties — Cases and Materials* 749-750 (3d ed. 1991).

The Convention is enforced by the European Commission on Human Rights, the Council of Ministers, and the European Court on Human Rights. Individual applications first go to the European Commission of Human Rights at Strasbourg. The Commission examines the applications to see whether local remedies have been exhausted. The Commission will consider first whether the application alleges a violation of the Convention. If it does not, then the application will be dismissed. The Commission will next consider whether the application presents sufficient facts to establish that a right defined in the Convention has been breached. If not, the application will be rejected as "manifestly ill-founded." The Commission may also choose to reject an application if it is unsigned, is an abuse of the right to petition, is "substantially the same as a matter which has already been examined by the Commission or has already been submitted to another procedure of international investigation or settlement and it contains no relevant new information." The Commission's decision to reject an application is final.[5]

The Commission next establishes the facts and drafts a report expressing its opinion, which is not legally binding, on the existence of a breach of the Convention. The Commission then encourages parties to reach a friendly settlement. If these efforts fail, the Commission determines whether there has been a breach of the Convention. Its opinions are not per se legally binding on the parties. The case may subsequently be referred to the Court itself by either the Commission, a defendant state, a state bringing an application, or a contracting party whose nation is an alleged victim. In practice, most cases that reach the Court are referred to it by the Commission. No individual can bring a matter directly to the Court. Identified elements that might be influential in the Commission's referral decision include whether the case raises a point of interpretation that has not previously arisen, whether the Commission is divided as to whether there has been a violation, or whether a case is perceived to have particularly serious political implications.[6]

The Court's judgment, which is binding, is normally declaratory. If the Court finds that a breach of the Convention has occurred, it brings into operation the defendant state's obligation in international law to make reparation. However, the Court may always award "just satisfaction" to the injured if the internal law of the defendant state allows only partial reparation.

The whole procedure can take up to five years between the registration of the application and the Court's final ruling. Although this is a slow procedure, "the primary purpose of state and individual applications is not to offer an international remedy for individual victims of violations of the Convention but to bring to light violations of an inter-state guarantee."[7]

The role of the European Court is of particular importance for several reasons. First, the volume of cases brought to the Court has increased over the years and has raised more complex jurisprudential issues than those that came

---

[5] *Id.* at 757-758.

[6] J.G. Merrills, *The Development of International Law by the European Court of Human Rights* 4 (2d ed. 1993).

[7] *Id.* at 761.

before the court in earlier years. Second, the Court is the longest standing international human rights court; it is considered the model against which other regional courts can be measured. Finally, the jurisprudence of the court has influenced the normative development of other parts of the international human rights system.[8] The Convention itself has a fundamental role in the European legal system as it has gradually acquired the status of a "constitutional instrument of European public order in the field of human rights."[9]

The critical privacy provision in the European Convention on Human Rights is Article 8. The language in Article 8 of the ECHR is similar to Article 12 of the Universal Declaration of Human Rights.

ECHR Article 8

Article 8 — Right to Respect for Private and Family Life

1. Everyone has the right to respect for his private and family life, his home and his correspondence.

2. There shall be no interference by a public authority with the exercise of this right except such as is in accordance with the law and is necessary in a democratic society in the interests of national security, public safety or the economic well-being of the country, for the prevention of disorder or crime, for the protection of health or morals, or for the protection of the rights and freedoms of others.

John Wadham, *Human Rights and Privacy — The Balance*

Cambridge Symposium (March 2000)[10]

1. The Rule of Law

A core concept in Convention jurisprudence is the rule of law. No matter how desirable the end to be achieved, no interference with a right protected under the Convention is permissible unless the citizen knows the basis for the interference because it is set out in an ascertainable law. In the absence of such detailed authorisation by the law, any interference, however justified, will violate the Convention. . . . No such interference can be permitted by executive rules alone.

To be "prescribed by law" or "in accordance with law" means that there must be an ascertainable legal regime governing the interference in question. The Strasbourg court explained the concept in *Sunday Times v. United Kingdom* (1979) 2 EHRR 245 at paragraph 49: "Firstly, the law must be adequately accessible: the citizens must be able to have an indication that is adequate

---

[8] The Inter-American Court, *e.g.*, has frequently referred to judgments of the European Court. *Cf.* H.J. Steiner & P. Alston, *International Human Rights in Context* 598 (1996).

[9] J. Polakiewicz & V. Jacob-Foltzer, *The European Human Rights Convention in Domestic Law*, 12 Hum. Rts. L.J. 65, 125 (1991).

[10] This article is taken from a speech given to the Cambridge Symposium in March 2000. It is available at <*http://www.liberty-human-rights.org.uk/mhrp6j.html*>.

in the circumstances of the legal rules applicable to a given case. Secondly, a norm cannot be regarded as a 'law' unless it is formulated with sufficient precision to enable the citizen to regulate his conduct".

The common law may be sufficiently clear for this purpose and statute law or regulation is not necessary. . . .

It is not acceptable for an interference with a Convention right to occur without any legal regulation. . . .

2. Legitimate Aims

In order to provide a defence to a claim under the Convention any interference by a public authority with a Convention right must be directed towards an identified legitimate aim. . . . The sorts of aims which are legitimate are the interests of public safety, national security, the protection of health and morals and the economic well-being of the country or the protection of the rights and freedoms of others. . . .

3. Proportionality

The third important concept which the Strasbourg institutions use when assessing whether a Convention right has been improperly violated is that of proportionality: the test of whether the interference is "necessary in a democratic society".

Although a few rights in the Convention are absolute, most are not. The Convention approach is to decide whether a particular limitation from a right is justified in the sense of being "proportionate to the legitimate aim pursued."

This means that even if a policy which interferes with a Convention right might be aimed at securing a legitimate aim of social policy, for example, the prevention of crime, this will not in itself justify the violation if the means adopted to secure the aim are excessive in the circumstances. . . .

Where the Convention allows restrictions on rights it requires them to be justified by a legitimate aim and proportional to the need at hand, that is, "necessary in a democratic society". The case law interprets this to mean that there must be a "pressing social need" for the interference. . . . [T]he state's desire to protect a legitimate aim does not allow it to restrict the right of the individual disproportionately — the state cannot use a sledgehammer to crack a nut. . . .

4. Article 8. Right to Respect for Private and Family Life

Article 8 protects the right to respect for a person's private and family life, home and correspondence. The majority of the case law is concerned with defining "private life", "family life", "home" and "correspondence". Article 8 has been used in a wide range of contexts: from phone tapping to the use of medical records in court; from the rights of children whose parents are deported to the right to have records altered, to the rights of transsexuals to have their status recognised on official records; from the right to protection from aircraft noise to the right to practise one's sexuality. The Court has held that the essential object of Article 8 is to protect the individual against arbitrary action by the public authorities.

The Court has also held the right to respect for private life contains both positive and negative aspects — not just that the state should refrain from interference but also that it has an obligation to provide for an effective respect for private life. . . .

4.1. Private Life

In *Niemietz v Germany* (1992) 16 EHRR 97 the concept of private life was held to cover the right to develop one's own personality as well as one's right to create relationships with others. The Court held, at para. 29, that, in defining "private life" for the purposes of Article 8:". . . it would be too restrictive to limit the notion to an 'inner circle' in which the individual may live his own personal life as he chooses and to exclude therefrom entirely the outside world not encompassed within that circle. Respect for private life must also comprise to a certain degree the right to establish and develop relationships with human beings". . . .

4.2. Home

The concepts of home life and private life may overlap. In *Niemietz v. Germany* (1992) 16 EHRR 97 the Court extended the notion of "privacy" to include some places of work. The case involved a search by the police of a lawyer's office. The Court held that the article protected his office space. The lawyer's office was protected because the Court accepted that one's private life was carried on both at "home" and, at time, elsewhere, including the office.

4.3. Correspondence

The right to respect for one's correspondence is a right to uninterrupted and uncensored communication with others. In the telephone-tapping case, *Malone v. United Kingdom* (1984) 7 EHRR 14 the Court found that the British government violated Article 8 when it intercepted the phone calls of the applicant, an antique dealer convicted of receiving stolen goods. The Court reasoned that, because the government did not have statutory procedures for monitoring the phone calls of private citizens, it was not acting in accordance with the law. The Court said, at paragraph 79: "In view of the attendant obscurity and uncertainty as to the state of the law in this essential respect, . . . the law of England and Wales does not indicate with reasonable clarity the scope and manner of exercise of the relevant discretion conferred on the public authorities. To that extent, the minimum degree of legal protection to which citizens are entitled under the rule of law in a democratic society is lacking". . . .

3. ECHR CASE LAW ON ARTICLE 8

Article 8, which addresses the right to privacy in family life, home, and correspondence, has been invoked by individuals in a number of landmark privacy decisions involving issues such as sexual and reproductive freedom, search and seizure, wiretapping, and electronic surveillance.

(a) Privacy and Law Enforcement

P.G. & J.H. v. United Kingdom

E.C.H.R., 9/25/2001

Principal Facts

The applicants are both British nationals.

On 28 February 1995, D.I. Mann received information that an armed robbery of a Securicor cash collection van was going to be committed on or around 2 March 1995 by the first applicant and B. at one of several possible locations. Visual surveillance of B.'s home began the same day. No robbery took place.

By 3 March, however, the police had been informed the robbery was to take place "somewhere" on 9 March 1995. In order to obtain further details, D.I. Mann prepared a report applying for authorisation to install a covert listening device in B.'s flat. On 4 March 1995, the Chief Constable gave oral authorisation and a listening device was installed in a sofa in B.'s flat the same day; the Deputy Chief Constable gave retrospective written authorisation on 8 March 1995. On 14 March 1995, the police requested itemised billing for calls from the telephone in B.'s flat. On 15 March 1995, B. and others who were with him in his home discovered the listening device and abandoned the premises. The robbery did not take place.

The applicants were arrested on 16 March 1995 in a stolen car containing two black balaclavas, five black plastic cable ties, two pairs of leather gloves, and two army kitbags.

As they wished to obtain speech samples to compare with the tapes, the police applied for authorisation to use covert listening devices in the applicants' cells and to attach listening devices to the police officers who were to be present when the applicants were charged. Written authorisation was given by the Chief Constable and samples of the applicants' speech were recorded without their knowledge or permission. An expert concluded it was "likely" the first applicant's voice featured on the taped recordings and "very likely" the second applicant's voice featured on them.

B. and the applicants were charged with conspiracy to rob. During their trial, evidence derived from the use of the covert listening devices was deemed admissible . . . .

. . . 34. The applicants complained that covert listening devices were used by the police to monitor and record their conversations at a flat, that information was obtained by the police concerning the use of a telephone at the flat and that listening devices were used while they were at the police station to obtain voice samples. They invoked Article 8 of the Convention. . . .

B. Concerning Information Obtained About
the Use of B.'s Telephone

42. It is not in dispute that the obtaining by the police of information relating to the numbers called on the telephone in B.'s flat interfered with the private lives or correspondence (in the sense of telephone communications) of the applicants who made use of the telephone in the flat or were telephoned

from the flat. The Court notes however that metering, which does not *per se* offend against Article 8 if for example done by the telephone company for billing purposes, is by its very nature to be distinguished from the interception of communications which may be undesirable and illegitimate in a democratic society unless justified. . . .

"In Accordance with the Law"

44. The expression "in accordance with the law" requires, firstly, that the impugned measure should have some basis in domestic law; secondly, it refers to the quality of the law in question, requiring that it should be accessible to the person concerned, who must moreover be able to foresee its consequences for him, and that it is compatible with the rule of law.

45. Both parties agreed that the obtaining of the billing information was based on statutory authority, in particular, section 45 of the Telecommunications Act 1984 and section 28(3) of the Data Protection Act 1984. The first requirement therefore poses no difficulty. The applicants argued that the second requirement was not fulfilled in their case, as there were insufficient safeguards in place concerning the use, storage and destruction of the records.

46. . . . In this case, the information obtained concerned the telephone numbers called from B.'s flat between two specific dates. It did not include any information about the contents of those calls, or who made or received them. The data obtained, and the use that could be made of it, were therefore strictly limited.

47. . . . [T]he Court is not persuaded that the lack of such detailed formal regulation raises any risk of arbitrariness or misuse. Nor is it apparent that there was any lack of foreseeability. Disclosure to the police was permitted under the relevant statutory framework where necessary for the purposes of the detection and prevention of crime and the material was used at the applicants' trial on criminal charges to corroborate other evidence relevant to the timing of telephone calls. It is not apparent that the applicants did not have an adequate indication as to the circumstances in, and conditions on, which the public authorities were empowered to resort to such a measure.

48. The Court concludes that the measure in question was "in accordance with the law".

"Necessary in a Democratic Society"

[The Court did not have to analyze the issue of proportionality under Article 8 (2) as it was not raised by the applicants.] . . .

51. The Court concludes that there has been no violation of Article 8 of the Convention in respect of the applicants' complaints about the metering of the telephone in this case.

C. Concerning the Use of Listening Devices in the Police Station
1. The Parties' Submissions

52. The applicants complained that their voices were recorded secretly when they were being charged in the police station and when they were held in their cells. They submitted that it was irrelevant what was said, which

ranged from the giving of personal details to a conversation about football instigated by a police officer. They considered that it was the circumstances in which the words were spoken which was significant and that there was a breach of privacy if the speaker believed that he was only speaking to the person addressed and had no reason to believe the conversation was being broadcast or recorded. The key issue in their view was whether the speaker knew or had any reason to suspect that the conversation was being recorded. In the present case, the police knew that the applicants had refused to provide voice samples voluntarily and sought to trick to them into speaking in an underhand procedure which was wholly unregulated, arbitrary and attended by bad faith. It was also irrelevant that the recording was used for forensic purposes rather than to obtain information about the speaker, as it was the covert recording itself, not the use made of it, which amounted to the breach of privacy.

53. The applicants further submitted that the use of the covert listening devices was not "in accordance with the law" as there was no domestic law regulating the use of such devices and no safeguards provided within the law to protect against abuse of such surveillance methods. They rejected any assertion that the police could rely on any general power to obtain and store evidence.

54. The Government submitted that the use of the listening devices in the cells and when the applicants were being charged did not disclose any interference, as these recordings were not made to obtain any private or substantive information. The aural quality of the applicants' voices was not part of private life but was rather a public, external feature. . . .

55. Assuming that there was an interference with any right under Article 8, the Government contended that it was justified under the second paragraph as necessary in a democratic society to protect public safety, prevent crime and/or protect the rights of others. . . .

2. The Court's Assessment

The Existence of an Interference with Private Life

56. Private life is a broad term not susceptible to exhaustive definition. The Court has already held that elements such as gender identification, name and sexual orientation and sexual life are important elements of the personal sphere protected by Article 8. . . . Article 8 also protects a right to identity and personal development, and the right to establish and develop relationships with other human beings and the outside world. . . . There is therefore a zone of interaction of a person with others, even in a public context, which may fall within the scope of "private life".

57. There are a number of elements relevant to a consideration of whether a person's private life is concerned in measures effected outside a person's home or private premises. Since there are occasions when people knowingly or intentionally involve themselves in activities which are or may be recorded or reported in a public manner, a person's reasonable expectations as to privacy may be a significant, though not necessarily conclusive factor. A person who walks down the street will, inevitably, be visible to any member of the public who is also present. Monitoring by technological means of the same

public scene (e.g. a security guard viewing through close circuit television) is of a similar character. Private life considerations may arise however once any systematic or permanent record comes into existence of such material from the public domain. It is for this reason that files gathered by security services on a particular individual fall within the scope of Article 8 even where the information has not been gathered by any intrusive or covert method. . . .

59. The Court's case-law has, on numerous occasions, found that the covert taping of telephone conversations falls within the scope of Article 8 in both aspects of the right guaranteed, namely, respect for private life and correspondence. While it is generally the case that the recordings were made for the purpose of using the content of the conversations in some way, the Court is not persuaded that recordings taken for use as voice samples can be regarded as falling outside the scope of the protection afforded by Article 8. A permanent record has nonetheless been made of the person's voice and it is subject to a process of analysis directly relevant to identifying that person in the context of other personal data. . . .

60. The Court concludes therefore that the recording of the applicants' voices when being charged and when in their police cell discloses an interference with their right to respect for private life within the meaning of Article 8 §1 of the Convention.

Compliance with the Requirements of the Second Paragraph of Article 8

61. The Court has examined, firstly, whether the interference was "in accordance with the law." As noted above, this criterion imports two main requirements: that there be some basis in domestic law for the measure and that the quality of the law is such as to provide safeguards against arbitrariness.

62. It recalls that the Government relied as the legal basis for the measure on the general powers of the police to store and gather evidence. While it may be permissible to rely on the implied powers of police officers to note evidence and collect and store exhibits for steps taken in the course of an investigation, it is trite law that specific statutory or other express legal authority is required for more invasive measures, whether searching private property or taking personal body samples. The Court has found that the lack of any express basis in law for the interception of telephone calls on public and private telephone systems and for using covert surveillance devices on private premises does not conform with the requirement of lawfulness. It considers that no material difference arises where the recording device is operated, without the knowledge or consent of the individual concerned, on police premises. The underlying principle that domestic law should provide protection against arbitrariness and abuse in the use of covert surveillance techniques, applies equally in that situation.

63. . . . [A]t the relevant time, there existed no statutory system to regulate the use of covert listening devices by the police on their own premises.

The interference was not therefore "in accordance with the law" as required by the second paragraph of Article 8 and there has been a violation of this provision. In these circumstances, an examination of the necessity of the interference is no longer required. . . .

NOTES & QUESTIONS

1. ***Reasonable Expectation of Privacy.*** Reread paragraph 57 of the decision. What does the Court mean? Compare the scope of the Court's conception of "reasonable expectation of privacy" with the approach set out in *Katz v. United States* (Chapter 4). Is one approach more protective of privacy than the other? How does the introduction of new technology for surveillance affect the analysis?

2. The European Court, because it considers identification evidence as a processing of personal data (*see* paragraph 59), will necessarily conclude that such activities implicate the right to privacy. Once again, this approach may be contrasted with the approach in the United States.

3. ***Pen Registers.*** Consider paragraph 46 of the decision. Would the Court's decision have been different if the police had intercepted the contents of the phone calls or the identity of the persons who made or received them? Compare this case with the U.S. Supreme Court case *Smith v. Maryland* (Chapter 4). How do the outcomes differ? Would surveillance pursuant to the Pen Register Act provisions of the ECPA, Title III, 18 U.S.C. §§ 3121-3127 (Chapter 4) satisfy the requirements of Article 8?

4. ***Wiretapping Laws Around the World.*** Numerous countries have laws governing wiretapping and electronic surveillance. Based on David Banisar and Simon Davies's broad survey of the privacy laws around the world, electronic surveillance laws differ greatly from country to country.[11] Some examples include:

   - *India.* Wiretapping in India is governed by the Indian Telegraph Act. Only designated officials can issue wiretap orders and intercepted telephone calls cannot be used as primary evidence in court. However, there have been numerous reported wiretapping abuses by the government.
   - *Japan.* Wiretapping is a violation of Japan's Constitution and is restricted by several laws. However, in 1999, based on "strong pressure by the United States government," Japan enacted a law authorizing wiretapping for various drug, gun, gang, and smuggling crimes.[12]
   - *Peru.* Peru has a strict law prohibiting electronic surveillance: "[A] person who violates personal or family privacy, whether by watching, listening to or recording an act, a word, a piece of writing or an image using technical instruments or processes and other means, shall be punished with imprisonment for not more than two years." Penal Code, art. 154. However, as David Banisar and Simon Davies observe:

     > [T]here have been constant abuses of wiretap authority by the government Peru's National Intelligence Service (Servicio Nacional de Inteligencia or SIN), headed by a close adviser to the president Vladimiro Montesinos. The SIN conducted widespread surveillance and illegal phone tapping of government ministers and judges assigned to constitutional cases, beginning in the early 1990s. Army agents used sophisticated Israeli

---

[11] The information about the wiretapping laws that follows is adapted from Banisar & Davies, *Global Trends in Privacy Protection, supra.*
[12] *See id.*

phone-tapping equipment to monitor telephone conversations, and copies of the conversations were delivered to Montesinos. The SIN maintains close ties with the U.S. Central Intelligence Agency, including a covert assistance program to combat drug trafficking. The SIN allegedly conducted a nationwide surveillance campaign with the sole purpose of intimidating political opposition figures. In 1990, an opposition congressman's house was blown up after he delivered a congressional report on domestic surveillance of opposition politicians, journalists, human rights workers and companies suspected of tax evasion.[13]

- *Russian Federation.* A 1995 Act requires judicial authorization for electronic surveillance. Another Act requires a warrant for surveillance by the secret services. In 1998, based on the public disclosure that the Federal Security Service was drafting a system to require ISPs to enable government surveillance of Internet use without a warrant, protections of privacy were strengthened.
- *Singapore.* Singapore has few protections of privacy, and the government engages in widespread surveillance. In 1986, Prime Minister Lee Kwan Yew declared:

  > I am often accused of interfering in the private lives of citizens. Yet, if I did not, had I not done that, we wouldn't be here today. And I say without the slightest remorse, that we wouldn't be here, we would not have made economic progress, if we had not intervened on very personal matters — who your neighbor is, how you live, the noise you make, how you spit, or what language you use. We decide what is right, never mind what the people think. That's another problem.[14]

- *Canada.* Canada criminalizes illegal electronic surveillance. Law enforcement officials must obtain court orders to engage in wiretapping. Wiretapping for national security purposes requires a warrant.

Note the great disparities in approaches and attitudes toward electronic surveillance. Also note that although many countries have laws regulating electronic surveillance, they differ greatly on the enforcement of those laws. To what extent do these various approaches satisfy the principles set out in Article 12 of the Universal Declaration of Human Rights?

(b) Privacy and Identification

B. v. France

E.C.H.R., 03/25/1992 Series A no. 232-C

The applicant before the Court, a French citizen, was registered with the civil status registrar as of male sex, with the forenames Norbert Antoine. Miss B. (referred in the judgment in the feminine, in accordance with the sex claimed by her) "adopted female behavior from a very early age" and was "noticeably homosexual" until the time she decided to undergo a surgical

---

[13]*Id.* at 79-80.
[14]*Id.* at 87.

operation in 1972 to modify the appearance of her external genital organs. Miss B., after deciding in 1978 to get married with a man, had to bring proceedings before a French court to have the Court hold that, "registered in the civil status register of [her] place of birth as of male sex, [she was] in reality of feminine constitution; . . . declare that [she was] of female sex; . . . order rectification of [her] birth certificate; . . . [and] declare that [she should] henceforth bear the forenames Lyne Antoinette". The French Court dismissed her action concluding that "the change of sex was intentionally brought about by artificial processes", that "the application of Norbert [B.] cannot be granted without attacking the principle of the inalienability of the status of individuals". Miss B. then appealed her case before the Bordeaux Court of Appeal and the French Court of Cassation (Supreme Court) which both dismissed Miss B.'s appeal.

A. Alleged Violation of Article 8

43. According to the applicant, the refusal to recognise her true sexual identity was a breach of Article 8. . . .

She argued that by failing to allow the indication of her sex to be corrected in the civil status register and on her official identity documents, the French authorities forced her to disclose intimate personal information to third parties; she also alleged that she faced great difficulties in her professional life. . . .

45. Miss B. argued that it was not correct to consider her application as substantially identical to those of Mr Rees and Miss Cossey previously before the Court.

Firstly, it was based on new scientific, legal and social elements.

Secondly, there was a fundamental difference between France and England in this field, with regard to their legislation and the attitude of their public authorities.

Thus the application of the very criteria stated in the above-mentioned judgments of 17 October 1986 and 27 September 1990 would have led to a finding of a violation by France, as French law, unlike English law, did not even acknowledge the appearance lawfully assumed by a transsexual. . . .

1. Scientific, Legal and Social Developments

. . . 48. The Court considers that it is undeniable that attitudes have changed, science has progressed and increasing importance is attached to the problem of transsexualism.

It notes, however, in the light of the relevant studies carried out and work done by experts in this field, that there still remains some uncertainty as to the essential nature of transsexualism and that the legitimacy of surgical intervention in such cases is sometimes questioned. The legal situations which result are moreover extremely complex: anatomical, biological, psychological and moral problems in connection with transsexualism and its definition; consent and other requirements to be complied with before any operation; the conditions under which a change of sexual identity can be authorised (validity, scientific presuppositions and legal effects of recourse to surgery, fitness for life with the new sexual identity); international aspects (place where the operation is performed); the legal consequences, retrospective or otherwise, of such a change (rectification of civil status documents); the opportunity to choose a different forename; the confidentiality of documents and information mentioning the change; effects of a family nature (right to marry, fate of an existing marriage, filiation), and so on. On these various points there is as yet no sufficiently broad consensus between the member States of the Council of Europe to persuade the Court to reach opposite conclusions to those in its *Rees* and *Cossey* judgments.

2. The Differences Between the French and English Systems

50. In the Government's opinion, . . . the Court could not depart in the case of France from the solution adopted in the Rees and Cossey judgments. The applicant might no doubt in the course of her daily life experience a number of embarrassing situations, but they were not serious enough to constitute a breach of Article 8. At no time had the French authorities denied transsexuals the right to lead their own lives as they wished. . . .

51. The Court finds, to begin with, that there are noticeable differences between France and England with reference to their law and practice on civil status, change of forenames, the use of identity documents, etc. . . .

(a) Civil Status
(i) Rectification of Civil Status Documents

52. The applicant considered the rejection of her request for rectification of her birth certificate to be all the more culpable since France could not claim, as the United Kingdom had done, that there were any major obstacles linked to the system in force.

The Court had found, in connection with the English civil status system, that the purpose of the registers was not to define the present identity of an individual but to record a historic fact, and their public character would make the protection of private life illusory if it were possible to make subsequent corrections or additions of this kind. This was not the case in France. Birth certificates were intended to be updated throughout the life of the person concerned, so that it would be perfectly possible to insert a reference to a judgment ordering the amendment of the original sex recorded. Moreover, the only persons who had direct access to them were public officials authorised to do so and persons who had obtained permission from the procureur de la République; their public character was ensured by the issuing of complete copies or extracts. France could therefore uphold the applicant's claim without amending the legislation; a change in the Court of Cassation's case-law would suffice.

53. In the Government's opinion, French case-law in this respect was not settled, and the law appeared to be in a transitional phase.

54. In the Commission's opinion, none of the Government's arguments suggested that the Court of Cassation would agree to a transsexual's change of sex being recorded in the civil status register. It had rejected the appeal in the present case on the grounds that the applicant's situation derived from a voluntary choice on her part and not from facts which had existed prior to the operation.

55. . . . It is true that the applicant underwent the surgical operation abroad, without the benefit of all the medical and psychological safeguards which are now required in France. The operation nevertheless involved the

irreversible abandonment of the external marks of Miss B.'s original sex. The Court considers that in the circumstances of the case the applicant's manifest determination is a factor which is sufficiently significant to be taken into account, together with other factors, with reference to Article 8.

(ii) Change of Forenames

56. The applicant pointed out that the law of 6 Fructidor Year II prohibited any citizen from bearing a surname or forename other than those recorded on his or her birth certificate. In the eyes of the law, her forename was therefore Norbert; all her identity documents (identity card, passport, voting card, etc.), her cheque books and her official correspondence (telephone accounts, tax demands, etc.) described her by that name. Unlike in the United Kingdom, whether she could change her forename did not depend on her wishes only; Article 57 of the Civil Code made this subject to judicial permission and the demonstration of a "legitimate interest" capable of justifying it. . . . Miss B. knew of no decision which had regarded transsexualism as giving rise to such an interest. In any event, the Libourne tribunal de grande instance and the Bordeaux Court of Appeal had refused to allow her the forenames Lyne Antoinette. . . .

58. . . . To sum up, the Court considers that the refusal to allow the applicant the change of forename requested by her is also a relevant factor from the point of view of Article 8. . . .

(b) Documents

59. (a) The applicant stressed that an increasing number of official documents indicated sex: extracts of birth certificates, computerised identity cards, European Communities passports, etc. Transsexuals could consequently not cross a frontier, undergo an identity check or carry out one of the many transactions of daily life where proof of identity is necessary, without disclosing the discrepancy between their legal sex and their apparent sex.

(b) According to the applicant, sex was also indicated on all documents using the identification number issued to everyone by [the National Institute for Statistics and Economic Studies (INSEE)]. . . . This number was used as part of the system of dealings between social security institutions, employers and those insured; it therefore appeared on records of contributions paid and on payslips. A transsexual was consequently unable to hide his or her situation from a potential employer and the employer's administrative staff; the same applied to the many occasions in daily life where it was necessary to prove the existence and amount of one's income (taking a lease, opening a bank account, applying for credit, etc). This led to difficulties for the social and professional integration of transsexuals. . . .

60. The Commission agreed substantially with the applicant's arguments. In its opinion the applicant, as a result of the frequent necessity of disclosing information concerning her private life to third parties, suffered distress which was too serious to be justified on the ground of respect for the rights of others. . . .

(c) Conclusion

63. The Court thus reaches the conclusion, on the basis of the abovementioned factors which distinguish the present case from the Rees and

Cossey cases and without it being necessary to consider the applicant's other arguments, that she finds herself daily in a situation which, taken as a whole, is not compatible with the respect due to her private life. Consequently, even having regard to the State's margin of appreciation, the fair balance which has to be struck between the general interest and the interests of the individual has not been attained, and there has thus been a violation of Article 8 . . . .

The respondent State has several means to choose from for remedying this state of affairs. It is not the Court's function to indicate which is the most appropriate.

NOTES & QUESTIONS

1. The Court's holding is unclear as to what is the violation of Article 8. In addition, it leaves the respondent State free to choose the means for remedying the violation of privacy. How do you think France, or generally any State, should change its current administrative practices? Allow transsexuals to rectify their civil status document? Change their first name? Have the statement or indication of sex deleted from the documents and identity papers for use in daily life? What would be the factors you would take into account?

   The following dissent from the judgment provides one answer:

   DISSENTING OPINION OF JUDGE PETTITI

   . . . The European Convention on Human Rights does not impose any obligation on the High Contracting Parties to legislate on the question of rectification of civil status in connection with transsexualism, even in application of the theory of positive obligations for States (case of *X v. the Netherlands*). Thus several member States have not enacted any legislation relating to transsexualism. The various national laws on the point show a great variety of criteria and mechanisms.

   In any event, member States who wish to confront these problems have a choice between the legislative path and the case-law path, and in this sensitive area, dependent on very diverse social and moral situations, the margin of appreciation allowed to the State is a wide one.

   Whichever path is chosen, legislative or by means of case-law, the State remains free to define the criteria for recognition of cases of intersexualism or true transsexualism, dependent upon undisputed scientific knowledge. A national court can take a decision on the basis of such criteria without violating the Convention. . . .

   If there is a field where States should be allowed the maximum margin of appreciation, having regard to moral attitudes and traditions, it is certainly that of transsexualism, having regard also to developments in the opinions of the medical and scientific experts.

   A solution by means of case-law may be a legitimate choice for the State to make. If the development of case-law makes it possible for domestic law to respond to undeniable cases, making it possible for rectification of civil status to take place, . . . it appears to be consistent with Article 8 to regard this case-law method as in accordance with the requirements of that Article.

   . . . Even if the member State agrees to rectification, it remains free to restrict the conditions for it and its consequences in civil law, if it does not systematically refuse applications in all such cases. . . .

> Conclusion: in the present state of French law and the status of the family, and taking into account the rights of others, it is apparent that the case-law path is the one which best respects Article 8 of the Convention, subject to the margin of appreciation allowed to the State.

2. Should the regulation of transsexualism remain within the competence of each State, taking into account the traditions and moral views of each State? What would be the impact on transborder data flow?
3. How is the situation of transsexuals dealt with in the United States with respect to identity documents disclosing an individual's sex?
4. Should the mention of sex be deleted from all identification documents (driver's license, national IDs, private company's identification cards, passports, etc.) to avoid any discrimination between transsexual and non-transsexual persons? Are there other types of personal data that are currently subject to such treatment?

(c) Privacy, Records, and Computer Databases

ROTARU v. ROMANIA

E.C.H.R., 5/4/2000

Principal Facts

The applicant, Aurel Rotaru, a Romanian national, was born in 1921 and lives in Bârlad (Romania).

In 1992 the applicant, who in 1948 had been sentenced to a year's imprisonment for having expressed criticism of the communist regime established in 1946, brought an action in which he sought to be granted rights that Decree no. 118 of 1990 afforded persons who had been persecuted by the communist regime. In the proceedings which followed in the Bârlad Court of First Instance, one of the defendants, the Ministry of the Interior, submitted to the court a letter sent to it on 19 December 1990 by the Romanian Intelligence Service, which contained, among other things, information about the applicant's political activities between 1946 and 1948. According to the same letter, Mr Rotaru had been a member of the Christian Students' Association, an extreme right-wing "legionnaire" movement, in 1937.

The applicant considered that some of the information in question was false and defamatory—in particular, the allegation that he had been a member of the legionnaire movement—and brought proceedings against the Romanian Intelligence Service, claiming compensation for the non-pecuniary damage he had sustained and amendment or destruction of the file containing the untrue information. . . .

[The claim the applicant filed was rejected by the Romanian courts.] These . . . courts held that they had no power to order amendment or destruction of the information in the letter of 19 December 1990 as it had been gathered by the State's former security services, and the Romanian Intelligence Service had only been a depositary.

[The applicant lodged his complaint in 1995 with the European Commission of Human Rights.]

In . . . 1997 the Director of the Romanian Intelligence Service [recognized] that the information about being a member of the "legionnaire" movement referred not to the applicant but to another person of the same name.

In the light of that letter the applicant sought a review of the Bucharest Court of Appeal's [last] judgment of . . . 1994 and claimed damages. [T]he Bucharest Court of Appeal quashed the judgment of 15 December 1994 and declared the information about the applicant's past membership of the "legionnaire" movement null and void. . . .

The Facts

I. Relevant Domestic Law . . .

[G. Law no. 187 of 20 October 1999 provides:

(1) All Romanian citizens, and all aliens who have obtained Romanian nationality since 1945, shall be entitled to inspect the files kept on them by the organs of the Securitate. . . . This right shall be exercisable on request and shall make it possible for the file itself to be inspected and copies to be made of any document in it or relating to its contents.

(2) Additionally, any person who is the subject of a file from which it appears that he or she was kept under surveillance by the Securitate shall be entitled, on request, to know the identity of the Securitate agents and collaborators who contributed documents to the file.]

The Law . . .

II. Alleged Violation of Article 8 of the Convention

1. The applicant complained that the RIS [Romanian Intelligence Service] held and could at any moment make use of information about his private life, some of which was false and defamatory. He alleged a violation of Article 8 of the Convention. . . .

A. Applicability of Article 8

3. The Court reiterates that the storing of information relating to an individual's private life in a secret register and the release of such information comes within the scope of Article 8 § 1. . . .

The Court has already emphasised the correspondence of this broad interpretation with that of the Council of Europe's Convention of 28 January 1981 for the Protection of Individuals with regard to Automatic Processing of Personal Data, which came into force on 1 October 1985 and whose purpose is "to secure . . . for every individual . . . respect for his rights and fundamental freedoms, and in particular his right to privacy with regard to automatic processing of personal data relating to him" (Article 1), such personal data being defined in Article 2 as "any information relating to an identified or identifiable individual."

Moreover, public information can fall within the scope of private life where it is systematically collected and stored in files held by the authorities. That is all the truer where such information concerns a person's distant past.

4. In the instant case the Court notes that the RIS's letter of 19 December 1990 contained various pieces of information about the applicant's life, in

particular his studies, his political activities and his criminal record, some of which had been gathered more than fifty years earlier. In the Court's opinion, such information, when systematically collected and stored in a file held by agents of the State, falls within the scope of "private life" for the purposes of Article 8 § 1 of the Convention. That is all the more so in the instant case as some of the information has been declared false and is likely to injure the applicant's reputation.

Article 8 consequently applies.

B. Compliance with Article 8
1. Whether There Was Interference

6. The Court points out that both the storing by a public authority of information relating to an individual's private life and the use of it and the refusal to allow an opportunity for it to be refuted amount to interference with the right to respect for private life secured in Article 8 § 1 of the Convention.

Both the storing of that information and the use of it, which were coupled with a refusal to allow the applicant an opportunity to refute it, amounted to interference with his right to respect for family life as guaranteed by Article 8 § 1.

2. Justification for the Interference

7. The cardinal issue that arises is whether the interference so found is justifiable under paragraph 2 of Article 8. That paragraph, since it provides for an exception to a right guaranteed by the Convention, is to be interpreted narrowly. While the Court recognises that intelligence services may legitimately exist in a democratic society, it reiterates that powers of secret surveillance of citizens are tolerable under the Convention only in so far as strictly necessary for safeguarding the democratic institutions.

8. If it is not to contravene Article 8, such interference must have been "in accordance with the law", pursue a legitimate aim under paragraph 2 and, furthermore, be necessary in a democratic society in order to achieve that aim. . . .

11. The Commission considered that domestic law did not define with sufficient precision the circumstances in which the RIS could archive, release and use information relating to the applicant's private life. . . .

The Court must . . . determine whether Law no. 14/1992 on the organisation and operation of the RIS, which was likewise relied on by the Government, can provide the legal basis for these measures. [Law no. 14/1992 grants broad authority to the Romanian Intelligence Services to gather information to protect the national security and made such information secret.] In this connection, it notes that the law in question authorises the RIS to gather, store and make use of information affecting national security. The Court has doubts as to the relevance to national security of the information held on the applicant. Nevertheless, it reiterates that it is primarily for the national authorities, notably the courts, to interpret and apply domestic law and notes that in its judgment of 25 November 1997 the Bucharest Court of Appeal confirmed that it was lawful for the RIS to hold this information as depositary of the archives of the former security services.

That being so, the Court may conclude that the storing of information about the applicant's private life had a basis in Romanian law. . . .

15. As regards the requirement of foreseeability, the Court reiterates that a rule is "foreseeable" if it is formulated with sufficient precision to enable any individual — if need be with appropriate advice — to regulate his conduct. The Court has stressed the importance of this concept with regard to secret surveillance in the following terms:

> The Court would reiterate its opinion that the phrase "in accordance with the law" does not merely refer back to domestic law but also relates to the quality of the "law," requiring it to be compatible with the rule of law, which is expressly mentioned in the preamble to the Convention. . . The phrase thus implies — and this follows from the object and purpose of Article 8 — that there must be a measure of legal protection in domestic law against arbitrary interferences by public authorities with the rights safeguarded by paragraph 1. . . Especially where a power of the executive is exercised in secret, the risks of arbitrariness are evident. . . .
>
> Since the implementation in practice of measures of secret surveillance of communications is not open to scrutiny by the individuals concerned or the public at large, it would be contrary to the rule of law for the legal discretion granted to the executive to be expressed in terms of an unfettered power. Consequently, the law must indicate the scope of any such discretion conferred on the competent authorities and the manner of its exercise with sufficient clarity, having regard to the legitimate aim of the measure in question, to give the individual adequate protection against arbitrary interference.

16. The "quality" of the legal rules relied on in this case must therefore be scrutinised, with a view, in particular, to ascertaining whether domestic law laid down with sufficient precision the circumstances in which the RIS could store and make use of information relating to the applicant's private life.

17. The Court notes in this connection that section 8 of Law no. 14/1992 provides that information affecting national security may be gathered, recorded and archived in secret files.

No provision of domestic law, however, lays down any limits on the exercise of those powers. Thus, for instance, domestic law does not define the kind of information that may be recorded, the categories of people against whom surveillance measures such as gathering and keeping information may be taken, the circumstances in which such measures may be taken or the procedure to be followed. Similarly, the Law does not lay down limits on the age of information held or the length of time for which it may be kept.

Section 45 empowers the RIS to take over for storage and use the archives that belonged to the former intelligence services operating on Romanian territory and allows inspection of RIS documents with the Director's consent.

The Court notes that this section contains no explicit, detailed provision concerning the persons authorised to consult the files, the nature of the files, the procedure to be followed or the use that may be made of the information thus obtained.

18. It also notes that although section 2 of the Law empowers the relevant authorities to permit interferences necessary to prevent and counteract threats to national security, the ground allowing such interferences is not laid down with sufficient precision.

19. The Court must also be satisfied that there exist adequate and effective safeguards against abuse, since a system of secret surveillance designed to protect national security entails the risk of undermining or even destroying democracy on the ground of defending it.

In order for systems of secret surveillance to be compatible with Article 8 of the Convention, they must contain safeguards established by law which apply to the supervision of the relevant services' activities. Supervision procedures must follow the values of a democratic society as faithfully as possible, in particular the rule of law, which is expressly referred to in the Preamble to the Convention. The rule of law implies, *inter alia,* that interference by the executive authorities with an individual's rights should be subject to effective supervision, which should normally be carried out by the judiciary, at least in the last resort, since judicial control affords the best guarantees of independence, impartiality and a proper procedure.

20. In the instant case the Court notes that the Romanian system for gathering and archiving information does not provide such safeguards, no supervision procedure being provided by Law no. 14/1992, whether while the measure ordered is in force or afterwards.

21. That being so, the Court considers that domestic law does not indicate with reasonable clarity the scope and manner of exercise of the relevant discretion conferred on the public authorities.

22. The Court concludes that the holding and use by the RIS of information on the applicant's private life was not "in accordance with the law," a fact that suffices to constitute a violation of Article 8. . . .

23. There has consequently been a violation of Article 8.

NOTES AND QUESTIONS

1. Referring to paragraphs 17 and 19 of this decision and its requirements, consider how the national security surveillance claims are treated under Article 8 of the ECHR and under the U.S. Foreign Intelligence Surveillance Act (FISA), as amended by the USA-PATRIOT Act (*see* Chapter 4). Which legal regime provides a more effective means of oversight?
2. Which other provisions in U.S. law regulate the collection of similar information by the police?

(d) Privacy and Place

NIEMIETZ V. GERMANY

E.C.H.R., 12/16/1992

. . . As To the Facts

I. The Particular Circumstances of the Case

6. Mr Niemietz lives in Freiburg im Breisgau, Germany, where he practises as a lawyer (*Rechtsanwalt*). . . .

10. In the context of [criminal] proceedings the Munich District Court issued, on 8 August 1986, a warrant to search the law office of the applicant and his colleague and the homes of Ms D. and Ms G. [The warrant was issued to

find out who sent a letter, signed by a "Klaus Wegner" insulting a judge. One of the places to be searched was the law office of Gottfried Niemietz.] Those searching neither found the documents they were seeking nor seized any materials. . . .

12. The homes of Ms D. and Ms G. were also searched; documents were found that gave rise to a suspicion that the letter to Judge Miosga had been sent by Ms D. under an assumed name. . . .

II. Relevant Domestic Law

18. Article 13 para. 1 of the Basic Law (*Grundgesetz*) guarantees the inviolability of the home (*Wohnung*); this provision has been consistently interpreted by the German courts in a wide sense, to include business premises. . . .

19. Article 103 of the Code of Criminal Procedure provides that the home and other premises (*Wohnung und andere Räume*) of a person who is not suspected of a criminal offence may be searched only in order to arrest a person charged with an offence, to investigate indications of an offence or to seize specific objects and provided always that there are facts to suggest that such a person, indications or objects is or are to be found on the premises to be searched.

21. . . . An unauthorised breach of secrecy by a lawyer is punishable by imprisonment for a maximum of one year or a fine (Article 203 para. 1(3) of the Criminal Code). A lawyer is entitled to refuse to give testimony concerning any matter confided to him in a professional capacity (Article 53 para. 1(2) and (3) of the Code of Criminal Procedure). The last-mentioned provisions, in conjunction with Article 97, prohibit, with certain exceptions, the seizure of correspondence between lawyer and client. . . .

As to the Law

I. Alleged Violation of Article 8 of the Convention

26. Mr Niemietz alleged that the search of his law office had given rise to a breach of Article 8 (art. 8) of the Convention. . . .

A. Was There an "Interference"?

27. In contesting the Commission's conclusion, the Government maintained that Article 8 did not afford protection against the search of a lawyer's office. In their view, the Convention drew a clear distinction between private life and home, on the one hand, and professional and business life and premises, on the other.

28. . . . The Court . . . [has doubts] as to whether this factor can serve as a workable criterion for the purposes of delimiting the scope of the protection afforded by Article 8 (art. 8). Virtually all professional and business activities may involve, to a greater or lesser degree, matters that are confidential, with the result that, if that criterion were adopted, disputes would frequently arise as to where the line should be drawn.

29. The Court does not consider it possible or necessary to attempt an exhaustive definition of the notion of "private life". However, it would be too restrictive to limit the notion to an "inner circle" in which the individual may live his own personal life as he chooses and to exclude there from entirely the

outside world not encompassed within that circle. Respect for private life must also comprise to a certain degree the right to establish and develop relationships with other human beings.

There appears, furthermore, to be no reason of principle why this understanding of the notion of "private life" should be taken to exclude activities of a professional or business nature since it is, after all, in the course of their working lives that the majority of people have a significant, if not the greatest, opportunity of developing relationships with the outside world. This view is supported by the fact that . . . it is not always possible to distinguish clearly which of an individual's activities form part of his professional or business life and which do not. Thus, especially in the case of a person exercising a liberal profession, his work in that context may form part and parcel of his life to such a degree that it becomes impossible to know in what capacity he is acting at a given moment of time. . . .

30. As regards the word "home", appearing in the English text of Article 8, the Court observes that in certain Contracting States, notably Germany . . . , it has been accepted as extending to business premises. Such an interpretation is, moreover, fully consonant with the French text, since the word "domicile" has a broader connotation than the word "home" and may extend, for example, to a professional person's office.

In this context also, it may not always be possible to draw precise distinctions, since activities which are related to a profession or business may well be conducted from a person's private residence and activities which are not so related may well be carried on in an office or commercial premises. A narrow interpretation of the words "home" and "domicile" could therefore give rise to the same risk of inequality of treatment as a narrow interpretation of the notion of "private life" (see paragraph 29 above).

31. More generally, to interpret the words "private life" and "home" as including certain professional or business activities or premises would be consonant with the essential object and purpose of Article 8, namely to protect the individual against arbitrary interference by the public authorities. . . .

32. To the above-mentioned general considerations, which militate against the view that Article 8 is not applicable, must be added a further factor pertaining to the particular circumstances of the case. The warrant issued by the Munich District Court ordered a search for, and seizure of, "documents"—without qualification or limitation—revealing the identity of Klaus Wegner. . . .

33. Taken together, the foregoing reasons lead the Court to find that the search of the applicant's office constituted an interference with his rights under Article 8 (art. 8).

B. Was the Interference "in Accordance with the Law"?

. . . [The Court considered that the search was lawful in terms of Article 103 of the Code of Criminal Procedure (see paragraph 19 above).] . . .

C. Did the Interference Have a Legitimate Aim or Aims?

36. . . . [T]he Court finds that . . . the interference pursued aims that were legitimate under Article 8 (2), namely the prevention of crime and the protection of the rights of others, that is the honour of Judge Miosga.

D. Was the Interference "Necessary in a Democratic Society"?

. . . It is true that the offence in connection with which the search was effected, involving as it did not only an insult to but also an attempt to bring pressure on a judge, cannot be classified as no more than minor. On the other hand, the warrant was drawn in broad terms, in that it ordered a search for and seizure of "documents", without any limitation, revealing the identity of the author of the offensive letter; this point is of special significance where, as in Germany, the search of a lawyer's office is not accompanied by any special procedural safeguards, such as the presence of an independent observer. More importantly, having regard to the materials that were in fact inspected, the search impinged on professional secrecy to an extent that appears disproportionate in the circumstances; it has, in this connection, to be recalled that, where a lawyer is involved, an encroachment on professional secrecy may have repercussions on the proper administration of justice and hence on the rights guaranteed by Article 6 of the Convention. In addition, the attendant publicity must have been capable of affecting adversely the applicant's professional reputation, in the eyes both of his existing clients and of the public at large.

E. Conclusion

38. The Court thus concludes that there was a breach of Article 8. . . .

NOTES & QUESTIONS

1. The ECHR case law requires that a governmental measure be taken "in accordance with a law." Is this a significant limitation on the activities of government? Compare this with the authority created by federal wiretap law to conduct electronic surveillance in the United States. Which approach is preferable?

2. Article 8 presents a multifactor approach to judicial review of privacy complaints. How does this approach compare with the "reasonable expectation of privacy" analysis generally followed by the courts in the United States? How are these factors derived? Could they be codified in a civil code system of law?

B. DATA PROTECTION FRAMEWORKS

1. INTRODUCTION

The Privacy Guidelines of the Organization for Economic Cooperation and Development (OECD) and the requirements of the EU Data Protection Directive have significantly influenced the development of privacy law, both in Europe and around the globe. In this section we consider how the two frameworks address key problems in information privacy. We consider the OECD Guidelines and EU Data Directive side by side to illustrate the similarities between the frameworks.

(a) OECD Guidelines

On September 23, 1980, the Organization for Economic Cooperation and Development (OECD), a group of leading industrial countries concerned with global economic and democratic development, issued guidelines for privacy protection in the transfer of personal information across national borders. These are the Guidelines on the Protection of Privacy and Transborder Flows of Personal Data.[15] The OECD Privacy Guidelines set out eight key principles for the protection of personal information.

First is the principle of *collection limitation:* there should be limits to the collection of personal data; any such data collected should be obtained by lawful means and with the consent of the data subject, where appropriate. Second is the principle of *data quality:* collected data should be relevant to a specific purpose, and be accurate, complete, and up-to-date. Third is the principle of *purpose specification:* the purpose for collecting data should be settled at the outset. The fourth principle, *use limitation,* works in tandem with the third: the use of personal data ought to be limited to specified purposes, and data acquired for one purpose ought not be used for others. The fifth principle is *security:* data must be collected and stored in a way reasonably calculated to prevent its loss, theft, or modification. The sixth principle is *openness:* there should be transparency with respect to the practices of handling data. The seventh principle is *individual participation:* individuals should have the right to access, confirm, and demand correction of their personal data. The eighth and last principle is *accountability:* those in charge of handling data should be responsible for complying with the principles of the privacy guidelines.

In developing the guidelines, the OECD worked closely with the Council of Europe, which was at that time drafting its own Convention on Privacy. Examination of both the Guidelines and the Convention will show that they have much in common, as well as pointing to the general concern for individual privacy protection that arose in the late 1970s. Since the Guidelines' release, many OECD countries have enacted laws to implement them. Although the OECD Guidelines are nonbinding on signatories, the eight privacy principles have been incorporated into privacy laws around the globe.

(b) European Union Data Protection Directive

The European Union Data Protection Directive of 1995 [16] establishes common rules for data protection among Member States of the European Union. The Directive was created in the early 1990s and formally adopted in 1995.

---

[15] Available at *<http://www1.oecd.org/dsti/sti/it/secur/prod/PRIV-EN.htm>*. OECD Declaration on Transborder Data Flows (1985) is available at *<http://www1.oecd.org/dsti/sti/it/secur/prod/e_dflow.htm>*. For a comparison of U.S. privacy law to the OECD guidelines, see Joel R. Reidenberg, *Restoring Americans' Privacy in Electronic Commerce,* 14 Berkeley J.L. & Tech. 771 (1999).

[16] Directive 95/46/EC of the European Parliament and of the Council of 24 October 1995 on the Protection of Individuals with Regard to the Processing of Personal Data and on the Free Movement of Such Data, available at *<http://europa.eu.int/eur-lex/en/lif/dat/1995/en_395L0046.html>*.

Although prior to the adoption of the Directive, many EU countries had broad national privacy legislation, protections did diverge. The Directive's purpose, somewhat paradoxically, is to facilitate the free flow of personal data within the EU. An increased harmonization of the privacy laws of various European nations would enable the free flow of goods and services, labor and capital.

The Directive imposes obligations on the processors of personal data. It requires technical security and the notification of individuals whose data are being collected, and outlines circumstances under which data transfer may occur. The Directive also gives individuals substantial rights to control the use of data about themselves. These rights include the right to be informed that their personal data are being transferred, the need to obtain "unambiguous" consent from the individual for the transfer of certain data, the opportunity to make corrections in the data, and the right to object to the transfer. Data regulatory authority, enforcement provisions, and sanctions are also key elements of the directive. Following passage of the Directive, the various national governments of the EU amended their own national data protection legislation to bring it into line with the Directive.

The Directive extends privacy safeguards to personal data that are transferred outside of the European Union. Article 25 of the Directive states that data can only be transferred to third countries that provide an "adequate level of data protection." As a result implementation focuses on both the adoption of national law within the European Union and the adoption of adequate methods for privacy protection in third party countries.[17]

Directives are a form of EU law that is binding for Member States, but only as to the result to be achieved. They allow the national authorities to choose the form and the methods of their implementation and generally fix a deadline for it. Therefore, the rules of law applicable in each Member State are the national laws implementing the directives and not the directive itself. However, the directive has a "direct effect" on individuals: it grants them rights that can be upheld by the national courts in their respective countries if their governments have not implemented the directive by the set deadline. A directive thus grants *rights* rather than creates obligations, and they are enforceable by *individuals* rather than by public authorities. There lies the distinction made between vertical and horizontal direct effect. "Vertical effects" means that the rights established by a directive flow from the European Union to citizens of the EU. Where a violation occurs, citizens may petition EU institution and their national government that has adopted (or "transposed") a directive into national law. But this does not create a right for one citizen of the EU to bring an action against another citizen. For this to occur ("horizontal effects") there must be national law or an EU regulation in place. Whereas the EU "regulations" or Treaty provisions are able to confer rights on private individuals and impose obligations on them, directives can only confer rights on

---

[17] EPIC, *Privacy and Human Rights* 2000, at 9-16. For perspectives on the EU Directive, *see* Peter P. Swire & Robert E. Litan, *None of Your Business: World Data Flows, Electronic Commerce, and the European Privacy Directive* (1998); Spiros Simitis, *From the Market to the Polis: The EU Directive on the Protection of Personal Data,* 80 Iowa L. Rev. 445 (1995); *Symposium: Data Protection Law and the European Union's Directive: The Challenge for the United States,* 80 Iowa L. Rev. 431 (1995).

individuals against the State; they cannot impose on them obligations in favor of the State or other individuals. Directives are only capable of "vertical" direct effect, unlike Treaty provisions and regulations which are also capable of "horizontal" direct effect.

Directives are enacted in the context of the European Community (EC)'s competences, the EC being one of the legal entities that is part of the European Union. It means that their scope is limited to the area of competence of the EC. The EU Data Directive, as a result, does not cover activities which fall outside the scope of E.C. law, such as the data processing operations concerning public security, defense, State security, and the activities of the State in areas of criminal law. *See, e.g.,* EU Data Directive, Article 3(2). In such cases, the only authorities that may promulgate enforceable legislation are the Member States. The European Union, however, can voice its concerns on data protection and privacy issues through its "Justice and Home Affairs" branch, regarding police and judicial cooperation in criminal matters, with particular attention being paid to terrorism, trafficking in persons, offences against children, drug trafficking, arms trafficking, corruption, and fraud. This branch, under the direction of the EU Council,[18] can take common positions defining the approach of the EU to a particular matter, or framework decisions to harmonize national legislation, or even establish conventions, although each Member State can always oppose these decisions and not implement them into national law.

2. GENERAL PROVISIONS

OECD GUIDELINES: PURPOSE, SCOPE, AND DEFINITIONS

Purpose. The preface to the OECD Guidelines explains the necessity and importance of the Guidelines:

> The development of automatic data processing, which enables vast quantities of data to be transmitted within seconds across national frontiers, and indeed across continents, has made it necessary to consider privacy protection in relation to personal data. Privacy protection laws have been introduced, or will be introduced shortly, in approximately one half of OECD Member countries (Austria, Canada, Denmark, France, Germany, Luxembourg, Norway, Sweden and the United States have passed legislation. Belgium, Iceland, the Netherlands, Spain and Switzerland have prepared draft bills) to prevent what are considered to be violations of fundamental human rights, such as the unlawful storage of personal data, the storage of inaccurate personal data, or the abuse or unauthorised disclosure of such data.
>
> On the other hand, there is a danger that disparities in national legislations could hamper the free flow of personal data across frontiers; these flows have greatly increased in recent years and are bound to grow further with the widespread introduction of new computer and communications technology.

---

[18] The EU Council is the group of delegates of the Member States, each State being represented by a government minister who is authorized to commit his government.

Restrictions on these flows could cause serious disruption in important sectors of the economy, such as banking and insurance.

For this reason OECD Member countries considered it necessary to develop Guidelines which would help to harmonise national privacy legislation and, while upholding such human rights, would at the same time prevent interruptions in international flows of data. They represent a consensus on basic principles which can be built into existing national legislation, or serve as a basis for legislation in those countries which do not yet have it.

The Recommendation was adopted and became applicable on 23rd September, 1980. . . .

General Recommendations. The Guidelines provide a series of general recommendations for their implementation: First, member countries should "take into account in their domestic legislation the principles concerning the protection of privacy and individual liberties set forth in the Guidelines." Second, member countries should, when creating privacy protections, avoid "unjustified obstacles to transborder flows of personal data." Third, member countries should cooperate in the implementation of the Guidelines. Fourth, member countries should agree "on specific procedures of consultation and co-operation for the application of these Guidelines."

Definitions. Three central terms that are used throughout the Guidelines are defined as follows:

> *a)* "data controller" means a party who, according to domestic law, is competent to decide about the contents and use of personal data regardless of whether or not such data are collected, stored, processed or disseminated by that party or by an agent on its behalf;
>
> *b)* "personal data" means any information relating to an identified or identifiable individual (data subject);
>
> *c)* "transborder flows of personal data" means movements of personal data across national borders. Part I.1.

Scope. The Guidelines "apply to personal data, whether in the public or private sectors, which, because of the manner in which they are processed, or because of their nature or the context in which they are used, pose a danger to privacy and individual liberties." However, the Guidelines state that they should not be interpreted narrowly to prevent their application to different categories of personal data or different protective measures. Further, the Guidelines need not exclude personal data which do not contain "any risk to privacy and individual liberties." Finally, the Guidelines need not only apply to "automatic processing of personal data."

Exceptions of the Guidelines in Parts II and III, "including those relating to national sovereignty, national security and public policy, should be: *a)* as few as possible, and *b)* made known to the public."

The Guidelines provide a floor of protection; member countries can adopt more stringent protections: "These Guidelines should be regarded as minimum standards which are capable of being supplemented by additional measures for the protection of privacy and individual liberties."

EUROPEAN UNION DATA PROTECTION DIRECTIVE: ARTICLES 1-5, 24, 32-33

Object of the Directive. Under Article 1, the Directive provides that "Member States shall protect the fundamental rights and freedoms of natural persons, and in particular their right to privacy with respect to the processing of personal data." However, in implementing these protections, Member States should avoid restricting or prohibiting "the free flow of personal data between Member States."

Definitions. Article 2 defines a number of terms used throughout the Directive:

(a) "personal data" shall mean any information relating to an identified or identifiable natural person ("data subject"); an identifiable person is one who can be identified, directly or indirectly, in particular by reference to an identification number or to one or more factors specific to his physical, physiological, mental, economic, cultural or social identity;

(b) "processing of personal data" ("processing") shall mean any operation or set of operations which is performed upon personal data, whether or not by automatic means, such as collection, recording, organization, storage, adaptation or alteration, retrieval, consultation, use, disclosure by transmission, dissemination or otherwise making available, alignment or combination, blocking, erasure or destruction;

(c) "personal data filing system" ("filing system") shall mean any structured set of personal data which are accessible according to specific criteria, whether centralized, decentralized or dispersed on a functional or geographical basis;

(d) "controller" shall mean the natural or legal person, public authority, agency or any other body which alone or jointly with others determines the purposes and means of the processing of personal data; where the purposes and means of processing are determined by national or Community laws or regulations, the controller or the specific criteria for his nomination may be designated by national or Community law;

(e) "processor" shall mean a natural or legal person, public authority, agency or any other body which processes personal data on behalf of the controller;

(f) "third party" shall mean any natural or legal person, public authority, agency or any other body other than the data subject, the controller, the processor and the persons who, under the direct authority of the controller or the processor, are authorized to process the data;

(g) "recipient" shall mean a natural or legal person, public authority, agency or any other body to whom data are disclosed, whether a third party or not; however, authorities which may receive data in the framework of a particular inquiry shall not be regarded as recipients;

(h) "the data subject's consent" shall mean any freely given specific and informed indication of his wishes by which the data subject signifies his agreement to personal data relating to him being processed.

Scope. Pursuant to Article 3, the Directive applies "to the processing of personal data wholly or partly by automatic means." It also applies to nonautomatic processing that involves a "filing system."

The Directive does not apply to the processing of personal data "in the course of an activity which falls outside the scope of Community law."

Further, it does not apply "in any case to processing operations concerning public security, defence, State security (including the economic well-being of the State when the processing operation relates to State security matters) and the activities of the State in areas of criminal law." Finally, the Directive does not apply to the processing of personal data "by a natural person in the course of a purely personal or household activity."

Jurisdiction and Choice of Law. Article 4 provides rules for choice of law. Recall from the definitions above that a "controller" determines the purposes of the processing of personal data while a "processor" does the actual processing for the controller. In other words, the entity desiring to use the information (controller) may employ another entity (processor) to process the data according to its purposes. Pursuant to Article 4:

> 1. Each Member State shall apply the national provisions it adopts pursuant to this Directive to the processing of personal data where:
>
>> (a) the processing is carried out in the context of the activities of an establishment of the controller on the territory of the Member State; when the same controller is established on the territory of several Member States, he must take the necessary measures to ensure that each of these establishments complies with the obligations laid down by the national law applicable;
>> (b) the controller is not established on the Member State's territory, but in a place where its national law applies by virtue of international public law. . . .
>> (c) the controller is not established on Community territory and, for purposes of processing personal data makes use of equipment, automated or otherwise, situated on the territory of the said Member State, unless such equipment is used only for purposes of transit through the territory of the Community.

According to these provisions, the Member State's law where the controller is established would apply. If the controller is established in multiple Member States, then it must comply with the laws of each Member State. This means that it must follow the most stringent of the protections among the Member States in which it is established. Pursuant to Article 4.1(c), if the controller is not established in any Member State (e.g., is established in the United States or another non-EU country) but "makes use of equipment, automated or otherwise" within the territory of a Member State, then it is subject to the laws of that Member State. However, if the equipment is only used for "purposes of transit" through the Member State, then it is exempt from such laws.

Implementation by Member States. The Directive provides general parameters for legislation by each Member State, which must pass its own laws and regulations to carry out the general dictates of the Directive. As Article 5 states: "Member States shall, within the limits of the provisions of this Chapter, determine more precisely the conditions under which the processing of personal data is lawful." Member States must "adopt suitable measures to ensure the full implementation of the provisions of this Directive." Article 24.

Further, Member States must establish sanctions for the infringement of provisions adopted pursuant to the Directive.

Time Frame for Implementation. Pursuant to Article 32, Member States must promulgate laws and regulations to comply with the Directive within three years of the Directive's adoption. Further, "Member States shall, however, grant the data subject the right to obtain, at his request and in particular at the time of exercising his right of access, the rectification, erasure or blocking of data which are incomplete, inaccurate or stored in a way incompatible with the legitimate purposes pursued by the controller."

Reports on Implementation. Under Article 33, "[t]he Commission shall report to the Council and the European Parliament at regular intervals, starting not later than three years after the date referred to in Article 32 (1), on the implementation of this Directive, attaching to its report, if necessary, suitable proposals for amendments. The report shall be made public." Further:

> The Commission shall examine, in particular, the application of this Directive to the data processing of sound and image data relating to natural persons and shall submit any appropriate proposals which prove to be necessary, taking account of developments in information technology and in the light of the state of progress in the information society.

NOTES & QUESTIONS

1. *The Underlying Philosophy of the EU Data Directive.* Consider the following argument by Joel Reidenberg:

   > The background and underlying philosophy of the European Directive differs in important ways from that of the United States. While there is a consensus among democratic states that information privacy is a critical element of civil society, the United States has, in recent years, left the protection of privacy to markets rather than law. In contrast, Europe treats privacy as a political imperative anchored in fundamental human rights. European democracies approach information privacy from the perspective of social protection. In European democracies, public liberty derives from the community of individuals, and law is the fundamental basis to pursue norms of social and citizen protection. This vision of governance generally regards the state as the necessary player to frame the social community in which individuals develop and in which information practices must serve individual identity. Citizen autonomy, in this view, effectively depends on a backdrop of legal rights. Law thus enshrines prophylactic protection through comprehensive rights and responsibilities. Indeed, citizens trust government more than the private sector with personal information.[19]

   As you examine the various provisions of the EU Data Directive and the OECD Guidelines throughout this chapter, consider how the overall approach of European democracies toward protecting differs from that of the United States. Are there ways in which the approaches are similar? To the

---

[19]Joel R. Reidenberg, *E-Commerce and Trans-Atlantic Privacy*, 38 Hous. L. Rev. 717, 730-731 (2001).

extent that the approaches are different, think about why such differences exist.

2. *Personal Data Under the EU Data Directive.* The EU Data Directive's definition of "personal data" (Art. 2(a)) is one of the keys to understanding the scope and application of the Directive as it only applies to the processing of personal data. Although a more precise definition might simplify the application of data protection across the EU, this formulation reflects the diversity in Member States' laws. To help interpret the concept, the Directive's recitals recommend that "account should be taken of all the means likely reasonably to be used either by the controller or by any other person to identify the said person." The recitals also advise that the data protection rules should not be applicable to "data rendered anonymous in such a way that the data subject is no longer identifiable" Preamble # 26. As a result, the determination of the scope of "personal data" constitutes a crucial issue when enforcing data protection rules, particularly in the online context. Can an e-mail be considered a "personal data"? What about a dynamic IP address? Clickstream information? Cookies? Log files?

In which cases could a person be "indirectly" identified by reference to factors such as his "physical, physiological, mental, economic, cultural or social identity"? If a set of data does not refer to an identified or identifiable person, would there still be circumstances where this person's data could be considered "personal data"?

Compare the notion of "personal data" with the notion of "personally identifiable information" found in U.S. privacy laws. Are they identical?

3. *EU Data Directive Jurisdiction and Clickstream Data.* Article 4 provides jurisdictional criteria to determine the liability of data controllers. How could you determine such liability if the processing pertains to clickstream data that we assume as qualifying as "personal data"? Would an allocation not be preferable in such case? According to which criteria?

Consider Joel Reidenberg and Paul Schwartz:

> The clickstream data generated by on-line activities is initially processed by an Internet access or service provider. The bits and bytes are then shared with a myriad of parties to on-line service transactions. The localization of relevant processing activities may be quite variable. Consequently, the determination by various Member States of their authority to apply national law to all or parts of the clickstream will have a significant impact on the development of on-line services.[20]

4. *Electronic Communication and the Processing of Personal Data.* Personal data processed in connection with electronic communications are the subject of a specific directive (Directive 2002/58/EC concerning the processing of personal data and the protection of privacy in the electronic communications sector). This directive, the Directive on Privacy and Electronic

---

[20]Joel R. Reidenberg & Paul M. Schwartz, *Online Services and Data Protection Law: Regulatory Responses* (EUR-OP:1998) <*http://europa.eu.int/comm/internal_market/en/dataprot/studies/regul .htm*>.

Communications, establishes specific protections covering electronic mail, telephone communications, traffic data, calling line identification, and unsolicited communications. Member states are expected to transpose the Directive before October 31, 2002.

Like the EU Data Directive, the EU Directive on Privacy and Electronic Communications is intended to harmonize national law in Europe. As Article I explains:

> This Directive harmonises the provisions of the Member States required to ensure an equivalent level of protection of fundamental rights and freedoms, and in particular the right to privacy, with respect to the processing of personal data in the electronic communication sector and to ensure the free movement of such data and of electronic communication equipment and services in the Community.

The Directive sets out a strong presumption in favor of communications privacy:

> Article 5 - Confidentiality of the communications
> 1. Member States shall ensure the confidentiality of communications and the related traffic data by means of a public communications network and publicly available electronic communications services, through national legislation. In particular, they shall prohibit listening, tapping, storage or other kinds of interception or surveillance of communications and the related traffic data by persons other than users, without the consent of the users concerned, except when legally authorised to do so in accordance with Article 15(1). This paragraph shall not prevent technical storage which is necessary for the conveyance of a communication without prejudice to the principle of confidentiality.

But there has already been some dispute concerning the Article 15(1) provision that may allow for access to electronic communications. That provision states:

> Member States may adopt legislative measures to restrict the scope of the rights and obligations provided for in Article 5, Article 6, Article 8(1), (2), (3) and (4), and Article 9 of this Directive when such restriction constitutes a necessary, appropriate and proportionate measure within a democratic society to safeguard national security (i.e. State security), defence, public security, and the prevention, investigation, detection and prosecution of criminal offences or of unauthorised use of the electronic communication system, as referred to in Article 13(1) of Directive 95/46/EC. To this end, Member States may, inter alia, adopt legislative measures providing for the retention of data for a limited period justified on the grounds laid down in this paragraph. All the measures referred to in this paragraph shall be in accordance with the general principles of Community law, including those referred to in Article 6(1) and (2) of the Treaty on European Union.

Recall the approach taken in the United States under the Electronic Communications Privacy Act for interception (Chapter 4). How does that compare with the approach set out in the EU Directive? What about Article 8 of the European Convention of Human Rights?

5. *Location Data and Itemized Billing.* The Directive on Privacy and Electronic Communications contains several interesting new privacy provisions. Article 9 covers location data:

> 1. Where location data other than traffic data, relating to users or subscribers of public communications networks or publicly available electronic communications services, can be processed, such data may only be processed when they are made anonymous, or with the consent of the users or subscribers to the extent and for the duration necessary for the provision of a value added service. The service provider must inform the users or subscribers, prior to obtaining their consent, of the type of location data other than traffic data which will be processed, of the purposes and duration of the processing and whether the data will be transmitted to a third party for the purpose of providing the value added service. Users or subscribers shall be given the possibility to withdraw their consent for the processing of location data other than traffic data at any time.

Another provision concerns itemized billing:

> Article 7 - Itemised billing
> 1. Subscribers shall have the right to receive non-itemised bills.
> 2. Member States shall apply national provisions in order to reconcile the rights of subscribers receiving itemised bills with the right to privacy of calling users and called subscribers, for example by ensuring that sufficient alternative privacy enhancing methods of communications or payments are available to such users and subscribers.

How do these provisions compare with the EU Data Directive, the OECD Guidelines, or the various sectoral laws in the United States? Why do you think the European Union has adopted these specific measures?

6. *The EU Directive and Cookies.* Article 6 of the Privacy and Electronic Communications Directive regulates the collection of traffic data, including "cookies":

> 1. Traffic data relating to subscribers and users processed and stored by the provider of a public communications network or publicly available electronic communications service must be erased or made anonymous when it is no longer needed for the purpose of the transmission of a communication without prejudice to paragraphs 2, 3 and 5 of this Article and Article 15(1).
> 2. Traffic data necessary for the purposes of subscriber billing and interconnection payments may be processed. Such processing is permissible only up to the end of the period during which the bill may lawfully be challenged or payment pursued.

The provider may process the data for marketing purposes "if the subscriber or user to whom the data relate has given his/her consent." But users or subscribers must be given the opportunity to withdraw their consent for the processing of traffic data at any time and the service provider must inform the subscriber or user of the types of traffic data which are processed and of the duration of such processing, prior to obtaining consent.

What do you think the impact of the EU Directive on Privacy and Electronic Communications will be on the use of cookies? Are cookies still permissible?

7. ***Personal Data Under the OECD Guidelines.*** Consider also the definition of
"personal data" in the OECD Guidelines — "any information relating to an
identified or identifiable individual (data subject)." The explanatory memo
that follows the Guidelines states:

> The terms "personal data" and "data subject" serve to underscore that the
> Guidelines are concerned with physical persons. The precise dividing line be-
> tween personal data in the sense of information relating to identified or iden-
> tifiable individuals and anonymous data may be difficult to draw and must
> be left to the regulation of each Member country. In principle, personal data
> convey information which by direct (e.g. a civil registration number) or indi-
> rect linkages (e.g. an address) may be connected to a particular person.

   In another section of the explanatory memo, the OECD rejects an approach that would extend privacy protection to business enterprises, associations, and groups:

> [T]he Guidelines reflect the view that the notions of individual integrity and
> privacy are in many respects particular and not be treated in the same way as
> the integrity of a group of persons, or corporate security and confidentiality. . . .
> The scope of the Guidelines is therefore confined to data relating to individu-
> als and it is left to Member countries to draw dividing lines and decide policies
> with regard to corporations, groups, and similar bodies.

3. BASIC DATA PROCESSING PRINCIPLES

OECD GUIDELINES: BASIC PRINCIPLES

Collection Limitation Principle

There should be limits to the collection of personal data and any such data
should be obtained by lawful and fair means and, where appropriate, with the
knowledge or consent of the data subject.

Data Quality Principle

Personal data should be relevant to the purposes for which they are to be used,
and, to the extent necessary for those purposes, should be accurate, complete
and kept up-to-date.

Purpose Specification Principle

The purposes for which personal data are collected should be specified not
later than at the time of data collection and the subsequent use limited to the
fulfillment of those purposes or such others as are not incompatible with those
purposes and as are specified on each occasion of change of purpose.

Use Limitation Principle

Personal data should not be disclosed, made available or otherwise used for
purposes other than those specified in accordance with [the purpose specification principle] except: *a)* with the consent of the data subject; or *b)* by the
authority of law.

Security Safeguards Principle

Personal data should be protected by reasonable security safeguards against such risks as loss or unauthorised access, destruction, use, modification or disclosure of data.

Openness Principle

There should be a general policy of openness about developments, practices and policies with respect to personal data. Means should be readily available of establishing the existence and nature of personal data, and the main purposes of their use, as well as the identity and usual residence of the data controller.

Individual Participation

An individual should have the right:

a) to obtain from a data controller, or otherwise, confirmation of whether or not the data controller has data relating to him;

b) to have communicated to him, data relating to him (i) within a reasonable time; (ii) at a charge, if any, that is not excessive; (iii) in a reasonable manner; and (iv) in a form that is readily intelligible to him;

c) to be given reasons if a request made under subparagraphs*(a)* and *(b)* is denied, and to be able to challenge such denial; and

d) to challenge data relating to him and, if the challenge is successful to have the data erased, rectified, completed or amended.

Accountability Principle

A data controller should be accountable for complying with measures which give effect to the principles stated above. . . .

NOTES & QUESTIONS

1. *The OECD Guidelines and the Fair Information Practices.* How do the OECD Guidelines compare with the articulation of Fair Information Practices in the HEW Report of 1973 (Chapter 6)? Is either framework more comprehensive? More detailed? Which framework would be easier to comply with? To enforce?

   Several privacy commentators have observed that the concept of Fair Information Practices continues to play a vital role in understanding the development of information privacy law even though specific conceptions of the principles vary. David Flaherty has proposed more than a dozen principles that could be considered Fair Information Practices.[21]

2. The detailed explanatory memorandum of the OECD Privacy Guidelines may be found in Marc Rotenberg, ed., *Privacy Law Sourcebook* 329-352 (EPIC 2002).

3. *The Worldwide Influence of the OECD Guidelines.* The OECD Privacy Guidelines are nonbinding on members of the OECD. Nonetheless, they have had a significant impact on the development of national law in North America, Europe, and East Asia.[22]

---

[21] *See* David H. Flaherty, *Protecting Privacy in Surveillance Societies* (1989).

[22] For an analysis of privacy laws around the world, *see, e.g.,* EPIC & Privacy International, *Privacy and Human Rights* (2002); Banisar & Davies, *Global Trends in Privacy Protection, supra.*

For example, in Australia, a proposal in the mid-1980s to adopt a national identity card (called the "Australia Card") created a public outcry. The proposal was defeated, and as a result, Australia enacted a Privacy Act in 1988. The Act establishes 11 privacy principles based on the OECD Guidelines.[23]

New Zealand enacted a Privacy Act in 1993 that regulates information collection and use in both the public and private sectors. It adopts 12 principles based on the OECD Guidelines.

In Japan, a 1988 act regulates electronic personal information maintained by the government. The Act adopts many of the OECD Guidelines, including the collection limitation principle, the purpose specification principle, and the openness principle.

South Korea's Act on the Protection of Personal Information Managed by Public Agencies of 1994, which regulates electronic personal data maintained by the government, follows a number of OECD Guidelines such as the collection limitation principle, the data quality principle, the openness principle, and the purpose specification principle.

The privacy provisions in the U.S. Cable Act of 1984, discussed in Chapter 6, incorporate many of the elements of the OECD Guidelines. Why do you think the OECD Guidelines have had such a worldwide influence? In *Regulating Privacy,* Colin Bennett suggests that "policy convergence" has played a significant role in the development of privacy laws around the globe.[24] Do you think the Internet will further contribute to policy convergence?

EUROPEAN UNION DATA PROTECTION DIRECTIVE: ARTICLES 6-11

Principles Relating to Data Quality. Article 6 provides that Member States must ensure that data be (a) "processed fairly and lawfully"; (b) "collected for specified, explicit and legitimate purposes and not further processed in a way incompatible with those purposes"; (c) "adequate, relevant and not excessive in relation to the purposes for which they are collected and/or further processed"; (d) "accurate and, where necessary, kept up to date"; (e) "kept in a form which permits identification of data subjects for no longer than is necessary for the purposes for which the data were collected."

Criteria for Making Data Processing Legitimate. Under Article 7, before data may be processed, Member States must ensure that:

(a) the data subject has unambiguously given his consent; or

(b) processing is necessary for the performance of a contract to which the data subject is party or in order to take steps at the request of the data subject prior to entering into a contract; or

(c) processing is necessary for compliance with a legal obligation to which the controller is subject; or

(d) processing is necessary in order to protect the vital interests of the data subject; or

---

[23] Banisar & Davies, *Global Trends in Privacy Protection, supra,* at 18.
[24] Colin J. Bennett, *Regulating Privacy* (1992).

(e) processing is necessary for the performance of a task carried out in the public interest or in the exercise of official authority vested in the controller or in a third party to whom the data are disclosed; or

(f) processing is necessary for the purposes of the legitimate interests pursued by the controller or by the third party or parties to whom the data are disclosed, except where such interests are overridden by the interests for fundamental rights and freedoms of the data subject which require protection under Article 1.

Restricted Processing of Special Categories of Data. Article 8 restricts the processing of certain categories of personal data—"personal data revealing racial or ethnic origin, political opinions, religious or philosophical beliefs, trade-union membership, and the processing of data concerning health or sex life."

There are a number of exceptions. Such data may be processed if: (a) the data subject explicitly consents; (b) "processing is necessary for the purposes of carrying out the obligations and specific rights of the controller in the field of employment law in so far as it is authorized by national law providing for adequate safeguards"; (c) processing is necessary to safeguard the data subject's "vital interests"; (d) subject to certain limits, by an organization with a political, philosophical, religious, or trade union aim; (e) processing of data made public by the data subject or necessary to exercise or defend legal claims. Further, the Article 8 restrictions do not apply when the data are necessary "for the purposes of preventive medicine, medical diagnosis, the provision of care or treatment or the management of health-care services" and where the processing is by a health professional subject by national laws to maintain patient confidentiality.

Member States may, for reasons of "substantial public interest" make further exceptions to the ones included in Article 8. The Commission must be notified of all derogations.

Criminal Justice System Data Processing. Article 8 also provides special rules governing the processing of data relating to the criminal justice system:

> Processing of data relating to offences, criminal convictions or security measures may be carried out only under the control of official authority, or if suitable specific safeguards are provided under national law, subject to derogations which may be granted by the Member State under national provisions providing suitable specific safeguards. However, a complete register of criminal convictions may be kept only under the control of official authority. Article 8.5.

National Identification Numbers. The Directive leaves the issue of national identifiers to the discretion of Member States: "Member States shall determine the conditions under which a national identification number or any other identifier of general application may be processed." Article 8(7).

Processing of Personal Data and Freedom of Expression. Pursuant to Article 9, Member States may depart from the restrictions discussed above for the "processing of personal data carried out solely for journalistic purposes or the purpose of artistic or literary expression only if they are necessary to reconcile the right to privacy with the rules governing freedom of expression."

Notice to the Data Subject. When data are collected from the data subject, Article 10 provides that Member States must notify the data subject of the following information:

(a) the identity of the controller and of his representative, if any;
(b) the purposes of the processing for which the data are intended;
(c) any further information such as

— the recipients or categories of recipients of the data,
— whether replies to the questions are obligatory or voluntary, as well as the possible consequences of failure to reply,
— the existence of the right of access to and the right to rectify the data concerning him. . . .

According to Article 11, when data are collected about the data subject, but not obtained directly from her, Member States must either at the time the data are recorded or prior to the time the data are first disclosed to a third party notify the data subject of:

(a) the identity of the controller and of his representative, if any;
(b) the purposes of the processing;
(c) any further information such as

— the categories of data concerned,
— the recipients or categories of recipients,
— the existence of the right of access to and the right to rectify the data concerning him. . . .

Article 11 makes an exception to the notice if the data are processed "for statistical purposes or for the purposes of historical or scientific research" and the notification of the data subject would be impossible or very difficult. However, in these circumstances, Member States must "provide appropriate safeguards."

NOTES & QUESTIONS

1. *Opt-In Versus Opt-Out.* Does the EU Directive adopt an opt-in or opt-out regime? Why does the distinction not appear in the text?
2. *The Fair Information Practices, OECD Guidelines, and the EU Directive.* Can you reconcile the HEW Fair Information Practices with the EU Directive's provisions? How about the OECD Guidelines with the EU Directive's provisions?
3. *Article 8.* Article 8 of the Data Directive provides for a special treatment for data that are particularly sensitive to data subjects. Think about the data that are considered "sensitive" by the Directive. Would you have added more? Why are financial data not in the list? How does the EU Data Directive regulate children's personal data?
4. *Harmonization and Article 8.* Consider the following argument by Peter Swire:

> Although the Directive has led to significant convergence in data protection laws, harmonization is far from complete. Actual enforcement does not

take place under the Directive itself. Instead, national laws are being enacted to implement the Directive. These laws will differ in both large and small ways from each other. The level of enforcement effort will also undoubtedly vary by country, due both to differences in views about proper policy and differing levels of enforcement resources and experience. . . .

"Sensitive" data is defined in article 8 as "personal data revealing racial or ethnic origin, political opinions, religious or philosophical beliefs, trade-union membership, and the processing of data concerning health or sex life." The general provisions of article 8 are quite strict, banning all processing of sensitive data except in enumerated circumstances such as receiving "explicit consent" for processing from the individual. Moreover, several provisions in article 8 allow the Member State to set even stricter rules. For instance, Member States can provide that even with "explicit consent" they will not allow processing of categories of sensitive data.

The potential lack of harmonization on sensitive data may have more far-reaching implications than appear at first glance. The reason is that some sensitive data might be included in an enormous range of databases. For example, human resources records might easily include information about health insurance or trade-union membership. Credit card records and other payment information might reveal purchases of pharmaceuticals or other health-related purchases. Purchases from book stores, visits to web pages, or subscriptions to periodicals might reveal political opinions or religious affiliation. In all of these instances, a routine method for processing data, which otherwise complies with the Directive, might be subject to non-harmonized national laws that prohibit such processing. Organizations that design their systems for the ordinary case might not have an infrastructure in place to process sensitive data legally.[25]

5. In 2002 the United States Senate considered privacy legislation for the Internet that recognized a category of "Sensitive Personally Identifiable Information" and distinguished opt-in and opt-out requirements based on this dividing line. It is reasonable to conclude that the EU Data Directive had some influence on this legislative proposal in the United States Congress. In what other areas of privacy law would you anticipate a similar "dialogue" over the structure of new privacy regimes?

4. THE DATA SUBJECT'S RIGHTS

EUROPEAN UNION DATA PROTECTION DIRECTIVE: ARTICLES 12-15

Right of Access. Article 12(a) provides that every data subject be guaranteed the right to obtain from the data controller "at reasonable intervals and without excessive delay or expense" the following: (1) "confirmation as to whether or not data relating to him are being processed and information at least as to the purposes of the processing, the categories of data concerned, and the recipients or categories of recipients to whom the data are disclosed"; (2)

---

[25] Peter P. Swire, *Of Elephants, Mice, and Privacy: International Choice of Law and the Internet,* 32 Int'l L. 991, 1002-1003 (1998).

"communication to him in an intelligible form of the data undergoing processing and of any available information as to their source"; (3) "knowledge of the logic involved in any automatic processing of data concerning him at least in the case of the automated decisions referred to in Article 15 (1)."

Right to Correct Inaccurate Information. If data are incomplete or inaccurate, the data subject shall have the right to rectify, erase, or block the processing of the data. *See* Article 12(b). Further, any third parties to whom the data were disclosed shall be notified of the errors and restricted in the same manner from processing of the data. *See* Article 12(c).

Exemptions and Restrictions. Article 13 provides that Member State may restrict the scope of the obligations and rights provided for in Articles 6(1), 10, 11(1), 12, and 21 when it is necessary to protect:

> (a) national security;
> (b) defence;
> (c) public security;
> (d) the prevention, investigation, detection and prosecution of criminal offences, or of breaches of ethics for regulated professions;
> (e) an important economic or financial interest of a Member State or of the European Union, including monetary, budgetary and taxation matters;
> (f) a monitoring, inspection or regulatory function connected, even occasionally, with the exercise of official authority in cases referred to in (c), (d) and (e);
> (g) the protection of the data subject or of the rights and freedoms of others.

When data are processed for the purpose of scientific or statistical research, are not used to make decisions about the data subject, and "where there is clearly no risk of breaching the privacy of the data subject," member states may restrict by way of a legislative measure the rights provided for in Article 12.

Right to Object. Pursuant to Article 14, the data subject shall be granted the right to "object at any time on compelling legitimate grounds relating to his particular situation" in cases referred to in Article 7(e) (processing for tasks carried out in the public interest) and Article 7(f) (processing for legitimate interests pursued by the controller or third parties). If the objection is justified, the processing of the data subject's data must cease. *See* Article 14(a).

Additionally, the data subject can object to:

> the processing of personal data relating to him which the controller anticipates being processed for the purposes of direct marketing, or to be informed before personal data are disclosed for the first time to third parties or used on their behalf for the purposes of direct marketing, and to be expressly offered the right to object free of charge to such disclosures or uses. Article 14(b).

Member States must take measures to ensure that data subjects know about their rights to object.

Right Not to Be Subject to Certain Automated Decisions. An automated decision is one made based not on personal judgment but upon an automated processing technique using an individual's personal data. Article 15 of the

Directive restricts the instances in which automated decisions can be made about data subjects:

> Member States shall grant the right to every person not to be subject to a decision which produces legal effects concerning him or significantly affects him and which is based solely on automated processing of data intended to evaluate certain personal aspects relating to him, such as his performance at work, creditworthiness, reliability, conduct, etc. Article 15(1).

There are some exceptions: (1) if the automated decision is made pursuant to a contractual arrangement with the data subject; (2) if "there are suitable measures to safeguard his legitimate interests, such as arrangements allowing him to defend his point of view"; or (3) if it "is authorized by a law which also lays down measures to safeguard the data subject's legitimate interests."

NOTES & QUESTIONS

1. The right of access has always been a critical element of privacy laws. In the modern era, the Fair Credit Reporting Act of 1970 made the right to access a credit report a central feature of the statute. How does Article 12 in the EU Data Directive compare?
2. Article 12(1) contains this interesting provision: "Member States shall guarantee every data subject the right to obtain from the controller: . . . knowledge of the logic involved in any automatic processing of data concerning him at least in the case of the automated decisions referred to in Article 15 (1)." Why should a data subject have the right to access the "logic" of a data processing as well as the data? Are there any similar concepts in U.S. law?

5. SUPERVISORY AUTHORITY AND INDIVIDUAL REMEDIES

One of the most important differences between the European and U.S. privacy regimes is the general right for individuals whose privacy has been infringed by the violation of data protection rules to go before a judge to obtain compensation from the breaching company or individual. This is a general right established by the Directive. In the United States, such claims are typically based on sectoral privacy laws or common law privacy tort theories.

Another critical difference is the presence of "supervisory authorities"—privacy agencies that are responsible for investigating privacy complaints, issuing annual reports, and serving as a privacy ombudsman. There is no similar agency in the United States, although the Federal Trade Commission has played an increasingly important role in privacy matters.

EUROPEAN UNION DATA PROTECTION DIRECTIVE: ARTICLES 16-19, 21-23, 28

Confidentiality of Processing. Pursuant to Article 16:

> Any person acting under the authority of the controller or of the processor, including the processor himself, who has access to personal data must not process them except on instructions from the controller, unless he is required to do so by law.

Security of Processing. Under Article 17, the controller must implement appropriate measures to protect against accidental or unlawful destruction, loss, alteration, unauthorized disclosure, unauthorized access, and unlawful processing of personal data. "Having regard to the state of the art and the cost of their implementation, such measures shall ensure a level of security appropriate to the risks represented by the processing and the nature of the data to be protected." Article 17(1). The processing of data "must be governed by a contract or legal act binding the processor to the controller." The contract must state that "the processor shall act only on instructions from the controller" and that the processor implement appropriate measures to protect the security of the data as set forth in paragraph 1 of Article 17. Article 17(3).

Supervisory Authority. Article 28 requires that each Member State shall establish one or more public authorities to monitor the application of the laws and regulations adopted pursuant to the Directive. "These authorities shall act with complete independence in exercising the functions entrusted to them." Article 28(1). Supervisory authorities must be consulted when creating the rules and regulations for the protection of individuals' rights with regard to data processing. Article 28(2). The supervisory authority shall have the following powers: (1) investigative powers; (2) "effective powers of intervention"— the ability to express opinions before the carrying out of processing operations, the ability to order the blocking, erasure, or destruction of data, the ability to warn or admonish the controller, and the ability to refer the matter to national parliaments or other political institutions; and (3) powers to engage in legal proceedings when rules and regulations adopted pursuant to the Directive are violated. If the supervisory authority's decisions are objected to, they may be appealed in the courts. Article 28(3).

The supervisory authority shall hear individual claims concerning the protection of her rights regarding the processing of personal data. Article 28(4). Further, the supervisory authority shall "hear claims for checks on the lawfulness of data processing lodged by any person when the national provisions adopted pursuant to Article 13 of this Directive apply." Article 28(4). The supervisory authority must issue public reports on its activities at regular intervals. Article 28(5).

Members and staff of the supervisory authority must be subject to a "duty of processional secrecy with regard to confidential information to which they have access." This duty applies even after their employment has terminated. Article 28(7).

Obligation to Notify the Supervisory Authority. Under Article 18, the "controller" (the entity determining the purposes of the data processing) must notify the "supervisory authority" before carrying out any partly or wholly automatic processing operation. If certain conditions are met, Member States may enact rules exempting controllers from notifying the supervisory authority (or simplifying the notification). Such conditions include: (1) where processing operations are unlikely to "affect adversely the rights and freedoms of data subjects" and Member States have specified detailed information concerning the processing; (2) where the controller appoints a "personal data protection official" who is responsible for "ensuring in an independent manner the internal application of the national provisions taken pursuant to this Directive" and "for keeping the register of processing operations carried out by the controller, containing the items of information referred to in Article 21(2)."

Contents of the Notification to the Supervisory Authority. Article 19 describes the contents of the notification to the supervisory authority as required by Article 18. The notification must include

> (a) the name and address of the controller and of his representative, if any;
> (b) the purpose or purposes of the processing;
> (c) a description of the category or categories of data subject and of the data or categories of data relating to them;
> (d) the recipients or categories of recipient to whom the data might be disclosed;
> (e) proposed transfers of data to third countries;
> (f) a general description allowing a preliminary assessment to be made of the appropriateness of the measures taken pursuant to Article 17 to ensure security of processing.

Publicizing of Processing Obligations. Pursuant to Article 21, Member States must publicize processing operations. Further:

> Member States shall provide that a register of processing operations notified in accordance with Article 18 shall be kept by the supervisory authority. The register shall contain at least the information listed in Article 19 (1) (a) to (e). The register may be inspected by any person. . . . Article 21(2).

Individual Remedies. Pursuant to Article 22, "Member States shall provide for the right of every person to a judicial remedy for any breach of the rights guaranteed him by the national law applicable to the processing in question."

Further, Article 23 requires that Member States "shall provide that any person who has suffered damage as a result of an unlawful processing operation or of any act incompatible with the national provisions adopted pursuant to this Directive is entitled to receive compensation from the controller for the damage suffered."

NOTES & QUESTIONS

1. ***A U.S. Data Protection Authority?*** Would you support the creation of a federal data protection authority in the United States? What are the benefits and drawbacks of such an authority? What alternatives to a privacy agency exist and how would you measure their effectiveness?[26]
2. ***The FTC as a Data Protection Authority?*** Steven Hetcher argues that the Federal Trade Commission is evolving into a federal data protection authority:

> In the short history of the Internet, there has been a major shift — a norm cascade — toward norms that are more respectful of privacy. The transition

---

[26] For the background on the proposal to create a federal privacy agency in the United States, see Marc Rotenberg, *In Support of a Data Protection Board in the United States,* 8 Gov't Info. Q. 79-94 (Spring 1991).

has been from a Wild West world in which Web sites acted with near impunity in collecting whatever personal data they could, to a world in which a significant percentage of Web sites are explicitly addressing privacy concerns. . . .

Reacting to this sub-optimal social situation, the FTC promoted the fair information practice principles. The FTC then used threats to induce Web sites to adopt these principles. The FTC created a large-scale collective action problem for the Web site industry, where none had existed before. It did this by creating a collective good that the industry would be interested to promote, the avoidance of congressional legislation. The agency threatened to push for legislation unless the industry demonstrated greater respect for privacy. Some of the large sites in turn threatened to withhold advertising from smaller sites with whom they do business, if these sites were not more respectful of consumer privacy. The result of this network of threats by the FTC and large Web sites is a new situation in which there is no longer a uniform norm of disrespect for privacy. . . . On the whole, this represents a significant increase in the degree to which Web sites are subject to governmental regulation with regard to their data-collection practices. Accordingly, the FTC is fairly viewed as a nascent, de facto federal privacy commission.[27]

Recall the cases you read about in Chapter 6 involving the FTC's enforcement efforts of privacy policies. Has the FTC performed well in its current role? How would you compare the FTC's authority to investigate unfair or deceptive trade practices with European data protection authority to enforce substantive provisions in the EU Data Directive?

One example of the limitations in the FTC's jurisdiction is the issue of workplace privacy. Jack Karns argues that a special agency should be created to address issues involving privacy in the workplace. Karns argues: "With the evolution of privacy rights under common law concepts, it has been a difficult transition to bring within the reach of traditional legal theories modern methods of conducting business transactions and handling personal matters." Karns further contends that the FTC is not the appropriate agency to handle these problems:

As for current agencies, such as the Federal Trade Commission ("FTC"), this body is charged with regulating unfair and deceptive trade, and this creates the question as to whether privacy protection falls within this agency's enabling legislation. The business community, in general, supports the delegation of work related privacy issues to the FTC given its well established involvement in business regulation. But is this position self serving, and would it really protect the worker adequately?. . . . [T]he FTC is not well situated to take on this aspect of the regulatory task and that a comparable consumer and worker oriented agency with separate and distinct enabling legislation is needed to protect fundamental constitutional rights in this area.[28]

---

[27] Steven Hetcher, *The De Facto Federal Privacy Commission,* 19 J. Marshall J. Computer & Info. L. 109, 130-131 (2000).

[28] Jack Karns, *Protecting Individual Online Privacy Rights: Making the Case for a Separately Dedicated, Independent Regulatory Agency,* 19 J. Marshall J. Computer & Info. L. 93, 95-96 (2000).

3. ***Effective Privacy Regimes.*** There is a complicated interplay between rights of private enforcement and authority granted to public agencies. It is possible to construct privacy regimes that make private enforcement impractical and agency oversight ineffective. What lessons might be learned from the experience in the United States, Europe, and elsewhere about the development of effective privacy regimes?[29]

4. ***Privacy Commissioners in Other Countries.*** In addition to EU countries, a number of other countries have privacy commissioners. For example, similar to the United States, Canada has a Privacy Act to regulate personal information in government records (*see* Chapter 6 for the U.S. Privacy Act). The Canadian Privacy Act adopts many of the Fair Information Practices. In contrast to the U.S. Privacy Act, the Canadian version is supervised by a privacy commissioner, who can investigate complaints and initiate judicial review. Canada also has privacy commissioners for each of its provinces. New Zealand's Privacy Act establishes a privacy commissioner with independent oversight powers. Switzerland's 1992 Federal Act of Data Protection establishes a Federal Data Protection Commission. Hong Kong's Personal Data (Privacy) Ordinance, which became effective in 1996, created the Office of the Privacy Commissioner. The Privacy Commissioner has significant powers; the Commissioner can initiate investigations, require the users of personal data to publicize how their data is processed, and issue codes to facilitate compliance with the Ordinance.[30] For several years, the Privacy Commissioner of Hong Kong was one of the most effective in the world.

C. INTERNATIONAL TRANSFERS OF DATA

We live today in a global economy that is becoming increasingly dependent upon information. The Internet has enabled a dramatic increase in international communication and commerce. As a result, personal information increasingly flows across the borders of different nations around the world. Each nation has its own set of privacy laws and regulations. This raises at least two difficulties. First, differing levels of protection might interfere with the smooth and efficient flow of personal information between countries. There is thus a need for harmonization or convergence of approaches to regulating the processing of personal data. Second, countries seeking to protect the privacy of their citizens must depend upon the protections accorded by other countries since a vast amount of personal data flows out of its borders to these other countries. The OECD Guidelines and the EU Data Directive both contain rules for transborder data flows — the flow of information between different countries.[31]

---

[29] *See generally* EPIC & Privacy International, *Privacy and Human Rights: An International Survey of Privacy Laws and Developments* (EPIC 2002).

[30] For more information about Hong Kong's privacy commissioner, see <*http://www.pco .org.hk*>.

[31] For more about transborder data flows, see Joel R. Reidenberg, *Resolving Conflicting International Data Privacy Rules in Cyberspace,* 52 Stan. L. Rev. 1315 (2000).

1. ADEQUATE LEVEL OF PROTECTION

OECD GUIDELINES: TRANSBORDER DATA FLOWS

Domestic Processing. OECD Guideline 15 provides that "Member countries should take into consideration the implications for other Member countries of domestic processing and re-export of personal data."

Security of Transborder Data Flows. Member countries should ensure that transborder data flows (including transit through the member country) are "uninterrupted and secure."

Restrictions on Transborder Data Flows. Member countries should avoid restricting transborder data flows with another member country except if that country "does not yet substantially observe these Guidelines or where the re-export of such data would circumvent its domestic privacy legislation." If a member country has protections of certain categories of personal data and another member country has no equivalent protection, then the member country may impose restrictions on the transborder flows of these categories of data.

Openness of Transborder Data Flows. Member countries should avoid adopting measures in the name of protecting privacy "which would create obstacles to transborder flows of personal data that would exceed requirements for such protection." In other words, protection of privacy affecting transborder data flows must be well-tailored to protect the privacy interests involved and must not be overbroad.

EUROPEAN UNION DATA PROTECTION DIRECTIVE: ARTICLES 25-26, 29-30

Transborder Data Flows. Article 25 governs when Member States may permit the flow of personal data to other countries. This provision has particular relevance for the United States, because it governs the level of privacy protections other countries must have in place for data transfers to occur:

1. The Member States shall provide that the transfer to a third country of personal data which are undergoing processing or are intended for processing after transfer may take place only if, without prejudice to compliance with the national provisions adopted pursuant to the other provisions of this Directive, the third country in question ensures an adequate level of protection.

2. The adequacy of the level of protection afforded by a third country shall be assessed in the light of all the circumstances surrounding a data transfer operation or set of data transfer operations; particular consideration shall be given to the nature of the data, the purpose and duration of the proposed processing operation or operations, the country of origin and country of final destination, the rules of law, both general and sectoral, in force in the third country in question and the professional rules and security measures which are complied with in that country.

3. The Member States and the Commission shall inform each other of cases where they consider that a third country does not ensure an adequate level of protection within the meaning of paragraph 2.

4. Where the Commission finds, under the procedure provided for in Article 31 (2), that a third country does not ensure an adequate level of protection within the meaning of paragraph 2 of this Article, Member States shall take the measures necessary to prevent any transfer of data of the same type to the third country in question.

5. At the appropriate time, the Commission shall enter into negotiations with a view to remedying the situation resulting from the finding made pursuant to paragraph 4.

6. The Commission may find, in accordance with the procedure referred to in Article 31 (2), that a third country ensures an adequate level of protection within the meaning of paragraph 2 of this Article, by reason of its domestic law or of the international commitments it has entered into, particularly upon conclusion of the negotiations referred to in paragraph 5, for the protection of the private lives and basic freedoms and rights of individuals.

Member States shall take the measures necessary to comply with the Commission's decision.

Derogations. Article 26(1) provides for certain exceptions to Article 25. Transfers of personal data to a third party country that does not ensure an adequate level of protection under Article 25(2) may still take place on condition that:

(a) the data subject has given his consent unambiguously to the proposed transfer; or

(b) the transfer is necessary for the performance of a contract between the data subject and the controller or the implementation of precontractual measures taken in response to the data subject's request; or

(c) the transfer is necessary for the conclusion or performance of a contract concluded in the interest of the data subject between the controller and a third party; or

(d) the transfer is necessary or legally required on important public interest grounds, or for the establishment, exercise or defence of legal claims; or

(e) the transfer is necessary in order to protect the vital interests of the data subject; or

(f) the transfer is made from a register which according to laws or regulations is intended to provide information to the public and which is open to consultation either by the public in general or by any person who can demonstrate legitimate interest, to the extent that the conditions laid down in law for consultation are fulfilled in the particular case.

A Member State may also authorize transfers of personal data to third countries without an adequate level of protection where protection of the privacy and individual freedoms "result from appropriate contractual clauses." Article 26(2). If a Member State does authorize such a transfer, it must notify the Commission and other Member States. Member States or the Commission may object, and the Commission may take appropriate measures following the procedure in Article 31(2). "Where the Commission decides, in accordance with the procedure referred to in Article 31(2), that certain standard contractual clauses offer sufficient safeguards as required by paragraph 2, Member States shall take the necessary measures to comply with the Commission's decision."

Working Party. Article 29 provides for the creation of a "Working Party on the Protection of Individuals with regard to the Processing of Personal Data."

The Working Party "shall have advisory status and act independently." It shall be composed of a representative of the supervisory authorities in each Member State and a representative of the Commission. Decisions made by the Working Party are made by a simple majority of the representatives. The Working Party elects a chairman who serves for two years.[32]

Article 30 describes the tasks of the Working Party. The Working Party, among other things: (1) examines questions concerning the uniform application of national measures adopted under the Directive; (2) provides an opinion to the Commission on the level of protection in the Community and in third countries; and (3) advises the Committee on any additional measures to safeguard the rights of individuals with regard to data processing. The Working Party should inform the Commission of any "divergences likely to affect the equivalence of protection for persons with regard to the processing of personal data in the Community." The Commission must inform the Working Party of the action it takes in response to the Working Party's recommendations in a public report. The Working Party also must draw up an annual public report regarding the protections regarding processing of personal data in the Community and in third countries.

NOTES & QUESTIONS

1. *Article 25.* Article 25 enables the European Union to block the transfer of personal information on European citizens processed in third party countries that fails to meet the requirements of "adequacy." What do you think the reason is behind this requirement? Is this an example of an "extra-territorial" application of European law? To what extent do the United States and other countries regulate the practices of companies based elsewhere, but providing goods and services in domestic markets?

2. *Adequate Level of Protection.* Adequate protection does not necessarily mean "equivalent" protection. The Article 31 Committee has provided some clarifications on the meaning of "adequate" protection.

> For its part, the Committee regards it as necessary to be even-handed in implementing the provisions of the Directive that deal with third countries. The Committee express its commitment to the principle of non-discrimination and recall that the general principle of equality, of which the prohibition of discrimination on grounds of nationality is a specific enunciation, is one of the fundamental principles of Community law. This principle requires that similar situations shall not be treated differently unless differentiation is objectively justified. The Committee also recalls obligations emanating from other international instruments, in particular the European Convention of Human Rights. Article 14 of the ECHR requires that the rights and freedoms set forth in the Convention (which include the right to respect for privacy — Article 8) be secured without discrimination on any ground, including *inter alia* national origin.
>
> The Committee also regards it as important to be able to judge different situations on their merits and not to regard the equal treatment principle as

---

[32] Several recent reports from the Article 29 Working Party can be found in Marc Rotenberg, *Privacy Law Sourcebook* 434-559 (EPIC 2002).

imposing a single model on third countries. Such an interpretation of the principle would fly in the face of the deliberately flexible wording of Article 25 (which requires "adequate" protection in third countries and which allows circumstances to be judged on a case by case basis) and of the need to take into account different countries' varied approaches to achieving effective data protection. This approach means that adequacy findings may sometimes be made despite certain weaknesses in a particular system, provided of course that such a system can be assessed as adequate overall, for example because of compensating strengths in other areas. The principle of equal treatment does not mean that allowances made to take account of the particular traditions of one country, as described above, are automatically applicable to or acceptable in the cases of other third countries. It does mean that assessments of adequacy should be made broadly by reference to the same standard. . . .[33]

How is the "adequacy" determination made, i.e., what factors are considered?

3. *Canada's Personal Information Protection and Electronic Documents Act (PIPEDA).* In 2001, a sweeping new privacy law became effective in Canada. The Act, called the Personal Information Protection and Electronic Documents Act (PIPEDA), S.C. 2000 ch. 5 (Can.), governs all entities that collect personal information on Canadians. PIPEDA phases in its protections, and in 2004, it will extend to all "personal information" used in connection with any commercial activity. *Id.* § 4(1)-(2). The Act applies to all personal information collected prior to the enactment of PIPEDA, and it does not exempt non-Canadian entities. The PIPEDA is based on the OECD Guidelines and the Canadian Standards Association (CSA) Model Code for the Protection of Personal Information, which articulated ten privacy principles. PIPEDA requires that the individual must consent prior the collection, use, or disclosure of personal data. *See id.* sched. 1, § 4.3. It also incorporates the OECD purpose specification principle, security safeguard principle, openness principle, accountability principle, and data quality principle, among others.

On December 20, 2001, the EU Commission issued a Decision that Canada's PIPEDA provides an adequate level of protection:

> The Canadian Act covers all the basic principles necessary for an adequate level of protection for natural persons, even if exceptions and limitations are also provided for in order to safeguard important public interests and to recognize certain information which exists in the public domain. The application of these standards is guaranteed by judicial remedy and by independent supervision carried out by the authorities, such as the Federal Privacy Commissioner invested with powers of investigation and intervention. Furthermore, the provisions of Canadian law regarding civil liability apply in the event of unlawful processing which is prejudicial to the persons concerned.[34]

---

[33] Text on Non-Discrimination adopted by the Article 31 Committee (May 31, 2000).

[34] Commission Decision of 20 December 2001 Pursuant to Directive 95/46/EC of the European Parliament and of the Council on the Adequate Protection of Personal Data Provided by the Canadian Personal Information Protection and Electronic Documents Act, C(2001) 4539, available at <*http://www.europa.eu.int/comm/internal_market/en/dataprot/adequacy/index.htm*>.

PIPEDA may have substantial effects on transborder flows between Canada and the United States. According to some commentators:

> Although Canada's privacy laws certainly apply to covered organizations located in Canada, a more difficult question is raised when trying to determine their effects on companies located solely within the United States that happen to collect, use, or disclose the personal information of Canadians. . . . PIPEDA will certainly affect American companies. This is because of PIPEDA's secondary data transfer requirements which force Canadian companies to incorporate the Act's privacy requirements into all contracts which contemplate the transfer of Canadians' personal information to U.S. or other foreign companies. But to date Canadian law provides mixed guidance on how it will address the extraterritorial effects of the Act.[35]

4. ***The Effects of the EU Data Directive on Other Countries.*** Consider the following observation by Peter Swire:

> The Directive undoubtedly increases the level of harmonization within the European Union by requiring every Member State to create a data protection agency and implement detailed statutes. In some significant, but difficult to measure way, passage of the Directive has also put pressure on other countries to adopt similar legislation. A wide range of countries with extensive trade relations with the European Union might be found to lack adequate protection of privacy and thus might encounter limits on the transfers of personal information. The last few years have seen data protection laws enacted or seriously considered in European countries outside of the European Union and in far-flung countries such as Argentina, Brazil, Canada, and New Zealand. In conversations with persons knowledgeable about these developments, it is clear that the Directive has played a prominent role in encouraging such legislation. The possible finding of inadequate protection has also been used as an argument for enacting new privacy legislation in the United States.[36]

How did the United States respond to the EU Data Directive? Consider the materials in the next section.

2. SAFE HARBOR ARRANGEMENT BETWEEN THE EUROPEAN UNION AND THE UNITED STATES

There are substantial differences in the privacy protections set out in the OECD Guidelines/EU Directive and the approach in the United States. Pursuant to Article 25 of the EU Directive, transfers of personal data about European citizens can be blocked if third party countries (such as the United States) do not provide "an adequate level of protection."

---

[35] Juliana M. Spaeth, Mark J. Plotkin & Sandra C. Sheets, *Privacy, Eh!: The Impact of Canada's Personal Information Protection and Electronic Documents Act on Transnational Business,* 4 Vand. J. Ent. L. & Prac. 29 (2002).

[36] Peter P. Swire, *Of Elephants, Mice, and Privacy: International Choice of Law and the Internet,* 32 Intl. L. 991, 1002 (1998).

As Joel Reidenberg observes:

The European Directive exerts significant pressure on U.S. information rights, practices and policies. The Directive facilitates a single information market place within Europe through a harmonized set of rules, but also forces scrutiny of US data privacy. In this context, the lack of legal protection for privacy in the United States threatens the flow of personal information from Europe to the United States. At the same time, the EU Directive is having an important influence on privacy protection around the world and leaves Americans with legal protections as second class citizens in the global marketplace. . . .

The European Directive requires the national supervisory authorities in each of the Member States and the European Commission to make comparisons between European data protection principles and foreign standards of fair information practice. The European Directive further requires that foreign standards of fair information practice be "adequate" in order to permit transfers of personal information to the foreign destination.

For the United States, this means that both national supervisory authorities and the European Commission must assess the level of protection offered in the United States to data of European origin. Because the United States lacks directly comparable, comprehensive data protection legislation, the assessment of "adequacy" is necessarily complex. The European Commission and national supervisory authorities recognize that the context of information processing must be considered to make any determination of "adequacy."

Under the European Directive, the national data protection supervisory authorities and the European Commission must report to each other the non-European countries that do not provide adequate protection. This bifurcated assessment of foreign standards means that intra-European politics can play a significant role in the evaluation of US data practices. While a European level decision is supposed to apply in each Member State, the national supervisory authorities are independent agencies and will still have a degree of interpretive power over any individual case.

The end result for the United States and for American companies is that US corporate information practices are under scrutiny in Europe and under threat of disruption when fair information processing standards are not applied to protect European data. Some commentators have predicted that any European export prohibition might spark a trade war that Europe could lose before the new World Trade Organization. While, in theory, such a situation is possible, an adverse WTO ruling is unlikely.

Even with the difficulties of the European approach, countries elsewhere are looking at the European Directive as the basic model for information privacy, and significant legislative movements toward European-style data protection exist in Canada, South America, and Eastern Europe. . . . In effect, Europe through the European Directive has displaced the role that the United States held since the famous Warren and Brandeis article in setting the global privacy agenda. . . .[37]

While Reidenberg prefers the approach of the EU Data Directive and welcomes it as a great incentive to improve U.S. privacy law as well as privacy reg-

---

[37]Joel Reidenberg, *The EU Data Protection Directive: Implications for the U.S. Privacy Debate* (2001), available at <*http://energycommerce.house.gov/107/hearings/03082001Hearing49/Reidenberg 104.htm*>.

ulation around the world, Peter Swire and Robert Litan are less sanguine about the Data Directive. According to Swire and Litan, "there is also the possibility that strict data protection rules in Europe, coupled with less strict rules in other countries, will pose a competitive disadvantage for Europe. The risk is that Europe will fall behind in creating the information society." [38] One possible solution would be for the United States to adopt comprehensive privacy legislation. Swire and Litan observe that "[t]o American sensibilities . . . [adopting omnibus privacy legislation] might easily seem an unnecessary regulatory intrusion into how an organization should manage its own information." [39] As a result, the authors note, the EU will be forced to compromise: "As it has become more clear to the Europeans that the United States and other countries will not pass comprehensive privacy laws, European officials have become more willing to find workable contract and other [self-regulatory] solutions." [40]

In response to Swire and Litan, Robert Gellman argues that self-regulatory solutions will be inadequate:

> The United States is now awash in overlapping privacy self-regulatory mechanisms that were developed at great expense and with great effort. Yet not one of them meets all of the fair information practices included in the Directive. It is unclear whether market forces alone can produce an adequate form of self-regulation or can induce anyone but major international players to comply. Contracts may be even more expensive and more complicated. Multinational companies like IBM and EDS may require thousands of contracts and an army of lawyers to satisfy EU regulators. [41]

Reidenberg contends that although the EU must make compromises, the United States must also make some as well:

> For the European side, the United States posed a major problem. American law did not provide comparable protections to European standards, and fair information practices in the United States were rather spotty. Yet, European regulators did not want to cause a disruption in international data flows. The prospect of change in U.S. law seemed remote, and the European Commission would have serious political difficulty insisting on an enforcement action against data processing in the United States prior to the full implementation of the European Directive within the European Union. Similarly, while transposition remained incomplete, an aggressive enforcement strategy by a national supervisory authority could have hampered the national legislative debates on transposition. Safe Harbor offered a mechanism to delay facing tough decisions about international privacy and, in the meantime, hopefully advance U.S. privacy protections for European data.
>
> On the U.S. side, the Department of Commerce faced strong pressure from the American business community to block the European Directive. The United States was not prepared to respond to the Directive with new privacy rights and wanted to prevent interruptions in transborder data flows. Safe

---

[38] Peter P. Swire & Robert E. Litan, *None of Your Business: World Data Flows, Electronic Commerce, and the European Privacy Directive* 151 (1998).

[39] *Id.* at 178.

[40] *Id.* at 173.

[41] Robert Gellman, *Book Review,* 32 Geo. Wash J. Intl. L. & Econ. 179, 186 (1999) (reviewing Swire & Litan, *None of Your Business*).

Harbor became a mechanism to avoid a showdown judgment on the status of American law and defer action against any American companies.[42]

In 1998, the U.S. Department of Commerce began negotiations with the EU Commission to formulate a "safe harbor" agreement to ensure that the United States met the EU Data Directive's "adequacy" requirement in Article 25. In July 2000, the negotiations yielded the Safe Harbor Arrangement as well as other supportive documents elaborating on the principles, such as letters and a list of Frequently Asked Questions.

(a) Safe Harbor Arrangement: Basic Principles

SAFE HARBOR PRIVACY PRINCIPLES

U.S. Department of Commerce (July 21, 2000)

The European Union's comprehensive privacy legislation, the Directive on Data Protection (the Directive), became effective on October 25, 1998. It requires that transfers of personal data take place only to non-EU countries that provide an "adequate" level of privacy protection. While the United States and the European Union share the goal of enhancing privacy protection for their citizens, the United States takes a different approach to privacy from that taken by the European Union. The United States uses a sectoral approach that relies on a mix of legislation, regulation, and self-regulation. Given those differences, many U.S. organizations have expressed uncertainty about the impact of the EU-required "adequacy standard" on personal data transfers from the European Union to the United States.

To diminish this uncertainty and provide a more predictable framework for such data transfers, the Department of Commerce is issuing this document and Frequently Asked Questions ("the Principles") under its statutory authority to foster, promote, and develop international commerce. The Principles were developed in consultation with industry and the general public to facilitate trade and commerce between the United States and European Union. They are intended for use solely by U.S. organizations receiving personal data from the European Union for the purpose of qualifying for the safe harbor and the presumption of "adequacy" it creates. Because the Principles were solely designed to serve this specific purpose, their adoption for other purposes may be inappropriate. The Principles cannot be used as a substitute for national provisions implementing the Directive that apply to the processing of personal data in the Member States.

Decisions by organizations to qualify for the safe harbor are entirely voluntary, and organizations may qualify for the safe harbor in different ways. Organizations that decide to adhere to the Principles must comply with the Principles in order to obtain and retain the benefits of the safe harbor and publicly declare that they do so. For example, if an organization joins a self-regulatory privacy program that adheres to the Principles, it qualifies for the safe harbor.

---

[42]Joel R. Reidenberg, *E-Commerce and Trans-Atlantic Privacy,* 38 Hous. L. Rev. 717, 739-740 (2001).

Organizations may also qualify by developing their own self-regulatory privacy policies provided that they conform with the Principles. Where in complying with the Principles, an organization relies in whole or in part on self-regulation, its failure to comply with such self-regulation must also be actionable under Section 5 of the Federal Trade Commission Act prohibiting unfair and deceptive acts or another law or regulation prohibiting such acts. *(See the annex for the list of U.S. statutory bodies recognized by the EU.)* In addition, organizations subject to a statutory, regulatory, administrative or other body of law (or of rules) that effectively protects personal privacy may also qualify for safe harbor benefits. In all instances, safe harbor benefits are assured from the date on which each organization wishing to qualify for the safe harbor self-certifies to the Department of Commerce (or its designee) its adherence to the Principles in accordance with the guidance set forth in the Frequently Asked Question on Self-Certification.

Adherence to these Principles may be limited: (a) to the extent necessary to meet national security, public interest, or law enforcement requirements; (b) by statute, government regulation, or case law that create conflicting obligations or explicit authorizations, provided that, in exercising any such authorization, an organization can demonstrate that its non-compliance with the Principles is limited to the extent necessary to meet the overriding legitimate interests furthered by such authorization; or (c) if the effect of the Directive or Member State law is to allow exceptions or derogations, provided such exceptions or derogations are applied in comparable contexts. Consistent with the goal of enhancing privacy protection, organizations should strive to implement these Principles fully and transparently, including indicating in their privacy policies where exceptions to the Principles permitted by (b) above will apply on a regular basis. For the same reason, where the option is allowable under the Principles and/or U.S. law, organizations are expected to opt for the higher protection where possible.

Organizations may wish for practical or other reasons to apply the Principles to all their data processing operations, but they are only obligated to apply them to data transferred after they enter the safe harbor. To qualify for the safe harbor, organizations are not obligated to apply these Principles to personal information in manually processed filing systems. Organizations wishing to benefit from the safe harbor for receiving information in manually processed filing systems from the EU must apply the Principles to any such information transferred after they enter the safe harbor. An organization that wishes to extend safe harbor benefits to human resources personal information transferred from the EU for use in the context of an employment relationship must indicate this when it self-certifies to the Department of Commerce (or its designee) and conform to the requirements set forth in the Frequently Asked Question on Self-Certification. Organizations will also be able to provide the safeguards necessary under Article 26 of the Directive if they include the Principles in written agreements with parties transferring data from the EU for the substantive privacy provisions, once the other provisions for such model contracts are authorized by the Commission and the Member States.

U.S. law will apply to questions of interpretation and compliance with the Safe Harbor Principles (including the Frequently Asked Questions) and relevant privacy policies by safe harbor organizations, except where organizations have committed to cooperate with European Data Protection Authorities. Unless otherwise stated, all provisions of the Safe Harbor Principles and Frequently Asked Questions apply where they are relevant.

"Personal data" and "personal information" are data about an identified or identifiable individual that are within the scope of the Directive, received by a U.S. organization from the European Union, and recorded in any form.

NOTICE: An organization must inform individuals about the purposes for which it collects and uses information about them, how to contact the organization with any inquiries or complaints, the types of third parties to which it discloses the information, and the choices and means the organization offers individuals for limiting its use and disclosure. This notice must be provided in clear and conspicuous language when individuals are first asked to provide personal information to the organization or as soon thereafter as is practicable, but in any event before the organization uses such information for a purpose other than that for which it was originally collected or processed by the transferring organization or discloses it for the first time to a third party.[43]

CHOICE: An organization must offer individuals the opportunity to choose (opt out) whether their personal information is (a) to be disclosed to a third party or (b) to be used for a purpose that is incompatible with the purpose(s) for which it was originally collected or subsequently authorized by the individual. Individuals must be provided with clear and conspicuous, readily available, and affordable mechanisms to exercise choice.

For sensitive information (i.e. personal information specifying medical or health conditions, racial or ethnic origin, political opinions, religious or philosophical beliefs, trade union membership or information specifying the sex life of the individual), they must be given affirmative or explicit (opt in) choice if the information is to be disclosed to a third party or used for a purpose other than those for which it was originally collected or subsequently authorized by the individual through the exercise of opt in choice. In any case, an organization should treat as sensitive any information received from a third party where the third party treats and identifies it as sensitive.

ONWARD TRANSFER: To disclose information to a third party, organizations must apply the Notice and Choice Principles. Where an organization wishes to transfer information to a third party that is acting as an agent, as described in the endnote, it may do so if it first either ascertains that the third party subscribes to the Principles or is subject to the Directive or another adequacy finding or enters into a written agreement with such third party requiring that the third party provide at least the same level of privacy protection as is required by the relevant Principles. If the organization complies with these requirements, it shall not be held responsible (unless the organization agrees otherwise) when a third party to which it transfers such information processes it in a way contrary to any restrictions or representations, unless the organization knew or should have known the third party would process it in such a

---

[43] It is not necessary to provide notice or choice when disclosure is made to a third party that is acting as an agent to perform task(s) on behalf of and under the instructions of the organization. The Onward Transfer Principle, on the other hand, does apply to such disclosures.

contrary way and the organization has not taken reasonable steps to prevent or stop such processing.

SECURITY: Organizations creating, maintaining, using or disseminating personal information must take reasonable precautions to protect it from loss, misuse and unauthorized access, disclosure, alteration and destruction.

DATA INTEGRITY: Consistent with the Principles, personal information must be relevant for the purposes for which it is to be used. An organization may not process personal information in a way that is incompatible with the purposes for which it has been collected or subsequently authorized by the individual. To the extent necessary for those purposes, an organization should take reasonable steps to ensure that data is reliable for its intended use, accurate, complete, and current.

ACCESS: Individuals must have access to personal information about them that an organization holds and be able to correct, amend, or delete that information where it is inaccurate, except where the burden or expense of providing access would be disproportionate to the risks to the individual's privacy in the case in question, or where the rights of persons other than the individual would be violated.

ENFORCEMENT: Effective privacy protection must include mechanisms for assuring compliance with the Principles, recourse for individuals to whom the data relate affected by non-compliance with the Principles, and consequences for the organization when the Principles are not followed. At a minimum, such mechanisms must include (a) readily available and affordable independent recourse mechanisms by which each individual's complaints and disputes are investigated and resolved by reference to the Principles and damages awarded where the applicable law or private sector initiatives so provide; (b) follow up procedures for verifying that the attestations and assertions businesses make about their privacy practices are true and that privacy practices have been implemented as presented; and (c) obligations to remedy problems arising out of failure to comply with the Principles by organizations announcing their adherence to them and consequences for such organizations. Sanctions must be sufficiently rigorous to ensure compliance by organizations.

NOTES & QUESTIONS

1. The process for EU approval of the Safe Harbor agreement began with the EU Parliament, which commented on the efficacy of the agreement by issuing a nonbinding resolution. The EU Parliament rejected the Safe Harbor agreement by a vote of 279 to 259 because of concerns over the adequacy of U.S. protections and numerous loopholes.[44] An excerpt of the EU Parliament's resolution is included in section B below. The ultimate decision on whether the EU would approve the Safe Harbor agreement rested in the EU Commission. Since the EU Parliament's resolution was nonbinding on the Commission, on July 26, 2000, the Commission approved the Safe Harbor

---

[44]Steven R. Salbu, *The European Union Data Privacy Directive and International Relations*, 35 Vand. J. Transnat'l L. 655, 678-679 (2002). There were 22 abstentions.

agreement.[45] Below is the letter transmitting the Commission's decision along with an excerpt from the decision.

LETTER FROM COMMISSION SERVICES TRANSMITTING THE EUROPEAN COMMISSION'S ADEQUACY FINDING[46]

EUROPEAN COMMISSION
Internal Market DG
Director-General
Brussels, 28.01.00 4074
DG Markt/E-1 D(2000)168

Mr. Robert LaRussa
Under Secretary for International Trade of
the United States Department of Commerce
Washington D.C. 20230
United States of America

Dear Mr. LaRussa,

Thank you for your letter of 17 July with which you enclosed the "Safe Harbor Privacy Principles" and the frequently asked questions and answers (the principles) issued by the Department of Commerce on 21 July and related material concerning enforcement by public bodies in the United States. I am pleased to inform you that the Commission, exercising the powers conferred on it by Article 25.6 of the Data Protection Directive (95/46/EC), has found that these arrangements would provide adequate protection for the purposes of Article 25.1 of the Directive regarding the transfer of personal data to countries outside the European Union. I enclose a copy of the Commission decision C(2000) 2441 for your information. The Member States are required to comply with decisions of the Commission taken on the basis of Article 25.6.

The Commission Decision

The decision provides that data controllers in the EU can transfer personal data processed in accordance with Member States law, without providing additional safeguards to ensure their protection, to US-based organisations declaring their adherence to the "safe harbor" principles, provided that they are subject to the statutory powers of a public body empowered to investigate complaints and to obtain relief against unfair or deceptive practices or otherwise effectively ensure compliance with the principles. The effect of this decision is also that any requirements for the prior authorisation of transborder data transfers as provided for under Member State law will be waived, or that approval will be automatically and promptly granted, as regards such transfers to organisations qualifying for the safe harbor. The Directive and Member States' laws implementing it still of course govern the lawfulness of processing in the EU, and

---

[45] *See id.* at 679-680.
[46] Available at <*http://www.export.gov/safeharbor/EUletter27JulyHeader.htm*>.

Article 25.6 decisions do not affect that in any way. This means that violations of Member State laws by data exporters can result in the blocking of data transfers, notwithstanding the existence of relevant Article 25.6 decisions.

List of Participating US-Based Organisations

The Commission welcomes the fact that the Department of Commerce will provide for the maintenance of a list, to be made publicly available and kept up to date on a regular basis, of the US-based organisations which have declared their adherence to the "safe harbor" principles and which notify this to the Department of Commerce or the organisation the Department designates for this purpose. We note also that the Department of Commerce or its designee will make public any proper and final adverse determinations notified to it pertaining to non-compliance with the principles by a "safe harbor" organisation or to other events that might bring to an end an organisation's participation in the "safe harbor", such as a takeover or a merger. This will ensure transparency and clarity about which US-based organisations enjoy "safe harbor" benefits.

Date of Entry into Effect

Member States are required to ensure that the decision is effective 90 days after its notification to them. After this, US organisations self-certifying their adherence to the "safe harbor" will be assured of "safe harbor" benefits from the date that they notify the Department of Commerce (or its designee) and publicly announce that they have taken the measures necessary to comply with the principles. The Commission and the Member States recognise that US organisations will need some time to consider whether to participate in the "safe harbor" and, if so, to implement privacy policies to put the principles into effect. During the course of our discussions, Member States have demonstrated their willingness to use the flexibility offered by Article 26 of the Directive to avoid interruptions in data flows, so as not to call into question the good faith efforts being made to secure adequate protection for data transferred from the EU. The Commission and the Member States have confirmed their willingness to continue to use this flexibility during the implementation phase of the "safe harbor", so that US organisations have time to decide whether to participate in the "safe harbor" and (if necessary) to update their information processing policies and practices accordingly. . . .

In deciding whether to participate in the "safe harbor", organisations should consider that the "safe harbor" represents clear advantages over the existing situation, in terms of speedier transfers, lighter administrative burdens and greater legal certainty. These advantages will benefit the EU transfers of data as well as the US recipients. US organisations may of course join the "safe harbor" at any time, but we consider that the resulting benefits represent strong arguments for their entering the "safe harbor" as quickly as possible. . . .

Complaint Procedures

It can be expected that claims will arise from time to time that an organisation which has entered the "safe harbor" is not in fact complying with the "safe harbor" principles. As for all cases where complaints concern recipients falling within the scope of a decision taken on the basis of Article 25.6 of the

Directive, it will be for the appropriate US bodies to determine whether such claims are founded and if so, to ensure that the organisation takes the measures necessary to come into compliance with the principles as quickly as possible, or is removed from the "safe harbor". Reliance on US enforcement arrangements to ensure a good general level of compliance with the principles is a fundamental aspect of the "adequacy" finding. As indicated by Article 2 of the decision, evidence that any enforcement body in the United States responsible for compliance with the principles is failing to secure compliance may trigger action by the Commission, in consultation with the Member States through the Article 31 Committee, and after informing the Department of Commerce, to reverse, suspend or limit the scope of the decision with respect to such enforcement body. Measures to suspend specific data transfers for reasons connected with compliance problems in the United States can be taken at the national level only in the circumstances and in the manner set out in Article 2, paragraph 1. Moreover, such measures can have only a temporary effect, pending a resolution of the problem by the appropriate enforcement bodies in the United States. These arrangements as a whole reflect our shared twin objectives of avoiding the interruption of transborder data flows and maintaining high data protection standards.

Jurisdiction

During our dialogue, you raised with me the concerns of US industry about the possible effects of the "safe harbor" as regards jurisdiction and applicable law in the European Union. I would like to confirm that it is the Commission's intention that participation in the "safe harbor" does not change the *status quo ante* for any organisation with respect to jurisdiction, applicable law or liability in the European Union. Moreover, our discussions with respect to the "safe harbor" have not resolved nor prejudged the questions of jurisdiction or applicable law with respect to websites. All existing rules, principles, conventions and treaties relating to international conflicts of law continue to apply and are not prejudiced in any way by the "safe harbor" arrangement.

Use of Contracts — Commission Decisions Based on Article 26 of the Data Protection Directive

I should also add that the establishment of the "safe harbor" does not affect the ability of Member States to authorise transfers on the basis of safeguards adduced by the data exporter in accordance with Article 26.2. This means organisations not wishing to qualify for the "safe harbor" could put in place the safeguards necessary for transfers of personal data from the EU to the United States by means of binding written agreements between the transferers and the recipients of data. The Commission may approve model clauses for such agreements under Article 26.4 of the Directive which are binding on the Member States. The Commission and the Member States are of the view that the "safe harbor" principles may be used in such agreements for the substantive provisions on data protection. Such agreements may need to include other provisions on issues such as liability and enforcement, on which decisions have not yet been taken. . . .

It is also important to recall that the "safe harbor" reflects a number of features which may be unique to the US constitutional model and legal system and which were taken into account in the US context, but which are not necessarily present outside this context. We continue to prefer legally binding data protection rules, for which the Directive and the OECD guidelines must remain our principal benchmarks and any proposal to regard the "safe harbor" as providing adequate protection outside the US context would have to be examined by the Commission in the light of all the relevant circumstances. . . .

COMMISSION DECISION FINDING THE SAFE HARBOR TO PROVIDE ADEQUATE PROTECTION

C (2000) 2441 (July 26, 2000) [47]

Adequate Level of Protection. Pursuant to the Commission's Decision:

> The adequate level of protection for the transfer of data from the Community to the United States recognised by this Decision, should be attained if organisations comply with the Safe Harbor Privacy Principles for the protection of personal data transferred from a Member State to the United States (hereinafter "the Principles") and the Frequently Asked Questions (hereinafter "the FAQs") providing guidance for the implementation of the Principles issued by the Government of the United States on 21.07.2000. Furthermore the organisations should publicly disclose their privacy policies and be subject to the jurisdiction of the Federal Trade Commission (FTC) under Section 5 of the Federal Trade Commission Act which prohibits unfair or deceptive acts or practices in or affecting commerce, or that of another statutory body that will effectively ensure compliance with the Principles implemented in accordance with the FAQs.

The Commission's Decision states that two government bodies in the United States are "empowered to investigate complaints and to obtain relief against unfair or deceptive practices as well as redress for individuals" in instances of noncompliance with the Safe Harbor Principles. These bodies are (1) the FTC and (2) the U.S. Department of Transportation. The Decision notes that the FTC's jurisdiction is limited in a number of respects:

> The Federal Trade Commission acts on the basis of its authority under Section 5 of the Federal Trade Commission Act. The jurisdiction of the Federal Trade Commission under Section 5 is excluded with respect to: banks, saving and loans and credit unions; telecommunications and interstate transportation common carriers, air carriers and packers and stockyard operators. Although the insurance industry is not specifically included in the list of exceptions in Section 5, the McCarran-Ferguson Act leaves the regulation of the business of insurance to the individual states. However, the provisions of the FTC Act apply to the insurance industry to the extent that such business is not regulated by State law. The FTC retains residual authority over unfair or deceptive practices by insurance companies when they are not engaged in the business of insurance. EU Commission Decision, Annex VII.

---

[47] These documents are also available at: <*http://www.europa.eu.int/comm/internal_market/en/dataprot/wpdocs/index.htm*>. Other interesting documents that are part of the Safe Harbor Arrangement may be found at: <*http://www.export.gov/safeharbor/sh_documents.html*>.

The U.S. Department of Transportation "institutes cases based on its own investigations as well as formal and informal complaints received from individuals, travel agents, airlines, US and foreign government agencies." EU Commission Decision, Annex VII.

According to the Decision:

> Sectors and/or data processing not subject to the jurisdiction of any of the government bodies in the United States listed in Annex VII to this Decision should fall outside the scope of this Decision.

List of Participating Organizations. According to the Commission, organizations adhering to the Safe Harbor principles and FAQs must be able to be known to data subjects, data exporters, and data protection authorities. The U.S. Department of Commerce must issue a "public list of organisations self-certifying their adherence to the Principles implemented in accordance with the FAQs."

Relevant Documents for the Safe Harbor Principles. In addition to the Safe Harbor Principles, the Commission concluded that a number of other documents establish that there is an "adequate level of protection" in the United States. These documents include a letter from the FTC, a letter from the U.S. Department of Transportation, and a memorandum on damages for breaches of privacy and explicit authorizations in U.S. law. *See* EU Commission Decision, Article 1(1).

Conditions Relating to the Transfer of Data. Article 1(2) of the EU Commission decision sets forth the following conditions that must be met in relation to each transfer of data:

> (a) the organisation receiving the data has unambiguously and publicly disclosed its commitment to comply with the Principles implemented in accordance with the FAQs, and
> (b) the organisation is subject to the statutory powers of a government body in the United States listed in Annex VII to this Decision which is empowered to investigate complaints and to obtain relief against unfair or deceptive practices as well as redress for individuals, irrespective of their country of residence or nationality, in case of non-compliance with the Principles implemented in accordance with the FAQs.

These conditions "are considered to be met for each organisation that self-certifies its adherence to the Principles implemented in accordance with the FAQs." Article 3. The organization must inform the U.S. Department of Commerce of its public disclosure pursuant to Article 2(a) above and must identify the government body that will investigate complaints and provide redress for violations pursuant to Article 2(b) above.

Suspension of Data Flows with Participating Organizations. Under Article 3 of the Commission's decision:

> 1. Without prejudice to their powers to take action to ensure compliance with national provisions adopted pursuant to provisions other than Article 25

of Directive 95/46/EC, the competent authorities in Member States may exercise their existing powers to suspend data flows to an organisation that has self-certified its adherence to the Principles implemented in accordance with the FAQs in order to protect individuals with regard to the processing of their personal data in cases where:

> (a) the government body in the United States referred to in Annex VII to this Decision or an independent recourse mechanism within the meaning of letter a) of the Enforcement Principle set out in Annex I to this Decision has determined that the organisation is violating the Principles implemented in accordance with the FAQs; or
>
> (b) there is a substantial likelihood that the Principles are being violated, there is a reasonable basis for believing that the enforcement mechanism concerned is not taking or will not take adequate and timely steps to settle the case at issue, the continuing transfer would create an imminent risk of grave harm to data subjects, and the competent authorities in the Member State have made reasonable efforts under the circumstances to provide the organisation with notice and an opportunity to respond.

The suspension shall cease as soon as compliance with the Principles implemented in accordance with the FAQs is assured and the competent authorities concerned in the Community are notified thereof.

Member States must immediately inform the Commission of measures adopted pursuant to the above provisions. If there is evidence that the U.S. governmental body responsible for ensuring compliance with the Safe Harbor Principles is not "effectively fulfilling its role," then the Commission will inform the U.S. Department of Commerce and may draft measures to suspend the Commission's decision or limit its scope. Article 3(4).

Evaluation of Implementation of the Commission's Decision. Pursuant to Article 4, the Commission will evaluate the implementation the Commission's decision within three years.

NOTES & QUESTIONS

1. ***Frequently Asked Questions.*** Along with the Decision, a series of frequently asked questions (FAQs) summarizes the Decision and provides information to companies and individuals seeking to comply with the Safe Harbor agreement.[48] Some of the FAQs include:

> **Are the standard contractual clauses compulsory for companies interested in transferring data outside the EU?**
> No. The standard contractual clauses are neither compulsory for businesses nor are they the only way of lawfully transferring data to countries outside the EU.

---

[48]Standard contractual clauses for the transfer of personal data to third countries — frequently asked questions, available at <*http://europa.eu.int/comm/internal_market/en/dataprot/news/clauses2faq.htm*>.

First of all, organisations do not need contractual clauses if they want to transfer personal data to recipients in countries which have been recognised by the Commission as providing adequate protection of data. This is the case of transfers to Switzerland, Hungary or U.S. based companies adhering to the Safe Harbor Privacy Principles issued by the U.S. Department of Commerce. . . .

Can companies still rely on different contracts approved at national level?

Yes. The standard contractual clauses do not prejudice past or future contractual arrangements authorised by national Data Protection Authorities pursuant to national legislation. . . .

Can companies implement the standard contractual clauses in a wider contract and add specific clauses?

Yes. Parties are free to agree to add other clauses as long as they do not contradict, directly or indirectly, the standard contractual clauses approved by the Commission or prejudice fundamental rights or freedoms of the data subjects. It is possible, for example, to include additional guarantees or procedural safeguards for the individuals (e.g. on-line procedures or relevant provisions contained in a privacy policy, etc.). All these other clauses that parties may decide to add would not be covered by the third party beneficiary rights and would benefit from confidentiality rights where appropriate. . . .

2. ***The Efficiencies of the EU Data Directive for U.S. Businesses.*** There has been some criticism of the inefficiences for U.S. businesses created by having to comply with the EU Data Directive. However, consider the following argument by Robert Gellman:

For all the consternation about the Directive, everyone — including the United States — will benefit because it exists. The Directive will solve the same problem for third countries that it solves for Europe: how to function in a multi-jurisdictional environment characterized by differing local privacy rules. If there were no Directive then it would be necessary for U.S. companies seeking business in Europe to independently address the same privacy issues fifteen times in EU member states rather than once. If there were no Directive U.S. businesses would demand that one be developed to open EU markets to foreign information processors. The absence of an EU directive harmonizing data protection laws would be a greater barrier to trade.[49]

3. ***Dual System of Data Protection.*** Does a dual system of data protection rules comply with the clause in the OECD Guidelines that prohibits discrimination on the ground of nationality?

4. ***Financial Data.*** Why does financial data fall outside the scope of the Safe Harbor Arrangement? What is so specific about this kind of data that justifies such temporary exemption? How would you frame safe harbor guidelines for such data? What are the interests at stake? Which U.S. authority should regulate the protection of financial data? The same question

---

[49] Robert Gellman, *Book Review*, 32 Geo. Wash J. Intl. L. & Econ. 179, 186 (1999) (reviewing Swire & Litan, *None of Your Business*).

could be asked concerning the insurance industry or the telecommunications industry whose regulation is left to the individual States.

5. Can you think about any case where international trade might conflict with the Safe Harbor Arrangement? Is there not a discrimination between U.S. and European companies, the latter being subject to more onerous data protection requirements than their counterparts?

6. *Convergence.* Recall Colin Bennett's argument at the beginning of this chapter on policy convergence in the privacy realm. The Safe Harbor Arrangement appears to provide strong support for Bennett's hypothesis. Which of the facts identified by Bennett do you think contributed to the outcome here? What are we to make now of "American exceptionalism"?

(b) Critiques of the Safe Harbor Arrangement

EUROPEAN PARLIAMENT RESOLUTION ON THE DRAFT
COMMISSION DECISION ON THE ADEQUACY OF THE PROTECTION
PROVIDED BY THE SAFE HARBOUR PRIVACY PRINCIPLES

European Parliament (July 5, 2000)[50]

C. whereas in the United States:

(a) there is not at present any generally applicable legal data protection in the private sector and virtually all data are currently processed without specific guarantees of judicial protection;

(b) there are, however, numerous legislative proposals pending before Congress and the President of the United States himself recently referred to the need for further legislative measures, while the Federal Trade Commission expressed the same opinion in its third report to Congress on the functioning of the system of self-regulation in the electronic marketplace;

(c) the guidelines approved by the OECD (signed by the USA in 1980 and ratified at the Ottawa OECD Conference in September 1998) must in any case be applied in the area of personal data protection. . . .

D. whereas, rather than encouraging a legislative approach, the U.S. Department of Commerce intends to propose to companies "safe harbour privacy principles" (and the Frequently Asked Questions (FAQs) arising from such principles), which:

(a) will apply only to personal data of EU origin, with the status of the voluntary "standard" suggested to the businesses intending to receive data from the EU, but are binding on those businesses that opt to adhere to them and are enforceable by private dispute resolution bodies and government bodies with powers to obtain relief against unfair or deceptive practices;

(b) relate only to firms which fall within the competence of the Federal Trade Commission and the Department of Transportation (so that, for example, firms in the banking and telecommunications sectors are excluded);

---

[50]Available at *<http://www.europa.eu.int/comm/internal_market/en/dataprot/adequacy/index .htm>*.

(c) are subject to exceptions (FAQ 15) as regards public record and publicly available data (e.g. land register, telephones, tax declarations, electoral rolls), which are protected by Community legislation;

(d) use ambiguous terms such as "organisation" (which may refer both to businesses and business conglomerates) and "explicit authorisations" (which allow exemptions to the principles);

(e) do not provide a right of effective, personal appeal to a public body (FAQ 11);

(f) do not allow it to be concluded with certainty that it will be possible to obtain compensation for individual damage suffered as a result of possible violations of the safe harbour principles. . . .

NOTES & QUESTIONS

1. ***Dual Data Processing Systems.*** If U.S. companies have to comply domestically with more stringent rules with respect to the personal data coming from the European Union, they would have to implement a dual system of processing, one for the personal data collected in the United States, another one for the data from EU origin. Will such dual data processing system not become more burdensome and costly than the implementation of a uniform system?

2. ***Dissatisfaction with the Safe Harbor Principles.*** Consider the following comment by Steven Salbu:

   > As some domestic observers question whether the United States has given up too much, the concern of the EU Parliament is that the United States has given away too little. Driven by fears that the Safe Harbor Principles lack meaningful enforcement mechanisms, the EU Parliament's fears seem to have some merit, given the slow pace at which U.S. companies have responded to the provisions. As of a March 2001 report, a mere two dozen or so U.S. companies had registered as Safe Harbor compliant. By August 2001, the number had risen to about seventy, a miniscule portion of all U.S. firms. Perhaps partially in response to concerns that meaningful data flow controls under the Privacy Directive may fizzle, the European Union is pressing implementation forward.[51]

3. ***The Ratcheting-Up Effect.*** Greg Schaffer has observed a "ratcheting up" effect in the relationship between the United States and Europe in the area of privacy policy.[52] As a consequence of laws in Europe that safeguard privacy, it is more likely today that similar laws will be adopted in the United States or at least that United States firms will improve their privacy protection. This is a surprising observation since the popular view of the global economy is that there is a "race to the bottom," a tendency for trade to lead to a reduction in regulatory authority. Why do you think this dynamic occurs in the privacy realm?

---

[51] Steven R. Salbu, *The European Union Data Privacy Directive and International Relations*, 35 Vand. J. Transnatl. L. 655, 684 (2002).

[52] See Gregory Shaffer, *Globalization and Social Protection: The Impact of EU and International Rules in the Ratcheting Up of U.S. Privacy Standards*, 25 Yale J. Intl. L. 1 (2000).

4. ***Remedying the EU Parliament's Concerns.*** The European Parliament's major concerns regarding the Safe Harbor Principles are the absence of an individual right of judicial appeal and the failure to have an agreement to oblige companies to pay compensation for unlawfully processed data. How could a system of judicial remedy be implemented in the United States?

5. ***Absence of Safe Harbor.*** Without the Safe Harbor Arrangement, U.S. firms would have been subject to the national data protection laws in Europe. Large U.S. firms have complied with these requirements for many years, and presumably could continue to operate in Europe without Safe Harbor. Who, then, does Safe Harbor benefit?

YVES POULLET, *THE SAFE HARBOR PRINCIPLES:*
AN ADEQUATE PROTECTION?

IFCLA International Colloquium, Paris, France (June 2000)[53]

1. The phenomenon of transborder data flows is increasing, particularly between E.U. Member States and the U.S. Many explanations might be given: the first one is definitively the Internet traffic: more than 70% of the web sites are located in North America. The fact that the use of telecommunications networks is cheaper there and the huge capacity of these networks justify that more than 40% of the European telecommunications traffic is running through U.S. networks. To these explanations it might be added that the concentration movement as regards companies creates an increasing need for large central data banks about employees and their use world-wide. Finally, more and more people are traveling around the world and generate multiple data which are processed within information systems often managed from U.S.

2. The "Safe Harbor Principles" have been developed in that context as an answer to the fears raised up as regards the privacy protection. This answer has been enacted by the Department of Commerce after a wide public consultation of various groups including, not only companies but also consumers and civil liberties associations. The subtitle of the "Safe Harbor Principles": "Elements of Effective Self-Regulation for Privacy Protection" clearly indicates that the American point of view deeply differs from the European one insofar the privacy protection is considered as sufficiently ensured through self-regulation, and not through a legislative approach considered by the U.S. Government as inadequate and costly. . . .

9. In the first place we would like to highlight a lack of coherence between, on the one hand, the requirement to monitor compliance with the "safe harbor" principles by an institution such as the FTC and, on the other hand, the scope of the Safe Harbor. This covers areas over which the FTC does not appear to have competence, such as, for example, telecommunications, data concerning employees, data concerning pharmaceutical data.

In the second place, the conditions for applying the Safe Harbors are limited by particularly wide ranging exceptions, which include legislative texts, administrative regulations or case-law decisions which create contradictory

---

[53] *<http://www.droit.fundp.ac.be/textes/safeharbor.pdf>.*

obligations or envisage explicit authorisations. These exceptions give rise to uncertainty with regard to the scope of the principles, and weaken the principle of legal security, which is essential for the interpretation of the applicable principles. . . .

10. Although it notes some progress here and there in the formulation of the principles, nevertheless the absence of any precise definition of the fundamental concepts must be underlined. Thus, without claiming to be exhaustive, the concept of personal data is defined vaguely by reference to the scope of the directive, but this reference does not state whether the "Safe Harbor Principles" will give the concept the same very broad scope given by Article 2(a). The concept of third party itself is not defined, and does the concept of consent, fundamental in principle 2: "Choice," require the same conditions as those called for by Article 2(h) of the directive. The "sensitive" data, especially broadened in relation to the previous versions of the Safe Harbour, is defined as data "specifying" and not, in the broad sense of the directive, as data "revealing" data of a medical, health, ethnic, racial, etc. nature.

11. As regards now the principles to be enacted and considered essential by the Article 29 Group's documents already quoted, certain doubts might be addressed as regards two principles, namely the principle of the legitimate purpose (purpose limitation principle) and the principle of access.

Considering the first principle, its compliance is essential. It is important that the purposes of a personal data processing are adequately defined and that the purposes have a certain legitimacy in relation to the mission of the company or the administration in its relations with persons concerned with the data. . . .

22. Although the American system does represent innovative and courageous solutions for ensuring an effective protection of the European personal data, we think that certain serious reservations ought to be expressed in connection with the adequacy of the protection that could be afforded by Safe Harbor and the declaration by a public or private body that these are being complied with.

These reservations are justified as follows:

1. The scope remains vague and is subject to interpretation.

2. The "Safe Harbor" principles concern only data covered by the directive and not all data processed by American organisations. As a consequence, for European data they introduce a system of exception which risks being little known and poorly respected in reality.

3. The "Safe Harbor" principles disregard the principle of determined legitimate purpose. This introduces risks regarding the conditions for application of the other principles.

4. The "Safe Harbor" principles give too relative a scope to the right of access and as a result leave organisations the opportunity to shirk their duty with regard to transparency too easily.

5. Application of the "Safe Harbor" principles rests on case law or on the intervention of numerous self-regulation bodies, the uniformity of interpretation of which is not guaranteed by any official authority. In particular, the competence of the F.T.C. in the matter is too indirect to guarantee it.

6. The enforcement of compliance with the Safe Harbor depends on complicated mechanisms, some of which are of doubtful quality. In particular, self

certification by the organisation itself may be surrounded by guarantees regarding the possibility of disputing compliance before independent authorities but the quality of independence of these authorities is poorly defined and the way in which the organisations are under the control of these organisations, unspecified.

7. Generally, the American approach is based on the intervention of private Alternative Dispute Resolution institutions which, one can only note, are in the early stages of their existence, with the result that their operation makes little impression, and finally that their investigative powers are inadequately defined.

8. Lastly, it is regrettable that the person concerned is ultimately poorly provided for. It is up to him to verify whether the American body which deals with the data is in a position of compliance or not, it is up to him to find, and to refer the matter to, the appropriate independent control authority to study his case, it is up to him to put forward the arguments of his application. In this connection, assistance and support from the militant American human rights or defence of freedom organisations would have been useful but their intervention is not envisaged nor is it very probable, since these organisations were created initially for the defence of American, not European citizens.

**JOEL R. REIDENBERG, *E-COMMERCE
AND TRANS-ATLANTIC PRIVACY***

38 Hous. L. Rev. 717, 744-746 (2001)

For the national supervisory authorities in Europe, Safe Harbor poses a weakening of European standards. . . .

. . . Safe Harbor weakens European standards for redress of data privacy violations. Under the European Directive, victims must be able to seek legal recourse and have a damage remedy. The U.S. Department of Commerce assured the European Commission that Safe Harbor and the U.S. legal system provided remedies for individual European victims of Safe Harbor violations. The European Commission expressly relied on representations made by the U.S. Department of Commerce concerning available damages in American law. The memorandum presented by the U.S. Department of Commerce to the European Commission, however, made misleading statements of U.S. law. For example, the memorandum provides a lengthy discussion of the privacy torts and indicates that the torts would be available. The memorandum failed to note that the applicability of these tort actions to data processing and information privacy has never been established by U.S. courts and is, at present, purely theoretical. Indeed, the memorandum cites the tort for misappropriation of a name or likeness as a viable damage remedy, but all three of the state courts that have addressed this tort in the context of data privacy have rejected it. Safe Harbor is also predicated on dispute resolution through seal organizations such as TRUSTe. Yet, only one seal organization, the ESRB, proposes any direct remedy to the victim of a breach of a privacy policy, and other organizations' membership lists look like a "Who's Who" of privacy scandal-plagued companies.

Lastly, the enforcement provisions of Safe Harbor rely on the FTC. Even if the FTC has jurisdiction to enforce Safe Harbor, the assertion that the FTC will give priority to European enforcement actions is hard to believe. First, although the FTC has become active in privacy issues recently, the agency's record of enforcing the Fair Credit Reporting Act, one of the country's most important fair information practices statutes, is less than aggressive. Second, were the FTC to devote its limited resources to the protection of Europeans' privacy, Americans should and would be offended that a U.S. government agency — charged with protecting American consumers — chose to commit its energies and U.S. taxpayer money to the protection of European privacy in the United States against U.S. businesses at a higher level than the FTC asserts for the protection of Americans' privacy.

Sadly, though, for many American companies even these weakened European standards impose substantially greater obligations than U.S. law. In particular, the notice, choice, access, and correction requirements are only sporadically found in U.S. law. As a result, pitifully few American companies have subscribed to Safe Harbor; indeed, as of June 21, 2001, fewer than fifty-five companies had signed up.

The upshot of these sui generis standards, the unenthusiastic reception by American companies, and enforcement weaknesses is a likelihood that the national supervisory agencies will be dissatisfied with Safe Harbor and the Member States will face great political pressure to suspend Safe Harbor once transposition is completed. Thus, for e-commerce, the utility of Safe Harbor is rather dubious. . . .

NOTES & QUESTIONS

1. The European Commission's decision C(2000) 2441 finding the safe harbor to provide adequate protection provides that "[t]he 'safe harbor' created by the Principles and the FAQs, may need to be reviewed in the light of experience, of developments concerning the protection of privacy in circumstances in which technology is constantly making easier the transfer and processing of personal data and in the light of reports on implementation by enforcement authorities involved." Could you think of any technological developments that could justify such changes and of the changes which would then be required?

2. The issue of the enforceability of the Safe Harbor Arrangement might soon arise as the exchange of letters between the Commission and the U.S. Department of Commerce on the implementation of the Safe Harbor Arrangement might be interpreted by European and/or United States judicial authorities as having the substance of an international agreement adopted in breach of Article 300 of the Treaty establishing the European Community and the requirement to seek Parliament's assent. How would you rule on this issue if you were the judge of a U.S. jurisdiction?

3. Joel Reidenberg believes that there are steps the United States could take to address growing concerns about the adequacy of Safe Harbor. He concluded his congressional testimony with these recommendations:

> Congress needs to act to establish a basic set of legal protections for privacy in the United States. Any such regulation must recognize that technologies will be essential to assure privacy protections in the global environment across divergent sets of rules. In fact, technical decisions are not

policy neutral. Technical decisions make privacy rules and, more often than not, these rules in the United States are privacy invasive. For technology to provide effective privacy protection, three conditions must be met: (a) technology respecting fair information practices must exist; (b) these technologies must be deployed; and (c) the implementation of these technologies must have a privacy protecting default configuration. Legal rights in the United States should provide an incentive structure that encourages these developments.

In conjunction with the establishment of a legal baseline in the United States, Congress should promote the negotiation of a "General Agreement on Information Privacy" within the World Trade Organization framework. Whether desired or not by various interest groups and countries, the WTO will be unable to avoid confronting international privacy issues as a result of the biennial ministerial conferences and the inevitable trade-in-services agenda. Many of the core differences among nations on the implementation of privacy principles touch upon fundamental governance and sovereignty questions. These types of problems will only be resolved at an international treaty level like the WTO.[54]

Do you agree with Reidenberg? What other steps could be taken to safeguard privacy in a global economy?

3. ALTERNATIVE SOLUTIONS TO THE SAFE HARBOR

STANDARD CONTRACTUAL CLAUSES FOR THE TRANSFER OF PERSONAL DATA TO THIRD COUNTRIES: FREQUENTLY ASKED QUESTIONS

Can US-based organisations that have joined the "Safe Harbor" use the standard contractual clauses to receive data from the EU?

As a general rule, standard contractual clauses are not necessary if the data recipient is covered by a system providing adequate data protection such as the "Safe Harbor." However, if the transfer concerns data that is not covered by their "Safe Harbor" commitments, use of the standard contract clauses is one way of providing the necessary safeguards.

Can US-based companies that have not joined the "Safe Harbor" use the relevant "Safe Harbor" rules under the contract?

Yes, provided that they also apply the three mandatory data protection principles in the Annex (applicable to all countries of destination): the purpose limitation, restrictions on onward transfers and the right of access, rectification, deletion and objection.[55]

---

[54] Joel Reidenberg, *The EU Data Protection Directive: Implications for the U.S. Privacy Debate*, Available at *<http://energycommerce.house.gov/107/hearings/03082001Hearing49/Reidenberg104.htm>*.

[55] Available at *<http://europa.eu.int/comm/internal_market/en/dataprot/news/clauses2faq.htm>*.

NOTES & QUESTIONS

1. Two European online auction web sites (*iBazar.be* and *iBazar.fr*) recently merged with eBay. The iBazar registered users received early November 2001 an e-mail explicitly asking them to give their consent to have their personal user file shared with eBay. The e-mail explains that their data will be processed by *eBay.fr* and *eBay.nl,* and that to consent, they have to agree to (1) eBay's terms of use and privacy notice; and (2) the transfer of their "data" to eBay's servers in the United States. The e-mail adds that if they do not give their consent "within a few days," their iBazar personal subscriber file will be blocked and not available to them anymore. In a short FAQ, the e-mail provides that iBazar asks its users to consent to the transfer of their data to U.S.-based servers because "the online auction service of the future Web site *eBay.be* and *eBay.fr* will be provided by eBay International AG based in Europe, that, however, eBay International AG has recourse to the platforms and technical services of eBay Inc., and that the personal data that you have communicated to us will soon be transferred to its servers based in the United States."

   Why did *ibazar.be* and *ibazar.fr* use the opt-in mechanism to get the consent of its subscribers? Is there any legal provision? Where do you need to look for such a provision? Which data protection regulations will be applicable to the *iBazar.be* and *iBazar.fr* subscribers? Assuming that eBay Inc. has not signed the Safe Harbor Guidelines, how are iBazar subscribers' personal data protected if they are to be transferred to eBay's servers based in the United States? Are the standard contractual clauses mentioned above useful to answer the question? Will the iBazar subscribers' personal data have a privileged treatment compared to the *eBay.com* subscribers even after they have consented to the sharing of data envisaged in the aforementioned e-mail? Do you think this e-mail should have been written more clearly? That it omitted to mention some important details? Why?

2. *DRM and International Privacy Protection.* The development of new tools for Digital Rights Management (DRM), which provide publishers with technological controls over the use of digital works, is likely to raise new privacy concerns as individual user information is recorded and monitored to determine whether consumers are complying with the terms of a new digital product. Consider a hypothetical company DigitoMusico that provides online music to consumers all around the world for a very modest rate. DigitoMusico takes advantage of a new technique that monitors over the Internet every single use of every song that it provides to its customers. It is able to determine with virtual certainty whether the device that plays a song is owned by the person who purchased the song and also whether the song is playing on two devices owned by the same person simultaneously. What issues does this raise under the EU Data Directive or the OECD Privacy Guidelines? What about the Safe Harbor Arrangement? If Digito-Musico is based in Spain, does it matter for privacy purposes whether its customers are in Europe, the United States, or Canada?

3. *Post 9-11 Antiterrorism Measures.* In the introduction to the 2002 report on Privacy and Human Rights, Sarah Andrews notes that many of the

antiterrorism measures adopted by governments after September 11 have had a negative impact on privacy:

> In response to the events of that day, specific anti-terrorism measures have been introduced in Australia, Austria, Canada, Denmark, France, Germany, India, Singapore, Sweden, the United Kingdom and the United States. Another significant development was the passing, in May 2002, of the European Union's Electronic Communications Privacy Directive. This Directive allows European Union member states to enact laws requiring Internet Service Providers, and other telecommunications operators, to retain the traffic and location data of all people using mobile phones, text messaging, landline telephones, faxes, e-mails, chatrooms, the Internet, or any other electronic communication devices, to communicate. Such data retention schemes are already in place in Belgium, France, Spain and the United Kingdom and have been proposed in the Netherlands. In New Zealand a law granting significant new interception authority to law enforcement is also pending.[56]

Andrews concludes:

> Among all of these measures, it is possible to identify a number of trends including: increased communications surveillance and search and seizure powers; weakening of data protection regimes; increased data sharing; and increased profiling and identification. While none of the above trends are necessarily new; the novelty is the speed in which these policies gained acceptance, and in many cases, became law.[57]

To what extent do you believe that governments are required to "trade" privacy for security? In what sense do antiterrorism measures enhance privacy? In what respects might they diminish privacy?[58]

4. *Convergence Revisited. Again.* In 1992, Colin Bennett argued for convergence. In 1996 he found flaws in the convergence theory, noting that the United States in particular had failed to follow a general movement toward data protection based on Fair Information Practices. What do you think Bennett might say today? What are your own views? Do you anticipate privacy norms becoming more similar in the years ahead?

5. *The Future of Information Privacy.* In December 2000, the leaders of the institutions of the European Union gathered in Nice to sign the European Union Charter of Fundamental Rights.[59] The Charter of Fundamental Rights sets out in a single text, for the first time in the European Union's history, the whole range of civil, political, economic, and social rights of European citizens and all persons living in the European Union. Article 8 of the Charter, concerning Protection of Personal Data, states:

> 1. Everyone has the right to the protection of personal data concerning him or her.

---

[56] Electronic Privacy Information Center & Privacy International, *Privacy and Human Rights: An International Survey of Privacy Laws and Developments* iii (2002).

[57] *Id.*

[58] For a thoughtful examination of the relationship between privacy and security, see Ronald J. Daniels, Patrick Macklem, & Kent Roach, *The Security of Freedom: Essays on Canada's Anti-Terrorism Bill* (2001).

[59] Available at *<http://www.europarl.eu.int/charter/default_en.htm>*.

2. Such data must be processed fairly for specified purposes and on the basis of the consent of the person concerned or some other legitimate basis laid down by law. Everyone has the right of access to data which has been collected concerning him or her, and the right to have it rectified.

3. Compliance with these rules shall be subject to control by an independent authority.

At the end of the nineteenth century, Brandeis and Warren described a new legal right to privacy. At the beginning of the twenty-first century, the European Union has set out a new right to information privacy. How well do you think these few sentences capture the spirit of privacy protection, the experience of the twentieth century, and the challenges that may lie ahead?

TABLE OF CASES

TABLE OF
AUTHORITIES

Courtney, Jeremiah, *Electronic Eavesdropping, Wiretapping and Your Right to Privacy,* 26 Fed. Comm. B.J. 1 (1973), 281

Craig, John D.R., Privacy and Employment Law (1999), 638

Curcio, Louis A. and Andrew B. Buxbaum, Note, *When You Can't Sell to Your Customers, Try Selling Your Customers (But Not Under the Bankruptcy Code),* 8 Am. Bankr. Inst. L. Rev. 395 (2000), 551

Daniels, Ronald J., Patrick Macklem, & Kent Roach, The Security of Freedom: Essays on Canada's Anti-Terrorism Bill (2001), 762

Dann, Michael, *The Fifth Amendment Privilege Against Self-Incrimination: Extorting Evidence from a Suspect,* 43 S. Cal. L. Rev. 597 (1970), 277

Dash, Samuel, Richard Schwartz, & Robert Knowlton, The Eavesdroppers (1959), 281, 323

Davies, Simon & David Banisar, *Global Trends In Privacy Protection: An International Survey of Privacy, Data Protection, and Surveillance Laws and Developments,* 18 J. Marshall J. Computer & Info. L. 1 (1999), 688, 700, 701, 725, 726

DeCew, Judith W., In Pursuit of Privacy: Law, Ethics, and the Rise of Technology (1997), 38, 47

Dendy, Geoff, Note, *The Newsworthiness Defense to the Public Disclosure Tort,* 85 Ky. L.J. 147 (1997), 91, 108

Dienes, C. Thomas, *Protecting Investigative Journalism,* 67 Geo. Wash. L. Rev. 1139 (1999), 79, 80

Diffie, Whitfield & Susan Landau, Privacy on the Line: The Politics of Wiretapping and Encryption (1998), 281, 323, 345

Directive of the European Parliament and the Council of Europe on the Protection of Individuals with Regard to the Processing of Personal Data and on the Free Movement of Such Data (1996), 25

Donlinko, David, *Is There a Rationale for the Privilege Against Self-Incrimination,* 33 UCLA L. Rev. 1063 (1986), 277

Dripps, Donald A., *Self-Incrimination and Self-Preservation: A Skeptical View,* 1991 U. Ill. L. Rev. 329, 277

Duby, Georges, *Foreword,* in A History of the Private Life I: From Pagan Rome to Byzantium (Paul Veyne ed. & Arthur Goldhammer trans. 1987), 26

Earl-Hubbard, Michele L., Comment, *The Child Sex Offender Registration Laws: The Punishment, Liberty Deprivation, and Unintended Results Associated with the Scarlet Letter Laws of the 1990s,* 90 Nw. U. L. Rev. 788 (1996), 399

Edelman, Peter B., *Free Press v. Privacy: Haunted by the Ghost of Justice Black,* 68 Tex. L. Rev. 1195 (1990), 117

Electronic Privacy Information Center & Privacy International, Privacy and Human Rights: An International Survey of Privacy Laws and Developments (2001), 316, 715, 725

_____, Privacy and Human Rights: An International Survey of Privacy Laws and Developments (2002), 735, 762

Ellis, Jr., Dorsey D. *Damages and the Privacy Tort: Sketching a "Legal Profile,"* 64 Iowa L. Rev. 1111 (1979), 90

Emerson, Thomas I., *The Right of Privacy and Freedom of Press,* 14 Harv. C.R.-C.L. L. Rev. 329 (1979), 117

Epstein, Richard A., *Privacy, Publication, and the First Amendment: The Dangers of First Amendment Exceptionalism,* 52 Stan. L. Rev. 1003 (2000), 135

_____, *The Legal Regulation of Genetic Discrimination: Old Responses to New Technology,* 74 B.U. L. Rev. 1 (1994), 263

Ernst, Morris L. & Alan U. Schwartz, Privacy: The Right to Be Let Alone (1962), 6

Etzioni, Amitai, The Limits of Privacy (1999), 38, 457

Felcher, Peter L. & Edward L. Rubin, *Privacy, Publicity, and the Portrayal of Real People by the Media,* 88 Yale L.J. 1577 (1979), 90

Feldblum, Chai, *Medical Examinations and Inquiries Under the Americans with Disabilities Act: A View from the Inside,* 64 Temp. L. Rev. 521 (1991), 656

Feldman, Daniel L., *The "Scarlet Letter Laws" of the 1990s: A Response to Critics,* 60 Alb. L. Rev. 1081 (1997), 399

Firestone, Marvin & Fillmore Buckner, *"Where the Public Peril Begins" 25 Years After Tarasoff,* 21 J. Legal Med. 187 (2000), 238

Flaherty, David H., Protecting Privacy in Surveillance Societies (1989), 25, 725

_____, Privacy in Colonial New England (1972), 673

Fogel, Stephen M. et al., *Survey of the Law on Employee Drug Testing,* 42 U. Miami L. Rev. 553 (1988), 638

Franklin, Marc A., *A Constitutional Problem in Privacy Protection: Legal Inhibitions on Reporting of Fact,* 16 Stan. L. Rev. 107 (1963), 117

Freiwald, Susan, *Uncertain Privacy: Communication Attributes After the Digital Telephony Act,* 69 S. Cal. L. Rev. 949 (1996), 337

Fried, Charles, *Privacy,* 77 Yale L.J. 475 (1968), 31

Froomkin, A. Michael, *Flood Control on the Information Ocean: Living with Anonymity, Digital Cash, and Distributed Databases,* 15 J.L. & Comm. 395 (1996), 402, 430

_____, *The Metaphor Is the Key: Cryptography, the Clipper Chip, and the Constitution,* 143 U. Pa. L. Rev. 709 (1995), 344

_____, *The Constitution and Encryption Regulation: Do We Need a "New Privacy"?,* 3 N.Y.U. J. Legis. & Pub. Pol'y 25 (1999), 345

Funk, T. Markus, *The Dangers of Hiding Criminal Pasts,* 66 Tenn. L. Rev. 287 (1998), 389

Gandy, Oscar H., Jr., The Panoptic Sort: A Political Economy of Personal Information (1993), 492

_____, *Exploring Identity and Identification in Cyberspace,* 14 Notre Dame J.L. Ethics & Pub. Pol'y 1085 (2000), 401, 506

Garfinkel, Simson, Database Nation: The Death of Privacy in the 21st Century (2000), 180, 448, 493

Gavison, Ruth, *Feminism and the Public/Private Distinction,* 45 Stan. L. Rev. 21 (1992), 47

_____, *Privacy and the Limits of Law,* 89 Yale L.J. 421 (1980), 32

Gellman, Robert M., *Prescribing Privacy: The Uncertain Role of the Physician in the Protection of Patient Privacy,* 62 N.C. L. Rev. 255 (1984), 246

_____, *Book Review,* 32 Geo. Wash J. Int'l L. & Econ. 179 (1999), 742

_____, *Does Privacy Law Work?* in Technology and Privacy: The New Landscape (Philip E. Agre & Marc Rotenberg eds. 1997), 475

Gerety, Tom, *Redefining Privacy,* 12 Harv. C.R.-C.L. L. Rev. 233 (1977), 32

Gerstein, Robert S., *Intimacy and Privacy,* in Philosophical Dimensions of Privacy: An Anthology (Ferdinand David Schoeman ed., 1984), 32

Gewirtz, Paul, *Privacy and Speech,* 2001 Sup. Ct. Rev. 139 (2001), 135

Gilles, Susan M., *All Truths Are Equal, But Are Some Truths More Equal Than Others?,* 41 Case W. Res. L. Rev. 725 (1991), 128

Gilliom, John, Surveillance, Privacy, and the Law: Employee Drug Testing and the Politics of Social Control (1994), 638

_____, Overseers of the Poor: Surveillance, Resistance, and the Limits of Privacy (2001), 484

Gindin, Susan E., *Lost and Found in Cyberspace: Informational Privacy in the Age of the Internet,* 34 San Diego L. Rev. 1153 (1997), 493

Ginsburg, Douglas H., *Genetics and Privacy,* 4 Tex. Rev. L. & Pol. 17 (1999), 262

Giordano, Philip, *Invoking Law as a Basis for Identity in Cyberspace,* 1998 Stan. Tech. L. Rev. 1, 428

Glancy, Dorothy J., *The Invention of the Right to Privacy,* 21 Ariz. L. Rev. 1 (1979), 4, 6

_____, *At the Intersection of Visible and Invisible Worlds: United States Privacy Law and the Internet,* 16 Santa Clara Computer & High Tech. L.J. 357 (2000), 493

Godkin, E.L., *The Right to Privacy,* The Nation (Dec. 25, 1890), 5

_____, *The Rights of the Citizen: IV. To His Own Reputation,* Scribner's Magazine (1890), 5

Goodenough, Oliver R., *Go Fish: Evaluating the Restatement's Formulation of the Law of Publicity,* 47 S.C. L. Rev. 709 (1996), 162

Gormley, Ken, *One Hundred Years of Privacy,* 1992 Wis. L. Rev. 1335, 3

Gostin, Lawrence O. & James G. Hodge, Jr., *Piercing the Veil of Secrecy in HIV/AIDS and Other Sexually Transmitted Diseases: Theories of Privacy and Disclosure in Partner Notification,* 5 Duke J. of Gender L. & Pol'y 9 (1998), 226

_____, *Personal Privacy and Common Goods: A Framework for Balancing Under the National Health Information Privacy Rule,* 86 Minn. L. Rev. 1439 (2002), 216

Gostin, Lawrence O., *Health Information Privacy,* 80 Cornell L. Rev. 451 (1995), 179, 231

Grant, Rebecca & Colin J. Bennett eds., Visions of Privacy: Policy Choices for the Digital Age (2000), 61

Green, M., The Mount Vernon Street Warrens: A Boston Story, 1860-1910 (1989), 5, 6

Greenawalt, R. Kent, *Silence as a Moral and Constitutional Right,* 23 Wm. & Mary L. Rev. 15 (1981), 277

Greenberg, Thomas R., Comment, *E-Mail and Voice Mail: Employee Privacy and the Federal Wiretap Statute,* 44 Am. U. L. Rev. 219 (1994), 336

Grier, Manton M., Jr., *The Software Formerly Known as "Carnivore": When Does E-Mail Surveillance Encroach Upon a Reasonable Expectation of Privacy?,* 52 S.C. L. Rev. 875 (2001), 336

Gross, Hyman, *The Concept of Privacy,* 42 N.Y.U. L. Rev. 34 (1967), 25, 32

Gurak, Laura J., Persuasion and Privacy in Cyberspace: The Online Protests over Lotus Marketplace and the Clipper Chip (1997), 55

Haag, Ernest Van Den, *On Privacy,* in Nomos XII: Privacy 149 (J. Ronald Pennock & J.W. Chapman eds. 1971), 32

Habermas, Jürgen, The Structural Transformation of the Public Sphere (Thomas Burger trans. 1991), 26

Halpern, Sheldon, *The Right of Publicity: Maturation of an Independent Right Protecting the Associative Value of Personality,* 46 Hastings L.J. 853 (1995), 162

Hammitt, Harry A. & David L. Sobel, & Mark S. Zaid, eds., Litigation Under the Federal Open Government Laws (EPIC 2002), 462

Harris, D.J., S.H. Bailey, & B.L. Jones, Civil Liberties — Cases and materials (3d ed., 1991), 691, 692

Hatch, Mike, *HIPAA: Commercial Interests Win Round Two,* 86 Minn. L. Rev. 1481 (2002), 216

Health Privacy Project, Report: Genetics and Privacy: A Patchwork of Protections (2002), 204, 263

Hemholtz, R.H. et al. The Privilege Against Self-Incrimination: Its Origins and Development (1997), 278

Hertzel, Dorothy A. Note, *Don't Talk to Strangers: An Analysis of Government and Industry Efforts to Protect Child's Privacy Online*, 52 Fed. Comm. L.J. 429 (2000), 562

Hess, Jennifer A. & Dan L. Burk, *Genetic Privacy: Constitutional Considerations in Forensic DNA Testing*, 5 Geo. Mason U. Civ. Rts. L.J. 1 (1994), 267

Hetcher, Steven, *The De Facto Federal Privacy Commission*, 19 J. Marshall J. Computer & Info. L. 109 (2000), 734

_____, *The FTC as Internet Privacy Norm Entrepreneur*, 53 Vand. L. Rev. 2041 (2000), 547

_____, *Changing the Social Meaning of Privacy in Cyberspace*, 15 Harv. J. L. & Tech. 149 (2001), 547

_____, *Norm Proselytizers Create a Privacy Entitlement in Cyberspace*, 16 Berkeley Tech. L.J. 877 (2001), 547

Hill, Alfred, *Defamation and Privacy Under the First Amendment*, 76 Colum. L. Rev. 1205 (1976), 117

Hodge, Jr., James G. & Lawrence O. Gostin, *Personal Privacy and Common Goods: A Framework for Balancing Under the National Health Information Privacy Rule*, 86 Minn. L. Rev. 1439 (2002), 216

_____, *Piercing the Veil of Secrecy in HIV/AIDS and Other Sexually Transmitted Diseases: Theories of Privacy and Disclosure in Partner Notification*, 5 Duke J. of Gender L. & Pol'y 9 (1998), 226

Hoffman, Sharona, *Preplacement Examinations and Job-Relatedness: How to Enhance Privacy and Diminish Discrimination in the Workplace*, 49 U. Kan. L. Rev. 517 (2001), 620

Hudson, Dennis L. & George B. Trubow, *The Right to Financial Privacy Act of 1978: New Protection from Federal Intrusion*, 12 John Marshall J. Prac. & Proc. 487 (1979), 530

Inness, Julie C., Privacy, Intimacy, and Isolation (1992), 32

Jacob-Foltzer, V. & J. Polakiewicz, *The European Human Rights Convention in Domestic Law*, 12 Hum. Rts. L. J. 65 (1991), 693

Jacobson, Peter D., *Medical Records and HIPAA: Is it Too Late to Protect Privacy?*, 86 Minn. L. Rev. 1497 (2002), 216

Janger, Edward J., *Muddy Property: Generating and Protecting Information Privacy Norms in Bankruptcy*, 44 Wm. & Mary L. Rev. __ (2002), 552, 553

Janger, Ted & Paul M. Schwartz, *The Gramm-Leach-Bliley Act, Information Privacy, and the Limits of Default Rules*, 86 Minn. L. Rev. 1219 (2002), 536

Jennings, E. Judson, *Carnivore: U.S. Government Surveillance of Internet Transmissions*, 6 Va. J. L. & Tech. 10 (2001), 366

Jourard, Sidney M., *Some Psychological Aspects of Privacy*, 31 L. & Contemp. Probs. 307 (1966), 32

Jurata, Jr., John A., Comment, *The Tort That Refuses to Go Away: The Subtle Reemergence of Public Disclosure of Private Facts*, 36 San Diego L. Rev. 489 (1999), 126

Kahn, Jonathan, *Bringing Dignity Back to Light: Publicity Rights and the Eclipse of the Tort of Appropriation of Identity*, 17 Cardozo Arts & Ent. L.J. 213 (1999), 163

Kalven, Jr., Harry, *Privacy in Tort Law — Were Warren and Brandeis Wrong?*, 31 Law & Contemp. Probs. 326 (1966), 3, 117

Post, Robert C., *Rereading Warren and Brandeis: Privacy, Property, and Appropriation,* 41 Case W. Res. L. Rev. 647 (1991), 168

_____, *The Social Foundations of Privacy: Community and Self in the Common Law Tort,* 77 Cal. L. Rev. 957 (1989), 66, 90, 101

_____, *The Social Foundations of Defamation Law: Reputation and the Constitution,* 74 Cal. L. Rev. 691 (1986), 136

_____, *Three Concepts of Privacy,* 89 Geo. L.J. 2087 (2001), 27

_____, *Encryption Source Code and the First Amendment,* 15 Berkeley Tech. L.J. 713 (2000), 344

Pritts, Joy, Janlori Goldman, Zoe Hudson, Aimee Berenson, & Elizabeth Hadley, The State of Health Privacy: An Uneven Terrain (A Comprehensive Survey of State Health Privacy Statutes), at http://www.healthprivacy.org, 208, 209, 210, 261

Privacy International & Electronic Privacy Information Center, Privacy and Human Rights: An International Survey of Privacy Laws and Developments (2001), 316, 715, 725

_____, Privacy and Human Rights: An International Survey of Privacy Laws and Developments (2002), 735, 762

Prosser, William L., *Privacy,* 48 Cal. L. Rev. 383 (1960), 18, 65

Rachels, James, *Why Privacy Is Important,* in Philosophical Dimensions of Privacy: An Anthology (Ferdinand David Schoeman ed., 1984), 32

Rada, Maureen P., Note, *The Buckley Conspiracy: How Congress Authorized the Cover-Up of Campus Crime and How It Can Be Undone,* 59 Ohio St. L.J. 1799 (1998), 616

Radin, Margaret Jane, Contested Commodities (1996), 511

Rackow, Sharon H., Comment, *How the USA PATRIOT Act Will Permit Governmental Infringement Upon the Privacy of Americans in the Name of 'Intelligence' Investigations,* 150 U. Pa. L. Rev. 1651 (2002), 341

Rao, Radhika, *Property, Privacy, and the Human Body,* 80 B.U. L. Rev. 359 (2000), 260

Ray, Nathan E., *Let There Be False Light: Resisting the Growing Trend Against an Important Tort,* 84 Minn. L. Rev. 713 (2000), 155

Regan, Priscilla M. Legislating Privacy: Technology, Social Values, and Public Policy (1995), 22, 40, 281, 323, 459, 469, 470, 483, 564, 673

Reidenberg, Joel R. & Paul M. Schwartz, Online Services and Data Protection Law: Regulatory Responses (EUR-OP:1998), 721

_____, Data Privacy Law (1996), 3, 24

Reidenberg, Joel R., *E-Commerce and Trans-Atlantic Privacy,* 38 Hous. L. Rev. 717 (2001), 720, 743, 758

_____, *Privacy in the Information Economy: A Fortress or Frontier for Individual Rights?,* 44 Fed. Comm. L.J. 195 (1992), 525, 565

_____, *Resolving Conflicting International Data Privacy Rules in Cyberspace,* 52 Stan. L. Rev. 1315 (2000), 59, 735

_____, *Restoring Americans' Privacy in Electronic Commerce,* 14 Berkeley J. L. & Tech. 771 (1999), 714

_____, *Setting Standards for Fair Information Practice in the U.S. Private Sector,* 80 Iowa L. Rev. 497 (1995), 57, 507, 687

_____, *Lex Informatica: The Formulation of Information Policy Rules Through Technology,* 76 Tex. L. Rev. 553 (1998), 512

_____, *The EU Data Protection Directive: Implications for the U.S. Privacy Debate* (2001), available at <http://energycommerce.house.gov/107/hearings/ 03082001 Hearing49/Reidenberg104.htm>, 741, 760

Reiman, Jeffrey H., *Privacy, Intimacy, and Personhood, in* Philosophical Dimensions of Privacy: An Anthology 300 (Ferdinand David Schoeman, ed. 1984), 36

Roach, Kent, Ronald J. Daniels, & Patrick Macklem, The Security of Freedom: Essays on Canada's Anti-Terrorism Bill (2001), 762

Rodriguez, Alexander L., Comment, *All Bark, No Byte: Employee E-Mail Privacy Rights in the Private Sector Workplace,* 47 Emory L.J. 1439 (1998), 674

Rosen, Jeffrey, *A Cautionary Tale for a New Age of Surveillance,* N.Y. Times Magazine (Oct. 7, 2001), 316

Rosen, Jeffrey, The Unwanted Gaze: The Destruction of Privacy in America (2000), 32, 677

Rosenhan, D.L. & Terri Wolff Teitelbaum, Kathi Weiss Teitelbaum, & Martin Davidson, *Warning Third Parties: The Ripple Effects of Tarasoff,* 24 Pac. L.J. 1165 (1993), 238

Rotenberg, Marc, ed., Privacy Law Sourcebook (EPIC 2001), 23, 553, 738

Rotenberg, Marc, & Philip E. Agre, eds., Technology and Privacy: The New Landscape (1997), 493

Rotenberg, Marc, *Fair Information Practices and the Architecture of Privacy (What Larry Doesn't Get),* 2001 Stan. Tech. L. Rev. 1, 44. 23, 431, 471, 513, 566

_____, *In Support of a Data Protection Board in the United States,* 8 Gov't Info. Q. 79-94 (1991), 733

_____, *Privacy and Secrecy After September 11,* 86 Minn. L. Rev. 1115 (2002), 483

Rothstein, Mark A., *The Law of Medical and Genetic Privacy in the Workplace, in* Genetic Secrets: Protecting Privacy and Confidentiality in the Genetic Era 281 (Mark A. Rothstein ed., 1997), 656

Rubin, Edward L. & Peter L. Felcher, *Privacy, Publicity, and the Portrayal of Real People by the Media,* 88 Yale L.J. 1577 (1979), 90

Rule, James B., Private Lives and Public Surveillance: Social Control in the Computer Age (1974), 492

Salbu, Steven R., *The European Union Data Privacy Directive and International Relations,* 35 Vand. J. Transnat'l L. 655 (2002), 746, 747, 755

Samuelson, Pamela, *Privacy as Intellectual Property?,* 52 Stan. L. Rev. 1125 (2000), 511

Schauer, Frederick, *Reflections on the Value of Truth,* 41 Case W. Res. L. Rev. 699 (1991), 128

Scheppele, Kim Lane, Legal Secrets: Equality and Efficiency in the Common Law (1988), 42

Schulhofer, Stephen J., *Some Kind Words for the Privilege Against Self-Incrimination,* 26 Val. U. L. Rev. 311 (1991), 277

Schwartz, Alan U. & Morris L. Ernst, Privacy: The Right to Be Let Alone (1962), 6

Schwartz, Gary T., *Explaining and Justifying a Limited Tort of False Light Invasion of Privacy,* 41 Case W. Res. L. Rev. 885 (1991), 155

Schwartz, Paul M. & Joel R. Reidenberg, Data Privacy Law (1996), 3, 25

_____, Online Services and Data Protection Law: Regulatory Responses (EUR-OP: 1998), 721

Schwartz, Paul M. & Ted Janger, *The Gramm-Leach-Bliley Act, Information Privacy, and the Limits of Default Rules,* 86 Minn. L. Rev. 1219 (2002), 536

Schwartz, Paul M., *Free Speech Versus Information Privacy: Eugene Volokh's First Amendment Jurisprudence,* 52 Stan. L. Rev. 1559 (2000), 583

_____, *Privacy and Democracy in Cyberspace,* 52 Vand. L. Rev. 1609 (1999), 35, 547, 564, 583

Symposium, *Data Protection Law and the European Union's Directive: The Challenge for the United States,* 80 Iowa L. Rev. (1995), 715

Symposium, *Privacy,* 31 L. & Contemp. Probs. 251-435 (1966), 22

Symposium, *The Right to Privacy One Hundred Years Later,* 41 Case W. Res. L. Rev. 643-928 (1991), 6

Symposium, *Cyberspace and Privacy—A New Legal Paradigm?,* 52 Stan. L. Rev. 987 (2000), 493

Thompson, William C., *DNA Testing,* in 2 Encyclopedia of Crime and Punishment 537 (David Levinson, ed. 2002), 267, 268

Thomson, Judith Jarvis, *The Right to Privacy,* 4 Philosophy & Public Affairs 295 (1975), 40

Tribe, Laurence, American Constitutional Law (2d ed. 1988), 305

Trubow, George B. & Dennis L. Hudson, *The Right to Financial Privacy Act of 1978: New Protection from Federal Intrusion,* 12 John Marshall J. Prac. & Proc. 487 (1979), 530

True, John M. & Edward M. Chen, Pauline T. Kim, *Common Law Privacy: A Limit on an Employer's Power to Test for Drugs,* 12 Geo. Mason U. L. Rev. 651 (1990), 638

Turkington, Richard C. & Anita L. Allen, Privacy Law: Cases and Materials (2002), 3

Turkington, Richard C., *Confidentiality Policy for HIV-Related Information: An Analytical Framework for Sorting Out Hard and Easy Cases,* 34 Vill. L. Rev. 871 (1989), 247

Turn, Rein & Willis H. Ware, *Privacy and Security Issues In Information Systems* (RAND, July 1976), 55

U.S. Dep't of Health, Education & Welfare, Records, Computers, and the Rights of Citizens: Report of the Secretary's Advisory Comm. on Automated Personal Data Systems (1973), 23, 448, 470

U.S. General Accounting Office, Report to the Chairman, Subcomm. on Social Security, Comm. On Ways and Means, House of Representatives: Social Security: Government and Commercial Use of the Social Security Number is Widespread (Feb. 1999), 449

Volokh, Eugene, *Freedom of Speech and Information Privacy: The Troubling Implications of a Right to Stop People from Speaking About You,* 52 Stan. L. Rev. 1049 (2000), 110, 128, 389, 582

Wade, John W., *Defamation and the Right to Privacy,* 15 Vand. L. Rev. 1093 (1962), 90

Wald, Patricia M., *The Freedom of Information Act: A Short Case Study in the Perils and Paybacks of Legislating Democratic Values,* 33 Emory L.J. 649 (1984), 463

Walker, John Kent Jr., Note, *Covert Searches,* 39 Stan. L. Rev. 545 (1987), 278

Ware, Willis H. & Rein Turn, *Privacy and Security Issues In Information Systems* (RAND, July 1976), 55

Warren, Samuel & Louis Brandeis, *The Right to Privacy,* 4 Harv. L. Rev. 193 (1890), 3, 6, 55, 116, 512

Wasserstrom, Silas J. & Louis Michael Seidman, *The Fourth Amendment as Constitutional Theory,* 77 Geo. L.J. 19 (1988), 278

Wefing, John B., *Employer Drug Testing: Disparate Judicial and Legislative Responses,* 63 Albany L. Rev. 799 (2000), 638

Weissenberger, Glen, Federal Evidence (1996), 219

Westin, Alan, Privacy and Freedom (1967), 19, 22, 28, 509

Westin, Alan & Michael A. Baker, Databanks in a Free Society: Computers, Record-Keeping and Privacy (1972), 22, 459, 469

Whitaker, Reg, The End of Privacy: How Total Surveillance is Becoming a Reality (2000), 492

Winn, Peter A., *Confidentiality in Cyberspace: The HIPAA Privacy Rules and the Common Law,* 33 Rutgers L.J. 617 (2002), 232

Winner, Langdon, *Victory for Computer Populism,* Technology Review (1990), 55

Winnick, Raphael, *Searches and Seizures of Computers and Computer Data,* 88 Harv. J.L. & Tech. 75 (1994), 355

Zaid, Mark S. & Harry A. Hammitt, David L. Sobel, eds., Litigation Under the Federal Open Government Laws (EPIC 2002), 460

Zimmerman, Diane L., *Requiem for a Heavyweight: A Farewell to Warren and Brandeis's Privacy Tort,* 68 Cornell L. Rev. 291 (1983), 128

_____, *False Light Invasion of Privacy: The Light That Failed,* 64 N.Y.U. L. Rev. 364 (1989), 155

_____, *Real People in Fiction: Cautionary Words About Troublesome Old Torts Poured into New Jugs,* 51 Brook. L. Rev. 355 (1985), 117

Zuriek, Elia & David Lyon, eds., Computers, Surveillance, and Privacy (1996), 493

INDEX